THE ENCYCLOPEDIA OF
POLITICAL SCIENCE

Volume

1

THE ENCYCLOPEDIA OF
POLITICAL SCIENCE

George Thomas Kurian, EDITOR IN CHIEF

James E. Alt
Simone Chambers
Geoffrey Garrett
Margaret Levi
Paula D. McClain
ASSOCIATE EDITORS

Prepared with the assistance of the American Political Science Association

CQ PRESS

A Division of SAGE
Washington, D.C.

CQ Press
2300 N Street, NW, Suite 800
Washington, DC 20037

Phone: 202-729-1900; toll-free, 1-866-4CQ-PRESS (1-866-427-7737)

Web: www.cqpress.com

Cover design: Anne C. Kerns, Anne Likes Red, Inc.
Cover photos: Protest in India: Associated Press, Mustafa Quraishi; Afghan women vote: Associated Press, Alexandra Boulat; Japanese Parliment: Kyodo; U.S. Supreme Court: Jarek Tuszynski, Wikimedia Commons, CC-BY-SA-3.0; Iraqi Kurdish women militia: Associated Press, Hasan Sarbakhshian
Maps: International Mapping Associates
Composition: C&M Digitals (P) Ltd.

♾ The paper used in this publication exceeds the requirements of the American National Standard for Information Sciences—Permanence of Paper for Printed Library Materials, ANSI Z39.48-1992.

Printed and bound in the United States of America

14   13   12   11   10   1   2   3   4   5

Library of Congress Cataloging-in-Publication Data

The encyclopedia of political science/George Thomas Kurian, editor-in-chief.
    5 v. cm.
Includes bibliographical references and index.
ISBN 978-1-933116-44-0 (alk. paper)
    1. Political science—Encyclopedias. I. Kurian, George Thomas. II. Title.

JA61.E513 2011
320.03—dc22

                                                                    2010036238

CONTENTS

~

VOLUME 1

VOLUME 2

VOLUME 3

VOLUME 4

VOLUME 5

ALPHABETICAL TABLE OF CONTENTS

THEMATIC TABLE OF CONTENTS

CULTURE, MEDIA, AND LANGUAGE

DEMOCRACY AND DEMOCRATIZATION

ETHICS AND POLITICAL CORRUPTION

EUROPEAN POLITICS AND SOCIETY

FEDERALISM AND LOCAL POLITICS

INSTITUTIONS AND CHECKS AND BALANCES

INTEREST GROUPS AND LOBBIES

INTERNATIONAL RELATIONS

POLITICAL PSYCHOLOGY

POLITICAL THEORY

POLITICS AND SOCIETY

QUALITATIVE/QUANTITATIVE METHODS

RACE, ETHNICITY, AND POLITICS

RIGHTS AND FREEDOMS

SCIENCE, TECHNOLOGY, AND POLITICS

WAR, PEACE, AND TERRORISM

BIOGRAPHIES

ABOUT THE EDITORS

EDITOR IN CHIEF

George Thomas Kurian is founder and president of the Encyclopedia Society. Born in India, he emigrated to the United States in 1968. Over the past twenty years, he has produced more than twenty-three encyclopedias and thirty-one other reference books, including atlases, dictionaries, almanacs, annuals, chronologies, desk references, and anthologies.

ASSOCIATE EDITORS

James E. Alt is Frank G. Thomson Professor of Government at Harvard University. He is author, coauthor, or coeditor of *The Politics of Economic Decline* (Cambridge University Press, 1979), *Political Economics* (University of California Press, 1983), *Perspectives on Positive Political Economy* (Cambridge University Press, 1990), *Competition and Cooperation* (Russell Sage, 1999), and *Positive Changes in Political Science* (University of Michigan Press, 2007). He also has published numerous articles in scholarly journals. He is the founding director of Harvard's Center for Basic Research in the Social Sciences (now the Institute for Quantitative Social Science). He is or has been a member of the editorial boards of the *American Journal of Political Science, British Journal of Political Science, Political Studies, American Political Science Review,* and other journals and is a former member of the Political Science panel of the National Science Foundation. He was a Guggenheim fellow (1997–1998) and is a member of the American Academy of Arts and Sciences.

Simone Chambers is a professor in the Department of Political Science at the University of Toronto. She is author of *Reasonable Democracy: Jurgen Habermas and the Politics of Discourse* (Cornell University Press, 1996) and the coeditor of *Deliberation, Democracy, and the Media* (Rowman and Littlefield, 2000) and *Alternative Conceptions of Civil Society* (Princeton University Press, 2001). Chambers has published articles on deliberative democracy, the Frankfurt School, constitutional theory, civil society, rhetoric and the public sphere in such journals as *Political Theory, Journal of Political Philosophy, Constellations,* and *Perspectives on Politics.* She teaches the history of political thought, critical theory, democratic theory, continental thought, and public law.

Geoffrey Garrett is founding CEO of the United States Studies Centre and professor of political science at the University of Sydney. He was previously president of the Pacific Council on International Policy in Los Angeles and before that dean of the International Institute at the University of California, Los Angeles. He has served on the faculties of Oxford, Stanford, and Yale universities and the Wharton School of the University of Pennsylvania. Garrett is author of *Partisan Politics in the Global Economy* and editor of *The Global Diffusion of Markets and Democracy,* both published by Cambridge University Press, and he has published more than fifty articles in the world's leading social science journals on the politics of globalization and European integration.

Margaret Levi is Jere L. Bacharach Professor of International Studies, Department of Political Science, University of Washington, Seattle and, jointly, chair in politics, United States Studies Centre at the University of Sydney. She is director of the CHAOS (Comparative Historical Analysis of Organizations and States) Center and formerly the Harry Bridges Chair and Director of the Harry Bridges Center for Labor Studies. She served as president of the American Political Science Association (2004–2005) and was elected to the American Academy of Arts and Sciences in 2001. She was a Guggenheim fellow (2002–2003) and a Phi Beta Kappa Visiting Scholar (2006–2007). Levi's many publications include *Consent, Dissent, and Patriotism* (1997), *Of Rule and Revenue* (1988), and the multi-authored *Analytic Narratives* (1998) and *Cooperation Without Trust* (2005). In 1997 she became the co–general editor of the Trust series for Russell Sage Foundation Press, in 1999 the general editor of *Cambridge Studies in Comparative Politics,* and in 2006 the general editor of the *Annual Review of Political Science.*

Paula D. McClain is professor of political science, public policy, and African American studies at Duke University. She is codirector of the Center for the Study of Race, Ethnicity and Gender in the Social Sciences at Duke. She directs the American Political Science Association's Ralph Bunche Summer Institute hosted by Duke University and funded by the National Science Foundation and Duke University. Her primary research interests are in racial minority group politics, particularly interminority political and social competition, and urban politics, especially public policy and urban crime. Her articles have appeared in numerous journals, most recently the *Journal of Politics, American Political Science Review, Urban Affairs Review,* and the *Du Bois Review: Social Science Research on Race.*

CONTENT EDITORS

Micah Altman is senior research scientist in the Institute for Quantitative Social Science in the Faculty of Arts and Sciences at Harvard University, archival director of the Henry A. Murray Research Archive, and nonresident senior fellow at the Brookings Institution.

Kevin G. Barnhurst is a professor in the Department of Communication at the University of Illinois at Chicago and chair of the Political Communication Division of the International Communication Association.

Janet M. Box-Steffensmeier is the Vernal Riffe Professor of Political Science, courtesy professor of sociology, and director of the program in statistical methodology at Ohio State University.

Susan Burgess is professor of political science and women's and gender studies at Ohio University.

Ladislav Cabada is the Jean Monnet Chair and Associate Professor in the Department for Politics and International Relations and also is on the faculty of philosophy and arts at the University of West Bohemia in Pilsen, Czech Republic.

Tihomir Cipek is professor of political science at the University of Zagreb in Croatia and former president of the Croatian Political Science Association.

Louis DeSipio is associate professor of political science and chair of Chicano/Latino studies at the University of California, Irvine.

Joyce Gelb is professor emerita of political science at the City University of New York.

Michael T. Gibbons is associate professor of political science in government and international affairs at the University of South Florida.

Michael Gilligan is associate professor of politics at New York University.

Michael Goodhart is associate professor of political science and women's studies at the University of Pittsburgh.

Sean Q. Kelly is professor of political science at California State University, Channel Islands in Camarillo, California.

Joseph L. Klesner is professor of political science and associate provost at Kenyon College.

George Klosko is the Henry L. and Grace Doherty Professor in the Department of Politics at the University of Virginia.

Rose McDermott is professor of political science at Brown University and a fellow at the Radcliffe Institute for Advanced Study at Harvard University.

Andrew Murphy is associate professor of political science at Rutgers University, New Brunswick.

J. Mitchell Pickerill is coeditor of "The State of American Federalism" annual issue of *Publius: The Journal of Federalism* and an associate professor in the Department of Political Science at Washington State University.

Peter Rutland is the Colin and Nancy Campbell Professor in Global Issues and Democratic Thought, professor of government, and professor of Russian and Eastern European studies at Wesleyan University in Middletown, Connecticut.

Reeta Tremblay is vice president (academic) pro tempore at Memorial University of Newfoundland and president-elect of the Canadian Political Science Association. Beginning January 1, 2011, she will be vice president (academic) and provost at the University of Victoria.

Gul Gunver Turan is professor of economics (retired) in the faculty of economics at Istanbul University.

Ilter Turan is a professor of political science in the Department of International Relations at Istanbul Bilgi University in Turkey.

James J. Wirtz is dean of the School of International Graduate Studies, Naval Postgraduate School, Monterey, California.

Joseph F. Zimmerman is professor of political science in the Rockefeller College of the State University of New York at Albany.

BOARD OF EDITORIAL CONSULTANTS AND ADVISERS

Lisa Anderson
School of International and Public Affairs, Columbia University

Judith Baer
Texas A&M University

Karen Beckwith
Case Western Reserve University

Lance Bennett
University of Washington

Richard Bensel
Cornell University

Adam Berinsky
Massachusetts Institute of Technology

Kenneth Bickers
University of Colorado at Boulder

Catherine Boone
University of Texas at Austin

Henry E. Brady
Goldman School of Public Policy, University of California, Berkeley

Lawrence Broz
University of California, San Diego

Cornell Clayton
Washington State University

Joseph Cooper
Johns Hopkins University

Neta C. Crawford
Boston University

Martha Crenshaw
Center for International Security and Cooperation, Stanford University

Christian Davenport
Kroc Institute for International Peace Studies, University of Notre Dame

Henry A. Dietz
University of Texas at Austin

Peter Eisinger
The New School for Management and Urban Policy

Barbara Farnham
Institute of War and Peace Studies, Columbia University

H. George Frederickson
University of Kansas

John Freeman
University of Minnesota

William A. Galston
University of Maryland

Shirley Geigers
Savannah State University

Kim Geron
California State University East Bay

James L. Gibson
Washington University in St. Louis

Benjamin Ginsberg
Center for the Study of American Government, Johns Hopkins University

John C. Green
Bliss Institute of Applied Politics, University of Akron

Paul Gronke
Reed College

Fen Osler Hampson
Norman Paterson School of International Affairs, Carleton University

Jeffrey Herbst
Colgate University

Jennifer Hochschild
Harvard University

Michael Howlett
Simon Fraser University

John Ishiyama
University of North Texas

Shanto Iyengar
Stanford University

Simon Jackman
Stanford University

Stathis N. Kalyvas
Yale University

Richard S. Katz
Johns Hopkins University

William R. Keech
Duke University

Anthony King
University of Exeter

Jack Knight
Duke University

Paul A. Kowert
Rutgers, The State University of New Jersey

Yves Laberge
Institut québécois des hautes études internationales

Jack S. Levy
Rutgers, The State University of New Jersey

Mark Irving Lichbach
University of Maryland

Baodong Liu
University of Utah

Burdett A. Loomis
University of Kansas

Stephen Macedo
Princeton University

Cathie Jo Martin
Boston University

Gregory E. McAvoy
University of North Carolina at Greensboro

Joseph P. McCormick II
Penn State–York Campus

Wayne McIntosh
University of Maryland

Graham T. T. Molitor
Public Policy Forecasting

Andrew Moravcsik
Princeton University

Elinor Ostrom
Indiana University–Bloomington

Paul Quirk
University of British Columbia

David Brian Robertson
University of Missouri–St. Louis

Allan Rosenbaum
Florida International University

Marc Howard Ross
Bryn Mawr College

Bo Rothstein
Göteborg University

M. Elizabeth Sanders
Cornell University

Joanna Vecchiarelli Scott
Eastern Michigan University

Kathryn Sikkink
University of Minnesota

Jack Snyder
Institute of War and Peace Studies, Columbia University

Manfred B. Steger
Royal Melbourne Institute of Technology

Sidney Tarrow
Cornell University

Charles Tilly
Columbia University

Aili Mari Tripp
University of Wisconsin–Madison

Joan C. Tronto
University of Minnesota

Ashutosh Varshney
Brown University

Eduardo A. Velasquez
Washington & Lee University

David Vogel
University of California, Berkeley, Haas School of Business

Barbara F. Walter
Graduate School of International Relations and Pacific Studies, University of California, San Diego

Graham Wilson
Boston University

INTERNATIONAL BOARD OF EDITORIAL ADVISERS

Luc Sindjoun
African Association of Political Science

Rainer Baubock
Austrian Political Science Association

Andre Blais
Canadian Political Science Association

Yun-han chu
Chinese Association of Political Science

Tihomir Cipek
Croatian Political Science Association

Ladislav Cabada
Czech Political Science Association

Peter Kurrild-Klitgaard
Danish Political Science Association

Ken Newton
European Consortium for Political Research (ECPR)

Niilo Kauppi
Finnish Political Science Association

Gideon Doron
Israel Political Science Association

Lars Svasand
Norwegian Political Science Association

Maura Adshead
Political Science Association of Ireland

Antonio L. Rappa
Political Science Association of Singapore

Ilter Turan
Turkish Political Science Association

LIST OF AUTHORS

~

Samer N. Abboud
Arcadia University

Christiana Abraham
University of the West Indies, St. Augustine Campus

Seth Abrutyn
Institute for Research on World-Systems, University of California, Riverside

Karen Ruth Adams
University of Montana

John Agnew
University of California, Los Angeles

Robert Agranoff
School of Public and Environmental Affairs, Indiana University

John S. Ahlquist
Florida State University

Arif Akgul
Turkish Monitoring Center for Drugs and Drug Addiction

Eşref Aksu
Victoria University of Wellington

John H. Aldrich
Duke University

C. Fred Alford
University of Maryland

Fidelis Allen
University of Port Harcourt

William B. Allen
Michigan State University

Doreen K. Allerkamp
School of Social Sciences, University of Mannheim

Dennis Altman
La Trobe University

Micah Altman
Harvard University

Rudy B. Andeweg
Leiden University

Eva Anduiza
Autonomous University of Barcelona

Stephen C. Angle
Wesleyan University

Andrew L. Aoki
Augsburg College

Kai Arzheimer
Johannes Gutenberg–Universität Mainz

Katrin Auel
University of Oxford

Julia Bader
German Development Institute

Kate Baldwin
Columbia University

Terence Ball
Arizona State University

Jordon B. Barkalow
Bridgewater State College

Robert Bates
Harvard University

Jeeyang Rhee Baum
Kennedy School of Government, Harvard University

Murat Bayar
University of Georgia

Virginia Parish Beard
Hope College

Mary Beth Beazley
Michael E. Moritz College of Law, Ohio State University

Karen Beckwith
Case Western Reserve University

Sonu S. Bedi
Dartmouth College

Betsi Beem
University of Sydney

Nasser Behnegar
Boston College

Daniel Béland
Johnson-Shoyama Graduate School of Public Policy (University of Saskatchewan campus)

David S. Bell
School of Politics and International Studies, University of Leeds

Paul Bellamy★
New Zealand Parliamentary Library

Farid Samir Benavides-Vanegas
Campus for Peace, Universitat Oberta de Barcelona, Spain

Andrew Bennett
Georgetown University

★Views expressed are those of the author and do not necessarily represent official views of the New Zealand Parliamentary Library.

Kenneth Benoit
Trinity College Dublin

Ramiro Berardo
*School of Government and Public
Policy, University of Arizona Consejo
Nacional de Investigaciones Científicas y
Técnicas-Argentina*

John C. Berg
Suffolk University

Henrik Berglund
Stockholm University

Kenneth A. Betsalel
University of North Carolina at Asheville

David J. Betz
King's College London

Rajani Bhatia
University of Maryland

Ron J. Bigalke Jr.
University of Pretoria

Simon Birnbaum
Stockholm University

Amanda Bittner
Memorial University of Newfoundland

Amy E. Black
Wheaton College

Paul Blackledge
*Reader, School of Social Sciences, Leeds
Metropolitan University*

Charles P. Blair
Federation of American Scientists (FAS)

Nebojsa Blanusa
University of Zagreb, Croatia

Charles R. Boehmer
University of Texas at El Paso

John R. Bokina
University of Texas–Pan American

Julio Borquez
University of Michigan, Dearborn

Erin L. Borry
University of Kansas

Jocelyn M. Boryczka
Fairfield University

Tanja A. Börzel
*Otto Suhr Institute for Political Science Freie
Universität Berlin*

Jason R. Bossie
Temple University

Denise M. Bostdorff
College of Wooster

Chiara Bottici
New School for Social Research

Janet Box-Steffensmeier
Ohio State University

Richard Boyd
Georgetown University

Megan Bradley
Saint Paul University

David A. Bray
Goizueta Business School

Corey Brettschneider
Brown University

Christian Breunig
University of Toronto

Mark D. Brewer
University of Maine

Jamal Donaldson Briggs
University of North Carolina at Charlotte

John Brigham
University of Massachusetts, Amherst

Rebecca E. Bromley-Trujillo
Michigan State University

Stephen Eric Bronner
Rutgers, The State University of New Jersey

Sarah M. Brooks
Ohio State University

Courtney Brown
Emory University

Aaron-Andrew P. Bruhl
University of Houston Law Center

William I. Brustein
Ohio State University

Dovile Budryte
Georgia Gwinnett College

Cynthia Burack
Ohio State University

Susan Burgess
Ohio University

Walter Dean Burnham
*Frank C. Erwin, Jr. Centennial Chair in
State Government, University of Texas*

Andrew Calabrese
University of Colorado

Karen Callaghan
Texas Southern University

Pamela Camerra-Rowe
Kenyon College

Paul Cantor
University of Virginia

Tereza Capelos
University of Surrey, Guildford

Daniele Caramani
University of St. Gallen

Thomas E. Carbonneau
Pennsylvania State University

M. Cathy Carey
Western Kentucky University

Leah Carmichael
University of Georgia

Julio F. Carrión
University of Delaware

Jeffrey N. Carroll
Temple University

Jamie L. Carson
University of Georgia

Marcio A. Carvalho
Fundacao Getulio Vargas

Terrell Carver
University of Bristol

Brian Caterino
Independent Scholar

Matthias Catón
World Economic Forum

Sezgin S. Cebi
Kadir Has University

Marco Cesa
*School of Advanced International Studies,
Johns Hopkins University*

Benoit Challand
New School for Social Research

Audrey R. Chapman
University of Connecticut School of Medicine

Evan Charney
Duke University

Thomas Cieslik
Tecnológico de Monterrey

Nevim Çil
*Ministry of Justice in Hamburg Department
Anti-Discrimination Unit Cultural Diversity*

David Cingranelli
Binghamton University, SUNY

David Ciuk
Michigan State University

Cornell W. Clayton
Washington State University

Patrick Cloos
Université de Montréal

Kevin Coe
University of Arizona

Simchi Cohen
University of California, Los Angeles

Josep M. Colomer
*Higher Council for Scientific Research
(CSIC), Barcelona*

David B. Conklin
The Chelsea School

Walter D. Connor
Boston University

Aaron Cooley
University of North Carolina at Chapel Hill

Jerome E. Copulsky
Goucher College

David Cortright
University of Notre Dame

Bezen Balamir Coskun
Zirve University

John C. Courtney
*Johnson-Shoyama Graduate School of Public
Policy, University of Saskatchewan*

David Cowan
St. Andrew's University

Claudiu Craciun
*National School of Political Studies and
Public Administration, Bucharest, Romania*

Tobin L. Craig
*James Madison College, Michigan State
University*

Martha Crenshaw
*Center for International Security and
Cooperation (CISAC), Stanford University*

William W. Culver
State University of New York at Plattsburgh

Michael S. Cummings
University of Colorado Denver

K. Amber Curtis
University of Colorado

Brent Cusher
Rhodes College

Richard Dagger
University of Richmond

Dennis Dalton
Barnard College, Columbia University

Jennifer E. Dalton
York University

David Darmofal
University of South Carolina

Noah Dauber
Colgate University

Christian Davenport
University of Notre Dame

Isabel David
*Instituto Superior de Ciências Sociais
e Políticas–Technical University of Lisbon*

Laurence Davis
National University of Ireland, Maynooth

Robert Dayley
College of Idaho

Massimo De Angelis
*School of Humanity and Social Sciences,
University of East London*

Sybille Reinke de Buitrago
IFSH, Universität Hamburg

Rodolfo O. de la Garza
Columbia University

Filippo Del Lucchese
Brunel University–West London

Philippe De Lombaerde
*United Nations University–Comparative
Regional Integration Studies (UNU-CRIS)*

Jasper de Raadt
VU University Amsterdam

Jaap H. de Wilde
University of Groningen

Eliot Dickinson
Western Oregon University

Henry A. Dietz
University of Texas at Austin

Rekha Diwakar
Goldsmiths, University of London

A.G. Dizboni
Royal College of Canada

Nives Dolšak
University of Washington

Jorge Dominguez
Harvard University

Janet L. Donavan
University of Colorado

Charles F. Doran
*Johns Hopkins School of Advanced
International Studies, Washington, D.C.*

Donald A. Downs
University of Wisconsin–Madison

John Duggan
University of Rochester

David A. Dulio
Oakland University

John Duncan
Trinity College, University of Toronto

O. P. Dwivedi
University of Guelph

David M. Edelstein
*Edmund A. Walsh School of Foreign Service,
Georgetown University*

Rita Kiki Edozie
*James Madison College at Michigan State
University*

George Ehrhardt
Appalachian State University

Mette Eilstrup-Sangiovanni
University of Cambridge

Eldon J. Eisenach
University of Tulsa

Rainer Eisfeld
University of Osnabrueck

Rabab El-Mahdi
American University in Cairo

Miriam Fendius Elman
Maxwell School, Syracuse University

Kjell E. Engelbrekt
Stockholm University

Jacob F. English
Marquette University

Richard N. Engstrom
Kennesaw State University

John H. Evans
University of California, San Diego

Joám Evans Pim
University of Santiago de Compostela

Barbara Farnham
Columbia University

Henry Farrell
George Washington University

Christina Fattore
West Virginia University

Jörg Faust
German Development Institute

Joseph Femia
University of Liverpool

Kathy E. Ferguson
University of Hawai'i

Leela Fernandes
University of Michigan, Ann Arbor

Marco Fey
Peace Research Institute Frankfurt

Bonnie N. Field
Bentley University

G. Borden Flanagan
American University School of Public Affairs

Curtis Fogel
University of Guelph

Carolyn Forestiere
University of Maryland, Baltimore County

Carly Hayden Foster
Southern Illinois University of Edwardsville

Russell Arben Fox
Friends University

Ronald Francisco
University of Kansas

Mary Francoli
*School of Journalism and Communication,
Carleton University*

Volker K. Frank
*University of North Carolina
at Asheville*

Benedikt Franke
*St. John's College, University of
Cambridge*

Julian H. Franklin
Columbia University

Leonard Freedman
University of California, Los Angeles

Siegrun Fox Freyss
California State University, Los Angeles

Earl H. Fry
Brigham Young University

Timothy Fuller
Colorado College

Matteo Fumagalli
Central European University (Budapest)

Sean Gailmard
University of California, Berkeley

John A. Garcia
University of Michigan

Monica Gariup
Zayed University

Christian Garland
Independent Scholar

Graeme Garrard
Cardiff University

Bryan Garsten
Yale University

George Gavrilis
University of Texas at Austin

Joyce Gelb
City University of New York

Bobbi Gentry
Millikin University

Daniel B. German
Appalachian State University

Ryan Gibb
University of Kansas

Michael T. Gibbons
University of Southern Florida

Tobias T. Gibson
Westminster College

Eytan Gilboa
Bar-Ilan University

Itzhak Gilboa
*Bar-Ilan University and University of
Southern California*

J. Ramon Gil-Garcia
*Centro de Investigación y Docencia
Económicas, Mexico*

Anthony Gill
University of Washington

Michael Allen Gillespie
Duke University

Bruce Gilley
Portland State University

Ryan R. Gladwin
University of Edinburgh

Marlies Glasius
Universiteit van Amsterdam

Andrew Glencross
University of Aberdeen

Christian Göbel
*Centre for East and South-East Asian
Studies, Lund University*

Mark Gobeyn
Bradley University

Doug Goldenberg-Hart
Senior Acquisitions Editor, CQ Press

Loren Goldman
University of Chicago

Sheldon Goldman
University of Massachusetts, Amherst

Jack A. Goldstone
*School of Public Policy, George Mason
University*

Michael Goodhart
University of Pittsburgh

Victoria Gordon
Western Kentucky University

Norbert Götz
*Institute of Contemporary History, Södertörn
University*

Mark A. Graber
University of Maryland

Robert Grafstein
University of Georgia

Jim Granato
University of Houston

Shannon Granville
Independent Scholar

Peter Gratton
University of San Diego

Marko Grdesic
University of Wisconsin–Madison

Donald P. Green
*Institution for Social and Policy Studies,
Yale University*

Marcus E. Green
Otterbein University

Samuel R. Greene
Catholic University of America

Michael F. Gretz
New School for Social Research

Ramona June Grey
University of Montana

Vsevolod Gunitskiy
Columbia University

John G. Gunnell
*Distinguished Professor, Emeritus, State
University of New York at Albany; Research*

Associate, Affiliated Faculty, Department of
Political Science, University of California,
Davis*

Asha Gupta
University of Delhi

Sandy Brian Hager
York University

Michael W. Hail
Morehead State University

Leonard Hammer
Independent Scholar

John Mark Hansen
University of Chicago

Wendy L. Hansen
University of New Mexico

Jean-Baptiste Harguindéguy
Pablo de Olavide University

Gardenia Harris
Illinois State University

Ralph Hartsock
University of North Texas Libraries

Colin Harvey
Queen's University Belfast

Silja Häusermann
University of Zurich

Mary Hawkesworth
*Rutgers, The State University of
New Jersey*

Reuven Y. Hazan
Hebrew University of Jerusalem

Andrew Heard
Simon Fraser University

David Hedge
University of Florida

Jorge Heine
Balsillie School of International Affairs

Rabih Helou
University of Maryland

Manfred Henningsen
University of Hawai'i at Manoa

James J. Hentz
Virginia Military Institute

Francisco Herreros
*Institute for Public Goods and Policies
(CSIC)*

Michael C. Herron
Dartmouth College

Ghaidaa Hetou
Rutgers, The State University of New Jersey

Neil Hibbert
University of Saskatchewan

Alexander Hicks
Emory University

John Higley
University of Texas at Austin

Peter Hilger
University of Helsinki

Alexandra Elizabeth Hoerl
Wabash College

Samuel B. Hoff
Delaware State University

Sean O. Hogan
RTI International

Stephen Holmes
School of Law, New York University

Arthur Holst
Widener University

Marc Hooghe
University of Leuven

Dana Howard
Brown University

Peter Hudis
Oakton Community College

Louisa S. Hulett
Knox College

Andrew Hurrell
Oxford University

Stephen R. Hurt
Oxford Brookes University

Iza Hussin
University of Massachusetts, Amherst

Patrick H. Hutton
University of Vermont

Jacques E. C. Hymans
University of Southern California

Petronela Iacob
Central European University (Budapest)

Joanne Ibarra
University of Texas at Austin

Simon Jackman
Stanford University

William G. Jacoby
Michigan State University

Farah Jan
*Rutgers, The State University of
New Jersey*

Kenneth Janda
Northwestern University

Lee Jarvis
Swansea University

Erin K. Jenne
Central European University (Budapest)

David C. Johnston
Columbia University

Michael Johnston
Colgate University

Charles W. B. Jones
University of Western Ontario

Randall J. Jones Jr.
University of Central Oklahoma

Joseph Jupille
University of Colorado

Ronald Kahn
Oberlin College

Akis Kalaitzidis
University of Central Missouri

Mark E. Kann
University of Southern California

Daniel Kapust
University of Georgia

Richard S. Katz
Johns Hopkins University

Michael Keaney
*Helsinki Metropolia University of Applied
Sciences*

Christine Keating
Ohio State University

William R. Keech
Duke University

Anthony Kelly
University of Southampton

Norm Kelly
Australian National University

Hans Keman
VU Univerity Amsterdam

James Alan Kendrick
Duke University

Haroon A. Khan
Henderson State University

L. Douglas Kiel
University of Texas at Dallas

Youngmi Kim
Central European University (Budapest)

Edward King
Concordia University

Kristy M. King
Whitman College

Shannon King
College of Wooster

Edgar Kiser
University of Washington

Robert Klemmensen
Syddansk Universitet

Joseph L. Klesner
Kenyon College

Stephan Klingebiel
German Development Institute

George Klosko
University of Virginia

Aysegul Komsuoglu
Istanbul University

Jonathan Koppell
Yale School of Management

Karina Kosiara-Pedersen
University of Copenhagen, Centre for Voting and Parties

Spyros Kosmidis
University of Essex

Dirk Kotzé
University of South Africa

Michael E. Kraft
University of Wisconsin–Green Bay

Jeffrey Kraus
Wagner College

Martin Kreidl
Masaryk University

Charles A. Kromkowski
University of Virginia

Paul James Kubicek
Oakland University

Mirjam Künkler
Princeton University

George Thomas Kurian
President, Encyclopedia Society

Yves Laberge
Independent Scholar, Quebec City

Gladys Lang
University of Washington

Kurt Lang
University of Washington

Margaret Meek Lange
Independent Scholar

Stephen J. Lange
Morehead State University

George R. La Noue
University of Maryland, Baltimore County

Tom Lansford
University of Southern Mississippi

Jeffrey Larsen
Science Applications International Application; Larsen Consulting Group LLC

Jennifer L. Lawless
Women and Politics Institute, American University

Regina G. Lawrence
Manship School of Mass Communication, Louisiana State University

David L. Leal
University of Texas at Austin

J. Wesley Leckrone
Widener University

André Lecours
University of Ottawa

Theresa Man Ling Lee
University Of Guelph

Fabrice Lehoucq
University of North Carolina at Greensboro

Gary Lehring
Smith College

Stephan Leibfried
Bremen University

Julia Leininger
German Development Institute

Yphtach Lelkes
Stanford University

Howard H. Lentner
City University of New York

Eric K. Leonard
Shenandoah University

Eduardo Leoni
IBGE—Brazilian Institute of Geography and Statistics

Paul Lermack
Bradley University

David Levi-Faur
Hebrew University

Alan Levine
American University

Daniel C. Lewis
University of New Orleans

Mark Irving Lichbach
University of Maryland

Joel A. Lieske
Cleveland State University

Mary Liston
Faculty of Law, University of British Columbia

Baodong Liu
University of Utah

Gerhard Loewenberg
University of Iowa

Joseph Losco
Ball State University

Todd R. Lowery
University of Maryland

Robert C. Lowry
University of Texas, Dallas

Cyanne E. Loyle
University of Maryland

Thorsten Luhde
Federal Ministry of Finance (Germany)

Sander Luitwieler
Erasmus University Rotterdam

Arthur Lupia
University of Michigan

Michael Lusztig
Southern Methodist University

Willem Maas
York University

David MacDonald
University of Guelph

Eric MacGilvray
Ohio State University

Scott MacLeod
Simon Fraser University

Allan MacNeill
Webster University

James Magee
University of Delaware

Lars Magnusson
Uppsala University

Deanna Malatesta
Indiana University–Purdue University Indianapolis

Laura Mamo
San Francisco State University

Cecilia G. Manrique
University of Wisconsin–La Crosse

Joseph R. Marbach
La Salle University

Raffaele Marchetti
LUISS Guido Carli University

Lee Marsden
University of East Anglia

Cathie Jo Martin
Boston University

Guy Martin
Winston-Salem State University

Janet M. Martin
Bowdoin College

Sherry L. Martin
Cornell University

Andrew D. Mason
University of Southampton

Geoffroy Matagne
University of Liege

Lawrence C. Mayer
Texas Tech University

Sebastián Mazzuca
Harvard University

Erin McAdams
College of Charleston

Keally McBride
University of San Francisco

Michael McCann
University of Washington

James M. McCormick
Iowa State University

Rose McDermott
Brown University

Tony McGann
University of California, Irvine and University of Essex

James W. McGuire
Wesleyan University

Iain McLean
Nuffield College, Oxford University

Michael McNamara
Cape Breton University

Peter McNamara
Utah State University

Richard J. Meagher
Randolph-Macon College

John Medearis
University of California, Riverside

Jérôme Melançon
University of Alberta, Augustana Campus

Jiri S. Melich
Kazakhstan Institute of Management, Economics, and Strategic Research (KIMEP)

Raymond Mercado
Duke University

Jonathan Mercer
University of Washington

John M. Meyer
Humboldt State University

Ellen Mickiewicz
Duke University

Andrea Migone
Simon Fraser University

Mark C. Miller
Clark University

Maren Milligan
Oberlin College

Henry Milner
Université de Montréal

Fathali M. Moghaddam
Georgetown University

Benoit F. Monange
Institut d'Etudes Politiques de Grenoble

Philippe Mongin
Centre National de la Recherche Scientifique & Ecole des Hautes Etudes Commerciales

Michael Moran
School of Social Sciences, University of Manchester

Jo Moran-Ellis
Center for International Studies in Social Policy and Social Services, Bergische Universität Wuppertal

Luis Moreno
Spanish National Research Council (CSIC)

Irwin L. Morris
University of Maryland

Rebecca B. Morton
New York University

Michael Mosher
University of Tulsa

Jennifer E. Mosley
School of Social Service Administration, University of Chicago

Gary Mucciaroni
Temple University

Gerardo L. Munck
School of International Relations, University of Southern California

Michael C. Munger
Duke University

Andrew Murphy
Rutgers, The State University of New Jersey

Fortunato Musella
University of Naples Federico II

Ella K. Myers
University of Utah

Todd Myers
Grossmont College

Amarjit S. Narang
Indira Gandhi National Open University

Wissam Nasr
Columbia University

Karl-Heinz Nassmacher
Institute of Social Sciences Carl von Ossietzky University of Oldenburg

Pervaiz Nazir
University of Cambridge

Cary J. Nederman
Texas A&M University

Jorge Nef
University of Guelph

Eric Nelson
Missouri State University

Roderick P. Neumann
Florida International University

James Newman
Idaho State University

Kate Nicholls
National University of Singapore

Eric Novotny
U.S. Civilian Research & Development Foundation

J. M. Norton
University of Georgia

Hannu Nurmi
University of Turku

Adam W. Nye
Pennsylvania State University

Herbert Obinger
Bremen University

Edith Obinger-Gindulis
Bremen University

Aron Octavian
Central European University (Budapest)

Niall Ó Dochartaigh
School of Political Science and Sociology, National University of Ireland, Galway

Ismaila Odogba
University of Wisconsin–Stevens Point

Muhamad S. Olimat
University of South Florida, St. Petersburg

David M. Olson
University of North Carolina at Greensboro

Laura Olson
Clemson University

Barry O'Neill
University of California, Los Angeles

Susan Marie Opp
Colorado State University

Danny Osborne
University of California, Los Angeles

Jeffery L. Osgood Jr.
West Chester University of Pennsylvania

Diana Owen
Georgetown University

John E. Owens
University of Westminster

Isik Ozel
Sabanci University, Istanbul

Fania Oz-Salzberger
University of Haifa

Jan Pakulski
University of Tasmania

Kari Palonen
University of Jyväskylä

Niccole M. Pamphilis
Michigan State University

Joel Parker
University of Texas at Austin

Michael Parkin
Oberlin College

John M. Parrish
Loyola Marymount University

Rick Parrish
West Texas A&M University

Eleonora Pasotti
University of California, Santa Cruz

Juliano Pasqual
Fundacao Getulio Vargas

Benjamin J. Pauli
Rutgers, The State University of New Jersey

Bruce G. Peabody
Fairleigh Dickinson University

Colin D. Pearce
University of Guelph–Humber

Malte Pehl
College of Charleston

Riccardo Pelizzo
Griffith University

Daniel Pellerin
National University of Singapore

Glenn E. Perry
Indiana State University

Ravi Perry
Clark University

Leylâ Pervizat
Haliç University in Istanbul

Steven Peterson
Penn State University

Jon Pevehouse
University of Wisconsin

J. Mitchell Pickerill
Washington State University

Mark A. Pickup
Centre for Research Methods in the Social Sciences, University of Oxford and Simon Fraser University

Jean-Benoit Pilet
Université libre de Bruxelles

Pietro Pirani
University of Western Ontario

Wm. C. Plouffe Jr.
Independent Scholar

Andrew Poe
Amherst College

Jonathan T. Polk
University of Georgia

Mark A. Pollack
Temple University

Colin Provost
School of Public Policy, University College London

Sue Pryce
University of Nottingham

Hermann Pünder
Bucerius Law School (Hochschule für Rechtswissenschaft)

Elizabeth Rholetter Purdy
Independent Scholar

Kurt Pyle
Michigan State University

George H. Quester
University of Maryland

John Quigley
Michael E. Moritz College of Law, Ohio State University

Andrea Quinlan
University of Saskatchewan

Kirk A. Randazzo
University of South Carolina

Anthony L. Rappa
Singapore Institute of Management (SIM) University

Claire E. Rasmussen
University of Delaware

Dennis C. Rasmussen
Tufts University

Carsten Rauch
Peace Research Institute Frankfurt

Clyde Ray
Villanova University

David Rayside
University of Toronto

James H. Read
College of St. Benedict and St. John's University

Chad Rector
George Washington University

Robert B. Reich
University of California, Berkeley

Blanka Říchová
Charles University in Prague

Jean-Marc Rickli
Geneva University Strategic Studies Group

Valéry Ridde
Centre de recherche du CHUM, Université de Montréal

Steven C. Roach
University of South Florida

Ian Roberge
Glendon College, York University

Andrew Roberts
Northwestern University

Neil Robinson
University of Limerick

Stephen R. Rock
Vassar College

Joseph Romance
Drew University

Richard Rose
University of Aberdeen

Susan Rose-Ackerman
Yale University, Law School and Department of Political Science

Steven Rosefielde
University of North Carolina at Chapel Hill

David H. Rosenbloom
City University of Hong Kong

Bo Rothstein
University of Gothenburg

Thomas R. Rourke
Clarion University

Stephen R. Routh
California State University, Stanislaus

Paul S. Rowe
Trinity Western University

Molly Ruhlman
Temple University

Mark Rush
Williams School of Commerce, Economics and Politics, Washington and Lee University

Peter Rutland
Wesleyan University

Thomas Saalfeld
University of Bamberg

Filippo Sabetti
McGill University

Marcelo Saguier
Latin American School of Social Sciences

Joseph C. Santora
Thomas Edison State College

Austin Sarat
Amherst College

Meredith Reid Sarkees
American University

Larry Savage
Brock University

Marian Sawer
Australian National University

William C. Schaniel
University of West Georgia

Marc Schattenmann
Advisory Council, Das Progressive Zentrum, Berlin

Gary Schaub Jr.
Air War College

Kay Lehman Schlozman
Boston College

Vivien A. Schmidt
Boston University

Saundra K. Schneider
Michigan State University

Julian Schofield
Concordia University

David Schultz
Hamline University

Chris Matthew Sciabarra
New York University

Jason Scorza
Fairleigh Dickinson University

Kyle Scott
University of North Florida

David O. Sears
University of California, Los Angeles

Nicholas J. Seaton
Public Opinion Research Laboratory, University of North Florida

Susan K. Sell
George Washington University

Jeffrey Shantz
Kwantlen Polytechnic University

Paul Sharp
University of Minnesota, Duluth

Steve Sheppard
University of Arkansas

Kenneth A. Shepsle
Institute for Quantitative Social Science, Harvard University

David A. Shirk
University of San Diego

Gordon Shockley
School of Community Resources and Development, Arizona State University

Carisa R. Showden
University of North Carolina at Greensboro

Peter M. Siavelis
Wake Forest University

Katri Sieberg
University of Tampere

Carlos Nunes Silva
Institute of Geography and Spatial Planning, University of Lisbon

Marian Simms
Deakin University

J. P. Singh
Georgetown University

Henry B. Sirgo
McNeese State University

Richard M. Skinner
Rollins College

Jonathan Slapin
University of Houston

Brian Slocock
University of West of Scotland

Dennis Smith
Loughborough University

Martin J. Smith
University of Sheffield

Stephen Smith
University College London

T. C. Smith
Albright College

Anand E. Sokhey
Ohio State University

M. Scott Solomon
University of South Florida

Albert Somit
Southern Illinois University

Robert Speel
Penn State Erie, Behrend College

James H. Spencer
University of Hawai'i at Manoa

Clemens Spiess
Heidelberg University

Peter J. Spiro
Beasley School of Law, Temple University

Hendrik Spruyt
Northwestern University

Lavinia Stan
St. Francis Xavier University

Lyndsey Stanfill
Ohio State University

Koen Stapelbroek
Erasmus University Rotterdam

Jennifer A. Steen
Arizona State University, School of Government, Politics and Global Studies

Manfred B. Steger
Royal Melbourne Institute of Technology

Peter J. Steinberger
Reed College

John Steinbruner
University of Maryland

Jennifer Sterling-Folker
University of Connecticut

Garth Stevenson
Brock University

Judith Hicks Stiehm
Florida International University

Brian Stipelman
Dowling University

Daniel Stockemer
University of Ottawa

Gregory W. Streich
University of Central Missouri

Heinz Sünker
Center for International Studies in Social Policy and Social Services, Bergische Universität Wuppertal

Thomas C. Sutton
Baldwin-Wallace College

Gert Tinggaard Svendsen
Aarhus University

Donald G. Tannenbaum
Gettysburg College

Gregory Tardi
Institute of Parliamentary and Political Law

Shira Tarrant
California State University, Long Beach

Sidney Tarrow
Cornell University

Steven Tauber
University of South Florida

Rodrigo Tavares
United Nations University–Institute on Comparative Regional Integration Studies (UNU-CRIS)

Sarah Taylor
New School for Social Research

Joanne Tetlow
Comptroller of Maryland

Göran Therborn
University of Cambridge

Michael Thom
Michigan State University

Aaron Thomas
University of California, Los Angeles

Michael J. Thompson
William Paterson University

Chris Thornhill
University of Glasgow

Paul W. Thurner
Department of Political Science, University of Munich (LMU)

Martina Topić
University of Zagreb, Croatia

Cirila Toplak
University of Ljubljana, Slovenia

Pier Domenico Tortola
University of Oxford

Lee Trepanier
Saginaw Valley State University

Lily L. Tsai
Massachusetts Institute of Technology

Mark Tunick
Wilkes Honors College

Jack Turner
University of Washington

Nadia Urbinati
Columbia University

Jennifer (van Heerde) Hudson
University College London

Abigaile Marguerite VanHorn
Purdue University

Tatiana Vashchilko
University of Rochester

Francisco José Veiga
Universidade do Minho (Portugal)

Peter Vermeersch
University of Leuven

Matías Vernengo
University of Utah

Steven Vertovec
Max-Planck-Institute for the Study of Religious and Ethnic Diversity

John R. Vile
Middle Tennessee State University

Barbara Vis
VU University Amsterdam

Wim J. M. Voermans
Leiden University, the Netherlands

John von Heyking
University of Lethbridge

Matthew Voorhees
Hartwick College

F. Peter Wagner
University of Wisconsin–Whitewater

Amentahru Wahlrab
University of Texas at Tyler

Claire Wallace
University of Aberdeen

Jennifer E. Walsh
Azusa Pacific University

Henry Kiragu Wambuii
University of Central Missouri

Lena Wängnerud
University of Gothenburg

James F. Ward
University of Massachusetts, Boston

Andrew J. Waskey
Dalton State College

Georgina Waylen
University of Sheffield

Ronald Weed
University of New Brunswick

David L. Weeks
Azusa Pacific University

Gregory Weeks
University of North Carolina at Charlotte

David L. Weiden
Indiana University–Purdue University Indianapolis

Richard R. Weiner
Rhode Island College

Howard J. Wiarda
University of Georgia

Erik Wibbels
Duke University

Wesley W. Widmaier
Centre for Governance and Public Policy/ Griffith Asia Institute, Griffith University

Nelson Wikstrom
Douglas Wilder School of Government and Public Affairs, Virginia Commonwealth University

Harold L. Wilensky
University of California, Berkeley

Brent M. Will
Temple University

Kenneth C. Williams
Michigan State University

Russell Alan Williams
Memorial University of Newfoundland

Graham K. Wilson
Boston University

Matthew S. Winters
University of Illinois

James J. Wirtz
Naval Postgraduate School

Christopher Wlezien
Temple University

Albert B. Wolf
University of California, Irvine

Kerri Woods
University of York

Kent Worcester
Marymount Manhattan College

Jeff Worsham
West Virginia University

Melike Wulfgramm
Bremen University

James S. Wunsch
Creighton University

Harald Wydra
St Catharine's College, University of Cambridge

Vineeta Yadav
University of Notre Dame

Richard M. Yon
U.S. Military Academy

Dannagal Goldthwaite Young
University of Delaware

Dana Zartner
Tulane University

Claudia Zilla
Stiftung Wissenschaft und Politik (SWP), German Institute for International and Security Affairs

Joseph F. Zimmerman
Rockefeller College, University at Albany

Roukayatou Zimmermann
Deutsches Institut für Entwicklungspolitik (DIE)

Catherine Zuckert
University of Notre Dame

Michael Zuckert
University of Notre Dame

Benjamin Zyla
University of Ottawa

PREFACE

Man is by nature a political animal.

—Aristotle

The Encyclopedia of Political Science (TEPS) is an ambitious survey of the world of politics at the beginning of the twenty-first century. TEPS, developed by the Encyclopedia Society and CQ Press with the assistance of the American Political Science Association (APSA), is an authoritative resource for political scientists and students of politics throughout the world. It assembles more than 1,500 signed articles by contributors from nearly forty countries, making it one of the largest encyclopedias on political science published to date.

Politics has many definitions, all of which are explored in this work. *Merriam-Webster's Collegiate Dictionary* offers one of the classic and broadest definitions of politics as the quest for good government. Politics is thus one of the most consequential of collective human activities and, next to religion, possibly the oldest. The search for good government has engaged humans from the time they formed groups and communities; modern political science brings an unprecedented toolbox of conceptual and empirical instruments to this search. Hence, political science is one of the world's most interdisciplinary disciplines—there is scarcely any area of human life untouched by it. Political science impinges on and is influenced by public administration, electoral processes, economics, religion, legal systems, societal ethos, education, technology, science, and a host of other related activities and disciplines. Politics is about power: who wields it, how it should be used, and the relationship between the ruler and the ruled. Because politics determines the pathways to power, it also serves as the gateway to history: what is politics today is history tomorrow.

Every discipline requires a flagship resource that professionals, teachers, and students can use. TEPS is designed to be such a foundational resource for political science. It is primarily a synchronic encyclopedia that presents the state of the art by assembling and distilling ideas. This is the function defined by the old Latin term for encyclopedias, *Notitia*. TEPS is also a diachronic encyclopedia that presents the foundations and historic evolution of political ideas, concepts, and theories. This is the function defined by the Latin term *Summa*. Political science is driven by ideas and concepts, values and theories, as well as philosophers and thinkers. Politics represents the confluence of theory and praxis. On the one hand, ideologies form the bedrock of political science. But politics also exists

as an empirical science, especially in the arena of government and elections. TEPS devotes a considerable number of entries both to the nomothetic, or abstract, side of political science and to the empirical side.

The appearance of TEPS at the beginning of the twenty-first century is significant because the end of the twentieth century brought enormous challenges to politics. Quantitatively, the universe of political science has expanded. The global electorate—the number of voters eligible to vote in free elections—is now 3.8 billion, compared to just 87 million at the beginning of the twentieth century. This means that more people have become stakeholders in the political process throughout the world. There are 193 sovereign nations in the world, compared to 35 at the beginning of the twentieth century, and more of them are democratic than ever before. There are 1.7 million political officeholders and elected officials in the world. The number of universities with political science departments has decupled and so has the number of political science scholars and political science media and associations.

The qualitative changes have been equally impressive. The world of politics is continually buffeted by remarkable events and transformed in unlikely ways. The sovereignty of the nation-state has been eroded by endogenous and exogenous forces, including the growing globalization of a borderless world from without and centrifugal ethnic, nationalist, religious, and linguistic forces from within. The very lexicon of politics has changed, and the sources of collective identity have been recast. New concerns and issues such as the environment have challenged the primacy of such older concerns as economic inequality. Solidarities animated by gender, race, ethnicity, religion, and language have challenged the old dichotomies based on the traditional Left/Right polarities. The Internet has transformed political communications and is competing with the ballot box as an agent of political change. *Vox Populi* has become *Twitter Populi*.

TEPS is not merely concerned with change. Although change forces us to view the world as a moving target, there are enduring themes in politics that remain as urgent in the twenty-first century as they did in Athens in the second century B.C. The institutional and constitutional bases of politics and the loci, exercise, and legitimacy of power confront political scientists as much today as they did in Aristotle's time. Political corruption and cronyism are as rampant today as they were in ancient Rome. Politics is about power, and Lord Acton's dictum that power corrupts, absolute power corrupts absolutely, holds true today. Other enduring themes include the rule of law, modernization, demography, revolution, reform and restoration, tradition, convergence, value systems, lifestyles, class and ethnic conflicts, religious conflicts, the homogenization of cultures, and the preservation of diversity. These colliding political ideas and movements have blurred the traditional tidy boundaries of political science and in some cases have caused them to disappear altogether. Political science, like politics itself, has become borderless. Political science now represents the union of law, economics, anthropology, media studies, women's studies, sociology, law, history, theology, international relations, statistics, technology, and philosophy. Political scientists import ideas from other disciplines and, in turn, export ideas to them, but, on balance, political science is a net importer of ideas. On an ideological level, the traditional and convenient binary divisions (Left/Right, North/South, domestic/international) that once constrained innovative scholarship have disappeared or no longer hold as much currency. TEPS thus maps the enlarged terrain of political science as we move into the twenty-first century.

There are large areas of political life and culture not covered or explained by political theory. These include the imponderable and unpredictable dilemmas, the problems and paradoxes, that make the study of politics a formidable undertaking. It is the task of political scientists in the twenty-first century to deal with these problems. Among them are:

Problem 1. Why does it appear that injustice persists even under the best legal systems and in the best governed nations and under the best constitutions? Do the foibles and frailties of human nature—including corruption, scandals, and blunders—make the quality of any political system no better than the quality of its politicians?

Problem 2. From whence comes the force of the status quo and inertia in political evolution, the almost pathological resistance to change in human nature?

Problem 3. Is it power alone that corrupts, or does powerlessness corrupt just as much?

Problem 4. Why does politics, like religion, seem to be a source of disunity as much or even more than of unity, and why are divisions in democracies perhaps even more prevalent than under other political systems?

Problem 6. Do the Eurocentric assumptions of political science about political beliefs and behavior, such as theories about sovereignty, nationalism, and political ethics, have relevance in the Third World, or do they actually contribute to failed and rogue states like Somalia in Africa and Afghanistan in the Middle East?

Problem 7. Why do class and ethnic groups radically diverge on their political ideologies and philosophical stances despite sharing a common political system? As Gilbert and Sullivan famously said, "Why are some men born Tory and others born Whig?"

Problem 8. How are conventional notions of civil rights, citizenship, and nationality scrambled and reassembled in the presence of large groups of undocumented immigrants in industrialized countries?

As in all social sciences, there are no absolutes in political science. Every political system, every form of government, and every method of determining the popular will ever devised by man is flawed—some more than others. In Plato's philosophy, all forms of government are only shadows of the ultimate ideal government in the unseen realm. The task of the political scientist is to bridge the gap between the shadows and the ideal.

Political science is not merely an academic discipline, and political scientists do not just study the anatomy of politics. Political science is renewed with every political administration and with every major political event and with every political leader. Influential political leaders construct their own -isms (Fidelism/Castroism, Maoism, Gandhism, Reaganism, and so on) so that the political philosophies and ideologies that undergird the discipline have to be reinvented constantly. Further, political science is arguably so important in the scheme of human knowledge because of its normative function. As problems emerge in the body politic, political science suggests remedies, probes into causes, and provides solutions. TEPS is designed to frame the issues, problems, and challenges and to provoke a polygonal effort to suggest solutions.

ARCHITECTURE

The value of an encyclopedia resides not merely in its contents but in what the French call *ordonnance*—the selection, classification, and arrangement of entries and the placement of navigational aids. TEPS is a strict A–Z encyclopedia that follows the principles of alphabetization in the *Chicago Manual of Style*. Each entry of more than five hundred words carries a bibliography that includes journal articles. Most entries carry cross references to related entries. Readers are also advised to consult the Thematic Table of Contents that appears in the frontmatter. This is a map of the entries in the book organized by subject matter or subfield. Within each theme, there are six classes of entries, each weighted and assigned a length based on its importance.

Class 1, Core Articles: These are wide-ranging articles that define a field or major analytic concerns and include commentary, discussion, interpretation, and comprehensive reviews of literature. They are designed as *tours d'horizon* to lay the groundwork for all other entries.

Class 2, Long Interpretive Essays: These delve substantively into key issues, concepts, ideas, and theories or develop a particular argument or thesis.

Class 3, Short Descriptive Essays: These deal with the less theoretical and programmatic aspects of the discipline but have no commentary.

Class 4, Breakout Articles: These are derivatives from core articles that examine and explore particular aspects of a topic.

Class 5, Lexical Entries: These are designed to provide useful definitions of unusual terms and concepts.

Class 6, Biographies: No biographies of living persons (with a few exceptions) are included in this category, but the nearly three hundred biographies cover the seminal thinkers and figures in the formation of political science as it is today and will be in the coming century.

APSA ASSISTANCE

TEPS was produced and published with the assistance of the American Political Science Association (APSA), the world's largest professional organization for the study of politics and political science. It is a privilege the editorial board and publisher have taken seriously, and we have tried to meet the high standards of scholarship that such a collaboration demands. The APSA nominated the five members of the editorial board, and APSA's membership formed the principal source for contributors.

When I approached Michael Brintall, executive director of APSA, with the idea of producing the first major political science encyclopedia of the twenty-first century, he warmly embraced the vision and offered the full support of the organization. But for his positive response and unwavering commitment, TEPS would never have become a reality.

EDITORIAL ORGANIZATION

Three elements determine the strength and quality of an encyclopedia. The first is the credentials of the contributors—any encyclopedia is only as good as its contributors. We assembled one of the finest teams of political science scholars, based on the recommendations of the editorial board. The contributors were drawn from a host of disciplines in the social sciences and humanities as well as political science. All were chosen for the originality and importance of their contributions. They were also chosen from more than forty countries to ensure that the breadth and range of interpretations match the needs of a global information age. The selection of articles and the mix of authors represent an attempt to strike a balance among various schools of thought, regions of the world, gender identities, and ideological emphases.

The second element of strength in an encyclopedia is the editorial board. We had three levels in place. The principal, or working, editorial board consisted of five members nominated by the APSA: James E. Alt, Simone Chambers, Geoffrey Garrett, Margaret Levi, and Paula D. McClain. Core articles in TEPS bear the impress of their careful review and input. To bring such a vast work to completion, even more help was needed, and we are most grateful for all the work of the content editors who reviewed long and short essay entries. We also thank the larger seventy-two–member board of editorial consultants and advisers and the international board of editorial advisers, which was drawn from political science associations from around the world to assist the editor in chief in choosing contributors from outside the United States. Together, these boards shepherded the project and enlisted the best possible contributions from universities and associations across the globe. The full list of members of these three boards appears in the preceding pages.

The last element of strength is the publisher. CQ Press has remained for many decades the premier political science publisher in the United States, and its imprint guarantees the integrity of a work. Over the four years TEPS was in the making, I had the privilege of working with a number of veteran publishers and editors at CQ Press, including John Jenkins, the president; Andrea Pedolsky, editorial director; and Doug Goldenberg-Hart, acquisitions editor. Doug is an experienced reference book editor, and his editorial skills and dedication kept the project on track during its extended gestation. The development editing team was led initially by January Layman-Wood; followed by Nancy Matuszak, who helped to bring the project successfully to its home stretch; Andrea Cunningham; and John Martino. Finally, at the Encyclopedia Society, managing editor Sarah Claudine Day worked on the project from beginning to end.

Our collective mission for TEPS was not merely to create an encyclopedia that is original, accurate, and comprehensive but also one that conveys through its 1,500 entries some of the vitality and excitement of the world of political science and politics and offers vibrant cutting-edge interpretations and insights.

We welcome and earnestly solicit feedback in the form of comments, suggestions, and corrections for future editions. Please address them to me (gtkurian@aol.com) or to the publisher (iencypolisci@cqpress.com).

GEORGE THOMAS KURIAN
Editor in Chief
August 2010

INTRODUCTION
～

The *Encyclopedia of Political Science* offers scholars and students easy access to the essential concepts in political science in the early twenty-first century. Organized by traditional subfields, such as political theory, comparative politics, international relations, and public policy, it also incorporates those fields that have emerged more recently, for example, race and ethnicity, gender studies, and political economy. In addition, the content reflects the blurring of boundaries increasingly prevalent in political science—whether this occurs in association with cultural studies, neurology, history, or economics. Biographical entries provide a sense of the history of the discipline, and methodological entries suggest the variety of approaches—sometimes used singly and sometimes in combination—available for studying politics. There is material that gives background on countries, theorists, and theories, and there are entries on terms that everyone should know and entries on terms only specialists require.

Diversity in practice characterizes political scientists in their research and teaching, and the editors of this text have tried to respect and illuminate this pluralism. We endeavored to be sensitive to controversies and disagreements over methods, approaches, and models of the world while providing access to what has become an increasingly specialized subject. We also paid attention throughout to enduring questions and topics, such as war and peace, democratization, political development, and ethnic conflict—topics that cut across the subfields of the discipline—while making room to cover some novel initiatives at the cutting edge of research in the field. We recognize that at any time such an encyclopedia as this is necessarily a snapshot, but we have tried to reflect the ways in which political science, like other fields of inquiry, is constantly evolving in reaction both to debates among scholars and to developments in the real world of politics.

DEVELOPMENT OF POLITICAL SCIENCE AND ITS CLASSICAL FIELDS

The introduction to *The Encyclopedia of Political Science* should contain a short history of the development of the discipline of political science. Yet one is not easy to construct, given the various views on what the discipline is. According to Farr (1988), if one understands political science as the "more-or-less empirical study of practical politics," then Aristotle is the beginning. If perceived as the study of *realpolitik*, then Machiavelli gets the nod. If focused on the character of the modern state,

then Hobbes is central. If one considers the study of politics a science, then Hume and others in the Scottish Enlightenment might be considered its "founders." Finally, if one thinks of it as an academic discipline with a school devoted to the study of politics, then John W. Burgess should be considered the founder of American political science, and "everything before the School of Political Science founded at Columbia University in 1880 will be 'pre-history'" (Farr 1988: 1178).

Ira Katznelson and Helen Milner (2002: 6) suggest that the many narratives of the development of the discipline "often overlook deep continuities that have made up political science during its first century as an organized discipline." They reiterate the familiar retelling of the history of political science—"[a]n early legal-formal constitutionally oriented discipline was supplanted by a more scientific, behavioral impulse" (p. 7). Later, behavioralism was replaced by a post-behavioral stage with multiple methods but with a view toward unification of the discipline through a method-specific research program. They argue that even these approaches to the history of the discipline "are both too simple and too complex." The simplicity results "from the tendency to overstate the internal consistency of a given period within and across subfields," while the complexity results "because their periodization tends to miss the manner in which American political science has been continuous across epochs" (p. 7). These historical narratives identify the study of the state with the first epoch, the study of power with the middle epoch, and the study of choice with the latest epoch (p. 7). This characterization of the growth of the discipline of political science nicely captures Anglo-Saxon approaches, particularly in the United States and Great Britain, but many of the themes and issues tend to occur, if in somewhat different forms and languages, throughout the world.

This particular orientation to the history of political science, based on the study of concepts, differs from that of Charles Merriam in his 1925 book, *New Aspects of Politics,* which viewed the development of the discipline through the lens of analytical methods. Merriam divided the development of political science into four periods—the a priori and deductive method (1850 and earlier); historical and comparative method (1850–1900); observation, survey, and measurement (1900–); and the beginnings of the psychological treatment of politics in the 1920s (Merriam 1925 as quoted in Farr 1988: 79).[1]

Merriam's construction of the discipline of political science prompted a response some years later from Bernard Crick. In *The American Science of Politics* (1959), Crick articulated the perspective of many British political scientists. He believed that American political science was trading in a false scientism "that seeks universally applicable general theories, a scientism that arguably masks its actual role as an American ideology" (Adcock and Bevir 2005). He argued that the increasing focus on scientism by American political scientists came at the expense of older modes of thought, for example, history and philosophy.

What this brief discussion suggests is the difficulty of providing a definitive history of the development of the discipline given the wide variety of perspectives about what political science is and should do. One attempt to create an overview is found in this encyclopedia's article, "Political Science, History of," by John G. Gunnell, who uses a democratic narrative as the overarching theme. Other approaches are equally plausible.

Yet despite the lack of consensus on the development of the discipline, some consensus can be reached on the classic subfields that developed over time, as reflected in the subfields offered by most political science departments (Kaufman-Osborn 2006). These classic subfields are:

1. **The politics of a country or region.** Whether this is British, French, Latin American, Chinese, or American depends on the location of relevant universities and practitioners. Each has its own distinctive history. We shall use as an example **American politics**, which incorporates the study of political behavior, public opinion, elections, electoral structure, institutions, political parties, and different levels of government—national, state, local, urban—in the United States. The subfield embraces writings from the founding and early development of the United States—The Federalist Papers (and some of the Anti-Federalist papers) and John Adams, Thomas Paine, and Alexis de Tocqueville, among others. Classic early academic texts include Woodrow Wilson's *Congressional Government: A Study in American Politics* (1885), James Bryce's *The American Commonwealth* (1888), and Arthur Bentley's *The Process of Government* (1908).

2. **Comparative politics** began as a field that encompassed two things: "area" studies of countries and regions other than one's own and comparisons of governmental institutions, including legislatures, electoral systems, and prime ministers versus presidents, among countries. Currently, the subfield focuses not only on the politics of countries around the globe but also on concepts and how they apply across countries, for example, democratization and tolerance, among others. The institutional and ideological foundations of the modern national state are central concerns of comparative politics (Boix and Stokes 2007). While Aristotle studied the development of constitutions and John Andrews published *A Comparative View of the French and English Nations, in Their Manners, Politics and Literature* in 1785, "modern" books incorporating "comparative politics" into their titles probably date from 1961 with the publication of *Comparative Politics: Notes and Readings* by Bernard E. Brown and Roy C. Macridis.

3. **International relations** is the study of relations among nation-states (countries) and the organization of the international system via public, private, and nongovernmental institutions. The field originated in the early twentieth century as the United States expanded its influence around the world, but its intellectual origins date back far earlier to Thucydides and Clausewitz. Contemporary academic scholarship begins with such works as Alfred Zimmern's *The Study of International Relations* (1931) and Harold D. Lasswell's *World Politics and Personal Insecurity* (1935).

4. **Political theory** is an interdisciplinary endeavor of theoretical inquiry and philosophical reflection on political interactions among humans whose center of gravity is at the humanities end of the discipline of political science. Political theory includes classical political philosophy and such contemporary theoretical concerns as postmodernism, critical theory, and constructivism. Until the mid-1970s political theory, as practiced within political science, was dominated by the exegetical study of classical texts in the history of Western political thought. Since the publication of John Rawl's *A Theory of Justice* (1971), however, political theory has increasingly turned to normative theory and ethical and moral concerns about politics. This move has seen issues of justice and equity, democracy, liberalism, secular and religious ways of life, identity and difference, and the good life take center stage. Classical texts, such as Plato's *Republic,* Hobbes's *Leviathan,* and John Stuart Mill's *On Liberty,* still make up the canon of political theory, and every specialist still needs to be conversant with this history, but contemporary research focuses heavily on moral and normative questions facing modern political communities. Will Kymlicka's *Contemporary Political Philosophy: An Introduction* (2002) is widely regarded as the best overall statement of the state of the field today.

5. **Public administration** (and, later, **public policy**), whose early boundaries were defined by Woodrow Wilson's famous 1887 essay, "The Study of Administration," studies the role of bureaucracy in society and the role of administrators in bureaucracies. Whereas Wilson, according to Donald Kettl (1993), is generally considered the father of the *study* of administration, Alexander Hamilton is identified as the person responsible for the *practice* of American public administration. From its roots in the reform and scientific management movements, the Institute of Public Administration (later to become Syracuse University's Maxwell School) introduced formal training in public administration. Over time, the subfield of public policy—with its emphasis on the interactions that produce outcomes rather than on the bureaucratic process per se—developed from its foundations in public administration. Public administration began as a subfield of political science, but in recent years, it and public policy are often housed in separate schools focused more on the practice of government than the study of politics.

6. Public law and judicial politics consist of a number of areas of study with a mix of methodological approaches. Public law and constitutional law are associated with the study of the courts, beginning with the U.S. Supreme Court. Martin Shapiro (1993: 363) indicates that until the 1950s, "public law" was thought to contain three distinct entities—constitutional law, administrative law, and international law—linked, respectively, to American politics, public administration, and international relations. Classic constitutional texts include *John Marshall and the Constitution: A Chronicle of the Supreme Court* (1919) and *The Constitution and What It Means Today* (1920), both by Edwin S. Corwin. Behaviorism ushered in the study of judicial behavior/judicial politics, and the focus shifted away from the decisions made by the courts to the process and behavior of the judges and justices making those decisions.

Changes in the nature of politics and the dynamism of political science have led to the development of additional subfields, including race, ethnicity, and politics; gender and politics; and lesbian, gay, bisexual, and transgendered politics. These subfields are now quite robust, with intellectually stimulating research, and the concerns raised by scholars in these areas are increasingly incorporated into the more traditional subfields.

There has also been increasing attention paid to the subfield of methods, with a focus on how to study politics rather than on what to study. In addition, political economy, political psychology, and other subfields that emphasize cross-disciplinary approaches have become permanent features of many modern political science departments.

All of these developments, both the most recent and the longest past, reflect the evolution of the discipline to better respond to the enduring questions of politics, resolve the dissensus over how best to answer these questions, explore new frontiers in the study of politics, and reflect on real and pressing political and governmental issues of the day.

ENDURING QUESTIONS

Although political science as a modern discipline did not emerge until the second half of the nineteenth century, the study of politics is often thought to have started in ancient Greece and especially in Athens during the tumultuous years spanning the transition from Athenian city-state democracy to Alexander the Great's global empire. The grand themes of war and peace, dictatorship and democracy, wealth and poverty, and interests and values were taken up by such thinkers as Thucydides, Plato, and Aristotle and studied in their own right, which is to say independent of cosmology, religion, and mysticism. Many of the questions and themes that engaged these ancient thinkers still occupy the contemporary agenda. This is not because no progress has been made since the ancient Greeks or because there is no cumulative knowledge in the social sciences. Far from it. A great deal more is known today than was known by the ancient Greeks both at the individual level of the citizen and the aggregate level of states. The enduring questions are enduring not because there are

not good answers to them; often there are. They are enduring because each and every political community has to confront and deal with them anew.

WAR AND PEACE

War is a constant in human history. Yet the questions that everyone wants answered are: Why do states go to war, and how do we achieve peace? The answers depend on the findings to related questions, chief among them how to understand and explain relations among states. As Carl von Clausewitz famously stated, war is a continuation of international politics by other, violent means.

Why do states act the way they do? Is the international system anarchic, and, if it is, is the anarchy governed by strategic logic? Or are there rules, written and unwritten, that work to effectively regulate the international sphere? The nature of the international order still poses the same enduring questions that puzzled Thucydides (why did the Peloponnesians go to war?), but an ever-changing set of circumstances poses new challenges to every generation of scholars attempting to solve the puzzle of war.

Chief among these different circumstances are the development of human rights and globalization. Human rights and their defense, codification, proliferation, and enforcement, as well as globalization of communication, markets, and politics, raise perennial issues concerning the relation of the macro and micro in human relations, interaction, and regulation. War and peace not only direct our gaze to the many questions concerning international relations but also to questions about inward-looking versus outward-looking state policy. In political science, whether to spend money and effort internationally or domestically is often referenced in shorthand as "guns or butter?" Why and under what circumstances do states invest in defense and security rather than welfare, infrastructure, and job training? To put it another way: What role and effect do security questions have on political decisions and domestic policy? How do national and international spheres interact on political grounds?

For a list of articles related to these topics, the reader should see the following Thematic Table of Contents headings: **Foreign Policy; Globalization and Politics; International Security and Arms Control**; and **War, Peace, and Terrorism.**

DICTATORSHIP AND DEMOCRACY

Plato and Aristotle were very interested in regime types and regime change. It would be an understatement to say that the choice of form of government has been central and still is central to political science. Classifying regimes and explaining how and why regimes crumble, are overthrown, explode into civil strife, stabilize, reform, stagnate, and evolve are core activities of modern political science. This is a rich and diverse area framed by an implicit (sometimes explicit) normative dichotomy between dictatorship as something to be avoided and democracy as something to be admired. Modern political science is a global phenomenon that thrives in democracies, and so it is unsurprising that this regime type has a special place within the study of politics. Indeed, all of American politics as a subfield could in some sense be understood as the study of democracy.

From micro-level questions about why people vote the way they do to macro questions of why democracies do not seem to wage wars against each other, the role of the citizen in democracy is key. Voting and political participation are the most obvious arenas in which to study why and when democratic citizens act and with what consequences. However, these only touch the tip of questions, puzzles, and issues opened up by the question "What is a citizen?"

But as much as political science has been enthralled with democracy, it has also been fascinated by how democratization occurs and how democracies endure or break down. The question of regime transition moves beyond the citizen to the forces within which citizens move and which in turn move citizens—power, authority, legitimacy, and law are core political concepts without which the political world could not begin to be explained. They are also contested concepts, with scholars disagreeing about what they mean. More important, scholars disagree about how these forces work and behave in the empirical world. This disagreement has been hugely productive in political science, powering creative empirical research as well as theoretical insight.

For a list of articles related to these topics, the reader should see the following Thematic Table of Contents headings: **Comparative Politics; Democracy and Democratization; Nation and State**; and **Representation and Electoral Systems.**

WEALTH AND POVERTY

Aristotle noted that the most stable regimes almost always have a large middle class and hence a relatively egalitarian distribution of income and wealth. Since his time we have been trying to figure out in regard to both output and input how and in what ways economic questions connect to political ones. On the output side we ask about the impact of economic policy and, especially, the large role played by redistributive policies on the life and structure of the political community. All governments across the spectrum redistribute to some degree, but some redistribute to the rich and some to the poor. The forms and variation are enormous. Can we account for this variation? On the input side we want to know how different economic regimes and existing distributions of wealth affect, shape, and, indeed, determine politics. Harold Lasswell went so far as to argue that politics is the study of who gets what, when, and why—the causes and consequences of political decisions over the distribution of economic output.

While the distribution of economic output is an enduring theme in political science, gender, race, culture, ethnicity, and religion increasingly have also become significant categories in the analysis of social stratification and political choices over them. How interest and belief both shape and are shaped by politics and were always the subject of political study, as well as the attention to additional modes of stratification, raises new questions about the sources and effects of interests and beliefs.

For a list of articles related to these topics, the reader should see the following Thematic Table of Contents headings: **Gender and Politics; Political Economy; Politics and Society;** and **Politics of Oppression; Race, Ethnicity, and Politics**.

INTERESTS AND VALUES

Both output and input questions can be framed by general theoretical paradigms that place economic interest more or less at the center of analysis. The classic example of a configured economic interest lies in class analysis, and one alternative is contemporary rational choice, which emphasizes the individual as the key actor. Political science has thrived and developed in states that value freedom and equality as well as democracy. How such values are instantiated through politics is a common theme in modern political science. While specific interests are not necessarily opposed to certain values, how they interact and the weight we ought to give each in our explanations are perennial themes of political science.

For a list of articles related to these topics, the reader should see the following Thematic Table of Contents headings: **Ethics and Political Corruption; Ideologies; Interest Groups and Lobbies; Political Behavior;** and **Political Concepts**.

CONSENSUS AND DISSENSUS

While almost all political scientists believe that what they study should have consequences for understanding and possibly improving the world in which we live, there is nonetheless sharp disagreement about how to best promote such understanding. For some political science is a means to comment on contemporary events, but for most it provides a means for analyzing the enduring questions already discussed and the concepts implicated by those questions, for example, power, influence, conflict, and institutional design. The contestation over concepts and the disagreement over what kinds of interests—class, individual, or group identity—motivate action and how those interests interact with values have already been noted. Decisions in regard to concepts, interests, and values inform the kind of analysis used for the problem under investigation.

Probably one of the greatest and most long-lasting divides is among those who believe that analysis necessarily requires statistical methods and formal (that is, mathematical) theories and those who emphasize context, sensitivity, and nuance through fieldwork, archives, and the texts of great political thinkers. Increasingly, many young scholars are using all of these tools. Nevertheless, the way departments are organized, heated debates over appropriate qualifications to receive a doctorate, and the controversies that raged in the heyday of the "Perestroika" movement among political scientists (following the new openness of Gorbachev's Soviet Union)[2] all suggest a continuing qualitative/quantitative divide.

Beyond methodological disputes are enduring differences over substantive questions. Political science still can boast relatively few, if any, "laws of politics," which is understandable given that politics involves human interactions with its multiplicity of actors, strategies, and issues. Barriers to agreement are created by the lack of appropriate data for arbitrating contradictory claims. For example, there is consensus that power is a key concept for political science, but still no one is clear about just what it is or how to study it. The "community power" debate that raged in the 1960s and 1970s still lacks resolution.[3] "Non–decision making," hegemony, and other—so far—nonobservable influences on what people believe it is possible to do make it difficult to empirically refute (if one is so inclined) Robert Dahl's pluralistic conception of power distribution. Yet, as noted below, there is beginning to be progress on the sources of preferences and beliefs, the key to understanding who has power and how power relations are maintained.

By limiting the focus to certain tractable aspects of power, such as minimum winning coalitions and agenda control in legislatures, there has been considerably more success in understanding who has power in given contexts and circumstances under particular sets of rules. Yet, while there are certainly findings in these domains, detractors object to the narrowing of the question and to the overreliance on technique. Increasing the science at the expense of the politics—and vice versa—remains the deep challenge for the discipline—and was one even before Bernard Crick raised the issue.

Political scientists largely share a consensus over the key issues in politics. It is the conceptualization and measurement of those issues that generate debate. What does it mean for citizens to trust government or for government to be trustworthy? We know government effectiveness rests at least in part on its capacity to deliver services and to obtain legitimacy. But how do we define, let alone measure, government capacity or legitimacy? Recent research is beginning to make headway on these issues as well as further illuminate solutions to the enduring questions and puzzles of political science. In the process, new political science questions are coming to the fore.

For a list of articles related to these topics, the reader should see the following Thematic Table of Contents headings: **Comparative Politics; Federalism and Local Politics; Institutions and Checks and Balances; Political Concepts; Political Theory;** and **Qualitative/Quantitative Methods.**

POLITICAL SCIENCE AND POLITICS

Before turning to the frontiers of political science research, there is one more divide we must address. As the previous subsection mentioned, one major source of discord in political science is the tension between its scientific ambitions and its political relevance. The "scientism," the rigorous scientific ambitions of many American political scientists, remains one of its enduring features from the invariably critical perspectives of political scientists in most other countries and by more policy-oriented students of politics in the United States.

Political science was publicly criticized in the wake of the events of September 11, 2001, for being too concerned with the often esoteric debates within the discipline and for not focusing enough on generating and disseminating real-world relevant information and analysis that could better inform the public and improve policymaking. This followed a similar critique a

decade earlier following the sudden and unpredicted collapse of communism that caught most political scientists, let alone the general public, off guard. In turn, these public criticisms struck many political scientists as ironic given the common feeling in the discipline that scholars of the Middle East and the former Soviet bloc have always been too close to policy issues and too far from disciplinary concerns.

Nonetheless, the visibility and trenchant nature of post–Cold War and post-9/11 attacks on political science laid bare an important tension inside the discipline between academic rigor and policy relevance. The leaders of the discipline invariably present a motherhood-and-apple-pie public face, saying that rigor and relevance are complementary, not conflicting, goals and that the discipline supports both in equal measure. There is little denying, however, that many political scientists, and the discipline as a profession, value academic rigor over policy relevance. This is born out in what gets published in the major journals and book series, who gets the best jobs and the biggest promotions in the political science job market, and, less formally, in who is held in the highest esteem by their peers.

The problem of relevance has its roots in a larger question of scholarship: the creation of knowledge and the contexts of discovery. It is not just a problem for disciplines that seek scientific rigor. It is a problem for all scholarly disciplines that want to push the knowledge envelope. What makes political science particular in this respect is not that it seeks rigor over relevance, it is that its topic is especially practical in the Aristotelian sense. Thus, the discipline's desire to be as scientific as possible—against a backdrop in which most people in the world feel they already have some understanding of the politics around them—creates a serious tension between rigor and relevance.

Political scientists are committed to generalization over specificity in the objects of their analysis and to explaining the broadest possible range of phenomena with the fewest possible explanatory variables. Put simply, parsimonious generalization is the discipline's gold standard. An example is Barrington Moore's infamous dictum (and, before him, Aristotle): no middle class, no democracy. This approach also necessarily entails focusing on independent variables—in this case, the presence or absence of an effective middle class—more than on dependent variables—whether or not a country transitions into a stable democracy.

The contrast with a discipline such as history that embraces the idiosyncratic and the fine-grained is stark. The general public is often fascinated by the works of historians precisely because of their complexity and subtlety but frustrated by the abstractions of political science.

Consider perhaps the closest political scientists have come to a scientific law of politics—Maurice Duverger's thesis that countries with winner-take-all election systems such as the United Kingdom and the United States will have only two political parties. The theoretical reasoning behind Duverger's law is elegant. Voters know that supporting third parties that cannot win an election means wasting their votes, so rational voters would not vote for third parties even if they more closely match the voters' policy preferences than the existing two parties. Knowing this, politicians who might be tempted to form third parties do not do so, preferring to stay members of the existing parties and working to broaden their electoral appeal. In equilibrium, therefore, the United States and Great Britain should have only two major and enduring political parties—as has been the case for the preponderance of their histories as electoral democracies.

But there are some stunning exceptions to Duverger's law that have had major real-world consequences. Democrat Bill Clinton was elected U.S. president in 1992 because a third-party candidate, Ross Perot, ran and ran very well, winning almost 20 percent of the vote and taking more votes from Republican George H. W. Bush than from Clinton. This allowed Clinton to win the White House on not much more than 40 percent of the vote. In Great Britain, Margaret Thatcher won a landslide re-election in 1983 on an even lower vote share because a new party, the Liberal Democrats (LibDems), won more than a quarter of the vote and took more votes from the Labour opposition than from Thatcher's Conservatives. Both elections not only violated Duverger's law, they also violated the normal understanding of majority rule. The elections also resulted in long-lived governments that had far-reaching consequences not only for the United Kingdom and United States but also for the world. Had George H. W. Bush been re-elected in 1992 or had Thatcher been defeated in 1983, the world we live in might be quite different today.

Do these exceptions, so important in the real world, make Duverger's law much less relevant if not invalidated? Journalists and historians might well say yes. They might also then ask rhetorically: If political science cannot deliver on its scientific aspirations here on the terrain the discipline itself considers most favorable, what hope does the science of politics have in explaining more complex phenomena such as political change in nondemocracies or decisions about war or terrorism?

Many political scientists would demur, however. They would say that the 1992 American and 1983 British elections are wholly consistent with Duverger's logic, exceptions that prove the rule. Third parties cannot hope to win in first-past-the-post elections. The folly of Perot and the Liberal Democrats was exposed, and third parties receded in subsequent elections (until 2010 in Britain, with the jury still out at the time of writing as to whether the country will revert back to hewing closer to two parties in the future or change the electoral system to accommodate third parties like the LibDems).

There are two lessons to learn from this simple example. First, it is actually not a fair criticism to say that political scientists do not concentrate on phenomena of real-world relevance. In fact, the most important work in the discipline is invariably focused on questions that historians, journalists, governments, and citizens would agree are the most important to the operation of the real world—how democracy works, how political transitions work, and how countries interact with each other.

Second, political scientists do tend to value parsimonious generalization more highly than do journalists and the public. As a discipline with scientific aspirations that are frequently quite high, it is entirely appropriate that political science seek to generate lawlike generalizations. It is equally important, however, that the discipline take seriously the exception as well as the rule—either to stimulate further scientific inquiry or to focus attention on important outcomes that do not rest easily within accepted theoretical models. Put differently, political scientists are right to analyze the most important political phenomena with the highest level of rigor they can apply with a view to achieving the highest degree of generalization they can. They just need to be aware that this is not the only way to study politics.

This leads to another general comment on the rigor-relevance debate. The closer political scientists get to the real world of politics, the less important developing lawlike generalization becomes and the more the political scientists come to resemble historians focused on specific outcomes and interested in explaining them as thoroughly as possible. This is clearest in the United States, the country with the world's largest collection of professional political scientists. Here there is a clear division of labor between academic teaching and research taking place in universities and colleges and policy-relevant analysis being done in think tanks. Political scientists in policy positions (including former U.S. secretaries of state Madeleine Albright and Condoleezza Rice) have become common enough to warrant a renewed attention to their role in the discipline, harking back to the debates over the origins of the discipline itself and to the concerns of a famous political scientist who became president: Woodrow Wilson.

Specialization is less feasible in smaller countries with fewer political scientists. As a result, the boundaries between academic political science and think tank political science tend to be more blurred outside the United States than within its borders. This, among other things, helps explain why there is less commitment to the "science" of politics outside the United States than in it. British governments, for example, still tend to draw heavily on Oxbridge and the University of London for policy advice, whereas U.S. administrations rely much more heavily on think tank expertise.

For a list of articles related to these topics, the reader should see the following Thematic Table of Contents headings: **Political Change**; **Public Policy**; and **Representation and Electoral Systems**.

FRONTIERS OF POLITICAL SCIENCE RESEARCH

The rigor-relevance divide is a real one, but it is also true that some of the most politically and policy-relevant work in political science is being done as a result of recent methodological and analytical advances using new tools and data from multiple sources. Field experiments now inform the work of the World Bank and major foundations in their efforts to alleviate poverty. Game theory has long influenced security decisions, but in some of its new guises it may have useful consequences for a wider range of problems. Ethnographic, historical, and qualitative data more generally are being used to test major propositions in political science and enrich policymaking.

Solid research design requires reliance on appropriate concepts for the problem and subjection of propositions to tests that determine their validity, the scope of their generalizability, and the extent to which they can illuminate other problems and domains. Some of the most exciting contemporary political science research combines solid research design with substantively interesting questions. A casual overview of titles in recent issues of the *Annual Review of Political Science* (ARPS), which is a good source for recent developments in the study of politics, suggests that the subfield of international relations, for instance, is focused on enduring issues involving the causes and consequences of conflict and, more recently, on post-conflict reconstruction. Titles like "The Politics of Effective Foreign Aid," "Rationalist Approaches to Conflict Prevention and Resolution," "The Prosecution of Human Rights Violations," "Treaty Compliance and Violation," "Domestic Terrorism: The Hidden Side of Political Violence," and "Bargaining Failures and Civil War" make this clear.

Comparative politics emphasizes accountability, which spans a range of topics from the political economy of development and democratization to how electoral and political institutions affect the ability of voters to control politicians. Again, ARPS article titles suggest the richness of the field: "Parliamentary Control of Coalition Governments," "Representation and Accountability in Cities," "Accountability in Coalition Governments," "Political Order and One-Party Rule," "Legislative Obstructionism," "Variation in Institutional Strength," "Quality of Government: What You Get," "Democratization and Economic Globalization," "Redistricting: Reading Between the Lines," "Negative Campaigning," and "Elections Under Authoritarianism," to name a representative sample of work.

Within the field both the impacts of real-world developments like the recent rise in inequality in many nations ("Origins and Persistence of Economic Inequality," "The Politics of Inequality in America: A Political Economy Framework," and "The Institutional Origins of Inequality in Sub-Saharan Africa") can be seen, as well as the impact of newly available tools to assist in, for instance, the analysis of geography ("The Geographic Distribution of Political Preferences," "Immigration and Social Policy in the United States," and "Regionalism"). Issues of race and gender also appear frequently, as do other subjects that reflect even newer developments in the discipline.

The frontier of political science research, however, is not wholly driven by substantive concerns. Progress also reflects the interdependent development of theory, evidence, and tools. Political science as a discipline has always been self-conscious about its methods, and the frontier includes both endless diversification and new forms of reintegration of the discipline's theoretical and methodological toolkit. Three articles from a recent *Annual Review of Political Science* (volume 13, 2010) illustrate how persistent methodological divides are being overcome at the same time that new sources of data are being used. In a piece on the new political history, Julien Zelizer emphasizes what political science can learn from the

historical research on the nineteenth century or on the rise of conservatism. Evan Lieberman stresses explicit means to overcome the qualitative-quantitative divide by using historical data for purposes of testing political science theory. Lisa Wedeen, who relies on ethnographic field work, argues that "interpretive social science does not have to forswear generalizations or causal explanations" and that "ethnographic methods can be used in the service of establishing them."

Historical and ethnographic data and analysis are sweeping political science, but so are other types of information. William Butz and Barbara Toomey (2006) identify six areas of innovation in data and tools that are pushing at the frontiers of social sciences: laboratory and field experimentation, international replication, longitudinal data, improved statistical methods, and (beginning to cross disciplinary boundaries into political science) geographic information tools, and biosocial science.

For a list of articles related to these topics, the reader should see the following Thematic Table of Contents heading: **Qualitative/Quantitative Methods.**

The spread of experimental methods for examining causal effects is particularly noteworthy. Experiments are no longer just about game theory, risk and decision science, and social psychology, as Butz and Toomey put it, but now "the objects of inquiry span all the social sciences, including the origins and impacts of ethnic conflict, group and team behavior in organizations, and the nature and consequences of trust and reciprocity in interpersonal and international relations." Equally striking is the development of harmonized cross-sectional survey data, critical for distinguishing among local, regional, and universal phenomena. In political science such studies include the International Social Survey Program (ISSP) and the World Values Survey, respectively, 43- and 81-country repeated compendiums of social and political issues and values, as well as several comparative election studies and the Luxembourg Income Study, with its exceptionally fine-grained household income and spending data. At the same time it has become more common to develop longitudinal surveys, which either collect information about the same persons (observations) over many years or many times over shorter periods. Such panel studies can document the importance of accumulated life experience as well as study things like campaigns in which individual responses, treatments (like campaigning), and controls (for example, polls) interact continuously over time.

These experimental and longitudinal developments are not independent of the growth of Internet surveys, which can reach around the world to seemingly endless respondents who want to participate. Of course, this creates new problems: statisticians face the challenge of dealing with possible bias from respondent self-selection. At the same time, these developments cross subfield boundaries. For example, worldwide data increase the integration of geographic information science with, for example, international relations, in which political geography affects international conflict and cooperation, globalization, international commerce, and democratization. These are just some of the ways in which political science is, as said earlier, both specialized and interactive and growing and changing. Perhaps the online edition of this encyclopedia will increasingly have articles on the impact of biology and neuroscience, which could, as Butz and Toomey put it, "[A]lter understandings about sexual orientation, criminal responsibility, prospects for marriage as a social institution, and even the nature of moral obligation."

CONCLUSION

This short discussion of the discipline of political science—its history, its current subfields and methods, and its emerging subfields, modes of analysis, and testing procedures—reveals the wide range of questions and concerns that characterize the field. Transforming the huge number of concepts and terms into an encyclopedia is no easy task, especially given our desire to make it useful to students, specialists, and the interested policymaker, among others. By necessity, the most attention has been focused on core ideas and controversies, but, as this essay suggests, political science is ever evolving. It also is centrifugal. In an effort to become more like a science, some practitioners are on the cutting edge of research methods. In an effort to provide deeper understanding of enduring problems, some scholars merge political analysis with what can be learned from philosophy, history, anthropology, and psychology. In an effort to become relevant, some use the best tools at hand to focus on immediate political problems.

Although many of the frontier concerns of political science may seem over the horizon, this encyclopedia offers useful tools for becoming familiar with an increasingly dynamic field of political science. Its capacity to respond to change with its online edition marks it as useful well into the future.

JAMES E. ALT
SIMONE CHAMBERS
GEOFFREY GARRETT
MARGARET LEVI
PAULA D. MCCLAIN
Associate Editors

REFERENCES

Adcock, Robert, and Mark Bevir. "The History of Political Science." *Political Studies Review* 3 (2005): 1–16.

Andrews, John. *A Comparative View of the French and English Nations, in Their Manners, Politics and Literature*. London: printed for T. Longman, and G. G. J. and J. Robinson, 1785.

Bachrach, Peter, and Morton S. Baratz. "Two Faces of Power." *American Political Science Review* 56, 4 (1962): 947–952.

———. "Decisions and Nondecisions: An Analytical Framework." *American Political Science Review* 57, 3 (1963): 632–642.

Bentley, Arthur. *The Process of Government: A Study of Social Pressures*. Chicago: University of Chicago Press, 1908.

Boix, Carles, and Susan C. Stokes. "Overview of Comparative Politics." In Robert E. Goodin, ed. *The Oxford Handbook of Political Science*. Oxford, UK: Oxford University Press, 2007.

Brown, Bernard E., and Roy C. Macridis. *Comparative Politics: Notes and Readings*. New York: Macmillan, 1961.

Bryce, James. *The American Commonwealth*. London and New York: Macmillan, 1888.

Butz, William P., and Barbara Boyle Torrey. "Some Frontiers in Social Science." *Science* 312, 5782 (2006): 1898–1900.

Corwin, Edwin S. *John Marshall and the Constitution: A Chronicle of the Supreme Court*. Toronto: Glasgow, Brook, 1919.

———. *The Constitution and What It Means Today*. Princeton: Princeton University Press, 1920.

Crick, Bernard. *The American Science of Politics: Its Origins and Conditions*. Berkeley: California University Press, 1959.

Dahl, Robert A. *Who Governs? Democracy and Power in an American City*. New Haven: Yale University Press, 1961.

Deutsch, Morton, and Catarina Kinnvall. "What is Political Psychology?" In K. Monroe, ed. *Political Psychology*. Mahwah, N.J.: Erlbaum, 2002.

Dryzek, John S., Bonnie Honig, and Anne Phillips. "Overview of Political Theory." In Robert Goodin, ed. *The Oxford Handbook of Political Science*. Oxford, UK: Oxford University Press, 2007.

Farr, James. "The History of Political Science." *American Journal of Political Science* 32, 4 (November 1988): 1175–1195.

Katznelson, Ira, and Helen V. Milner, eds. *Political Science: The State of the Discipline*. Centennial Edition. New York: W. W. Norton and Company, and Washington, D.C.: American Political Science Association, 2002, 1–26.

Kaufman-Osborn, Timothy V. "Dividing the Domain of Political Science: On the Fetishm of Subfield." *Polity* 38, 1 (January 2006): 41–71.

Kettl, Donald F. "Public Administration: The State of the Field." In Ada Finifter, ed. *Political Science: The State of the Discipline II*. Washington, D.C.: American Political Science Association, 1993, 407–428.

Kymlicka, Will. *Contemporary Political Philosophy: An Introduction*. Oxford, UK: Oxford University Press, 2002.

Lasswell, Harold D. *World Politics and Personal Insecurity*. New York: McGraw-Hill, 1935.

Lieberman, Evan S. "Bridging the Qualitative-Quantitative Divide: Best Practices in the Development of Historically Oriented Replication Databases." *Annual Review of Political Science* 13 (2010): 37–59.

Lukes, Steven. *Power: A Radical View*. London: Macmillan, 1974.

Merriam, Charles E. *New Aspect of Politics*. Chicago: University of Chicago Press, 1925.

Rawls, John. *A Theory of Justice*. Cambridge: Belknap Press of Harvard University Press, 1971.

Shapiro, Martin, and Ada Finifter, eds. "Public Law and Judicial Politics." In *Political Science: The State of the Discipline II*. Washington, D.C: American Political Science Association, 1993, 363–381.

Wedeen, Lisa. "Reflections on Ethnographic Work in Political Science." *Annual Review of Political Science* 13 (2010): 255–272.

Wilson, Woodrow. *Congressional Government: A Study in American Politics*. Boston: Houghton Mifflin, 1885.

Zelizer, Julian E. "What Political Science Can Learn from the New Political History." *Annual Review of Political Science* 13 (2010): 25–36.

Zimmern, Alfred. *The Study of International Relations*. Oxford, UK: Clarendon Press, 1931.

NOTES

1. The initial interest took place in the decades between the first and second world wars, according to Deutsch and Kinnvall; for others its origins are in the 1940s. Serious psychological research did not occur until World War II, however.

2. This is the name of a movement in American political science to encourage more openness in response to what its members perceived as a hegemony of rational choice theory and a general narrowing of questions and scope in the discipline.

3. See, for example, Dahl 1961, Lukes 1974, and Bachrach and Baratz 1962, 1963.

ENTRIES: A–C

Abortion and Politics

By the early twenty-first century, abortion has come to be one of the most heated political issues in the world. In many Western nations, abortion is a divisive issue between the political left and the political right, with those on the left supporting the rights of the mother to control her reproductive life. Abortion opponents, on the other hand, label abortion as murder, often insisting that the rights of the unborn child begin at the moment of conception. An estimated fifty million abortions are performed yearly in various parts of the world, and at least twenty million of those are considered illegal. Around one-half of all abortions are performed under conditions detrimental to the mother's health, and many lead to chronic health problems, loss of fertility, and a woman's loss of life. In countries where abortion laws are the most restrictive, approximately one-fourth of all pregnancies are illegally terminated.

HISTORY

Until the turn of the nineteenth century, abortion before quickening—the point at which the mother feels the baby move—was generally legal in the United States and Europe. Quickening was generally believed to occur around the twelfth week of pregnancy. The use of quickening as the point of viability could be traced back to the ancient Greeks and Romans. Historically, some abortions were performed with the assistance of friends, family members, midwives, doctors, or apothecaries. Self-induced abortions, which had a low success rate, were attempted through a variety of methods that included applications of herbs and ointments to the skin, vigorous internal or external massage, insertion of foreign objects, stomach binding, running, lifting, leaping, excessive exercise, starving, bleeding, blistering, hot and cold baths, emotional distress, fretting, excessive laughing, purging, and vomiting. If all other methods failed, women sometimes resorted to infanticide.

By the mid-nineteenth century, the male-dominated medical profession had co-opted the birthing process. In the United States, the American Medical Association, founded in 1847, led the campaign to make abortion illegal. The move sent desperate women underground, and the number of self-induced and "back alley" abortions increased. Over time, outlawing abortion evolved into outlawing all methods of birth control.

The issue of abortion returned to the front burner in the mid-twentieth century when scores of babies with massive deformities were born to mothers who had contracted German measles or taken the tranquilizer drug thalidomide. Consequently, many countries passed laws legalizing abortions. In 1994, the United Nations Conference on Population and Development signaled a global shift toward improving the quality of life for women and produced new policies on family planning and abortion around the world.

THE UNITED STATES

Birth control was outlawed in a number of states until the 1960s, when the second wave of the feminist movement swelled in response to the publication of Betty Friedan's *The Feminine Mystique* in 1963, and the U.S. Supreme Court held in *Griswold v. Connecticut,* 381 U.S. 479 (1965), that a constitutional right to privacy guaranteed married couples access to birth control. This right was extended to single couples in *Eisenstadt v. Baird,* 405 U.S. 438 (1972). Building on the right to privacy, *Roe v. Wade,* 410 U.S. 113 (1973), confirmed the right to privacy. In *Roe,* Justice Harry Blackmun developed the trimester method of determining a timetable for legal abortions based on the development of the fetus. Abortions were generally legal in the first trimester but restricted in the second and third trimesters.

The rise of conservatism in the 1980s added heat to the abortion debate. Under presidents Ronald Reagan and George H. W. Bush, views on abortion became a litmus test for appointment to the Supreme Court. Congress began attaching abortion riders to unrelated bills and regularly renewed the Hyde Amendment of 1976, which banned Medicaid-financed abortions. This antiabortion stance had grave consequences for women in developing nations because Congress appropriated foreign aid with restrictions that limited access to family planning as well as to abortion. After a respite from abortion restrictions in foreign aid under Bill Clinton, George W. Bush renewed them in 2001. Although the Supreme Court has continued to narrowly uphold *Roe v. Wade,* states were given authority to limit access to abortion in *Webster v. Reproductive Health Services,* 492 U.S. 490 (1989), and *Planned Parenthood of Southeastern Pennsylvania v. Casey,* 505 U.S. 833 (1992).

One of the most controversial aspects of the abortion battle has been the conflict between abortionist opponents, who claim that the right to protest outside abortion clinics is guaranteed by the First Amendment, and prochoice advocates, who object to practices that limit entry to family planning and abortion clinics. After an increase in violence and the murder of two abortion-providing physicians, the Supreme Court held in *NOW v. Scheidler,* 510 U.S. 249 (1994), that states could pass laws designed to deter violence with increased fines and punishment. As a result of violence and ongoing controversy, 87 percent of all counties in the United States have been left without abortion services. The appointment of John Roberts as chief justice of the Supreme Court in 2005 raised conservative hopes that *Roe v. Wade* would eventually be overturned.

ASIA

In countries such as China and India, abortion is viewed as an acceptable means of controlling exploding populations. Both countries have liberal abortion policies, and women are more likely to abort female fetuses. Most Chinese women are restricted by the government's one-child policy. As of 2005, the male to female birth ratio in China was 120 boys for every 100 girls, equating to an estimated thirty-two million more boy than girls. India's birth ratio as of 2001 was 108 boys for every 100 girls. In Asian cultures, males are traditionally perceived as more valuable because they are honor bound to take care of aging parents. Such traditional thinking lingers despite modern lifestyle changes.

Abortions are performed less often in developing countries than in developed countries because high infant mortality rates and a need for cheap labor in the agricultural sector result in high fertility rates. In East Timor, for example, the poorest country in the world, with a per capita income of only US$400, the infant mortality rate is 45.89 children per one thousand live births and the fertility rate is 7.8 children per woman. In comparison, the infant mortality rate in the United Kingdom is 4.85 per one thousand live births and the fertility rate is 1.9 births per woman. In Japan, the infant mortality rate is 2.79 children per one thousand live births, with a fertility rate of 1.34 per woman.

EUROPE

In the transition countries of eastern Europe, former Soviet bloc nations are struggling economically as they attempt to reinvent themselves. Abortion on demand was prevalent under socialism because it was believed to increase the productivity of women. However, some restrictions have now been instituted, in part because of the influence of the Catholic Church. In Poland, for instance, the church was successful in overturning liberal abortion laws and removing sex education from classrooms in 1993. Three years later sex education was reintroduced, and some restrictions on abortion were removed.

Antiabortion forces within the church have been most successful in Ireland, where all abortions are illegal. Conversely, in France, where more than 80 percent of the population is Catholic, abortion rights have been guaranteed since 1974. Elsewhere in Europe, abortions are legal up to the twelfth week of pregnancy in Austria, Belgium, Bulgaria, the Czech Republic, Denmark, Germany, the Netherlands, Norway, Slovakia, Sweden, and Russia. Limited access to abortion is available in Britain, Finland, Hungary, Portugal, Spain, and Switzerland.

AFRICA AND THE MIDDLE EAST

While Cape Verde, South Africa, and Tunisia allow unrestricted abortions, most other African nations retain restrictive and old colonial laws, as well as ineffective family planning, both of which contribute to high numbers of abortions. According to the World Health Organization, an estimated 4.2 million African women seek unsafe abortions each year, with thirty thousand maternal deaths resulting.

African women suffer disproportionately from unsafe abortion practices. While 10 percent of the world's abortions occur in Africa each year, its women comprise half of the resultant deaths. In countries where abortion is legal, maternal death rates are much smaller. For instance, South Africa's number of deaths due to unsafe abortions fell by 90 percent from 1984 to 2001, after that country legalized abortion.

Eighty percent of the countries in North Africa and the Middle East outlaw abortion in some fashion: 21 percent prohibit abortion under all circumstances, 55 percent prohibit abortion except to save the woman's life, and 24 percent allow abortion to preserve the woman's physical or mental health. The restrictive laws and, in many cases, lack of effective family planning programs contribute to the number of unsafe abortions and related deaths in this region.

In 1992, the Syrian Family Planning Association and International Planned Parenthood Federation's Arab World Regional Office hosted a regional conference on unsafe abortion and sexual health. The attendees agreed that unsafe abortion was a major public health problem throughout the region. They determined the need to review policies and provide better family planning.

Lack of effective family planning services, including the availability of contraception, contributes to higher rates of abortion. For instance, abortions in Turkey decreased as the availability of family planning programs increased. Similarly, Tunisia legalized abortion for all women in 1973. Since then, the number of unsafe abortions has drastically decreased, as have the number of maternal deaths. For every one thousand women of reproductive age in 1990, eleven received abortions. By 2003, this number had dropped to seven out of every one thousand women of reproductive years.

See also *Health Care Policy; Law and Society; Multiple Streams Theory; Privacy Rights; Social Policy.*

. . . . ELIZABETH RHOLETTER PURDY

BIBLIOGRAPHY

Dabash, Rasha, and Farzaneh Roudi-Fahimi. "Abortion in the Middle East and North Africa." Washington, D.C.: Population Reference Bureau, 2008. www.prb.org/pdf08/MENAabortion.pdf.

Guilmoto, Christophe Z. *Characteristics of Sex-Ratio Imbalance in India, and Future Scenarios.* Report presented at the 4th Asia Pacific Conference on Reproductive and Sexual Health and Rights, Hyderabad, India, October 2007.

Knudsen, Lara M. *Reproductive Rights in a Global Context.* Nashville, Tenn: Vanderbilt University Press, 2006.

Neft, Naomi, and Ann D. Levine. *Where Women Stand: An International Report on the Status of Women in 140 Countries, 1997–1998.* New York: Random House, 1997.

Reagan, Leslie J. *When Abortion Was a Crime: Women, Medicine, and Law in the United States, 1867–1973.* Berkeley: University of California Press, 1997.

Riddle, John M. *Contraception and Abortion: From the Ancient World to the Renaissance.* Cambridge, Mass.: Harvard University Press, 1992.

Sanger, Alexander. *Beyond Choice: Reproductive Freedom in the 21st Century.* New York: Public Affairs, 2004.

Stalcup, Brenda, ed. *Women's Suffrage.* San Diego: Greenwood, 2000.

Stetson, Dorothy McBride, ed. *Abortion Politics, Women's Movements, and the Democratic State.* New York: Oxford, 2001.

"Unsafe Abortion the Scourge of African Women." IRIN News, January 10, 2010, www.irinnews.org/report.aspx?reportid=58537.

World Health Organization. *Unsafe Abortion and Associated Mortality in 2003.* Geneva: World Health Organization, 2007.

Zhu, Wai Xing, Li Lu, and Therese Hesketh. "China's Excess Males, Sex Selective Abortion, and One Child Policy: Analysis of Data from 2005 National Intercensus Survey." London: *BMJ*, April 2009, www.bmj.com/cgi/reprint/338/apr09_2/b1211.pdf.

Absentee Voting

Absentee voting is a process that provides people the opportunity to cast a ballot even if they are unwilling or unable to appear at a polling station. Absentee voting is common in developed democracies, such as the United States, Japan, and the nations of western Europe. A variety of procedures can be used in absentee voting, including early voting, voting by mail, and casting ballots by fax or over the Internet. For instance, in the United States, members of the military who are deployed outside of their home regions are given absentee ballots that may be mailed without postage to their precincts, while in the United Kingdom, postal ballots are freely given on request. In addition, voters in countries that allow absentee balloting may cast their votes up to six weeks prior to an election. One of the principal challenges in absentee voting is ensuring the secrecy of the ballot and preventing fraud. Consequently, most countries require that the authenticity of absentee ballots be certified by witnesses or electoral officials. This form of voting is recognized as a means to increase voter turnout and prevent disenfranchisement of citizens who physically cannot appear at a polling station.

See also *Disenfranchisement; Voting Procedures; Voting Rights and Suffrage.*

. . . .   TOM LANSFORD

Absolutism

Absolutism is a historical term for a form of government in which the ruler is an absolute authority, unrestricted by any other institution, such as churches, estates, a constitution, laws, or opposition.

The Reformation of the sixteenth and seventeenth centuries caused erosion of monarchical power and the rise of libertarian democratic sentiment in feudal Europe. Political philosophers of the period reacted by introducing concepts of the natural law or the divine right of kings. Although contradictory, both concepts claimed that unquestionable rule by a single person was the best form of government. According to Thomas Hobbes, human beings ceded authority to a ruler in exchange for security, which kept society together. Jacques-Benigne Bossuet argued that God vested the monarch with the right to rule in order to protect society and that rebelling against the monarch would mean challenging God.

Absolutism is characterized by the end of feudal partitioning, unification and centralization of the state, rise of professional standing armies and professional bureaucracies, and the codification of state laws. The general rise of state power was demonstrated by expensive lifestyles of absolute monarchs who identified with the state ("*L'État c'est moi*" claimed Louis XIV of France). Absolutist monarchs attempted to intervene personally in every area; welfare of the state was therefore determined by their (in)competence.

Absolutist monarchs held nobility under political control by keeping them permanently at luxurious courts and arbitrarily distributing payable honorary duties and titles, while noble estates were managed by exploitative officials. The enormous increase in state expenses was addressed by modernization of tax systems and mercantilism that favored the emerging bourgeoisie. Monarchs considered absolute rulers include Louis XIII (reigned 1610–1643) and Louis XIV of France (r. 1643–1715), Ivan the Terrible (r. 1547–1584) and Peter the Great of Russia (r. 1682–1725), Leopold I of Austria (r. as Holy Roman Emperor 1658–1705), and Charles XI (r. 1660–1697) and Charles XII of Sweden (r. 1697–1718).

Absolutism went through several historical stages, such as *early* absolutism, *confessional* absolutism, *court* absolutism, and *Enlightened* absolutism. Frederick I of Prussia (r. 1740–1786), the Hapsburg emperors of Austria (Marie-Thérèse, r. 1740–1780, and her son Joseph II, r. 1780–1790), and Catherine the Great of Russia (r. 1762–1796) ruled as absolute monarchs in eastern Europe while implementing reforms based on Enlightenment ideas. Enlightened absolutism was commonly justified as a provider of better living conditions for its subjects.

Following bourgeois revolutions in America and France, absolutism and constitutionalism became principal opposing political concepts in the West. The Jacobin terror during the French Revolution (1789–1799) demonstrated that political freedom was threatened also by democratic absolutism. To early-nineteenth-century rightist political thinkers, the French Revolution, instead of abolishing absolutism, was therefore rather a struggle between the monarch and the people over sovereignty, and French *Republicanism*, Napoleon's *imperialism*, and *constitutionalism* were merely forms of absolutism.

Mid-nineteenth-century liberals considered the rising proletariat as another dangerous form of absolutism and argued against radicals' demand of universal suffrage. By 1848, a general consensus on constitutionalism was reached, and the method of its implementation became the principal matter of political controversy. While the term *absolutism* remained a commonly used pejorative, especially in France and England, in Germany the Hegelian Idealism relegated it to historiography from the 1830s on.

In the early twentieth century, research on absolutism as a historical concept was conceived in contemporary terms. Historians' views on the extent of absolutism among European monarchs vary. Some argue that a considerable number of monarchs achieved absolutist control over their states. Others question the very existence of absolutism, arguing that most absolutist monarchs had comparable power over their subjects to any other rulers, and they point to the gap between the absolutist rhetoric and the reality, especially to many absolutist monarchs' incapability to successfully address their constant financial difficulties.

See also *Authority; Monarchy; Tyranny, Classical.*

. . . . CIRILA TOPLAK

BIBLIOGRAPHY

Blänkner, Reinhard. *"Absolutismus" und "moderner Staat": Eine begriffsgeschichtliche Studie zur Geschichtswissenschaft und zur politischen Theorie in Deutschland 1830 bis 1890.* Göttingen, Germany: Vandenhoeck and Ruprecht, 1993.

Böing, Günther, ed. *Die Weltgeschichte.* Freiburg im Breisgau, Germany: Herder, 1971.

Davies, Norman. *Europe, a History.* London: Pimlico, 1997.

James, Alan. *The Origins of French Absolutism, 1598–1661.* New York: Pearson Longman, 2006.

Treasure, Geoffrey, and Russell Richards. *The Making of Modern Europe: 1648–1780.* New York: Routledge, 2003.

Academic Freedom

Academic freedom refers primarily to the rights of faculty and students to provide instruction and inquiry in academic institutions without restrictions on their analysis or fear of negative consequences. Although the term is more frequently applied to higher education, it is used also in public schooling, though it is often controversial in this context.

ORIGINS AND ESSENCE OF ACADEMIC FREEDOM

Academic freedom developed in the Middle Ages with the maturation of European universities, which during this time experienced exceptional freedom because the philosopher, scholar, and student aimed to be consecrated to the service of truth, and such freedom was regarded as divine sanction. By the 1800s, the principles of *Lehrfreiheit* (freedom of inquiry), *Lernfreibeit* (freedom to learn), and *Freiheit der Wissenschaft* (conduct research) had arisen in German universities, which eventually influenced what constitutes a genuine research university in the United States.

Experienced in varying degrees worldwide, academic freedom has been based throughout its history on the belief that it is beneficial to society for truth to be pursued. Academic freedom means typically that faculty members of an institution possess the prerogative of communication, expression, inquiry, and study. In American higher education, for instance, it has been primarily professors who have defended the right to pursue—without concern about being dismissed from their position—knowledge and truth through their publications, research, and teaching. Throughout the world, this concept also has been extended to students who require the right to question faculty propositions without concerns of negative repercussion.

ENSHRINING FREEDOM IN ACADEMIC INSTITUTIONS

Higher education institutions have defended their right to be the final arbitrators in making conclusive decisions concerning the content and method of both the research and teaching that engages students. Elementary and secondary teachers, too, have employed the term *academic freedom* for their particular rights, especially during the 1960s, to determine the content of courses taught and select departmental curricula. It is also common for educators and students to seek the freedom to engage in various political and social activities. Academic freedom for university professors necessitates the institutional component of tenure, the acknowledgement of the right of a teacher to an appointment based on demonstration of competence. The appointment is continuous unless incompetence, moral turpitude, or neglect is demonstrated, and is integral to the institution as a whole because it sustains the principles of "free search for truth and its free exposition" through professional experience (e.g., an educator may teach without fear of penalty for pursuing ideas that conflict with the institution or general society).

Although academic freedom is varied in practice and theory worldwide, it is the general expectation in Western society and is regarded positively in developing countries of Africa, the Far East, and the Middle East. For example, the German Constitution specifically grants academic freedom, as "art and science, research and teaching are free. Freedom of teaching does not absolve from loyalty to the constitution." The institutional component to academic freedom in the United States was famously expressed in 1957 when Justice Felix Frankfurter established a foundation for academic freedom in the United States. Based on a statement of the Open Universities in South Africa, Justice Frankfurter opined,

> It is the business of a university to provide that atmosphere which is most conducive to speculation, experiment, and creation. It is an atmosphere in which there prevail "the four essential freedoms" of a university—to determine for itself on academic grounds who may teach, what may be taught, how it shall be taught, and who may be admitted to study" (*Sweezy v. New Hampshire,* 354 U.S. 234 [1957]).

As the "common good" of the institution of higher learning "depends upon the free search for truth and its free exposition," the individual component of academic freedom encompasses the entitlements of both teacher and student (although to a lesser extent for the latter).

IMPORTANT CHARTERS FOR ACADEMIC FREEDOM

"The 1940 Statement of Principles on Academic Freedom and Tenure" (drafted and approved by the Association of American Colleges and Universities) established three aspects of academic freedom for an institution to ensure in "fulfilling its obligations to its students and to society": (1) "the teacher is entitled to full freedom in research and in the publication of the results," (2) "the teacher is entitled to freedom in the classroom in discussing his/her subject," and (3) when a professor "writes as a citizen, he/she should be free from institutional censorship or discipline" (American Association of University Professors, 3). Essentially the institutional and individual components should function harmoniously, as institutions should provide an atmosphere of complete freedom for educators to conduct research and publish the conclusions, as long as their performance is sufficient in other academic responsibilities. While without this academic freedom it can be argued that educators are unable to fulfill their service of pursuing and communicating truth, teachers should, however, be careful to avoid discussion of controversial matters unrelated to the subject at hand.

"The 1940 Statement of Principles" did not demand religious institutions to implement this form of academic freedom, as "limitations of academic freedom because of religious or other aims of the institution should be clearly stated in writing at the time of the appointment." The statement is perhaps intentionally ambiguous in assuming that certain limitations would exist, seeking to regulate these limitations through the obligation of honest and immediate disclosure. As granted by the limitations clause, religious institutions would have liberty to implement their own principles of academic freedom. Religious institutions that require their faculty to sign statements of faith merely formalize a mode of voluntary association that develops naturally at other institutions where such requirements do not exist. Consequently, statements of faith intrinsically considered do not limit genuine academic freedom.

Such declarations of academic freedom are prevalent worldwide. For example, "The Magna Charta Universitatum" of 1988, signed by Rectors of European Universities, states that,

> [T]he university is an autonomous institution at the heart of societies differently organized because of geography and historical heritage; it produces, examines, appraises and hands down culture by research and teaching. To meet the needs of the world around it, its research and teach must be morally and intellectually independent of all political authority and economic power (1).

Originally signed by twenty-nine European countries, the 1999 Bologna Process reinforced the academic ideals laid out within the Magna Charta and has continued to gain popularity with forty-six participating countries.

See also *Education Policy; Education Policy, Higher; Freedom of Speech.*

. . . . RON J. BIGALKE JR.

BIBLIOGRAPHY
Aby, Stephen H., and James C. Kuhn IV, comps. *Academic Freedom: A Guide to the Literature.* Westport, Conn.: Greenwood, 2000.
Alstyne, William W. Van, ed. *Freedom and Tenure in the Academy.* Durham, N.C.: Duke University Press, 1993.
American Association of University Professors. "1940 Statement of Principles on Academic Freedom and Tenure with 1970 Interpretative Comments," n.d., www.aaup.org/AAUP/pubsres/policydocs.
Baade, Hans W., and Robinson O. Everett, eds. *Academic Freedom: The Scholar's Place in Modern Society.* Dobbs Ferry, N.Y.: Oceana, 1964.
Beale, Howard K. *A History of Freedom of Teaching in American Schools.* New York: Scribner's, 1941.
Byse, Clark, and Louis Joughin. *Tenure in American Higher Education.* Ithaca, N.Y.: Cornell University Press, 1959.
De George, Richard T. *Academic Freedom and Tenure: Ethical Issues.* Lanham, Md.: Rowman and Littlefield, 1997.
Hamilton, Neil W. *Academic Ethics: Problems and Materials on Professional Conduct and Shared Governance.* Westport, Conn.: Praeger, 2002.
Hofstadter, Richard, and Walter P. Metzger. *The Development of Academic Freedom in the United States.* New York: Columbia University Press, 1955.
Kirk, Russell. *Academic Freedom: An Essay in Definition.* Chicago: Henry Regnery, 1955.
MacIver, Robert M. *Academic Freedom in Our Time.* New York: Columbia University Press, 1955.
Magna Charta Observatory. "The Magna Charta Universitatum," 1988, www.magna-charta.org/pdf/mc_pdf/mc_english.pdf.
Pincoffs, Edmund L., ed. *The Concept of Academic Freedom.* Austin: University of Texas Press, 1972.
"354 U.S. 234 (1957) Sweezy v. New Hampshire" Washington, D.C.: The Supreme Court Historical Society, n.d., www.supremecourthistory.org.

Accountability

In political science, the term *accountability* refers to an actor's acknowledgment and assumption of responsibilities specific to a role—including the responsibility to report and justify the consequences of actions taken within the scope of the role—and the existence of sanctions for failing to meet these responsibilities. A is therefore accountable to B when "A is obliged to inform B about A's (past and future) actions and decisions, to justify them, and to suffer punishment in the case of eventual misconduct," as political scientist Andreas Schedler noted in his 1999 article "Conceptualizing Accountability."

The concept of accountability thus entails monitoring of behavior, justification of behavior, and enforcement of good behavior. The monitoring and justification aspects of accountability constitute what is often referred to as *answerability*. Answerability involves the ability to ask actors about (1) *what* they have done and (2) *why* they have done so. In other words, there is an informational dimension as well as an argumentative dimension to answerability. Both dimensions of answerability require accurate information and are improved by transparency of actions.

Accountability requires not only answerability for behavior but also enforcement of good behavior. To have accountability as well as answerability, there must also be institutions for enforcing good behavior that fulfills official responsibilities. Without some way of punishing bad behavior, government agents that shirk their responsibilities cannot be held to account.

Political, public, or governmental accountability is the ability of citizens, societal actors, or other state actors to hold government officials and agents responsible for their actions in their official capacities. Successful institutions of governmental accountability specify the official duties of government agents, establish a sense of obligation in government agents to fulfill their responsibilities, and create incentives that motivate government officials to act in the public interest, punishing them when they pursue their own private interests at the expense of the public interest and rewarding them to make pursuing the public interest in their own interests as well. Political accountability is, in essence, about the need and the ability to restrain the power of government.

Some define political accountability to include only relationships in which public officials have a legal obligation to answer to those holding them accountable, and those holding public officials accountable have a legal right to impose sanctions. Others note that actors are empowered by either formal institutions or informal rules to sanction and reward government agents for their activities or performance.

THEORIES OF ACCOUNTABILITY

Models of accountability are derived from two main bodies of theoretical literature: principal-agent theory and theories of moral responsibility. While the models highlight different factors in the process of holding actors accountable, they are not necessarily incompatible with each other.

Principal-agent models of accountability posit relationships in which the *principal* (such as an employer or a voter) selects an *agent* (an employee, for example, or a local official) to choose actions that benefit the principal's interest. The relationship between the principal and agent is conceptualized as a contractual relationship between two autonomous actors. Mutually agreed terms of the contract determine the responsibilities for which the principal holds the agent accountable. Whether the principal can actually hold the agent accountable depends on whether the principal has ways of enforcing the contract.

Scholars have applied agency theory to model the conditions under which government agents might increase accountability by making their actions more observable to constituents: the implications of accountability as an equilibrium state, as well as a set of mechanisms used when accountability as an equilibrium fails and the consequences of successfully functioning sanctioning mechanisms when citizens have incorrect information.

In contrast to principal-agent models of accountability that focus on issues of contract choice, information asymmetries, and mechanisms for dismissing and punishing agents, theories of moral responsibility and group solidarity focus on the ways in which groups and communities establish duties and obligations for their members. Expectations and standards established by the group determine the responsibilities for which groups hold members accountable. Moral responsibility models of accountability focus on internal feelings of obligation and duty that groups inculcate in their members. Accountability in these models conceptualizes actors as fulfilling their responsibilities in part because they feel duty-bound to do so. In addition to the negative social sanctions that groups can apply to discourage misbehavior, theories of moral responsibility also highlight positive external and internal rewards for fulfilling responsibilities, such as group expressions of gratitude to individuals, the awarding of social and moral standing, and internal feelings of pride and identification within individuals.

TYPES OF ACCOUNTABILITY

One way to distinguish between different types of political or governmental accountability is to look at the different things that government is held accountable for doing. For what kind of behavior are government actors being held accountable? *Performance accountability,* for example, refers to the ability of citizens, first, to observe whether the government is implementing its policies effectively and efficiently, and, second, to hold them to account for their behavior. *Policy-making accountability,* on the other hand, refers to the ability of citizens to ensure that government policies are representative and reflect the preferences of the population.

A distinction can be made also between accountability *for* something and accountability *to* someone. Government accountability in a democratic system, for example, can either be conceptualized as the responsibility of government officials for representing majority preferences and implementing the government's policies effectively, or conceptualized as the responsibility of government officials to answer for its behavior to citizens.

Accountability also can be typologized in terms of *who* holds government actors accountable. In *vertical* accountability, citizens and societal actors such as civic groups, voluntary associations, and mass media seek to hold the government officials above them accountable. In *horizontal* accountability, agencies and offices within the state, such as auditing agencies, oversight commissions, or the legislative branch, oversee other branches or offices within government. A relatively new body of literature also discusses *external* accountability, or the role of international institutions in helping to hold national governments accountable for their performance and representation of public interests. Organizations such as the European Union, for example, can establish institutions that help eastern European countries to consolidate democracy and build rule of law by insulating parts of a new democracy's weakly institutionalized legal system from domestic political interest groups.

Scholarly attention to the accountability of powerful, international nongovernmental political actors such as the World Bank and the International Monetary Fund also has been increasing. These organizations command vast political and economic resources and have an enormous influence on the policies and actions of governments that receive resources from them. Their accountability remains, however, a matter of both academic and political debate. Within this debate are questions such as whether these organizations are or should be accountable to the governments that provide funding for their projects, to the governments that receive funding for development, or to the citizens of recipient countries whom these projects are intended to help.

INSTRUMENTS AND MECHANISMS OF ACCOUNTABILITY

Principal-agent and moral responsibility models of governmental accountability identify several necessary functions for an effective system of accountability. Systems of governmental accountability should include instruments or mechanisms for all parties to agree upon and acknowledge the official responsibilities of government actors. It may also be important for these instruments to establish feelings of duty and obligation among government officials. Systems of government accountability should also include ways for obtaining accurate information about the behavior and performance of government actors, as well as ways of rewarding and punishing their behavior.

Political systems vary widely in the type and strength of the institutions they have for ensuring governmental accountability. Institutions that are created to contribute to governmental accountability may not operate successfully or may function for purposes other than accountability. Elections, for example, are often considered a key element of accountability in democratic systems. Yet they may function as opportunities for citizens to choose a "good type" of political leader who feels morally responsible for fulfilling official duties, one who will act on behalf of voters regardless of incentives for reelection. Moreover, instruments and mechanisms for establishing obligation, providing information, and punishing misbehavior can contribute to systems of governmental accountability without being sufficient for ensuring accountability.

BUREAUCRATIC INSTITUTIONS OF ACCOUNTABILITY

One category of institutions that contribute to accountability are bureaucratic or administrative institutions, such as performance targets and auditing offices, that enable one set of government actors to monitor and sanction another set. Institutions such as bureaucratic performance reviews at fixed intervals are formal, top-down mechanisms involving hierarchical authority. "Modern officialdom" is characterized by the "supervision of lower offices by the higher ones." Bureaucratic institutions of meritocratic selection and promotion, training programs, and selective recruitment from particular universities or elite social groups also can lead to informal bureaucratic norms emphasizing loyalty and collective identity, which help to foster a sense of duty among bureaucrats to put collective goals above individual ones.

Other administrative and bureaucratic institutions of accountability include institutions of horizontal accountability, which consist of state institutions that oversee and sanction public agencies and other branches of the government. One classic example of horizontal accountability is the checks-and-balances relationship between legislative, executive, and judiciary branches of government, which are supposed to constrain and monitor each other. Other examples include auditing agencies, anticorruption commissions, ombudsmen, central banks, and personnel departments. As part of the government itself, however, these institutions can find it difficult to establish legally authorized or actual autonomous oversight and sanctioning abilities.

DEMOCRATIC MECHANISMS OF ACCOUNTABILITY

Another category of institutions that contribute to government accountability involve an active role by citizens themselves. In the eighteenth and nineteenth centuries, John Stuart Mill and other political philosophers came to the conclusion that representative democracy could provide "accountable

and feasible government." In a democracy, citizens would be capable of and responsible for "controlling the business of government." In democratic models, citizens—rather than higher-level officials—become the "principals" supervising local officials. Democratic mechanisms and instruments of accountability include elections, constitutions and legislatures, and corporatism and other arrangements for incorporating citizen participation and oversight in the policy-making and policy implementation processes, and civil society institutions such as protections for free press and voluntary associations.

ELECTIONS

Elections that are free and fair enable citizens to elect officials they believe to be responsive and responsible. People who want to be officials have to communicate their positions and objectives to the public. An informed public can then sanction them for failing to meet their responsibilities and obligations by voting them out of office.

Although elections can in theory serve as an important mechanism for accountability, there is a difference between the existence of electoral democracy and a government that is actually accountable for the policies that it produces and implements. While a minimalist definition of electoral democracy simply requires competitive elections with broad suffrage where institutionalized political parties take turns in office, an accountable democratic government is closer to what Robert Dahl calls a "polyarchy"—an electoral democracy that also guarantees the existence of alternative information sources and civil liberties. These additional institutions ensure the ability of voters to obtain accurate information about official behavior and to sanction them appropriately.

Elections also have a number of shortcomings if used as the primary or only mechanism for accountability to citizens. They occur infrequently, so voters have little control over elected officials between elections. Voters can only vote entire parties or candidates out of office instead of exercising more finely tuned sanctions on party or candidate behavior or decisions on a specific issue.

CONSTITUTIONS AND LEGISLATURES

Even in consolidated democracies, bureaucratic officials are unelected and cannot be held accountable to voters through elections. Constitutions can authorize legislatures to hold unelected civil servants accountable by holding hearings and organizing investigations.

CORPORATISM AND CITIZEN OVERSIGHT OF BUREAUCRACY

Institutions such as public hearings, advisory councils, and consultation committees increase transparency of information to citizens and incorporate citizen participation and oversight over the making of bureaucratic regulations and administrative statutes. An ombudsman can provide information to voters or negotiate with the bureaucracy on behalf of citizens who register complaints about the behavior of bureaucrats.

It is often assumed that consolidated democracies with competitive elections are enough to ensure high levels of policy-making accountability, but because of the ambiguities that always exist in laws and statutes, much policy making is often done in practice by the bureaucrats who are responsible for implementing the policy. As a result, policy-making accountability requires institutions that require bureaucrats to consult with citizens and interest groups who have relevant interests or special expertise such as corporatism before issuing administrative statutes to resolve gaps and ambiguities in legislation. Building these kinds of institutions to ensure policy-making accountability in new democracies such as countries in eastern Europe can often be far more difficult than setting up national elections and political parties.

This view, however, is controversial. In the past, the working assumption has been that the bureaucracy needs to be apolitical and professional in order to ensure a degree of state autonomy. Shielded from political considerations, bureaucrats should be able to implement policies and laws impersonally, fairly, and efficiently.

CIVIL SOCIETY INSTITUTIONS

Free press and citizen organizations also help to inform the public about the behavior of government actors and to sanction government actors for misconduct through influencing public opinion and voting. As providers of information, a free press and active civil society act as institutions that assist citizens in holding government actors accountable, but because government actors are legally obliged to answer to citizens rather than these societal actors, civil society organizations and the press are not necessarily considered agents of accountability.

DECENTRALIZATION AND DEMOCRATIC ACCOUNTABILITY

Theories of decentralization posit that decentralization of fiscal, administrative, and political authority can increase democratic accountability. Local governments are thought to be more likely than higher levels to have better information about what citizens need and want. Decentralizing authority to local governments also should make it clear to citizens whom they should hold responsible for performance and economic development. Local autonomy over taxation and expenditures also may allow citizens to sanction local governments for poor fiscal performance and public goods provision. Local governments who have to compete for tax revenues from firms and individuals who move to the localities that provide the best policies and public services cannot afford to misuse public funds or run deficits that force them to raise taxes.

On the other hand, decentralization also can have negative effects on other outcomes that may be important to governmental performance and representativeness. Decentralization can result in the hijacking of local government by local elites. Local governments may not have sufficient resources or expertise to resolve complex problems that have causes external to the locality.

Moreover, decentralization in practice often reduces overall government accountability by obscuring how responsibilities are actually allocated among different levels of government and making government authority more complex.

FORMAL JUDICIAL OR LEGAL ACCOUNTABILITY

In systems with rule of law, these institutions include constitutional tribunals that rule on the constitutionality of government actions and legislation. Court action and judicial review are also mechanisms that citizens can use to hold the government accountable.

INFORMAL INSTITUTIONS OF ACCOUNTABILITY

In nondemocratic or transitional systems where formal institutions of accountability are weak, citizens may still be able to hold government officials accountable through informal institutions of accountability. Officials in these systems may not fear elections or sanctions from higher levels of the state, but they can become enmeshed in social obligations established by solidary communities such as ethnic groups, religious organizations, or nationalist movements.

Solidary groups, based on shared moral standards and obligations rather than simply shared interests, can offer moral standing as an incentive to officials for performing well and providing public goods and services responsibly. Their activities also can offer forums for government officials to publicize their good behavior and public praise for this behavior as a reward. Higher moral standing can be an important source of soft power for government officials. In contrast to formal institutions of accountability such as elections and performance contracts, which are officially authorized for the purpose of holding officials accountable, the norms and obligations provided by solidary groups that help to establish a sense of obligation, transmit information about the behavior of public officials, and sanction misbehavior are informal in the sense that they evolved or were created to maintain the solidarity of a social group. They are not officially authorized or intended to enable citizens to hold government officials accountable, but do so nevertheless.

EMPIRICAL IMPLICATIONS

Systems and institutions of accountability can have important effects on other significant political, economic, and social outcomes. Effective institutions of accountability can help to constrain corruption and the extent to which officials can deviate from the responsibilities of their office. Political systems with governmental accountability may experience more legitimacy, trust in government, and voluntary compliance from citizens with state demands such as tax collection and military draft. Institutions of accountability have been found to make financial crises less likely and affect economic output.

See also *Bureaucracy; Centralization, Deconcentration, and Decentralization; Checks and Balances; Civil Society; Principal-agent Theory; Rule of Law; Transparency.*

. . . . LILY L. TSAI

BIBLIOGRAPHY

Dahl, Robert A. *A Preface to Democratic Theory.* Chicago: The University of Chicago Press, 1956.

Evans, Peter. *Embedded Autonomy: States and Industrial Transformation.* Princeton, N.J.: Princeton University Press, 1995.

Evans, Peter B., Dietrich Rueschemeyer, and Theda Skocpol. *Bringing the State Back In*. Cambridge: Cambridge University Press, 1985.

Fearon, James D. "Electoral Accountability and the Control of Politicians: Selecting Good Types versus Sanctioning Poor Performance." In *Democracy, Accountability, and Representation,* edited by Adam Przeworski, Susan C. Stokes, and Bernard Manin, 55–97. New York: Cambridge University Press, 1999.

Ferejohn, John. "Accountability and Authority: Toward a Theory of Political Accountability." In *Democracy, Accountability, and Representation,* edited by Adam Przeworski, Susan C. Stokes, and Bernard Manin, 131–153. New York: Cambridge University Press, 1999.

Fox, Jonathan A., and L. David Brown, eds. *The Struggle for Accountability: The World Bank, NGOs, and Grassroots Movements.* Cambridge: MIT Press, 1998.

Hechter, Michael. *The Principles of Group Solidarity,* Berkeley: University of California Press, 1988.

Kaufman, Daniel, Aart Kraay, and Massimo Mastruzzi. "Governance Matters III: Governance Indicators for 1996–2002." World Bank Policy Research Working Paper No. 3106, June 30, 2003.

Laver, Michael, and Kenneth A. Shepsle. "Government Accountability in Parliamentary Democracy." In *Democracy, Accountability, and Representation,* edited by Adam Przeworski, Susan C. Stokes, and Bernard Manin, 279–296. New York: Cambridge University Press, 1999.

Mainwaring, Scott, and Christopher Welna, eds. *Democratic Accountability in Latin America.* Oxford: Oxford University Press, 2003.

Manzetti, Luigi. "Political Manipulations and Market Reforms Failures." *World Politics* 55 (April 2003): 315–160.

Mill, John Stuart. "Considerations on Representative Government." In *Utilitarianism, Liberty, and Representative Government,* edited by H. B. Acton, 229–230. London: Dent, 1951.

Moe, Terry. "The New Economics of Organization." *American Journal of Political Science* 28, no. 4 (1984): 739–777.

Moreno, Erika, Brain F. Crisp, and Matthew S. Shugart. "The Accountability Deficit in Latin America." In *Democratic Accountability in Latin America,* edited by Scott Mainwaring and Christopher Welna, 79–154. New York: Oxford University Press, 2003.

O'Donnell, Guillermo. "Delegative Democracy." *Journal of Democracy* 5 (January 1994): 55–69.

———. "Horizontal Accountability in New Democracies." *Journal of Democracy* 9, no. 3 (1998): 112–126.

Rodden, Jonathan. *Hamilton's Paradox: The Promise and Peril of Fiscal Federalism.* New York: Cambridge University Press, 2006.

Rose-Ackerman, Susan. *From Elections to Democracy: Building Accountable Government in Hungary and Poland.* Cambridge: Cambridge University Press, 2005.

Schedler, Andreas. "Conceptualizing Accountability." In *The Self-Restraining State: Power and Accountability in New Democracies,* edited by Andreas Schedler, Larry Diamond, and Marc F. Plattner, 13–28. Boulder, Colo.: Lynne Rienner, 1999.

Schedler, Andreas, Larry Diamond, and Marc F. Plattner, eds. *The Self-Restraining State: Power and Accountability in New Democracies.* Boulder, Colo.: Lynne Rienner, 1999.

Schumpeter, Joseph A. 1942. *Capitalism, Socialism, and Democracy.* New York: Harper and Row, 1975.

Seabright, Paul. "Accountability and Decentralization in Government: An Incomplete Contracts Model." Centre for Economic Policy Research Discussion Paper no. 889, London, 1996.

Shearer, Teri. "Ethics and Accountability: From the For-Itself to the For-the-Other." *Accounting, Organizations, and Society* 27, no. 6 (2002): 541–573.

Sklar, Richard L. "Developmental Democracy." *Society for Comparative Studies in Society and History* 29 (October 1987): 686–714.

Smiley, Marion. *Moral Responsibility and the Boundaries of Community: Power and Accountability from a Pragmatic Point of View.* Chicago: University of Chicago Press, 1992.

Stokes, Susan C. "What Do Policy Switches Tell Us about Democracy." In *Democracy, Accountability, and Representation,* edited by Adam Przeworski, Susan C. Stokes, and Bernard Manin, 98–130. New York: Cambridge University Press, 1999.

Tsai, Lily. *Accountability without Democracy: Solidary Groups and Public Goods Provision in Rural China.* New York: Cambridge University Press, 2007.

Weber, Max. *Wirtschaft und Gesellschaft.* Tubingen, Germany: Mohr, 1922.

———. 1904–1911. *Economy and Society: An Outline of Interpretive Sociology.* Edited by Guenther Roth and Claus Wittich. New York: Bedminster, 1968.

Addams, Jane

American social worker, educator, suffragist, and social and political activist and commentator, Jane Addams (1860–1935) was born in Illinois. She is best known for cofounding Hull House in 1889 with friend Ellen Gates Starr. This revolutionary settlement house was located in Chicago's predominantly immigrant area. Addams used her influence to fight for decreases in infant mortality, and for childhood immunizations; children's literacy; better sanitation; and the rights of women, factory workers, tenants, newsboys, railroad workers, and midwives. She waged protracted campaigns against disease, truancy, prostitution, drug use, and alcoholism. A staunch advocate for peace, she also helped to redefine roles for women of the late nineteenth and early twentieth centuries.

After leaving Women's Medical College of Philadelphia for health reasons, Addams traveled to Europe in 1893. In London, she visited Toynbee Hall, a settlement house that became the model for Hull House. Addams gathered a revolving group of her friends of both sexes at Hull House, which boasted day nurseries, a kindergarten, boys and girls clubs, a gym, public baths, and a swimming pool. Hull House brought theater, concerts, and extension courses on a range of subjects into the lives of Chicago's poor immigrants.

Addams became involved in local politics to promote her causes, engaging in direct battle with Chicago's political machine. She was named sanitation inspector and served on the Board of Education and various committees. She also served on a number of national committees and made history by nominating Theodore Roosevelt as presidential candidate for the Progressive Party in 1912. Addams soon became disillusioned with Roosevelt and supported Democrat Woodrow Wilson in 1916 because of his promise to keep the United States out of World War I (1914–1918). When Wilson was unable to fulfill that promise, Addams broke with the Democratic Party and voted for Socialist candidate Eugene Debs in 1920.

World War I changed the public's image of Addams. Her propeace stance during a time of world war and high national patriotism resulted in Addams, once one of the most admired women in the country, becoming one of the most reviled. In 1929, Addams was named president for life of the Women's International League for Peace and Freedom. In 1931, she shared the Nobel Peace Prize with fellow peace advocate Nicholas Murray Butler. Three years later, however, her reputation suffered again when she was identified as a dangerous radical by Elizabeth Patrick Delling in *The Red Network: A Who's Who and Handbook of Radicalism for Patriots.*

Jane Addams first became involved in politics to promote personal causes but made a national impact on social issues.

SOURCE: Library of Congress

Addams' early written work appeared as essays to promote her views on social causes. Such was the case with *A Modern King Lear* (written in 1894 but not released publicly until 1912), a controversial essay about the 1894 Pullman strike. Her major works include *Democracy and Social Ethics* (1902), a commentary on the conflict between American democratic ideals and the realities of the Industrial Revolution, and *Newer Ideals of Peace* (1907), a rejection of Enlightenment theory, as well as the autobiography in *Twenty Years at Hull House* (1910), *The Second Twenty Years at Hull House* (1930), and numerous later works.

See also *Nobel Peace Prize; Progressiveism.*

. . . . ELIZABETH RHOLETTER PURDY

BIBLIOGRAPHY
Addams, Jane. *Forty Years at Hull House.* New York: Macmillan, 1935.
Davis, Allen F. *American Heroine: The Life and Legend of Jane Addams.* Chicago: Ivan R. Dee, 2000.
Elshtain, Jean Bethke. *Jane Addams and the Dream of American Democracy: A Life.* New York: Basic Books, 2002.
Knight, Louise W. *Jane Addams and the Struggle for Democracy.* Chicago: University of Chicago Press, 2005.
Lasch, Christopher, ed. *The Social Thought of Jane Addams.* Indianapolis: Bobbs-Merrill, 1965.

Additional Member System

The additional member system is an electoral process that combines both constituency and proportional voting. Voters may cast two ballots, the first for a representative of their geographic region and the second for a political party. Individual representatives are elected in the traditional first-past-the-post method, while the party vote is used to allocate seats among party lists. The additional member system is common in western Europe for balloting for national or regional representative bodies. For instance, in the Scottish Parliament, seventy-three seats are elected through the first-past-the-post system and the remaining fifty-six are chosen through party lists. Variations of the system include the mixed-member proportional process, which allows additional seats to be awarded to the parties that gain the highest number of seats in the proportional voting. This offsets victories in individual constituencies and ensures that the composition of elected bodies is roughly proportional. The system is designed to ensure that small parties are better able to compete against larger and better-funded groupings. However, the use by some countries of minimum thresholds, as high as 5 percent of the vote, continues to prevent some smaller parties from gaining seats.

See also *Electoral Formulas; First Past the Post; Representative Systems.*

. . . . TOM LANSFORD

Adjudication

Adjudication is a mechanism by which disputes or controversies are peacefully resolved. It is a method of conflict resolution wherein an official and formal declaration of a legal judgment or determination is rendered in a tribunal proceeding. Societies can resolve conflicts among parties in a variety of ways without recourse to formal adjudications: legislative statutory enactment of policies, mediation and arbitration in employment disputes or labor-management clashes, persuasion, compromising and negotiation among parties to a contract, marriage counseling, or even parental discipline. The diverse methods of conflict resolution can be classified according to two dimensions: the level of formality of the proceedings and the level of governmental involvement in the proceedings. The higher the level of each, the more the method displays the hallmarks of adjudication.

Both the courts and regulatory administrative agencies engage in formal adjudication. In terms of the raw numbers adjudications in the United States, agencies engage in far more than the courts do. Nevertheless, the archetypal adjudication is found in the court system, and adjudication procedures in administrative agencies increasingly resemble adjudication in the courts. The delivery of justice to aggrieved parties has been at the heart of adjudication from ancient times, but the contemporary era has developed a specific archetype of adjudication: a tribunal that establishes the facts in a dispute, assesses the relevant law and attendant guiding rules and principles, and then applies the law to the facts. Claims of all parties to the dispute are duly weighed and considered, and there are avenues for appeal by the parties of the final decision. The presiding judge must be impartial and have no vested interest in the outcome.

In the American system, courts are organized into trial and appeals courts. Both types of courts engage in adjudication, albeit with different underlying dynamics. Trial courts possess original jurisdiction; that is, they are the initial courts to hear cases. There is much variation among different court jurisdictions and judicial systems in the rules of evidence that guide and structure the establishment of the facts in trial courts. Appeals courts have appellate jurisdiction; that is, they hear appeals from parties who lost in a trial court or in a lower appeals court. Appellate courts, which are composed of a multiple judge panel, do not reconsider the facts and do not retry the case; instead, they assess the fairness of trial court proceedings by ascertaining whether the law and legal procedures were followed properly. They review trial court procedures and rulings (for example, the admissibility of evidence) for congruence with statutory and constitutional obligations. In other words, they review previous court proceedings and assess whether those court proceedings were fair.

Trial and appellate courts hear and resolve both civil and criminal cases. Criminal adjudications revolve around murder, rape, robbery, assault, embezzlement, extortion, and other acts that bring harm to society and are violations of the penal code. In criminal adjudications the government brings the legal action against the defendant. Alternatively, civil cases revolve around disputes between private parties and potential violations of private rights—the state is typically not a party in such disputes. These private disputes typically are over personal welfare, property, or finances. Judicial responses in such cases involve a judge's declaration ordering certain actions be taken or some amount of pecuniary compensation to be awarded.

For a process of adjudication to proceed, two conditions must be met: the court must have the legal right to hear the case (jurisdiction) and the parties must have the right to bring the case before the court (standing). Jurisdictions for courts stem primarily from statutes and constitutions laying out what specific types of disputes or types of parties to a dispute fall under the purview of particular courts. The jurisdictional requirement reinforces the main function of the courts—to protect the rights of individuals. At the core of standing is that the plaintiff has suffered an actual injury or harm to a legally protected interest. Such a harm or injury must be clear and concrete and particularized to that plaintiff, and it also must be actual or immanent, not merely hypothetical or speculative. The standing requirement distinguishes the courts' role from the role of the legislature, which is to promote the public interest and society in general. In other words, adjudications by the courts focus on more individualized-level dispute resolution, whereas the public policy-making process as conducted by legislatures focuses on more generalized-level disputes. Nevertheless, class-action lawsuits, such as those brought

against the tobacco industry because of its health effects, tend to blur the line between the two.

See also *Administrative Courts; Trial Courts.*

. . . . STEPHEN R. ROUTH

BIBLIOGRAPHY

Baum, Lawrence. *American Courts: Process and Policy,* 4th ed. Boston: Houghton Mifflin, 1998.

Carp, Robert A., Ronald Stidham, and Kenneth L. Manning. *Judicial Processes in America.* 6th ed. Washington, D.C.: CQ Press, 2004.

Melone, Albert P., and Allan Karnes. *The American Legal System: Foundations, Process, and Norms.* Los Angeles: Roxbury, 2003.

Murphy, Walter F., C. Herman Pritchett, Lee Epstein, and Jack Night. *Courts, Judges, and Politics: An Introduction to the Judicial Process.* Boston: McGraw-Hill, 2006.

Porto, Brian L. *May It Please the Court: Judicial Processes and Politics in America.* New York: Longman, 2001.

Warren, Kenneth F. *Administrative Law in the Political System,* 4th ed. Boulder, Colo.: Westview, 2004.

Administration, International

See *International Administration.*

Administrative Courts

Administrative courts are judicial bodies that adjudicate cases involving disputes that arise under administrative law—that is to say, disputes over the government's exercise of its public authority. Administrative law regulates the exercise of authority by executive officials (administrative acts); it also lays out the correctives or remedies when public officials violate those rules. Administrative courts are distinct from general courts as they focus solely on these types of public law disputes, whereas general courts may deal with both private law disputes (conflicts between private citizens or private entities) and public law controversies. Administrative courts typically play a more prominent role in countries with a history of civil law systems that feature elaborate legal codes (such as France and other countries in continental Europe) than in nations with a common law tradition where many legal principles are taken from prior judicial rulings (such as Great Britain, some other nations in the British Commonwealth, and the United States).

A CLASH OF INTERESTS

At the heart of administrative court litigation is a clash involving the private interests of a citizen on one side and the public interest as advanced by organs of the state on the other. Ultimately a country's decision to have a specialized system of administrative courts is based on a policy decision about the best way to render and ensure justice and fairness in administration. Citizens or corporations unhappy with a governmental agency decision concerning, for example, welfare eligibility, old-age or disability entitlements, immigration status, level of tax liability, the granting of a broadcasting license, or the ability to develop a wetlands area, need a forum for resolving this type of conflict between their private interest and the public entity. Should there be a separate set of courts with specialized jurisdiction only on this type of case, or should general courts with broader jurisdiction and less-specialized judges have this type of private-public dispute fall within their purview?

SEPARATIST VERSUS INTEGRATIONIST ORIENTATIONS

Liberal democracies have settled on two approaches for addressing this foundational question—the separatist and the integrationist. A leading example of the separatist orientation is found in France, which features a well-developed administrative courts arrangement. French administrative courts engage in close judicial oversight of public agency actions. All administrative decisions produced by executive officials may be subject to review by the Conseil d'État (Council of State), which sits at the apex of an administrative court system of lower tribunals and intermediate courts of appeals that adjudicate these public law disputes. This particular court possesses much authority, independence, and prestige in the French legal system, and there is no comparable analogue to it in either Great Britain or the United States. Through its myriad decisions, the Conseil d'État has developed abiding legal precedents and principles concerning administrative power as exercised by the state; its jurisprudence constitutes a viable check to executive power but also lends legitimacy to various state actions.

Proponents of the separatist approach point to these courts' specialization and expertise in administrative law (and specific administrative areas) as the major advantages over general courts. With the growth of the modern administrative state and regulation of more private sector activities (and the resultant heavier administrative caseload for general courts) these courts are well positioned to manage the caseload and clarify the legal principles shaping the relationship between the individual citizen and the authority of the state bureaucracy. However, critics argue that administrative courts are inherently adverse to long-established views of individual liberty and freedom, primarily because such courts may have a tendency to defer to the state using judicial criteria that favor of the exercise of executive power.

The integrationist model is typically found in Anglo-American countries with their accompanying common law systems. This approach posits that a nation only needs one kind of court to resolve disputes arising from both private and public law—legal rules and principles should be equally applicable to both realms without an artificial distinction between the two. Thus, there is no need for a second set of specialized courts; ordinary courts are completely adequate and proper in rendering administrative justice. Proponents of this approach also contend that having a separate apparatus of administrative courts ineluctably leads to jurisdictional confusion and procedural problems for judges and litigants in trying to determine in which court should litigation be situated. With only one group of courts, such "territorial" problems are not an issue and the judicial structure is helpfully simplified for all involved. Questions revolving around the appropriate scope of administrative discretion resist easy resolution; this uncertainty becomes even more acute when having another set of courts adjudicating administrative disputes. As well, at a more theoretical level, the integrationist model postulates the fundamental notion that both the government and the people should obey the same laws—both components of society must be held accountable to the law by the same set of judges, judicial standards, and legal principles.

CONVERGENCE

In practice, however, countries that have attempted to use just one set of courts to handle all disputes over time have dropped their conceptual purity and begin to use some specialized forms of administrative courts. Caseload burdens and the need for judicial expertise in substantive policy areas often work to increase the number of administrative courts. Whether the ordinary judicial system can accommodate these types of specialized administrative disputes is an important determinant of a state ultimately choosing to have this second structure of courts. A prime example of this is the United States, where several administrative courts in the federal government specifically handle litigation stemming from areas of patents, copyright, customs, and taxes. Most of these courts were created by the U.S. Congress under its powers under Article I of the Constitution, as opposed to the more familiar general federal court system established by Article III that constitute the judicial branch. The judges appointed by the president to these courts do not enjoy the lifetime tenure of Article III federal judges. The decisions of these courts, however, are reviewable on appeal to the Article III courts (i.e., the U.S. Courts of Appeals and the U.S. Supreme Court).

A derivative form of administrative courts can be found within some U.S. executive branch agencies that have their own internal administrative tribunals (conducted by ostensibly independent administrative law judges) to help more expeditiously resolve disputes over administrative decisions. Judicial review by appeal to an Article III court remains available to disputants after exhausting the appeals process through these administrative tribunals and agency appeal boards.

See also *Adjudication; Administrative Law; Administrative State; Conseil d'État; Regulation and Rulemaking; Trial Courts.*

. . . . STEPHEN R. ROUTH

BIBLIOGRAPHY

Abraham, Henry J. *The Judicial Process: An Introductory Analysis of the Courts of the United States, England, and France,* 7th ed. New York: Oxford University Press, 1997.

Derbyhire, J. Denis, and Ian Derbyshire. *Political Systems of the World.* New York: Palgrave Macmillan, 1996.

Legomsky, Stephen H. *Specialized Justice: Courts, Administrative Tribunals, and a Cross-national Theory of Specialization.* New York: Oxford University Press, 1990.

Melnick, R. Shep. *Regulation and the Courts: The Case of the Clean Air Act.* Washington, D.C.: Brookings Institution, 1983.

Rabkin, Jeremy. *Judicial Compulsions: How Public Law Distorts Public Policy.* New York: Basic Books, 1989.

Shapiro, Martin. *Who Guards the Guardians? Judicial Control of Administration.* Athens: University of Georgia Press, 1988.

Warren, Kenneth F. *Administrative Law in the Political System,* 4th ed. Boulder, Colo.: Westview, 2004.

Administrative Law

Administrative law is the body of law that deals with the procedures, authority, and actions involved in public administration. It incorporates the various powers, responsibilities, duties, and functions of public agencies and agency officials in the attempted advancement of their respective missions, along with judicial decisions that help structure these exercises of authority. The expansion and progression of administrative law have been concomitant with the growth of the administrative state in the twentieth century as governmental bureaucracy has developed to deal with pressing social, economic, and political problems emanating from modern society. In other words, at its core, administrative law is the branch of law that regulates the exercise of authority by executive branch officials.

A focus of much of administrative law is on the protocols and procedures to which government agencies must adhere to take legal and constitutionally acceptable actions that affect private parties. Thus, it can be said that the corpus of administrative law is composed of efforts to ensure that governmental agencies effectively implement public policies designed to advance the public interest, and at the same time to guarantee that the liberty of private interests are safeguarded from possible and potential administrative infringements. Rephrased, administrative law is a fluid and ever-evolving area of law that endeavors to reconcile and synthesize public and private interests—agencies are in place to help government fulfill its mission, but they may not violate individual liberties.

In the American context at the federal level, there are four main sources of administrative law: the U.S. Constitution, the Administrative Procedure Act of 1946 (APA), particular agency enabling acts, and administrative common law. The APA is a federal law that directly lays out the procedures agencies must follow and creates the legal structure for review by the federal courts of agency actions. At the core of motivation behind the enactment of the APA was Congress's wish to not allow executive agencies so much leeway in the conduct of their duties that executive agents would be able to drift away from congressional intentions and desires in the law that the executive was implementing. The great and abrupt growth of the administrative state under President Franklin Roosevelt communicated to Congress the need for such structures as the APA to rein in and guide executive actions. Similar legislative concerns are manifested also in the drafting of agency enabling acts that set out the boundaries of agency authority and purpose and the use of the legislative veto. The actual, day-to-day implementation of public policy and enforcement of laws remains a continuing source of political and institutional tension between the executive branch and the Congress.

Agencies are the entities that actually execute the laws that the legislature has enacted, and they engage in several types of activities when enforcing these laws. These agency activities include the regulation of private conduct, the disbursement of entitlements, the management of governmental property, the granting of licenses and permits, engaging in investigations and gathering of information, and the making of public policy. The vast majority of what agency officials do ends up having important consequences on the lives of private parties, by preventing them or allowing them to engage in a particular action, or giving them or taking away some form of benefit. Two important sets of actions that agencies engage in when performing such activities are rulemaking and the issuance of an order after an adjudication of a dispute. Rulemaking is essentially where an agency promulgates a general rule or regulation that is filling in the details of statutory policy and that rule possesses the force of law. The issuance of an administrative order is more specifically tailored to a particular dispute in which a private party is required, after an administrative hearing, to conform to the law by doing or refraining from doing certain things.

There is variation among liberal democracies in their respective administrative law structures. For example, administrative law in France and Sweden is administered by a system of highly developed separate administrative courts that are distinct from ordinary courts in that they focus solely on public law disputes. Such administrative courts are more readily seen and stronger in countries with a history of civil law legal systems than in nations with a common law legal heritage (such as the United States and Great Britain). The purpose of these courts is to closely oversee public agency actions. In the French system, all administrative decisions produced by executive officials are subject to review by the Conseil d'État (Council of State), which sits at the apex of this system of administrative lower tribunals and intermediate courts of appeals. This particular court possesses much authority, independence, and prestige in the French legal system, and there is no comparable analogue to it in either the United States or Great Britain. Through its myriad decisions over the past two hundred years, the Conseil d'État has developed abiding legal precedents and principles concerning administrative power as exercised by the state. Thus, the leading administrative court in France constitutes a viable check to executive power, as well as lending legitimacy to various state actions. The judiciary's use of administrative law is a leading method by which bureaucrats can be held accountable and to ensure executive fidelity to the law and correct procedures.

Some controversy and ongoing questions revolve around agency activities and how administrative law has developed to deal with those concerns. A variety of nations have opted for an external watchdog of an ombudsman to help assist in scrutinizing potentially problematic actions taken by government administrators. The ombudsman is an appointed public official who has the authority to investigate accusations of corrupt, incompetent, or incorrect actions taken by bureaucrats. This oversight mechanism started in Scandinavia and has filtered out over time to other European democracies and to the European Union, but its full potential is yet to be seen.

In the United States, an important worry is that the scope of agency action has worked to undermine the separation-of-powers system—legislative, executive, and judicial—as laid out in the Constitution. The U.S. Supreme Court has held that it is constitutionally permissible for executive agencies to exert authority that one normally associates with the legislative and judicial branches as long as judicial review of agency decisions is available to the affected parties and agencies operate only in areas that are clearly under their regulatory jurisdiction and expertise. Thus, this merging of governmental powers is constitutionally satisfactory as long as appropriate safeguards are kept in place.

Of special concern in these separation-of-powers considerations is the delegation doctrine. The delegation doctrine prohibits excessive delegation of discretionary powers by the Congress to federal agencies. The major question here is where exactly is the threshold when the U.S. Congress has delegated too much authority to an agency so that the agency is actually legislating the law, and not the Congress itself? From the 1940s to the present, the delegation doctrine has become essentially dormant in the federal courts and does not pose much of a constraint on Congress, with Congress giving healthy amounts of leeway to agencies in the implementation of federal law. As long as some type of intelligible principle is articulated in the relevant law to generally guide the implementing agency, the courts will uphold the agency action as meeting the requirements of the delegation doctrine and is thus constitutional.

See also *Administrative Courts; Delegation, Theories of; Regulation and Rulemaking.*

. . . . STEPHEN R. ROUTH

BIBLIOGRAPHY

Breyer, Stephen G., Adrian Vermeul, Richard B. Stewart, and Cass Sunstein. *Administrative Law and Regulatory Policy: Problems, Texts, and Cases.* New York: Aspen, 2006.

Cass, Ronald A., Colin S. Driver, and Jack M. Beermann. *Administrative Law: Cases and Materials.* New York: Aspen, 2006.

Funk, William F., and Richard H. Seamon. *Administrative Law: Examples and Explanations,* 3rd ed. New York: Aspen, 2009.

Hall, Daniel E., and John Feldmeier. *Administrative Law: Bureaucracy and Democracy,* 4th ed. Upper Saddle River, N.J.: Prentice Hall, 2008.

Strauss, Peter L. *Administrative Justice in the United States,* 2nd ed. Durham, N.C.: Carolina Academic Press, 2002.

Warren, Kenneth F. *Administrative Law in the Political System,* 4th ed. Boulder, Colo.: Westview, 2004.

Administrative State

The term *administrative state* denotes political systems in contemporary developed nations with rationally organized, technically oriented government agencies that play large, central, and powerful roles in the formulation of public policy and the implementation of government services, constraints, functions, and programs. The term came into common usage in political science with the publication of Dwight Waldo's classic 1948 book *The Administrative State.* The administrative state developed from a variety of historical causes including the rise of the twentieth century welfare-warfare state, market failures in capitalist economies, and socialist economic organization.

THE BUREAUCRACY

A chief characteristic of the administrative state is the development of a new and relatively independent power center in government, typically referred to as "the bureaucracy," that is difficult for chief executives, legislatures, and courts to control.

Independence develops from the selection of tenured administrative personnel based on technical expertise (merit), the scope of administrative tasks and the detailed knowledge they require, and the continuous operation of administrative units regardless of changes in their leadership and staff. Such units are difficult for legislators, elected and politically appointed executives, and courts to supervise and hold accountable due to their technical expertise, knowledge of and adherence to routine, scope of activity, and limited transparency.

The organization of administrative units in the administrative state is typically bureaucratic; that is, incorporating specialization, hierarchy, expertise, impersonality, and large size. Specialization of units is by jurisdiction and function. Ministries or departments are generally the largest units. Smaller units are called *agencies,* and subunits are called *bureaus.* Jurisdictional specialization is manifested in such units as Ministries or Departments of Labor, Commerce, Agriculture, and Interior, among others. Specialization by function forms the basis of units devoted to such matters as defense; national security; crime control; education; nuclear power; welfare; and economic, environmental, and social regulation, as well as for overhead administrative activities such as budgeting, procurement, and personnel administration.

These categories are not wholly distinct—overlaps are common and one person's regulation may be another's service, as in the case of measures for consumer protection. Hierarchy reaching upward through political appointees in the administrative units to the various offices of the chief executive and culminating with the president, premier, or prime minister promotes coordination of the administrative component as a whole. Expertise, sometimes referred to as "technorationality," results from specialization and the selection of administrative personnel based on merit. Impersonality, which contributes to procedural regularity and continuity of operations, is promoted by organizations based on positions rather than on persons (e.g., individual administrators), adherence to comprehensive procedural rules for decision making and other actions, and communication in writing. Large size is a function of the broad range of policies and activities dealt with by the administrative state.

SEPARATION OF POWERS VERSUS PARLIAMENTARY SYSTEMS

In separation-of-powers systems, the administrative state is at odds with the governmental design because administrative units combine all three functions of government: execution, legislation, and adjudication. Execution of legal mandates is the primary function of administrative units. However, they also legislate in a generic sense by enacting rules setting regulatory standards that have the force of law. Administrative units also adjudicate a wide variety of economic conflicts, such as whether a labor or advertising practice is fair. The collapse of the separation of functions into a modern nation's administrative component and its individual units is an inevitable outgrowth of expansion in the scope of governmental activity. Legislatures lack the capacity to draft laws with detailed standards for a host of economic, social, and other activities and environmental and other conditions subject to governmental regulation. Similarly, court systems would require dramatic expansion to deal effectively with all the conflicts resolved through administrative adjudication. Because agencies exercise executive, legislative, and adjudicatory functions, they are apt to be subject to some degree of direction and oversight by each branch of government, sometimes dictating conflicting courses of action.

The administrative state in parliamentary systems is more in keeping with the governmental design because the legislative and executive functions are fused in the sense that the political executive is formally a creature of the legislature. Nevertheless, the elective governmental institutions and courts may lack the capacity to exercise close direction over the whole range of administrative operations.

See also *Bureaucracy; Bureaucratic Authoritarianism; State, Functions of the; State, The.*

. . . . DAVID H. ROSENBLOOM

BIBLIOGRAPHY

Barker, Ernest. *The Development of Public Services in Western Europe.* Hamden, Conn.: Archon, 1966.

Chapman, Brian. *The Profession of Government.* London: Unwin University Books, 1959.

Jacoby, Henry. *The Bureaucratization of the World.* Berkeley: University of California Press, 1973.

Kettl, Donald. *The Transformation of Governance.* Baltimore: Johns Hopkins University Press, 2002.

Morestein Marx, Fritz. *The Administrative State.* Chicago: University of Chicago Press, 1957.

Rohr, John A. *To Run a Constitution: The Legitimacy of the Administrative State.* Lawrence: University Press of Kansas, 1986.

Rosenbloom, David H., and Howard McCurdy, eds. *Revisiting Waldo's Administrative State.* Washington, D.C.: Georgetown University Press, 2007.

Van Riper, Paul P. "Administrative State." In *International Encyclopedia of Public Policy and Administration,* edited by Jay Shafritz, 71–77. Boulder, Colo.: Westview, 1998.

Wilson, James Q. *Bureaucracy.* New York: Basic Books, 1989.

Adorno, Theodor W.

Theodor Wiesengrund Adorno (1903–1969) was a German music theorist, literary critic, philosopher, social psychologist, and sociologist. Born in Frankfurt to a family of musicians, Adorno started to write as a music critic at a very early age. His name is, however, primarily linked to the Frankfurt school, the group of intellectuals working within the framework of the Frankfurt Institute for Social Research, of which he is considered to be one of the central exponents. The essays he wrote in the 1930s in the *Zeitschrift für Sozialforschung,* the main organ of the institute, combine formal music analysis with a sociological critique.

With Adolf Hitler's rise to power, Adorno, together with other members of the institute, migrated to the United States, first to New York and then to California. During these years Adorno collaborated with philosopher and sociologist Max Horkheimer, with whom he wrote the influential *Dialectic of Enlightenment* (1944). In this book, written after the advent of Nazism and their experience of American mass society, the

authors developed a harsh critique of Western rationality by arguing that the latter, far from realizing the Enlightenment's promise of emancipation, had turned into a radical form of domination. In so doing, they suggested that the entire Western Enlightenment was ultimately based on an instrumental concept of reason and domination over nature that could result in the opposite of reason—that is, myth and barbarism. Adorno returned to Frankfurt in 1949 and contributed to reopening the Institute for Social Research.

Although Adorno would try, in particular in his later *Negative Dialectics* (1966), to investigate the way in which rationality could escape the dialectic of Enlightenment, thus avoiding the nightmare of total domination, his work remained devoted to critiquing late capitalist societies. In particular, Adorno's writings on mass culture contain a powerful critique of the way in which culture and other everyday practices can become the vehicle of ideological forms of domination.

Adorno also promoted and took part in empirical studies, which was in line with the multidisciplinary character of the Frankfurt school research program. One of the most prominent works of Adorno's in this field is the collaborative *Authoritarian Personality* (1950). This study combines insights from psychoanalysis with sociological research in an attempt to provide an explanation for the rise of authoritarianism.

Due to the importance he gave to factors such as culture and psychology, Adorno, like other exponents of the Frankfurt school, exercised an important function in the renewal of Western Marxism, as well as in the opening of new fields of investigation into the sociology of culture.

See also *Enlightenment Political Thought; Frankfurt School; Horkheimer, Max; Marxism; Political Theory.*

. . . . CHIARA BOTTICI

BIBLIOGRAPHY

Adorno, Theodor W. 1966. *Negative Dialectics.* London: Routledge, 1990.

———. *The Culture Industry: Selected Essays on Mass Culture,* edited by J. M. Bernstein. London: Routledge, 1991.

———. *The Adorno Reader,* edited by Brian O'Connor. Oxford, U.K.: Blackwell, 2000.

———. *Essays on Music.* Berkley: University of California Press, 2002.

Adorno, Theodor W., Betty Aron, William Morrow, Maria Hertz Levinson, Else Frenkel-Brunswik, Daniel J. Levinson, and R. Nevitt Sanford. 1950. *The Authoritarian Personality.* New York: Norton, 1969.

Adorno, Theodor W., and Max Horkheimer. 1944. *Dialectic of Enlightenment.* London: Verso, 1997.

Adverse Selection and Moral Hazard

Adverse selection and moral hazard are informational imperfections potentially presented in any activity or transaction because of asymmetric information about involved risks. *Adverse selection* is a possibility that actors undertake an activity or transaction based on actors' characteristics unobservable for others (these are informed actors because they know their own characteristics). If the decisions of informed actors adversely affect other uninformed actors participating in the same activity or transaction, then adverse selection is present.

Moral hazard is a possibility that informed actors might undertake an activity or transaction more risky than uninformed actors' original belief. If such activity or transaction is undertaken, and uninformed actors cannot observe it, then moral hazard is present. For example, if a state borrows money from an international organization, then the state has more information about its own current and future risks than does the lender. Adverse selection arises from the possibility of using borrowed funds in the ways that would lead to difficulties in repaying the loan. Alternatively, moral hazard arises if that state, which had intended to use borrowed funds in a less risky way, experiences a change in government, and the new government uses the borrowed funds for riskier purposes.

See also *Ethics, Political.*

. . . . TATIANA VASHCHILKO

Advertising, Political

Political advertising encompasses a broad array of strategies in which paid media is used to communicate political messages to the public. Although most commonly associated with candidates' campaign commercials, political advertising has developed into a massive industry in which various political actors (e.g., parties, advocacy groups) use a host of media such as radio, television, and the Internet to deliver carefully packaged messages directly to voters. Research has provided important insights into the use and effect of political ads, although some intriguing questions have yet to be fully resolved.

EARLY AMERICAN USAGE

Political advertising has developed considerably since its early use in the first American elections. Campaign advertisements were initially limited to handbills, newspaper ads, and, later, radio spots, but the advent of television significantly enhanced the ability of candidates to make direct appeals to the public. The 1952 U.S. presidential election featured the first series of televised candidate commercials which, although relatively simple, signaled a new era in political advertising. Over time, television spots became more ubiquitous, increasingly sophisticated, and, in some cases, more alarming. U.S. presidential candidate Lyndon B. Johnson's 1964 "Daisy" ad, for example, shocked many with contrasting images of a little girl and an atomic mushroom cloud—so much so that, although it only ran once, the media replayed it multiple times on evening newscasts. Since then, there have been many notable spots, including presidential candidate Ronald Reagan's 1984 "Morning in America" ad, which used positive imagery to inspire voters, and his "Bear in the Woods" ad, which invoked fears of a foreign enemy—both themes that would be reused in subsequent campaigns. In 1988 the "Willie Horton" ad promoting the campaign of U.S. presidential candidate George H. W. Bush stirred controversy by allegedly including implicit racial cues, and, in 2000, an ad in which the word *rats* flashed briefly across the television screen during a voiceover

regarding U.S. presidential candidate Al Gore's prescription drug plan raised questions about the possible use of subliminal techniques in political advertising.

The American political advertising industry has expanded beyond presidential candidates to include a host of other political actors. It is now common for many candidates across all levels of elected office to spend large portions of their budgets on creating and airing ever more sophisticated advertising campaigns. In terms of buying air time, estimates show that congressional and gubernatorial candidates spent nearly $2 billion during the 2006 campaign alone. Political advertising has further expanded to include advocacy groups who now routinely sponsor "issue ads" that promote a policy—often implicitly tied to a candidate—without explicitly offering an endorsement. Candidates benefit from the issue being promoted without having to pay for the ad or being held accountable for what is said.

NEW VENUES

Political advertising also has expanded to new venues. Campaigns are now using the Internet to create somewhat unorthodox pieces, such as animated spots or comedic skits that are intended to be distributed through a viral network of supporters. Individual citizens also have started producing their own Web-based political ads, some of which have gained considerable attention on the Internet. In addition, the 2004 U.S. presidential candidates pioneered a technique called "phantom advertising" in which they created ads that, rather than being aired, were sent to media outlets in the hopes that they would be included in stories about the campaign. American political advertising is an expanding enterprise that appears to be on the cusp of another profound change.

These trends and practices have started to have some influence on political advertising in other Western democracies. Growing similarities are due, in part, to the fact that American political consultants have increasingly exported their strategies to parties and candidates in other countries. While this has raised concerns about the "Americanization" of campaigns in places like Britain, Canada, and France, differences in campaign spending laws, party systems, and political culture have kept political advertising in these countries from completely replicating the American model.

RESEARCH ON ADVERTISING EFFECTS

Scholarly interest in political advertising has produced valuable insights into the nature and strategic use of ads as well as their effect on the public. Political ads have been usefully categorized based on their tone (e.g., positive, negative), approach (e.g., attack, contrast), and substance (e.g., issue, image). This work, along with massive collection and cataloging efforts, has provided the necessary foundation for understanding various aspects of political advertising.

One such area of research concerns the motivations that drive political actors in their strategic use of advertisements. Research has shown, for example, that candidates are more likely to use attack ads when they are involved in a tight race. Otherwise, they are inclined to promote their candidacy with contrasting or positive messages. However, challengers

IS THIS YOUR PRO-FAMILY
TEAM FOR 1988 ?

DUKAKIS   HORTON

Dear Fellow Marylander:

By now, you have heard of the Dukakis/Bentsen team.

But have you heard of the Dukakis/Willie Horton team?

This is the real team which voters, in particular pro-family
voters, should be concerned about because it's the Dukakis/Willie
Horton team which really tells what you can expect if Mike
Dukakis is elected in November.

You see, Willie Horton is the Massachusetts killer Dukakis
released as part of his prison furlough program for first degree
murderers sentenced to life without parole. Like fifty-eight of
his fellow killers, he decided not to return to prison when his
weekend of fun was over.

Like many of his fellow escapees, Horton committed further
violent crimes while on his "extended" furlough. In Horton's
case, he came to Maryland to ply his trade.

The Dukakis/Horton story began on the night of October 26,
1974 when Horton robbed a gas station in Massachusetts. Horton,
on parole at the time for assault with intent to murder, wasn't
satisfied with merely robbing the 17 year-old station operator.
So, he stabbed the boy 19 times, stuffed him into a trash can and
left the boy to die.

Horton was captured and convicted of armed robbery and
first-degree murder in May of 1975. Unfortunately for honest
citizens, Massachusetts' new governor Mike Dukakis had, several
weeks earlier, vetoed the death penalty bill in Massachusetts.
Horton was sentenced to life imprisonment without parole.

Thus was the Dukakis/Horton team born.

By 1986, Horton was receiving weekend furloughs from
Dukakis. After one of his "weekend vacations" Horton,
surprisingly enough, failed to return to custody.

Horton was able to run as a direct result of his teammate
Mike Dukakis' actions. You see, in 1975 the Massachusetts'

(Over, please)

Paid for by Maryland Republican Party. Contributions are not deductible for federal income tax purposes.

As part of a its advertising campaign, the Maryland Republican Party issued a letter to its members linking then-governor Michael Dukakis with murderer Willie Horton in an effort to discredit Dukakis.

SOURCE: AP Images

are generally more likely than incumbents to run negative ads because challengers need to make the case for replacing the incumbent. Furthermore, although previous research suggested that candidates avoid discussing issues "owned" by—significantly identified with—their opponent's party, more contemporary work suggests that candidates may, at times, use ads to engage in issue dialogue, particularly when races are close.

The effect of negative advertising has received considerable scholarly attention. Initially, attack ads were thought to depress voter turnout by decreasing feelings of political efficacy and satisfaction with the electoral process. Subsequent research has argued, however, that negative political ads can actually stimulate participation by providing salient and compelling information while motivating people to act against the concerns raised in the ad. This tension in the literature may be explained, at least in part, by the possibility that low levels of negativity spur participation while a saturation of negative ads drives it down. Furthermore, researchers have shown that the effects of negative advertising likely are conditioned by factors including the source of the negativity and the individual characteristics of voters, such as gender and race.

Researchers also have explored how voters are affected by political advertising more generally. Although most people claim to dislike political ads, a number of studies have shown that ads can be significantly informative. In fact, voters seem to learn more about candidates and issues from political ads than they do from newspaper or television coverage. This is because ads are succinct, shown repeatedly, and designed to be memorable, thus enhancing their reception, particularly among those who may be less interested in other forms of campaign news. However, while people may learn from political ads, the evidence suggests that ads do more to activate and reconfirm political beliefs than they do to persuade people to vote one way or another. This does not mean that political ads have little strategic value. In fact, this solidifying of beliefs seems to be quite important, as evidenced by the finding that, in general, advertising expenditures are positively associated with levels of voter support. Unfortunately, research on the ultimate impact that advertising has on election outcomes has been plagued by difficulties in measuring exposure to ads and controlling other influences in the campaign environment. So, while it is clear that political ads can have some effect on voters, questions remain about their overall role in determining electoral outcomes.

See also *Advocacy Groups; Campaigns; Public Opinion.*

. . . . MICHAEL PARKIN

BIBLIOGRAPHY

Ansolabehere, Stephen, and Shanto Iyengar. *Going Negative: How Political Advertisements Shrink and Polarize the Electorate.* New York: Free Press, 1995.

Brader, Ted. *Campaigning for Hearts and Minds: How Emotional Appeals in Political Ads Work.* Chicago: University of Chicago Press, 2006.

Brians, Craig L., and Martin P. Wattenberg. "Campaign Issue Knowledge and Salience: Comparing Reception from TV Commercials, TV News, and Newspapers." *American Journal of Political Science* 40, no. 1 (1996): 172–193.

Franz, Michael M., Paul B. Freedman, Kenneth M. Goldstein, and Travis N. Ridout. *Campaign Advertising and American Democracy.* Philadelphia: Temple University Press, 2007.

Geer, John G. *In Defense of Negativity: Attack Ads in Presidential Campaigns.* Chicago: University of Chicago Press, 2006.

Goldstein, Kenneth, and Travis A. Ridout. "Measuring the Effects of Televised Political Advertising in the United States." *Annual Review of Political Science* 7 (2004): 205–226.

Kaid, Lynda Lee, and Anne Johnston. *Videostyle in Presidential Campaigns: Style and Content of Televised Political Advertising.* Westport, Conn.: Praeger, 2001.

West, Darrel M. *Air Wars: Television Advertising in Election Campaigns, 1952–2004,* 4th ed. Washington, D.C.: CQ Press, 2005.

Advise and Consent

The U.S. Constitution, in Article II, Section 2, mandates that the Senate engage in advice and consent with presidential appointments to the executive and judicial branches. This constitutional provision is notably brief and vague pertaining to this Senate responsibility, and this has led to a variety of conflicts between presidents and senators over what constitutes the proper manner of fulfilling this congressional task. The Constitution states that it is the president who formally chooses and nominates appointees to fill vacancies to important posts in the federal government, and it is the Senate's duty to confirm or reject such nominations after reviewing them. Advice and consent is a prime example of the constitutional framework of the separation of powers among the three branches of the federal government being layered over with checks and balances. These checks and balances result ultimately in a sharing of power at times between the executive and legislative branches—in this instance, the president has the sole power of appointment, but the Senate can check that authority with its power to reject those nominations.

Working from the original phrasing in the Constitution and subsequent enactments by the Congress, the Senate must consent to presidential appointments to the following types of offices: Supreme Court justices, all other lower federal judges, Cabinet secretaries, subcabinet executive branch posts, ambassadors, and other upper-tier governmental positions. In the twenty-first century, the Senate annually receives roughly twenty thousand such nominations. The great majority of these votes are on military promotions or civilian appointments to executive branch agencies (e.g., the Public Health Service) and these are routinely approved with no challenge or controversy and minimal Senate attention. There are about one to two thousand nominations to higher-level posts that do have more significant policy implications associated with them (i.e., the position has some manner of policy-making authority), and the probability of senatorial opposition increases. That being said, the Senate still usually approves them with little difficulty.

To be confirmed and to legally take office, a nominee must receive a vote of approval by a majority of senators present and voting. Almost all nominees are approved in the Senate by unanimous consent, typically a voice vote, with little to no debate. A recorded roll call vote where it is clear how a particular senator voted on a nomination constitutes only a small percentage of all of these confirmation votes.

Some types of offices usually garner greater levels of Senate opposition than others wherein senators wish to have their preferences accounted for by the president. Judicial appointments, particularly to the Supreme Court, with their lifetime tenure and increasingly prominent policy implications of federal court decisions, have been shown to ratchet up senators' willingness to reject a nominee. The inverse is generally true for executive branch vacancies where appointees only serve for the time that their appointing president is in power—more deference is shown by senators to those selections of the president. Many senators consider it appropriate for the president to be given the greatest leeway in picking executive branch appointments, especially his Cabinet secretaries.

The onus is on opponents of a nomination to advance why the nominee should be rejected—opponents must establish the grounds for opposition to a nomination. There historically have been four primary grounds of opposition. The first three concern the nominee's personal character—competence and qualifications for the position to which the nominee has been appointed, potential conflicts of interest, and ethics. The fourth focuses on the nominee's policy views and ideology. The legitimacy of policy-based and ideological opposition to a nominee

remains a source of continuing controversy. The first three are generally considered to be valid or acceptable reasons, the fourth less so. Resistance to a nomination commonly emanates from senators who are members of the opposition party and who are ideologically distant from the appointing president.

From the 1960s onward, the greater frequency of divided government and expanded organized interest group mobilization with these appointments has worked to reinforce and increase the institutional tensions between the Senate and the White House with this advice and consent duty. When a controversy erupts over a nomination, overt hostility between these two branches has become the current norm. A strategy now more readily seen in the contemporary era compared to the past is senators' greater willingness to obstruct presidential appointments by keeping nominees from ever receiving a confirmation floor vote. Commonly seen tactics as part of this general strategy include the relevant Senate committee not holding hearings nor considering a nomination at all (a necessary step before a floor vote can occur) and the use of holds and filibusters on specific nominees by individual senators that directly prevent a floor vote.

See also *Cabinets and Cabinet Formation; Checks and Balances; Executive, The; Judicial Selection and Nomination; Supreme Court.*

· · · · · · · · · · · · · · · · · STEPHEN R. ROUTH

BIBLIOGRAPHY

Abraham, Henry J. *Justices, Presidents, and Senators: A History of U.S. Supreme Court Appointments from Washington to Clinton*, rev. ed. Lanham, Md.: Rowman and Littlefield, 1999.

Epstein, Lee, and Jeffrey A. Segal. *Advice and Consent: The Politics of Judicial Appointments.* New York: Oxford University Press, 2005.

Fisher, Louis. *Constitutional Conflicts between Congress and the President*, 4th ed., rev. Lawrence: University of Kansas Press, 1997.

Harris, Joseph P. *The Advice and Consent of the Senate: A Study of the Confirmation of Appointments by the United States Senate.* Berkeley: University of California Press, 1953.

Mackenzie, G. Calvin. *The Politics of Presidential Appointments.* New York: Free Press, 1981.

Advocacy Coalition Networks

Advocacy coalition networks, as conceptualized by Paul A. Sabatier and Hank Jenkins-Smith (1993), consist of groups of people who share a common belief system and participate in nontrivial, coordinated activities to transform their beliefs into public policy. Similar to iron triangles or policy whirlpools, advocacy coalition networks include organized interest groups, executive agencies, and members of relevant legislative committees. However, unlike the traditional conceptions of coalition groups, advocacy coalition networks recognize that many more participants are active in seeking to influence public policy, including members of the media, academic researchers, policy analysts, and comparable political actors at multiple levels of government. Advocacy coalition networks also differ from broader issue networks in that the participants of the coalition are united around shared core and secondary policy beliefs rather than a more encompassing focus on a particular policy area.

Advocacy coalition networks operate in wider policy subsystems that include all actors who are involved in a particular policy area. This includes active participants in advocacy coalitions, as well as potential *latent* actors who may be mobilized in the future. In addition to coalition participants, the policy subsystem may include *neutral* actors who become involved through technical expertise and knowledge, such as bureaucrats and academics. Policy subsystems usually include several (typically two to four) advocacy coalition networks that compete to influence policy makers, but some *quiescent* subsystems may only have a single coalition. Because coalitions are united by shared belief systems, they should be relatively stable over time, especially when the policy debate centers on core beliefs and values.

In 2002, Miles Burnett and Charles Davis provided a ready example from their analysis of the policy subsystem of U.S. national forest policy from 1960 to 1995. They identified three active coalitions. The first coalition was a commodity production coalition consisting of lumber firms, mill workers, some administrators in the U.S. Forest Service, local government officials, and members of Congress from districts economically affected by timber policy. The second coalition, pursuing conservation and environmental protection, consisted of environmental groups, water quality agencies, state and local fish and game departments, some U.S. Forest Service employees, and members of Congress who support conservation policies. The final coalition, formed around the principles of multiple use and sustained yield, includes forestry associations, the U.S. Department of Agriculture, the U.S. Bureau of Land Management, and some U.S. Forest Service employees. Each coalition utilized varying strategies, from venue shopping to using policy information to attract media attention, all aimed at influencing policy outcomes affecting national forests.

ADVOCACY COALITION NETWORKS IN THE POLICY PROCESS

Advocacy coalition networks play a central role in Sabatier and Jenkins-Smith's framework of the policy process, the *advocacy coalition framework (ACF)*. The ACF was developed as an alternative to the traditional stages model, which was seen as too simplistic and linear to be an accurate description of the policy process, and too limited in its utility to show causal mechanisms and generate testable hypotheses. The ACF focuses on the roles of information and belief systems and tracks policy change advocacy coalition networks within policy subsystems over long periods (usually a decade or more).

Under the ACF, minor or secondary aspects of policy can change as coalitions compete within a policy subsystem to influence decisions of sovereign policy makers. Importantly, advocacy coalition networks engage in policy-oriented learning, processing both technical policy information and political feedback, to update their strategies as well as secondary aspects of their belief systems. Incremental change can result from this type of policy-oriented learning. Major, nonincremental policy changes are unlikely without significant shifts in factors external to the subsystem, like socioeconomic conditions, public

attitudes, governing coalitions, and constitutional structures. Still, significant external shocks do not necessitate major policy change. Rather, minority or nondominant coalitions must skillfully use these external perturbations to gain an advantage in the subsystem that would allow them to institute core policy changes that would not have been possible under the previously dominant coalition.

APPLICATIONS AND CRITIQUES OF THE ADVOCACY COALITION FRAMEWORK

Developed around environmental politics in the United States, most studies using the ACF have addressed policy subsystems such as auto pollution control, public lands policy, and water policy. However, it also has been applied successfully to other policy areas, including national security, education, and drug policy. Though it was developed with the U.S. political system in mind, it has been used to analyze policy change in international settings as well, including roads policy in Britain, water quality policy in the Netherlands, and gender discrimination policy in Australia.

Through these varied applications, several critiques and modifications to the original framework have been offered. A 1996 study of the education policy by Michael Mintrom and Sandra Vergari noted the difficulty in predicting when major policy change might occur because external shocks were, themselves, not a sufficient cause. Several studies have suggested also that more attention be paid to issues of collective action because the primary focus of the framework centers on coalitions of varied political actors. Several applications of the ACF have found less stable coalitions than the framework originally hypothesized, leading to a distinction between *nascent* and *mature* policy subsystems. In newly formed subsystems, coalitions may be much more fluid as the stakes of the policy area may be initially unclear. As more information is generated, coalitions should become more stable and entrenched.

Finally, although advocacy coalition networks have been conceptualized under the auspices of the ACF, similar concepts of coalitions and issue networks have been used also in other frameworks of the policy process. In the *multiple streams* framework of agenda setting, John Kingdon (1984) noted that "policy communities" made up of bureaucrats, congressional staffers, think-tank researchers, and academics centered around a single policy area play a crucial role in generating policy solutions and alternatives. Policy entrepreneurs, meanwhile, actively pursue policy change by matching these solutions to emerging problems and political conditions. In Frank Baumgartner and Bryan Jones's (1993) *punctuated equilibrium* framework, groups of interests compete to exert influence in a policy subsystem. These interests actively seek to structure the decision-making authority to give themselves a policy monopoly or dominant control that leads to incremental policy change. Major policy change results from minority interests successfully altering the policy image to give themselves control over the policy subsystem. Concepts similar to advocacy coalition networks are even prominent in policy innovation and diffusion models, where issue networks and advocacy groups play a strong role in diffusing new ideas from one governmental entity to another.

See also *Coalition Formation; Interest Groups and Lobbies; Public Policy Development.*

. . . . DANIEL C. LEWIS

BIBLIOGRAPHY

Baumgartner, Frank R., and Bryan D. Jones. *Agendas and Instability in American Politics.* Chicago: University of Chicago Press, 1993.

Burnett, Miles, and Charles Davis. "Getting Out the Cut: Politics and National Forest Timber Harvests, 1960–1995." *Administration and Society* 34, no. 2 (2002): 202–228.

Heclo, Hugh. "Issue Networks and the Executive Establishment." In *The New American Political System,* edited by Anthony King, 87–124. Washington, D.C.: American Enterprise Institute, 1978.

Kingdon, John W. *Agendas, Alternatives, and Public Policies.* Boston: Little, Brown, 1984.

Mintrom, Michael, and Sandra Vergari. "Advocacy Coalitions, Policy Entrepreneurs, and Policy Change." *Policy Studies Journal* 24, no. 3 (1996): 126–148.

Sabatier, Paul A., and Hank Jenkins-Smith. *Policy Change and Learning: An Advocacy Coalition Approach.* Boulder, Colo.: Westview, 1993.

Schlager, Edella, and William Blomquist. "A Comparison of Three Emerging Theories of the Policy Process." *Political Research Quarterly* 49, no. 3 (1996): 651–672.

Advocacy Groups

In political science, advocacy groups form a subgroup of interest groups. Interest groups can represent the self-interest of their members or a broader public interest. Public interest groups also are called advocacy groups in that they seek to promote a common or collective good. But this definition is not universally shared. Some scholars, including Ross Stephens and Nelson Wikstrom (2007), assign the term *public interest groups* to lobbying organizations that represent the interest of governmental entities, such as the National League of Cities.

Another ambiguity involves the legitimacy of advocacy activities. Traditionally, scholars have accepted advocacy groups as essential components of pluralist democracy, while more recently issue advocacy has been associated with negative forms of political communication.

BRIEF HISTORY

Advocacy groups can trace their origin to political movements in the nineteenth century. Organizations with dedicated leaders and dues-paying members emerged to pursue a variety of political causes and seek fundamental constitutional changes, such as the abolition of slavery or suffrage for women. Improved literacy made it possible to print newspapers and pamphlets to mobilize supporters and educate the public.

Advocacy groups survived over time by adapting their goals and tactics to changing political conditions. The NAACP, for instance, was founded in 1909 to promote civil rights, as well as educational and economic opportunities, for people of color. After women obtained the right to vote in 1920, activists reconstituted themselves as the League of Women Voters to educate women about their new right, as well as to promote good government reforms.

Advocacy for animals, plants, and unique landscapes has its roots in the nineteenth century as well. The idea of conservation and the creation of national parks established a foundation for the contemporary environmental movement. Today, the high-tech revolution and new forms of communication have made the mobilization of supporters much easier, but also has facilitated the spread of misinformation.

SCOPE, PURPOSE, AND IRS RULES

The organizational structure of advocacy groups varies, depending on the cause they are championing. Some are international in scope, and they may have offices in major world cities. U.S. advocacy groups with a national focus tend to have their headquarters in the Washington, D.C., area, with chapters spread across the country. Quite a few groups promote statewide, regional, or local causes, and their geographical presence is limited accordingly.

The incorporation of advocacy groups is regulated by state law, while tax-exempt status comes under the purview of the Internal Revenue Service (IRS). The tax code makes two distinctions that delineate the limits imposed on lobbying and political involvements of advocacy groups. One is the distinction between section 501(c)(3) and 501(c)(4) organizations.

Those 501(c)(3) entities, including foundations, have to be organized and operated for purposes such as religious, charitable, educational, scientific, or cultural objectives. Among tax-exempt organizations, 501(c)(3) groups enjoy the most favorable tax treatment. Not only are they exempt from the federal income tax, but they also can accept tax deductible donations.

In return for the favorable tax treatment, 501(c)(3) entities are limited in their advocacy work and lobbying. In 1934, new tax law stipulated that "no substantial part" of the organization's activities could be used to influence the legislative process. In 1976, Congress passed legislation that allowed 501(c)(3) organizations either to continue under the "no substantial part" clause or under new rules that set specific dollar amounts depending on the size of the organization. Congress and the IRS settled on generous limits to avoid violating First Amendment rights. The 501(c)(3) groups can work also within IRS rules by presenting their advocacy work as educational efforts and by using volunteers rather than paid lobbyists to speak to legislators. They also can create 501(c)(4) subsidiaries.

The appropriate Internal Revenue Code for tax-exempt organizations that want to make advocacy their major mission is section 501(c)(4). It covers entities that seek to promote general social welfare and civic improvements. The activities have to support a public-serving cause; they cannot be of a membership-serving nature. Financial support for 501(c)(4) comes in the form of dues and non-tax-deductible donations from members who believe in the cause. Major 501(c)(4) groups have foundations as affiliates, to which tax-deductible donations for educational and other appropriate purposes can be directed.

The second important distinction in the federal tax code is between (1) lobbying and seeking to influence the policymaking process versus (2) partisan political activities and electioneering. Neither 501(c)(3) nor 501(c)(4) organizations can engage in election activities, by which the IRS means explicitly supporting or opposing candidates running for political office. However, for more direct electoral involvement, 501(c)(4) entities can create political organizations under section 527. The Federal Election Campaign Act of 1971 (FECA), as amended, limits the amount of money section 527 entities can spend for or against candidates. However, FECA created new ambiguities, which the Supreme Court tried to resolve by distinguishing between *express advocacy*, such as mentioning a candidate, and *issue advocacy*, or focusing on a policy issue. The express form of political communication falls under FECA, but issue advocacy does not.

See also *Interest Groups and Lobbies; Political Action Committee (PAC); Public Interest Groups.*

. . . . SIEGRUN FOX FREYSS

BIBLIOGRAPHY

Berry, Jeffrey M. *The Interest Group Society,* 3rd ed. New York: Longman, 1997.

Boris, Elizabeth T., and Jeff Krehely. "Civic Participation and Advocacy." In *The State of Nonprofit America,* edited by Lester M. Salamon, 299–330. Washington, D.C.: Brookings Institution, 2003.

Dwyre, Diana. "Campaigning Outside the Law: Interest Group Issue Advocacy." In *Interest Group Politics,* 6th ed., edited by Allan J. Cigler and Burdett A. Loomis, 141–159. Washington, D.C.: CQ Press, 2002.

Fowler, Linda L., Constantine J. Spiliotes, and Lynn Vavreck. "Group Advocacy in the New Hampshire Presidential Primary." In *The Interest Group Connection: Electioneering, Lobbying, and Policymaking in Washington,* 2nd ed., edited by Paul S. Herrnson, Ronald G. Shaiko, and Clyde Wilcox, 89–111. Washington, D.C.: CQ Press, 2005.

O'Neill, Michael. *The Third America. The Emergence of the Nonprofit Sector in the United States.* San Francisco: Jossey-Bass, 1989.

Skocpol, Theda. "How Americans Became Civic." In *Civic Engagement in American Democracy,* edited by Theda Skocpol and Morris P. Fiorina, 27–80. Washington, D.C.: Brookings Institution, 1999.

Smucker, Robert. *The Nonprofit Lobbying Guide,* 2nd ed. Washington, D.C.: Independent Sector, 1999.

Stephens, G. Ross, and Nelson Wikstrom. *American Intergovernmental Relations: A Fragmented Federal Polity.* New York: Oxford University Press, 2007.

Affirmative Action

Redistribution of wealth and other benefits is a common function of government. Controversies over the extent of redistribution are the principal basis of politics in many countries. When this redistribution is based on characteristics acquired at birth, such as race, ethnicity, caste, or gender, controversy often increases because the redistribution may exacerbate group rivalries and be inconsistent with other values, such as equal protection of the law. Such redistribution is often called *affirmative action*. Economist Thomas Sowell, the principal scholar comparing such policies, has identified them in such diverse counties as India, Malaysia, Nigeria, Sri Lanka, and the United States. Additionally, more limited versions exist in Britain, Canada, France, New Zealand, and Pakistan.

The origins of affirmative action vary by country. In the United States, the Fourteenth Amendment to the Constitution and almost all civil rights laws prohibit discrimination and require governments and many private entities to treat all persons equally. As the civil rights movement changed from advocacy of race-blind equal opportunity programs to race-conscious programs, which some saw as necessary to achieve proportional representation, affirmative action became the preferred tool in the areas of employment, higher education, public education, and voting rights. Such policies are now deeply embedded in both the public and private sector of American life as a device to overcome the legacies of past discrimination, create diversity, and attract political support from under-represented groups. In India and Malaysia, affirmative action programs began under British colonial rule and have survived independence and expanded their coverage. In India, during the 1950s and 1960s free secondary school opportunities and, in some states, free books, supplies, and meals were offered to members of select castes and tribes. Later, university slots were preserved for them. Such actions helped to unite various Hindu castes behind Hindu political parties. In Malaysia, nationalist parties sought to reduce the influence of Chinese and Indians in that country by providing education and employment benefits to the native Malay and *bumipateras* or "sons of the soil" populations.

The controversy over affirmative action programs stems from several factors. First, most legal systems, including the United Nations (UN) Charter, proclaim the principle of equal treatment for all individuals. When affirmative action programs promote equal treatment or when they promote preferences, sometimes called *reverse discrimination*, has received careful study. Such studies are complex and often not welcomed by some stakeholders who often have strong association with group identities and politics.

Second, disagreements exist over which groups should benefit from affirmative action programs. In many countries, such as Britain and New Zealand, the policies benefit demographic minorities, but in some cases the number of beneficiaries has spread to encompass populations not envisioned at the programs' inception. In the United States, for example, the moral driver for affirmative action has been the more than three-hundred-year history of mistreatment of African Americans and Native Americans. The principal beneficiaries, however, often have been white women, as well as Asian Americans and Hispanic Americans, some of whom faced discrimination based on national origin or ancestry while others are more recent immigrants. In India and Malaysia, the majority of the population is entitled to preferences.

Third, affirmative action programs may be justified as temporary remedies, but in fact the inequalities that the programs are designed to address are difficult to eliminate. In the United States, judicial rulings require that governments (but not private organizations) must have a compelling interest to use racial classifications by making findings that they are remedying discrimination for which they are responsible. Affirmative action programs also must be narrowly tailored to remedy that discrimination, which may restrict the scope of beneficiary groups and benefits, but litigation to enforce those judicial principles is often lengthy and costly to undertake.

For all of these reasons, affirmative action programs remain controversial in the countries that have adopted them. Elites sometimes see affirmative action as a moral undertaking, but the preferences rarely threaten their status. Further, they see these programs as useful symbolic policies adding to social stability or as marketing tools to obtain votes or to sell products. Beneficiary groups seek to expand the reach of affirmative action programs. As these programs become bureaucratically institutionalized, they develop infrastructures supported by government, corporate, foundation, and educational funds. Opponents are rarely so well organized or funded. They often have majority public opinion support, however, and can invoke with some sympathy in legal forums defending the principle of equal protection.

The global economy and the growing migration of peoples are likely to leave most countries increasingly multiethnic and multireligious. This will add to the difficulty of reconciling the political value of eliminating inequalities with the legal value of treating individuals equally. Whatever it may be called in the future and whatever form it takes, something like affirmative action programs will continue to be controversial in a number of countries worldwide.

See also *Caste System; Civil and Political Rights; Civil Rights Movement; Discrimination; Economic, Social, and Cultural Rights; Positive Discrimination; Racial Discrimination; Reverse Discrimination; Segregation and Desegregation; Xenophobia.*

. . . . GEORGE R. LA NOUE

BIBLIOGRAPHY

Becker, Gary S. *The Economics of Discrimination.* Chicago: University of Chicago Press, 1971.

Callister, Paul. *Special Measures to Reduce Ethnic Disadvantage in New Zealand: An Examination of their Role.* Wellington, N.Z.: Institute of Policy Studies, 2007.

Galanter, Marc. *Competing Inequalities: Law and the Backward Classes in India.* Berkeley: University of California Press, 1984.

Graham, Hugh D. *The Civil Rights Era: Origins and Development of National Policy 1960–1972.* New York: Oxford University Press, 1990.

Guinier, Lani, and Gerald Torres. *The Miner's Canary: Enlisting Race, Resisting Power, Transforming Democracy.* Cambridge, Mass.: Harvard University Press, 2002.

Kymlicka, Will. *Multicultural Citizenship: A Liberal Theory of Minority Rights.* New York: Oxford University Press 1995.

Jesudason, James. *Ethnicity and the Economy: The State, Chinese Business, and Multinationals in Malaysia.* Kuala Lumpur: Oxford University Press, 1989.

Leiter, Samuel, and William M. Leiter. *Affirmative Action and Anti-discrimination Law and Policy.* Albany: State University of New York, 2002.

Skrentny, John David. *The Ironies of Affirmative Action: Politics, Culture, and Justice in America.* Chicago: University of Chicago Press, 1996.

Sowell, Thomas. *Affirmative Action around the World: An Empirical Study.* New Haven, Conn.: Yale University Press, 2004.

Thernstrom, Stephan, and Abigail Thernstrom. *America in Black and White: One Nation Indivisible.* New York: Simon and Shuster, 1997.

Aflaq, Michel

A Greek Orthodox Christian Syrian, Michel Aflaq (1910–1989) became one of two founders, along with his Muslim countryman, Salah al-Din Bitar, of the Baath (Ba'th; "rebirth" or "resurrection") Party in the early 1940s. He was regarded as the party's leading thinker. Aflaq considered Egyptian president Gamal Abdel Nasser to be a charismatic leader for the Arabs and, with the idea that Baathists could play a leading role in what he saw as the beginning of a pan-Arab

state, lent his support to the formation of the United Arab Republic (UAR) in 1958. However, Baathists were disappointed with their actual role in the UAR, leading some of them, not including Aflaq, to endorse its breakup in 1961. Aflaq participated in abortive attempts to form another UAR in 1963, following Baathist coups in both Iraq and Syria.

He gave up his position as Secretary General of the National (i.e., pan-Arab) Command in 1965, and took refuge in Europe and Brazil after a radical military faction of the Baath, which he opposed, took power in Damascus in 1966. After the Baathist takeover in Iraq in 1968, Aflaq returned to the Middle East, at first living mainly in Beirut before moving to Baghdad, where he became Secretary General of the Iraqi-sponsored Baathist National Command (a bitter rival to the Syrian-backed National Command). The position was essentially symbolic. Aflaq allegedly converted to Islam late in life.

Aflaq was involved in politics from childhood, as his nationalist father suffered imprisonment both by the Ottomans, who ruled the country until 1918, and by France, to whom the League of Nations assigned Syria as a mandated territory. At age eighteen, he went to Paris to study history, philosophy, and literature at the Sorbonne, where he established an Arab student organization before returning home in 1932. Aflaq worked as a history teacher in secondary school for the next ten years. In Paris, he was influenced by Marxist ideas and even contributed to a communist periodical, but never joined the Communist Party, about which he apparently had reservations. Eventually, in his own words, he "became disenchanted and felt betrayed" when the Popular Front government of Leon Blum in France failed to end France's colonialist policies. This caused Aflaq to think instead of creating a synthesis of socialism and Arab nationalism.

His three attempts to win a seat in the Syrian parliament during the 1940s failed, apparently at least in part because of electoral fraud, resulting in Aflaq's disillusionment with the democratic route to change. His political activities led to imprisonment for short periods. Aflaq briefly held a cabinet position as minister of education in 1949, after which he decided to play the role of party philosopher rather than office holder. He published numerous essays and short stories portraying the ills of traditional Arab society and calling for change along socialist, democratic, and nationalist lines. Aflaq was not a dynamic speaker but he was effective in talking to small groups, with whom his interaction is said to have been much like that with students during his teaching days. He was noted for his "frugal" lifestyle and for refraining from using his influence for personal gain.

See also *Baathism; Middle Eastern Politics and Society; Pan-Arabism and Pan-Islamism.*

. . . . GLENN E. PERRY

BIBLIOGRAPHY

Aflak [Aflaq], Michel. *Choice of Texts from the Ba'th Party Founder's Thought.* N.p.: Arab Ba'th Socialist Party, 1977.

Aflaq, Michel. *In the Cause of the Baath: The Complete Political Writings of Michel Aflaq,* 2009, http://albaath.online.fr/index.htm.

Babikian, N. Salem. "A Partial Reconstruction of Michel Aflaq's Thought: The Role of Islam in the Formulation of Arab Nationalism." *The Muslim World* 67 (October 1977): 280–294.

Binder, Leonard. *The Ideological Revolution in the Middle East.* New York: Wiley, 1964.

Devlin, John F. "Aflaq, Michel." In *Political Leaders of the Contemporary Middle East and North Africa: A Biographical Dictionary,* edited by Bernard Reich, 32–39. New York: Greenwood, 1990.

Khadduri, Majid. *Arab Contemporaries: The Role of Personalities in Politics.* Baltimore: Johns Hopkins University Press, 1973.

Africa, Anglophone

See *Anglophone Africa.*

Africa, Francophone

See *Francophone Africa.*

Africa, Health Policy in

See *Multiple Streams Theory.*

Africa, Postindependence

See *Postindependent Africa, Politics and Governance in.*

African Political Economy

African political economy is a field of study within political science that analyzes the relationship between the state and the market in Africa. This field is generally geographically delimited to include only sub-Saharan Africa. The major preoccupation of scholarship in this discipline has been analyzing the role of the state in promoting economic growth and poverty alleviation.

THE FAILURE OF STATE-LED DEVELOPMENT

As sub-Saharan African countries gained independence (primarily in the 1950s and 1960s), policy makers and scholars alike emphasized the importance of the state in driving development in the new African countries. Due to the weakness of the indigenous capitalist classes in these countries, it was assumed the state would lead the development process. In both socialist countries, like Tanzania, and more market-oriented countries, like Nigeria, the state subsidized industries, manipulated exchange rates, and restricted international trade with the goal of encouraging industrialization.

However, by the early 1980s, the failures of the prevailing development strategy had become clear. Most countries in Africa were experiencing a decline in growth rates, an erosion of per capita income, and an increase in external debt. A World Bank investigation into the economic crisis laid the blame squarely on the interventionist policies adopted by African governments. The publication, which became known as the Berg Report (World Bank, 1981), argued that these policies had undermined the functioning of the market and had created bloated public sectors.

The major puzzle motivating academic research was why African governments had not abandoned these interventionist policies once it became obvious they were not stimulating growth. The key insight of the political economy literature was that governments often secured political gains from economic mismanagement. Robert Bates (1981) influentially argued that governments had incentives to distort the operation of the economy to secure cheap food for organizationally powerful urbanites at the expense of the rural population. Richard Sandbrook (1985) emphasized that African leaders depended on the disbursement of patronage to maintain political support, which resulted in poor policy choices and incompetent administration.

STRUCTURAL ADJUSTMENT AND EXTERNAL ACCOUNTABILITY

In response to the recommendations of the Berg Report, the World Bank and the International Monetary Fund (IMF) decided to make future loans to African governments conditional on a reduction in state intervention in the economy. The structural adjustment programs (SAPs) countries were required to adopt in return for new loans involved cutting the fiscal deficit, devaluing exchange rates, and liberalizing trade policy. The prescribed policies were highly contentious within Africa. The United Nations Economic Commission for Africa challenged the Berg Report's explanation for the economic crisis, instead blaming colonialism and Africa's subordinate position in the global economy. Many countries experienced "IMF riots" in which citizens protested against the austerity measures proscribed by the SAPs. However, in the face of balance-of-payments crises, most African countries eventually had little choice but to adopt SAPs.

The political science literature on structural adjustment focused on the interaction between regime type and economic reform. The initial consensus was that SAPs could only be implemented by authoritarian governments, because draconian measures were necessary to implement unpopular economic reforms. However, Nicolas van de Walle (2001) demonstrated that authoritarian governments were not any more successful in implementing reform than their democratic counterparts in Africa. He argued that both autocrats and democratically elected leaders depend on the allocation of patronage to remain in power. As a result, they have all resisted reducing public sector employment, even as they have cut educational and medical programming. Although a few countries, such as Ghana, have experienced sustained growth following economic reform, SAPs have brought limited benefits overall.

STATE CAPACITY AND PARTICIPATORY DEVELOPMENT

In the aftermath of structural adjustment, the new consensus was that African governments needed to play a greater constructive role in fostering development; they could not simply engage in fewer negative interventions. Governments must—at a minimum—provide basic law and order if they are to encourage their citizens to be economically productive. In addition, economic development requires public investment in infrastructure, education, and health. Both academics and policy makers emphasized the need to build the capacity of African states to deliver basic goods and services to their citizens. This view corresponded with the United Nations' development of the Millennium Development Goals, which commit member states to increasing access to primary education and basic health care.

Furthermore, in contrast to the earlier consensus that citizen participation would hinder economic reform, the new argument was that citizens should drive the development process because they had an interest in ensuring economic improvement and poverty alleviation. International agencies adopted the mantra of "participatory development" in the hope that domestic pressure would be more successful than external pressure in encouraging economic development.

As a result, many observers were optimistic about the reintroduction of multiparty elections and the decentralization of government in Africa during the 1990s. Democratization and decentralization were thought to increase citizens' ability to demand development. In a similar vein, the proliferation of nongovernmental organizations (NGOs) and civil society associations was encouraged as means of delivering development.

Later studies have been more uncertain about the developmental impact of democracy and participation. David Stasavage (2005) demonstrates that democratization is associated with increased government spending on primary education. However, many scholars have argued that elections and NGOs simply provide new venues for preexisting political practices; established politicians will stay in power by disbursing patronage to their supporters, rather than providing programming with broad welfare benefits.

Certainly, neither donor conditionality nor domestic participation has initiated a quick recovery of African economies. In contrast, recent research has found that structural factors, such as ethnic diversity and geography, explain a significant component of African governments' poor performance in providing public goods. A longer view of the development process may be necessary, given the importance of historical factors in explaining Africa's weak economic performance.

See also *African Union; Authoritarianism, African; Political Economy; Postindependent Africa, Politics and Governance in.*

. . . . KATE BALDWIN

BIBLIOGRAPHY

Ake, Claude. *Democracy and Development in Africa.* Washington, D.C.: Brookings Institution, 1996.

Bates, Robert. *Markets and States in Tropical Africa: The Political Basis of Agricultural Policies.* Berkeley: University of California Press, 1981.

Chabal, Patrick, and Jean-Pascal Daloz. *Africa Works: The Political Instrumentalization of Disorder.* Bloomington: International African Institute, in association with James Currey and Indiana University Press, 1999.

Habyarimana, James, Macartan Humphreys, Daniel Posner, and Jeremy Weinstein. *Coethnicity: Diversity and the Dilemmas of Collective Action.* New York: Russell Sage Foundation, 2009.

Herbst, Jeffrey. *States and Power in Africa: Comparative Lessons in Authority and Control.* Princeton, N.J.: Princeton University Press, 2000.

Mkandawire, Thandika, and Adebayo Olukoshi, eds. *Between Liberalisation and Oppression: The Politics of Structural Adjustment in Africa.* Dakar, Senegal: Codesria, 1995.

Sandbrook, Richard. *The Politics of Africa's Economic Stagnation.* Cambridge: Cambridge University Press, 1985.

Stasavage, David. "Democracy and Education Spending in Africa." *American Journal of Political Science* 49 (April 2005): 343–358.

van de Walle, Nicholas. *African Economies and the Politics of Permanent Crisis, 1979–1999.* New York: Cambridge University Press, 2001.

World Bank. *Accelerated Development in Sub-Saharan Africa: An Agenda for Action* ("Berg Report"). Washington, D.C.: World Bank, 1981.

African Political Thought

Modern African political thought refers to the political theories and ideologies enunciated in the speeches, autobiographies, writings, and policy statements of African statesmen and scholars. It varies according to historical circumstances and constantly changing African and world political environments. Political theory and political practice are inextricably linked, which makes for six distinctive periods of African history, each with its own dominant theories: indigenous Africa; imperial Africa; colonial Africa; and (early, middle, and late) modern or postcolonial Africa.

EARLY MODERN AFRICAN NATIONALISM

Early modern African nationalism was developed in the late nineteenth century by British-educated elites in West Africa. In Sierra Leone, James Africanus B. Horton, a doctor of medicine, challenged racist theories and argued that Africans were as capable of achieving "civilization" as Europeans, both biologically and psychologically. He advocated the development of "modern" states in Africa. In Liberia, Edward Wilmot Blyden, politician, writer, and diplomat, developed an ideology of racial pride and nonacculturation and advocated African development through an authentic indigenous Africa, based on an African personality, history, and culture. He also called for the establishment of a West African state. In the Gold Coast [Ghana], Joseph E. Casely Hayford, a lawyer, advocated modernization from indigenous African roots. He believed that African nations, civilization, and political institutions could be revived and modernized to cater to modern needs in an "African way." He also called for the creation of a West African nation.

PAN-AFRICANISM

The next major movement in African political thought, pan-Africanism, was prominently promoted by the African Diaspora—scholars and activists of African descent living in other nations. Pan-Africanism is a political and cultural ideal and movement born in the 1900s aimed at regrouping and mobilizing Africans in Africa and in the Diaspora against foreign domination, oppression, and discrimination. Political pan-Africanism is linked to African nationalism (i.e., the struggle for independence), while economic pan-Africanism is linked to the struggle against imperialism and neocolonialism. The major proponents of pan-Africanism in North America were W. E. B. Du Bois, Marcus Garvey, Paul L. Robeson, and George Padmore. The so-called back to Africa movement (i.e., the return of the African slaves to their continent of origin) mainly advocated by Garvey, led to the creation of Sierra Leone in 1801 and Liberia in 1817. Cultural pan-Africanism was expressed through *Négritude,* a cultural movement reasserting African culture, values, and traditions as part of the common heritage of mankind. Négritude emerged in France in the 1930s among African and Afro-Caribbean elites, notably Aimé Césaire, Léon-Gontran Damas, and Léopold Sédar Senghor.

MODERN AFRICAN NATIONALISM

Modern African nationalism is a political ideal and movement aimed a liberating Africans from European colonial political domination, cultural oppression, social exclusion, and economic exploitation. The goal was to achieve political independence as a prelude to economic independence. In Kwame Nkrumah's words, "Seek ye first the political kingdom and all else will be added unto you." The challenge of African nationalism was to build viable nations out of more than fifty artificially created states, most of which attained independence in the 1960s.

AFRICAN SOCIALISM

African socialism is a radical form of African nationalism. Influenced by Marxism-Leninism (though officially non-Marxist), African socialism rejects capitalism as being alien to African culture and traditions. Instead, it is based on the African tradition of *communalism,* according to which the group takes precedence over the individual. The socialist model of development includes a state-led development strategy based on planning, land reform, industrialization, and the nationalization of the economy. The foreign policy of African Socialist states is pan-Africanist. The African countries (and leaders) who adopted this ideology between 1960 and 1970 were Algeria (Ahmed Ben Bella); Ghana (Kwame Nkrumah, 1962); Guinea (Ahmed Sékou Touré); Mali (Modibo Keïta), and Tanzania (Julius K. Nyerere, 1968). Senegal (Léopold Senghor) and Kenya (Jomo Kenyatta) paid lip service to African socialism but did not actually implement it.

AFRICAN THEORIES OF REVOLUTION

Frantz Fanon, a French-born psychiatrist from Martinique who joined the Algerian revolution, posits that under the guidance of revolutionary intellectuals, the peasantry is a revolutionary force in Africa. He argues that it is only through violence that the colonized people can achieve their freedom. For Fanon (1968), decolonization is a violent revolution that destroys the social and political structures of the colonial regime, liberates consciousness, and creates a new man. He argues that violence is a cleansing force, but that it must be accompanied by political education if it is to be truly emancipatory.

Amilcar Cabral, an agronomist and leader of the liberation struggle in Guinea-Bissau, sees culture as a form of resistance to foreign domination. Cabral (1972) argues that culture is a weapon against the imperialist power; it becomes the instrument through which people reclaim their history. For him, the main goal of the liberation movement is not only national independence and the defeat of colonialism, but also the economic,

social, and cultural progress of the people. This can occur only when foreign domination has been totally eliminated.

AFRICAN MARXIST REGIMES

The period 1969 to 1975 saw the emergence of African Marxist regimes—many of them military—which adopted Marxism-Leninism as the state ideology. However, in general, the self-proclaimed "Marxist" African leaders did not genuinely believe in this ideology but simply used it an instrument of political domination and control of the people. The African countries (and leaders) who adopted this ideology were Angola (Agostinho Neto and José Eduardo dos Santos); Benin (Mathieu Kérékou); Congo-Brazzaville (Marien Ngouabi, Joachim Yhombi-Opango, and Denis Sassou-Nguesso); Ethiopia (Mengistu Haile Mariam); Guinea-Bissau (Luís Cabral and João Bernardo Vieira); Madagascar (Didier Ratsiraka); Mozambique (Samora Machel and Joaquim Chissano); Namibia (Sam Nujoma); Somalia (Mohammed Siad Barre); and Zimbabwe (Robert Mugabe), 1980–1995. Marxism as a state ideology was officially abandoned everywhere in Africa by 1996.

AFRICAN POPULIST REGIMES

Emerging in the early 1980s, African populism borrows elements of both African socialism and Marxism-Leninism, and places the people at the center of democracy and development in Africa. Its main policy is to satisfy the basic needs of the peasantry, the largest and poorest social class in Africa. African populist regimes advocate popular democracy and people-centered development. African populist regimes include Burkina Faso (Thomas Sankara); Ghana (Jerry Rawlings); Libya (Muammar Qaddafi) since 1977; and Zimbabwe (Robert Mugabe) since 1995.

AFRICAN THEORIES OF DEMOCRACY AND DEVELOPMENT

Three African scholars (Claude Ake, Daniel Osabu-Kle, and Mueni wa Muiu) have recently developed Africa-centered theories of democracy and development.

Nigerian scholar-activist Claude Ake notes that in the postindependence era, the African elites have privatized the African state for their own benefit, leading to the marginalization of the African people. Ake (1996, 1) argues that "the problem is not so much that development has failed as that it was never really on the agenda in the first place." Like the populists, he advocates popular development (in which people are the end, agent, and means of development), and popular democracy (which emphasizes political, social, and economic rights).

Ghanaian scholar Daniel Osabu-Kle (2000) starts from the assumptions that indigenous African political culture was essentially democratic and consensual, based on the accountability of the rulers to the people. He argues that only a democracy compatible with the African cultural environment (i.e., a modernized form of Africa's indigenous democracy) is capable of achieving the political conditions for successful development in Africa.

Mueni wa Muiu introduces a new paradigm to study the African state. According to *A New Paradigm of the African State: Fundi wa Afrika* (2009), the current African predicament may be explained by the systematic destruction of African states and the dispossession, exploitation, and marginalization of African people through successive historical processes (from the trans-Atlantic slave trade to globalization). Muiu argues that a new, viable, and modern African state based on five political entities—the Federation of African States—should be built on the functional remnants of indigenous African political systems and institutions and be based on African values, traditions, and culture.

See also *African Union; Pan-Africanism; Postindependent Africa, Politics and Governance in.*

. . . .   GUY MARTIN

BIBLIOGRAPHY

Ake, Claude. *Democracy and Development in Africa*. Washington, D.C.: Brookings Institution, 1996.

Boele van Hensbroek, Pieter. *Political Discourses in African Thought, 1860 to the Present*. Westport, Conn.: Praeger, 1999.

Cabral, Amilcar. *Revolution in Guinea*. New York: Monthly Review Press, 1972.

Fanon, Frantz. *The Wretched of the Earth*. New York: Grove, 1968.

Idahosa, P. L. E. *The Populist Dimension to African Political Thought*. Trenton, N.J.: Africa World Press, 2003.

Muiu, Mueni wa, and Guy Martin. *A New Paradigm of the African State: Fundi wa Afrika*. New York: Palgrave Macmillan, 2009.

Mutiso, Gideon-Cyrus M., and S. W. Rohio, eds. *Readings in African Political Thought*. London: Heinemann Educational Books, 1975.

Nkrumah, Kwame. *Towards Colonial Freedom: Africa in the Struggle against World Imperialism*. London: Heinemann, 1962.

Nyerere, Julius K. *Ujamaa: Essays on Socialism*. London: Oxford University Press, 1968.

Osabu-Kle, Daniel. *Compatible Cultural Democracy: The Key to Development in Africa*. Toronto: UTP Higher Education, 2000.

Rosberg, Carl G., and Thomas M. Callaghy, eds. *Socialism in Sub-Saharan Africa: A New Assessment*. Berkeley: Institute of International Studies/ University of California, 1979.

Young, Crawford. *Ideology and Development in Africa*. New Haven, Conn.: Yale University Press, 1982.

African Politics and Society

Throughout this entry, *Africa* refers to sub-Saharan Africa, the region south of the Saharan Desert that is bounded in the north and west by Mauritania; in the east by Eritrea, Ethiopia, Sudan, and Somalia; and in the south by the Republic of South Africa.

The contemporary political history of Africa is marked by imperialism, the expulsion of foreign powers and settler elites, and the postindependence travails of its roughly fifty states.

IMPERIALISM

Africa was among the last regions of the globe to be subject to imperial rule. In the so-called scramble for Africa, as described by Thomas Pakenham in his 1991 book of that title, the British and French seized major portions of the continent; Belgium, Germany, Italy, Portugal, and Spain seized lesser holdings as well. During the imperial era, most of Africa's people were subject to the rule of bureaucrats in London, Lisbon, and Paris rather than being ruled by leaders they themselves had chosen. Two states in Africa had long been independent: Ethiopia from time immemorial and Liberia since 1847. In 1910, the

settlers of South Africa succeeded in securing independence from British bureaucrats.

European immigrants settled in several territories: Kenya in the east, the Rhodesias in the center, and portions of southern Africa. Conflicts between the settler populations and colonial bureaucrats characterized the politics of the colonial era, as white settlers strove to control the colonial governments of these colonies and to dominate their native populations.

While Africa's peoples fought against the seizure of their territories, they lacked the wealth, organization, and weaponry to prevail. The situation changed, however, during World War I (1914–1918) and World War II (1939–1945). The wars eroded the capacity and will of Europeans to occupy foreign lands, while economic development increased the capacity and desire of Africa's people to end European rule.

During World War II, the allied powers maintained important bases in Africa, some poised to support campaigns in the Mediterranean and others to backstop armies fighting in Asia. After World War II, the colonial powers promoted the development of African export industries, seeking thereby to earn funds to repay loans contracted with the United States to finance the war. The increase in exports led to the creation of a class of prosperous farmers and the rise of merchants and lawyers who provided services to the export industries. As World War II gave way to the cold war, the United States began to stockpile precious metals and invested in expanding Africa's mines, refining its ores, and transporting its precious metals overseas. That Africa's economic expansion took place at the time of Europe's decline prepared the field for its political liberation. The one was prospering while the other was not, and their relative power shifted accordingly.

NATIONALIST REVOLT

Among the first Africans to rally against European rule were urban elites, whose aspirations were almost immediately checked by resident officials of the colonial powers. Workers who staffed the ports and railways that tied local producers to foreign markets soon joined them. In the rural areas, peasants rallied to the struggle against colonial rule, some protesting intensified demands for labor and the use of coercion rather than wage payment to secure it. Among the primary targets of the rural population were the chiefs, who had been tasked by colonial rulers with taxing the profits of farmers and regulating the use of their lands. Thus did the Kenya Africa Union support dock strikes in Mombasa and the intimidation of chiefs in the native reserves. Similarly, the Convention Peoples' Party backed strikes in the Gold Coast (now Ghana) port cities of Tema and Takoradi, while seeking to "destool" chiefs inland.

Adding to the rise of nationalist protest was global inflation. Reconstruction in Europe and rearmament in the United States ran up against shortages of materials and higher prices in global markets. Throughout Africa and the developing world, consumers rallied to protest against these increases, tending to blame them on European monopolies—such as in Ghana, where the people focused their anger on the United Africa Company—or local trading communities—such as the Indian merchants in Kenya or Lebanese traders in Sierra Leone.

After its independence, Kwame Nkrumah (second from right) became prime minister of Ghana. Within a few years, he amassed substantial power before being toppled by a military coup in 1966.

SOURCE: © Bettmann/Corbis

The economic development of Africa thus transformed the social composition and political preferences of its people. It was in the postwar period, however, that independence was achieved by the vast majority of Africa's people. At first, political liberty arrived in a trickle—to the Sudan in 1956 and Ghana in 1957. Soon thereafter independence came as a flood, with twenty-nine French- and English-speaking states securing independence from 1960 to 1965, the Portuguese territories in the mid-1970s, and the settler redoubts of southern Africa in the last decades of the twentieth century.

THE POSTINDEPENDENCE PERIOD

The optimism of the nationalist period very quickly gave way to pessimism, as governments that had seized power turned authoritarian or were displaced by military regimes. Ghana's experience was emblematic of this early postindependence trend. Ghana had been among the first African countries to attain self-governance (1954) and then independence (1957). Both events were celebrated not only in Africa but throughout the globe. In 1960, a change in the constitution gave Kwame Nkrumah, as head of state, the power to dismiss civil servants, judges, and military officers without the authorization of parliament. In 1963, the president acquired the power to detain persons charged with political crimes and to try their cases in special courts. When, in 1964, Nkrumah proclaimed the ruling party the sole legal party in Ghana, he both followed and gave impetus to the trend toward single-party rule on the continent. When, in 1966, Ghana's military toppled the Nkrumah regime, Ghana joined Sudan, Benin, Togo, and the Central African Republic—all states in which the national military had overthrown a civilian regime (in 1958, 1962, 1963, and 1965 respectively). Following the military's overthrow of Nkrumah's government in Ghana, armed forces drove civilian governments from power in Burkina Faso, Nigeria, and Burundi in 1966, and Congo in 1968. By the mid-1970s, the military held power in one-third of the nations of sub-Saharan Africa.

By the mid-1970s, the politics of Africa had turned authoritarian. Only four states in Africa—Botswana, Gambia, Mauritius, and Senegal—retained multiparty systems. Figure 1 captures this turn to authoritarianism in postindependence Africa.

LATE-CENTURY POLITICS

The politics of late-century Africa was marked by two major trends. The first was the return to multiparty politics;

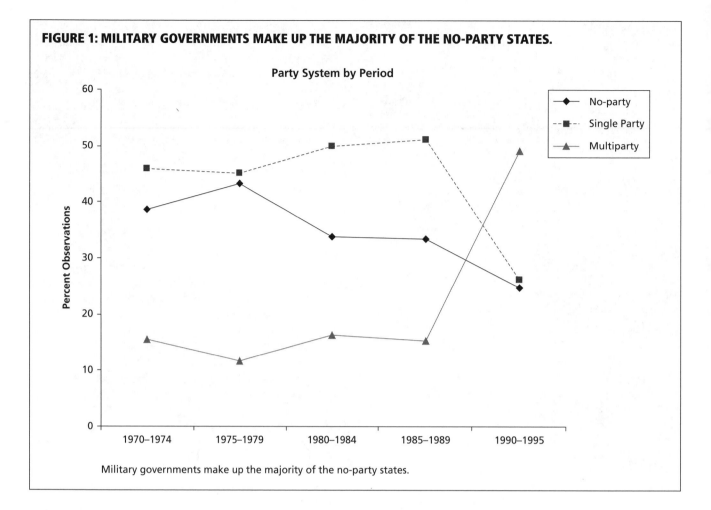

FIGURE 1: MILITARY GOVERNMENTS MAKE UP THE MAJORITY OF THE NO-PARTY STATES.

Party System by Period

Military governments make up the majority of the no-party states.

the second, an increase in political violence. These trends had common origins in global political and economic crises.

Beginning with the rise in oil prices following the Yom Kippur war of 1973, the economies of the advanced industrial nations fell into deep recession. As a result of declining growth in these nations, Africa's export earnings declined. Private income fell, and so too did government revenues.

Some economies initially eluded economic decline: those that produced oil, of course, and others that produced crops, such as coffee, whose prices rose when frost and war drove two major exporters from global markets. Those countries blessed with rich natural endowments—Zambia, with its copper deposits, or Zaire, with copper, cobalt, and gold—could borrow and thus postpone cuts in spending. In the mid-1980s, their incomes also collapsed. In the early 1980s, the U.S. Federal Reserve had precipitously increased the rate of interest, sharpening the level of recession. The subsequent collapse of the Mexican peso led to an end of private lending to developing economies. When in 1986 Arab countries increased oil production in an effort to revive the growth of the industrial economies, Africa's oil exporters experienced a decline in earnings. With this last blow, virtually all economies of the continent fell into recession.

In the recession, Africa's citizens experienced increased poverty; so too did their governments. The result was a decline

in the quality of public services. Most African governments secured their revenues from taxes on trade. Given the decline in exports, they could respond to the fall in revenues either by freezing salaries and cutting their payrolls or by running deficits, which lowered the real earnings of public servants by increasing prices. Children attended schools that lacked text books. Teachers were often absent, seeking to supplement their salaries with earnings from private trade. In clinics and hospitals, patients suffered from the lack of medicines and the absence of staff. Soldiers went unpaid.

In response, the citizens of Africa began to turn against their governments. Parents and children protested the decline in the quality of schools, hospitals, and clinics. Business owners targeted the erratic supply of water and electricity and the crumbling systems of transport and communications. Discontent with the decline in public services was heightened by the disparity in fortunes between those with power and those without. High-ranking officials could send their children to schools abroad or secure medical treatment in London, Washington, or Paris. The political elite could recruit and pay their own security services, purchase private generators, and maintain private means of transport. In general, those who ruled could escape the misery that befell others. As the economies of African states collapsed, citizens increasingly called for reform, particularly the restoration of multiparty politics and an increase in the power of the masses relative to the power of those who governed.

Opposition to Africa's authoritarian regimes also mounted from abroad. Governments had fallen into debt, and foreign creditors increasingly demanded that the governments adopt reform policies aimed at reigniting economic growth on the continent. Governments that were accountable to their people, the creditors argued, would be less likely to prey upon private assets, distort private markets, and favor public firms over private enterprises. Led by officials of the World Bank, economic technocrats began to join with local activists in demanding political reform.

In the later decades of the twentieth century, Africa's political elites thus faced challenges from home and abroad. To a remarkable degree, military and single-party regimes proved able to hold onto power until a second global shock—the fall of communism—destabilized many African regimes. Western governments had tolerated repressive practices in Africa nations in exchange for support in the cold war, but after the collapse of the Soviet Union, Western governments no longer urged their economic technocrats to release loans to repressive governments. They were willing to let fall those African elites whose services they no longer required.

In response to increased pressures from home and abroad, some governments reformed. As shown in Figure 1, whereas more than 80 percent of Africa's governments had been no party (largely military) or single-party systems in the mid-1980s, by the mid-1990s, multiparty systems prevailed in nearly one-half of African countries. Other governments, however, reacted by intensifying the level of repression. In Togo, the armies of President Gnassingbé Eyadéma fired on civilians who had gathered in the streets of Lomé, the national capital, to protest his rule. In Liberia, Rwanda, and Sierra Leone, thugs hired by the governing parties harassed and harried those who sought to displace them. In Burundi, the military, once displaced from power, slaughtered the civilians who had seized it, while in neighboring Rwanda, the government unleashed a program of mass killing, seeking to eradicate those who opposed it.

Since the late twentieth century, military coups have become rare, and multiparty elections the norm in Africa. In addition, the continent has become more peaceful, with civil wars ending in Angola, Burundi, Liberia, Mozambique, Rwanda, Somalia, and, less certainly, Congo. In the mid-1990s, economic growth returned for the first time since the 1980s, apparently sparked by the increased demand for primary products resulting from economic growth in China and India, as well as the return of private investment, much by companies from South Africa. When measured in terms of peace and prosperity, however, the nations of Africa still occupy the lower rungs of the global community. For the first time in several decades, there have been distinct signs of political and economic progress in the continent.

ETHNICITY

Some have attributed Africa's slow growth to ethnic diversity; others attribute its political instability to conflict among ethnic groupings. Many observers thus contend that ethnicity is at the roots of Africa's development crisis.

The evidence, however, suggests several flaws in this argument. Though some argue that ethnic diversity weakens the capacity of people to agree on the allocation of shared resources, others argue that ethnic groups mobilize resources in support of their communities by, for example, sponsoring the educations of promising young people, building schools and clinics, and conferring recognition on those who use their wealth in support of their communities. There are large literatures on the local funding of schools in Kenyan communities and of the funding of scholarships by Ibo communities in eastern Nigeria. In addition, while ethnic groups may compete for power, in most African nations this competition is peaceful. As in the urban centers of the advanced industrial countries, politics in Africa may pit one ethnic group against another, but these rivalries, while colorful, rarely lead to violence.

Recent research suggests the conditions under which conflicts among ethnic groups *can* become violent. One such condition occurs when small groups capture power and employ it to extract wealth from others. Such was the case in Burundi under the rule of Michel Micombero or in Liberia under Samuel Doe. To remain in power, such groups may have to rule by fear, thereby cowing or decimating their political opposition. In addition, when one ethnic group is sufficiently large to form a political majority on its own, others may come to fear the prospect of political exclusion and so choose to revolt, as did the Tutsi in Rwanda and the Gio and Mano in Liberia. The statistical evidence for this phenomenon is not robust in cross-national data, but qualitative accounts and data on within country variation offer fairly consistent support for it.

In Africa, as elsewhere, normal politics involves the management of differences among ethnic groups. Only in special circumstances do political forces align so as to transform these rivalries into political violence.

See also *African Political Economy; Authoritarianism, African; Colonialism; Ethnocentrism; Imperialism; Nationalism; Party Systems, Comparative; Poverty.*

. . . . ROBERT BATES

BIBLIOGRAPHY
Abernethy, David B. *The Dynamics of Global Dominance: European Overseas Empires, 1415–1980.* New Haven, Conn.: Yale University Press, 2000.
Austin, Dennis. *Politics in Ghana, 1946–60.* Oxford: Oxford University Press, 1964.
Bates, Robert H. *Essays on the Political Economy of Rural Africa.* Berkeley: University of California Press, 1987.
———. *Open Economy Politics.* Princeton, N.J.: Princeton University Press, 1997.
———. *When Things Fell Apart: State Failure in Late-century Africa.* New York: Cambridge University Press, 2008.
Bates, Robert H., and Irene Yackovlev. "Ethnicity, Capital Formation, and Conflict: Evidence from Africa." In *The Role of Social Capital in Development: An Empirical Assessment,* edited by Christiaan Grootaert and Thierry Van Bastelaer, 310–340. New York: Cambridge University Press, 2002.

Collier, Paul. "The Political Economy of Ethnicity." In *Proceedings of the Annual Bank Conference on Development Economics,* edited by B. Pleskovic and J. E. Stigler, 387–399. Washington D.C.: World Bank, 1999.

Collier, Paul, Robert H. Bates, A. Hoeffler, and Steve O'Connell. "Chapter 11: Endogenizing Syndromes." In *The Political Economy of African Economic Growth, 1960–2000,* edited by B. Ndulu, Paul Collier, Rorbert H. Bates, and Steve O'Connell. Cambridge: Cambridge University Press, 2007.

Collier, Ruth Berins. *Regimes in Tropical Africa: Changing Forms of Supremacy, 1945–1975.* Berkeley: University of California Press, 1982.

Easterly, William, and Ross Levine, "Africa's Growth Tragedy: Policies and Ethnic Divisions." *Quarterly Journal of Economics* 112 (November 1997): 1203–1250.

Fearon, James D., and David D. Laitin. "Ethnicity, Insurgency and Civil War." *American Political Science Review* 97 (February 2003): 75–90.

Hodgkin, Thomas. *Nationalism in Colonial Africa.* New York: New York University Press, 1956.

Kaplan, Robert D. "The Coming Anarchy." *The Atlantic Monthly* 273 (February 1994): 44–76.

Meredith, Martin. *The State of Africa: A History of Fifty Years of Independence.* London: Free Press, 2005.

Miguel, Edward, and Mary Kay Gugerty. "Ethnic Diversity, Social Sanctions, and Public Goods in Kenya." *Journal of Public Economics* 89, no. 11–12 (2005): 2325–2368.

Murshed, S. Mansoob, and Scott Gates. "Spatial-Horizontal Inequality and the Maoist Insurgency in Nepal." Paper comissioned by the Department for International Development, London, 2003.

Pakenham, Thomas. *The Scramble for Africa: The White Man's Conquest of the Dark Continent from 1876 to 1912.* London: Weidenfeld and Nicolson, 1991.

Uchendu, Victor C. *The Igbo of Southeast Nigeria.* New York: Holt, Rinehart, and Winston, 1965.

World Bank. *Sub-Saharan Africa: From Crisis to Sustainable Growth.* Washington, D.C.: World Bank, 1989.

———. *Governance and Development.* Washington, D.C.: World Bank, 1991.

African Union

The *African Union (AU)* is an intergovernmental, international organization created in 2002 with the purpose of securing democracy, human rights, and a sustainable economy in Africa, especially by bringing an end to intra-African conflict and creating an effective common market. The AU was formed as a successor of the Organization of African Unity (OAU). The OAU, founded in 1963 on the principles of state sovereignty and noninterference, drew criticism throughout the 1990s for its lack of intervention as conflicts erupted in several African countries.

The idea of creating the AU emerged in the mid-1990s and resulted in the adoption of the Sirte Declaration by the OAU's heads of state and government. The declaration, issued in September 1999, called for the establishment of an African Union with a view to accelerating the process of integration on the continent. In the following year, the Constitutive Act of the African Union was signed in Lomé, Togo, and the organization was officially launched in Durban in July 2002. Fifty-three countries in Africa are members of the AU (all African countries but Morocco).

OBJECTIVES AND PRINCIPLES

The AU is guided by fourteen objectives designed to enhance political cooperation and economic integration, ranging from greater unity and solidarity between the countries and peoples of Africa to promotion of democratic principles and good governance to protection of human rights to coordination and harmonization between the regional economic communities.

The attainment of these objectives is to be achieved through the observance of a number of fundamental principles, in accordance with which the AU shall function. Included among these principles are the participation of African people in the AU activities; the promotion of self-reliance within the AU's framework; the promotion of gender equality and of social justice; respect for the sanctity of human life; the prohibition of the threat of or use of force; the establishment of a common defense policy; and the condemnation and rejection of unconstitutional changes of government. Unlike its antecessor, the AU has recognized the right to intervene without consent in internal conflicts, in cases in which circumstances are grave, "namely war crimes, genocide, and crimes against humanity" (Constitutive Act, article 4-h). On February 3, 2003 this provision was amended to include "serious threats to legitimate order." Regarding the economic integration of Africa, the AU bases itself on the *Treaty Establishing the African Economic Community* (Abuja Treaty), signed in 1991 (came into effect in 1994). The treaty envisaged that the community must be established mainly through the coordination, harmonization, and progressive integration of the activities of the Regional Economic Communities (RECs)—the subregions of Africa.

ORGANIZATIONAL STRUCTURE

According to the Constitutive Act of the AU (2002) and the Protocol Relating to the Establishment of the Peace and Security Council of the AU (2002), the organs of the organization are: (1) Assembly, comprised of heads of state. It meets at least once a year and is the AU's main decision-making body. Its members elect an AU chair, who holds office for one year. (2) Executive Council, comprised of foreign affairs ministers or other ministers designated by member states. The Executive Council is responsible to the Assembly. (3) Commission, composed by a chair, a deputy and the commissioners holding individual portfolios, which manages day-to-day tasks and implements AU policies. (4) Peace and Security Council (PSC), a body set up in 2004, which serves as a collective security and early warning arrangement to respond to conflict and crisis (through preventive diplomacy, early warning, peacemaking, peacekeeping, peace enforcement, peace building, and humanitarian action). The PSC has fifteen member states, elected for two or three year terms, with equal voting rights; .(5) Pan-African Parliament, established in March 2004 to ensure the participation of African peoples in governance, development, and economic integration of the continent. This body debates continentwide issues and advises AU heads of state. It currently exercises oversight and has advisory and consultative powers only, but there are plans to grant it legislative powers in the future. (6) Economic, Social, and Cultural Council (ECOSOCC), established in 2005, which seeks to build partnerships between African governments and civil society. ECOSOCC includes

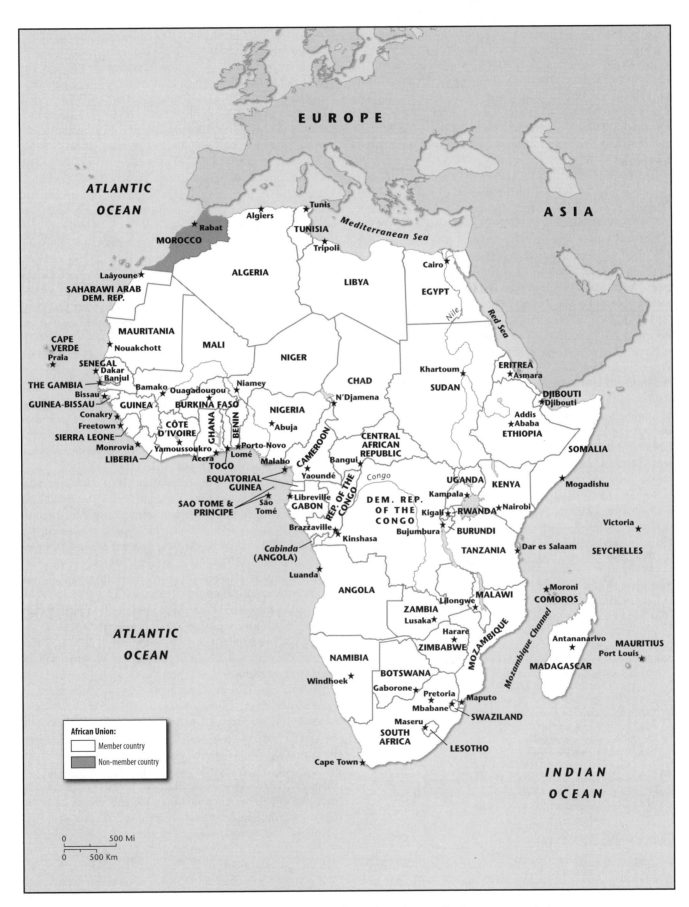

EUROPE

ASIA

ATLANTIC OCEAN

Tunis

★ Algiers

★ Rabat
MOROCCO

TUNISIA

★ Tripoli

Mediterranean Sea

Cairo ★

Laâyoune ★

SAHARAWI ARAB
DEM. REP.

ALGERIA

LIBYA

EGYPT

Nile

Red Sea

MAURITANIA

★ Nouakchott

MALI

NIGER

Khartoum ★

SUDAN

ERITREA
★ Asmara

CAPE
VERDE
Praia
★

SENEGAL
★ Dakar
★ Banjul

Bamako ★ Ouagadougou ★

Niamey ★

CHAD

N'Djamena ★

DJIBOUTI
★ Djibouti

THE GAMBIA
Bissau ★
GUINEA-BISSAU

GUINEA

BURKINA FASO

NIGERIA

Addis
★ Ababa
ETHIOPIA

Conakry ★
Freetown ★
SIERRA LEONE

CÔTE
D'IVOIRE

GHANA

BENIN

Abuja ★

CENTRAL
AFRICAN
REPUBLIC

SOMALIA

Monrovia ★
LIBERIA

Yamoussoukro ★
Accra ★

TOGO

Porto-Novo ★
Lomé

Malabo ★

Bangui ★

Mogadishu ★

EQUATORIAL
GUINEA

CAMEROON

Yaoundé ★

Congo

UGANDA

KENYA

SAO TOME &
PRINCIPE

São
Tomé ★

★ Libreville
GABON

REP. OF THE CONGO

DEM. REP.
OF THE
CONGO

Kampala ★

Kigali ★
RWANDA

Nairobi ★

Victoria ★

Brazzaville ★

Bujumbura ★
BURUNDI

SEYCHELLES

Cabinda
(ANGOLA)

Kinshasa ★

TANZANIA

Dar es Salaam ★

Luanda ★

ANGOLA

Lilongwe ★
MALAWI

Moroni ★
COMOROS

ZAMBIA

Lusaka ★

Harare ★

MOZAMBIQUE

Mozambique Channel

Antananarivo ★

MAURITIUS
Port Louis ★

ATLANTIC
OCEAN

NAMIBIA

ZIMBABWE

MADAGASCAR

Windhoek ★

BOTSWANA

Gaborone ★

Pretoria ★

Maputo ★

Mbabane ★
SWAZILAND

Maseru ★

SOUTH
AFRICA

LESOTHO

INDIAN
OCEAN

Cape Town ★

African Union:
Member country
Non-member country

0   500 Mi
0   500 Km

Member states of the African Union focus on ending intra-African conflict and creating an effective common market.

African social groups, professional groups, nongovernmental organizations (NGOs), and cultural organizations. (7) African Court of Justice and Human Rights, which came about as the result of a merger between the regional African Court on Human and Peoples' Rights and the AU Court of Justice. The court is located in Arusha, Tanzania. And (8) financial institutions. The AU charter names three bodies: the African Central Bank, the African Monetary Fund, and the African Investment Bank.

Besides these key institutions, the AU's activities are supported as well by a Panel of the Wise, a Continental Early Warning System (CEWS), an AU Standby Force, a Peace Fund, and the New Partnership for Africa's Development (NEPAD). NEPAD is a comprehensive development plan that addresses key social, economic, and political priorities in a coherent and balanced manner. It was adopted at the thirty-seventh session of the Assembly of Heads of State and Government of the AU in July 2001 in Lusaka, Zambia.

The AU has adopted various key documents establishing norms at the continental level to supplement those already in force when it was created. These include the African Convention on Preventing and Combating Corruption (2003); the Protocol to the African Charter on Human and Peoples' Rights on the Rights of Women in Africa (2003); the African Union Non-Aggression and Common Defense Pact (2005); the African Youth Charter (2006); the Charter for African Cultural Renaissance (2006); the African Charter on Democracy, Elections, and Governance (2007); and the African Charter on Statistics (2009).

For an organization that only became operational in 2002, and unlike the OAU, the AU has demonstrated a strong political willingness to engage with decisive issues such as conflict resolution and economic development. Its resource capacity is limited, however, which encourages dependency on foreign funds.

See also *African Political Economy; African Political Thought; African Politics and Society; Pan-Africanism; Regional Security.*

. . . . RODRIGO TAVARES

BIBLIOGRAPHY
African Union. *Constitutive Act of the African Union,* Togo, July 11, 2000. Addis Ababa, Ethiopia: African Union, 2000.
————. *The Protocol Relating to the Establishment of the Peace and Security Council of the African Union,* July 2, 2002. Durban, South Africa: African Union 2002, www.africa-union.org/root/AU/organs/psc/Protocol_peace%20and%20security.pdf.
Francis, David. *Uniting Africa: Building Regional Peace and Security Systems.* Aldershot, U.K.: Ashgate, 2006.
Makinda , Samuel M., and Wafula Okumu. *The African Union: Challenges of Globalization, Security and Governance.* London: Routledge, 2008.
Murithi, Timothy. *The African Union; Pan-Africanism, Peacebuilding and Development.* Aldershot, U.K.: Ashgate, 2005.

Afro-Marxism

Afro-Marxism refers to the adoption by postcolonial governments in Africa of Marxist-style models of social and economic development supported through links with Communist Party–led governments such as the Soviet Union and Cuba. Afro-Marxism is characterized by centralized political decision making, typically within a one-party state, economic collectivization or nationalization of productive property and industry, and the direction of a national culture, often without regard for the cultures of ethnic minorities, by the ruling party. It is to be distinguished from *African socialism,* which refers to the perspective that traditional African communities exhibit characteristics, including social relations and sharing of resources, that reflect a form of indigenous socialism based on local communal organization and practices. African socialism offered an alternative to the "scientific" or authoritarian socialism of Afro-Marxism, which was based on models borrowed from Soviet or Maoist regimes.

For many Africans involved in liberation movements and struggles against colonialism, Marxism, especially the example of the Russian Revolution (1917), offered a model for the launching of economic and political revolutions. This revolutionary model, in which a seizure of national power provides a lever for rapid industrialization, held great appeal throughout the twentieth century within numerous newly liberated African countries. As postcolonial governments looked for means by which to "catch up" with the industrial might of the former colonial powers, the approach of socialism, especially statist socialism or Marxism, seemed to provide both a potentially effective political program and an ideological justification for statist reorganization of the economy. It seemed to offer a distinct alternative to the exploitative and oppressive political economic regimes of imperialist rule.

The history of such movements in Africa dates especially to the movements against colonialism from the middle or late twentieth century. Important examples of Afro-Marxist movements and systems include the Popular Movement for the Liberation of Angola (MPLA) and the Liberation Front of Mozambique (FRELIMO), which took power in those former Portuguese colonies in 1975. Between 1974 and 1991 a socialist government under Lieutenant Colonel Haile Mengitsu ruled Ethiopia. In addition, numerous Marxist parties and organizations have been active in several African countries, including South Africa, where the South African Communist Party played a significant part in the downfall of the apartheid regime.

Among the most notable proponents of Afro-Marxism are Amilcar Cabral (Guinea-Bissau and Cape Verde), Samora Machel (Mozambique), Michel Micombero (Burundi), Agostinho Neto (Angola), and Thomas Sankara (Burkina Faso). Robert Mugabe of Zimbabwe, who took power in 1980 through an armed struggle movement deploying some elements of Marxist-Leninist ideology, has positioned himself as a defender of African autonomy from Western corporate interests while subjecting his population, especially the poor and his political opponents, to ongoing repression and punishment.

Afro-Marxism played an important part in bringing about the end of the apartheid regime in South Africa. Angolan (MPLA) forces, backed by Cuban troops along with forces of the South West Africa People's Organization (SWAPO), pushed back the South African forces that invaded Angola.

The stalemate forced the South African government to take part in negotiations that eventually led to the independence of Namibia and indeed played a major part in the collapse of the apartheid regime in 1994.

Afro-Marxism held out a promise of self-sufficiency, equality, economic development, and prosperity. In practice, most examples of Afro-Marxism failed to deliver much in any of these areas. Also, many leaders who had advocated the more moderate African socialism fell back on authoritarian forms of Soviet-style government when attempting to implement their policies. Economic development primarily directed wealth into the hands of the new elite, which consisted of leading members of the ruling party.

Western versions of socialism, especially Soviet-inspired systems, were often inapplicable to the specific social circumstances of less industrialized countries, whose labor base was often concentrated in agricultural or resource-extractive industries. Similarly, Afro-Marxism failed to draw on local governance practices to organize social and productive life and instead relied on the centralized statist models of Sovietism.

The collapse of the Soviet Union and the Soviet systems in Eastern Europe in the late 1980s and early 1990s, along with the passing of Maoism and China's embrace of capitalism by the late twentieth century, all dealt severe blows to Afro-Marxist regimes. The loss of aid and trade ties with the Soviet economies left Marxist governments in Africa desperate for aid from Western capitalist governments and international financial organizations like the International Monetary Fund and World Bank. At the same time, China maintains aid and investment in many African countries and seeks to expand its influence on the continent. China's financial connections with the regime in Sudan has been highly criticized by human rights activists and commentators. While China has attempted to develop its influence, it has not supported or encouraged the development of communist regimes or parties as the Soviet Union did. Governments also became more vulnerable to the pressures of Western governments and institutions to accept structural adjustment programs, including the privatization of government works and lands.

See also *Apartheid; Communism; Marxism.*

. . . . JEFFREY SHANTZ

BIBLIOGRAPHY
Babu, A. M. *African Socialism or Socialist Africa?* London: Zed, 1981.
Higgins, Nicholas P. *Understanding the Chiapas Rebellion: Modernist Visions and the Invisible Indian.* Austin: University of Texas Press, 2004.
Mbah, Samuel, and I. E. Irigariwey. *African Anarchism: The History of a Movement.* Tucson, Ariz.: Sharp, 2001.
Nyerere, Julius. *Freedom and Socialism: A Selection of Writings and Speeches, 1965–1967.* Dar es Salaam: Oxford University Press, 1968.
———. *Ujaama: Essays on Socialism.* London: Oxford University Press, 1977.

Agenda Control

Agenda control may be defined as the ability to affect the way in which alternatives enter collective decision making. While agenda control is important generally, it plays a special role in the rational-choice-based theory of democratic institutions (or the "new institutionalism"). It has two major but somewhat different roles. One is the ability to regulate what alternatives are allowed to be considered at all; the other is in controlling the manner in which alternatives are considered, such as the order of voting.

PATH DEPENDENCE IN THE ABSENCE OF MAJORITY-RULE VOTING EQUILIBRIUM

A distinction may be drawn between when there is a majority-rule voting equilibrium—roughly speaking, an outcome that a majority in society prefers to all others—and when there is no such an equilibrium. The first case is the famous median voter result and its variants. The second case is when there is a majority cycle with no alternative that can win a majority over all others.

In the latter case, what wins depends on the order in which alternatives come up, as Charles R. Plott (1967) showed, and hence agenda control is exceedingly important. Richard McKelvey (1976) and Norman Schofield (1983) then demonstrated that there is a path of choices that makes it possible to get from any possible starting point to any logically possible policy imaginable; hence, the outcome is called *path dependent*. This massive extent of potential effects put agenda control at the center of inquiry for new institutionalist theories, for whoever controlled the agenda controlled the outcome, getting almost literally any outcome the controllers desired.

Plott's work also shows how agenda control of this form can matter. Plott, Cohen, and Levine (1978) were asked to devise a method for choosing among planes for a club for those who enjoy flying airplanes. Plott and Levine devised an agenda that secured Levine's most preferred outcome, even though a majority preferred something else. Plott, Cohen, and Levine (1978) then devised a series of game theoretic experiments to show this point in another way. By clever application of agenda control, they could induce the subjects in the experiment to choose any kind of pizza toppings the Plott and company desired, including "chocolate pizza" (which they used in the title of their article).

MAJORITY-RULE EQUILIBRIA VERSUS REVERSION POINTS

The most important positive result about majority rule is that it will select the ideal point of the median voter, because that it is the majority-rule equilibrium when a median exists. In Duncan Black's median voter theorem (1958), the agenda is assumed to be open, the median voter can therefore propose a preferred outcome at some point, and that alternative then will defeat any and every other proposal. Thomas Romer and Howard Rosenthal (1978) examined the case when an individual (or group) can select which alternatives may to be considered. They find that, at the extreme, agenda control power will pull the outcome away, sometimes substantially, from the median voter outcome.

For example, in many locales, the school board may propose a tax rate to pay for schools for the coming year. Voters then vote it up or down. Given this ability to limit the choice set of the voters drastically, it is not surprising that the agenda controller can shape the outcome. It is not complete control, however, as in the case where there is no majority-rule equilibrium. The final result reflects, in effect, a balancing between the preferences of the median voter, the preferences of the agenda controller, and what is called the *reversion point*—what would happen if the proposal of the agenda controller is defeated. The reversion point is not always the status quo. To use the school board example, if the school board's new tax rate is rejected, the school budget may not revert to last year's budget—it may fall to zero. The prospect of essentially shutting down the schools would give the school board tremendous bargaining power as the agenda controller to obtain an outcome it desires. In general, the more extreme the reversion point, the greater the control held by the agenda controller.

WIDE APPLICATIONS

This relatively straightforward result has been applied in many settings. For example, committees in the U.S. Congress have "gatekeeping power" in their jurisdiction. That is, they have a set of policies that are granted to them, their policy jurisdiction. In many circumstances, they decide whether there will be any consideration of change to the status quo in their jurisdiction at all. By "keeping the gates closed"—that is, reporting out no proposal for new policy in that area—the Congress as a whole cannot change policy. (In reality, there are of course limits to this power.) Conversely, they can "open the gates" by reporting a bill out from committee to the floor. In some cases, the bill has a "closed" rule, which means that no amendments are permitted. Thus, in such cases, the committee has strong agenda control in the sense analyzed by Romer and Rosenthal. Shepsle (1979) developed a model of Congress along these lines.

Furthermore, when the two chambers in the U.S. Congress pass different forms of similar legislation, the bills are often referred to a conference committee to work out the differences. The bill designed by the conference committee then returns to the floor of both chambers for final consideration with no amendments permitted, another instance of such agenda control. In many parliaments, the government (that is, the party or parties that form the operative majority and appoint a cabinet of ministers) often reports bills from the cabinet to the legislature with no amendments permitted. Thus, this form of agenda control has many important applications to democratic institutions around the world.

See also *Agenda Setting; Equilibrium and Chaos; New Institutionalism; Voting Behavior.*

. . . . JOHN H. ALDRICH

BIBLIOGRAPHY

Black, Duncan. *The Theory of Committees and Elections.* Cambridge: Cambridge University Press, 1958.

McKelvey, Richard D. "Intransitivities in Multidimensional Voting Models and Some Implications for Agenda Control." *Journal of Economic Theory* 12 (1976): 472–482.

McKelvey, Richard D., Peter C. Ordeshook, and Peter Ungar. "Necessary and Sufficient Conditions for Voting Equilibria in Continuous Voter Distributions." *SIAM Journal of Applied Mathematics* 39 (1980): 161–168.

Mckelvey, Richard D., and Norman Scofield. "Structural Instability of the Core." *Journal of Mathematical Economics* 15 (1986): 179–198.

Plott, Charles R. "A Notion of Equilibrium and Its Possibility under Majority Rule." *American Economic Review* 57 (September 1967): 787–806.

———. "Path Independence, Rationality, and Social Choice." *Econometrica* 41 (November 1973): 1075–1091.

Plott, Charles R., Linda Cohen, and Michael Levine. "Communication and Agenda Influence: The Chocolate Pizza Design." In *Coalition Forming Behavior: Contributions to Experimental Economics,* vol. 8, edited by H. Sauermann, 329–357. Tubingen, Germany: Mohr, 1978.

Plott, Charles R., and Michael Levine. "A Model of Agenda Influence on Committee Decisions." *American Economic Review* 68 (March 1978): 146–160.

Romer, Thomas, and Howard Rosenthal. "Political Resource Allocation, Controlled Agendas, and the Status Quo." *Public Choice* 33 (Winter 1978): 27–43.

Schofield, Norman. "Generic Instability of Majority Rule." *Review of Economic Studies* 50 (1983): 695–705.

Shepsle, Kenneth A. "Institutional Arrangements and Equilibrium in Multidimensional Voting Models." *American Journal of Political Science* 23, (February 1979): 27–59.

Agenda Setting

Agenda-setting theory rests on the assumption that while most citizens depend on the news media for their political information, the media seem to have surprising little impact on actually altering voters' attitudes about a given issue. Instead, agenda-setting theory posits that the media's power of persuasion is indirect in nature. According to Bernard Cohen in his 1963 book, *The Press and Foreign Policy,* even though "the press may not be successful much of the time in telling people what to think, it is stunningly successful in telling its readers what to think about" (13). That is, by covering certain issues and ignoring others, the news media create a political agenda (i.e., determine what issues are important and what issues are not), which the public then internalizes as its own set of priorities. Thus, the media's and the public's agendas merge into one, so that what the media find to be noteworthy and in turn promote as important through news coverage is eventually mirrored by citizens.

Sociologists Kurt Lang and Gladys Engel Lang (1966), two of the pioneers of media effects research, put it this way: "The mass media force our attention onto certain issues by covering or promoting certain issues and individuals, which then suggests what we should think about, know about, have feelings about" (468). Or in the simplest of terms, try not to think about pink elephants after *Good Morning America,* the *NBC Nightly News, 20/20,* and *Nightline* all run news segments on them.

EARLY RESEARCH

Although over a century ago journalist Walter Lippman captured the essence of agenda setting with his phrase "the world outside, and the pictures in our heads" (referring to the fact that people are more responsive to the pseudo-environment of mental images created by the media than they are to reality), early communication research focused on assessing direct media effects, not the more subtle indirect ones. Therefore, empirical confirmation of agenda-setting effects did not occur until the last few decades of the twentieth century. The classic agenda-setting study was conducted by Maxwell McCombs and Donald E. Shaw in 1972. McCombs and Shaw interviewed one hundred undecided voters in and around Chapel Hill, North Carolina, combining voters' attitudes about various policy concerns with a content analysis of television and the print media's coverage on those same issues. Though the authors found a strong correspondence between the media's and the voters' agendas, McCombs and Shaw could not fully support their conclusion that news coverage was shaping voters' policy agendas over an alternative explanation: that the news media were simply successful in tailoring news coverage to reflect the actual issue interests of audience members. More research was needed.

Using experimentation, Shanto Iyengar and Donald Kinder presented strong evidence that the news media set the public agenda. In a series of experiments described in their now classic book, *News That Matters* (1987), the researchers manipulated media content, thereby controlling which issues participants were exposed to. Participants in the experiments were shown what they believed were regular newscasts from the 6 o'clock evening news, when in fact the newscasts had been carefully edited to include or omit specific stories. The results indicate classic agenda-setting effects. For example, participants who were exposed to stories about the inadequacy of funding for the U.S. military were more likely to consider this issue to be important, even though prior to the study they were unconcerned about military spending. For participants in the control condition—those who did not view the military spending story—the importance they assigned to military funding remained unchanged.

AGENDA SETTING AND PRIMING

Agenda-setting effects are not limited to focusing the public's attention on particular problems; they also can change the measures that people use to evaluate those issues. Iyengar and Kinder found evidence of a *priming* effect; that is, issues that the media stress become the issues that voters use to later evaluate political candidates. For instance, exposure to television stories that linked the economic downturn in the 1980s to the president's performance primed viewers to use this standard of economic performance in their subsequent evaluations of the president. Thus, if the news media consistently suggest that an economic downturn is the result of poorly crafted presidential policy, the public will come to believe overwhelmingly that the president has caused that economic downturn. On the other hand, when television coverage discounts the president's role in the state of the economy, so will viewers.

Therefore, by deciding what issues to cover, the media set the public agenda, which in turn influences the importance citizens ascribe to the reported issues. By elevating certain issues over others or "priming" those issues, the media influence citizens' evaluations of political actors and alter the criteria by which political players are judged. That is, priming, as some political scientists use the term, causes a greater influential weight to be attached to an issue once it receives media coverage. Voters' prior attitudes toward these issues are then more likely to predict their political candidate evaluations if they have been primed by the media. For example, attitudes in support of the Nicaraguan contras were twice as important in determining President Ronald Reagan's popularity after media coverage of the Iran-Contra scandal than they were prior to coverage, as Jon Krosnick and Donald Kinder argued in 1990. Because the media emphasized the Iran-Contra affair, citizens' evaluations of President Reagan were more likely to be based on this issue than others. The first is an example of media *agenda setting;* the second is an example of media *priming.*

ROLE REVERSAL

While an overwhelming number of legitimate issues and ideas circulate at any one time, one of the major dilemmas journalists face is deciding what issues to cover and what not to cover, and how much coverage to devote to any given issue. As Michael Delli Carpini noted in 2005, "given the inherent constraints on covering everything of potential import, public journalists argue that citizens themselves, rather than (or in addition to) elites, should set the agenda." Thus, a reversal of agenda setting occurs when journalists listen to citizens to understand what aspects of the social and political world are important to them.

In a comprehensive study of Britain's 1997 general election campaign, Pippa Norris and her colleagues (1999) found that political parties, not citizens, set the agenda, thus limiting the power of the media to directly boost attention to an issue. A similar study by Heinz Brandenburg (2004) of the 2002 Irish election campaign found that political parties such as Fianna Fáil are the main agenda setters and that the media follow. Although media outlets such as *The Irish Times* also influenced party communications, these effects were small and infrequent. Thus, campaigns seem to foster different agenda-setting dynamics.

In conclusion, most research to date has focused on either documenting the actual phenomenon of agenda setting or exploring the psychology of agenda setting—that is, the media's impact on the public agenda and the subsequent consequences for citizens' attitudes and opinions. For the most part, thirty years and more than 200 studies later, Bernard Cohen's classic observation still holds true: "The press may not be successful much of the time in telling people what to think, but it is stunningly successful in telling its readers what to think about" (1963, 13). And, to this we might add (in Cohen's words) "that by altering citizens' issue priorities and voters' subsequent policy and vote choices, the media indirectly reshape the political landscape and ultimately the democratic process."

See also *Media and Politics; Media Bias; Media Effect.*

. . . .   KAREN CALLAGHAN

BIBLIOGRAPHY

Brandenburg, Heinz. "Manipulating the Dimensions. A Comparative Study of Campaign Effects on Media Agenda Formation." Paper presented at the European Consortium for Political Research Joint Sessions, Uppsala, Sweden, April 2004.

Cohen, Bernard. *The Press and Foreign Policy.* Princeton, N.J.: Princeton University Press, 1963.

Delli Carpini, Michael. "News from Somewhere: Journalistic Frames and the Debate over Public Journalism." In *Framing American Politics,* edited by Karen Callaghan and Frauke Schnell, 21–53. Pittsburgh: University of Pittsburgh Press, 2005.

Iyengar, Shanto, and Donald Kinder. *News That Matters.* Chicago: University of Chicago Press, 1987.

Iyengar, Shanto, Donald Kinder, Mark D. Peters, and Jon A. Krosnick. "The Evening News and Presidential Evaluations." *Journal of Personality and Social Psychology 46* (1984): 778–787.

Krosnick, Jon, and Donald Kinder. "Altering the Foundations of Support for the President through Priming." *American Political Science Review 84* (1990): 497–512.

Lang, Kurt, and Gladys Engel Lang. "The Mass Media and Voting." In *Reader in Public Opinion and Communication,* 2nd ed., edited by Bernard Berelson and Morris Janowitz, 455–472. New York: Free Press, 1966.

Lippman, Walter. *Public Opinion.* New York: MacMillan, 1922.

McCombs, Maxwell. "A Look at Agenda Setting: Past, Present, and Future." *Journalism Studies 6* (2005): 543–557.

McCombs, Maxwell, and Donald E. Shaw. "The Agenda Setting Function of the Mass Media." *Public Opinion Quarterly 36* (1972): 176–187.

Norris, Pippa, John Curtice, David Sanders, Margaret Scammell, and Holli A. Semetko. *On Message: Communicating the Campaign.* London: Sage, 1999.

Agrarianism

Agrarianism is a political and philosophical orientation that emphasizes the purported moral virtue, practical wisdom, environmental sustainability, and political usefulness of agricultural pursuits, in particular when such pursuits are practiced by large numbers of people, preferably by their own labor on land they own or who at least exercise some authority over themselves. Many proponents of agrarianism do not embrace all or even most particulars of this orientation, seeing it instead as merely an appropriate label for those who see value in farming and a more rustic or "simple" rural life as opposed to more commercial or urban transactions and lifestyles. However, agrarianism as a broad challenge to various complex forms of economic and political organization has deep roots, extending back centuries to the writings of Roman landowners, as well as having played a particularly important role in developing approaches to modern republican thought in several nations.

AFFILIATION WITH CONSERVATISM, POPULISM, AND LOCALISM

By looking to rural living conditions and mostly self-sufficient economies—in particular those maintained by minimal technology and in accordance with traditional family and community practices—as a superior form of social organization, the one best able to inculcate in human beings the moral goods necessary for a fulfilled life, agrarianism seems closely associated with various forms of conservatism. Many of those who have expressed agrarian sentiments in the wake of the Industrial Revolution have consciously, and some very explicitly, presented themselves as conservatives. Agrarianism, in the writings of some, has invoked mostly lost premodern social structures, like the remnants of the feudal order long preserved—despite enclosure laws—in Great Britain, or the yeoman farmer/freeholder ideal treasured by early settlers in the English colonies, an ideal perpetuated in early-nineteenth-century America by republican thinkers like Thomas Jefferson and John Taylor of Caroline. Other, more recent agrarian thinkers have presented themselves as lamenters of a traditional, regional agrarian way of life lost in the midst of socioeconomic growth and demographic and technological change. This would be the case in the United States of the "Vanderbilt" or "Southern Agrarians," including poets and authors like John Ransom, Allen Tate, and Robert Warren, who mourned and, to a degree, raged against the passing of the primarily agricultural "Old South" as President Roosevelt's responses to the Great Depression (1929–1939), such as the Tennessee Valley Authority, used federal power and dollars to bring industrial work in impoverished parts of the United States.

However, by looking to the capacity of individuals to own, work, and make a sustainable living off of land labored upon by themselves, agrarianism also is closely associated with populist revolts; for example, the People's or Populist Party in the United States from the 1880s through the early 1900s was overwhelmingly shaped by the hopes and demands of rural voters from the American South, Midwest, and Great Plains. Consequently, the agrarian orientation also may align with certain progressive demands from that era, including greater democratic control over banks, railroads, and other corporate institutions whose decisions greatly affect the ability of farmers to independently decide on their own economic actions. Hence, agrarianism is both radical and reactionary, and it has historically encouraged ambitious reforms aimed at limiting corporate power and distributing land, as well as rhetorical and political approaches to civic life that privilege the countryside, the "heartland," as more authentic, closer to historical virtues, and thus a better gauge of how people ought to use their freedom.

One common feature of both radical and reactionary ways of speaking of agrarianism, however, is its localism—its belief in the importance of keeping human affairs limited to a scale small enough that local knowledge will be sufficient to address the concerns of daily life. Such localism is usually expressed along with an anticorporate perspective, visible today in the frequent hostility to globalization and free trade felt by those who live in and represent the agricultural sectors of Europe, North America, and East Asia, and in particular to a distrust or at least an ambiguous relationship with agribusinesses and large, often corporate farm and ranch operations. While such industrial farms and feedlots in fact provide the great bulk of the food consumed in industrialized nations around the world, agrarian thinking usually sees the globalization of agriculture as undermining the real value of farming.

FOUR ASPECTS OF MODERN AGRARIAN CLAIMS

The specifics of modern agrarian claims usually include several particular elements:

First, morally, farming teaches an economy of limits, patience, shared work, and seasonal dependence, thus schooling those who are raised in agricultural environments in a perspective that will help them deal more respectfully with others, be less demanding and less self-concerned in addressing problems, be more willing to share with others and form associations with them to accomplish goals, be more generous with their time and resources, and remain pious in the face of challenges to their faith.

Second, practically, rural life and agricultural work teach good physical and mental habits and instruct those who devote themselves to—or are at least raised in environments shaped by—farming in a multitude of practical skills that involve animal husbandry, nutrition, construction, and so forth.

Third, environmentally, agrarian occupations teach one about the needs of the planet and about nourishing soil, irrigation, crop rotation, and the like, and as such communicate ideas of stewardship between natural resources and human beings far more thoroughly than can those occupations that have no contact with agriculture, thus leaving those so employed to learn about the natural world through tourism or indirect education at best, or perhaps not at all.

Fourth, politically, being a landowner (the ideal agrarian arrangement) or a farm laborer teaches, through habituation, personal responsibility but also civic humility, keeping the mind focused on practical as opposed to abstract possibilities. It also teaches, through the experience of tending to one's stewardship and working visibly through the slow cycle of growing food and feeding oneself, independence of mind and an unwillingness to allow one's economic or social life to be controlled by powers over which the individual has direct say.

CONCLUSION

The environmental claims made on behalf of the agrarian orientation are for the most part a product of late-twentieth-century reflections on the nature of the natural world and the agricultural use of it. The three other sets of claims all have direct antecedents in the writings of Roman agrarians such as Cato the Elder, Cicero, Varro, Virgil, and others, all of whom associated the ownership and operation of a farm (though not, it should be noted, the life of the slaves who did most of the work on said farms) with economic independence, humility, a strong work ethic, physical heartiness, and a determination to resist tyranny. These varying points, echoed down the centuries, have been used in the history of many Western nations to suggest that the task of agricultural work must be preserved for the sake of the moral health, political liberty, and environmental resources of the nation. Jefferson famously claimed that "those who labor in the earth are the chosen people of God." While relatively few advocates of agrarianism today would use Jefferson's exact words, his sentiments remain prevalent.

See also *Progressivism*.

. . . .   RUSSELL ARBEN FOX

BIBLIOGRAPHY
Berry, Wendell. *The Unsettling of America: Culture and Agriculture.* San Francisco: Sierra Club, 1977.
———. *The Art of the Commonplace: The Agrarian Essays of Wendell Berry.* Edited by Norman Wirzba. Washington, D.C.: Counterpoint, 2002.
Carlson, Allan. *The New Agrarian Mind: The Movement toward Decentralist Thought in 20th-Century America.* New Brunswick, N.J.: Transaction, 2000.
Goodwyn, Lawrence. *The Populist Moment: A Short History of the Agrarian Revolt in America.* Oxford: Oxford University Press, 1978.
Hanson, Victor Davis. *The Other Greeks: The Family Farms and the Agrarian Roots of Western Civilization.* New York: Free Press, 1995.
Jackson, Wes. *New Roots for Agriculture.* Lincoln: University of Nebraska Press, 1985.
McCoy, Drew R. *The Elusive Republic: Political Economy in Jeffersonian America.* New York: Norton, 1980.
Twelve Southerners. *I'll Take My Stand: The South and the Agrarian Tradition.* Introduction by Louis D. Rubin Jr. Baton Rouge: Louisiana State University Press, 1977.
Vitek, William, and Wes Jackson, eds. *Rooted in the Land: Essays on Community and Place.* New Haven, Conn.: Yale University Press, 1996.

Agrarian Socialism

See *Lipset, Seymour Martin.*

AIDS, Politics of

From the discovery of a new epidemic disease among healthy young men in the United States in 1981, acquired immune deficiency syndrome, or AIDS, has been a very political disease. The new disease was first described as *gay-related immune deficiency,* an association that has affected the course of the disease ever since. The perception that AIDS was primarily a disease of promiscuous male homosexuals slowed government response in the United States and created considerable moral panic worldwide.

Today perhaps thirty-five million people are infected with human immunodeficiency virus or HIV, the cause of AIDS, a minority of whom has access to the complex antiretroviral drugs that can control, but not treat, the disease. In parts of southern Africa, the virus has infected more than a quarter of the young adult population, reducing life expectancy and creating enormous strains on social and health services. The long-term effects on social stability and development are not yet well understood, and it is not known how deaths from AIDS are a factor in ongoing instability in countries such as the Congo and Zimbabwe.

While the first major medical and governmental responses to HIV and AIDS came in developed countries where public health and gay movements were more established, it became apparent that AIDS was far more severe in some of the world's poorest countries, above all in sub-Saharan Africa. In 1986, the World Health Organization established the Global Program on AIDS, which in the early 1990s was replaced by UNAIDS, a program intended to promote coordination across all United Nations agencies. In 2000 there was a specific debate on the impact of AIDS on the peace and security in Africa in the UN Security Council, followed by two special sessions of the General Assembly to address the global crisis. A commitment to combating HIV is specifically mentioned in the United Nation's Millennium Development Goals as well.

Responses to the AIDS epidemic were strongest in countries that combined government commitment to fighting the disease with strong civil society organizations, and Brazil, Thailand, and Uganda are often cited as exemplars of good responses. However, the situation in Uganda has become far more complex over recent years, as moralism has affected what was originally a very effective prevention program.

The politics around treatments and prevention are rather different. As antiretroviral drugs (ARVs) have become more effective, access to them has become a major concern, with considerable tension between major pharmaceutical companies and governments over supply and access to generic drugs. The provision of ARVs are testing international trade and property agreements, with a gradual acceptance that profits and intellectual property should not be barriers to providing lifesaving medicines.

Prevention, on the other hand, requires a change to intimate behaviors, mainly sexual but also drug-related and needle usage, which many governments are reluctant to acknowledge. Although intravenous drug and needle users and homosexual men are the most vulnerable demographics in many countries, especially in Asia, Latin America, and the former Soviet Union, programs directed to educate and assist these groups are often underfunded, as prevention is often hampered by laws and social stigma. For example, the money made available by the Bush administration through the President's Emergency Plan for AIDS Relief required an emphasis on abstinence education as a preventive measure instead of promoting safe sexual practices, and there is considerable controversy about the effectiveness of abstinence on stemming sexual disease.

The most controversial responses to the epidemic came in South Africa, where after years of dilatory response South African President Thabo Mbeki expressed skepticism about the role of HIV in causing AIDS and the effectiveness of ARVs. It is estimated that President Mbeki's denial resulted in more than three hundred thousand deaths that could have been prevented had the South African government made readily available drugs, which generated the most significant grassroots AIDS movement to date: the Treatments Action Campaign. AIDS policies started to change toward the end of Mbeki's term in office, but it remains an unfortunate reminder of the negative importance of government inaction and denial.

South African activism drew heavily on earlier examples of AIDS treatment and prevention from Western countries, especially the United States, which pioneered community mobilization in result to the epidemic and introduced global symbols such as the red ribbon and the label "People living with AIDS." The AIDS epidemic remains a case study of globalization, both in terms of the spread of discourses and treatment.

See also *Gender and Politics; Health Care Policy; Lesbian, Gay, Bisexual, and Transgender Rights; Mutiple Streams Theory.*

. . . . DENNIS ALTMAN

BIBLIOGRAPHY

Altman, Dennis. *Power and Community: Organizational and Cultural Responses to AIDS.* London: Taylor and Francis, 1994.

Barnett, Tony, and Alan Whiteside. *AIDS in the Twenty-First Century: Disease and Globalization.* New York: Palgrave Macmillan, 2003.

De Waal, Alex. *AIDS and Power: Why There Is No Political Crisis—Yet.* New York: Zed Books, 2006.

Epstein, Helen. *The Invisible Cure: Africa, the West, and the Fight against AIDS.* New York: Farrar, Straus and Giroux, 2007.

Fourie, Pieter. *The Political Management of HIV and AIDS in South Africa: One Burden Too Many?* New York: Palgrave Macmillan, 2006.

Lieberman, Evan. *Boundaries of Contagion: How Ethnic Politics Have Shaped Government Responses to AIDS.* Princeton, N.J.: Princeton University Press, 2009.

Pisani, Elizabeth. *The Wisdom of Whores: Bureaucrats, Brothels, and the Business of AIDS.* New York: Norton, 2008.

Poku, Nana K. *AIDS in Africa: How the Poor Are Dying.* Cambridge, U.K.: Polity Press, 2005.

Alienation, Political

Political alienation is an umbrella term that captures a set of negative attitudes about politics that are distributed in systematic ways across the mass public. Higher concentrations of alienated individuals are often located in socially subordinated, marginalized, and politically under-represented groups. Broadly defined as a loss of confidence in political actors and institutions, mass political alienation can lead citizens to challenge regime legitimacy and can compromise regime stability over the long term. This entry provides an overview of ongoing debates about how to define political alienation, what causes it, how it influences individual and mass political participation, the consequences for governance, and prescriptive measures to restore citizens' confidence in elected officials. Although levels of political alienation have varied historically and across different types of government, this entry focuses on advanced industrialized democracies in the post–World War II era.

Though political alienation has a long intellectual history and is particularly indebted to Marx, contemporary research interest in political alienation deepened with the second wave of democratization following World War II (1939–1945) as political scientists tried to forecast potential for long-term regime stability. The debate continued to flourish in the 1960s and 1970s as political scientists and political elites sought to understand the causes—and predict the long-term consequences—of the mass movements for social justice unfolding in Western democracies. Attributed to "culture shift," characterized by an increase in elite-challenging attitudes about government and more activist modes of political participation, these social justice movements became institutionalized in new policies and government agencies. Nevertheless, public confidence in government and voter turnout continued to decline with each ensuing decade.

DEFINING AND MEASURING POLITICAL ALIENATION AND SUPPORT

Ada Finifter's work is a common starting point for political scientists interested in political alienation. Finifter (1970) defined four separate attitudinal dimensions of political alienation—powerlessness, meaningless, normlessness, and isolation. Powerless citizens express the belief that political elites are not attentive to voters' concerns, and that there is little that they can do to influence political outcomes. Politics is meaningless when elite decision making is seen as senseless, unpredictable, and random. Citizens find that politics is normless when political elites break the rules of the game. Normlessness also is referred to as political distrust or cynicism. Isolated individuals reject the norms and values of the dominant political culture.

National and cross-national surveys of mass political attitudes and behavior conducted over four decades commonly include items designed to measure each of these four dimensions. In their 2000 volume on disaffection in political life cross-nationally, Putnam, Pharr, and Dalton used *The Harris Poll* measures of individual respondents' disagreement or agreement with the following statements to establish a common framework that links how this concept is measured in North America to analogous efforts in the European and Japanese contexts: "The people running the country don't really care what happens to you"; "Most people with power try to take advantage of people like yourself"; "You're left out of things going on around you"; "The rich get richer and the poor get poorer"; "What you think doesn't count very much anymore" (9).

These basic survey questions have been used to probe how much citizens' perceptions of elites are an artifact of the institutions and specific political contexts that determine their range of action. Finifter's (1970) definition of political alienation captures both specific and diffuse (regime) support. *Specific support* refers to attitudes about particular politicians and parties; *diffuse support* captures attitudes about the political regime and political processes. Scholars debate how closely the two different types of support are related. Though correlated, specific and diffuse support can vary independently of one another; voters can distrust elected officials and still support democracy. David Easton (1965) has argued that lack of specific support, left unaddressed for a long period, could translate into a lack of regime support.

Governments that enjoy high levels of legitimacy and regime support enjoy greater ease in making and enforcing unpopular decisions in the short term that will be of long-term benefit to the common good. High levels of diffuse support accumulate over time to constitute a "reserve of goodwill" that is slow to exhaust and sustains regimes through times of political and economic crisis. Similarly, political losers who are confident in the knowledge that there will be political change in the long-run and can find alternative outlets for exercising political voice are more likely to remain engaged with politics.

DECLINING POLITICAL SUPPORT ACROSS ADVANCED INDUSTRIAL DEMOCRACIES

Americans entered the twenty-first century with less confidence in all branches of government and political institutions (e.g., parties and elections) than in the late 1960s. Similar trends are evident cross-nationally in Canada, France, Germany, Great Britain, Italy, Japan, and Sweden. This long decline in public confidence in politics has been correlated with a decline in voter turnout, a loosening of partisan identification and a corresponding increase in independent voters, and an increase in unconventional forms of political participation when political elites cannot be held accountable through the ballot box. The duration of these trends have led scholars to ask, "Are skeptical publics an enduring feature of democracy?" (Dalton

2006, 254). If so, understanding the roots of discontent may give guidance for improving how democracy works.

The increase in political alienation has been attributed to various reasons: widening disparities between voter preferences and policy outcomes; the inability of the state to maintain a fine balance between policies that protect workers while promoting an environment conducive to economic growth; corruption scandals that reveal collusion between government and business elites at the cost of the well-being of everyday voters; media coverage of political scandals; negative campaigning that focuses on personal attacks; the decline in civic engagement and a corresponding erosion of social capital; and changing public values. All of these factors predict change along one or more dimensions of political alienation to some degree.

Further complicating efforts to understand and respond to deepening public cynicism are the remaining unresolved questions from the 1960s and 1970s about theoretical and empirical links between politically alienated attitudes and the modes of political action that they produce among different social groups in different political contexts. Political alienation can produce a range of behaviors from apathy—or withdrawal from politics—to protest voting and, ultimately, rebellion. Conversely, political alienation also can deepen engagement when angry citizens mobilize for positive democratic change.

CONCLUSION

Research that attends to the behavioral outcomes of different attitudinal dimensions of political alienation has found that the demobilizing effects of powerless and meaninglessness, can be offset by the mobilizing potential of political cynicism. Russell J. Dalton (2006) finds that contemporary political cynics are also highly supportive of political rights and participatory norms. Similarly, Ronald Inglehart (1990) finds that when political alienation is characterized by a high level of political cynicism, it is correlated with elite-challenging attitudes that foster an increase in public demands for direct participation in democracy. Despite a decline in public confidence in politics, overwhelming majorities (90 percent) across established democracies agree that democracy is the best form of government. There is considerable evidence that alienated publics in established democracies counterbalance potentially corrosive effects of political distrust with mass actions that reinforce and deepen democratic norms. The politically alienated in democracies can take actions designed to hold officials publicly accountable while demanding greater citizen participation in making the decisions that govern them.

See also *Corruption and Other Political Pathologies; Democracies, Advanced Industrial; Democracy and Corruption; Mobilization, Political; Protests and Demonstrations.*

. . . . SHERRY L. MARTIN

BIBLIOGRAPHY

Almond, Gabriel, and Sidney Verba. *The Civic Culture.* Princeton, N.J.: Princeton University Press, 1963.

Anderson, Christopher, and Yuliya V. Tverdova. "Winners, Losers, and Attitudes toward Government in Contemporary Democracies." *International Political Science Review* 22, no. 4 (2001): 321–338.

Citrin, Jack. "Comment: The Political Relevance of Trust in Government." *American Political Science Review* 68 (September 1974): 973–988.

Dalton, Russell J. *Citizen Politics: Public Opinion and Political Parties in Advanced Industrial Democracies.* Washington, D.C.: CQ Press, 2006.

Easton, David. *A Systems Analysis of Political Life.* New York: Wiley, 1965.

Finifter, Ada W. "Dimensions of Political Alienation." *American Political Science Review* 64 (June 1970): 389–410.

Herring, Cedric. "Alienated Politics and State Legitimacy: An Assessment of Three Neo-Marxian Theories." *Journal of Political and Military Sociology* 15 (1987): 17–31.

Inglehart, Ronald. *Culture Shift in Advanced Industrial Society.* Princeton, N.J.: Princeton University Press, 1990.

———. *Modernization and Postmodernization: Cultural, Economic and Political Change in 43 Nations.* Princeton, N.J.: Princeton University Press, 1997.

Miller, Arthur. "Political Issues and Trust in Government." *American Political Science Review* 68 (September 1974): 951–972.

———. "Rejoinder to 'Comment' by Jack Citrin: Political Discontent or Ritualism." *American Political Science Review* 68 (September 1974): 989–1001.

Nachmias, David. "Modes and Types of Political Alienation." *The British Journal of Sociology* 25, no. 4 (1974): 478–493.

Putnam, Robert D. *Making Democracy Work: Civic Tradition in Modern Italy.* Princeton, N.J.: Princeton University Press, 1993.

Putnam, Robert D., Susan J. Pharr, and Russell J. Dalton. "Introduction: What's Troubling the Trilateral Democracies?" In *Disaffected Democracies: What's Troubling the Trilateral Countries,* edited by Pharr and Putnam, 3–30. Princeton, N.J.: Princeton University Press, 2000.

Schyns, Peggy, and Christal Koop. "Political Cynicism: Measurement, Characteristics and Consequences of a Growing Phenomenon." Paper presented at the annual meeting of the International Society of Political Psychology, Classical Chinese Garden, Portland, OR, July 2007, www.allacademic.com/meta/p204693_index.html.

Southwell, Priscilla L. "The Effect of Political Alienation on Voter Turnout, 1964–2000." *Journal of Political and Military Sociology* 36, no. 1 (2008): 131–145.

Alighieri, Dante

Dante Alighieri (1265–1321), best known as a poet because of his *Divine Comedy,* was also an active participant and observer of late medieval Italian city-state politics and the writer of *Monarchy,* a substantial work on political theory.

Born in Florence, Dante embraced the active political life of his city. As a supporter of the White Guelf party, he served on several councils from 1295 and served in 1300 as one of six priors who constituted the executive body in Florence. In October 1301, Dante's active political life ended when the rival Black Guelf party seized power in Florence through a coup. Dante was banished from the city and never returned to Florence. During the final twenty years of his life, Dante abandoned the White Guelf party and instead became an observer of Italian political culture as he traveled throughout northern Italy. Both through his experience in Florence and his travels in the region, Dante witnessed firsthand the coercive effects of factional strife and outside meddling on public order in Italian cities. While the exact date of its composition is uncertain, *Monarchy,* his response to the instability of the political system in Italy, was most likely completed in the final years of his life and almost certainly after 1314.

The chief purpose of *Monarchy* was to provide a solution to the endemic political instability that Dante viewed as the key

scourge of his time. While the subject matter was undoubtedly inspired by his personal experiences, the text itself focuses on first principles. In Book One, Dante argues that for human society to thrive it required the establishment of a world ruler whose authority was supreme over all other sovereigns. Only such a ruler could ensure the peace that was a prerequisite for mankind's fulfillment of God's plan for humanity. Book Two turns to history to show that ancient Rome served such a role for humankind in the past and was serving God's purpose at its height. The final book turns to the contemporary political system and makes the case that the Holy Roman Emperor's power came directly from God and was independent of the pope. In making this case, Dante examines and refutes the key arguments in favor of papal authority in secular affairs. At their core, the three books of *Monarchy* argue that the key to peace in the thirteenth century and ultimately mankind's ability to fulfill its role in God's cosmic order depended on the reestablishment of a universal supreme political power through the institution of the Holy Roman Emperor.

Scholars have criticized *Monarchy* as unrealistically utopian in an age when imperial authority was in decline and the text as repetitive. It certainly is medieval in organization and structure. Written in Latin, it draws heavily on Aristotelian thought and is permeated with biblical examples. In some ways *Monarchy* might best be seen as complementing Dante's better-known *Divine Comedy.* If *Divine Comedy* sought to provide readers with a path to salvation in the next life, *Monarchy* sought to provide readers with a model that would ensure peace in this life.

See also *Italian Political Thought; Political Theory.*

. . . .   ERIC NELSON

BIBLIOGRAPHY

Gilson, Etienne. *Dante the Philosopher.* Translated by David Moore. New York: Sheed and Ward, 1949.

Shaw, Prue, ed. and trans. *Dante: Monarchy.* Cambridge: Cambridge University Press, 1996.

Alker, Hayward R.

American scholar Hayward Alker (1937–2008) held the John A. McCone Chair in International Relations at the University of Southern California (USC), where he specialized in the history of international relations theory, computational research methodologies, conflict resolution, and world order studies. In his 1997 book, *The Future of International Relations,* international affairs expert Iver Neumann named Alker one of twelve most influential thinkers in international relations.

Alker was born in New York City in 1937 and raised in Greenwich, Connecticut. He earned his bachelor's degree in mathematics from Massachusetts Institute of Technology (MIT) in 1959 and a doctorate in political science from Yale University in 1963. He stayed to teach at Yale and became a full professor at the age of twenty-nine. In 1968, Alker returned to MIT as a political science professor and remained there until joining USC in 1995. His career was marked also by distinguished visiting professorships, including a 1989 appointment as the first Olaf Palme professor at the universities of Uppsala and Stockholm and a 1996 fellowship to study chaos theory at the Santa Fe Institute. Alker served as president of the International Studies Association from 1992–1993 and of the Institute of Defense and Disarmament Studies. He was also an adjunct faculty member of the Watson Institute.

Alker's wide-ranging contributions to his field include pioneering work on North-South dynamics within the United Nations, computational linguistics, mathematical modeling in the social sciences, the analysis of complex systems, social theory, and peace research. He was also responsible for pathbreaking work on bringing humanistic traditions back into the study of international relations. His many publications include *Mathematics and Politics* (1965), *Rediscoveries and Reformations: Humanistic Methodologies for International Studies* (1996), and the coauthored *Journeys through Conflict: Narrative and Lessons* (2001). He integrated mathematics and humanities into his investigations of artificial intelligence, globalism, and game theory. His last project, which he led at the Watson Institute, was on the dialectics of world orders.

See also *Conflict Resolution; International Relations; International Relations Theory.*

. . . .   GEORGE THOMAS KURIAN

BIBLIOGRAPHY
Alker, Hayward. *Mathematics and Politics.* New York: Macmillan, 1965.
———. *Rediscoveries and Reformulations: Humanistic Methodologies for International Studies.* Cambridge: Cambridge University Press, 1996.
Alker, Hayward, Karl Wolfgang Deutsch, and Antoine H. Stoetzel. *Mathematical Approaches to Politics.* New York: Wiley, 1973.
Alker, Hayward, Ted Robert Gurr, and Kumar Rupesinghe, eds. *Journeys through Conflict: Narratives and Lessons.* Lanham, Md.: Rowman and Littlefield, 2001.
Alker, Hayward, and Bruce M. Russett. *World Politics in the General Assembly.* New Haven, Conn.: Yale University Press, 1965.
Neumann, Iver, and Ole Waever. *The Future of International Relations, Masters in the Making.* New York: Routledge, 1997.

Allegiance

Allegiance, following Scottish philosopher David Hume, can be defined as loyalty and obedience to magistrates. Allegiance, however, can be owed not just to leaders and states, but to a range of institutions, ideals, and people. Examining the concept of allegiance raises questions such as to whom or what is allegiance owed; from what does allegiance derive; is allegiance absolute; can one have multiple allegiances or is there one that supersedes all others; and what happens if allegiances conflict? Once such questions are raised, it is clear that allegiance has a long history in Western and Eastern philosophies, religions, and politics. In the ancient world, questions of allegiance are examined and expressed in Sophocles' *Antigone,* the Confucian notion of filial piety, Plato's dialogues on the trial and death of Socrates, Diogenes the Cynic's declaration that he is a citizen of the world, and Jesus' edict to "render unto Caesar the things which are Caesar's, and unto God what are God's." In the modern era,

questions of allegiance become intertwined with the social contract theory of English philosopher John Locke, which posits consent as the source of allegiance, and the contrasting views of Hume and English philosopher and statesman Edmund Burke, who suggest that one owes allegiance to one's state, customs, and traditions not because one promised but because they were inherited from previous generations and provide stability and continuity in the present. And in the contemporary era, themes of allegiance are explicit in debates surrounding nationalism, patriotism, civil disobedience, and conscientious objection.

TO WHOM OR TO WHAT IS ALLEGIANCE OWED?

Allegiance can be owed to institutions such as nation-states or churches, as well as to the ideals and principles, such as liberty, democracy, or a particular faith, that institutions embody and represent. Besides institutions, allegiance also can be owed to persons, such as political or religious leaders, or even to fellow compatriots, believers, ethnics, or to all of humanity. In addition to external entities, allegiance can be pledged internally to one's conscience which, in turn, may be guided by higher laws derived from nature, reason, or religion.

Like American philosopher Henry David Thoreau, pastor Martin Luther King Jr., Indian spiritual and political leader Mohandas Gandhi, and other conscientious objectors, one may ultimately decide to disobey civil laws and statutes if they violate one's deeply held sense of justice. As such, civil disobedience is an expression of allegiance to a higher law that transcends civil laws and ensures that one is not complicit in the injustice they oppose. Thus, allegiance to a state can conflict with allegiance to one's conscience, as well as to subnational units (e.g., a local community) or to supranational entities and ideals (e.g., diasporas or loyalty to humanity).

ON WHAT IS ALLEGIANCE FOUNDED?

Allegiance can be founded on chosen or unchosen sources, with classical and contemporary liberals defending the former and communitarians the latter. Chosen allegiance derives from consent (either express or tacit) that is central to social contract theory. Express consent, following Locke and English revolutionary Thomas Paine, is a promise one makes to grant authority to and obey a government provided that, in return, the government protects the liberties, rights, and common good of its citizens. Free will is a central element of express consent and can be found in the oath recited at naturalization ceremonies in the United States, in which new citizens pledge their allegiance to the Constitution and foreswear their former national allegiances. Tacit consent also produces allegiance, but does so indirectly, as in Socrates' explanation that he implicitly promised to obey the laws of Athens when he chose to live there and benefit from its protection. Tacit consent may be reinforced through socialization rituals, such as when millions of public schoolchildren in the United States begin their school day with the Pledge of Allegiance or when their French counterparts are prohibited from displays of religious identity in order to reinforce a secular national identity.

In 1778, George Washington signed an oath of allegiance to the Congress of the United States. Washington's express consent granted authority to and his obedience toward the new government.

SOURCE: The Granger Collection, New York

Unchosen allegiance, in contrast, derives not from a promise but from social necessity, birth, and traditions. The traditions that form the community or nation into which one is born give that person predetermined identities and duties of allegiance prior to the exercise of free will. Upon maturing, communitarians allow that persons may continue to adhere to those identities, traditions, and allegiances or may modify them within limits, but they are likely to remain deeply constitutive of their identity. Some political and ethnoreligious identities and allegiances are passed on in this fashion. Politically, communitarians and conservatives often echo Burke's defense of custom, tradition, and the "little platoons" that give people their sense of history and social obligations. Ethnoreligiously, this can be found in allegiance to one's group that may be held in higher regard than allegiance to one's state, especially if the group is subject to persecution or discrimination by the state.

IS ALLEGIANCE SINGULAR OR PLURAL; HOW IS CONFLICT RESOLVED?

Contemporary liberal theorists generally suggest that loyalty to a state rests on adherence to a set of unifying civic principles and ideals that diverse people can consent to, but add that individuals can have a multiplicity of identities, social roles, groups, and institutions to which they owe allegiance.

Depending on the context, individuals can modify and alter the priority of these allegiances. Thus, multiple allegiances are not inherently problematic because this reflects the multiple identities of the self. If there is a conflict between two or three entities to which individuals owe allegiance (e.g., one's country, faith, or ethnic group), contemporary liberals generally allow individuals the freedom to choose which one is primary, and if necessary defend their right to engage in civil disobedience even in subtle forms such as abstaining from reciting the Pledge of Allegiance for religious reasons.

For communitarian and conservative theorists, individuals typically do not have unlimited freedom to decide which allegiance takes priority if their allegiance to the state conflicts with an allegiance to some other entity or belief. As a result, states are typically granted the authority to compel compliance with the laws or limit the rights of those who wish to engage in civil disobedience. Further, communitarian and conservative theorists generally suggest that loyalty to a state rests on a thicker set of shared moral values, and they add that individuals have a limited ability to modify their identities and allegiances. Because subnational or supranational allegiances are potentially disruptive, they must be subsumed under a unifying national allegiance. This is one reason why John F. Kennedy was asked whether his Roman Catholic faith would supersede his allegiance to the Constitution if he were elected president of the United States. However, despite some tensions caused by plural allegiances, the federalist structure of Canada and the European Union allow subnational, national, and supranational allegiances to coexist.

See also *Authority; Burke, Edmund; Civic Engagement; Civil Society; Communitarianism; Hume, David; Liberal Theory; Locke, John; Nation; Nationalism; Social Contract; Socialization, Political; Tradition.*

. . . . GREGORY W. STREICH

BIBLIOGRAPHY

Hume, David. "Of the Original Contract." In *Hume's Moral and Political Philosophy,* edited Henry D. Aiken, 356–372. New York: Hafner, 1948.

Locke, John. *Second Treatise of Government,* edited by Richard Cox. Arlington Heights, Ill.: Croft Classics, 1982.

Nussbaum, Martha. *For Love of Country: Debating the Limits of Patriotism,* edited by Joshua Cohen. Boston: Beacon, 1996.

Alliances

Alliances, or formal associations between two political bodies to further their common interests, are one of the most recurrent phenomena in the field of international politics. Most definitions of alliance focus on four basic elements: its *formal* nature (based on a treaty signed by states), its *cooperative* dimension (states agree to join forces to pursue some common goal), its *external* orientation (alliances are usually against states outside their own membership), and its *military* character (the content of cooperation is related to security). Overall, this conception is a correct one, albeit of a limited nature.

POWER AGGREGATION MODEL

Most scholars believe that underlying all alliances are the convergent interests of the individual member and that the interests in question are directly linked to *security,* broadly defined as protection against a powerful enemy. Thus an alliance is simply—or mostly—the union of the forces of those who, fearing that they are incapable of dealing with the enemy on their own, decide to cooperate with other states in the same situation. This is the essence of the *power aggregation* model, which is probably the most common interpretation of alliances. It should be pointed out that balance of power theory, and alliance theory, clearly overlap. As stated by Hans Morgenthau in 1973, alliances are nothing more than a means whereby states maintain an approximately equal distribution of power; as such, alliances are a particular manifestation of the more general state behavior known as "balancing." This classical view has been partly modified by noticing that the behaviour of states is not based on the need to balance power but to deal with *threats,* as described by Stephen Walt (1987): In deciding whether a given state represents a threat to our security, we need to take account not only of its aggregate power, but also of its geographical proximity, its offensive power, and its aggressive intentions.

BALANCING VERSUS BANDWAGONING

However, states do not always unite against a state that threatens them. Sometimes, on the contrary, they form alliances with the latter, thus adopting a policy known as *bandwagoning.* The dichotomy of balancing versus bandwagoning has been hotly debated, and there is no agreement on which represents the most common behavior, in empirical terms. To further complicate matters, scholars such as Randall Schweller (1994) argue that the term *bandwagoning* should be used to refer to alliance not with the state posing the threat, but simply with *strong* states. From this perspective, the most important factor affecting alignment is the compatibility of various different states' political objectives rather than the power (or threat) imbalance: If one state is satisfied with the status quo, it will join a conservative alliance, even if the latter is the strongest force. On the other hand, a revisionist state will be driven more by the desire for "profit" than by the desire for security, and thus will align itself with the strongest revisionist power in ascendance at the time.

TOOLS OF MANAGEMENT

All those views, despite their differences, share the same conception of alliances as aggregation of power. Yet, alliances also can be seen as something profoundly different; i.e., as *tools of management.* A rapid survey of the most important alliances from 1815 to 1945 led Paul Schroeder to conclude in 1976 that the wish to aggregate power against a threat is not always of vital importance for the creation of an alliance; that all alliances work, to a certain degree, restricting and controlling the actions of the allies themselves; and that certain alliances may be employed in order that even an adversary joins our side and is thereby constrained by the alliance itself. Those ideas have brought to the forefront the fundamental issue of interallied relations, shedding light on their ambiguous nature. Accordingly, some political scientists, such as Patricia Weitsman (2004), have expanded the role of threat in the creation and functioning of alliances to include threats posed by one's ally. Others, such as Jeremy Pressman (2008), have focused on how states use alliances to restrain their partners, thereby preventing war.

The most important contribution, however, comes from Glenn Snyder's (1997) *alliance security dilemma.* In every alliance, states tend to oscillate between two opposite fears—abandonment and entrapment. The former concern is that an ally abandons us, either directly (by abrogating a treaty, for example) or indirectly (by denying its diplomatic support during a crisis). The latter refers to the risk of being drawn into a war provoked by an intransigent or reckless ally. The common response to the fear of abandonment is to "get closer" to the ally; that is, to increase those incentives that may induce the ally into keeping its initial pledge. The usual response to the fear of entrapment is to "get away"; that is, to reduce one's obligations or threaten to withdraw one's support. If a state chooses to get closer, it reduces the risk of abandonment but increases the risk of entrapment; on the other hand, if a state chooses to get away, the opposite will be true. Thus, the policies adopted to prevent abandonment make entrapment that much more likely, just as the policies designed to avoid entrapment make abandonment more likely.

A TYPOLOGY OF ALLIANCES

All this points at a striking variety of types of alliance, as can be seen not only in the degree to which the various members condition the behavior of the others, but also in the tone of their relations, which may vary from tense to cordial, and from a position of reciprocal support to one of mutual diffidence. One way of dealing with such a variety is by means of a typology of alliances, based on two dimensions, one internal and one external. The first allows one to distinguish between *symmetric* and *asymmetric* alliances, according to whether power relations between the allies are balanced or skewed in favor of one of them, respectively. In the second dimension, we have *homogeneous* and *heterogeneous* alliances, depending on whether members respond to converging constraints and opportunities, or on whether they react to diverging constraints and opportunities, respectively.

Combining these classes of alliance, four types are obtained. In the *aggregation* alliance (homogeneous and symmetric), decisions are taken by mutual consent, and both parties obtain reasons for satisfaction from their collaboration. In the *guarantee* alliance (homogeneous and asymmetric), although the weaker party's interests are safeguarded, the content of the agreements reflects first of all the major ally's preferences. In the *hegemonic* alliance (heterogeneous and asymmetric), the two parties are in divergent positions, and the imbalance in power relations allows the major ally to drag the other ally along, imposing solutions that are at least partially damaging for the latter. And in the *deadlocked* alliance (heterogeneous and symmetric), the members, who have equal bargaining power and hold positions that are difficult to reconcile, end up paralyzing each other.

See also *Autonomy; Balance of Power; Bandwagoning; Power.*

. . . . MARCO CESA

BIBLIOGRAPHY

Cesa, Marco. *Allies Yet Rivals: International Politics in 18th Century Europe.* Translated by Patrick Barr. Standford, Calif.: Standford University Press, forthcoming.

Liska, George. *Nations in Alliance. The Limits of Interdependence.* Baltimore: Johns Hopkins University Press, 1962.

Morgenthau, Hans J. *Politics among Nations: The Struggle for Power and Peace,* 5th ed., rev. New York: Knopf, 1973.

Pressman, Jeremy. *Warring Friends: Alliance Restraint in International Politics.* Ithaca, N.Y.: Cornell University Press, 2008.

Schroeder, Paul W. "Alliances, 1815–1945: Weapons of Power and Tools of Management." In *Historical Dimensions of National Security Problems,* edited by Klaus Knorr, 227–262. Lawrence, Kan.: Allen, 1976.

Schweller, Randall L. "Bandwagoning for Profit: Bringing the Revisionist State Back In." *International Security* 19, no. 1 (1994): 72–107.

Snyder, Glenn H. *Alliance Politics.* Ithaca, N.Y.: Cornell University Press, 1997.

Weitsman, Patricia A. *Dangerous Alliances: Proponents of Peace, Weapons of War.* Stanford, Calif.: Stanford University Press, 2004.

Walt, Stephen M. *The Origins of Alliances.* Ithaca, N.Y.: Cornell University Press, 1987.

Almond, Gabriel

Born in Rock Island, Illinois, American political scientist Gabriel A. Almond (1911–2002) was one of the most influential scholars in comparative politics during the 1950s and 1960s, when he was the first chair of the Social Science Research Council's Committee on Comparative Politics. His work stood out as a pioneering attempt to achieve a truly comparative framework for the study of politics, one that encompassed non-Western countries and thus broke with the European focus of much prior research in comparative politics.

Almond received his PhD in political science in 1938 from the University of Chicago, where he studied with Charles Merriam and Harold Lasswell, two of the main representatives of what became known as the Chicago School of Political Science. After teaching at Brooklyn College (now part of City University of New York) and working for the U.S. government during World War II (1939–1945), Almond returned to academia and taught at Yale University (1946–1950, 1959–1963), Princeton University (1950–1959), and Stanford University (1963–1976).

Almond's most important work consisted of a series of publications, starting in the mid-1950s, in which he formulated a structural-functional approach to the study of political development. He saw the political system as comprised of *structures,* such as political parties, legislatures, and bureaucracies, which performed distinct *functions,* such as articulating and aggregating the preferences of citizens, making and implementing public policy, and maintaining overall political stability. Drawing on the distinction between structures and functions, he developed a broad typology of varieties of democratic and nondemocratic political systems. This framework was applied by many researchers to developing countries in Latin America and particularly to the countries of Asia and Africa that achieved independence following World War II.

Almond also wrote a pioneering book on political culture. *The Civic Culture* (1963), coauthored with Sidney Verba, was a pathbreaking work that demonstrated the potential of comparative studies using survey research. It distinguished three kinds of citizen orientation toward politics: parochial, subject, and participant. It argued that a civic culture, composed of a balanced mixture of individuals from all three orientations, was the most conducive to democracy.

Later in his career, in *Crisis, Choice, and Change* (1973), Almond sought to develop an integrated theory of political change by combining his structural-functional approach with other approaches that put more emphasis on the role of political leaders, choice, and contingency. The goal of this work, he wrote, was to connect the theory of statics provided by a structural-functional approach to a theory of dynamics.

Almond became a professor emeritus at Stanford in 1976 and continued to write and publish. His later research included works on the intellectual history of, and the ongoing debates within, political science and comparative politics. Almond's prolific career spanned seven decades, and his achievements were well recognized. Among other things, he was elected to the American Academy of Arts and Sciences in 1961, served as president of the

American Political Science Association in 1965 to 1966, and was elected to the National Academy of Sciences in 1977.

See also *Development, Economic; Politics, Comparative.*

. . . . GERARDO L. MUNCK

BIBLIOGRAPHY

Almond, Gabriel A. *A Discipline Divided: Schools and Sects in Political Science.* Newbury Park, Calif.: Sage, 1990.

Almond, Gabriel A., and James S. Coleman, eds. *The Politics of the Developing Areas.* Princeton, N.J.: Princeton University Press, 1960.

Almond, Gabriel A., Scott C. Flanagan, and Robert J. Mundt, eds. *Crisis, Choice, and Change: Historical Studies of Political Development.* Boston: Little, Brown, 1973.

Almond, Gabriel A., and G. Bingham Powell Jr. *Comparative Politics: Systems, Processes, and Policy.* Boston: Little, Brown, 1978.

Almond, Gabriel A., and Sidney Verba. *The Civic Culture; Political Attitudes and Democracy in Five Nations.* Princeton, N.J.: Princeton University Press, 1963.

Munck, Gerardo L., and Richard Snyder. *Passion, Craft, and Method in Comparative Politics.* Baltimore: Johns Hopkins University Press, 2007.

Alternate Delegate

An *alternate delegate* is someone appointed or elected to act as a substitute if a delegate is absent or otherwise cannot fulfill the required duties at a political meeting, conference, or session. Alternate delegates are seated with their delegation and attend all meetings and functions. If they replace a delegate, alternates also engage in debate and vote on matters. In the U.S. political system, alternate delegates are chosen along with delegates to participate in party nominating conventions. Selection as an alternate delegate is generally considered an honor or a reward for contributions to the party. For instance, at the 2008 Republican National Convention, there were 2,380 delegates, with 2,227 alternates. Alternates may be selected by the delegate they replace, by the state delegation, or through a party election. Like delegates, alternates usually have to commit to a candidate prior to the convention (unless the candidate releases the delegates or unless they are formally classified as uncommitted). Requirements to be an alternate delegate vary from state to state, but generally candidates are required to be at least eighteen years old, a party member, and a resident of the district that they represent for a specified time prior to their selection.

See also *Candidate Selection; Political Participation.*

. . . . TOM LANSFORD

Althusius, Johannes

Johannes Althusius (1557–1638) was born in Diedenshausen in Westphalia. After studying in Cologne, Paris, Geneva, and Basel, he took a doctorate in both civil and ecclesiastical law at Basel in 1586. In the same year he accepted a position on the law faculty at the Reformed Academy in Hebron. Upon the publication of his most famous work, *Politica,* in 1603, Althusius was offered the position of Syndic in Emden, East Frisia, where he guided the city until his death in 1638. Althusius had tremendous influence in this city for thirty-five years, a city that was one of the first in Germany to accept the Reformed articles of faith.

His appointment at Emden, and its association with the Reformation, reflect his intellectual debt to John Calvin. Like Calvin's *Institutes of the Christian Religion,* Althusius argued in *Politica* that all power and government come from God, and civil authorities cannot use their power to serve any ends other than God's. Thus, a citizen's first allegiance is to God. *Politica* was widely embraced by the Dutch, who saw it as a theoretical justification for their revolt against the Spanish. While not generally recognized in the modern canon, *Politica* was a divisive force during its time.

Althusius calls for a unifying covenant, a covenant that is quite different from the social contract of Thomas Hobbes or John Locke. The covenant must be agreed to by all who enter it. Althusius is accused of transforming all public law into private law with his idea of covenant. He preserves this distinction, but recognizes the connection and symbiotic relationship between the two.

Althusius finds the origins of his federal design, and understanding of covenant, in the Bible and bases the design on biblical lessons: (1) The federal design is based on a network of covenants beginning with the original covenant between God and man on which all others are based. (2) The classical biblical commonwealth was a federation of tribes tied to one another by covenant that functioned as a unifying set of laws between the tribes. (3) The Bible ends with a restoration of the tribal system on a global scale in which each nation is able to preserve its own integrity while supporting a common covenant. Althusius' biblical observations served as the inspiration for his theoretical work that confronted the problem of divisible sovereignty. For a federal system to work, sovereignty must be divided among the constituent parts while still binding the parts to the whole. Althusius addressed this problem by relying on a covenant that would bind the sovereign parts to a sovereign whole. This arrangement mirrors the symbiotic relationship that exists between private law and public law.

Althusius' work contributed to the intellectual reputation of the Reformation. He wrote in direct refutation of the theory of indivisible sovereignty as understood by Jean Bodin. The idea of a single sovereign and self-determination could not be reconciled until Althusius introduced his theory of federalism with the covenant as its central feature.

See also *Calvin, John; Protestant Political Thought; Reformation Political Thought.*

. . . . KYLE SCOTT

BIBLIOGRAPHY

Althusius, Johannes. *Politica.* Translated by Frederick S. Carney, with a foreword by Daniel J. Elazar. Indianapolis: Liberty Fund, 1995.

Althusser, Louis

Louis Althusser (1918–1990) was a French philosopher who attempted to reconcile Marxism with structuralism. His works influenced Marxist thought in the West.

Althusser was born in Birmandries in French Algeria and was educated in Algiers, Marseilles, and Lyon, where he attended the Lycee du Parc. In 1939 he was admitted to the Ecole Normale Superieure (ENS), the French academy for teachers, but he was conscripted into the French Army. Althusser would later observe how Machiavelli thought conscription helped establish national identity. Althusser was captured and spent five years in a German concentration camp, most of that time in Stalag XA, located in Schleswig. After the war, he entered the ENS.

While at ENS, Althusser suffered from and was treated for clinical depression. In 1948, Althusser joined the Community Party and completed his master's thesis on the German philosopher Georg Wilhelm Friedrich Hegel. Althusser became a tutor at ENS and spent his entire academic career there, eventually becoming a professor of philosophy.

Althusser rose to prominence in the mid-1960s through the publication of his works in which he attempts to reinterpret the ideas of philosopher Karl Marx. *For Marx* (1969) (first published as *Pour Marx* in 1965 by Francois Maspero, Paris) was a collection of articles that had been previously been published in *La Pen* and *La Nouvelle Critique* and was regarded as the seminal text in the school of structuralist Marxism. Althusser viewed Marxism as a revolutionary science. While Marx, in his writings, argued that all aspects of life were dependent on the superstructure of economic production (economic determinism), Althusser believed that the foundations of societies were based on one of three processes: economic practice, politico-legal practice, and ideological practice. In the 1970 essay "Ideology and Ideological State Apparatuses: Notes toward an Investigation," Althusser (2001) emphasizes the scientific aspects of Marxism, in particular its investigation of how societal structures determine lived experience. These *structures* determined history, but their importance and relationship to one another varied with circumstances. Therefore, at different times particular *practices* might be dominant. He also cited the existence of ideological state apparatuses, which include the family, mass media, religious institutions, and education. He suggested that these apparatuses are agents of repression and inevitable. Therefore, it is impossible to escape ideology.

Althusser contended that there were differences between the "young" and the "mature" Marx, that what he called an "epistemological break" had taken place in the 1840s, and that the mature Marx was more "scientific" than he had been as a younger writer. Althusser believed that Marx had been misunderstood because his work had been considered as a whole, rather than as the product of distinct intellectual periods. However, Althusser would later backtrack on the timing of this break in Marx's work. In his 1969 essay "Preface to Capital Volume One," Althusser (2001) concedes that the scientific approach is only found in the *Critique of the Gotha Programme,* which Marx wrote in 1875. Later, in 1976's "Elements of Self Criticism," Althusser suggested that this "break" was a process rather than a clearly defined event. Another work in a similar vein was *Lire le Capital,* a collection of essays by Althusser and some of his students published in 1965, based on a seminar about Marx's *Das Kapital* conducted by Althusser at the ENS.

Althusser's career essentially came to an end in 1980 when he murdered his wife, Helene. He was declared unfit to stand trial and was institutionalized until 1983. During the last years of his life, Athusser wrote two versions of his autobiography, *Les Faits* (*The Facts*) and *L'Avenir dure Longtemps* (*The Future Lasts a Long Time*), which were published posthumously in 1992 as a single volume: *The Future Lasts Forever: A Memoir.*

See also *Communism; Hegel, Georg W. F.; Marx, Karl; Marxism; Marxist Parties.*

. . . .   JEFFREY KRAUS

BIBLIOGRAPHY
Althusser, Louis. *For Marx,* translated by Ben Brewster. London: Penguin, 1969.
———. "Elements of Self-Criticism." In *Essays in Self-Criticism,* translated by Grahame Lock, 101–162. London: New Left, 1976.
———. *The Future Lasts Forever: A Memoir,* edited by Oliver Corpet and Yann Moulier Boutang, translated by Richard Veasey. New York: New Press, 1993.
———. "Ideology and Ideological State Apparatuses: Notes toward an Investigation." In *The Norton Anthology of Theory and Criticism,* edited by Vincent B. Leitch, 1483–1509. New York: Norton, 2001.
———. 1971. "Preface to Capital Volume One." In *Lenin and Philosophy and Other Essays.* New York: Monthly Review Press, 2001.
Althusser, Louis, and Etienne Balibar. *Lier le Capital.* Paris: François Maspero, 1965.
Elliott, Gregory. *Althusser: The Detour of Theory.* New York: Verso, 1987.
Ferretter, Luke. *Louis Althusser.* Routledge Critical Thinkers. London: Routledge, 2006.
Montag, Warren. *Louis Althusser.* Hampshire, U.K.: Palgrave Macmillan, 2003.
Resch, Robert Paul. *Althusser and the Renewal of Marxist Social Theory.* Berkeley: University of California Press, 1992.
Smith, Steven B. *Reading Althusser: An Essay on Structural Marxism.* Ithaca, N.Y.: Cornell University Press, 1984.

Amendments, Constitutional

See *Constitutional Amendments.*

Americanization

The term *Americanization* refers to the perceived spread and absorption of presumed American values, practices, methods, beliefs, and symbols. This definition is important because some things taken to be American are not in fact of American origin. Further, critics of Americanization sometimes wrongly overestimate the spread of Americanization, the rate of absorption, and the American desire to promote presumed American things.

In 1835, sociologist Alexis de Tocqueville laid out the essence of American identity, comprising a combination of populism, egalitarianism, liberty, individualism, and laissez-faire. Equally important was a distrust of big government and a belief that local power was more responsive to people's needs. These values have more recently been dubbed the "American Creed," based on a form of "dissenting Protestantism." The creed comprises five elements, which Samuel Huntington (2004) lists as individual rights, the people as the legitimate source of political power, government limited by law and the people, a belief in limited or small government, and private property.

DOMESTIC AMERICANIZATION

Americanization includes domestic and international variants. Domestically, the term refers to the socialization of immigrants to the United States. Philip Bell defines it as "a process by which an alien acquires our language, citizenship, customs, and ideals" (1998, 1). Acculturation, however, does not necessarily lead to assimilation, as studies of Jewish and other immigrants have shown. Americanization domestically is not as assimilatory as its founders originally suggested, and some states such as Florida, California, and Texas have informal policies of Spanish-English bilingualism. In 2000, some forty-seven million people, or 18 percent of the population, spoke a language other than English at home. Images of the melting pot have been replaced by the salad bowl or mixed salad, suggesting tolerance for cultural diversity and multiculturalism. Ideals of religious and cultural freedom can be seen as new forms of Americanization, where respect for difference is celebrated.

Americanization must be seen as a two-way street. It involves the assimilation of foreign cultures and peoples, the transformation of cultural products, and their export outside America's borders. The United States is a massive consumer of culture as well as a producer of it. Americans have been highly receptive to foreign influences and immigrants, which has affected the creation of new forms of culture, movies, food, fashions, architecture, science, and so on. As Richard Pells (2005) argues,

> It is precisely these foreign influences that have made America's culture so popular for so long in so many places. American culture spread throughout the world because it has habitually drawn on foreign styles and ideas. Americans have then reassembled and repackaged the cultural products they received from abroad, and retransmitted them to the rest of the planet. (190)

INTERNATIONAL AMERICANIZATION

Americanization also has international dimensions. American variants of democracy, trade liberalization, and culture are often seen as attractive outside America's borders, and perceived American practices are often spontaneously adopted and reinterpreted in different cultural contexts. Thus, America not only projects hard military power, as Joseph Nye (2008) has shown, but the soft power of cultural attraction and diplomacy as well. Historically, Americanization involved the spread of democratic institutions and the promotion of free trade. This began in the 1850s with America's opening of Japan for international trade, later culminating in its "open door" policies for the Asia-Pacific in the 1890s. It also coincided with the spread of Wilsonian liberal democracy after 1919. After

World War II (1939–1945), the U.S. government promoted a mixture of democracy, free trade, international institutions to regulate trade, new international markets, opening of closed economic systems, currency convertibility, access to world markets and materials, and a reduction in domestic barriers to trade. Institutions such as the International Monetary Fund, the World Bank, the United Nations, and the General Agreement on Tariffs and Trade all promoted an economic agenda favored by America and its allies.

In parts of Latin America and Central Europe, a form of economic Americanization was expressed in the 1990s through the Washington Consensus, a World Bank project that sought to reduce social spending and increase the level of privatization. *Americanization* is sometimes used as shorthand for large-scale industrialization or assembly-line manufacturing, like Fordism. As such, Americanization can figure as a stand-in for Westernization or globalization, even if in today's economic climate the majority of manufactured goods are produced outside of the United States. America's massive domestic market has enabled American industries to create products at home before trialing them abroad. This has further been facilitated by the fact that more than one billion people speak English, making the "American" language of business and culture a global language.

People outside the United States may pick and choose what elements of American culture they consume. For the most part, people are conditioned by their families, local cultures, and circumstances, which allows them to filter and select what they want and don't want. The success of Americanization often lies in the ability of corporate mass culture to adapt and change to suit local needs rather than forcing the same product on everyone. There is considerable variation in how American values, practices, methods, beliefs, and symbols are adopted. Some authors now reject the idea of American cultural imperialism, pointing instead to a more nuanced and complex model of reappropriation, negotiation, and creolization. One might therefore see Americanization as a "tool box," a series of resources that can be selected or rejected by cultural and national groups as they see fit, depending on what elements of Americanization suit their cultures. As such, it makes more sense to speak of Americanization as being polyvalent, comprising military, economic, cultural, and other characteristics, some of which may seem more attractive than others. Americanization as a process must also be seen as dynamic and in constant evolution. What *America* and *Americanization* mean is subject to continual discussion with each new generation of Americans.

See also *Assimilation; Globalization; Individualism.*

. . . . DAVID MACDONALD

BIBLIOGRAPHY
Bell, Philip. *Americanization and Australia.* Crow's Nest, Australia: University of New South Wales Press, 1998.
Bruno, Rosalind, and Hyon Shin. *Language Use and English-Speaking Ability: 2000.* Washington, D.C.: U.S. Census Bureau, October 2003.
Fluck, Winfried. "California Blue: Americanization as Self-Americanization." In *Americanization and Anti-Americanism: The German Encounter with*

American Culture after 1945, edited by Alexander Stephan, 221–237. New York: Berghahn, 2005.

Huntington, Samuel. *Who Are We? The Challenges to America's National Identity.* New York: Simon and Schuster, 2004.

Ignatieff, Michael, ed. *American Exceptionalism and Human Rights.* Princeton, N.J.: Princeton University Press, 2006.

Katzenstein, Peter, and Robert Keohane, eds. *Anti-Americanisms in World Politics.* Ithaca, N.Y.: Cornell University Press, 2006.

Kohut, Andrew, and Bruce Stokes. *America against the World: How We Are Different and Why We Are Disliked.* New York: Holt, 2007.

Nye, Joseph. *The Powers to Lead.* New York: Oxford University Press, 2008.

Pells, Richard. "Double Crossings: The Reciprocal Relationship between American and European Culture in the Twentieth Century." In *Americanization and Anti-Americanism: The German Encounter with American Culture after 1945*, edited by Alexander Stephan, 189–201. New York: Berghahn, 2005.

Rifkin, Jeremy. *The European Dream.* London: Tarcher Penguin, 2004.

Rivas, Darlene. "Patriotism and Petroleum: Anti-Americanism in Venezuela from Gomez to Chavez." In *Anti-Americanism in Latin America and the Caribbean,* edited by Alan McPherson, 84–112. New York: Berghahn, 2006.

Seltzer, Robert, and Norman Cohen. *The Americanization of the Jews.* New York: New York University Press, 1995.

Amicus Curiae Briefs

Amicus curiae is Latin, meaning "friend of the court." Amicus briefs are submitted to the Supreme Court by a party that is not directly involved in a case. The briefs offer support for a particular party to a case. An amicus curiae brief often will illustrate relevant legal matters that briefs submitted by those directly involved fail to address. These briefs can be submitted at two stages of the Supreme Court decision-making process: when the justices are deciding if they will hear a case and after the Court has decided to hear the case on merits. Usually, permission must be granted by either party, or the Supreme Court, for an amicus curiae brief to be submitted. Legal representatives of government, however, need not obtain permission to submit a brief. It is exceptionally rare for an amicus brief not to gain the permission of the party or of the Court. Most legal scholars believe that amicus briefs impact the Supreme Court's decisions. Research suggests that amicus briefs have a positive impact on the likelihood that a case will be selected for a decision on the merits. Additionally, arguments made in the accompanying briefs often are found in the opinions of the Court, suggesting that the justices are willing to adopt the reasoning suggested in amicus briefs.

See also *Supreme Court.*

. . . . TOBIAS T. GIBSON

BIBLIOGRAPHY

Caldeira, Gregory A., and John R. Wright. "Organized Interests and Agenda Setting in the U.S. Supreme Court." *American Political Science Review* 82 (1988): 1109–1127.

———. "Amici Curiae before the Supreme Court: Who Participates, When, and How Much?" *Journal of Politics* 52 (1990): 782–806.

Collins, Paul M., Jr. *Friends of the Supreme Court: Interest Groups and Judicial Decision Making.* New York: Oxford University Press, 2008.

Hansford, Thomas G. "Information Provision, Organizational Constraints, and the Decision to Submit an Amicus Curiae Brief in a U.S. Supreme Court Case." *Political Research Quarterly* 57 (2004): 219–230.

Analytic Narrative

The expression *analytic narrative* sounds like an oxymoron. A narrative can be defined as a report of human actions and resulting events that makes the temporal order of these actions and events clear, with the primary purpose of making them intelligible to the public. There seems to be no concept of analysis that fits narratives; if anything, they are syntheses (of description and account, art and knowledge, entertainment and instruction). Still, analytic narrative has become a tag in today's social sciences, especially in the "political economy" literature that flourishes at the crossroads of economics, politics, and history. Usually, analytic narrative means little more than storytelling with significant theoretical underpinnings (for an example, see Dani Rodrick's 2003 publication *In Search for Prosperity: Analytic Narratives on Economic Growth*). A few users of the expression are keenly aware of the paradox it raises, and for them it means no less than a new approach to history, one that would be capable of reconciling the narrative mode of this discipline with the model-building activity of theoretical economics and politics. Prominent in this group are Robert H. Bates, Avner Greif, Margaret Levi, Jean-Laurent Rosenthal, and Barry R. Weingast, whose 1998 *Analytic Narratives* is the most sustained attempt to make sense of the tag, both in terms of methodological theorizing and concrete applications. This entry reviews this contribution before expanding on the issues more broadly.

CASE STUDIES: MEDIEVAL GENOA TO THE INTERNATIONAL COFFEE ORGANIZATION

During the Middle Ages, the city-state of Genoa underwent a succession of peaceful consulate system, civil war between the leading families, and civil peace under a new political system, the *podesteria*. Historians' best narratives fail to explain this sequence satisfactorily, and furthermore, to discern all the relevant questions. For instance, the first period was accompanied with a variable pattern of maritime activity in terms of raids and conquered possessions that also needs explaining. Avner Greif responds by constructing two extensive form games of perfect information involving the clans as strategic players. The first explores the clans' trade-off between maintaining mutual deterrence and participating in maritime operations. It accounts both for the variability within the first period and—using external threat as the variable parameter—its collapse into civil war. The second game, which the *podestà* enters as a player, rationalizes his stabilizing effect in the third period. Subgame perfect equilibrium is used to solve both games. Each period is first described in a pretheoretic narrative to clarify the open problems, second analyzed in a corresponding model, and third discussed and checked in another narrative that uses the theoretical language of the second stage.

The problem for a classic historian is understanding why France and England followed such different paces of institutional change in the seventeenth and eighteenth centuries: one country keeping the absolutist monarchy throughout while the other gradually established representative government. Jean-Laurent Rosenthal's answer emphasizes the two countries' difference in fiscal structure. Given that the product of taxes was mostly spent on wars, Rosenthal investigated how a country's style of warfare relates to its political regime. His argument combines standard narrative parts with the use of an extensive form game that is formalized in an appendix. The two players, the king and the elite (an abstraction representing the French and English parliaments, and the provincial estates where they existed in France) enjoy separate fiscal resources and try to make the best of them in fighting profitable wars. The king alone has the power of launching a war, and if he exerts it, the elite decide whether to participate financially. Because most wars need joint funding, there is a free rider problem that is more acute when the fiscal resources are shared than when they are in one player's hands; when the prediction that wars are the more frequent, the higher the king's share of fiscal resources. For Rosenthal, France's absolutism was a case of sharing, whereas England's representative government was one of near control by the elite. Rosenthal's model can be tested on the two countries and, if confirmed, will illuminate the connection between their warfare and political regimes. However, it is unclear what it contributes to the initial question of their different paces of political change.

In the nineteenth century, there was a trend in the West to reform military service to more or less universal conscription. Standard histories emphasize democratization and military efficiency, but military efficiency is unclear, and against democratization, reforms took place either before (in Prussia) or later (in France and the United States) than universal suffrage prevailed. Starting from these objections, Margaret Levi narrates the changes in French and American regulations, attending not only to the chronological problem but also to the technical forms of buying out one's military duty (substitution, replacement, commutation). Her narrative is analytic to the extent that it relies on an informal model in the spirit of formal political economy. The main actors are the government, which strives to employ the population efficiently, the constituents, who are divided into social classes with distinctive preferences, and a pivotal legislator, who aligns himself on the coalition prevailing among the classes. Hypothesized changes in the preferences of the government and the middle classes account for the observed change in regulations that is sensitive to its fine-grained features.

Historians of the United States have long been puzzled by the relative stability of the federation of the states through the decades before the Civil War (1861–1865). Classical historians argue that slavery became a divisive issue only after a certain period, and that the Democratic Party following Andrew Jackson managed a successful coalition of Southern and Northern interests. Others put forward local political issues and changing economic conditions. Barry R. Weingast combines these factors into a narrative that stresses explicit political arrangements, especially the "rule of balance" between slave and free states (they should remain equal in number to preserve the South's veto power in the Senate). Crises typically occurred when a new state was admitted. The first newly admitted state brought about a compromise that helped resolve the second, but this did not work with the third. To keep an effective balance despite the continuing expansion to the West, the slave economy should have developed beyond its feasible limits; this is why conflict became unavoidable. Weingast's explanatory narrative accommodates three formal models: one of the spatial brand of mathematical politics and the other two of the extensive form brand of game theory. These models fully clarify his claim that the rule of balance was necessary to maintain federal stability.

From 1962 to 1989, the International Coffee Organization (ICO) regulated coffee prices by setting export quotas to its members, notably Brazil and Colombia, which were the main producers. The birth of the ICO raises strategic issues that Robert H. Bates addresses in an original format of narrative. He recounts the same event three times: Brazil and Colombia unsuccessfully tried to gather other coffee producers; they brandished the communist threat to trap the United States, their main consumer, into their cartel organization; despite congressional reservations, the United States accepted the deal when Brazil and Colombia's large coffee-selling companies supported it. Each partial narrative is followed by a formal argument—not an actual proper model—that supports it but leaves an explanatory residual that motivates the next narrative step. Bates's discussion of the operations of ICO involves the same alternation.

SIMILARITIES AND DIFFERENCES AMONG CASE STUDIES

There is much common ground between the previous five studies: Each begins with a set of historical problems that generally emerge from a critique of the extant literature (only the ICO case is too recent for such a reflective start). The problems often concern fine temporal patterns and variations that previous scholarship simply took for granted. A clear answer is finally given, which a modeling effort has contributed to shape, and the authors' methodology emphasizes not only explanation but also empirical testing. This is because their explanatory hypotheses, especially when they are duly formalized, deductively entail more than just the chosen explanandum. There is room for independent testing, ideally by varying parameters such as Rosenthal's fiscal sharing ratio, but also less formally as when Greif supports his account of *podesteria* in Genoa by discussing the form it took elsewhere. It is evident from the authors' related contributions that they believe to have uncovered theoretical patterns that can be transferred successfully. For an example, see Greif's (2004) "A Theory of Endogenous Institutional Change" in which he highlights Genoa as a particular case. Still, it is dubious that the studies rely on genuine lawlike regularities, and *Analytic Narratives* (Bates et al. 1998) explicitly distances them from Carl Hempel's 1965 *Aspects of Scientific Explanation*. An unresolved methodological issue is to locate the new genre between this extreme construal and its alternatives, or put more simply, to decide of what the generality of the suggested explanations really consists.

The dissimilarities between the studies in *Analytic Narratives* (Bates et al. 1998) are no less striking, as they relate to the very concept that supposedly unites them. Greif and Bates develop a clear scheme of alternation between narration and analysis, with a ternary rhythm in Greif and more iterations in Bates (and correspondingly, more modeling in the former than the latter). In this conception, *analytic narrative* cannot mean a narrative that is also analytic but a dual genre in which narratives and analyses cooperate for a common explanatory purpose while keeping their distinct identities. The two components exchange positions—the problems stemming sometimes from one, sometimes from the other, and similarly with the solutions—and influence each other linguistically but are never blurred. What conceptions the other contributors promote is not so explicit. Levi and Rosenthal introduce their technical concepts and hypotheses before proceeding to the narrative, whose foremost function seems to provide empirical evidence to check the hypotheses. Faithful to this hypothesis-testing conception, Levi carefully states the historical facts separately from the explanation they contribute to, but Rosenthal blurs the limits between the two, as if he were after the integrated form that Greif and Bates precisely exclude, i.e., a narrative-made analytic. Exemplifying still another conception, Weingast introduces his hypotheses at the outset, but without technicalities, and his later models serve only to clarify part of them. In a sense, they confirm the narrative rather than the other way round.

IDEAL TYPES AND GAME THEORY

From this overview, one can distinguish four ideal-types of analytic narratives: alternation, hybridation, hypothesis-testing, and supplementation. This classification is new to the methodology of analytic narratives and is conceptually unrelated to, and arguably more significant than, the form and intensity of the modeling effort, which are also quite variable in *Analytical Narratives*. As comparisons across the book show, the formalized model may be solved to variable degrees of detail, depending on its inner complexity and, more subtly, the way it is used. The mathematical demands are not the same if the account is targeted at one or more historical situations and at a few or many selected features of these situations. Also the model may be constructed for the purpose, as in Greif, Rosenthal, and Weingast, or borrowed from the shelf, as in Bates. Levi's study does not involve a formal modeling stage, and critics like Jon Elster (2000) have complained that such borderline cases were little more than standard narratives. Arguably, only modeling in principle and not actual modeling—this proposed distinction parallels a classic one in the philosophy of explanation—is essential to analytic narratives. In politics, international relations, and military strategy, the new genre was predated by heuristic sketches rather than mathematical applications. Many of these sketches can be filled out, and it would seem arbitrary to keep them outside the door. Some topics have already gone through two stages of technicalities. Thus, the 1914 diplomatic crisis was analyzed strategically first at a semiformal level by Jack Levy (1990/91) and second within a full-fledged model by Frank Zagare (2009).

To return to the *Analytical Narratives* contributors (Bates et al. 1998), their most obvious common ground is perhaps their involvement with game theory. Granting the plan of subjecting history to some theoretical framework, this one recommended itself to Greif, Levi, Weingast, and Rosenthal, given their chosen cases. Empirical existence can be claimed for the collectives—clans, states, countries, social classes, or interests—they deal with. Furthermore, in the historical circumstances, these collectives could plausibly be endowed with feasible sets of actions, preferences, and strategic calculations. Game theory was perhaps not so appropriate for Rosenthal's wide-ranging explananda; he can employ it only after lumping together—e.g., in the "elite"—a large number of very different actors. Within game theory, *Analytical Narratives* claims a special status for extensive forms of perfect information and subgame perfection. Granting that the latter is a powerful equilibrium concept for the former, the two contentious issues are how analytic narrators would solve extensive forms under imperfect information and why they should not sometimes employ normal forms. To see these alternative forms at work, take O. G. Haywood's (1954) penetrating analysis of World War II (1939–1945) battles in terms of two-person zero-sum games—the first application ever made of a game-theoretic technique to history.

The *Analytical Narratives* contributors make occasional use of social choice theory, and they could have resorted more to decision theory, at least in the basic form of an expected utility apparatus. These two blocks are integral parts of the mathematical corpus of rational choice theory (RCT), so it is appropriate that the debate over analytic narratives has centered on their association with the compound rather than just game theory. Elster (2000) claims that *Analytical Narratives* fails because the standard already-telling objections to RCT become absolutely irresistible in the contributors' case. For instance, the problem of checking for the actors' motivations, given that they are not observed but conjectured from overt behavior, is dramatized by the information lacunae that are the historians' lot. Bates, Greif, Levi, Rosenthal, and Weingast respond both by defending RCT for lack of better alternatives and arguing that their applications do not worsen its case.

Some academics do agree with Bates, Greif, Levi, Rosenthal, and Weingast but would emphasize more than they do the relativity of success and failure. In social sciences generally, RCT has preferential explananda: human actions and their proximate consequences, when the actors are individuals or can be regarded as such, perform some deliberation or calculation, and their desires can be disentangled from their beliefs. The closer its case stands to this ideal point, the more promising the analytic narrative, and conversely, cases that depart on too many dimensions are bound to failure. A paradoxical consequence is that analytic narratives perform well in those areas in which ordinary narratives already do; this is because RCT and ordinary narratives share roughly the same preferential explananda.

These are the objective conditions, as it were, and there are others relative to the intellectual context. A convincing analytic narrative needs rooting into traditional history. There should be a problem neglected by the historians, but this problem, once brought to light, should attract them, and their inadequate records should be adequate enough for the solution arrived at analytically to be double-checked. This is a knife's edge, and there could be few candidates that survive in the end.

CONCLUSION

Philippe Mongin's 2009 analytic narrative of the Waterloo campaign in June 1815 in "A Game-Theoretic Analysis of the Waterloo Campaign and Some Comments on the Analytic Narrative Project" is meant to provide a decently favorable case along these stringent lines. (Campaign narratives and military applications generally appear to be a fertile area for the new genre.) Mongin starts from a gap in the extant narratives: They do not properly explain why Napoleon weakened himself before his decisive battle against Wellington by sending Grouchy's detachment against Blücher. This failure at answering a major historical question by ordinary means suggests a RCT model. Beside the contextual condition, the objective conditions are met paradigmatically—the explanandum being a single man's action, taken deliberatively in a limited context of uncertainty to achieve a seemingly transparent objective of victory. Mongin introduces a zero-sum game of incomplete information in normal form. At the unique equilibrium, Napoleon's strategy consists in dividing his army, sending out Grouchy to prevent Blücher from joining Wellington. Eventually, nature played against Napoleon, and Grouchy messed up the orders, so the ex post failure is compatible with ex ante rationality. This is the claim of the pro-Napoleonic literature but rejuvenated by the technical apparatus. Here, the analytic narrative plays an arbitration role between historians, but elsewhere, it will provide them with new conclusions and, most importantly, new explananda to consider.

See also *Discourse Analysis; Event History and Duration Modeling; Hierarchical Modeling; Historical Method, Comparative.*

. . . .   PHILIPPE MONGIN

BIBLIOGRAPHY

Bates, Robert H., Avner Greif, Margaret Levi, Jean-Laurent Rosenthal, and Barry R. Weingast. *Analytic Narratives.* Princeton, N.J.: Princeton University Press, 1998.

———. "The Analytic Narrative Project." *American Political Science Review* 94 (September 2000): 696–702.

Brams, Steven J. *Game Theory and Politics.* New York, Free Press, 1975.

Elster, Jon. "Rational Choice History: A Case of Excessive Ambition." *American Political Science Review* 94 (2000): 685–695.

Ferejohn, John. "Rationality and Interpretation: Parliamentary Elections in Early Stuart England." In *The Economic Approach to Politics,* edited by Kristen R. Monroe, 275–305. New York: Harper Collins, 1991.

Gardiner, Patrick L., ed. *The Philosophy of History.* Oxford: Oxford Unversity Press, 1974.

Greif, Avner. *Institutions and the Path to Modern Economy.* Cambridge: Cambridge University Press, 2006.

Greif, Avner, and David Laitin. "A Theory of Endogenous Institutional Change." *American. Political Science Review* 98, no.4 (2004): 633–652.

Haywood, O. G., Jr. "Military Decision and Game Theory." *Journal of the Operations Research Society of America* 2, no. 4 (1954): 365–385.

Hempel, Carl G. *Aspects of Scientific Explanation, and Other Essays in the Philosophy of Science.* New York: Free Press, 1965.

Levy, Jack S. "Preferences, Constraints, and Choices in July 1914." *International Security* 15 (Winter 1990/91): 151–186.

Maurer, John H. "The Anglo-German Naval Rivalry and Informal Arms Control, 1912–1914." *Journal of Conflict Resolution* 36 (1992): 284–308.

Mongin, Philippe. "A Game-Theoretic Analysis of the Waterloo Campaign and Some Comments on the Analytic Narrative Project." *Les Cahiers de Recherche* 915. Jouy-en-Josas, France: HEC School of Management, 2009.

Myerson, Roger B. "Political Economics and the Weimar Disaster." *Journal of Institutional and Theoretical Economics* 160 (2004):187– 209.

O'Neill, B. "Game Theory Models of War and Peace." In *Handbook of Game Theory II,* edited by Robert J. Aumann and Sergiu Hart, 1010–1013. Amsterdam: Elsevier, 1994.

Roderick, Dani., ed. *In Search for Prosperity: Analytic Narratives on Economic Growth.* Princeton, N.J.: Princeton University Press, 2003.

Zagare, Frank C., "Explaining the 1914 War in Europe: An Analytic Narrative." *Journal of Theoretical Politics* 21 (2009): 63–95.

Anarchism

The term *anarchism* comes to us from the Greek *anarkhos,* defined as "without a ruler." While seemingly uncomplicated, the question of whether and how societies might live peacefully without a ruler is at the core of anarchist theory and practice.

HISTORICAL ROOTS

Until French writer Pierre-Joseph Proudhon embraced them in his 1840 book *What Is Property?,* the words *anarchy* and *anarchism* were pejorative terms for the chaotic and conflictual condition said to result from the absence of a ruler. While Proudhon was the first self-proclaimed anarchist, the political theory of anarchism is conventionally traced back to William Godwin's *Enquiry Concerning Political Justice,* published in 1793. Although never using the label, Godwin rejected the artificial and coercive authority of the state in favor of a natural, egalitarian society. Anarchist thought can then be traced through a number of European and American writers of the late nineteenth and early twentieth centuries, including Mikhail Bakunin, Peter Kropotkin, Benjamin Tucker, and Emma Goldman.

Anarchism is much more, however, than the creation of these individuals. Kropotkin himself argues that "[a]narchy does not draw its origin from . . . any system of philosophy" but represents one of "two currents of thought and action [that] have been in conflict in . . . [all] human societies . . . from all times there have been Anarchists and Statists" (Horowitz 1964, 145–147).

AN ANARCHIST ORIENTATION

Understood in this way, anarchism is less an intellectual tradition than it is a distinctive spirit, or an *orientation,* defined by antipathy to domination and coercion—especially, but not solely, by the state—and a vision of an alternative free of domination. This understanding casts a wide net, drawing together not only avowed anarchists, but many earlier thinkers, activists, and movements. Various interpreters and historians have characterized Lao Tzu, Aristippus, Zeno, Diogenes, Jesus, and the Anabaptists, for example, as sharing an anarchist orientation. It is also reflected in many literary and cultural works. Perhaps surprisingly, this understanding also expands the scope of contemporary anarchism. While there has been a notable reemergence of self-proclaimed anarchists in recent years, the pejorative connotation of anarchy as "chaos" remains influential. As a consequence, many in the alternative globalization, antiwar, indigenous autonomy, radical environmental, and radical feminist movements share an anarchist orientation, yet eschew the label—often describing themselves as *antiauthoritarian* instead.

In contrast to the artificial, coercive power of the state and other institutions that they reject, anarchists counterpoise a more natural and informal basis—Kropotkin calls it "mutual aid"—for social harmony and agreement. Although anarchists characterize this alternative vision in diverse ways, its role is vital. As a consequence, while some who are truly anarchists do not identify themselves using with the label, others who do promote the term are not properly understood as anarchists. Philosopher Robert Paul Wolff's widely read *In Defense of Anarchism* offers a prominent example of this. Wolff unequivocally rejects the legitimacy of the state, arguing that it conflicts with individual moral autonomy, which he takes to be "the fundamental assumption of moral philosophy" (Wolff 1970, 12). Yet Wolff makes no actual defense of anarchism; he offers no sense of how a society might be sustained without the state. As a result, he makes no argument for dismantling or overthrowing states or rulers, despite their avowed illegitimacy.

INDIVIDUAL VERSUS COMMUNITY?

If, as Emma Goldman has argued, anarchism stands for both "the sovereignty of the individual" and "social harmony," anarchists both past and present can be differentiated by their relative emphasis on the individual or community. Often this reflects differences in their views of property and capitalist economic organization. At one end of the spectrum, individualist anarchists regard private property as the basis for a noncoercive society. At the other, anarchist communists reject capitalism and private property as a central form of domination in modern society. Other differences exist. While the historical preoccupation of anarchism has been the abolition of state rule, many contemporary anarchists have sought to expand the rejection of "rule" to hierarchies of race, gender, and species.

ANARCHISM'S INFLUENCE AND RELEVANCE

The legacy and contemporary relevance of anarchism depends on the viewpoint from which it is assessed. As a comprehensive theory and revolutionary movement, anarchism can be understood literally as *utopian*—it exists nowhere—and has been unsuccessful in reconstructing any large-scale society in its image. Moreover, such an anarchist theory relies on a dichotomy: On one side is the coercive power of the state and other rejected forms of rule; on the other are social sanctions and other informal sources of power acceptable with a liberated society. Yet theorists from Alexis de Tocqueville and John Stuart Mill to Michel Foucault have argued that the latter can be at least as domineering as the former. If so, both normative and empirical bases for such a dichotomy become questionable.

By contrast, the influence of an anarchist orientation has been widespread. Bakunin and other nineteenth-century anarchists offered a remarkably prescient critique of the perils of the proletarian state envisioned by Marx. During the twentieth century, anarchists have been a fount of energy and inspiration to labor organizing and the creation of cooperative institutions, to resistance during the Spanish Civil War (1936–1939), and to education reform movements. In recent decades, as Uri Gordon has argued, an anarchist orientation has been central to many grassroots political movements, opposing domination in a wide variety of forms. It also has promoted an ethos of *direct action* rather than attempting to influence policy makers and other institutional actors.

Rather than condemning anarchism to the dustbin of history, the inability to truly liberate society has continued to nurture anarchists' critical and reconstructive vision. In this sense, paraphrasing Kropotkin, there will *always* be anarchists.

See also *Anarchy; Authority; Bakunin, Mikhail; Goldman, Emma; Kropotkin, Peter.*

. . . . JOHN M. MEYER

BIBLIOGRAPHY
Carter, April. *The Political Theory of Anarchism.* London: Routledge and Kegan Paul, 1971.
Godwin, William. 1793. *Enquiry Concerning Political Justice.* Oxford: Oxford University Press, 1971.
Goldman, Emma. *Anarchism and Other Essays,* 3rd rev. ed. New York: Mother Earth, 1917, http://sunsite.berkeley.edu/Goldman/Writings/Anarchism/anarchism.html.
Gordon, Uri. *Anarchy Alive! Anti-authoritarian Politics from Practice to Theory.* London: Pluto, 2008.
Horowitz, Irving Louis, ed. *The Anarchists.* New York: Dell, 1964.
Kropotkin, Peter. *Mutual Aid: A Factor of Evolution,* edited and with an introduction by Paul Avrich. London: Penguin, 1972.
Marx, Karl. "After the Revolution: Marx Debates Bakunin." In *The Marx-Engels Reader,* 2nd ed., edited by Robert C. Tucker, 542–548. New York: Norton, 1978.
Miller, David. *Anarchism.* London: J.M. Dent, 1984.
Proudhon, Pierre-Joseph. 1840. *What Is Property?* Cambridge: Cambridge University Press, 1994.
Sheehan, Sean M. *Anarchism.* London: Reaktion, 2003.
Wolff, Robert Paul. *In Defense of Anarchism.* New York: Harper Colophon, 1970.
Woodcock, George. *Anarchism: A History of Libertarian Ideas and Movements.* New York: World Publishing, 1962.

Anarchy

The term *anarchy* derives from ancient Greek where it originally meant "absence of a leader." In current usage we can distinguish between two main meanings: anarchy in the strict sense means absence of a chief or a government, while in the broader sense it denotes a condition of disorder and chaos.

THE DEFINITION: ABSENCE OF GOVERNMENT OR DISORDER?

Although the two meanings of the term *anarchy* are often intermingled in common language, it is important to distinguish between them at the conceptual level. In technical usage, it would be better to limit the usage to the strict meaning. While the term *anarchy* in the sense of disorder is superfluous (other possible words for it being *chaos, mess,* and *disarray*), the strict meaning is necessary because we otherwise lack a single word to denote the third possibility between the existence of a government and pure chaos. In other words, *anarchy* is needed to denote the fact that order is possible even in absence of an orderer.

This definition has three main corollaries. First, most scholars agree that anarchy does not mean lack of organization, although disputes may arise as to the degree of centralization that is compatible with anarchy (e.g., for some a noncoercive form of government is compatible with anarchy). This is very clear in primitive acephalous (literally, "headless") societies and in the case of the society of sovereign states: In both cases, we have anarchical societies that display a high degree of organization even in the absence of a common government.

Second, anarchy does not only mean absence of the state. Anarchy means absence of coercive and centralized governments, of which the state is only one of the possible forms (other examples being empires or hierarchically ordered tribes). The reason why anarchy came to mean hostility to the state is that, since its rise, the modern sovereign state appeared as the culminating point of political life, the alternative to it being anarchy. This is clear in social contract theories that counterpoise the civil society to a hypothetical anarchical state of nature, thus supporting the passage from the denotation of absence of government to its frequent connotation of disorder. Such an opposition is however more a normative and therefore disputable model of social order than a description of the actual origins of the state.

Third, anarchy is both a descriptive and a prescriptive concept. In the first sense, it denotes a state of things, such as the condition of the acephalous societies mentioned above, while, in the second, it means an ideal that must be pursued. The anarchic ideal is characterized by the central emphasis it puts on the concept of freedom, so much so that some have claimed that this word summarizes the sense of the entire anarchic doctrine.

FORMS OF ANARCHY: THE ANARCHIC IDEAL

Although the anarchic ideal is recurrent in different cultures and epochs, it is in the nineteenth and twentieth century when a number of revolutionary movements emerged in many Western countries that Western anarchism as a distinct political doctrine emerged. Pierre-Joseph Proudhon is usually recognized as the first to have defined himself as an anarchist, which led many to consider him the father of modern anarchism.

Anarchists are united by their refusal of coercive forms of authority, be they political or religious, and their plea for voluntary and spontaneous forms of organizations that follow a bottom-up logic. Yet, many different and variegated forms of anarchism exist, and they can be grouped according to the different ends and means of their political proposals. With regards to the *ends,* there is a broad distinction between individualist

and social approaches. The usual example of a strict individualist credo is the theory of the German philosopher Max Stirner, who argued that freedom can have no other principle and end than the self and its egoism. Individualist anarchism developed mainly in the United States, where anarchism has often been coupled with the free market (an example being the so-called *anarcho-capitalism*).

On the opposite side stand those approaches that see the realization of the self as possible only within and through the society. Distinct approaches among these are communists, such as the Russian Peter Kropotkin, and collectivists, such as Michael Bakunin, who favored a form of communism of production but recognized some space for the individual enjoyment of the fruits of labor. Behind the different forms of anarchism stand radically different conceptions of freedom: The idea that freedom is to be realized individually (Stirner) or that it can only be achieved in common because, as Bakunin observed, one cannot be free in a society of slaves because their slavery prevents the full realization of one's own freedom.

With regards to the *means* through which anarchy is to be realized, most anarchists agree that they must be homogenous to the ends: If the aim is freedom, it can only be realized through free means. Differences emerge as to the way in which they must be conceived: (1) Some favored forms of rebellion or revolution, (2) others valued more nonviolent means such as education, while (3) others, taking an intermediate route, looked for an alliance with workers' organizations such as trade unions, which can both educate the masses and provide the infrastructures for the reorganization of society (see in particular the French and Spanish anarcho-syndicalism).

Among the first, there must be a further distinction between those who trust the spontaneity of revolution and others who believe in the "propaganda by the deeds"; that is, either local rebellions that could stimulate masses elsewhere toward a general revolution or single individual acts of violence, like assassination of political leaders. While the recourse to violence is very much controversial among anarchists, most of them agree on the importance of education for the creation of an anarchical society. Among those who emphasized education are antiviolence writers such as the Russian Leo Tolstoy or contemporary pacifist and ecological movements.

In the decades surrounding the turn of the twenty-first century, political and technological transformations have lead to a resurgence of interest in anarchism. On the one hand, the decline in popularity of Marxism in the 1990s created a sort of vacuum in the radical left. This is linked also to the fact that the collapse of the Soviet Union showed that the anarchists were right in their critique of Marxists: a workers' state cannot but reproduce the same logic of every state, where a minority of state bureaucrats rule over the majority of people. Nevertheless, the main reason for the resurgence of interest in anarchism is linked to the technological developments of the past few decades, which are usually referred to as globalization. The rise of network forms of social, economic, and political organizations, in particular through the World Wide Web and associated technologies, have somehow proved what modern political theory has always been reluctant to recognize: order is possible without an orderer.

See also *Anarchism; Authority; Freedom; Social Contract; Tyranny, Classical.*

. . . . CHIARA BOTTICI

BIBLIOGRAPHY

Bakunin, Mikhail. *Bakunin on Anarchy: Selected Works by the Activist-Founder of World Anarchism.* New York: Vintage, 1972.

Bull, Hedley. *The Anarchical Society: A Study of Order in World Politics.* London: Macmillan, 1977.

Call, Lewis. *Postmodern Anarchism.* Lanham, Md.: Lexington, 2002.

Crowder, George. *Classical Anarchism: The Political Thought of Godwin, Proudhon, Bakunin, and Kropotkin.* New York: Oxford University Press, 1992.

Day, Richard J. F. *Gramsci Is Dead: Anarchist Currents in the Newest Social Movements.* London: Pluto, 2005.

Guérin, Daniel. *Ni dieu, ni Maître. Anthologie de l'anarchisme.* Paris: La Decouverte, 1999.

Kropotkin, Pyotr. *The Essential Kropotkin.* London: Macmillan, 1976.

Malatesta, Errico. *Errico Malatesta: His Life and Ideas.* London: Freedom, 1965.

Miller, David. *Anarchism.* London: Dent, 1984.

Proudhon, Pierre-Joseph. *What Is Property?* Cambridge: Cambridge University Press 1994.

Stirner, Max. *The Ego and Its Own.* Cambridge: Cambridge University Press, 1995.

Anglophone Africa

Anglophone Africa refers primarily to sub-Sahara African states colonized by the British Empire in the late nineteenth and early twentieth century. English is the most widely spoken language in independent Africa, and twenty of Africa's fifty-three countries use English as their official lingua franca. With the exceptions of South Africa (1700s–1910—dates for colonization) and the island nation of Mauritius (1810–1968), the British colonies scattered on the Western Coast of Africa are the earliest: the Gambia (1664–1965), Sierra Leone (1787–1961), and Nigeria (1861–1960), the largest country by population in Africa, along with Ghana (1874–1957). Lesotho, entirely landlocked within South Africa, was also an earlier colony (1867–1966).

The later wave of colonization, following the Berlin Conference of 1885 (also referred to as the "Scramble for Africa"), includes the southern countries of Botswana (1885–1966), Zimbabwe (1890–1980), Malawi (1891–1964), Zambia (1891–1964), and Swaziland (1902–1968). The largest countries by population, besides Nigeria, are all in east Africa: Kenya (1885–1963), Uganda (1885–1965), and Tanzania (1918–1964), while the largest by land area is the Sudan (1899–1956). Of these sixteen countries, only Tanzania, the Sudan, and Zimbabwae are not among the member states of the British Commonwealth.

Other countries may be included in Anglophone Africa either due to their use of English or their colonial heritage. Liberia is an English-speaking African country that was not colonized by the British but was purchased by the American colonization society to act as a homeland for freed African American slaves. The northern portion of Somalia (though not internationally recognized as the Republic of Somaliland) was colonized by the British from 1884 to 1960. Egypt is also a formerly British-colonized African country but is Arabic-speaking. Namibia is an English-speaking, formerly German-colonized country; Cameroon is a Francophone African country whose Northeastern region uses English as its lingua franca due to joint British colonial administration with Nigeria (1916–1961). Both Cameroon and Namibia belong to the present-day Commonwealth, as do English-speaking Sierra Leone and Rwanda.

DECOLONIZATION AND QUICK DEMOCRATIC REVERSAL

During the decolonization period (primarily the 1960s), Britain created local government councils and national legislative council institutions in its former colonies to use as vehicles for influencing the eventual shape of the independent democratic governments. Established as liberal democracies at independence, most countries reformed the British Westminster parliamentary system to evolve presidential hybrid systems. Since the early 1970s, with the exception of Botswana, the Gambia, and Mauritius, Anglophone Africa's liberal democracies have suffered democratic reversals, beginning with the constriction of multiparty regimes into one-party states and continuing with the ousting of democratic governments by military regimes. Examples include,

- *Tanzania:* The leadership of the first prime minister, Julius Nyerere, paved the way for the 1965 referendum that transitioned the Westminster parliamentary system into the self-styled, Ujaama one-party "democracy."
- *Kenya:* By 1966, federalism was discontinued and transformed into a one-party regime by the first majority party, the Kenyan African Nationalist Union (KANU).
- *Nigeria:* A tripartite federalist, Westminster parliamentary regime was ousted by a military coup in 1966 after just seven years, despite the notable leadership of its first president, Nnamdi Azikiwe; first prime minister, Sir Tafewa Balewa; and western region premier, Obafemi Awolowo.
- *Ghana:* One of the continent's first independent democracies in 1957, its liberal democratic regime was ousted in a coup in 1968 after a metamorphosis toward one-party socialism under the the pan-Africanist leadership of West Africa's first independence nationalist, Dr. Kwame Nkrumah, and his populist Congress Peoples Party (CPP).
- *The Sudan:* A Westminster parliamentary regime from 1956 until 1969 gave way to the single-party military regime of Jafar Numeiri (1969–1985) due to war, instability, and the dominance of the northern Muslim Sudanese to the exclusion of the non-Muslim South.
- *Uganda:* A democratic regime led by President Milton Obote was overthrown in a 1971 coup by General Idi Amin.

THIRD WAVE OF DEMOCRATIZATION

By the end of the cold war in the 1990s, what political scientist Samuel Huntington has called the "Third

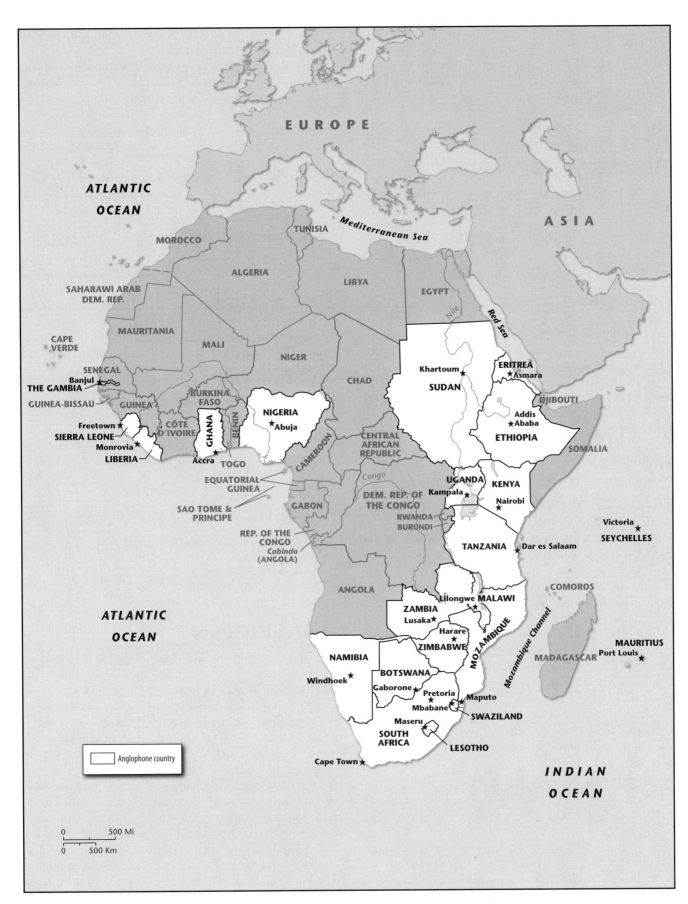

The term "Anglophone Africa" refers to English-speaking African nations influenced by British colonialism.

Wave of Democratization" spread to Anglophone Africa. Zambia's 1990–1991 prodemocracy Movement for Multi-party Democracy (MMD) in 1991 was first to reestablish democracy through the leadership of former union leader Fredrick Chiluba, who replaced Kenneth Kaunda's UNIP one-party regime. Kenya formally restored multiparty elections in 1992 under President Daniel Arap Moi, but only in 2001 did the National Rainbow Coalition (NARC) finally oust KANU regime dominance and usher in a genuine democratic transition. Nigeria underwent a redemocratization period between 1979 and 1983, and another in 1993, but did not truly reachieve democracy until its 1999 military-led elections that resulted in its fourth republic, the Obasanjo regime. In the midst of these transitions, the Gambia underwent a military coup in 1994, but soon reestablished multiparty elections in 1997.

South Africa's transition to democracy was significant in both African and world politics. The country's 1948 establishment of a multiparty democracy for white settlers led by National Party (NP) dominance and the establishment of formal white minority rule was not truly a democracy, as it excluded most of the nation's population. Although the African National Congress (ANC) was founded in 1912 to embark upon (black) majority rule, only in 1990, under the new leadership of President F. W De Klerk, did a pact between the NP and the ANC's Nelson Mandela result in the first full-suffrage election. The 1994 election was an ANC electoral victory, installing Nelson Mandela as the first black African president, and completing South Africa's democratic transition.

LEVELS OF DEMOCRACY IN ANGLOPHONE AFRICA

Only a few Anglophone African countries are classified as *free* democracies with the highest political rights and civil liberties. These countries have established liberal democratic institutions and play more than nominal reference to human rights. The domains of power reserved for the military or other actors not accountable to the electorate are absent, and government systems in these democracies have achieved both vertical and horizontal accountability that constrain executive power and protect constitutionality, legality, and the democratic process. The regimes extend provisions for political and civic pluralism, as well as individual and group freedoms, as individuals are able to frequently exercise their rights to citizenship in obtaining unfettered and just access to the democratic system. Examples include,

- *Botswana's* Botswana Democratic Party's (BDP) continuous democracy
- *Ghana's* recent turnover electoral victory by President Attah-Mills's National Democratic Coalition (NDC) party
- *South Africa's* 1994 liberal democratic constitution (CODESA) that extends rights to gays and lesbians
- *Mauritius's* ethnically plural consensus democracy
- *Lesotho's* experiments in proportional representation to extend voting rights more fully to minorities,

These are all characteristics of the substantive democratic deepening among these countries.

Several of Africa's largest Anglophone countries remain only partially free, including Nigeria, Kenya, and Tanzania, whose large, multiethnic, complexly forged socioeconomic contexts foster certain limitations in fully consolidating liberal democracy. The Sudan and Zimbabwe, on the other hand, are infamously known for their "not-free" statuses with the worst political rights and civil liberty regimes on the African continent. Sudan ended its thirty-year war with the non-Muslim south in a bifederal unity government in 2004, but then emerged the Darfur crisis, during which the Sudanese militarized regime (National Islamic Front—NIF) chose a military option to subvert the Darfuran militant resistance. The effect on Sudanese democracy of an April 2009 ICC indictment of President Omar Bashir for human rights abuses against Sudanese citizens remains to be seen. Zimbabwe also is considered a not-free democracy due to party dominance and the exclusion of opposition by President Robert Mugabe's Zimbabwe African National Union (ZANU) regime. A February 2009 government of national unity coalition between ZANU and the opposition party Movement for Democratic Change (MDC), led by Prime Minister Morgan Tzviringirai, held promise and hope for the consolidation of democracy in Zimbabwe.

See also *Democracy and Democratization; Francophone Africa; Lusophone Africa; Postindependent Africa, Politics and Governance in.*

. . . . RITA KIKI EDOZIE

BIBLIOGRAPHY

Edie, Carelene. *Politics in Africa: A New Beginning.* Belmont, Calif.: Wadsworth, 2003.

Edozie, Rita Kiki. *Reconstructing the Third Wave of Democracy: Comparative African Democratic Politics.* Lanham, Md.: University Press of America, 2008.

Freedom House, "Freedom in the World: Country Report," 2009, www.freedomhouse.org/template.cfm?page=1.

Animal Rights

The idea that animals have rights develops almost solely within Western intellectual traditions. Vegetarianism based on respect for animals in non-Western cultures was almost always based on religious asceticism. Philosophical vegetarianism seems first to have appeared in classical Greek thought with the quasi-theological work of Pythagoras and the neo-Platonists, Plutarch, and Porphyry. Throughout ancient antiquity and the Middle Ages, however, Western philosophy and theology, under the influence of Aristotle and the Bible, assumed that animals existed for the convenience of humanity. Although heretical sects like the Jewish Christians in the early church and several Manichean movements in late antiquity and the Middle Ages were vegetarian, they sought purification of the human soul rather than the welfare of animals. The Protestant Reformation gave greater recognition to the earthly suffering and future resurrection of animals, especially in the more radical sects, which were particularly strong in

England. This new sensitivity to animals, along with Enlightenment humanitarianism and Romantic naturalism, prepared the animal welfare movements of the nineteenth century.

Bernard Mandeville, Frances Hutcheson, David Hume, Jean Jacques Rousseau, and other figures of the Enlightenment advanced the ideas of compassion and sympathy that brought them close to animal rights. Indeed English philosopher Jeremy Bentham, counting only aggregates of pain and pleasure, famously said ". . . the question is not, Can they reason?, nor Can they talk? But, Can they suffer?" But like all the major writers of this period, Bentham the radical was too much a prisoner of deeply embedded custom and tradition to carry thoughts like this through to a logical conclusion (i.e., principled vegetarianism). In the nineteenth century, some transcendentalists such as Henry David Thoreau moved to principled vegetarianism and a more general respect for animals and nature.

The modern theory of animal rights, as well as the movement to secure them, really begins with the 1975 publication of *Animal Liberation* by Peter Singer. Singer, himself a utilitarian, systematically worked out the full implications of Bentham's thought on animals: If every sentient individual is to count as one, then the suffering of a nonhuman animal counts no less than that of a human. The interests of animals must thus be accorded equal respect. Not to do so is *specieism,* a term that Singer popularized, holding that the modern movement for liberation focused until then on racism and sexism should extend also to the liberation of animals from specieism. Singer reviewed at length the horrors of factory farming and the torments of animals in biomedical research, all but a tiny fraction of which he showed to be pointless, repetitious, or misleading. For factory farming, Singer's remedy is vegetarianism. For the evils of research, limit animal testing to what is truly urgent. His test for urgency is whether the experimenters would be willing to take human infants of six months or younger and mentally defective adults as the subjects of their experiments. Such entities, Singer holds, have no more preference for life than animals.

The great alternative to Singer and utilitarianism is the rights approach, the classic text for which is Tom Regan's *The Case for Animal Rights* (1983). Regan begins by observing that no responsible thinker has ever held that we may treat animals in any way we please and then elaborates on the full meaning of that common intuition. He dismisses as inadequate the idea that cruelty is to be ruled out merely because of its alleged "indirect effect" in hardening human hearts in their treatment of each other. Utilitarianism is excluded also because it treats individual sentient beings as mere receptacles for units of utility, which may then be abstracted and aggregated and can thus sacrifice justice to individuals to maximize an aggregate. Respect for animals as individuals requires taking each subject-of-a-life as a locus of "inherent value" or subjectivity and recognizing that this inherent value is equal for every subject-of-a-life. This rights approach goes beyond Singer's utilitarianism in admitting no exceptions to vegetarianism and condemning all experimentation on animals as inherently wrong and unnecessary in the long run. Although Regan confines full subjectivity to mammals of a year or more in age, he

admits that the circle of rights may be extended, and other theorists have done so.

More recently Christine M. Korsgaard has argued that humans cannot value their own sensible nature without valuing that of animals as well. Julian H. Franklin has deepened the foundations of the rights position by showing that Kant's categorical imperative logically includes all sentient beings among its beneficiaries, not only humans, even though rational beings alone are subject to its obligations.

See also *Children's Rights; Enlightenment Political Thought; Kant, Immanuel; Utilitarianism.*

. . . . JULIAN H. FRANKLIN

BIBLIOGRAPHY

Franklin, Julian H. *Animal Rights and Moral Philosophy.* New York: Columbia University Press, 2005.

Korsgaard, Christine M. *The Sources of Normativity.* Cambridge: Cambridge University Press, 1996.

Regan, Tom. *The Case for Animal Rights.* Berkeley: University of California Press, 1983.

Singer, Peter. *Animal Liberation.* New York: HarperCollins, 1975.

Annexation

See *Occupation and Annexation.*

Anthems, National

See *National Anthems.*

Anthony, Susan Brownell

American political reformer and "Napoleon of the women's rights movement," Susan B. Anthony (1820–1906) was born in Massachusetts. Over the course of a sixty-year career as a reformer, Anthony traveled an average of thirteen thousand miles (twenty-one thousand kilometers) a year to garner support for women's causes. Her reformist nature was nurtured from an early age by her activist Baptist mother and her abolitionist father, a liberal Quaker who had been run out of the local meeting house for allowing young people to hold dancing lessons in his attic.

At age fifteen, Anthony began teaching in her father's school during summer breaks. The part-time job turned into a full-time profession three years later when her father became impoverished during a financial recession. In 1848, Anthony's career as a reformer was launched when she joined the local chapter of the Daughters of Temperance. She also became an ardent abolitionist, expressing her support for the controversial John Brown. She did not, however, take part in the first women's rights convention held in Seneca Falls, New York, in 1848 under the leadership of Elizabeth Cady Stanton and Lucretia Mott. Although her interest in women's rights was ignited after her parents and sister returned from Seneca Falls, it was not until reformer Amelia Bloomer introduced her to suffragists Stanton and Lucy Stone in 1851 that Anthony became actively involved in the fledgling movement.

Anthony and Stanton became lifelong friends and colleagues, actively lobbying for women's suffrage, abolition, and equal rights for women and African Americans, often under the auspices of the American Equal Rights Association, which they cofounded. To promote their views, they published the radical newspaper, *The Revolution,* from 1868 to 1870.

The women's movement split amid the furor over the Fifteenth Amendment, ratified in 1870, which guaranteed suffrage to black men but not to women. Anthony and Stanton formed the National Woman Suffrage Association (NWSA) in 1869. The breech among the women's groups was healed over the next two decades. In 1890, NWSA merged with the American Woman Suffrage Association, which under the leadership of Lucy Stone had supported the Fifteenth Amendment, to create the National American Woman's Suffrage Association. It was not until the 1960s that the women's movement and civil rights movement again supported one another's struggle for equal rights.

Anthony wrote a number of articles and speeches, most notably *The True Woman* (1859) and the *Declaration of the Rights of Woman* (1876) with Stanton and Matilda Jocelyn Gage. Anthony's most significant work was her contribution to the multiauthored six-volume *History of Woman's Suffrage* published between 1881 and 1922. In 1896, with Anthony's consent, Husted Harper authored a two-volume biography of her; a third volume was published after Anthony's death.

In 1872, Anthony challenged the ban on female suffrage by voting illegally. She was arrested and convicted. The decades-long collaboration of Anthony and Stanton culminated in 1920 when the ratification of the Nineteenth Amendment, known familiarly as the Susan B. Anthony Amendment, gave white women the right to vote. Neither woman lived to experience the success that had taken seventy-two years to accomplish.

See also *Women's Rights; Women's Suffrage.*

. . . . ELIZABETH RHOLETTER PURDY

BIBLIOGRAPHY

DuBois, Ellen Carol, ed. *The Elizabeth Cady Stanton–Susan B. Anthony Reader: Correspondence, Writings, Speeches.* Boston: Northwestern University Press, 1992.

Harper, Ida Husted. *Life and Work of Susan B. Anthony.* Reprint of 1898–1908 eds. New York: Arno, 1969.

Harper, Judith E. *Susan B. Anthony: A Biographical Companion.* Santa Barbara, Calif.: ABC-CLIO, 1998.

Sherr, Lynn. *Failure Is Impossible: Susan B. Anthony in Her Own Words.* New York: Times Books, 1995.

Ward, Geoffrey C. *Not for Ourselves Alone: The Story of Elizabeth Cady Stanton and Susan B. Anthony.* New York: Knopf, 1999.

Anti- and Alter-globalization Movements

The anti-globalization movement is a social movement that opposes neoliberal corporate-led globalization as advanced by corporations, neoclassical economists, and key global institutions such as the World Bank, the International Monetary Fund (IMF), and the World Trade Organization (WTO). The movement asserts that the current form of globalization, which is based on economic integration through trade, investment, and financial flows, is not beneficial to the majority of the world's population nor to the environment. Its goal is to ensure that globalization's burden does not fall on workers, communities, the environment, women, and other more marginalized sectors of society. This movement is part of what is known as *new social movements.* That is, movements that are cross-class—advocate a myriad of issues rather than being one-issue specific—and transnational in terms of demands, focus, and even organizational forms. This cross-borders movement first came to light and became known by the term *anti-globalization* movement after staging mass demonstrations in Seattle, Washington, in 1999. However, some scholars argue that the roots of this kind of cross-border citizens' activism against global economic trends can be found decades if not centuries earlier during European colonialism and antislavery movements. According to these scholars, there are several hundred years of movements that, with varying degrees of success, made international linkages on specific issues related to cross-borders economic integration.

The *alter-globalization* movement, which is a less-known term sometimes used interchangeably with *anti-globalization* to delineate the same thing, has a lot of commonalities with the latter. That is, both anti- and alter-globalization movements emphasize a shared conception of neoliberalism as a global project harmful to the majority of the world population and the environment. The terms were coined to distinguish a current of thought and activism that is not opposed to globalization as a multidimensional and often inevitable process linking people together; rather, it is to emphasize the need for a different form of globalization whereby this process and its different composites of telecommunication leaps, global governance, and economic logic work for the benefit of the majority of the world's population and not a minority of corporations. Many of the activists and groups involved in this movement are not necessarily against capitalism, rather they want to use to use it in a way that can enhance prosperity with better distribution of resources and opportunities. Initiatives such as *fair trade,* corporate codes of conduct, flexible migration laws, and free use of the Internet are examples of what this movement and its different groups work on.

For the contemporary anti-globalization and alter-globalization movements, three episodes have been seminal to putting it center stage within living-room discussions as much as academic and policy-making debates: the Seattle protests of 1999, the Genoa protests of 2001, and the antiwar demonstrations in 2003 in multiple cities. While other demonstrations targeting neoliberal global policies were organized earlier—during World Bank and IMF meetings (including Berlin in 1988 and Madrid in 1994)—and later (Washington, D.C., in 2000, G8 meetings in different European cities early in the new millennium), these three episodes were the largest and most confrontational. They stirred academic debate about the limitation of the nation-state both as an actor and as a target for contention, and the impact and potential of global civil society and transnational activism and movements. The movement adopted a discourse of unified neoliberalism as a master frame, and accordingly devised and included a cultural framing process that universalizes its shortcomings and alternatives to the movement itself.

ORGANIZATIONAL FORMS

Not only has the anti-globalization movement ushered in new concepts and cultural frames, but it also emphasized new forms of organization. Observers such as Carlos Azambuja (2003) describe the movement as:

> . . . [dis]organization that has no hierarchical structure or operational center, consisting of just "us," in whose interventions thousands of organizations come together horizontally to protest, in one way or another, the current world order. They can grow infinitely without anyone having to give up his individuality to any hierarchical structure. (1)

The movement has been conceptualized as a network. A network in this analysis is a wider concept that potentially includes social movements but also nongovernmental organizations (NGOs), professional unions, and the media. Networks make great use of information technology and are characterized by alliances forged between groups with disparate political and ideological affiliations, and by the great diversity in the backgrounds of their members. These loose horizontal forms of organization, the cross-class nature of the movement (intellectuals, students, workers, professionals), along with the diverse ideological leanings of participants and their demands (environmentalists, feminists, Marxists, anarchists, liberal-humanists) put it within the category of new social movements. Using changes in technology, innovative protest styles, information politics, and analytical advances, this movement created debates about the changing nature of contentious politics in the new millennium. The debates ranged from a post–nation-state era to global policing and the demise of political parties.

IMPACT

The anti-globalization movement marked a growing space for extraparliamentary politics and the rising number and diversified tactics of different movements that could be adopted and adapted by others, including the range of alliances, organizational forms, and framing dissent. The movement also gave rise to transnational or global civil society forums pioneered in the World Social Forum (WSF). The first WSF, held in 2001, convened in Porto Alegre, Brazil, with the intention to provide a counterevent to the World Economic Forum in Davos, Switzerland. Since then the social forums have been replicated on a regional level (European and Asian Social Forums). The forum is held under the slogan "Another World Is Possible," which summarizes the common outlook of the various participants advocating alternatives for the neoliberal model on different issues.

The WSF, which is attended by individual activists, social movement representatives, NGOs, and some leftist political parties, is meant to serve as a global rally against corporate-led globalization and a meeting point where delegates can exchange experiences and coordinate and plan campaigns.

For instance, the WSF was a rallying point for worldwide dissent against the U.S. invasion of Iraq, with protests held in different cities on February 15, 2003. Hence, what came to be called the *antiwar movement* since 2003 is in fact an extension of the anti-globalization movement in terms of participants, tactics, and aspired universality. Thus, the emergence of antiwar movement, which was the biggest campaign and most successful mobilization attempt (in terms of size at least) of the anti-globalization movement, has marked the retreat of the latter.

See also *Contentious Politics; Globalization; Globalization and Development; Modernization; Protests and Demonstrations.*

. . . . RABAB EL-MAHDI

BIBLIOGRAPHY

Azambuja, Carlos I. S. "The New Face of the Anti-globalization Movements," 2003, www.cubdest.org/0312/cazambuje.html.

Ayres, Jeffery. "Framing Collective Action Against Neoliberalism: The Case of the 'Anti-globalization' Movement." *Journal of World-Systems Research* (Winter 2004): 11–34.

Broad, R., ed. *Global Backlash: Citizen Initiatives for a Just World Economy.* Lanham, Md.: Rowman and Littlefield, 2002.

Cavanagh, John, Jerry Mander, Sarah Anderson, Debi Barker, and Maud Barlow. *Alternatives to Economic Globalization: A Better World Is Possible.* San Francisco: Berrett-Koehler, 2002.

della Porta, Donatella, and Sidney Tarrow. "After Genoa and New York: The Anti-global Movement, the Police, and Terrorism." *Items and Issues: Social Science Research Council* (Winter, 2001): 9–11.

Edelman, Marc. "Social Movements: Changing Paradigms and Forms of Politics." *Annual Review of Anthropology* 30 (2001): 285–317.

Keck, Margret, and Kathryn Sikkink. *Activists beyond Borders: Advocacy Networks in International Politics.* New York: Cornell University Press, 1998.

Khagram, Sanjee, James Riker, and Kathryn Sikkink, eds. *Restructuring World Politics: Transnational Social Movements, Networks, and Norms.* Minneapolis: University of Minnesota Press, 2002.

Anticlericalism

Anticlericalism is an attribute of a political movement or ideology that refers to animosity or opposition to the established religious leadership, often associated with broad disapproval of the public role of religion. While secularism describes the dissociation of religion and public life, anticlericalism seeks the deliberate limitation and reversal of the influence of religious leaders through legal and behavioral constraints. Anticlericalism was a foundational premise of many of the revolutionary movements from the Protestant Reformation of the 1500s to the Iranian White Revolution of the 1960s and continuing in various forms to the present day.

Anticlericalism arose originally in European politics in response to the power of the Roman Catholic papacy and clergy in the Middle Ages. The Reformation challenged the power of the Roman Catholic Church as the sole interpreter of doctrine and practice, and it led parts of northern Europe to break with the church, sparking almost a century of warfare. For example, Martin Luther's major works beginning in 1520 directly challenged the authority and sanctity of the Roman Catholic priesthood and the papacy. As a result, the Peace of

Westphalia of 1648 committed the nations of Europe to refrain from attempting to enforce Roman Catholic orthodoxy and, more generally, introduced the principle of *cuius regio, eius religio,* under which the religion of the leader was made the religion of the people.

Nevertheless, the Roman Catholic Church remained a powerful force in Europe and colonial areas up to the modern age. In countries such as France, Italy, and Spain that had resisted the Reformation, the clergy was commonly associated with conservative and monarchical power, while radical and leftist forces typically espoused anticlerical attitudes as a form of opposition to the dominant classes.

Enlightenment Europe brought many new anticlerical forces to power. The Jacobin movement that inspired the French Revolution (1789–1799) was ardently opposed to the established power of the church in addition to its opposition to aristocracy and monarchy. Acts of the revolutionary National Assembly up to and including the 1790 Civil Constitution of the Clergy led to the confiscation of church property and dissolved religious orders.

Anticlericalism was equally a force in colonial resistance movements. For example, a persistent theme of Mexican politics has been the limitation of the power of the Roman Catholic clergy through deliberate anticlerical policies, such as article 27 of the 1917 Mexican constitution (since amended), which forbid the church from owning property. Early postcolonial constitutions specifically laid out restraints on the church, and church properties were held by the revolutionary governments with a view toward redistribution of these assets.

The totalitarian movements of the 1930s brooked no dissent from any societal force and the religious establishment was no exception. Marx's famous dictum that "religion is the opiate of the masses" inspired an antagonism toward religious authorities in most all communist states from the Soviet Union to Cuba. Fascist movements in Italy and Germany in the 1930s were more ambiguously anticlerical, combining a vague tolerance of religion with a desire to subordinate and persecute clergy should they present a strong philosophical challenge to chauvinistic nationalism. In non-Christian contexts, movements of both the left and the right have likewise pursued an anticlerical bent, from Maoist suppression of the Buddhist religion in China to the enforced secularism in Kemalist Turkey and Iran under Muhammad Reza Shah.

Anticlericalism remains a part of many modern and secularizing political movements and has had an important influence on many feminist and structuralist analyses. For example, leading feminist theologian Rosemary Radford Ruether has criticized traditional religion and the hierarchy of the Roman Catholic Church and the Vatican. Likewise in critical texts on colonialism such as that of Frantz Fanon's *The Wretched of the Earth,* organized religion is castigated for its role in perpetuating relationships of dominance. The resurgence of religion as a militant force, beginning in the 1990s and demonstrated in the attacks of September 11, 2001, in the United States, also has led many to argue that it is inherently regressive and should be subordinated to liberal norms.

See also *Reformation Political Thought; Religion and Politics; Roman Catholic Social Thought; Secularism.*

. . . . PAUL S. ROWE

BIBLIOGRAPHY

Barnett, S. J. *Idol Temples and Crafty Priests: The Origins of Enlightenment Anticlericalism.* New York: St. Martin's, 1999.

Burleigh, Michael. *Sacred Causes: The Clash of Religion and Politics, from the Great War to the War on Terror.* New York: Harper Collins, 2007.

Dykema, Peter A., and Heiko A. Oberman, eds. *Anticlericalism in Late Medieval and Early Modern Europe.* Leiden, Netherlands: E. J. Brill, 1993.

Fanon, Frantz. *The Wretched of the Earth.* Translated by Richard Philcox. New York: Grove, 2004.

Sanchez, Jose. *Anticlericalism: A Brief History.* Notre Dame, Ind.: University of Notre Dame Press, 1972.

Anti-democratic Thought

The term *democracy* originated in classical Athens and combines the ancient Greek words *demos,* meaning "the people," and *kratein,* meaning "to rule." From that time, anti-democratic arguments have taken a variety of forms, though some commentators (e.g., Dahl 1989) maintain that all of them are reducible to knowledge claims, or the "idea of guardianship," according to which one person or group of people knows better than the rest how to maximize the interests of the community. This seems a rather simplistic way to characterize anti-democratic thought. A more subtle approach is to make use of the analytical categories developed by A. O. Hirschman in his study of "reactionary" thought (1991): *perversity, futility,* and *jeopardy.*

HISTORY

In classical Athens, where democracy originated, "the people" of necessity encompassed the poor and uneducated, and democracy was often identified with the rule of the mob or the rabble. Both Plato and Aristotle held it in contempt as a degenerate form of governance, subordinating reason to passion, polarizing rich and poor, and generating both instability and imprudence. Instead, Aristotle and other writers extolled the virtues of a "mixed constitution," in which rule by the many is balanced in some formal way by the influence of the wealthy and literate minority. This was the model of government that emerged from the ancient world, one where popular power was restricted by mutual checks and the rule of law. The word *democracy* fell into disuse, except as a synonym for internal dissension and majority tyranny. Even the framers of the American constitution drew a distinction between a *democracy,* which they feared, and a *republic,* another name for the "mixed" or "balanced" regime they favored.

The present vogue for democracy really dates from the French Revolution (1789–1799), whose more radical protagonists appealed to "the people" as an undiluted source of power. Democracy soon lost its toxic connotations and came to be associated with the classical republican tradition that had long challenged the monarchical institutions of Europe. In its new incarnation, democracy could no longer be dismissed as mob rule. It was now seen to include representative parliaments, the separation of powers, the rule of law, and civil rights. Gradually, the idea of democracy became a dominant standard by which regimes were judged. But, despite the supposed taming of the democratic beast, the rehabilitation of democracy led to the revival of anti-democratic thought.

PERVERSITY THESIS

The *perversity thesis* holds that radical reformers likely will produce the exact opposite of what they intended. Society is seen as an infinitely complex system of causal chains, making the consequences of disruptive change entirely unpredictable. In the aftermath of the French Revolution, romantic conservatives such as Edmund Burke formulated a version of the perverse effect in their attacks on the revolution and its egalitarian pretensions. They saw society as an organic whole, more easily damaged than improved, and the divisive individualism, the incessant and ignorant questioning implicit in democracy, would—in their view—unleash chaos. But nature abhors a power vacuum. A demagogic elite, unrestrained by inherited customs, would seize power and rule with an iron fist. Democracy would transmute into tyranny, albeit one that might reflect the base and foolish preferences of the majority. The dream of liberation would become a nightmare of repression.

In the middle part of the nineteenth century, even liberals who were sympathetic to democracy fretted over its tyrannical potential. It was commonly believed that the multiple sources of authority in traditional society, which served to preserve a measure of pluralism and individual eccentricity, would eventually be swept aside by the growing power of the people, who would tolerate no activities that did not originate in popular mandate. Alexis de Tocqueville argued that this dissolution of the intermediate structure of authority could leave the individual isolated and vulnerable, unable to resist the ubiquitous and absolute power of the state.

FUTILITY THESIS

By the end of the century, the fear of democratic tyranny had receded, and a new type of critic emerged. Motivated more by cynicism than anxiety, the classical elitists (Vilfredo Pareto, Gaetano Mosca, and Robert Michels) argued that the oppressive effects of democracy had not come to pass because democracy itself was impossible. No matter what the constitution says, the inherent dynamics of human interaction always will prevent the masses from exercising power. This was the *futility thesis*. Pareto used psychological factors to explain this "law" of oligarchy, while Mosca and Michels stressed organizational factors, but they all agreed on the existence of an immanent hierarchical order of things, which meant that so-called democratic institutions were, at best, exercises in futility, and, at worst, expressions of rank hypocrisy.

JEOPARDY THESIS

The elitists seemed to understand democracy in a "pure" sense, where all government decisions are presumed to emanate from some clearly defined popular will. That democracy in this sense could never exist was, to some observers, merely a statement of the obvious. Nevertheless, the inexorable extension of the franchise in the early part of the twentieth century convinced many people that democracy, even in diluted form, was still a threat, if not to liberty then to other values held dear. This is the *jeopardy thesis*—the idea that progressive reform always will incur a cost. While democracy may bring some benefits to the common people, it extinguishes cultural creativity and belittles heroic and noble deeds. It destroys economic efficiency and elevates mass appetites and prejudices above mental rigour. Such arguments were quite common before World War II (1939–1945) turned democracy into a "hurrah" word, signifying nothing but approbation.

Traditional conservatives such as the poet T. S. Eliot insisted that "high" culture was threatened by the vulgar tastes of the masses, who would use democratic mechanisms to impose their debased values. Social coherence also would suffer, as equality of opportunity, an inevitable concomitant of democracy, would create a society of strangers, devoid of historical memory. Thinkers on the radical right, especially fascists, were inspired by Nietzsche's diatribes against "slave-morality" and mass mediocrity. In their eyes, democracy was a complicated bundle of decadent values—individualism, pacifism, materialism, egalitarianism—which was eroding cultural vitality and the collective spirit.

CONCLUSION

The rising tide of democratization and democratic rhetoric that swept through the international community during the latter half of the twentieth century has left the remaining explicitly anti-democratic regimes marooned in global public disapproval. All of the reactionary criticisms that justify such regimes are rarely taken seriously by political scientists or indeed most educated people throughout the world. Nevertheless, some observers, in contemplating how the democratic ethos tends not toward excellence but rather toward the lowest common denominator, point out that the tradition of anti-democratic thought contains at least some grains of truth. After all, even the most beneficial changes entail loss. However, such is the power of the democratic idea that, nowadays, even neofascists feel obliged to claim affinity with it.

See also *Authority; Democracy; Democracy and Corruption; Democratic Theory; Greek Democracy, Classical; Tyranny of the Majority and Minority Rights.*

. . . . JOSEPH FEMIA

BIBLIOGRAPHY

Dahl, Robert A. *Democracy and Its Critics,* New Haven, Conn.: Yale University Press, 1989.

Femia, Joseph. *Against the Masses: Varieties of Anti-democratic Thought since the French Revolution.* Oxford: Oxford University Press, 2001.

Griffin, Roger. *The Nature of Fascism.* London: Pinter, 1991.

Hirschman, Albert O. *The Rhetoric of Reaction: Perversity, Futility, Jeopardy.* Cambridge, Mass.: Harvard University Press, 1991.

Holmes, Stephen. *The Anatomy of Antiliberalism.* Cambridge, Mass.: Harvard University Press, 1993.

Meisel, James Hans. *The Myth of the Ruling Class.* Ann Arbor: University of Michigan Press, 1958.

Saward, Michael. *The Terms of Democracy.* Cambridge, U.K.: Polity Press, 1998.

Anti-Semitism

Semites are both Jews and Arabs who emerged from a common ancestral and geographical setting in the Middle East. However, *anti-Semitism* refers specifically to prejudice against Jews as a religious, ethnic, or racial body. It can include a wide range of attitudes and expressions, from individual hostility to legal discrimination and violence against Jews as a group.

Like so many stereotypes, anti-Semitism is based on a myth—one with the power to influence individual attitudes toward Jews and their place in society and, collectively, to impact the larger culture. It has no basis in fact or reason, but its acolytes make vague references to historical or pseudo-scientific genetic arguments in support of their prejudices. Accusations against Jews of two millennia ago, or toward some individual Jew today, are portrayed as the collective responsibility of all Jews as a people, who must be punished by strong measures, up to and including genocide.

Religious anti-Semitism attacks Jews as being responsible for the death of Jesus, and for practicing their minority faith, which is portrayed as the devil's product. It promises a cessation of persecution if Jews give up their faith and assimilate into an approved religion.

Racial anti-Semitism identifies Jews as a genetically distinct race. They are an innately subhuman race that can never assimilate with the superior culture but conspire to pollute the more advanced Aryan race and control the world, its government, and its economy. They must be stopped at all costs. A recent variant is geographic, based in opposition to Zionism and the existence of the state of Israel. Radical Islam and its allies use motifs from anti-Semitic Europe in pursuit of their political goals. All forms of anti-Semitism have been used to justify discrimination and persecution of Jews.

ORIGINS

The term *anti-Semitism* was concocted by German agitator Wilhelm Marr in about 1880 to indicate hatred of the Jews. Marr favored their forced expulsion from German soil. Jews had faced persecution, enslavement, and dispersion for their monotheism since ancient times. Egypt, Babylonia, Assyria, and Alexandrine Greece were early conquerors. However, modern anti-Semitism had its origins in the Roman Empire. In protecting their rituals and beliefs from the Romans, the Jews raised several rebellions against Roman rule, which gave them the reputation of agitators who were threats to imperial stability. When the Romans finally defeated the Jews in 70 CE, their temple was razed, and they were dispersed throughout the empire.

Shortly before this, Jesus preached and died as a Jew living under Roman rule. He was tried in a Jewish court for blasphemy and turned over to the Romans for punishment, which the Roman governor decreed would be execution. By the fourth century the belief emerged among Christians that Jews who were not followers of Jesus were willful unbelievers in the truth, and responsible for his death. After the Emperor Constantine I began the process that made Christianity the official religion of the Roman Empire, this belief was translated into persecution.

During the Middle Ages, nontoleration became a cornerstone of religious policy, and Jews were increasingly identified as usurers and punished in many ways for their refusal to convert, culminating in the violence and murder committed by mobs against various Jewish communities during eight Crusades (intermittently from 1096–1273). In 1215, Pope Innocent III decreed that Jews were to wear a special badge to mark their inferior status whenever they went out. In 1242, Pope Gregory IX was persuaded by an investigating committee of Paris theologians to denounce the Talmud—a fourth-century commentary on rabbinic tradition, Jewish life, and law—as blasphemous and ordered all copies to be burned. Urban Jews were forced to live in special areas, or *ghettos,* and they were restricted in economic and social life; some of these restrictions lasted until the end of the nineteenth century. As early as 1144, charges were brought against Jews of blood libel, the supposed Jewish drinking of blood of murdered Christian children. When the Black Death swept Europe in the fourteenth century, rumors spread that the Jews were the cause of the plague, and many were massacred. During the Protestant Reformation in the sixteenth century, German theologian and religious reformer Martin Luther, disappointed that the Jews would not convert to his religious views, denounced them as severely as he denounced medieval popes, calling for their property to be confiscated and for their expulsion.

LATER DEVELOPMENTS

Under Napoleonic rule, following the French Revolution (1789–1799), Jews were offered the opportunity to participate fully in European political, economic, and social life. The defeat of Napoleon in 1815 brought such advances to a temporary halt, but by 1870 many nations of western Europe granted full citizenship to all Jews. However, anti-Semitism lingered. In 1893 Alfred Dreyfus, a Jewish captain in the French army, was falsely convicted of treason by a military court. The evidence against Dreyfus had been faked by two fellow officer, and his conviction was supported by leading French conservatives in the army, the Catholic Church, and anti-Semitic writers, such as Edouard Drumont. The efforts of the noted author, Émile Zola, played a central role in reversing Dreyfus' unjust conviction in 1899, although it took another seven years for him to be restored to the French army. If the Dreyfus affair indicated that anti-Semitism was not eradicated, it came at a time when the conditions of life for most Jews in western Europe had vastly improved.

Destruction of property and massacres of Jews, called *pogroms,* began in Russia in 1881. The pogroms were instigated by the government to divert the discontent of dissatisfied workers and peasants toward the usual convenient scapegoats, the Jews. Tsarist agents produced a notorious forgery, the *Protocols of the Elders of Zion*, which purported to reveal a secret Jewish plot to dominate the world. This work emerged in the United States, where anti-Semitism was so strong in some powerful quarters that it became a factor in blocking the immigration of Jews from Europe to the United States, which

Nazi leader Adolf Hitler seemed willing to allow until shortly before World War II (1939–1945) began.

The most virulent and systematically organized form of government-sponsored racial anti-Semitism emerged in Nazi Germany from 1933 to 1945. Following a pattern of gradual escalation, the regime passed the Nuremberg Laws in 1935, which removed Jews from the protection of German law. Jews were excluded from German public life, including business and education, intermarriage with Germans was prohibited, their property was seized, and finally they were imprisoned and forced into slave labor or murdered outright in death camps. As Nazi forces conquered other nations, the Jews in the rest of Europe were doomed, and by 1945 an estimated six million Jews were massacred, executed, or starved to death.

CURRENT ANTI-SEMITISM

After the war, the exposure of the death camps led to the framing of the United Nations Declaration of Human Rights and a series of trials of former Nazis complicit in mass murder. Christian religious leaders also have made efforts to end religious anti-Semitism.

Still, the racial variety persists today, perpetuated by Holocaust deniers, small gangs, and tiny political parties in many parts of the non-Muslim world. In the Middle East, geographic anti-Semitism is encouraged by governments seeking the destruction of the state of Israel, conceived as a Jewish collectivity. This is intertwined with the activities of Muslim extremists who denounce the Judeo-Christian West.

See also *Genocide; Holocaust; Zionism.*

. . . . DONALD G. TANNENBAUM

BIBLIOGRAPHY

Abel, Ernest L. *The Roots of Anti-Semitism.* Cranbury, N.J.: Fairleigh Dickinson University Press, 1973.

Brustein, William I. *Roots of Hate: Anti-Semitism in Europe before the Holocaust.* New York: Cambridge University Press, 2003.

Carmichael, Joel. *The Satanizing of the Jews: Origin and Development of Mystical Anti-Semitism.* New York: Fromm International, 1992.

Hay, Malcolm. *Thy Brother's Blood: The Roots of Christian Anti-Semitism.* New York: Hart, 1975.

Katz, Jacob. *From Prejudice to Destruction, Anti-Semitism, 1700–1933.* Cambridge, Mass.: Harvard University Press, 1980.

Kleg, Milton. *Hate, Prejudice, and Racism.* Albany: State University of New York Press, 1993.

Laquer, Walter. *The Changing Face of Antisemitism: From Ancient Times to the Present Day.* New York: Oxford University Press, 2006.

Lewis, Bernard. *Semites and Anti-Semites: An Inquiry into Conflict and Prejudice.* London: Norton, 1986.

Lindemann, Albert S. *Esau's Tears: Modern Anti-Semitism and the Rise of the Jews.* New York: Cambridge University Press, 1997.

Wyman, David. *Abandonment of the Jews: America and the Holocaust, 1941–1945.* New York: Pantheon, 1984.

Antitrust Policy

Antitrust polices are government regulations prohibiting abusive monopolistic practices of market power. A significant number of countries have developed antitrust statutes and maintain an active program of antitrust enforcement. Countries based on a market economy generally enforce policies that prevent uncompetitive businesses and discourage dishonest policies within an industry, in addition to other policies that do not benefit the public. In various forms, these policies represent a vital means of regulating competition and form the basis of many public policies in regard to business.

The primary intent of competition policy is the general protection of the market economy. Antitrust policies in Europe were a primary focus of discussion following World War II (1939–1945) to restrict anticompetitive agreements and practices and some noncompetitive mergers. They were enforced through international agreements and national laws. The European Commission filed thousands of decisions involving company agreements and practices for trade in the Common Market. The decisions of the European Commission are based on Articles 85 and 86 of the 1957 Treaty of Rome, which address typical competition restrictions. Article 85 provides a nonexhaustive listing of anticompetitive practices that will be automatically void for "companies aimed at fixing prices, sharing markets, or exchanging confidential information in defiance of the elementary rules of competition and of the interests of the citizens of the European Union." Whereas Article 85 has a provision for exemption if specific conditions are satisfied, Article 86 does not. Article 86 prohibits abuse of a dominant position (i.e., economic strength preventative of effective competition) that may affect trade between member states and provides a nonexhaustive listing of abusive practices, such as "unfair purchase or selling prices" and "limiting production markets or technical development to the prejudice of customers."

Governments in the European Union and the United States may intervene to restrict or dissolve a *monopoly* (a single firm that sells output for which no close substitute exists) because the unregulated profit-maximizing monopoly model demonstrates output reduction and increased market power. The argument against monopoly is based on efficiency; some monopolies are believed to create inefficient use of resources as compared to a competitive equilibrium.

To prevent an incipient monopoly, governments regulate mergers to avoid concentration of the market and to allow new competitors to enter into the market. The merger of two companies, or the acquisition of one company by another, may be proposed for two reasons. The merger may have the favorable outcome of creating lower prices, which would increase capital of the two companies and make the combined company a stronger competitor. Or the merger could reduce competition, giving the combined company an opportunity to sell at higher prices.

BACKGROUND OF TRUSTS

During the industrialization of the United States, the emergence of railroads afforded industries and individuals the ability to conduct business and travel in spite of distances that previously had prevented such efforts. As transportation competition increased, the railroad industry consolidated finances. In the late 1880s and early 1900s, powerful and influential financiers, such as Jay Gould, Edward H. Harriman, James J. Hill, Leland Stanford, and Cornelius Vanderbilt, consolidated their corporations, as competition during the age of industrialization increased. The outcome essentially was a form of monopolization. When these trusts obtained a controlling share of an industry, they formed a monopoly that could dominate the industry, preventing other companies from competing against the monopoly. By 1890, the oil and railway industries in particular were restricting competition and establishing price controls, organizing their networks of businesses in trusts that concealed the extent of the monopoly.

U.S. ANTITRUST LEGISLATION

The U.S. government enacted the Sherman Antitrust Act of 1890 against the large monopolistic trusts of the late nineteenth century. The law prohibited monopolization and trusts, as well as restrained trade. The vague language of the law ineffectively discouraged anticompetitive business practices. Furthermore, the act did not create an independent commission to investigate allegations of antitrust law abuses. U.S. presidents Theodore Roosevelt and William Howard Taft strictly enforced antitrust laws on the basis of the Sherman Act.

Congress later passed the Clayton Act of 1914 (a supplement to the Sherman Act) to assist the government in preventing monopolies. The Clayton Act listed specific illegal practices— several that were not prohibited specifically by the Sherman Act—such as the practice of *tying contracts,* which required a consumer to purchase another product before being able to purchase the desired product, and *price discrimination,* or selling the same product at different prices to different customers (though some industries, such as air travel, are allowed to practice price discrimination). Other prohibitions of the act included *exclusive dealing* (selling of a product if a consumer agrees not to buy from other producers of the same product) and *interlocking directorates,* in which at least one director serves on two boards of directors of competing companies.

The Federal Trade Commission Act of 1914 created a federal body whose purpose is to oversee markets, with the intent of enforcing antitrust laws. The Federal Trade Commission (FTC) has the power to block *horizontal mergers* (merging of firms that produce similar products or services) and *vertical mergers* (merging of firms that produce different products or services with an input-output relation in the production of one specific product. Input-output relation is a circular dependency of capital, entrepreneurship, labor, and land resources (input), and the sale of goods and services to consumers (output). The two 1914 acts established a solid foundation for modern antitrust law enforcement. The intent of antitrust legislation is to discourage abuse of the market economy through practices such as exclusive dealing arrangements, exclusive territories, predatory pricing, price discrimination, refusals to deal, resale price maintenance, and tie-in sales. Antitrust laws enforce competitive limitations upon firms for the benefit of the public (e.g., labor laws) and to be fair to consumers (e.g., regulating the sale of inferior products at higher prices) and potential competitors (such as small businesses).

DEVELOPMENTS IN U.S. ANTITRUST POLICY

Not until the mid-1960s did antitrust economics undergo vast reform in the American postwar industrial economy. The conglomerate merger wave in the 1960s—the "Go-Go Years" of the stock market that inaugurated an era of company acquisitions beyond their central industries—involved firms that were entirely disparate in business activities. Many of these conglomerate firms were unsuccessful in managing companies within different countries and markets.

Throughout the late 1970s and early 1980s, there were substantial developments in antitrust enforcement and research into strategic business practices. New antitrust thinking emerged that countered the long-held idea that conglomerate firms were anticompetitive. Both England and the United States essentially witnessed a rebirth of laissez-faire philosophy regarding government regulations. An unprecedented number of merger and acquisition activities occurred in the 1980s, and they generally involved using debt capital to purchase a firm, then selling certain components of the firm to pay the debt. The outcome was a sudden increase of buyouts executed without consideration of corporate strategy and at a relatively high cost of capital, which in turn resulted in the early 1990s in widespread bankruptcies of companies unable to pay the inflated interest of high-leverage costs. The sectoral mergers of the 1990s primarily affected banking, defense, health care, and telecommunications. In the 1990s, government regulation demonstrated a more aggressive attitude against anticompetitive mergers and practices. The twenty-first century has been characterized by increased government regulation of the accounting, power utility, and security industries.

Governments enforce antitrust laws in the interest of maintaining an efficient society by ensuring competitive markets. Government enforcement of these laws necessitates identifying and banning those corporate practices that may discourage competition. The U.S. Department of Justice and the FTC, for instance, review all potential mergers of companies that may become monopolistic or anticompetitive; legal approval must be granted before the merger is completed. If the primary reason for a proposed merger is a favorable outcome of lower prices (as in the cases of XM and Sirius Radio), which will be efficient for society and fair to consumers and potential competitors, the merger will be granted legal approval. If the merger will result in less competition and an opportunity for the merging firms to increase prices, then it will not be granted legal approval. (An example of this is the proposed Staples and Office Depot merger, which was blocked by the FTC because it would allow the companies to control prices.) Antitrust laws grant the government power to ban anticompetitive practices, and even to divide a monopoly into two companies. Such decisions can be overturned by federal appeals court, sometimes with new stipulations (as was the case with Microsoft in 2001–2002).

See also *Economic Policy Formulation; Regulation and Rulemaking.*

. . . . RON J. BIGALKE JR.

BIBLIOGRAPHY

American Bar Association. *ABA Section of Antitrust Law, Antitrust Law Developments,* 6th edition. Chicago: ABA Book Publishing, 2007.

Armentano, Dominick T. *Antitrust and Monopoly: Anatomy of a Policy Failure.* New York: Wiley, 1982.

Bain, Joe Staten. *Barriers to New Competition: Their Character and Consequences in Manufacturing Industries.* Cambridge: Harvard University Press, 1956.

Berle, Adolf A., Jr., and Gardiner C Means. *The Modern Corporation and Private Property.* New York: Macmillan, 1932.

Brozen, Yale. *Concentration, Mergers, and Public Policy.* New York: Macmillan, 1982.

Chamberlain, Edward H. *The Theory of Monopolistic Competition.* Cambridge, Mass.: Harvard University Press, 1933.

Howard, Marshall C. *Antitrust and Trade Regulation.* Englewood Cliffs, N.J.: Prentice Hall, 1983.

Lai, Loi Lei, ed. *Power System Restructuring and Deregulation: Trading, Performance and Information Technology.* New York: Wiley, 2001.

Letwin, William. *Law and Economic Policy in America: The Evolution of the Sherman Antitrust Law.* New York: Random House, 1965.

Mason, Edward Sagendorph. *Economic Cooperation and the Monopoly Problem.* Cambridge, Mass.: Harvard University Press, 1957.

Posner, Richard A. *Antitrust Law: An Economic Perspective.* Chicago: University of Chicago Press, 1976.

Robinson, Joan. *The Economics of Imperfect Competition.* London: Macmillan, 1933.

Stigler, George J. *The Organization of Industry.* Homewood, Ill.: Richard D. Irwin, 1968.

Williamson, Oliver E. *The Economic Institutions of Capitalism.* New York: Free Press, 1985.

Apartheid

Apartheid is an Afrikaans word meaning "separateness." It was the official government policy in South Africa from 1948 until a negotiated transition that culminated in the first democratic elections in 1994. In 1976, the UN General Assembly recognized apartheid as a crime against humanity. The idea of racial segregation was not new; similar policies had been introduced in different parts of South Africa long before the Union of 1910.

KEY ASPECTS

Apartheid was adopted by the National Party (NP), which came to power in South Africa in 1948. It was built on the growth of Afrikaner nationalism and increasing economic hardship for parts of the Afrikaner population. A new intellectual elite known as the *Broederbond,* which at the time was a secret organization, was central to the promotion of Afrikaner nationalism. The main architect of apartheid policy was H. F. Verwoerd, who was Minister of Native Affairs during the early 1950s and later became prime minister. One of the central tenets of the apartheid system was the Population Registration Act introduced in 1950. This law required all citizens to have their racial group officially recorded. Decisions were clearly arbitrary in some cases and often were disputed. Race was determined by skin color, but other criteria, such as language and social status, were considered also.

Another of the major laws passed was the Group Areas Act in 1950. This clearly designated areas of land for each of the four racial groups (white, coloured, Indian, and native). The consequence of this law was that huge numbers of people were

forcibly relocated. Africans were forced to travel for work and basic goods and services, but the pass law system ensured close regulation of such movements. Later this policy was extended to become the homelands approach. Residents of these "independent" homelands were no longer afforded South African citizenship.

The NP also played on white fears of *miscegenation,* which is the interbreeding of races. The Mixed Marriages Act (1949) and the Immorality Act (1950) outlawed marriage and extramarital sex between different races. The system became ever more pervasive with the introduction in 1953 of "*petty apartheid,*" which involved racial segregation in public places such as restaurants, lavatories, beaches, hotels, and public transport.

OPPOSITION TO APARTHEID

Opposition to apartheid was strongly organized within South Africa itself. During the 1950s, the African National Congress (ANC) forged an alliance with other organizations and adopted a policy of defiance. One peaceful demonstration against the pass law system resulted in the deaths of sixty-nine people in Sharpeville on March 21, 1960. The government reacted by banning all the major resistance groups in 1960. The ANC then formed *Umkhonto we Sizwe* (Spear of the Nation), which developed a guerrilla warfare strategy. Soon after, in 1963, many of the ANC's leaders, including Nelson Mandela, were arrested and tried for planning a violent revolution against the state.

There was also international pressure from the antiapartheid movement. However, key governments such as the United States and United Kingdom continued to see South Africa as an ally in the cold war. Moreover, many leading economies maintained their economic links with South Africa, and it was only during the 1980s that significant economic sanctions were imposed.

A SYSTEM UNDER PRESSURE

Apartheid came under strain during the 1970s due to domestic economic pressures and a renewal of resistance politics. There was a revival of black trade unionism, and the ideology of the black consciousness movement inspired a new generation of black South Africans. Demonstrations against the compulsory use of Afrikaans in black schools began in Soweto in June 1976 and spread across the country. Meanwhile, sections of the business community began to question the economic viability of the apartheid system given the restrictions on labor and inequality in education. As a result, in 1984 attempts at constitutional reform of the system were introduced, including the tricameral parliament. However, the idea of separate development was maintained, and the mass mobilization tactics of the United Democratic Front increased civil unrest.

NEGOTIATED TRANSITION

In 1989, F. W. de Klerk became the final apartheid-era president and began negotiating a settlement. In 1990, he released Mandela and the other political prisoners and unbanned all the liberation movements. Despite high levels of political violence, a period of negotiation ensued under the banner of The Convention for a Democratic South Africa (CODESA).

The ANC, NP, and a number of other, though not all, South African political organizations took part in CODESA. In April 1994, South Africa's first democratic elections were held, and Nelson Mandela was elected as president.

See also *Discrimination; Race and Racism; Segregation and Desegregation.*

. . . . STEPHEN R. HURT

BIBLIOGRAPHY

Barber, James. 1999. *South Africa in the Twentieth Century: A Political History—In Search of a Nation State.* Oxford, U.K.: Blackwell, 1999.

Dubow, Saul. *Racial Segregation and the Origins of Apartheid in South Africa, 1919–36.* Basingstoke, U.K.: Macmillan, 1989.

Guelke, Adrian. *Rethinking the Rise and Fall of Apartheid.* Basingstoke, U.K.: Palgrave Macmillan, 2005.

Lipton, Merle. *Capitalism and Apartheid: South Africa, 1910–86.* Aldershot, U.K.: Wildwood House, 1986.

O'Meara, Dan. *Forty Lost Years: The Apartheid State and the Politics of the National Party 1948–1994.* Randburg, South Africa: Ravan Press, 1996.

Sparks, Allister. *The Mind of South Africa: The Story of the Rise and Fall of Apartheid.* London: Mandarin, 1991.

Waldmeir, Patti. *Anatomy of a Miracle: The End of Apartheid and the Birth of the New South Africa.* London: Viking, 1997.

Apparentement

Apparentement is the French term for an electoral procedure that is designed to increase the participation of small parties in countries that use proportional voting systems. Proportional electoral systems often have thresholds that require parties to gain a certain percentage of the vote to secure representation. Small parties may be unable to gain the necessary 3 to 5 percent. Apparentement permits minor parties to form electoral coalitions or groupings. The parties continue to be listed separately and generally campaign separately, but they combine their total votes. This increases the chances that the parties will gain representation. If the cartels win seats, those seats are allocated according to predetermined agreements or by proportionality, depending on the country. The system is used in continental Europe, including Switzerland and the Netherlands, some areas of Latin America, and Israel. In France, prior to electoral reforms in 1951, the system was used by centrist parties in an effort to prevent parties at either political extreme from gaining majorities in the Assembly. Studies reveal that apparentement typically reduces disproportionality in electoral systems. Nonetheless, apparentement coalitions are often unstable, especially if member parties find themselves excluded from representation in successive elections.

See also *Europe, Democracy in; European Parliament; European Political Thought; Political Parties.*

. . . . TOM LANSFORD

Appeasement

Appeasement is an influence strategy employed by states in relations with adversaries. Most students of appeasement define it as a policy of easing tensions and avoiding war by eliminating an opponent's grievances. Others, however, define it as a strategy of systematic concessions, and concessions are the means by which the strategy is implemented. Thus, terms frequently associated with appeasement include *inducements, positive sanctions, conciliation,* and *accommodation.* Appeasement may be considered a subcategory of *engagement.* The principal mechanism by which appeasement seeks to influence an opponent's behavior is satiation—satisfying its hunger for land, status, or something else it values. But policy makers may also intend for appeasement to work through *reassurance* (convincing an insecure adversary that one's own intentions are benign) or *socialization* (demonstrating the proper way to behave in international society).

Because it seeks to modify an adversary's behavior through promises and rewards, rather than threats and punishments, appeasement is often regarded as the antithesis of, and an alternative to, deterrence. However, scholars have long recognized that coercive and noncoercive approaches can, and perhaps should, be combined in mixed influence strategies.

WHY DO STATES PURSUE APPEASEMENT?

States pursue appeasement policies for a variety of reasons. In some cases, the objective may be short term or tactical—e.g., to conserve resources or buy time in order to rearm so that an adversary may be confronted more effectively. Appeasement may also serve to test the motives of a state whose intentions are ambiguous. In other cases, the goal may be strategic, such as to eliminate the possibility of war with an adversary, or even to transform a relationship from hostility to friendship. The pursuit of appeasement policies is frequently encouraged by the absence of a feasible alternative or by opposition to other options, domestically or internationally.

DOES APPEASEMENT WORK?

Appeasement is often regarded as being futile and dangerous. It is considered to be futile because, it is believed, an adversary cannot be placated through concessions. Indeed, concessions are commonly thought to increase the adversary's appetite for additional gains, leading it to make further demands. Appeasement is regarded as being dangerous because it allegedly undermines the credibility of deterrent threats. Accommodation of the adversary convinces it that the appeasing state is weak and irresolute. Should the state decide to stand firm and resist additional demands, its threats to defend its interests are not believed. Deterrence fails and war results. These concerns were central to the strategy of containment pursued by the United States during the cold war, motivating U.S. policy makers to vigorously counter efforts by the Soviet Union and other communist states to expand their influence.

The conventional wisdom regarding appeasement is derived mainly from the experience of Britain and France during the 1930s, when the leaders of those countries attempted unsuccessfully to avert a war with Nazi Germany. Many scholars have argued that Anglo-French conciliation of Germany—reflected particularly in the Munich Agreement of September 1938—caused Hitler to discount French and British promises to defend Poland, leading him to attack that country in September 1939. In a minority opinion, other scholars have disputed this interpretation. Arguing that Hitler regarded the outcome at Munich as a crushing defeat in which he himself shrank from the prospect of war, they contend that he found Anglo-French threats to defend Poland credible but, determined not to back down again, he decided to attack anyway. In some cases, appeasement has succeeded. Perhaps the most notable instance involves British conciliation of the United States after 1895; within a period of roughly a decade, the government of Great Britain was able to fundamentally transform the relationship between the two countries, not merely eliminating the possibility of an Anglo-United States war, but also securing diplomatic and strategic cooperation from the United States.

The success or failure of any effort at appeasement must be evaluated in terms of its objectives. Frequently, an appeasement policy has both minimum and maximum aims. Some may be attained, while others may not, so that the policy may be a partial success and a partial failure. Britain and France failed to prevent war with Nazi Germany, but according to some scholars, they did succeed in buying time for Britain to rearm. American efforts to avoid war with the Soviet Union during the latter stages of World War II (1939–1945) secured that goal, although the cost—Soviet domination of large portions of eastern and central Europe—was high and the U.S.-Soviet cooperation in the postwar world so desired by U.S. President Franklin Roosevelt never materialized.

WHY DOES APPEASEMENT SUCCEED OR FAIL?

Factors important to determining whether appeasement succeeds or fails include the nature of the adversary, the inducements offered by the appeasing state and the adversary's perception of them, and the presence or absence of other reasons for the adversary to respond favorably to the policy. Generally speaking, appeasement is most likely to succeed when the adversary's aims are limited, when the adversary is motivated by insecurity rather than greed, when the concessions that are offered address the adversary's concerns directly and fully, and when there exist other reasons—for example, domestic political pressures—for the adversary to accept the concessions and modify its behavior.

See also *Containment; Deterrence.*

. . . . STEPHEN R. ROCK

BIBLIOGRAPHY
Baldwin, David. "The Power of Positive Sanctions." *World Politics* 24 (October 1971): 19–38.
Beck, Robert J. "Munich's Lessons Reconsidered." *International Security* 14 (Fall 1989): 161–191.
Cortright, David, ed. *The Price of Peace: Incentives and International Conflict Prevention.* Lanham, Md.: Rowman and Littlefield, 1997.
Kennedy, Paul M. *Strategy and Diplomacy, 1870–1945: Eight Studies.* London: George Allen and Unwin, 1983.
Mommsen, Wolfgang J., and Lothar Kettenacker, eds. *The Fascist Challenge and the Policy of Appeasement.* London: George Allen and Unwin, 1983.
Press, Daryl G. "The Credibility of Power: Assessing the Credibility of Threats during the 'Appeasement' Crises of the 1930s." *International Security* 29 (Winter 2004/05): 136–169.
Richardson, J. L. "New Perspectives on Appeasement: Some Implications for International Relations." *World Politics* 40 (April 1988): 289–316.
Ripsman, Norrin M., and Jack S. Levy. "The Realism of Appeasement during the 1930s: Buying Time for Rearmament." Paper presented at International Studies Association, San Diego, Calif., March, 2006.
Rock, Stephen R. *Appeasement in International Politics.* Lexington: University Press of Kentucky, 2000.
Small, Melvin, and Otto Feinstein, eds. *Appeasing Fascism: Articles from the Wayne State University Conference on Munich after Fifty Years.* Lanham, Md.: University Press of America, 1991.

Appropriation

Appropriation is the actual legislative act of designating money. By constitutional design, the U.S. Congress must pass a law in order to spend money: "No money shall be drawn from the Treasury, but in Consequence of Appropriations made by Law" (U.S. Constitution, Article I, Section 9). Appropriations can occur through an annual appropriations act accounting for discretionary spending or by permanent law accounting for direct spending. Approximately two-thirds of federal spending is direct spending that covers most federal entitlement programs. The remaining one-third is discretionary spending that must go through an authorization process before being funded. The House and Senate Committees on Appropriations have jurisdiction over the appropriation bills. Generally, there are three types of appropriations: regular, continuing, and supplemental. *Regular* appropriations are the annual budgetary appropriations (i.e., the setting of the annual budget) and cover most of the federal spending. *Continuing* appropriations are enacted if Congress cannot pass the regular appropriations bill in time and allow for government entities to continue functioning. *Supplemental* appropriations provide for additional funds at a later date that is not accounted for in the regular appropriations bills. The president also can exercise his power over appropriations by vetoing the appropriations law passed by Congress.

See also *Budgeting; Legislative Hearings; Monetary Policy.*

. . . . SUSAN MARIE OPP

Approval Voting

Approval voting is an electoral system that allows voters to indicate their preferences for multiple candidates in elections. All candidates are listed on a ballot, and voters may indicate their preference or vote for one or more of the candidates. Hence, in a contest with five candidates, a voter could vote for between one and five of the office seekers. The candidate who receives the majority of votes is the winner. The system was designed to provide a better means of indicating public sentiment in elections by alleviating concerns that individuals might waste their ballots by voting for a candidate that might not appear capable of winning. In addition, if two or more candidates appealed to the same group, voters could indicate their support for all of them. Proponents have argued that approval voting would reduce the impact of negative voting because voters are less likely to vote against a candidate. Advocates also assert that approval voting would more strongly encourage candidates to reach across party or ideological lines. The system was first proposed in the 1970s, and has been used in some nongovernmental bodies, but it has not been used extensively at the governmental level.

See also *Voting Behavior; Voting Procedures.*

. . . . TOM LANSFORD

Aprismo

Aprismo is a political philosophy developed by Víctor Raúl Haya de la Torre, the dominant political figure of twentieth century Peru. Derived from his political party (APRA— *Alianza Popular Revolucionaria Americana,* or Popular Revolutionary American Alliance), aprismo emerged in the 1920s and the 1930s as a response to both imperial capitalism and European Marxism. Haya argued that for "Indoamerica" (Latin America), imperialism had to be viewed as the first stage of capitalism, and that the feudal class persisted in alliance with imperial capitalism. Its strident anti-American tone emerged in its maximum goals, enunciated in 1928, and then modified as a minimal plan in 1932. Over the following decades, Haya developed extensive modifications to his theory.

To Haya de la Torre's followers, aprismo was a full-fledged political philosophy that brought together the best ideas of such disparate thinkers as Karl Marx, Albert Einstein, Arnold J. Toynbee, and many others. To his detractors, aprismo was little more than a hodgepodge of ideas that offered little to improve Peru. APRA's image as a party rigidly unwilling to compromise prevented it from winning a presidential election until 1985, after Haya de la Torre had died.

See also *Imperialism; Marxism.*

. . . . HENRY A. DIETZ

Aquinas, Thomas

See *Thomas Aquinas.*

Arab–Israeli Relations

The relationship between Arabs and Israel has been hostile not only since the birth of the Jewish state in 1948, but from the foundation of political Zionism in the 1890s. This resulted from a fundamental conflict over Palestine, where the Zionist movement aspired to establish Israel. Palestine had long been Arab territory, and Arabs saw their existence there threatened.

The United Nations plan for the partitioning of Palestine in 1947 led to civil war between the Jewish and Arab communities of Palestine. When the British completed their withdrawal from Palestine in May 1948, Jewish forces already occupied part of the proposed Arab state, and about two hundred thousand Arabs had become refugees. Upon the declaration of the state of Israel, Egypt, Transjordan (Jordan), Iraq, Lebanon, and Syria sent troops into Palestine, purportedly to protect the Arab Palestinians. This First Arab-Israeli War (1948–1949) turned into a disaster for the Arabs, leaving Israeli forces in control of 78 percent of Palestine and, due to the flight or expulsion of many Arab Palestinians, only a small Arab minority.

Although Israel and the adjoining Arab states concluded armistice agreements in 1949, violence continued. Further wars followed in 1956 (the Sinai War), 1967 (the Six-Day War), 1973 (the October War), and 1982 (the Lebanon War). Though not directly involving Arab states, Arab-Israeli warfare has been endemic in Lebanon since the 1970s. Guerrilla attacks by Hezbollah forced Israel's withdrawal from Lebanon in 2000. An air and land war by the Israelis against Hezbollah in 2006 met fierce resistance and, some say, produced Israel's first military failure. In addition, Palestinian uprisings began in 1987 and, after subsiding in the mid-1990s, resumed more bloodily in 2000.

The 1967 War was a major turning point. Following an intense crisis, Israel quickly defeated its neighbors and occupied parts of Egypt (Sinai), the rest of mandatory Palestine (the Gaza Strip and the West Bank, including East Jerusalem), and southwestern Syria (the Golan Heights). Following this, Israel announced that it had no territorial aspirations, and the Arab states accepted the idea of peace in return for withdrawal. However, Israelis began to establish new Jewish settlements and then rejected calls for full withdrawal.

ARAB GOVERNMENTS AND THE CONFLICT

The role of Arab governments has always been complicated. With the Arab public opposing Israel, governments sought legitimacy by seeming to support this cause and by using the issue as a weapon against each other. They were rarely serious about confronting Israel, however. In 1948, what looked like an attempt to prevent Israel's emergence had more to do with Egyptian-Transjordanian rivalry. Transjordan had a secret arrangement with the Israelis to divide up the area of the proposed Arab state and, except in the Old City of Jerusalem, avoided combat with its apparent enemy. In 1967, popular sentiment forced King Husayn to go to war with his tacit ally and to lose part of his kingdom in order to save the rest. While publicly rejecting peace, Egypt responded favorably to mediation attempts during the 1950s. To dispel accusations of softness, Egypt allowed itself to be pulled into a crisis in 1967 by letting Israel attack. This is a prime example of what scholar Michael Barnett (1988) calls "impression management" and "symbolic entrapment," where one entity preempts a peaceful solution (that may make it appear weak) rather than an attack. While using the issue as a legitimacy resource, Arab regimes have not been willing to subordinate their own interests for the sake of the Palestinian cause. While Egypt and Syria went to war in 1973, this was to jump-start a peace settlement that would hopefully get their own territories back, not to liberate Palestine.

Significant changes in Arab-Israeli relationships have occurred in recent years. Egypt made peace with Israel in 1979 to obtain full Israeli withdrawal from its territory. The Oslo Accords of 1994 led to the establishment of a Palestinian Authority and the hope of a two-state solution to the Palestine problem. Although the process broke down six years later, it provided King Husayn an opportunity to conclude formal peace with Israel. Under American pressure, Mauritania also established diplomatic relations with Israel in 1999. An Israeli trade office was set up in Qatar in 1996. Israeli offices established in Morocco, Oman, and Tunisia were closed in 2000. The Arab boycott of Israel, declared by the Arab League in 1945, has withered over time.

With militantly anti-Israel Islamist forces growing and non-Arab Iran taking the lead in opposing Israel, unstable Arab regimes have become desperate for a settlement in order to appease popular passions. Consequently, a Saudi initiative of 2002, adopted unanimously by an Arab League summit but rejected by Israel, articulates the willingness of all Arab states to establish normal diplomatic ties with Israel in return for full withdrawal and a Palestinian state. Many Israelis fear that continuing to rule Palestinians eventually will doom them as a Jewish state, and yet they want to keep much of the West Bank and to impose limits on the independence of any Arab Palestinian state. They are also unwilling to consider the return of a substantial number of Palestinian refugees to Israel.

See also *Arab League; Arab Political Thought; Islamic Political Thought; Jewish Political Thought; Palestine; Zionism.*

. . . . GLENN E. PERRY

BIBLIOGRAPHY

Barnett, Michael N. *Dialogues in Arab Politics.* New York: Columbia University Press, 1988.

Hudson, Michael C. *Arab Politics: The Search for Legitimacy.* New Haven, Conn.: Yale University Press, 1979.

Kazziha, Walid. "The Impact of Palestine on Arab Politics." In *The Arab State,* edited by Giacomo Luciani, 306–309. Berkeley: University of California Press, 1990.

Kurtulus, Ersun. "The Notion of a 'Pre-emptive War:' The Six Day War Revisited." *Middle East Journal* 61 (Spring 2007): 220–239.

Morris, Benny. *Righteous Victims: A History of the Zionist-Arab Conflict, 1881–2001.* New York: Vintage, 2001.

Novo, Joseph. *King Abdallah and Palestine: A Territorial Ambition.* New York: St. Martin's, 1996.

Rubin, Barry. *The Arab States and Palestine.* Syracuse, N.Y.: Syracuse University Press, 1981.

Shlaim, Avi. *Collusion across the Jordan: King Abdullah, the Zionist Movement, and the Partition of Palestine.* Oxford, U.K.: Clarendon, 1988.

———. *The Iron Wall: Israel and the Arab World,* 2nd ed. Norton, 2001.

Smith, Charles D. (2004). *Palestine and the Arab-Israeli Conflict: A History with Documents,* 5th ed. New York: Bedford/St. Martin's, 2004.

Arab League

The Arab League, the full name of which is the League of Arab States, is a regional interstate organization headquartered in Cairo. Founded in 1945 by seven Arab states to strengthen their ties and preserve their independence, the League now has twenty-two members: Algeria, Bahrain, Comoros, Djibouti, Egypt, Iraq, Jordan, Kuwait, Lebanon, Libya, Mauritania, Morocco, Oman, Palestine (represented by the Palestine Liberation Organization), Qatar, Saudi Arabia, Somalia, Sudan, Syria, Tunisia, the United Arab Emirates, and Yemen. Three member states—Comoros, Somalia, and Djibouti—according to the usual criteria, are not Arab countries, although they

have cultural and historical connections to the Arab world. Normally the dominant member, Egypt was suspended from the organization from 1979 to 1989 because of its peace treaty with Israel, and the organization's headquarters moved to Tunis until 1990, when it returned to Cairo.

The Arab League grew out of popular demands for Arab unity. It also was a response to the rivalries of Arab leaders, as the British-allied Hashimite rulers of Transjordan (now Jordan) and Iraq hoped to form a larger entity in the Fertile Crescent and put another member of their family on the throne of Syria. British Foreign Minister Anthony Eden gave his government's go-ahead to the idea of Arab unity in 1941, and this was followed by Transjordanian and Iraqi proposals for Greater Syria and Fertile Crescent unions, respectively. Such ideas evoked opposition from other Arab states, particularly Egypt, which did not want a new rival to its primacy in the Arab world, and the Saudi ruling family, which had overthrown Hashimite rule in the Hijaz two decades earlier and feared a future attempt at restoration. Thus, in order to counter Hashimite proposals, Egyptian Prime Minister Mustafa al-Nahhas invited representatives of the Arab states to meet in Alexandria in 1944. The result was the conclusion of an Alexandria Protocol calling for the formation of a League of Arab States, which was accomplished with the signing of the pact (or covenant) of the organization at a meeting in Cairo in February of the following year. While the pact gave lip service to the possibility of "closer cooperation," the formation of the Arab League was in fact a victory for the principle of state sovereignty.

Each member of the League wields one vote in its main organ, the council. Meetings are held on the level of either foreign ministers or heads of state. The principle of unanimity prevails, in that decisions made by a mere majority are not binding on members not voting for those decisions. A secretariat, headed by a Secretary-General (Amr Musa since 2001), is chosen by the council by a two-thirds vote, and an Economic and Social Council also exists. An Arab parliament, without legislative authority and of uncertain significance, was established in 2005.

The Arab League's goal of political and military cooperation, as in the case of the Treaty of Joint Defense and Economic Cooperation of 1950, has been hindered by persistent divisions among the organization's members. But the League has engaged in numerous mediation efforts and has organized peacekeeping forces, such as in Kuwait in 1961 and Lebanon in 1976. The League has established specialized agencies for cooperation in a variety of nonpolitical matters, including science and technology, administrative development, research, labor, agricultural development, satellite communications, broadcasting, and investment. It maintains information centers throughout the world.

See also *Middle Eastern Politics and Society; Organization of Petroleum Exporting Countries (OPEC); Pan-Arabism and Pan-Islamism; Sovereignty.*

. . . .   GLENN E. PERRY

BIBLIOGRAPHY

Dean, Lucy, ed. "League of Arab States." In *The Middle East and North Africa 2009*, 55th ed., 1386–1397. London: Routledge, 2008

Hasou, Tawfig Y. *The Struggle for the Arab World: Egypt's Nasser and the Arab League.* London: KPI, 1985

Hassouna, Hussein A. *The League of Arab States and Regional Disputes: A Study of Middle East Conflicts.* Dobbs Ferry, N.Y.: Oceana, 1975.

Khalil, Muhammad. *The Arab States and the Arab League: A Documentary Record. Vol. II. International Affairs.* Beirut: Khayats, 1962.

MacDonald, Robert W. *The League of Arab States: A Study in Regional Organization.* Princeton, N.J.: Princeton University Press, 1965.

Arab Political Economy

The Arab political economy revolves around three main axes: (1) economic growth and structural transformation (developments in different sectors of the economy), (2) state structures and economic policy, and (3) domestic socioeconomic actors. Beginning in the seventeenth century, the Arab world has been drawn into a global economy dominated by the European powers. The need of the Ottoman Empire (1299–1922) to raise revenues to support its administrative and military reforms resulted in the introduction of private property. As a result, over time local notables and tax collectors gained the rights to enough property to allow some to establish commercial estates equivalent to large commercially owned farms. These estates propelled agricultural export trade with Europe and the Arab world's subsequent integration into the global economy.

A series of Ottoman reforms in the 1800s, which were practiced in other Arab countries such as Morocco, further entrenched the institution of private property in the empire.

Tax collection and administration were reformed so that more revenues could be absorbed by the central state, and these reform efforts had as a direct consequence the rise of a propertied elite that was shaped by agricultural export growth. Agriculture also attracted large sums of foreign investment into the empire, making this sector the most important in shaping the political-economic landscape of the Arab world during this period.

After the collapse of the Ottoman Empire, the colonial state was introduced into the Arab world, with repressive apparatuses strengthened by European support that allowed these states to enjoy relative autonomy in relation to society. These structures gave rise to further capitalist reforms throughout the Arab world. During colonialism, public education and public service were introduced into the Arab political-economic sphere. Owing to these reforms, in the 1930s a professional—but not propertied—middle class emerged. Thus the colonial state entrenched the interests of the landowning classes while introducing this new middle class.

The postcolonial state in the Arab world, emerging from independence movements in the 1950s and 1960s, featured dramatically altered political-economic patterns. A process of radical class restructuring occurred through which the historically marginalized groups—workers, farmers, and small landowners—were integrated into the postcolonial state's economic policy planning, while the historically advantaged groups—large land-owning elites—faced economic discrimination. Varying policies of agrarian reform and import substitution industrialization (ISI) benefited the formerly marginalized groups and shored up the new middle class though mass education and bureaucratic expansion. The postcolonial state, underpinned by ISI policies, created and absorbed the major productive, commercial, and financial assets of the countries into the state structure.

The introduction of oil revenues throughout much of the Arab world further concentrated political and economic power into the state, allowing the state to foster a new elite that would be dependent on the distribution of oil revenues. This also introduced the "Dutch Disease," the exploitation of natural resources at the expense of the development of a manufacturing sector. Taken together, these processes gave rise to the emergence of rentier states, states that derive a substantial amount of revenues from the rents of one resource, and this arrangement has shaped state-society relations since the 1960s. This form of corporatism has functioned to subordinate various socioeconomic groups to the state, precluding the potential for effective class-based political opposition. As a result, throughout the Arab world political and economic power remains concentrated in the hands of those actors that are embedded in the state's corporatist mosaic.

The gradual transition away from state-led development toward market-led growth has seen the rise of economic actors that have directly benefited from economic liberalization policies enacted since the 1990s. Contemporary political-economy landscapes are shaped by these liberalization policies and also by a number of socioeconomic challenges.

Demographically, the Arab world is one of the youngest regions in the world. As populations grow, urbanization rates are increasing rapidly. The collapse of state-led development and a growing, urbanized population has meant that unemployment is increasing throughout the region, particularly among youth. Additionally, the pressures of democratization are echoed both from within by domestic actors and from without by Western countries. Emerging sectors such as tourism and finance have begun to displace traditional export sectors in some countries, particularly the Gulf Arab countries. Finally, the challenges of regional and global integration will serve as the context in which future Arab political-economic landscapes will be shaped.

See also *Arab Political Thought; Economic Development, State-led; Economic Policy Formulation; Economic Systems, Comparative.*

. . . . SAMER N. ABBOUD

BIBLIOGRAPHY

Ayubi, Nazih N. *Over-stating the Arab State: Politics and Society in the Middle East.* London: I. B. Tauris, 1995.

Chaudhry, Kiren Aziz. *The Price of Wealth: Economics and Institutions in the Middle East.* Ithaca, N.Y.: Cornell University Press, 1997.

Henry, Clement M., and Robert Springborg. *Globalization and the Politics of Development in the Middle East.* New York: Cambridge University Press, 2001.

Heydemann, Steven. *Networks of Privilege in the Middle East: The Politics of Economic Reform Revisited.* New York: Palgrave Macmillan, 2004.

Owen, Roger. *The Middle East in the World Economy, 1800–1914.* London: I. B. Tauris, 1993.

Owen, Roger, and Sevket Pamuk. *A History of Middle East Economies in the Twentieth Century.* Cambridge, Mass.: Harvard University Press, 1999.

Richards, Alan, and John Waterbury. *A Political Economy of the Middle East.* Boulder, Colo.: Westview, 2008.

Rivlin, Paul. *Arab Economies in the Twenty-first Century.* New York: Cambridge University Press, 2009.

Arab Political Thought

Like all intellectual landscapes, the history and trajectory of Arab political thought must be contextualized within specific cultural, social, legal, and religious periods. Arab political thought has evolved against the backdrop of three dramatic settings: the rise of Islam and the eventual absorption of many Arab lands into the Ottoman Empire (1299–1922); the Western setting and the colonial experience; and the postcolonial setting and modern Arab statehood. The five phases of Arab political thought include the pre-Ottoman phase; the early Ottoman phase (1299–1798); the liberal phase (1789–1939); the nationalist phase (1940–1967); and the contemporary, postnationalist phase.

Pre-Ottoman Arab philosophers were heavily influenced by both the rise of Islam and the translation of Greek works into Arabic, and they were concerned with questions of political organization and the nature of sovereign power. Al-Farabi developed a theory of the state that was to be adopted in Europe more than seven centuries later. He argued that under unjust conditions, people would gather together and agree to renounce rights to a sovereign who served as a protector of the community. He also argued that to live peacefully, groups needed to be formed along recognizable bonds, such as geography, culture, or language. Al-Ghazali advanced these ideas and contended that the innate human need for belonging would naturally produce forms of social and political organization bound by laws and a sovereign power. More than a hundred years later, Ibn Jama'a wrote that a sovereign could only maintain power through force and that the people would only accept the rule of the sovereign if the sovereign could exercise this force. This period was characterized by concerns over questions of sovereignty, power, and political organization and, in particular, with how these questions could be reconciled with various schools of Islamic jurisprudence.

The early Ottoman phase was shaped by the influential Arab philosopher Ibn Khaldun. In his work, he related the rise of the state to that of society. According to Ibn Khaldun, as society developed throughout history it needed increasingly complex forms of organization. The state, he believed, was inseparable from society. Arab thought during this phase was predominantly concerned with questions of political and religious authority and the obligations of the sovereign to society. Sayyid Murtada al-Zabidi, for example, drew an important distinction between the legitimacy of the caliphate, which was earned by religious merit, and the sultanate, which was earned by force. Because the Ottoman empire was a Sunni Muslim state, questions concerning the application of Islamic law, the treatment of non-Muslim communities, and intra-Muslim relations with other non-Sunni sects dominated Arab political thought during this period.

The liberal phase witnessed the secularization of Arab political thought and reflected the Arab experience with European colonialism and modernity. This period was defined by the emergence of nationalist thought, which asserted that the commonalities of certain groups meant that they formed a political community. Three conceptions of political community are identifiable in this period: religious, territorial, and ethnolinguistic nationalism. This liberal phase served as the midwife to more complex forms of Arab nationalism that dominated Arab political thought until 1967. Arab nationalism articulated Arabs as a single cultural, social, ethnic, and linguistic community that should be brought under the organization of a central Arab state and drew on various ideological currents, including fascism and socialism.

The contemporary phase of Arab political thought is defined by three factors that emerged in the aftermath of the defeat of Arab armies by Israel in the 1967 war: the collapse of socialism as an ideological model; the discrediting of secular Arab nationalism that had emerged during the liberal phase; and the reintegration of religious discourse into mainstream Arab political thought. This contemporary phase, characterized by modern, independent Arab states, is further defined by growing social, economic, and geopolitical trends in the Arab world, including growing population rates, the presence of Israel, increasing Western encroachment, the rise of Islamism, and the persistence of authoritarianism.

See also *Al-Farabi; Islamic Political Thought; Middle-Eastern Politics and Society.*

. . . . SAMER N. ABBOUD

BIBLIOGRAPHY
Abu-Rabiʻ, Ibrahim M. *Contemporary Arab Thought: Studies in Post-1967 Arab Intellectual History.* London: Pluto, 2004.
Browers, Michaelle. *Democracy and Civil Society in Arab Political Thought: Transcultural Possibilities.* Syracuse, N.Y.: Syracuse University Press, 2006.
Choueiri, Youssef M. *Arab Nationalism: A History—Nation and State in the Arab World.* Malden, Mass.: Blackwell, 2000.
Hourani, Albert H. *Arabic Thought in the Liberal Age, 1798–1939.* Cambridge: Cambridge University Press, 1983.

Arab Socialism

Arab socialism is the name given to an ideology that was particularly prevalent in the Arab world in the 1960s, combining Arab nationalism with policies designed to favor the less privileged segments of society—notably involving land reform, a planned economy, subsidized prices for necessities, and the nationalization, in whole or in part, of large business enterprises. It represented an attack both on economic underdevelopment and extreme inequality. The term *Arab socialism* emphasized the ideology's allegedly distinctive features in comparison with other kinds of socialism. Although socialist ideas appeared in the Arab world as early the late nineteenth century, the notion of a specifically Arab kind of socialism seems to have originated with the Baath Party and later was embraced by the regime of President Gamal Abdel Nasser of Egypt (after 1958, the United Arab Republic, UAR). The term also was applied in Arab countries such as Libya and Algeria that at that time were described as "progressive," or "liberated." It tended to be an expression of Arab nationalism and, with its rejection of capitalism and communism, of nonalignment in the cold war.

ORIGINS OF EGYPT'S ARAB SOCIALISM

Characterized by pragmatism, the Nasser regime gradually evolved from a vague emphasis on social justice and democracy and opposition to feudalism and monopoly and the domination of capital in 1952 to fully embracing Arab socialism in the early 1960s. A first step in this direction was the enactment in 1952 of an Agrarian Reform Act that limited ownership to two hundred faddans (slightly more than two hundred acres or eighty-one hectares) and providing small plots for previously landless peasants, but in the beginning the regime showed signs of favoring private enterprise. Then nationalization occurred in several specific circumstances, as in the case of the Suez Canal Company in 1956 and in 1960 some leading banks. By the late 1950, references to a "socialist, democratic, and cooperative society" abounded, and the first of a series of five-year plans went into effect in 1960.

Nationalization of large enterprises accelerated during 1961, thus completing the transition to Arab socialism. The state took possession of all banks, insurance companies, and forty-four companies involved in various sectors and acquired a 50 percent interest in eighty-six other enterprises. The maximum ownership in some companies was set at LE10,000 (US$1,825).

Other nationalization followed during subsequent months. Thus Egypt's economy became one of the most statist outside the communist world, although it left considerable room for small-scale private ownership, particularly in agriculture. The maximum salary was set at LE5,000 (US$912), and the tax on incomes more than LE10,000 (US$1,825) at 90 percent. Maximum land ownership per individual was reduced to one hundred faddans (forty hectares) and eventually to fifty faddans.

ARAB SOCIALISM AND COMMUNISM

Emphasis was given to contrasts between Arab socialism and communism. Listing seven major differences between the two, Nasser's confidant, Mohamed Heikal (Muhammad Haykal), began by arguing that Arab socialism rejects the communist solution of "proletarian dictatorship" and the elimination of classes through violence in favor of giving the underprivileged their rightful share of property "within a framework of national unity" without resorting to bloodshed. Unlike the communist equation of property with exploitation, he described the Arab socialist belief in property earned through work, which indeed should be extended to as many people as possible.

Some observers have questioned the depths of Nasser's socialist transformation. As there was not enough land to go around, most peasants remained landless, and landholding families retained much of their property and dominated local politics. News of continuing "feudalism" in 1966 created a sensation, followed by steps to rectify this. Some explain this by pointing to a leadership that came disproportionately from the equivalent of the Russian kulak class or, in a few cases, from big landholding families. Marxists talked about the rise of a new class of privileged technocrats and a new "state bourgeoisie" and pointed to the evasion of progressive taxes.

SEEKING INDIGENOUS ROOTS

Arab socialists generally sought to establish that their ideology had indigenous roots. Islam in particular came to be interpreted by Arab socialists as having had socialist principles that had been disregarded in subsequent centuries. Nasser argued that all religions "call for social justice." For example, he maintained that gross inequality could not have emerged if the Islamic requirement of giving 2.5 percent of one's wealth each year to the poor had been followed.

DECLINE OF ARAB SOCIALISM

With Nasser's death in 1970 and succession by Anwar Sadat, Arab socialism gradually faded away. Sadat adopted the idea of *infitah* (opening) to capitalist investment. State controls over the economy have been removed slowly and land reform undone. Nasser's social revolution has largely been reversed.

See also *Arab Political Economy; Arab Political Thought; Communism; Ideologies, Political; Socialism.*

. . . . GLENN E. PERRY

BIBLIOGRAPHY
Ansari, Hamid. *Egypt: The Stalled Society.* Albany: State University of New York Press, 1986.
Binder, Leonard. *In a Moment of Enthusiasm: Political Power and the Second Stratum in Egypt.* Chicago: University of Chicago Press, 1978.

Dekmejian, H. Hrair. *Egypt under Nasir: A Study of Political Dynamics.* Albany: State University of New York Press, 1971.

Hanna, Sami A., and George H. Gardner, eds. *Arab Socialism: A Documentary Survey.* Salt Lake City: University of Utah Press, 1969.

Ismael, Tareq Y. *The Arab Left.* Syracuse, N.Y.: Syracuse University Press, 1976.

Karpat, Kemal H., ed. *Political and Social Thought in the Contemporary Middle East,* 2nd ed. New York: Praeger, 1982.

Khadduri Majid. *Political Trends in the Arab World: The Role of Ideas and Ideals in Politics.* Baltimore: Johns Hopkins University Press, 1970.

O'Brien, Patrick. *The Revolution in Egypt's Economic System: From Private Enterprise to Socialism, 1952–1965.* London: Oxford University Press, 1966.

Arbitration

Arbitration is a long-standing form of adjudication that seeks to provide more economical, less formal, quicker, and more expert trial proceedings. The process was recognized in the ancient world, mentioned in the Quran, and served as a model for rabbinical courts. George Washington referred to it in his will. Although it is meant to be an alternative to judicial litigation, arbitration more closely resembles court proceedings than structured negotiation mechanisms, like mediation. Under contemporary perceptions, arbitration is more than an ancillary form of adjudication. In *Scherk v. Alberto-Culver Co.,* 417 U.S. 506 (1974), the U.S. Supreme Court deemed arbitration vital to international commerce; in *Rodriguez v. Shearson/Am. Express, Inc.,* 490 U.S. 477 (1989), it proclaimed arbitration instrumental to fulfilling the promise of constitutional due process.

The improper operation of judicial processes has made arbitration necessary. As former Chief Justice Warren Burger stated, judicial litigation takes too long, costs too much, and can decimate human relationships. Ordinary legal rights fall by the wayside. Faced with dwindling social resources and political deadlock, the Supreme Court chose to advocate for privatized justice and the submission of civil disputes to arbitration.

Arbitration in the United States is governed by the Federal Arbitration Act (FAA). Enacted in 1925, the FAA contains provisions establishing the validity of arbitration agreements and enforceability of arbitral awards. The legislation embodies a "hospitable" federal policy on arbitration. The case law has added substantially to its content over the years. More than forty U.S. Supreme Court opinions establish that the federal law of arbitration preempts conflicting state laws (making the FAA the exclusive national law of arbitration); the act applies to the vast majority of employment arbitration agreements despite the exclusion in FAA § 1, and arbitral proceedings are the equal of judicial trials for litigating claims. Moreover, arbitrations are isolated events with no general impact. The court also has determined that statutory claims can be submitted to arbitration, thereby substantially increasing the jurisdictional range of arbitration. In *Penn Plaza v. Pyett,* 129 S. Ct. 1456 (2009), for example, the Supreme Court ruled that arbitrators could decide civil rights claims.

In a word, arbitration thrives in U.S. law. It is greatly favored by courts and legal doctrine. The case law makes it exceedingly difficult to void arbitration agreements or nullify arbitral awards. California and neighboring states dissent from the general consensus by invalidating arbitration in adhesionary

circumstances. The federal preemption doctrine, however, keeps the dissension in check by giving the federal support of arbitration its full doctrinal impact.

Arbitration is structurally resilient and adaptive. It seeks solutions and avoids impasse. Its ethic is pragmatic. Proposed congressional legislation, buttressed by some lobbying groups and a small minority of academic commentators, threatens the current practice by prohibiting arbitration in unilateral contracts. The wholesale invalidation of predispute arbitration agreements in adhesionary sectors could compromise the basic legitimacy of arbitration by creating the erroneous impression that arbitration is an abusive process that caters solely to the richest and most powerful parties. The U.S. Supreme Court's depiction is more accurate: Arbitration supplies meaningful access to an effective means of redressing grievances through third-party decision making.

Arbitration also has wide currency in global commerce. It recently expanded its reach to the mixed political-commercial issues of investment between developed and developing countries. European democracies, like France and England, have embraced arbitration particularly in matters of transborder commerce, giving it—for the time being—somewhat less play in the internal administration of justice. Arbitral adjudication has taken hold in Latin America and China. Despite some resistance and a few flaws, it is the most universal and effective extant adjudicatory process.

See also *Adjudication; Supreme Court.*

. . . .   THOMAS E. CARBONNEAU

BIBLIOGRAPHY

Born, Gary B. *International Commercial Arbitration,* 2 vols. Boston: Kluwer Law International, 2009.

Burger, Warren. "Our Vicious Legal Spiral." *Judges Journal* 16, (Fall 1977): 23.

Carbonneau, Thomas E. *The Law and Practice of Arbitration,* 3rd ed. Huntington, N.Y.: Juris, 2009.

Edmonson, Larry E. *Domke on Commercial Arbitration,* 3rd ed., 2 vols. St. Paul, Minn.: West, 2009.

MacNeil, Ian R. *American Arbitration Law.* Oxford: Oxford University Press, 1992.

Searle Civil Justice Institute. "Consumer Arbitration before the American Arbitration Association" (Preliminary Report). Chicago: Searle Center on Law, Regulation, and Economic Growth, Northwestern University School of Law, March 2009.

Archives, National

See *National Archives.*

Arendt, Hannah

Hannah Arendt (1906–1975) was born in Hanover, Germany, to a secular Jewish middle-class family. Dedicated to study early on, Arendt completed a doctoral dissertation in 1929 at Heidelberg University. During this same period, Arendt became increasingly preoccupied with the issue of German Jewish identity in response to rising anti-Semitism. She began writing a biography of Rahel Varnhagen, who was a Jewish salon hostess in Berlin in the early 1800s. Although the work

During her career as a political thinker, Hannah Arendt capably blended historical analysis with philosophical reflection on topics including anti-Semitism and totalitarianism.

SOURCE: AP Images

was not published until 1958, it marked the start of Arendt's lifelong career as a political thinker who showed a unique gift of blending historical analysis with philosophical reflection. In 1933, with the Nazis' rise to power, Arendt fled to Paris and worked in a number of Jewish refugee organizations. In 1940, Arendt and her second husband, Heinrich Blüche, left Paris as it fell under German control. They eventually made their way to New York in 1941, and Arendt became an American citizen in 1951. By then her academic career was taking off, and she became one of the most influential but controversial thinkers of the twentieth century.

Arendt's first major publication in English was *The Origins of Totalitarianism* in 1951. This large volume, which is divided into three parts, traces the historical conditions that set the stage for the rise of totalitarianism under the broad themes of anti-Semitism and imperialism. What made the book controversial at the time was the third part, which paints Nazism and Stalinism with the same stroke, which was totalitarianism. On this important point, Arendt based her argument on philosophical rather than historical grounds. Totalitarianism as such is characterized by "ideological thinking," which in essence is a form of radical idealism that is sustained by a closed system of logic. It is the mind working in singularity rather than in plurality. Hence totalitarianism can only thrive in societies

where individuals are completely isolated from one another. This observation led her to write what many consider to be her most original contribution to political thought, *The Human Condition,* in 1958. In it Arendt put forth a concept of action as direct interaction between individuals without any intermediary. Speech is thus the quintessential action and is what makes us distinctly human. Freedom and human plurality are realized through action.

Yet it was Arendt's later analysis of a related subject that proved to be even more controversial. This was the question of individual responsibility in totalitarian movements and the occasion was the Eichmann trial in 1961. As its firsthand observer, Arendt concluded that the former Nazi henchman Adolf Eichmann was no Mephistopheles nor Faust. Rather, Arendt observed in her *Eichmann in Jerusalem,* "he *merely,* to put the matter colloquially, *never realized what he was doing* . . . It was sheer thoughtlessness . . . that predisposed him to become one of the greatest criminals of that period" (1964, 287–288). To some, this pronouncement understated the magnitude of Eichmann's crime. However, in Arendt's last but incomplete major work, which was published posthumously in 1978 as *Life of the Mind,* thinking is identified as an internal dialogue that everyone can and should have with oneself at all times and as such, it is a moral obligation that no one can evade. Eichmann's defense that he was a "mere functionary" following orders from above was therefore inexcusable.

Since the late 1980s, scholarship on Arendt has flourished significantly on both sides of the Atlantic and beyond. Her continued appeal may be related to the fact in her lifetime, she had never lent herself to the political cause of either the liberal or the communist camp. Arendt is thus seen by many to be particularly pertinent to the post–cold war world of our time, including a vision of participatory democracy that is not right-based.

See also *Stalinism; Totalitarianism.*

. . . .   THERESA M. LEE

BIBLIOGRAPHY

Arendt, Hannah. *Eichmann in Jerusalem: A Report on the Banality of Evil,* rev. and enl. ed. Harmondsworth: Penguin, 1964.

———. "Thinking and Moral Considerations." *Social Research* 38 (1971): 417–446.

———. "On Hannah Arendt." In *Hannah Arendt: The Recovery of the Public World,* edited by Melvyn A. Hill, 301–339. New York: St. Marin's, 1979.

———. *Lectures on Kant's Political Philosophy,* edited by Ronald Beiner. Chicago: University of Chicago Press, 1982.

Canovan, Margaret. *Hannah Arendt: A Reinterpretation of Her Political Thought.* Cambridge: Cambridge University Press, 1992.

d'Entreves, Maurizio Passerin. "Hannah Arendt." In *The Stanford Encyclopedia of Philosophy,* edited by Edward N. Zalta. Stanford, Calif.: Metaphysics Research Lab, Center for the Study of Language and Information, 2006, http://plato.stanford.edu/entries/arendt.

Honig, Bonnie, ed. *Feminist Interpretations of Hannah Arendt.* University Park: Pennsylvania State University Press, 1995.

Villa, Dana, ed. *The Cambridge Companion to Hannah Arendt.* Cambridge: Cambridge University Press, 2000.

Young-Bruehl, Elizabeth. *Hannah Arendt: For Love of the World.* New Haven, Conn.: Yale University Press, 1982.

Aristotle

Aristotle (384–322 BCE) was born in Stagira, in Northern Greece. His father, Nicomachus, was court physician to Amyntas III, king of Macedon, and Aristotle maintained close connections to the Macedonian regime throughout his life. At the age of seventeen, he traveled to Athens, to study in Plato's Academy, where he stayed for twenty years, until Plato's death in 347. After he left the Academy, Aristotle's travels included returning to Macedon to tutor the future Alexander the Great. He returned to Athens, in 336, to open his own school, the Lyceum, where he stayed until the death of Alexander the Great in 323.

The corpus of Aristotle's works that have come down to us are not finished products, prepared for publication, but were composed in connection with his school, most likely for use in lecturing. Aristotle also wrote dialogues, which were renowned for their literary qualities, but aside from fragments that have been recovered, these were all lost. Aristotle's works encompass an enormous range of subjects, including logic, scientific studies of the natural world, metaphysics, ethics, and politics. His *Politics* has a strong claim to being the first extant work of political science.

Aristotle's moral and political philosophy shows the strong influence of Plato, and he provides powerful, detailed answers to important questions that Plato raised. But Aristotle clearly broke with Plato in important respects, notably in rejecting the latter's conception of *forms* or *ideas* that exist apart from their instances in the material world. In *Politics,* Aristotle departs from Plato most significantly in detailed examination of existing political forms, which he is willing to consider more or less on their own terms. In Book II of the work, Aristotle presents a harsh—although frequently clearly misguided—critique of Plato's *Republic* and *Laws,* generally in regard to what he views as these works' excessive utopianism.

In *Politics,* Aristotle explores the *polis* in its entirety, including different kinds of *poleis* and their distinctive features, factors that lead to the stability and instability of different forms. He also subjects the *polis* to moral inquiry, including what it means for human beings to live in it, and how it contributes to their well-being. In addition to the *polis* as it exists, Aristotle considers ideal representatives at different levels, ranging between ideal states unconstrained by actual circumstances, to remedying defects in existing states. In Book IV of the work, he presents a powerful argument for a relative ideal, a state that achieves the important end of social-political stability, based on rule by the middle class—as opposed to the political instability occasioned by rule of either the rich or the poor.

In composing *Politics,* Aristotle drew on studies of 158 different Greek constitutions. One of these studies, a book-length analysis of the constitution of Athens, by either Aristotle or his students, is extant. Aristotle demonstrates impressive command of the history and workings of innumerable specific cases. The *polis* existed in myriad forms, while the Greek world was torn by constant tumult, revolution, and change.

His studies of different instances—primarily of democracies, oligarchies, and tyrannies—compared and contrasted across numerous dimensions, provide a wealth of empirical analysis perhaps unmatched until relatively recent times.

See also *Greek Political Thought, Ancient; Plato.*

. . . . GEORGE KLOSKO

BIBLIOGRAPHY

Aristotle. *The Complete Works of Aristotle: The Revised Oxford Translation,* 2 vols, edited by Jonathan Barnes. Princeton, N.J.: Princeton University Press, 1984.

Keyt, David, and Fred Miller, eds. *A Companion to Aristotle's Politics.* Oxford, U.K.: Blackwell, 1991.

Kraut, Richard. *Aristotle.* Oxford: Oxford University Press, 2002.

Mulgan, Richard. *Aristotle's Political Theory.* Oxford, U.K.: Clarendon, 1977.

Newman, William L., ed. *The Politics of Aristotle,* 4 vols. Oxford, U.K.: Clarendon, 1887–1902.

Armenian Genocide

The Armenian Genocide is often cited as the first genocide of the twentieth century, carried out against the Armenian population of the Ottoman Empire during World War I (1914–1918). Many in Turkey, however, dispute that the event should be considered genocide, and it remains a controversial topic both within Turkey and internationally.

ARMENIANS UNDER THE OTTOMAN EMPIRE

Armenians, a Christian people, had long lived in the territory of the Ottoman Empire in eastern Anatolia and in cities such as Istanbul. Until the late nineteenth century, Armenians were referred to as *millet-i sadıka* (loyal nation) by the Ottomans. Like other minorities, they were free to practice their religion and had their own courts, although they were also subject to heavy taxes and denied rights granted to Muslims. In the late 1800s, increasingly despotic rule by the Ottoman sultan combined with Russian claims to act as a protector of Christian peoples in the Ottoman Empire led some Armenians to clamor for independence. Armenian unrest was forcefully put down by the government, resulting in tens of thousands of deaths from 1894 to 1897.

In 1909, the Ottoman Empire came under the control of the Young Turks, a movement within the bureaucracy and military that advocated reform within the Ottoman Empire. However, by 1913 the Committee of Union and Progress (CUP), a more militant and nationalistic faction among the Young Turks, gained control over the government. The CUP was led by Ismail Enver Pasha, Mehmed Talat Pasha, and Ahmed Djemal Pasha, all individuals who have been accused of being behind the Armenian genocide.

WORLD WAR I AND GENOCIDE

In 1914, the Ottoman Empire joined World War I and attacked Russian forces. The Russians defeated the Ottomans. Some Armenians who lived in the area—there were Armenians on both sides of the Ottoman-Russian border—assisted Russian forces. The Ottoman government, however, accused the

Armenians *en masse* of being in league with the Russians, making them an enemy of the state. This would provide the pretext for the genocide.

The genocide began in 1915. First, Armenians in the army were disarmed, placed into labor battalions, and then killed. On April 24, 1915, Armenian intellectuals in Istanbul were arrested and deported by the government. They were eventually executed. (April 24 thus serves as the day of commemoration by those who acknowledge the genocide.) This was followed in May 1915 by a Temporary Law on Deportation, which gave the government the right to deport anyone it deemed a threat to national security. Several months later, a Temporary Law of Expropriation and Confiscation was passed, giving the government the right to seize Armenian property. Throughout 1915, the Ottoman authorities expelled the Armenians in eastern Anatolia from their homes, told them they would be relocated, and then marched them off to concentration camps in the desert between Jerablus and Deir ez-Zor, where many would perish due to lack of food and water. In other cases, Armenians were drowned, raped, or simply shot on sight by local Turks and Kurds, who acted with impunity.

According to many sources, the CUP created an administrative unit (*Teshkilai Mahusuna*) and special "butcher battalions," manned by violent criminals released from prison, to ensure that actions against the Armenians were carried out. Estimates are that between one and one and a half-million (of the roughly two and a half million Armenians in the Ottoman Empire) perished. Official Turkish records, published in 2008, indicate that nearly a million Armenians disappeared between 1914 and 1918.

Hundreds of eyewitnesses, including American missionaries and German military advisers (who were on the Ottoman side during the war) documented various massacres. For example, the German ambassador wrote to Berlin in 1916 that the Ottoman government sought "to resolve its Armenian question by the destruction of the Armenian race" (Hovannisian, 1992, xii). U.S. Ambassador to the Ottoman Empire Henry Morgenthau wrote in 1915 that "deportation of and excesses against peaceful Armenians is increasing and from harrowing reports of eyewitnesses it appears that a campaign of race extermination is in progress under a pretext of reprisal against rebellion" (Winter, 2003, 150). The *New York Times* ran more than one hundred articles on the plight of the Armenians in 1915, and many prominent Americans, including former President Theodore Roosevelt and orator and politician William Jennings Bryan, spoke out against it.

The Ottoman government, when not denying the massacres, claimed that they were driven by the needs of the war. Some Ottoman officials who refused to comply with orders were dismissed, and Turks who protected Armenians risked death themselves. Survivors of the genocide would find refuge in Russia, the Middle East, and, eventually, in Europe, North America, Africa, and Australia, making Armenians one of the world's largest diaspora groups.

After the war, the Ottoman Empire was defeated, and its wartime leaders were put on trial, often *in absentia*. In 1919,

a Turkish court convicted many Ottoman officials for war crimes, claiming that "the disaster visiting the Armenians was not a local or isolated event. It was the result of a premeditated decision taken by a central body . . . and the immolations and excesses which took place were based on oral or written orders issued by that central body" (Balakian, 2003, 339). This court functioned while Turkey was still occupied by Western powers. Later, Turkish army officer Mustapha Kemal (later Ataturk) organized Turkish resistance to foreign occupation, creating the Republic of Turkey in 1923 and securing the release of war criminals held by the British.

CONTEMPORARY CONTROVERSIES

The Armenian genocide remains a very sensitive issue. While Armenians have lobbied for international recognition of the crime committed against them, the Turkish government refuses to acknowledge that the actions taken against the Armenians consistute a genocide. In its view, the Armenian claims of more than a million dead are wildly inflated, and those deaths that did occur among Armenians, Kurds, and Turks were the result of localized activity carried out during the war due to civil conflict. In this interpretation, there was no systematic, centralized campaign to eliminate Armenians. Others, however, would seek to justify actions taken against Armenians as necessary for the Turkish war effort, as Armenians were deemed to be unreliable. Many individuals, such as the Nobel-prize winning Turkish author Orhan Pamuk, who have spoken of the Armenian genocide, have been brought before Turkish courts for "insulting Turkishness." Efforts within Turkey to examine the issue have been subjected to harassment by the government, although some Turkish scholars, such as Turkish historian Taner Akcam, are willing to acknowledge that a genocide against Armenians did occur. Internationally, Turkey's refusal to acknowledge the Armenian genocide is held up by some as a reason not to admit Turkey to the European Union.

See also *Genocide; Nationalism; War Crimes.*

. . . . PAUL JAMES KUBICEK

BIBLIOGRAPHY
Akcam, Taner. *A Shameful Act: The Armenian Genocide and the Question of Turkish Responsibility.* New York: Metropolitan Books, 2006.
Balakian, Peter. *The Burning Tigris: The Armenian Genocide and America's Response.* New York: Harper Collins, 2003.
Bloxham, Donald. *The Great Game of Genocide: Imperialism, Nationalism, and the Destruction of the Ottoman Armenians.* Oxford: Oxford University Press, 2005.
Hovannisian, Richard, ed. *The Armenian Genocide: History, Politics, Ethics.* New York: St. Martin's, 1992.
———. *Remembrance and Denial: The Case of the Armenian Genocide.* Detroit: Wayne State University Press, 1999.
Suny, Ronald G. *Looking toward Ararat: Armenia in Modern History.* Bloomington: Indiana University Press, 1993.
Winter, Jay, ed. *America and the Armenian Genocide.* Cambridge: Cambridge University Press, 2003.

Arms, Freedom to Bear

See *Freedom to Bear Arms.*

Arms Control

Arms control is both a process and a result. On the one hand, it involves the conscious and dedicated effort by two or more parties (typically nation-states) to negotiate an improved security relationship. On the other, arms control is often manifested by an agreement to regulate some aspect of the participating states' military capabilities or potential. The agreement may apply to the location, amount, readiness, or types of military forces, weapons, or facilities, but always presupposes cooperation or joint action among the participants regarding their military programs.

While not as centrally important today as it was during the second half of the twentieth century, arms control, in its broadest definition that encompasses not only traditional negotiations and agreements but also nonproliferation, counterproliferation, and disarmament, still has a role in a globalizing world that has ongoing security concerns. Arms control and other cooperative security initiatives should be seen as part of a nation-state's foreign policy toolbox, available when necessary to enhance a state's security, but seldom the only tools available; they complement rather than substitute for diplomatic, economic, and coercive military actions.

Arms control was born during the cold war to stall the military conflict primarily between the former Soviet Union, and its satellite states, and the United States long enough for the West to win. With the end of the cold war in 1991, the world experienced a flush of optimism and arms control activity that reached its zenith in the mid-1990s as formal agreements and cooperative measures were signed and entered into force with astounding speed. Both sides codified lower numbers of forces to ensure that the cold war was really over, but eventually arms control found a place dealing with the new concerns of proliferation, regional instability, and economic and environmental security. The value of arms control appeared to be growing in the new world, as states attempted to stem the illegal proliferation of weapons of mass destruction to rogue nations or groups and to meet their security needs in a multipolar, more interdependent world.

By the late 1990s, arms control had lost its luster for the United States and had become less important to a national security stance that no longer recognized the importance of such policies in the globalizing post–cold war world. The arrival of President George W. Bush in 2001 and the attacks of September 11 put the country on a war footing against a dramatically different kind of enemy. Arms control, at least from an American perspective, seemed passé, if not dead, a stance the Bush administration encouraged.

With the 2008 election of President Barack Obama, however, the United States restored arms control to its formerly central place in American diplomacy, and the international security agenda facing the new president required renewed attention to this policy approach. The Obama administration also saw arms control as a good way to try to restore better relations with Russia after several years of increasing antagonism.

WHAT IS ARMS CONTROL?

Arms control can be defined as any agreement among states to regulate some aspect of their military capability or potential. Proponents of the concept believe that while the negotiating methods, regions of concern, and weapons involved may have changed, the underlying principles and objectives of arms control remain relevant today. The arms control process is intended to serve as a means of enhancing a state's national security; it should not be pursued as an end unto itself. Arms control also should be distinguished from disarmament, the rationale for which is that armaments have been the major cause of international instability and conflict, and only through reductions in the weaponry of all nations can the world achieve peace. Proponents of disarmament have an overall goal of reducing the size of military forces, budgets, explosive power, and other aggregate measures.

COOPERATIVE SECURITY

Arms control falls under the rubric of cooperative security, a concept that has been used to outline a more peaceful and idealistic approach to security. One commonly accepted definition of *cooperative security* is a commitment to regulate the size, technical composition, investment patterns, and operational practices of all military forces by mutual consent for mutual benefit. Cooperative security is slightly different in meaning than collective security or collective defense. *Collective security* is a political and legal obligation of member states to defend the integrity of individual states within a group of treaty signatories, whereas *collective defense* is more narrowly defined as a commitment of all states to defend each other from outside aggression. By contrast, cooperative security can include the introduction of measures that reduce the risk of war, measures that are not necessarily directed against any specific state or coalition, a definition that definitely includes arms control.

DISARMAMENT

The classical practices underlying disarmament can be found almost as far back as the beginnings of recorded Western history. Early practices were largely postconflict impositions of limitations on military force by the victor upon the vanquished. However, there were also examples of efforts to avoid conflict by cooperating to demilitarize likely regions of contact and restrict the use of new and destructive technologies. Efforts to impose some degree of order on interstate conflict focused on the advance of legal standards toward just war. Another series of efforts included demilitarizing colonial forces and avoiding distant conflicts. The period of the late nineteenth and early twentieth centuries was marked by dramatic increases in the lethality of warfare and a parallel move toward bounding the employment of new weapons. Efforts were made to ban the use of certain systems and munitions, limit numbers of advanced systems deployed, and restrict the geographic employment of forces.

Traditionally then, *disarmament* was used to indicate the full range of endeavors to reduce and restrict military weapons and forces through a wide variety of means, from cooperation

Jimmy Carter and Leonid Brezhnev shake hands at the signing of the SALT II Treaty in Vienna, Austria. The treaty was part of a nuclear arms control effort between the United States and the Soviet Union.

SOURCE: © Bettmann/Corbis

to imposition. These efforts included the demilitarization or deconfliction of potential regions of conflict, postconflict limitations on state forces and weapons, as well as attempts to limit and eliminate new and destructive technologies. Efforts also included regulating the conduct of warfare, from determinations of noncombatant status to precepts of just and moral uses of armed force. Until the early 1960s, the concept of *disarmament* was broadly used as an umbrella under which all of these arrangements and means of implementation could reside.

ARMS CONTROL

Arms control belongs to a group of closely related views whose common theme is peace through the manipulation of force, and is but one of a series of alternative approaches to achieving international security through military strategies.

The centrality of the concept of disarmament was supplanted by the term *arms control* early in the nuclear age. World War II (1939–1945) saw the introduction of what many

described as the "ultimate weapon," or the atomic bomb, as well as near-global technologies of delivery. With the failure of early proposals to either eliminate or internationalize control over atomic weapons, the focus shifted toward limiting their development and spread and controlling their use and effects. Western academics and policy analysts soon realized that disarmament in the literal sense of eliminating nuclear weapons was not going to happen; these weapons had become a long-term reality of the international system. Thus, as they began examining these weapons and nuclear strategy, they adopted a preference for terminology that directly captured efforts to come to grips with "controlling" these weapons.

In the mid-1950s, policy makers began rethinking an approach that had emphasized general and complete disarmament and considered instead limited, partial measures that would gradually enhance confidence in cooperative security arrangements. Thus, more modest goals under the rubric of arms control came to replace the propaganda-laden disarmament efforts of the late

1940s and early 1950s. International security specialists began using the term *arms control* in place of *disarmament*, which they felt lacked precision and smacked of utopianism. The seminal books on the subject published in the early 1960s all preferred *arms control* as a more comprehensive term. Austrian scholar Hedley Bull differentiated the two as follows: disarmament is the reduction or abolition of armaments, while arms control is restraint internationally exercised upon armaments policy—not only the number of weapons, but also their character, development, and use.

The concept and theory of arms control was developed by a small number of academic study groups in the United States and Great Britain, who published the three seminal works on arms control in 1961. *Strategy and Arms Control,* by Thomas Schelling and Morton Halperin, reflected the findings of a 1960 summer study group organized under the auspices of the American Academy of Arts and Sciences. The basic premise of this book was that cooperative arrangements with adversaries could have the same objectives as sensible military policies in reducing the likelihood of war. The authors were influenced by the work of another member of the summer study, Donald G. Brennan, who served as editor of *Arms Control, Disarmament, and National Security.* Similarly, *The Control of the Arms Race: Disarmament and Arms Control in the Missile Age,* by Hedley Bull, was based on a series of symposia held at Oxford University in 1960. These three works form the essential basis for understanding modern arms control theory.

The arms control perspective was perhaps best expressed by Schelling and Halperin when they framed the arms control construct as follows:

> We believe that arms control is a promising . . . enlargement of the scope of our military strategy. It rests essentially on the recognition that our military relation with potential enemies is not one of pure conflict and opposition, but involves strong elements of mutual interest in the avoidance of a war that neither side wants, in minimizing the costs and risks of the arms competition, and in curtailing the scope and violence of war in the event it occurs. (1)

Arms control in the nuclear age was framed as a component part of an overall military and national security strategy—an instrument of policy and an adjunct to force posture, not a utopian or moral crusade. It captured the more cooperative side of policy, focusing not on imposition but on negotiation and compromise, recognizing the shared interest in avoiding nuclear conflict.

ARMS CONTROL IN THE COLD WAR

EARLY COLD WAR MULTILATERAL EFFORTS

Multilateral efforts early in the cold war sought to affect the control of nuclear weapons by limiting the physical scope of the weapons, their testing, and their further technological development and proliferation. Multilateral agreements prior to the 1970s banned placing nuclear weapons in Antarctica, outer space, or the earth's seabed. Regional nuclear-weapon-free zones also were established during this period in Latin America and later in the South Pacific, Africa, Southeast Asia, and Central Asia. Early restrictions on atmospheric testing were supplemented by efforts to ban all atmospheric tests and eventually all weapons test explosions, even underground. The early multilateral efforts were capped by the 1968 Nuclear Nonproliferation Treaty (NPT) that sought to prevent future additions to the nuclear club by establishing a framework for additional multilateral efforts extending to biological and chemical weapons and other arenas of arms control. The NPT also paid service to its disarmament heritage by containing a clause calling on all nuclear weapons states to seek the eventual elimination of their nuclear arsenals.

With the establishment of the NPT regime, the primary focus of arms control focus during the second half of the cold war centered on bilateral strategic controls between the United States and the Soviet Union. The meaning of arms control subsequently narrowed to a focus on the formal negotiating process, characterized by staged, multipart negotiation, implementation, and verification phases.

THE SALT ERA

The first effort of the bilateral U.S.-Soviet nuclear arms control process led to the Strategic Arms Limitation Talks (SALT) and three treaties—an Interim Agreement on Offensive Weapons and Anti-Ballistic Missile Treaty (both signed in 1972, together called SALT I), and the 1979 SALT II treaty. Cold war tensions and a dangerous and expensive nuclear arms race, whose potential ramifications had been made evident by the Cuban Missile Crisis, spurred both the United States and the Soviet Union in the 1960s into a series of cooperative measures and steps toward bilateral cooperation to limit future strategic systems. With the development of sufficient capabilities in national technical means of unilateral verification, formal bilateral negotiations on SALT began in 1969. SALT I froze the total number of deployed intercontinental ballistic missiles on both sides and limited the total number of maritime strategic systems that could be deployed. It also limited the development and deployment of future antiballistic missile systems and restricted defense technologies. The two sides agreed on the outline of a follow-on agreement at the Vladivostok Summit in 1974. Subsequent negotiations led to SALT II, which placed an aggregate limit on deployed strategic launch vehicles and also limited the number of systems that could be equipped with multiple warheads.

THE START ERA

The second series of negotiations between the United States and the Soviet Union addressed force reductions through the Strategic Arms Reduction Talks (START), leading to the START I and START II treaties and the elimination of an entire class of weapons through the Intermediate-Range Nuclear Forces (INF) Treaty. Beginning simultaneously with the SALT talks, a broader series of East-West efforts had addressed the reduction of tensions between the North Atlantic Treaty Organization (NATO) and the Warsaw Pact. By 1987, the INF treaty negotiations came to fruition, and both sides' intermediate-range missiles were withdrawn and destroyed. A key legacy of this agreement, in addition to its precedent for elimination of an entire category of weapon systems, was its reliance on on-site inspection teams to verify missile removal and destruction on the other side's territory.

The START talks began in 1982 and proceeded alongside an extensive series of nuclear confidence-building measures addressing risk reduction and data sharing. The 1992 START I Treaty required measured reductions in both nuclear weapons and delivery vehicles, with intrusive verification provisions to ensure compliance. The bilateral nuclear arms control process was so firmly established that even with the dissolution of the Soviet Union in 1991, the two sides were still able to quickly negotiate the 1993 START II Treaty, in which both sides agreed to further reduce their nuclear arsenals. In addition, cooperative efforts succeeded in consolidating control of Soviet nuclear systems in the Russian Republic and initiating a broad effort known as *cooperative threat reduction measures* to reduce the chances of proliferation from the former Soviet Union. At the 1997 Helsinki summit meeting, both countries committed themselves to continue the strategic arms reduction process to even lower levels of nuclear warheads through a START III round, but this plan was obviated by the 2002 Moscow Treaty (officially the Strategic Offensive Reductions Treaty, or SORT).

THE MOSCOW TREATY AND BEYOND

The Moscow Treaty called for continued reductions in both sides' arsenals of deployed strategic warheads, but with no formal verification measures to ensure compliance. Given that START was scheduled to expire in December 2009, and SORT in December 2012, the two states began negotiations on a replacement strategic agreement in earnest after Barack Obama became president of the United States in 2009.

MULTILATERAL ARMS CONTROL SUCCESSES

Arms control has not been solely focused on bilateral U.S.-Soviet strategic issues since the 1970s. There have been parallel efforts under way in multiple other fields, often led by the United Nations Conference on Disarmament. These multilateral discussions were not as highly charged politically as the bilateral efforts, but they did achieve several notable accomplishments. For example, in 1972 the world agreed to ban the production, stockpiling, and use of biological and toxin weapons (the Biological Weapons Convention), and in 1993 it agreed to a similar treaty on chemical weapons (the Chemical Weapons Convention). NATO and the Warsaw Pact came to an agreement on conventional force levels, composition, and disposition in the Conventional Forces in Europe Treaty in 1990. A Comprehensive Test Ban Treaty was signed in Geneva in 1996 (although it has not yet entered into force), and discussions are still ongoing regarding a global Fissile Materials Cutoff Treaty. A series of nuclear-weapon-free zones has essentially denuclearized the entire Southern Hemisphere. A coalition of states and nongovernmental organizations led the effort to ban landmines in 1997 (the Ottawa Convention), and several informal groupings of states were created to prevent the proliferation of weapons of mass destruction technologies through organizations such as the Zangger Committee, the Australia Group, the Wassenaar Arrangement, and the Nuclear Suppliers Group.

ARMS CONTROL AND DISARMAMENT TODAY

The agenda of existing, active efforts in the arena of arms control and disarmament remains extensive. The potential for nuclear proliferation—whether materials, components, systems, weapons, or expertise—keeps nuclear arms control on the agenda. Small arms and light weapons remain outside of any effective controls. Other weapons with catastrophic potential—particularly biological and chemical—while subject to international controls and even bans, remain a threat due to further development and possible proliferation. Far-reaching technological developments have opened up entire new arenas of potential and actual military development in areas such as information technology and outer space. Ongoing arms control efforts—unilateral, bilateral, and multilateral, formal and informal, between nations and non-state parties in some cases—are addressing this wide agenda.

The U.S.-Russian strategic arms control implementation process will take decades to complete. This is a massive, difficult, expensive, and often contentious process, and it will be compounded with each new increment of cuts. The added factor of dealing with strategic defenses will complicate this bilateral endgame, at least in the short term, but it also holds the potential—at least to some observers—of being the only route to the continued safe drawdown of the two strategic nuclear arsenals. In addition, the United States and Russia have yet to address the additional nonstrategic nuclear weapons that are included in their arsenals, which will even further complicate bilateral arms controls. Similar cooperative efforts to dismantle, control, and destroy former Soviet chemical and biological weapons and capabilities extend the scope and horizons of the bilateral strategic arms control effort. The highly formal cold war bilateral arms control process will certainly be altered, but it is far from over.

We also can expect a continuation of multilateral arms control and disarmament efforts, particularly toward halting and reversing the proliferation and development of nuclear, biological, and chemical weapons. Work remains to be done in fully implementing the NPT and the Comprehensive Test Ban Treaty, and in improving the implementation of the Biological and Chemical Weapons Conventions.

Regional arms control and disarmament efforts are just emerging. Europe has long addressed security cooperation, confidence-building, and conventional arms control issues, and that effort will persist as the region continues to stake out its future course. Other regions have adopted nuclear-weapon-free zones, and some have established regional cooperative programs on a range of economic, political, and security issues. New and emerging arenas for arms control and disarmament include existing efforts among some states and nonstate actors to address controls or bans on small arms, at least academic discussion of controls on advanced conventional weapons, and emerging venues of military interest—and thus arms control interest—in space and cyberspace. All of these efforts are only in their infancy.

Humankind has a long legacy of attempts to limit the potential and destructive results of warfare. Today, as modern technologies threaten massive destruction and suffering, nations will continue to strive for humane and measured applications of force. As long as weapons remain tools of international relations, citizens of those nations will be involved in arms control and disarmament. For nearly three generations, policy development and intellectual advancement in the field of international relations have focused on the role of arms control and used the specialized language developed for that purpose. This field of international policy will remain viable and vital into the foreseeable future.

See also *Arms Race; Conflict Resolution; Nuclear Club; Nuclear Proliferation and Nonproliferation; Weapons of Mass Destruction.*

. . . . JEFFREY LARSEN

BIBLIOGRAPHY

Arbotov, Alexei, and Rose Gottemoeller. "New Presidents, New Agreements? Advancing U.S.-Russian Strategic Arms Control." *Arms Control Today* (July-August 2008), www.armscontrol.org/act/2008_07-08/CoverStory.

Arms Control Association. *Arms Control and National Security: An Introduction.* Washington, D.C.: Arms Control Association, 1989.

Bernstein, Paul. "International Partnerships to Combat Weapons of Mass Destruction." Occasional Paper 6. Washington, D.C.: National Defense University, May 2008.

Blechman, Barry, ed. *Unblocking the Road to Zero: Perspective of Advanced Nuclear Nations.* Nuclear Security Series. Washington, D.C.: Henry L. Stimson Center, February 2009.

Brennan, Donald G., ed. *Arms Control, Disarmament, and National Security.* New York: George Braziller, 1961.

Brown, Harold. "Is Arms Control Dead?" *Washington Quarterly* 23, no. 2 (2000): 171–232.

Bull, Hedley. *The Control of the Arms Race: Disarmament and Arms Control in the Missile Age.* New York: Praeger, 1961.

Burns, Richard Dean, ed. *Encyclopedia of Arms Control and Disarmament,* 3 vols. New York: Scribner's, 1993.

Campbell, Kurt M., Robert J. Einhorn, and Mitchell B. Reiss, eds. *The Nuclear Tipping Point: Why States Reconsider Their Nuclear Choices.* Washington, D.C.: Brookings Institution, 2004.

Carter, Ashton B., William J. Perry, and John D. Steinbruner. *A New Concept of Cooperative Security.* Washington, D.C.: Brookings Institution, 1992.

Daalder, Ivo, and Jan Lodal. "The Logic of Zero: Toward a World without Nuclear Weapons." *Foreign Affairs* 87 (November-December 2008): 80–95.

Dunn, Lewis A., and Victor Alexxi. "Arms Control by Other Means." *Survival* 42, no. 4 (2000): 223–238.

Gaddis, John Lewis. *Cold War Statesmen Confront the Bomb: Nuclear Diplomacy Since 1945.* New York: Oxford University Press, 1999.

Gray, Colin S. *House of Cards: Why Arms Control Must Fail.* Ithaca, N.Y.: Cornell University Press, 1992.

Kaye, Dalia Dassa. *Talking to the Enemy: Track Two Diplomacy in the Middle East and South Asia.* Santa Monica, Calif.: RAND, 2007.

Krepon, Michael, and Dan Caldwell. *The Politics of Arms Control Treaty Ratification.* New York: Palgrave Macmillan, 1992.

Larsen, Jeffrey A., ed. *Arms Control.* Boulder, Colo.: Lynne Rienner, 2002.

———. "Neo-Arms Control in the Bush Administration." *Disarmament Diplomacy* 80 (Autumn 2005): 49–54.

———. "Arms Control and the Obama Administration: Coming in from the Cold." *Strategic Insights* 8 (April 2009), www.nps.edu/Academics/centers/ccc/publications/OnlineJournal/2009/Apr/larsenApr09.html.

Larsen, Jeffrey A., and Gregory J. Rattray, eds. *Arms Control Toward the 21st Century.* Boulder, Colo.: Lynne Rienner, 1996.

Larsen, Jeffrey A., and James M. Smith. *Historical Dictionary of Arms Control and Disarmament.* Lanham, Md.: Scarecrow, 2005.

Larsen, Jeffrey A., and James J. Wirtz, eds. *Arms Control and Cooperative Security.* Boulder, Colo.: Lynne Rienner, 2009.

Levi, Michael A., and Michael E. O'Hanlon. *The Future of Arms Control.* Washington, D.C.: Brookings Institution, 2005.

Lindemyer, Jeff. "Memorandum to President-Elect Obama: A New Arms Control and Non-proliferation Agenda." Washington, D.C.: Center for Arms Control and Non-proliferation, June 2008, www.policyarchive.org/bitstream/handle/10207/11816/Memorandum%20to%20President-elect%20Obama%20%20A%20New%20Arms%20Control%20and%20Non-Proliferation%20Agenda.pdf?sequence=1.

Platt, Alan. *The Politics of Arms Control and the Strategic Balance.* Santa Monica, Calif.: RAND, 1982.

Schelling, Thomas, and Morton Halperin. *Strategy and Arms Control.* New York: Twentieth Century Fund, 1961.

Schultz, George P., William J. Perry, Henry A. Kissinger, and Sam Nunn. "A World Free of Nuclear Weapons," *Wall Street Journal,* January 4, 2007, http://online.wsj.com/article/SB116787515251566636.html.

Sims, Jennifer E. *Icarus Restrained: An Intellectual History of Nuclear Arms Control 1945–1960.* Boulder, Colo.: Westview, 1990.

Trachtenberg, Marc. "Arms Control: Thirty Years On." *Daedalus: Journal of the American Academy of Arts and Sciences* 120 (Winter 1991): 203–216.

Woolf, Amy F., Mary Beth Nikitin, and Paul K. Kerr. *Arms Control and Nonproliferaiton: A Catalog of Treaties and Agreements.* CRS Report for Congress no. RL33865. Washington, D.C.: Congressional Research Service, February 10, 2009.

Arms Race

An *arms race* is generally understood as a process of competitive acquisition of weaponry. The domestic and international forces driving an arms race may be as era-defining as global ideological rivalry or as idiosyncratic as the preferences of an admiral's spouse, but evidence of hostility between the racers is a definitional requirement, usually including an assertion on each side that the buildups are necessary because of the growing arsenal of the opponent.

Arms racers are often pairs of nation-states, but interactive arming may occur also between alliances, within nation-states, between armed services, within armed services, or among nonstate actors. One example of complex interactions among more than two nation-states is trilateral arming among China, the United States and the Soviet Union during the cold war era. Arms racing may precede war, substitute for war, or grow out of unresolved issues following war, but as a rule, weapons production during wartime is not considered arms racing.

Races are identified by the names of the participants (e.g., U.S.-Soviet Arms Race) as well as by the nature of the weaponry (e.g., the nuclear arms race). Arms races also may be distinguished according to whether they are essentially qualitative or quantitative. Qualitative arms racing means that participants compete to develop higher *quality, more effective* arsenals. Qualitative races are characterized by weapons whose accuracy, range, and lethality change quickly and by rapid research and development of new weapons technologies. Quantitative racing is competition in *numbers* of existing weaponry. Arms control specialists find that quantitative races are easier to limit by agreement than qualitative races. Rapidly moving qualitative races also facilitate agreement, but only in obsolescent technologies.

CONCEPTUALIZATIONS

Arms races are conceptualized in several ways. One view is that arms racing can be understood as a mechanistic process like the motion of billiard balls but capable of generating unanticipated and undesired effects such as World War I (1914–1918), or a nuclear war catalyzed by a crisis. Other analysts see arms racing as tacit but intelligent communication, in which acquisition of weapons systems becomes a coded conversation. This view assumes that adversaries know and understand each other's political goals and that new weaponry becomes reasonably well known on both sides, perhaps by open testing.

A policy instrument conceptualization views arms racing as a device to achieve political-economic goals, foreign and domestic, deliberately and rationally. Arms racing also may be conceived as a less rational result of internal bureaucratic forces: domestic political and economic bargaining, competition among military services, incremental decision making, and failure to discard old programs, such as the U.S. horse cavalry. In this view the arms buildup is a result of a military-industrial complex grafted onto the legislature. Large-scale weapons systems are seen as fruit of a patronage system and may have little to do with the outside world. Choice of adversary is then mostly a historical accident and may be altered to meet domestic political, including electoral, needs.

Some scholars, such as Brian Eslea (1985), understand arms racing in part or in whole as an aberrant consequence of psychological pressures on decision making, so that racing is propelled by misperception, genuine psychopathology, or imperatives of gender on decision making. Larger theoretical arguments about interstate conflict dynamics have posited a role for competitive armaments processes in catastrophe theory, in the intersection of competition for resources and political alliances as well as in escalation of disputes to crises and thence to war. The fact that arms races often originate in or precipitate territorial disputes leads to the inclusion of contiguity (close proximity, usually understood as a shared border) and geostrategic data in many explanations.

EXAMPLES OF ARMS RACES

Soviet Union-United States, 1948–1989

Israel-rejectionist states, various dates; e.g., 1957–1966

India-Pakistan, various; 1957–1964

Chile-Peru, 1868–1879

England-Germany, 1898–1914

ARE ARMS RACES RISKY?

Under what circumstances is arms racing dangerous? When is it stabilizing? Deterrence theorists assert that some arms races contribute to conflict stabilization, hence to peace (deterrence stability). Intriligator and Brito argue (1984) that for some constellations of weaponry, racing leads to peace. Power equilibrium hypotheses and power transition arguments also can be developed in which military power is used to restore balance and order. Similar arguments apply to horizontal proliferation as potentially stabilizing. Racing also may preserve peace at least temporarily by substituting another arena for competition.

However, arms races may be deterrence-stable (in the sense that ratios of weapons remain constant while the arsenals grow),

while being neither mechanically stable, nor crisis-stable. Arms races may then be war precursors in the long term because mechanical instability can occur within deterrence stability or other forms of stability.

Some types of arms races are probably more hazardous than others. Observers cannot avoid the conclusion that racing in weapons of mass destruction (WMD)—chemical, biological, nuclear, radiological—is inherently dangerous. Arms racing in nuclear weapons is risky even if tightly controlled, simply because of the inevitable environmental contamination before, during, and after the arms race, and because of the risks of accidental detonation, loss, theft, and diversion. As weapons proliferate, into whose hands they may devolve becomes a more urgent question. The specter of the "terrorist" use of WMD looms large, but it should not obscure the risk that status quo powers themselves may not be reasonable users of WMD.

Does arms racing itself risk interstate war? Arms racing may be perilous because it can be a method of maximizing arsenals before initiating a war (risk of a long and severe war). Alternatively, arms racing may be misunderstood by a potential adversary as signaling imminent attack when none is intended (risk of an accidental war). Arms racing from a position of notable inferiority may even invite preemptive attack (deterrence failure).

Arms racing is not typical nation-state behavior. Scholars come to contrasting conclusions about the political consequences of arms racing, depending on variations in their original assumptions, definitions of terms, conceptualizations, and initial political conditions. Outcomes are affected by dynamic factors such as power transitions and the type and form of the race and by specifics such as the nature of the weaponry, as well as the risks taken in deployment, such as instituting automatic launch-on-warning mechanisms. On balance, the risk posed by arms racing in general cannot be given a single answer.

The social science term *arms racing,* understood as unstable escalatory processes, is now established in the natural sciences as well, especially in the context of evolutionary theory. In biology, arms racing is understood as an interactive process of adaptive defense and offense, against pathogens, parasites or predators. For instance, in a predator-prey pair, racing prey animals evolve resistance to predator toxins, while predators evolve more effective poisons, capturing the social science concepts of dyadic relationships and action-reaction spirals.

See also *Arms Control; Cold War; Nuclear Club; Nuclear Proliferation and Nonproliferation.*

. . . . T. C. SMITH

BIBLIOGRAPHY

Bueno de Mesquita, Bruce, and David Lalman. "Arms Races and the Opportunity for Peace." *Synthese* 76 (December 2004): 263–283.

Choucri, Nazli, and Robert C. North. *Nations in Conflict: National Growth and International Violence.* San Francisco: W. H. Freeman, 1975.

Cohn, Carol. "Sex and Death in the Rational World of Defense Intellectuals," *Signs* 12 (Summer 1987): 687–718.

Dror, Yehezkel. *Crazy States: A Counterconventional Strategic Problem.* Millwood, N.Y.: Kraus, 1980.

Eslea, Brian. *Fathering the Unthinkable: Masculinity, Scientists and the Nuclear Arms Race.* Wolfeboro, N.H.: Longwood, 1985

Feshbach, Murray. *Ecological Disaster: Cleaning Up the Hidden Legacy of the Soviet Regime: A Twentieth Century Fund Report (Russia in Transition).* New York: Twentieth Century Foundation, 1994.

Gray, Colin. *The Soviet-American Arms Race.* Lexington, Mass.: Lexington Books, 1976.

Hoffman, David. *The Dead Hand: The Untold Story of the Cold War Arms Race and Its Dangerous Legacy.* New York: Doubleday, 2009.

Holsti, Ole. *Crisis Escalation War.* Montreal: McGill-Queen's University Press, 1972.

Holt, Robert, Brian L. Job, and Lawrence Markus. "Catastrophe Theory and the Study of War." *Journal of Conflict Resolution* 22 (June 1978): 171–208.

Huntington, Samuel. "Arms Races: Prerequisites and Results." *Public Policy* 7 (1958): 41–86.

Intriligator, Michael, and Dagobert Brito. "Can Arms Races Lead to the Outbreak of War?" *Journal of Conflict Resolution* 28 (March 1984): 63–84.

Klare, Michael. "The Next Great Arms Race." *Foreign Affairs* 72 (Summer 1993): 136–152.

Mintz, Alex, and Michael D. Ward. "The Political Economy of Military Spending in Israel." *American Political Science Review* 83 (June 1989): 521–533.

Richardson, Lewis F. *Arms and Insecurity: A Mathematical Study of the Causes and Origins of War.* Pittsburgh: Boxwood, 1960.

Singer, J. David, and Melvin Small. "Alliance Aggregation and the Onset of War 1815–1945." In *Quantitative International Politics: Insights and Evidence,* edited by J. David Singer, 247–286. New York: Free Press, 1968.

Smith, T. C. "Arms Race Instability and War." *Journal of Conflict Resolution* 24 (June 1980): 253–284.

Wallace, Michael. "Armaments and Escalation: Two Competing Hypotheses." *International Studies Quarterly* 26 (March 1982): 37–56.

Wright, Quincy. *A Study of War.* Chicago: University of Chicago Press, 1942.

York, Herbert. *Race to Oblivion.* New York: Simon and Schuster, 1970.

Zinnes, Dina A. "The Expression and Perception of Hostility in Pre-war Crisis: 1914." In *Quantitative International Politics: Insights and Evidence,* edited by J. David Singer, 85–119. New York: Free Press, 1968.

Arnold, Thurman Wesley

Thurman Arnold (1891–1969) was a lawyer, judge, law professor, political theorist, and assistant attorney general in charge of antitrust initiative in the Roosevelt administration. His two principal books are *The Symbols of Government* (1935) and *The Folklore of Capitalism* (1937).

Arnold contends that humans are primarily irrational, governed not by reason but by the need to tell stories and cast people into familiar roles in order to make sense of the world. Successful political action requires discovering the folklore of a people (including ideas, symbols, and ceremonial action) and advocating change within its context, to make new ideas seem like the fulfillment of old promises. Arnold's work is devoted to exposing the folklore that governed American life during the Great Depression (1929–1939), to pave the way for a new folklore that justified an American welfare state.

Arnold's theory focuses on the relationship between ideas and organizations. He argues that theory has no meaning apart from its attachment to organizations and that the primary purpose of theory is not to reflect truth but to provide morale. No organization can function for long without the legitimacy (and attendant morale) provided by its folklore. The ability of an organization to respond effectively to changing circumstances depends on the flexibility of that folklore to respond to tensions between original purposes and new obligations. Sometimes the tension is reconciled through elaborate ceremonies (Arnold's most famous detailed analysis of this is a look at the Sherman Antitrust Act of 1890) or the creation of sub-rosa institutions to meet needs not legitimated under the dominant folklore (e.g., bootlegging during Prohibition in the 1920s). Substantive change is possible only in times of institutional collapse, and even then innovation must account for the existential authority of the old folklore.

Arnold's principal works analyze the folklore behind political governance (the U.S. Constitution) and economic governance (capitalism). In *The Folklore of Capitalism,* generally regarded as his most important work, Arnold's central goal is to expose the business corporation in the United States as essentially a form of feudal government, a fact obscured by capitalist folklore. He accomplishes this through systematic analyses of the symbols of taxation, the personification of the corporation, and the nature of U.S. antitrust and corporate reorganization laws. Ultimately, Arnold attempts to justify an active welfare state and a regulatory apparatus that forces corporations to recognize their public obligations.

Folklore paved the way for Arnold's appointment in 1938 as assistant attorney general, in charge of the antitrust division. Arnold revolutionized the division, introducing new legal tactics and new ways of thinking about the role of trusts in American economic life. His goal was not to attack the size of corporations per se but the restraints of trade created by them that negated competition and harmed the consumer. Arnold enjoyed considerable success until the defense buildup during World War II (1939–1945) ended the political support for his initiatives. He resigned in 1943 and after a brief judgeship went on to found the law firm Arnold, Fortas & Porter.

See also *Antitrust Policy; New Deal.*

. . . .   BRIAN STIPELMAN

BIBLIOGRAPHY

Arnold, Thurman. *The Symbols of Government.* New Haven, Conn.: Yale University Press, 1935.

———. *The Folklore of Capitalism.* New Haven, Conn.: Yale University Press, 1937. Reprint, Frederick, Md.: Beard Books, 2000.

Aron, Raymond

Raymond-Claude-Ferdinand Aron (1905–1983) was a French scholar and journalist who, in postwar France, opposed the intellectual left.

Aron, the son of Gustave Aron, a Jewish law professor, studied at the Ecole Normale Superieure (ENS), the French academy for teachers, from 1924 to 1928. In 1928 Aron had the highest score on the aggregation in philosophy (a competitive civil service examination offered in France). He was awarded a doctorate in 1930.

In 1930, Aron went to Germany, where he was a lecturer at the University of Cologne until 1931 and a researcher from 1931 to 1933 at the Maison Academique in Berlin. He married Suzanne

Gauchon in 1933. Aron was awarded his doctorate during this time, completing his thesis on the philosophy of history.

With the rise of Adolph Hitler and anti-Semitism in Germany, Aron returned to France. He became a philosophy professor at the Lycee of Le Havre. He returned to Paris in 1934, becoming the secretary at the Center of Social Documentation at the ENS.

In 1939, Aron began teaching social philosophy at the University of Toulouse, but left to join the French Air Force when World War II (1939–1945) began. Following the fall of France in 1940, Aron escaped to London, where he became part of the Free French movement and the editor of their newspaper, *La France Libre*. He edited the paper until 1944.

Following the liberation, Aron returned to France to teach sociology at the Ecole Nationale d'Administration (ENA) and the Paris Institute of Political Studies. In 1955 he became a professor of political science as a member of the Faculty of Letters at the Sorbonne, a post he held until 1968. He was an opponent of the French student movement of May 1968. In 1970 he became a professor of sociology at the College de France.

In addition to his teaching, Aron became a columnist in 1947 for *Le Figaro*, a conservative daily newspaper. He wrote for the paper for thirty years, becoming one of the nation's leading columnists. When the paper was purchased by Robert Hersant, a conservative newspaper publisher allied with French President Valery Giscard d'Estaing, Aron resigned. He moved to *L'Express*, a weekly news magazine, where he wrote columns from 1977 until his death.

Aron's scholarship was in the fields of economics, philosophy, political science, and sociology. He wrote more than forty books during his lifetime, in which he supported the classical liberal tradition of freedom and private property, challenging the views of those on the ideological left, especially those of his classmate at the ENS, Jean-Paul Sartre.

In *The Opium of the Intellectuals* (published as *L'opium des intellectuels* in 1957), Aron's thesis was that Marxism is a "mental opium" and was based on false myths. In particular he noted the Marxist belief that history was progressive and liberating, although the Marx-inspired Soviet regime was based on totalitarian controls. The second Marxist myth he challenged was the role that philosopher Karl Marx assigned to the proletariat—that of the saviors of humanity; Aron contended that all most workers wanted was a middle class (bourgeoisie) standard of living.

Scholar Reed Davis notes that, in international relations, Aron subscribed to what he called "the idea of reason, an image of society that would truly be humanized." Aron hoped that the possibility of nuclear war would lead to an end to power politics.

See also *French Political Thought; Marx, Karl; Marxism; Sartre, Jean-Paul.*

. . . . JEFFREY KRAUS

BIBLIOGRAPHY

Anderson, Brian C. *Raymond Aron: The Recovery of the Political.* Lanham, Md.: Rowman and Littlefield, 1998.

Aron, Raymond. *The Opium of the Intellectuals.* London: Secker and Warburg, 1957.

———. *Memoirs: Fifty Years of Political Reflection.* Translated by George Holoch. New York: Holmes and Meier, 1990.

Colquhoun, Robert. *Raymond Aron.* Beverly Hills, Calif.: Sage, 1986.

Davis, Reed. "Liberalism and Cold War Diplomacy in the Thought of Raymond Aron." Paper presented at the annual meeting of the International Studies Association, March, 2006.

Mahoney, Daniel J. *The Liberal Political Science of Raymond Aron: A Critical Introduction.* Lanham, Md.: Rowman and Littlefield, 1992.

Arrow's Paradox

See *Voting Cycles and Arrow's Paradox.*

Articles of Confederation

The Articles of Confederation were the original constitution of the United States and were developed and adopted during the conflict with Great Britain. In 1776, the delegates of the thirteen colonies met as a Continental Congress to adopt the Declaration of Independence and plan the Revolutionary War (1776–1783). Led by John Dickinson of Delaware and Pennsylvania, the Congress formed a committee to draft the articles that would guide the new nation.

The document was ratified July 9, 1778, by ten of the original thirteen colonies. New Jersey later ratified the Articles of Confederation on November 26, 1778, and Delaware followed on February 23, 1779. Maryland ratified them two years later on March 1, 1781, after seeking concessions from several large states, including any claims on lands to Maryland's west. With the Revolutionary War's resolution in April 1783, numerous interest groups began to call for revision of the Articles.

Article II included the foundational principle of the document: "Each state retains its sovereignty, freedom, and independence, and every power, jurisdiction, and right, which is not by this Confederation expressly delegated to the United States, in Congress assembled." The Articles, thus, granted the national government limited powers and made it fiscally dependent on the former colonies, now states, which also controlled the militia.

The Articles constituted the U.S. Congress as a single branch of government, and each state selected congressional delegates, who voted as states, not as individuals. Measures needed nine of thirteen votes to pass Congress, but any fundamental alterations in national policy or changes to the Articles required a unanimous vote. Several attempts to change the Articles prior to the adoption of the new Constitution were prevented by a single state.

The weak central government created under the Articles contributed to significant financial trouble for the new nation because states could not be compelled to pay their debts. Without necessary resources, the government could not address economic and military challenges—from the encroachments of the British on the borders set by the Treaty of Paris (1783) to those of the Spanish on the southern borders of the United States and raids by Native Americans on the western frontier. The United States also possessed only limited power to regulate commerce and resolve tariff wars between the states. Inflation and an economic depression after the Revolutionary War led to new efforts to revise the Articles.

In January 1786, Virginia called for a meeting of the states in Annapolis to discuss modifying the Articles, but only five states attended. In 1787, the Congress convened in Philadelphia to draft amendments. Only Rhode Island did not attend. After determining that the Articles of Confederation were insufficient for guiding the new nation, the Philadelphia convention proposed a new constitution, and a protracted struggle between Federalists and Anti-Federalists erupted. Ratification presented an early constitutional crisis for the new republic, but after extensive debate, the U.S. Constitution was adopted in 1787.

See also *Checks and Balances; Constitutions and Constitutionalism.*

. . . . MICHAEL W. HAIL

BIBLIOGRAPHY

Articles of Confederation, n.d., www.state.gov/r/pa/ho/time/ar/91719.htm.

Bloom, Allan, ed. *Confronting the Constitution.* Washington, D.C.: AEI Press, 1990.

Bradford, Melvin E. *Original Intentions: On the Making and Ratification of the United States Constitution.* Athens: University of Georgia Press, 1993.

Jensen, Merrill. *The Articles of Confederation: An Interpretation of the Social-Constitutional History of the American Revolution.* Madison: University of Wisconsin Press, 1970.

McDonald, Forest. *Novus Ordo Seclorum: The Intellectual Origins of the Constitution.* Lawrence: University of Kansas Press, 1985.

Asian American Identity and Groups

The term *Asian American* originated as a political statement. Inspired by other social movements of the era, activists of the late 1960s and early 1970s coined the term to reflect a new identity. An example of what Michael Omi and Howard Winant, in their 2007 work *Racial Formation in the New Millennium,* have labeled a racial formation, this Asian American identity was a declaration of self-determination and part of an effort to overcome oppression. The story of that identity is an ongoing one that can relay much about the power of race in the United States.

THE EMERGENCE OF AN ASIAN AMERICAN IDENTITY

Americans with ancestral roots in Asia had often been called *orientals,* but there was little sense of a common—a panethnic—identity among them before the 1960s. In some cases, there had even been concerted efforts at ethnic "disidentification." For instance, many Japanese Americans worked to disassociate themselves from Chinese Americans during intense anti-Chinese campaigns in the late nineteenth century, and many Chinese Americans returned the favor when public hatred of the Japanese reached a fever pitch during the 1940s. These efforts were to little avail, however. Although the initial restrictive immigration laws, such as the Chinese Exclusion Act (1882) had originally named specific nationalities, over time, all Americans of Asian ancestry found themselves the targets of discriminatory treatment.

Realizing this, 1960s activists began to call themselves Asian Americans. Because there had been little immigration from Asia for more than three decades, young adults were usually the grandchildren of immigrants, and for these third-generation youth, similarities between subgroups greatly overshadowed the differences. While those differences had been important to their immigrant grandparents, the younger generation had a very different frame of reference. For them, the "homeland" was the United States, where they experienced prejudice that did not distinguish between Asian subgroups. Japanese Americans, for example, subject to the derogatory term *chinks* (a slur at the Chinese) recognized that bigots cared little for ethnic distinctions. Many came to believe that Chinese, Japanese, Koreans, and others of Asian ancestry should emphasize a common, *panethnic* identity: Asian American.

Superficially, *Asian American* resembled the older *oriental* category, but the differences were substantial. *Oriental* was little more than a descriptive category and had not served as a unifying idea that could draw individuals of different ancestries together. *Asian American,* on the other hand, was explicitly promoted as a collective identity, emphasizing the shared experiences and geographical roots experiences of all Asian-ancestry Americans. To proclaim an Asian American identity was to assert the power to define oneself, which many activists emphasized by calling theirs a "yellow power" movement. Although *yellow power* faded as a rallying cry, an Asian American identity spread rapidly.

THE NEW IMMIGRATION AND THE TRANSFORMATION OF ASIAN AMERICA

As this new identity was growing, dramatic changes in immigration created new challenges. In 1965, the Hart-Celler Act repealed the national origins quotas that had greatly favored western and northern Europeans, replacing them with family reunification preferences that ended an era in which race served as a central component to immigration policy. This created much greater opportunity for Asian immigration, much of it coming from areas that had not previously sent large numbers to the United States. Wars in Korea and Southeast Asia also created connections through which increasing numbers of newcomers would move to the United States. The result was rapid growth and diversification of the Asian American population, so that by 2000, Japanese Americans, who had been the largest subgroup in 1970, had been surpassed by Chinese, Filipino, (Asian) Indian, Korean, and Vietnamese Americans. Asian Americans as a group had grown from less than 1 percent in 1970 to a little over 4 percent of the total population by 2000.

Immigration also brought great socioeconomic diversity. From 50 to 60 percent of Cambodian, Hmong, and Laotian Americans had less than a high school diploma in 2000, while more than 40 percent of Chinese, Filipino, Indian, Japanese, and Korean Americans had a bachelor's degree or higher, with the percentage reaching a stunning 64 percent for Asian Indians (in all cases, figures are for individuals twenty-five or older).

Perhaps most importantly, immigration transformed the Asian American population into one that was predominantly foreign-born—almost two-thirds, according to Census 2000. Thus, for a substantial number of Asian Americans, their sense of identity was likely to be shaped by experiences in another country. Third-generation Asian Americans, who were the driving force behind the creation of an Asian American identity, were by the mid-2000s a distinct minority. Can a panethnic identity survive in a population that does not have the shared experiences that characterized Asian America in the mid-1960s?

THE FUTURE OF AN ASIAN AMERICAN IDENTITY

A common identity may survive, but not unchanged. The Pilot National Asian American Political Survey (PNAAPS) found that half or more of each Asian subgroup surveyed identified panethnically at times, but immigrants and their children were more likely to identify first in ethnic terms—such as being a Korean or a Vietnamese American. But, although they usually identified primarily in ethnic terms, around half of all PNAAPS respondents expressed a sense of linked fate—meaning what happens to other Asian American groups would affect them as well—and felt that Asian Americans shared a common culture.

This sense of interconnected fates creates bonds that strengthen panethnic identification. Common problems can be more effectively combated when Asian American subgroups form a coalition, and a panethnic identity can make coalition-building easier. Subgroups will not always coexist peacefully, but they sometimes will find it in their interest to join together.

If the children and grandchildren of immigrants find growing acceptance in society, however, an Asian American identity may not take deep root. The more that Asian Americans can move into all ranks of society, the more likely it is that their ethnic or panethnic identity will recede in importance and become an option that they will exercise or ignore as they wish.

If Asian Americans continue to be viewed as foreigners, however—even when their families have lived in the United States for three or more generations—they would have little choice but to embrace a separate identity. A strengthening Asian American panethnicity would be evidence that racial distinctions continue to carve deep divisions within American society.

See also *Coalition Formation; Identity, Politics of; Immigration, Effects on Intergroup Relations; Pan-ethnicity; Racial Discrimination.*

. . . . ANDREW L. AOKI

BIBLIOGRAPHY

Espiritu, Yen Le. *Asian American Panethnicity: Bridging Institutions and Identities.* Philadelphia: Temple University Press, 1992.

Hing, Bill Ong. *Making and Remaking Asian America through Immigration Policy, 1850–1990.* Stanford, Conn.: Stanford University Press, 1993.

Lien, Pei-et, M. Margaret Conway, and Janelle Wong. *The Politics of Asian Americans: Diversity and Community.* New York: Routledge, 2004.

Omi, Michael, and Howard Winant. *Racial Formation in the New Millenium,* 3rd ed. New York: Routledge, 2007.

Reeves, Terance J., and Claudette E. Bennett. "We the People: Asians in the United States." *Census 2000 Special Reports.* Washington, D.C.: U.S. Census Bureau, 2004.

Asian Political Thought

Asian political thought is political thought produced, shaped, and adapted to explain, justify, or reform political conditions within the cultures throughout Asia. These highly diverse traditions of political thought are contrasted with the rights-based political thought associated with the traditions of classical and modern liberal thought that has its geographical center in western Europe and North America. Whereas the rights-based traditions of the Atlantic community tend to emphasize the individual, democracy, and economic liberty, Asian political thought is viewed to favor the community, rulership and guidance by spiritual or political elites, and social purposes over economic rights.

The richness of both the Asian and Atlantic traditions makes these generalizations the target of scholarly and political criticism, but some political elites and political scientists have found these generalizations useful for political, research, or explanatory purposes. An understanding of what Asian political thought means for modern political science can be gathered by exploring the approach Western scholarship has taken to Asian political thought, surveying the religious traditions behind Asian political thought, examining the encounter of Asia with the West and the impact of Western dominance on Asian political thought, chronicling the Asian reaction to Western imperialism and decolonization, and assessing the impact of globalization on Asian political thought.

WESTERN ORIENTALISM

Greek historian Herodotus made the first known mention of the continent of Asia in his writings. The Persians, the first Asians by this reckoning, were characterized as loving freedom too little in comparison with the Greeks. The general tone of Herodotus' reflections would later reverberate throughout Western scholarship on Asia. The most notable thinkers who focused on Asia as a place lacking freedom were German philosophers Georg Friedrich Wilhelm Hegel and Karl Marx. Hegel viewed Asia as the place where only the despot was free. Marx identified the Asiatic mode of production as being a mode of production that differed from feudalism based on the centralized control of the modes of production associated with irrigation agriculture. German American historian Karl Auguste Wittfogel built upon Marx's theory. Wittfogel argued that the bureaucracies that were essential to Asia's irrigation works and managing large hydraulic works crushed civil society and resulted in a mode of government he called "oriental despotism." He contended that modern communist societies followed the model of oriental despotism and would be even more repressive.

Not all European understandings of Asian culture were so negative. Jesuit missionaries found much that was admirable in Chinese and Japanese society and tried to reconcile the secular religion of Confucianism with Christianity. The Vatican rejected these attempts; the Magisterium, the governing body of the Catholic Church, found ancestor worship to be incompatible with Christianity. The Catholic condemnation of Confucianism commended Confucianism to freethinking Enlightenment intellectuals such as German philosopher and mathematician Gottfried Leibniz and French writer Voltaire as a nontheocratic source of ethical behavior and social order. French physician and writer Francois Bernier found within the Chinese tradition a model of an ethically justifiable and practical absolutist government that resonated with the European practice of absolute monarchy exemplified by Louis XIV. Interestingly, Bernier, who spent time in the Mughal Empire, characterized India as a plurality of what would today be described as kleptocracies.

Palestinian American literary critic Edward Said's concept of *orientalism* addressed the tendency to idealize or demonize Asian societies. Said, a scholar focusing on western Asia, identified Western images of the Orient to be tools in an imperialistic project of domination. Owing much to French postmodernist philosopher Michel Foucault, Said saw the process of knowledge production as intimately related to the quest for power. The image of the other, from this perspective, may have very little to do with the reality of the other, but is instead a reflection of needs of the one creating the image. According to this view, the accumulation of knowledge of Western societies about Asia may tell us less about Asian political realities than the role Asia played for Western societies as an enemy or an idealized other.

Bernard Lewis, a prominent scholar of western Asia who has been criticized as a practitioner of orientalism by Said, argues that Said is overblown in his characterization of Western efforts to produce knowledge about Asia as aiding and abetting imperialism. Instead of being rooted in the project of imperialism, the quest for knowledge about Asia is rooted in the project of humanism. A rejection of religious dogma lay at the foundation of humanism and opened the way to explore other cultures. Lewis characterizes Said's efforts to bring into question the efforts of Westerners to understand other cultures as a form of *intellectual protectionism* that would reserve discourse about a culture to those within the boundaries of that culture alone.

Some political science scholars such as Lucian Pye and Samuel Huntington have tried to use political culture as a means of explaining political behavior. These efforts have roots in the Western social science tradition beginning with German sociologist and political economist Max Weber's analysis of how different religious belief systems would either hinder or facilitate the development of capitalism. Weber found both Hinduism and Confucianism to contain aspects that worked against the rationalization process necessary for the development of capitalism.

From Weber and his intellectual heirs' perspective, the ideas of a culture manifest themselves in the social psychology of a society and have serious impact on political and economic outcomes. For example, Pye has worked on a nuanced exploration of theories of power and authority to uncover how a preference for authoritarian government interacts with different family structures in various Asian cultures. From a similar perspective emphasizing culture, Huntington has attempted to develop a theory of global politics with civilizations at the center of managing world order. Huntington's thesis brings into doubt the universal validity of Western conceptions of human rights and democratic governance. Concerns about limited government and individual liberty are construed to be the product of a unique Western political heritage.

In contrast to the line of reasoning pursued by the scholars mentioned above, Amartya Sen, an Indian Nobel Prize winner in economics, has been highly critical of the narratives that have associated Asian values with authoritarianism and Western civilization with freedom. He insists that a more careful examination of history will reveal lines of reasoning amicable with a universal value of freedom in Hindu, Buddhist, Confucian, and Islamic traditions. For Sen, universal values are possible, and Asian political thought is diverse enough that it is a misguided enterprise to characterize it as radically different from the political traditions of the West. Instead, Sen would have us seek the foundations of a universal ethic in the human quest for freedom.

THE ROOTS OF ASIAN ORDER

Sen's search for a universal ethic needs to contend with the great diversity of ontological and political assumptions contained within the traditions of Asian political thought. The briefest examinations of east, south, and west Asian thought reveal substantial differences in worldviews.

Many scholars, such as Roger Ames and David Hall, view Chinese political thought as being radically immanent. This approach to politics puts a premium on maximizing the value of the constituent parts of a political community without a transcendent source of order or appraisal, such as a God separate from the cosmos. *Confucianism, Taoism,* and *Legalism* represent different ways of achieving political order within this radically immanent context.

Confucianism emphasized rituals, relationships, and humanity as the source of social harmony and contended that the sage must widen the cosmos by realizing humanity through creative actions. Taoism took a critical stance toward the artificial order proposed by the Confucians and taught that a path of not-knowing and not-doing would better preserve a harmonious social balance. The legalists approached the problem of order from a less subtle approach to social harmony and argued for the judicious use of punishments and rewards to secure political order.

Throughout Chinese history, a hybrid of Confucian and legalist principles dominated the massive bureaucracy put in place to administer the empire. Mandarins, scholarly elites selected through a competitive testing process, filled the positions of this bureaucracy from the Han Dynasty (206 BCE to 220 CE) down through the end of the Qing Dynasty (1644–1912). The Confucian ideology also made inroads into Japan, Korea, and Vietnam, forming an important part of the intellectual superstructure of those societies up to the present.

If the Chinese worldview is radically immanent, *Hinduism* can be appropriately classified as a radically transcendent worldview with some important consequences for the sociopolitical world. The Hindu faith focuses on the ultimate

L. K. Advani, president of India's Bharatiya Party, sits below a poster of the influential Bhagavad Gita. The ancient Hindu text serves as a foundation for political authority in Asian political thought, with its insistence that a ruler follow his or her duty wherever it leads.

SOURCE: AP Images

purpose of human life as being the achievement of *moksha,* or liberation from an endless cycle of rebirths. Rebirths are caused by *karma* that will bring one either closer or farther away from this ultimate goal. Following the *dharma* (law) of one's *varna* (caste)—whether *Brahmins* (priests), *Kshastriyas* (warriors and rulers), *Vaishyas* (merchants, artisans, and cultivators), or *Sudras* (workers)—is essential to making progress toward liberation.

This transcendently grounded vision of Hinduism allowed for a highly realistic, power-centered approach to politics to emerge, exemplified by the political thinker Kautilya, the alleged author of the *Arthashastra* and adviser to Chandragupta, the founder of the Mauryan dynasty (322–185 BCE). Contemporaneous texts, such as the *Bhagavad Gita,* strengthened this bias by making it clear that a ruler must follow his duty wherever it leads him. This Hindu understanding of rulership spread

throughout Southeast Asia only to be blended with Buddhist and Islamic worldviews as a foundation for political authority.

Buddhism, a reform movement within Hinduism that minimized the importance of the caste system and focused more intently on achieving liberation from suffering through enhancing awareness, was the vehicle by which Chinese, Japanese, Korean, Southeast Asian, and Tibetan civilizations were exposed to a radically transcendent vision of liberation. The Chinese would prove to be exceptionally adept at adapting this transcendent message for the purposes of meeting the demands of the immanent world through the Mahayana variation of the Buddha's path. This tradition, unlike Theravada Buddhism that became prominent in Southeast Asia, down-played the other worldly aspects of Buddhism along with monasticism as the sole source of enlightenment and emphasized finding enlightenment in the here and now through living ordinary life. The Buddhist message proved to be attractive and found wide acceptance in Japan and Korea. By providing a comprehensive approach to deal with the suffering of individuals, Buddhism in its various guises played a powerful role as a tool for quelling the discontent that could cause social disorder.

Unlike the Buddha's path of liberation, an act of submission to a revealed authority grounds Islam. Muhammad, the seal of the prophets, disclosed through his actions, sayings, and recitation of God's word revealed in the Quran, God's will regarding the order of human community. The *sharia,* or Islamic law, spread itself through the swords and trade networks of the faithful. Revelation and the intimacy of God's rulership of his followers offered clarity of insight into the divine will. This insight into the divine will made conflict with idolatrous communities a religious duty rather than a simple question of political and economic gain. The interpretation of God's law is the core of Islamic political thought.

The faith of Islam spread to South Asia and, through its encounter with the unyielding infidels, the Hindus, Islam learned a tolerance uncharacteristic of a purist application of God's word. This tolerance facilitated the spread of Islam throughout Southeast Asia mostly through trade networks as opposed to the sword. Threats to Islamic and Hindu identities would result in a revival of conflicts as elites attempted to reassert their group's cohesion.

The interactions of Asian belief systems demonstrate both plasticity and form. The dynamism of this process makes it difficult to assess the potential of a thought system's ability to yield solutions to any set of emerging political problems and makes the study of the political effects of these traditions highly dependent upon context. Sometimes a lack of attractive institutional structures opened the door for another worldview to expand its influence as the earlier Buddhist communities did against a relatively ossified Hinduism. Sometimes the failure to adjust to a changing environment resulted in the elimination of a political community and worldview, as was the case of the Buddhist community in India during the Islamic invasions. Authority, community, and creative responses to challenges were central to the spread and survival of Asian political traditions.

ENCOUNTER WITH THE WEST AND WESTERN DOMINANCE

As the European states reached out to Asia in the sixteenth century, they encountered a world of greater wealth, population, and resources than the world from which they came. Trading outposts and missionaries would play an important role in giving Europeans access to the markets of China, India, Japan, and Southeast Asia, and thereby to the center of global power at that time, even as the core civilizations of the region looked upon the Europeans as barbarians from the sea.

Fragmented political organization allowed the Europeans to establish footholds throughout Asia, taking advantage of local rivalries as best they could. The Dutch established themselves in Indonesia; the Spanish established themselves in the Philippines; and the English, French, and Portuguese battled for influence in India. Dutch, English, and Portuguese interests initially penetrated Japan, but in response to a perceived threat from foreign powers, the Tokugawa Shogunate closed off contact with the European world with the exception of limited access for the Dutch. China's great centralized bureaucracy effectively managed European relations on its own terms.

By 1800, European states had substantial influence over 35 percent of the globe. By the beginning of the twentieth century, European powers had gained control of 85 percent of the globe, with only Ethiopia, Iran, Japan, Siam, Turkey, and the nations of North and South America retaining independence. Political and religious divisions within India eventually enabled the British to incorporate it into the British Empire by the time Queen Victoria became Empress of India in 1858. The French gained a dominant foothold in Indo-China by 1857. China's defeat by the British in the Opium Wars (1839–1842 and 1856–1860) and the establishment of a series of unequal treaties combined with a series of internal crises such as the Taiping, Muslim, and Bandit rebellions weakened the Qing dynasty so substantially that the dynasty collapsed by 1911. In 1854, Japan was opened up to Western trade by the Black Ships of Commodore Matthew Perry of the United States and began a path of modernization that would enable it to join the European powers in the game of imperialism.

REACTION TO THE WEST AND THE SEARCH FOR A MODERN IDENTITY

China's reaction to the challenge of the West was slow. Traditional Confucian teachings prevailed through the 1860s. Success in subduing the major rebellions threatening the Qing dynasty supported a belief in the effectiveness and vitality of the received tradition. From the 1860s to the 1890s, China embraced a *ti-yung* reformism that emphasized preserving the essence (*ti*) of Chinese culture while using the contrivances (*yung*) of Western culture to strengthen the dynasty by building arsenals and railroads. The defeat by Japan in the Sino-Japanese War (1894–1895) led to a movement focused on reinterpreting Chinese essence. Reformers such as Kang Youwei and his student, Liang Qichao, argued that the essence of Confucianism was the ability to manage change.

They led efforts to help China evolve into a constitutional monarchy, but an alliance of the empress dowager and a variety of conservative forces across the nation stopped these reform efforts.

The revolution of 1911 overthrew the Qing Dynasty and ushered in an era that would reject Confucianism completely in favor of Western ideas. The writings of Lu Xun, which characterized Confucianism as a form of cannibalism and embraced an evolutionary metaphor, capture the rejection of tradition. In his political thought, revolutionary Chinese leader Sun Yat-sen attempted to implement principles of government based on such influences as Charles Darwin, the British Fabians, Alexander Hamilton, Henry George, Abraham Lincoln, Marxism, and a variety of other Western and non-Western resources as a means of resisting Western imperialism. A decidedly nonliberal view played a more important role in formulating the ideology that dominated China's future. Marxist-Leninist thinkers such as Li Dazhao and Chen Duxiu played an important role in formulating this ideology.

Japan embraced Western ideas more quickly than China. This embrace had much to do with the quick overthrow of the Tokugawa Shogunate and the restoration of the Emperor Meiji as the center of the Japanese state. Thinkers such as Fukuzawa Yukichi laid the foundation of Western learning, but practical political leaders would imitate Western constitutional, industrial, and military institutions to set Japan on the path of modernization.

The Japanese defeat of Russia in the Russo-Japanese War in 1905 signaled to the colonized people of Asia that the Europeans were not invincible. Japan's experiment with constitutional government wrestled unsuccessfully with military and industrial forces, setting the country on an ultranationalistic path. Kita Ikki, Okakura Kakuzo, and Shumei Okawa, as well as philosophers associated with the Kyoto school, framed this imperial path in terms of a Pan-Asian crusade against Western colonial powers. Japan's efforts to build an Asian Co-Prosperity Sphere, a regional order with Japan replacing the European powers as the center of authority, ultimately failed as a function of its own colonial mismanagement and the superior industrial and military strength of its enemies. A constitution of American design implemented with a Japanese sensibility replaced the emperor system that blended the Japanese traditions of Confucianism, Shinto, and Zen, with extreme nationalism.

English dominance of South Asia spawned a nationalist movement seeking to return to a genuinely Hindu identity. Figures in this movement included a wide range of political thinkers and actors such Vivekananda, Sri Aurobindo, Savarkar, Rabindranath Tagore, and Mohandas Gandhi. The nature of this identity varied according to its interpreter. Savarkar focused on the revival of the warrior spirit. Rabindranath Tagore advocated a cosmopolitanism rejecting all nationalisms. Gandhi embraced the doctrine of *satyagraha,* a nonviolent approach to overcoming injustice. Gandhi's philosophy played a central role in securing India its independence from Great Britain.

The separation from Great Britain did not separate South Asia from the political thought dominating Western political discourse at that time. Jawaharlal Nehru, the first prime minister of India, embraced liberalism and socialism as a means of finding a way for his society to make progress. A commitment to humanism and science molded the secular state that Nehru played such an important role in constructing. Socialist theory similarly influenced the Muslim majority areas of South Asia, but Pakistan embraced firmly its Islamic identity instead of secularism. Islamic countries in Southeast Asia followed similar paths.

Socialism had influence throughout the emancipating colonial world, but the more revolutionary ideology of Marxism-Leninism took center stage in various civil wars and wars of liberation. The victory of the communists in the Chinese civil war (1945–1949) empowered Mao Zedong to become a leading Asian Marxist theorist. Mao embraced a political pragmatism that enabled him to move from a Stalinist approach to heavy industrialization to an anarchistic decentralization during the Cultural Revolution (1966–1976). Revolutionaries such as Cambodia's Pol Pot, North Korea's Kim Il Sung, and Vietnam's Ho Chi Minh would wield Marxist concepts in a similarly creative fashion. These Marxist experiments to build new worlds had incredibly high human costs.

Academic theorists throughout Asia embraced more nuanced Marxist lenses to examine the problem of underdevelopment in the non-Western world. Japanese scholars such as Otsuka Hisao and Uno Kozo developed the foundations of world systems theory independently and simultaneously with the Western scholars Andre Gunder Frank and Immanuel Wallerstein. Economic and political events weakened the intellectual attractiveness of Marxist thought throughout Asia.

The economic success of states such as Hong Kong, Japan, Singapore, South Korea, and Taiwan, which embraced relatively liberal economic regimes, and the collapse of the socialist block in Europe raised serious questions about the effectiveness of socialism or Marxism to help developing countries to modernize. China and states in Southeast Asia began to experiment with market liberalization with positive effect. Though some of these states embraced democratization, China and Singapore, as well as others, remained skeptical about the value of the full range of civil liberties for social well-being.

GLOBALIZATION AND CONTEMPORARY CHALLENGES

The end of the cold war opened up the world to greater economic, social, and political integration underneath the emerging liberal international order. Francis Fukuyama's *The End of History and the Last Man* (1992) argued that the triumph of liberal democracy had ended the search for a comprehensive political ideology and, with that end, ushered in the final universal ideology. Doubts about the desirability of Western-style liberal democracy are the beginning of modern Asian political thought.

Asian leaders such as Singapore's first prime minister, Lee Kuan Yew; longtime Malaysian prime minister Mahathir Mohamad; Singapore scholar and diplomat Kishore Mahbubani; and others critiqued Western cultures as being disrespectful of authority, destructive to the family, too contentious, too concerned about individual civil liberties and not concerned enough about the rights of the community, and too dismissive of the role of elites in creating the conditions that would serve the economic and cultural needs of the community. These critics believed Asian values could cure these Western maladies. The economic success of the East Asian Tigers (Hong Kong, Singapore, South Korea, and Taiwan), Japan, Thailand, and Malaysia made many in the West find much to admire in these Asian values.

The Asian financial crisis of 1997 and 1998 revealed some of the weaknesses of the authority/family/community-based paradigm previously credited for the strength of Asian societies and economies. Concerns about cronyism, the stifling of innovation, and the inability of economies to respond to market conditions replaced previous admiration for social order, family values, and harmony.

In recent years, strong economic growth rates in India and China and the need to provide social stability in the midst of economic development have led some to look to the traditional cultures of Asia as an anchor in a storm. China's call for a "harmonious society" and its own "peaceful rise" in the global community most clearly owe a great deal to the traditional values of Confucianism. The role of Hindu nationalism in India, Buddhist nonviolence and social activism in Bhutan, Myanmar, Tibet, Thailand, and other historically Buddhist countries, and Islamic fundamentalism and the traditional and modern response to this phenomenon throughout Southeast Asia, just to name a few examples, make it evident that Asian political thought will continue to be an important and dynamic part of the Asian political landscape.

It is also important to note that Western scholars are mining the political traditions of Asia for materials to deal with contemporary political problems. Roger Ames and David Hall find common ground between the Confucian tradition and the thought of the American pragmatist and progressive John Dewey to help further a universal democratic project. Peter Hershock looks inside the Buddhist tradition and demonstrates the relevance of the conceptions of karma and emptiness for a full spectrum of public policy problems. Daniel Bell explores the different meanings of human rights in a Western and east Asian context. Richard Nisbett examines the foundations for how Westerners and east Asians perceive the world differently. His work lends scientific credibility to those who discern profoundly different approaches to political and social problems in the various cultural regions—even as he affirms the possibility of the convergence of Western and Eastern values.

Asian critics of the Asian values thesis, such as former South Korean president Kim Dae Jung and former Taiwan president, Lee Teng-hui, give credence to Nisbett's hypothesis about convergence. These advocates of democracy perceive the Asian values argument as a means of attacking fundamental human rights and perceive these rights to exist in the broader intellectual heritages of their respective civilizations. Coming into this debate at the liberal end of liberal democracy, Chinese political scientist Liu Junning perceives parallels between the Chinese philosophical tradition of Taoism and the Western classical liberal tradition. A growing classical liberal think-tank movement throughout the Asia Pacific region demonstrates the practical basis for such theoretical endeavors. Just as classical liberal ideas have Asian allies and advocates, progressive strains of Western thought focused on environmentalism and global justice find resonance among local activists such as Thai activist Sulak Sivaraksa, who argues that Buddhist ethical teachings require advocacy for the rights of indigenous peoples that are in alignment with these broader social movements. If the present multicultural intellectual climate is preserved, the cross-fertilization of political ideas likely will yield regionally interesting hybrids of Western and Asian political thought, even if it fails to produce a homogenous political thought grounded in a universal conception of human rights.

See also *Asia Pacific Region Politics and Society; Buddhist Political Thought; Chinese Political Thought; Confucian Political Thought; Gandhism; Hindu Political Thought; Islamic Political Thought; Kautilya; Kita Ikki; Lu Xun; Oriental Despotism; Pye, Lucian; Satyagraha; Uno Kozo; Weber, Max.*

. . . . TODD MYERS

BIBLIOGRAPHY
Ames, Roger, and David Hall. *The Democracy of the Dead: Dewey, Confucius, and the Hope for Democracy in China.* Chicago: Open Court, 1999.
Angle, Stephen C. *Human Rights and Chinese Thought: A Cross-Cultural Inquiry.* Cambridge: Cambridge University Press, 2002.
Aydin, Cemil. *The Politics of Anti-Westernism in Asia: Visions of World Order in Pan-Islamic and Pan-Asian Thought.* New York: Colombia University Press, 2007.
Barlow, Tani E. *New Asian Marxisms.* Durham, N.C.: Duke University Press, 2002.
Barr, Michael D. *Cultural Politics and Asian Values: The Tepid War.* London: Routledge, 2002.
Bell, Daniel A. *Beyond Liberal Democracy: Political Thinking for an East Asian Context.* Princeton, N.J.: Princeton University Press, 2006.
———. *China's New Confucianism: Politics and Everyday Life in a Changing Society.* Princeton, N.J.: Princeton University Press, 2008.
Berger, Mark T. *The Battle for Asia: From Decolonization to Globalization.* London: Routledge, 2003.
Bruun, Ole, and Michael Jacobsen, eds. *Human Rights and Asian Values: Contesting National Identities and Cultural Representations in Asia.* Richmond, U.K.: Curzon, 2000.
Clarke, John James. *Oriental Enlightenment: The Encounter between Asian and Western Thought.* London: Routledge, 1997.
Fukuyama, Francis. *The End of History and the Last Man.* New York: Free Press, 1992.
Gress, Daniel. *From Plato to NATO: The Idea of the West and Its Opponents.* New York: Free Press, 1998.
Heisig, James W, and John C. Maraldo, eds. *Rude Awakenings: Zen, the Kyoto School, and the Question of Nationalism.* Honolulu: University of Hawaii Press, 1995.
Hershock, Peter. *Buddhism in the Public Sphere: Reorienting Global Interdependence.* New York: Routledge, 2006.
Huntington, Samuel. *The Clash of Civilizations and the Remaking of World Order.* New York: Simon and Schuster, 1998.
Jensen, Lionel M. *Manufacturing Confucianism: Chinese Traditions and Universal Civilization.* Durham, N.C.: Duke University Press.
Loy, David. *A Buddhist History of the West: Studies in Lack.* Albany: State University Press of New York, 2002.

Mahbubani, Kishore. *Can Asians Think? Understanding the Divide between East and West.* Southroyalton, Vt.: Steerforth, 2002.
Nisbett, Richard E. *The Geography of Thought: How Asians and Westerners Think Differently . . . and Why.* New York: Free Press, 2003.
Pines, Yuri. *Envisioning Eternal Empire: Chinese Political Thought of the Warring States Era.* Honolulu: University of Hawaii Press, 2009.
Pye, Lucian W. *Asian Power and Politics: The Cultural Dimension of Authority.* Cambridge, Mass.: Belknap Press of Harvard University Press, 1985.
Sen, Amartya. *Development as Freedom.* New York: Anchor, 2000.
Sharma, Jyotirmay. *Hindutva: Exploring the Idea of Hindu Nationalism.* New York: Penguin Global, 2004.
Sivaraksa, Sulak. *Conflict, Culture, and Change: Engaged Buddhism in a Globalizing World.* Boston: Wisdom, 2005.
Williams, David. *Defending Japan's Pacific War: The Kyoto School Philosophers and Post-White Power.* New York: Routledge Courzon, 2004.

Asia Pacific Region Politics and Society

Scholars have recognized that, despite free elections, leaders in new democracies may not be accountable to their citizens. One reason for this is that the state apparatus is difficult to control. Authoritarian rulers use bureaucracies to pursue their objectives. In doing so they create complex institutional structures that are not necessarily brought to heel once elections occur and new governments are in place. The transition to democracy thus also involves a complex struggle over controlling the state apparatus and thereby enhancing accountability.

In posttransition Asia, politicians have chosen to pursue two primary types of proaccountability mechanisms, or reform paths: formalized/institutional and informal/social. The institutional mechanisms include laws such as Administrative Procedure Acts (APAs) that constrain the bureaucracy with various requirements when making policy, legislative oversight, and judiciaries. The social, societal, or informational mechanisms, in turn, include independent agencies, civil society organizations, and the media.

At their core, each of these mechanisms is about *sanctions.* National legislatures in Japan, South Korea, and Taiwan, for example, have passed APAs to open up central bureaucracies and their policy-making processes by legalizing and formalizing accountability measures. In each case, in addition to APAs, the judiciary also plays a crucial role, as politicians can decentralize monitoring of the bureaucracy by using judicial review of administrative actions (i.e., giving citizens the right to sue).

Another path that governments can take is increasing citizen participation through informal or social accountability mechanisms, through which citizens function as watchdogs, impose sanctions, and can even activate institutionalized punishment mechanisms. Interestingly, international organizations (IOs) such as the World Bank or foreign aid agencies such as U.S. Agency for International Development (USAID) have often supported such measures, which coincide with general decentralization efforts.

This entry presents the different ways that politicians try to restructure the state with the aim of increasing accountability. First the range of major mechanisms of control available to politicians, as discussed in the literature, is reviewed. Next comes discussion of the trends in their use in Asia during the past two decades. Then the disparate research programs that constitute the literature on state accountability and democratization are synthesized into a more coherent framework. The goal is to clarify the relationships between the actors and link them to the types of control mechanisms chosen to increase accountability.

THE ASIAN EXPERIENCE

Given the two main types of proaccountability measures—formalized/institutional and informal/social—where does Asia fit in? Asia is a fruitful region to study questions of accountability because the region includes states facing common problems unfolding within differing political institutional contexts. South Korea, for instance, had a large developmental state that had supported the maturation of the private sector, but at the expense of other concerns. Taiwan was similar to South Korea but with policies favoring a particular partisan constituent: the Kuomintang (KMT, the dominant party in Taiwan for fifty years until recently). The Philippines is somewhat different from either of these countries; even though its bureaucracy had been a source of patronage prior to transition, the executives continue to rely on it as a means of controlling their agents posttransition. What these three countries share in common is that leaders following democratic transitions faced a governance dilemma: how to rein in a central bureaucracy that had long favored a restricted set of interests? In all these cases, and as one can imagine in many other posttransition states, politicians face a similar problem of reorienting an entrenched bureaucracy. Thus, holding free and fair elections, while critical, only addresses the *representation* aspect of democracy but not necessarily the *responsiveness* aspect. After all, central bureaucracies are responsible for implementing laws that elected members of the legislature pass.

From the recent experiences of states in Asia, it is apparent that some states have more options than others. The choice of which reform path to follow appears to rest on two factors: capacity and institutional openness. Tom Ginsburg (2001) observes that states with significant preexisting bureaucratic capacity, such as Japan and Korea, face a choice concerning the degree to which they want to open the bureaucracy. States without strong bureaucratic systems—that is, those lacking high-capacity bureaucracies—seem to have opted for decentralization. This option appears especially popular in assuaging fears of corruption and carryover from autocratic regimes, because it physically moves the location of much of the bureaucratic interaction. Additionally, states pursuing decentralization are able to exploit international organization involvement—especially the World Bank—to help with decentralization and increasing social accountability.

The key cases of formal or institutional adopters are Japan, South Korea, and Taiwan. South Korea and Taiwan opened up their bureaucracies significantly, while Japan did so more modestly as a result of institutional constraints. The political tradeoff that these three states faced between more or less openness in an APA or Administrative Procedure Law (APL)

is very different from the challenges facing newly democratizing states such as the Indonesia and the Philippines. These states are more concerned with general governance issues. In cases like these, note Jose Edgardo Campos and Joel Hellman (2005), "the decision to decentralize is sparked by strong reactions to a prolonged period of highly authoritarian rule" (238).

But what specific measures have states adopted? Table 1 summarizes the key example countries for each of the major categories. Japan, South Korea, and Taiwan represent cases of formal, institutionalized accountability measures (or "vertical" accountability). South Korea and Taiwan have formally opened their bureaucracies much more extensively than Japan, which has used the APL primarily to delegate some monitoring functions to the courts. Indonesia and the Philippines have both followed a path of decentralization and increasing social accountability measures, largely with the aid of the World Bank. The Philippines is further down this path, given the length of time since transition, but Indonesia appears to be following suit.

It should be noted that in none of these cases are such measures fully effective at preventing politicians or bureaucrats from evading their intent. Perhaps it is inevitable that these measures will never live up to their full potential, but the amount of slack given and accepted is nonetheless noteworthy.

MINI COUNTRY REVIEWS

The remainder of this entry briefly looks at the various mechanisms used in posttransition Asia to increase accountability. As noted, Japan, South Korea, and Taiwan are the three best examples of heavily institutionalized mechanisms of control, whereas Indonesia and the Philippines, as well as India, to some extent, have followed a more decentralized, social accountability route, often with the help of organizations such as the World Bank. That said, it is important to bear in mind that even with laws on the books, some scholars remain skeptical about full implementation or full closure in all of these countries.

THE PHILIPPINES

The Philippines is a good example of the range and variety of measures leaders may undertake. The overthrow of the Marcos dictatorship in 1986 led to a major push for decentralization of Filipino politics. In 1991, the state undertook massive decentralization aimed at moving government downward—to create "responsive and accountable local governance structures." The government was not only responding to internal pressures for decentralization. The USAID also was pushing for decentralization in the Philippines, arguing that movement toward the local level is good for democracy. The World Bank also has been involved in supporting the use of the Citizen Report Card, as well as in promoting interaction and aid at the local level. It has identified local capacity building and performance monitoring as two areas of priority for its work at the local level.

In addition to these shifts, the Filipino government has implemented informal/social accountability mechanisms at all

TABLE 1: MAJOR EXAMPLES OF TYPES OF ACCOUNTABILITY MEASURES IN ASIA

FORMAL AND MORE OPEN	FORMAL AND LESS OPEN	DECENTRALIZED AND SOCIAL
South Korea, Taiwan	Japan	Philippines (early) Indonesia (late)

levels. Ombudsmen were introduced in 1994 and now exist at every level of local government. The key document in the Philippines is the Local Government Code of 1991. The intent of this document was to "break the self-perpetuating nature of centralized power" particularly after Marcos, notes Malcolm Russell-Einhorn (2007). Key formal accountability measures now include "right to information" provisions, rights of initiative and referendum, public hearings for key decisions, establishment of village development councils, and the right to petition to prioritize debate of legislation.

Despite sweeping reforms—both formal and informal attempts to increase the informational mechanisms—follow-through has been incomplete. The statute is vague about how public hearings should be conducted and contains no provisions for notice of hearings. Local governments are not required to release information.

In fact, many APAs fail to specify public notice and comment requirements. Russell-Einhorn (2007) writes that there are "local special bodies that serve as critical advisory groups on particular issues, including those dealing with health, public safety, education, infrastructure procurement, or local development. . . . These groups can propose, not approve or monitor initiatives or compel information" (217).

That said, it is noteworthy that some scholars see "bureaucratic tradition" as limiting accountability throughout the region (including in Thailand and Indonesia). Like Japan, South Korea, and Taiwan, opening up the bureaucracy—particularly after a nondemocratic regime shored it up—is one of the key challenges in creating long-term accountability in many of new democracies, including the Philippines.

INDONESIA

Indonesia has followed a similar, if more gradual, path as the Philippines. Emerging from authoritarian rule, it has sought to increase accountability by decentralizing. "Big Bang" decentralization began in 2001. This first round of decentralization included shifting control over civil servants to the local rather than central government. The World Bank has had a strong role in these efforts, particularly in promoting local and district involvement. For example, the World Bank is exploring a Justice for the Poor initiative, which is a decentralized, community participation approach, according to John Ackerman (2005, 44).

Formal administrative procedures reform also has made headway recently in Indonesia. In April 2008, an expanded Freedom of Information Act passed and will be fully implemented by 2010. This law requires that bureaucratic institutions make at least biannual public updates and promptly disseminate information relating to public order or services. The World Bank lobbied for this bill along with Indonesian civil society organizations.

Other measures of note include anticorruption laws that, since 1998, have provided access to information and freedom of the press. As with the Philippines, there are active advocacy campaigns supported by IOs, but they are not yet as well developed, given the relatively short time since transition.

THAILAND

Like many other states in Southeast Asia, Thailand had a long history of military authoritarianism. Observers saw the 1997 constitution as a chance to implement progressive reforms. Civil society groups played a role in drafting it, and accordingly constitutional provisions included seven new proaccountability institutions. These include creation of a National Counter Corruption Commission, independent electoral commission, ombudsman, constitutional court, administrative court, environmental review board, and consumer review board. Formal accountability measures include "right to information" provisions—sections 58 and 59 of the 1997 constitution.

In addition to the 1997 changes, a Thai decentralization law passed in 1999. Although the government has been slow to implement this law, it formally calls for local collection of taxes, a major new provision. There are also questions about the potential vague or contradictory provisions of such local government laws, further hindering effective decentralized governance and accountability. While the hallmarks of the decentralized, social, and informational accountability-oriented reform path are present in Thailand, as in the Philippines and Indonesia, bureaucratic traditions have proved difficult to break.

INDIA

Like the Philippines, India's accountability measures have been largely of the social and informational variety. Formal accountability measures include "right to information" provisions. Additionally, the Indian government has implemented accountability measures in a highly decentralized way. In 1992 and 1993, the Indian constitution was amended to create more levels of government, including at the federal, state, and municipal levels. Civil society groups have used this massive decentralization to bring government, as well as accountability measures, closer to the people.

This said, there has been a major push within India to promote local and community involvement in policy as well as to work with nongovernmental organizations at those levels. Additionally, India is experimenting in some cities with using a World Bank Citizen Report Card. The initial city-level experiment involved Bangalore in 1994. Other accountability measures vary by state or even municipality. For example, Kerala has a program designed to empower local councils, based on highly participatory village-based planning, while Goa has adopted a much more liberal Right to Information Act.

JAPAN

Japan's accountability measures have been largely formal in nature. Japan recodified its APL in 1995 and 1997. This set up an Administrative Appeals Commission under the prime minister to handle nonjudicial appeals. These courts can revoke or alter administrative depositions but have rarely done so in practice. While a Japanese Freedom of Information Act exists, it has many loopholes and has thus proved largely "toothless," observes Ginsburg (2002, 253–254).

The Japanese case represents a very formalized system, but one that is used only at the behest of a strong ruling party. The dominance of the Liberal Democratic Party (LDP) has provided little incentive to open up the policy-making process through open provisions as seen in the South Korean case or other, more decentralized regimes. Ginsburg (2001) finds that the Japanese bureaucracy after the APL has kept the policy-making process relatively closed but has lightened monitoring and control mechanisms by involving the courts more extensively. However, it appears that the courts see only the cases that are relatively less important to politicians.

IO involvement in Japan is relatively limited in relation to its more decentralized neighbors (there are antibribery reports issued on Japan and South Korea by the Organization for Economic Cooperation and Development). This institutional reality—centralized LDP dominance—makes Japan a special case of formal accountability measures, in which politicians with unusually long time horizons do not see any advantage to opening up the bureaucracy or even to protecting themselves in times when they are out of office.

SOUTH KOREA

Opening up South Korean bureaucracy and increasing accountability have followed a similar path as in Japan. Ginsburg (2001) notes that these reforms are seen partly as resulting from Japanese influence in general, and its recently adopted APL in particular, but also as a result of democratization and a desire for the bureaucracy to be more responsive to a broader set of interests. Specifically, in transitions in which the executive's preferences are aligned with the status quo elements in the bureaucracy—as in South Korea and Taiwan initially—governments prefer continuity in structure and process and so opt for strengthening or maintaining executive control. But where the government is facing a bureaucracy with divergent preferences and has legislative support for reform, it chooses to attack these entrenched interests and achieve greater accountability with control mechanisms such as an APA. Unlike countries such as the Philippines and Thailand, South Korean reforms are primarily highly institutionalized, rather than being oriented toward decentralization and social accountability.

The core reform law was the 1994 APA (amended in 1997) that restricted the bureaucracy's discretion over the policy-making process. Administrative reform had been in the works for almost a decade, following a failed 1987 attempt at an APL. In 1994, South Korea passed a law creating an administrative appeals court. Then, in 1995, a reform to the 1994 law referred to the court all appeals against the government and empowered it to "revoke or alter administrative dispositions as necessary" (Administrative Appeals Act, Article 6–2, in Ginsburg, 2001, 606).

The South Korean APA requires advance public notice and comment, which opens up the policy process to those interests that have not been previously aligned with the ruling party. The 1996 Disclosure of Information Held by Public Authorities law, which is subject to judicial review, significantly opens up policy making. Through these and other related reforms, the South Korean bureaucracy and policy process have grown much more open and are subject to greater oversight by a wider range of actors, including courts and independent actors such as ombudsmen.

TAIWAN

Like South Korea, Taiwan's reforms have focused on formalizing institutional structures and processes for increasing accountability. Administrative reforms were driven by the need for the ruling party (the KMT) to change its image from one of entrenched corruption and favoritism toward wealthy private interests to one of "clean government." To do so, the party had to rein in the very bureaucracy that had long served as the cornerstone of its power.

Taiwan's 1999 APA requires public notice and comment of all proposed regulations and that agencies investigate administrative action appeals and notify all relevant parties of their decisions. A Freedom of Information provision is another major feature of Taiwan's APA. This requires that most agencies disclose information to the public upon request. The APA also allows formal adjudication, whereby parties have the right to present evidence and cross-examine witnesses at an oral hearing. Additionally, the 1994 amendments to the Administrative Litigation Law established an administrative court. Taiwan's 1998 Administrative Litigation Act, in turn, allows judicial review of administrative actions.

CONCLUSION

There seem to be two primary paths for increasing accountability in the Asian experience during the past twenty years. One path—followed by Japan, South Korea, and Taiwan—is highly institutionalized, although there is significant variation between these three cases. The Japanese bureaucracy is still relatively insulated compared with South Korea and Taiwan, but these three countries nonetheless contrast sharply with the more decentralized systems of Indonesia and the Philippines. IOs, particularly the World Bank, appear much more willing and able to assist with these more decentralized paths.

The literature has tended to focus on one or the other path and variation within that path. Thus far largely unexplored are the equally important questions of why these appear to be substitutes and the conditions under which states select a particular set of tools. Are decentralization and social accountability chosen only out of necessity? Alternatively, if this proves to be a more common path outside of Asia, the question arises as to whether a "Japan" would ever choose such a path, and if so when? Is social accountability really a second choice, behind the more preferred alternative of an APA? Or is it more likely that these states prefer to pursue these types of "good governance" building measures and in doing so sometimes conclude that IO assistance (particularly World Bank) will ease some of their burden? Determining the circumstances under which states will opt for administrative reform, the path they will follow if they do pursue such reforms, and the particular tools they will select under different conditions all represent potentially fruitful avenues for future research.

To some extent, time will tell about the progression of the decentralized cases. Accountability along the decentralization path appears to hinge on two factors: the effectiveness of decentralization and the strength of civil society groups, including those with IO assistance. Presumably increases in both of these should aid accountability, but in some countries this seems like a lot on which to hang one's hat.

See also *Accountability; Centralization, Deconcentration, and Decentralization; Institutionalism, Comparative; International Organization.*

. . . . JEEYANG RHEE BAUM

BIBLIOGRAPHY

Ackerman, John M. "Social Accountability for the Public Sector: A Conceptual Discussion." In *Social Development Paper 82.* Washington, D.C.: World Bank, 2005.

Baum, Jeeyang Rhee. "Presidents Have Problems Too: The Logic of Intrabranch Delegation in East Asia." *British Journal of Political Science* 37, no. 4 (2007): 659–684.

Baum, Jeeyang Rhee. *Responsive Democracy: Increasing State Accountability in East Asia.* Ann Arbor: University of Michigan Press, forthcoming.

Bennett, Colin J. "Understanding Ripple Effects: The Cross-national Adoption of Policy Instruments for Bureaucratic Accountability." *Governance: An International Journal of Policy and Administration* 10, no. 3 (1997): 213–233.

Campos, Jose Edgardo, and Joel S. Hellman. "Governance Gone Local: Does Decentralization Improve Accountability." In *East Asia Decentralizes: Making Local Government Work,* 237–252. Washington, D.C.: World Bank, 2005.

Geddes, Barbara. *Politician's Dilemma: Building State Capacity in Latin America.* Berkeley: University of California Press, 1994.

Ginsburg, Tom. "Dismantling the 'Developmental State'? Administrative Procedure Reform in Japan and Korea." *American Journal of Comparative Law* 49, no. 4 (2001): 585–625.

———. "Comparative Administrative Procedure: Evidence from Northeast Asia." *Constitutional Political Economy* 13, no. 3 (2002): 247–264.

Goetz, Anne Marie, and John Gaventa. "Bringing Citizen Voice and Client Focus into Service Delivery." Working Paper 138. Brighton, U.K.: Institute of Development Studies, 2001.

Iszatt, Nina T. "Legislating for Citizens' Participation in the Philippines." LogoLink Report. Brighton, U.K.: Institute of Development Studies, July 2002.

Kaufmann, Daniel. "Myths and Realities of Governance and Corruption." In *Global Competitiveness Report 2005–2006,* 81–98. Washington, D.C.: World Bank, 2005.

McGee, Rosemary. "Legal Frameworks for Citizen Participation: Synthesis Report." LogoLink Report. Brighton, U.K.: Institute of Development Studies, 2003.

Moreno, Erica, Brian F. Crisp, and Matthew Shugart. "The Accountability Deficit in Latin America." In *Democratic Accountability in Latin America,* edited by Scott Mainwaring and Christopher Welna, 79–131. Oxford: Oxford University Press, 2003.

O'Donnell, G. "Horizontal Accountability in New Democracies." In *The Self-Restraining State: Power and Accountability in New Democracies,* edited by Andreas Schedler, Larry Diamond, and Marc F. Plattner, 29–52. Boulder, Colo.: Lynne Rienner, 1999.

———. "Horizontal Accountability: The Legal Institutionalization of Mistrust." In *Democratic Accountability in Latin America,* edited by Scott Mainwaring and Christopher Welna, 34–54. Oxford: Oxford University Press, 2003.

Russell-Einhorn, Malcolm. "Legal and Institutional Frameworks Supporting Budgeting and Accountability in Service Delivery Performance." In *Performance Accountability and Combating Corruption,* edited by Anwar Shah, 183–232. Washington, D.C.: World Bank, 2007.

Smulovitz, Catalina, and Enrique Peruzzotti. "Societal and Horizontal Controls: Two Cases of a Fruitful Relationship." In *Democratic Accountability in Latin America,* edited by Scott Mainwaring and Christopher Welna, 309–331. Oxford: Oxford University Press, 2003.

Stokes, Susan. *Mandates and Democracy: Neoliberalism by Surprise in Latin America.* Cambridge: Cambridge University Press, 2001.

———. "Perverse Accountability: A Formal Model of Machine Politics with Evidence from Argentina." *American Political Science Review* 99, no. 3 (2005): 315–325.

Wolfe, Robert. "Regulatory Transparency, Developing Countries, and the Fate of the WTO." Paper presented at the meeting of the International Studies Association, Portland, Ore., March 2003.

Assassinations, Political

Political assassination involves the targeted killing of people, often but not always those who hold positions of political authority or political office. Typically, those who carry out such killings have a political or ideological motivation, although they range across the political spectrum, both right wing and left. While some assassination attempts have been carried out by individual sociopaths, the figure of the insane assassin has often been used to downplay or marginalize the larger political basis of the event. Political assassinations are directed or carried out also by members of states against civilians.

The term *assassin* has its origins in a militant Islamic secret society, Hashshashin, active in the Middle East between the eighth and fourteenth centuries. Motivated by religious and political reasons, this Shiite sect killed members of the Sunni elite. The first organized group to systematically use murder as a political weapon, they also were feared by invading Crusaders.

Assassination probably has always been a tool of politics. Among the earliest documented attempts is the attempted assassination of Chinese Emperor Qin Shi Huang around 210 BCE. The assassination of Julius Caesar in 44 BCE stands as one of the most famous early recorded assassinations. The number of political assassinations grew with the emergence and development of the modern nation-state. In the early modern period in Russia, four emperors—Ivan VI, Peter III, Paul I, and Alexander II—were killed in a span of less two hundred years. Democratic regimes have experienced political assassinations as well as totalitarian regimes. In the United States, assassins killed four presidents—Abraham Lincoln, James Garfield, William McKinley, and John F. Kennedy—and made attempts to kill others. Political assassinations are often tactics used by insurgent groups that lack the means to challenge a state's military apparatus. Groups that have used assassination as a tool in larger sociopolitical struggles in the late twentieth century include, the Provisional IRA (Irish Republican Army) since 1969, the leftist Red Brigades in Italy in the 1970s and 1980s, and Hezbollah.

With the internationalization of politics, assassinations carried out for local reasons have had wide-ranging impacts. The assassination of Archduke Franz Ferdinand by Serb nationalist Gavrilo Princip in 1914 is generally viewed as the spark that set off World War I (1914–1918). The assassination of Rwandan President Juvenal Habyarimana and Cyprien Ntaryamira, the Hutu president of Burundi, in 1994, their airplane shot down as it prepared to land in Kigali, is identified as the incident that launched the genocide in Rwanda.

Activists also have been targets for political assassination. Human rights activist and philosopher of nonviolence, Mohandas Gandhi, was shot on January 30, 1948, by Nathuram Godse for seeking peace between Hindus and Muslims in India. Civil rights leader Martin Luther King Jr. was killed in 1968 by James Earl Ray while in Memphis to assist striking sanitation workers. King's assassination, which was widely viewed as an attack on the civil rights movement as a whole, set off waves of rioting in several major American cities. During the 1970s, U.S. Senate hearings revealed that political assassinations against leftist and black power activists had been carried out by agents of the Federal Bureau of Investigation (FBI) as part of their counterintelligence program (COINTELPRO).

Critics of state violence point out that more people have been killed through state actions than have been killed by non-state assassins. Critics of states are certainly not lacking when it comes to martyrs. The Haymarket martyrs, Joe Hill, Frank Little, Gustav Landauer, Sacco and Vanzetti, the Kronstadt sailors, and the Maknovists of Ukraine are only a few of the poor and working-class victims of state violence. The administrations of U.S. presidents Bill Clinton and George W. Bush have sanctioned political assassinations, including against elected political leaders such as Mullah Omar. State-sanctioned assassinations have been cloaked in euphemisms such as targeted strikes or extrajudicial executions. Recent assassinations carried out by the U.S. government include the killing of Abu Musab al-Zarqawi and Sheikh Abd-al-Rahman by guided bombs against a so-called safe house outside of Baghdad.

Assassinations have long been advocated by political theorists, including those whose works are still highly regarded. Sun Tzu argued, on military grounds, for the use of assassinations in his book *The Art of War*. In his classic of political theory, *The Prince*, Niccolò Machiavelli argued the utility of assassination.

One of the most notorious treatises on political assassination comes from the anarchist Sergei Nechaev in his pamphlet *Catechism of the Revolutionist*. Nechaev's work inspired Bolshevik leader Vladimr Lenin. Anarchism stands as the political philosophy most associated with advocacy of political assassination in part because of the theory of "propaganda of the deed" in which some anarchists proposed assassinations as means to inspire the exploited to mobilize against elites. Figures like Ravachol and Emile Henry during the nineteenth century and Leon Czolgosz, who assassinated President McKinley in 1901, are among the most famous anarchist assassins. In fact few

anarchists have even advocated violence. The characterization stems largely from the startling bombings and assassinations that arose from the despair of the 1890s. Many anarchists, such as Leo Tolstoy, have argued that political assassinations primarily serve to strengthen the state and provide a potent excuse for the state to increase repression and control of the population. Political assassinations, for Tolstoy, do little to inspire the people and represent little more than cutting off one of the hydra's heads. A new leader always emerges to take the place of the one assassinated.

See also *Anarchy; Coup d'Etat; Machiavelli, Niccolò; Nonviolence; Tolstoy, Leo.*

. . . . JEFFREY SHANTZ

BIBLIOGRAPHY

Gross, Michael L. *Moral Dilemmas of Modern War: Torture, Assassination, and Blackmail in an Age of Asymmetric Conflict.* Cambridge: Cambridge University Press, 2010.

Iqbal, Zaryab, and Christopher Zorn. "Sic Semper Tyrannis? Power, Repression, and Assassination since the Second World War." *The Journal of Politics* 68 (2006): 489–501.

Lentz, Harris M. *Assassinations and Executions: An Encyclopedia of Political Violence, 1865–1986.* Jefferson, N.C.: McFarland, 1988.

———. *Assassinations and Executions: An Encyclopedia of Political Violence, 1900 through 2000.* Jefferson, N.C.: McFarland, 2002.

Nelson, Michael. *Guide to the Presidency.* Washington, D.C.: CQ Press, 2008.

Snitch, Thomas H. "Terrorism and Political Assassinations: A Transnational Assessment, 1968–80." *Annals of the American Academy of Political and Social Science* 463 (September 1982): 54–68.

Assembly, Freedom of

See *Freedom of Assembly.*

Assimilation

Assimilation is the name of a process in which cultural minorities change their practices, values, or behavior in order to become more like members of the majority or dominant group among which they live. Assimilation may occur in the absence of state intervention, as the result of choices made by individual members of minority groups (albeit in a context where there are often benefits that accompany assimilation and that provide incentives to make that choice), or it may be a product of state policies that are specifically designed to bring it about; for example, when a state forbids the speaking of a minority language in schools.

Assimilationist policies are often distinguished from integrationist policies or practices. Sometimes assimilation is regarded as a process in which minority cultural groups abandon *all* of their distinctive values and practices, in effect relinquishing their particular identities, while *integration* involves members of these groups merely giving up *some* of their particular values and practices to become more like members of the dominant group. Alternatively, integration may be viewed as a two-way process that, unlike assimilation, requires change on both sides. Whereas assimilation requires minority cultural groups to change their values, practices, or behaviors to fit in with those of the dominant group, integration involves a process of *mutual* adjustment.

An integrated society is in turn often contrasted with one in which different cultural groups lead parallel lives in the same society. So understood, integration requires members of different groups to come into meaningful contact with each other, to lead more of their lives together. This is sometimes an effort to promote community cohesion and greater trust between groups.

A powerful argument in favor of assimilationist policies is that such policies may be required to foster a single, shared culture, and that a single, shared culture is either necessary for, or at least conducive to, the stability of a state. Theorists of nationalism have sometimes appealed to this idea to justify policies that are designed to promote a shared national identity among citizens and even to restrict immigration to prevent that identity from being eroded. Those on the left of the political spectrum also may have reason to value a shared national identity, for it has been argued that such an identity is important to secure widespread support for redistribution on grounds of social justice.

Alternatively, a powerful argument against assimilationist policies is that they are either oppressive or counterproductive. Political theorist Iris Young (1990), for example, claims that assimilated groups suffer from cultural imperialism. When a policy of assimilation is pursued, the dominant cultural group will see themselves as objectively superior and cultural minorities will internalize a sense of inferiority. This argument may not always be successful, however. Assimilationist policies can be directed toward practices that are themselves oppressive, such as forced marriage and female genital mutilation. A policy of assimilation, however, need not be premised or implemented on the idea that the dominant culture is superior, and may be pursued through a range of initiatives that are not clearly oppressive. Examples include requiring immigrants to learn the language in which public affairs are conducted or requiring that state schools focus on the history, geography, and literature of the dominant group.

See also *Individual and Society; Segregation and Desegregation; Xenophobia; Young, Iris Marion.*

. . . . ANDREW D. MASON

BIBLIOGRAPHY
Modood, T. *Multiculturalism: A Civic Idea.* Cambridge, U.K.: Polity Press, 2007.
Young, Iris. *Justice and the Politics of Difference.* Princeton, N.J.: Princeton University Press, 1990.

Association, Freedom of

See *Freedom of Association.*

Astell, Mary

English philosopher, educator, and theologian, Mary Astell (1666–1713) was born in Newcastle, England, but moved to London when she was orphaned by the age of 18. When she was 23, William and Mary were crowned in England after the Glorious Revolution of 1688. Astell had been educated by her uncle, Ralph Astell, who influenced her royalist beliefs, and she remained a loyal Tory.

In London, Astell embarked on a career as a commissioned pamphleteer. Her entire body of work was condensed into an eleven-year period. Her early works are strongly polemical, expressing contempt for democracy, religious toleration, separation of church and state, and patriarchy. Astell has been identified as the "first English feminist," one of her most quoted lines being "If all Men are born free, how is it that all Women are born slaves?"

Astell believed that individuals of all classes should be educated beyond basic skills and that women need to find their own voices. Although critical of the theories of John Locke and leading Enlightenment figures who dominated the political thought of Europe, Astell extended those theories to women. She contended that women, like men, were both intelligent and rational and deserved the benefits of education.

Astell's views on the roles of women was highly influenced by the French *salonnieres,* particularly Madeleine de Scudery, and by French philosopher René Descartes. Believing that education was a viable alternative to what was doomed to be unhappy marriages, Astell argued that females should be trained to support themselves. In 1694, Astell articulated her evolving views in *A Serious Proposal to the Ladies for the Advancement of the True and Greatest Interest by a Lover of Her Sex.* The book presented Astell's radical proposal that her wealthy friends finance the founding of a college for women.

In 1697 she wrote *A Serious Proposal to the Ladies for the Advancement of Their True Greatest Interest,* recommending a religious order where women could retire to study and support one another without the permanent commitment of a nunnery. British writer Daniel Defoe was so taken with Astell's proposal that he demanded that Parliament make it a felony for men to solicit women in these secluded areas.

Astell's proposal for higher education for women was received with skepticism, and she turned her attention to the Chelsea Charity School, created to educate the daughters of English veterans. She was particularly interested in educating orphans who needed to support themselves. Her involvement in this project continued until 1724.

Astell was a devout Anglican. Her correspondence with John Norris, a prominent Platonic philosopher, was published in 1695 as *Letters Concerning the Love of God.* Astell and Norris both criticized what they viewed as John Locke's rejection of religion. Astell's theological views were further articulated in 1705 in *The Christian Religion, As Profess'd by a Daughter of the Church of England.*

In 1700, *Some Reflections upon Marriage, Occasion'd by the Duke and Duchess of Mazarine's Case* was published. Astell was interested not only in justifying the Duchess's decision to leave her cruel and jealous husband but in pointing out that marriage was inherently unequal. Astell did not, however, exonerate women. She insisted that both sexes shared the blame for perpetuating the inequities.

See also *Education Policy; Enlightenment Political Thought; Feminism; Women's Representation; Women's Rights*

. . . . ELIZABETH RHOLETTER PURDY

BIBLIOGRAPHY

Hill, Bridget, ed. *The First English Feminist: Reflections upon Marriage and Other Writings by Mary Astell.* Adlershot, U.K.: Gower, 1986.

Hunt, Margaret, Margaret Jacob, Phyllis Mack, and Ruth Perry, eds. *Women and the Enlightenment.* New York: Haworth, 1984.

Smith, Florence M. *Mary Astell.* New York: Columbia University Press, 1916.

Springborg, Patricia. *Mary Astell: Theorist of Freedom from Dominion.* New York: Cambridge University Press, 2005.

Sutherland, Christine Mason. *Eloquence of Mary Astell.* Calgary, A.B.: University of Calgary, 2005.

Asylum Rights

Asylum is protection offered by a government to persons who face persecution in their home country for reasons including race, religion, nationality, membership in a particular social group, or political opinion. It is possible to separate discussion of asylum rights from the question of international refugee protection. Such a distinction is, however, unhelpful, and modern analysis of asylum rights should be framed in the context of wider global refugee debates. The treatment of refugees and asylum-seekers has become a defining feature of the modern age. The protection and promotion of human rights have particular significance for these groups. While the concept of asylum has ancient origins, the right to seek asylum gained international recognition in the Universal Declaration of Human Rights 1948. Article 14(1) provides that "everyone has the right to seek and to enjoy in other countries asylum from persecution." The concept gained further acknowledgement in the American Declaration of the Rights and Duties of Man 1948, the American Convention on Human Rights 1969, the Organisation for African Unity Convention on the Specific Aspects of Refugee Problems in Africa 1969, the African Charter on Human and Peoples' Rights 1981, the Arab Charter on Human Rights 1984, and the European Union Charter of Fundamental Rights 2000. The right to seek asylum is to be found in a range of international instruments; the challenge is establishing whether refuge is in fact being provided. Possessing a right to seek asylum, or even a right to leave your country of origin, is important, but states remain firmly wedded to notion that granting entry is a foundational sovereign "right" of the state.

The 1951 Convention Relating to the Status of Refugees and the 1967 Protocol Relating to the Status of Refugees are the legal instruments that have gained widespread acceptance in the international community. Provision is made for the definition of *refugee*, as well as protections and guarantees that attach to that status. The definition contains several elements. First, the person must be outside the country of origin and be unable or unwilling to avail of state protection. Those displaced within their own countries are therefore not refugees for convention purposes. Internally displaced persons can be particularly vulnerable (and are more numerous globally), yet in international legal terms they are not refugees. Second, the person must have a "well-founded fear of being persecuted." This test combines the objective (well-founded) and the subjective (fear) with the prospective "being persecuted." Many refugee determination systems are therefore concerned with establishing what might happen to the person upon return to the country of origin. This is not enough to establish a claim to refugee status. The person must also demonstrate a fear of being persecuted for a reason stated in the convention: race, religion, nationality, membership of a particular social group, or political opinion. Debate continues on these grounds, as well as how inclusively they should be interpreted. The 1951 Convention provides protections ranging from legal status and employment to housing and social security. The guarantee of particular significance is that of *nonrefoulement,* the prohibition of expulsion or return (Article 33(1)). The principal objective of refugees is not to be returned to face persecution, and this legal obligation is intended to reflect that fact. The obligation contained in the convention is not absolute and contains an exception that relates to security and those who have committed serious crimes.

The 1951 Convention remains the cornerstone of international refugee protection. In terms of institutional protection, the United Nations High Commissioner for Refugees (UNHCR) operates as the international "guardian" of refugee protection. UNHCR figures reveal 10.5 million refugees of concern to that organization, with more than 50 percent in Asia and 20 percent in Africa. The number of internally displaced persons is approximately double that, standing at twenty-six million in 2008 (UNHCR 2010).

International human rights law, with its focus on the person, is of significance. Although the guarantees do not often refer expressly to this group, by implication they are applicable as *human* rights. For example, the International Covenant on Civil and Political Rights 1966 and the International Covenant on Economic, Social and Cultural Rights 1966 contain important guarantees of relevance to any discussion of asylum rights. At the regional level, in Europe, the European Convention on Human Rights 1950 is notable. For example, Article 3 has evolved into an important guarantee against return of those who can show substantial grounds to believe there is a real risk they will be tortured or subjected to inhuman or degrading treatment or punishment. National constitutional protections also will be of relevance in determining the rights asylum-seekers might avail of.

The rights of refugees and asylum-seekers are now well-established in international law. The reality of refugee protection and asylum rights is often markedly different. The problem of effective implementation and enforcement remains, and negotiating the politics of asylum and human displacement is one of the most pressing challenges of our time.

See also *Ethnic Cleansing; Refugees; Religious Persecution.*

. . . . COLIN HARVEY

BIBLIOGRAPHY

Harvey, Colin. "Dissident Voices: Refugees, Human Rights and Asylum in Europe." *Social and Legal Studies* 9, no. 3 (2000): 367–396.

———. *Seeking Asylum in the UK: Problems and Prospects.* London: Butterworths, 2000.

———. "Refugees, Asylum Seekers the Rule of Law and Human Rights." In *The Unity of Public Law,* edited by David Dyzenhaus, 201–224. Oxford, U.K.: Hart. 2004.

Hathaway, James. *The Rights of Refugees under International Law.* Cambridge: Cambridge University Press, 2005.

Hathaway, James C., and Colin J. Harvey. "Framing Refugee Law in the New World Disorder." *Cornell International Law Journal* 34, no. 2 (2001): 257–320.

UNHCR: The UN Refugee Agency, 2010, www.unhcr.org.

Asymmetric Wars

Asymmetric wars are historically armed conflicts in which one actor has significantly more power, usually a larger military or navy, which subsequently compels a weaker opponent to undertake unconventional strategies or tactics to overcome the quantitative or qualitative power deficit. Asymmetric wars were typically guerilla conflicts that emphasized the use of insurgent attacks to disrupt supply lines and weaken an enemy's morale. Small groups would use the weapons or materials at hand to attempt to inflict the maximum political and military damage. Consequently, asymmetric warfare involves the use of limited resources to result in attacks or impacts that are largely out of proportion to the weapons used. In contemporary military doctrine, asymmetric warfare is defined as any conflict in which an actor seeks to exploit the weaknesses of an opponent by concentrating resources or weapons against vulnerabilities.

THE HISTORY OF ASYMMETRIC WARFARE

Throughout history, people have reacted to invasion and occupation by powerful actors by engaging in armed insurrections and attacking outposts or by small deployments in battles in which the rebels could gain numeric equality, or even superiority. Such maneuvers came to be known as "hit-and-run" tactics. While asymmetric warfare is not synonymous with guerilla campaigns, insurgency groups typically used these tactics against occupying powers or domestic governments.

Chinese author Sun Tzu wrote in the sixth century BCE about asymmetric wars in his classic treatise on military conflict, *The Art of War.* In the second century BCE, the Parthians used asymmetric warfare against the Seleucid Empire (and later the Romans). During the Middle Ages, Scottish knight and resistance leader William Wallace effectively combined guerilla tactics with conventional warfare against the English. After the Treaty of Westphalia (1648), nation-states gained a monopoly on the legitimate use of force, and the customs and rules of military conflict became increasingly formalized. Native Americans used asymmetric warfare against the better-armed European colonial forces, and their tactics were subsequently used by both sides during the French and Indian War (1754–1763) and by the Americans during the Revolutionary War (1775–1783). In the Napoleonic Wars (1795–1815), small units of Anglo-Spanish forces conducted raids and attacks on French posts during the Peninsula Campaign, prompting the deployment of ever-larger numbers of troops.

Through the imperial era of the 1800s, colonial forces endeavored to counter hit-and-run tactics by indigenous fighters through superior weapons, scorched-earth policies, and attrition. During the Second Boer War (1899–1902), the Boer conventional troops were initially defeated by the British, but then launched a guerilla campaign with between twenty thousand and thirty thousand fighters, forcing the continued deployment of five hundred thousand imperial soldiers. Victory was achieved only through a ruthless strategy of concentration camps and destruction of crops. British adventurer, scholar, and soldier T. E. Lawrence popularized asymmetric war as a viable strategy against a conventional enemy during the Anglo-Arab campaign against the Ottoman Empire in World War I (1914–1918). The national liberation conflicts of the post–World War II era were mainly asymmetric wars, pitting insurgents using guerilla tactics against better armed and trained colonial conventional forces. Through the cold war, both superpowers supported subnational combatants in a series of proxy wars. During the Vietnam War (1961–1974), the U.S. military devoted considerable efforts to develop countermeasures against asymmetric tactics, with limited success. The Soviet Union likewise failed to counter an insurgency movement in Afghanistan during its occupation in the 1980s.

ASYMMETRIC WARFARE AND TERRORISM

Terrorism evolved into the most substantial asymmetric threat in the 1990s and 2000s. A range of substate actors used political violence against civilian and military targets in low-intensity conflicts in areas such as Northern Ireland, Spain, and the Middle East. By the late 1990s, catastrophic attacks, including the 1998 twin bombings of U.S. embassies in Kenya and Tanzania, attested to the growing capability of terrorist groups to inflict substantial damage to civilian targets (and were an extension of the main point of asymmetric wars, the targeting of the enemy's greatest vulnerabilities). The September 11, 2001, al-Qaida attacks on the United States, which killed more than three thousand people, were the deadliest and most devastating strikes against the continental United States in recent history. The attacks demonstrated the ability of a small band to inflict major losses against a more powerful opponent by using materials often not perceived as weapons (hijackers turned aircraft into flying missiles that used the kinetic energy in the buildings to expand the devastation of the strikes).

In Operation Enduring Freedom in 2001 and 2002, the U.S. military and its coalition partners used asymmetric warfare to defeat the Taliban regime in Afghanistan that had harbored the leadership of the al-Qaida network. Allied military forces used tactical air power and missile strikes, in combination with the indigenous anti-Taliban Northern Alliance, against the numerically superior Taliban conventional forces. The Taliban was overthrown after two months. The U.S.-led invasion of Iraq in 2003 employed a similar mix of precision-guided weaponry and an invasion force of 168,000 that was outnumbered by the defending Iraqi forces (more than 430,000 troops, including paramilitary forces, but not reserves). While the coalition quickly achieved a military victory, a widespread insurgency, combining both traditional hit-and-run tactics and terrorism, proved the continuing utility of asymmetric tactics against conventional forces. Other contemporary examples of asymmetric warfare include the tactics used by Hamas and Hezbollah against Israel or the attacks of Chechen rebels against Russian troops.

See also *Insurgency; Insurrection and Insurgency; Terrorism, Political.*

. . . . TOM LANSFORD

BIBLIOGRAPHY

Arreguin-Toft, Ivan. *How the Weak Win Wars: A Theory of Asymmetric Conflict.* New York: Cambridge University Press, 2005.

Asprey, Robert B. *War in the Shadows: The Guerilla in History.* New York: William Morrow, 1994.

Barnett, Roger W. *Asymmetrical Warfare: Today's Challenge to U.S. Military Power.* Washington, D.C.: Brassey's, 2003.

Mack, Andrew J. R. "Why Big Nations Lose Small Wars: The Politics of Asymmetric Conflict." *World Politics* 27 (January 1975): 175–200.

Metz, Steven, and Douglas V. Johnson II. *Asymmetry and U.S. Military Strategy: Definition, Background, and Strategic Concepts.* Carlisle Barracks, Pa.: Strategic Studies Institute/U.S. Army War College, 2001.

Atlantic Charter

The Atlantic Charter was an agreement by U.S. President Franklin Delano Roosevelt and British Prime Minister Winston Churchill that set forth the two countries' war aims and laid out their vision of a post–World War II world. The charter was drafted at the Atlantic Conference, a secret meeting held August 9 through 12, 1941, aboard two warships (HMS *Prince of Wales* and USS *Augusta*) anchored in Ship Harbour, Newfoundland, Canada. The secrecy was due to fears that German submarines would target Roosevelt and Churchill.

The Atlantic Conference was the first of nine face-to-face meetings that the two leaders would have during World War II (1939–1945). Joining Roosevelt and Churchill were high-ranking government officials and military officers, who discussed military strategy and the challenges of supplying Great Britain under the Lend-Lease Act (Public Law 77–11). The law, enacted by Congress in March 1941, allowed the United States to transfer weapons to "any nation vital to the defense of the United States."

The Atlantic Charter was issued as a joint declaration by the two leaders on August 14, 1941, at a time when the British were fighting Nazi Germany and the United States was still neutral. A statement that accompanied the declaration noted that the leaders,

> have considered the dangers to world civilization arising from the policies of military domination by conquest upon which the Hitlerite government of Germany and other governments associated therewith have embarked, and have made clear the stress which their countries are respectively taking for their safety in the face of these dangers.

The two nations agreed to eight common principles: (1) the United States and United Kingdom would not seek territorial gains from the war; (2) territorial changes would not take place that were not in accord with the wishes of the people affected; (3) people have the right to choose their form of government, and national sovereignty should be restored to those from which it was taken forcibly; (4) the lowering of trade barriers for all nations; (5) global collaboration to secure improved labor standards, economic advancement, and social security; (6) freedom from fear and want; (7) freedom of travel on the high seas; and (8) aggressor nations should be disarmed and a "permanent system of general security" should be established.

The principles were reminiscent of Woodrow Wilson's Fourteen Points and reflect the "four freedoms"—freedom of speech, freedom of religion, freedom from want, and freedom from fear—of President Roosevelt's 1941 State of the Union address.

In an August 21, 1941, message to Congress, Roosevelt asserted that "the declaration of principles at this time presents a goal which is worthwhile for our type of civilization to seek." The Axis powers (Germany, Italy, and Japan) saw the charter as a potential alliance between the two nations.

On September 24, 1941, the Soviet Union and the governments in exile of Belgium, Czechoslovakia, Greece, Luxembourg, the Netherlands, Norway, Poland, Yugoslavia, and the Free French movement adopted the principles of the Atlantic Charter. In less than three months, following the Japanese attack on Pearl Harbor, the United States entered the war.

The Atlantic Charter would serve as the basis for the establishment, after World War II, of the United Nations and the Bretton Woods agreements that created the International Monetary Fund and the International Bank for Reconstruction and Development.

See also *International Monetary Fund (IMF); United Nations (UN).*

. . . . JEFFREY KRAUS

BIBLIOGRAPHY

Borgwardt, Elizabeth. *A New Deal for the World: America's Vision for Human Rights.* Cambridge, Mass.: Belknap Press of Harvard University Press, 2005.

Brinkley, Douglas, and David R. Facey-Crowther, eds. *The Atlantic Charter.* New York: St. Martin's, 1994.

Morton, H. V. *Atlantic Meeting.* New York: Dodd, Mead, 1943.

Wilson, Theodore A. *The First Summit; Roosevelt and Churchill at Placentia Bay 1941,* rev. ed. Lawrence: University Press of Kansas, 1991.

At-Large Elections

In *at-large elections,* members are chosen to represent an entire political unit, as opposed to a single district or ward. At-large elections are most commonly used in the United States in local or regional balloting. Proponents of at-large balloting contend the system allows members to take a broader view of policy and not become tied to the narrow interests of a single ward or district. The system emerged in Great Britain in the eighteenth century, but was replaced by the use of single district voting in the 1800s in response to concerns over the capacity of at-large representatives to respond to constituent needs in individual districts and wards. In the United States, the system became widespread in the late 1800s as a progressive reform to reduce the power of corrupt political bosses. Later, during the civil rights movement, at-large systems were implemented in the Southern

States in an effort to reduce the political power of minority groups. A series of civil rights court cases and national legislation have significantly reduced the use of at-large balloting in America, while the system never gained widespread use outside of Great Britain and the United States. Today, at-large elections are used by only about 6 percent of democratic countries.

See also *Electoral Reform; Minority Representation; Representative Systems; Voting Procedures.*

. . . . TOM LANSFORD

Attorney General

The role of the attorney general is to provide legal expertise and support to the government. A number of nations, from Canada to Kenya, possess an office or ministry of the attorney general. The responsibilities and institutional constraints of these offices vary by country and political context. In some countries, the office is ministerial, dealing mainly with routine litigation, while in others it is much more politicized with a diverse array of functions.

Most nations formally under British rule established an office of attorney general. Some countries codified the office in their constitutions or by statute, while others did not. There are also differences in terms of which branch of government the office is located in and the appointment process. In the United States, the attorney general is appointed by the president and confirmed by the Senate. In contrast, the Canadian attorney general is a member of Parliament appointed by the prime minister.

The office of attorney general has a long history that has roots in medieval England, when the "king's attorney" represented the Crown's interests in court. In 1472, the title of attorney general was used for the first time with the appointment of William Hussee, and in 1673 the attorney general became an official member of parliament in England.

Before independence from Britain, each American colony had an attorney general who served as a liaison to the English attorney general. Their duties varied from colony to colony. The first recorded appointment to the office in America was Richard Lee of Virginia in 1643. The English established similar offices in other locations throughout the British Empire to serve the interests of the Crown.

The office of attorney general is not explicitly discussed in the U.S. Constitution. It was established by the Judiciary Act of 1789 as part of the executive branch. Early in U.S. history, the office of attorney general was informally structured, low paying, and undemanding. Over the years the responsibilities of the office slowly increased. It was not until 1870, however, that Congress established the Department of Justice. As head of the department, the attorney general could better coordinate legal policy by overseeing governmental litigation. In the twenty-first century, the U.S. attorney general administers the Department of Justice, represents the government, and offers advice on legal issues, as well as plays an important role consulting the president on judicial nominations.

The office of state attorney general in the United States is older than the national office. After independence, the office was incorporated into the new state governments. The state attorney general became the chief legal officer of the state, giving legal advice, drafting legislation, writing advisory opinions, and litigating causes that are in the public interest. Through multistate litigation and filing amicus curiae briefs in federal court, state attorneys general have been able to shape and refine national domestic policy. Also, the definition of what is in a state's interest has expanded significantly, allowing state attorneys general to influence policy on issues ranging from environmental pollution to consumer protection.

The office of attorney general, at both the state and national level, plays a critical role in the U.S. government. As the country has grown, the attorney general has been delegated more responsibilities and functions. In turn, these changes have increased the office's prominence and policy-making potential.

The policy-making potential of the office has become more salient in other countries as well. In some nations, individual attorneys general have begun to conceptualize their role more expansively. This may lead to a new public and scholarly interest in attorneys general as political actors.

See also *Law and Society; Legislature-court Relations; Rule of Law; Supreme Court.*

. . . . ADAM W. NYE

BIBLIOGRAPHY
Bellot, Hugh H. L. "The Origin of the Attorney-General." *Law Quarterly Review* 25 (1909): 400–411.
Clayton, Cornell W. *The Politics of Justice: The Attorney General and Making of Legal Policy.* Armonk, N.Y.: M.E. Sharpe, 1992.
———. "Law Politics and the New Federalism: State Attorneys General as Policymakers." *Review of Politics* 56, no. 3 (1994): 525–554.
Meador, Daniel J. *The President, the Attorney General, and the Department of Justice.* Charlottesville, Va.: White Burkett Miller Center of Public Affairs, 1980.
Provost, Colin. "State Attorneys General, Entrepreneurship, and Consumer Protection in the New Federalism." *Publius* 33, no. 2 (2003): 37–53.
Ross, Lynne M., ed. *State Attorneys General: Powers and Responsibilities.* Washington, D.C.: Bureau of National Affairs, 1990.
Scott, Ian. "Law, Policy, and the Role of the Attorney General: Constancy and Change in the 1980s." *University of Toronto Law Journal* 39, no. 2 (1989): 109–126.

Auditing

See *Program Evaluation and Auditing.*

Augustine of Hippo

Aurelius Augustine (354–430), or Saint Augustine, was a theologian and father of the Christian church. His autobiographical *Confessions* (c. 397) and *City of God against the Pagans* (413–427) shaped medieval European ideas about political order, freedom, soul, inner life, will, sin, evil, just war, history, time, religion, immortality, love, and God. His thought is influential across all Christian denominations, especially perhaps Calvinism, and extends into the contemporary age even among secular thinkers. Examples of his influence include French philosopher René Descartes' meditations, the express imitation of Augustine used by French thinker Jean-Jacques Rousseau in formulating his own *Confessions* (1782), the Augustinian overtones in French political philosopher Alexis de Tocqueville's diagnosis of the democratic soul, and German-Jewish political theorist Hannah Arendt's understanding of the "banality of evil" and of natality.

Augustine was born in the North African town of Thagaste. At age sixteen he was sent to Carthage for a liberal arts education, which included rhetoric. At eighteen he read ancient Roman philosopher Marcus Tullius Cicero's now-lost work, *Hortensius,* and the evocation of wisdom contained in the text converted Augustine to philosophy. He joined the Manichean sect but eventually left them on account of their lack of philosophical rigor and their understanding of evil as a substance. Augustine famously argued evil is instead a deficient cause. He moved to Rome, Italy, where he embarked on a career teaching rhetoric. There he met Ambrose, the bishop of Milan, and discovered the books of the Platonists. Platonism enabled Augustine to understand scripture, as conveyed through Ambrose's sermons, in their allegorical as well as literal senses. He no longer considered scripture as simplistic and converted to Christianity in 386.

In 388 Augustine returned to North Africa and became bishop of Hippo in 395. During this time, civil wars convulsed the Roman Empire. Imperial authorities had been enforcing religious conformity as a means of preserving political unity since the Theodosian Code (a legal code) began to be compiled in 312. Augustine was drawn into a conflict between Christians and Donatists, a kind of Puritan sect, which frequently took violent form. He at first opposed banning the Donatists but in 411 changed his mind. Augustine's justification of the coercion of heretics has led many commentators to regard him as the Inquisition's first theorist, though more recent scholarship has shown that Augustine considered his decision a prudent response to an emergency situation in which the line between a religious sect and its violent political wing became blurred. In addition, Augustine thought only Donatist bishops should be arrested and that violence should be punished by beatings with wooden rods, the punishment that teachers of the day meted out to students, instead of the death penalty or beatings by iron rods as required by the Theodosian Code.

Alaric, the Visigoth king, entered Rome in 410, which prompted Roman aristocrats to blame Rome's collapse on Christians whose humility undermined the courage and allegiance to the fatherland. In response, Augustine argued in *City of God* that Christianity better protects civic virtue because of the importance it places on faith and justice, instead of the "noble lie" of antiquity. Politics not guided by genuine virtue, rooted in faith, is governed by the lust of domination (*libido dominandi*), which was the real cause of political ruin, including that of Rome. The contrast between faith and *libido dominandi* marks the difference between the symbols of the city of God and the earthly city. The theme of the two cities asks whether political society is something sacred, something profane, or some intermingling of the two. This is also the central question of contemporary politics when the appropriate relationship of religion and politics is considered, and the degree to which communities of faith can share the same political principles with those outside their communities.

See also *Arendt, Hannah; Cicero, Marcus Tullius; Just War Theory; Reformation Political Thought; Religion and Politics; Rousseau, Jean-Jacques; Thomas Aquinas; Tocqueville, Alexis de.*

. . . . JOHN VON HEYKING

BIBLIOGRAPHY

Augustine. *Confessions,* translated by F. J. Sheed. Indianapolis: Hackett, 1970.

Augustine. *City of God against the Pagans,* translated by R. W. Dyson. Cambridge: Cambridge University Press, 1998.

Arendt, Hannah. *Love and Saint Augustine,* edited by Joanna Vecchiarelli Scott and Judith Chelius Stark. Chicago: University of Chicago Press, 1996.

Brown, Peter. *Augustine of Hippo,* rev. ed. London: Faber and Faber, 2000.

Elshtain, Jean Bethke. *Augustine and the Limits of Politics.* Notre Dame, Ind.: University of Notre Dame Press, 1995.

Fitzgerald, Allan D., ed. *Augustine through the Ages: An Encyclopedia.* Grand Rapids, Mich.: Eerdmans, 1999.

Heyking, John von. *Augustine and Politics as Longing in the World.* Columbia: University of Missouri Press, 2001.

Australian Ballot

The Australian Ballot is one form of the *secret ballot,* a method of voting where the voter's choices are confidential. The purpose of the secret ballot is to ensure that voters will not be subjected to undue influence, as their vote will not be known to anyone else.

This voting method is known as the *Australian Ballot* because it originated in Australia during the 1850s. With this particular ballot, all candidate names are preprinted on a ballot provided by the government and given to the voter at the poll site. The voters then fill out their ballot in private.

In the United States, prior to the introduction of the Australian ballot, political parties and others would print ballots and distribute them to voters. In Great Britain and Australia, voters would hand in signed voting papers indicating their choice and their own name and address. The *open vote* made it possible to determine how voters cast their ballots, subjecting voters to bribery or intimidation.

INTRODUCTION OF THE AUSTRALIAN BALLOT

The introduction of the secret ballot was influenced by Chartism, a British working-class movement that advocated secret ballot elections. John Basson Humffray, a native of Wales and a member of the Chartist movement, moved to Victoria in Australia, where he became the leader of the Ballarat Reform League, an organization established to protest the colonial government's treatment of gold miners. One of the league's demands was the introduction of the secret ballot. Following an armed rebellion, the demands of the miners, including the call for the secret ballot, would soon me met.

The secret ballot was first adopted in Victoria, Australia, in December 1855, when the colony's Legislative Council agreed to include the secret ballot in the new self-governing colony's election law. Henry Samuel Chapman devised the system of the government-printed ballot, whose use spread across Australia over the next two decades.

The Australian ballot would be adopted in New Zealand (1870), Great Britain (1872), Canada (1874), and Belgium (1877). By 1896, all but four American states had introduced the Australian system (Brent 2005, 9).

See also *Ballot Design; Election Monitoring; Electoral Reform; Electoral Rules; Electoral Systems; Electronic Voting; Voting Machines and Technology.*

. . . . JEFFREY KRAUS

BIBLIOGRAPHY

Brent, Peter. "The Secret Ballot—Not an Australian First." 2005, www.enrollingthepeople.com.

Fredman, Lionel E. *The Australian Ballot: The Story of an American Reform.* East Lansing: Michigan State University Press, 1958.

Wigmore, John Henry. *The Australian Ballot Systen as Embodied in the Legislation of Various Countries.* Boston: C.C. Soule, 1889.

Autarky

Autarky means self-sufficiency, or nonattachment, especially in relation to economics. In economic literature it refers to a closed economy. The term should not be confused with *autarchia*, which is the act of self-ruling. Autarky is understood both as a theoretical construct of comparative advantage and as economic self-sufficiency. Autarky is a foundational concept in the doctrine of comparative advantage. David Ricardo sought to enhance Adam Smith's theory of absolute advantage by means of the principle of comparative advantage and trade that Robert Torrens originated. Ricardo thereby introduced into economic literature the theory of comparative cost advantage in international trade. For the purpose of independence from international influence, autarkic countries should be self-sufficient and not engaged in international trade. Historical examples of autarky just prior to the beginning of World War II (1939–1945) include Fascist Italy when the League of Nations sanctioned an embargo, Hitler's expressed desire for Germany in the Hossbach Memorandum, and Spain following an Allied embargo subsequent to its civil war.

Autarky, however, is quite rare in the current age. China is an example of a country that pursued a policy of almost entire autarky until recently, and it was not until the 1970s that India began the process of eliminating powerful trade barriers. Even North Korea, which is perhaps the only current autarky, practices some trade with China and Japan. Modern countries that have pursued autarky through the substitution of domestic production for imports have reduced themselves to inefficiency and poverty, compared to those countries that are competitive in foreign trade. The population demand for production of a full range of goods at competitive prices is impossible to be achieved by any country. It is because trade is beneficial to society that higher commodity prices do not eliminate the doctrine of comparative advantage.

See also *Free Trade; Sanctions and Embargoes; Trade Diplomacy.*

. . . . RON J. BIGALKE JR.

BIBLIOGRAPHY

Bardhan, Pranab K. *Economic Growth, Development and Foreign Trade: A Study in Pure Theory.* New York: Wiley, 1970.

Dobb, Maurice H. *Theories of Value and Distribution since Adam Smith.* London: Cambridge University Press, 1973.

Jones, Ronald W., and Peter B. Kenen, eds. *Handbook of International Economics*, vol. 1. Amsterdam: North-Holland, 1984.

Seers, Dudley, ed. *Dependency Theory: A Critical Assessment.* London: Frances Pinter, 1981.

Steedman, Ian, ed. *Fundamental Issues in Trade Theory.* London: Macmillan, 1979.

Authoritarianism, African

Authoritarianism is a form of political governance in which a ruler exercises absolute control over a state or group of people with the ultimate goal being preservation of power. In Africa, in addition to the elected presidents who have usurped power and turned themselves into presidents for life, military dictators are another category of authoritarians. Wherever military coups have occurred and a military oligarchy *(junta)* has taken power, a strong autocrat has always managed to emerge with the help of supportive military forces. Three such cases are those of President Muammar Qaddafi of Libya (1969 to present), former strongman Idi Amin Dada of Uganda (1971–1979), and former president Jerry Rawlings of Ghana (1979–2000). This prevailing style of autocracy has earned African authoritarianism the alternative title of *personal rule*.

While authoritarianism can take many different forms, African authoritarianism has three main characteristics. The first is a high level of violence and political intimidation against perceived opponents of the regime. Visible proof here is the openly meted police brutality against perceived opposition. A related element is the denial of government services and constitutionally guaranteed rights to those seen as opposing the regime.

The second distinctive feature is a high level of embedment in the existing social and cultural environment. The third is a remarkably low appeal to ideology. African authoritarian rulers have sought to portray themselves as cultural icons and to embed their governments in preexisting cultural structures.

At the height of his authoritarian rule, former president Daniel arap Moi of Kenya (1978–2002) sought to apply the "Nyayo" philosophy of peace, love, and unity as a tool for mobilization of the masses. Beyond rallying around the ruling KANU party however, what most legitimized his authority to the masses was his appeal to the African traditional custom of respect for elders. Posing as a traditional African elder, complete with the title *mzee* (Swahili for elder), Moi was able to put in place a formidable patron-client system that strongly legitimized his position and brought him support, even in the face of increasing international pressure and a budding political opposition to his rule. President Moi's predecessor, President Jomo Kenyatta, served for more than 14 years as a patron to various localized constituencies, including ethnic groups and women's organizations. In Libya, Muammar Qaddafi has successfully appealed to his country's strong Islamic background and has held on to power by portraying himself as one of the respected Islamic prophets.

Although the development of authoritarianism in modern African states can partly be traced back to the colonial administrations that preceded them and whose structures they inherited, it can be argued that African authoritarianism preceded European colonialism. Precolonial Africa had a fair share of authoritarian rulers like Shaka, head of the Zulu people. In essence, what European colonialism did was to introduce more political structures to endow the practice of authoritarianism. Such emergent political structures include restrictive economic and political structures, easy to manipulate court systems, a rubber-stamping legislature essential for legitimizing the actions of an authoritarian leader, and even a structured bureaucracy that could be employed to enforce the whims of the authoritarian ruler.

Further, ensuing tribalism as a result of colonial divide-and-rule strategies helped enhance the role of modern African authoritarian rulers as defenders and all-able benefactors of their people, regardless of constitutional stipulations. Through a combination of hero worship, open nepotism, and corruption using the resources of the state, a formidable system of client-patron relationships has taken shape in many African states. In so doing, the authoritarian rulers have become strongly entrenched in government.

A distinct outcome of African authoritarianism in almost all cases has been the deterioration of African economies, given the state's incompetence and heightened corruption that breeds restrictive monopolies to benefit the elite. Despite the continent's abundance of natural resources, noticeably few African countries can claim a plausible takeoff in industrialization. African authoritarian rulers and their henchmen have repeatedly stolen their countries' resources and turned them into personal property, to the detriment of their people. A case in point is the late Mobutu Sésé Seko of the Democratic Republic of Congo (formerly Zaire) who presided over the historical looting of his country's natural resources and who became one of the richest men on the continent at a time when extreme poverty continued to ravage his country.

Agriculture, which is the backbone for many African economies, has suffered also due to neglect and exploitation of the mostly subsistent farmers based in the rural areas. With no reliable means of income, many in the continent have sunk to unprecedented levels of poverty. While President Robert Mugabe's country of Zimbabwe was once considered to be Africa's most successful agricultural state, more than twenty-eight years of Mugabe's authoritarian rule, and a no-holds-barred approach to preservation of his power by eliminating any source of organized opposition, has left the country dilapidated and scrounging for food, amid high levels of poverty.

See also *African Political Thought; African Politics and Society: Postindependent Africa, Politics and Governance in.*

. . . . HENRY KIRAGU WAMBUII

BIBLIOGRAPHY

Ayittey, George B. N. *Africa Betrayed.* New York: St. Martin's, 1992.

N'Diaye, Boubacar, Abdoulaye Saine, and Mathurin Houngnikpo. *Not Yet Democracy: West Africa's Slow Farewell to Authoritarianism.* Durham, N.C.: Carolina Academic Press, 2005.

Schraeder, Peter J. *African Politics and Society: A Mosaic in Transformation.* Boston: Bedford/St. Martin's, 2000.

Tordoff, William. *Government and Politics in Africa,* 4th ed. Bloomington: Indiana University Press, 2002.

Authoritarianism, Bureaucratic

See *Bureaucratic Authoriatarianism.*

Authority

Defining political authority is a useful exercise for it raises the central problems of political theory. There is therefore no easy way to discuss authority without encountering important controversy. Rather than supply a settled definition of authority, what follows discusses the central questions that such an attempt inevitably raises.

DEFINING POLITICS

To understand political authority, it is necessary first to try to define *politics.* The most influential modern definition described the modern state as "a human community that (successfully) claims the monopoly of the legitimate use of physical force within a given territory" (Weber 2004). Weber sought to define politics in a purely descriptive, value-free manner. Notice that the state has authority not just because it has a monopoly of violence, but because its monopoly is claimed, successfully, to be legitimate. There seems to be a difference, intuited by most, between genuine authority and mere force. Where genuine authority *obliges* us, force alone merely compels. But what adds legitimacy to force, and turns it into authority? What's the difference between authoritative force and merely successful force? Weber abstains from giving legitimacy value-content. Legitimacy may be viewed in many ways, but the state, as a state, is successful in advancing its claim to it, whatever that claim may be. Legitimate force is force that has succeeded in advancing its claim to legitimacy. This applies, therefore, to force that has merely succeeded in controlling minds as well as bodies. But this means that, in Weber's terms, authority is power, or rather, that there is no intelligible content to authority, if by *authority* we seek something other than power that has managed to mobilize or indoctrinate.

AUTHORITY AND JUSTICE

To understand authority beyond mere power, we enter the world of normative political theory. If we try to avoid normative issues by defining authority in terms of a political process, we are faced with having to ground our choice of process. Do we require that authority be legitimated by democratic, rather than nondemocratic processes? Why? We immediately find a value-judgment, a view of justice, operating as a hidden premise: Authority must be democratic, for democracy is just. Claims about what counts as genuine authority are conceptually inseparable from claims about justice.

To investigate authority is to investigate justice, about which there is a distinguished history of ideas. Rather than attempt a survey here, it may be useful to suggest, as a preview of such a survey, one point of comparison that sheds light on the question of authority. The following presentation is meant to be highly provisional, an invitation to first steps.

Arguments about justice, and therefore genuine authority, are often grounded in assertions about the purpose of government. Justice means accomplishing a particular end, which then defines the nature of authority and its limits. For example, the purpose of Socrates' utopian city in *The Republic* appears to be the greatest possible fulfillment of the basic human types consistent with the greatest possible harmony of the types with each other. To create and manage a city that accomplishes this, he argues, a ruler is needed who has the greatest possible wisdom about human types, their fulfillment and education, and their relations to each other. This ruler also needs tremendous power in the areas of education and procreation. True authority, then, has to combine these particular powers with this particular wisdom: a philosopher-king. Both his particular wisdom (about the human good) and these particular powers (to turn individuals into harmonious fellow citizens) are necessary to achieve the city's purpose, which defines justice. Only this union of power and wisdom then, embodied in a philosopher-king, has genuine authority. It is precisely in the avowed unlikelihood of such a union that Plato's subtle subversion of all actual political authority consists.

SOCIAL CONTRACT THEORY

For social contract theorists, power becomes authority not only by virtue of the purpose it serves, but by virtue of its origin in consent. The premise of all social contract theory is natural equality, variously understood. For Hobbes, we are equally vulnerable to violent death, for example, while for Locke we are equal in our authority over ourselves, but in both cases equality means that no one has natural authority over others. Authority must be created, by agreement among equals, and this necessitates a social contract. Legitimate authority is merely conventional, but created on natural grounds (our equality), and for the sake of natural ends (our survival and prosperity, for example). A particular kind of convention, then, is necessary for power to have genuine authority.

Once the requirement of free consent has been satisfied, the scope and nature of authority is determined, again, by the purpose for which the contract was created. The purpose of government for Hobbes is safety; authority is created to impose peace on a violently competitive state of nature. The sovereign power can justly claim authority only if it can achieve its purpose, and the powers that are inherent to its authority are all those that are necessary for doing so. Hobbes's sovereign is justly absolute—just authority must be understood to be unlimited—for only absolute power can ensure the safety of the commonwealth. Safety is near the heart of Locke's view of the purpose of government—protection of life, liberty, and estate—but he argues that, given the dangers of tyranny, safety can only be ensured through limited government. Locke's

authority is justly limited, because the purpose of government makes such limits necessary. Should government overstep those limits, it oversteps its authority, because in overstepping its limits it vitiates the purpose for which it was created, in the name of which the citizens gave their consent. Early liberal thought is about further articulating those limits and their institutional consequences (e.g., separation of powers, Bill of Rights).

THE ANTI-LIBERAL CRITIQUE

For anti-liberal thinkers such as Marx (and to a lesser extent, Rousseau) it is the absence of a natural purpose for politics, and the injustice of its actual purposes, that destroys the claim to authority of modern regimes. For Marx, the state is the handmaiden of the exploiting class and can have no genuine authority. Politics is the appropriation of the monopoly of violence for class warfare. There can be no political justice, and therefore no political authority. Justice begins when class exploitation, and with it politics and the modern state, ends; the natural or authentic end of our species, species-being, is antithetical to the historical ends of politics. For Nietzsche, finally, there are no natural ends of any kind, therefore no justice or genuine authority, nor injustice or genuine oppression. There is only will to power. Power often masquerades as authority, and the struggle to define authority by defining justice is a principal arena of the struggle for power. In Nietzsche we see the fullest development of the implications hinted at in Weber, and expounded at length in Machiavelli, that authority is merely successful power.

See also *Justice and Injustice; Normative Theory; Politics; Social Contract.*

. . . . G. BORDEN FLANAGAN

BIBLIOGRAPHY

Hamilton, Alexander, John Jay, James Madison, and Clinton Rossiter. *The Federalist Papers,* edited by Charles R. Kesler. New York: Signet Classics, 2003.

Hobbes, Thomas. *Leviathan,* edited by Edwin Curley. Indianapolis: Hackett, 1994.

Locke, John. *Two Treatises of Government,* edited by Peter Laslett. Cambridge: Cambridge University Press, 1999.

Machiavelli, Niccolò. *The Prince,* translated by Harvey Mansfield Jr. Chicago: University of Chicago Press, 1985.

Marx, Karl, and Friedrich Engels. "The Communist Manifesto." In *The Marx-Engels Reader,* 2nd ed., edited by Robert C. Tucker. New York: Norton, 1978.

Mill, John Stuart. *"On Liberty" and Other Writings,* edited by Stefan Collini. Cambridge: Cambridge University Press, 1989.

Montesquieu, Charles. *The Spirit of the Laws (Cambridge Texts in the History of Political Thought),* edited by Anne M. Cohler, Basia Carolyn Miller, and Harold Samuel Stone. Cambridge: Cambridge University Press, 1989.

Nietzsche, Friedrich. *Beyond Good and Evil,* translated by Walter Kaufmann. New York: Vintage, 1966.

Plato. *The Republic of Plato,* translated and edited by Allan Bloom. New York: Basic Books, 1991.

Rawls, John. *A Theory of Justice: Original Edition.* New York: Belknap Press of Harvard University Press, 2005.

Rousseau, Jean-Jacques. *The Basic Political Writings,* translated and edited by Donald A. Cress. Indianapolis: Hackett, 1987.

Weber, Max. *The Vocation Lectures: Science as a Vocation, Politics as a Vocation,* edited by David S. Owen and Tracy B. Strong, translated by Rodney Livingstone. Indianapolis: Hackett, 2004

Autocracy

Autocracy is a form of government in which a single person has unlimited authority to exercise power. The word comes from two ancient Greek words, *auto-* ("self") and *-cracy* ("rule" from *kratia*). Modern authors are more likely to use the term *authoritarian* than *autocracy*, which is commonly used by some to describe ancient regimes that prevailed in backward societies without legal and political institutions to protect individuals.

PREVALENCE OF AUTOCRACY IN HISTORY

Until the advent of modern government, beginning with the American Revolution (1776–1783), almost all governments were autocratic governments ruled by tribal chiefs, kings, or emperors, with the exception of the ancient Greek democracies. Autocratic rulers have usually been accepted as the sole source of legitimate power, unless a competing autocrat were accepted as more just or successful or legitimate. The autocrat is not limited by constitutional or popular restraints or by political opposition. If any opposition arises, it is usually not tolerated and is eliminated.

The ancient empires of the Assyrians, Babylonians, Egyptians, and Persians were fully autocratic. Various dynasties of ancient China were ruled by individuals in whom the power of their political system was centered. The Inca in Peru or various other empires around the world were without a doubt autocratic. Many autocracies were also theocracies because the exercise of power by the autocrat was based on some claim to divine right. The Buddhist theocracies or those of the Mayans were autocratic but also theocratic. It was mainly the Greek democracies that opposed autocratic government.

Even today autocratic governments exist in many places. Arab sheikdoms of the Persian Gulf region can be described as autocratic; although their rule often appears to be benign, it is still very strong. This can have administrative advantages because decisions can often be achieved without having to engage in exhausting battles with interest groups or opposition parties that exist in democratic states. Thus, a decision to adopt green technology can be made by the ruler even if other interests are hurt.

THEORETICAL DISCUSSIONS OF AUTOCRACY: ARISTOTLE TO HOBBES

Aristotle in his discussions of the forms or constitutions of government in his books *Ethics, Rhetoric,* and *Politics* defined *monarchy* and *tyranny* as rule by a single individual. The difference between a monarch and a tyrant lay in the object of concern of the autocrat. It was the people in the case of the monarch but self-interest in the case of the tyrant. Because tyrants have often masked their political actions, it has been difficult at times to distinguish them from monarchs.

Niccolò Machiavelli supported *absolutism,* which was similar to autocracy. He wanted a centralizing power in the hands of an absolute ruler as a solution for the violent strife between the various city-states that was wracking Renaissance Italy. Without a firm hand there would be no peace, and in that regard he counseled an ethic of success in the exercise of power. However, even Machiavelli was like many in autocratic regimes. The more the society matures, the less willing many are to tolerate unrestrained power in a single ruler.

Jean Bodin, author of *Six Books of the Commonwealth* (*Les Six livres de la République*), defined *sovereignty* as the absolute and perpetual power vested in a commonwealth. For him, a prince who was sovereign was only accountable to God. This vision of the autocratic state found its fulfillment in King Louis XIV's reign (1643–1715), where the loss of liberty stimulated the quest of the Baron de Montesquieu for liberty (*Spirit of the Laws*), ending with federalism as an antidote. However, as Aristotle observed in *Politics,* autocracy tends to be unstable.

Thomas Hobbes was an advocate of an absolute monarchy. In *Leviathan* (1651), he used the idea of a social contract to place all power into the hands of a single sovereign who would keep the peace among men who would otherwise be in a "state of nature," which was "a war of all against all" with lives that were "solitary, poor, nasty, brutish, and short." His absolute sovereign, if not an autocrat, is described as one who functions like an autocrat even if the sovereign power is vested in a legislative body.

AUTOCRACY AND DEMOCRACY IN MODERNITY

In more recent centuries, the tsars of Russia, the absolutist rulers of eighteenth-century Europe including the Sultan of Turkey, and many of the smaller kingdoms or dukedoms of Europe were autocrats. The Russian emperors employed the title *autocrat*. The title came from the Byzantine Empire as a translation of *imperator* (emperor). In modern times it has been used also as a title for the Emperor of Japan. Some monarchs have ruled in an autocratic fashion, but with diminished power due to growing restraints.

However, the rise of liberal democracy, a partial revival of elements of ancient Greek democracy, brought most of the hereditary forms of autocracy to an end. Replacing autocracy that placed power in the hands of a single individual have been forms of authoritarianism.

Authoritarianism is absolutist, but it rests on the principle that authority per se is legitimate and must be obeyed. Authoritarianism uses ideological elements to enlist the whole population of a state into its service. The rulers of such regimes then aspire to be autocrats or become autocrats. Adolph Hitler, Benito Mussolini, Joseph Stalin, and others used ideology and party to gather absolute power to become autocratic totalitarian rulers. Rulers like Idi Amin Dada of Uganda, Muammar al-Qaddafi of Libya, and El Hadj Omar Bongo Ondimba of Gabon have used tribal power supported by their personal ideology to justify their autocratic rule. Some modern autocratic rulers have assumed the trappings of democratic legitimacy.

The rise of democratic government has not ended its competition with autocracy. In times of stress people may seek refuge in autocracy for the sake of peace and prosperity as both Machiavelli and Hobbes recognized. Or those with authoritarian personalities may trade freedom for autocratic rule.

Autocracy can appear in areas of life other than civil politics. Religious organizations, businesses, management styles (e.g., Theory X), or family life may be dominated by autocratic persons or groups.

See also *Bodin, Jean; Hobbes, Thomas; Machiavelli, Niccolò.*

. . . . ANDREW J. WASKEY

BIBLIOGRAPHY

Downing, Brian. *Military Revolution and Political Change: Origins of Democracy and Autocracy in Early Modern Europe.* Princeton, N.J.: Princeton University Press, 1993.

Friedrich, Carl J. *Totalitarian Dictatorship and Autocracy.* Cambridge, Mass.: Harvard University Press, 1965.

Roller, Matthew B. *Constructing Autocracy: Aristocrats and Emperors in Julio-Claudian Rome.* Princeton, N.J.: Princeton University Press, 2001.

Rotberg, Robert. *Ending Autocracy, Enabling Democracy: The Tribulations of Southern Africa, 1960–2000.* Washington, D.C.: Brookings Institution, 2002.

Tullock, Gordon. *Autocracy.* Leiden, Netherlands: E.J. Brill, 1987.

White, Ralph K. *Autocracy and Democracy: An Experimental Inquiry.* New York: Harper, 1960.

Autogestion

Autogestion, a term used especially among French- and Spanish-language worker movements, refers to workers' self-management and workplace control. Forms of activity undertaken by autogestion movements include workers' cooperatives, workers' councils, and syndicalism or revolutionary unionism.

The notion of autogestion makes an early appearance in the works of the French anarchist Pierre-Joseph Proudhon in the nineteenth century. Perhaps the most extensive expression of autogestion occurred in Barcelona under anarchist direction during the Spanish Revolution (1936–1939). In France during the 1960s and 1970s the writings of social theorist André Gorz were particularly influential in mobilizations over demands for workers' self-control. The 1973 worker occupation and self-management of the LIP clockwork factory in France was the most influential moment in the autogestion movement during the cold war period. It sparked international movements for libertarian socialism and anarchist communism, which advocated autogestion as a grassroots working-class alternative to party-led forms of socialism and communism.

During the twenty-first century, autogestion has become an important working-class response to the closure of factories in Argentina following the economic crisis of 2001. The recovered factory movement has involved the takeover of numerous workplaces, which have restarted production on a democratically controlled, cooperative basis by employees, after employers had abandoned them.

See also *Anarchism; Proudhon, Pierre-Joseph.*

. . . . JEFFREY SHANTZ

Autogolpe

Autogolpe is a Spanish term translated as "self-coup." An autogolpe occurs when a seated president seizes power, often with the assistance of the military, and shuts down the legislature and other branches of government so as to govern with no opposition. It is not the same as a *golpe de estado* (coup d'etat), which generally involves a military overthrowing a president and taking power for itself.

Autogolpes are not common events. The best-known took place in Peru in April 1992, when President Alberto Fujimori (elected in 1990) took power with the backing of the military and closed the Peruvian congress and the judicial system. His seizure of power was preceded by acrimonious relations with the congress over congressional attempts to limit Fujimori's power, debates over economic policy, and ongoing problems with the judiciary. Fujimori was a minority president; his party held only 32 of the 175 seats in the legislature. In his address that announced the autogolpe, Fujimori recited a list of grievances as justifying the coup; a poll carried out a day or two after the coup found that 80 percent of the populace supported it.

See also *Bureuacratic Authoritarianism; Coup d'Etat.*

. . . . HENRY A. DIETZ

Autonomy

Autonomy, or self-government, is an ancient term that seems to have gained wide currency only in the second half of the twentieth century. It derives from the Greek word *autonomia,* which combines the words for self (*auto*) and law (*nomos*). To be autonomous, then, is to live according to laws one gives to oneself.

In both ancient Greek and in contemporary usage, *autonomy* figures in two different kinds of political discussions. In the first kind, autonomy may be a property of political units, such as cities, counties, provinces, or states. This was apparently the dominant usage of the term among the Greeks, who were concerned with the autonomy of the *polis*—the self-governing city-state. This usage persists, but is probably less common now than the second, which takes autonomy to be a possible and perhaps desirable feature of the individual person's life. In this case, autonomy is of particular interest to political philosophers, who often explore the relationship between personal autonomy and government. They may ask, for instance, whether government is more likely to promote individual autonomy by leaving people alone or by taking steps to help them become (more) autonomous.

POLITICAL AUTONOMY

Autonomy of the first kind—the autonomy of the self-governing political unit—was closely related in Greek thought to the concept of autarky (from *autarkeia*), or self-sufficiency. For a *polis* or state to be self-governing, according to the usual argument, it must be free to chart its own course, independent of the will of other political units. If it is to be truly independent, however, it will have to meet all, or almost all, of its own material needs; otherwise it will find itself dependent on those who provide it with food and other vital resources. Such a *polis* will be autonomous in name only.

Contemporary discussions of political autonomy sometimes touch on this connection between autonomy and autarky, but they are more likely to concentrate on the relations of political units and subunits. In some cases the question is how much control over its own affairs a sovereign state can or should surrender, yet remain autonomous, when it joins an entity such as the United Nations or the European Union. In other cases, political autonomy is primarily a problem of the relations between a region or subunit and the overarching political unit in which it finds itself. Familiar examples include Quebec's relationship with Canada, the Kurds' relationship with Iraq, and the place of Scotland and Wales within the United Kingdom. Often the region or subunit wants full autonomy, to be achieved by secession, but sometimes arrangements are made to keep it within the larger political unit while granting it control over local matters that directly concern those who inhabit the subunit. Arrangements of this kind recognize what is often called *regional* or *provincial* autonomy.

PERSONAL AUTONOMY

Autonomy as a property of political units may have been the primary sense in which ancient writers used the term, but there is at least one important reference to personal autonomy in Greek literature. This occurs in Sophocles' tragedy *Antigone,* when the Chorus refers to the title character as *autonomos:* "true to your own laws" (Sophocles 2001, 36). This concept seems not to have played a major part in Western philosophy, however, until the eighteenth century. French Enlightenment philosopher Jean-Jacques Rousseau did not use the term, but his brief discussion of "moral liberty" has overtones of autonomy, as when he proclaims that "the impulse of appetite alone is slavery, and obedience to the law one has prescribed for oneself is freedom" (Rousseau 1978). Rousseau's admirer, German philosopher Immanuel Kant, developed this assertion into a distinction between autonomy and *heteronomy,* or being ruled by others—including rule by one's own irrational desires.

Whether autonomy is necessarily a good thing—and what exactly it is—has been the subject of much discussion and debate in the past fifty years or so. The point of departure for these debates is often British philosopher Isaiah Berlin's lecture, "Two Concepts of Liberty." There Berlin connects the desire for autonomy to the "retreat to the inner citadel" (Berlin 1969, 135)—that is, the desire for self-mastery that is achieved by withdrawing into isolation and self-denial. Most other writers, however, take a more positive view of autonomy. In Stanley Benn's account, for example, autonomy is a character ideal that leads the individual to try to form a consistent and coherent set of beliefs, albeit a set that must continually be adjusted in light of critical reflection.

Personal autonomy is frequently taken to be an ideal of the liberal tradition. Autonomy is certainly at home within liberalism, which greatly values individual liberty, but it is by no means clear that it is an exclusively liberal ideal. Nevertheless, some critics of liberalism, including some feminists, have complained that autonomy is an individualistic concept that deflects attention from the importance of community and social relations, especially caring relations. Parents, for example, should be less concerned with their autonomy than with the needs of their dependent children.

In response, supporters of autonomy as an ideal agree that it is an individualistic concept, but they deny that it is the kind of individualism that ignores or even erodes important social relations. Personal autonomy is something that individuals *exercise,* but they can exercise it only when their capacity for self-government has been sufficiently *developed.* Yet developing that capacity is something that no one can do alone. In other words, no person can *be* autonomous unless others help that person to *become* autonomous. One of the things the autonomous person should realize, then, is the importance of protecting and nurturing those relationships—and the other conditions—that protect and promote autonomy. What the role of government should be in this attempt to further autonomy has become one of the principal concerns of political philosophers.

See also *Autarky; Berlin, Isaiah; Greek Political Thought, Ancient; Individual and Society; Kant, Immanuel; Rousseau, Jean-Jacques; Self-determination; Sovereignty.*

. . . . RICHARD DAGGER

BIBLIOGRAPHY

Benn, Stanley. *A Theory of Freedom.* Cambridge: Cambridge University Press, 1988.

Berlin, Isaiah. "Two Concepts of Liberty." In *Four Essays on Liberty,* edited by Isaiah Berlin, 118–172. Oxford: Oxford University Press, 1969.

Christman, John, ed. *The Inner Citadel: Essays on Individual Autonomy.* Oxford: Oxford University Press, 1989.

Christman, John, and Joel Anderson, eds. *Autonomy and the Challenges to Liberalism: New Essays.* Cambridge: Cambridge University Press, 2005.

Dworkin, Gerald. *The Theory and Practice of Autonomy.* Cambridge: Cambridge University Press, 1988.

Hannum, Hurst. *Autonomy, Sovereignty, and Self-Determination: The Accommodation of Conflicting Rights,* rev. ed. Philadelphia: University of Pennsylvania Press, 1996.

Haworth, Lawrence. *Autonomy: An Essay in Philosophical Psychology and Ethics.* New Haven, Conn.: Yale University Press, 1986.

Kant, Immanuel. 1785. *Groundwork of the Metaphysic of Morals.* Translated by Mary Gregor. Cambridge: Cambridge University Press, 1998.

Lindley, Richard. *Autonomy.* Basingstoke, U.K.: Macmillan, 1986.

Nedelsky, Jennifer. "Reconceiving Autonomy: Sources, Thoughts, and Possibilities." *Yale Journal of Law and Feminism* 1 (Spring 1989): 7–36.

Rousseau, Jean-Jacques. 1762. *On the Social Contract,* edited by Roger Masters and translated by Judith Masters. New York: St. Martin's, 1978.

Schneewind, J. B. *The Invention of Autonomy: A History of Modern Moral Philosophy.* Cambridge: Cambridge University Press, 1998.

Sophocles. *Antigone.* Translated by Paul Woodruff. Indianapolis: Hackett, 2001.

Young, Robert. *Personal Autonomy: Beyond Negative and Positive Liberty.* London: Croom Helm, 1986.

Baathism

The starting point for understanding the ideology of the Arab Baath (also Ba'ath or Ba'th; Arabic for "resurrection" or "renaissance") Socialist Party, is its slogan, "Unity, Freedom, Socialism." Generally known as the *Baath,* it emerged in the early 1940s in Syria, but sometimes is considered a successor to another Syrian organization, the League of National Action, which dates back to 1932. The party spread to other Arab countries, particularly in the Fertile Crescent region. Its ideology represents an articulation of Arab nationalist and anticolonial thinking then ubiquitous in the area, especially among young educated people of modest origin.

The precise date of the founding of the party is subject to some controversy, as two separate groups, largely made up of high school students, appeared almost simultaneously under the name Arab Baath Party. One of these soon disappeared, with its members joining the group led by two Syrian high school teachers, Michel Aflaq and Salah al-Din al-Bitar. The party added the word *socialist* to its name when it merged with the Arab Socialist Party of Akram Hourani, a prominent agitator for peasants' rights in the Hama district of Syria (who broke away from that party in 1962). A national convention adopted a constitution for the Baath Party, which later changed its name to Socialist Baath Party, in 1947.

The Baath eventually gained influence in electoral politics in Syria during the mid-1950s and later became the ruling party of Syria following a Baathist coup in 1963. Baathists also took power in Iraq in 1963, only to be overthrown later in the same year. Another coup in 1968 ushered in a period of Baathist rule in Iraq that endured until the American invasion of 2003, when the party was banned. Baathists (or ex-Baathists) apparently have played a significant role in the anti-American insurgency in the country since then. The Baath had considerable support in Jordan during the 1950s, particularly among the Palestinian population, but declined as a result of the regime's repressiveness and its own factionalism.

ONE ARAB NATION

Placing the word *unity* first in its slogan served to stress the idea, widely shared with others, of the Arabs as a nation with an "eternal mission"—distinct but not superior to other nations—that must unite. Party terminology stresses the oneness of the Arab nation by having a pan-Arab *National Command*, while each country-level subdivision is known as a *Regional Command*. Dedication to this idea, together with threats from communists and "reactionaries," led Baathists in 1958 to seek union with Egypt, whose leader, President Gamal Abdul Nasser, recently had gained heroic stature among Arab nationalists after his nationalization of the Suez Canal Company and subsequent survival of an invasion by Israel, Britain, and France. Baathists also hoped to provide the ideology and leadership for the new United Arab Republic (UAR), but soon were disillusioned by being left on the sidelines, leading many of them to support its breakup in 1961.

The Arabs' relationship to Islam remained an important part of their national identity, sometimes even for Christian Arabs, during the ascendancy of secular Arab nationalism. But while a connection between Islam and the Arab "spirit" was recognized, the Baathist concept of unity stresses the equality of Arabs without distinction of religion. Consequently, it has sometimes had a strong appeal to minority religious sects. In Syria, this led to a strong influx of the small, previously disadvantaged Alawi sect into the party's ranks and the emergence of a Baathist regime in which it is dominant. In Iraq, the Sunni Baathists who took power made considerable progress in bringing Shiites into the party. And yet the tendency of those in power to rely on cronies and blood relatives, especially when faced with threats, resulted ironically in regimes with a highly sectarian character. In Iraq, in particular, Iran's Islamic Revolution (1979) inspired many Shiites and put the loyalty of others in question, thus undermining the idea of nonsectarianism. As Shiite revolts were brutally suppressed, this accentuated the equation of Baathism with the Sunni Arab in a way that belied the nonsectarian nature of the ideology.

FREEDOM

The word *freedom* in Baath Party usage carries multiple implications. It connotes freedom from the colonialism that dominated much of the Arab world when the party first emerged, as well as from continuing subordination to outside powers (that is, the freedom of the nation). Baathists have been committed to the slogan of nonalignment while cooperating pragmatically with particular big powers.

Freedom also seemed to refer originally to freedom for the individual. Baathists gave strong support for such democratic principles as the direct election of members to the Syrian parliament and female suffrage in the late 1940s. But Baathist regimes have come to power through military coups in both Syria and Iraq, and each regime has been highly authoritarian. Although the Syrian and Iraqi Baathist regimes established fronts in which some other parties were allowed to participate, those have had no real power. In effect, both Syria and Iraq have been single-party regimes, with the Baath organized along Leninist lines of "democratic centralism" (from cells at the bottom to a secretary general at the top). In reality, the power structure has been personalistic, with informal networks of cronies and relatives more important than any political party.

SOCIALISM

Socialism always was subordinate to unity in the hierarchy of Baathist goals. Baathist socialist ideology, like other versions of *Arab socialism,* stresses the need to end exploitation and promote social justice. It advocates nationalization of big enterprises while leaving much of the economy in the hands of small owners. It calls for limits on ownership of agricultural land. The party's constitution, adopted in 1947, declares "property and inheritance" to be "natural rights . . . protected within the limits of the national interest." In practice, the Baathist regimes of Syria and Iraq brought formerly underprivileged people to power and established relatively statist economies, although both implemented some economic liberalization in the 1980s.

Although Baathist regimes generally received much backing from communist countries, the Baath Party was always anticommunist, due to the Baathists' ideology and their unwillingness to tolerate other political groups in their countries. They sometimes collaborated with Western powers against communism, as in the case of the U.S. Central Intelligence Agency's 1963 help in bringing the Baath to power in Iraq and implementing an anticommunist pogrom. Like other proponents of socialism, both Baathist regimes pursued policies of land reform and nationalization but never attempted to abolish all private ownership.

FROM BAATH TO BAATHS

Factionalism, based on both personal rivalries and ideological differences, has plagued the Baath. The period of Syrian-Egyptian unity brought several splits, as Bitar and Hourani, but not Aflaq, endorsed secession from the UAR in 1961. With the Baath coming to power in Syria in 1963, factionalism remained rampant. A leftist military faction of the party (sometimes called the *Neo-Baath* and tending to come from the countryside), much influenced by Marxism and pursuing a particularly militant anti-Israel policy, carried out a coup against the existing Baathist regime in 1966. This was overthrown by a pragmatic, "corrective movement" under Hafiz al-Asad in 1970, during which Asad, also a Baathist, took power. The Baathist group that came to power in Iraq in 1968 became a rival to the Syrian regime, leading to the emergence of two rival National Commands and of rival Regional Commands in some countries, analogous to the competition between pro-Moscow and pro-Beijing communist parties. This rivalry seems basically to represent personal and geopolitical conflicts more than any disagreement over ideology

or policy. Enmity between Baathist Syria and Baathist Iraq became so intense that the former supported Iraq's enemy in the Iraq-Iran War (1980–1988) and then joined the anti-Iraqi coalition in 1991.

The Baath seems largely to belong to the past. By the early twenty-first century, both socialism and the goal of pan-Arab unification lost their former widespread appeal, as had secularism. The Syrian Baathist regime in 2009 was more a personalistic than a party dictatorship. Considering anti-Baathist attitudes of the now-empowered Shiite majority in Iraq, the restoration of the Baath there seems unthinkable. Only minor Baathist parties exist in other Arab countries, such as Yemen, Bahrain, Lebanon, Sudan, and Mauritania.

See also *Arab Socialism; Middle Eastern Politics and Society; Pan-Arabism and Pan-Islamism.*

. . . . GLENN E. PERRY

BIBLIOGRAPHY

Abu Jaber, Kamel S. *The Arab Ba'th Socialist Party.* Syracuse, N.Y.: Syracuse University Press, 1966.

Baram, Amazia. *Culture, History, and Ideology in the Formation of Ba'thist Iraq, 1968–1989.* New York: St. Martin's, 1991.

Devlin, John F. *The Ba'th Party: A History from Its Origins to 1966.* Stanford, Calif.: Hoover Institution Press, 1976.

———. "The Baath Party: Rise and Metamorphosis." *The American Historical Review* 96 (December 1991): 1396–1407.

Kaylani, Nabil A. "The Rise of the Syrian Baath 1940–1958: Political Success, Party Failure." *International Journal of Middle East Studies* 3 (January 1972): 3–23.

Marr, Phebe. *The Modern History of Iraq,* 2nd. ed. Boulder, Colo.: Westview, 2004.

Olson, Robert. *The Ba'th and Syria, 1947 to 1982: The Evolution of Ideology, Party, and State.* Princeton, N.J.: Kingston, 1982.

Rabinovich, Itmar. *Syria under the Ba'th 1963–1966: The Army-Party Symbiosis.* New Brunswick, N.J.: Transaction, 1972.

Roberts, David. *The Ba'th and the Creation of Modern Syria.* New York: St. Martin's, 1987.

Seale, Patrick. *The Struggle for Syria: A Study of Post-War Arab Politics, 1945–1958.* New Haven, Conn.: Yale University Press, 1987.

Bachrach, Peter

Peter Bachrach (1918–2007) was a political scientist and a prominent analyst of participatory democracy.

Born in Winnetka, Illinois, Bachrach earned his bachelor's degree from Reed College in Portland, Oregon, and a PhD in political science from Harvard University in 1951. He joined the faculty of Bryn Mawr College in 1946. In 1968, he moved to Temple University, where he remained until his retirement in 1988. In 1980, he was a visiting professor at the Graduate School of the City University of New York.

Bachrach is best known for his 1962 article, "Two Faces of Power," which he coauthored with Morton S. Baratz. Published in the *American Political Science Review,* it is the most widely cited article in the discipline of political science. In their article, Bachrach and Baratz argued that a lack of controversy may reflect latent power conflicts.

According to Bachrach, prevailing institutions and political processes could limit the decision-making abilities and the formation and articulation of concerns among disenfranchised groups in society. While most power theorists of the time studied decisions, Bachrach contended that power also could be reflected in "nondecisions." That is, that some actors had so much influence in the political process that they could block decisions that would be adverse to their interests from even being considered. According to Bachrach and Baratz, "power is also exercised when A devotes his energies to creating or reinforcing social and political values and institutional practices that limit the scope of the political process to public consideration of those issues which are comparatively innocuous to A" (948). They asserted that this power meant that demands for change can be suffocated before they are even voiced. Non-decision-making, therefore, constituted a "second face" of power.

See also *Elite Theory; Power.*

. . . . JEFFREY KRAUS

BIBLIOGRAPHY
Bachrach, Peter. *The Theory of Democratic Elitish: A Critique.* Boston: Little, Brown, 1967.
Bachrach, Peter, and Morton S. Baratz. "Two Faces of Power." *American Political Science Review* 56 (December 1962): 947–952.
———. *Power and Poverty: Theory and Practice.* New York: Oxford University Press, 1970.
Bachrach, Peter, and Elihu Bergman. *Power and Choice: The Formulation of American Population Policy.* Lexington, Mass.: Lexington Books, 1973.
Bachrach, Peter, and Aryeh Botwinick. *Power and Empowerment: A Radical Theory of Participatory Democracy.* Philadelphia: Temple University Press, 1992.

Bagehot, Walter

Walter Bagehot (1826–1877) was an economist and political journalist and one of the most influential writers on the British constitution until recent times. Bagehot is so important that other commentators have treated his doctrines, published in 1867, as if they were part of the unwritten constitution itself.

Bagehot was born into a banking family in Somerset in southwestern England. Bored by banking, he turned to journalism and edited *The Economist* from 1861 until his death. His main legacy is a pair of books: *The English Constitution* (1865) and *Lombard Street* (1873), a study of the role of the central bank. Bagehot's writing is clear and persuasive, and his influence is still apparent today: the United Kingdom's politics correspondent for the modern *Economist* writes under the penname "Bagehot" (pronounced *badge-ot*).

In *The English Constitution,* Bagehot's target is political philosopher Charles-Louis Montesquieu's claim that the United Kingdom's liberty is due to a separation of powers. He argues that Montesquieu (and perhaps the American Federalists) got England completely wrong. (Like many Victorians, Bagehot failed to distinguish between England and the United Kingdom and was thus insensitive to Scotland and Ireland.) The "efficient secret" of the English constitution was the cabinet, a "buckle" that joined the "dignified" (the formal institutions of governance: church, Parliament, and above all the monarchy) to the "efficient" part of the constitution. According to Montesquieu and the Federalists, the key to liberty lies with the separation of powers. According to Bagehot, it lies with concealing the efficient part of government (the cabinet operating through its control of the House of Commons) behind the dignified façade of crown and establishment. Power was fused, not separated. The executive ran the country through its control of both the permanent officials and (normally) the majority of seats in the House of Commons. Because of the doctrine of parliamentary supremacy, whereby statutes trump all other forms of law, the judiciary also occupied a subordinate role. There was no judicial review of either legislation or executive acts in Bagehot's constitution.

Bagehot was contemptuous of the monarch and her heir, calling them "a retired widow and an unemployed youth." But he thought that having an ordinary family at the head of state was advantageous to social order. People would, he believed, follow the lives of the retired widow and the unemployed youth with interest, and not concern themselves with the efficient part of government, which could be left to competent statesmen.

Curiously, successive British monarchs have learned their constitution from Bagehot, despite his evident contempt for the royal family's intelligence. Even more curiously, so have most subsequent constitutional commentators. Though a liberal free trader, Bagehot was a profound anti-democrat. His constitutional doctrine may be summarized as this: The royalty and the aristocracy are too stupid to rule—"It is as great a difficulty to learn business in a palace as it is to learn agriculture in a park" (Bagehot 2008, 107)—as are the working and lower-middle class. Government should therefore remain in the hands of educated people who are well-informed on current events and politics.

See also *British Political Thought; Enlightenment Political Thought; Monarchy; Montesquieu, Charles-Louis.*

. . . . IAIN MCLEAN

BIBLIOGRAPHY
Bagehot, Walter. 1873. *Lombard Street.* Indianapolis: Library of Economics and Liberty, 2001, www.econlib.org/library/Bagehot/bagLom.html.
———. 1865. *The English Constitution.* Glenside, N.Z.: Forgotten Books, 2008.

Bahro, Rudolf

Rudolf Bahro (1935–1997) is principally known as a green politician and thinker, and particularly as an advocate of eco-socialism and of a spiritual and psychological path to political transformation. He was born in 1935 in Bad Flinsberg, Lower Silesia, now part of Poland. He grew up in East Germany, and lost his mother, sister, and brother in World War II (1939–1945). As a youth he joined the East German Democrat Party and studied at Humboldt University in Berlin. He then worked as a journalist and as an official of the Union of Scientific Employees, a post from which he was dismissed in 1967 for publishing an article that was critical of the party.

On the crushing of the Prague Spring in 1968, Bahro wrote what would be published in 1977 as *The Alternative in Eastern Europe,* in which he presented a critique of East European communism, particularly its materialism and its destructive growth-based economic aims, which mirrored those of Western Europe. He was arrested and imprisoned for this publication, causing an international outcry and campaign for his release.

In 1979 he was deported to West Germany, where he joined the German Greens (*Die Gruen*). He argued for a synthesis of red and green political and economic principles, but he rejected many traditional Marxist ideas. His argument is best articulated in his 1984 book *From Red to Green,* arguably his best-known work.

Although associated with the green political movement, Bahro was deeply critical of the "realist" sections of the green movement that sought electoral victory within the existing political system rather than pursuing more wholesale change. He argued that change at the spiritual and psychological level was necessary to overturn the ecologically destructive patterns of living accepted in the postindustrial West. Like Arne Naess, the founder of *deep ecology,* Bahro worked from an uncompromising biocentric viewpoint and was interested in the spiritual dimensions of green thinking. In 1985, after increasing frustration with the party's strategy, he left the Die Gruen over a dispute about policy on animal testing: Bahro and his partner Christine Schröter would not accept the party's compromise position that called for a ban on animal testing but allowed for exceptions in the field of medical research.

In the years after his split with Die Gruen, Bahro further developed his ideas on the spiritual and psychological dimensions of social ecology, moving further from traditional democratic politics. From 1990, he was professor of social ecology at Humboldt University. His thought tended increasingly toward an authoritarian approach as the only viable practical solution to environmental problems, to the dismay of many on the left of the green movement. This approach is evident in his last book, *Avoiding Social and Ecological Disaster: The Politics of World Transformation* (1994).

Bahro was diagnosed with cancer in 1995 and died two years later.

See also *Environmental Political Theory; Green Parties.*

. . . . KERRI WOODS

BIBLIOGRAPHY
Bahro, Rudolf. *From Red to Green.* London: Verso, 1984.
———. *Avoiding Social and Ecological Disaster: The Politics of World Transformation.* Bath, U.K.: Gateway, 1994.
Frankel, Boris. *The Post-industrial Utopians.* Cambridge, U.K.: Polity Press, 1987.
Ulf, Wolter, ed. *Rudolf Bahro: Critical Responses.* New York: M. E. Sharpe, 1980.

Bakunin, Mikhail

Russian revolutionary Mikhail Bakunin (1814–1876), who popularized the term *anarchy* and whose work was instrumental in the early development of the anarchist movement, was born in Tver, Russia, to an established noble family. He was primarily a person of action who participated in numerous uprisings in Europe, most notably the Lyon uprising of 1870. A proponent of pan-Slavism in his youth, Bakunin turned to anarchism through his contact with the working-class movements.

In his writings, Bakunin argues that external legislation and authority lead to the enslavement of society. All civic and political organizations are founded on violence exercised from the top down as systematized exploitation. Political law is understood by Bakunin, who served many years in prison and exile, as an expression of privilege. He rejects all legislation, convinced that it must turn to the advantage of powerful minorities against the interests of subjected majorities. Laws, inasmuch as they impose an external will, must be despotic in character. For Bakunin, political rights and democratic states are flagrant contradictions in terms. States and laws only denote power and domination, presupposing inequality. Where all govern, he once suggested, no one is governed. Where all equally enjoy human rights, the need for political rights dissolves. In such instances the state as such becomes nonexistent.

Like Pierre-Joseph Proudhon, Bakunin envisions future social organizations as economic rather than political. He sees society as organized around free federations of producers, both rural and urban. Any coordination of efforts must be voluntary and reasoned. For example, Bakunin viewed trade unions not merely as economic institutions but as the "embryo of the administration of the future," and he argued that workers should pursue cooperatives rather than strikes. Recognizing the impossibility of competing with capitalist enterprises, he called for the pooling of all private property as the collective property of freely federated workers' associations. These ideas would serve as the intellectual impetus for anarcho-syndicalism and its vision of the industrial syndicate as the seed of the future society.

Bakunin's famous disagreements with Karl Marx over the role of the state in the transition to socialism initiated a rift within the International Working Men's Association (IWMA), or First International, which led to the eventual expulsion of the anarchists and IWMA's dissolution by Marx's supporters, partly as a means to keep it out of anarchist hands. Bakunin's central conflict with Marx was that an authoritarian revolutionary movement, as Marx espoused, would inevitably initiate an authoritarian society after the revolution. For Bakunin, if the new society is to be nonauthoritarian, then it can only be founded upon the experience of nonauthoritarian social relations. During his battle with Marx in 1871, Bakunin's supporters in the IWMA asked, How can an egalitarian and free society be expected to emerge from an authoritarian organization? His concerns were vindicated by the direction taken decades later following the Russian Revolution (1917).

Bakunin's tireless work within the First International laid the groundwork for the development of flourishing anarchist movements in Italy, Spain, and several countries of Latin America, including the syndicalist movements that contributed to the Spanish Revolution (1936).

See also *Anarchism; Marx, Karl; Proudhon, Pierre-Joseph.*

. . . . JEFFREY SHANTZ

BIBLIOGRAPHY

Mendeel, Arthur P. *Roots of Apocalypse.* New York: Praeger, 1981.

Saltman, Richard P. *Social and Political Thought of Michael Bakunin.* Westport, Conn.: Greenwood, 1983.

Balance of Power

Balance of power in international relations refers to the effort by states, in the face of a threat to security projected by a hostile, powerful third state, to offset aggression through association. The balance of power operates most effectively in a central system of three to five member states—neither too few nor too many—and roughly equal power, so that each state possesses enough weight to count in the balance. Small or weak states bandwagon because they cannot balance larger states. Historically, in a system of virtually perpetual warfare among states, as occurred in the seventeenth century, any increase in power would trigger a new balance. Modern conditions, where peace usually prevails, require an increase in both threat and power to trigger the formation of a new balance. Powerful Germany is no threat to Belgium; Belgium does not need to balance Germany and does not try. Nor does Canada seek to balance the United States, which is ten times its size in terms of gross national product or population.

Why do alliances form within a balance-of-power framework? Conservative-realists argue that alliances form to counter a common external threat. Liberal-idealists argue that alliances form among like-minded governments with a similar cultural and institutional outlook. Stressing instead the role of institutions such as the United Nations, liberals, like postmodernists, tend to emphasize the shortcomings and contradictions of the balance of power to the point of rejection. Constructivists replace interest with identity, making balance-of-power calculations difficult.

Neorealism subscribes to the idea of anarchy or independence among states, thus permitting a balance of power to operate. But more recent theories of hegemony require that the notion of hierarchy replace anarchy as a core concept; one state is dominant, the others are subordinate. In terms of assumption and operation, hegemony and balance of power are incompatible.

When force is used to preserve security, peace may be undercut. Critiques of the shortcomings of the balance of power fail to distinguish its separate impact on security and peace. Although the balance of power probably has deterred many aggressors, it admittedly has failed to stop all wars. But it has preserved the security of the major states, such as in the alliance of Britain, the United States, and the Soviet Union against Nazi Germany and Imperial Japan in World War II (1939–1945). It also has preserved the decentralized nation-state system from military takeover.

When facing rising and declining power in the system, the balance of power gives off the wrong signals. Rising power internal to the state can never be halted; declining power can never be permanently bolstered. Prior to World War I (1914–1918), rising Germany should not have been isolated and encircled; the war arose from an attempt by the

system to constrain Germany's power rather than accommodate Germany's rise with legitimate role adjustment before it was too late, that is, before the "bounds of the system" shattered its expectations of continued rise and future opportunity for role gratification. Prior to World War II, declining Germany should have been balanced immediately; it had no role deficit, and Hitler's territorial demands were inherently aggressive. While preserving security, such a dynamic equilibrium requires a strategy of adaptation to cope with the legitimate role aspirations of rising power, and a strategy of opposition and balance to deal with potentially expansionist behavior. Democracies can use balance and dynamic equilibrium to their advantage, but, as Henry Kissinger has noted, such thinking does not come easily to the democratic mind.

See also *Alliances; Coalition Formation; Foreign Policy Role; Power; Power Cycle Theory.*

. . . . CHARLES F. DORAN

BIBLIOGRAPHY

Doran, Charles F. *Systems in Crisis: New Imperatives of High Politics at Century's End.* Cambridge: Cambridge University Press, 1991.

Haas, Ernst B. "The Balance of Power: Prescription, Concept, Propaganda." *World Politics* 5 (1953): 446–477.

Kissinger, Henry. *Diplomacy.* New York: Touchstone, 1994.

Mearsheimer, John J. *The Tragedy of Great Power Politics.* New York: Norton, 2001.

Rosecrance, Richard. *Action and Reaction in World Politics.* Boston: Little, Brown, 1963.

Walt, Steven. *The Origins of Alliances.* Ithaca, N.Y.: Cornell University Press, 1987.

Wight, Martin. *Power Politics.* London: Continuum International, 2002.

Balkans

The term *Balkans* is typically used to refer to the peninsula in southeastern Europe that includes the present-day countries of Albania, Bulgaria, Greece, Romania, and the lands of the former Yugoslavia (Bosnia-Herzegovina, Croatia, Kosovo, Macedonia, Montenegro, Serbia, and Slovenia). Once referred to as European Turkey or Rumeli, the present appellation comes from the Balkan mountains of Bulgaria, which were mistakenly believed to divide the entire peninsula from continental Europe. Besides its geographical meaning, the Balkans has, since the mid-nineteenth century, carried secondary connotations of violence, savagery, and primitivism that have led some scholars to prefer the designation southeastern Europe.

THE TERRITORY AND ITS HISTORY

The lands of the Balkans are more than 70 percent mountainous, which has helped to produce two of its defining characteristics: its mixture of cultures and religions and its position as a relatively undeveloped borderland of empires. The Balkans have long been home to a variety of different cultures— Albanian, Greek, Roman, Slav, and Turkish, among others—and religions—Catholic, Jewish, Muslim, and Orthodox. The intermingling of these cultures and religions was the trait that most distinguished the region to later visitors from mainland Europe.

The region began to assume its modern form as a borderland of the Ottoman Empire, which became the main regional power in the fifteenth century and was only gradually pushed out over the course of the nineteenth and early twentieth centuries. A distinctive characteristic of Ottoman rule was its millet system, which granted a degree of self-government to religious groups even as all state offices were held by Muslims. One consequence of the millet system was the preservation of the region's multiculturalism, as well as the creation of a significant Muslim minority made up largely of ethnic Slavs and Albanians who converted.

In the nineteenth century, local intellectuals picked up European concepts of the nation and nationalism and began to apply them to the region. Though they initially encountered difficulties in creating Croat, Greek, or Serb identities from predominantly peasant and religious cultures, ultimately they managed to cobble together the official cultures, languages, and histories of the lands that exist today and at the same time extinguish many of the microcultures that existed up until then (e.g., Morlachs, Vlachs). These nationalists began to lead increasingly successful revolts against the deteriorating Ottoman Empire, producing the independent states of Bulgaria, Greece, Romania, and Serbia, while the territories of Bosnia-Herzegovina, Croatia, and Slovenia were subsumed into the Austro-Hungarian Empire.

The meeting of nationalist ambitions with the diversity of cultures and the difficulty of classifying residents as members of one or another national group led to frequent inter-Balkan conflicts. As the great powers attempted to resolve these conflicts, they became entangled, and it was the assassination of the Austrian Archduke Franz Ferdinand in Sarajevo by a Slav nationalist that helped to ignite World War I (1914–1918).

The end of the war led to a clarification of the region's boundaries with the states of Albania, Bulgaria, Greece, and Romania assuming near their modern forms, and the Kingdom of Yugoslavia (or the South Slavs) being created out of Albanians, Bosniaks, Croats, Slovenes, Macedonians, Montenegrins, and Serbs, with the Serbs playing the leading role. It was Yugoslavia that proved the most volatile of the Balkan states, and it broke apart during World War II (1939–1945). The war was marked by brutal score-settling, particularly between Serbs and Croats, and frequently exceeding rational war aims. The communist partisan leader Josip Broz Tito managed to restore Yugoslavia to more or less its prewar borders by promulgating a myth of national resistance to the Nazis and clamping down on nationalist sentiment.

THE WARS OF YUGOSLAV SUCCESSION

In contrast to the hard-line communist regimes that emerged after the war in neighboring Albania, Bulgaria, and Romania, postwar Yugoslavia pursued an independent course both in foreign policy (helping to form the nonaligned movement) and in domestic affairs, where it ultimately pioneered a unique form of worker self-management. This economic and political liberalization led many to expect the country to weather the fall of communism in 1989 better than other communist nations.

In fact, the transition unleashed the bloodiest fighting in Europe since World War II. Though the relatively homogeneous Slovenia managed to extract itself from Yugoslavia with minimal violence, moves by Croatia, and particularly Bosnia-Herzegovina, to declare their independence met resistance from Serb minorities in those republics. These Serbs were backed by the remnants of the Serb-controlled Yugoslav People's Army and paramilitary militias. Efforts to carve out territory by Serbs and Croats in Bosnia, egged on by ultranationalist leaders, led to ethnic cleansing and genocide, with Muslims bearing the brunt of atrocities. The massacre of eight thousand Bosnian Muslims at Srebrenica in the presence of a UN peacekeeping force and the bombing of multiethnic Sarajevo by Serb forces focused world attention on the region.

Though Western powers had been quick to recognize the new independent republics, they were slow to react to the fighting. One reason was the attribution of the conflict to "ancient hatreds," a theory propounded by Croat and Serb nationalists and backed by many Western politicians. The theory, however, did not explain why the region had become multicultural in the first place, why much of its history was peaceful, nor the high rates of ethnic intermarriage in postwar Yugoslavia.

Public revulsion at the slaughter, however, ultimately prompted the Western powers to intervene against Serb aggression in Bosnia and force the three sides to sign the Dayton Agreement (1995) that ended the fighting and led to a UN-sponsored, NATO-led mission enforcing the peace in Bosnia. Hostilities, however, later resumed in Kosovo, with Kosovar Albanians turning to violent resistance against Serb oppression and then facing massive retaliation. Ultimately, NATO intervened through a bombing campaign against Serbia in 1999, which led to UN administration and ultimately independence for Kosovo.

AFTERMATH OF THE CONFLICT

The final balance of these wars was horrific. The death toll has been estimated at slightly more than one hundred thousand, and perhaps two million people were displaced from their homes. Mass rape, torture, and attempted genocide compounded the trauma, with Bosnian Muslims bearing the lion's share of the suffering. However, the effects of the war differed dramatically by territory. While Slovenia and, to a lesser extent, Croatia managed to reform their economies and turn themselves toward Europe, the other republics have faced rockier paths. Serbia democratized in 2000, but its economy remains marked by the entangling of the security forces and organized crime, its politics by significant ultranationalist forces, and its integrity by the secession of both Montenegro and Kosovo. Bosnia continues under international administration and is de facto divided into ethnic zones with efforts at resettlement and interethnic cooperation meeting scant success. Though successful in attaining its independence, Kosovo still has not been recognized by several major powers and faces an economy in shambles.

There have been significant and productive debates in political science about the causes of these wars and what could have been done to prevent them. A key issue has been who is to blame. On one side stand those who single out volitional individuals or groups, especially the Serb leader Slobodan Milošević and the Croatian leader Franjo Tuđman and their allies who stirred up ethnic hatred. Some have rather pointed blame at the Slovenes or even the international community (either for recognizing the independent republics too soon or not intervening early enough).

On the other side are those who point to structural forces. Susan Woodward, for example, emphasizes how persistent economic decline and state weakness left citizens dependent on national groups for security guarantees. Still others have focused on the structure of communist-era federalism and the military, the improper sequencing of regional and national elections, the dangers of democratization without prior liberalization, and even the clash of civilizations.

There also have been enlightening debates about the justice and practicality of international involvement in civil wars and genocides. Particular attention has been devoted to the proper deployment of international peacemaking and peace-keeping operations, given the failures of a UN force without robust engagement policies and the apparent successes of more forceful interventions by NATO. The formation of the International Criminal Tribunal for the former Yugoslavia, which saw the first indictment of a sitting head of state and was a precedent for the International Criminal Court, also spawned a large literature on the efficacy of trials for war criminals. Critics argue that it has engaged in selective and politically inspired prosecutions, while supporters argue that it did provide justice for the victims of the war and removed important obstacles to democratization. Finally, there have been fierce debates about the normative desirability of international support for secession and state breakup versus respect for state sovereignty, both with respect to the start of the war and as a precedent for other regions. What was a tragedy for the people of Yugoslavia has led to a flourishing literature in political science.

See also *Clash of Civilizations; Democracy and Democratization; European Politics and Society; Genocide; Humanitarian Intervention; International Criminal Court (ICC) (ICC); Transitional Regimes; Transitology.*

. . . . ANDREW ROBERTS

BIBLIOGRAPHY
Mazower, Mark. *The Balkans: A Short History.* New York: Modern Library, 2000.
Ramet, Sabrina P. *Thinking about Yugoslavia: Scholarly Debates about the Yugoslav Breakup and the Wars in Bosnia and Kosovo.* Cambridge: Cambridge University Press, 2005.
Woodward, Susan L. *Balkan Tragedy: Chaos and Destruction after the Cold War.* Washington, D.C.: Brookings Institution, 1995.

Ballot Design

Ballot design generally refers to the ways in which candidates and contests are arranged on electoral ballots of various types. Ballot design first received widespread attention in 2000, when the U.S. presidential election was decided in part by contested results in a county that used a *butterfly ballot* of allegedly poor design. Two groups in the United States that have paid particular attention to ballot design are Design for Democracy (an initiative of AIGA, the professional association for design) and the Brennan Center for Justice at New York University School of Law. On an international level, the ACE Electoral Knowledge Network (www.aceproject.org), begun in 1998, seeks to expand transparency of elections and increase trust in their credibility. Affiliated with the United Nations and the International Institute for Democracy and Elections Assistance, the ACE Project compiles information about election processes and tries to identify best practices.

U.S.-style democracies may be more susceptible to ballot design issues for a variety of reasons. Responsibility for ballot design is usually not centralized and is often assigned to partisan officials who lack design expertise. Further, frequent changes in election regulations and technology create opportunities for new mistakes in design.

BALLOT DESIGN ISSUES IN THE UNITED STATES

In the United States, voters elect officeholders from the president to the county coroner, and may vote also in contests tied to their residence in school or water districts that cross various jurisdictional lines. Ballot challenges may make ballot design a moving target until shortly before election day. Further, ballots must be adjusted for each new election, which will have different categories of contests, numbers of contestants, and ballot styles. Best practices in design recommend that ballots be tested with users before elections, but timing considerations may make testing difficult.

Ballot design may affect electoral results in two ways. First, design flaws can mislead voters and cause them to miscast votes or fail to cast votes in certain contests. Second, every choice mechanism, even if perfectly designed, favors one choice over another. As Thaler and Sunstein (2008) have noted, there is no such thing as a neutral choice mechanism. The consequences of this reality are often called *primacy effect* or *position bias,* but perhaps a better term is *position impact,* because any effect on the vote is not necessarily the result of conscious or unconscious prejudice.

DESIGN FLAWS

Design flaws may lead voters to skip a contest or to vote for the wrong candidate. In a 2006 congressional contest in Florida, ballot designers placed the two-candidate congressional race on the same screen as a six-candidate gubernatorial contest. Norden et al. (2008) reported that 13.9 percent of the voters did not vote in the contest, compared to only 2.5 percent of voters who voted in the same contest on different ballots. Similarly, many King County, Washington, voters skipped a 2009 referendum contest that appeared at the bottom of a column of voting instructions.

A ballot that requires voters to behave in a counterintuitive way may mislead voters, despite the presence of accurate instructions. Most voters obey their intuitive, "automatic systems" instead of reading directions. This kind of problem can be exacerbated by overly complex voting technologies such as

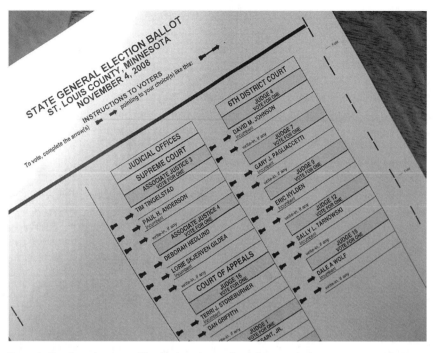

Paper ballots have been used in elections for much of the twentieth century. Voters first used pull-lever machines and, later, punch card methods to cast their ballot.

SOURCE: AP Images

An Indonesian official holds up a checked presidential election ballot in 2009 bearing the faces of the candidates. While electronic ballots are growing in use in the twenty-first century, a variety of ballot styles remain in use.

SOURCE: Getty Images

POSITION IMPACT

It is axiomatic that for every contest on every ballot, one candidate's name— usually the top name on the list—will be the first name that the voter sees. Scholars theorize that seeing a candidate's name first may cause a voter to think of that candidate in a more positive light or to make that candidate the standard against which all others are judged. Krosnick and others (2004) have argued that this effect can swing as much as 3 percent of the vote. Whether or not this psychological effect exists, it is a physical reality that on some ballots, the names of certain candidates will be in more conspicuous positions than the names of others.

Despite controversy as to the existence and effect of position impact, ballot regulations seem to take it into account. In some states, the law requires that candidate names rotate from precinct to precinct or district to district, so that each candidate's name appears in each position on approximately the same number of ballots. In other states, in contrast, the ballot rules seem to ensure that any possible position impact benefits the two dominant parties. In these states, candidates of lesser-known parties may be symbolically and literally moved to the fringe of the ballot. Voters who are distracted from or who cannot find their original choice may vote for a different candidate or not vote in a particular contest at all.

Position impact is less likely to affect a voter in a presidential election or other significant contest. But when voters reach the less-significant, or *down-ticket*, contests, they may be unwilling to expend the time and energy needed to give all candidates equal consideration, or to search diligently for the candidate they had originally planned to select. These voters consciously choose the candidates they select—or consciously choose not to vote in a particular contest—but that conscious choice may have been influenced by the positions of the various candidates in the contest. Because small differences can change the outcome of an election, position impact has almost certainly affected the results of some elections.

punch-card ballots. The most infamous example of this kind of problem is the so-called *butterfly ballot,* which was used in Palm Beach County, Florida, in 2000.

INTERNATIONAL BALLOT DESIGN ISSUES

Ballot design varies from country to country and from electoral system to electoral system. In some parliamentary elections, a ballot paper may be a single preprinted sheet on which the voter selects the party of choice; in others, the voter casts two votes: one for a particular candidate, and one for the preferred party. In countries with lower literacy rates, elections officials may use pictures of candidates or party symbols to help make it easier for voters to identify their choices.

Andrew Reynolds and Marco Steenbergen (2006) report that Latin American countries tend to include symbols, colors, and photographs on their ballots and that party and candidate symbols may be found on ballots in southern Europe and in former British colonies of Asia and the Caribbean. They argue that seemingly innocuous symbols assigned to candidates can have a direct impact on voters. They report that in Tanzanian elections, candidates who were randomly assigned the symbol of a gardening hoe seemed to receive a significant benefit compared to candidates who were randomly assigned the symbol of a Western-style house. Some theorize that anti-Western, proagrarian attitudes aided the "hoe" candidates and hurt the "house" candidates. Eventually, the symbols were abandoned after allegations that the house symbol was being deliberately assigned to candidates of the nonruling party.

POSSIBLE SOLUTIONS

Design for Democracy, the Brennan Center, the ACE Project, and others have recommended best practices to avoid design flaws, including reducing visual clutter, using plain language in voting instructions, and following design principles that recognize how voters intuitively move through documents. For example, electronic ballots should include only one contest on each computer screen. On a paper ballot, candidates in a single contest should be listed in a single column. The ACE Project specifically recommends using party symbols in all environments and using photographs on ballots in societies with lower literacy rates and where party affiliations frequently change. Most importantly, best practices include conducting usability testing to verify the effectiveness of the ballot design. Rotation of candidate names, while not yet widely recommended, can help to mitigate position impact, as well as the impact of some design flaws.

Perfect ballots cannot be guaranteed, but elections officials who follow best practices can greatly reduce the number of design flaws and increase the effectiveness of and confidence in voting systems.

See also *Absentee Voting; Campaigns; Election Monitoring; Electronic Voting; Voting Behavior; Voting Machines and Technology; Voting Procedures.*

. . . . MARY BETH BEAZLEY

BIBLIOGRAPHY

Alvarez, R. Michael, Betsy Sinclair, and Richard L. Hasen. "How Much Is Enough? The 'Ballot Order Effect' and the Use of Social Science Research in Election Law Disputes." *Election Law Journal* 5, no. 1 (2006): 40–56.

Bain, Henry M., and Donald S. Hecock. *Ballot Position and Voter Choice.* Detroit: Wayne State University Press, 1957.

Brady, Henry E., Michael C. Herron, Walter R. Mebane Jr., Jasjeet Singh Sekhon, Kenneth W. Shotts, and Jonathan Wand. "'Law and Data': The Butterfly Ballot Episode." *PS: Political Science and Politics* 34 (March 2001): 59–69, www.jstor.org/stable/1350311.

Brockington, David. "A Low Information Theory of Ballot Position Effect." *Political Behavior* 25 (March 2003): 1–27, www.jstor.org/stable/3657312.

Bullock, Charles S., III, and Richard E. Dunn. "Election Roll-off: A Test of Three Explanations." *Urban Affairs Review* 32, no. 1 (1996): 71–86, http://uar.sagepub.com/cgi/content/abstract/32/1/71.

California Electrical Code, sec, 13112(a) (2003).

Garber, Andrew. "Thousands of King County Voters Apparently Missed I-1033 on the Ballot." *Seattle Times,* November 4, 2009.

Herrnson, Paul S., Richard G. Niemi, Michael J. Hanmer, Benjamin B. Bederson, and Frederick C. Conrad. *Voting Technology: The Not-So-Simple Act of Casting a Ballot.* Washington, D.C.: Brookings Institution, 2008.

Ho, Daniel E., and Kosuke Imai. "Shaken, Not Stirred: Evidence on Ballot Order Effects from the California Alphabet Lottery, 1978–2002." Harvard Law School Public Law and Legal Theory Research Paper Series, Paper No. 89; Princeton University Program in Law and Public Affairs, Paper No. 04–001, http://ssrn.com/abstract=496863.

Krosnick, Jon A., Joanne M. Miller, and Michael P. Tichy. "An Unrecognized Need for Ballot Reform: The Effects of Candidate Name Order on Election Outcomes." In *Rethinking the Vote: The Politics and Prospects of American Election Reform,* edited by Ann N. Krigler, Marion R. Just, and Edward J. McCaffery, 51–74. New York: Oxford University Press, 2004.

Laskowski, Sharon J., Marguerite Autry, John Cugini, William Killam, and James Yen. *Improving the Usability and Accessibility of Voting Systems and Products.* Special Publication 500–256. Washington, D.C.: National Institute of Standards & Technology, 2004.

Lausen, Marcia. *Design for Democracy: Ballot + Election Design.* Chicago: University of Chicago Press, 2007.

Miller, Joanne M., and Jon A. Krosnick. "The Impact of Candidate Name Order on Election Outcomes." *Public Opinion Quarterly* 62 (1998): 291–330.

Norden, Lawrence, David Kimball, Whitney Quesenbery, and Margaret Chen. *Better Ballots.* New York: Brennan Center for Justice, 2008, www.brennancenter.org/content/resource/better_ballots.

Ohio Const. art. V, § 2a.

Ohio Revised Code, sec. 3505.03.

Reynolds, Andrew, and Marco Steenbergen. "How the World Votes: The Political Consequences of Ballot Design, Innovation, and Manipulation." *Electoral Studies* 25, no. 3 (September 2006): 570–598.

Roth, Susan King. "Disenfranchised by Design: Voting Systems and the Election Process." *Information Design Journal* 9, no. 1 (1998): 1–8.

Thaler, Richard H., and Cass R. Sunstein. *Nudge: Improving Decisions about Health, Wealth, and Happiness.* New Haven, Conn.: Yale University Press, 2008.

Baltic States

The term *Baltic states* refers to the countries of Estonia, Latvia, and Lithuania. Formerly republics in the Soviet Union, each became independent in 1991. Unlike most other former Soviet states, they established liberal democracies and market economies, and they are unequivocally pro-Western in their orientation. In 2004, all three states joined the European Union (EU) and the North Atlantic Treaty Organization (NATO).

These countries are frequently grouped together because of their geographic proximity on the southern shores of the Baltic Sea, their common history under Soviet rule, and their small size. Lithuania, about the size of West Virginia and with

The Baltic states of Estonia, Latvia, and Lithuania were once republics in the former Soviet Union.

a population of 3.4 million people, is the largest of the three. Latvia has 2.3 million people; Estonia's population is only 1.3 million. However, the titular peoples of the Baltic states are ethnically distinct and have different national histories. Lithuanians and Latvians speak Indo-European Baltic languages, but they are not mutually intelligible. Estonians speak a Finno-Urgic language that is closely related to Finnish. Lithuanians, as part of the Polish-Lithuanian Commonwealth (1569–1795), ruled over most of the region in the sixteenth and seventeenth centuries, and are overwhelmingly Catholic. Estonia and large parts of Latvia are primarily Lutheran, a reflection of their connections to the Hanseatic League and the Danish and Swedish empires. By the early nineteenth century, however, all three peoples fell under Russian domination.

BALTIC STATES DURING THE WORLD WARS

After World War I (1914–1918), all three Baltic states declared themselves independent and successfully fought independence wars against both Germans and Bolshevik (Soviet) authorities. Although they tried to establish democratic governments in the interwar period, these did not take root. Political paralysis led to a coup in Lithuania in 1926, and economic problems led to the rise of extreme nationalist groups in Estonia and Latvia. These groups, aided by paramilitary forces, in these two states seized power in bloodless coups in 1934, overturning weak but democratically elected governments. Foreign threats, emanating from Germany, Poland, and the Soviet Union, also were invoked by some to justify the creation of more powerful governments.

Estonia, Latvia, and Lithuania lost their independence in June 1940 as a consequence of Soviet invasion. Afterward, the Soviets rigged elections in all three countries, after which communist authorities in each government formally applied to join the Soviet Union. They became republics within the formally federal Soviet state. However, this takeover was deemed illegitimate both internationally and by large segments of the local population. In 1941, all were conquered by invading German forces, and most of their sizeable Jewish populations (especially in Lithuania and Latvia) perished in the Holocaust. In 1944, when Soviet authorities (re)invaded as they pushed the Germans back, many Balts fought against the Red Army; some were still combating Soviet authorities into the early 1950s.

RISE AND FALL OF SOVIET RULE

Soviet rule was harsh in the Baltic states, particularly in Estonia and Latvia, where tens of thousands of people were deported to other parts of the Soviet Union. In turn, large numbers of ethnic Russians emigrated to the region, particularly to Latvia and Estonia. For example, by 1989 ethnic Estonians comprised only 61 percent of Estonia's population; ethnic Latvians were a bare majority, 52 percent, in their republic. Many feared that they would lose their culture and language because of Soviet (Russian) control. However, thanks to their previous development and relatively skilled population, the Baltic republics were the most prosperous region in the Soviet Union.

Lithuania's new President Dalia Grybauskaite, second from right, stands with her predecessor, Valdas Adamkus, second from left, during her 2009 inauguration ceremony in Vilnius, Lithuania. Once a Soviet republic, Lithuania obtained its independence in 1991.

SOURCE: AP Images

When Soviet leader Mikhail Gorbachev launched his reforms of glasnost and democratization in the late 1980s, it allowed people to discuss their history and form independent political groups. Peoples in the Baltic states began to demand an accounting for the past and political changes for the future. They pointed to their forceful and (in their view) illegal incorporation into the Soviet Union, threats to their language and culture, and environmental damage caused by Soviet rule. In an unprecedented display of civic activism under the Soviet Union, more than two million people from all three countries formed a 400-mile (640-kilometer) human chain in August 1989 to mark the sixtieth anniversary of the Nazi-Soviet Pact, which had facilitated the Soviet takeover.

By spring 1990, in order to win local elections, even local communist leaders were agitating for independence from the Soviet Union. Over the course of the next year, these states issued declarations of sovereignty and eventually independence, and independence referendums were overwhelmingly approved by voters. There was, however, some violence in

Latvia and Lithuania in January 1991, which was instigated by Soviet troops stationed in the Baltics. The example of the Baltics would encourage other Soviet peoples to demand their independence as well, making the Baltic republics crucial actors in the dissolution of the Soviet Union. Ultimately, Gorbachev refused to endorse major military operations to squash the independence movements. By September 1991, Moscow recognized their independence, which Baltic leaders asserted was a rightful restoration of their status as sovereign states.

INDEPENDENT BALTIC STATES

Since gaining independence, the Baltic states rank as the most successful of the former Soviet states in terms of consolidating democratic governments and creating vibrant, market-oriented economies. After protracted negotiations, Russian troops pulled out of the region in 1994. By the mid-1990s, all three states had well-functioning parliamentary democracies, with tensions over citizenship and language status for Russian-speaking minorities resolved, due largely to international mediation and pressure. After a period of economic hardship in the early 1990s, governments in the Baltic states implemented market-based economic reforms and reoriented their economies westward. By the late 1990s, their economies began to rebound, with Estonia, thanks to its ties to Finland, becoming a high-tech leader for all the postcommunist world. In 2004, all three joined the EU and NATO, which they considered important both for economic reasons and for protection against any political or military threat from Russia.

See also *Europe, Democracy in; European Politics and Society; Glasnost; Soviet Union, Former.*

. . . . PAUL JAMES KUBICEK

BIBLIOGRAPHY

Lane, Thomas. *Lithuania: Stepping Westward.* New York: Routledge, 2001.

Lieven, Anatol. *The Baltic Revolution: Estonia, Latvia, Lithuania, and the Path to Independence.* New Haven, Conn.: Yale University Press, 1993.

Misiunas, Romuald, and Rein Taagepera. *The Baltic States: Years of Dependence 1940–1990.* Berkeley: University of California Press, 1993.

O'Connor, Kevin. *The History of the Baltic States.* Westport, Conn.: Greenwood, 2003.

Pabriks, Artis, and Aldis Purs. *Latvia: The Challenges of Change.* New York: Routledge, 2001.

Smith, David. *Estonia: Independence and European Integration.* New York: Routledge, 2001.

Banana Republic

In his 1904 novel, *Cabbages and Kings,* the author O. Henry first referred to a "banana republic," and the resulting image of a corrupt, fruit-dependent country came from his own impressions of Honduras at the turn of the twentieth century. Over time, however, the term has transcended its specific historical, temporal, and geographical origins. It now typically refers to a small and poor country (generally, but not exclusively, Central American or Caribbean) that is deemed backward, weak, and unequal, and is ruled by a corrupt elite closely tied to foreign interests. Those foreign investors, in turn, show a proclivity to appeal to their home government (especially the United States) to intervene if their investments seem at risk.

The reference to bananas reflected (and in many cases, continues to reflect) the dominance of a limited number of agricultural exports, particularly the fruit industry, and the political influence of foreign investors. The most prominent example was the United Fruit Company, which wielded tremendous power over a number of governments in the first half of the twentieth century in countries like Guatemala and Honduras. All national leaders, elected or not, were faced with a company that was the largest single land owner, employer, and tax payer, which had built its own infrastructure, encouraged the crushing of internal dissent and bought off or intimidated government officials at all levels, thus severely limiting any efforts at social, political, or economic change.

See also *Corruption and Other Political Pathologies; Corruption, Political; Elites, Political; Trade Diplomacy.*

. . . . GREGORY WEEKS

Bandwagoning

In electoral politics, *bandwagoning* refers to supporting a candidacy or political position because it is already popular. This *bandwagon effect* can occur because the popularity of a preference is seen as evidence for its rightness. Individuals who "join the bandwagon" often free-ride by sharing the benefits of the victory without having shared the costs to accomplish it.

In foreign policy, bandwagoning is a strategy in which states seek to increase their security or prosperity by aligning with a strong regional or global power, whether through official alliance agreements or more informally through increased economic and political ties. A term popularized by Kenneth Waltz in his 1979 *Theory of International Politics,* bandwagoning is often presented as the opposite of *balancing,* which can be defined as a strategy of increasing national security by siding against the dominant actors in the system.

Bandwagoning (in the foreign policy sense) may be undertaken for a number of reasons, ranging from self-preservation in a crisis to an opportunistic desire to free-ride on the success of others. Historically, bandwagoning is more likely to be undertaken by smaller and less powerful actors, which explains why theories of great and middle powers focus on balancing behavior. Bandwagoning is also more likely to occur near the end of major wars, when the winning alliance has nearly secured its victory. Traditionally, fear of bandwagoning and attempts to thwart it have influenced foreign policy far more than the actual practice of bandwagoning. Superpower relations during the cold war, for instance, were shaped in part by a fear of falling geostrategic dominoes at their periphery.

See also *Alliances; Balance of Power.*

. . . . VSEVOLOD GUNITSKIY

Banfield, Edward C.

Edward C. Banfield (1916–1999) was a political scientist who is best known for three books: *The Moral Basis of a Backward Society* (1958), *The Unheavenly City* (1970), and *The Unheavenly City Revisited* (1974).

Banfield grew up on a farm in Bloomfield, Connecticut. He attended the Connecticut State College at Storrs (now the University of Connecticut) and received a bachelor's degree in English in 1938. Following graduation, Banfield held a variety of government jobs. He began with the U.S. Forest Service, then moved to the New Hampshire Farm Bureau in 1939. From 1940 to 1947, Banfield worked in public relations for the U.S. Farm Security Administration (FSA), a New Deal era agency.

During his time at the FSA, Banfield was admitted to the University of Chicago, where he studied planning and cities. He received his PhD in political science in 1952 from the University of Chicago and then joined its faculty. He remained there until 1959, when he moved to Harvard University. Banfield remained at Harvard until his retirement, except for a four-year stint (1972–1976) at the University of Pennsylvania.

While initially a supporter of Franklin Roosevelt and the New Deal, Banfield increasingly became skeptical of government's growing social welfare role. Reviewing his experience with the FSA, he concluded that assistance to the poor had not improved the lives of the recipients, and in some cases had made their lives worse.

He was critical of liberal ideas, especially the use of federal aid to relieve urban poverty. He argued that culture was the cause of urban poverty, and that federal aid would ultimately fail because it targeted the wrong problem. Indeed, he suggested that federal assistance could make the problems of urban poverty worse. His work was often criticized as "blaming the victim" for their situation.

With scholar Martin Meyerson, Banfield challenged the proliferation of high-rise public housing projects in Chicago and other cities around the country, warning that they would have the unintended consequence of racially isolating the urban poor. His point of view would be vindicated during the 1990s, as public housing authorities around the country began demolishing these high-rises, replacing them with less dense-packed garden apartments and town houses.

Banfield's *The Moral Basis of a Backward Society* is about a poor village of Chiramonte in southern Italy. In explaining why the village was poor, Banfield coined the term, *amoral familism,* a phenomenon that he described as families in the village distrusting one another to the point where they could not cooperate. He compared this town with Gunlock, Utah, a small Mormon town he had studied in the early 1950s. In contrast to Chiramonte, Gunlock prospered because the farmers of the town cooperated with one another. This led Banfield to conclude that culture, not the absence of financial support, explained why the Italian town did not prosper.

In *The Unheavenly City,* he contended that the so-called urban crisis of the time was misunderstood. He suggested that many aspects of the crisis were not problems, and that some problems (traffic congestion) could be managed easily, while others (crime and racism) would be difficult to manage. While acknowledging that racism was a problem, he contended that urban poverty was more a case of class prejudice than race prejudice.

Banfield's influence was extensive, with several future leading conservative scholars among his students: Christopher DeMuth, Bruce Kovner, Thomas Sowell, and James Q. Wilson. Banfield also served as an advisor to President Richard M. Nixon, heading the Presidential Task Force on Model Cities.

See also *New Deal; Urban Economic Development; Urban Housing; Urban Inequality and Poverty.*

. . . .   JEFFREY KRAUS

BIBLIOGRAPHY

Banfield, Edward C. *The Unheavenly City.* Boston: Little, Brown, 1970.
———. *The Unheavenly City Revisited: A Revision of the Unheavenly City.* Boston: Little, Brown, 1974.
Banfield, Edward C., and Laura Fasano. *The Moral Basis of a Backward Society.* Glencoe, Ill.: Free Press, 1958.
Banfield, Edward C., and Martin Meyerson. *Politics, Planning, and the Public Interest.* Glencoe, Ill.: Free Press, 1955.
Banfield, Edward C., and James Q. Wilson. *City Politics.* Cambridge, Mass.: Harvard University Press/MIT Press, 1963.
Kesler, Charles R., ed. *Edward C. Banfield: An Appreciation.* Claremont, Calif.: Henry Salvatori Center for the Study of Individual Freedom in the Modern World, 2002.
Meyerson, Martin, and Edward C. Banfield. *Boston: The Job Ahead.* Cambridge, Mass.: Harvard University Press, 1966.

Banks, Jeffrey S.

Jeffrey Scot Banks (1958–2000) was a scholar who made wide-ranging contributions to economics and political science. He received his BA in political science from the University of California Los Angeles in 1982 and his PhD in social science from the California Institute of Technology in 1986. Banks began his career at the University of Rochester and was promoted to full professor of economics and political science in just five years. He left Rochester in 1997 to join the faculty at the California Institute of Technology, where he remained until his death due to complications from the treatment of leukemia. Banks' productivity as an academic was prodigious: At the time of his death, he had published forty-three articles and two books—with an additional book and eight additional articles published posthumously.

Banks' work had an impact in a large number of fields, including game theory, social choice theory, economic theory, international relations, experimental economics, and political economy. In game theory, his work with Joel Sobel produced the concept of divine equilibrium, used to sharpen theoretical predictions in mathematical models of strategic interaction. In social choice, Banks characterized the outcomes possible as a result of varying the order in which bills are considered (this is now known as the "Banks set"); he contributed to the understanding of the conditions under which majority voting leads to stable outcomes; and with David Austen-Smith, he authored a two-volume book that has provided students and researchers with much-improved access to the cutting edge of the field. In economic theory, his work with Rangarajan Sundaram expanded our knowledge of optimal decision rules when faced with a set of choices with uncertain outcomes. In international relations, Banks established general results on the probability of war, importing the techniques from the literature on mechanism design in economics. In experimental economics, Banks and coauthors John Ledyard and David Porter analyzed the performance of markets in the face of uncertain demand or supply. Perhaps the largest impact of Banks' work was in the field of political economy. With David Austen-Smith, Banks made seminal contributions to our understanding of elections and government formation in parliamentary systems and of the effect of strategic voting on the probability that majority voting leads to the "correct" outcome. With John Duggan, Banks established foundational results for general legislative bargaining games. On the topic of elections, Banks (by himself and with various coauthors) elucidated the effect of small costs due to deviations from campaign platforms, the impact of uncertainty about voting behavior on candidate positions, and the influence of future elections on political outcomes in the present.

See also *Economic Theories of the State; Game Theory; International Relations Theory; Political Economy; Social Choice Theory.*

. . . . JOHN DUGGAN

BIBLIOGRAPHY
Austen-Smith, David, and Jeffrey S. Banks. "Elections, Coalitions, and Legislative Outcomes." *American Political Science Review* 82 (1988): 405–422.
———. "Information Aggregation, Rationality, and the Condorcet Jury Theorem." *American Political Science Review* 90 (1996): 34–45.
———. *Positive Political Theory I: Collective Preference.* Ann Arbor: University of Michigan Press, 1999.
———. *Positive Political Theory II: Strategy and Structure.* Ann Arbor: University of Michigan Press, 2005.
Banks, Jeffrey S. "Sophisticated Voting Outcomes and Agenda Control." *Social Choice and Welfare* 1 (1985): 295–306.
———. "Equilibrium Behavior in Crisis Bargaining Games." *American Journal of Political Science* 34 (1990): 599–614.
———. "Singularity Theory and Core Existence in the Spatial Model." *Journal of Mathematical Economics* 24 (1995): 523–536.
Banks, Jeffrey S., and John Duggan. "A Bargaining Model of Collective Choice." *American Political Science Review* 94 (2000): 733–788.
Banks, Jeffrey S., John O. Ledyard, and David P. Porter. "Allocating Uncertain and Unresponsive Resources: An Experimental Approach." *Rand Journal of Economics* 20 (1989): 1–25.
Banks, Jeffrey S., and Joel Sobel. "Equilibrium Selection in Signaling Games." *Econometrica* 55 (1987): 647–661.
Banks, Jeffrey S., and Rangarajan K. Sundaram. "Denumerable-armed Bandits." *Econometrica* 60 (1992): 1071–1096.

Bargaining

See *Negotiations and Bargaining.*

Barker, Ernest

Sir Ernest Barker (1874–1960) was a British scholar of the early twentieth century and a noted authority on classical political philosophy. Barker was the oldest of seven children born to a farm family in rural England. He was noted for his hard work and exceptional intellect. Barker received his PhD from Oxford University, where he was fellow of several colleges and served on the history faculty for twenty-one years. Barker was principal of Kings College, London; held the first Rockefeller funded chair in political science; and was fellow of Peterhouse at Cambridge University from 1928 until his retirement in 1939. Barker was knighted in 1944 for his contribution to the Books Commission of the Allied Ministers of Education.

Barker's most noted work, *The Political Thought of Plato and Aristotle,* was published when he was thirty-two years old and became an enduring foundational work in classical political philosophy. Barker produced exceptional quality work throughout his life. Forty years after *The Political Thought of Plato and Aristotle,* Barker published his translation of Aristotle's *Politics,* which remains a classic in the field and is still widely read today. By the close of his career, his work was published in canonical collections of current political thought, alongside Peter Kropotkin, Georg Wilhelm Friedrich Hegel, and Bertrand Russell.

Barker, as underscored by Professor Jean Stapleton, "lectured on the social and political ideas of European civilization in historical perspective" and notably did so in a lecture commemorating the 700th anniversary of Albertus Magnus' first lectures on Aristotle in a European university. Barker's works on *The Character of England* and *Traditions of Civility* continue to reflect his European outlook on civilization, which he held with ever greater conviction throughout his life. The European perspective was the shared cultural foundation of the West and, was fundamentally combined, for Barker, with a sense of Englishness. Barker was not only an English patriot, but a Burkean intellectual whose politics were those of the Liberal Party, though with a qualified conservatism. The foundation of Barker's thought should be understood as being twofold, first in his Platonism and second in his perspective on Christendom.

As Barker noted in his introduction to Aristotle's *Politics,* "the translation has been a labour of love, and a permanent consolidation of such leisure as was left to the writer, from the autumn of 1940 to the spring of 1945, among the anxiety and duties of war." Barker credits Sir Richard Livingston for the encouragement for his translation of *Politics,* and Barker acknowledged the debt to Merton College by dedicating the work to the Warden and Fellows of Merton College, for it was they who "gave him the opportunity of a scholar's life, when it elected him to a Prize Fellowship in Classics in 1898."

Barker is a foundational writer in the tradition of English political thought. Barker's work on classical political philosophy makes him a seminal authority in the discipline, but his work on Western civilization and English political culture make him indispensable for understanding the clash of civilizations that defines our present time.

See also *Aristotle; British Political Thought; Hegel, Georg W. F.; Kropotkin, Peter; Plato; Russell, Bertrand.*

. . . . MICHAEL W. HAIL

BIBLIOGRAPHY
Aughey, Arthur. *The Politics of Englishness.* Manchester, U.K.: Manchester University Press, 2008.
Barker, Ernest. *Greek Political Theory: Plato and His Predecessors.* London: Methuen, 1925.
———. *The Character of England.* Oxford, U.K.: Clarendon, 1947.
———. *The Politics of Aristotle.* New York: Oxford University Press, 1958.
———. *The Political Thought of Plato and Aristotle.* New York: Russell and Russell, 1959.
———. *Reflections on Government.* London: Oxford University Press, 1967.
———. *Traditions of Civility.* Hamden, Conn.: Archon, 1967.
———. *Political Thought of England.* Westport, Conn.: Greenwood, 1980.
Stapleton, Julia. *Englishness and the Study of Politics: The Social and Political Thought of Ernest Barker.* New York: Cambridge University Press, 1994.

Barrès, Maurice

Maurice Barrès (1862–1923), French novelist and nationalist politician whose eclectic career exerted a major influence on his generation, was born in Charmes sur Moselle, France, in a traditionalist family. His father was a member of the Napoleonic imperial guard.

Barrès began legal studies at the faculty of Nancy (Lorraine) before continuing his academic training in Paris in 1883. His work as a journalist in *Jeune France* (Young France) allowed him to frequent the symbolist artistic circles of Paris. In 1888, he published *Sous l'oeil des barbares,* the first volume of his trilogy *Le culte du moi* (The Cult of the Self), followed by *Un homme libre* (1889) and *Le jardin de Bérénice* (1891). He was considered the leading authority of the individualist, exalting the quest of new sensations and the satisfaction of senses.

In parallel to his literary activity, Barrès was elected as a deputy of Nancy at the French National Assembly in 1889 and retained his seat in the legislature until 1893. Rebelling against the establishment, he became a member of the nationalist-populist party of Georges Boulanger. This political involvement was one of the expressions of his ideological evolution toward patriotism and traditionalism. The lyrical transcendence of the ego by "historical roots" and "the land and the deaths" was visible also in his new literary trilogy *Le roman de l'énergie nationale* (*Les déracinés,* 1897; *L'appel au soldat,* 1900; *Leurs figures,* 1902) and in *La cocarde,* the short-lived newspaper he launched in 1894.

During the Dreyfus Affair—in which a French Jewish military officer Alfred Dreyfus was accused of being a German spy in 1894 and deported to Guyana—Barrès became one of the leading authorities of the *anti-Dreyfusards.* He joined the ultranationalist *Ligue des patriotes* (League of Patriots) created by Paul Déroulède and wrote a series of violent anti-Semitic articles.

In 1906, Barrès was elected to the *Académie française* (French Academy) and as deputy of Paris. In parliament, he opposed Jean Jaurès, founder of the French Socialist Party, by refusing to allow burial of the writer Émile Zola, a defender of Dreyfus, at the *Panthéon.* Despite their political differences, Barrès was one of the first to show his respect at Jaurès's tomb after his assassination by a French nationalist because of Jaurès opposition to a new war against Germany.

Succeeding Déroulède as head of the *Ligue* in 1914, Barrès became an important figure in World War I (1914–1918), emphasizing the importance of revenge against the pan-Germanist policy of the Kaiser. Such propaganda provoked harsh debates with pacifists, although the majority of French opinion was in favor of war. Barrès's private notebooks, however, revealed he was very circumspect about the outcome of the war.

Diverging from Charles Maurras, the monarchist leader of the antiparliamentarist *Action française* (French Action), Barrès revised some of his earlier assumptions after the war by reincluding French Jews as one of four components of the French national essence, alongside traditionalists, Protestants, and socialists.

See also *Anti-Semitism; French Political Thought.*

. . . . JEAN-BAPTISTE HARGUINDÉGUY

BIBLIOGRAPHY
Curtis, Michael. *Three against the Third Republic: Sorel, Barres, and Mauras.* Princeton, N.J.: Princeton University Press, 1959.
Doty, Charles Stewart. *From Cultural Rebellion to Counter-revolution.* Athens: Ohio University Press, 1976.
Soucy, Robert. *Fascism in France: The Case of Maurice Barres.* Berkeley: University of California Press, 1972.

Bartholomew of Lucca

See *Ptolemy of Lucca.*

Basque Separatism

The Basque region (País Vasco) lies in the northern part of Spain on the border with France. Basque separatism reflects the Basques' desire to establish an independent state that encompasses four Spanish regions—Vizcaya, Guipúzcoa, Álava (together País Vasco), and Navarra—plus three French regions—Labourdi, Basse-Navarre, and Soule. The father of Basque separatism is Sabino Arana, founder of the Basque Nationalist Party.

Several arguments are made for the creation of an independent Basque state. Supporters note that Basques are the oldest European nation, constituting an independent ethnic group that has historically inhabited four Spanish regions. Some point to their unique language of unknown origin that lacks any clear link to other languages.

In the Basque language, the name of their country is Euskal Herria (the people of Euskare), the language is Euskara, and one who speaks Basque is Euskaldun. What is not Euskara is Erdara, and one who does not speak Euskara is Erdaldun.

The Basque language is one of the most powerful means of enforcing separatism in the Basque region. For example, ETA

(Euskadi Ta Askatasuna), the armed face of Basque separatism, rejected race as a reason for separatism but took the language instead. The region also has formal autonomy (following the Statutory of Autonomy from 1979 and the law enforcing Euskara from 1982). The region is divided into two parts: the Autonomous Community of Basque, in which the Basque language is equal to Spanish, and Navarra, where Basque is the second official language after Spanish. In French regions inhabited by Basques, the language is not officially recognized because the French consider France to be one country with one language and one nation.

One of the foundations of Basque separatism lies in the legacy of the *fueros* (an organization with traditional laws, administering life inside the *fuero*), which emerged in the eighteenth century from Aragon, Cataluña, Mallorca, and Valencía, but not from Basque. Fueros established relations with internal institutions functioning inside the fueros, such as the General Assembly (Juntas Generales). In Navarra, these councils established executive committees that played a role similar to the executive position of modern government.

Difficulties in maintaining autonomy in the form of fueros were encountered, and in 1839 the fueros were terminated. From that year until the civil war in 1936, Basques engaged in a national movement. With the emergence of the dictatorship of General Primo de Rivera (1923–1930), the establishment of the Republic in 1931, and the civil war in 1936, the Basque Provinces (Vizcaya, Guipúzcoa, and Álava) achieved autonomy. Navarra remained a separate autonomous province due to its mixed inhabitants, a situation which continues today.

General Francisco Franco Bahamonde (known as General Franco) persecuted and oppressed Basque nationalists along with Republicans. He did not recognize any national identity other than Spanish, and he sentenced Basque opponents to death. The oppression of Franco's regime led to the creation of ETA in 1958. ETA is primarily a separatist organization, but it is often perceived as a terrorist network because it directly attacks the authorities. Its primary target is not civilians, but civilians have become victims. Franco's death in 1975 brought a return to democracy and autonomy for the Basques (with general elections in 1977, confirmation of the constitution in 1978, and the Statutory on the Autonomy of the Basque in 1979). ETA, however, continues to fight for independence, with the goal of establishing an independent Basque state.

See also *Nation; Nationalist Parties; Terrorism, Political.*

. . . . MARTINA TOPIĆ

BIBLIOGRAPHY

Conversi, Daniele. *The Basques, the Catalans, and Spain: Alternative Routes to Nationalist Mobilisation.* London: Hurst, 1997.

Del Giorgio, J. F. *The Oldest Europeans: Who Are We? Where Do We Come From? What Made European Women Different?* N.p.: A.J. Place, 2006.

Hooper, John. *The Spaniards: A Portrait of the New Spain.* London: Penguin, 1986.

Kurlansky, Mark. *The Basque History of the World.* New York: Walker, 1999.

Lecours, Andre. *Basque Nationalism and the Spanish State.* Reno: University of Nevada Press, 2007.

Payne, Stanley G. *A History of Spain and Portugal, Vol. II.* Chicago: University of Wisconsin Press, 1973.

Pérez-Agote, Alfonso. *The Social Roots of Basque Nationalism.* Reno: University of Nevada Press, 2006.

The Political Constitution of the Spanish Monarchy: Promulgated in Cádiz, the Nineteenth Day of March. N.d., www.cervantesvirtual.com/servlet/SirveObras/c1812/12159396448091522976624/index.htm.

Bassett, Reginald

Reginald Bassett (1901–1962) was an English political scientist who started out on the left, being a member of the Independent Labour Party in his youth. He turned to the right in 1931, when Labour Prime Minister J. Ramsay MacDonald became head of a coalition government dependent on the votes of conservatives and cutting public expenditure in the face of the Great Depression (1929–1939). This political progression made Bassett's writings critical of the prevailing Marxist-inspired criticisms of parliamentary government put forth by British political theorists Harold Laski; G. D. H. Cole; and Sir Oswald Mosley, who led the British Union of Fascists from 1932 to 1940.

Bassett left school young to work as an office clerk, and at the age of twenty-five he won a scholarship to study at Oxford. After graduation he spent fifteen years as an Oxford extramural tutor. In 1945 he became a tutor for trade union studies at the London School of Economics. In 1950 he received a tenured post in the Department of Government and was a professor there at the time of his death.

In *The Essentials of Parliamentary Democracy* (1935), Bassett endorsed the value of parliamentary tradition of government by discussion and consent. He interpreted parties as offering contrasting alternatives for policy, which were then resolved by compromises around a central position. Bassett offered a dynamic interpretation of how parties and politicians adapted to events rather than following ideologies to potentially revolutionary or counter-revolutionary extremes. The result was that while policies altered, a cross-party political consensus was maintained.

The victory in World War II (1939–1945) revived respect for established institutions of democracy among British academics. By the early twenty-first century, much of Bassett's book appeared consistent with mainstream political science, just as it was with Whiggish nineteenth century British views. It shows its age in not allowing for the prospect of Parliament turning into an arena in which parties competed for votes by rancorously attacking their adversaries rather than deliberating about policies and party leaders, and television becoming more important than Parliament as the chief sphere of politics. At the time of its publication, *Essentials of Parliamentary Democracy* was an overt challenge to class conflict theories of British government and to Britons who sympathized with undemocratic forms of government in the Soviet Union, Nazi Germany, or fascist Italy. No attention is given in the book to the New Deal, the domestic reform program instituted by U.S. President Franklin D. Roosevelt.

Bassett continued with his revisionist approach to contemporary history with studies of the absence of League of Nations action against Japan when it annexed Manchuria (*Democracy and Foreign Policy*, 1952) and of the events that led to Ramsay MacDonald resigning as the Labour prime minister and reassuming office as a National Government prime minister (*Nineteen Thirty-One: Political Crisis,* 1958). Bassett's papers are deposited in the London School of Economics archive.

See also *British Political Thought; Cole, George Douglas Howard; Laski, Harold Joseph; Parliamentary Democracy.*

. . . . RICHARD ROSE

BIBLIOGRAPHY
Bassett, Reginald. *The Essentials of Parliamentary Democracy.* London: Macmillan, 1935.
————. *Democracy and Foreign Policy.* London: Longmans, 1952.
————. *Nineteen Thirty-One: Political Crisis.* London: Macmillan, 1958.

Baudrillard, Jean

Jean Baudrillard (1929–2007) was a French social, cultural, and political theorist; a philosopher; and a sociologist. Even though he has usually been presented as a representative for French postmodern theory and sometimes associated with poststructuralism, post-Marxism, and other contemporary schools of thought, Baudrillard was able to develop a very particular frame of analysis, characterized throughout his large collection of writings by a sharp and provocative critique of the impact of consumerism, the media, and other technologies in the social and political arenas.

Baudrillard was born in Reims, France. After concluding his thesis in sociology, *Le Système des objets* (*The System of Objects*), he joined the faculty of the Université de Paris-X Nanterre, which was considered one of the most radically oriented French institutions during the 1960s. Baudrillard aligned with colleagues and students in the buildup of the May 1968 events, which led to an unprecedented general strike that brought the French government to the verge of collapse. He remained at Nanterre until 1986, when he transferred to Institut de Recherche et d'Information Socio-Économique (IRIS) at the Université de Paris-IX Dauphine. Distancing himself from academic orthodoxy, his works became increasingly popular and reached a wide international readership.

Beginning with his early works, Baudrillard took on the structuralist semiotic tradition, further developing and applying the notion of *self-referentiality*. However, as he considered objects could never be fully comprehended, they would produce a form of delusion (or seduction) among subjects seeking absolute knowledge. As a consequence, individuals and societies would fall into a form of simulated reality or *hyperreality* driven by a showcase of images, codes, information, and entertainment. This simulation shapes human behavior, providing an experience of such intensity that "actual" life is shadowed. In addition to explaining consumer dynamics (the acquisition of symbols) and the associated reification of the self, Baudrillard applied this framework to political analysis. The cold war (*The Illusion of the End,* 1992), the Gulf War (*The Gulf War Never Happened,* 1995) and the September 11, 2001, attacks on the United States (*The Spirit of Terrorism,* 2002) were examined in three of his most controversial essays.

In these three works, politics and history are presented as sheer illusions. In Baudrillard's view, in the same way the system of nuclear deterrence made it impossible for the cold war to actually take place, halting historical progress, the Gulf War also was viewed as a "weak event," a media creation closer to a video game than to a genuine war. He presented this simulated kind of warfare as, as he stated in *The Spirit of Terrorism,* "the continuation of the absence of politics by other means" (34). The September 11 attacks would be a gruesome example of a *strong* or *absolute* event, a symbolic inversion of the rules of the game (with the sole aim of disrupting it), brought about as a violent reaction to the expansion of the post–cold war New World Order.

Baudrillard's rhetoric received considerable criticism, which was often stimulated by his provocative and at times exaggerated style. Critics have argued that some of Baudrillard's works actually provide grounds for justifying terrorism. Others have seen his denial of reality as a form of instant revisionism or cynical skepticism. Nevertheless, his views generated a large following and led to the creation of the *International Journal of Baudrillard Studies* in 2004.

See also *Consumer Society; French Political Thought.*

. . . . JOÁM EVANS PIM

BIBLIOGRAPHY
Baudrillard, Jean. *Simulacra and Simulation.* Ann Arbor: University of Michigan Press, 1994.
————. *The Gulf War Never Happened.* Oxford, U.K.: Polity Press, 1995.
————. *The Illusion of the End.* Stanford: Stanford University Press, 1994.
————. *The Spirit of Terrorism: And Requiem for the Twin Towers.* London: Verso, 2002.
Butler, Rex. *Jean Baudrillard: The Defense of the Real.* Thousand Oaks, Calif.: Sage, 1999.
Kellner, Douglas, ed. *Jean Baudrillard: A Critical Reader.* Oxford, U.K.: Blackwell, 1994.

Bauer, Otto

Otto Bauer (1881–1938) was one of Austria's most prominent twentieth-century social-democratic statesmen. Born in Vienna, Austria-Hungary, he was expected to take over his father's textile business but instead dedicated himself to the cause of Marxism.

Bauer was both a brilliant theoretician and a man deeply engaged in real-world politics. He earned a doctorate in law from the University of Vienna in January 1906 and in the following year became secretary of the social-democratic faction in parliament. He was editor of the social-democratic *Arbeiterzeitung* (*Workers' Newspaper*), for which he also regularly wrote articles, and helped found the influential Austro-Marxist journal *Der Kampf* (*The Struggle*). His first major work, *The Nationalities Question and Social Democracy* (1907), is considered a classic Marxist study of the dual forces of socialism and nationalism. He viewed modern nations as communities of character (*Charaktergemeinschaften*) that emerged out of communities of fate (*Schicksalsgemeinschaften*) and argued that conflict among the dozen nations comprising the Austro-Hungarian Empire was due primarily to class struggle.

Bauer fought in World War I (1914–1918), was captured on the eastern front by the Russians, and survived three years as a prisoner of war. Upon his return to Austria after the war, he resumed activity in the Social Democratic Party and served from 1918 to 1919 as foreign minister in the first revolutionary Austrian government. In this official capacity, he advocated Austrian unification with Germany and even signed a secret annexation agreement because, like many socialists at the time, he believed it would lead to greater solidarity among the proletariat. The Allies, however, subsequently forbade unification in the 1919 Treaty of Saint-Germain.

Among Bauer's collected works, *The Austrian Revolution* (1923) stands out as a particularly insightful and detailed analysis of the role of class in Austria's transition from multinational empire to modern nation-state. Always a fierce defender of the working class, Bauer and others in the left wing of the Social Democratic Party declared in the 1926 Socialist Declaration of Linz that, should social democracy not be realized through peaceful and democratic means, they would not rule out "defensive violence" to achieve their ends. In addition to being the intellectual leader of the Social Democratic Party, he served from 1929 until 1934 as a representative in parliament.

Following a brief civil war in February 1934, in which the leadership of the Social Democratic Party was arrested and imprisoned, Bauer fled to Czechoslovakia. Austrian Chancellor Engelbert Dollfuss subsequently banned the Social Democratic Party and its trade unions and suspended constitutional democracy. A failed Nazi attempt to overthrow the government that resulted in Dollfuss's assassination in July 1934 marked the end of the First Austrian Republic and the beginning of the ignominious period of authoritarian government known as Austrofascism. Bauer did not live to see the rebirth of social democracy in the Second Austrian Republic after World War II (1939–1945). He died in exile in Paris, France, on July 4, 1938, four months after Austria had been annexed by Nazi Germany, with Europe headed toward a catastrophic war and much of what he had worked for torn asunder.

See also *Marxism; Social Democracy.*

. . . .   ELIOT DICKINSON

BIBLIOGRAPHY
Bauer, Otto. *Kapitalismus und Sozialismus nach dem Weltkrieg.* Vienna: Wiener Volksbuchhandlung, 1931.
———. *The Austrian Revolution.* New York: Burt Franklin, 1970.
———. "Fascism." In *Austro-Marxism,* edited by Tom B. Bottomore and Patrick Goode. Oxford, U.K.: Clarendon, 1978.
———. *The Question of Nationalities and Social Democracy.* Minneapolis: University of Minnesota Press, 2000.
Braunthal, Julius. *Otto Bauer: Eine Auswahl aus Seinem Lebenswerk.* Vienna: Verlag der Wiener Volksbuchhandlung, 1961.

Bayesian Analysis

Bayesian analysis generally refers to statistical analysis that relies on Bayes' theorem. *Bayes' theorem* provides a solution to the general problem of induction, explaining how to rationally update prior beliefs in light of evidence so as to yield posterior beliefs. In statistical inference, if θ is a parameter of interest, then Bayes' theorem implies that if $p(\theta)$ is the researcher's a priori probability density over θ (or a priori mass function, in the case of a discrete parameter), and $p(\gamma|\theta)$ is the likelihood function for some data γ, then the posterior probability density $p(\theta|\gamma)$ is proportional to the likelihood multiplied by the prior density. Bayesian statistical inference consists of computing, summarizing, and communicating features of the posterior density. Once considered controversial because of the subjectivism implicit in specifying a prior density, Bayesian analysis has become popular in recent years via the widespread availability of relatively powerful computers and algorithms (e.g., Markov chain Monte Carlo algorithms) that generate arbitrarily precise characterizations of posterior densities, making Bayesian analysis feasible for statistical models with large numbers of parameters or nonstandard probability distributions. Examples in political science include the analysis of roll-call data, hierarchical models, and multinomial choice models.

See also *Hierarchical Modeling; Quantitative Analysis; Roll-call Analysis; Statistical Analysis.*

. . . .   SIMON JACKMAN

BIBLIOGRAPHY
Gelman, Andrew, John B. Carlin, Hal S. Stern, and Donald B. Rubin. *Bayesian Data Analysis,* 2nd ed. Boca Raton, Fla.: Chapman Hall/CRC, 2004.
Gill, Jeff. *Bayesian Methods: A Social and Behavioral Sciences Approach.* Boca Raton, FL: Chapman Hall/CRC, 2002.
Jackman, Simon. "Bayesian Analysis for Political Research." *Annual Review of Political Science* 7 (2004): 483–505.

Beard, Charles A.

Charles A. Beard (1874–1948), born to a prosperous family in Indiana and educated at DePauw University, was one the most important historians of the twentieth century. He was influential among scholars, a sought-after public speaker, and a writer for the nonacademic world. Beard is probably most famous for his ability to align significant academic research with a progressive concern about politics. His most famous work, *An Economic Interpretation of the Constitution of the United States* (1913), looked past high-minded political theory or simple hagiography of the Founders to assert that economic interests best explain the drafting of the U.S. Constitution and its ratification. Indeed, throughout his life, Beard was insistent on exploring the economic forces that could explain American history. This often made him controversial among the public audience that he sought. Although many later historians repudiated his ideas, he remains an important historian who influenced generations of readers to think more realistically about American history and the men and women who shaped it.

Beard traveled to England and was a founder in 1899 of the progressive Ruskin House at Oxford, which dealt with labor education. Throughout his life, he remained concerned with public affairs and maintained a progressive desire to end injustice. He eventually became a distinguished and popular professor of history at Columbia University. His resignation from Columbia, in protest over the treatment of antiwar faculty in

1917, added to his fame. Later he was involved in the founding of the New School for Social Research in New York.

Beard, who always had a lively interest in politics, was elected president of the American Political Science Association in 1926 and the American Historical Association in 1933. He continued to write, often with his wife Mary Beard, popular histories of the United States. These include the two-volume *The Rise of American Civilization* (1927) and its two sequels *America in Midpassage* (1939) and *The American Spirit* (1943), as well as the *Basic History of the United States* (1944). In the late 1940s he developed a strong isolationist streak and wrote highly critical books about Franklin Roosevelt and what he believed were Roosevelt's authoritarianism and duplicitous efforts to force the United States into World War II (1939–1945). Even though these views are largely rejected, they reveal a man who was always critical in the best sense of that word. Beard never accepted the conventional wisdom and kept a skeptic's eye on the world.

Although many of Beard's judgments have been subjected to rigorous subsequent research that, in the end, undermines his conclusion, Beard remains a vital figure in American history and student of politics. His efforts to bring economic questions to the forefront of political thought are now an accepted way of approaching U.S. history. Even his critics recognize the worth of the questions he asked and the answers he sought. Beard will always be remembered as a writer who sought to balance objective historical research with a progressive's desire for social justice.

See also *Economic Theories of the State.*

. . . . JOSEPH ROMANCE

BIBLIOGRAPHY

Barrow, Clyde W. *More Than a Historian: The Political and Economic Thought of Charles A. Beard.* New Brunswick, N.J.: Transaction, 2000.

Brown, Robert E. *Charles Beard and the Constitution.* Westport, Conn.: Praeger, 1979.

Hofstadter, Richard. *The Progressive Historians: Turner, Beard, Parrington.* Chicago: University of Chicago Press, 1992.

Martin, James J. "Charles A. Beard: A Tribute." *Journal of Historical Review* 3 (Fall 1982): 239–258.

Beauvoir, Simone de

French novelist and political activist and critic, Simone Ernestine Lucie Marie Bertrand de Beauvoir (1908–1986) was born in Paris into a bourgeois family. She is best known for her nonfiction work, *The Second Sex* (1949), in which she argued that women had become "the other" after centuries of being compared with the male norm. Like Mary Wollstonecraft before her, Beauvoir observed that women were bullied into viewing themselves as inferior beings dependent on the males around them, and she proclaimed that women were not born as such but became so through socialization. Her declaration has remained controversial as feminists and other scholars debate the issue of nature versus nurture.

Published during the "feminist wasteland" that followed the grant of women's suffrage in Western democracies in the

Simone de Beauvoir's controversial work *The Second Sex* asserted that women were made to feel inferior to and dependent on men through socialization.

SOURCE: Getty Images

early twentieth century, *The Second Sex* issued a wake-up call to women around the world. The book combined with Beauvoir's lectures in the United States to provide the foundation for the second wave of American feminism that began with the publication of Betty Friedan's *The Feminine Mystique* in 1963. By the 1970s, Beauvoir had revaluated earlier political positions and endorsed the right to reproductive freedom and lobbied for laws to protect women from domestic violence.

Rebelling against her Catholic upbringing, Beauvoir's body of work endorsed *existentialism,* the notion that individuals are responsible for their own fate. She did not believe in God and rejected the rationalist concepts of classical liberalism that had been dominant in Western political thought since the Enlightenment. Beauvoir refused to accept the notion that human nature was formed by either society or the mode of production, arguing that individuals form their own nature.

Beauvoir received attention for her nontraditional decades-long relationship with fellow writer Jean Paul Sartre, her mentor, friend, and lover, whom she met as a student at the Sorbonne in 1926. Despite her commitment to Sartre, Beauvoir refused to marry or to give birth. In addition to Sartre, Beauvoir's worldview was heavily influenced by philosophers G. W. F. Hegel, Edmund Husserl, Karl Marx, Jean-Jacques Rousseau, and by the groundbreaking work of psychiatrist Sigmund Freud.

In 1945, Beauvoir and Sartre joined fellow existentialist writer Maurice Merleau-Ponty in founding the highly respected French political journal, *Les Temps Moderne.* Beauvoir's first novel, *She Came to Stay* (1943), was followed by *Ethics of Ambiguity* (1948), which was a critique of Hegel's views on the individual. In 1951, Beauvoir published a scathing criticism of the Marquis de Sade, *Must We Burn Sade?* and continued the critique in *Djamila Boupacha* (1962). Repudiating monogamy, Beauvoir had a tempestuous affair with American novelist Nelson Algren and penned a fictionalized version of the affair in *The Mandarins* (1954).

Beauvoir was a prolific writer for more than forty years. Among her many works, she addressed the issue of death both personally and philosophically in *All Men Are Mortal* (1946), *A Very Easy Death* (1966), and *A Farewell to Sartre* (1984) and dealt with the realities of aging in *Coming of Age* (1972).

See also *Feminism; Feminist Movement; French Political Thought; Wollstonecraft, Mary; Women's Suffrage.*

. . . . ELIZABETH RHOLETTER PURDY

BIBLIOGRAPHY
Bainbrigge, Susan. *Writing against Death: The Autobiographies of Simone de Beauvoir.* New York: Rodopi, 2005.
Beauvoir, Simone de. *The Second Sex.* New York: Knopf, 1975.
Card, Claudia, ed. *The Cambridge Companion to Simone de Beauvoir.* New York: Cambridge University Press, 2003.
Scarth, Fredrika. *The Other Within: Ethics, Politics, and the Body in Simone de Beauvoir.* Lanham, Md.: Rowman and Littlefield, 2004.
Schole, Sally J. *On Beauvoir.* Belmont, Calif.: Wadsworth, 2000.

Beccaria, Cesare

Cesare Beccaria (1738–1794), a key figure of the Italian Enlightenment, established his reputation as a political writer with *On Crimes and Punishments,* published anonymously in 1764. Widely read in the eighteenth century, the pamphlet was prominent in debates on penal reform in Europe and colonial America.

Born in Milan, Beccaria was sent, at the age of eight, to a Jesuit school in Parma, where his "sentiments of humanity" were "stifled by eight years of fanatical and servile education" (Beccaria 2008, xvii) as he later recalled. After studying law at the University of Pavia from 1754 to 1758, he returned to Milan and frequented the city's literary salons. There he befriended Pietro Verri, a writer and intellectual who founded his own circle in 1761, bringing Beccaria with him.

Beccaria traced his "conversion to philosophy" to this milieu with readings of, among others, Charles-Louis de Secondat Montesquieu's *Persian Letters* (1721) and Claude-Adrien Helvétius' *De l'esprit* (*On the Mind,* 1759). Beccaria's first work, a study of currency problems in the Milanese state published in 1762, grew out of this experience. His writings, like others of the coterie, aimed to influence a receptive Habsburg administration in Lombardy.

In *On Crimes and Punishments,* Beccaria combined social contract theories with utilitarianism to criticize existing criminal jurisprudence, which he held to be unnecessarily cruel, ineffective, arbitrary, and too often muddled with religious notions such as the expiation of sin. For Beccaria, laws sometimes unfairly protected the particular interests of class

and clergy, in part through the "terrible and perhaps unnecessary right" (2008, 43) to property. A more just social order, he argued, would craft laws to achieve "the greatest happiness shared among the greatest number" (9).

In Beccaria's view, laws should be written clearly and enforced by impartial judges. Trials should be public and by a jury of one's peers, and punishments prompt and proportional to the crimes committed. Beccaria argued that detentions prior to trial must be made on the basis of law rather than at the sovereign's whim and that torture should be eliminated because it was unreliable in securing accurate information and constituted a punishment prior to the determination of guilt. Long prison sentences and hard labor were to be used for serious crimes. The death penalty was to be abolished as an ineffective deterrent and gross spectacle that was illegitimate under the very terms of the social contract.

In Italy, *On Crimes and Punishments* was attacked by a Benedictine friar, Ferdinando Facchinei, who denounced its contractualist postulates and branded Beccaria a socialist. Nonetheless, the pamphlet saw several editions in the span of two years. Parisian *philosophes* championed the text, praised Beccaria as a "defender of humanity," and invited him to Paris in 1766. A French translation appeared in 1765, followed shortly by editions in other European languages. A substantial commentary by Voltaire further raised the book's visibility.

Catherine II sought Beccaria's guidance in reforming Russia's criminal codes, but his shyness forced him to retreat from the public spotlight. He taught economics in Milan for two years, wrote briefly on aesthetics, and took various positions in the Lombard administration, for which he wrote numerous policy recommendations. In a 1792 report, Beccaria reaffirmed the ineffectiveness of capital punishment and added a further reason for its abolition: namely, its irrevocability in the event of an erroneous execution.

See also *Bentham, Jeremy; Capital Punishment; Social Contract; Utilitarianism.*

. . . . AARON THOMAS

BIBLIOGRAPHY
Beccaria, Cesare. *On Crimes and Punishments and Other Writings,* edited by Richard Bellamy, translated by Richard Davies. Cambridge: Cambridge University Press, 1995.
———. *On Crimes and Punishments and Other Writings,* edited by Aaron Thomas, translated by Aaron Thomas and Jeremy Parzen. Toronto: University of Toronto Press, 2008.
Maestro, Marcello. *Cesare Beccaria and the Origins of Penal Reform.* Philadelphia: Temple University Press, 1973.
Venturi, Franco. *Italy and the Enlightenment: Studies in a Cosmopolitan Century,* translated by Susan Corsi. London: Longman, 1972.
Young, David. "Cesare Beccaria: Utilitarian or Retributivist?" *Journal of Criminal Justice* 11, no. 4 (1983): 317–326.

Beer, Samuel Hutchison

Samuel Hutchison Beer (1911–2009) was an Eaton professor of the science of government at Harvard University and one of America's most distinguished political scientists, especially renowned for his writings on British politics and American federalism.

Beer received his undergraduate education at the University of Michigan, graduating with a bachelor of arts in 1932, and was a Rhodes Scholar at Oxford University from 1932 to 1935. After working as an occasional speech writer for Franklin Roosevelt from 1935 to 1936, Beer became a reporter for the *New York Post* in 1936 and worked as a writer at *Fortune* magazine from 1937 to 1938.

Beer's long career at Harvard University, begun as a graduate student in 1938, was interrupted by his service as a captain in the American military during World War II (1939–1945). After finally receiving his PhD from Harvard in 1943, he returned to the university after the war, teaching there until his retirement in 1981. For more than thirty years his lecture course, Western Thought and Institutions, the longest-running of Harvard's famous postwar general education courses, was an inspiration to thousands of students, among them such notables as Henry Kissinger and William Rehnquist.

Beer published his Harvard dissertation as *The City of Reason* (1949), a work of political theory drawing on the philosophy of A.N. Whitehead and defending liberalism against the totalitarian threat. His *Treasury Control: The Co-ordination of Financial and Economic Policy in Great Britain* (1956) was a penetrating look into what had previously been the secretive workings of a key institution of the British cabinet. In 1965 his masterful study of British political parties and reigning ideologies, *Modern British Politics: A Study of Parties and Pressure Groups* (the first American edition was titled *British Politics in the Collectivist Age*) appeared. Arguing, among other things, that great moral ideas continue to shape political conflict in the age of interest groups, it is considered one of the most influential studies of British politics ever written, winning the Woodrow Wilson Foundation Award in 1966. Subsequent publications include *The British Political System* (1974) and *Britain against Itself: Political Contradictions of Collectivism* (1982). The latter traces the self-defeating pluralism, political overload, and "scramble for benefits" of 1970s British politics to the end of an inherited culture of deference and the erosion of class as a basis for party support. In 1993 Beer published *To Make a Nation: The Rediscovery of American Federalism,* in which he argued that the historical origins of American federalism do not support the conservative or "states' rights" view of the system.

While teaching and publishing, Beer continued to be active in American politics, serving as national chair of Americans for Democratic Action from 1959 to 1962. He was elected president of the American Political Science Association (APSA) in 1977. During congressional deliberations on the impeachment of President Bill Clinton in 1998, Beer testified before the House Committee on the Judiciary, arguing against the use of impeachment as a partisan political weapon.

Intellectually vigorous and productive until his death in 2009 at age 97, Beer devoted his later research and writings to the search for an American public philosophy adequate to challenges of governance in the twenty-first century.

See also *British Political Thought; Federalism; Political Theory; States' Rights.*

. . . . STEPHEN HOLMES

BIBLIOGRAPHY

Beer, Samuel. *The City of Reason.* Cambridge, Mass.: Harvard University Press, 1949.

————. *Treasury Control:* The Co-ordination of Financial and Economic Policy in Great Britain. Oxford: Oxford University Press, 1956.

————. *Modern Political Development.* New York: Random House, 1973.

————. *Britain against Itself: The Political Contradictions of Collectivism.* Norton, 1982.

————. *Modern British Politics: Parties and Pressure Groups in the Collectivist Age.* Norton, 1982. First published as *Modern British Politics: A Study of Parties and Pressure Groups,* London: Faber and Faber, 1965, and as *British Politics in the Collectivist Age,* New York: Knopf, 1965.

————. *To Make a Nation: The Rediscovery of American Federalism.* Cambridge, Mass.: Harvard University Press, 1993.

Behavior, Political

See *Political Attitudes and Behavior.*

Behavioral Game Theory

Behavioral game theory is a recent approach that adapts game theory to explain and accommodate experimental results that violate typical game theoretic predictions. Game theory applies mathematical analysis to understand human behavior. In particular, game theory assumes that individuals will attempt to form best response strategies to what they believe a partner or opponent will do. The analysis relies on some assumptions, including that individuals are self-interested actors who plan ahead and maximize their expected utility (try to obtain the best possible outcome, given constraints).

One limitation to testing game theory is that many of its predictions are based on variables that are difficult or impossible to observe empirically: personal costs, preferences, strategies, and information. The use of experimental economics allows experimenters to specify these factors and to vary them systematically or to hold them constant in order to observe whether the predicted effects occur. Results from laboratory experiments have frequently been in conflict with game theoretic predictions. These disparities occur in a number of dimensions—all of which call into question key assumptions in game theory. Larry Samuelson argues that the role of experimental results that challenge existing theory is to indicate how to make improvements. Behavioral game theory generalizes the theory by relaxing assumptions that experiments highlight as questionable to incorporate these findings.

Laboratory experiments reveal that instead of being purely self-interested, additional considerations often affect strategies and decisions. *Other-regarding behavior,* or a concern for fairness, is frequently apparent. Subjects often offer too much in ultimatum bargaining games—games in which a player proposes a share of an amount of money to another who can either accept the proposal or reject it, leaving nothing for either player. This tendency has been seen as a concern for fairness either in terms of a desire for equality or in guessing that the responder will reject an unfair offer.

Experiments also reveal that people do not engage in as much backward induction as game theory would predict. Most players will go no further than two steps of iterated reasoning. Theorists have argued that we should not expect to see subgame-perfect game theoretic behavior, as economists themselves have to work to derive the "proper" proposals in bargaining games. Others note that as a player doubts that an opponent is selecting best response strategies, that player's choice of strategy can vary also. Behavioral game theory has a number of ways to account for these tendencies. Behavioral game theory extends game theory to incorporate the bounded rationality and learning that are seen in the laboratory. Quantal response analysis depicts a form of bounded rationality in which players use decision rules where probabilities for choices of action are positively, but imperfectly, related to payoffs. Players can form beliefs about the probability that an opponent will play any given strategy. If a player is completely random, not responsive to expected payoffs, we should expect a wide distribution of results. When players are completely responsive to payoffs, the results converge to the Nash equilibria. This type of extension allows understanding and analysis of behavior that should not occur according to standard game theoretic results.

See also *Game Theory.*

. . . . KATRI SIEBERG

BIBLIOGRAPHY

Binmore, Kenneth, G., John Gale, and Larry Samuelson. "Learning to Be Imperfect: The Ultimatum Game." *Games and Economic Behaviour* 8, (1995): 56–90.

Binmore, Kenneth, Avner Shaked, and John Sutton. "A Further Test of Noncooperative Bargaining Theory: Reply." *American Economic Review* 78 (September 1988): 837–839.

Bolton, Gary, and Axel Ockenfels, "ECR: A Theory of Equity, Reciprocity, and Competition." *American Economic Review* 90 (March 2000): 166–193.

Camerer, Colin F. *Behavioral Game Theory: Experiments in Strategic Interaction.* Princeton, N.J.: Princeton University Press, 2003.

———. "Behavioral Game Theory: Predicting Human Behavior in Strategic Situations." In *Advances in Behavioral Economics,* edited by Colin F. Camerer, George Lowenstein, and Matthew Rabin, 374–392. New York: Princeton University Press, 2004.

Capra, C. Monica, Jacob K. Goeree, Rosario Gomez, and Charles A. Holt. "Anomalous Behavior in a Traveler's Dilemma?" *American Economic Review* 89 (June 1999): 678–690.

Goeree, Jacob K., and Charles A. Holt. "Ten Little Treasures of Game Theory and Ten Intuitive Contradictions." *American Economic Review* 91 (December 2001): 1402–1422.

Kirchsteiger, Georg. "The Role of Envy in Ultimatum Games." *Journal of Economic Behavior and Organization* 25 (December 1994): 373–389.

McKelvey, Richard D., and Thomas R. Palfrey. "An Experimental Study of the Centipede Game." *Econometrica* 60 (July 1992): 803–836.

Nagel, Rosemarie. "Unraveling in Guessing Games: An Experimental Study." *American Economic Review* 85 (December 1995): 1313–1326.

Palfrey, Thomas R. "McKelvey and Quantal Response Equilibrium." In *Positive Changes in Political Science: The Legacy of Richard D. McKelvey's Most Influential Writings,* edited by John Aldrich, James Alt, and Arthur Lupia, 425–441. Ann Arbor: University of Michigan Press, 2007.

Roth, Alvin E. "Bargaining Experiments." In *The Handbook of Experimental Economics,* edited by John H. Kagel and Alvin E. Roth, 253–348. Princeton, N.J.: Princeton University Press, 1995.

Samuelson, Larry. "Economic Theory and Experimental Economics." *Journal of Economic Literature* 43, (March 2005): 65–107.

Schotter, Andrew, Avi Weiss, and Inigo Zapater. "Fairness and Survival in Ultimatum and Dictatorship Games." *Journal of Economic Behavior and Organization* 31, no. 1 (October 1996): 37–56.

Bellarmine, Robert

Cardinal and Doctor of the Church, Jesuit Robert Bellarmine (1542–1621) became a leading Catholic theologian and controversialist who is best known for his defense of Catholic doctrine and for his theory of indirect papal authority in temporal affairs. Born in Montepulciano, Italy, Bellarmine made his first vow as a Jesuit in 1560. After studying Aristotelian philosophy and Thomistic theology, Bellarmine was sent by the Jesuit Father General to Louvain, where his focus on the defense of Catholic doctrines took shape as he taught theology in a university city on the front line of the Catholic response to Reformers.

In 1576, Bellarmine returned to Rome to teach English and German Catholic missionaries. He continued in this position until 1588, and it was during this period that he published *Disputationes de Controversiis Christianae Fidei adversus hujus temporis haereticos* (1586–1593). This examination of Protestant theology was an unusually balanced assessment for the time designed to better equip Catholic missionaries in disputes rather than score rhetorical points in polemical exchanges. The work also was wide ranging and, in conjunction with his *De translatione Imperii Romani* (1584), provided the first clear statement of his ideas about the nature of papal authority.

In the 1590s, Bellarmine was appointed to important positions first within the Society of Jesus and then within the papal court, culminating in his being named cardinal in 1599 by Clement VIII (1592–1605). Under Pope Paul V (1605–1621), Bellarmine became a leading advocate for the church in a series of controversies concerning papal authority, especially a dispute caused by James I of England's requirement of an oath of allegiance from all his subjects in 1607. The issues at stake in these disputes ultimately resulted in Bellarmine fully articulating his theory of papal authority, perhaps best expressed in his *Tractus de potestate Summi Pontificis in rebus temporalibus adversus Gulielmum Barclaeum* (1610), written in response to Scottish royalist and Catholic William Barclay's assertions in support of absolute royal authority. In *Tractus,* Bellarmine advocated a sophisticated theory of papal authority that granted the pontiff indirect power in temporal affairs. Bellarmine defined papal authority within narrow limits. He granted the pope sovereign jurisdiction over all Christians and over all temporal matters when they affected spiritual matters, but he carefully distinguished between ordinary and direct jurisdiction and the extraordinary jurisdiction that the pope possessed over secular rulers. According to Bellarmine, the pope possessed temporal authority over secular rulers only to protect the souls of the faithful and only after he had exhausted all other remedies. Even then the pope's power remained indirect: he could admonish, excommunicate, and, if all else failed, remove subjects from their obligations to their secular ruler, but under no circumstances could a pope work to remove a ruler from power. In an age of uncompromising polemical exchanges between promoters of papal and secular authority, Bellarmine's was a carefully balanced theory that ultimately pleased neither group. Bellarmine died in 1621 but was canonized as a defender of the church only in 1930.

See also *Papacy; Roman Catholic Social Thought.*

. . . .   ERIC NELSON

BIBLIOGRAPHY

Bellarmine, Robert. *Opera Omnia,* 12 vols, edited by Justinus Fèvre. Paris: Vivès, 1870–1874.

Brodrick, James. *Robert Bellarmine, Saint and Scholar.* London: Blackwell, 1961.

Bentham, Jeremy

Jeremy Bentham (1748–1832), inventor of the term *international,* was one of the greatest political and legal philosophers of his time. As the founder of utilitarianism, he has remained a controversial figure in the history of political thought, subject to much praise and criticism at once. His greatest follower, John Stuart Mill, described him as a "one-eyed man who offered philosophy a new method of analysis," while his most notable critic, Karl Marx, referred to him as an "insipid, pedantic, leather-tongued oracle of the commonplace bourgeois intelligence of the nineteenth century." Whether or not they approved of his views, none of the influential political thinkers of the last two centuries could afford to ignore this great philosopher.

Born in London, Bentham was the son of a wealthy lawyer. He too studied law but never practiced it, preferring instead to focus on law "as it ought to be." He remained a committed advocate of judicial and political reform throughout his life. His Panopticon project, for example, is among the most innovative prison reform proposals of all time. His persistent criticism of and elaboration on "political fallacies" was intended to pave the way for meaningful political reform. Bentham's normative views were distinctively secular on the one hand and grounded on an exploration of existing practice on the other. During the American and French revolutions, he rejected the idea of natural rights. Bentham's thought is frequently associated with legal positivism.

Bentham is most famous (and notorious) for his concept of "utility" aimed at calculating and, by implication, manipulating human motivations. For him, it is possible to rank order the motives for human action according to their preeminence. "Purely social" motives are morally best, followed by semisocial, asocial, and dissocial motives. Asocial motives (i.e., self-interest) are the most common, uniform, and powerful, followed by semisocial, purely social, and dissocial motives. Every human action, in Bentham's view, is ultimately motivated by a desire to gain pleasure and avoid pain. Even when one acts benevolently toward another, one does so because one finds pleasure in helping the other person. Ultimately, for Bentham, the degree of pleasure is calculable through the use of such variables as intensity, duration, or extent—a

Jeremy Bentham, founder of utilitarianism, believed that the motivation behind every human action was to gain pleasure and avoid pain.

SOURCE: Getty Images

principle known as *felicific calculus.* Taken together, these ideas led Bentham to systematize his famous normative agenda: "the greatest happiness of the greatest number."

Bentham published his most well-known concise treatment of utility, *An Introduction to the Principles of Morals and Legislation,* in 1789. He was a prolific yet somewhat disorganized writer, with a crowded intellectual agenda. He never married and reportedly lived an eccentric life. When he died in London in 1832, he left behind some seventy thousand unpublished manuscript pages contained in some eighty wooden boxes. The first comprehensive collection of Bentham's works was published posthumously by John Bowring in eleven volumes in 1843. The organization and editing of his original work still continues today under the auspices of the University College London's Bentham Project.

See also *Mill, John Stuart; Natural Rights; Utilitarianism.*

. . . .   EŞREF AKSU

BIBLIOGRAPHY

Bentham, Jeremy. *The Works of Jeremy Bentham,* edited by John Bowring. Edinburgh, U.K.: William Tait, 1843.

Harrison, Ross. *Bentham.* London: Routledge and Kegan Paul, 1983.

Hoogensen, Gunhild. *International Relations, Security and Jeremy Bentham.* London: Routledge, 2005.

Parekh, Bhikhu. *Jeremy Bentham: Ten Critical Essays.* London: Cass, 1974.
Schofield, Philip. *Utility and Democracy: The Political Thought of Jeremy Bentham.* Oxford: Oxford University Press, 2006.
Steintrager, James. *Bentham.* London: Allen and Unwin, 1977.

Bentley, Arthur Fisher

Arthur Fisher Bentley (1870–1957) was an American political scientist and philosopher who worked in the fields of epistemology, logic, and linguistics. Along with his colleague, philosopher and psychologist John Dewey, Bentley also contributed to the development of a behavioral methodology of political science. Bentley, however, did not gain wide recognition in the field until forty years after the publication of his most noted work, *The Process of Government* (1908). This book laid the foundation of the study of groups by breaking with the pre–World War I (1914–1918) traditions of political science research.

Bentley also influenced the Chicago school in the development of value-free, objective analyses. His idea that process-based behavioralism is a basic feature of contemporary pluralist and interest groups later became central to political science. He held that interactions of groups are the basis of political life and rejected statist abstractions. Bentley asserted that group activity was the fundamental datum available to describe and understand the social behavior of people. He sought an end to reliance on all prior ideas, ideals, and concepts, and what he derisively called "mind stuff." He believed that what groups were, what they did, and what they sought should not be distorted through biased observation and description or through anticipatory conceptual frameworks or limiting paradigms. Government in its various forms was one such group activity manifested publicly.

Bentley's concern was to outline methods, not to obtain results, and his method was only a research protocol, not a philosophical system. The term *Bentleyan* was added to the political science lexicon as a description of activity free of "mind stuff" but with purposes and goals contained in the activity and stated in its description. The key to Bentley's analysis was his use of the term *activity* as a synonym for interest. Bentley himself was against definitions, which he held to be limiting.

Bentley found the thought of German philosopher Karl Marx too rigid and abstract, although he was interested in economics and the economic life. Like Austrian scholar Ludwig Gumplowicz, whom he admired, Bentley found that the only possible solution of the social question lay in a harmonious cooperation of the social groups as far as that was possible. Bentley was a reformer despite his stubborn skepticism. He relied on American progressivism and the constitutional rules that helped to make government benign and curbed the striving for dominance by any one group. He viewed government as extending beyond formal governing institutions to include associations and corporations, and he urged the elimination of notions of sovereignty and the state from political investigation.

None of Bentley's later works focused on politics, government, or economics, with the exception of *Relativity in Man and Society* (1926), in which he argued that social scientists should apply a space-time approach and relativism in their investigations. All human action needed to be placed in the social context of its period. His last book was *Knowing and the Known* (1949), a collaboration with John Dewey.

Bentley was honored in 1953 by the American Political Science Association. In 1954 the American Humanist Association voted him Humanist of the Year.

See also *Dewey, John; Group Relations; Group Theory.*

. . . . GEORGE THOMAS KURIAN

BIBLIOGRAPHY
Kress, Paul F. *Social Science and the Idea of Process: The Ambiguous Legacy of Arthur F. Bentley.* Chicago: University of Chicago Press, 1970.
Ratner, Sidney. "Arthur F. Bentley, 1870–1957." *Journal of Philosophy* 55 (July 1958): 573–578.

Berelson, Bernard R.

Bernard R. Berelson (1912–1979) was an American behavioral scientist who made significant contributions to communication research, voting studies, and population policy. Born in Spokane, Washington, on June 2, 1912, Berelson graduated from Whitman College in 1936 and received a PhD from the University of Chicago in 1941. In 1944 he became a project director at the Columbia University Bureau of Applied Social Research. In 1951 he joined the Ford Foundation in California and popularized behavioral sciences as a director. Berelson also guided the establishment of the Center for Advanced Study in Behavioral Sciences at Stanford University in California in 1952.

Berelson wrote or edited twelve books in social and behavioral sciences, including *The People's Choice* (1944; coauthored with Paul E. Lazarsfeld and Hazel Gaudet), and published more than ninety articles. He contributed a very important chapter on the meaning of the voting process in a democracy in *Voting: A Study of Opinion Formation in a Presidential Campaign* (1986), which he coauthored with Lazarsfeld and William McPhee. He highlighted the fact that most voters are not acquainted with political reality and respond to irrelevant social influences. He stated that "a democracy sets different requirements for different individuals and an electoral system must achieve a balance between various segments of society."

Berelson was highly organized and goal-oriented. He preferred writing in a direct and jargon-free style. He was greatly concerned about the practical, ethical, and value implications of scientific research. For example, in his last publication, he dealt with various ethical issues involved in government efforts toward influencing fertility. He showed great respect for the rights of the people in studies such as *Paths to Fertility Reduction: The Policy Cube* (1977) and *The Condition of Fertility Decline in Developing Countries, 1965–75* (1978). He held the firm belief that rapid population growth suppressed social and economic development and, therefore, all efforts should be made to lower population growth in global interest.

Berelson was convinced that well-researched and evidence-based findings could make a significant practical difference in knowledge-based societies. He encouraged collaboration between research scientists and policy makers. For instance, he evaluated various family planning interventions in Bangladesh, South Korea, Taiwan, and Thailand and sought to convince the governments of these countries that such interventions also could be politically and socially acceptable. He even established a journal called *Studies in Family Planning.* He played a pioneer role in promoting *World Leaders Declaration on Population,* which was presented at the United Nations in 1967.

Berelson served as a member of the U.S. Commission on Population Growth and the American Future. He excelled at summarizing important scientific works. Fourteen of his articles were published posthumously in a volume edited by John A. Ross and W. Parker Mauldin in 1988. This volume also included Berelson's full bibliography. Berelson remained the president of the Population Council until 1974, when he resigned due to disagreements with John D. Rockefeller III—the founder and chair of the council. However, Berelson continued as a senior fellow until his death in 1979.

See also *Lazarsfeld, Paul F.; Voting Behavior.*

. . . . ASHA GUPTA

BIBLIOGRAPHY

Granberg, Donald, and Soren Holmberg. "The Berelson Paradox Reconsidered: Intention-Behavior Changers in the U.S. and Swedish Election Campaigns." *The Public Opinion Quarterly* 54 (Winter 1990): 530–550.

Mauldin, W. Parker. "Bernard Berelson: 2 June 1912–25 September 1979." *Studies in Family Planning* 10 (October 1979): 259–262.

Ross, John A., and W. Parker Mauldin, eds. *Berelson on Population.* New York: Springer-Verlag, 1988.

Sills, David L. "In Memoriam: Bernard Berelson, 1912–1979." *The Public Opinion Quarterly* 44 (Summer 1980): 274–275.

Berle, Adolf Augustus

Adolf Augustus Berle (1895–1971) was an American corporate lawyer, political advisor, diplomat, academic educator, and scholar. Berle's astonishingly wide-ranging and prestigious career began after his completion of a law degree at the age of twenty-one at Harvard University. Already cast into public life at the age of twenty-four, Berle joined Woodrow Wilson as a representative of the American delegation at the Treaty of Versailles (1919). In a moment of characteristic political intuitiveness, Berle eventually resigned in protest of the Versailles settlement, warning that the treaty would serve as the cause to further wars as opposed to a lasting peace.

After establishing himself as a successful corporate lawyer in New York, Berle then turned to academia, eventually earning a professorship in corporate law at Columbia University in 1927, a post he would hold until his retirement in 1963. The remainder of Berle's time in academia would be balanced with a series of high-profile government appointments. The most important of these include various positions as a political advisor to presidents Franklin D. Roosevelt and John F. Kennedy, in addition to serving as assistant secretary of state (1938–1944) and ambassador to Brazil (1945–1946).

Berle's diverse career is reflected in the broad scope of his scholarly interests, which include extensive writing on political economy, Latin American affairs, and New York State politics. His most influential and important contribution has been his work on American capitalism, particularly in the realm of corporate governance. Coauthored with economic historian Gardiner Means, Berle's *The Modern Corporation and Private Property* (1932) still stands as the central reference point in studies of the relations between key actors within the joint stock company. The main argument of this study is that the historical rise of the corporation from the middle of the nineteenth century has transformed American capitalism by gradually separating ownership from control and power from private property.

Berle's work on corporate governance was interested in changes that had taken place that led to an empowerment of a managerial class separate from labor and capital, its position bolstered by the growing concentration of wealth in the corporate sector and the increasing dispersion of stock ownership across society. Concerned with the implications of managerial power and uncertainties over whose interests it was meant to serve, Berle recommended that certain legal limits be placed on management so that its power should be exercised in the interests of those subjected to its growing influence, including shareholders, employees, and civil society. Through the advancement of the proper legal framework, Berle believed that a culture of corporate responsibility could be instilled that directed managerial power toward the benefit of public interest and society as a whole. In his unique position as architect and practitioner of *corporate liberalism,* a form of capitalism that purports to be a middle way between the unbridled free market and state socialism, Berle stands as one of the most important political and academic figures of his era.

See also *Capitalism and Democracy; Political Economy; Property Rights.*

. . . . SANDY BRIAN HAGER

BIBLIOGRAPHY

Berle, Adolf A. *Power without Property: A New Development in American Political Economy.* New York: Harcourt, 1959.

———. *Navigating the Rapids, 1918–1971: From the Papers of Adolf A. Berle.* New York: Harcourt, 1973.

Berle, Adolf A., and Gardiner Means. *The Modern Corporation and Private Property.* London: Transaction, 1932.

Mizruchi, Mark S. "Berle and Means Revisited: The Governance and Power of Large U.S. Corporations." *Theory and Society* 33, No. 5 (2004): 579–617.

Schwarz, Jordan A. *Liberal: Adolf A. Berle and the Vision of an American Era.* New York: Free Press, 1987.

Van Apeldoorn, Bastiaan, and Laura Horn. "The Marketisation of European Corporate Control: A Critical Political Economy Perspective." *New Political Economy* 12, no. 2 (2007): 211–235.

Zeitlin, Maurice "Corporate Ownership and Control: The Large Corporation and the Capitalist Class." *American Journal of Sociology* 79, no. 5 (1974): 1073–1119.

Berlin, Isaiah

Born in the Latvian capital of Riga, Isaiah Berlin (1909–1997) was a leading liberal political theorist and historian of ideas. Focusing on themes of liberty and pluralism, Berlin contends that because human life is characterized by incompatible but equally legitimate goals, a just political order will embrace the natural diversity of human choices rather than imposing one fixed ethical system.

In 1917, Berlin's family moved to Petrograd during the Russian Revolution. They returned to Riga in 1920 and emigrated to London in 1921. Berlin attended Corpus Christi College, Oxford, and was appointed a lecturer at New College in 1932. That same year he received a Prize Fellowship at All Souls, the first Jew to receive such a high honor. During World War II (1932–1945), Berlin worked for the British government in New York (1940–1942), Washington, D.C. (1942–1945); and Moscow (1945–1946), but he remained at Oxford throughout his academic career.

Berlin was knighted in 1957, the same year he was elected Chichele professor of social and political theory at Oxford. In 1966 he became the founding president of Wolfson College, Oxford, and from 1974 to 1978 served as president of the British Academy. He retired from Oxford in 1975. During his life, Berlin also received the prestigious Order of Merit, as well as the Agnelli, Erasmus, Lippincott, and Jerusalem prizes.

Berlin's most well-known work of political theory is his essay "Two Concepts of Liberty" (1958), in which he distinguishes between positive and negative liberty. He defines negative liberty as the absence of external constraints on one's behavior and positive liberty as the capacity for self-determination. Although these two concepts may appear similar, negative liberty is characterized by the absence of external obstacles, whereas positive liberty requires the presence of a self-determining rational will.

According to Berlin, positive liberty carries a danger of totalitarianism because its advocates are "monists" who contend that there is only one way of acting authentically human and those who behave otherwise are slaves to their passions or ignorance. This provides a justification for those who consider themselves wise to oppress those they perceive to be enslaved to their own appetitive impulses. When the enlightened have overcome the irrational empirical selves of these misguided individuals, their real selves finally will emerge to pursue their true interests, which inevitably will harmonize with those of their enlightened educators. Tracing the history of this positive liberty, Berlin shows how dictators of all ideologies, from Plato's philosopher-kings to the Nazis, have used this notion to justify the suppression of diversity in the name of their monistic conceptions of the good life.

Berlin sees negative libertarians as pluralists who maintain that there is a range of ways to act authentically human and that persons should be as free as possible from external constraints to pursue their own ideas of the good life. Many of the choices required may be incommensurable, yet for Berlin the ability to decide for oneself from among these competing values is the core of human dignity. Even so, Berlin argues that the pursuit of negative liberty also may become oppressive, as when a pure free market allows some actors to dominate others economically.

See also *Liberal Theory; Libertarianism.*

. . . . RICK PARRISH

BIBLIOGRAPHY

Berlin, Isaiah. *The Power of Ideas,* edited by Henry Hardy. Princeton, N.J.: Princeton University Press, 2001.

———. *Liberty,* edited by Henry Hardy. Oxford: Oxford University Press, 2002.

Gray, John. *Isaiah Berlin.* Princeton, N.J.: Princeton University Press, 1997.

Ignatieff, Michael. *Isaiah Berlin: A Life.* New York: Henry Holt, 1998.

Bernstein, Eduard

Born in Berlin, Eduard Bernstein (1850–1932) was a leading German social-democratic politician and theorist. His life is a microcosmic reflection of the first century of the German Social Democratic Party (SPD). Like the German labor movement itself, Bernstein started out as a socialist eclectic, then "converted" to Marxist orthodoxy, only to return to an eclectic position that espoused a nonrevolutionary, democratic socialism that recognized Marxism as only one among several important theoretical sources.

Bernstein grew up in Berlin in modest circumstances. After a short career as a bank clerk, he joined the SPD in 1872 as a campaign speaker and pamphleteer. Expelled from Germany in 1878 as a result of German Chancellor Bismarck's repressive antisocialist laws, Bernstein settled in Zurich, Switzerland, from where he edited *Der Sozialdemokrat,* the rallying point of the underground SPD press. After his expulsion from Switzerland, Bernstein continued the periodical from London, where he cultivated close contacts with Friedrich Engels and leaders of the British socialist Fabian Society. When Engels died, Bernstein served as his literary executor and was widely regarded as one of the leading Marxist voices in Europe.

Thus, it came as a shock to his party comrades when Bernstein launched a series of tough criticisms against Marxist theory. In several articles and books between 1896 and 1900, Bernstein rejected the central Marxist dogma of the inevitable collapse of capitalist society and the ensuing revolutionary seizure of power by the working class. In his view, Marx and Engels had painted an unrealistic picture of a revolutionary "final goal." Bernstein advocated an "evolutionary" road to socialism through peaceful, parliamentary means centered on success at the ballot box and gradual democratic reforms. Stressing the tight connection between means and ends, he insisted that the extension of democracy required democratic methods. He argued that the SPD ought to broaden its narrow working-class base and appeal to the middle class as well, becoming a genuine people's party. Finally, rejecting the Marxist view that liberalism and socialism constituted diametrically opposed worldviews, Bernstein urged socialists to consider themselves the legitimate heirs of liberalism and embrace the

Enlightenment language of citizenship, human rights, rule of law, and universal ethics.

Although Bernstein's views became the cornerstones of modern European social democracy after World War II (1939–1945), they were severely condemned by various European Marxists, including Vladimir Lenin in Russia and Rosa Luxemburg and Karl Kautsky in Germany. When the Bolsheviks seized power in Russia in 1917, Bernstein emerged as one of their earliest and fiercest critics, warning that Lenin's brand of Soviet communism was based on the erroneous belief in the "omnipotence of brute force." He predicted, correctly as it turned out, that the Soviet regime represented an odd repetition of the old despotism of the tsars that would lead Russia into a "social and economic abyss." Bernstein held high political posts in the German Weimar Republic (1918–1933), including as undersecretary of the treasury. During his parliamentary tenure (1920–1928), he concentrated on matters of taxation and foreign affairs while maintaining his busy journalistic schedule.

See also Democratic Socialism; German Political Thought, Foundations of.

. . . . MANFRED B. STEGER

BIBLIOGRAPHY

Bernstein, Eduard. *The Preconditions of Socialism,* edited and translated by Henry Tudor. Cambridge: Cambridge University Press, 1993. Originally published as *Die Voraussetzungen des Sozialismus und die Aufgaben der Sozialdemokratie,* Stuttgart: Dietz, 1899.

———. *Selected Writings of Eduard Bernstein, 1900–1921,* edited and translated by Manfred B. Steger. Atlantic Highlands, N.J.: Humanities International, 1996.

Gay, Peter. *The Dilemma of Democratic Socialism: Eduard Bernstein's Challenge to Marx.* New York: Columbia University Press, 1952.

Steger, Manfred B. *The Quest for Evolutionary Socialism: Eduard Bernstein and Social Democracy.* Cambridge: Cambridge University Press, 1997.

Bicameralism

See *Unicameralism and Bicameralism.*

Bill of Rights

A *bill of rights* is a list of legally protected rights or immunities enjoyed by citizens or holders of public office. The English Bill of Rights (1689) was drawn up during the Glorious Revolution of 1688 that ended repressive Stuart rule and brought William and Mary to the English throne. It lists such protections as the right to trial by jury, freedom of speech (for members of Parliament only), the right to keep and bear arms (for Protestants only), and other limited rights and immunities.

A century later, a more sweeping and inclusive Bill of Rights was added to the United States Constitution in 1791, as the first ten amendments to the Constitution. These amendments were added as an afterthought, for the Founders who met in Philadelphia in the summer of 1787 did not believe that a bill of rights needed to be included in the newly drafted document. This view was, however, hotly disputed during the course of the ratification debate of 1787 and 1788.

Most Anti-Federalist opponents of the proposed constitution, and some strong Federalist supporters of the new constitution, including Thomas Jefferson, decried the absence of a bill of rights in the document drafted in Philadelphia. The Anti-Federalists hammered the point home: Without a bill of rights, the new constitution created a system that is republican in name only. A bill of rights would serve as a reminder to rulers and citizens alike that the government's authority is limited by its citizens' inviolable liberties. Didn't England's Glorious Revolution result in a bill of rights to which King William agreed to abide? Didn't the American Revolution of 1776 deserve no less a guarantee? For what was the revolution fought, if not to preserve American rights and liberties? The Anti-Federalists believed that if rights and liberties are to be properly protected, the nature and extent of those liberties must be fixed from the outset. The goodwill or solicitude of rulers or representatives was not to be relied on for very long, if at all. Unless checked by the law and an active and vigilant citizenry, those to whom power is entrusted will abuse it sooner or later. Without an explicit "declaration of rights" to protect "the democratical part" of the citizenry, wrote the pseudonymous Anti-Federalist pamphleteer Brutus (thought by most to be Robert Yates), "the plan is radically defective in a fundamental principle, which ought to be found in every free government" (Brutus 2003, 453–454). Because the arguments in favor of such a declaration are so clear and compelling, its omission is an ominous portent, revealing the malign designs of the Federalists: "so clear a point is this," Brutus added, "that I cannot help suspecting, that persons who attempt to persuade people, that such reservations were less necessary under this constitution, than under those of the states, are willfully endeavoring to deceive, and to lead you into an absolute state of vassalage" (453).

Anti-Federalist objections to the absence of a bill of rights grew louder over the course of the ratification debate. Writing as "Publius" in *The Federalist,* Alexander Hamilton first derided these objections as confused and incoherent (No. 38). Later, in *Federalist* (No. 84), he felt obliged to respond, albeit reluctantly and under the heading of "miscellaneous points." Hamilton wrote, "The most considerable of these remaining objections is that the plan of the convention contains no bill of rights." He replied by noting that several state constitutions, including New York's, are also without bills of rights. Acknowledging the force of the Anti-Federalists' answer to this objection—namely, that no separate bill of rights is needed because provisions for protecting those rights are incorporated into the texts of the state constitutions—Hamilton asserted that the same is true of the new federal constitution as well. "The truth is, after all the declamation we have heard, that the constitution is itself in every rational sense, and to every useful purpose, A BILL OF RIGHTS." Yet the bill of rights that Hamilton tried to tease out of the text is a motley assortment of legal guarantees, prohibitions, and definitions. The "privileges" of *habeas corpus* and jury trials are affirmed (although there is no requirement that the jury be composed of one's peers), and the prohibition of titles of nobility (Art. I, sec. 9) Hamilton offered as positive proof of the rights-respecting character of the new constitution. But, in any event, Hamilton added, a bill of rights is out of place in a republican constitution. Harking back to Magna Carta (1215) and the 1689 English Bill of Rights, Hamilton said that "bills of rights are in their origin, stipulations between kings and their subjects," and therefore have no place in a truly republican constitution.

Hamilton's argument fell on deaf ears. Although the proposed constitution was eventually ratified by all thirteen states, several did so on the condition that a bill of rights be added as soon as possible. The bill of rights drafted by James Madison and adopted in 1791 explicitly enumerated the rights to freedom of religion, speech, press, assembly, and other protections.

By no means a static and unchanging enumeration of rights, the 1791 Bill of Rights—like the Constitution to which it is attached—has been subjected to repeated reinterpretation. The original (or originally intended) meanings of free speech, due process, "takings," and a host of other rights have been modified in the course of American legal and political history. Successive U.S. Supreme Court cases have expanded the scope and range of the rights enumerated in the Bill of Rights. The First Amendment, in particular, has been the object of interpretive dispute and controversy. For example, freedom of speech and the press has been expanded to mean freedom of expression of various sorts, including artistic and other nonverbal forms of expression. And the Second Amendment, which originally appeared to apply only to members of militias, was in 2008 reinterpreted by the Supreme Court to apply to all law-abiding adult citizens.

See also *Constitutional Amendments; Freedom of the Press; Freedom of Religion; Freedom of Speech.*

. . . . TERENCE BALL

BIBLIOGRAPHY

Amar, Akhil Reed. *The Bill of Rights: Creation and Reconstruction.* New Haven, Conn.: Yale University Press, 1998.

Brant, Irving. *The Bill of Rights: Its Origin and Meaning.* Indianapolis: Bobbs-Merrill, 1965.

Brutus. "Letters of Brutus." In *The Federalist: With Letters of Brutus,* edited by Terence Ball, 433–534. Cambridge: Cambridge University Press, 2003.

Bryner, Gary C., and A. D. Sorenson, eds. *The Bill of Rights: A Bicentennial Assessment.* Provo, Utah: Brigham Young University, 1993.

Hamilton, Alexander, James Madison, and John Jay. *The Federalist: With Letters of Brutus,* edited by Terence Ball. Cambridge: Cambridge University Press, 2003.

Hand, Learned. *The Bill of Rights.* Cambridge, Mass.: Harvard University Press, 1958.

Hickok, Eugene W., Jr., ed. *The Bill of Rights: Original Meaning and Current Understanding.* Charlottesville: University Press of Virginia, 1991.

Lacey, Michael J., and Knuud Haakonsson, eds. *A Culture of Rights: The Bill of Rights in Philosophy, Politics, and Law—1791 and 1991.* Cambridge: Cambridge University Press, 1991.

Martin, Robert W. T. *The Free and Open Press: The Founding of American Democratic Press Liberty, 1640–1800.* New York: New York University Press, 2001.

Murphy, Paul L. *The Meaning of Freedom of Speech: First Amendment Freedoms from Wilson to F.D.R.* Westport, Conn.: Greenwood, 1972.

Rutland, Robert Allen. *The Birth of the Bill of Rights, 1776–1791,* rev. ed. Chapel Hill: University of North Carolina Press, 1983.

Stone, Geoffrey R., Richard A. Epstein, and Cass R. Sunstein, eds. *The Bill of Rights in the Modern State.* Chicago: University of Chicago Press, 1992.

Bill of Rights, International

See *International Bill of Rights.*

Binomial Electoral System

The binomial electoral system is a unique legislative electoral system used in Chile. The system is part of the comprehensive reform of the Chilean political system imposed by Augusto Pinochet's dictatorship, which was defeated in a popular plebiscite in 1988. The binomial system remains the military government's primary and most controversial institutional legacy.

In designing the binomial system, the military government sought to transform Chile's historic multiparty system by reducing the number of political parties, diminish the power of the left, and provide electoral benefits for the right. Reformers assumed that a small-magnitude (i.e., seats per district) system would reduce the number of political parties, purportedly enhancing stability; however, they knew a single-member district system would shut the right out of congress. Reformers opted for the binomial system to balance the transformational and electoral interests of the military and rightist parties.

Under the binomial electoral system, each party or coalition can present two candidates in each of the sixty Chamber of Deputies and nineteen Senate districts. The system uses open lists, where voters indicate a single preference from one of the two-seat lists. Though preference votes are candidate-centered, list votes are first pooled together to determine how many seats each list wins. Seats are then awarded to individual candidates based on their rank order using the D'hondt counting method, which means that the first-place list in a district can only win both seats if it more than doubles the vote total of the second-place list. If it does not, each of the top two lists wins a single seat. In most districts the two largest coalitions (the center-left Concertación and the right-wing Alianza) split the seats, because the only way for a leading coalition to win both is to outpoll its nearest competitor by two to one.

The binomial system failed its initial goal of reducing the number of political parties. Rather, parties now compete as multiparty coalitions but maintain separate identities and electoral bases. The system has provided disproportionate benefits for the right. Because the Concertación would require a supermajority in most districts to double the electoral power of the right, and the Concertación's level of electoral support has hovered around 55 percent and the Alianza's at around 40 percent, in functional terms the coalitions simply divide seats in most districts, providing an electoral bonus for the right. The system also has succeeded in marginalizing the non-Concertación left, or any small party that fails or refuses to strike an electoral bargain with one of the two major coalitions.

Although the first four postauthoritarian Chilean presidents proposed reform of the system, opposition from rightist parties stymied reforms. Proponents of the system contend that it has brought stability and governability to Chile, arguing that small magnitudes have helped transform the historically fractious party system by providing incentives for the formation of two long-standing multiparty coalitions. Critics argue that it provides a lock on power for the two main coalitions, excludes small parties, and limits representation and accountability, given its tendency to concentrate the power over candidate selection in the hands of elites.

See also *Candidate Selection; Electoral Reform; Electoral Systems.*

. . . . PETER M. SIAVELIS

BIBLIOGRAPHY

Magar, Eric, Marc R. Rosenblum, and David J. Samuels. "On the Absence of Centripetal Incentives in Double-member Districts: The Case of Chile." *Comparative Political Studies* 31, no. 6 (1998): 714–739.

Rabkin, Rhoda. "Redemocratization, Electoral Engineering, and Party Strategies in Chile, 1989–1995." *Comparative Political Studies* 29, no. 3 (1996): 335–356.

Siavelis, Peter M. "Continuity and Change in the Chilean Party System: On the Transformational Effects of Electoral Reform." *Comparative Political Studies* 30, no. 6 (1997): 651–674.

———. "The Hidden Logic of Candidate Selection for Chilean Parliamentary Elections." *Comparative Politics* 34, no. 4 (2002): 419–438.

Valenzuela, J. Samuel, and Timothy Scully. "Electoral Choices and the Party System in Chile: Continuities and Changes at the Recovery of Democracy." *Comparative Politics* 29, no. 4 (1997): 511–527.

Bioethics and Politics

The ethics of scientific technologies and medical practices have always been controversial, and society as a whole has largely decided that a modicum of collective control of science and medicine should be enforced. Debates about this control have come to be generally called *bioethical* debates, but clarity requires distinctions between three distinct subdebates. The first is *clinical bioethics,* which is the microapplication of government and institutional policy to the evaluation of the ethics of human experimentation and the treatment of patients in hospitals. For example, every university that conducts research on humans has an institutional review board that applies government ethics policy to individual research proposals, and every hospital must have a bioethicist (or equivalent) on call to resolve ethical dilemmas. A second is *regulatory bioethics,* wherein groups of professionals make ethical recommendations to government officials on issues outside those considered by clinical ethics. Most influential in this category have been various government bioethics commissions over the years, which have made ethical recommendations to elected and unelected government officials about issues such as reproductive cloning, the definition of death, and the treatment of the subjects of medical research. A third category is *cultural bioethics.* Here, the debate is not necessarily about policies that should be enacted, but rather about how the society should morally evaluate developments in science and medicine. For example, there is a bioethics debate that takes place in the media over whether genetically enhancing children should be considered morally licit.

These three bioethical debates are differently political. Clinical ethics is fairly apolitical, in that the ethics required by the government has not been challenged by any group.

Regulatory bioethics has until recently been fairly apolitical, largely because people with views not in concert with scientific or medical interests were marginalized from participation in these forums. For example, it has been claimed that not a single member of U.S. president Bill Clinton's federal bioethics commission was opposed to the destruction of embryos, which certainly required making sure that not all views available in society were represented in the commission. With the advent of the George W. Bush administration, a different group of scholars were put in charge of the federal bioethics commission, more of whom were opposed to destroying embryos. The result is that what was once a fairly technocratic enterprise of advising the bureaucratic state from a "neutral" ethical perspective became challenged by social movements in the public sphere, particularly on beginning and end-of-life issues. For instance, the appointment of the commissioners to these once obscure commissions has been the subject of press releases, petitions, and challenges.

Cultural bioethics was always political in the broader sense of debate in the public sphere that results in consensus formation. While the issues at stake and the professions involved in shaping this debate have changed since the 1960s, its "politicization" has been constant. For example, whether reproductive cloning is moral is political, and all sorts of social movements, interest groups, and academics are involved in trying to convince the public to accept one position or another.

Bioethical debate is not old enough for consensus to have developed on terminology. However, most scholars would say that there are bioethical *issues* (e.g., reproductive cloning) that can be the subject of political activity, such as campaigns to enact legislation, but that *bioethics* and *bioethical debate* refer to the activity of professionals, not ordinary citizens. Moreover, while members of many different professions participate in the three distinct bioethical debates, there is widely acknowledged to be a distinct and dominant profession named *bioethics,* made up of *bioethicists* who exclusively participate in these debates. The general ethical approach of the bioethics profession—in contrast to other professions in the debate, such as theology—is to embody liberal democratic procedural ideals. Typically bioethicists claim to not be trying to promote their own values in these debates, but rather are trying to help patients clarify their own values (clinical ethics), or to clarify and utilize what they take to be the common moral principles of Western civilization (regulatory ethics.) Unlike other experts whose expertise is thought to give them an appropriate voice in politics, like climatologists, the very notion that there are ethical experts has always been controversial.

See also *Biology and Political Science; Science Policy; Science, Technology, and Politics.*

. . . . JOHN H. EVANS

BIBLIOGRAPHY

Brown, Mark B. "Three Ways to Politicize Bioethics." *American Journal of Bioethics* 9, no. 2 (2009): 43–54.

Callahan, Daniel. "Bioethics and the Culture Wars." *Cambridge Quarterly of Healthcare Ethics* 14 (2005): 424–431.

Dzur, Albert W., and Daniel Levin. "The 'Nation's Conscience': Assessing Bioethics Commissions as Public Forums." *Kennedy Institute of Ethics Journal* 14, no. 4 (2004): 333–360.

Engelhardt, H. Tristram, Jr. "Bioethics as Politics: A Critical Reassessment." In *The Ethics of Bioethics: Mapping the Moral Landscape,* edited by Lisa A. Eckenwiler and Felicia G. Cohn, 118–133. Baltimore: Johns Hopkins University Press, 2007.

Evans, John H. *Playing God? Human Genetic Engineering and the Rationalization of Public Bioethical Debate.* Chicago: University of Chicago Press, 2002.

Kass, Leon R. "Reflections on Public Bioethics: A View from the Trenches." *Kennedy Institute of Ethics Journal* 15, no. 3 (2005): 221–250.

Biology and Political Science

Almost from its inception, mainstream political science has insisted that, for all practical purposes, human nature, and, hence, political behavior, is shaped by culture. This basic tenet carries with it three corollaries: (1) humans have no innate political tendencies; (2) our political behavior is solely the product of learning and socialization (in short, of *nurture*); (3) human nature (and, thus, human political behavior) is malleable. This is traditionally referred to as the *standard social science model.*

Starting in the mid-1960s, this long-dominant paradigm has been challenged by a more biologically oriented approach, usually termed *biopolitics.* (While others have used the term *biopolitics* with variant meanings, such as Michel Foucault or Morley Roberts, this entry will use the term in its more restricted sense, to describe the current interest in the relationship between the life sciences and the study of politics, beginning, as is generally accepted, in the 1960s.) Yes, culture is important, its advocates agree, but so are the genetically transmitted behavioral inclinations our species has evolved, as social primates, over literally millions of years. Consequently, they insist, *both* nature *and* nurture must be taken into consideration.

From this disagreement on first principles there flow important differences as to how political scientists can most fruitfully study and understand political behavior. A concise examination of these differences may be the most effective way of familiarizing the reader with the key premises on which the biopolitical approach is based. The most important include the following.

GENETIC FACTORS AS BEHAVIORAL INFLUENCES

As mentioned above, mainstream political science dismisses these entirely. From an evolutionary, biopolitical perspective, however, we share quite a few behavioral traits with other social primate species. Among the most politically important of these are: a proclivity for hierarchical social and political structures characterized by dominance and submission (and unequal access to the good things of life); status seeking; aggression; xenophobia; and nepotistic favoritism.

HISTORICAL EVIDENCE AS A BASIS FOR PREDICTING FUTURE BEHAVIOR

Standard evolutionary theory holds that, barring mutation or some profound environmental change, the behaviors a species has evolved are likely to remain largely unchanged over lengthy periods. Thus, as those in biopolitics see it, when efforts to alter or even prohibit "undesirable" social and political behaviors have been consistently unsuccessful in the past, similar attempts are not likely to be any more effective in the future. They see trying to "change human nature" as analogous to asking a leopard to change its spots.

Having greater faith in the malleability of human nature, mainstream political science is more likely to discount past behavioral patterns. Conceivably, this time the leopard might be induced—or compelled—to alter its coloration. Why, then, not try?

USE OF PRIMATOLOGICAL DATA

If, according to the accepted wisdom, human behavior is shaped almost entirely by culture and socialization, knowledge about other species, no matter how akin to ours, serves no useful purpose. On the other hand, if our genetic legacy often meaningfully influences how we act, the study of closely related species becomes most relevant. For instance, primatologists have used their research on our nearest relatives in the animal kingdom to consider the evolutionary roots of human behavior, from aggression to altruism. Political scientists, for their part, have explicitly explored how an understanding of primates might inform our theorizing about human politics and ethics.

RESEARCH METHODOLOGY

The study of human behavior from an evolutionary perspective emerged from ethology, a discipline guided by the dictum that, to understand how and why an organism acts as it does, we must study its actual behavior in its natural setting. Both mainstream political science and biopolitics accept experiments as a valid means of inquiry. The latter, however, insists the experiment should mirror, to the extent possible, the challenges and environment the subject(s) would encounter under real-life conditions. For this reason, it is skeptical about the validity of experiments in which subjects, human or other, are placed in a patently artificial setting and are asked to perform tasks that lack meaningful consequences. Biopolitics, with its ethologically derived emphasis on actual behavior, sees survey research, by and large, as a research instrument of last resort.

THE FORMULATION OF PUBLIC POLICY

Here, some examples illustrate how a biological perspective might inform policy choices. Evolutionary change almost always entails a tradeoff. Greater size requires greater caloric intake; speed comes at the cost of endurance; a massive protective carapace or shell leads to lessened mobility. Given their neo-Darwinian orientation, those in biopolitics tend to think less in terms of a "solution" to problems like human "vices" and more in terms of what is to be gained and lost by a particular policy. These trade-offs have not been adequately considered, for example, in the ill-fated Eighteenth Amendment to the U.S. Constitution (which prohibited the sale of alcohol); in the interminible "war on drugs"; or in the consistently futile efforts, literally over the centuries, to prohibit prostitution.

To elaborate on the last example, Michael McGuire and Margaret Gruter examine the almost certain failure of anti-prostitution laws. McGuire and Gruter note the value of an evolutionary inquiry:

> Both sexes have dispositional tendencies to reproduce, and reproduction-related behavior (e.g., flirting, experimentation with one's and other's bodies) begins during adolescence. . . . In effect, both sexes are predisposed and well prepared to engage in sexual behavior. It follows that attempts to control sexual behavior will be only partially successful, a point to which the high frequency of teenage sexual encounters, abortions, and adult extramarital affairs attests. (2003, 35)

Given this, what policy suggestions follow? Because prostitution is unlikely to be completely suppressed given human impulses, then limited legalization may make the most sense. This would call for registration of sex workers, making sure that sexually transmitted diseases are controlled, reducing criminal involvement, bringing the workers into the recognized workforce. Of course, some aspects of prostitution would remain outside the law—such as human trafficking and child prostitution. The authors cite Holland and Nevada as localities where successful regulation has taken place.

TOWARD THE FUTURE

Launched, as noted above, in the mid-1960s, the biology-and-politics enterprise received official recognition from the International Political Science Association in 1973 with the creation of the eponymous Research Committee #12. After considerable debate over the wisdom of a separate professional organization, the Association for Politics and the Life Sciences was established in 1980, and the first issue of its journal, *Politics and the Life Sciences,* was published in 1982.

As yet, to be sure, a sizable majority of political scientists continues to see political behavior as fundamentally, if not exclusively, the product of culture, socialization, and individual experience. Over the past decade or so, however, a neo-Darwinian approach has been fostering a steadily growing amount of research in anthropology, psychology, social psychology, sociology and, most recently, economics. Conceivably, this may eventually be the case in political science, historically quite susceptible to intellectual trends in its sister social sciences.

See also *Bioethics and Politics; Foucault, Michel Paul; Political Ecology; Sociobiology and Politics.*

. . . . ALBERT SOMIT AND STEVEN PETERSON

BIBLIOGRAPHY
Blank, Robert H., and Samuel M. Hines Jr. *Biology and Political Science.* New York: Routledge, 2001.
Dahl, Robert A. *On Democracy.* New Haven, Conn.: Yale University Press, 1998.
Degler, Carl. *In Search of Human Nature.* New York: Oxford University Press, 1991.
De Waal, Frans B. M. *Peacemaking among Primates.* Cambridge, Mass.: Harvard University Press, 1989.
McGuire, Michael, and Margaret Gruter. "Prostitution: An Evolutionary Perspective." In *Human Nature and Public Policy: An Evolutionary Approach,* edited by Albert Somit and Steven A. Peterson, 29–40. New York: Palgrave Macmillan, 2003.
Piano, Aili, Arch Puddington, and Mark Y. Rosenberg, eds. *Freedom in the World 2006.* New York: Freedom House, 2006.
Schubert, Glendon, and Roger D. Masters, eds. *Primate Politics.* Lanham, Md.: University Press of America, 1991.
Somit, Albert, and Steven A. Peterson. *Darwinism, Dominance, and Democracy.* Westport, Conn.: Praeger, 1997.
———. "Review Article: Biopolitics after Three Decades—A Balance Sheet." *British Journal of Political Science* 28 (1998): 559–571.
Vanhanen, Tatu. *Democratization.* New York: Routledge, 2003.

Bisexual Movement

See *Lesbian, Gay, Bisexual, and Transgender Movement, Comparative.*

Blackstone, William

Sir William Blackstone (1723–1780) was an English jurist and legal scholar whose exposition of English common law continues to resonate in courtrooms in the early twenty-first century. His *Commentaries on the Laws of England,* published over four volumes beginning in 1765, was a comprehensive yet accessible treatise on the history of common law that proved critical to jurists in both England and the colonies of America. Blackstone's *Commentaries* is still cited in American courts of law as one of the foremost influences on the American Founders and a cornerstone of the U.S. Constitution.

Born in London, Blackstone studied at Oxford before being admitted to the bar in 1746. He both practiced and taught law to little major public acclaim until the 1756 publication of his *An Analysis of the Laws of England,* a work comprising many of his lectures at Oxford. In 1761 he was appointed as a counsel to the Crown and was elected to the House of Commons, where he exhibited a mostly Tory ideology. He was knighted in 1770 and appointed as a justice to the Court of Common Pleas, the last formal position he would hold.

Many of these appointments can be traced to the fame Blackstone experienced as a result of the success of his collected lectures. His *Commentaries* was well received in Europe, where it was translated into many languages, and in America, where its first publication in 1771 met with widespread acclaim for its utility in summarizing the legal tradition of England and how it might be applied to a new political landscape. The work was divided into four legal subjects: the "Rights of Persons" (or individuals), the "Rights of Things" (or property law), "Private Wrongs," and "Public Wrongs." Taken together, the volumes encompass an able introduction to the common law tradition for the aspiring lawyers Blackstone instructed and a ready framework for the American Founders in justifying the Declaration of Independence and, later, the construction of the Constitution. While luminaries such as British philosopher John Locke, American founding father Thomas Paine, and other Enlightenment thinkers provided abstract justifications for the natural rights of the colonists, the *Commentaries* offered a crucial practical vindication of and design for an independent legal system in America.

While Blackstone's influence has waned in the realm of contemporary legal thought, there can be little doubt concerning the pivotal role he played during the debates during and after the American constitutional convention of 1787, during which his work was frequently invoked for both Federalist and anti-Federalist causes. Furthermore, the *Commentaries* acted as a layman's barricade for the tradition of English common law against encroaching parliamentary legislation, just when such a defense was most needed. These twin contributions alone enshrine Blackstone as a pillar of legal theory, earning him praise and criticism from later philosophers such as Jeremy Bentham and John Austin.

See also *Common Law; Constitutional Law; Law and Society; Locke, John; Paine, Thomas; Political Law.*

. . . . CLYDE RAY

BIBLIOGRAPHY

Blackstone, William. *Commentaries on the Laws of England,* 4 vols, edited by Wayne Morrison. Oxford, U.K.: Clarendon, 2001.

Boorstin, Daniel J. *The Mysterious Science of the Law: An Essay on Blackstone's Commentaries.* Chicago: University of Chicago Press, 2001.

Plucknett, Theodore F. T. *A Concise History of the Common Law.* London: Butterworth, 1956.

Warden, C. Lewis. *The Life of William Blackstone.* Charlottesville, Va.: Michie, 1938.

Blame Management

See *Scandals and Blame Management, Political.*

Blanqui, Louis-Auguste

Louis-Auguste Blanqui (1805–1881) was a French republican activist and legendary revolutionary conspirator. Intellectually precocious as a youth, he studied law and medicine at the University of Paris, though he never earned a degree. Coming of age during the repressive Bourbon restoration, he abandoned his studies in favor of the secret societies of the republican underground, sealing his commitment to abet popular insurrections against all conservative governmental regimes. Despite repeated arrests, trials, and lengthening prison sentences for his subversive activities, Blanqui managed to participate in all of the major Parisian popular uprisings of the early nineteenth century—those of 1830, 1832, 1839, and 1848. By mid-century he had become widely known as an insurgent leader willing to sacrifice himself for the republican cause.

Blanqui's subversive political activism was a quasi-religious vocation. As a professional revolutionary, he promoted not only an egalitarian republic, but also a society free of religious obscurantism that perpetuated social injustice. His politics drew on the moral implications of his radical atheism: the value of righteous struggle against oppression now, whatever the odds. Sympathetic to a vaguely conceived notion of a social republic, he had little interest in the theory of collectivism then gaining ground in Europe, and he kept his distance from the First Workingmen's International Association, whose practical projects to advance the labor movement threatened to displace the activist style of confrontation and revolt on which the revolutionary tradition had relied.

Blanqui's reputation among left-wing militants was compromised toward mid-century, when a former comrade in arms publicly accused him of having betrayed his coconspirators to the police in the abortive uprising of 1839. Blanqui recovered his stature during the Second Empire among radical republican youth, who looked to him as a mentor. In this guise, the aging Blanqui initiated his young followers into the rites and rituals of the revolutionary tradition. Many of them would come to play leading roles in the Paris Commune of 1871. By then, Blanqui had been imprisoned once more. The refusal of the French provisional government to trade him for all the priests of Paris held hostage by the commune suggests the proportions his legend had by then assumed. Ironically, he was freed upon his election to the Chamber of Deputies in 1879 as the emblem of the campaign for the amnesty of the Communards in the name of national reconciliation. Revered across a broad spectrum of the political left, Blanqui returned to Paris to live in tranquility until his death on New Year's Day 1881.

In the twentieth century, Blanqui assumed a place in the pantheon of heroes of the French Communist Party as a founding father of its cause. His remarkable life elicited the interest of sympathetic historians and literary critics, who idealized his role in the revolutionary tradition. That portrait was challenged by a more critical biographer, Maurice Paz, who pointed to Blanqui's rigid authoritarianism and his psychological need for the adulation of his disciples.

See also *French Political Thought; Revolutions.*

. . . . PATRICK H. HUTTON

BIBLIOGRAPHY

Bernstein, Samuel. *Blanqui.* Paris: Maspero, 1970.

Decaux, Alain. *Blanqui, l'insurgé.* Paris: Perrin, 1976.

Dommanget, Maurice. *Auguste Blanqui: Des origines à la révolution de 1848.* Paris: Mouton, 1969.

Hutton, Patrick. *The Cult of the Revolutionary Tradition: The Blanquists in French Politics.* Berkeley: University of California Press, 1981.

Paz, Maurice. *Un Révolutionnaire professionnel, Auguste Blanqui.* Paris: Fayard, 1984.

Bloc

A *bloc* is a coalition of individuals, groups, or parties in a democratic system. Electoral blocs are common in multiparty, parliamentary systems. Depending on the national political structure, a bloc may be formed prior to an election through a formal or informal agreement. The bloc then contests the balloting as a unified group in an effort to gain a majority in the legislature. Electoral blocs may be created for a single election, or they may be more stable and span multiple cycles. The membership of blocs can change from election to election. For instance, in Ukraine, the core of the Yulia Tymoshenko Electoral Bloc was the same two parties through three rounds of parliamentary elections between 2002 and 2008, although other members of the bloc joined other groupings. Parliamentary blocs also may be formed through formal accords whereby parties and individual legislators agree to support each other. Such coalitions are often necessary in parliamentary systems in which no single party gains a majority of seats in the legislature. Informal blocs may form to advance an issue or policy and then dissolve. In the United States, bipartisan blocs often emerge on regional or policy issues.

See also *Block Vote; Trade Blocs.*

. . . . TOM LANSFORD

Bloch, Ernst

Ernst Bloch (1885–1977) was a German-Jewish Marxist political philosopher. His work can appear overly esoteric at times, infused as it is with what may be called a "messianic" political theology that sits uncomfortably with standard versions of Marxism and their dismissal of such "idealist" utopian dreaming. For Bloch, however, the limitless scope of the human imagination is the very keynote of human beings' continual striving to reshape and remake the world as it is into what it might yet be.

Bloch lived through the most tumultuous and bloody decades of the twentieth century, over the course of which he produced a vast body of work that has reached an arguably smaller readership than is deserved. His magnum opus and most famous work, the monumental three-volume study, *The Principle of Hope* (1954–1959), brings together a dizzying array of conceptual and thematic motifs discernable throughout the rest of his writings. Bloch's political philosophy can be broadly described as nondoctrinaire, thoroughly heterodox Marxism, but one richly textured by a messianic consciousness that absorbs and refines the apparently utopian possibilities glimpsed in the most everyday phenomena and the political conclusions that can be drawn from them.

Bloch's unorthodox and reflexive philosophy had a not unproblematic reception during his own lifetime. It was curiously and somewhat incongruously accommodated—temporarily at least—by the official state wisdom of East Germany. Bloch's actual political decisions sometimes were inconsistent as well, the most notorious of these being his defense of the Moscow Show Trials of 1937 (a series of staged trials of political opponents of Soviet dictator Josef Stalin) after his return from exile in the United States. In 1961 Bloch finally fell out with the German Democratic Republic for good, remaining in West Germany for the rest of his life.

Central to Bloch's political philosophy is his theory of the "not yet" (*noch-nicht*); that is, the persistent and recurrent critical consciousness that indicts its own time as falling short of the possibilities both real and imagined that could yet come into being. This emancipatory demand of the "not-yet-become," so frequently and easily dismissed as wishful thinking, is for Bloch an inescapable and elemental force throughout human history. In this and other regards Bloch shares a distinct affinity with German cultural critic Walter Benjamin's no less elusive messianic philosophy of hope. The time of the "not yet" is for Bloch anterior to the present; an advanced state of perceiving a future world yet to come while recognizing the existing shape of things to be neither infinite nor unchangeable. Such a total critique of existing society—indeed reality—cannot obviously be set out by or co-opted into any standard political program. Instead it can be expressed in theoretical reflection and culture on the one hand and popular social movements seeking to inaugurate widespread social and political change on the other.

Bloch offers a rich body of work linking seemingly disparate cultural and political fragments together into a unifying and consistent (but never doctrinaire) whole. Removed from the false certainties of orthodox Marxism, his philosophy of hope remains noncontemporaneous with both his time and the present day, and yet in spite of this—or indeed perhaps because of it—it is more illuminating than ever.

See also *German Political Thought; Marxism; Utopias and Politics.*

. . . . CHRISTIAN GARLAND

BIBLIOGRAPHY

Bronner, Stephen. "Utopian Projections: In Memory of Ernst Bloch." In *Not Yet: Reconsidering Ernst Bloch,* edited by Jamie Owen Daniel and Tom Moylan, 165–174. London: Verso, 1997.

Daniel, Jamie Owen, and Tom Moylan, eds. *Not Yet: Reconsidering Ernst Bloch.* London: Verso, 1997.

Hudson, Wayne. *The Marxist Philosophy of Ernst Bloch.* London: Macmillan, 1982.

Kellner, Douglas. "Ernst Bloch, Utopia, and Ideology Critique." *Illuminations—The Critical Theory Project,* 1997, www.gseis.ucla.edu/faculty/kellner/Illumina%20Folder/kell11.htm.

Block Vote

Block voting is an electoral system used by multimember electoral wards or districts in which voters cast as many votes as there are seats in the area. In one form of the system, citizens may cast their votes for candidates irrespective of the party affiliation of the office seekers. In another form of block voting, voters cast ballots for a party, and representatives are chosen through proportionality. The system was developed to increase the representation of smaller political parties and reward groupings with effective organizations and popular candidates. However, several countries that used block voting discovered that the system weakened major parties and led to the proliferation of smaller groupings. It also had the opposite effect and tended to result in overwhelming and decisive electoral victories when voters concentrated their ballots on a single popular party. For instance, in multiple block voting elections in Mauritius, the winning party won every seat in parliament despite only winning about 65 percent of the vote. Consequently, during the twentieth century, countries such as Australia, the Philippines, and the United Kingdom either abandoned the method or created mixed systems that combined block voting with first-past-the-post elections.

See also *Electoral Systems; First Past the Post.*

. . . . TOM LANSFORD

Blogs and Bloggers

The term *blog* is a contraction of the term *Weblog,* a page with numerous chunks of content arranged from newest to oldest. It is one of many forms of social media or networking available to people on the Internet since August 1998, which also includes Web forums, podcasts, YouTube, Facebook, and so on. A blog is found in what has come to be known as the *blogosphere,* a public sphere or space of opinions and discussions that is radically open to the voices of massive numbers of people. Thus a blog is any space on the Internet where one can voice opinions, thoughts, and ideas in a very open manner on any topic or subject matter. They are easily created and easily updated Web sites that allow an author or authors to publish instantly to a large audience from any Internet connection. The term *blog* may be used as a noun or as a verb.

A blogger is a person who engages in the act of blogging, which is the act of writing opinions, thoughts, and ideas in any public space on the Internet. This involves making posts, replying to posts, and providing various audio and video links within a Weblog page.

As a result of the pervasiveness of blogging, several new terms have entered the lexicon including *splog,* a fake blog that has no substantive content, just spam (unsolicited commercial messages); *splogsplosion,* an explosion of spam e-mails; Twitter, a free social networking *microblogging* service that allows the *twitterer* to send brief (140 character) notes to other Twitter members on the Internet and on other digital devices such as a cell phone; and *vlog,* a video-based or video-oriented blog.

CHARACTERISTICS

Blogs are the fastest growing sites on the Internet during the first decade of the twenty-first century. Technorati, the leading blog tracking and searching site, has reported that as of December 2007 they have counted the existence of 112 million blogs, with 120,000 new blogs being created every day. Over the three-year period for which data is available, the growth was from nine million in 2005 to thirty-two million in 2006 to eighty million in 2007. There are believed to be 1.2 million postings per day, which amounts to seventeen per second. The major languages of the blogosphere are Chinese, English, Farsi, and Japanese.

POSITIVE ASPECTS

The attention garnered by blogs and their sheer numbers signal their importance. Trend spotters listen to the "key conversations" among the informed and passionate writers and readers of these blogs. The viral aspect of the blog (the ease and speed at which posts zip around the Internet) shows the potential for such a tool in politics as well as in business communications.

Bloggers are some of the most cutting-edge content creators online at the beginning of the twenty-first century because they state their opinions without fear. The power of the blog comes from the ability to allow individuals to express themselves worldwide almost instantly. It is indeed the cheapest, quickest, and easiest way to gain a Web presence. Through blogs ordinary people have the (1) opportunity to share knowledge and experience, (2) potential to educate and entertain, (3) ability to quickly disseminate news and information to a mass readership, and (4) possibility of generating revenue.

As bloggers recount everyday experiences and exchange advice on familiar problems, they often incorporate outside sources, linking to interesting stories from both online and offline publications. What takes place in blogs is not just personal journaling but also thinking and learning. Blogs present a broad range of varied and contradictory opinions and a wealth of information about topics from the minutia of life to global issues. Activists use blogging as a means of fostering political awareness, including blogathons wherein users can blog for a good cause and for various charity events.

Other proponents of blogs see it as a great format for delivering up-to-the-minute news on constantly updated pages across the World Wide Web. The community of bloggers acts as a cadre of fast fact-checkers that quickly root out fraudulent claims. Bloggers can be faster than traditional media when posting accounts of natural disasters, terrorist attacks, or how well *American Idol* participants performed.

Some believe that blogs increase cultural diversity by allowing a wide variety of opinions to propagate and decreasing barriers to cultural and political participation. Blogs have a tendency to reflect our common humanity by showing us that we can assert our individuality and yet we are not alone.

NEGATIVE ASPECTS

For all the good that blogs may provide, there are problems associated with their constant use. With the millions of conversations taking place, information overload is inevitable. How does one sort through the chatter to find relevant, substantive, and trustworthy conversations? Beyond the sheer number, issues regarding the nature of the quality, reliability, and finality of data and information obtained from these blogs raise important questions. Their credibility, objectivity, and representativeness also have been questioned. As a result, calls to create guidelines or rules for blogging have been made, but to many, this amounts to censorship.

IMPACT ON POLITICAL NEWSMAKING

One of the major aspects of blogging deals with its impact on political newsmaking. For example, on December 5, 2002, at Strom Thurmond's 100th birthday party Trent Lott said,

> I want to say this about my state: When Strom Thurmond ran for president, we voted for him. We're proud of it. And if the rest of the country had followed our lead, we wouldn't have had all these problems over all these years, either.

Because Thurmond had explicitly supported racial segregation in that presidential campaign, the statement was widely interpreted to mean that Lott also supported racial segregation. The comment, initially broadcast on C-SPAN, was largely ignored by the mainstream media. However, when political blogs picked up on it, the mainstream media followed suit, leading to Lott's resignation from Republican Senate leadership.

Another example of blogs' impact on the media is blog swarming—the relentless criticism of bloggers on an individual or group that causes a change in action by the individual or group. Former CBS anchor Dan Rather was said to have been stung by blog exposure over his use of forged documents in a report about President George W. Bush's Air National Guard service, hastening Rather's retirement. The negative buzz about Supreme Court nominee Harriet Miers and her qualifications for the job caused her to withdraw her nomination. A blog swarm about the demonic-looking photo of Condoleeza Rice in *USA Today* in October 2005 caused the newspaper to remove the doctored photo.

OTHER ASPECTS

The world of the Internet is a ripe area for study, and attempts to harness it are often seen as a way of curtailing the entrepreneurial spirit. The legal system has had to develop rules for dealing with blogs—users must treat blog posts as business records that can be subpoenaed and, therefore, posts need to be saved, stored, and handed over to litigators in the event of legal action. However, the world of the blog to date is largely a free-for-all, with undefined rules and many players.

See also *Internet and Politics.*

. . . . CECILIA G. MANRIQUE

BIBLIOGRAPHY
Armstrong, Jerome, and Markos Moulitsas Zúniga. *Crashing the Gate.* White River Junction, Vt.: Chelsea Green, 2006.
Barlow, Aaron. *The Rise of the Blogosphere.* Westport, Conn.: Praeger, 2007.
Bausch, Paul, Matthew Haughey, and Meg Hourihan. *We Blog.* Indianapolis: Wiley, 2002.
Berkman, Robert. *The Art of Strategic Listening.* New York: Paramount Market, 2008.
Bruns, Axel. *Blogs, Wikipedia, Second Life, and Beyond.* New York: Peter Lang, 2008.
Flynn, Nancy. *Blog Rules: A Business Guide to Managing Policy, Public Relations, and Legal Issues.* New York: American Management Association 2006.
Forrester, Duane, and Gavin Powell. *How to Make Money with Your Blog.* New York: McGraw-Hill, 2008.
Kelly, Christopher. *Two Bits.* Durham, N.C.: Duke University Press, 2008.
Richardson, Will. *Blogs, Wikis, Podcasts.* Thousand Oaks, Calif.: Corwin, 2006.
"Social Web Sites Face Transparency Questions," *Winona Daily News,* March 23, 2009.

Bobbio, Norberto

Norberto Bobbio (1909–2004), a prominent legal and political philosopher, was instrumental in developing Italian legal positivism and made significant contributions to democratic theory. Committed to the rule of law, he was an important voice of the reformist and liberal-democratic left in Italy.

Born and educated in Turin, Bobbio obtained degrees in jurisprudence and philosophy in the early 1930s and taught law and political science from 1935 to 1984, the year in which he was nominated lifetime senator. Although raised in a middle-class environment that welcomed fascism against the perceived threat of socialist revolution, he associated with leading antifascist intellectuals and liberal socialists from the clandestine groups Justice and Liberty and the Action Party, helping to found the latter in 1942. He was jailed for brief periods in 1935 and 1943 for antifascist activities.

In early writings, Bobbio distanced himself from the predominant currents of idealism represented by Benedetto Croce and Giovanni Gentile, briefly sketched phenomenological approaches to legal science and sociology, and elaborated a theory of social personalism aimed at transcending individualism and collectivism. In the 1940s he criticized existentialism as an apolitical and decadent philosophy, arguing that its tendency toward solipsism and antirationalism undercuts its own focus on action and individual responsibility, notions crucial in the democratic struggle against fascist dictatorship.

Upon fascism's demise, Bobbio engaged in debates over the shape of the new Italian political order. Increasingly influenced by Carlo Cattaneo's positivism, he argued for secular and tolerant politics, liberal democratic rights and institutions, economic and social rights, and domestic and international federalism. After an unsuccessful candidacy to the Constituent Assembly in 1946, he withdrew from politics to concentrate on research and teaching. He propounded a "neo-Enlightenment" rationalism that substituted theoretical rigor and empirical study for idealism's speculative abstractions. Against efforts to revive natural law theories, Bobbio launched Italian legal positivism in the 1950s through a synthesis of logical positivism and Hans Kelsen's pure theory of law—a perspective he supplemented in the 1970s with a sociological account of how law functions in advanced industrial societies.

Bobbio consistently defended liberal democracy against Marxist critics—such as Galvano Della Volpe and Palmiro Togliatti in the 1950s and Antonio Negri in the 1970s—who tended to denigrate citizenship rights as bourgeois ephemera and ignore concrete mechanisms of political rule. He advanced a "minimal" definition of democracy outlining certain "rules of the game" for arriving at collective decisions nonviolently, such as universal and equal suffrage, majority rule with minority rights, and the freedoms of expression and association. To redress democracy's many "broken promises," such as the persistence of oligarchies, Bobbio called for representative institutions to permeate civil society (bringing democratic principles to other domains where collective decisions are made) and an extension of welfare state protections.

With the development of nuclear weapons, Bobbio questioned conventional theories of "just war." Viewing state sovereignty as a primary cause of war, he urged the construction and democratization of international institutions such as the United Nations to safeguard human rights and resolve disputes nonviolently—a notion he termed *legal pacifism.*

Alarmed by increasing economic inequality and the persistence of authoritarian impulses in Italian politics, Bobbio argued in the 1990s for the continuing salience of the political distinction between left and right, and aligned himself with what he viewed as the left's long-standing project of realizing justice and liberty.

See also *Civil and Political Rights; Democratic Socialism; Democratic Theory; Economic, Social, and Cultural Rights; Italian Political Thought; Just War Theory; Kelsen, Hans; Liberal Democracy; Positive Theory.*

. . . . AARON THOMAS

BIBLIOGRAPHY

Anderson, Perry. "The Affinities of Norberto Bobbio." *New Left Review* 170 (July-August, 1988): 3–6.

Bellamy, Richard. *Modern Italian Social Theory.* Stanford, Calif.: Stanford University Press, 1987.

Bobbio, Norberto. *The Philosophy of Decadentism,* translated by David Moore. Oxford: Oxford University Press, 1948.

———. *Politica e cultura.* Turin, Italy: Einaudi, 1955.

———. *The Future of Democracy,* edited by Richard Bellamy, translated by Roger Griffin. Minneapolis: University of Minnesota Press, 1987.

———. *Which Socialism? Marxism, Socialism and Democracy,* edited by Richard Bellamy, translated by Roger Griffin. Minneapolis: University of Minnesota Press, 1987.

———. *Democracy and Dictatorship: The Nature and Limits of State Power,* Translated by Peter Kennealy. Minneapolis: University of Minnesota Press, 1989.

———. *The Age of Rights,* translated by Allan Cameron. Cambridge: Cambridge University Press, 1996.

———. *Left and Right: The Significance of a Political Distinction,* translated by Allan Cameron. Chicago: University of Chicago Press, 1996.

———. *Il problema della Guerra e le vie della pace,* 4th ed. Bologna, Italy: Il Mulino, 1997.

Greco, Tommaso. *Norberto Bobbio: Un itinerario intellettuale tra filosofia e politica.* Rome: Donzelli, 2000.

Urbinati, Nadia. "Liberalism in the Cold War: Norberto Bobbio and the Dialogue with the PCI." *Journal of Modern Italian Studies* 8, no. 4 (2003): 578–603.

Bodin, Jean

One of the most influential French political thinkers of the sixteenth century, Jean Bodin (1529/1530–1596) was a product of his times. Born in Angers, France, he studied and then taught law at the University of Toulouse in the decade before the outbreak of the French Religious Wars (1559–1598). In the 1560s, as France descended into political and religious civil war, Bodin practiced law as an *avocat* in Paris. Two publications in the 1560s brought him public notoriety. The first, *Methodus ad facilem historiarum cognitionem* (*Method for the Easy Comprehension of History,* 1566), advocated the comparative study of all legal codes in the search for the strongest on a specific topic. The second, *Response aux paradoxes de M. Malestroit* (*Response to the Paradoxes of Malestroit,* 1568), addressed the relatively new but pressing problem of price inflation.

In 1571, Bodin entered the household of the Duc d'Alençon, the king's brother, and in 1576 he took part in a meeting of the Estates General of France called by Henry III during a crisis point in the sectarian and political conflicts of the religious wars. In the same year he published his seminal work in political philosophy, *Les six livres de la république* (*Six Books of the Republic*), which advocated a political system that concentrated power in a hereditary monarch. In 1587, he became *procureur au roi* for the town of Laon and was an active participant in the Catholic League, which first rebelled against Henry III and then sought to thwart the accession of the Protestant Henry

IV to the throne of France. Despite his participation in the Catholic League, he wrote in 1588 the controversial *Colloquim Heptaplomeres,* which made the case for religious tolerance. The *Colloquim* only appeared in print posthumously in 1596.

Bodin's single most important contribution to political thought was his transformation of the study of public law through a new definition and demarcation of supreme power in his *Les six livres.* His basic premise was that sovereignty was indivisible. He was less concerned with the origins of this power than with its practice. Key to this idea was a theory of ruler sovereignty that entirely concentrated high power in one individual or group and rejected the idea that power could be shared or distributed among separate agents. Thus, Bodin argued that royal servants were delegated authority and possessed no power of their own. Indeed, royal power was only limited by customary law insomuch as prudence and good government made respect for custom and natural law advantageous to the sovereign. It should be noted, however, that Bodin chose to construct his powerful sovereign using the model of a patriarchal family rather than mystical theories of the royal persona upon which other French political thinkers drew. His ideas proved particularly influential in the half century after the first publication of the *Les Six livres* in 1576 and continued to influence thinkers like Thomas Hobbes and Jean-Jacques Rousseau.

See also *Absolutism; French Political Thought; Sovereignty.*

. . . . ERIC NELSON

BIBLIOGRAPHY

Bodin, Jean. *Selected Writings on Philosophy, Religion, and Politics,* edited by Paul Lawrence Rose. Geneva: Droz, 1980.

———. *Bodin: On Sovereignty,* edited by Julian H. Franklin. Cambridge: Cambridge University Press, 1992.

Franklin, Julian H. *Jean Bodin and the Rise of Absolutist Theory.* Cambridge: Cambridge University Press, 1973.

Boff, Leonardo

Leonardo Boff (1938–) is a recognized Brazilian theologian, philosopher, ecologist, and social critic who has written more than sixty books. He is best known for being one of most outspoken and controversial pioneers of the Latin American Liberation Theology (LALT) movement, which argued that the focus of theology should be the direct relationship that exists between faith and liberating sociopolitical action. In *Salvation and Liberation* (1984), Leonardo and his brother Clodovis Boff posited that LALT is a novel way of approaching theology because it develops a rigorous theological discourse of social, political, and economic liberations. As such, for Boff and the LALT movement, social and political theory became an essential tool for theology, along with its more traditional dialogue partner, philosophy.

Boff was born in 1938 in Concórdia, Brazil. In 1959 he entered the Franciscan Order and in 1964 became an ordained priest. Subsequently, he went to Europe to continue his studies and received a doctorate in philosophy and theology from the

Ludwig-Maximilian University of Münich in 1970. He came to the forefront of the liberation theology movement with the publication of his *Jesus Christ Liberator: A Critical Christology for Our Time* (1978), in which he examines Christology through the historical Jesus and demonstrates the direct relationship between spirituality and political commitment to the poor. Following the arguments of Peruvian theologian Gustavo Gutiérrez in Gutiérrez's seminal 1973 *A Theology of Liberation*, Boff asserted repeatedly in his writings that the first step of the theological process is historical praxis, which is only then followed by a second step of reflection on praxis in light of faith. For this reason, he and other liberationists readily used political theory—Marxism, dependency theory, and critical theory—to interpret the sociopolitical setting, asserting that theology must reflect on orthopraxis (right practice) and not simply orthodoxy (right doctrine). While critics charged this method of politicizing the Christian faith and advocating communism, violent revolution, and atheism, Boff and other LALT adherents responded that all theology is implicitly political and that LALT, in contrast, simply speaks of politics explicitly.

Boff gained notoriety for applying the methods of LALT not only to the social situation but also to the institution of the church. In his *Ecclesiogenesis: The Base Communities Reinvent the Church* (1977), he argued that the grassroots base ecclesial communities movement was revolutionizing the church. However, in *Church, Charism, and Power: Liberation Theology and the Institutional Church* (1981), he directly critiqued the Roman Catholic Church's appropriation of political and symbolic power to control the masses, vehemently contending that this power needs to be decentralized. The Vatican responded in 1984 through the Congregation for the Doctrine of the Faith, led by Cardinal Joseph Ratzinger (later Pope Benedict XVI), by silencing Boff for ten months. Boff submitted, but when he was threatened with silencing again in 1992, he refused to abide and reluctantly left the priesthood. Undaunted, he continued to write and further developed arguments he had begun supporting feminism and the ordination of women in *The Maternal Face of God: The Feminine and Its Religious Expressions* (1979). He also discussed the application of LALT to ecological issues in *Ecology and Liberation* (1993) and *Cry of the Earth, Cry of the Poor* (1995).

Boff has taught at numerous universities in Brazil, been a visiting professor at Lisbon, Basel, Salamanca, Heidelberg, and Harvard universities, and served as an editor of numerous journals. He is currently professor emeritus of ethics, philosophy of religion, and ecology at the State University of Rio de Janeiro.

See also *Latin American Political Thought; Liberation Theology; Religion and Politics.*

. . . . RYAN R. GLADWIN

BIBLIOGRAPHY
Boff, Leonardo. *Jesus Christ Liberator: A Critical Christology for Our Time,* translated by Patrick Hughes. Maryknoll, N.Y.: Orbis, 1978.
———. *Church, Charism, and Power: Liberation Theology and the Institutional Church,* translated by John W. Diercksmeier. New York: Crossroad, 1985.
———. *Ecclesiogenesis: The Base Communities Reinvent the Church.* Maryknoll, N.Y.: Orbis, 1986.
———. *The Maternal Face of God: The Feminine and Its Religious Expressions,* translated by Robert R. Barr and John W. Diercksmeier. San Francisco: Harper and Row, 1987.
———. *Ecology and Liberation: A New Paradigm,* translated by John Cumming. Maryknoll, N.Y.: Orbis, 1995.
———. *Cry of the Earth, Cry of the Poor. Vol. 1 Ecology and Justice,* translated by Phillip Berryman. Maryknoll, N.Y.: Orbis, 1997.
Boff, Leonardo, and Clodovis Boff. *Salvation and Liberation,* translated by Robert R. Barr. Maryknoll, N.Y.: Orbis, 1984.
Cox, Harvey. *The Silencing of Leonardo Boff: The Vatican and the Future of World Christianity.* Oak Park, Ill.: Meyer-Stone, 1988.
Gutiérrez, Gustavo. *A Theology of Liberation: History, Politics, and Salvation,* translated by Caridad Inda and John Eagleson. Maryknoll, N.Y.: Orbis, 1973.

Bolshevism

Bolshevism refers to a movement for Marxist socialist revolution spearheaded by the Bolshevik Party in Russia. Its founder was Vladimir Lenin, and as a consequence, Bolshevism is often viewed as synonymous with *Leninism.* Leninism, however, has more of a theoretical component than Bolshevism and aspires to be a more complete political ideology.

Bolshevism was born at the Second Congress of the Russian Social Democratic Labor Party (RSDLP) in 1903. Lenin advocated a more active and committed party membership of professional revolutionaries, which stood in contrast to the trade union–based membership of other social democratic parties at that time. He forced a split in the party, and, after political maneuvering that assured his faction the majority of the seats in the RSDLP's leading bodies, he named his group the Bolsheviks (from the Russian word *bol'shinstvo,* meaning majority). They were opposed by the Mensheviks (from the Russian word *men'shinstvo,* meaning minority) led by, among others, Julius Martov and Grigorii Plekhanov. However, it was not until the Seventh Congress of the RSDLP in 1917 that the term *Bolshevik* officially appeared in the party title. In 1918 the party was renamed the Russian Communist Party (Bolsheviks) and in 1925, under the Soviet Union, became the All-Union Communist Party (Bolsheviks). The term *Bolshevik* officially disappeared in 1952, when the party name was changed to the Communist Party of the Soviet Union.

The basis of the Bolshevik position was a strategy that emphasized the role of a "vanguard party" of professional revolutionaries who were committed to a Marxist socialist revolution. Those who were inactive or not wholly committed to the movement were excluded from membership. The party committed itself to raising class consciousness among the working class and rejected the view that the Russian workers needed to cooperate with the middle class to bring political change to Russia. It professed to be a party of a "new type," based on democratic centralism. This means that members participate in the formation of policy and election of leaders, but after a policy has been decided, all party members are commanded to carry it out loyally. In power, the Bolsheviks aspired to create a "dictatorship of the proletariat," in which the party would rule in the name of the working class and ferret out class enemies.

With the victory of the Bolshevik Party in the Russian Revolution of November 1917 and formation in Moscow of the Communist International in 1921, Bolshevism became the model for other communist parties. Later under Joseph Stalin, it was associated with his policies of rapid industrialization, collectivization of agriculture, socialism in one country, and complete subordination of all other social groups to the interests of the party. Over time, Bolshevism became associated with the Soviet form of communism in which the state did not wither away, as Karl Marx predicted, but instead played a leading role in modernizing the economy and a repressive function in ensuring control over political and social life.

Many Marxist thinkers have been critical of Bolshevism. The Mensheviks argued for more evolutionary movement to communism and thought the Bolshevik idea of bringing developed socialism to agrarian Russia premature in Marxist terms and politically infeasible. Rosa Luxemburg opposed in principle the idea of a centralized party organization that would impede the independent activity of the working class. Leon Trotsky and, later, the Trotskyites of the Fourth International viewed Bolshevism as appropriated by Stalin and turned, into a degenerate form of communism. They argued for greater participation of the membership, more control over the leadership of the party, and more emphasis on the global scope for revolutionary action. While one could maintain that Bolshevism should not be equated with "true communism" as envisaged by Marx, the fact is that only parties based on Bolshevik principles of organization have managed to seize power.

See also *Communism; Democratic Centralism; Leninism; Marxism.*

. . . . PAUL JAMES KUBICEK

BIBLIOGRAPHY

Besancon, Alain. *The Intellectual Origins of Leninism,* translated by Sarah Matthews. Oxford, U.K.: Blackwell, 1981.

Dan, Fedor. *The Origins of Bolshevism.* New York: Harper and Row, 1964.

Kolakowski, Leszek. *Main Currents of Marxism,* 3 vols, translated by Paul S. Falla. Oxford, U.K.: Clarendon, 1978.

Tucker, Robert. *The Lenin Anthology.* New York: Norton, 1973.

Ulam, Adam. *The Bolsheviks: The Intellectual and Political History of the Triumph of Communism in Russia.* New York: Macmillan, 1965.

Bonald, Louis-Gabriel-Ambroise, vicomte de

Louis-Gabriel-Ambroise, vicomte de Bonald (1754–1840) was a French counterrevolutionary writer, conservative polemicist, and statesman. He lived a quiet life in provincial obscurity until the French Revolution (1789–1799), when he fled into exile to join the Army of the Condé to fight against the armies of revolutionary France. During these years, Bonald lived in Heidelberg, Germany, where he wrote his first major theoretical work, *Théorie du pouvoir politique et religieux* (1796).

Following the Restoration of the monarchy in France with the defeat of emperor Napoleon Bonaparte, Bonald sat as a deputy for the Aveyron department in the French National Assembly, supporting the Ultra-Royalist faction (the Ultras). This was the majority faction in the assembly during the reign of the moderate, constitutional monarchy of Louis XVIII, who considered the Ultras more royalist than he. Louis was succeeded as king in 1824 by his reactionary brother Charles X, who was himself an Ultra. Charles supported the enactment of many conservative laws during his reign, including the Anti-Sacrilege Act (1825), which provided for capital punishment for some acts of blasphemy and sacrilege against the Catholic Church. Bonald defended this law in the National Assembly, where he also defended laws restricting freedom of the press. He argued for the repeal of the French Revolutionary law that legalized divorce, a stance he defended in his essay *On Divorce* (*Du divorce,* 1801). Bonald was a supporter of capital punishment and was fiercely hostile to democracy, liberalism, and industrialization, against which he campaigned tirelessly as both a lawmaker and a writer. He was eventually appointed a minister of state and made a peer before retiring from politics in 1830 with the abdication of Charles X. He died a decade later.

As a writer, Bonald sought to explain and justify philosophically what he campaigned for politically as a member of the assembly. Conceptually, he started from a complete rejection of methodological individualism—the idea that fully-formed humans with reason and identity and agency pre-exist society, which has been created by humans to further their interests. Bonald believed that it was not individuals who constitute society, but society that constitutes individuals. Because the modern age has put the individual before society, it has instituted a form of life fundamentally and dangerously incompatible with society, as the events of the 1790s so graphically demonstrated. Unless the individual is wholly subordinated to and subsumed within society, social disintegration and political anarchy will be ever-present dangers.

Bonald also believed that just as men do not create societies, so they do not invent languages. This is because the creation of a language presupposes the existence of a language. From this Bonald drew the conclusion that only God could create language, and he implanted it humans. Given these views, it is not surprising how much Bonald's ideas were admired by French philosopher Auguste Comte, the so-called father of sociology, whose own "science of society" started from the same assumption of methodological holism.

See also *Comte, Auguste; French Political Thought.*

. . . . GRAEME GARRARD

BIBLIOGRAPHY

Bonald, Louis-Gabriel-Ambroise, vicomte de. *Oeuvres complètes,* 3 vols, edited by Abbé Migne. Paris: Migne, 1859–1864.

———. *Théorie du pouvoir politique et religieux,* edited by Colette Capitan. 1796. Reprint, Paris: Union générale d'éditions, 1965.

———. *Démonstration philosophique du principe constitutif de la société: Méditations politiques tirées de l'Evangile.* Paris: Librairie philosophique J.Vrin, 1985.

———. *On Divorce,* translated and edited by Nicholas Davidson, foreword by Robert Nisbet. New Brunswick, N.J.: Transaction, 1992.

Klinck, David. *The French Counterrevolutionary Theorist, Louis de Bonald (1754–1840).* New York: Peter Lang, 1996.

Reedy, W. Jay. "The Traditionalist Critique of Individualism in Post-revolutionary France: The Case of Louis de Bonald." *History of Political Thought* 16, no. 1 (1995): 49–75.

Toda, Michel. *Louis de Bonald: Théoricien de la Contre-Révolution.* Clovis, France: Étampes, 1997.

Bookchin, Murray

Murray Bookchin (1921–2006) was perhaps the most significant and widely read English-language anarchist thinker of the post–World War II era. His work also made significant contributions to political thought in relation to a range of issues aside from anarchism, including radical ecology, the history of the 1936 Spanish Revolution, neo-Marxism, and urban studies. His writings influenced a variety of political movements and tendencies, including the New Left movement of the 1960s and 1970s, environmentalism, and municipalism.

Bookchin's most significant political contributions centered on his theoretical integration of ecological concerns with anarchist philosophy. He argued that environmental destruction was an outcome of authoritarian social relations and class hierarchies within capitalist societies that allowed for the massive exploitation of common resources to serve the ends of privately controlled profit. Ending ecological damage could not occur through statist reforms that left structures of exploitation intact, but required a fundamental rearrangement of social life along antiauthoritarian lines. Bookchin signaled this concern in his groundbreaking work *Our Synthetic Environment* (1952), which was largely overlooked because of its radical conclusions.

Bookchin's anarchist approach to radical ecology is termed *social ecology* and still provides an influential perspective within environmentalist circles. As a social ecologist, Bookchin argues that radical activism, to be dark green, must be informed most decisively by the moral considerations surrounding each manifestation of struggle. He argues that the capitalist mode of production and hierarchically rationalized workplaces have only negative consequences for workers as a class and for the environment. Bookchin's critique further engages a direct confrontation with productivist visions of ecological or socialist struggles that, still captivated by illusions of progress, accept industrialism and capitalist technique while rejecting the capitalist uses to which they are applied. The ecological conclusion reached by Bookchin is revealed in the assertion that the sources of conflicting interests in society must be confronted and overcome in a revolutionary manner. This means that the earth can no longer be owned and must become a shared commons. These statements represent crucial aspects of radical alliances between ecological and labor movements beyond a limited "jobs versus environment" construction. Bookchin offers social ecology as an alternative to notions of deep ecology that argued that humans as a species should be held accountable for ecological destruction. Deep ecologists seek a mystical transformation of individual consciousness in which people, without regard to social context, status, or opportunity, are called to abandon industrial civilization. Such an approach was anathema to Bookchin because it overlooked the structures of inequality within class societies, holding poor people as accountable for ecological damage as corporate executives and elites who consumed vastly greater resources.

During the 1990s, Bookchin became increasingly critical of anarchist movements. His book *Social Anarchism or Lifestyle Anarchism* (1996), which criticized anarchists for confining their activities to subcultural or countercultural enclaves, shocked anarchist communities of North America, becoming one of the most controversial books in a long line of controversial literature. For Bookchin, contemporary anarchists have forsaken the revolutionary tradition of anarchism, preferring to become, in his view, just another bohemian subculture with no interest in confronting the powers of state and capital. He suggested that contemporary anarchism represents a fatal retreat from the social concerns (and communal politics) of classical anarchism into episodic adventurism (confrontation with authorities) and a decadent egoism. This unfortunate transformation threatens to make anarchism irrelevant at precisely the moment when it is most needed as a counterforce to globalization and the social dislocations engendered by neoliberal policies.

Bookchin's distancing from anarchism grew over the last years of his life as he increasingly turned to his new theoretical innovation *libertarian municipalism.* Libertarian municipalism argued for a strategic shift in community organizing toward involvement in municipal politics as the most immediate and local venue for formal political engagement. Many anarchists viewed this as a retreat into reformism and came to disregard Bookchin as an anarchist.

See also *Anarchism; Anarchy; Environmental Political Theory.*

. . . . JEFFREY SHANTZ

BIBLIOGRAPHY

Biehl, Janet. *The Murray Bookchin Reader.* London: Cassell, 1997.

Bookchin, Murray. *Post-scarcity Anarchism.* New York: Ramparts, 1971.

———. *The Ecology of Freedom: The Emergence and Dissolution of Hierarchy.* Montreal: Black Rose, 1982.

———. *The Philosophy of Social Ecology: Essays on Dialectical Naturalism.* Montreal: Black Rose, 1996.

———. *Social Anarchism or Lifestyle Anarchism: An Unbridgeable Chasm.* San Francisco: AK Press, 1996.

Shantz, Jeff. "Radical Ecology and Class Struggle: A Re-consideration." *Critical Sociology* 30, no. 3 (2004): 691–710.

———. *Radical Ecology and Social Myth: The Difficult Constitution of Counterhegemonic Politics.* Saarbrucken, Germany: VDM Verlag, 2008.

Boundary Making and Boundary Disputes

Although marking and disputing territory date back to premodern tribes, the formal study of boundary making and boundary disputes came of age in the nineteenth and twentieth centuries as the number of sovereign states and colonial territorial possessions multiplied. With them came thousands of miles of new borders that had to be sorted out, affixed, defended, and policed. Lord Curzon—former viceroy of British colonial India, foreign minister, geographer, and explorer—reflected this urgency in a 1907 lecture in Oxford (later published as *Frontiers,* 1908) as he described the difficulties of affixing and policing the borders of Britain's colonial possessions against bandits, warlords, and rival empires. He lamented that substantive understanding of how to create stable, safe borders was in short supply. More than one hundred years later, geographers, historians, and political scientists are still attempting to make sense of the dynamics of interstate boundaries.

LOCATING A BOUNDARY

In its most technical form, boundary making consists of the delimitation and demarcation of a boundary. *Delimitation* refers to the definition of a boundary in a treaty, map, or other formal document. Improvements in survey techniques, printing, and longitude measurement in eighteenth-century Europe generated more detailed maps that proved essential for state makers wishing to craft precise boundaries between sovereign territories.

Demarcation refers to the physical marking of the boundary on the ground with signs, pyramids, posts, or fences. Engineers, diplomatic representatives, and local residents descend on the border with maps and survey tools in hand after delimitation is completed to physically mark where one state's sovereignty ends and another's begins. While good survey teams are essential to a proper demarcation, so too are knowledgeable locals familiar with topography and toponymy (place names). However, local populations aren't always happy to have a new border in their vicinity and may resist state makers' attempts to partition territory and restrict access to it. In the nineteenth century, locals along the newly delimited border between Greece and the Ottoman Empire conspired to provide the demarcation commission with false place names, with the result that clusters of villages wound up on the wrong side of the boundary.

Some borders are delimited but never complete demarcation. Many African state borders, for example, were affixed on maps and certified in treaties but have been marked only at official crossings.

While traditional approaches to boundary making focused on geographic factors and mapping techniques, subsequent approaches in political geography and political science shifted the focus to boundary maintenance—the processes and strategies states use to regulate and restrict territorial access.

BOUNDARIES AS INSTITUTIONS

Before moving on to define boundary disputes, it is prudent to note exactly what the term *boundary* means. Boundaries—or borders—have been defined as lines of separation or legally binding divisions between modern states. Yet, boundaries are also institutions of state authority. State authorities check passports at official crossings, collect customs taxes on imported goods, police against border jumping and illegal migration,

and take measures to suppress the flow of contraband. States may administer their side of a boundary unilaterally or they may pool their resources and coordinate their activities with their neighbor's border authorities. Some states may demilitarize boundaries as military threats from neighboring states decline, while intensifying border policing against nonstate actors such as traffickers, illegal migrants, and insurgents. For example, the United States and the European Union are investing in high-technology equipment and border barriers to prevent the entry of illegal migrant workers.

Given these dynamics, border disputes have two dimensions—functional and territorial. Functional disputes arise when one state perceives that its territory and security are being adversely affected by the administration of its neighbor's boundary. For instance, if border guards on one side neglect their duties, the entire boundary zone may attract smuggling and violent activity. Even though functional boundary disputes are relatively common, most research focuses on territorial disputes.

TERRITORIAL DISPUTES

Territorial disputes are defined as overlapping territorial claims by one or more states. Ongoing boundary disputes in this category include conflicting Indo-Pakistani claims over Kashmir and Israel's occupation of the Golan Heights taken from Syria in the 1967 Six-Day War. Territorial disputes are by no means confined to large territories. Between 1895 and 1963, U.S.-Mexican relations repeatedly soured because of the Chamizal, a disputed stretch of land along the Rio Grande barely the size of a few football fields.

The study of territorial disputes has rapidly expanded in recent years, particularly in political science. While there is no consensus on what causes or intensifies territorial disputes, a number of prominent explanations include the following variables: (1) the strategic value of territory (e.g., the British-Spanish dispute over Gibraltar); (2) resources contained by the territory (e.g., the multicountry dispute over the oil-rich Spratly Islands in the Pacific); (3) long-standing historical claims (e.g., Saddam Hussein once declared Kuwait to be Iraq's long-lost thirteenth province); (4) the correspondence between borders and ethnic-group boundaries (e.g., millions of ethnic Albanians reside near, but outside Albania's boundaries); (5) a ruler's likelihood of experiencing domestic backlash for the handling of a territorial dispute (e.g., Kyrgyz government officials resolved a territorial dispute with China but subsequently faced major political opposition and protest for "giving away" national territory).

Not all territorial disputes are indivisible, and some boundary disputes get resolved. In 1982, Israel handed back the Sinai to Egypt following a United States–brokered peace treaty. In the 1990s, the International Court of Justice adjudicated a long-standing dispute over the Aouzou Strip between Chad and Libya. In the beginning of the twenty-first century, China resolved border disputes with several neighboring states in order to improve the security situation in its outlying provinces.

Although boundary making and boundary disputes have conventionally been treated as separate categories, they are both contentious processes with overlapping dynamics.

See also *Political Geography; Regional Security.*

. . . . GEORGE GAVRILIS

BIBLIOGRAPHY

Andreas, Peter. "Redrawing the Line: Borders and Security in the Twenty-first Century." *International Security* 28, no. 2 (Fall 2003): 78–111.

Black, Jeremy. *Maps and History: Constructing Images of the Past.* New Haven, Conn.: Yale University Press, 1997.

Fravel, Taylor M. "Regime Insecurity and International Cooperation: Explaining China's Compromises in Territorial Disputes." *International Security* 30, no. 2 (2005): 46–83.

Gavrilis, George. *The Dynamics of Interstate Boundaries.* New York: Cambridge University Press, 2008.

Gelb, Leslie H. "The Three State Solution." *New York Times,* November 25, 2003.

Hassner, Ron. "The Path to Intractability: Time and the Entrenchment of Territorial Disputes." *International Security* 31 (Winter 2006/07): 107–138.

Huth, Paul. *Standing Your Ground: Territorial Disputes and International Conflict.* Ann Arbor: University of Michigan Press, 1996.

Jones, Stephen B. *Boundary-making: A Handbook for Statesmen, Treaty Editors, and Boundary Commissioners.* Washington D.C.: Carnegie Endowment for International Peace, Division of International Law, 1945.

Kahler, Miles, and Barbara F. Walter, eds. *Territoriality and Conflict in an Era of Globalization.* New York: Cambridge University Press, 2006.

Lattimore, Owen. *Studies in Frontier History: Collected Papers, 1928–1958.* London: Oxford University Press, 1962.

Malmberg, Torsten. *Human Territoriality: A Survey of Behavioural Territories in Man with Preliminary Analysis and Discussion of Meaning.* New York: Mouton, 1980.

Newman, David, ed. *Boundaries, Territory, and Post-modernity.* London: Frank Cass, 1999.

Ratner, Stephen R. "Drawing a Better Line: Uti Possidetis and the Borders of New States." *American Journal of International Law* 90, no. 4 (1996): 590–624.

Sahlins, Peter. *Boundaries: The Making of France and Spain in the Pyrenees.* Berkeley: University of California Press, 1991.

Bourdieu, Pierre

Pierre Bourdieu (1930–2002) was a French sociologist who approached politics sociologically, outside of the perspective of politicians, in order to study the social conditions of its access.

Bourdieu's interest in politics and sociology began in the mid-1950s, during his military service in Algeria. During this time, he adopted a militant posture toward the necessity of Algerian independence. Neutrality was an impossible position for Bourdieu; he felt that it led to the defense and strengthening of the status quo. An example of his militant attitude is found in his book *The Weight of the World* (1993), which seeks at once to unveil the suffering of those who are excluded by society and to give them the possibility to understand and express themselves.

According to Bourdieu, sociology has its own *habitus* (set of physiological, psychological, and social habits) and

develops in relation to the position of the same individual in other fields of social life. The political field is one of many in the social world; it is shaped by political agents, individuals, and groups who can produce effects within it. These agents who claim to speak in the name of social groups share the sentiment (tied to their gender, education, and class) that they have the right and the competence to speak and be heard in political matters. This belief is central to their desire to act in the political field.

Bourdieu also found that those who lack political and post-secondary education tend to believe that they do not know enough about politics to have the right to have their voices heard and feel that they do not understand enough to make the right decisions. In this manner, social positions and ideas are reproduced by being defined, one generation after another, by a small group of individuals with the opposite belief.

Bourdieu argued that relations of antagonism and collaboration between representatives within the political field are more important in shaping their allegiances than their relations to the electorate. Politicians commonly confuse their attempts to maintain their influence and power with their attempts to act on behalf of those they can only represent by defending their own position. As a result, when members of social movements attempt to become political agents, they face the difficulty of being heard, but also often are affected by the attempt of their representatives to neutralize them because of the threat they represent to their position in the political field. Representation can then be seen as a form of usurpation of power.

Throughout the 1990s, Bourdieu attempted to give a voice to the social movements in Europe. He advocated for the creation of collectives of intellectuals, such as his own movement centered around the journal *Liber-Raisons d'agir.* His political interventions followed his suggestion that intellectuals should work together and with social movements to help them in developing a criticism of their situation, expressing their demands, giving them weapons to fight the dominant opinion (i.e., neoliberal ideology), and unveiling its contradictions and its violence. Bourdieu thus highlighted the interdependency of the freedom of intellectuals and of the freedom of all social agents.

See also *Social Movements; Social Movements, Comparative; Sociobiology and Politics.*

. . . . JÉRÔME MELANÇON

BIBLIOGRAPHY

Bourdieu, Pierre. *Language and Symbolic Power,* edited and introduced by John B. Thompson, translated by Gino Raymond and Matthew Adamson. Cambridge, Mass.: Harvard University Press, 1991.

———. *The Weight of the World: Social Suffering in Contemporary Society.* 1993. Reprint, Stanford, Calif.: Stanford University Press, 1999.

———. *Propos sur le champ politique.* Lyon, France: Presses Universitaires de Lyon, 2000.

———. *Political Interventions: Social Science and Political Action,* edited by Franck Poupeau and Thierry Discepolo, translated by Gregory Elliot. London: Verso, 2008.

Wacquant, Loïc, ed. *Pierre Bourdieu and Democratic Politics: The Mystery of Ministry.* Cambridge, U.K.: Polity Press, 2005.

Boycott

To *boycott* is to abstain from or act together in abstaining from using, buying, or dealing with as an expression of protest or disfavor or as a means of coercion. The term is derived from a campaign of ostracism on Captain Boycott, leveled by the Irish Land League in 1840. After refusing to lower tenant rents, the Irish Land League, whose mission was to ensure fair rents for all, organized all workers to cease granting services to Captain Boycott, such as selling goods in stores, delivering mail, and harvesting his land. This ultimately resulted in his isolation and forced him to leave his position in Ireland to return to England.

Boycotting continues to be seen by many as an effective strategy, and it is employed in many forms. Most forms of boycott are short term and used to rectify a single event of injustice. However, some forms of boycott are long term and are used as part of larger organizational or structural form of protest. Examples include systematic *disinvestment,* such as the international call for the withdrawal of businesses from South Africa during the Apartheid era and the call for consumers to purchase items based on fair trade.

See also *Collective Action and Mobilization; Trade Diplomacy.*

. . . . JEFFREY N. CARROLL

Brinkmanship

In international politics, *brinkmanship* refers to the calculated escalation of threats against adversaries to achieve foreign policy aims.

The term was introduced by U.S. Secretary of State John Foster Dulles, who advocated such a policy against the Soviet Union, defining it as "the ability to get to the verge [the brink] without getting into the war." It is a challenge in the form of a credible threat, whether real or perceived, designed to compel an adversary to back down or to deter it from pursuing an undesirable course of action. It also may involve a deliberately created crisis to generate political or military leverage over an opponent.

Brinkmanship is an important (if sometimes implicit) component of bargaining models of war, and has parallels to hostile bargaining models in economic theory, such as in the widely cited "ultimatum game." Soviet and U.S. nuclear policy during the early decades of the cold war, culminating in the 1962 Cuban missile crisis, displayed elements of brinkmanship. Crises that never erupt into full-scale conflicts are often cited as instances of brinkmanship, although it is often difficult to separate the influence of actor choices (e.g., deliberate threat escalation) from other factors like the relative capability of the states involved.

See also *Cold War; Diplomacy; Negotiations and Bargaining.*

. . . . VSEVOLOD GUNITSKIY

King John signs the Magna Carta in 1215. The Magna Carta set a precedent for limited government and established the traditional rights of English subjects.

SOURCE: The Granger Collection

British Political Thought

The British tradition of political thought represents a complex puzzle of intellectual history. Admirers like the French political commentator Baron de Montesquieu praised the British monarchy and its system of checks and balances as the very pinnacle of freedom in his 1748 *Spirit of the Laws,* whereas less than a half-century later critics like British political writer and activist Thomas Paine and many of the American revolutionaries portrayed the British system as the abyss of tyranny. The irony, however, is that even those most vehemently critical of the British system of government have appealed to principles within the British tradition itself to justify their objections. Even so, these institutions and ideals have not been effortlessly achieved. They are the end products of centuries of struggles and settlements—religious and secular—that have shaped the contours of present-day Britain and left an indelible imprint on modern concepts of liberty, constitutionalism, and representative government. Both in terms of its practices as well as its principles, Britain is responsible for some of the greatest accomplishments in Western political theory.

MAGNA CARTA, CIVIL WAR, INTERREGNUM, AND RESTORATION

The notion of the traditional rights of English subjects dates at least back to Magna Carta in 1215, which secured from King John certain concessions for both the feudal barons and the people and set the precedent that the monarch's power is limited and the king himself subject to law. Although its principles were regularly violated and even forgotten altogether in the intervening centuries, Magna Carta nonetheless served as a reference point for later arguments on behalf of limited government, the rule of law, and fundamental rights retained by the people.

Magna Carta's precedent of limited government was in stark contrast to later absolutist theories like those espoused by James I (England) and VI (Scotland). His *The True Law of Free Monarchies* (1603) maintained that the powers of the monarch were unlimited because they descended from God by means of divine succession. These absolutist ideas were perpetuated by his son and successor, Charles I, and undoubtedly contributed to the latter's conflicts with Parliament and decades of religious and civil turmoil. The English Civil War (1642–1651) led to the defeat and execution of Charles I in 1651, the establishment of the Commonwealth, and, eventually, Oliver Cromwell's Protectorate (1653–1658). Although this protracted struggle between the British monarchs and Puritan-controlled parliaments was one of the bloodiest periods in English history, it was also one of the most intellectually fertile.

The defining work of this era was English political philosopher Thomas Hobbes's magisterial *Leviathan* (1651). Hobbes's pessimistic view of human nature and his suspicion of anarchy and civil war were undoubtedly colored by the experience of being driven into exile along with Charles II and many of his royalist supporters. While agnostic as to the question of who should ultimately be sovereign, *Leviathan* is the most influential statement of modern social contract theory and the natural rights thinking that shaped the British tradition for centuries to come.

According to Hobbes, sovereignty arises when individuals flee the vagaries of a state of nature and agree to alienate all of their liberties, save their right of self-preservation, to an impartial sovereign. Having authorized its power, they are bound to obey the law because the security provided by even the most tyrannical sovereign is still preferable to the state of nature's abominable "war of all against all." Hobbes begins his argument in *Leviathan* with liberal assumptions of individual natural rights but manages to turn these ideas into a defense of virtually unlimited sovereign power. For these reasons, as well as Hobbes's irreverent treatment of Christianity, *Leviathan* was condemned by both Puritan advocates of consent theory and royalist defenders of the divine right of kings.

Hobbes's writings were not the only influential political ideas during the Civil War and Interregnum. Consent theory came to the foreground in the Putney Debates (1647) between representatives of Cromwell's Army Council and more radical segments of the army influenced by the Protestant Levellers.

The Leveller's proposed constitution, an *Agreement for the People,* promised nearly universal male suffrage, reformed electoral districts, a parliament popularly elected every two years, religious freedom, and an end to debtor's prison. The majority of the regiments of the army were eventually persuaded to accept the more conservative *The Heads of the Proposals,* submitted by Henry Ireton for the Army Council, which secured property rights against redistribution and upheld traditional privileges.

JOHN LOCKE AND THE GLORIOUS REVOLUTION

The Restoration of Charles II in 1660 brought an end to decades of civil war. Although Charles II continued his father's heavy-handed rule, as evidenced by the Clarendon Codes enforcing religious conformity and his dissolution of several parliaments that sought to pass Exclusion Acts forbidding a Catholic successor, his unpopularity never reached the level that had led to his father's execution. His brother James II, who succeeded him on the throne in 1685, was not so fortunate, however, and was dethroned in 1688 and replaced by the Protestant Mary II and William III in 1689. This Glorious Revolution and the settlement that produced it were milestones in the development of English liberty. William and Mary's assent to the principles of the 1689 Bill of Rights established Britain as a constitutional monarchy and formalized many of the personal liberties enshrined a century later in the American Bill of Rights.

English philosopher John Locke's (1632–1704) political writings were deeply intertwined with these events. Published in 1689, Locke's *First Treatise of Government* was nominally a refutation of Sir Robert Filmer's *Patriarcha* (1680), disposing once and for all of the patriarchal idea that political authority derives from the right of dominion originally given to Adam by God. After dismissing the historical absurdity that latter-day monarchs hold their title from an unbroken line of succession, Locke more affirmatively stipulates in the *Second Treatise of Government* that government originates when individuals in the state of nature agree to surrender some of their rights to better secure their life, liberty, and property. Whenever governments become tyrannical—ruling in their own interest, rather than the public interest—individuals have a right of revolution to alter or abolish them. Contrary to Hobbes, Locke insists that allowing individuals this appeal to heaven does not lead to perpetual civil war because individuals are inclined to put up with many petty abuses before making a revolution, and that far from devolving back into a Hobbesian state of nature pitting individual against individual, the right of revolution merely restores sovereignty to the community as a whole, who might then form a new government more to their liking. In addition to Locke's liberal emphasis on the political value of individual consent, the *Second Treatise* also posits that our right to property is natural and inviolable because we have mixed our labor with the natural commons.

Although there remains some controversy about the actual date of composition of Locke's *Second Treatise,* the discovery that it was in all likelihood written before the Glorious Revolution of 1688—rather than afterward as had always been assumed—gave credence to Locke's reputation as the apostle of revolutionary politics. While few of Locke's ideas were wholly original, his writings crystallized the theory of a social contract between sovereign and subjects from which the latter might extricate themselves based on the performance of the former, as well as the notion that individuals cannot be obligated without their consent. Locke's writings have become a bulwark of limited government premised on individual rights to life, liberty, and property, and they did much to influence the American Revolution (1776–1783), the Declaration of Independence, and the liberal tradition in America.

CLASSICAL REPUBLICANISM AND "COUNTRY" VERSUS "COURT"

With its doctrine of natural rights, a social contract, religious toleration, and the sanctity of private property, Lockean liberalism has been one of the most important strands of Anglo-American political thought. However, only belatedly have revisionist scholars come to appreciate that an older ideology of classical republicanism also may have shaped opposition to the arbitrary power of kings and courts. The republican James Harrington in the seventeenth century and neo-Harringtonian "Country" thinkers like Algernon Sidney, John Trenchard and Thomas Gordon in *Cato's Letters,* and Bolingbroke in the eighteenth century were all captivated by classical, Roman, and Florentine republican authors. According to this classical republican ideology, liberty is threatened by the corruption bred in the luxury of courts and by monarchs who rule through patronage, partisanship, standing armies, faction, and the promotion of moneyed interests. By way of contrast, liberty is maintained only by cultivating austere republican and participatory virtues that are easily corrupted by proximity to absolute power. Intellectual historians and political theorists continue to debate the relative influence in the Anglo-American tradition of "classical republican" or "civic humanist" political thinking vis-à-vis more familiar Lockean or Enlightenment notions of individuals endowed with natural rights.

THE SCOTTISH ENLIGHTENMENT

The second half of the eighteenth century brought a flowering of commercial prosperity and intellectual life in the major urban centers of Scotland. The most influential thinker associated with this Scottish Enlightenment was David Hume, who challenged many of the basic assumptions of social contract thinking and the idea that governments could have arisen purely from the consent of subjects. For Hume, moral traditions, laws, and justice developed over time in response to particular circumstances and the overall utility of society. Private property, justice, and the rule of law arose because they maximized predictability and minimized uncertainty. Hume's *Enquiries Concerning Human Understanding* (1748) and *Concerning the Principles of Morals* (1751), his *Essays Moral and Political* (1741–1742), as well as his multivolume *History of England* (1754–1762) were defining works of eighteenth-century philosophy.

Hume's protégé, Adam Smith, expanded on the idea of a moral sense that was implicit in Hume's writings. Smith's two great works of moral philosophy, *A Theory of Moral Sentiments* (1759) and *An Inquiry into the Nature and Causes of the Wealth of Nations* (1776) describe the extended order of a market society that was the product of individual activity but not of deliberate design. The latter work in particular has had a tremendous influence on the social sciences, particularly among economists. Smith was a trenchant critic of mercantilism, protectionism, and monopoly. Smith's fundamental insight was that nations' wealth was created by free trade and the division of labor, rather than by their hoarding of bullion or specie. He contended that government should limit itself to the role of impartial arbiter between the various interests of society. Smith was an early defender of the policy of laissez-faire economics and the miracles of coordination accomplished by the "invisible hand" of the marketplace. Unlike many of his libertarian appropriators, however, Smith acknowledged that a market society was vulnerable to moral and intellectual deterioration among its citizenry and that governments might legitimately take steps to prevent this.

Hume, Smith, and later thinkers of the Scottish Enlightenment held, first, that manners and institutions are best understood in terms of historical progress and, second, that commerce is the single most important driving force behind historical development. These ideas influenced Karl Marx's historical materialism. In addition, the Scottish *stadial* view of history gave way to the distinction between "civilized" commercial societies and "barbarous" premodern nations. While Hume and Smith saw development mainly in liberal, progressive terms, Scottish philosopher and historian Adam Ferguson was an outlier in voicing classical republican misgivings about the tendency of modern commercial societies to succumb to individualism, apathy, and self-interest. In *An Essay on the History of Civil Society* (1767), Ferguson complains that commerce saps the martial spirit by which liberty is maintained and that commercial societies incline toward luxury, civic malaise, and decline.

THE FRENCH REVOLUTION AND THE RIGHTS OF MAN

The French Revolution of 1789 and ensuing turmoil on the continent left an imprint on the British tradition. While more radical English thinkers like Richard Price and Thomas Paine embraced the ideals of the French Revolution and argued for similar reforms to the British monarchy, the metaphysical natural rights espoused by the French revolutionaries provoked a backlash in more conservative circles. Despite his long-standing reputation as a leading figure among the Rockingham Whigs and his liberal stance on behalf of conciliation with the American colonies and the Irish and Indian questions, Edmund Burke, in his *Reflections on the Revolution in France* (1790), repudiated the French Revolution and the metaphysical doctrines of natural rights and social contractarianism upon which it rested.

Subsequent exchanges between Burke and Paine, whose *Rights of Man* (1791) was a trenchant critique of Burke's *Reflections,* get directly to the heart of one of the major tensions within the British tradition, namely, a disagreement between the more empirical, institutional, or sociological understanding of liberty represented by thinkers like David Hume and Edmund Burke and the more radical social contractarian ideas that see liberty as grounded in natural law and natural rights. Neither Hume nor Burke denied the importance of the traditional liberties of British subjects. Nonetheless, both objected to the idea that one could appeal to reason or abstract natural laws to justify those liberties. For Burke especially, such universalistic appeals to reason and natural laws were liable to undermine the particular traditions on which true liberty depended. Likewise for Hume, the idea of an original contract was a logical and historical absurdity, and the only reliable guides in politics were the experience and moral practices of common life.

Another celebrated eighteenth-century exchange between British writer and philosopher Mary Wollstonecraft and Burke captures a different dimension of this tension. Faulting Burke for his defense of tradition and opposition to the French Revolution in her *Vindication of the Rights of Men* (1790), Wollstonecraft subsequently argued in *A Vindication of the Rights of Women* (1792) that all human beings—not just men—are deserving of their God-given rights and that the vast majority of societal conventions are invoked to infantilize women, to create false and unnatural distinctions, and to prevent women from acceding to their moral duties as citizens.

UTILITARIANISM AND REFORM

Arguably the single most influential thinker in nineteenth-century England was Jeremy Bentham, whose philosophical challenge to custom and inherited institutions gave rise to the various nineteenth-century reform movements that did so much to rationalize and democratize Britain's political system. Bentham's major philosophical contribution was the doctrine of utilitarianism. According to Bentham, public policy should aim to secure the greatest good for the greatest number as determined by aggregating the utility of the various parties. Utility afforded a superior benchmark for public policy than mere custom or tradition.

Benthamic philosophical radicalism marks a departure from two key assumptions of the British tradition. First, Bentham's emphasis on legal reform challenged the conviction that Britain's inherited traditions are reliable supports for liberty. Whereas many appealed to British liberties as originating in an ancient constitution or feudal law—and jurists like Edward Coke and William Blackstone had extolled the common law's congeniality for liberty—Bentham notably demurred. The common law was an "Augean stable" of anachronisms, fictions, and absurdities that needed to be purged and reestablished on more defensible rational grounds. Bentham's second major challenge was to the idea of individual liberties as grounded in metaphysical natural rights. The notion that individuals are endowed with natural rights by virtue of their common humanity was "nonsense upon stilts." To the contrary, as Hume, Burke, and other more empirically minded thinkers in the British tradition had argued earlier, liberties arise only from concrete political arrangements.

Both of these assumptions about liberty are shared by Bentham's most formidable nineteenth-century legatee, John Stuart Mill. Like Bentham, Mill tried to elucidate principles of representative government, law, opinion, and political economy on rationally defensible grounds. And again following Bentham, the ultimate appeal on these issues for Mill was utility, albeit in the somewhat broader sense of humankind's permanent interests as a group of progressive beings. As Mill argues in *On Liberty* (1859), although the state has a right to regulate activities that inflict concrete harms on others, it has no business interfering in matters such as speech, expression, opinion, or other actions that pertain only to individuals themselves. Liberty of thought and opinion is most conducive to the spontaneity and individuality that pull the human race forward.

The irony is that despite his theoretical and political efforts on behalf of democratizing reforms, Mill's arguments are in important respects anti-democratic. Indeed his thought is illustrative of the fundamental tension between liberty and democracy in nineteenth-century social and political thought. Inspired by the writings of the French social theorist Alexis de Tocqueville, whose *Democracy in America* Mill widely championed upon its publication in 1835, Mill feared the vapid conformity and collective mediocrity that arises in a democratic age. The greatest threat to liberty was no longer the overbearing influence of democratic majorities but the sociological dynamics of "tyrannical public opinion." Even if democratic individuals enjoy legal freedoms of speech or expression, they are still subject to the powerful coercion of society itself. Thus for Mill, true or effective freedom requires more than just the absence of legal coercion. While negative liberty is a necessary condition for cultivation, progress, and development, it is not a sufficient condition, and for this Mill looks to a stimulating diversity of social conditions. Mill's concept of liberty marks a decisive advance beyond Hobbesian or classical liberal definitions of freedom as nothing more or less than the absence of restraint.

Nineteenth- and twentieth-century liberalism by and large followed in the footsteps of Mill and other theorists of positive liberty, who believed that the state had an active and affirmative role in cultivating the freedom, autonomy, and development of modern citizens. The new liberalism of Thomas Hill Green and Leonard Trelawny Hobhouse, as well as various strands of Fabian socialism, are premised on similar assumptions that true freedom requires underlying power or capabilities in order to make good use of formal liberties.

CONCLUSION

While ideas of liberty and popular government are recurrent themes in the British tradition, there is enormous variation even within that tradition itself. Liberty is variously conceived as negative and positive, empirical and metaphysical, and as originating from sources as diverse as historical traditions and institutions, the common law, abstract natural laws and natural rights, and the participatory republican traditions of antiquity. Despite the social conflicts that gave birth to these ideals and practices, what can hardly be disputed is the profound influence that the British tradition as a whole has had on the development of liberty, constitutionalism, participatory government, and human rights in the modern world.

See also *Bentham, Jeremy; Burke, Edmund; Constitutions and Constitutionalism; Divine Right of Kings; Enlightenment Political Thought; Hobbes, Thomas; Hume, David; Locke, John; Magna Carta; Mill, John Stuart; Natural Rights; Paine, Thomas; Republicanism, Classical; Scottish Enlightenment; Smith, Adam; Utilitarianism.*

. . . . RICHARD BOYD

BIBLIOGRAPHY

Armitage, David, ed. *British Political Thought in History, Literature, and Theory, 1500–1800.* Cambridge: Cambridge University Press, 2006.

Ashcraft, Richard. *Revolutionary Politics and Locke's "Two Treatises of Government."* Princeton, N.J.: Princeton University Press, 1986.

Bentham, Jeremy. *Principles of Morals and Legislation.* Buffalo, N.Y.: Prometheus, 1988.

Burke, Edmund. *Reflections on the Revolution in France,* edited by J. G. A. Pocock. Indianapolis: Hackett, 1987.

Halevy, Elie. *The Growth of Philosophic Radicalism.* London: Faber, 1928.

Hobbes, Thomas. *Leviathan,* edited by Richard Tuck. Cambridge: Cambridge University Press, 1996.

Hume, David. *Essays: Moral, Political and Literary.* Indianapolis: Liberty Press, 1985.

Locke, John. *Two Treatises of Government,* edited by Peter Laslett. Cambridge: Cambridge University Press, 1988.

Macpherson, Crawford B. *Political Theory of Possessive Individualism: Hobbes to Locke.* Oxford, U.K.: Clarendon, 1962.

Mill, John Stuart. *On Liberty and Other Essays,* edited by John Gray. New York: Oxford World Classics, 1991.

Pocock, J. G. A. *The Ancient Constitution and the Feudal Law.* Cambridge: Cambridge University Press, 1957.

Pocock, J. G. A., Gordon Schochet, and Lois Schwoerer, eds. *The Varieties of British Political Thought, 1500–1800.* Cambridge: Cambridge University Press, 1996.

Walzer, Michael. *The Revolution of the Saints.* Cambridge: Harvard University Press, 1965.

Bryce, James

The career of British statesman and historian James Bryce (1832–1922) covered the reign of Queen Victoria, the American Civil War (1861–1865) and its aftermath, and extended until after the end of World War I (1914–1918). Bryce was born in Belfast, Northern Ireland; raised in Scotland; and educated at Glasgow, Heidelberg, and Oxford universities. His activities spanned the worlds of scholarship, politics, and diplomacy. He was a practicing lawyer, a professor of law at Oxford, a liberal member of the House of Commons (1880–1907), a member of the House of Lords as Viscount Bryce, and from 1907 to 1913 the British ambassador to the United States. In an era when travel was slow and imposed many obstacles, Bryce observed life and politics firsthand in many countries throughout the world and published articles and books about his travels.

Bryce's two-volume *The American Commonwealth* (1888) was a pioneering study for its time of the institutions of American politics, drawing on his travels there from the presidency of Ulysses S. Grant onward, as well as on written sources. Like French political thinker Alexis de Tocqueville, Bryce was attracted to study America because it was the leading example of democracy. As Bryce wryly noted, any European who wished to recommend or disparage democracy could point to the United States because it offered plenty of facts to warrant either praise or blame. Bryce's approach emphasized describing American politics without explicitly theorizing, as Tocqueville had done. Bryce was sympathetic but often critical, likening American political parties to two bottles with identical labels and both empty. He also wrote a chapter about why highly qualified men were never elected to the presidency.

Bryce believed that the best way to gain knowledge of political behavior was to become directly involved in politics and study one's colleagues. That knowledge could be amplified by studying history and institutions and using comparison to identify similarities and differences in political institutions and practices. These principles were applied in his last book, the two-volume *Modern Democracies* (1921). The geographical scope was limited to Australia, Canada, France, New Zealand, Switzerland, and the United States, countries of which he had firsthand knowledge. Democracy was defined as a system in which the majority of qualified citizens ruled. In keeping with the thought of the time, Bryce did not regard restrictions of the voting franchise on the grounds of race or gender as a disqualification from calling a government democratic.

Bryce held government office from 1885 to 1906 under three different prime ministers. He also prepared reports for the British government on subjects as diverse as secondary education, World War I atrocities, and principles for founding a League of Nations. He also served on the International Court at the Hague. His term as ambassador to the United States overlapped with the presidencies of Theodore Roosevelt, William Howard Taft, and Woodrow Wilson. Bryce was also a president of the British Academy and a member of the Alpine Club.

See also *Democracy; Democratic Theory; Tocqueville, Alexis de.*

. . . . RICHARD ROSE

BIBLIOGRAPHY

Bryce, James. *The American Commonwealth,* 2 vols. London: Macmillan, 1888.

———. *Modern Democracies,* 2 vols. London: Macmillan, 1921.

Fisher, H. A. L. *James Bryce,* 2 vols. London: Macmillan, 1927.

Ions, Edmund S. *James Bryce and American Democracy, 1870–1922.* London: Macmillan, 1968.

Buddhist Political Thought

As the world's third largest religion (with an estimated 400 million adherents), Buddhism is an important political force from Sri Lanka through Southeast Asia to Taiwan and Japan. Theological differences, however, make Buddhist political thought quite different from that of either Christianity or Islam. Those religions demand that believers bring the material world into line with a supernatural truth, producing calls for a government to tailor its policies by divine commandments, for example, to ban birth control or regulate marriage. Buddhism argues that actions flow organically from a state of being. Proper behavior is the result of being in harmony with the universe, not from consciously following a written code of laws.

THE CHARACTER OF THE RULER

Applied to the political realm, this belief suggests that the important questions are ones about the state of government, not about policy choice. If society is properly governed, then the government's policies will, by definition, be proper. To assess the state of government, Buddhist political thought focuses on two things: the character of the ruler and the relationship between the ruler and the *Sangha* (the community of monks).

The first of these must be seen in the context of Buddhism's long association with kingly rulers. While Guatama started the faith by rejecting his princely inheritance, the subsequent reign of King Ashoka (274–236 BCE) laid the foundations for Buddhist governance. Scriptures remember him for the way he ended his wars of conquest after converting to Buddhism and the respect he is said to have shown for his subjects. As the faith spread across Asia, other regions absorbed this model of society ruled by a devout and compassionate king as ideal.

In theory, this makes Buddhist political thought sympathetic to arguments for social justice and nonviolence, but in practice, Buddhist teachings are used to support a variety of contingent preferences. For example, scholars have struggled for decades to identify a coherent political agenda behind the Japanese political party *Komeito*, which was founded as an explicitly Buddhist party and advertises itself as promulgating a "middle way" in politics. Even the basic insistence on respecting all life is subject to change, as in the violent rhetoric of contemporary Sri Lankan Buddhism or the way Japanese Buddhist sects of the 1920s justified their country's militarism. Some Buddhist sects explicitly avoid any hint of politics, like the Compassionate Relief Society, one of Taiwan's most visible Buddhist sects. In other words, knowing an individual is Buddhist does not help us predict what policy preferences that person will carry into a voting booth.

THE *SANGHA* AND BUDDHIST NATIONALISM

Most Buddhist sects do not share the current Sri Lankan willingness to accept violence, but feelings of nationalism are widespread among Buddhists across Asia. This comes from the second component of Buddhist political thought, its call for a close relationship between ruler and the *Sangha*. After converting, King Ashoka patronized Buddhist temples extensively, paying for their establishment throughout his territory. In return, the monks he supported glorified his rule to the peasants in their communities. Not only did this meet the needs of both king and *Sangha*, it also resonates with Buddhist cosmology. A belief in karma and rebirth implies a society in which lay people improve their karma by supporting monks; the *Sangha*, in turn, guide the people by their progress toward enlightenment. In this schema, the king's responsibility is to ensure that both sides fulfill their roles: By collecting taxes and supporting religious institutions, he helps peasants do their duty, by keeping order in the *Sangha,* he prevents the disunity that robs the people of guidance.

Following this model, Buddhist organizations and the state evolved in symbiosis throughout Asia; the *Sangha* legitimized the state in prayer and sermon in return for support and protection from political rulers. Rulers co-opted Buddhist organizations with a mix of coercion and rewards, razing recalcitrant temples and subsidizing cooperative ones, offering them authority over the lay population and over rival monks. This bargain served both parties: The monks enjoyed financial support from the government and protection against the rise of competing temples, and their sermons legitimized rulers' places at the top of social hierarchies.

This integration of Buddhist thinkers into the state also roots their politics to a sense of place, strengthening its nationalist flavor. Monks in as diverse contexts as Nichiren in thirteenth-century Japan and Soma in the twentieth-century Sri Lanka have made parallel arguments that their nation is a chosen vehicle for embodying the "true" Buddhist path. Doing so, they argue, will cure the nation of its existing weaknesses and fend off foreign dangers.

This close relationship between Buddhists and the state is still true in the modern world. During the period of authoritarian rule in Taiwan, for example, the Nationalist Party co-opted Buddhist political activity by forcing temples to operate in the context of a state-created umbrella organization. When the government was considering the end of martial law (and incidentally allowing religious freedom), the official Buddhist association weighed in *against* the idea. The unsuccessful protest against state repression by Burmese monks, compared to the strength of Catholic liberation movements in Poland and Latin America or Islamic opposition to secular rule in the Middle East, is another example of how Buddhist political thought lacks external truths from which to sustain criticism of the state. Similarly, Buddhism remains a powerful force for government legitimization in Thailand and Cambodia. In short, while predicting individual policy preferences among Buddhists, it is possible to predict a willingness to support their rulers.

CONCLUSION

Buddhist political thought, however, has struggled with the emergence of democracy. Its conservative beliefs in hierarchy and support for the state offer little guidance to voters comparing the policy agendas of competing parties. In both Thailand and Sri Lanka, explicitly Buddhist political parties collapsed under a public backlash; the Japanese *Komeito* party officially disowned its religious heritage under public pressure in 1970. Strains of *engaged Buddhism,* which stress compassionate public service instead of withdrawal or obedience, are spreading across East Asia. If their growth continues, they may provide a new Buddhist perspective on politics, but that remains to be seen.

See also *Asian Political Thought; Religion and Politics.*

. . . . GEORGE EHRHARDT

BIBLIOGRAPHY

Berkwitz, Stephen. "Resisting the Global in Buddhist Nationalism: Venerable Soma's Discourse of Decline and Reform." *Journal of Asian Studies* 67 (February 2008): 73–106.

Hardacre, Helen. "State and Religion in Japan." In *Nanzan Guide to Japanese Religions,* edited by Paul Swanson and Clark Chilson, 274–288. Honolulu: University of Hawaii Press, 2006.

Jackson, Peter. *Buddhism, Legitimation, and Conflict—The Political Functions of Urban Thai Buddhism.* Singapore: Institute of Southeast Asian Studies, 1989.

Lewis, Todd. "Buddhism: The Politics of Compassionate Rule." In *God's Rule: The Politics of World Religions,* edited by Jacob Neusner, 233–256. Washington D.C.: Georgetown University Press, 2003.

Ling, Trevor. "Review Essay: Religion and Politics in South and Southeast Asia." *History of Religions* 20 (February 1981): 281–287.

Madsen, Richard. *Democracy's Dharma: Religious Renaissance and Political Development in Taiwan.* Berkeley: University of California Press, 2007.

Philpott, Daniel. "Explaining the Political Ambivalence of Religion." *American Political Science Review* 101 (August 2007): 505–526.

Reynolds, Frank. "Dhamma in Dispute: The Interactions of Religion and Law in Thailand." *Law and Society Review* 28, no. 3 (1994): 433–452.

Queen, Christopher S., and Sallie B. King, eds. *Engaged Buddhism: Buddhist Liberation Movements in Asia.* New York: State University of New York Press, 1994.

Budgeting

The term *budgeting* refers to the process of allocating financial resources to serve public purposes. A government's budget is essentially a summary statement of all planned revenues and expenditures for the coming fiscal cycle. This statement enables the bureaucracy to collect and spend money. This brief definition alludes to two fields of research on public budgeting: political science and public administration.

Political science is interested in budgeting because a budget is a fundamental output of political systems and serves as a key indicator of governments' public policy commitments. Because the process of budgeting entails taking away money from some segments of society (taxation) and giving it to others (expenditures), budgets are contentious and the result of an often hard-fought political process. Broadly speaking, political scientists contend that the outcome of the budget process is determined by the choices of political actors involved in budgeting as well as the formal and informal rules governing the decision-making process.

In political science, the substantive focus of the vast literature concentrates on three major topics: (1) the size of the budget, especially in relation to the overall size of the economy (i.e., government expenditures as percentage of gross domestic product); (2) the balance of the budget: planned revenues (mostly originating from taxation) minus expenditures; and (3) the composition of public budgets: spending across governmental functions such as defense, social security, and health care.

Similarly, the field of public administration is fascinated by budgeting because of the formidable and complex task to formulate, implement, and monitor the execution of a budget. The technical process of administering a budget entails forecasting, accounting, reporting, and auditing of revenue and expenditures streams. The organization of budgeting is characterized by tremendously diverse and specialized programs and structures, as well as high technical demands. As a consequence of an interest in the technical aspects of budgeting, public administration generally focuses on specific budgeting systems or detailed budgeting problems. Public administration lags somewhat behind political science in developing a comparative and generalized theoretical framework of budgeting.

The public administration literature on public budgeting concentrates on two major research topics: (1) policy analysis and (2) the study of institutional arrangements that provide public services. Consequently, a substantial part of this literature attempts to fuse both topics and is concerned with devising appropriate and efficient budgetary systems. In the past decades, some of the major budgetary systems can be classified under the following labels: *program-based budgeting, zero-based budgeting,* and, more recently, *performance-based budgeting,* which attempts to bring businesslike practices, such as accrual budgeting, to public management. Moreover, a vast empirical literature, mostly generated by economists, is devoted to revenue forecasting; that is, the attempt to predict future revenues by identifying the consequences of future macroeconomic developments under existing laws (taxation). Forecasting serves as a tool for medium-term and long-term planning.

Because scholarly work on budgeting in political science and public administration overlap less and less, this entry concentrates on outlining core conceptual aspects and theoretical advances on the politics of budgeting. The main focus, as in much of the classic work on budgeting, is on the politics of public spending. Studies of the politics of budgeting move beyond a simple vision of budgeting as devising a document on how to collect and spend citizens' monies and instead recognizes that budgeting is a political endeavor. Budgeting is the allocation of a scarce resource—money. This process demands trade-offs among competing policy alternatives and political interests. The outcome of these trade-offs is a manifestation of a government's policy priorities, as well as a reflection of power among individual budget actors. Money spent according to the budget holds two broad societal consequences: It allows citizens to observe whether their preferences are fulfilled (accountability), and it fuels the economy. Given these features of budgeting, political scientists are interested in the decision-making process—the rules for confrontation and compromise—and in the actors who determine budget outcomes.

TERMINOLOGY

In general, a government's commitment to spend monies is outlined regularly (often annually) in one or a series of laws. While there is some variation on the exact terminology across countries, this commitment is a government output and called *appropriations.* For the United States, researchers also refer to *budget authority*—that is the authority granted per congressional vote and presidential approval to an agent of government to spend money. Once these commitments are honored and the money is actually spent, we speak of *outlays* or *expenditures* (i.e., outcomes). In general, fiscal policy, deficits, and surpluses are captured by expenditures.

Some governments separate their current operations and capital expenditures. A core function of this division is to identify how borrowing or current account surpluses are translated into investments in capital assets, such as physical infrastructure. By doing so, governments can show that public spending moves beyond simple consumption. While advocates of *capital budgeting* claim that this process encourages long-term planning, critics argue that capital budgets misstate governments' financial positions. Many developing countries and most American states employ capital budgeting. However, in practice, there is large variation on how the capital and operating budgets are related to each other.

Three more distinctions are noteworthy. Within a budget, one can draw a distinction between *entitlements* and *discretionary spending*. Based on authorizing legislation, entitlements mandate payments, often to eligible individuals, by an agency. Thus, outlays depend on exogenous circumstances, such as economic well-being, and are independent of the amount appropriated to a program in the previous budget. For example, unemployment benefits comprise of a series of set eligibility requirements, but the economic climate and the number of people claiming benefits determine the actual withdrawal of financial resources. As a consequence for budgeting, entitlement spending needs to be forecast for the coming fiscal year by government agencies. Moreover, an effective change in entitlement spending is not pursued in the budget itself but in separate legislation modifying existing eligibility requirements. In contrast to entitlements, discretionary spending is public expenditure over which budget makers decide by reoccurring (mostly annual) appropriations.

Second, a government's budget may be delineated along organizational units, such as ministries and departments, or across programmatic functions. Budget items are grouped programmatically when they are identified by government activities in relation to a specific set of policy objectives. Proper classification can be tricky. For example, should a nursing school operated by a public hospital be classified under health or education? To overcome these problems and generate internationally comparable standards, the United Nations, in corporation with the International Monetary Fund, the Organization for Economic Cooperation and Development, and the World Bank, developed a conceptual structure, the System of National Accounts, in 1993 to provide international standards for the measurement of the market economy. Specifically for budgets, classification of the functions of government (COFOG) categorizes activities according to socioeconomic objectives, such as defense, health, and public order.

Finally, an increasing number of countries, especially developed ones, have moved from *cash-based budgeting* to *accrual accounting* since the 1990s. Under the cash basis, a transaction is recorded at the time the payment or receipt occurs. Accrual accounting, on the other hand, records a transaction when an action producing revenues or spending takes place and not when this action is paid for. In short, accrual accounting records change in ownership, while cash-based budgeting tracks exchange of monies. Clearly, for large-scale governmental infrastructure projects, the time difference between both occurrences might be large, thus making a comparison between cash and accrual-based, or even mixed budgets, challenging.

POLITICS OF BUDGETING

In his famous call for a theory on government resource allocation, V. O. Key (1940) asked why government should allocate a certain amount of money to a specific government function over all others. While the normative element of this question was initially addressed by economists based on the principles of efficiency and equity—e.g., Paul Samuelson (1954)—a seminal theoretical response by a political scientist was Aaron Wildavsky's (1964) *The Politics of the Budgetary Process.*

Wildavsky argued that budgets and the programs within it change only incrementally over time. Incrementalism holds that budget makers respond to the remarkable complexity of distributing the shares of a budget across programs by making small corrections to the status quo. Given the financial, temporal, and cognitive constraints on bureaucrats and policy makers, the budgetary decision-making process is simplified by the concepts of *base* and *fair share*. Base essentials mean that previous allocation to a program are expected to be matched in the current year. Fair share denotes the idea that new funding should be distributed roughly equally across agencies and programs. In short, the current budget is largely determined by last year's size and content.

Incrementalism conceptualizes budgeting as a negotiation process among a regular set of political actors including bureaucrats, as well as policy makers from the executive and legislative branches. While entitlements and budget rules may contribute to incremental changes in budgets, bargaining within the expectations of base and fair share among political actors is identified as the key feature for composing a new budget. Because incrementalism builds on decision-making theory, the budgeting process is perceived as open, pluralist, and conflict-free.

Incrementalism has been challenged on empirical and theoretical grounds since the mid-1970s. First, scholars charged that incrementalism is too conceptually vague and too descriptive for providing insightful theoretical contributions. Second, scholars also discovered that large differences in the magnitude of budget changes at both the programmatic and the overall budget level occur. Some budgets rise and fall dramatically. Incrementalism cannot account for the empirical reality of large-scale changes in budgets.

Among the first to theorize on the occurrence of both incremental and nonincremental change was John Padgett (1980). He argued that budget decisions are made serially. Decision makers engage in an ordered search through a limited set of alternatives. They inquire sequentially through different budget options until they can match a solution reflecting both the merits of a program and the perception of the overall fiscal climate. In aggregate, his decision-making model suggests that most programs only change marginally in any given year, but on some occasions, policy makers radically alter the size of a program.

In public policy, Bryan Jones and Frank Baumgartner (2005) contend that incrementalism is one element of a more comprehensive model of budgeting based on punctuated equilibrium theory. Their core argument is that individuals as well as organizations possess a limited capacity to process information. As a consequence, policy makers only concentrate on and prioritize a small set of budgetary issues. Budget issues that receive disproportionate attention change dramatically because policy makers are prone to under- and over-respond to changes in the exogenous environment. Those unattended budget items, however, remain largely unchanged. Overall, their model predicts that budgetary changes are characterized by periods of stability that are occasionally interrupted by large-scale shifts in resources. In short, the punctuated equilibrium model of Baumgartner and Jones combines incrementalism and dramatic changes under a unified model of budgetary choice.

This model originated from insights on the American political system. Several other studies across a variety of advanced democracies and levels of government find strong empirical evidence that budgeting at the subnational and national level is predominantly highly incremental but sometimes interrupted by very large and often consequential budgetary changes. Jones and colleagues (2009) assess the accumulated evidence across several advanced industrialized democracies and assert that the punctuated nature of budgetary changes offers a strong empirical generalization. Taken together, these empirical verifications of the punctuated equilibrium model indicate the need for theorizing on processes generating extreme change in budgeting research.

A third approach studying the politics of budgeting emerges out of comparative political economy and rational choice institutionalism during the 1990s. The main focus of this literature is on budget balance, while incrementalism and public policy theories concentrate on spending patterns. Comparative political economists aim to identify rules generating balanced budgets and conceive budgeting along two problems: *principal-agent* and *common-pool*. In both cases, the literature identifies the self-interest of policy makers as the core problem of efficient and effective budgeting.

In the principal-agent framework, citizens (principal) delegate the authority to tax and spend to politicians (agent) and, after making their spending decisions, politicians (principal) delegate the implementation to bureaucrats (agent). In both principal-agent relationships (citizen-politician and politician-bureaucrat), the literature assumes that the preferences between principal and agent do not overlap. For example, voters may prefer more education spending while politicians and bureaucrats would rather spend money on nice offices. Principal-agent problems thus may lead to inefficient budgeting and more public spending.

In the common-pool resource problem, the common resource (money) is generated by general taxation of all citizens. However, policy makers are assumed to spend this money on specific purposes without regard to the depletion of the overall budget. For example, agricultural ministers are said to obtain and distribute as many agricultural subsidies as possible without considering the overall shape of the budget. Theoretically, the common-pool framework predicts that the aggregation of all individual excessive spending decisions lead to large government budgets, deficits, and debt increases.

The political economy literature on budgeting argues that both problems—principal-agent and common-pool—can be alleviated by constructing the appropriate fiscal rules and political institutions. Jürgen Von Hagen (2006) outlines three sets of rules: legislative and constitutional constraints on budgetary aggregates, political institutions fostering accountability, and procedural rules of the budgeting process.

Legislative and constitutional constraints on budgetary aggregates entail balanced budget constraints, debt and deficit limits, as well as taxation and spending restrictions. Large variation in the specifics and enforceability of these rules prevail across countries and subnational entities. While rare at the national level, among the most prominent and widely studied restrictions are those imposed by the European Monetary Union and American states. The empirical evidence on the effectiveness of these rules, however, is weak.

A significant amount of scholarly work considers the impact of political institutions, most prominently certain electoral rules of a political system, as a key influence on budgeting. This line of inquiry suggests that political competition and accountability allow voters to resolve the principal-agent problem of budgeting. When elections are competitive and personal, voters are able easily to identify and punish politicians and political parties who diverge from citizens' preferences. There is a lively theoretical and empirical debate on other consequences of electoral rules. To a large extent, the discourse concentrates on the distinction between majoritarian and proportional electoral systems.

Procedural rules of the budget process lay out the interactions within and between the legislative and executive branches of government. Budgeting generally proceeds along a tight time schedule of formulation, enactment, execution, and assessment (the budget cycle). With some exceptions (most notably the United States), the executive branch dominates all four stages of the budget process and often manages the process within its hierarchical structures. In presidential systems, as well as multiparty collation governments, budgets also are formulated and enacted either via negotiation or by reliance on established contracts, such as coalition agreements. Overall, the process of budgeting might be fairly fragmented, specialized, and opaque to the outside observer. It is a common call in the literature, as well as among international organizations, to make the budgeting process more transparent.

Taken together, the political economy literature on budgeting proposes the following institutional solutions to the principal-agent problem: increase the accountability of the agents and increase the transparency of the budget process. Greater accountability might be achieved through electoral institutions that bring candidates closer to voters or by policy makers screening viable candidates for the top bureaucratic positions. How well these solutions works is still in debate. This is partly due to the fact that cross-national data on budget procedures and practices has been collected systematically only since the 1990s and for only a small group of countries.

Three solutions are delineated for the common-pool problem. First, a strong finance minister might be able to check excessive spending. Attributes of a strong finance minister include possessing the ability to propose a budget, being chief negotiator with individual spending ministers, and being able to unilaterally cut individual spending items. Second, a fiscal contract outlining targets might limit individual overindulgence. Third, a budget process that requires first settlement on overall spending and then considers the distribution of funds might limit government spending. While empirical evidence for advanced democracies is mixed so far, recent observations suggest that an increasing number of countries strengthened the role of the finance minister in the budget process.

DISCUSSION

It is helpful to contrast the three approaches to the study of budgeting—incrementalism, punctuated equilibrium, and political economy—in regard to their conception of actors, choice, and institutions. All three approaches ask how political actors engage with each other in various institutional settings in order to decide on a budget. Substantively, the first two approaches concentrate on appropriations, while political economy is more interested in outlays and deficits.

Theoretical approaches to budgeting based on political economy clearly name the actors in the budgeting process. Most commonly, a game theoretical model identifies an interaction between a pair of the following actors: voters, government, spending ministers, and the bureaucracy. In contrast, incrementalism and punctuated equilibrium scholarship relies on the amorphous group known as policy makers or focuses on the executive organization. The last two approaches often understand budgeting as a fairly open process with different actors providing diverse inputs at the various stages of the process. As a consequence of each approach, political economy might miss important actors in the budgeting process due to its restrictive assumptions, while the other two approaches' vagueness might hinder developing generalizable insights.

Political science's theoretical development in budgeting research is accommodated by two models of individual choice. Political economy relies on the postulates of rational choice theory and assigns preferences and expected utilities to individual budgeting actors. In contrast, incrementalism and punctuated equilibrium develop within bounded rationality and contend that, in budgeting, imperfect decision-making conditions produce imperfect solution searches and foster a reliance on temporally available heuristics. While its simplicity and the ability to generalize self-interested strategic behavior allow the political economy approach to develop a unified body of research, bounded rationality more accurately reflects on choices and actions of the actors in the budgeting process.

Finally, all three approaches also vary in their assessment of political institutions. The political economy approach attributes core causal effects to the macro-institutional setting, such as the system of government and electoral system. However, this approach is rightfully concerned with the possible endogenity of institutions: governments can choose both budgets and the fiscal rules that outline the budgeting process. Incrementalism and punctuated equilibrium theories follow detailed fiscal rules more closely and often perceive institutions as part of the organizational features of the budgeting process. In all of the research on budgeting, political scientists and public administration scholars are searching for a budget process that produces efficient allocation and fair political representation.

See also *Incrementalism; Political Economy; Punctuated Equilibrium.*

. . . . CHRISTIAN BREUNIG

BIBLIOGRAPHY

Guess, George M., and Lance T. LeLoup. *Comparative Public Budgeting: Global Perspectives on Taxing and Spending.* Albany: State University of New York Press, 2010.

Hallerberg, Mark. "Fiscal Rules and Fiscal Policy." In *Handbook of Public Administration,* edited by B. Guy Peters and Jon Pierre, 393–401. London: Sage, 2003.

Hallerberg, Mark, Rolf Strauch, and Jürgen von Hagen. *Fiscal Governance in Europe.* New York: Cambridge University Press, 2009.

Jones, Bryan D., and Frank R. Baumgartner. "A Model of Choice for Public Policy." *Journal of Public Administration Research and Theory* 15, no. 3 (2005): 325–351.

Jones, Bryan D., Frank R. Baumgartner, Christian Breunig, Christopher Wlezien, Stuart Soroka, Martial Foucault, Abel Francois, et al. "A General Empirical Law of Public Budgets: A Comparative Analysis." *American Journal of Political Science* 53, no. 4 (2009): 855–873.

Key, Vladimer O., Jr. "The Lack of a Budgetary Theory." *American Political Science Review* 34, no. 6 (1940): 1137–1144.

Kraan, Dirk-Jan. *Budgetary Decisions: A Public Choice Approach.* New York: Cambridge University Press, 1996.

Padgett, John F. "Bounded Rationality in Budgetary Research." *American Political Science Review* 74 (1980): 354–372.

Poterba, James M., and Jürgen von Hagen. *Fiscal Institutions and Fiscal Performance.* Chicago: University of Chicago Press, 1999.

Samuelson, Paul A. "The Pure Theory of Public Expenditure." *Review of Economics and Statistics* 36 no. 4 (1954): 387–389.

Shah, Anwar. *Budgeting and Budgetary Institutions.* New York: World Bank, 2007.

Von Hagen, Jürgen. "Political Economy of Fiscal Institutions." In *Oxford Handbook of Political Economy,* edited by Barry R. Weingast and Donald Wittman, 464–478. Oxford: Oxford University Press 2006.

Wehner, Joachim. "Assessing the Power of the Purse: An Index of Legislative Budget Institutions." *Political Studies* 54, no. 4 (2006): 767–785.

Wildavsky, Aaron. *The Politics of the Budgetary Process.* Boston: Little, Brown, 1964.

———. *Budgeting: A Comparative Theory of Budgetary Processes.* Boston: Little, Brown, 1975.

Bukharin, Nikolai Ivanovich

Russian Marxist theorist and revolutionary, Nikolai Ivanovich Bukharin (1888–1938) was an important figure in the early history of the Soviet Union. He is most famously credited with the development of gradualist New Economic Policy (NEP) in the 1920s, but this policy was abandoned by Joseph Stalin, and Bukharin was eventually arrested and executed.

Bukharin joined the Bolshevik Party in 1906 as student, but his studies were interrupted by arrests and eventual exile. He settled in Austria and Switzerland, where he participated in activities with other exiled Russian Marxists, including

Vladimir Lenin. As a young man, Bukharin produced two major works, *The Economic Theory of the Leisure Class* (1914) and *The World Economy and Imperialism* (1915). The latter analyzed the clash between nation-states and the internationalization of capital, of which the latter, according to Bukharin, was producing networks of state capitalist trusts. Lenin wrote an approving introduction to the work and would become an important patron to Bukharin in his rise through the party's ranks.

Bukharin returned to Russia in 1917 and was elected to the Bolshevik Party's Central Committee three months before the Bolshevik Revolution (1917). He assumed many leadership positions, including editor of the party newspaper, *Pravda* (*Truth*), from 1917 to 1929, and head of the Communist International from 1926 to 1929.

In the first years of communist rule, he was more radical, clashing with Lenin on such issues as concluding a peace with Germany and defending the rapid move to a communist system under "war communism." He produced *The Economics of the Transition* (1920), which grappled with the issue of how to create a communist state.

By the early 1920s, Bukharin had moderated his position, joining with Stalin in favoring a more gradual and peaceful evolution to communism, which was to be known as the New Economic Policy (1921–1929). Lenin, prior to his death in 1924, praised Bukharin as one of the party's most brilliant thinkers. Bukharin defended NEP in *The Road to Socialism and the Worker Peasant Alliance* (1925). NEP foresaw a limited role for markets in an economy in which the "commanding heights" of industry would be dominated by the state. Bukharin hoped that socialism would gradually emerge through the NEP. However, by 1929, Stalin turned against the NEP as too gradual and too capitalist, and Bukharin lacked the political power to challenge Stalin successfully. He was gradually removed from positions of leadership and was expelled from the party altogether in 1937. After a show trial on charges of treason, he was executed in 1938.

After the tragedy of Stalinism, Bukharin's views were reevaluated in a more positive light by many on the political left in the West and reformers in the Soviet Union as the "road not taken," a possible means to produce a more humane communism. Ideas of the NEP influenced Mikhail Gorbachev, who, as the last Soviet leader (1985–1991), politically rehabilitated Bukharin in 1988.

See also *Bolshevism; Lenin, Vladimir Ilich; Marxism.*

. . . . PAUL JAMES KUBICEK

BIBLIOGRAPHY
Coates, Ken. *The Case of Nikolai Bukharin.* Nottingham, U.K.: Spokesman, 1982.
Cohen, Stephen F. *Bukharin and the Bolshevik Revolution: A Political Biography.* New York: Oxford University Press, 1980.
Gluckstein, Donny. *Tragedy of Bukharin.* London: Pluto, 1994.
Haynes, Michael. *Nikolai Bukharin and the Transition from Capitalism to Socialism.* New York: Holmes and Meier, 1985.
Weitz, Eric D., and Nicholas N. Kozlov. *Nikolai Ivanovich Bukharin: A Centenary Appraisal.* New York: Praeger, 1990.

Bull, Hedley

Hedley Bull (1932–1985) was one of the major figures in the modern academic study of international relations and taught at the London School of Economics, The Australian National University, and Oxford University. One of the key figures in the English School of International Relations, he is best known for the idea that states form among themselves an "international society." Bull began his early work by analyzing the common framework of rules and institutions that developed within the anarchical society of the classical European state system. For Bull, this society was anarchical in that there was no common power to enforce law or to underwrite cooperation, but it was a society in so far as states were conscious of common rules and values, cooperated in the working of common institutions, and perceived common interests in observing these rules and working through these institutions. As against the realist emphasis on the material structures of the international system, Bull saw international society as built around a historically created, and evolving, structure of common understandings, rules, norms, and mutual expectations. But as against later liberal constructivists, he retained realism's concern with power and its emphasis on the central role of the balance of power.

Bull's approach in his most famous book, *The Anarchical Society: A Study of Order in World Politics* (1977) involved three elements. There is an *analytical* approach (what is order, and what are the minimum conditions that would have to exist before any society could be meaningfully so described?); a *historical* approach (how far can one isolate and identify an acceptance of these conditions in the evolving practices of states?); and a *normative* approach (on which minimum conditions of coexistence might the holders of sharply conflicting values be able to agree?). The subsequent task was to map and explain the changing normative constitution of international society—in particular the move from a limited pluralist society of states built around coexistence to a liberal solidarist society of states united by denser institutional forms and by stronger moral and legal ties.

Bull also established a reputation as one of the most important early theorists of arms control. He was closely involved in the early years of the Institute for Strategic Studies in London and, in *The Control of the Arms Race* (1961), he attacked arguments for general and complete disarmament. He argued instead that the most important goal should be the stability of a strategic relationship rather than any particular level of armaments and that the greatest efforts should be devoted to stabilizing the structure of nuclear deterrence and agreeing on the methodologies, technologies, and shared understandings to produce that end.

Although his work on strategy was dominated by the cold war, Bull believed that the transition from a European to a global international society represented a more fundamental historical development. In his later work—especially *The Expansion of International Society* (1985)—he explored relations between the European and non-European world. He traced five stages in what he called the "revolt against Western dominance"—the struggle for equal sovereignty, the anticolonial revolution, the struggle for racial equality, the fight for economic justice, and the struggle for cultural liberation—and he analyzed the impact of what had by then become known as the third world on the institutions of international society.

See also *Arms Control; Arms Race; European Political Thought; International Relations; International Relations Theory; International Relations: Worldviews and Frameworks.*

. . . . ANDREW HURRELL

BIBLIOGRAPHY
Alderson, Kai, and Andrew Hurrell, eds. *Hedley Bull on International Society.* London: Macmillan, 2000.
Bull, Hedley. *The Anarchical Society: A Study of Order in World Politics.* New York: Columbia University Press, 1977.
Roberts, Adam. "Bull, Hedley Norman (1932–1985)." In *Oxford Dictionary of National Biography,* edited by Brian Harrison, 27. Oxford: Oxford University Press, 2004.

Bunche, Ralph Johnson

Ralph Johnson Bunche (1903–1971) was an American political scientist and diplomat known for his work with the United Nations (UN). He was the first African American to earn a doctorate from Harvard University and to win the Nobel Peace Prize. He was awarded the Medal of Freedom, America's highest civilian honor, in 1963.

Bunche was born in Detroit, Michigan. He graduated summa cum laude from the University of California–Los Angeles in 1927 and then received his master's degree and doctorate in government and international relations from Harvard University. From 1936 to 1938, Bunche conducted postdoctoral research (as a Social Science Research Council Fellow) at the London School of Economics and at the University of Cape Town in South Africa. As a result of his research, he became known as a leading expert on colonialism.

While still a graduate student, Bunche joined the faculty at Howard University and taught there until 1942. He was appointed to Harvard University in 1950, but he resigned in 1952 having never actually taught there. In 1953 he was elected the president of the American Political Science Association.

Bunche joined the National Defense Program Office (later the Office of Strategic Services, the forerunner of the Central Intelligence Agency) as a senior analyst on Africa and Asia in 1941 and worked there until 1944. He then joined the U.S. Department of State and, in 1945, became the first African American to head a division of a federal agency when he became the acting chief of the Division of Dependent Area Affairs.

Bunche helped write the UN Charter and served as a member of the U.S. delegation to the first UN General Assembly in 1946. In 1947 he became the director of the UN's trusteeship division. Three years later Bunche received the Nobel Peace Prize for his work in negotiating the agreements that ended the 1948–1949 war between the newly established state of Israel and its Arab neighbors. Over the next two decades, Bunche presided over the UN conference on the peaceful uses of atomic energy and organized and directed UN peacekeeping operations in the Middle East, Lebanon, the Congo, Yemen, and Cyprus.

Bunche was an active scholar and participant in the civil rights movement. In 1931 he helped organize a protest against a segregated performance of *Porgy and Bess* at the National Theater in Washington, DC. His work as codirector of the Institute of Race Relations at Swarthmore College resulted in his writing *A World View of Race* (1936). In 1935 he organized a conference at Howard University on President Franklin D. Roosevelt's New Deal domestic reform program and its impact on African Americans. In February 1936, Bunche cofounded the Negro National Congress, which held its first meeting in Chicago; Bunche would leave this organization in 1938 after it was taken over by the Communist Party. From 1938 to 1940, he worked with Gunnar Myrdal, the Swedish sociologist, on his study of African Americans that culminated with Myrdal's *An American Dilemma: The Negro Problem and Modern Democracy* (1944). In 1949 Bunche was awarded the National Association for the Advancement of Colored People's (NAACP) Spingarn Medal, the organization's highest honor. President Harry S. Truman offered Bunche the position of assistant secretary of state, but he declined because of the segregated life in Washington, DC. Bunche participated in the 1963 March on Washington, at which he introduced famed activist Martin Luther King Jr., and he helped to lead the 1965 civil rights march organized by King.

Bunche served as a member of the Board of Trustees of the Rockefeller Foundation (1955–1971), as a member of the New York City Board of Education (1958–1964), and as a member of the Board of Overseers of Harvard University (1960–1965). Suffering from heart disease and diabetes, Bunche resigned as UN undersecretary-general on October 1, 1971. He died on December 9, 1971.

See also *Civil Rights Movement; Race and Racism; United Nations (UN); U.S. Politics and Society: African American Political Participation; U.S. Politics and Society: African American Social Movements.*

. . . . JEFFREY KRAUS

BIBLIOGRAPHY
Bunche, Ralph J. "French Administration in Togoland and Dahomey." PhD diss., Harvard University Graduate School, 1934.
———. *The Political Status of the Negro in the Age of FDR.* Edited with an introduction by Dewey W. Grantham. Chicago: University of Chicago Press, 1973.
Henry, Charles P., ed. *Ralph J. Bunche: Selected Speeches and Writings.* Ann Arbor: University of Michigan Press, 1995.
———. *Ralph Bunche: Model Negro or American Other?* New York: New York University Press, 1999.
Kugelmass, J. Alvin. *Ralph J. Bunche: Fighter for Peace.* New York: Julian Messner, 1952.
Rivlin, Benjamin, ed. *Ralph Bunche: The Man and His Times.* New York: Holmes and Meier, 1990.
Urquhart, Brian. *Ralph Bunche: An American Life.* New York: Norton, 1993.

Bureaucracy

Bureaucracy refers to an organization or a set of organizations designed to carry out a specialized set of tasks, often on a massive scale. In political science, as well as the general public discourse, the term generally refers to the characteristics and workings of government organizations, although studies on bureaucracies have borrowed generously from research on economics and business organization.

Bureaucrats are people who work in bureaucracies. Tasks that are entrusted to bureaucrats range from simple administrative ones, such as typing or photocopying, to the implementation of complex policy goals, such as reducing air pollution or maintaining national defense. Thus, the subjects of studies of bureaucracy have ranged from street-level bureaucrats, such as doctors, teachers, soldiers, and social workers, to very powerful bureaucrats, such as army generals, monetary policy regulators, and attorneys general.

While executive and legislative bodies are responsible for making policy and judicial bodies are responsible for interpreting policy, bureaucracies are generally responsible for the implementation of policy. Studies of policy implementation examine how bureaucratic decision making is influenced by policy-making preferences, as well as political, economic, and social institutions. Within political science, such studies are typically part of the subfield discipline known as *public administration*, although the term *public management* has been used as well. However, some scholars have suggested that the term *public management* applies more specifically to studies of how to make public agencies more efficient and market oriented.

Although bureaucracies have been endemic throughout history, the origin of their analysis in the social sciences is generally traced back to the work of German social theorist Max Weber. Weber stated in 1946 that the use of bureaucratic organizations had grown over time because of their technical superiority over any other form of organization. According to Weber, several organizational features of bureaucracies ensured their technical superiority, most notably the consistent application of rules and the placement of appointed officials with expertise within a hierarchical structure. Most modern bureaucracies contain these features, but each feature receives different emphasis, according to each country and bureaucratic culture.

THE APPLICATION OF RULES

Bureaucratic organizations apply rules and deliver services efficiently because they do so according to sets of rules and without regard to the varying concerns of individual people, argued Weber. When bureaucracies begin to treat each client according to criteria other than specific rules, such as the person's socioeconomic status, resources are wasted on determining outcomes for each client. Additionally, erratic application of the rules also diminishes the credibility of the agency itself, as people will learn over time that particular clients are favored over others. In *The Politics of Bureaucracy* (1995), political science scholar B. Guy Peters argues that many non-Western societies have been unable to implement a consistent interpretation of rules within public bureaucracies because clients expect to barter, to some extent, over final decisions or to use their status in society as leverage.

However, while a consistent application of the rules is generally a desired result, this does not necessarily mean that bureaucrats always will know precisely how to behave and do their job. According to James Q. Wilson in *Bureaucracy: What Government Agencies Do and Why They Do It* (1989), most government agencies have goals that they want to accomplish, but the more vague these stated goals are and the less easily they are translated into tasks, the more the behavior of bureaucrats will come to depend on other factors. For example, the collective goals of a police department might be to "protect the public" and "uphold the law," but people will have different interpretations as to how to achieve these rather broad goals. Additionally, these goals do not necessarily dictate how a police officer should deal with, for example, a belligerent panhandler on the street. Thus, the particular circumstances will be important as the officer attempts to bring the situation under control. Herbert Simon, in his 1947 book *Administrative Behavior*, argued that the uncertainty of such situations is precisely what causes bureaucrats to follow rules and routines. According to Simon, because policy outcomes arising out of bureaucratic action are often difficult to determine or observe, structured and organized behavior helps to reduce uncertainty and preserve stability within the organization.

Wilson also argues that when agency goals are unclear, behavior may come to depend on the professional training of the bureaucrats in question. In antitrust or competition law, economists tend to favor breaking up concentrations of market power when they are economically inefficient, whereas attorneys are more likely to favor such breakups when the law has been broken. Finally, when an agency has multiple constituencies with competing interests, bureaucrats may feel pulled in different directions. For example, an agency charged with regulating air pollution may have to weigh the benefits of clean air against the potential costs to business of pollution abatement. Dissatisfaction with agency actions may lead certain constituents to seek formal rule changes from the legislature overseeing the agency, in turn, sending conflicting signals to the bureaucrats themselves.

Several examples exist of administrative cultures that strongly emphasize an adherence to written laws and rules. Such systems have been characterized as following the Hegelian civil service, or *Rechtsstaat* model, a model that requires senior civil servants to be trained in law. Countries with such systems, such as France, Germany, and Italy, accord civil servants a high level of respect, and future civil servants are trained in administrative law in prestigious institutions, such as France's École Nationale d'Administration. Government scholar Christopher Hood has referred to civil servants in such systems as *trustees* of the government, acting in an autonomous fashion (2002). However, in contrast to the Weberian ideal of impartial expertise, French civil servants can be highly political, and many French politicians are former civil servants. Similarly, in Germany and Italy a lack of impartiality among civil servants may clash with the need to follow rules closely.

The Rechtsstaat model of civil service has been contrasted with the *public interest* model found in Australia, Canada, New Zealand, the United Kingdom, and the United States. In these countries, there is not the same emphasis on administrative law as in Rechtsstaat countries, and consequently, there is less adherence to the notion of rigidly following rules. According to Hood, public employees act more as "battle troops" to carry out the political will of the political incumbent. Despite this characterization, the degree to which the civil service is politicized varies considerably across these countries. For example, British civil servants have traditionally been considered to be neutral, working for the incumbent government, whereas in the United States, political appointees come and go with each presidency, and often are added or subtracted from particular agencies as presidents see fit.

SPECIALIZATION AND EXPERTISE

Weber observed that bureaucracies were made more efficient by the selection of people with technical expertise in the organization. This expertise enables bureaucrats to perform their tasks in a specialized fashion and to apply strict criteria to their decision-making processes. In addition to his observations, Weber also argued that bureaucratic organizations should recruit and select personnel based on merit and expertise in order to ensure an independent and consistent application of bureaucratic rules. Once granted some autonomy in action as well, bureaucrats could use their specialized knowledge, free from political interference. As Murray Horn argues in *The Political Economy of Public Administration: Institutional Choice in the Public Sector* (1995), legislatures often "tie their hands" by limiting their ability to interfere with the inner workings of bureaucracies, thus enhancing the credibility of both the politicians and the bureaucrats. Fabrizio Gilardi (2002) demonstrates that many western European nations created independent regulatory agencies with the purpose of overseeing newly privatized energy and telecommunication companies.

Weber's argument that bureaucrats should be selected according to merit has been echoed by other scholars, but historically, patronage concerns have often trumped merit concerns. In the United States in the 1830s, President Andrew Jackson implemented what became known as the *spoils system*, whereby loyal party workers were given high-ranking government jobs on a rotating basis. The system was created to eliminate what Jackson saw as a pattern of wealthy elites receiving the majority of federal appointments. This system of spoils or patronage enabled average party workers to obtain government jobs. While Weber's ideal bureaucrat held a fixed term so that employment could not be arbitrarily terminated by political executives, administration turnover in the spoils system meant wholesale personnel changes across bureaucratic agencies, as party workers were rewarded for their loyalty with government jobs. Office holders were generally accountable to the politicians they helped elect, but populists, progressives, and urban reformers viewed the spoils system as a corrupt method of giving plum jobs to unqualified representatives of special interests.

Along with this negative perception of the spoils system, several events in the late nineteenth century resulted in the slow conversion of the American federal bureaucracy to a merit-based system from a patronage system. First, Congress passed the Pendleton Act in 1883, which required that federal jobs gradually come to be filled according to merit and qualification. Second, in 1887, political science scholar and future president Woodrow Wilson claimed in "The Study of Administration," that it should be the job of American administrators to neutrally and faithfully implement the policy directives of politicians. Wilson's article supported the idea that bureaucrats could work free of political influence and that administration could be separated from politics. The U.S. Congress had Wilson's ideas in mind when it passed the Interstate Commerce Act of 1887 and established the Interstate Commerce Commission with the purported aim of independently regulating the nation's railroads. However, depleted resources, vague statutory goals, and competing constituent influence all indicated how difficult it could be to separate politics from administration in bureaucratic policy making.

Although the complete separation of policy implementation or administration from politics has been an elusive, if not an impossible, goal to achieve, policy makers and scholars agree that there are some areas of policy making, such as macroeconomic monetary policy, in which bureaucratic independence from politicians is a concern of paramount importance. Conventional wisdom suggests that if politicians had direct control over the money supply and interest rates, they would print more money to finance their projects and would lower interest rates to engineer economic booms. The main consequence of both activities would of course be soaring inflation, which would diminish the credibility of any political commitments toward stable monetary policy. The United States Federal Reserve, the European Central Bank, the Bank of England, and the Bundesbank are just a few of the major, formally independent central banks.

HIERARCHY

Finally, according to Weber, expert bureaucrats applying a rational-legal framework had to be placed in a hierarchical setting to function properly. In a hierarchical setting, bureaucrats would work in a disciplined fashion toward common objectives set forth by the head administrators. Any other setting might result in the failure of bureaucrats to work coherently toward the same goals.

Weber's observations caused other scholars to seek to explain why, over the course of history, hierarchies had emerged as the most common type of organizational structure. In his landmark 1937 article "The Nature of the Firm," British economist Ronald Coase posited that, for private firms, hierarchy was efficient because it limited the transaction costs that business entrepreneurs would have to incur otherwise. In the absence of a hierarchy, the business entrepreneur must negotiate contracts with others to purchase input products and labor. If extensive bargaining must take place to negotiate each contract, time and resources are wasted in the process.

A hierarchical structure eliminates the need for costly bargaining by setting rules and, in the words of political scientist Terry Moe in his 1984 article "The New Economics of Organization," "substitutes authority relations for market relations."

Although hierarchies serve to promote efficiency by reducing transaction costs, they also introduce into public and private organizations a new range of organizational dilemmas, known broadly as principal-agent problems. Moe states that

> the principal-agent model is an analytic expression of the agency relationship, in which one party, the principal, considers entering into a contractual agreement with another, the agent, in the expectation that the agent will subsequently choose actions that produce outcomes desired by the principal (756).

However, agents have an incentive to misrepresent their true skills, and the manager may find it difficult to select the best candidate. This is a problem of asymmetric information, known as *adverse selection*. Second, the degree to which a principal can monitor the work behavior of the hired agent varies considerably across jobs. For example, a police captain cannot monitor what uniformed officers actually do on the streets at all times, if at all. The less observable the agent's behavior, the more that agent can shirk the obligation to the principal. Additionally, when the principal hires an agent with specialized expertise to perform a complex task, the agent can exploit that information advantage to either shirk or perform the task in any preferred manner. This problem, known as *moral hazard,* is also a problem of asymmetric information.

The principal-agent framework has been employed broadly throughout political science and public administration research, particularly to depict the relationships between politicians and bureaucrats. William Niskanen, applying economic principles of utility maximization to bureaucrats, argued in his 1971 work *Bureaucracy and Representative Government* that information asymmetries between bureaucrats and legislatures were particularly problematic because knowledgeable bureaucrats could request exorbitant budgets from legislators, who, due to their lack of expertise, do not know the true cost of performing the bureaucratic tasks. Niskanen's work, although highly influential, was criticized by many scholars as overly broad and flawed. Patrick Dunleavy followed Niskanen by maintaining in *Democracy, Bureaucracy, and Public Choice* (1991) that, rather than pursuing budget maximization, decision makers in bureaucracies follow a bureau-shaping strategy, most notably by separating the service delivery functions of the agency—or *line agency functions*—from the policy-making aspects of the agency. As a result, over time the agency's core functions are more narrowly defined, and it actually faces fewer subsequent budget constraints. In turn, Dunleavy's research was criticized by David Marsh, Martin Smith, and David Richards in their 2000 article, "Bureaucrats, Politicians, and Reform in Whitehall: Analyzing the Bureau-shaping Model." Marsh, Smith, and Richards found that the bureau-shaping model did not explain the creation of many, highly specialized government agencies

in the United Kingdom, known as the *next-step agencies.* The authors argue that this effective hiving off of duties into other newly created agencies did not originate among bureaucrats, but was imposed by Prime Minister Margaret Thatcher and her cabinet.

The research of Marsh, Smith, and Richards raises the question of how and why politicians attempt to control bureaucrats, a particularly salient question in a separation-of-powers system, such as the United States, where Congress, the president, and the courts vie for control over the direction of bureaucratic policy making. In *The Administrative Presidency* (1983) Richard Nathan emphasized how the president can influence bureaucratic outputs through the powers of appointment and reorganization; studies done by B. Dan Wood and Richard Waterman empirically demonstrate this (1994). Additionally, in a 2005 study, David Lewis found that presidents also manipulate the number of appointees and civil servants, particularly in agencies that clash with the president.

Much research also has been devoted to illustrating the U.S. Congress's alleged ability to steer bureaucratic behavior. Congress is responsible for crafting the legislation from which agencies are born and, as a result, it has significant authority over how agencies are designed. Matthew McCubbins, Roger Noll, and Barry Weingast (aka McNollgast) have stressed the importance of this function, arguing in a 1987 article that Congress embeds particular administrative procedures into agency design in order to ensure that bureaucratic behavior does not deviate too far from congressional intent. Since their influential work was written, several scholars (e.g., David Epstein and Sharyn O'Halloran, 1996; Evan Ringquist, Jeff Worsham, and Marc Allen Eisner, 2003) have attempted to refine the work of McNollgast by showing that agency authority delegated by Congress also depends on the salience and complexity of the issue, the presence of divided government within Congress, and the ability of affected constituents to organize.

However, many scholars have focused also on the ability of American bureaucracies to be autonomous and to display greater independence of political control. In a 1976 study, Joel D. Aberbach and Bert A. Rockman found through surveys that Nixon administration bureaucrats were suspicious of his domestic policy agenda, particularly those bureaucrats that administered social regulatory programs. In *Bureaucracy, Politics, and Public Policy* (1984), Francis Rourke argues that bureaucrats can develop knowledge and expertise that can then be used independently of political principals. Additionally, agencies with large or important constituencies may have enough political cover to act contrary to the wishes of the president or Congress. In *The Forging of Bureaucratic Autonomy* (2001), Daniel Carpenter also emphasizes the ability of entrepreneurial agency heads to cultivate coalitions as the key to bureaucratic autonomy.

BUREAUCRATIC REFORMS

In the latter half of the twentieth century, public management reforms were driven by high levels of government debt, but also by the conservative ideals of leaders such as Ronald Reagan and Margaret Thatcher. Many countries in Europe and elsewhere implemented changes to the structure of civil servant contracts and to budgeting decisions. These changes also represented a desire to bring free-market principles into government—greater flexibility was sought in civil servant contracts to reward and punish bureaucrats according to their performance. Thus, for example, countries such as Australia, New Zealand, and the United Kingdom introduced programs whereby bureaucrats were hired according to performance-related contracts for a variable number of years, as opposed to being appointed for life. Moreover, budgeting procedures also were transformed in order to stimulate agency performance and enhance efficiency. Budgets are increasingly drawn up according to evaluations of agency performance, and many countries have instituted auditing procedures as well to monitor how money is spent once it is allocated. Finally, many countries passed legislation, such as the Government Performance and Results Act in the United States in 1993, to allow formal evaluation of bureaucratic behavior through the use of performance indicators and measurement.

In western Europe, the regulation of business gradually shifted away from direct control of nationalized industries by the executive to the creation of independent regulatory agencies. The shift to autonomous agencies represented a decision by governments to interfere less in markets while delegating important regulatory decisions to bureaucrats with specialized expertise. In his 1996 book *Regulating Europe*, Giandomenico Majone documented the proliferation of independent regulatory agencies as the European Union's emergence as a regulatory state. The creation of such agencies also represented a shift toward more market-oriented economies, as state-owned enterprises were jettisoned in favor of an arrangement whereby the new agencies oversee private utilities and energy companies. Similar changes occurred in the United States in the late 1970s, despite the long-standing prevalence there of independent regulatory agencies. Widespread deregulation in transportation and utilities sectors of business resulted in the dismantling of regulations that were considered favorable for existing large businesses, but destructive to competition and consumers.

While these elements of the *new public management* have been widespread throughout the industrialized world, they have been implemented to varying degrees across countries. What accounts for this variation? In *Public Management Reform: A Comparative Analysis* (2004), Christopher Pollitt and Geert Bouckaert posit that in majoritarian and centralized (unitary) governments, public sector reforms tend to be implemented most rapidly and most broadly, while in consensual and decentralized (federal) governments, such reforms move more slowly and with more limited scope. First, because everyone's interests are represented in a consensual government, it is easier for those opposed to reforms to block their passage. Second, because power is dispersed from the federal government to regional governments in a federal system, it is more difficult for the executive in a federal system to impose

nationwide reforms. Thus, majoritarian, centralized governments like New Zealand and the United Kingdom could implement far-reaching reforms. An oft-mentioned instance of such change occurred in the United Kingdom in 1986 when Prime Minister Margaret Thatcher responded to policy disagreements with the Greater London Council by simply abolishing it, along with several other county councils. On the other hand, more consensual and federal systems, such as Belgium and Germany, did not experience the same level of change. Additionally, countries like Belgium, France, and Italy are characterized as having risk-averse bureaucratic cultures in which attempts to introduce performance-related civil servant contracts are fiercely resisted by bureaucrats.

Public sector reforms such as privatization, contracting out, pay for performance, and performance measurement have helped some governments realize significant savings and improve government performance, but public management scholars also emphasize that these reforms can be difficult to implement and may yield mixed results. For example, it may be difficult to develop indicators that reliably assess public sector performance, which also makes it difficult to link salary and budgets to performance. To the extent that reliable indicators can be developed, close linkage with budget or salary may give bureaucrats incentives to manipulate their numbers or ignore other important indicators. Finally, as numerous public administration scholars have noted, the procedures of implementing public policy are often concerned with values other than efficiency, such as equity or fairness.

See also *Civil Service; Performance Management; Regulation and Rulemaking; Weber, Max.*

. . . . COLIN PROVOST

BIBLIOGRAPHY
Aberbach, Joel D., and Bert A. Rockman. "Clashing Beliefs within the Executive Branch: The Nixon Administration Bureaucracy." *American Political Science Review* 70 (June 1976): 502–522.
Carpenter, Daniel. *The Forging of Bureaucratic Autonomy.* Princeton, N.J.: Princeton University Press, 2001.
Coase, Ronald. "The Nature of the Firm." *Economica* 4 (November 1937): 386–405.
Dunleavy, Patrick. *Democracy, Bureaucracy, and Public Choice.* New York: Prentice Hall, 1991.
Epstein, David, and Sharyn O'Halloran. "Divided Government and the Design of Administrative Procedures: A Formal Model and an Empirical Test." *Journal of Politics* 58 (May 1996): 373–397.
Gilardi, Fabrizio. "Policy Credibility and Delegation to Independent Regulatory Agencies: A Comparative Empirical Analysis." *Journal of European Public Policy* 9 (December 2002): 873–893.
Hood, Christopher. "Control, Bargains and Cheating: The Politics of Public-Service Reform." *Journal of Public Administration Research and Theory* 12 (July 2002): 309–332.
Horn, Murray. *The Political Economy of Public Administration: Institutional Choice in the Public Sector.* Cambridge: Cambridge University Press, 1995.
Lewis, David. "Staffing Alone: Unilateral Action and the Politicization of the Executive Office of the President." *Presidential Studies Quarterly* 35 (September 2005): 496–514.
Majone, Giandomenico. *Regulating Europe.* London: Routledge, 1996.
Marsh, David, Martin Smith, and David Richards. "Bureaucrats, Politicians, and Reform in Whitehall: Analyzing the Bureau-shaping Model." *British Journal of Political Science* 30 (2000): 461–482.

McCubbins, Matthew, Roger Noll, and Barry Weingast. "Administrative Procedures as Instruments of Political Control." *Journal of Law, Economics, and Organization* 3 (Autumn 1987): 243–277.

Moe, Terry. "The New Economics of Organization." *American Journal of Political Science* 28 (November 1984): 739–777.

Nathan, Richard. *The Administrative Presidency.* New York: Wiley, 1983.

Niskanen, William. *Bureaucracy and Representative Government.* Chicago: Aldine/Atherton, 1971.

Peters, B. Guy. *The Politics of Bureaucracy,* 4th ed. White Plains, N.Y.: Longman, 1995.

Pierre, J. *Bureaucracy in the Modern State: An Introduction to Comparative Public Administration.* Aldershot, U.K.: Edward Elgar, 1995.

Pollitt, Christopher, and Geert Bouckaert. *Public Management Reform: A Comparative Analysis,* 2nd ed. New York: Oxford University Press, 2004.

Ringquist, Evan, Jeff Worsham, and Marc Allen Eisner. "Salience, Complexity and the Legislative Direction of Regulatory Bureaucracies." *Journal of Public Administration Research and Theory* 13 (April 2003): 141–164.

Rourke, Francis E. *Bureaucracy, Politics, and Public Policy.* 3rd ed. Boston: Little, Brown, 1984.

Simon, Herbert. *Administrative Behavior.* New York: Macmillan, 1947.

Weber, Max. "Bureaucracy." In *From Max Weber: Essays in Sociology,* edited by H. H. Gerth and C. Wright Mills, 196–244. London: Routledge and Kegan Paul, 1948.

Wilson, James Q. *Bureaucracy: What Government Agencies Do and Why They Do It.* New York: Basic Books, 1989.

Wilson, Woodrow. "The Study of Administration." *Political Science Quarterly* 2 (June 1887): 209–210.

Wood, B. Dan, and Richard Waterman. *Bureaucratic Dynamics: The Role of Bureaucracy in a Democracy.* Boulder, Colo.: Westview, 1994.

Bureaucratic Authoritarianism

Bureaucratic authoritarianism is a type of authoritarian regime that features rule by an alliance of military leaders, civilians with technical expertise (especially in economic policy), and leading business sectors. These regimes are hypothesized to form under certain conditions where a nation is attempting to industrialize and faces popular agitation or unrest that makes it difficult for elites to maintain order. The original paradigms of the bureaucratic-authoritarian regime were Latin American countries of the 1960s, Latin American regimes in the 1970s and 1980s, as well as East Asian countries that have provided the opportunity for political science to test the theories proposed about their development.

ORIGIN OF THE CONCEPT

Guillermo O'Donnell coined the term *bureaucratic authoritarianism* in *Modernization and Bureaucratic-Authoritarianism* (1973), which examined the military regimes of South America that made economic performance a key component of their legitimation formulae. O'Donnell argued that the modern authoritarian regimes that came to power in Brazil (1964) and Argentina (1966) were supported by a coalition of military officers, civilian technocrats, and big business (especially multinational firms) that sought to move beyond the populist, distribution-oriented politics previously prevalent in those societies. The new regimes sought to replace distributional conflict with a more technocratic, bureaucratic approach to making economic policy.

Scholars using this concept criticized modernization theory for failing to predict the emergence of military regimes in some of the developing world's most advanced economies. Political development theorists following the modernization paradigm had associated higher levels of economic development with greater political pluralism and hence higher probabilities of democratic advancement. O'Donnell observed that Latin America's most economically advanced countries had fallen to nondemocratic rule in the 1960s and offered an alternative explanation that linked economic development with authoritarianism in late developers.

FEATURES OF BUREAUCRATIC AUTHORITARIANISM

Specifically, he suggested that in late-developing countries following the *import-substituting industrialization (ISI)* model—which promoted economic development by protecting and subsidizing local production of manufactured goods previously imported from already industrialized countries—the political power of lower-class and middle-class urban groups (especially the urban working class) grew as their numbers increased and as populist politicians developed coalitions that relied on their support. As the market for consumer goods became saturated due to the success of the first, "horizontal" stage of ISI, those economies required "deepening" into the production of capital goods and consumer durables in order to further economic growth.

Such heavy industries required investments by foreign capital. International investors were discouraged from entering these economies, however, where populist politics, featuring popular sector agitation and economic nationalism, prevailed. O'Donnell identified an "elective affinity" between the military, concerned about the implications for domestic order in the face of popular sector mobilization, and civilian technocrats, who sought military support for the adoption of orthodox economic policies. From this affinity, coup coalitions were formed, leading to authoritarian regimes in which the military chose to rule as an institution (rather than via personalist rule by a single strongman), but brought civilian technocrats—especially economists and engineers—into key roles managing the nation's economic development.

This alliance of the military and civilian technocrats is the key characteristic of bureaucratic authoritarianism. O'Donnell's conceptualization of bureaucratic authoritarianism stresses political exclusion of the masses, a highly technocratic policy-making process shared by the military and civilian experts, and rule that benefits transnational business and permits the country to further engage in the global economy.

EMPIRICAL INVESTIGATIONS

Originally developed to apply to Argentina and Brazil, the concept of bureaucratic authoritarianism was subsequently used by many scholars of Latin America to apply to military regimes that emerged in Chile and Uruguay in 1973 and to a second military regime that came to power in Argentina in 1976. As the Brazil, Chile, and Uruguay regimes, and the later military government of Argentina, evolved, attempts by scholars to refine the theory and to use it to predict the evolution of Latin American dictatorships produced valuable empirical research on patterns of political development in Latin American but failed to extend the theory. Scholars paid substantial attention to the idea that the degree of threat posed to the coup coalition partners by popular sector agitation could predict the severity of repression, the commitment to economic orthodoxy, the country's economic performance, and the unity both of the military institution and the coup coalition after the seizure of power.

However, as Karen Remmer and Gilbert Merkx convincingly demonstrated, actual events in the four countries of South America's Southern Cone did not bear out these hypotheses. For example, Brazil's relatively low precoup threat levels were nevertheless associated with initial fiscal orthodoxy while relatively high threat levels in Argentina in the 1970s and in Uruguay were followed by unorthodox fiscal policies under the military regimes that seized power. High threat levels led to low initial military unity in Uruguay but high initial unity in post-1976 Argentina.

The concept of bureaucratic authoritarianism has been applied with modifications to industrializing economies in East Asia, particularly South Korea, the Philippines, and Indonesia. As the model has been applied more broadly and critiqued by comparative politics scholars, the elements that have proven most useful remain two: (1) The prediction of modernization theory that democracy would result from economic development proved too optimistic, as many late industrializers opted for (often harsh) authoritarian rule during the initial phases of their heavy industrialization, and (2) when threatened by popular sector mobilization military officers, civilian technocrats, and business elites could agree on the merits of imposing a dictatorship that emphasized apparently rational, technical decision making based on objective criteria and the exclusion of the political interests of the broader public.

In the later evolution of regimes labeled as bureaucratic-authoritarian, this early unity of the coup partners typically dissolved, however, because politics did invade the decision-making process in the form of interservice rivalries within the military and suspicions of private sector investors that state enterprises operated by military and civilian technocrats threatened to crowd them out of the economy. Internal rivalries eventually led the Argentine military regime to attempt to forge unity by seizing the Falklands (Malvinas) Islands from the British, a failed venture that hastened the regime's downfall. Prominent critics of the Brazilian regime in the 1980s came to include industrialists concerned about the growing control of the economy by military and civilian technocrats at the head of state enterprises.

CONCLUSION

While the classic examples of bureaucratic-authoritarian regimes have given way to renewed democracies, the concept has continued to be used as an "ideal-type" or a tendency toward which certain regimes gravitate. The *autogolpe* (self-coup) of Peru's president Alberto Fujimori in 1992 is seen by some as a variant on the bureaucratic-authoritarian tradition; others have targeted postcommunist Russia under Vladimir Putin as a regime whose democratic elections are in tension with an alliance among politicians, business leaders, and secret police that tends toward bureaucratic authoritarianism.

See also *Autogolpe; Bureaucracy; Latin American Political Economy; Military Rule; Modernization; Newly Industrializing Countries (NIC).*

. . . . JOSEPH L. KLESNER

BIBLIOGRAPHY

Collier, David, Ed. *The New Authoritarianism in Latin America.* Princeton, N.J.: Princeton University Press, 1979.

Im, Hyug Baeg. "The Rise of Bureaucratic Authoritarianism in South Korea." *World Politics* 39, no. 2 (1987): 231–257.

Linz, Juan J. "Totalitarian and Authoritarian Regimes." In *Handbook of Political Science, Vol. 3, Macropolitical Theory,* edited by Fred I. Greenstein and Nelson W. Polsby, 175–411. Reading, Mass.: Addison-Wesley, 1975.

Malloy, James M., ed. *Authoritarianism and Corporatism in Latin America.* Pittsburgh: University of Pittsburgh Press, 1977.

O'Donnell, Guillermo A. *Modernization and Bureaucratic-Authoritarianism: Studies in South American Politics.* Berkeley: Institute of International Studies, University of California, 1973.

———. "Reflections on the Patterns of Change in the Bureaucratic-Authoritarian State." *Latin American Research Review* 13, no. 1 (1978): 3–28.

———. "Tensions in the Bureaucratic-Authoritarian State and the Question of Democracy." In *The New Authoritarianism in Latin America,* edited by David Collier, 285–318. Princeton, N.J.: Princeton University Press, 1979.

Remmer, Karen L., and Gilbert W. Merkx. "Bureaucratic-Authoritarianism Revisited." *Latin American Research Review* 17, no. 2 (1982): 3–40.

Robison, Richard. "Authoritarian States, Capital-Owning Classes, and the Politics of Newly-Industrializing Countries: The Case of Indonesia." *World Politics* 41, no. 1 (1988): 52–74.

Shevtsova, Liliia Fedorovna. "The Limits of Bureaucratic Authoritarianism." *Journal of Democracy* 15, no. 3 (2004): 67–77.

Burke, Edmund

Irish statesman and philosopher Edmund Burke (1729–1797) was born in Dublin, Ireland, to a Catholic mother and Protestant father. After graduating from Trinity College, Dublin, and briefly studying law in London, Burke entered the British Parliament in 1756, where he served for several decades among the Rockingham branch of the Whig party.

Burke's purely philosophical writings range from *A Vindication of Natural Society* (1756), widely read at the time as a defense of anarchism, to his treatment of aesthetics in *A Philosophical Enquiry into the Origin of Our Ideas of the Sublime and Beautiful* (1757). Although Burke's philosophical writings are worthy accomplishments, he is best remembered for his political speeches and writings in which he synthesized abstract questions of political philosophy with the details and exigencies of practical politics.

On the basis of his *Reflections on the Revolution in France* (1790), Burke is widely considered to be the founder of Anglo-American conservatism. Even before the French Revolution (1789–1799) had devolved into the Reign of Terror (1793–1794), Burke indicted the zeal of the French revolutionaries and accurately predicted some of the revolution's later excesses. He objected to the French Revolution's irreligious character, its invocation of metaphysical doctrines of natural rights, and its hostility to custom or tradition. *Reflections* strikes many readers as antidemocratic, as Burke not only complains about the leveling and disordering effects of the French Revolution but also defends aristocratic values such as chivalry, honor, and duty.

The conservative dimensions to Burke's *Reflections* have tended to overshadow his advocacy of other patently liberal causes. Burke defended a policy of conciliation toward the American colonies. Because the colonies had evolved a national identity distinct from Britain, it would be wrong to resist their efforts to separate themselves and pursue liberty in their own way. Likewise, Burke felt considerable sympathy for his native Ireland and argued for toleration of Irish Catholics. Burke led the impeachment of Warren Hastings, director of the British East India Company, whose maladministration and abuses of power threatened the lives and liberties of Britain's Indian subjects. In the case of the French Revolution, Burke defended himself against charges of inconsistency in his 1791 "Appeal from the Old to the New Whigs," identifying a consistent emphasis on the value of liberty running throughout all of his major speeches and writings.

Burke's "Speech to the Electors of Bristol" (1774) outlines what has come to be known as the Burkean theory of political representation. For Burke, the duty of a good representative is not just to mirror the interests and desires of constituents but to make disinterested decisions about the public good.

Mostly neglected in the late nineteenth and early twentieth centuries, Burke was rediscovered by American political theorists during the cold war. American conservatives like Russell Kirk rehabilitated Burke as a natural law thinker to anchor their defense of traditional American values against the irreligion and immorality of communist totalitarianism. More recently, however, Burke's liberal face has reemerged as many postcolonial political theorists have taken a fresh look at his criticism of the conduct of British imperialism in India.

See also *Conservatism; Imperialism.*

. . . .   RICHARD BOYD

BIBLIOGRAPHY
Burke, Edmund. *Selected Letters of Edmund Burke,* edited by Harvey
    Mansfield. Chicago: University of Chicago Press, 1984.
————. *Reflections on the Revolution in France,* edited by J. G. A. Pocock.
    Indianapolis: Hackett, 1987.
————. *Pre-revolutionary Writings,* edited by Ian Harris. Cambridge:
    Cambridge University Press, 1993.
Canavan, Francis P. *The Political Reason of Edmund Burke.* Durham, N.C.:
    Duke University Press, 1960.
Mansfield, Harvey C. *Statesmanship and Party Government: A Study of Burke
    and Bolingbroke.* Chicago: University of Chicago Press, 1965.
O'Brien, Conor Cruise. *The Great Melody.* Chicago: University of Chicago
    Press, 1992.

Burnham, James

American political theorist James Burnham (1905–1987) was one of the most influential anticommunist thinkers of the cold war era. Like many anticommunists, he started out as a Trotskyite, but eventually he moved away from Trotskyism and began a slow journey to the right. He became a mentor to American

conservative political commentator William F. Buckley Jr. and a founding editor at the conservative *National Review,* where he remained until he was felled by a stroke in 1987. He has been described by Richard Brookhiser, an American journalist and historian, as the "first neoconservative."

Burnham was unique among conservative thinkers. Unlike other conservatives who based their theories on religion, tradition, or natural law, he was rigorously empirical and influenced by the so-called realist school of politics. He sought to discover universal laws of politics and apply them to foreign policy and cultural change. He was generally supportive of free enterprise and limited government. He was neither a member of the old right nor the neocon right and was not a doctrinaire believer in laissez-faire. Burnham's views on congressional supremacy; his partial support for Joseph McCarthy, a U.S. senator who made accusations that the U.S. government had been infiltrated by communists; and his views on race place him broadly on the paleoconservative spectrum.

From 1930 to 1934, Burnham and American philosopher Philip Wheelwright co-edited a review entitled *Symposium.* In 1932 he and Wheelwright published a textbook titled *Introduction to Philosophical Analysis.* At this time Burnham became acquainted with philosopher and Marxist Sidney Hook, his colleague at New York University. Burnham's articles in *Symposium* impressed Hook and Russian Marxist revolutionary Leon Trotsky. After The Nazi-Soviet Non-Aggression Pact of 1939, in which Germany and the Soviet Union agreed to settle any differences amicably without war, Burnham broke with the Socialist Workers Party.

Burnham's next intellectual phase began in 1941 with the publication of *The Managerial Revolution,* a study in which he theorized that the world was witnessing the emergence of a new ruling class, the managers, who would soon replace the capitalists and the communists. *The Managerial Revolution* was a political and socioeconomic work, but it was also Burnham's first foray into global geopolitics. In it he sketched that the world would become tripolar with three strategic centers: (1) North America; (2) north-central Europe; and (3) west Asia, North Africa, and East Asia, including Japan and China. He predicted that Russia would break up, the British Empire would be liquidated, and the United States would become a superpower. In 1943, as his ideas expanded, he published his first analysis of political science, *The Machiavellians.* Based on the study of Italian political theorist Niccolò Machiavelli, Burnham deduced that (1) all politics is a struggle for power among individuals and groups; (2) political analysis is concerned with things as they are, not what they ought to be; (3) there is a distinction between formal meaning and real meaning; (4) political person is driven by self-interest and instinct, not by logic; (5) political elites are concerned only with the aggrandizement of power and they hold power by force and fraud; (6) all societies are divided into the rulers and the ruled; and (7) the ruling classes shift over time in their membership and goals.

After World War II (1939–1945), Burnham became the chief critic of the policy of containment, which was devised by advisor George Kennan for President Harry S. Truman's administration in an effort to curtail the spread of communism. Burnham criticized containment from the ideological right, arguing for a more aggressive strategy that called for the liberation of Eastern Europe to undermine Soviet power. Decades later President Ronald Reagan adopted Burnham's confrontational approach, which resulted in the collapse of the Soviet Empire and thus vindicated Burnham's views.

Burnham wrote *The Struggle for the World* (1947) and *The World We Are In* (1967), both of which were broad comprehensive analyses of the beginning of the cold war, the nature of the communist threat to the world, Soviet leader Joseph Stalin's ambitions, and the strategy for a U.S. victory. He expanded his ideas in *The Coming Defeat of Communism* (1950) and *Containment or Liberation?* (1952). As early as 1962 he predicted a U.S. defeat in the Vietnam War (1959–1975). Burnham was also broadly pessimistic about the future of the West. In his *Suicide of the West* (1964), he argued that the West had passed the apex of its power and would decline soon.

See also *Communism; Containment; Hook, Sidney; Marxism; Political Theory; Trotsky, Leon.*

. . . . GEORGE THOMAS KURIAN

BIBLIOGRAPHY
Francis, Samuel. *Power and History: The Political Thought of James Burnham.* Lanham, Md.: University Press of America, 1984.
———. *Thinkers of Our Time: James Burnham.* London: Claridge, 1999.
Kelly, Daniel. *James Burnham and the Struggle for the World: A Life.* New York: Intercollegiate Studies Institute, 2002.

Business Cycles, Political

Political business cycles occur when political motivations induce politicians to take actions that cause macroeconomic fluctuations. Cycles may be *opportunistic,* as when pre-election stimulus enhances incumbents' reelection prospects, or *partisan,* as when incoming parties reverse the policies of predecessors.

OPPORTUNISTIC MODELS

Models of opportunistic political business cycles appeared in the 1970s. William Nordhaus (1975) argued that incumbent politicians manipulate the economy to enhance reelection prospects. Specifically, expansionary macroeconomic policies are used to stimulate the economy and lower the unemployment rate prior to an election, and myopic voters respond by voting for the incumbent party. Given the model's expectational Phillips curve, inflationary consequences of the pre-election expansion are largely delayed until after the election, when contractionary policies are used to reduce inflation.

The Nordhaus model generated much interest and research, but ultimately was a victim of the rational expectations revolution. Nordhaus had assumed adaptive expectations. In his model pre-election stimulus produced favorable outcomes only because it was not anticipated. In essence, voters were repeatedly tricked in successive electoral cycles.

In a second phase of the political business cycle literature, models incorporated rational expectations, which rule out systematic expectational errors. Rogoff and Sibert (1988) developed a rational opportunistic model in which asymmetric information replaced voter myopia in explaining electoral cycles in macroeconomic policy variables. Voters have rational expectations but are unsure of the "competence" of politicians. The model can produce an equilibrium in which incumbent politicians increase government spending in pre-election periods in an effort to signal competence (ability to produce a higher level of government services with a given revenue). Rogoff (1990) later developed a similar model where the incumbent strategically manipulates the composition of expenditures in pre-electoral years, by favoring items that are more visible to the electorate.

PARTISAN MODELS

In partisan models, political business cycles are due to party differences in ideology and economic goals. According to the pioneering work of Douglas Hibbs (1977), left-wing parties are relatively more concerned with unemployment than inflation, while the opposite is true for right-wing parties. These concerns reflect the preferences of the parties' core constituencies. Consequently, left-wing parties are expected to pursue more expansionary policies when in office. This results in a cycle in which the level of activity and inflation varies with the ideology of the incumbent.

The length of the cycle depends on the way expectations are modeled. Under adaptive expectations, the partisan effect can be long-lasting. But, under rational expectations, cycles are short-lived and depend on electoral surprises. In rational partisan models, business cycles are driven by partisan differences and uncertainty about electoral outcomes. For example, a left-wing policy maker whose election was not fully anticipated can stimulate the economy and reduce unemployment, but this effect will disappear once inflation expectations adjust. Thus, partisan cycles will be temporary, with the strongest impacts occurring after elections.

EMPIRICAL RESEARCH

The empirical literature on political business cycles is quite extensive. Overall, there is little evidence of systematic opportunistic cycles in economic outcomes, such as unemployment and output, in developed countries. The evidence is stronger for policy instruments, especially fiscal aggregates, which favors models that adopt the rational expectations assumption. Results of tests of the partisan political business cycle for the United Sates and for Organization for Economic Cooperation and Development (OECD) countries also favor rational expectations models, but the effects are somewhat stronger for outcomes than for policy instruments.

The lack of empirical evidence of opportunistic cycles in economic outcomes induced a change in the focus of research toward political budget cycles; that is, cycles in some component of the government budget. Several studies find evidence of political budget cycles in both developed and, especially, in developing countries. According to Brender and Drazen (2005), that finding is driven by the experience of "new democracies," where voters are inexperienced with electoral politics or lack the information required to detect fiscal manipulations. When only "established democracies" are considered, there is no evidence of political budget cycles. In contrast, Alt and Lassen (2006) show that, conditioning on fiscal transparency, electoral cycles are present also in a sample of nineteen OECD countries, all of which are old democracies. They identify a persistent pattern of political budget cycles in low(er) transparency countries, while no such cycles can be observed in high(er) transparency countries.

Analyzing the effects of political budget cycles on reelection prospects, Brender and Drazen (2008), conclude that election year deficits do not help the incumbent get reelected. Changing the composition of spending or targeting some voters at the expense of others may be more effective ways of increasing reelection prospects.

See also *Constituency; Incumbency; Political Economy; Political Economy, Comparative.*

. . . . FRANCISCO JOSÉ VEIGA

BIBLIOGRAPHY

Alesina, Alberto. "Macroeconomic Policy in a Two-party System as a Repeated Game." *Quarterly Journal of Economics* 102, no. 3 (August 1987): 651–678.

Alesina, Alberto, Nouriel Roubini, and Gerald Cohen. *Political Cycles and the Macroeconomy.* Cambridge: MIT Press, 1997.

Alt, James, and David Lassen. "Transparency, Political Polarization, and Political Budget Cycles in OECD Countries." *American Journal of Political Science* 50 (July 2006): 530–550.

Brender, Adi, and Allan Drazen. "Political Budget Cycles in New versus Established Democracies." *Journal of Monetary Economics* 52 (October 2005): 1271–1295.

———. "How Do Budget Deficits and Economic Growth Affect Reelection Prospects? Evidence from a Large Panel of Countries." *American Economic Review* 98 (December 2008): 2203–2220.

Chappell, Henry, and William Keech. "Party Differences in Macroeconomic Policies and Outcomes." *American Economic Review* 76 (May, 1986): 71–74.

Hibbs, Douglas. "Political Parties and Macroeconomic Policy." *American Political Science Review* 71 (December 1977): 1467–1487.

Nordhaus, William. "The Political Business Cycle." *Review of Economic Studies* 42 (April 1975): 169–190.

Rogoff, Kenneth. "Equilibrium Political Budget Cycles." *American Economic Review* 80 (March 1990): 21–36.

Rogoff, Keneth, and Anne Sibert. "Elections and Macroeconomic Policy Cycles." *Review of Economics Studies,* 55 (January 1988): 1–16.

Business Preference Formation

The scholarly literature on the formation of employers' preferences seeks to understand how managers conceptualize their interests in public policy. Three debates anchor this literature. First, scholars diverge on the relative importance of economic conditions and institutional constraints in guiding human action. A second debate concerns the level of analysis at which corporate preferences are formulated: Some believe that business interests are largely defined and acted on at the micro firm level, while others believe that preferences are formed in the collective deliberative processes of national employers associations. A third debate reflects on the appropriate causal agent in constructing preferences—employers may autonomously formulate their policy positions or they may follow the lead of government policy entrepreneurs.

These debates suggest four broad causal determinants of preference: economic characteristics of firms and sectors, firms' internal institutions for evaluating public policy, business associations (and other institutional vehicles for firm coordination), and government structures and agents that shape employers' positions on public policy.

First, some analyses derive employers' political preferences from the economic characteristics of the firm or structure of the industry to which it belongs. This economic model of preference underlies public choice and many pluralist theories, and assumes that individuals are motivated by readily apparent material circumstance.

Second, institutional analyses suggest that decision making almost always occurs under conditions of bounded rationality in which full information is not available. Institutional permutations within the firm deliver quite different competitive strategies, which, in turn, lead to very different preferences for public policy. Companies' positions on policy issues depend, in part, on the firms' organizational capabilities for gathering information; therefore, firms with in-house policy experts have different preferences from those firms without such experts. Company policy experts like Powell and DiMaggio (1991) bring ideas from the external community of policy makers back to others within the firms, a process called *boundary spanning.* Companies with government affairs offices also tend to be more supportive of government policies, because these units increase collaboration between business and government.

Third, some scholars highlight the importance of business organization to employers' preferences for economic and social policy outcomes. Corporatist employers' associations, for example, are more likely than pluralist associations to produce business positions that are supportive of social welfare spending. Corporatist associations bring employers together to discuss their broader, shared concerns and bind firms to negotiated outcomes; therefore, members will be more willing to commit to longer-term goals, even if these goals detract from shorter-term interests. Hall and Soskice (2001) argue that the institutional profiles of different "varieties of capitalism" also bring employers to assume quite different policy preferences across settings.

Finally, the state influences the formation of business preferences in both long-term structural and short-term strategic ways. Institutional structures of government (such as constitutional structure and veto points) shape the manner in which employers can press their claims on government; for example, separation of powers and federalism generally translate into greater business resistance to government, because these permit managers to try to influence successive veto points until they find a sympathetic hearing. Political entrepreneurs also may seek to mobilize business allies in support of specific pieces of legislation; in these cases, political leaders lead employers to form specific policy positions.

See also *Business Pressure in Politics; Constitutional Systems, Comparative; Lobbying.*

. . . . CATHIE JO MARTIN

BIBLIOGRAPHY

Dobbins, Frank. *Inventing Equal Opportunity.* Princeton, N.J.: Princeton University Press, 2009.

Grier, Kevin, Michael Munger, and Brian Roberts. "The Determinants of Industry Political Activity, 1978–1986." *American Political Science Review* 88 (December 1994): 911–926.

Hall, Peter, and David Soskice, eds. *Varieties of Capitalism.* New York: Oxford University Press, 2001.

Hillman, Amy, Gerald Keim, and Doug Schuler. "Corporate Political Activity: A Review and Research Agenda." *Journal of Management* 30, no. 6 (2004): 837–857.

Martin, Cathie Jo. *Stuck in Neutral.* Princeton, N.J.: Princeton University Press, 2000.

Martin, Cathie Jo, and Duane Swank. "Does the Organization of Capital Matter?" *American Political Science Review* 98 (November 2004): 593–611.

McConnell, Grant. *Private Power and American Democracy.* New York: Alfred Knopf, 1966.

Powell, Walter, and Paul DiMaggio. *The New Institutionalism in Organizational Analysis.* Chicago: University of Chicago Press, 1991.

Streeck, Wolfgang. *Social Institutions and Economic Performance.* Beverly Hills, Calif.: Sage, 1992.

Business Pressure in Politics

In any capitalist system the issue of business pressure in politics is central to the viability of the market economy and to the viability of governments as institutions capable of making decisions in the public interest. The issue is particularly pressing in the most important political constellation in the modern world, capitalist democracy; that is, in social systems that claim to combine capitalist economics (allocation through the market and private ownership of productive resources) with democratic government. In capitalist democracy, if business pressure subverts the capacity of government to rule in the public interest, then the claim to democracy is hollow. Conversely, if democratic politics creates hostility to business, then the viability of the market order is endangered.

THREE VIEWS OF BUSINESS PRESSURE

Three views of the role of business pressure have dominated debate for more than a generation. First, a structural account of business power holds that the very existence of corporate property and business control of investment decisions means that democratic government is always powerfully constrained by corporate preferences. Business thus does not have to exert overt "pressure" to exercise great influence. The most powerful statement of this view comes from American political scientist Charles Lindblom (2002). Second, a view heavily influenced by the pluralist tradition holds that, while business can be powerful, to exercise this power, it must compete successfully with other interests, this success varies, and the effectiveness of business pressure thus varies, by historical period, sector, and issue. The most influential modern statement of this view comes from David Vogel (1989). Finally, a pessimistic view of the capacity of business to exercise influence in the market economy dates from the work of economic historian, Joseph Schumpeter, in his classic, *Capitalism, Socialism, and Democracy* (1943). On this view, the rationalizing culture of democracy constantly undermines the legitimacy of business authority, surrounding it with critics and creating an increasingly hostile cultural environment.

CHANGING MODES OF BUSINESS LOBBYING

What is without doubt is that the modes of business pressure in politics have changed greatly in recent decades. Three developments are particularly important. First, business increasingly has to formally organize to exert pressure over the political process; informal elite lobbying through private, personal contact is much less important than it was a generation ago. This is reflected in the increasingly professional character of business lobby groups, such as the business roundtable in the United States, an organizational form now widely copied across the capitalist democracies. Second, business pressure has to be conducted under conditions of increasing formal regulation. The most striking instance is the growing regulation of business contributions to party and election finance. As business money has assumed increasing importance to campaigning politicians, the conditions under which it can be solicited have been subjected to more and more stringent formal controls. The third change in the last generation is the rise of the large, single corporation as a sophisticated political actor. The biggest corporations typically have interests that are too complex to be easily accommodated by traditional collectively organized forms of business pressure, such as trade associations. They also typically have the resources to build in-house expertise and lobbying capacity. The rise of public affairs or government relations departments within large firms is thus one of the most distinctive recent developments in the world of business pressure.

The rise of the giant firm as a political actor is connected to another development of the past generation: the multinational organization of business as a political actor. Business has long crossed national borders, but the surge of globalization in the past generation also has prompted a surge in the globalization of business pressure. The best known examples are multinational institutions designed to provide both a forum for business to identify its interests, and a means of turning the consciousness of common interests into political pressure. For example, the European Round Table of Industrialists now speaks for the business elite in the European Union. Dutch political economist Bastian Van Apeldoorn (2000) has shown that it was central to the creation of the common European currency, the euro. The Transatlantic Business Dialogue, more ambitiously still, organizes a group of the thirty or so of the largest U.S. and European corporations. And since 1971, the World Economic Forum has provided an even more ambitious setting for the global distillation of business interests. The forum is best known for its annual meeting in Davos, but its more important work is conducted in numerous working parties and meetings that join together the global business elite throughout the year.

THE PROBLEMS OF BUSINESS LOBBYING

Business pressure in the politics of capitalist democracies remains profoundly important—a statement to which even the most committed pluralist could assent. But business faces great problems, of which three are particularly pressing. First, it faces acute problems of collective action. Firms are simultaneously divided by the competitive pressures of a market economy and yet driven by the need to cooperate for the purpose of exercising political pressure. The globalization of business life has made collective action both more necessary and more difficult and has made more acute the tension between global outlook and interests and national jurisdictions. Second, business faces numerous new competitors and critics in civil society: environmental and consumer organizations, critics of its employment practices, and intellectual critics of the very foundation of business life in parts of the media and the higher education system. Finally, the great global financial crisis that began in 2007 in the United States damaged the claims of key parts of the business order, in the financial sector, to be able to conduct its affairs prudently, greatly increased state control and ownership of many enterprises, and raised large questions about the scale of reward enjoyed by many in the business elite. For the first time in a generation, business has found itself on the defensive politically across much of the advanced capitalist world. Nevertheless, the largest business corporations have formidable resources to organize that defense.

See also *Business Preference Formation; Campaign Finance; Capitalism and Democracy.*

. . . .   MICHAEL MORAN

BIBLIOGRAPHY
Graz, Jean-Christophe. "How Powerful Are Transnational Elite Clubs? The Social Myth of the World Economic Forum." *New Political Economy* 8, no. 3 (2003): 321–340.
Lindblom, Charles. *Politics and Markets: The World's Political-Economic Systems.* New York: Basic Books, 1977.
———. *The Market System: What It Is, How It Works, and What to Make of It.* New Haven, Conn.: Yale University Press, 2002.
Schumpeter, Joseph. 1943. *Capitalism, Socialism, and Democracy.* London: Allen and Unwin 1976.
Van Apeldoorn, Bastian. "Transnational Class Agency and European Governance: The Case of the European Round Table of Industrialists." *New Political Economy* 5, no. 2 (2000): 157–181.
Vogel, David. *Lobbying the Corporation: Citizen Challenges to Business Authority.* New York: Basic Books, 1978.
———. *National Styles of Regulation: Environmental Policy in Great Britain and the United States.* Ithaca, N.Y.: Cornell University Press, 1986.
———. *Fluctuating Fortunes: The Political Power of Business in America.* New York: Basic Books, 1989.
———. *Kindred Strangers: The Uneasy Relationship between Politics and Business in America.* Princeton, N.J.: Princeton University Press, 1996.

By(e)-election

By-elections (also spelled *bye elections* and known as *special elections* in the United States) are used to fill legislative vacancies arising during a term and between regular elections. In general the vacancy transpires due to the death or resignation of the holder of a public office, but sometimes it may happen when incumbents are deemed ineligible to continue their public duties. By-elections also occur when the results of a general election are invalidated due to voter irregularities or recall. About sixty-four countries worldwide use by-elections for all legislative vacancies, and this list includes various types of political systems. Countries ranging from China to Poland, New Zealand to Malta, and South Africa to Iran all avail by-elections when needed.

Historically, by-elections played a crucial role. During the time of Charles II, members of parliament in England had no limit to their duration. For that reason, by-elections were the prime source of recruiting new members to the parliament.

To better comprehend the significance of by-elections, one has to acknowledge their functions for the political system. By-elections perform several purposes, extending beyond the apparent objective of filling vacant legislative seats. Voter turnout is usually low for most by-elections in comparison to general elections. Not all by-elections prove important, but some have consequences for the legislature, political parties, election campaigns, governance, and the media. By-elections can sometimes prove an important way of recruitment of new representatives; they have led to turnover of as much as 10 percent in some British parliaments. By-elections also have created a route for parties to bring back leading frontbenchers defeated in the previous general election. The political ramifications following key contests have had considerable impact on subsequent events—and indeed on subsequent by-elections. The special elections in the Unites States have a minor impact on the political system due to a range of factors, namely, (1) the U.S. system consists of periodic fixed-term elections; (2) particular outcomes do not effect the timings of the general elections; and (3) U.S. House of Representative elections for all members are held every two years, with one-third of the members of the Senate elected for six-year terms every two years. Additionally, the United States is a two-party system in which special elections do not typically promote the minority party.

In general, by-election results are unfavorable for the governing party. Though certain by-elections have proven to be critical tests for minor parties, increasing their legislative strength, shaping expectations about party fortunes, and increasing the credibility of challenges to the established two-party system. By-elections, in contrary to general elections, embolden citizens to vote for the other party—the less significant party—which they would not vote for in general elections when their vote might change the political party in power. By-election victories for the governing party boost its popularity and support, while a loss leads to the disheartening of party supporters and sometimes divisions in party lines. Nevertheless, by-elections can provide significant political consequences for the political parties as well as the political system.

See also *Electoral Rules; Electoral Systems; Representation and Representative; Representative Systems.*

. . . .   FARAH JAN

BIBLIOGRAPHY
Butler, David. "By-elections and Their Interpretations." In *By-elections in British Politics,* edited by Chris Cook and John Ramsden, 1–12. London: UCL Press, 1997.
Feigert, Frank B., and Pippa Norris. "Do By-elections Constitute Referenda? A Four-country Comparison." *Legislative Studies Quarterly* 15 (May 1990): 183–200.

Cabinets and Cabinet Formation

The British essayist Walter Bagehot, in *The English Constitution,* famously defined the cabinet as a "combining committee—a *hyphen* which joins, a *buckle* which fastens the legislative part of the State to the executive part of the State" (Bagehot, 1867, 68). As such, the concept does not travel far outside parliamentary systems of government, but one needs to amend it only slightly to give it wider applicability: It is the most senior constitutional body, politically responsible (to parliament or president or both, depending on the political system) for directing the state bureaucracy. The cabinet is part of the broader concept of the government; not all (junior) ministers are cabinet ministers. In the United Kingdom, for example, of over one hundred ministers, only about a quarter are in the cabinet.

CABINET STRUCTURE

With regard to the cabinet function, the constitutional conventions are for it to deliberate collectively and for each cabinet minister's voice to count equally. Together, collective decision making and ministerial collegiality form an ideal type of cabinet government, with existing cabinets often deviating from one or both of these norms. Both collectiveness (the arena of decision making) and collegiality (the distribution of power) are dimensions of the cabinet's structure.

Dutch coalition cabinets, for example, are still close to the ideal type, with a cabinet that meets at least weekly for several hours, during which proposals are actually debated and sometimes amended, and with a prime minister whose formal powers are constrained by being the leader of only one of the political parties in the governing coalition. In the United States, the experience is completely different in both respects: although there is a "Cabinet Room" in the White House, and most newly elected presidents promise to use it, the president primarily deals with individual department secretaries bilaterally, and the cabinet as such rarely meets to deliberate on government policy. In addition, since the president is not only the chair of this cabinet but also the person to whom secretaries answer, the president holds a very powerful position. In this way, the U.S. cabinet is probably closest to the seventeenth-century origins of the cabinet as a set of individual advisers to

the (British) monarch. That collectiveness and collegiality are linked in the two examples above does not mean that the two dimensions can be collapsed. A prime minister can be dominant but exercise powers within meetings of the full cabinet (as is the case in Swedish single-party cabinets); or the prime minister can really be simply "a first among equals" without the cabinet serving as the principal venue for deliberating and deciding government policy (as seems to be the case in the Swiss Federal Council, where the position of prime minister rotates and ministers enjoy considerable autonomy).

Both collectivity and collegiality were confused in the (primarily British) debate about prime ministerial versus cabinet government, which led to the inconclusiveness of that debate. Recently this debate has broadened into the hypothesis that most countries with parliamentary systems of government are witnessing a trend of "presidentialization." Presidentialization occurs when prime ministers become less dependent on their political parties, fight more personalized election campaigns, and have more power over other ministers within the cabinet. This last aspect of presidentialization need not be the result of the prime minister being given more formal powers or resources; a greater need for coordination within the government, the internationalization of political decision making with the prime minister attending international summit meetings, and the tendency of the media to personalize government are also contributing factors to presidentialization. Others have criticized the ill-defined nature of the presidentialization thesis and have found little evidence for it.

Table 1 illustrates the poles of the two dimensions, on both of which intermediate positions can be discerned. Between collective and fragmented cabinets, for example, are segmented cabinets in which cabinet committees play an important role, especially where cabinet committees enjoy some degree of autonomy from the full cabinet. With regard to the distribution of power within cabinets, the intermediate position between monocratic and collegial cabinets takes hold when an inner cabinet dominates decision making. During 1970s and 1980s, for example, Canadian cabinets had both strong cabinet committees, which were even allocated their own budget at times, and an inner cabinet in the form of the Operations Committee of the Priority and Planning Committee. In Canada, an inner cabinet was set up because the cabinet itself had

TABLE 1: TWO DIMENSIONS OF CABINET GOVERNMENT

DISTRIBUTION OF POWER	ARENA OF DECISION MAKING	
	Fragmented	Collective
Monocratic	e.g., U.S. presidential cabinets	e.g., Swedish single-party cabinets
Collegial	e.g., the Swiss cabinet	e.g., Dutch coalition cabinets

grown too large, but this need not be the only reason. Many coalition cabinets have an inner cabinet or coalition committee, bringing together the leaders of the governing parties to prevent intracoalition conflicts from threatening the survival of the government.

CABINET FORMATION

By convention, a new cabinet is said to take office with each parliamentary or presidential election, with a change of party composition, or with a change of the head of government. Although the latter two changes can occur without elections, this is rare and usually intended as an interim solution after a cabinet crisis, to take care of government until the next scheduled or early elections are held. If the cabinet is monocratic, the president or the prime minister of a single-party cabinet forms the cabinet without much interference from others. In practice, however, even such cabinets are often coalitions of sorts: prime ministers must unite their own party and appease rival factions by appointing rival-party leaders to cabinet positions; presidents in presidential systems often want to broaden support in the legislature to ease passage of their proposals by inviting politicians from outside their own party to join the cabinet.

Where cabinets are based on a coalition of parties, their formation usually involves intensive negotiations between party leaders. An extensive body of literature, primarily based on rational choice theory, seeks to explain the outcome of the formation process in terms of the cabinet's party composition. Much less attention has been given to the allocation of particular portfolios to coalition parties. In 1996, Michael Laver and Kenneth Shepsle argued that the cabinet's policies are determined by this portfolio allocation as each party sets the agenda for the government departments that are led by a minister from its own ranks, in fact assuming that all cabinets are both collegial and fragmented. Scholars who argue instead that collective decision making plays an important role in cabinets have recently drawn attention to the fact that, increasingly, the cabinet formation results in a written coalition agreement replacing the individual parties' election manifestos as the basis for policy making; in the 1940s, 33 percent of European coalition cabinets had such a document, compared with 81 percent of such cabinets in the 1990s. In some cases the documents are quite comprehensive, with the record set by a coalition agreement of 43,550 words in Belgium (Müller

and Strøm, 2008). Given the negotiations involved, the cabinet formation can take quite a long time. Forming monocratic cabinets and single-party cabinets takes less time, as does the formation of coalition cabinets with a fixed-party composition (the Swiss "magic formula") or those based on a preelectoral coalition. In other cases, the number of viable alternative combinations of parties may prolong the bargaining process and produce several failed attempts before a new cabinet can take office.

See also *Coalition Formation; Coalition Theory.*

. . . . RUDY B. ANDEWEG

BIBLIOGRAPHY

Andeweg, Rudy B. "On Studying Governments." In *Governing Europe*, edited by J. Hayward and A. Menon, 39–60. Oxford: Oxford University Press, 2003.

Andeweg, Rudy B., and Arco Timmermans. "Conflict Management in Coalition Government." In *Cabinets and Coalition Bargaining*, edited by Kaare Strøm, Wolfgang C. Müller, and Torbjörn Bergman, 269–300. Oxford: Oxford University Press, 2008.

Bagehot, Walter. *The English Constitution*, 1867. Glasgow: Fontana/Collins, 1963.

De Winter, Lieven, and Patrick Dumont. "Uncertainty and Complexity in Cabinet Formation." In *Cabinets and Coalition Bargaining*, edited by Kaare Strøm, Wolfgang C. Müller, and Torbjörn Bergman, 123–157. Oxford: Oxford University Press, 2008.

Helms, Ludger. *Presidents, Prime Ministers, and Chancellors: Executive Leadership in Western Democracies.* New York: Macmillan, 2005.

Laver, Michael, and Kenneth A. Shepsle. *Making and Breaking Governments: Cabinets and Legislatures in Parliamentary Democracies.* Cambridge: Cambridge University Press, 1996.

Müller, Wolfgang C., and Kaare Strøm. "Coalition Agreements and Cabinet Governance." In *Cabinets and Coalition Bargaining*, edited by Kaare Strøm, Wolfgang C. Müller, and Torbjörn Bergman, 159–199. Oxford: Oxford University Press, 2008.

Moe, Ronald C. *The President's Cabinet: Evolution, Alternatives, and Proposals for Change.* New York: Novinka, 2004.

Neto, Octavio Amorim. "The Presidential Calculus: Executive Policymaking and Cabinet Formation in the Americas." *Comparative Political Studies* 39, no. 4 (2006): 415–440.

Webb, Paul, and Thomas Poguntke. "The Presidentialization of Contemporary Democratic Politics: Evidence, Causes, and Consequences." In *The Presidentialization of Politics*, edited by Thomas Poguntke and Paul Webb, 336–356. Oxford: Oxford University Press, 2005.

Caciquismo/Coronelismo

Caciquismo and *coronelismo* refer to informal political boss or chieftain systems in Latin America and Spain. The term *cacique* derives from a Caribbean indigenous word used at the time of the Spanish conquest. In Spain and Spanish-speaking Latin America, caciques are local bosses exercising power in informal and personalistic ways, often using violence or threats thereof to buttress their power. National officials often recognize the cacique's de facto authority in a locality and work through the cacique to distribute government largess. The officials rely on caciques to provide effective policing of the area the caciques control, which often leads to the determination that the political cost of challenging a cacique's authority would be excessive. Caciquismo has flourished in the larger Latin American nations, reflecting regionalism and the incapacity of central states to consolidate their authority across the nation. Most caciques emerge out of their communities because they possess sources of power such as access to land, loans needed by poor peasants to survive, or political connections.

Coronelismo refers to the variant of caciquismo practiced in Brazil, especially its rural northeast. In colonial Brazil, *coronel* was the highest rank in the colonial militia, to which local bosses sought to attach their armed followers.

See also *Latin American Politics and Society; Latino Politics.*

. . . . JOSEPH L. KLESNER

Caesarism

Named after the first Roman Emperor Julius Caesar (100–44 BCE), Caesarism connotes absolute rule, dictatorship, and use of military force. It is believed François Auguste Romieu, in his *Ere des Césars* (1850), first coined the neologism. Caesarism is the phenomenon of a political ruler's assertion of great political and military force at a time of national crisis, uniting the populace while avoiding constitutional limitations on executive power. As a political concept, Caesarism came into being with the rise of mass democracy after the French Revolution (1789–1799). Opposed to representative institutions and mediating elements between ruler and ruled, Caesarism, as Oswald Spengler stated in *Decline of the West*, is a return to formlessness. As institutions are emptied of meaning, the personal power of the Caesarist ruler becomes fundamental to the existence of the nation. Spengler calls Caesarism the period of contending states when gigantic private wars are fought to promote democracy for states without form and a history. Caesarism characterizes the new modern politics of mass democracy where the private individual absorbed in money effaces the national identities of tradition, institutions, and culture. The strong ruler steps into the anarchical abyss of mass democracy and money appealing to the primitive instincts of religion, race, and blood. Politics becomes infused with mysticism and secular religious symbols expressed in the mythic figure of the leader representing the people.

See also *Authoritarianism, African; Charisma; Religion and Politics; West, Decline of the.*

. . . . JOANNE TETLOW

Calhoun, John

Leading American politician and theorist, John Caldwell Calhoun (1782–1850) served as a South Carolina state representative, U.S. representative, U.S. senator, secretary of war and of state, and vice president of the United States. Calhoun's political writings reflect his responses to the great political problems of nineteenth-century America: the conflict over the Tariff Acts of 1828 and 1832, the slavery crisis, and the concentration of political power in the national government under President Andrew Jackson. All of these convinced Calhoun that America's constitutional foundations were in danger.

Calhoun addresses these dangers in his primary political writings. *A Disquisition on Government* (1851) looks at the nature of man and government in addition to expounding the doctrine of the concurrent majority—the right of significant interests to have a veto over the enactment or implementation of a public law. *A Discourse on the Constitution and Government of the United States* (1851) traces the constitutional foundation for the concurrent majority within the American political tradition and argued for its restoration. By recognizing and incorporating natural social divisions into a coherent whole, Calhoun contended that the concurrent majority ameliorates social and political tensions through deliberation and compromise, distinguishing it from the numerical majority that deals with these tensions through force.

Calhoun believed that the numerical majority fails to consider a political community's natural diversity. As a result, it can only assess preference through overall electoral victory, which overrates the homogeneity of the political environment. Moreover, the majority system supposes that the apparatus of voting can resolve all conflict, even when no consensus of opinion exists. The numerical majority attempts to control government at any cost by emphasizing political party at the expense of constitutional principles, and the numerical majority's inability to assess the true preferences of the citizenry threatens to undermine the electoral and constitutional foundations of republican government.

Calhoun's critique has been interpreted as evidence of a lack of concern for popular rule. He is seen as the protector of particular interests, especially slaveholders, and his defense of slavery as a "positive good" instead of a necessary evil is thought to derail America's liberal tradition. Calhoun is seen as overthrowing America's Lockean origins through a purposeful rejection of James Madison's politics, especially the emphasis on natural rights. But his defense of slavery is neither the most important nor the most consuming aspect of his political thought.

Focusing on the relationship between the *Disquisition* and the *Discourse* shows that Calhoun's focus is on liberty, the nature of the American union, constitutionalism, and states' rights. British philosopher and political theorist John Stuart Mill (1806–1873) applauds Calhoun's understanding of federal representative government as a means of providing for greater participation while avoiding conflict. Calhoun also provides a disincentive to the growth of a corruptive central governing authority. Lord Acton (1834–1902), British historian and moralist, finds in Calhoun's presentation of an authentic constitutional tradition a defense of democratic theory and the American union. Calhoun's political thought is central to an understanding of America's constitutional tradition.

See also *Natural Rights; States' Rights.*

. . . . JORDON B. BARKALOW

BIBLIOGRAPHY

Coit, Margaret L. *John C. Calhoun.* Englewood Cliffs, N.J.: Prentice-Hall, 1970.

Hemphill, Edwin W., ed. *Papers of John C. Calhoun,* 24 vols. Columbia: University of South Carolina Press, 1969.

Lence, Ross M. *The Political Philosophy of John C. Calhoun.* Indianapolis, Ind.: Liberty Fund, 1992.

von Holst, Herman E. *John C. Calhoun.* Englewood Cliffs, N.J.: Prentice Hall, 1970.

Wilson, Clyde N. *The Essential Calhoun.* New Brunswick, N.J.: Transaction, 2000.

Calvin, John

John Calvin (1509–1564), the most systematic Protestant theologian of the Reformation, has, through his writings, influenced the nature and scope of secular authority and the right of Christians to resist their rulers. Born in Noyon, France, Calvin studied liberal arts in Paris, law at Orléans, and then a humanist curriculum at the Collège Royal in Paris. In 1534, he fled to Basel, Switzerland, because of his association with evangelical figures. In Basel in 1536, he published a compendium of the Reformed faith titled *Institutes of the Christian Religion,* a work that he would continue to revise and expand throughout his life.

The *Institute's* success gained Calvin notoriety in evangelical circles, and he was recruited by Guillaume Farel (1489–1565) to help organize a Reformed church in Geneva. Enemies of Farel and Calvin secured their expulsion from Geneva in 1538, and Calvin moved to Strasbourg where he became leader of the French Reformed community and participated in religious dialogues among participants. In 1541, supporters in Geneva recalled Calvin who, using his practical experience heading a community in Strasbourg, created a new church ordinance and order of worship that became the basis of the Genevan reformation. He remained at the center of the Genevan church until his death.

Calvin's frequent revisions to his most important work, the *Institutes,* reveal an evolution in his political thought. In the first published edition in 1536, his views share much with those of the mature Martin Luther (1483–1546). Calvin offers a form of Luther's doctrine of the two kingdoms when he asserts that the state is charged only with maintaining external righteousness by regulating such acts as blasphemy and should not interfere with a believer's personal relationship with God. Calvin also largely agreed with Luther that all subjects owe political obedience to the authorities and should offer only passive resistance to even tyrannical rulers because God places all rulers in power. However, again following Luther's line of thinking by the mid-1530s, he accepted that "popular magistrates" in some circumstances may collectively resist tyrants.

By the 1539 and 1543 editions of the *Institutes,* Calvin's thought had evolved, reflecting his experiences as a participant in the civil life of Strasbourg and Geneva. Calvin expanded several sections on church organization where he advocated an aristocratic or mixed form of government. This shift had an impact on his view of civil polity. For the first time, he fully articulated a preference for mixed government, arguing that the divinely ordained form for ecclesiastical government must provide the model for civil polity. He also shifted his views on secular authority. No longer did he advocate clearly separate secular and ecclesiastical spheres. Instead he presented the Christian polity as a single whole in which both secular and ecclesiastical institutions derived their authority directly from God and cooperated to govern a polity of like-minded believers. This conceptualization of the Christian polity came out of Calvin's experiences and offered an influential new theory of the relationship between ecclesiastical and civil authorities in Reformed communities.

See also *Luther, Martin; Reformation Political Thought.*

. . . . ERIC NELSON

BIBLIOGRAPHY

Bouwsma, W. J. *John Calvin: A Sixteenth-Century Portrait.* Oxford: Oxford University Press, 1988.

Calvin, John. *John Calvin: Selections from his Writings,* edited by John Dillenberger. Garden City, N.Y.: Doubleday, 1971.

Höpfl, Harro. *The Christian Polity of John Calvin.* Cambridge: Cambridge University Press, 1982.

———. *Luther and Calvin on Secular Authority.* Cambridge: Cambridge University Press, 1991.

Calvinism

See *Calvin, John.*

Cambridge School

The *Cambridge school* refers to that coterie of intellectual historians educated at Cambridge University, chief among whom were Quentin Skinner and J. G. A. Pocock, whose work emphasized the importance of various contexts to the study of political thought. They sought by their approach to offer a new interpretation of the history of political thought that would avoid the confusions to which, they alleged, prevailing texualist modes of interpretation, above all, were prone.

Recent accounts of the school's genesis identify the work of Cambridge historian Peter Laslett as seminal to its creation. Laslett, who in 1949 published an edition of Sir Robert Filmer's (1588–1653) *Patriarcha,* showed in his research that Filmer's *Patriarcha* had been composed perhaps as early as 1630 but only published in 1679 to 1680, whereas his other writings had appeared in 1648. Thus Laslett pointed to "three contexts," or historical moments, that had to be considered before the historian could comprehend "what [Filmer] had intended and how he had been understood" at the time. Laslett subsequently established, with the publication in 1960 of his critical edition of John Locke's (1632–1704) *Treatises on Government,* that the *Treatises* had been written perhaps as early as 1681, several years before Locke published them anonymously in 1689. The setting of this date called into question the thesis that Locke's intention in writing the *Treatises* had been to make a post hoc apology for the Glorious Revolution of 1688, and permitted historians to consider the possibility that he had intended to advocate rebellion in England from the outset.

The emphasis Laslett's work placed on context provided by certain historical moments strongly influenced J. G. A. Pocock, a New Zealand–born graduate student then at Cambridge University under the tutelage of historian Herbert Butterfield.

Pocock's dissertation, expanded and published as *The Ancient Constitution and the Feudal Law* in 1957, declared itself to be an effort in the *history of historiography*, a term he would later apply to his life's work, but his best known and most influential contribution to the history of political thought would prove to be *The Machiavellian Moment*. First appearing in 1975, it argued for the existence of a continuity between the political thought of Machiavelli—seen as issuing in the revival of a "republican ideal" taken from Aristotle—and the "civic consciousness" of Puritan England and America during the Revolution. After holding teaching posts in New Zealand, Pocock emigrated to the United States, eventually settling at Johns Hopkins University, where in the mid-2000s he was the Harry C. Black Professor of History Emeritus.

Quentin Skinner, shortly after becoming a Fellow at Christ's Church College in Cambridge in 1962, published several articles on interpretive and methodological questions, the most important of which, "Meaning and Understanding in the History of Ideas," became the "manifesto of an emerging method" and closely associated with the approach of the Cambridge school as a whole. In "Meaning and Understanding," Skinner attacked textualist approaches to the history of political thought for often issuing in anachronism through neglect of external evidence crucial to interpretation of texts. Thus, for example, scholars who ignored the fact that contemporaries of Thomas Hobbes and Pierre Bayle had understood their intention "to deal both ironically and destructively with the prevailing theological orthodoxies" were in danger of erecting mythologies rather than writing histories of political thought. Likewise, Skinner criticized contextualists for wrongly presuming their accounts of social contexts and conditions as sufficient to supply an understanding of authorial intent. Instead, he stressed the importance of attending to the manner in which a word or idea was used in a given context, believing such recourse to linguistic conventions would reveal whether and to what extent political theorists adhered to or departed from the regnant ideas of their time. Accordingly, in his 1978 *The Foundations of Modern Political Thought*, Skinner sought to "construct a general framework within which the writings of the more prominent theorists can then be situated" and more fully understood. In 1996, Skinner became the Regius Professor of Modern History at Cambridge University.

See also *Political Discourse; Political Thought, Foundations of.*

. . . .   RAYMOND MERCADO

BIBLIOGRAPHY

Pocock, J. G. A. *The Ancient Constitution and the Feudal Law.* Cambridge: Cambridge University Press, 1987.

———. *The Machiavellian Moment.* Princeton: Princeton University Press, 2003.

———. "Quentin Skinner: The History of Politics and the Politics of History." *Common Knowledge* 10, no. 3 (Fall 2004): 532–550.

———. "Present at the Creation: With Laslett to the Lost Worlds." *International Journal of Public Affairs* 2, no. 2 (2006): 7–17.

Skinner, Quentin. "The Limits of Historical Explanations." *Philosophy* 4 (1966): 199–215.

———. *The Foundations of Modern Political Thought,* 2 vols. Cambridge: Cambridge University Press, 1978.

———. "Meaning and Understanding in the History of Ideas." *History and Theory* 8, no. 1 (1969): 3–53.

Tarcov, Nathan. "Quentin Skinner's Method and Machiavelli's *Prince.*" *Ethics* 92, no. 4 (July 1982): 692–709.

Tully, James, ed. *Meaning in Context: Quentin Skinner and His Critics.* Princeton: Princeton University Press, 1988.

Campaign Advertising

Campaign advertising is the use of paid-for political ads to communicate a political party or candidate's message to the public, in an effort to influence decision making and win votes. Campaign ads provide the opportunity to send carefully crafted, unadulterated messages directly to the electorate and are an integral component of the information environment in an election campaign. While campaign advertising is primarily associated with American-style, candidate-centered campaigns, campaign advertising also features in-party-centered systems found across Europe. In recent years however, nonparty-based organizations have increased their use of paid-for political advertising to influence ballot measures resulting from initiative or referendum processes. For example, in November 2008 California voters passed Proposition 8, a constitutional amendment banning gay marriage, after record breaking spending on advertising funded largely by religious groups, including $20 million from the Mormon Church. Across Europe, campaign advertising for the European No Campaign on the European Union (EU) Constitution was managed outside traditional party organizations and funded primarily by wealthy individuals from member states.

THE POSTMODERN CAMPAIGN

Proposition 8 illustrates another key feature of campaign advertising—the move from the modern campaign, where advertising was based predominantly on broadcast television and radio advertising, to the postmodern campaign, characterized by the use of advertising mediums driven by advances in information and communication technologies (e.g., the Internet, mobile phones, and social networking sites) to target ads to voters based on their self-identified most important issue. Using sophisticated databases and mapping technology like GeoVote and Voter Vault, parties and candidates are able to microtarget messages to individual voters based on sociodemographic characteristics, consumer behavior, and values, thus maximizing the opportunity to get the right message to the right voter. The Obama campaign in the United States successfully targeted younger voters in battleground states using mobile phone technology, and in the United Kingdom, the Tories have used Spotify, a music streaming service, to target a message on debt to young people and encourage them to vote Conservative in the next election.

Advances in information and communication technology pose problems for campaign advertising, which has been subject to extensive regulation. In the United States, campaign advertising for federal (national) office is regulated by the Federal Election Commission (FEC) and governed by key

Non-political party groups have become more active in political advertising, such as the campaign to pass Proposition 8 in California. Spending in support of the proposition to ban same-sex marriage far surpassed those against it, and voters passed the proposition into law.

SOURCE: AP Images

legislation including the Federal Elections Campaign Act (FECA; 1971, 1974) and the Bipartisan Campaign Reform Act (BCRA; 2002). The FEC is charged with maintaining transparency and accountability by regulating the source, disclosure, and sponsorship requirements of campaign advertisements. Since the BCRA, two standards are applied in regulating ads: express advocacy and electioneering communications. However, the electioneering communications standard only applies to campaign ads appearing on broadcast, cable, or satellite transmission, exempting many other advertising media: newspapers; direct mail; billboards or posters; and electronic media, including Internet websites, email, and social networking sites.

The regulatory focus on broadcast advertising stems from the growing number of, resources allocated to, and unintended consequences of (particularly) negative ads. The thirty-second television spot, the workhorse of campaign advertising, is the primary means by which citizens are exposed to campaign ads, and the use of spots for presidential and congressional elections has increased dramatically since 2000. Indeed, many critics claim the costs associated with the production and airtime required for television ads are largely responsible for the significant increases in campaign spending. This charge is not without merit: Fundraising for the 2008 election totaled over $3 billion for federal candidates, with fundraising in the presidential race alone up 80 percent from 2004. Presidential candidates Barack Obama and John McCain spent $440 million on national ads alone, producing some six hundred thousand airings.

Since 2000, the Wisconsin Advertising Project, using data from TNS Media Intelligence/Campaign Media Analysis Group, has made available data on the content, targeting, and frequency of political ads. This has helped provide some of the empirical evidence for perhaps the key debate surrounding campaign advertising: the increased use and consequences of negative ads. Scholars, politicians, pundits, and journalists have expressed concern for the (un)intended consequences of negative advertising on the health of representative democracy, and more specifically on voter learning, engagement, and turnout.

NEGATIVE ADS

While a dominant feature of recent U.S. elections, the use of negative ads is not a new phenomenon. In the 1964 presidential election, Lyndon Johnson's "Daisy Girl" television ad capitalized on Barry Goldwater's threat to use nuclear weapons in the ongoing U.S. conflict in Vietnam. The ad, which ran only once (bowing to Republican Party protest), contrasted a young girl playfully counting petals pulled from a flower in a field of daisies and a male voiceover counting down a nuclear launch; the girl was eventually subsumed in the blackened mushroom cloud. The controversial "Daisy Girl," former president George H. W. Bush's "Willie Horton" ad linking Michael Dukakis with murderer Willie Horton, and the 527 group's "Swift Boat Veterans" campaign ad attacking John Kerry's Vietnam service record are now classic examples of how negative ads can successfully influence the discourse, direction, and outcome of election campaigns.

However, there is some risk to negative advertising, because ads can backfire. In Britain, the Conservative Party's "Demon Eyes" ad aimed to reframe Tony Blair's broad smile and wide eyes, once considered positive attributes, to reveal his underlying insincerity and untrustworthiness. Whilst the Conservatives were censured by the Advertising Standards Agency for portraying Blair as sinister and dishonest, the ad also crystallized public opinion against the Tories, who, in the public's eyes, were seen as out of touch, unduly negative, and desperate.

Scholarly evidence from experimental and survey research on how negative ads impact mobilization and participation is mixed. Stephen Ansolabehere and Shanto Iyengar's (1995) benchmark study found that negative advertising suppresses turnout, particularly for the nonpartisan electorate, which may serve to incentivize candidates who benefit from low turnout to engage in this form of advertising. More recently, evidence suggests that negative advertising depresses the public mood, which has indirect and unequal effects on turnout. While the thirty-second spot has been vilified for increasing the perceived superficiality of the information environment and the so-called dumbing down of political discourse, a number of studies have found positive effects of negative advertising. With this, scholars have disputed the demobilization hypothesis with evidence suggesting that negative advertising can actually

Britain's Conservative Party issued this "demon eyes" ad to sway public opinion against Tony Blair and the Labour Party. It is one example of negative advertising, which can both sway voters and turn them off from voting.

SOURCE: AP Images

differences in conceptualization and measurement of negative advertising may contribute to the ongoing empirical debate over their impact on representative democracy.

See also *Campaign Finance; Campaigns.*

. . . .   JENNIFER (VAN HEERDE) HUDSON

BIBLIOGRAPHY
Ansolabehere, Stephen, and Shanto Iyengar. *Going Negative: How Attack Ads Shrink and Demobilize the Electorate.* New York: Free Press, 1995.
CNN Election Center. "Election Tracker: Ad Spending." CNN Politics. www.edition.cnn.com/ELECTION/2008/map/ad.spending/.
Dolan, Christopher J. "Two Cheers for Negative Ads." In *Lights, Camera, Campaign! Media, Politics, and Political Advertising,* edited by David A. Schwartz, 45–71. New York: Peter Lang, 2004.
Finkel, Steven E., and John G. Geer. "A Spot Check: Casting Doubt on the Demobilizing Effect of Attack Advertising." *American Journal of Political Science* 42, no. 2 (1998): 573–595.
Freedman, Paul, and Ken Goldstein. 1999. "Measuring Media Exposure and the Effects of Negative Campaign Ads." *American Journal of Political Science* 43, no. 4 (1999): 1189–1208.
Geer, John G. "Assessing Attack Advertising: A Silver Lining." In *Campaign Reform: Insights and Evidence,* edited by Larry M. Bartels and Lynn Vavreck. Ann Arbor: University of Michigan Press, 2000.
———. *In Defense of Negativity: Attack Ads in Presidential Campaigns.* Chicago: University of Chicago Press, 2006.
Goldstein, Ken, and Paul Freedman. "Lessons Learned: Campaign Advertising in the 2000 Elections." *Political Communication* 19, no. 5 (2002): 5–28.
Jamieson, Kathleen Hall, Paul Waldman, and Susan Scheer. 2000. "Eliminate the Negative? Defining and Redefining Categories of Analysis for Political Advertisements." In *Crowded Airwaves,* edited by James Thurber, Candice Nelson, and David Dulio, 44–64. Washington, D.C.: Brookings Institution Press, 2000.
Lau, Richard, and Lee Sigelman. "Effectiveness of Negative Political Advertising." In *Crowded Airwaves,* edited by James Thurber, Candice Nelson, and David Dulio, 10–43. Washington, D.C.: Brookings Institution Press, 2000.
Norris, Pippa. *A Virtuous Circle: Political Communications in Postindustrial Societies.* Cambridge: Cambridge University Press, 2000.
Stevens, Daniel. "The Relationship between Negative Political Advertising and Public Mood: Effects and Consequences." *Journal of Elections, Public Opinion, and Parties* 18, no. 2 (2008): 153–177.

stimulate turnout. Furthermore, John Geer (2000, 2006) has shown that negative ads hold a higher information content than positive ads, are more issue than trait or value oriented, and are more likely to be supported by evidence.

Some of the disparity in the findings about the impact of negative advertising stems from the debate over defining negativity. Many have argued that negative ads have a legitimate place in campaigns and elections because they make genuine contrasts between candidates (parties) on policy, ideology or traits, whereas "attack" advertising serve no other purpose than to malign and assail the opposition. Thus, on normative grounds, there appears to be little justification for limiting the use of negative ads, as they serve an important role in transferring information from the candidate or party to the voter; however, a similar case cannot be made for attack ads that stretch the boundaries between truth and fiction and serve to obfuscate the actuality of party, policy, or personal realities. A number of studies have failed to make this distinction, relying on a two-category comparison of positive versus negative ads in lieu of more refined categorization demarcating positive versus negative, comparative, or contrast ads, or comparing positive ads to attack ads across trait or issue appeals. Thus,

Campaign Finance

Campaign finance refers to money that is spent for purposes of political competition. In modern liberal democracies, such funds are not necessarily devoted to election campaigns. When senior scholars James Pollock and Louise Overacker began analyzing the role of money in politics, they started in the United States, looking at the money spent to influence the outcome of a federal election. Their starting point has dominated perception of the subject ever after. "Campaign funds" is the subject heading under which the Library of Congress catalogs all books dealing with money in politics and the classification is the major target of any U.S. scholar who approaches the subject.

During the second half of the twentieth century, U.S. political scientist Alexander Heard tried to bridge the glaring gap of perception between U.S. and foreign scholars when he created the broader term, *costs of democracy.* Arnold Heidenheimer, a European researcher, added the term *party finance,* and Europeans may have applauded this enlargement of perception. However, American author Delmer Dunn returned to the traditional trail and many others followed in the footprints of their forebears. To this day, for U.S. scholars, *campaign finance* is the name of the game.

Regulation of campaign funds varies among the democracies. Some (like the United States) regulate the flow of contributions into campaign coffers. Some limit candidate spending only, as the United Kingdom did between 1883 and 2000. Very rarely a political finance regime (like the Canadian system) stipulates rules for contributions and expenses, for candidates and parties. Currently, no democracy provides for full transparency of all campaign funds.

RAISING CAMPAIGN FUNDS

The financial support of policies, politicians, and parties is an expression of economic and political freedom, not necessarily the consequence of influence peddling or corrupt exchanges. Individual donations in small amounts provide about half of the total funds raised in the United States and Canada, much less of it in Germany and the United Kingdom. Only in the Netherlands and Switzerland, European politicians can collect a comparable share from signed-up party members. Even the traditional left-of-center mass-membership parties raise less than a quarter of their funds from this source.

Various alleys have been explored successfully to glean grassroots funding: recruiting party members, lotteries, direct mail drives, Internet or neighborhood solicitation, and social events at the local level. Whereas personal (door-to-door and peer) solicitation for political contributions was more frequent in the 1960s, it has been superseded by computerized mass mailings since the 1970s, and Internet appeals more recently. A public benefit program (preferably matching funds or tax credits) can ensure that political fundraising will not fall victim to competing nongovernmental organizations or charities. Because matching funds and tax credits require financial contributions by individual citizens, they are more suitable to participatory democracy than direct public subsidies (flat grants), which do not require specific efforts by parties or candidates.

Money from the business community (corporate donations) is no longer a real danger in most democracies. Both means of raising plutocratic funding (direct contributions as well as institutional fundraising) have declined, mostly because their proceeds have been substituted by public subsidies. Due to political action committee money and independent expenditures, the United States may be the most important exception to that rule.

A comparatively new source of political funding is public subsidies. As with any other kind of funding, specific problems accompany them (such as rules for access and distribution). However, in combination with other sources of revenue as well as rules to enforce fairness and legitimacy (e.g., the matching principle), according to Canadian scholar Khayyam Paltiel, state aid is a means of political funding that no modern democracy should forgo.

LEVELS AND ITEMS OF CAMPAIGN SPENDING

Knowledge of political spending has improved much during recent decades, but it is still limited to a few countries. In the two biggest democracies of our time (India and the United States), the bulk of all money spent for political purposes is deployed for campaigning. Any guess between 75 and 90 percent of the total funds available for political competition can be an adequate measure for the share of campaign funds. However, not even in Canada or the United Kingdom, two other important Anglo-Saxon democracies, do campaigns devour a comparable share of all political funds. In any *Parteienstaat, partitocrazia,* or party democracy of continental Western Europe (e.g., Germany, Italy, and Austria), most funds devoted to politics are used to pay for the routine operations of parties on the ground and in that nation's capital.

Many observers suggest that, over time, campaign spending has exploded. Paid television advertising, new campaign technology, and growing numbers of salaried experts are seen to have caused unavoidable financial needs. Political competitors may sink significant amounts of money into such items just because—thanks to citizens' generosity, public subsidies, or corrupt exchanges—they can afford to do so. Surprisingly enough, current levels of political spending fall short of earlier peaks. In gross domestic product adjusted terms, U.S. presidential campaigns cost less than 30 cents per citizen in the 1920s, in the 1950s, and in 2000; about 35 cents in the 1990s; some 50 cents in the Nixon years (1968–1972); and 80 to 95 cents for Franklin Roosevelt's reelection bids in 1936 and 1940. This supply-side theory of expenditure can be demonstrated for the United States, the United Kingdom, Canada, Germany, Japan, and Austria. In these countries, per capita expenses are now much lower than they used to be, due to shrinking revenue possibilities. This is quite in line with earlier observations made by Pollock, Overacker, and Heard.

SPEND AND WIN?

Journalists and scholars have frequently claimed that money wins elections. Clearly, people who spend more and more money on political competition expect that this will have some sort of impact. With the current commercial style of campaigning, money seems to be much more relevant today than in the times of mass parties and machine politics. Money buys access to communication (newspapers, radio, television, billboards, telephones, and mailings).

Statistical analysis in examining campaign finance has been greatly enhanced by the use of computers and the wealth of available data. For the 1979 Canadian election, Seymour Isenberg found evidence of a clear relationship between being first and spending the most, and he confirmed this for the 1980 election. Using more data and different modeling, Gary Jacobson also found "a clear connection between campaign spending and election results" in the United States. However, evaluating English constituencies, Ronald Johnston found no indication "that the level of spending is a major, let alone a dominant influence on the result."

Based on spending data and election results, spending is frequently analyzed as the cause of voting. However, it may well be that donating is a means of support and a bellwether of expected success, whereas spending is just a consequence of cash at hand, not the cause of success. Thus, a simple correlation between political money and electoral success is misleading. Campaign money is most productive when other factors make winning possible—and if so, it is definitely the voters' choice and not the politicians' cash that will decide the outcome of an election.

See also *Campaign Advertising; Campaigns; Nongovernmental Organizations (NGOs); Party Finance; Political Action Committee (PAC).*

. . . .   KARL-HEINZ NASSMACHER

BIBLIOGRAPHY
Alexander, Herbert E. *Financing the 1960 Election.* Princeton, N.J.: Citizens' Research Foundation, 1962.
———. *Financing Politics. Money, Elections, and Political Reform,* 4th ed. Washington, D.C.: Congressional Quarterly Press, 1992.
Heard, Alexander. *The Costs of Democracy.* Chapel Hill: University of North Carolina Press, 1960.
Magleby, David B., Anthony Corrado, and Kelly D. Patterson, eds. *Financing the 2004 Election.* Washington, D.C.: Brookings Institution Press, 2006.
Nassmacher, Karl-Heinz. *The Funding of Party Competition: Political Finance in 25 Democracies.* Baden-Baden, Germany: Nomos Verlag, 2009.
Overacker, Louise. *Money in Elections.* New York: Macmillan, 1932.
Paltiel, Khayyam Z. "Campaign Finance: Contrasting Practices and Reforms." In *Democracy at the Polls: A Comparative Study of Competitive National Elections,* edited by David Butler, Howard R. Penniman, and Austin Ranney, 138–172. Washington, D.C.: American Enterprise Institute, 1981.
Pollock, James K. *Party Campaign Funds.* New York: Knopf, 1926.
Sridharan, Eswaran. "Electoral Finance Reform: The Relevance of International Experience." In *Reinventing Public Service Delivery in India: Selected Case Studies,* edited by Vikram K. Chand, 363–388. New Delhi: Sage Publications, 2006.

Campaigning, Negative

See *Negative Campaigning.*

Campaigns

A *campaign* is an effort on the part of a candidate or organized group to convince a segment of the population to reach a particular decision. Said differently, campaigns reflect competition over ideas. The goal of any political campaign is for a candidate to be elected so that candidate can advance specific policy goals or political ideals. In a democratic system, candidates interested in attaining political office find it necessary to campaign in order to appeal to their respective constituencies in the period preceding an election. In a presidential, congressional, statewide, or local campaign, for instance, that effort typically involves convincing registered or likely voters to support one party's political candidate over the alternative. Ultimately, those candidates who are elected are often said to have run an effective campaign, while those who lose are viewed as running an ineffective or less successful campaign.

In nearly all cases, the process is much more complicated than this simple dichotomy would suggest, but this can be a useful starting place for thinking about the campaigning process.

Although all campaigns for elective office are unique or different, there are certain similarities in political campaigns regardless of which office a candidate is trying to attain. In many respects, the most important feature of a campaign is finding effective and innovative ways of increasing one's name recognition with likely or potential voters. This can involve meeting with small groups of voters face-to-face; giving speeches to larger crowds; sending out mailers listing one's qualifications for office; and advertising on billboards, radio, or television. While some strategists might claim that any name recognition is a good thing, the most effective campaigns are designed specifically to elicit a favorable response among voters regarding the candidate. Essentially, the candidate tries to generate a positive "brand" name that will be remembered favorably by the voters when they go to their polling place on election day. In this respect, campaigning is not unlike creating a favorable image for a popular laundry detergent or brand of shampoo that shoppers will want to purchase.

Another essential aspect of a successful campaign is the ability to raise money. Creating a favorable brand name is not an inexpensive endeavor. It is costly both in terms of time and money. As such, candidates need to raise substantial sums of money in order to wage an effective campaign for any political office. Not surprisingly, the higher the stakes, the greater the amount of money needed to win an election. Presidential candidates, for instance, often find it necessary to raise enormous sums of money during the primary stage of the campaign and are still not assured the nomination for office. Congressional candidates, in contrast, spend millions of dollars in attempts to be reelected to either the House or Senate. Sending out mailings, hiring operatives to assist with campaign efforts, and advertising on both radio and television are very expensive, and require candidates for political office to constantly raise money during their campaigns.

A third important feature of a successful political campaign involves crafting a message that will resonate with the voters. Candidates running for political office against an incumbent (one who already holds political office) have to convince voters both why the incumbent should not be reelected and why the challenger represents a more viable alternative. As such, a carefully constructed message targeted to a specific subset of voters who will help the candidate win is crucial. The message a candidate employs can vary based on whether it is a statewide or national race, the economic nature of the times, or which party currently is in power in government. During the 2008 presidential campaign, for instance, Democratic candidate Barack Obama campaigned on a message or theme of change. On election day, his message of change resonated with nearly 53 percent of the American voters who were tired of eight years of control by the Bush administration. In a similar fashion, candidates for Congress or statewide legislators can run on a similar message of change. The classic notion of "throwing the bums out" is often invoked in legislative campaigns to signify that the incumbents have lost touch with the voters and should be replaced with a new face—often one that represents change from the status quo.

While all of the above factors—name recognition, money, and a message that resonates with the voters—are necessary to win an election, they are not sufficient. In nearly all cases, the success of a candidate's campaign is also contingent upon the ability of staff, volunteers, and party activists to motivate people to turn out to vote on election day. Even candidates with a well-recognized name, lots of money, and a strong message are not guaranteed victory unless their supporters are encouraged to show up and vote. This is why voter registration efforts and get-out-the-vote drives are important components to a candidate's electoral success. Clearly, a candidate can do only so much in terms of motivating voters to participate in the election. Beyond that, it takes a well-organized and highly structured campaign staff as well as volunteers to encourage people to go to the polls. Since both party's candidates seek to maximize turnout, it is ultimately the candidate whose strategies and tactics are more effective who will be the victor at the end of the day.

PRESIDENTIAL CAMPAIGNS

In many respects, the presidential campaign has become the focal point of elections in the United States. Every four years, Americans focus their attention on the pomp and circumstance associated with the presidential campaign. There is probably no equivalent political event that generates as much attention and interest in this country and around the world. Candidates vying for the highest elective office in the land often are required to start their campaign relatively early to have a chance of earning the nomination during the primary stage of the campaign. In recent years, it has almost become the case that as soon as one presidential campaign ends, the next one begins. If a candidate is to have a chance at raising the hundreds of millions of dollars necessary to wage a successful campaign, securing the delegates necessary to capture the nomination, and increasing one's name recognition on a national level, it is not surprising that candidates need to begin campaigning as early as possible—in most cases, several years in advance.

Presidential campaigns occur in two stages. The first stage involves securing the party's nomination for president during the primary stage of the election, and the second stage pits both parties' nominees against one another in the general election. During the primary stage of the campaign, those starting early often have an advantage in terms of enhancing their name recognition, raising money, and securing commitments among delegates at the presidential conventions. It is at this stage of the process that candidates begin to craft a message for their campaign that will hopefully earn them the nomination. Although a frontrunner may emerge early on, there are often a number of potentially viable candidates seeking to earn the nomination during the primary campaign. Unlike the general election, the nomination stage is actually a series of elections. Thus, momentum plays a part in the primary process—winning a number of early contests can help propel a candidate to the nomination. As a result of limited resources, time, and other constraints, a gradual winnowing process occurs the longer the primary campaign continues. Ultimately, the slate of candidates is reduced to two or three after the initial caucuses and primaries occur. With additional primaries and caucuses held on various days, eventually only one candidate from each party is left, and that candidate ends up earning the most delegates and the respective party's nomination.

Once the nomination for each candidate is secured at the party's national convention, the general election campaign begins. This usually takes place around early September, right after Labor Day. This is the stage of the process when each party's presidential candidate attempts to "seal the deal" with the American voters. This task is complicated by the fact that many voters have already made up their minds about who they intend to vote for well before the general election campaign begins. Some evidence suggests that nearly two-thirds of the American voters have already decided whom they will vote for before the final two months of the general election campaign. As such, both party's candidates use whatever opportunities are available to reach out to undecided voters or weak "leaners" who might be convinced to vote for the opposing party's candidate. It is during this stage of the campaign process that presidential candidates begin releasing television advertisements in, and traveling to, the competitive or battleground states in an attempt to secure a majority of electoral votes to eventually win the presidency.

The media plays an important role during both stages of the presidential campaign, as they are the main audience for much of what the candidates do when running for the presidency. Since media outlets want to attract as many readers or viewers as possible, they tend to focus on the "horserace" aspect of the presidential campaign. In other words, they focus much of their attention on which presidential candidate is currently in the lead, what presidential polls look like on a day-to-day basis, and what issues emphasized by the candidates seem to be resonating the most with likely or potential voters. Given the enormous costs of political advertising, presidential candidates value as much free media time as possible. If their actions are being covered by the media on a daily basis, that is less money that the candidates have to spend themselves in order to get their names out or to advertise their positions to voters. Nearly all presidential candidates travel with an entourage of press correspondents so they will be there when breaking news happens on the campaign trail. Despite the fact that their messages are being filtered through the media, candidates still value the access granted to them by various media outlets.

The presidential campaign has changed dramatically since the early days of the American republic. During much of the nineteenth century, presidential campaigns were carried out primarily by the party organizations. Presidential candidates were often said to wage what was known as a front-porch campaign—they would sit on their front porches throughout the fall greeting anyone who would come by to talk with them. However, they rarely if ever campaigned themselves. President Theodore Roosevelt was among the first to change this tradition as he traveled around the country by train during the 1904 presidential campaign. Several years later, Franklin Roosevelt was the first presidential candidate to appear in person when the Democratic Party nominated him at their convention in 1932. Since that time, the presidential campaign has steadily evolved into more of a candidate-centered system that is more familiar in the modern age. As such, candidates are largely responsible for selecting their own campaign staffs, paid consultants, and advisers with less support from the political party organizations than was the case during the nineteenth century.

CONGRESSIONAL, STATE, AND LOCAL CAMPAIGNS

Not surprisingly, congressional, state, and local campaigns receive far less attention and coverage than presidential campaigns. With literally hundreds of races at these lower levels, it is difficult for any one race in particular to generate as much attention as the presidential campaign. Every four years, and wherever possible, congressional or statewide candidates seek to ride the coattails of the presidential candidates during the election campaign. For instance, candidates for congressional or statewide offices try to appear with their respective party's presidential candidates as much as they can during campaign visits to their district or state. Not only does this generate additional attention for their own campaigns, but it also offers a form of credible endorsement given that the presidential candidates are willing to appear on the same stage as the candidates running in these more localized races. Any type of "free" media coverage in this context is a good thing for statewide or congressional candidates since it reinforces the notion that they are both well-connected and important enough for the party's presidential nominee to spend time visiting with supporters in the local constituencies. These types of candidates can also benefit from the increase in turnout during presidential election years since voters tend to go to the polls in greater numbers every four years.

During off-year or midterm elections, congressional or statewide candidates have a more difficult time generating as much media attention as might occur during a presidential campaign. However, this is probably more reflective of the candidate-centered electoral system in the United States. As noted earlier for presidential campaigns, candidates for congressional, statewide, or local races often run individually due to the candidate-centered nature of U.S. campaigns. Political parties can offer valuable services, especially in terms of voter education campaigns and get-out-the-vote efforts, but the role of parties in these types of races is far more decentralized than it used to be. Although candidates for congressional or statewide offices run under one of the two party labels, they often formulate their own campaign messages and strategies and are not unified under one broad party platform. As such, congressional candidates may run as Democrats that are both moderate and more liberal just as Republican candidates may run who are both centrist and more conservative on the ideological spectrum.

DO CAMPAIGNS MATTER?

One question that repeatedly arises in the context of research on presidential elections is whether or not campaigns actually matter in terms of the overall election outcome. This is an important question that has been widely debated in the context of electoral politics in recent decades. To the casual observer, this question has a simple answer—of course campaigns matter. After all, why would politicians go to all the trouble of raising money, scheduling campaign visits, and debating their opponents if these activities had little or no impact on the outcome of the election? This is certainly a fair question. Time and resources are certainly scarce commodities for any candidate running for political office, and candidates do not want to waste them if they suspect they are not being allocated efficiently. Yet for all the logic underlying this inquiry, political scientists remain somewhat skeptical about whether campaigns matter for a variety of different reasons.

The main reason for this skepticism is the evidence from various forecasting models of presidential elections. Every four years, political scientists offer predictions about which party's presidential candidate will win the upcoming election through the use of a variety of forecasting models. While some of the models are relatively complex in terms of the number of explanatory variables, others are fairly simple and predictions are based on factors such as the current state of the economy and the overall approval level of the incumbent administration. As is often the case, these relatively straightforward models offer an accurate prediction of the election outcome to within one or two percentage points. Since these parsimonious models can often predict the outcome of the election without accounting for any specific campaign effects, the natural question that arises is how important can campaigns be in light of this highly suggestive evidence? Furthermore, there is considerable survey evidence suggesting that a large proportion of voters make up their minds about whom to vote for months before the election occurs, which casts additional doubt on the overall effectiveness of campaigns.

Although some scholars discount the importance of campaigns in light of the above findings, many others suggest that, in most cases, the effects of campaigns may simply be muted. For instance, it may be the case that campaigns matter, but that the effects of competing campaigns tend to cancel each other out over the course of the months preceding the election. Others suggest that campaigns matter, but the effects are felt only at the margins in close, competitive elections when the number of votes between the two candidates is relatively small. Still others believe that campaigns are very effective at helping undecided voters make up their minds, but that they have little effect on the early deciders or partisan leaners who rely almost exclusively on party affiliation as a cue for whom to vote for in the upcoming election. Regardless of the scholarly evidence, it would likely be difficult to find candidates willing to forgo their campaign efforts on the off chance that the efforts might actually make a difference in terms of predicting who would go on to win the election.

See also *Democracy; Political Parties; Primaries; Republic; Voter Registration Drive; Voting Behavior.*

. . . .   JAMIE L. CARSON

BIBLIOGRAPHY

Campbell, James E. *The American Campaign: U.S. Presidential Campaigns and the National Vote,* 2nd ed. College Station: Texas A&M University Press, 2008.

———. "Forecasting the Presidential Vote in the States." *American Journal of Political Science* 36 (May 1992): 386–407.

Gomez, Brad T., and J. Matthew Wilson. "Causal Attribution and Economic Voting in American Congressional Elections." *Political Research Quarterly* 56 (September 2003): 271–282.

Herrnson, Paul S. *Congressional Elections: Campaigning at Home and in Washington.* Washington, D.C.: CQ Press, 2008.

Holbrook, Thomas M. "Campaigns, National Conditions, and U.S. Presidential Elections." *American Journal of Political Science* 38 (November 1994): 973–998.

———. *Do Campaigns Matter?* Thousand Oaks: Sage Publications, 1996.

Jacobson, Gary C. *The Politics of Congressional Elections,* 7th ed. New York: Longman, 2009.

———. "Strategic Politicians and the Dynamics of U.S. House Elections, 1946–86." *American Political Science Review* 83 (1989): 773–793.

Kolodny, Robin. *Pursuing Majorities: Congressional Campaign Committees in American Politics.* Norman: University of Oklahoma Press, 1998.

Lewis-Beck, Michael S., and Tom W. Rice. "Forecasting Presidential Elections: A Comparison of Naïve Models." *Political Behavior* 6, no. 1 (1984): 9–21.

Sellers, Patrick J. "Strategy and Background in Congressional Campaigns." *American Political Science Review* 92 (1998): 159–171.

Sigelman, Lee, and Emmett H. Buell Jr. "You Take the High Road and I'll Take the Low Road? The Interplay of Attack Strategies and Tactics in Presidential Campaigns." *Journal of Politics* 65 (May 2003): 518–531.

Wlezien, Christopher, and Robert S. Erikson. "The Timeline of Presidential Election Campaigns." *Journal of Politics* 64 (November 2002): 969–993.

Campbell, Albert Angus

Albert Angus Campbell (1910–1980) is considered by many as the father of modern political behavior and survey research in the social sciences. His contributions extend from groundbreaking research in the early use of surveys, the establishment of the University of Michigan's Survey Research Center (SRC) after World War II (1939–1945), and the entrenchment of the National Election Studies (NES) as a national resource by the National Science Foundation. Campbell's impact in political science literature has been far-reaching, because of the methods and concepts developed and the standards set by his work, from the pathbreaking *The American Voter* to his final work, *The Sense of Well-Being in America.*

Born in Indiana, Campbell was one of six children, the son of a school principal who had been educated in Latin and Greek at the University of Michigan. The family moved to Portland, Oregon, where Campbell later attended the University of Oregon, receiving a BA and an MA in psychology. At Stanford University, he obtained his doctorate in experimental psychology. His transition to social psychology came after a series of career developments, including a position teaching social psychology at Northwestern University, a research fellowship from the Social Science Research Council to study social anthropology at Cambridge, and research in the Virgin Islands on the culture and personality of the black population of St. Thomas.

During World War II, Campbell left Northwestern to join the Division of Program Surveys in the Department of Agriculture in Washington, D.C., conducting national sample surveys to determine American reactions to the war. It was here that Campbell developed his skills and interests in the survey techniques that he would later apply to his academic research program. After the war, he moved, with a number of his colleagues from the division, to the University of Michigan, becoming the first director of the SRC, where the techniques developed in the division were continued in the academic setting. It was in this context that a program for studies in political behavior was developed, in which the SRC conducted election studies during the national elections every two years. This research program led to the publication of *The American Voter* (1960), a collaborative project that set the foundation for the field of political behavior.

The American Voter put forth concepts that have become synonymous with the Michigan school approach to political behavior, an approach that centers upon the individual and the psychology of voting. As a result of Campbell and his research team's efforts, the NES has become entrenched in the social sciences and a model for election studies around the world, facilitating the development of a large comparative literature in the study of voting behavior and public opinion.

Campbell was also involved in a rich and diverse research program, in which he gave insight on partisanship, attitudes toward social change, political institutions, racial attitudes, and issues in methodology and measurement, culminating in his final publication, *The Sense of Well-Being in America: Recent Patterns and Trends* (1980). He has had a seminal influence on the establishment of political behavior as a discipline in political science, as a result of his commitment to the development and improvement of survey research and the scientific approach to the study of politics, and his willingness to tackle the tough questions in society.

See also *Political Psychology; Public Opinion; Survey Research; Voting Behavior.*

. . . . AMANDA BITTNER

BIBLIOGRAPHY

Campbell, Angus. *The Sense of Well-Being in America: Recent Patterns and Trends.* New York: McGraw-Hill, 1980.

Campbell, Angus, Philip E. Converse, Warren E. Miller, and Donald E. Stokes. *The American Voter.* Chicago: Wiley, 1960.

Converse, Philip E. "On the Passing of Angus Campbell." *American Journal of Economics and Sociology* 40, no. 4 (1981): 341–342.

Coombs, Clyde H. "Angus Campbell, 1910–1980." In *Biographical Memoirs,* vol. 56, 43–52. Washington, D.C.: National Academy of Sciences, 1987.

Katz, Daniel. "In Memoriam: Angus Campbell, 1910–1980." *Public Opinion Quarterly* 45, no. 1 (1981): 124–125.

Camus, Albert

One of the most important figures associated with French existentialism, the Algerian-born Frenchman Albert Camus (1913–1960) made significant contributions to literature, philosophy, political analysis, drama, and journalism. An important critic of the capital punishment and totalitarianism, Camus won the Nobel Prize in Literature in 1957 and died in a car crash three years later.

In 1942 Camus published the novel *The Stranger* and the essay *The Myth of Sisyphus,* two classics associated with existentialism. The point of departure for both is that humans are often unable to make sense of the world. In the shadow of the death of God (and his surrogates), announced by German philosopher Friedrich Nietzsche in the late nineteenth century, justifiable belief in absolute certainty has become virtually impossible, and the world exceeds the ability to make complete sense of it. Nevertheless, humans seek fundamental meaning, which, in what seems to be a fundamentally meaningless world, constitutes the relationship that Camus terms "the absurd" and also invites humankind to face. However, unable to face meaninglessness, some speculatively posit fundamental meaning, committing "philosophical suicide," while others worry that life without fundamental meaning is not worth living and so consider actual suicide. In both cases, the absurd relationship that constitutes human existence in the world is denied. The challenge is to face the truth and seek meaning even though humans must continually fail, like the mythical Sisyphus who had to roll a boulder up a hill every day, only to have it roll back down each evening.

In Camus's *The Rebel* (1951), the argument shifted from a critical rejection of suicide to one of political murder. The modern discovery of revolutionary meaning within the historical process suggests that the strategic removal of those who stand in the way of a better future for all is justified. However, all futures are speculative, and if humans are seduced by the utopian promise of the future, humankind will sacrifice real individuals to what may never be, which would amount to a failure to understand the meaning of revolt. Revolt is legitimate only insofar as it is the rejection of a transgression of the limits of endurable subjugation. The point at which subjugation becomes unendurable is the point at which an individual understands that no one should have to tolerate it. Thus, the rebel's rejection contains an affirmation of human solidarity— "I rebel, therefore we exist"—that is inconsistent with the utopian promise of "we shall be" and its violent expediencies. To kill anyone is to violate the very principle on which the rebel stands. The challenge is to preserve the principle by resisting oppression, not to violate it by becoming another oppressor.

During the cold war, there seemed to be no alternative between world capitalism and world communism. Camus was critical of the latter, and *The Rebel's* critique of strategic violence read like an assault on revolutionary communism and its sympathizers. This elicited a counterattack from Camus's friend and philosopher Jean-Paul Sartre, and his colleagues, who continued to support communist possibilities against capitalist exploitation and imperialism. The ensuing debate, carried out in Sartre's journal *Les Temps modernes,* was very public and acrimonious, ending the friendship and dividing intellectuals throughout France and the world on essential issues of progressive politics and theory.

See also *Nietzsche, Friedrich; Sartre, Jean-Paul.*

JOHN DUNCAN

BIBLIOGRAPHY

Camus, Albert. *The Myth of Sisyphus, and Other Essays,* translated by Justin O'Brien. New York: Knopf, 1955.
———. *The Rebel,* translated by Anthony Bower. New York: Random House, 1956.
———. *The Stranger,* translated by Mathew Ward. New York: Knopf, 1993.
Sprintzen, David, and Adrian Van den Hoven, eds. *Sartre and Camus: A Historic Confrontation.* New York: Humanity Books, 2004.

Candidate Recruitment

Candidate recruitment refers to the rules employed by political parties through which possible candidates for elected office appear on the official electoral ballots (be it in list as well as in nonlist systems). Thus, the term has a more precise meaning in political science than *recruitment to the legislature,* which includes parties' rules for drafting elections as well as other factors operating in accession to parliamentary functions such as the legal rules governing eligibility or the electoral system. The recruitment of independent candidates, for instance, does not fall under candidate recruitment as political scientists study it.

Candidate recruitment is both a matter of who appoints candidates to run for elections and the effect of candidate recruitment procedures on who actually appears on the ticket. Within the former, political scientists analyze how many people are involved in the selection process and how much power the centralized authority wields. In respect to the latter, scholars have paid attention to two elements: the effect of candidate selection on the composition of parliaments, and its impact on the flourishing or wilting of party mobilization and cohesion, that is, on intraparty life.

INCLUSIVENESS AND POWER IN CANDIDATE RECRUITMENT

In recent political science literature, Reuven Hazan and Gideon Rahat propose the most comprehensive work on candidate recruitment in their 2001 work in *Party Politics.* The authors isolate two main questions to address when studying where lists are made within a party. The first element taken into account is the inclusiveness of the procedure, which distinguishes parties according to the number of persons involved in the candidate selection process. On that variable, parties may be ranged on a continuum going from very exclusive to totally inclusive (see Figure 1, p. 186).

The most exclusive way to select candidates is for the whole process to be controlled by one person, most of the time the party leader or the party president. Few examples of this logic can be found; it exists only in parties dominated by a charismatic and authoritarian leader, such as extreme-right parties (Front National in France, Vlaams Blok in Belgium). From that extreme point, procedures involve more and more participants. Slightly less exclusive is a system in which an oligarchy is in charge of drafting electoral ballots. Making the procedure more inclusive, candidates may be selected by party delegates designated by party members. More rarely, party members may also be directly involved, as in the recently founded Italian Democratic Party. Finally, the most inclusive

FIGURE 1: INCLUSIVENESS OF CANDIDATE SELECTION

Exclusive   **Inclusive**

←——→

One person   Oligarchy   Party delegates   Party members

---

system associates the electorate to the procedure, as is the case in the United States with primary elections. In Western democracies, the most frequent procedure to select candidates is to have party delegates in charge of candidate selection.

The recent dominant trend is to open the procedure to party members. In all Western democracies, there is growing pressure for more transparency and participation. Political parties are facing this demand and are adapting through opening their procedures, and in particular by making the way they select their leaders and their candidates more open. Many parties have, for example, abandoned recruiting candidates via selected party agencies and opted for full members' vote systems, or at least for giving their members a bigger say. Examples include the French *Parti Socialiste* or the British Labour Party. The impact of the democratization of candidate recruitment procedures is still unclear.

Apart from the degree of inclusiveness, the second element relevant to the study of candidate recruitment is the level of power wielded by those in charge of drafting electoral ballots. For this variable, one extreme is a system entirely controlled by the national party organs who select the candidates running in each constituency. Canadian parties function very much like this; the national party leader imposes some candidates in constituencies that have a chance to be won. On the other extreme, the party in the district with no veto power for national organs recruits the candidates. Between the two extremes are systems that have various rules involving both levels of power and differ on which level has the final word. In practice, in most Western parties, decentralized bodies usually dominate candidate selection; the national party organs usually have only a consultative role.

COMPOSITION OF PARLIAMENTS AND PARTY HEALTH

Numerous studies about candidate selection have demonstrated that electoral ballots are still far from being mirrors of society. Candidate recruitment is not equally open to all citizens. Michael Gallagher and Michael Marsh's 1988 study, *Candidate Selection in Comparative Perspective: The Secret Garden of Politics*, made clear that some members of certain categories have greater chances to become candidates and to enter parliament than others, beginning with incumbents who are more likely to be renominated than first-time candidates. Furthermore, candidates tend to have a stronger educational background and to be wealthier than the average. Thirdly, in lists systems only, parties usually try to have geographically balanced lists covering the whole constituency. Finally, ethnic

minorities and women are underrepresented on electoral lists. The recent trend toward a more open system of candidate selection has, in this respect, not proven able to unlock the access to parliamentary mandates. On the contrary, a more open system has even reinforced some bias, in favor of incumbents and of men. This trend is balanced, however, in some countries due to mandatory gender equality (e.g., French law imposes gender parity among candidates).

Some scholars have explored the impact of reforming candidate selection on intraparty life. The major line of interest on this issue splits into two opposing camps. Some contend that more inclusive procedures are potential sources of internal divisions. Others believe that more inclusive rules allow national leaders to enhance their control of party candidates and, as a consequence, the cohesion of their party. The first thesis is supported, among others, by Hazan, who judges in his 2002 work "Candidate Selection" that "candidates who are chosen by inclusive selectorate owe their loyalty to their voters in the candidate selection process, and not only to their party. [. . .] Democratizing candidate selection thus produces dual sources of legitimacy for candidates—party legitimacy and selectorate legitimacy" (119). As a result, intraparty discipline becomes weaker; party leaders lose control over their ministers of parliament and their potential candidates by transferring candidate selection to party members. By contrast, Richard Katz and Peter Mair believe democratizing candidate selection increases leaders' control. In their cartel party model, the top of the party could enhance its autonomy through the empowerment of the party basis. The core idea in their reflection is that party members are less ideological and more controllable than party activists. In that respect, attributing candidate selection to party members has not resulted in reducing the control of party leaders. On the contrary, it even strengthens their command by setting party activists aside.

CONCLUSION

Candidate recruitment has evolved significantly in the last twenty years. Since the early 1990s, political parties in established democracy have decided to open up the procedures for deciding who is going to stand for the party on the electoral ballot. Party members in particular have gained influence in the process, and in some cases voters have also been involved through open primaries copying the U.S. primary system. The change would be trivial if it was not expected to impact the quality of democracy and representation. Recent studies have shown that these changes have slightly affected the profile of candidates. Incumbents and well-known figures from outside politics have been more successful in convincing party members to select them. Party leaders have lost their ability to impose new faces on the ballot. Yet the party leadership is adapting quickly, and the changes provoked by democratizing candidate recruitment should not be overestimated.

See also *Candidate Selection; Party Discipline; Party Membership; Party Systems, Comparative.*

. . . . JEAN-BENOIT PILET

BIBLIOGRAPHY
Bille, Lars. "Democratizing a Democratic Procedure: Myth or Reality?" *Party Politics* 7, no. 3 (2001): 363–380.
Gallagher, Michael, and Michael Marsh. *Candidate Selection in Comparative Perspective: The Secret Garden of Politics.* London: Sage Publications, 1988.
Hazan, Reuven Y. "Candidate Selection." In *Comparing Democracies 2: New Challenges in the Study of Elections and Voting,* edited by Lawrence LeDuc, Richard G. Niemi, and Pippa Norris, 108–126. London: Sage Publications, 2002.
Hazan, Reuven Y., and Gideon Rahat. "Candidate Selection Methods: An Analytical Framework." *Party Politics* 7, no. 3 (2001): 297–322.
———. "The Influence of Candidate Selection Methods on Legislatures and Legislators: Theoretical Propositions, Methodological Suggestions, and Empirical Evidence." *Journal of Legislative Studies* 12, nos. 3–4 (2006): 366–385.
Katz, Richard S. "The Problem of Candidate Selection and Models of Party Democracy." *Party Politics* 7, no. 1 (2001): 277–296.
Katz, Richard S., and Peter Mair. "Changing Models of Party Organization and Party Democracy: The Emergence of the Cartel Party." *Party Politics* 1 (January 1995): 5–28.
Norris, Pippa, and Joni Lovenduski. *Political Recruitment: Gender, Race, and Class in the British Parliament.* Cambridge: Cambridge University Press, 1995.
Scarrow, Susan, Paul Webb, and David Farrell. "From Social Integration to Electoral Contestation: The Changing Distribution of Powers within Political Parties." In *Parties Without Partisan: Political Change in Advanced Industrial Democracies,* edited by Russell J. Dalton and Matthew P. Wattenberg. Oxford: Oxford University Press, 2000.

Candidate Selection

Candidate selection is one of the first things political parties must do before an election. Those who are eventually elected to office are the successful candidates whom the parties previously selected, and the ones who will subsequently determine what the party looks like and does. Because it is relatively easy for parties to alter, changes in candidate selection will affect politics inside both the party and the legislature, in expected and unexpected ways.

Candidate selection takes place almost entirely within parties. There are very few countries (e.g., Germany, Finland, Norway) where the legal system specifies criteria for candidate selection, and only in the United States does the system regulate the process. In most countries, the parties themselves determine the rules for the selection of candidates.

CRITERIA FOR CLASSIFICATION

In any analysis of candidate selection methods, the unit of analysis is a single party in a particular country at a specific time. Classification is based on four criteria: the selectorate, candidacy, decentralization, and voting versus appointment.

The selectorate is the body that selects the candidates and is classified according to its inclusiveness. At one extreme, the selectorate is the most inclusive (i.e., the entire electorate); at the other extreme, the selectorate is the most exclusive (i.e., a nominating entity of one leader). The middle of the continuum is when the selectorate consists of party delegates, such as a party convention. Candidacy defines who can present oneself as the candidate of a party. At the inclusive pole, every voter is eligible to stand as a candidate. As one moves toward the exclusive pole, one encounters a series of restrictive conditions, such as minimum length of membership. Party selection methods can be decentralized in two senses: *territorial,* that is, local selectorates nominate candidates; and *social,* that is, representation for such groups as women and minorities. Usually candidates are appointed in the exclusive selectorates, whereas inclusive selectorates vote to choose their candidates (see Figure 1, below).

POLITICAL CONSEQUENCES

Different candidate selection methods produce different consequences. For example, parties that use appointment methods balance representation better than parties that use voting systems. Territorial decentralization could lead to increased responsiveness of representatives to the demands of their particular constituencies. Concerning candidacy, parties can influence the composition of their party by adopting term limits. The selectorate, however, determines the most significant and far-reaching consequences. The political consequences of the

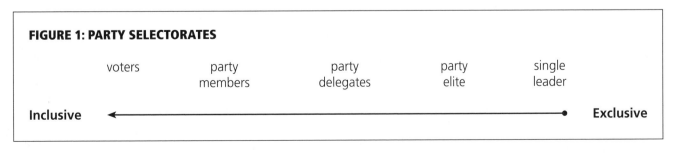

FIGURE 1: PARTY SELECTORATES

| voters | party members | party delegates | party elite | single leader |

Inclusive ←————————————————————————————————→ **Exclusive**

SOURCE: Hazan, Reuven Y., and Gideon Rahat. *Democracy Within Parties: Candidate Selection Methods and Their Political Consequences,* p. 35. Oxford: Oxford University Press, 2010.

inclusiveness of the selectorate are assessed according to four important aspects of democracy: participation, representation, competition, and responsiveness.

There is a difference between the quantity of participants and the quality of their participation. In terms of quantity, the more inclusive selectorates are the more participatory ones. The picture becomes less clear when analyzing the quality of membership. Although citizens perceive the adoption of more inclusive selectorates positively, most do not join parties. In addition, many of those who do join do not participate in their party's candidate selection process and are not affiliated for more than a short period.

Smaller, exclusive selectorates can balance representation. When selection is controlled by a party elite who appoints candidates—and to a lesser extent, when it takes place between party delegates who can be coordinated—there are more chances that ideological and social groups within the party will be allocated safe positions on the party list, or safe seats.

Party delegates are more competitive than primaries because of the shorter "distance" between candidates and their selectors. The party elite is expected to be even more competitive, but suffers from a lack of popular legitimacy and, to justify decisions, the party elite often presents a list largely composed of incumbents. A nonlinear relationship results between inclusiveness and competition: The most inclusive selectorates are moderately competitive, party delegates are the most competitive, and the more exclusive selectorates are the least competitive.

Inclusiveness also influences responsiveness. Legislators who are selected by a small selectorate, composed of party leaders, owe their positions to the party leaders and the legislators are likely to be party players. Legislators selected by larger party agencies are often party players but are also attuned to the interests of their power base. Legislators selected in primaries need to reach a massive, fluid audience and will behave more like individuals than team players.

CONCLUSION

The study of candidate selection reveals that more intraparty democracy does not necessarily lead to better democracy. For example, parties that select their candidates through primaries enjoy high levels of participation but have trouble balancing representation, fostering competition, or maintaining cohesion. Candidate selection can thus affect the essence of modern democratic politics.

See also *Electoral Rules; Political Participation; Political Parties; Selectorate.*

. . . . REUVEN Y. HAZAN

BIBLIOGRAPHY

Gallagher, Michael, and Michael Marsh, eds. *Candidate Selection in Comparative Perspective: The Secret Garden of Politics.* London: Sage Publications, 1988.

Hazan, Reuven Y. "Candidate Selection." In *Comparing Democracies*, edited by Lawrence LeDuc, Richard G. Niemi, and Pippa Norris. London: Sage Publications, 2002.

Hazan, Reuven Y., and Gideon Rahat. "Candidate Selection: Methods and Consequences." In *Handbook of Party Politics*, edited by Richard S. Katz and William J. Crotty. London: Sage Publications, 2006.

———. *Democracy Within Parties: Candidate Selection Methods and Their Political Consequences.* Oxford: Oxford University Press, 2010.

Narud, Hanne Marthe, Mogens N. Pedersen, and Henry Valen, eds. *Party Sovereignty and Citizen Control: Selecting Candidates for Parliamentary Elections in Denmark, Finland, Iceland, and Norway.* Odense: University Press of Southern Denmark, 2002.

Ohman, Magnus. *The Heart and Soul of the Party: Candidate Selection in Ghana and Africa.* Uppsala, Sweden: Uppsala University Press, 2004.

Rahat, Gideon. "Candidate Selection: The Choice Before the Choice." *Journal of Democracy* 18, no. 1 (2007): 157–170.

Ranney, Austin. "Candidate Selection." In *Democracy at the Polls*, edited by David Butler, Howard R. Penniman, and Austin Ranney. Washington, D.C.: American Enterprise Institute, 1981.

Siavelis, Peter M., and Scott Morgenstern, eds. *Pathways to Power: Political Recruitment and Candidate Selection in Latin America.* University Park: Pennsylvania State University Press, 2008.

Ware, Alan. *The American Direct Primary.* Cambridge: Cambridge University Press, 2002.

Capitalism and Democracy

Capitalism is a system of exchange that depends on the economic freedoms to own private property and to buy, sell, and invest the property as one wishes. Unless people can own and exchange property without worrying that a central authority will confiscate it, they will have little incentive to save and invest. Unless they can keep most of the fruits of their labors, they will also have little incentive to work hard.

Democracy is a system of governance that depends on the political freedoms to vote, speak one's mind and practice one's beliefs, assemble with others, and live without fear of arbitrary searches or punishment. Unless people feel secure in exercising these freedoms, they will be reluctant to criticize or oppose a government or its policies or to seek political change.

THE CONNECTION BETWEEN CAPITALISM AND DEMOCRACY

Capitalism and democracy are closely aligned. Capitalism emerged in Europe in the fourteenth century, and democracy emerged in the sixteenth century. With the collapse of Soviet communism, starting with the fall of the Berlin Wall in 1989, capitalism emerged as the dominant form of economic organization in most nations of the world, and democracy emerged as the dominant form of political organization. By the start of the twenty-first century, most major nations protected both the economic and the political freedoms of their citizens. As such, they exemplified *democratic capitalism.*

However, capitalism and democracy do not necessarily coexist. Capitalism is almost certainly a precondition for democracy, and economic freedom does seem to require political freedom. This is because the exercise of political rights requires that citizens possess a degree of economic dependence. When people have no choice but to depend on government for their sustenance, they are likely to be wary of dissenting from official orthodoxy out of fear that government could retaliate by taking away their livelihoods. No democracy in the world exists today that is not also capitalist.

Yet democracy may not be essential to capitalism. As China illustrates, economic freedom does not always require political freedom. Although China does not officially call itself capitalist, by the start of the twenty-first century, the country had emerged as the world's second largest capitalist nation after the United States. China's economic success stems in part from the economic freedoms it protects. However, China has not given its people political freedom.

DEMOCRATIC CAPITALISM VERSUS AUTHORITARIAN CAPITALISM

Some observers believe that capitalist nations inevitably become democratic over time because they generate middle classes that eventually demand a say in how they are governed. The history of capitalist development in England and the United States between the seventeenth and nineteenth centuries lends some support to this theory. As economic freedom and wealth spread first to major landholders, then to gentlemen farmers, and then to an emerging class of businessmen, these groups demanded ever-greater political freedom. Much the same pattern can be seen elsewhere around the world since then. Starting in the 1980s, as both Taiwan and South Korea gained wealth through trade and investment, their middle classes grew to the point that they sought political rights. By 2010, both nations were robust democracies.

Some believe on this basis that China will move toward democratic capitalism. But it seems just as likely that China's emerging middle class will not want to risk political instability that may threaten its economic gains, and will continue to support a leadership that is technically competent and committed to continued growth. China may thereby represent a new kind of system, *authoritarian capitalism*, that offers economic freedom without political freedom. The contest for the dominant form of economic and political organization in this century may be between democratic capitalism and authoritarian capitalism, just as it was between capitalism and communism during the latter half of the twentieth century.

Democratic capitalism appears to be in the lead. More nations than ever before call themselves "democracies." While in 1970 only about a third of the world's nations held free elections, by 2010 that number was closer to two-thirds. While in the 1970s fewer than fifty countries possessed the sort of civil liberties now associated with democracy, by the start of the twenty-first century nearly ninety did. Yet some of the places that call themselves democracies, such as Russia, are encumbered by endemic corruption, dominance by small elites, or one-party rule. Other putative democracies, such as Iran, are actually theocracies whose clergy make most important decisions.

TWO SCENARIOS OF THE FUTURE

Some observers believe that capitalism may ultimately threaten democracy even in strong democracies such as the United States, as intensifying competition among corporations spills over into politics. By this view, firms and industries seek competitive advantage over one another through laws and regulations that favor them over their rivals. They employ ever-increasing numbers of lobbyists, mounting campaign contributions, and costly media campaigns. This escalating arms race drowns out the voices of average citizens. It overwhelms political parties, voluntary associations, and nonprofit groups on which citizens previously depended to communicate their views to elected officials. Under this scenario, politics comes to represent the interests of companies and financial institutions and their executives and investors, more than the interests of ordinary people.

A more optimistic scenario holds that democracy will be enhanced by the instant-communication technologies of twenty-first century capitalism, such as the Internet, cell phones, blogs, text messaging, and social networking sites. These offer inexpensive means of connecting large numbers of people free from state control—allowing them to confer with one another, criticize political leaders, report abuses, mobilize opposition, and monitor vote rigging. Many observers attributed the surprise victory, in June 2008, of Lebanon's pro-Western March 14 movement over the pro-Iranian Hezbollah coalition to the widening use of new communication technologies, especially among younger people. Protests following Iran's election, soon thereafter, were similarly facilitated by new technologies. On the other hand, such technologies may give authoritarian states greater capacity to control their people.

It is impossible to know whether capitalism will overwhelm or strengthen democracy. What's certain is that the two systems interact in important ways and should be understood together.

See also *Business Pressure in Politics; Campaign Advertising; Democracies, Advanced Industrial; Democracy; Democracy, Future of; Democracy and Development; Emerging Democracies; Empire and Democracy; Interest Groups and Lobbies; Liberal Democracy; State Capitalism.*

. . . . ROBERT B. REICH

BIBLIOGRAPHY

Braudel, Fernand. *The Wheels of Commerce: Civilization and Capitalism, 15th–18th century*, vols. 1–3. New York: Harper and Row, 1979.

Friedman, B. *The Moral Consequences of Economic Growth.* New York: Knopf, 2005.

Friedman, M. *Capitalism and Freedom.* Chicago: University of Chicago Press, 1962.

Reich, R. *Supercapitalism: The Transformation of Business, Democracy, and Everyday Life.* New York: Knopf, 2007.

Yergin, D., and Stanislaw, J. *The Commanding Heights: The Battle between Government and the Marketplace That Is Remaking the Modern World.* New York: Simon and Schuster, 1988.

Capitalist Development

See *Development, Economic.*

Capital Punishment

The state's levy and administration of the penalty of death for criminal actions or conviction is called *capital punishment*. Capital punishment follows from regular legal procedures under due process of law, elements which distinguish it from extrajudicial executions. Capital punishment is generally on the decline around the globe, either because of a state's abolition or growing tendency to constrict its use.

Despite international criticism, the United States continues to allow capital punishment in states that have not outlawed it. A group in Columbia, South Carolina, demonstrates their support just prior to an execution.

SOURCE: © Bettmann/Corbis

supporters of capital punishment hesitate to cite states like the Democratic Republic of Congo, Iran, Saudi Arabia, China, or North Korea as examples of countries where the capital punishment is still applied. However, there is at least one more industrialized democracy, Japan, and several either democratic, or economically prosperous, countries such as India, South Korea, Taiwan, and Singapore, in which capital punishment still is part of the penal code. In the territory of Russia and the former Soviet States in central Asia, Turkmenistan alone has abolished the death penalty completely, although Russia, Kazakhstan, and Kyrgyzstan have moratoria in place. Africa presents a mixed picture, with eight fully and thirteen de facto abolitionist states, and twenty-six states that retain the death penalty. Most Asian nations retain the death penalty and no country in the Middle East—except the de facto abolitionist Israel—has decided to abandon judicially authorized state killing.

CAPITAL PUNISHMENT AROUND THE WORLD

The United States remains committed to the death penalty in the face of increasing criticism in the international arena and long after most other democratic nations have abandoned it. It is now a commonplace to note that the United States is alone among Western industrialized nations in executing its citizens. Today, Europe proclaims itself to be "death penalty free" and has succeeded in talking, and sometimes coercing, almost the whole of Eastern Europe into abolitionism. Abolitionists in Europe like to point out that the death penalty is unacceptable in a "civilized society." In addition, the Council of Europe in 1999 expressed its "firm conviction that capital punishment, therefore, has no place in civilised, democratic societies governed by the rule of law" (Council of Europe and Wohlwend). Further, in *Soering v. United Kingdom* (1989), European Court of Human Rights justice de Meyer put it simply when he said that capital punishment "is not consistent with the present state of European civilisation." Some believe that the civilizing process leads inexorably to rejection of legalized state killing. Europe, in this view, is a step ahead of the United States, which, along with the rest of the world, sooner or later will catch up.

From a global perspective, however, the United States does not seem that exceptional. While 111 nations have formally abolished or stopped using the death penalty, little more than one-fourth of the world's population lives in countries that have completely abolished it. Many

CAPITAL PUNISHMENT AND AMERICAN POLITICS

In the first decade of the twenty-first century, capital punishment continues to have an important place in U.S. politics and practice. Despite the recent reawakening of abolitionist activity, a majority of Americans in opinion polls say they favor capital punishment for persons convicted of murder. Yet capital punishment is perhaps less of a national phenomenon than it is a reflection of the distinctive history and politics of the American states in the so-called death belt, states such as Texas, Virginia, Oklahoma, Missouri, and Florida that together account for approximately two-thirds of all executions in the United States. Indeed, executions have become so commonplace that in some states, such as Texas and Virginia, it is difficult for abolitionist groups to mount a visible presence for every execution.

Motivations such as vengeance, retribution, and the simple justice of an eye-for-an-eye sort provide the basis for much of this popular support. This may reflect "a growing sense that capital punishment no longer needs to be defended in terms of its social utility. . . . The current invocation of vengeance reflects . . . a sense of entitlement to the death penalty as a satisfying personal experience for victims and a satisfying gesture for the rest of the community" (Simon, 1997, 13). Yet, as legal historian Stuart Banner rightly observes in Austin Sarat's book, *When the State Kills: Capital Punishment and the American Condition*,

Capital punishment . . . presents several puzzles. It gets more attention than any other issue of criminal justice, yet it is a minuscule part of our criminal justice system. It is very popular despite well-known shortcomings—it does not deter crime, it is inflicted in a systematically biased manner, it is sometimes imposed on the innocent, and it is quite expensive to administer. . . . It is often justified in simple retributive terms, as the worst punishment for the worst crime, but it is not hard to conceive of worse punishments, such as torture. . . . While capital punishment is intended to deter others, we inflict it in private, and allow prospective criminals to learn very little about it. (12)

It is not clear whether and when the United States will abolish capital punishment. This is, in part, a function of some distinctive aspects of the U.S. political system. Thus, Franklin Zimring, Gordon Hawkins, and Sam Kamin argue in their 2001 publication *Punishment and Democracy* that the more democratic penal policy making is, the more prone it is to be driven by punitivism, and the irrational and emotional motives often attributed to death penalty supporters. Their empirical case is the so-called "three strikes and you're out" legislation in California, but their hypothesis can be extended to capital punishment. To be sure, one has to be careful not to confuse "democracy" with "public participation in penal policy making." Throughout history, most authoritarian states, including socialist states, have used the death penalty liberally. This is not surprising since penal policy is a domain especially suitable for symbolic politics. Being "tough on crime" can be popular in any regime type.

Zimring, Hawkins, and Kamin also refer to popular participation in the penal policy-making process. The comparison between the United States and Europe, in this regard, is instructive. Observers have pointed out that American institutions are more "porous" and open to popular demands than European political structures. American institutions also expose many officials, particularly judges, to direct electoral competition which are, in Europe, staffed by career bureaucrats or disciplined party politicians. Additionally, American states allow penal policy to be made through referenda, such as the Californian three-strikes initiative, which would be unthinkable in most of Europe. As Joshua Micah Marshall puts it, "Basically, Europe doesn't have the death penalty because its political systems are less democratic, or at least more insulated from populist impulses, than the U.S. government" (12–15).

In spite of America's criminal justice populism, the last several years have seen a dramatic decline in both the number of people being sentenced to death and the number of executions administered in the United States. According to the Death Penalty Information Center, there were 276 death sentences handed down and 98 executions across the country in 1999; by 2005, the number of death sentences had declined to 125, and the number of executions shrunk to 60. These changes are, to some extent, a function of growing national concern about the possibility of executing the innocent. DNA-prompted exonerations have galvanized public attention and raised new doubts about the way the death penalty is administered.

Still, capital punishment remains a key part of American political life. It is caught up in, and sustained by, a series of contradictions in U.S. social and political attitudes. The power of the victims' rights movement in the United States arises, in part, from increasing distrust of governmental and legal institutions, yet it is to those very institutions that the families of victims must turn as they seek to ensure an adequate response to capital crimes. This same contradiction sometimes is revealed when jurors decide to impose the death penalty. Some jurors do so because they doubt that a life sentence will actually mean life, yet they can express this doubt by imposing a death sentence because they believe that appellate courts will ensure that state killing is used with great scrupulousness.

TRADITIONAL APPROACHES TO STUDYING CAPITAL PUNISHMENT

Much of the available research on the death penalty centers on the United States, which permits the federal government and state governments to use death as a punishment for homicide. Research traditionally focuses on three topics: (1) whether the death penalty deters, (2) whether it is compatible with contemporary standards of decency, and (3) whether it has been administered in a racially neutral or in a discriminatory manner.

DETERRENCE

Until relatively recently, the settled wisdom was that the death penalty did not produce a greater deterrent effect than life imprisonment. However, recent research has reignited the debate about deterrence. Hashem Dezhbakhsh and his colleagues suggest that each execution prevents approximately eighteen murders, while similar research by H. N. Macon and R. K. Gittings and Joanna Shepherd purports to show similar deterrent effects. In response, John Donohue and Justin Wolfers compare execution rates with homicide rates and contrasted U.S. trends to Canadian trends and conclude that there is considerable doubt about whether the death penalty has any deterrence effect at all.

Deterrence studies traditionally have used many different methodologies. Some examine murder rates before and after well-publicized executions; others compare murder rates in adjoining states, one with capital punishment, and the other without. In the 1970s, the economist Isaac Ehrlich conducted controversial research on the deterrent effect of capital punishment. It shows statistically significant deterrent effects and uses sophisticated statistical techniques to control for confounding variables. If Ehrlich is correct, execution did indeed save lives. He claims in his 1975 article "The Deterrent Effect of Capital Punishment," "On the average the trade-off between the execution of an offender and the potential victims it might have saved was on the order of magnitude of 1 to 8 for the period 1933–67 in the United States" (398). Ehrlich's research has been the object of sustained and rather persuasive criticism, such as that by Lawrence Klein and Richard Lempert, most of which focuses on the particular statistical techniques used. Today's controversy has reignited the effort to determine if the death penalty has distinct and discernible deterrent effects.

RETRIBUTION

The most powerful alternative justification suggests that even if the death penalty does not deter, one may justify it on retributive grounds or as a way of expressing a society's legitimate moral condemnation of heinous criminality. Researchers such as Neil Vidmar and Phoebe Ellsworth have conducted research on public opinion to determine whether this retributive attitude, and the death penalty that it supports, are compatible with contemporary standards of decency.

In deciding whether the American public supports the death penalty, social scientists have repeatedly documented strong support for capital punishment, which highly correlates with retributive attitudes. This suggests that it is a particular view of justice, rather than the death penalty's utility, that explains its persistence in the United States. However, research also demonstrates the malleability of this public embrace of capital punishment and its retributive justification.

In 1976, Austin Sarat and Neil Vidmar followed a hypothesis first advanced by Justice Marshall in *Furman v. Georgia* (1972) that found the more people know about the death penalty, how it works, and the evidence on deterrence, the less they support it. In 1993, William Bowers discovered that public support for capital punishment decreased dramatically when he presented survey respondents with alternative forms of punishment and asked them to choose which they preferred. Bowers found that people tend to accept the death penalty because they believe that currently available alternatives are insufficiently harsh. However, when people were asked whether they preferred the death penalty or life without parole combined with a restitution requirement, the expressed support for the death penalty fell considerably.

FAIR PROCESS AND NONDISCRIMINATION

The final traditional interest of scholars studying capital punishment is in the compatibility of capital punishment with democratic values. These researchers ask whether the state administers capital punishment fairly and, more particularly, in a racially nondiscriminatory manner. Efforts to answer this question often focus on the race of the offender. Scholars documented in rape and homicide cases, for example, that between 1930 and 1967 almost 50 percent of those executed for murder were black. However, this early research was unable to disentangle the impact of race from other supposedly legitimate factors on capital sentencing. Merely showing that the death penalty was more likely to be imposed on black defendants could not, in itself, establish that that difference was the result of racial discrimination.

In the mid-1980s, David Baldus and his colleagues undertook research designed to remedy this defect. Using sophisticated multiple regression techniques and a large data set, they aimed to isolate the effect of race on capital sentencing. First, they found no evidence of discrimination against black defendants because of their race in the period after *Furman v. Georgia* (1972). Second, they found strong effects for the victim's race. Taking over two hundred variables into account, Baldus and colleagues concluded that someone who killed a white victim was 4.3 times more likely to receive the death penalty

than if the victim was black. Even after the sustained efforts by the Supreme Court to prevent arbitrariness or racial discrimination in capital sentencing, juries seemed to still value the lives of white Americans more highly than the lives of African Americans and were, as a result, more likely to sentence some killers to die on the basis of illegitimate racial considerations.

The Baldus study was the highpoint of policy-relevant, empirically rigorous social science research on capital punishment; it spoke directly to issues that the U.S. Supreme Court had put at the heart of its death penalty jurisprudence and the study used the best social science methods. However, it did not persuade the Court. While the Court accepted the validity of the Baldus study, it concluded in *McCleskey v. Kemp* (1987) that such statistical evidence could not prove discrimination in any individual case. This rejection stunned those who believed that social science could help shape policy in the area of capital sentencing.

EMERGING RESEARCH TRENDS

Following *McCleskey v. Kemp* (1987), the U.S. Supreme Court became more conservative, unreservedly embracing the death penalty and rejecting what in earlier years seemed to be persuasive challenges rooted in social science research. Frank Munger, in a 1993 issue of *Law and Society Review*, asserts that after twenty years of research intent on influencing the Court's death penalty rulings, the *McKleskey* decision "has forced scholars to chart new courses. . . . Scholars have responded with research that is more deeply critical, more theoretically informed, and more broadly concerned about the culture and politics of the death penalty" (6).

Some of this new research focuses on analyzing the processing of capital cases, with special attention to how and why actors in the death penalty process behave as they do. Among the most important of these actors are jurors—ordinary citizens who must decide not only questions of guilt or innocence but also whether those found guilty of murder should be sentenced to life in prison or execution. Juror research, such as that done by Theodore Eisenberg and Martin Wells, Craig Haney and Mona Lynch, along with William Bowers and Benjamin Steiner, examined how jurors process the information provided to them, how they understand their responsibilities in capital cases, how they function in an atmosphere surrounded by the portrayal of violence, and how they balance their folk knowledge with the legal requirements of capital cases. In addition, Austin Sarat conducted research on lawyers and the lawyering process in capital cases, with special attention on the use of stories as persuasive devices and other narrative strategies. He also examined capital trials as events in which law attempts to put violence into discourse, and to differentiate state violence from the extralegal violence that it opposes.

David Garland's 1991 argument about the cultural impact of punishment has influenced other scholars. "Punishment," Garland contends, "helps shape the overarching culture and contribute to the generation and regeneration of its terms" (193). Punishment, he additionally notes, is a set of signifying practices with pedagogical effect that "teaches, clarifies, dramatizes, and authoritatively enacts some of the most basic moral-political categories and distinctions which help shape our symbolic universe" (195). Punishment teaches people how to think about categories like intention, responsibility, and injury, and it models the socially appropriate ways of responding to injury. What is true of punishment in general is particularly true for the death penalty. Scholars such as Émile Durkheim and George Herbert Mead, among others, contend that it is through practices of punishment that cultural boundaries are drawn, and solidarity is created through acts of marking difference between self and other, through disidentification as much as imagined connection.

The cultural politics of state killing has played a key role in shoring up distinctions of status and distinguishing particular ways of life from others. As a result, it is not surprising today the death penalty in the United States marks an important fault line in contemporary culture wars. Execution itself, the moment of state killing, is still today in the United States and some other nations an occasion for rich symbolization, for the production of public images of evil or of an unruly freedom whose only containment is in a state-imposed death.

See also *Beccaria, Cesare; Bonald, Louis Gabriel-Ambroise de; Crime Policy; Right to Life; Rule of Law; Sentencing Policy.*

. . . . AUSTIN SARAT

BIBLIOGRAPHY
Baldus, David C., George G. Woodworth, and Charles A. Pulaski Jr. *Equal Justice and the Death Penalty: A Legal and Empirical Analysis.* Boston: Northeastern University Press, 1990.
Bowers, William. "Capital Punishment and Contemporary Values: People's Misgivings and the Court's Misperceptions." *Law and Society Review* 27, no. 1 (1993): 157–176.
Bowers, William, and Benjamin Steiner. "Death by Default: An Empirical Demonstration of False and Forced Choice in Capital Sentencing." *Texas Law Review* 77, no. 3 (1999): 605–715.
Council of Europe, and Renate Wohlwend. "Europe: A Death Penalty-Free Continent." Council of Europe. http://assembly.coe.int/Main. asp?link=/Documents/AdoptedText/ta99/ERES1187.htm.
Dezhbakhsh, Hashem, Paul H. Rubin, and Joanna M. Shepherd. "Does Capital Punishment Have a Deterrent Effect? New Evidence from Postmoratorium Panel Data." *American Law and Economic Review* 5, no. 2 (2003): 344–376.
Donohue, John J., and Justin Wolfers. "Uses and Abuses of Empirical Evidence in the Death Penalty Debate." *Stanford Law Review* 58 (2005): 791.
Doyle, James. "The Lawyer's Art: Representation in Capital Cases." *Yale Journal of Law and the Humanities* 8 (1996): 417–450.
Ehrlich, Isaac. "The Deterrent Effect of Capital Punishment." *American Economic Review* 65, no. 3 (1975): 397–418.
Eisenberg, Theodore, and Martin Wells. "Deadly Confusion: Jury Instructions in Capital Cases." *Cornell Law Review* 79 (1993): 1–17.
Ellsworth, Phoebe, and Samuel Gross. "Hardening of Attitudes: Americans Views on the Death Penalty." *Journal of Social Issues* 50, no. 19 (1994): 48–71.
Fijalkowski, Agata. "Abolition of the Death Penalty in Central and Eastern Europe." *Tilburg Foreign Law Review* 9 (2001): 62–83.
Frankowski, Stanislav. "Post-Communist Europe." In *Capital Punishment: Global Issues and Prospects,* edited by Peter Hodgkinson and Andrew Rutherford. Winchester, UK: Waterside Press, 1996.
Garland, David. "Punishment and Culture: The Symbolic Dimension of Criminal Justice." *Studies in Law, Politics, and Society* 11 (1991): 191–224.
Gibbs, Jack. "Punishment and Deterrence: Theory, Research, and Penal Policy." In *Law and the Social Sciences,* edited by Leon Lipson and Stanton Wheeler. New York: Russell Sage, 1986.
Gross, Samuel. "Race and Death: The Judicial Evaluation of Evidence of Discrimination in Capital Sentencing." *UC Davis Law Review* 18, no. 4 (1985): 1275–1328.
Gross, Samuel, and Robert Mauro. "Patterns of Death: An Analysis of Racial Disparities in Capital Sentencing and Homicide Victimization." *Stanford Law Review* 37, no. 1 (1984): 27–153.
Haney, Craig, and Mona Lynch. "Clarifying Life and Death Matters: An Analysis of Instructional Comprehension and Penalty Phase Closing Arguments." *Law and Human Behavior* 21 (1997): 575–603.
Haney, Craig, Lorelei Sontag, and Sally Costanzo. "'Deciding to Take a Life': Capital Juries, Sentencing Instructions, and the Jurisprudence of Death." *Journal of Social Issues* 50, no. 2 (1994): 149–171.
Klein, Lawrence, B. Forst, and V. Filatov. "The Deterrent Effect of Capital Punishment: An Assessment of the Estimates." In *Deterrence and Incapacitation: Estimating the Effects of Criminal Sanctions on Crime Rates,* edited by Alfred Blumstein et al., 15–48. Washington, D.C.: National Academy of Sciences, 1977.
Lempert, Richard. "Desert and Deterrence: An Assessment of the Moral Basis of the Case for Capital Punishment." *Michigan Law Review* 79, no. 6 (1981): 1177–1255.
Macon, H. N. and R. K. Gittings. "Getting Off Death Row: Commuted Sentences and the Deterrent Effect of Capital Punishment." *Journal of Law and Economics* 46, no. 2 (2003): 453–78.
Mead, George Herbert. "The Psychology of Punitive Justice." *American Journal of Sociology* 23 (1918): 577–598.
Munger, Frank. "From the Editor." *Law & Society Review* 27 (1993): 5–8.
Sarat, Austin. "Between (the Presence of) Violence and (the Possibility of) Justice: Lawyering against Capital Punishment." In *Cause Lawyering: Political Commitments and Professional Responsibilities,* edited by Austin Sarat and Stuart Scheingold. New York: Oxford University Press, 1998.
———. "Speaking of Death: Narratives of Violence in Capital Trials." *Law & Society Review* 27 (1993): 19–58.
———. *When the State Kills: Capital Punishment and the American Condition.* Princeton: Princeton University Press, 2001.
Sarat, Austin, and Neil Vidmar. "Public Opinion, the Death Penalty and the Eighth Amendment: Testing the Marshall Hypothesis." *Wisconsin Law Review* 1 (1976): 171–206.
Shepherd, Joanna M. "Deterrence Versus Brutalization: Capital Punishment's Differing Impacts Among States." *Michigan Law Review* 104, no. 2 (2005): 203–256.
Simon, Jonathan. 1997. "Violence, Vengeance and Risk: Capital Punishment in the Neoliberal State." *Kolner Zeitschrift fur Soziologie und Socialpsychologie* 37: 279–301.
Vidmar, Neil, and Phoebe Ellsworth. "Public Opinion and the Death Penalty." *Stanford Law Review* 26, no. 6 (1974): 1245–1280.
Zimring, Franklin E. *The Contradictions of Capital Punishment.* New York: Oxford University Press, 2004.
Zimring, Franklin E., Gordon Hawkins, and Sam Kamin, eds. *Punishment and Democracy: Three Strikes and You're Out in California.* Chicago: Chicago University Press, 2001.

Caribbean

The *Caribbean* is a geographical region of the Americas consisting of the Caribbean Sea, its islands, and the surroundings coasts. Politically, the Caribbean consists of thirty-four territories, including sovereign states, departments, and dependencies. The total population of the region is about 37 million, with about 90 percent of the population situated in the region's sovereign states. While the countries of the Caribbean demonstrate a great deal of social, ethnic, and cultural diversity, they also share many common economic and political features that have defined their contemporary struggle for development. These features include a common history as plantation and slave societies, a shared dependence on agriculture (especially

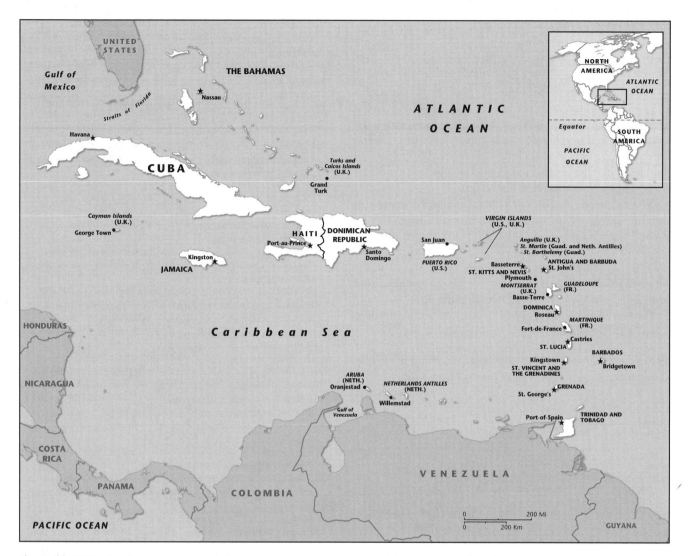

The Caribbean is a diverse region comprised of sovereign states, departments, and dependencies, with influences from colonizers Spain, England, France, and the Netherlands.

sugar), a relatively similar population and market size, and a long and difficult struggle for independence.

SETTLEMENT

By the late sixteenth century, Spain, England, France, and the Dutch had colonized most islands in the Caribbean. The temperate climate of the new colonies was particularly conducive to the development of lucrative agricultural exports, such as sugar. Thus, by the late seventeenth century, a lucrative plantation economy had developed in the region. As the European demand for Caribbean sugar exports increased over time, the demand for new sources of cheap plantation labor in the Caribbean also increased. In order to meet these demands, the colonizers turned to the slave trade in the eighteenth century. Massive numbers of African slaves were imported and sent to work on Caribbean plantations. Although slave revolts were common during this period, most were quickly suppressed. By the nineteenth century, most Caribbean territories had abandoned slavery as a practice. However, the legacy of African slavery continues to shape contemporary life and politics in the Caribbean.

SOVEREIGNTY AND INDEPENDENCE

Nationalism emerged in the Caribbean during the late nineteenth century. After a long and protracted struggle, all of the former Spanish colonies in the Caribbean had achieved independence by the year 1900, although Puerto Rico remains a self-governing unincorporated territory of the United States. As citizens of a self-governing territory, Puerto Ricans have U.S. citizenship, are entitled to vote at the federal level, and are subject to U.S. federal law. While Puerto Rico enjoys administrative autonomy similar to that of a U.S. state, it is not a state of the American union and has no voting representative in the U.S. Congress.

Suriname is the only Dutch colony to achieve independence as of 2007. The Netherlands's other former colonies, namely Aruba and the islands comprising the Netherlands Antilles (Saint Maarten, Curacao, Saba, Bonaire, and Saint Eustatius) are part of the Kingdom of the Netherlands. Aruba's governor is appointed by the Dutch monarch and serves as the de facto head of state. However, real executive authority in Aruba rests with the prime minister and parliament, which consists of twenty-one members elected by direct, popular vote. The Netherlands Antilles is a decentralized unitary state consisting of a governor and an elected Council of Ministers, headed by a prime minister. As a unified political entity, the Netherlands Antilles was scheduled to dissolve in 2008. However, dissolution of the Antilles has been postponed pending further negotiation regarding the future status of the territories.

Haiti, a former French colony, was the first country in the Caribbean to achieve independence in 1791 through a slave revolt led by Toussaint L'Ouverture. In a cruel twist of irony, it is the only French colony to achieve independence to date and it was already the poorest of all Caribbean countries when a 2010 earthquake devestated the capital Port au Prince and the surrounding area, killing hundreds of thousands.

The British case varies, with Jamaica, Trinidad, Barbados, and Guyana achieving independence in the mid-twentieth century. Today, several islands remain British Overseas Territories, including Anguilla, Montserrat, the Cayman Islands, the British Virgin Islands, and Turks and Caicos. These territories are under the sovereignty of the United Kingdom, but do not form part of the United Kingdom itself. Inhabitants have British citizenship, and the monarch appoints a governor to serve as de facto head of state for each territory, but the governor exercises little power over local affairs, which are governed instead by an elected parliament.

Like Haiti, many of the Caribbean islands that achieved independence, such as Guyana and Suriname, are also amongst the poorest in the region. In contrast, British Overseas Territories, such as the Cayman Islands and the British Virgin Islands, along with Aruba, boast the highest per capita incomes and account for 56 percent of the region's income. This trend has discouraged some islands from seeking total independence.

THE ECONOMY

A significant economic challenge for most Caribbean states and territories has been to break their dependence on primary agricultural exports, most notably sugar. Traditionally, Caribbean countries have relied heavily on a system of preferential access to European markets for export commodities such as sugar and bananas. Reliance on this export sector has limited financial returns, wages, industrialization, and regional competitiveness in global markets to the extent that, today, most Caribbean countries have large and persistent trade deficits. However, some countries have successfully diversified their markets. Curacao, Aruba, and Trinidad and Tobago have begun producing or refining oil. Guyana, Suriname, and Jamaica have developed their mining sectors. Puerto Rico is developing its manufacturing sector. The Cayman Islands, Aruba, and Curacao have developed a lucrative offshore banking sector, and almost all countries and territories in the Caribbean have developed tourism as a major industry, some to the virtual exclusion of almost any other economic activity. The economic result of this effort is mixed. Some countries, such as Trinidad and Tobago and Grenada, experienced significant economic growth during the late 1990s and early part of 2000. Others, like Jamaica and Haiti, continued to experience negative growth during this same period.

POLITICAL UPHEAVAL AND U.S. INTERVENTION

The twentieth century represented a long and difficult period of political struggle in the Caribbean. By the 1930s, most countries in the region experienced major political upheavals as labor leaders, trade unions, and students demanded social reform and greater participation in the political process. Charismatic and, at times, authoritarian leaders emerged from the movements, many of whom led their country to independence or dictatorship and ruin. These leaders include Alexander Bustamante and Norman Manley in Jamaica, Luis Muñoz Marín in Puerto Rico, Aimé Césaire in Martinique, Fidel Castro in Cuba, François Duvalier in Haiti, Rafael Trujillo in the Dominican Republic, and Maurice Bishop in Grenada.

Most of the Caribbean's experiments with political and social change, whether attempted through elections (as in Jamaica and Haiti), military coups (as in Grenada and the Dominican Republic), or open revolution (Cuba), elicited the attention of the United States, often in the form of direct or indirect military intervention. Since the Monroe Doctrine of 1823, the United States has maintained a strong interest in the Caribbean and, at times, has claimed and executed a right to intervene in its affairs. U.S. influence was particularly evident in 1899, when the United States intervened on the side of the Cubans in the Spanish-American War. In negotiating the subsequent terms of Cuban independence, the United States drafted the Platt Amendment to the newly formed Cuban constitution, which constitutionally enabled the United States to intervene in Cuban economic and political affairs. Following a prolonged period of civil war, political deadlock, and instability in the Dominican Republic, the United States invaded and occupied the country in 1916. In 1960, the United States began recruiting and training Cuban exiles to invade Cuba and overthrow the newly victorious revolutionary government of Fidel Castro. Launched in April 1961, the Bay of Pigs invasion proved disastrous for the United States when the invading force it supported was defeated by the Cuban National Guard in less than three days.

In 1965, U.S. troops were again deployed in the Dominican Republic to quell an uprising against dictatorial rule. In 1983, the United States invaded Grenada to remove left-wing leader Maurice Bishop. In 1994, and again in 2004, the United States invaded Haiti. Many Haitians accused the United States of arranging a coup d'état to remove democratically elected leader Jean-Bertrand Aristide.

REGIONAL INTEGRATION

By the 1990s, most countries of the Caribbean had attained political stability, with most countries transferring power through democratic elections (the notable exceptions being Haiti and Cuba). Except for a few cases, Caribbean countries have also experienced continuous economic growth, declining inflation rates, and climbing human development indexes. The region also continues to make positive steps forward through the Caribbean Community (CARICOM), which came into effect in 1973. CARICOM establishes a common market for member states. Currently, the organization boasts fourteen full members, and five associate members. In addition to establishing free trade and a common market in the Caribbean, CARICOM members have recently begun issuing CARICOM passports. CARICOM recently entered into *Petrocaribe,* an oil alliance with Venezuela that permits CARICOM members to purchase oil on conditions of preferential payments. Despite these significant political and economic achievements, more than one-third of the Caribbean's population continues to live below the poverty line. Unemployment rates remain high, and many countries continue to suffer under the weight of foreign debt.

See also *Colonialism; Latin American Political Economy; Monroe Doctrine; Poverty; Slavery; Trade Blocs.*

. . . . MICHAEL MCNAMARA

BIBLIOGRAPHY

Itam, Samuel, Simon Cueva, Erik Lundback, Janet Stotsky, and Stephen Tokarick. *Developments and Challenges in the Caribbean Region.* Washington, D.C.: International Monetary Fund, 2000.

Rogonzinski, Jan. *A Brief History of the Caribbean: From the Arawak and Carib to the Present.* New York: Plume, 2000.

West-Durán, Alan, ed. *African Caribbeans: A Reference Guide.* Westport, Conn.: Greenwood Press, 2003.

Carr, E. H.

Edward Hallett ("Ted") Carr (1892–1982) was a British political scientist and historian noted for his contributions to international relations theory. A graduate of Cambridge, Carr had a varied career that included service in the Foreign Office for more than twenty years and experience as a writer and assistant editor for *The Times.* He held several academic appointments and was the Woodrow Wilson Professor of International Relations at the University College of Wales and a fellow at Balliol College, Oxford.

Carr was a prolific author and his diplomatic experience colored his writing. He served as foreign officer in Riga, Latvia, after World War I (1914–1918) and the Russian Revolution of 1917 had a significant impact on his academic work. He emerged as one of Britain's foremost experts on Russian, and later Soviet, history. Among his earlier significant works were biographies of Russian writer Fyodor Dostoevsky, German philosopher Karl Marx, and Russian revolutionary Michael Bakunin, published between 1931 and 1937, each of which received critical praise.

Although Carr's opinion of the Russian Revolution was generally favorable, the Great Depression (1929) affirmed his growing distrust of liberal capitalism because of the social and economic inequalities apparent during it. In 1939, he published *The Twenty Years' Crisis,* an overview of international relations between 1919 and 1939. In it Carr expanded on the work of earlier theorists such as Thucydides and Niccolò Machiavelli and helped define the main tenets of classical realism within international relations theory by differentiating between realism and utopianism (idealism). Central to Carr's analysis was the significance of power in the development of global norms and ethics. He condemned idealism for its failure to incorporate the realities of contemporary international relations in visions of a utopia or ideal world. He further asserted that systemic war or revolution was often a necessary catalyst for significant social change, a contention rejected by his critics. However, he also initially advocated appeasement toward Nazi Germany, a position he revised in later editions of the book.

Carr's other significant works on international relations include *The Future of Nations: Independence or Interdependence?* (1941) and *International Relations Between the Two World Wars* (1955). In 1946, he began work on what turned out to be the seminal fourteen-volume *A History of the Soviet Union,* published over the next thirty-two years. Carr was criticized for minimizing the brutality and totalitarianism of successive Soviet regimes and for overemphasizing the progressive features of Soviet communism. Nonetheless, his work was one of the most comprehensive overviews of the rise of the country to superpower status, beginning with the revolution through World War II (1939–1945).

A series of Carr's Cambridge lectures were published in 1961 as *What is History?* In the essays, Carr analyzed the major contemporary schools of historiography. He argued against empiricism and instead contended that all historians employ a degree of subjectivity caused by their surroundings and the influences of the time period in which they live. Consequently, contemporary events and mores typically colored historians' perceptions of the past, a trend Carr warned strongly against. The book proved highly influential and shaped historiography for the next twenty years.

See also *International Relations; International Relations Theory; Machiavelli, Niccolò; Marx, Karl; Thucydides.*

. . . . TOM LANSFORD

BIBLIOGRAPHY

Cox, Michael, ed. *E. H. Carr: A Critical Appraisal.* London: Palgrave, 2000.

Haslam, Jonathan. *The Vices of Integrity: E. H. Carr, 1892–1982.* New York: Verso, 1999.

Jones, Charles. *E. H. Carr and International Relations: A Duty to Lie.* New York: Cambridge University Press, 1998.

Carter, Gwendolen M.

Gwendolen M. Carter (1906–1991) was a teacher, writer, and Africanist scholar best known for her work on South African politics. For over forty years, she was a pathbreaking authority on the politics and economy of southern Africa.

Carter received her doctorate from Harvard University in 1938 and taught at McMaster University in Hamilton, Ontario, Canada (1932–1935), Wellesley College (1938–1941), and Tufts University (1942–1943) before joining Smith College (1943–1964), Northwestern University (1964–1974), and the University of Florida (1984–1987). She was the president of the African Studies Association (1958–1959) and vice president of the American Political Science Association (1963–1964). She was also a trustee of the African-American Institute for over twenty years.

Carter's early work focused on European governance, but her attention shifted to Africa following a trip to South Africa in 1948. From then on, she was instrumental in bringing the study of Africa into the mainstream of comparative politics. She was one of the founders of African studies in the United States. Her work covered a critical period when apartheid had become institutionalized in South Africa and was unchallenged even in the West. Carter made many trips to South Africa, resulting in numerous publications, including the *Politics of Inequality: South Africa Since 1948* (1958), *Independence for Africa* (1960), *South Africa's Transkei: The Politics of Domestic Colonialism* (1967), and *Which Way Is South Africa Going?* (1980). She also edited several works on Africa, including the four-volume *From Protest to Challenge: A Documentary History of African Politics in South Africa, 1882–1964* (1972–1977), which chronicled the rise of nationalism and the struggle for equality in South Africa. The South African government subsequently canceled her permanent entry rights to the country.

In addition to her work on Africa, earlier in her career, Carter published a number of studies on international relations and politics. Her first book was *The British Commonwealth and International Security* (1947). She also coauthored (with John Herz) a textbook on *Major Foreign Powers* (1972) and wrote a series of books on governments, beginning with *Government and Politics in the 20th Century* (1961).

See also *African Political Economy; Apartheid.*

. . . .   GEORGE THOMAS KURIAN

BIBLIOGRAPHY

Utter, Glenn H., and Charles Lockhart. *American Political Scientists: A Dictionary.* Westport, Conn.: Greenwood Press, 2002.

Cartoons, Political

Political caricatures have a long tradition—the Egyptian pharaoh Akhnaton is often considered the first monarch caricatured, approximately thirty-three hundred years ago. Throughout their history, political cartoons have raised awareness and controversy, parodying important figures and bringing issues to the attention of the public.

POLITICAL CARTOONS IN THE EIGHTEENTH AND NINETEENTH CENTURIES

Perhaps the most famous political cartoon from the colonial era, "Join or Die," was created by Benjamin Franklin and published in the *Pennsylvania Gazette* on May 9, 1754. It shows a snake divided into eight pieces, symbolizing the isolation of the North American colonies' governments from the British monarchy an ocean away in Europe. In France, political cartoons became common in newspapers during the French Revolution (1789–1799), and have been common features in periodicals worldwide ever since.

German-born painter Thomas Nast (1840–1902) is often considered the "father of American caricature" because of politically provoking cartoons, many illustrating his opposition to U.S. president Andrew Johnson. Beginning in the mid-nineteenth century, his cartoons, published in *Harper's Weekly,*

skewered government corruption at the local, state, and national level. Nast also was the first to represent the Democratic Party with a donkey in 1870 and the Republican Party with an elephant in 1874, symbols still used to represents these parties in the twenty-first century.

In Canada, the most representative political cartoonist was Jean-Baptiste Côté (1832–1907), who opposed the Canadian Confederation and published satirical caricatures in the publication *La Scie.*

POLITICAL CARTOONS IN THE TWENTIETH CENTURY

In Belgium, cartoonist George Rémi (under the pseudonym Hergé) drew illustrated stories with a political background that are similar to political cartoons. Featuring teenaged hero Tintin, the first story pits his hero against the Stalinist regime and initially appeared in 1929 in a Belgian weekly paper supplement under the title "Tintin au pays des Soviets" ("The Adventures of Tintin, reporter for 'Le Petit Vingtième' in the Land of the Soviets"). The compiled album of the comic strips of this story was officially released in Belgium in 1973.

During the German occupation of Belgium during World War II (1939–1945), Hergé continued his illustrated stories in the Brussels daily *Le Soir.* His story "Le Secret de la Licorne" ("The Adventures of Tintin: Secret of the Unicorn") contained references to rationing and the black market in Brussels in 1942. Fascinated with the universe of Hergé, U.S. filmmaker Steven Spielberg produced a free adaptation of this story in 2010. Since their first publication, the stories of Tintin have sold hundreds of millions of copies and have been translated into sixty languages and dialects.

In France, comic heroes in children's magazines, such as the weekly *Journal Pilote,* often promoted a political or satirical message. The champion of these stories, Astérix, was a Gaul character created in 1959 by René Goscinny and Albert Uderzo. Although the action is set in Gaul in the year 50 BCE, there are countless references to contemporary French history and political culture, with such themes as occupation by a foreign army, in which the Roman army symbolizes the Nazis, and many inside jokes referencing modern French politicians. In the book *Le Combat des Chefs* (1966), a character adopting the famous pose of Napoleon (with his hand partly hidden inside his shirt) is considered a fool by the old Gaul druids because no one around him can figure out whom the character was trying to impersonate. Like Tintin's tales, the stories of Astérix have sold hundreds of millions of copies and have been translated into thirty languages.

In Chile in 1971, two young scholars—Ariel Dorfman of the United States and Armand Mattelart of Belgium—analyzed and decoded the hidden capitalist and imperialist ideologies in Disney comic strips published in Chilean newspapers, especially Donald Duck. The original Spanish version of their book, *How to Read Donald Duck: Imperialist Ideology in the Disney Comic,* was considered so subversive that it was banned after the Pinochet coup d'état in 1973; the two authors later reported that five thousand copies were thrown into the Pacific Ocean near Valparaiso.

Scott Adams created the comic strip character Dilbert in 1989. The character and his officemates illustrate the consequences of uncontrolled stewardship when poor leaders gain too much power, and its stories symbolize the absurdity and the contradictions of the bureaucracy in modern offices, like those Adams himself witnessed in Silicon Valley during the 1980s. Adams's insights are so thought provoking that several books on management have subsequently used his comic strips to exemplify specific management dos and don'ts. As of the early twenty-first century, Dilbert still appears in hundreds of newspapers and the cartoons are translated into a dozen languages.

POLITICAL CARTOONS AND CONTROVERSY IN THE TWENTY-FIRST CENTURY

In Denmark, on September 30, 2005, an international and interreligious controversy exploded when twelve cartoons depicting the Muslim prophet Muhammad as a Taliban-like terrorist with a black beard and a bomb inside his turban were published by the Danish newspaper *Jyllands-Posten*. Created by Kurt Westergaard, the cartoons were perceived as a provocation by many Muslims worldwide, and the immediate, violent reaction of some of these protesters was interpreted by Western observers as a sign of intolerance and fanaticism. As other newspapers around the globe reproduced these cartoons, the indignation and anger of protesters increased, and as a result, some European politicians asked newspapers not to mention or reproduce the cartoons, going against the normally respected freedom of the press.

Observers and scholars should be aware that while political caricatures can be seen as a sign of a healthy press and freedom of speech in democracies, they also frequently rely on clichés, common sense (in a sociological perspective), and sometimes prejudice, these cartoons can reinforce the usual clichés of "corrupt politicians" and "lazy bureaucrats."

ANIMATED FILMS AND ILLUSTRATED TEXTS

An essential part of popular culture, animated movies began as early as the first experiments in moving pictures, notably with Charles-Émile Reynaud, who invented the "praxinoscope" in 1876. Since then, many cartoon characters from comic strips have been transposed to film. Animated films have always enjoyed a large and durable circulation in movie theatres, from the golden age of cinema, when animated shorts were an integral part of the movie-going experience, to full-length films and television programs featuring popular animated characters.

During World War II, popular animated characters like Bugs Bunny and Daffy Duck appeared in films made for propaganda purposes. Among these animated shorts is the Warner Brothers's *Herr Meets Hare*, in which Bugs Bunny defies Nazi officer Hermann Goering. A decade later, the cold war stimulated countless cartoons and television series in the United States and elsewhere.

A less-studied genre in popular culture, some illustrated novels, especially those created by women, are meant to be subversive and politically engaging. The autobiographical book series *Persepolis* by Iranian writer Marjane Satrapi is a strong critique of the conservative interpretation of Islamic law found in Iran since 1978. First published in 2001, her books have been translated into many languages, and a critically acclaimed animated feature film of the same name was released in 2007.

See also *Censorship; Disinformation; Ideologies, Political; Media, Political Commentary in the; Media and Politics; Politics, Literature, and Film; Propaganda; Public Opinion; Television and Politics.*

. . . . YVES LABERGE

BIBLIOGRAPHY

Adams, Scott. *The Dilbert Principle*. New York, HarperBusiness, 1996.
Association of American Editorial Cartoonists. www.editorialcartoonists .com.
Dorfman, Ariel, and Armand Mattelart. *How to Read Donald Duck: Imperialist Ideology in the Disney Comic*. New York: International General, 1975.
HarpWeek. "The World of Thomas Nast." www.thomasnast.com.
Hergé [pseud.]. *The Adventures of Tintin: Secret of the Unicorn*. Lawrence, Kan.: Mammoth, 1942.
———. *Tintin: Reporter for "Le Petit Vingtième" in the Land of the Soviets*. Lawrence, Kan.: Mammoth, 2007.
Satrapi, Marjane. *Persepolis: The Story of a Childhood; The Story of a Return*. Pantheon Books, 2005.

Case Studies

A *case study* is one of several ways to conduct social and political science research. The term has several meanings in the research literature. Case study can be used to describe a unit of analysis (e.g., for an organization, a country, an event, or a person); a research method (generally as a qualitative inquiry); or a research strategy that investigates single or multiple cases using participant observations, interviews, surveys, and statistical data.

Some researchers have described the case study as an umbrella term for a group of research methods that focus an inquiry around a specific context. In this regard, for example, single or multiple case studies can include quantitative evidence based on multiple sources of evidence. Robert Yin, one of the prominent scholars who conceptualizes the term, points out that case studies should not be confused with qualitative research. He indicates that a case study can be based on any mix of quantitative and qualitative evidence, including experiments, surveys, and archival information. This definition is also supported by Siegfried Lamnek: "The case study is a research approach, situated between concrete data taking techniques and methodological paradigms." Case studies clearly address "what" (what happened) and "who" (who did it), and they also (descriptively) address the "how much" question. In some cases, instead of analyzing cause–effect relationships or generalizable truth within the study, researchers focus on the exploration and description of the situation. In other words, holistic understanding of the situation is more important in case studies. This type of research is multifaceted because it commonly involves analysis of data from multiple sources, with researchers examining single or multiple cases within a study.

Researchers from many disciplines, including social and natural sciences, use the case study method. Political science researchers use this method to describe or explain a situation or a phenomenon, explore an event, generate a new theory, test a theory in a certain environment, challenge a theory, or find applicable solutions for social problems. One of the major advantages of the case study method is its relation to everyday practices and applicability to real-life situations.

In case studies, the researcher can apply many theories in the research design but most commonly used theories are individual, organizational, and social. Individual theories, which focus on the personality, cognitive behavior, individual development, and interactions of a particular subject, can be applicable to political science research, especially the political psychology field. Organizational theories focusing on institutions, bureaucracies, organizational structure, and performance are commonly used in public policy and administration research in political science. Social theories that address urban development, group behavior, and cultural institutions are also applicable for political science research.

In terms of its history, the case study is not a new form of research. In fact, sociology and anthropology are credited with shaping the term as it is now conceptualized. However, case study research has its roots in a number of other areas as well: the clinical methods of medical doctors; the methods of journalists, historians, and anthropologists; and the qualitative descriptions provided by quantitative researchers such as Robert E. Park, Chicago sociologist and former newspaper reporter. Park was one of the most prominent scholars in shaping sociological case studies at the University of Chicago in the 1920s.

The debate between proqualitative and proquantitative became quite intense over the years, and the case study method has received many criticisms. In fact, when compared to statistics, case studies were considered to be unscientific by some scholars due to the rise of positivism and quantitative methods in social science research. The underlying philosophical assumptions in these case studies are exploration and description, which are considered a subjective issue by many. This type of comprehensive understanding involves an in-depth explanation of an entity, people, community, or a country that produces much more detailed information than a statistical analysis.

See also *Qualitative Methodologies; Quantitative Analysis.*

. . . . ARIF AKGUL

BIBLIOGRAPHY

Hamel, Jacques. *Case Study Methods.* Newbury Park, Calif.: Sage Publications, 1993.

Lamnek, Siegfried. *Qualitative Sozialforschung: Lehrbuch,* vol. 4. Weinhein, Ger.: Beltz Verlag, 2005.

Mills, Albert J., Durepos, Gabrielle, and Wiebe, Elden, eds. *Encyclopedia of Case Study Research.* Thousand Oaks, Calif.: Sage Publications, 2009.

Yin, Robert K. *Applications of Case Study Research,* 2nd ed. Thousand Oaks, Calif.: Sage Publications, 2003.

———. *Case Study Research, Design, and Methods,* 2nd ed. Newbury Park, Calif.: Sage Publications, 1994.

Caste System

The Indian caste system is primarily a division of human endeavor, yet the caste system also profoundly impacts Hinduism. A four-tiered system, the main castes of birth into the Hindu social system include: Brahmin (priestly class), Kshatriya (administrative class), Vaishya (mercantile class), Shudra (worker class), and Dalit (untouchables). Karma determines birth into one of the main castes, which means all of humanity is created unequal. Dalits are India's "hidden apartheid" and constitute approximately 20 percent (three hundred million) of India's population. The exploitation and oppression of the Dalits causes this population to occupy a position of perpetual economic and physical vulnerability, and condemnation of the Dalits varies from social ostracism to punitive violence.

However, many people have rallied to give Dalits the same rights as other Indians. Bhimrao Ramji Ambedkar was born an "untouchable" and became one of the most outspoken advocates for granting mutual rights to Dalits. He eventually advocated conversion to other religions, and in 1956, he and thousands of his followers converted to Buddhism as a rejection of Hinduism and its caste system. Udit Raj was also born an "untouchable," and he converted to Buddhism and labored against the social injustice of the Dalits. Although he was born Kshatriya, even Buddha condemned the caste system, as illustrated when he said, "Not by birth does one become an outcast . . . by deeds one becomes an outcast." Christian missionaries have been active in outreach ministries to the Dalits, and many Dalits converted to Christianity in the nineteenth and twentieth centuries.

Shortly after India's independence from Great Britain in 1947, it technically became illegal to discriminate on the basis of the caste system; however, such discrimination is not uncommon in modern India. Today, the caste system has a prevailing influence both economically and socially, especially in rural areas. In urban areas, the caste system is still defended but is less observable. The Buddhist religion, which began approximately 552 BCE, is a consequence of Hinduism, and therefore, some aspects of the caste system are practiced in Buddhist countries like Japan, Sri Lanka, and Tibet.

The caste system associated with Hinduism is not only the world's oldest social hierarchy; it is also an example of a traditional economy. Caste, custom, and heredity primarily determine allocation and ownership of available resources in this economy. According to the Hindu caste system, one should not attempt to alter one's destiny, but to commit life to one's current degree or estate in a way that is similar to the European feudal system. As an economic structure, the caste system is oppressive in restricting any opportunity to change one's occupational or social status.

According to Hinduism, people strive to achieve release from *samsara,* the cyclical process of death and rebirth, and consequently, the notion of *karma,* which is the law of cause and effect. The law of karma necessitates inevitable consequences in subsequent lives and is intimately associated with the social and economic structure of India. The original socio-religious system of India was Varnashrama Dharma, which did not restrict change in one's occupational or social status. However, the caste system is based upon *jati,* or birth, and identifies status in a rigid and hereditary manner.

The Varnashrama Dharma was not intended to be rigid, which is evident in the *Bhagavad-Gita* 4, a sacred Hindu scripture. Krishna, a Hindu deity, explained that he "established the four castes, which correspond to the different types of guna [quality] and karma." The class and stage divisions were established as the most effective means of engagement in eternal religious principles because they are based upon action and inaction in the material world. Ability, proclivity, and labor will control a person—not birth—and these qualities will be judged to determine social class. Social class will determine *dharma,* or moral duty, which is an essential doctrine of Hinduism. However, the distinguishing characteristic of Varnashrama Dharma and the contemporary caste system is the consideration of birth to determine social class, which is why Varnashrama Dharma is the historical basis for the modern caste system.

See also *Buddhist Political Thought; Gandhism; Hindu Political Thought; Indian Ocean Region.*

. . . . RON J. BIGALKE JR.

BIBLIOGRAPHY

Ambedkar, B. R. *The Untouchables.* Bangalore, India: Dalit Sahitya Akademy, 1948.

Aylett, Liz. *The Hindu Experience.* London: Hodder and Stoughton, 1992.

Cashdan, Elizabeth, ed. *Risk and Uncertainty in Tribal and Peasant Economies.* Boulder: Westview Press, 1990.

Hiro, Dilip. *The Untouchables of India.* London: Minority Rights Group, 1982.

Hopkins, Thomas J. *The Hindu Religious Tradition.* Belmont, Calif.: Wadsworth, 1971.

Keer, Dhananjay. *Dr. Ambedkar: Life and Mission.* Bombay: Popular Prakashan, 1990.

Krishan, Yuvraj. *The Doctrine of Karma: Its Origin and Development in Brahmanical, Buddhist, and Jaina Traditions.* Delhi: Motilal Banarsidass Publishers, 1997.

Mahar, J. Michael, ed. *The Untouchables in Contemporary India.* Tucson: University of Arizona Press, 1972.

Mayor, John N., ed. *India: Issues, Historical Background, and Bibliography.* Hauppauge, N.Y.: Nova Science Publishers, 2003.

Prabhavananda, Swami. *Bhagavad-Gita,* translated by Christopher Isherwood. New York: Barnes and Noble, 1995.

Castoriadis, Cornelius

Cornelius Castoriadis (1922–1997) was a French economist, psychoanalyst, and philosopher. A member of the Trotsky-ist Internationalist Communist Party at the end of World War II (1939–1945), Castoriadis broke away from the Fourth International due to its defence of the Soviet Union in 1948. Castoriadis's name is linked to the journal *Socialism or Barbarism,* which he cofounded with Claude Lefort. The journal was published between 1949 and 1965 and attracted activists and intellectuals such as Jean-François Lyotard. In those years, Castoriadis worked as an economist for the Organization for European Economic Cooperation (OEEC, later to become the OECD) and often wrote under pseudonyms such as Paul Cardan and Pierre Chaulieu.

The main contribution of *Socialism or Barbarism* was its critique of the Soviet Union as a form of state bureaucratic capitalism and of traditional Marxism for its ideological stiffness in its reading of advanced capitalist and bureaucratic societies. The unorthodox antiauthoritarian Marxist critique (sustaining at times a view close to council communism) developed by the journal exercised a deep influence on the social movements of May 1968 in France. The common thread of Castoriadis's political and intellectual life was indeed his unconditional defence of the *project of autonomy.*

The originality of Castoriadis's thinking lies in the combination of a theory of autonomy with a radical view of the social imaginary. In 1970, Castoriadis left his position in the OECD. In 1974 he became a practicing psychoanalyst, and in 1979 he was elected Director of Studies at Paris's École des Hautes Études en Sciences Sociales.

By autonomy, Castoriadis meant not only the possibility to give oneself one's own law, but more radically, the possibility to be at the origin of what will be and to know oneself as such. The project of autonomy is very difficult to realize, both at the individual and at the social level, because every society tends to mythologize the fact of being self-produced by attributing its origins to extrasocial sources such as gods and heroes. When a society recognizes that it is responsible for its own origins, that society accepts the possibility of chaos. This is why almost all known societies are heteronymous societies—societies that attribute their origins to something other.

Drawing insights from psychoanalysis, Castoriadis argued that the psyche is monadic since it is pure representational, affective, or unintentional flux; indeterminate; and, in principle, unmasterable. It is only through a process of socialization beginning with the first encounters with language that a social individual is created. If it is true that no society could ever exist without the single concrete individuals that sustain it, it is equally true that no individual could exist outside of the imaginary significations of the society to which the individual has been socialized.

If the individual depends on the imaginary significations of society, then a full realization of the project of autonomy needs to be pursued at the social level. Although this is very difficult to accomplish, the possibility always remains for a society and for the individuals that compose it to radically question the imaginary significations in which they live. Imagination is radical because it is at the origin of reality itself, but also because it can always potentially question its own products. Among the known societies that have been able to attain such an ideal, Castoriadis looked to ancient Greece, to which he attributed both the discovery of philosophy and politics.

See also *Lyotard, Jean-Francois; Organization for Economic Cooperation and Development (OECD); Trotsky, Leon.*

. . . . CHIARA BOTTICI

BIBLIOGRAPHY

Agora International. "Cornelius Castoriadis Agora International Website."
University of Michigan Library. www.agorainternational.org/.

Castoriadis, Cornelius. *Crossroads in the Labyrinth.* Cambridge. Mass.: MIT
Press, 1984.

———. *The Imaginary Institution of Society.* Cambridge: Polity Press, 1987.

———. *Philosophy, Politics, Autonomy.* New York: Oxford University Press,
1991.

———. *Political and Social Writings,* vols. 1–3. Minneapolis: University of
Minnesota Press, 1988–1993.

Casus Belli

Casus belli (Latin for "case for war" or "occasion for war") is the specific event, policy, or action that a state cites to justify going to war. Countries use a public justification for war in order to gain international support and to rally domestic support. Philosopher Hugo Grotius helped popularize the need to officially articulate a rationale prior to the start of hostilities as part of the development of just war theory (*jus ad bellum*). The existence of a casus belli, however, does not necessitate armed conflict; nations may still resolve disputes through peaceful means.

Traditional examples of widely accepted justifications for war include self-defense or the defense of an ally. For instance, Japan's attack on Pearl Harbor on December 7, 1941, was the casus belli for U.S. entry into World War II (1939–1945). The use of force on behalf of an international body such as the League of Nations or the United Nations is also widely now regarded as a legitimate casus belli.

Nations may promulgate a false or questionable casus belli in an attempt to gain global backing for military action. For example, critics of the 2003 U.S–led invasion of Iraq assert that the administration of President George W. Bush manipulated intelligence reports in order to make the regime of Saddam Hussein appear more of a threat.

See also *Grotius, Hugo; Just War Theory; Legitimate Violence; Statecraft; Strategy, Military.*

. . . . TOM LANSFORD

Catlin, George Edward Gordon

Although a native of England, George Edward Gordon Catlin (1896–1979) was a principal contributor to the transformation of American political science that took place during the 1920s.

At the beginning of World War I (1914–1918), Catlin left New College, Oxford, to join the London Rifle Brigade and serve in France. After his return to Oxford, his prize essay on Thomas Hobbes was published as a book in 1922. Although he was offered opportunities to remain in England, he chose, in 1924, to complete his graduate work in the United States at Cornell University, where he was instrumental in creating the political science department and was also offered a faculty position. A short time later, the Rockefeller Foundation and the Social Science Research Council invited him to go to New York City and study the issue of prohibition. He eventually published *Liquor Control* in 1931, a book that contributed to the movement to repeal the Eighteenth Amendment. While conducting this research, he met Charles E. Merriam and Harold Dwight Lasswell, prominent members of the Chicago school of political science. He subsequently became deeply involved with many American political scientists who were dedicated to propagating a new science of politics and whose perspective was linked to a commitment to practical application, which Catlin believed had been lacking in the English curriculum and its devotion to history and the traditional study of the state.

What in part attracted Catlin to the American scene was the growing emphasis on empirical research as well as the normative theory of democratic pluralism, which was becoming a central dimension of political science. His 1927 book, *The Science and Method of Politics,* advanced a conception of a rigorous science of politics, which, although ultimately dedicated to serving practical concerns, should distinguish between factual and ethical claims. It was also one of the first works to urge the application of economic theory to the analysis of political behavior. In 1930, Catlin published *A Study of the Principles of Politics,* which again emphasized the need to turn away from typical studies of political philosophy and the humanities and toward the development of a naturalistic interdisciplinary science of society. He continued, however, to argue—for example, in *Systematic Politics* (1962) and *Political and Sociological Theory and Its Applications* (1964)—that such a science should be devoted to the utilitarian goal of social change.

Catlin left Cornell to return to England in 1935, but he subsequently was a visitor at many colleges in the United States and elsewhere, including two years in Canada at McGill University. He published many scholarly articles and political essays and more than fifteen books, but much of his later life was devoted to practical politics and to causes such as peace and world government, the Atlantic community, the European market, and Indian independence. He was both a candidate for the Labour party in England and an adviser to Wendell Wilkie during the 1940 election in the United States. Catlin was knighted in 1970, and in 1972 he published his autobiography, *For God's Sake, Go!*

See also *British Political Thought; Lasswell, Harold Dwight; Merriam, Charles E.*

. . . . JOHN G. GUNNELL

BIBLIOGRAPHY

Gunnell, John G. "Political Science on the Cusp: Recovering a Discipline's
Past." *American Political Science Review* 99, no. 4 (2005): 597–609.

Caucus

A *caucus* is a general meeting of a political party or group. Within political science, the term has two distinct meanings. First, a caucus may refer to a party convention to select candidates or establish consensus on issues. Second, a caucus can be a policy- or issue-specific parliamentary grouping that exists either within a broader party or that often crosses party lines based on issue positions.

The term was first used in the United States to apply to the regular meetings of political parties at the local and state levels. At these sessions, party members would choose candidates and adopt common stances on policy matters. Caucuses provided a means for the party hierarchy to control candidate selection since political bosses typically handpicked the delegates. The use of primary elections to choose candidates was a progressive reform designed to open the system to greater public participation, and in the nineteenth and twentieth centuries many states replaced caucuses with primaries. In the United States, fourteen states still use some form of the caucus system to choose candidates. Caucuses have become more open and are held at the ward or district level. In addition, they are typically open to all registered members of a party. Attendees divide themselves according to their candidate preference and then engage in alternating periods of debate and voting until a winner emerges. The Iowa caucuses traditionally launch the U.S. presidential nomination process. Delegates are elected from all 1,784 precincts. Those delegates then meet at ninety-nine different county conventions (one for each county in the state) to choose the party's candidates for the presidency and Congress.

Within legislative bodies, caucuses are collective groups of individual representatives or political parties that organize themselves to advance specific interests and expand their influence. Sometimes known alternately as conferences, these groupings allow party members to organize around specific interests. Among countries that utilize the Westminster system, caucuses can be the collective membership of a party. These groupings are responsible for electing leaders, establishing rules, developing party positions on issues, and group discipline, especially on voting matters. For instance, in Canada the party caucus has the authority to elect the party leader, while in New Zealand the caucus even elects the members of the cabinet from a particular party. In the U.S. Congress and many state legislatures there is a caucus for each party. Congressional caucuses typically meet in closed-door sessions to chose leaders and formulate or debate policy positions. They further provide a means for organized ideological diversity in congressional parties. For example, conservatives within the Republican Party in the House of Representatives may join the Republican Study Committee while conservative Democrats have the Blue Dog Coalition. There are also a number of smaller caucuses based on policy issues. These caucuses can be bipartisan and may be open to members of both chambers such as the Congressional Czech Caucus or the Congressional Steel Caucus. Caucuses may be based on race or gender, including the Congressional Black Caucus and the Women's Caucus.

See also *Candidate Recruitment; Interest Groups and Lobbies; Party and Social Structure; Party Organization; Party Systems, Comparative; Westminster Model.*

. . . . TOM LANSFORD

BIBLIOGRAPHY
Baker, Ross K. *House and Senate*, 3rd ed. New York: Norton, 2001.
Bibby, John F. *Politics, Parties, and Elections in America*, 4th ed. Belmont, Calif.: Wadsworth, 2000.
Hammond, Susan Web. *Congressional Caucuses in National Policymaking.* Baltimore: Johns Hopkins University Press, 2001.
Mitchell, Austin. *Caucus: The New Zealand Parliamentary Parties.* London: University of London, 1968.
Skipper, John. *The Iowa Caucuses: First Tests of Presidential Aspiration, 1972–2008.* Jefferson, N.C.: McFarland, 2009.
Stewart, Charles. *Analyzing Congress.* New York: W. W. Norton, 2001.

Causal Inference

The modern scientific approach is based upon the search for answers to what causes observed phenomena. For instance, by establishing the causes of a given problem (low voter turnout), it is possible to seek answers for how to deal with or cure that problem (lower the barriers to voting). Research that establishes that one factor directly, or in combination with other factors, leads to observed effects is known as *causal inference.*

Causal inference is established through the construction and testing of hypotheses. A testable hypothesis may come from a theory seeking to explain why one variable (A) would have an effect upon a second variable (B). If the theory is sound, it will be supported by repeated observations where A causes B because changes in A cause changes in B (known as *covariation*). Causal inference is not equivalent to theory testing; for example, results from a randomized experiment may provide strong evidence that a medical treatment causes an effect, even in the absence of any underlying theory, but such controlled experiments are rare in political science. Without a solid theory, the simple observation that A and B change in tandem is an insufficient explanation and would be considered mere correlation.

For example, voter records may indicate that individuals in a particular constituency are relatively less likely to vote. In order to explain this phenomenon, political scientists would develop a possible causal hypothesis (e.g., people in this constituency are poorer or less educated and therefore are less likely to engage in registration and voting) and then test it using a data set. A causal relationship between income or levels of educational achievement and the act of voting are plausible in only one direction; the act of voting logically should have no causal effect on income or level of education.

See also *Causation and Correlation; Correlation; Experimental Design; Inference; Survey Techniques and Design.*

. . . . PAUL S. ROWE

Causation and Correlation

Political scientists are rarely content to simply describe political phenomena; they seek to explain them. These explanations are built upon correlation and causation between variables of interest. Two variables are *correlated* if certain values of one variable coincide with certain values of the other variable, or put differently, if change in one variable is associated with change in the other variable. Yet observing a correlation between two variables does not in itself mean that one causes the other. *Causality* means that values of one variable produce values of the other variable. In other words, an independent variable exerts causal influence on the dependent variable. To demonstrate a causal relationship between independent and dependent variables, one must show (1) that the two variables are correlated, (2) that the independent variable precedes the dependent variable in time, and (3) that the relationship is not *spurious*—the observed relationship between the two variables is not due to the influence of a third variable. Making a case for causality depends on strong theory that spells out how variables are related and anticipates possible spurious relationships. Careful research design is also important, especially in trying to account for time order of key variables.

. . . . JULIO BORQUEZ

See also *Causal Inference; Correlation; Experimental Design; Inference; Survey Techniques and Design.*

BIBLIOGRAPHY

Babbie, Earl R. *The Practice of Social Research,* 11th ed. Belmont, Calif.: Wadsworth, 2007.

Shively, W. Phillips. *The Craft of Political Research,* 5th ed. Upper Saddle River, N.J.: Prentice Hall, 2002.

Censorship

Censorship is the process of controlling or evaluating the content of books, films, newspapers, or art in an attempt to comply with social norms. It is usually overseen by a political, religious, or familial authority and sometimes results in the banning of content. It does not evolve with time; rather, this process adjusts itself according to the norms and consensus of a society. Often viewed as a negative, it is not necessarily bad; for instance, society as a whole generally agrees that pornography should not be accessible to minors.

How a society reaches consensus in determining what should be controlled or banned is a much discussed topic. Who should draw the line and determine what is or is not moral? Throughout the centuries, there have been leaders and governments that have controlled the dissemination of information, art, and correspondence, but scholars such as Noam Chomsky believe that even in democratic systems, pressure from well-funded and vocal groups can affect what is communicated in the public sphere.

THE DEFINITIONS OF CENSORSHIP

Censorship as a concept exists in such disciplines as psychoanalysis, law, political science, sociology, ethics, and media studies. Typically, it is defined as either (1) controlling or evaluating the contents of, for instance, a book or movie to be sure it's appropriate for the relevant audiences, or (2) forbidding or banning information considered by an authorized censor to be subversive, offensive, obscene, heretic, or against the official (often dominant) ideology.

The history of censorship is quite long, and the conditions surrounding its application have changed over time and as countries have evolved culturally. This is why censorship is a social and political issue as much as an ethical one. In a sense, censorship implicitly reveals the moral norms of, and limits set by, a society by banning specific images, words, and representations of situations and events deemed unacceptable to the public. Censorship issues also relate to the various distinctions between the public sphere and private life.

Those who seek total freedom of speech or lack confidence in governmental or religious institutions often contest censorship. Sometimes the media offer examples of censorship that appear to be abusive, unjustified, or the result of a lack of intelligence or artistic sensibility by the local authorities; for example, a movie may be forbidden in a country or a work of art may be refused as part of a gallery exhibit.

Societies exist in part on a foundation of unified thought and belief that allows individuals to live together in general harmony; however, at times, governments or law enforcement may feel the need to enforce that unity against ideas that may cause discontent or protest. To do so, these authorities may decide for the general population whether something is "good" or "bad" for it. Such actions illustrate the differences in taboos and acceptable levels of free speech, expression, and dissent among different governments, cultures, and societies. Government officials or other leaders in a particular society may feel that allowing access to some materials is too dangerous to their regimes or to the continued harmony of a locale, and too inflammatory in its content or in the reactions that it may inspire in the general populace. These officials may believe that the general population is not mentally mature enough or psychologically capable of being exposed to the content without incurring moral or psychological harm, or inciting dissent from a society's generally accepted rules and norms.

MOTION PICTURES

Motion pictures have faced censorship to varying degree since their beginnings in the late nineteenth century, but for the most part this existed at the local or state level. In the United States, the Motion Picture Production Code, better known as the Hays Code after its creator William H. Hays, was the first nationwide set of guidelines enumerating what was and was not acceptable material for a motion picture. The self-instituted rules were an attempt by the industry to hold off federal oversight and regulation following the Supreme Court ruling in *Mutual Film Corporation v. Industrial Commission of Ohio* (1915). The justices determined that films were a business and not an art form and, therefore, were not protected under the First Amendment, and local and state censorship bans proliferated in response. The guidelines were in place from 1930 until 1968 and mandated that films could not contain, among other things, any nakedness, interracial marriages, or depictions of homosexuality.

BOOK BURNING

One of the oldest forms of censorship is book burning. According to author Judith Kohl, the earliest case of book burning involved the Greek philosopher Anaxagoras, whose scientific works were considered heretical to the established religion of the time and were put to the torch around 450 BCE. This practice intensified with the invention of the printing press in 1435, and books became easily and quickly available to the general public.

In Nazi Germany of the early 1930s, minister of propaganda Josef Goebbels organized public book burnings that included works by Jewish authors such as Albert Einstein, Sigmund Freud, and Marcel Proust. In *Censorship: A World Encyclopedia*, Kohl writes that during the Nazi regime, "The works of many non-Jewish but liberal or communist authors were also consumed, including those of Thomas and Heinrich Mann, Arnold and Stefan Zweig, Havelock Ellis, Jack London, Upton Sinclair, and Émile Zola."

The Nazis were not the last to organize public book burnings. Kohl writes, "The Islamic revolution in Iran (1979) included the destruction of more than 5 million books." On February 14, 1989, Iranian leader Ayatollah Ruhollah Khomeini issued a *fatwa*, a kind of death warrant, after novelist Salman Rushdie wrote in his *Satanic Verses* that he no longer believed in Islam. Many Muslim communities around the world held public rallies at which copies of the book were burned. It was banned in South Africa and in Rushdie's native India, and copies were destroyed in many public libraries worldwide. In Berkeley at the University of California, a bookstore that carried the book was firebombed. The events parallel those of Ray Bradbury's novel *Fahrenheit 451*, first published in 1953, which depicts systematic book burning in a futuristic, totalitarian society.

PURPOSE OF CENSORSHIP

Could society exist without some form of censorship? Would values be protected without any form of control? Some family values groups are concerned about how prevalent violence and obscenity are in the media, and some of the key issues surrounding censorship in the early twenty-first century involve the Internet, where pornography and extremists sites proliferate.

The debate wages internationally. Journalism professor Hussein Amin writes about the situation in Egypt and Arab countries: "Overt censorship and self-censorship are commonplace in the Arab news media today and journalism education programs, just as the media themselves have, in fact, been recruited into a national enterprise for the production of propaganda." *Freedom of the press* as defined by most Westerners is not a universal value. According to international freedom-of-the-press advocate Reporters Without Borders, Burma, Cuba, the Maldives, the Seychelles, Tunisia, Vietnam, China, Pakistan, and Iran are among the most restrictive in regard to freedom of press.

CENSORSHIP AFTER 9/11

The events of September 11, 2001, on the U.S. East Coast were seen live worldwide, and had ripple effects across the globe. For instance, in the Gaza Strip, on September 14, Palestinian officials confiscated a videotape filmed by a U.S. camera operator covering a march of more than a thousand Palestinians celebrating the event while burning an Israeli flag and showing a poster of al-Qaida leader Osama bin Laden. The videotape was returned to the Associated Press two days later with portions erased. Also, in the United States, some video game–makers changed the contents of games involving plane crashes and skyscrapers in flames following 9/11 in what may be seen as a form of economic self-censorship, in that they realized the buying public was less likely to buy their products if this content remained.

See also *Family Values; Freedom of the Press; Freedom of Speech; Journalism, Political; Media Bias; Media, Political Commentary in the; Media and Politics; News, Construction of; Propaganda; Talk Radio; Television and Politics.*

. . . . YVES LABERGE

BIBLIOGRAPHY
American Library Association Intellectual Freedom Committee. "Gaza Strip." *Newsletter on Intellectual Freedom*, November 2001, 253.
American Library Association Intellectual Freedom Committee. "Video Games." *Newsletter on Intellectual Freedom*, November 2001, 252.
Amin, Hussein, "Freedom as a Value in Arab Media: Perceptions and Attitudes among Journalists," *Political Communication* 19, no. 2, (April 2002): 125–135.
Bernstein, Matthew, ed. *Controlling Hollywood. Censorship and Regulation in the Studio Era.* New Brunswick, N.J.: Rutgers University Press, 2000.
Blumer, Herbert. *Movies and Conduct.* New York: Macmillan, 1933.
Family Safe Media. "Preserving Family Values in a Media Driven Society." www.familysafemedia.com.
Foerstel, Herbert N. *Banned in the Media: A Reference Guide to Censorship in the Press, Motion Pictures, Broadcasting, and the Internet.* Westport, Conn.: Greenwood Press, 1998.
———. *Free Expression and Censorship in America: An Encyclopedia.* Westport, Conn.: Greenwood Press, 1997.
Heins, Marjorie. *Not in Front of the Children: "Indecency," Censorship and the Innocence of Youth.* New York: Hill and Wang, 2001.
Jones, Derek, ed. *Censorship: A World Encyclopedia*, 4 vols. London and Chicago: Fitzroy Dearborn, 2001.
Maltby, Richard. *Hollywood Cinema*, 2nd ed. Oxford: Blackwell, 2003.
Online Books. "Banned Books Online." University of Pennsylvania Library. www.digital.library.upenn.edu/books/banned-books.html.
Wallack, Lawrence, with Katie Woodruff, Lori Dorfman, and Iris Diaz. *News for a Change: An Advocate's Guide to Working with the Media.* Thousand Oaks, Calif.: Sage Publications, 1999.

Censure

Censure is the act of formally reprimanding a public official because of unethical or illegal conduct. In most democratic nations, censure is a legislative act, passed by majority vote to express a body's displeasure with a member or other public official. Censure is stronger than a rebuke, but is one step short of impeachment or removal from office. In some systems, censure may be enacted by simple majority vote, while others require a supermajority. The censure process may be specifically detailed in a nation's constitution, as is the case in Canada, or it may have its roots in tradition or the acquired powers of a legislature, as is true with the United States. In the U.S. Constitution, there is no explicit power to censure, but Congress does have the ability to approve nonbinding resolutions and establish rules of conduct and punish members. If a member of Congress is censured, they are removed from any leadership positions, including leadership of committees or subcommittees. In 1834, the Senate, under the control of the opposition Whigs, censured President Andrew Jackson, over his removal of deposits from the Bank of the United States.

However, three years later, the Democrat-controlled Senate voted to remove the censure.

See also *Impeachment.*

. . . . TOM LANSFORD

Center-periphery Relations (Federalism)

The center-periphery relations of interdependence are of the utmost importance for the understanding of politics in modern social life. This relationship not only refers to local and national contexts but extends to the international level as well. There is a center, or central zone, that impinges in various ways on those who live within the ecological domain in which the society exists. According to this *diffusionist* approach, the relationship to this central zone constitutes membership in society.

Such a relationship ought to be analyzed from the double perspective of centralization and peripheral accentuation. Center and periphery have often been considered in terms of subordination of the latter to the former. Likewise, a double dimension between horizontal and vertical relationships has been drawn when referring either to the strict geographical dimension or to a system of functional interaction. In the latter, a set of key decision-making powers form the center and the periphery is composed of participants in the interaction system who have the least influence on the central group and on the decision making. The relations of dominance and dependence are not restricted to their political forms but can also affect economic and social dimensions.

Theories of ethnocentrism and internal colonialism have stressed those abilities of state cores to implement programs of national assimilation over peripheral areas. William Graham Sumner coined *ethnocentrism* as the technical name for which one's own group is the center of everything, and all others are scaled down and rated with reference to it. Applied to territorial politics, ethnocentrism manifests in the disregard shown by the state core toward the economic development of the periphery.

Internal colonialism is viewed as a structure of social relations based on domination and exploitation among culturally heterogeneous groups within the state. Accordingly, the superordinate, or center, seeks to stabilize and monopolize its advantage over the subordinate, or periphery, by means of policies aimed at the institutionalization of a stratification system (e.g., developmental priorities given to cities to the detriment of resource-extractive rural areas). This is labeled as *cultural division of labor* and produces a reaction heightening cultural or ethnoterritorial distinctiveness in both core and periphery.

Modernization theory has pointed out that both processes of state formation and nation-building were accelerated by the development of industrial capitalism in Europe and North America in the nineteenth century. The enforcement of one central authority on peripheral regions or subordinated political groups, often socially and culturally different, seemed to be necessary. But, contrary to what was originally suggested, such centralization has often provoked a periphery accentuation and a subnational mobilization in quest for local autonomy.

In some industrial advanced democracies, political entrepreneurialism and clientelism in center-periphery relations have aimed at consolidating the territorial bases of power distribution and the preservation of channels of influence between central and local elites (e.g., Italy's First Republic until 1992). Often such power arrangements have been articulated by means of informal and "behind-the-door" arrangements, whereby subnational political actors have sought to secure their resources by means of sustaining political elites and parties at the central level. These exchange mechanisms have come increasingly under pressure to comply with the democratic principle of accountability in the intergovernmental relations between the central administration, the regions, and the local authorities. Multilevel governance is, therefore, increasingly shaped by the formalization of administrative arrangements, aimed at a more efficient planning and policy making, particularly in decentralized polities. The polycentric nature of many states and supranational political entities, such as the European Union, has provoked apparently divergent developments. Thus, if new economic policies have allowed for monetary centralization and a growing harmonization of single-market policies, the quest for policy decentralization also claims a political redistribution of powers according to the subsidiarity principle (decisions to be taken supranationally only if local, regional, or national levels cannot perform better).

At the international level, Immanuel Wallerstein has put forward the world-system approach that emphasizes a global rather that a state-centric perspective. It has been argued that since the sixteenth century, a capitalist world system was gradually formed having some European nations as core countries while other countries became subordinated and provided cheap labor and raw materials. Later on, other semiperipheral countries (e.g., the postcolonial United States) achieved some degree of industrialization and were less dominated by the economies of the core. This world-system approach has been criticized by its overriding analytical focus on the market and its emphasis on the overdetermination of the economic upon other political and social factors.

See also *Accountability; Autonomy; Centralization, Deconcentration, and Decentralization; Elites, Political; Ethnocentricism; Globalization; Governance; Intergovernmental Relations; Internal Colonialism; Modernization; Nation-building; Postcolonial Theory; State Formation; Subsidiarity; Sumner, William Graham.*

. . . . LUIS MORENO

BIBLIOGRAPHY

Mény, Yves, and Vincent Wright, eds. *Centre-Periphery Relations in Western Europe.* London: Allen and Unwin, 1985.

Rokkan, Stein, and Derek Urwin. *Economy, Territory, Identity: Politics of West European Peripheries.* Beverly Hills, Calif.: Sage Publications, 1983.

Shils, Edward. *Center and Periphery: Essays in Macrosociology.* Chicago: University of Chicago Press, 1975.

Wallerstein, Immanuel. *The Modern World-System. Vol. 1, Capitalist Agriculture and the Origins of the European World-Economy in the Sixteenth Century.* New York: Academic Press, 1974.

———. *The Modern World-System. Vol. 2, Mercantilism and the Consolidation of the European World-Economy, 1600–1750.* New York: Academic Press, 1980.

———. *The Modern World-System. Vol. 3, The Second Era of Great Expansion of the Capitalist World-Economy, 1730–1840s.* San Diego, Calif.: Academic Press, 1989.

Central Bank

Central banks are government or quasi-governmental agencies with a long history. For example, the Bank of England was chartered in the seventeenth century. But the prevalence and extensive policy-making authority of modern central banks is a post–World War II (1939–1945) phenomenon. While modern central banks vary in their institutional relationships with elected officials, their policy responsibilities typically include the development and implementation of monetary policy and regulation of the banking and, sometimes, the broader financial industry.

Monetary policy focuses on currency management. Monetary policy instruments available to central banks vary, but they may include authority over reserve requirements for commercial banks; the ability to lend directly to banks and, in some cases, other financial institutions; and the capacity to participate in open market operations (the purchase and sale of government securities). These responsibilities often include serving as a lender of last resort. Each policy tool is designed to influence the extent to which cash is available to commercial markets. Central banks manage the availability of financial resources in an effort to achieve their statutory policy goals. These goals often include stable prices, high employment, and economic growth.

POLITICS OF CENTRAL BANKING

The cross-national variation in central banks mirrors the cross-national variation in governmental systems. Some central banks have federal structures (such as the German *Bundesbank* or the American Federal Reserve System). Other central banks, like the Bank of England, have a centralized organizational structure. Finally, at least one central bank, the European Central Bank, is a multinational financial institution. Central banks also vary in the extent to which elected officials may manipulate or control them. In some cases, such as the case of the Federal Reserve, there is a considerable degree of both formal and actual independence. Federal Reserve governors are appointed for long terms (fourteen years), and neither Congress nor the president can remove a Federal Reserve governor before the end of the term without cause. Also, the Federal Reserve does not depend upon an annual budgetary allocation from Congress to cover its operating expenses. Not all central banks have these sorts of institutional protections against the encroachment of elected officials.

Central bank independence from the influence of elected officials is not trivial, nor is it an easy concept to measure. Political economists have long argued that politicians have strong electoral incentives to manipulate monetary policy.

Some argue that politicians use monetary policy to boost economic growth near elections; others contend that politicians manipulate monetary policy to achieve partisan goals. Political economists also argue that the political manipulation of monetary policy tends to induce inflation without producing significant long-term increases in income or employment. Substantial empirical evidence supports the presence of an inverse relationship between central bank independence and inflation, the variability of inflation, and the variability of interest rates. There is, however, little evidence of a strong relationship between central bank independence and real variables such as employment or income growth.

CENTRAL BANKS IN THE TWENTY-FIRST CENTURY

Research on the implications of central bank independence (CBI) flowed out of a time (and scholarly literature) focused on a highly inflationary economic environment (from the stagflation of the mid-1970s to hyperinflation in various countries during the final twenty-five years of the twentieth century). The deflationary pressures of the dramatic economic decline since 2008 are uncharted territory for central banks. The evidence for the macroeconomic significance of the relationship between elected officials and central banks is based on era in which significant inflation was widely common. It is not clear, for example, that actual CBI is positively associated with *deflation,* but in an economic era in which deflationary pressures may be far more significant—during or immediately after a global recession—the political and economic implications of CBI remain to be seen.

Also significant, the political and economic research on central banks has focused overwhelmingly on traditional monetary policy making. The extent to which an understanding of the political economy of central banking extends to contexts in which central banks take on increasing policy responsibilities—from additional oversight duties to increased lending to financial concerns besides commercial banks—remains to be seen.

See also *Economic Policy Formulation; International Monetary Fund (IMF); Macroeconomics; Monetary Policy; World Bank.*

. . . . IRWIN L. MORRIS

BIBLIOGRAPHY

Alesina, Alberto, Nouriel Roubini, and Gerald Cohen. *Political Cycles and the Macroeconomy.* Cambridge, Mass.: MIT Press, 1997.

Alesina, Alberto, and Lawrence H. Summers. "Central Bank Independence and Macroeconomic Performance: Some Comparative Evidence." *Journal of Money, Credit, and Banking* 25 (1993): 151–162.

Cukierman, Alex. "Central Bank Independence and Monetary Policymaking Institutions: Past, Present, and Future." *European Journal of Political Economy* 24 (2008): 722–736.

———. *Central Bank Strategy, Credibility, and Independence: Theory and Evidence.* Cambridge, Mass.: MIT Press, 1991.

Drazen, Allan. *Political Economy in Macroeconomics.* Princeton: Princeton University Press, 2001.

Morris, Irwin L. *Congress, the President, and the Federal Reserve: The Politics of American Monetary Policymaking.* Ann Arbor: University of Michigan Press, 2000.

Centralization, Deconcentration, and Decentralization

Centralization, deconcentration, and decentralization are concepts that describe different forms of administrative organization. Administrative deconcentration is the transfer of competences, or administrative powers, within the same institution; administrative decentralization is the transfer of competences between institutions with political and administrative autonomy. While *centralization,* or the concentration of power within the central government, answers the need of national unity, deconcentration and decentralization are two different ways to address sociogeographical diversity inside the country.

Most state structures include one or more subnational levels of administration, but states differ from each other in the way administrative powers are organized and in the degree of centralization of decision making. In recent decades, in most parts of the world, the move from traditional hierarchical forms of administration to forms of administration through the networks of alternative public and private organizations has reinforced previous trends towards deconcentration and decentralization.

DECONCENTRATION

Deconcentration is the transfer of competences or administrative powers between organizations inside the same entity, such as the state or municipalities. Taking the example of the state, deconcentration is the transfer of competences from central government entities or departments—those that have a jurisdiction over the entire national territory—to peripheral government entities, which have jurisdiction only over a part of the national territory. The central level retains the most important keys in the decision-making process, but its organs in the lower tiers may make decisions on less important issues. This is the case, for example, of central government departments in charge of the road network. They are responsible for the overall strategy and main decisions concerning planning and construction, while its regional departments are only in charge of road maintenance and implementation of decisions taken by the central department. Deconcentration only concerns entities inside the state. The state's aim with deconcentration is to bring public services closer to citizens without losing control of the decisions and resources applied by regional or local state departments.

In some cases, deconcentration can be used as a first step in a decentralization process, for example, when the state creates a regional tier where it didn't exist before. In such a case, the strategy can be to gradually deconcentrate those powers and resources—intended for transfer to the future regional self-government—to the regional departments of central government. In a second step, the new administrative tier is created and elections are held for its boards. In addition, other central government departments may also deconcentrate to peripheral regional departments; their competences will not be decentralized to the newly created regional government,

for example, but will have advantages in being geographically organized according to the same area and boundaries. Any central government department can be in this situation. Part of their competences will be transferred to the newly created form of regional government and part of the remaining competences can be deconcentrated to its regional offices.

DECENTRALIZATION

Decentralization is the transference of competences between different entities. It connotes the transfer of responsibilities, powers, and resources, from higher to lower level units of self-government and the direct management of local affairs by local populations through their elected local or regional representatives. The reasons to decentralize, the degree of decentralization, the number of administrative competences, and the amount of public resources assigned to local and regional governments vary from country to country. In most countries, administrative decentralization is done for a combination of political, economic, and social reasons—different from case to case. In some cases, the need to recognize and to respect political and cultural differences can lead to adopting forms of administrative or political decentralization (e.g., the creation of autonomous regions in Spain). In other cases, the specific geographical situation may require adopting these forms of decentralization (e.g., the case of islands or metropolitan areas).

Decentralization increases the opportunities for citizens to participate in local or regional public affairs, offering new conditions for participation and for public-private partnership, therefore reinforcing the involvement of local civil society in the management of its own affairs. With increased participation and with direct election of local or regional representatives, decentralization improves political accountability and increases transparency in public-policy decision making. Decentralization tends to increase institutional capacity and local empowerment, making local governments and local communities more competent to deal with their own affairs. As a consequence, administrative decentralization is thought to increase public service efficiency and responsiveness, and to achieve a better adjustment between citizens' preferences and public services. However, the number of administrative units or institutional fragmentation affect efficiency and responsiveness, since, for example, an excessive number of small units can be detrimental for the achievement of scale economies. On the other hand, large units may affect the relation between citizens and administrators and therefore the responsiveness of the regional government. Finally, decentralization may also allow local communities to counterweight decisions taken by the central government on issues likely to affect their local or regional well-being.

Decentralization processes may also have negative consequences. For example, decentralization can be responsible, in specific contexts, for macroeconomic instability, since the efforts made by the central government to reduce public sector expenditures or to increase public revenues may not be followed by similar efforts at the regional and local levels of self-government. Decentralization can also produce inequity in the amount and quality of public services delivered, according to the area of residence, in comparison with a situation in which the same services are delivered by central government based on common standards independent from the geographical location.

CONCLUSION

Centralization and decentralization have alternated as political and administrative models for the vertical organization of the state throughout the history of public administration. In the three decades after the end of World War II (1939–1945), administrative deconcentration prevailed in most industrialized countries as the preferred mechanism for the vertical organization of the state. In that period, there was strong state intervention with little or no delegation of powers and resources to entities outside the direct control of central government departments. However, in the 1980s and 1990s, the renewal and the dominance of the free market ideology on both sides of the Atlantic, as well as political demands for more public participation in decision making, led to reforms in the vertical organization of the state, which in part explains the general move toward political and administrative decentralization. Political changes from the 1990s onward consolidated political and administrative decentralization as the model for the organization of democratic states. Decentralization was seen, at the same time, as the best way for public administration to deal with the emerging forms of multilevel and multiactor governance, as the example of several member states of the European Union illustrates well.

See also *Centrally Planned Economy; Democratic Centralism; Local Politics; Public-private Dichotomy; Regions and Regional Government.*

. . . . CARLOS NUNES SILVA

BIBLIOGRAPHY
Amaral, Diogo Freitas, *Curso de Direito Administrativo,* 3rd ed, vol. 1. Coimbra, Portugal: Almedina, 2007.
Arzaghi, Mohammad, and J. Vernon Henderson. "Why Countries Are Fiscally Decentralizing." *Journal of Public Economics* 89 (July 2005): 1157–1189.
Aubry, François-Xavier. *La décentralistion contre l'État (L'État semi-centralisé).* Paris: Librarie Générale de Droit et de Jusrisprudence, 1992.
Bennett, Robert, ed. *Decentralization, Local Governments, and Markets: Towards a Post-welfare Agenda.* Oxford: Clarendon Press, 1990.
Burki, Shahid Javed, Guillermo Perry, and William Dillinger. *Beyond the Centre: Decentralizing the State.* Washington, D.C.: The World Bank, 1999.
Burns, Danny, Robin Hambleton, and Paul Hoggett. *The Politics of Decentralisation. Revitalising Local Democracy.* London: Macmillan, 1994.
Caupers, João. *A Administração Periférica do Estado,* Lisbon, Portugal: Aequitas/Editorial de Notícias, 1994.
Cohen, John, and Stephen Peterson. *Administrative Decentralisation: Strategies for Developing Countries.* West Hartford, Conn.: Kumarian Press, 1999.
Oates, Wallace E. "An Economist's Perspective on Fiscal Federalism." In *The Political Economy of Fiscal Federalism,* edited by Wallace E. Oates. Lanham, Md.: Lexington Books, 1977.
Page, Edwards, and Michael Goldsmith, eds. *Central and Local Government Relations: A Comparative Analysis of Western European Unitary States.* London: Sage Publications, 1989.
Tiebout, Charles M. "A Pure Theory of Local Expenditures." *Journal of Political Economy* 64, no. 5 (1956): 416–424.
Wolman, Harold. "Decentralization: What It Is and Why We Should Care." In *Decentralization, Local Governments, and Markets: Towards a Post-welfare Agenda,* edited by Robert J. Bennett. Oxford: Clarendon Press, 1990.

Centrally Planned Economy

In a centrally planned economy, the government decides which goods are produced, the quantity of the goods produced, the price at which the goods are sold, and the wages paid to laborers. The bureaucratic authority in a centrally planned economy takes responsibility for determining the maximal output for particular products. The bureaucracy orders manufacturers to produce at a given level and then manages the distribution network for those products. In a pure centrally planned economy, there is no private property and the government owns all of the physical assets in an economy such as factories, industrial machinery, land, and all facets of production. Workers in such an economy are paid a flat rate, set by the government, and buy goods at government-fixed prices. The same goods can be purchased from any state-run distribution center. Ideally, each good would available to each consumer.

THEORETICAL ADVANTAGES AND DISADVANTAGES OF CENTRALLY PLANNED ECONOMIES

Proponents of centrally planned economies argue that planned economies can allocate raw materials and other industrial inputs to producers more efficiently than market economies. Some of the wastes of a market economy are evidently absent due to central planning; competitive advertising, for instance, is relatively unnecessary. Another potential advantage of centrally planned economies is the ability of the state to correct what economists call *externalities,* which are socially undesirable outcomes arising from each individual and firm pursuing their own self-interest in the market. Since the government controls the economy, it can pursue environmental policies, achieve full employment, or prevent income disparities. These are all goals pursued by governments in market economies, but they have much less control than centrally planned economies. Finally, a centrally planned economy should, in theory, be able to avoid market shocks. A central planner may maintain full employment even when the economy is failing, because employment is decided by the state. Moreover, if disaster strikes, the state has the infrastructure in place to effectively redistribute food or raw materials as needed.

The criticism of centrally planned economies, however, is widespread, especially among economists. Some, like F. A. Hayek, argue on ideological grounds that removing decision making from producers and consumers is an affront to human freedom. More typically, critics have identified many practical problems with centrally planned economies. Proponents of free markets argue that no bureaucracy can match the ability of free markets to meet consumer demand. Individuals, pursuing their own self-interest, will seek the most efficient way to produce and purchase goods. Firms will seek the most efficient way to produce and distribute their goods in order to compete in the market.

Productivity growth is a driving force for economic growth, but centrally planned economies give little incentive for workers to increase their own efficiency. If workers are paid the same wage regardless of their output, they have no reason to work harder. Further, workers may seek to reduce their production to a minimum: workers or firms that consistently meet their quotas might be forced to produce more. The quality of industrial work often suffers because quota standards in centrally planed economies are typically quantitative, and thereby irresponsive to the market's demand for quality products. In market economies, consumers seek a balance between quality and quantity, and are free to choose between products.

The incentive structure of centrally planned economies not only stifles efficiency growth and quality; it also stifles innovation. First, innovation only happens in government institutions, not only because the government owns all the research and development institutions, but also because there is little incentive for individuals to invent or refine products. Second, there is a conflict of interest between innovators and manufacturers. Manufacturers must meet government-ordered quotas, and retooling due to research advances may slow production. Further, such advancements also cause governments to seek new or different resources, complicating chains of production and supply. Because of these production problems, critics frequently claim centrally planned economies lack the flexibility of efficient market economies.

OBSERVATIONS FROM HISTORICAL CENTRALLY PLANNED ECONOMIES

The two most prominent centrally planned economies in the twentieth century were the Soviet Union (roughly from 1928–1991) and China (1950s–late 1970s). During the cold war era, both states created public firms and severely limited privately owned property. Their bureaucracies assumed the responsibility for all significant manufacturing and agricultural output. Many critics of the Soviet Union blame its eventual economic collapse on the faults of the centrally planned economy. Its central planning proved inefficient in meeting consumer needs; rationing, shortages, and inferior quality were common and helped erode support for the regime. Peasants and workers responded by creating a robust black market to trade luxury, imported, or otherwise scarce goods, as they have in other centrally planned economies.

At the same time, the theoretical advantages of centrally planned economies were not observed. Waste in the Soviet Union far outstripped the wastefulness of its contemporary market economies. The central planners focused on heavy industry to achieve military goals and fulfill different social goals, but responded slowly to advances in light industry and consumer technology. Environmental quality deteriorated more quickly than in market economies. Despite the socialist rhetoric of equality, party officials and bureaucrats became an elite, which directed resources to themselves rather than the public good. If central planning allowed for the redistribution of food in famines, it also allowed for the creation of artificial famine as a political tool, most especially in the Ukraine from 1932 to 1933 when Josef Stalin required such a high quota of grain exports from the region that millions of Ukrainians starved.

CONCLUSION

In the early twenty-first century, pure central planning economies are rare; the Soviet Union collapsed in 1991, and China has gradually shifted from a planned to a mixed economy, beginning in earnest in the late 1970s. Nevertheless, most states engage in some economic planning. Typically, popularly elected governments have mandates to achieve high rates of employment. Governments may coordinate incentives for firms and individuals to produce different goods. In other states, firms cooperate with governments to set research and production levels in order to construct a home-country champion industry and compete against other international firms. Developing states may also pursue forms of central planning in order to limit imports, strengthen exporting firms, or otherwise achieve economic goals. Economies often combine elements of state planning with free markets to secure certain objectives. Thus, while the pure centrally planned economy is now rare, contemporary mixed economies reflect many of its elements.

See also *Bureaucratic Authoritarianism; Democratic Centralism; Dirigisme; Soviet Union, Former.*

. . . . RYAN GIBB

BIBLIOGRAPHY

Blyth, Marc. *Great Transformations: Economic Ideas and Political Change in the Twentieth Century.* New York: Cambridge University Press, 2002.

Cohn, Theodore H. *Global Political Economy: Theory and Practice,* 2nd ed. New York: Addison Wesley Longman, 2003.

Conquest, Robert. *The Harvest of Sorrow: Soviet Collectivization and the Terror-famine.* New York: Oxford University Press, 1986.

Hayek, F. A. *The Road to Serfdom: Text and Documents; the Definitive Edition,* edited by Bruce Caldwell. New York: Routledge, 2008.

O'Sullivan, Arthur, and Steven Sheffrin. *Macroeconomics: Principles and Tools,* 2nd ed. Upper Saddle River, N.J.: Prentice Hall, 2001.

Stilwell, Frank. *Political Economy: The Contest of Economic Ideas,* 2nd ed. London: Oxford University Press, 2006.

Wheelan, Charles. *Naked Economics: Undressing the Dismal Science.* New York: W. W. Norton, 2002.

Chamberlain, Houston Stewart

Houston Stewart Chamberlain (1855–1927) is widely regarded as an important contributor to German nationalist thought and anti-Semitic racism, and he had a direct influence on Adolf Hitler. His writings depict Jews as destroyers of civilization who represent absolute evil and Germans as a chosen people with a mission to defeat the Jews and rescue civilization.

Chamberlain was born in England. His mother died before he was a year old, and relatives in France raised him. His father, a rear admiral in the British navy, wanted him to follow a military career, but the young Chamberlain rejected this path. He was influenced by his Prussian private tutor to favor all things German: history, literature, and philosophy, and, later, the music of Richard Wagner. His formal university studies led to a degree in science, but he chose a career as an author.

Chamberlain's writings express his mission to save the world from the menace of Semitic materialism. Even his writings on Kant (1905) and Goethe (1912) reflect this perspective. The major thrust of his principal work first published in 1899, *Foundations of the Nineteenth Century,* is that race dominates history. Nations are political entities that create the context for the historical expression of a race. In his view, racial character determines the history of a people. At the center of world history through the ages is the clash between the Aryan or Germanic culture and the Semitic perspective, which Chamberlain regarded as materialistic and without cultural value.

The superiority of Western civilization stems largely from the positive influence of the Germanic races on history. For Chamberlain, these races included, inexplicably, Slavs, Celts, Greeks, and Latins as well as Germans—all heirs to ancient Greece and Rome. Semitic races, particularly the Jews, and institutions influenced by them, such as the Catholic Church, have typically acted to undermine Germanic superiority, as they once subverted the Roman Empire. Chamberlain uses spurious conjecture to conclude that Jesus was not a Jew, and he thinks that the Catholic Church diverted Christianity from its true path, a mistake not corrected until the Germanic influence of thinkers like Martin Luther emerged.

After England entered World War I (1914–1918) as an ally of those nations opposing Germany, Chamberlain accused his native country of treason to the Germanic ideal, and during the war he wrote a series of propaganda pieces favorable to the German cause. For this work he was awarded an Iron Cross, and the following year (1916) he became a German citizen.

In 1923, five years after Germany's defeat in World War I, Chamberlain met with Hitler, who was then head of the fledgling Nazi party. Chamberlain considered Hitler to be the promised leader he had earlier prophesied would reinfuse Germany with the spirit needed to reemerge as a world power. Later, in *Mein Kampf*, Hitler expressed his high regard for Chamberlain's views. In addition to Hitler, other leaders of Nazi Germany who claimed to have been influenced by Chamberlain include Hess, Goebbels, Himmler, and Rosenberg.

See also *Anti-Semitism.*

. . . . DONALD G. TANNENBAUM

BIBLIOGRAPHY
Chamberlain, Anna. *Meine Erinnerungen an Houston Stewart Chamberlain.* Munich: Beck, 1923.
Chamberlain, Houston S. *Foundations of the Nineteenth Century*, translated by John Lees, 2 vols. London: John Lane/The Bodley Head, 1910.
———. *Goethe.* Munich:Verlag, 1912.
———. *Immanuel Kant.* Munich: Bruckmann, 1905.
Field, Geoffrey G. *Evangelist of Race: The Germanic Vision of Houston Stewart Chamberlain.* New York: Columbia University Press, 1981.

Chancellor

Chancellor is a term used in some countries for a government minister or official. The chancellor is the head of government in Austria and Germany, having powers akin to a prime minister in a parliamentary system, but in other cases, the term is reserved for a lesser, more specialized official.

In ancient Rome, the chancellors, or *cancellarii*, sat in the courts of law at the *cancelli*, or lattice work screens, that separated the judge and council from the audience. Societies that trace their history back to Roman times frequently employ the term chancellor for ministers or judicial officials; however, the term is also employed anachronistically to high-ranking officials in the ancient Chinese and Egyptian empires.

The most powerful chancellors are those in Austria and Germany, where they are known as *bundeskanzler*, or federal chancellors. When Germany was first united under Chancellor Otto van Bismarck in 1871, the chancellor was appointed by the kaiser, or emperor, but after World War I (1914–1918), the chancellor was appointed by the German president. Then, after World War II (1939–1945), the introduction of democracy meant that the German chancellor would be selected by the *bundestag*, the lower house of parliament. In Austria, the president technically appoints the chancellor, but because government ministers must have the support of the National Council, the lower house of parliament, the president traditionally names the head of the largest party in the *Nationalrat* to be chancellor. In both countries, the chancellor is the head of government and exercises more political power than any other official. German and Austrian chancellors have similar powers to prime ministers in other parliamentary systems, such as that of Great Britain or Spain, meaning they appoint the cabinet, are responsible for submitting proposals to the parliament, and have the power to dismiss parliament and call for early elections. However, they are accountable to parliament, which means they can be removed if the parliament passes a vote of no confidence.

Elsewhere, chancellors serve a more subordinate role in government. In Switzerland, the federal chancellor is elected by the Swiss parliament, and heads the federal chancellery, the general staff of the seven-member executive Federal Council that makes up the Swiss government. This is more of an administrative position than a political position, as the Swiss chancellor participates in the meetings of the federal councilors with only a consultative vote and the primary responsibility is to prepare policy and activity reports. In the United Kingdom, the lord chancellor serves as the head of the English judiciary and the Department for Constitutional Affairs, and was, until 2006, speaker of the House of Lords. The chancellor of the exchequer is the minister responsible for the treasury, the equivalent to a minister of finance, and a very prominent official in British government. In Finland, the chancellor of justice supervises the legality of actions taken by government, and in Sweden, the chancellor of justice serves as the solicitor general. In several Latin American countries, the term chancellor is reserved for the minister or secretary in charge of foreign affairs. Chancellors also served as high-ranking state officials in the kingdoms of France, Denmark and the Polish-Lithuanian Commonwealth, and in imperial Russia, chancellor was the highest rank in the civil service.

In the United States, the only national-level office with such a title is the chancellor of the Smithsonian Institution, a ceremonial office held by the chief justice of the United States. Some states have a court of chancery who oversee equity cases, and the judges on these courts are known as chancellors. The term chancellor is also often employed as a title for a university academic official or the head of state departments of education.

See also *Parliamentary Government; Prime Minister (Head of Government).*

. . . . PAUL JAMES KUBICEK

BIBLIOGRAPHY

Hancock, M. Donald, and Henry Krisch. *Politics in Germany*. Washington, D.C.: Congressional Quarterly Press, 2009.

Helms, Ludger. *Institutions and Institutional Change in the Federal Republic of Germany*. New York: St. Martin's Press, 2000.

———. *Presidents, Prime Ministers, and Chancellors: Executive Leadership in Western Democracies*. New York: Palgrave, 2005.

Chaos

See *Equilibrium and Chaos*.

Charisma

Charisma is an exceptional quality that makes the very few people who possess it able to influence others by attracting their admiration and obedience. The term derives from ancient Greek and originally meant "gift." From Christian theology, where it designates a special gift given by God's grace, the concept has entered the political vocabulary through the reflection of German sociologist Max Weber. Weber appropriated the term to mean a certain quality of an individual personality by virtue of which the individual is set apart from ordinary human beings and treated as being endowed with exceptional powers.

Weber distinguished between three forms of authority according to the different sources of their legitimacy: (1) the *rational* authority is based on the belief in the legality of its commands, (2) the *traditional* authority rests on credence given to the sacredness of traditions, and, finally, (3) the *charismatic* authority stems from the faith in the extraordinary quality of a person. Whilst both the rational and traditional authorities are ordinary, because they can be subsumed under, respectively, discursively or historically grounded rules, charismatic authority goes beyond rules as it is based on the extraordinary gestures and qualities of the leader.

Examples of charismatic figures include Indian nationalist Mahatma Gandhi, Russian Communist leader Vladimir Lenin, British prime minister Winston Churchill, French president Charles de Gaulle, and Egyptian president Gamal Abdel Nasser.

See also *Authority; Caesarism; Cult of Personality; Leadership; Weber, Max*.

. . . . CHIARA BOTTICI

Chartism

Chartism was a democratic reform movement that emerged in Britain in the second third of the nineteenth century. The Chartists (those who advocated the Chartist program of reform) derive their name from the People's Charter, a document produced on May 8, 1838. The expressed purpose of this charter was the compulsion of the lower house of the British parliament toward political change and improvement through a restructuring of the constitution and citizens' rights. Historically, Chartism represents an important effort to increase and transform political representation through suffrage, thereby repairing the ills of a society disabled by low enfranchisement. As an ideology, Chartism was the conscious democratic struggle for improving of the lives of citizens in an industrialized economy.

ORIGINS

Chartism emerged in the context of widespread economic depression and political isolation of citizens outside the landed class. In 1831, the British electorate was composed of roughly half a million voters, as compared to a national population of nearly fourteen million. Landed elites maintained control of both economic development (even as Britain transitioned towards an industrial economy), as well as political power, through structuring districts and limiting the franchise. By means of such legislation as the Importation Act of 1815 (informally known as the Corn Laws), these elites maintained control over agricultural prices at the sacrifice of workers' wages and the balance of the economy writ large. A significant percentage of the British people were legally excluded from the development and execution of acts of state, leaving their interests underrepresented and creating conditions for abuse and class conflict.

The success of reformist Whigs in the general election of 1831 opened the possibility to alleviate these tensions. With the enactment of the Representation of the People Act of 1832 (the Reform Act), the British parliament ushered in transformations to the institutional arrangement of the political process. The new franchise extended political representation to the burgeoning business class, while, in addition, reducing the number of districts represented in the House of Commons. Such reforms disabled the institutional parameters that had encouraged the landed elites' sustained political power.

THE NEW POOR LAW AND THE PEOPLE'S CHARTER

Under these conditions, the political movement of Chartism emerged. While not yet a sustained national movement, local political activists (both trade unionists and middle-class reformers who were still excluded from the extension of the franchise) began to coalesce around the need for even further institutional reforms, perceiving universal suffrage as a means to enact these changes. These activists sought even wider-reaching reforms than most Whig party members were willing to endorse. Parliament responded to pressures for further reforms with the passage of the Poor Law Amendment Act of 1834 (the New Poor Law). And, while this New Poor Law did further extend the franchise to the middle class, it did not extend this right to the working class. Such political actions were perceived as creating incentives for class divisions through a restructuring of poor relief and workhouses, infringing on workers' rights and ignoring general demands for complete (adult male) suffrage.

Activists, following on a long tradition of democratic dissidence, responded by convening a parallel parliament (thus evoking both British and French democratic histories). Delegates to this convention would eventually produce what was known as the People's Charter. The charter consisted of six points of reform: complete adult (over age twenty-one) male suffrage, annual elections, secret ballots, abolition of property requirements for parliamentary service, pay allowances for all members of Parliament, and equal districts. Chartists argued that these transformations would correct the limitations of recent legislation, such as the First Reform Act and the New Poor Law, rectifying social inequalities produced by the then unrepresentative electorate. They claimed that such reforms would help to further the democratization of Britain, extending suffrage that was protected by transparent electoral institutions, and allowing all Britains representation in the House of Commons.

FRACTURE AND DECLINE

Initially, Chartism was not a reactive movement. Instead, Chartists conceived of themselves as engaging in traditional British politics, acting with a similar ethos as the Whig reformers, and aimed at the high ideals of repairing economic and political inequalities. Chartist leaders hoped to capitalize on the spirit of reform that had already begun to transform Britain's institutional structure. However, the conditions that encouraged a broad-based reform movement did not persist long. (Their demands, along with a petition of 1,280,000 signers, were rejected by the British parliament on July 12, 1839, by a 235–46 vote.) Growing class tensions between groups who had previously found common political ground began to limit the movement's success. Economic and health conditions worsened in metropolitan centers in the early 1840s, and divisions between the working and middle classes became magnified by the costs of depression (in combinations with the threats the New Poor Law imposed on the working class). In response, the remaining Chartist elites (those who, following parliamentary reaction, had not yet been imprisoned) transformed their tactics; some employed workers' strikes, others later encouraged armed uprisings. As these uprisings became more violent, and the British army began to confront rioters, the strength of the movement waned further. By 1848, while violent revolutions and political instability threatened much of Europe, tensions in Britain were already declining, without much hope for the successful implementation of Chartists's reforms.

HISTORICAL SIGNIFICANCE

While Chartists ultimately failed to meet their own political goals, the movement itself was successful in furthering the use of political channels for engaging in reformist—as opposed to revolutionary—action. Moreover, the demands for universal suffrage helped further conditions for democratization that extended beyond the movement itself.

The Chartist ideology is perhaps best known as an important early example of the expression of working-class consciousness attempting improvement and political change. Socialists and Marxists would later point to Chartism as evidence of sociological and world-historical transformations that signaled the decline of capitalism. However, the distinction between Chartism as social reform guided by humanitarian concerns for the costs of low representation, versus one of economic reform for worker's rights, only emerged as the national movement began to lose coherence and economic conditions created differing incentives for classes that had previously been unified under the early banner of reform.

See also *British Political Thought; Capitalism and Democracy; Electoral Reform; Radicalism; Socialism; Voting Rights and Suffrage.*

. . . . ANDREW POE

BIBLIOGRAPHY

Belchem, John. *Industrialization and the Working Class: The English Experience 1750–1900.* Portland, Ore.: Areopagitica Press, 1990.

Epstein, James, and Dorothy Thompson, eds. *The Chartist Experience Studies in Working-Class Radicalism and Culture, 1830–1860.* London: Macmillan, 1982.

Lovett, William, and John Collins. *Chartism: A New Organization of People.* Leicester: Leicester University Press, 1969. Reprinted with an introduction by Asa Briggs.

Taylor, Miles. *The Decline of British Radicalism, 1847–1860.* Oxford: Clarendon Press, 1995.

Thompson, Dorothy. *The Chartists: Popular Politics in the Industrial Revolution.* New York: Pantheon, 1984.

Thompson, E. P. *The Making of the English Working Class* London: Victor Gollancz, 1963.

Chauvinism

Chauvinism is extreme nationalism or excessive pride in an individual's group. The term originated with Nicolas Chauvin, a French soldier who exhibited a fanatical devotion to Napoleon Bonaparte and the French Empire. Initially the term referred to extreme pride in militarism, but through the 1800s, it became increasingly synonymous with patriotism and belief in the superiority of one's group or place. The ultranationalism of the 1800s among European states helped fuel imperialism by building on the social Darwinism of the era to create public support for expansion and colonialism. Chauvinism also contributed to the jingoism of the United States and other nations in the late nineteenth and early twentieth centuries. This period of chauvinism culminated in the cult of offense prior to World War I (1914–1918). During the cold war, political chauvinism developed an ideological component and was a tertiary factor in the struggle between Soviet-style communism and U.S. free market capitalism. Chauvinism increasingly has come to be used to describe extreme pride in one's race, ethnicity, or gender. During the women's rights movement of the 1960s and 1970s, male chauvinism was used to connote the sense of male superiority and entitlement. The term chauvinism became increasingly linked to genderism or other forms of discrimination toward women.

See also *Cold War; Colonialism; Misogyny; Nationalism.*

. . . . TOM LANSFORD

Checks and Balances

James Madison famously wrote in *Federalist* No. 10 that there are two ways to ward against the "dangerous vice" of political faction: "the one, by removing its causes; the other, by controlling its effects." The first of these options would require either destroying the liberty that allows factions to grow, an outcome Madison said is worse than the factions themselves, or requiring all citizens to have the same opinions and interests, a virtual impossibility. Because the underlying causes of factions cannot be removed, Madison argued for a political system—the U.S. Constitution—capable of controlling them. Even before Madison, Alexander Hamilton and John Jay wrote in support of the Constitution's separation of powers, and Montesquieu claimed that liberty is best protected through the construction of checks and balances. The division of the legislature into two chambers and the balancing of the presidency against the legislative branch mean that no one faction is likely to control the entire governing apparatus. In addition, federalism balances power of the states against the power of the central government and independent courts adjudicate disputes that arise between the various branches of government. Divided government, defined as no single party controlling all branches of government, demonstrates, as the norm in the United States, how well the Founders's ideas about government work.

The U.S. political system was designed to prevent one particular ideological faction from gaining control of the entire system of government, a situation that the Founders believed would lead to despotism. However, the checks and balances inherent in the U.S. system also create the possibility of gridlock. Because each branch of government must agree with all other branches for a bill to become a law, lawmaking is more difficult than it would be in a system with fewer checks and balances. This has led some to argue that a democratic system with fewer checks, such as Westminster parliamentary democracy, is superior. While normative arguments both in favor of and against checks and balances can and have been made, it is also possible to examine checks and balances from a positive perspective. Indeed, most political science literature of the last several decades has taken a positive, rather than normative, approach to checks and balances.

VETOES AND SUPERMAJORITIES

The ability of one branch of government to act as a check on another branch depends upon the power granted to it within the political system. Perhaps the strongest form of check is veto power, or the ability to block a bill from becoming law. George Tsebelis refers to actors with veto power as "veto players." He defines a *veto player* as any actor (individual or collective) in a political system whose assent is necessary to change the policy status quo. In the United States, the House, Senate, and the president are all veto players because no bill can pass without the support of all three. Tsebelis argues that as the number veto players within a political system grows, and as their preferences over policy become more ideologically diverse, it becomes more difficult to make new policy. In other words, the policy status quo becomes more difficult to change, and, therefore, more stable.

Veto power arises from two different sources. In some instances, actors such as the House, Senate, and president have constitutionally defined veto rights. Separation of powers systems, in which the president and the legislature are elected in different elections, and the president is not accountable to the legislature through a vote of confidence, by definition have several constitutionally defined, or institutional, veto players. In other political systems, veto rights emerge as part of the political process. In parliamentary democracies, where the government is elected by, and serves at the behest of, the lower house of parliament, there may be only one institutional veto player—formally the parliament itself (assuming there is no upper legislative chamber with veto power)—but numerous partisan veto players. In parliamentary democracies with multiparty systems, coalition governments are the norm. If no single party controls a majority of the seats in parliament, a coalition is likely necessary to pass laws. Each party in the governing coalition has the ability to block legislation by informing its members of parliament to vote against the bill. Tsebelis refers to these parties as partisan veto players, because the political system generates veto rights for parties through governing coalitions, despite the fact that the constitution does not provide them with a formal veto rights.

When examining checks and balances within a political system, it is necessary to consider both types of veto players. Federal separation-of-powers systems, such as the United States or Brazil, have several constitutionally defined veto players, while unitary parliamentary countries with multiparty coalition governments, such as the Netherlands and Israel, have many partisan veto players. The separation-of-powers systems have institutionalized checks and balances, while other systems generate checks through partisan coalitions. The effects, however, are the same. All else equal, the more actors with veto power, the more difficult it is to produce policy change.

In some instances, supermajority requirements can generate additional checks by making it easier for actors to veto legislation. In the U.S. Senate, for example, the filibuster rule means that a supermajority of sixty senators is required to pass important bills. Because Senate rules require sixty votes to cut off debate and hold a vote, forty senators can effectively block legislation. In the other cases, supermajorities are sometimes sufficient to overcome checks, thereby weakening them. Two-thirds supermajorities in the House and Senate can also override a presidential veto, meaning the president cannot block a bill when two-thirds of both houses desire to pass it. Similar veto override provisions exist in many presidential systems.

AGENDA SETTING AND PARLIAMENTARY OVERSIGHT

By definition, veto players are all alike in their ability to block legislation, but their powers may vary with regard to agenda setting. Although the term *agenda setting* may have a variety of meanings in everyday language, in works of formal theory it means something very specific: the ability to make a take-it-or-leave-it offer to another actor. Agenda setting, under this definition, is captured very nicely by the saying, "Congress proposes, the president disposes." In the American system, Congress is the agenda setter, meaning it can make a take-it-or-leave-it offer to the president. The president has no formal power to amend a bill that Congress has sent, and can only sign the bill into law or veto it. If the president wishes to make amendments to a bill, it would require a veto of the bill, then to find a member of Congress willing to reintroduce a new version of the bill in Congress, and subsequently hope the amendments survive the congressional process. The last part of this process is the least likely.

The opposite is true in a parliamentary democracy. In parliamentary systems, such as the United Kingdom, the government drafts legislation and makes a take-it-or-leave-it proposal to the parliament. Although a parliament can debate the merits of bills, there is usually little room for substantive amendments. Governments in parliamentary systems tend to get their way, leaving parliaments to complain that they are rubber stamps.

Agenda-setting rights grant an actor a great deal of power. Exactly how much power, though, depends upon precise decision-making rules as well as the ideological alignment of veto players. Agenda setters have more power when all veto players consider the status quo to be unsatisfactory. If everyone agrees that the current policy is inferior and that particular direction requires change, the actor possessing agenda-setting authority can simply propose the preferred policy. The other actors are then forced to compare the new proposal to the inferior status quo. In this instance, they agree to go along with the agenda setter's proposal. When there are one or more veto players whose preference is relatively close to the status quo policy, the power of the agenda setter diminishes. Assuming the agenda setter prefers a substantial change, the agenda setter will not be able to propose the preferred policy because the veto player close to the status quo will veto it. Instead, the agenda setter must propose a policy preferred by all veto players over the current policy.

The precise nature of formal agenda-setting authority varies greatly both within and across countries. For example, while it is generally the case that the U.S. Congress has formal agenda-setting authority, the president can make a take-it-or-leave-it offer to the Senate when appointing cabinet members and judges. The president makes appointments, but the Senate has the power to scrutinize and veto the appointees. The president, though, can temporarily bypass the requirement of Senate approval by making an appointment while the Senate is in recess. Likewise, the U.S. president has formal agenda-setting authority when negotiating foreign treaties. The president may negotiate a treaty with other countries, but the treaty must then be approved by a two-thirds vote in the Senate. The Senate cannot, however, amend the treaty.

In other countries, presidents have more formal powers to amend legislation than the American president, thereby reducing the agenda-setting power of the legislature. The Argentinean and Brazilian presidents, for example, can pass into law the sections of a bill they approve, and veto the sections they do not. In the United States, this procedure is referred to as a line-item veto, and it was briefly granted to President Clinton before the Supreme Court deemed it to be unconstitutional. In some countries, such as Brazil, the president has the right to initiate the budget, while in the United States all revenue bills must originate in the House.

In parliamentary systems, legislatures generally have fewer agenda-setting rights as the vast majority of bills come from the executive branch. However, there is significant variation in the powers of parliaments as well. Some parliaments, such as the Norwegian *Storting* and German *Bundestag,* have numerous permanent, specialized committees that participate in the drafting of legislation. In the United Kingdom, committees in the House of Commons, on the other hand, tend to be set up on an ad hoc basis and have significantly fewer powers. Parliaments and their committees also vary in their ability to oversee the executive. The European Affairs Committee of the Danish *Folketing* is often noted for its exceptionally high degree of oversight in the area of European Union affairs. While oversight committees in the United Kingdom tend to be weaker, question time in the House of Commons provides Parliament members of an opportunity for government oversight in a very public forum.

FEDERALISM AND BICAMERALISM

When discussing checks and balances, federalism and bicameralism are two political institutions that warrant special attention. *Federalism* is an arrangement that divides power among a federal government and its constituent states. Each level of government must have certain powers delegated to it, and these powers must be constitutionally protected. Federal bargains, by their nature, create checks on government authority. Some scholars have suggested that the checks and balances inherent in a federal system provide economic benefits by creating competition among states. Barry Weingast has argued that federalism helps preserve market economies by preventing government interference in the market. Others, like Daniel Triesman, however, have pointed to problems associated with decentralization. Regardless, when states have the ability to block legislation, they become another veto player in the political system and they may make policy change more difficult.

Bicameralism closely relates to federalism and can greatly impact policy making as well. States often have their interests represented through an upper chamber of a bicameral legislature, where they collectively have veto rights. This was case in the United States prior to the direct election of senators in 1913. Even though U.S. senators today represent citizens directly, rather than state governments, the states receive equal representation regardless of size in the Senate. In Germany, state representatives in the German upper house, the *Bundesrat,* have the ability to veto certain types of legislation passed by the lower house of parliament, the *Bundestag.* When the upper chamber can veto legislation and has policy preferences that differ from the lower chamber, policy stability becomes more likely due to the presence of an additional institutional veto player. Regardless of their effects on economic growth, federalism and bicameralism are likely to make policy change more difficult.

BUREAUCRATS AND JUDGES

After legislation has been written, bureaucrats must implement the law and judges may interpret it. The degree of freedom that judges and bureaucrats have with regard to interpretation and implementation relates to the checks and balances present within the political system. In systems with a greater number of checks and balances (more veto players), judges and bureaucrats have more discretion to interpret and implement the law. This is because politicians have limited ability to overturn what judges and bureaucrats do through the political process.

Judges, through their ability to interpret law, and bureaucrats, through their ability to implement policy, can influence policy outcomes. The delegation of powers to judges and bureaucrats creates a principal-agent problem for politicians. On the one hand, politicians rely upon these actors. Judges are needed to ensure that the law is followed, and they are required to interpret the law when situations arise that lawmakers did not originally anticipate. Bureaucrats are required for their policy expertise in particular areas. Legislators do not have the time or knowledge required to implement the laws that they write themselves. On the other hand, politicians cannot be sure that judges and bureaucrats desire the same policy outcomes they do. When judges and bureaucrats have different policy preferences than the politicians in power, the judges and bureaucrats may have some ability to reshape policy outcomes after the legislative process has been completed. This is known as *shirking*.

Politicians, though, are not completely powerless to prevent shirking. They have an arsenal of tools at their disposal to control judges and bureaucrats: Politicians can write more specific, detailed legislation *ex ante,* or they can monitor and punish shirking *ex post.* However, these tools are only effective to the degree that politicians can agree on how to use them. When there are fewer veto players, it is easier for politicians to enforce the policy outcome. Moreover, politicians are better able to overrule adverse judicial interpretations through the political process, something of great concern to judges who typically fear having their decisions overturned. The judiciary is also less independent when interpreting the law, and bureaucrats have less leeway when implementing it as the number of veto players and the ideological distance between them decreases.

GOVERNMENT AND REGIME STABILITY

Because the number of checks and balances present in a political system affects the ability of that system to produce new legislation, it also impacts a government's ability to handle crises. A political system with fewer checks can better respond to external crises than a system with many checks. When there are many veto players, they may not be able to agree on the best way to handle a crisis. This, in turn, may impact upon government stability. In parliamentary systems with coalition governments, a crisis may lead parties in a governing coalition to disagree, causing the government to collapse. This leads to the formation of a new government, and the possible dissolution of parliament and new elections. Therefore, in parliamentary systems, more veto players should mean less government stability.

In presidential systems, it is not possible to remove a president during the middle of a term for ideological reasons, although the possibility of impeachment for criminal activities does provide the legislature with some form of check. While parliamentary systems provide a constitutional mechanism to remove ineffective governments during a term, presidential systems do not. When a crisis arises in a presidential system with a great number of veto players, the system may be rendered immobile. This could potentially lead some to seek extraconstitutional means for change in the form of coups or revolution. Therefore, while high numbers of veto players in parliamentary democracy may lead to government instability, high numbers of veto players in presidential systems are likely to lead to regime instability and a greater likelihood of reversion to authoritarian regimes.

While there is little doubt today that parliamentary democracies are less likely to revert to authoritarian rule than presidential systems, there is still some debate about why. Some scholars believe that the features of presidential systems make them more susceptible to democratic breakdown, as the logic laid out here would suggest. Others, however, point out that it is difficult to know what leads to regime collapse because most presidential democracies also suffer from other maladies that increase the likelihood of authoritarian reversals, such as poverty, poor economic growth, and a history of previous military rule. Presidentialism tends to exist in countries where all forms of democracy are likely to fail, making it difficult to sort out the effects of presidentialism from these other variables. However, recent scholarship finds that while poor economic growth and, specifically, economic crises such as recessions are the primary cause of reversals to authoritarian rule, presidential systems are much less likely to undergo the process of democratic consolidation, leaving them much more vulnerable to shocks associated with economic crises than parliamentary systems. High numbers of veto players leads to policy gridlock in both parliamentary and presidential regimes; however, parliamentary systems offer a constitutional escape from the gridlock through the possibility of government collapse and the ability to call for new elections. Presidential systems do not offer such a release valve, and therefore presidential countries do not consolidate as democracies, leaving them more vulnerable to authoritarian reversal during times of crisis.

SUMMARY

The number of checks and balances in a political system has a tremendous impact on the policy-making process, which in turn affects other aspects of the political system, including the independence of judges and the ability of bureaucrats to implement policy. Lastly, checks and balances even impact the likelihood of government collapse and regime stability. In some circumstances, such as periods of strong economic growth, policy stability may be desirable; at other times, it may not be. Rather than constructing a normative argument about whether checks and balances are either inherently good or bad for democratic government, political science today often takes a positive approach to analysis of checks and balances, examining the underlying institutional sources of policy stability.

See also *Checks and Balances; Constitutional Systems, Comparative; Constitutions and Constitutionalism; Divided Government; Federalism; Parliamentary Democracy; Parliamentary Government; Westminster Model.*

. . . . JONATHAN SLAPIN

BIBLIOGRAPHY

Ackerman, Bruce. "The New Separation of Powers." *Harvard Law Review* 113, no. 3 (2000): 633–729.

Bawn, Kathleen. "Money and Majorities in the Federal Republic of Germany: Evidence for a Veto Players Model of Government Spending." *American Journal of Political Science* 43, no. 3 (1999): 707–736.

Cheibub, Jose. *Presidentialism, Parliamentarism, and Democracy.* Cambridge: Cambridge University Press, 2007.

Kiewet, D. Rodrick, and Matthew McCubbins. 1991. *The Logic of Delegation.* Chicago: University of Chicago Press, 1991.

Madison, James, Alexander Hamilton, and John Jay. *The Federalist Papers.* New York: Mentor/Penguin, 1961.

McCubbins, Matthew, Roger Noll, and Barry Weingast. "Administrative Procedures as Instruments of Political Control." *Journal of Law Economics and Organization* 3 (1987): 243–277.

———. "Structure and Process, Politics, and Policy: Administrative Arrangements and the Political Control of Agencies." *Virginia Law Review* 75 (1989): 430–482.

McCubbins, Matthew, and Thomas Schwartz. "Congressional Oversight Overlooked: Police Patrols versus Fire Alarms." *American Journal of Political Science* 28, no. 1 (1984): 165–179.

Riker, William. *Federalism: Origin, Operation, Significance.* Boston: Little, Brown, 1962.

Romer, Thomas, and Howard Rosenthal. "Political Resource Allocation, Controlled Agendas, and the Status Quo." *Public Choice* 33 (1978): 27–43.

Svolik, Milan. 2008. "Authoritarian Reversals and Democratic Consolidation." *American Political Science Review* 102, no. 2 (2008): 153–168.

Tiebout, Charles. "A Pure Theory of Local Expenditure." *Journal of Political Economy* 64 (1956): 416–424.

Triesman, Daniel. "Decentralization and Inflation: Commitment, Collective Action, or Continuity." *The American Political Science Review* 94, no. 4 (2000): 837–857.

Tsebelis, George. "Veto Players and Law Production in Parliamentary Democracies: An Empirical Analysis." *American Political Science Review* 93, no. 3 (1999): 591–608.

———. *Veto Players: How Political Institutions Work.* Princeton: Princeton University Press, 2002.

Tsebelis, George, and Jeanette Money. *Bicameralism.* New York: Cambridge University Press, 1997.

Weingast, Barry. "The Economic Role of Political Institutions: Market-Preserving Federalism and Economic Development." *Journal of Law, Economics, and Organization* 11 (1995): 1–31.

Children's Rights

Children's rights have become enshrined in the United Nations Convention on the Rights of the Child (UNCRC). Adopted in 1989, this declaration sought both to establish a concept of rights specific to children (ages seventeen and under) and to elaborate on that concept with regard to the specific rights that should be conferred on children by the state or society in which they live.

Although the principles underpinning these rights, and the specification of some of them, have been strongly contested at times, the UNCRC has nevertheless been adopted by most nations—only the United States and Somalia have not yet ratified the convention—and the UNCRC has acquired force through legislative expression in a number of countries. The United States is opposed to the convention because it fears that ratification could weaken national sovereignty and override parental rights. The points of contestation have emerged out of different cultural values, with some criticism that the UNCRC promulgates a Western, universal conceptualization of the child and of the place of the child in society. Further criticism orientates to a tension within the set of rights as established between protectionist and liberationist approaches to the matter of child rights. Finally, challenges stem from whether children need a specific set of rights or whether they should simply have extended to them the same human and civil rights to which adults can lay claim under the processes of the European Court of Human Rights and other supranational juridical institutions.

The specific provision for children reflects a duality of constructions: on the one hand, children as individual citizens with all the protections that brings, and on the other hand, children as dependents with the implications that carries for children's relationship to adults and to the state. The UNCRC has moved forward from the highly protectionist provisions of earlier formulations for children's rights such as that contained in the League of Nations in 1924 and the United Nations in 1959. A general characterization of the current UNCRC is that it addresses child rights in terms of the "3 Ps"—protection, participation, and provision. Under the protection rubric, children are assigned rights to protection *from* various harms that can be enacted by the state or which the state may fail to prevent (e.g., a right to freedom from violence and from abuse). What can be brought to the fore here is the approach of the "new" childhood studies and its view of the agency of the child in all dimensions of life against the "old" view dealing with the subordination of the child under parental interests. The provision rubric draws together those aspects of a child's life that are essential for a decent life: the right to health care, education, and a home. Finally, rights that relate to participation are those that seek to enable children's voices to be heard in processes of decision making and democratic participation. This new relationalization of protection, provision, and participation reflects the move from the socialization paradigm in childhood research to the new childhood studies in which the child is repositioned as a social actor and not as parents' property.

Consideration of the rights of children is highly relevant to questions concerning political socialization and political education, the theory and practice of democracy, and the politics of childhood. The UNCRC invites thoughts about the exercise of democracy not as something to be acquired at an age of majority but as something to be interwoven throughout the lifeworlds of all citizens across their lifetimes. Consequently, questions of how people become political, and are political, need to set aside assumptions of an apolitical status in childhood. This links to the issue of childhood politics. Childhood is itself a political construction and a political arena, and therefore a contested terrain. A rights perspective demands that children be afforded space, within that construction and arena, to be visible and heard by those with the power to affect daily and national life. Finally, the notion of political education then becomes one of education for political participation, not *about* democracy as a process reserved for adult engagement only.

See also *Universal Declaration of Human Rights.*

. . . . HEINZ SÜNKER AND JO MORAN-ELLIS

BIBLIOGRAPHY

Du Bois-Reymond Manuela, Heinz Sünker, and Heinz-Hermann Krüger, eds. *Childhood in Europe: Approaches, Trends, Findings.* New York: Peter Lang, 2001.

Hutchby, Ian, and Jo Moran-Ellis, eds. *Children and Social Competence: Arenas of Action.* London: Falmer Press, 1998.

James, Allison, and Alan Prout, eds. *Constructing and Reconstructing Childhood,* 2nd ed. London: Falmer Press, 1999.

Moran-Ellis, Jo, and Heinz Sünker. "Giving Children a Voice: Childhood, Power, and Culture." In *Symbolic Power in Cultural Contexts: Uncovering Social Reality,* edited by Jarmo Houtsonen and Ari Antikainen, 67–84. Rotterdam, the Netherlands: Sense Publishers, 2008.

Qvortrup, Jens, Marjatta Bardy, Giovanni Sgritta, and Helmut Wintersberger, eds. *Childhood Matters: Social Theory, Practice and Politics.* Aldershot, UK: Avebury, 1994.

Chinese Political Thought

Political thought has been an abiding concern of China's rich philosophical tradition for over twenty-five hundred years. Of course, much changed over this time span, including the nature of the Chinese polity along with relations to other peoples and other intellectual traditions. The twentieth century witnessed some of the most dramatic changes in all of China's history. Nonetheless, certain debates seem perennial, and various ideas continue to resurface. One example is the question of authoritative leaders versus authoritative standards or institutions. For many traditional thinkers in China, rule by a sage-king is an achievable and appropriate goal for politics, and it should result in harmonious flourishing for all. Objective standards play varying roles, but even in the twentieth century, it is rare to find a thinker who views standards merely procedurally, and countenances deep-seated pluralism, dissonance, or conflict: harmony or even uniformity are still widely sought. While twenty-first-century Chinese political thought is sure to undergo many changes—as Chinese thinkers reflect both on dramatic developments in Chinese society and their ongoing interactions with various foreign political philosophies—in all likelihood, political thought will also continue to be concerned with harmony, perfectionism, and similar ideas. As such, it may yet lead to new types of political institutions and political theories that will challenge the global hegemony of liberal democracy.

CLASSICAL POLITICAL THOUGHT

Classical Chinese political thought (pre-221 BCE) revolved around three sets of questions: (1) How should a state be organized and governed? In particular, who or what should the people be expected to take as authoritative? (2) What are the proper goals of governance? Which goals are most fundamental? (3) How are the answers to the previous questions justified? What renders the means and ends of governance legitimate?

Two types of answers dominate efforts for addressing the first question. First are those emphasizing adherence to some sort of objective standard (*fa*). Historians have labeled some but not all of the thinkers taking this approach as belonging to the school of standards (*fajia*), an older and misleading translation of which is "legalism." According to early chapters of the *Guanzi* (a collection of philosophical and other essays, begun in the early fourth century BCE and compiled around 26 BCE), for instance, if the people are well fed and put to work at tasks well suited to them, they are likely to accord with propriety and moderation. Yet, the author adds that rulers must "make clear the road to certain death," by which the author means "severe punishments" must be in place for those who go astray. In another chapter of the text, possibly by the same author, it states, "Those who shepherd the people desire them to be controllable. Since they desire them to be controllable, they must pay serious attention to standards (*fa*)." These standards are then enumerated, and include honoring ranks and ceremonial dress, giving salaries and rewards to the deserving, granting offices, and applying punishments. Standards, in short, mean objective criteria for punishment and reward. Legal codes are one sort of standard, but the *Guanzi* and many other texts make it clear that *fa* is understood more broadly than mere penal codes.

The main alternative to an emphasis on standards is the Confucian focus on virtuous rule and moral transformation. In the *Analects* (a collection of the sayings of Confucius and his school, begun shortly after 500 BCE), the dynamic of people identifying with and modeling themselves on the ruler permeates the text's understanding of governance. When asked whether a ruler should kill those who fail to follow the way (*dao*), Confucius responds, "You are there to govern; what use have you for killing? If you desire the good, the people will be good. The virtue of the gentleman is the wind; the virtue of the little people is the grass. The wind on the grass will surely bend it" (12:19). Unlike the emphasis put on punishments as one kind of standard in the *Guanzi,* the *Analects* here minimizes the importance of killing. This point is reinforced in perhaps the most famous saying in the text about governance: "Lead them with government and regulate them by punishments, and the people will evade them with no sense of shame. Lead them with virtue and regulate them by ritual, and they will acquire a sense of shame—and moreover, they will be orderly" (2:3).

These contrasting emphases—objective standards opposed to virtuous rule—can be found to varying degrees in all subsequent treatments of political thought. A related, and important, distinction is that between harmony (*he*) and uniformity (*tong*). Texts that stress objective standards tend also to demand strict uniformity with those standards and to leave little, if any, room for complaint or remonstrance. (One partial exception is the *Mozi,* a collection of essays by the philosopher Mozi and his school, begun in the late fifth century BCE. In one plausible reading, its objective standard of benefit is readily accessible to all, and thus could ground criticism of a leader who does not follow it.) Confucian texts, in contrast, emphasize individual judgment—at least among the cultivated—and despise uniformity. Drawing on the metaphors of balanced flavors in a soup or the blending of different notes in music, Confucians argue that harmony depends on situationally apt judgment. This enables the whole (of which one is a part) to flourish more than before. Confucian standards for judgment tend to be internal and based on virtue. While ritual propriety is important, Confucius makes clear that without an inner, emotional commitment, an external show of ritual is next to worthless.

There are various answers to the question of what grounds the objective standards found in texts like *Guanzi* and *Mozi*, as well as in two other famous collections of realist ideas from the classical period, *Shangjun Shu* and *Hanfeizi*. Especially in *Mozi*, one apparent answer is heaven (*tian*). This, however, is somewhat complicated. While *tian* once clearly referred to a religious entity, it eventually comes to be understood in more naturalistic terms. For the most part, classical philosophers of governance do not appeal to supernatural standards to justify their claims. Even in the *Mozi*, other chapters record that just as carpenters can use a compass to determine what is circular, so an understanding of the "will of heaven" leads one to reliably judge what is right. The striking thing about a compass is that no special knowledge is needed to use it: It is a public, objective standard for circles. If the will of heaven is to be analogous, then there must be a public, objective standard for right. Mysterious knowledge of the will of a deity does not sound like a good candidate for such a public, objective standard. The text offers an alternative, though, when it regularly speaks of maximally benefitting (*li*) the people as a standard. A neat way of resolving all these loose ends, then, is to conclude that the will of heaven is a metaphorical reference to the standard of benefit. Proper Mohist governance thus would ultimately be a matter of utilitarian judgment.

Along somewhat similar lines, the *Shangjun Shu* argues that "the greatest benefit to the people is order [*zhi*]," which is to implicitly accept that benefit is the standard by which theories of governance are judged. At the same time, it places particular stress on the collective character of benefit. In a war-torn world, the text relays, only when the state is strong can its inhabitants flourish. Those who act for their own interests rather than for the benefit of the state, therefore, are to be punished. One result of the fuzziness surrounding the idea of benefitting the people is that if clearer criteria can plausibly be seen as necessary conditions for benefitting the people, these criteria take center stage. A prime example is order. Disorder, it is natural to assume, is incompatible with the people's well-being, so rulers could concentrate on order and allow benefit to follow in its wake. Especially when combined with the idea that the people tend to be selfish and not understand what is really good for them, though, a focus on order can rapidly lead to tyranny. It is perhaps with this in mind that another early Confucian, *Xunzi*, maintained that "there is only governance by men, not governance by standards" (*Xunzi* 8). Just claiming to be virtuous is not enough, of course; in fact, Mencius famously asserted

that rulers who abandon their virtuous commitments can be treated like bandits and slain (*Mencius* 1B:8). Indeed, others saw that the doctrine of rule by virtue is by no means a panacea. The *Hanfeizi* argues that while objective standards and their attendant institutions will make no difference if the ruler is supremely good or supremely bad, for the vast majority of rulers, such institutions are critical (*Hanfeizi* 40).

POSTCLASSICAL THOUGHT

The general shape of political thought in the postclassical period (221 BCE–1911 CE) followed on the foundations classical political thought. Scholars have used the term *imperial Confucianism* to describe the philosophy-cum-state ideology that emerged. There was enormous institutional innovation, partly because of great social changes, but the mainstream Confucian discourse continued to see institutions and standards with secondary importance, compared to the cultivation of virtuous individuals. The language of *sage ruler* was regularly applied to emperors—not least by the emperors themselves—and rulers efforts to educate or transform their subjects sometimes led to horrific excesses. The idea that people were beholden to a standard of personal moral judgment was fleshed out; the source and justification of the judgment came to be seen as the underlying harmonious coherence (*li*) (also sometimes translated as "principle") of the cosmos.

One critical episode in this lengthy period was the failure of an ambitious program of top-down institutional reforms advocated by Wang Anshi (1021–1086), which led many subsequent Confucians to stress local institutions and local autonomy. A related trend, which both supported and was supported by the flourishing commercial economy of the sixteenth century and thereafter, was the increasing emphasis on legitimate personal (*si*) desires. A range of thinkers came to make explicit the importance of a legitimate sphere of personal concern, and this trend was one significant source of subsequent Chinese reflection about rights. Indeed, the Chinese term that came to be accepted as a translation of rights meant, to nineteenth-century Confucian thinkers, something close to "legitimate powers and interests."

Among the most significant political texts of the entire period was the trenchant manifesto *Waiting for the Dawn*, completed in 1663 by Huang Zongxi. Huang argues that a healthy polity is based on well-designed institutions (using *fa*, or standard, in a broad sense) like schools, property regimes, and ceremonies that train people to be social citizens, rather than selfish egoists. Huang contrasts these institutions with those promoted by recent rulers, which he characterizes as "anti-institutional institutions" (*fa* that are not *fa*): In this case, the educational system, property regime, and ceremonies are designed solely to glorify the one family who happens to occupy the throne—whether the family deserves it or not. Huang then famously asserts, "Should it be said that 'There is only governance by men, not governance by institutions [*fa*],' my reply is that only if there is governance by institutions can there by governance by men." He goes on to explain, "If the institutions of the early kings were still in effect, there would be a spirit among men that went beyond the institutions. If men were of the right kind, all of their intentions could be realized; and even if they were not of this kind, they could not slash deep or do widespread damage." Huang's argument may bring to mind the similar-sounding argument of Han Feizi, cited earlier, although for the most part Huang's institutions are designed to nurture people's good natures, rather than impose objective punishments along Han Feizi's lines. In any event, the tension between relying on virtuous rulers, and seeking to provide some sort of objective guidance or institution, clearly continued throughout the imperial period.

THE TWENTIETH CENTURY

A flourishing of political thought, under the twin stimuli of domestic challenges and encounters with foreign political philosophies, marked the last years of the Qing dynasty, which collapsed in 1911. The Russian Revolution of 1917 added further fuel to the fire, at a time when the nascent Republic of China was struggling with both internal and external threats. The nature and sources of political authority once again were topics of debate. Many now took it for granted that the goal was some sort of democracy in which the people were (at least in principle) sovereign. But who counted as "the people," how they were to be led or represented, and how collective versus individual goals were to be balanced, all were up for grabs. At a broader level, there was a debate between those who felt the answer could be in one or another "ism"—that is, an all-encompassing ideology like Marxism—and those who favored working more pragmatically, via institution building, on one problem at a time. A few decades later, after the founding of the People's Republic, similar issues were addressed in the contrast between "Red" (ideologically and morally pure) and "expert" (possessing technical expertise). In various ways, these twentieth-century debates resonated with classical rule-by-virtue versus rule-by-standards contention. Were morally advanced individuals the key to an ideal society? Or should objective standards of success, coupled with objective institutions, be society's political foundation? In cases of conflict, which had priority?

There was certainly no single answer offered to these questions by any of the groups constituting twentieth-century China's political landscape, ranging from *new Confucians* to nationalists to liberals to Marxists. However, the "isms" approach won out through much of the century, and Thomas Metzger has shown that Chinese political thinkers of all camps tended toward what he calls *epistemological optimism*, which is a confidence that the one, universally applicable moral and political truth is knowable, and so great that authority should be vested in those gifted individuals able to perceive this truth. Another way to put this would be to say that there is a strong utopian strand in much twentieth-century Chinese political thought, which has both pushed toward radical solutions and led to dissatisfaction with continued dissonance or piecemeal progress. Even Chinese liberals have, in many cases, envisioned harmonious societies in which individual self-realization goes hand-in-hand with the realization of the larger collectivity, which they

often called the larger self (*dawo*). From a Western perspective, they have leaned more towards the ideas of French Enlightenment philosopher Jean-Jacques Rousseau than toward those of British utilitarian philosopher John Stuart Mill.

Twentieth-century China was home to a number of creative Marxist political thinkers, the most famous of whom was Mao Zedong (1893–1976). Mao was instrumental in redefining the Marxist revolution so that peasants rather than urban workers were its foundation—a shift that was facilitated by the fact that the Chinese translation for *proletariat* literally meant "the class without property [*wuchan jieji*]." In philosophical essays like "On Practice" and "On Contradiction," Mao elaborated an understanding of knowledge and of political progress that emphasized the roles of experience and ongoing process, rather than abstract principles. Marxist theory certainly had a role, but pride of place went to individuals who are able to negotiate the dialectical relations between theory and concrete experience. The end result is a framework that allows leaders to claim authority to institute radical policies and even "permanent revolution"; neither objective standards nor rule of law could resist the claims to experiential insight on the part of individuals.

Some philosophers in the twentieth century have been more aware than others of the problems with utopianism. Mou Zongsan (1909–1995), a leader of the new Confucian movement, was not only aware of these problems, but also offered a particularly creative way out of the recurrent tension between personal virtue (or morality) and public standards (or politics). Mou's insight is that the relation between morality and politics is "dialectical." Rather than seeing a leader's political virtue as a direct extension of the leader's personal moral virtue, Mou argues that there needs to be an indirect relation between them. Politics and political virtue must develop out of morality, but nonetheless have an independent, objective existence. This means that human rights, for example, must have a basis in morality, but come to be measured by standards that are separate from moral standards. The converse is also true: Full moral virtue requires that which partly "negates its essential nature [*ziwo kanxian*]," namely objective structure (Mou, 59). Objective structures (like laws) are fundamentally different from the subjectively felt, internalized morality for which all should all individually strive. The concrete implication of this is that no matter what one's level of moral accomplishment, "insofar as one's virtue is manifested in politics, one cannot override the relevant limits (that is, the highest principles of the political world), and in fact must devote one's august character to the realization of these limits" (128). In short, sages cannot break the law or violate the constitution. Politics thus has its independence from morality.

Philosophers have differed in their evaluations of Mou's argument, but it can stand as an instance of the continuing creativity to be found in contemporary Chinese political thinking. China's dynamic society offers a crucible within which new ideas and new political forms may be forged and tested in coming years. To be sure, genuinely novel and intellectually challenging ideas do not form the majority of contemporary Chinese political discourse, but they are there on all sides of the spectrum. It remains to be seen whether robust political values and institutions will emerge as alternatives to more familiar models of Western political theory, just as the role is unforeseen for the Marxist, Confucian, liberal, and other traditions in future Chinese political thinking. Concerns with harmony and virtue are unlikely to disappear, but (as Mou's example shows) this by no means limits the future interest of whatever political institutions and theories emerge in China.

See also *Asian Political Thought; Confucian Political Thought; Maoism; Marxism; Political Culture; Social Order.*

. . . . STEPHEN C. ANGLE

BIBLIOGRAPHY

Angle, Stephen C. *Human Rights and Chinese Thought: A Cross-Cultural Inquiry.* New York: Cambridge University Press, 2002.

———. "Decent Democratic Centralism." *Political Theory* 33, no. 4 (August, 2005).

Bell, Daniel. *Beyond Liberal Democracy.* Princeton: Princeton University Press, 2006.

Brooks, E. Bruce. *The Original Analects: Sayings of Confucius and His Successors,* translated by A. Taeko Brooks. New York: Columbia University Press, 1998.

Creel, Herrlee G. *Shen Pu-Hai: A Chinese Political Philosopher of the Fourth Century BC.* Chicago: University of Chicago Press, 1974.

Dardess, John W. *Confucianism and Autocracy: Professional Elites in the Founding of the Ming Dynasty.* Berkeley: University of California Press, 1983.

De Bary, William Theodore. *The Trouble With Confucianism.* Cambridge, Mass.: Harvard University Press, 1991.

Ding, Yijiang. *Chinese Democracy After Tiananmen.* New York: Columbia University Press, 2001.

Elman, Benjamin A. *Classicism, Politics, and Kinship: The Ch'ang-Chou School of New Text Confucianism in Late Imperial China.* Berkeley: University of California Press, 1990.

Fewsmith, Joseph. *China Since Tiananmen: The Politics of Transition.* New York: Cambridge University Press, 2001.

Huang, Zongxi. *Waiting for the Dawn,* translated by William Theodore De Bary. New York: Columbia University Press, 1993.

Liu, James T. C. *Reform in Sung China: Wang An-shih (1021- 1086) and His New Policies.* Cambridge: Harvard University Press, 1959.

Metzger, Thomas. *A Cloud Across the Pacific: Essays on the Clash Between Chinese and Western Political Theories Today.* Hong Kong: Chinese University of Hong Kong Press, 2005.

Mou, Zongsan. *Zhengdao yu Zhidao* [The Way of Politics and the Way of Administration]. Taipei, Taiwan: Xuesheng Shuju, 1991.

Nathan, Andrew. *Chinese Democracy.* Berkeley: University of California Press, 1986.

Pan, Wei. "Toward a Consultative Rule of Law Regime in China." *Journal of Contemporary China* 12, no. 34 (2003).

Rickett, W. Allyn, trans. *Guanzi: A Study and Translation,* 2 vols. Princeton: Princeton University Press, 1985.

Saich, Tony, ed. *The Rise to Power of the Chinese Communist Party: Documents and Analysis.* Armonk, N.Y.: M. E. Sharpe, 1996.

Slingerland, Edward, trans. *Analects, with Selections from Traditional Commentaries.* Indianapolis: Hackett, 2003.

Wakeman, Frederic, Jr. *History and Will: Philosophical Perspectives of Mao Tse-tung's Thought.* Berkeley: University of California Press, 1973.

Womack, Brantly. "Party-State Democracy: A Theoretical Exploration." In *Mainland China After the Thirteenth Party Congress,* edited by King-yuh Chang, 11–29. Boulder: Westview Press, 1990.

Wood, Alan T. *Limits to Autocracy: From Sung Neo-Confucianism to a Doctrine of Political Rights.* Honolulu: University of Hawaii Press, 1995.

Zarrow, Peter. *Anarchism and Chinese Political Culture.* New York: Columbia University Press, 1990.

Christian Democratic Parties

Christian democracy is a label that has not been accurately defined, and it sometimes includes the more recent protestant parties of Scandinavia and Christen Demokratisch Appel (CDA) of the Netherlands, but this family of parties is usually assumed to be those of Catholic sensibility. As such, Christian democracy constitutes an influential group of parties with outliers in Latin America and in Asia (the Philippines). However, its heartland is the Old World: One of the main conservative movements in Western Europe at the end of World War II (1939–1945) was Christian democracy. This was not a sudden eruption onto the European stage, but the product of a long gestation and a slow acceptance of representative institutions by the Catholic Church as well as a current of thought that had roots in Catholic social teaching and in *papal encyclicals* (doctrinal briefs). Christian Democratic parties are not confessional parties, and they are probusiness. However, they are all located on the center left of the political spectrum and claim to be inspired by Catholic social teaching; consequently, they emphasize human dignity for all classes of people.

ROOTS OF CHRISTIAN DEMOCRATIC PARTIES

After the French Revolution (1789–1799), the Church of Rome found itself in opposition to the radical parties and to the revolutionaries of the left. However, the papacy recognized the plight of the new class of factory workers and, in the encyclical *Humanum genus*, rebuked the Western governments for stripping the workers of the protection given them by corporations and exposing them to the blast of the free market. These themes were developed, as were those of social Catholicism, by the encyclical from Pope Leo XIII in 1891, *Rerum Novarum*—seen as the founding document of the Christian Democrat movement, although it is differently interpreted. *Rerum Novarum* reiterated the Catholic Church's opposition to revolution, to socialism (which promoted rancor and resentment and attacked property), and to free market ideology. The capitalism attacked was of the sort propounded by J. S. Mill and Spencer that idealized the free market and regarded greed and avarice (akin to *usury* in Catholic thought) as the central motive in society. This encyclical promoted social welfare and trade-union protection for the workers and developed a positive view of the state. In Catholic political thought, the state had a big role in the way a community's interests can be legitimately defended and promoted. This encyclical also encouraged the development of Catholic social organizations, such as trade unions, and participation in secular Western institutions.

EARLY PARTIES

The impact of the encyclical *Rerum Novarum* was not immediate or dramatic, but it did inspire a number of movements, and the process of party-building, that was to come to fruition in the mid-century, was under way. Early experiments in Catholic Democratic Parties included Marc Sagnier's Sillon (founded in 1899) in France and the Zentrum in Germany (which polled 16.4 percent in 1914). In Italy, the Catholic dispute with the papacy prevented progress, and the pope condemned the Sillon in France in an authoritarian turn of policy that saw democracy and the nation as a threat in many cases.

French Christian democracy was not a force after the World War I (1914–1918), but the Zentrum emerged as one of the major governing parties of Weimar Germany, and in Italy, Don Luigi Sturzo founded the Partito Populare Italiano (PPI). Don Sturzo's PPI was influential in its teaching, and it polled 20 percent in 1919. In 1920, the PPI supported Mussolini before moving into opposition and being dissolved in 1926. Perhaps the most successful electorally was the Belgian *Parti catholique*, which polled 37 percent before World War II and was the major party in the country. In much of Europe, however, the main conservative or center-right perception was of a threat from communism and atheistic movements.

POST–WORLD WAR II SUCCESS AND CONTEMPORARY DECLINE

Many Catholics found themselves in resistance movements during the war, and the Vatican itself retreated from direct political involvement after 1945. During the reconstruction of Europe, the Christian Democrats emerged as a distinct force and as mass parties with a popular base. They were the main parties in France (*Mouvement républicain populaire* or MRP), Germany (*Christlich Demokratische Union* or CDU), Italy (*Democrazia Cristiana*), and Austria (*Österreichische Volkspartei*). One reason for this success is that they were seen as a bulwark against communism (Pius XII excommunicated Communist voters), but they also embraced the Atlantic Alliance and NATO as well as supporting the European welfare states and social protection. Christian Democratic ideas of the social market economy were influential and the slogan, "yes to a market economy, no to a market society" (often thought to be socialist in origin) sums up their outlook. Three Christian Democrats, Alcide de Gasperi of Italy, Konrad Adenauer of Germany, and Robert Schuman of France were seen as the founding fathers of European institutions (although others, notably the socialists, were equally involved). Although the MRP in France foundered under the impact of competition from de Gaulle's movements, it was one of the governing parties of the Fourth Republic contributing ministers to most governments. In Italy, the Christian Democrats were the principal governing party until 1992, and in Germany the CDU was in government from 1949 to 1998 (1969–1982 excepted). Likewise, in Benelux countries, Christian Democrats participated in governments from 1945 onward and in Austria, the Christian Democrats were the first party for most of the postwar period. There has, however, been a decline is support for Christian Democratic parties in Europe since the 1990. In Italy in 1993 to 1994, the Christian Democrats split four ways after successive party funding scandals and there is only a small center-left remnant. CDA has declined in the Netherlands, as have the Belgian French and Dutch-speaking Christian Democrats, although in France, the tradition is maintained within François Bayrou's small MoDem Party. No Christian

Democrats emerged as forces in Portugal or Spain after the fall of the dictatorships, and there is no Irish Party (although Fine Gael is affiliated). Christian Democrats are the dominant force in the European People's Party, and there is a Christian Democratic World Union movement (the Centrist Democrat International) with almost as many affiliates as the Socialist International. However, the movement is not homogenous and has decidedly different orientations on left-right issues in separate countries with the strongly Catholic countries being relatively conservative in inclination but with family and "church" issues, although generally conservative, also being prioritized differently. *Rerum Novarum* was celebrated by Pope John Paul II, who published the encyclical *Centisimus annus* in 1991, reiterating many of the same themes.

See also *Christian Socialism; Confessional Parties; Papacy; Religion and Politics; Religious Parties; Roman Catholic Political Thought.*

. . . . DAVID S. BELL

BIBLIOGRAPHY
Gilson, Etienne. *The Church Speaks to the Modern World: The Social Teachings of Pope Leo XIII.* New York: Doubleday, 1954.
Hanley, David, ed. *The Christian Democratic Parties: A Comparative Perspective.* London: Pinter, 1994.
Kaiser, Wolfram, and Michael Gehler, eds. *Christian Democracy in Europe Since 1945.* Routledge, London, 2004.
Kalyvas, Stathis N. *The Rise of Christian Democracy in Europe.* Ithaca: Cornell University Press, 1996.
McCarthy, David Matzko, ed. *The Heart of Catholic Social Teaching, Its Origins and Continuing Significance.* Grand Rapids, Mich.: Brazos, 2009.
Maritain, Jacques. *The Rights of Man and Natural Law.* London: Bles, 1958.
Wilensky, Harold L. "Leftism, Catholicism and Democratic Corporatism." In *The Development of Welfare States in Western Europe*, edited by Peter Flora and Arnold J. Heidenheimer. London: Transaction, 1981.

Christian Socialism

Christian socialism is an ideological perspective that believes that socialist political and economic policies—if not necessarily a fully socialist community or economy—are essential to living a Christian life. For Christian socialists, the message of Christianity is strongly egalitarian, encouraging all human beings to see themselves as brothers and sisters, condemning economic differences that allow the rich to exploit the poor, and generally disdaining the "profit mentality" and the principles of self-interest that are central to most defenses of free market economy. Hence, they see socialism, or at least some form of social democracy, as a natural concomitant to the Christian message. Similarly, they believe that being a member of a capitalist environment potentially implicates one in un-Christian practices; thus, an active resistance to certain elements of the liberal capitalist state, and attempts to reform those same elements, is the duty of every Christian.

Christian socialist movements or individual Christian socialist leaders, writers, or thinkers will occasionally explicitly link the practices of the original Christianity community formed following the death of Jesus with socialist teachings (e.g., by citing Acts 2:44–45: "All the believers agreed to hold everything in common: they began to sell their property and possessions and distribute to everyone according to his need;" (Revised English Bible). They will also sometimes associate Christian socialism as a whole with numerous egalitarian Christian communalist reforms and movements that have been attempted by different Christian churches, monastic orders, and dissident groups over the centuries (the Franciscans, the Mennonites, the Diggers during the English Civil War [1642–1651], the United Order practiced by the Mormons in nineteenth-century America, the Hopedale Community founded by Adin Ballou). For the most part, however, Christian socialist beliefs have of their roots in late-nineteenth-century Protestant social gospel teachings and, most particularly, the papal encyclical *Rerum Novarum* (On New Things). More than any other single writing, *Rerum Novarum* provided the foundation for numerous Christian democratic and Christian socialist parties throughout Europe.

Of course, these same sources also played an important role in the rise of progressivism in the United States and social solidarity and trade union movements through all the Western world, and have been embraced by numerous liberal, democratic, and egalitarian groups and parties. As such, Christian socialism has historically not been usually understood as a distinct, separate voice calling explicitly for a socialist revolution, but rather as a perspective aligned with other ideologies in seeking a gradualist or evolutionary (though occasionally necessarily confrontational) approach to securing progressive and ameliorative ends. Some Christian socialists hope to see those ends eventually result in a fully socialized economic environment and consider the liberal redistribution of wealth to be insufficient, whereas others see the Christian socialist perspective simply as one that can be realized in any sufficiently egalitarian economy (e.g., a capitalist society with strong welfare policies and key public goods—like transportation, education, and medical care—made accessible and affordable, or free, to all).

Various Christian socialist individuals and organizations have been closely entwined with major political parties throughout Western Europe (such as the Fabian Society and Labour Party in Great Britain, among others). The same holds for the mostly Catholic nations of Central and South America, although liberation theology, which has had its greatest impact in Latin America, is much more explicitly Marxist and revolutionary in its aims, despite being usually considered a branch of Christian socialist thought. Christian socialism has, like socialism in general, had a much smaller impact in the United States. Marx himself, it should be noted, was highly critical of Christian justifications for socialist reforms, calling Christian socialism "the holy water by which the priest consecrates the heart-burnings of the aristocrat."

See also *Capitalism and Democracy; Social Democracy; Socialism.*

. . . .   RUSSELL ARBEN FOX

BIBLIOGRAPHY

Ballou, Adin. *Practical Christianity: An Epitome of Practical Christian Socialism.* Providence, R.I.: Blackstone Editions, 2002.

Boyer, John. *Culture and Political Crisis in Vienna: Christian Socialism in Power 1897–1918.* Chicago: Chicago University Press, 1995.

Cort, John C. *Christian Socialism: An Informal History.* Maryknoll, N.Y.: Orbis, 1998.

Holland, Joe. *Modern Catholic Social Teaching: The Popes Confront the Industrial Age, 1740–1958.* Mahwah, N.J.: Paulist, 1993.

Lipset, Seymour Martin, and Gary Marks. *It Didn't Happen Here: Why Socialism Failed in the United States.* New York: Norton, 2000.

Norman, Edward R. *The Victorian Christian Socialists.* Cambridge: Cambridge University Press, 2002.

Phillips, Paul T. *A Kingdom of God on Earth: Anglo-American Social Christianity, 1880–1940.* University Park: Pennsylvania State University Press, 1996.

Wilkinson, Alan. *Christian Socialism: Scott Holland to Tony Blair.* London: SCM Press, 1998.

Church and State

Church and state refers to the institutional interaction between religious organizations and the formal governance within a country. As a topic of discussion, *church and state* differs from *religion and politics*. The latter deals with how individual or group beliefs, values, and norms influence power relations and policy outcomes within a polity. Church and state focuses on how official rules and secular-authority structures impact the operation of churches, and, conversely, how the institutional interests of church officials affect the operation of secular government.

DEFINING CHURCH AND STATE

A church is the institutional embodiment of a religious denomination, and as such, delineates the leadership roles and rules for governing behavior within the faith. A church should be considered analytically distinct from a religion, although each religion typically gives rise to a corresponding church. The term *church* typically has Christian connotations, referring primarily to the Catholic, Orthodox, and Protestant traditions. Most Western scholarship on church and state has focused on the Christian world, primarily Europe and the United States. Scholars studying non-Christian faith traditions sometimes prefer to use terms such as *mosque and state* (for Islam) or *temple and state* (for Eastern religions or Judaism).

State as defined in church-state studies, refers to the institutional and authoritative arrangements of a governing body within a nation. Following nineteenth-century German sociologist Max Weber's definition, a state typically maintains a monopoly over the use of coercion, which gives the state the ability to create and enforce rules and regulations within society. This power has significant consequences for religious organizations, and forms the basis for church-state relations. A state can craft rules that permit a limited number of official churches, making all other churches illegal. The state can also use its coercive powers to collect taxes to finance a church or demand a say in the appointment of church leaders or making of church policy. Alternatively, the state can impose various regulatory barriers to make it difficult for any church to operate within a country. Determining which churches, if any, receive special status and subsidization from the state is perhaps the central issue in church-state relations.

CHURCH-STATE RELATIONSHIP IN ERA OF "CHRISTENDOM"

The granting of official status, collection of religious taxes, and prohibitions on nonsanctioned churches have been the historical norm in European Christianity since the Edict of Milan in 312 CE. This edict provided Christianity with state financial support equal to that of traditional Roman pagan temples. As financial support for pagan religions dried up, Christianity effectively became the official state church of the Roman Empire. Upon the collapse of the Roman Empire and throughout the duration of the medieval era, the Christian Church (in both its Roman Catholic and Eastern Orthodox branches) relied, in part, upon financial support from various kings and nobles. In exchange for this much-needed support, the church would either sell leadership positions (bishoprics) to the nobility or allow kings to choose the leaders for these positions. Such control sometimes gave secular leaders veto power over official church proclamations, such as papal bulls. The Catholic Church also found ways to finance itself through a variety of other mechanisms when state authority was too weak to provide financial assistance.

One of the major disadvantages of state control over the church was that the church became corrupted for purposes of political power and secular financial gain, with some individuals gaining access to key church leadership positions without ever having read the Bible. Such corruption frequently gave rise to schismatic movements (e.g., Lollards, Hussites) that often required state force to crush.

The most successful and decisive schismatic movement in Christian history was Martin Luther's Protestant Reformation in the early 1500s. Initially, nobles simply chose between Catholicism and Lutheranism and imposed that particular religion on their citizenry. Thus, Lutheranism developed into a state church like its Catholic counterpart. The principal question relating to church-state relations in the sixteenth century became which religion a monarch would endorse and impose on their population.

The larger historical significance of Luther's Reformation (and the subsequent English Reformation in 1533) for church-state relations was that it gave legitimacy to a myriad of new denominations (e.g., Calvinists, Anabaptists) and created a burgeoning of religious pluralism in Europe. Religious pluralism initially gave rise to domestic and international conflict, such as the French Religious Wars (1562–1598) and the Thirty Years War (1618–1648). However, religious pluralism eventually pushed many European states to tolerate minority churches even while they formally endorsed a single religious establishment. France's Edict of Nantes (1589) and England's Acts of Toleration (1689) represented the initial movement toward religious liberty, although the former was repealed in 1685.

RELIGIOUS LIBERTY AND TOLERATION

Religious liberty is a form of church-state relation wherein multiple denominations are allowed to exist under government authority. A government may still maintain a state church, but other churches are granted some minimal level of freedom to own property and proselytize. The First Amendment of the United States Constitution took the concept of religious toleration to its logical conclusion by prohibiting the establishment of any official state religion at the federal level. While intense debate still surrounds what constitutes official government promotion of religion in the United States, the First Amendment created a model of church and state that eventually became the standard of religious freedom in the Christian world.

Despite an increasing trend toward religious freedom and toleration in the Western world, a number of states in Europe continue to maintain established churches either through official endorsement or via governmental subsidization. For example, Sweden recently ended the "state church" status of the Reformed Church but the state continues to heavily subsidize the daily operations of the church. The German government collects tithes (taxes) directly for the Lutheran Church and the Catholic Church. While Britain has reduced the amount of its financial subsidies to the Church of England, the archbishop of Canterbury, the head of the church, is still appointed by the monarch with input from Parliament. Low levels of church attendance in Europe have made relations between church and state a relatively moot policy issue. Despite the low salience of church-state policy in the public discourse, European governments continue to protect their state churches by making it legally difficult for various missionary movements (typically from the United States) to create a presence in the region. This is often done by prohibiting the construction of church buildings or making it difficult to gain tax-exempt status.

THE PROBLEM OF ISLAM AND NON-WESTERN RELIGIONS

An increasingly controversial phenomenon in European church-state relations concerns the growing presence of Islam. Given that Islam is a decentralized religion with no formal hierarchy, European governments have had difficulty accommodating Muslims in traditional church-state alliances, as there is no single voice to speak for Islam. Muslims have found it difficult to receive funding equivalent to that of other state-funded religions for their religious schools or programs in several countries. They have also faced difficulty in gaining recognition for their spiritual customs. The prohibition on headscarves in public schools in France represents a primary example of this. The U.S. model of a "wall of separation" between church and state—effectively meaning that the government does not endorse or publicly finance any specific church—has proved to be less difficult for Muslims, as they are treated similarly to Christian denominations in matters of public policy.

The concept of church and state is more ambiguous in non-Western contexts. Islam and many Eastern religions, such as Buddhism, do not share the hierarchical structure of Christianity, thus relations between church (mosque or temple) and state are more complex. For example, a diffusion of leadership within Islam makes it more difficult for the state to easily interact with the Muslim clergy, as there is not one unique point of contact (such as a pope or bishop). In many Islamic countries, the state will decree Islam to be the official religion and prohibit proselytization by non-Muslims. In some instances (such as Egypt and Saudi Arabia), the state will officially subsidize the Muslim clergy, mosques, or other important Islamic institutions even though many Muslim clergy and organizations exist without official state endorsement or subsidization. A similar situation exists in societies dominated by Eastern religions; while some governments may endorse various historical faith traditions, the decentralized nature of these religions makes it difficult for governments to strictly regulate every practitioner of that faith. The lack of formal religious hierarchies within these faith traditions has meant less scholarship on church and state as compared to religion and politics.

See also *Clericalism; Confessional Parties; Freedom of Religion; Laicite; Papacy; Protestant Political Thought; Reformation Political Thought; Religion and Politics; State Church; Theocracy; Toleration.*

. . . . ANTHONY GILL

BIBLIOGRAPHY

Ekelund, Robert B., Robert F. Hebert, Robert D. Tollison, Gary M. Anderson, and Audrey B. Davidson. *Sacred Trust: The Medieval Church as an Economic Firm.* Oxford: Oxford University Press, 1996.

Fetzer, Joel S., and J. Christopher Soper. *Muslims and the State in Britain, France and Germany.* Cambridge: Cambridge University Press, 2005.

Gill, Anthony. *The Political Origins of Religious Liberty.* Cambridge: Cambridge University Press, 2007.

_____. *Rendering unto Caesar: The Catholic Church and the State in Latin America.* Chicago: University of Chicago Press, 1998.

Monsma, Stephen V., and J. Christopher Soper. *The Challenge of Pluralism: Church and State in Five Western Democracies,* 2nd ed. Lanham, Md.: Rowman and Littlefield, 2008.

Segers, Mary C., and Ted G. Jelen. *A Wall of Separation?: Debating the Public Role of Religion.* Lanham, Md.: Rowman and Littlefield, 1998.

Stark, Rodney. *For the Glory of God: How Monotheism Led to Reformations, Science, Witch-Hunts, and the End of Slavery.* Princeton: Princeton University Press, 2003.

Tracy, James D. *Europe's Reformations, 1450–1650.* Lanham, Md.: Rowman and Littlefield, 1999.

Cicero, Marcus Tullius

Politician, philosopher, orator, lawyer, and poet, Cicero Marcus Tullius (106–43 BCE) is arguably the most important Roman political thinker.

Born in the Italian town of Arpinum, Cicero lived through the Social War, warfare between Marius and Sulla, and Sulla's dictatorship. The young Cicero studied law and encountered Stoicism, Skepticism, as well as academic philosophy. A brilliant orator, Cicero rapidly worked his way up the Roman *cursus honorum,* or course of magistracies, serving as consul in 63 BCE. While consul, Cicero suppressed Catiline's plot to overthrow the republic, putting to death several conspirators. In 58 BCE, he was exiled for executing Roman citizens; he returned in 57 BCE and favored Pompey in his increasingly violent political rivalry with Caesar. Following Caesar's invasion, Cicero fled Rome in 49 BCE, returning the following year after Caesar's victory at Pharsalus. Cicero helped lead

Influential Roman philosopher Cicero defined the republic as an affair of the people bound by right and advantage.

SOURCE: The Granger Collection, New York

senatorial opposition to Marc Antony after Caesar's assassination, delivering his famous *Philippics* against him in 44 BCE. Though Cicero hoped to play Caesar's adopted son, Octavian, against Antony, he was killed December 7, 43 BCE, following their reconciliation.

Cicero wrote many philosophical works dealing with a wide range of issues; his most important political works are the fragmentary *On the Republic* and *On the Laws,* and *On Duties.* In *On the Republic,* Cicero argues that the Roman constitution, mixing monarchy, aristocracy, and democracy, was the ideal constitution, and he famously defined the republic (*res publica*) as the *res populi,* or affair of the people bound by right and advantage; its defense against corruption lay in civic virtue and leadership. In *On the Laws,* Cicero describes the laws of his ideal republic, articulating a conception of natural law rooted in human and divine reason. In *On Duties,* Cicero discusses the three problems of ethics: the honorable, the expedient, and conflicts between the two. Cicero argues that the truly honorable is expedient; hence, there is no conflict between the two.

Cicero greatly influenced subsequent thought. Augustine of Hippo (354–430 CE) claimed that Cicero's *Hortensius* turned him toward philosophy and referenced *On the Republic* in *City of God;* the "Dream of Scipio," also from *On the Republic,* was of special influence in the Middle Ages. Cicero was a key figure in humanistic thought from the fourteenth to the sixteenth centuries, *On Duties* being especially influential. His writings would also inspire seventeenth-century English writers such as James Harrington and John Locke, and draw Thomas Hobbes's criticism in *Leviathan.* He influenced numerous eighteenth-century thinkers, including Francois-Marie Voltaire, David Hume, Edmund Burke, and Thomas Jefferson. Although his influence waned after the eighteenth century, Cicero now draws renewed attention due to interest in republicanism and civic virtue.

See also *Civic Humanism; Natural Law; Republic; Republicanism, Classical; Virtue Theory*

. . . .   DANIEL KAPUST

BIBLIOGRAPHY
Atkins, E. M. "Cicero." In *The Cambridge History of Greek and Roman Political Thought,* edited by Christopher Rowe and Malcolm Schofield. Cambridge: Cambridge University Press, 2000.
Cicero. *On the Commonwealth* and *On the Laws,* translated and edited by James E. G. Zetzel. Cambridge: Cambridge University Press, 1999.
———. *On Duties,* edited by Margaret Atkins, translated and edited by Miriam Griffin. Cambridge: Cambridge University Press, 1991.
Douglas, A. E. *Cicero.* Oxford: Oxford University Press, 1968.
Fuhrmann, Manfred. *Cicero and the Roman Republic,* translated by W. E. Yuill. Oxford: Basil Blackwell, 1992.
Wood, Neal. *Cicero's Social and Political Thought.* Berkeley: University of California Press, 1988.

Citizen Knowledge

Political knowledge is the factual information—and the skills for interpreting it—needed to act as an effective member of the *polis* or political community. From Plato to John Stuart Mill, political theorists have viewed political knowledge as a precondition for exercising citizenship—for taking part in community decision making. Since modern democracies extend citizenship to all adults, there is an expectation that they possess the necessary information and skills. Minimally, for representative democracy to function properly, those entitled to select representatives (i.e., voters in elections) need to have sufficient information and skill to evaluate leaders' performance, to compare parties' commitments against their own preferences, and to weigh the credibility of the commitments in light of their record in government.

TRADITIONAL PERSPECTIVES

Fulfilling the underlying principle of democracy, political equality thus becomes more than the right to vote and take part in politics; political equality requires being able to exercise the right knowledgeably. Traditionally, democratic theory has been concerned mainly with the effects of the distribution of power on political equality: knowledge focused on the manipulation of information by elites. As a result, political institutions and state policies are critically analyzed in terms of whether and how they block or distort—rather than foster—the dissemination of political knowledge. Concern with such dissemination was limited to policies and institutions involved with the political socialization of children and adolescents, through schools in particular, and their role in fostering support for democratic institutions.

THE RATIONAL CHOICE APPROACH

A different approach can be identified with the rational choice perspective. In his seminal 1957 volume, Anthony Downs pointed to "information asymmetries" resulting from the costs of acquiring needed information being inversely related to a person's economic resources. But rational choice thinkers have tended to view absence of political knowledge as an expression of "rational ignorance," rather than a public policy issue. Only recently has the presence or absence of knowledgeable democratic adult citizens been perceived as worthy of significant attention in research and public policy. The last two decades have produced important contributions to the understanding of a phenomenon termed political awareness, political sophistication, political information, and political literacy, as well as political knowledge. The main impetus has come from the accumulation of data showing that, despite rising levels of education, average levels of political knowledge are lower than that needed to meet the minimal expectations of universal adult citizenship—and declining. Already in 1964, Philip Converse observed that the average American citizen exhibited a low level of knowledge, lack of consistency between attitudes, attitude instability, and vacuous answers to open-ended questions. Thirty years later, Larry Bartels concluded that "the political ignorance of the American voter is one of the best documented data in political science."

There is no consensus, however, on what to make of this state of affairs, and the differences give rise to several different research agendas. The most profound debate centers on whether political ignorance matters. Downs noted that while citizens may act as rational consumers of information in a political market, their ignorance results in a "paradox" since they lose out on the benefits to be gained from an informed electorate. Some observers contest the ill effects of this voters' paradox, arguing that politically uninformed people follow social cues and rules of thumb to arrive at decisions; these decisions result in outcomes similar to those that would have been attained through the participation of informed people. Arend Lijphart disputes the premise that the views of those nonvoting out of ignorance do not differ substantially from those of voters, arguing that polled nonvoters have given the issues less thought than they would have if they had been mobilized to vote.

Evidence of such differences emerges from deliberative polls. Comparing the results of surveys conducted before and after participants are provided with relevant information in well over twenty deliberative polls conducted in North America, Europe, and Australia, James Fishkin and Robert Luskin report that deliberation almost always produces significant factual information gains and, often, changes in opinions. Underlying this approach is a critique over public opinion polling. On many issues, survey designers assume a level of knowledge that many respondents lack. Hence, the supposed reflection of popular opinion that polls provide is distorted because they are inaccurate, since poorly informed respondents, who are also generally poorer, will give answers they think are expected of them, and unrepresentative, since they are more likely not to answer.

POLITICAL KNOWLEDGE AND POLITICAL PARTICIPATION

A related literature has emerged examining the effects of political knowledge and how it serves as intermediary between opinions and voting. In particular, researchers have investigated differences between well-informed and poorly informed voters in the stability of their preferences when confronted with new information about candidates. As a rule, the more people are knowledgeable about politics, the more their expressed policy preferences will be consistent with their political values, and the more those who identify with a party, the more they will articulate policy preferences in line with those of the party.

A question addressed in the literature concerns how political knowledge is operationalized. One popular classification identifies three types of questions: Factual questions survey the processes of government, surveillance questions cover current office holders, and textbook questions get at historical and constitutional aspects. But some question this kind of typology. A school of thought has emerged taking a more subjective perspective on the "political." From this perspective, the widespread portrait of a politically uninformed and inattentive youth miss the "good news," namely attitudes about human relations and the environment which young people define as political. But there are problems with using attitudinal—as opposed to knowledge based—indicators, since they costlessly invite respondents to place themselves in a positive light.

Underlying this debate is an intensifying interest in the relationship between political knowledge and political participation. A great deal of empirical data link low levels of political knowledge to declining voter turnout, lack of party membership and identification, and distrust of politicians. Numerous studies show that more informed people are more likely to vote and engage in various forms of conventional, and even unconventional, political activity.

Such findings buttress calls for improved civic education, but tell us little about the effects of specific institutions. Electoral institutions, in particular, influence the accessibility, intelligibility, and usefulness of political information, and countries higher in civic literacy (the proportion of those with the knowledge to be effective citizens) tend to be high in electoral participation. Missing is the aggregate data to link specific institutional arrangements and levels of political knowledge. Cross-national survey questionnaires generally limit political knowledge questions to international events and processes. The contemporary challenge is to devise a battery of questions about government processes, office holders, and issues to be used in cross-national research.

See also *Citizenship; Civic Education; Mill, John Stuart; Voting Behavior*

. . . . HENRY MILNER

BIBLIOGRAPHY

Althaus, Scott. *Collective Preferences in Democratic Politics.* Cambridge: Cambridge University Press, 2003.

Bartels, Larry. "Uninformed Votes: Information Effects in Presidential Elections." *American Journal of Political Science* 40, no. 1 (February 1996): 194–230.

Converse, Philip. The nature of belief systems in mass publics. In David Apter ed., *Ideology and Discontent.* New York: Free Press, 1964.

Delli Carpini, Michael, and Scott Keeter. *What Americans Know about Politics and Why It Matters.* New Haven: Yale University Press, 1996.

Downs, Anthony J. *An Economic Theory of Democracy.* New York: Harper, 1957.

Fishkin, James. *The Voice of the People: Public Opinion and Democracy.* New Haven: Yale University Press, 1995.

Lijphart, Arend. "Unequal Participation: Democracy's Unresolved Dilemma." *American Political Science Review* 91, no. 1 (1997): 1–14.

Mill, John Stuart. *Representative Government.* London: Dent and Sons, 1910.

Milner, Henry. *Civic Literacy: How Informed Citizens Make Democracy Work.* Hanover, N.H.: University Press of New England, 2002.

Sniderman, Paul M., Richard A. Brody, and Philip E. Tetlock. *Reasoning and Choice.* New York: Cambridge University Press, 1991.

Zaller, John. *The Nature and Origins of Mass Opinion.* New York: Cambridge, 1992.

Citizenship

Defining *citizenship* has preoccupied social scientists for millennia. "It is clear that the first thing that must be sought is the citizen," wrote Aristotle, "for the city is a certain multitude of citizens. Thus what ought to be called a citizen and what the citizen is must be investigated" (Aristotle, 3:1). Like the *polis* of Aristotle's time, a modern state is a collection of citizens, defining citizenship requires investigation, and it is not always easy to determine what or who ought to be called a *citizen.* According to more recent commentary, there is "no notion more central in politics than citizenship, and none more variable in history, or contested in theory" (Shklar, 1).

DEFINITION

In its most fundamental sense, citizenship refers to membership within a political community. Today, this membership is most often expressed as a relationship between an individual and a sovereign state; for example, an individual can be a citizen of Canada or Brazil, but not a citizen within a company or private organization. Symbols such as a passport, or other identification documents issued by relevant state authorities, often represent citizenship as a form of state membership. Most people acquire citizenship in a particular state, at birth through the operation of nationality law. This means individuals are either commonly granted the nationality of the state in which they are born or granted citizenship based upon their father or mother's nationality. In the instance of individuals who do not acquire citizenship of the state in which they were physically born, such as immigrants, these persons may eventually acquire this state's citizenship through a process of naturalization, in which they are often required to have spent a minimum time period in the state, take an oath of allegiance, and potentially renounce a previously held foreign citizenship through denaturalization. Thus, the term citizenship, by these definitions, is a legal relationship between an individual and a political community (i.e., a state).

A related meaning of citizenship, going beyond the strictly legal relationship between an individual and a sovereign state, refers to the rights and duties that accompany a person's membership in a political community. This second meaning focuses on the political obligations of the citizen, since it refers to the individual not only obeying the state's law but also participating in the political process. For Aristotle, citizenship meant not only being ruled but also sharing in the ruling—a notion denouncing the proponents of absolute monarchy. For centuries, there have been debates about the distinction between citizens and subjects. Today the term *citizenship* is generally accepted in this political sense as restricted to individuals who are citizens of democratic regimes, in which they are considered to be active participants in their own state's political process. Essentially, while a person may be a legal citizen in a nondemocratic state retaining the proper passport proclaiming such legal citizenship, these citizens do not typically have the degree of influence or powers to exact political change within their states as practiced in democracies.

Theoretical work on defining citizenship is varied and voluminous; however, many authors distinguish between two strands captured under the terms *republican,* which is occasionally conflated with communitarian, and *liberal.* The republican concept of citizenship embraces Aristotle's views on political participation and civic self-rule. Italian Renaissance political philosopher Niccoló Machiavelli's description of Italian city-states encouraging national unity and open political engagement and debate, as well as 18th-century philosopher Jean-Jacques Rousseau's advocacy of the public's collective will to provide for the common good, also fall under the republican concept. By contrast, the liberal view of citizenship emphasizes an individual's adherence to the state's rule of law and the individual's liberty from state interference, thus a status rather than an activity.

Both versions are subject to the criticism that the distinction between public and private citizenship is artificial. They also fall prey to a multicultural critique that promotes differential rights for immigrants, minorities, or constituent nations; the possibility of group rights inherent in aboriginal self-government also arises. Such critiques question the extent to which citizenship, albeit a unitary status or a shared engagement, can operate within pluralist societies in which there is no singular entity with the ability to solely dictate the political or socioeconomic climate.

THE RISE OF CITIZENSHIP

DETERMINING CITIZENSHIP

Prior to any discussion of the rights that citizenship entails, it is common to discuss and determine the attribution of citizenship, and in particular the question of who has the power to grant or take away one's citizenship. Since the development of modern citizenship has been intimately connected with the development of sovereignty, the traditional view attributed citizenship to flow solely from state authority. In this vein, the 1930 Hague Convention specified that it "is for each State to determine under its own law who are its nationals."

However, during the next fifteen years, millions of individuals, not only in Germany but throughout Europe, were stripped of their citizenship as consequence of World War II (1939–1945). Due to the postwar large-scale European denaturalizations, the United Nations agreed, in the aftermath of the war, to limit sovereignty by specifying, in Article 15 of the Universal Declaration of Human Rights, that everyone is entitled to a citizenship and citizens cannot be arbitrarily deprived of their citizenship or denied the right to change it. Within such broad parameters of international law, however, individual state policies on the attribution of citizenship continue to differ substantially. All states employ some combination of *jus sanguinis* (attribution on the basis of descent) and *jus soli* (attribution on the basis of place of birth), but some are more restrictive while others more liberal. States frequently revise their laws and policies concerning such issues as dual nationality, immigration, and naturalization, all of which help determine who can acquire citizenship and who cannot.

Alongside varying policies on citizenship itself, the individual rights that comprise citizenship also change as state policies change. Thus, the meaning of the social rights tied to citizenship shifted in many states during the 1980s, away from concrete redistributive entitlements toward a simple emphasis on social inclusion and equal opportunity. Such changes altered the long-held perception that a state's duty was to provide basic economic entitlements to its citizens. Additionally, if shared citizenship implies an obligation to redistribute resources to fellow citizens, then the term citizenship is continuously transformed as the nature of welfare entitlements evolves.

EXAMINING THE RIGHTS OF CITIZENS

The rising interest in citizenship may be attributed to the term's common association with guaranteed rights and justices within a political community. T. H. Marshall's influential post–World War II definition of citizenship describes its development in terms of three distinct phases, with each phase characterized by individuals acquiring certain rights from the state. In this definition, *civil* rights (e.g., equality before the law, the right to own property and sign binding contracts, freedom of religion and of speech) led to an individual's *political* rights (e.g., the right to vote and run for office), which in turn led to *social* rights guaranteeing the right to a minimal level of social and economic welfare. Tension between the growth of individual entitlement, known as rights, and the demands of membership within particular communities, namely communal duties or shared obligations, often characterize contemporary democracies.

Authors focusing on the rise of globalization during the late 20th century complicate Marshall's model arguing that, due to the significant increases in foreign travel and immigration, the international human rights regime, rather than states, now guarantees civil rights to persons worldwide, and furthermore, many states grant social rights to individuals on the basis of residence rather than citizenship. Thus, some states appear to be extending civil and social rights to individuals within their community, regardless if they possess the political rights associated with citizenship.

However, contemporary developments in the late twentieth and early twenty-first century have, at times, contradicted this postnational thesis, at least in terms of social rights, as some states have restricted social rights to noncitizens and legal citizens—possibly as a means to limit transnational migration or reduce state expenditure and costs. Some states have excluded noncitizens from automatic access to education, nonemergency health care, or social benefit funding. Since the mid-twentieth and into the twenty-first century, certain states within the Middle East, South Asia, and Africa are significantly and frequently affected by cross-border refugee flows and internally displaced persons seeking to evade ongoing armed conflicts, ethnic violence, and insurgencies devastating their home states. Rising global refugee rates challenge host governments to abide by international standards but limit natural citizen rights. This challenge is heightened in many developing nations that cannot accommodate incoming immigrants or refugees with social rights, especially since most developing countries continue to struggle with supplying the basic, social, and political rights for their own legal citizen population.

Conversely, even legal citizens have lost some of their perceived or promised rights associated with their state's definition of citizenship or the international community's list of unalienable rights. Many state governments have privatized major institutions, adopting market fundamentalism, or an absolute reliance on a free market economy; this can interfere with a citizen's promise of equal and effective rights, as many persons cannot financially compete with private sector costs for health care or education. As such, while basic civil rights may still be protected for individuals, it appears more common for citizens of a wealthy or powerful state to fare better in retaining their social rights than those citizens residing in a poor or weak state. Indeed, citizenship of a wealthy and powerful state can be viewed as a valuable commodity.

Common to both Marshall's definition of citizenship and its postnational critiques is the premise that citizenship is a collection of rights. By these interpretations, citizenship is undeniably being challenged by the unbundling of rights accelerated by the processes of globalization. Individuals can increasingly choose services from different governments or pursue alternatives, rather than be constrained to accept government dictates in the regions where they have citizenship or reside. In the end, the tension between the universalist claims of human rights and the particularism of local identities and affiliations may be irreconcilable: The operation of every political community, short of a global one, involves processes of inclusion but also of exclusion.

DIFFERENT TRAJECTORIES OF CITIZENSHIP

In terms of citizen attribution rules and the rights associated with citizenship, the historical trajectories of citizenship among different states demonstrate significant variances. Such variation reflects the differences in historical processes of state- and nation-building and the rise and transformation of sovereignty.

CASE STUDY: U.S. CITIZENSHIP

In the United States, citizenship evolved in response to a range of factors, including efforts to restrict rights on the basis of race, ethnicity, and gender. Americans "long struggled over whether state or national citizenship is or should be primary. Many thought that question was settled by the Civil War or the New Deal, but it has resurfaced in recent political and legal debates" (Smith, 1997, 5). The early United States was far from a homogeneous body of citizens, and the states controlled citizenship until the Naturalization Acts of 1792 and 1795 established federal control. Even then, American citizenship meant a "double allegiance" to both state and nation. The naturalization acts made naturalization a federal responsibility, but the states continued to control voting rights and the extent of religious and racial discrimination. In some states, women and poor men could vote; in others, they could not. Some states permitted slavery, while others did not. Thomas Jefferson's claim that the U.S. Constitution established a "compact of independent nations" may be exaggerated, but it correctly described the differences in citizenship equality.

The U.S. Articles of Confederation established an underdeveloped central government, without a mechanism for enforcing its laws or collecting taxes, dependent on voluntary compliance by the states. The Constitution created a system of shared sovereignty between the federal government and the states, with the powers of the central government limited to those enumerated in the constitution and the states retaining sovereignty in all other areas. Over time, the federal government's authority grew primarily through expansive interpretations of the interstate commerce clause and the Fourteenth Amendment, which was a direct reversal of the U.S. Supreme Court's *Dred Scott* decision of 1857. The decision helped spark the American Civil War (1861–1865) by ruling that African Americans "are not included, and were not intended to be included, under the word 'citizens' in the Constitution, and can therefore claim none of the rights and privileges which that instrument provides for and secures to citizens of the United States." The *Dred Scott* ruling continued, "we must not confound the rights of citizenship which a State may confer within its own limits, and the rights of citizenship as a member of the Union. It does not by any means follow, because he has all the rights and privileges of a citizen of a State, that he must be a citizen of the United States." The decision was thus a decisive ruling against common national citizenship.

The Fourteenth Amendment was passed after the Civil War, in 1868, to guarantee all individual's born or naturalized in the United States with rights in all states, particularly the states in which slavery had just been abolished that were least likely to accept slaves as U.S. citizens. Though the amendment privileged national citizenship over state citizenship, the U.S. Supreme Court's decisions in the *Slaughterhouse Cases* (1873), the *Civil Rights Cases* (1883), and related rulings limited the amendment's impact. As the federal government abdicated its responsibility to protect rights, the Fourteenth Amendment's implementation and oversight reverted to the individual states. Racial policy, in particular, continued to be determined by separate states rather than the federal government. It was not until the 1920s that the Supreme Court reversed its restrictive doctrine and extended the range of citizenship rights for a wide range of civil rights and liberties—extensions prompted by social struggles for inclusion in the right to vote and right to employment.

Presently, citizenship questions and struggles for specific rights remain throughout the United States. Many social movements, including those pushing for equality on the basis of sexual orientation, continue to frame demands referencing the laws and definitions surrounding the term citizenship. Other inconsistencies include Puerto Rico since most Puerto Rican residents are U.S. citizens, but do not have full political rights, and nor do residents of Washington D.C. or several other U.S. territories. Comparable anomalies exist worldwide, highlighting the difficult nature of citizenship as a reflection of sovereignty. At the same time, the United States, like other federations, faces continuing tension between the ideal of equal citizenship and the reality of differential rights and privileges (e.g., lower tuition fees for local residents, or waiting times for access to health care or other benefits for citizens moving from another jurisdiction) accruing to members of its constituent jurisdictions.

CASE STUDY: EU CITIZENSHIP

The most dramatic development in the evolution of citizenship in postwar Europe has been the creation and growth of supranational rights captured under the concept of European Union (EU) citizenship. Citizens of EU's twenty-seven member states now hold EU citizenship as well as their own member state's national citizenship. Member states may no longer discriminate between their own citizens and those of other EU member states, who have acquired wide-ranging civic, political, and social rights throughout the territory of the European Union. Though treaties specify EU citizenship will not replace national citizenship, the European Court of Justice, in a series of judgments, has ruled, "Union citizenship is destined to be the fundamental status of Member States."

In contrast to U.S. citizenship, or indeed the citizenship of most contemporary states, the rise of EU citizenship is far more recent, motivated by economic integration coupled with a commitment to building a supranational political community. Proponents of further European integration actively promote the concept of an EU citizenship that supersedes member state nationality. Whereas member state citizenship remains primary in the European Union, in federal states such as the United States, state or provincial citizenship long ago ceased to dominate. The meaning of citizenship is far from uniform across Europe, however. Within national contexts, various views of citizenship and political community were important in developing the specific forms that national citizenship takes when it is translated into policies and institutions. Citizenship rights in most states generally evolved through a long process of political contestation between governments and citizens. Yet the rights that now comprise Union citizenship were simply introduced by treaties and bargaining among governments.

There are parallels between the rise of EU citizenship and the growth, in the nineteenth century, of a national layer of citizenship over existing municipal or regional versions. Before the French Revolution (1789–1799), which promoted the notion of popular sovereignty and spurred the creation of national citizenry, many of the rights characterizing today's citizens were provided by local municipalities; these included the rights of residence and employment, civil rights such as trial in local courts, and rights to participate in the political process. Notably, in German, the word for citizenship, *Bürgerschaft,* is the same term used to identify the parliaments of German cities, Bremen and Hamburg. Many municipalities even provided social rights. Establishing a "thin" EU citizenship over those same nation-state citizenships echoes the initially "thin" layer of nation-state citizenship rights over the existing structure of preexisting "thick" municipal citizenships. This parallels the development of federal citizenship in the United States.

RECONSIDERING THE MEANING OF CITIZENSHIP

Defining who has the right to have rights is a necessary first step for any political community. Rights need not be restricted to citizens; for example, every person enjoys human rights regardless of citizenship status, and in many states individuals enjoy rights even if they are not citizens. Nevertheless, full rights are restricted to citizens who, in a democracy, are the only ones authorized to change their rights.

The historical variability and theoretical contestation over citizenship has led to the concept being stretched far beyond its strict legal meaning, and even its broader political definition. Describing an emerging view of citizenship as relational, cultural, historical, and continent on socially constructed categories such as gender, race, or nationality, Charles Tilly defines citizenship as a continuing series of transactions between persons and agents of a state. Rights and obligations are enforceable uniquely by virtue of the person's membership in an exclusive category (the native born plus the naturalized) and the agent's relation to the state rather than any other authority. Meanwhile the journal, *Citizenship Studies,* states in its aims the desire to "move beyond conventional notions of citizenship, and treat citizenship as a strategic concept that is central in the analysis of identity, participation, empowerment, human rights and the public interest."

When conventional accounts of citizenship developed, it appeared relatively easy to distinguish between insiders and outsiders, and hence between candidates for citizenship and foreigners. Migrations were assumed to be permanent as immigrants moved to their destination country, became naturalized citizens, and broke ties with their country of origin. Increasingly, however, previously territorially fixed groups and individuals have gained access to various forms of mobility. In addition to the borderless movements of capital, goods, and ideas, people too move around to a much greater extent and with greater ease than was generally true in the past. Large groups of expatriate communities have been established, and members participate in the politics of their country of residence while at the same time sustaining connections to their country of origin. Such individuals maintain ties with more than one political community, and in many cases have access to dual citizenship, with full legal recognition as members of more than one political community.

In a world in which transnational moral and political obligations gain in importance and individuals claim membership and participate in multiple political communities, the view that territorially bounded sovereign states are the only source of civil society may become untenable. By its very nature, migration upsets the balance between insiders and outsiders, as newcomers seek to enter the political community. Despite universal or cosmopolitan hopes for a global citizenship, presently, achieving the legal status of citizen of the state remains important for immigrants, because only then do they enjoy full access to rights. More broadly, despite aspirations on the part of some for nation-states to wither away, it appears likely that for the foreseeable future the nation-state will remain the primary locus of citizenship.

See also *Citizen Knowledge; Dual Citizenship and Dual Nationality; Immigration Policy; Migration; Naturalization.*

. . . . WILLEM MAAS

BIBLIOGRAPHY

Aristotle. *The Politics,* translated by C. Lord. Chicago: University of Chicago Press, 1984.

Benhabib, Seyla. *The Rights of Others: Aliens, Residents, and Citizens.* Cambridge: Cambridge University Press, 2004.

Elkins, David J. *Beyond Sovereignty: Territory and Political Economy in the Twenty-first Century.* Toronto: University of Toronto Press. 1995.

Jacobson, David. *Rights Across Borders: Immigration and the Decline of Citizenship.* Baltimore: Johns Hopkins University Press, 1996.

Kettner, James H. *The Development of American Citizenship, 1608–1870.* Chapel Hill: University of North Carolina Press, 1978.

Kymlicka, Will, and Wayne Norman. "Return of the Citizen: A Survey of Recent Work on Citizenship Theory." *Ethics* 104 (1994): 352–381.

Maas, Willem. *Creating European Citizens.* Lanham: Rowman and Littlefield, 2007.

Marshall, T. H. *Citizenship and Social Class and Other Essays.* Cambridge: Cambridge University Press, 1950.

Shklar, Judith N. *American Citizenship: The Quest for Inclusion.* Cambridge Mass.: Harvard University Press, 1991.

Smith, Rogers M. *Civic Ideals: Conflicting Visions of Citizenship in U.S. History.* New Haven: Yale University Press, 1997.

Somers, Margaret R. *Genealogies of Citizenship: Markets, Statelessness, and the Right to Have Rights.* Cambridge: Cambridge University Press, 2008.

Soysal, Yasemin Nuhoglu. *Limits of Citizenship: Migrants and Postnational Membership in Europe.* Chicago: University of Chicago, 1994.

Tilly, Charles. 1995. "Citizenship, Identity, and Social History." *International Review of Social History* 40, no. 3 (1995): 1–17.

van Gunsteren, Herman. *A Theory of Citizenship: Organizing Plurality in Contemporary Democracies.* Boulder: Westview Press, 1998.

City-republic

The city, from which the notion of citizenship derives, is the most basic form of political community. In ancient, medieval, and early modern times, an array of self-governing city-republics existed where the vote of a broad electorate made many collective decisions. Most city-republics shared the following defining characteristics: small size in terms of both territory and population; relatively high degrees of internal harmony, as defined by the economic and ethnic characteristics of the members; and simple and soft forms of government based on the ease with which citizens could form a social majority supporting collective, enforceable decisions. The better-known cases can be found in Mesopotamia, the poleis of Greece, the German and Swiss territories, as well as a number of medieval Italian communes that have existed since the late Middle Ages.

The typical medieval city was formed by private associations of households organized to provide public goods such as the maintenance of a food supply, the administration of justice, and military defense. Local autonomy was a Roman tradition in some southern European towns, but it was also created by the privileges given to certain communes by their lords.

MEDIEVAL SELF-GOVERNED CITIES

One of the earliest meetings recorded of a representative assembly in Europe was in 1064, in Barcelona, Catalonia, for the approval by consensus and acclamation of public laws later compiled in the celebrated customs of the city (*Usatges*). Throughout the twelfth century, towns in northern Italy, led by their consuls, became autonomous from the emperor and church authorities. Bologna, Genoa, Pavia, Pisa, Siena, and many other communes organized themselves around an assembly of all the citizens, or harangue (*arengo*); these were open, inclusive, and popular events, allowing decisions by broad social consensus, as well as an occasion for public spectacle, processions, and festivities. Citizens approved the appointment of the consulate by acclamation or by indirect election. Regular elections to numerous offices were also held with the participation of most adult men.

In the case of Venice, the election of the *doge* (duke) by the entire population dates from 697 CE. For almost five hundred years, the assembly, or harangue, elected powerful doges. Beginning in 1172, the people's general assembly indirectly elected the great council (usually attended by about one thousand to fifteen hundred men, age thirty or older), which became the supreme authority, and the senate. From the thirteenth to the fifteenth century, the people's assembly had to ratify the council's election of the doge. Other elected offices, from the thirteenth century until 1789, included magistrates, procurators, advocates, and a high chancellor.

The citizens of Florence elected their rulers by broad popular suffrage for almost one hundred and fifty years, from 1291 on, as well as during shorter periods in the fifteenth and sixteenth centuries. The council of the people (with three hundred members) and the council of the commune (with two hundred members) were selected by a mixed procedure of people's election and appointment. The standard-bearer of justice, or *Gonfaloniere*, and the nine members of the lordship, or *Signoria*, were elected by a mixed system of voting and lots. Representatives of the sixteen quarters of the city, as well as by many other elected officers, formed the administration. Most adult men (over the age of twenty-five) voted and most voters were eligible for the administration.

While Geneva's liberties were codified by its bishop in 1387, the general council rejected papal authority, and in 1542 adopted a new institutional framework that lasted for more than two hundred years. The general council exerted legislative powers, including the ability to make laws, levy taxes, and make declarations of war and peace, as well as the power to annually elect, and hold accountable, the four syndics and other magistrates of the city. Approximately fifteen hundred to four thousand heads of family formed the general council, and most adult men were eligible to participate. In parallel, and increasingly in conflict with the former, the grand council (with two hundred members) and the petit council, which were controlled by a few traditional families, developed legislative initiative and nominated candidates for elected offices.

People's assemblies also governed many French municipalities in the late thirteenth century. Especially in the southern region of Languedoc, and more famously in towns like Montpelier and Nimes, among others, all heads of households (including widows), if they were natives or long-standing residents, attended "general assemblies of inhabitants." Attendance was commonly regarded as an obligation rather than a right. The assemblies elected proctors or syndics, as well as the collective consulate usually called the town body (*corps de ville*). Municipal offices were held for short terms of about two years.

MODERN COMPLEXITY AND DECLINE

The end of the republican regimes in the Italian communes has been attributed to frequent violence, disorder, and instability provoked by political factionalism, family feuds, and class conflicts. As new economic interests developed, the traditional predominance of artisans' guilds was defied, and the pattern of relatively peaceful fusion of old and new elements in society weakened. However, unregulated assemblies were replaced with more sophisticated rules. New institutional procedures were designed to accommodate varied social demands.

For example, for the election of their doge, the Venetians adopted an increasingly complicated procedure with up to nine stages of approval ballots and lots, which was conceived to ward off insincere voting and manipulative strategies. In Florence, an extremely complex procedure of elections was designed to prevent the fraudulent manipulation of the electoral process and to avert a few of the city's powerful families from domination over the commune. In many cities, some restrictions regarding reelection and office accumulation promoted openness and circulation of the appointees. Rulers and those in office stayed in their posts for short periods of only six months or a year.

Procedures like these aimed to promote the rotation of rulers, making manipulative strategies unviable and disallowing the concentration of power into a single group. However, in some cities, the association between popular participation in increasingly complex communities and rising instability was inescapable. Elections, factions or parties, and institutional stability became a difficult combination. Factionalism, family feuds, and class conflicts weakened republican self-government, as appropriate rules for consensus making were lacking. Northern Italian cities, deprived of protection by the fading Italian Empire, entered into frequent conflicts among themselves and with more powerful neighbors, including the duchy of Milan, and the papacy and kingdom of Naples. In most late medieval and early modern cities, the republican form of government was replaced with authoritarian, aristocratic rules, which eventually became supports for building new large and centralized states.

See also *Citizenship; Greek Democracy, Classical.*

. . . . JOSEP M. COLOMER

BIBLIOGRAPHY
Babeau, Albert. *Le village sous l'Ancien Régime.* Paris: Didier, 1882.
Brucker, Gene A. *Renaissance Florence.* Berkeley: University of California Press, 1983.
Colomer, Josep M. *Great Empires, Small Nations: The Uncertain Future of the Sovereign State.* London: Routledge, 2007.
Fazy, Henri. *Les constitutions de la République de Genève: Étude historique.* Paris: Librairie Fischbacher, 1890.
Finlay, Robert. *Politics in Renaissance Venice.* New Brunswick, N.J.: Rutgers University Press, 1980.
Fralin, Richard. *Rousseau and Representation: A Study of the Development of His Concept of Political Institutions.* New York: Columbia Unversity Press, 1978.
Guidi, Guidubaldo. *Il governo della città-repubblica di Firenze del primo Quattrocento,* 3 vols. Florence: Leo S. Olschki, 1981.
Lines, Marji. "Approval Voting and Strategy Analysis: A Venetian Example." *Theory and Decision* 20 (1986): 155–172.
Tilly, Charles, and Wim P. Blockmans, eds. *Cities and the Rise of States in Europe, AD 1000 to 1800.* Boulder: Westview Press, 1994.
Waley, Daniel. *The Italian City-Republics.* New York: Longman, 1988.

Civic Education

Civic education aims to promote and shape civic engagement by developing citizens' competencies (e.g., attitudes, skills, and knowledge) needed for participation in community, government, and politics.

CLASSIC CIVIC EDUCATION THEORIES

Theories of civic education can be traced back to ancient Greece, where Plato argued on behalf of the systematic moral education of young people for citizenship. In *The Republic,* Plato famously advocates the use of censorship and propaganda as instruments of civic education. In particular, he urges the elimination of most common myths (including those found with Homer, Hesiod, and the tragic poets) because of their portrayal of the gods and heroes as cruel, capricious, unjust, violent, deceitful, and vicious. He also recommends the use of "noble lies," such as the myth of metals, to accustom citizens to their proper roles in the highly hierarchical society he depicts.

Aristotle believed that civic education must be designed to match particular political constitutions, because the values and virtues required by citizens living under a despotic regime, for example, are very different from those required by citizens living under a democracy. Aristotle describes a scheme of civic education conceived to prepare the male children of citizens (not females or the male children of slaves or foreigners) for life under a mixed constitution in which citizens take turns ruling and being ruled according to law. In other words, they were to be prepared for lives of civic equality, sharing a capacity for moral excellence and sharing a responsibility for promoting the common good, rather than their own self-interests.

Civic education was given a more democratic slant in the eighteenth century by French philosopher Jean-Jacques Rousseau, who argued that teaching people how to be good citizens is a major role of government. A government fulfills this role by educating citizens regarding their civic duties and by teaching them how to discern the common good when they act in their capacity as sovereign people (i.e., when they make the laws under which they will be governed). Additionally, according to Rousseau, the government must make the laws beloved and respected by the people and must take care to correct and improve the mores, manners, customs, and morals of the people, so they will always love liberty and not become corrupt or slothful. Finally, Rousseau argues, government must take special care to manage the education of children, for respect for the law and the common good must be instilled from a very young age.

French writer and politician Alexis de Tocqueville, in the nineteenth century, takes a radically different view from previous theorists, arguing that the most effective form of civic education may be found not in formal schooling but through direct involvement in political life and the civic associations of one's community, such as religious congregations, clubs, and other voluntary organizations. In contrast with formal instruction in schools, which cultivates attitudes, knowledge, and skills that are not necessarily directly relevant to the learning context, participation in political life and civic associations informally cultivates the particular mores and attitudes directly needed by citizens in those contexts.

In the twentieth century, American philosopher, psychologist, and educator John Dewey reimagined schools themselves as experiential learning contexts that would help students develop practical experience in democratic problem solving. Schools would provide opportunities for the direct expression of democratic virtues and norms, and young citizens also would learn a scientific method of social inquiry that would allow them, later in life, to participate in broader discussions of public values and policies. Dewey's philosophy of civic education has one primary objective: to encourage and develop a culture of free inquiry that engenders and supports citizens as self-confident political and moral actors, both within and outside of formal academic institutions.

CIVIC EDUCATION TODAY

Methods of civic education employed today include, but are not limited to, study of government institutions and political processes, study of local and national history, instruction in civic character and values, and experiential or service learning activities. Contemporary educators, however, disagree about what methods of civic education should be employed by democracies and, indeed, whether civic education of any sort amounts to indoctrination or coercion.

Since the 1960s, numerous educators have embraced the importance of experiential learning and have argued for some form of mandatory community service or service learning as a form of civic education. Some critics have charged that such methods amount to requiring volunteerism. Theorists like Benjamin R. Barber and William Galston, however, do not recommend service as a form of do-goodism. Rather, their purpose is to prepare citizens for responsible membership in a community of interdependent equals through experiential learning, allowing the community itself to serve as a context for direct civic learning.

Although civic education can be distinguished conceptually from patriotic education, which is concerned primarily with promoting loyalty to a nation or state rather than active political participation, civic education often includes an element of patriotic education. Galston, for example, recommends a measure of patriotic indoctrination, moralizing, and the teaching of sentimental views of history, in order to strengthen the political order and develop individuals who can function effectively in, and actively support, their political community. Other thinkers, including Amy Gutmann and Jack Crittenden, reject this approach, and argue that young citizens must learn to participate in democratic deliberation in a pluralistic society and to stand apart, critically, from their own communities. They do not go so far, however, as to argue that civic education should promote full-fledged autonomy, as educational theorist Eamonn Callan does.

Some theorists, including Judith Shklar and Richard Flathman, have concluded that the character of individual citizens should be off-limits to government, thereby ruling out most forms of civic education. However, a decision not to provide formal civic education may itself be a kind of civic education, teaching young people that citizenship is not very important and ensuring the continued depreciation of the practice of citizenship. If civic values and virtues do not teach themselves, as Tocqueville argued, then perhaps, as political theorist Stephen Macedo insists, democracies must overcome their squeamishness about intervening in the character of citizens in order to protect themselves from antidemocratic adversaries.

See also *Citizenship; Civic Engagement; Dewey, John; Education Policy; Greek Political Thought, Ancient; Plato; Rousseau, Jean-Jacques; Tocqueville, Alexis de; Virtue Theory.*

. . . .   JASON SCORZA

BIBLIOGRAPHY

Barber, Benjamin R. *An Aristocracy of Everyone: The Politics of Education and the Future of America.* New York: Ballantine Books, 1992.

Callan, Eamonn. *Creating Citizens: Political Education and Liberal Democracy.* Oxford: Clarendon Press, 1997.

Crittenden, Jack. *Democracy's Midwife: An Education in Deliberation.* Lanham, Md.: Lexington Books, 2002.

Galston, William. "Political Knowledge, Political Engagement, and Civic Education." *Annual Review of Political Science* 4 (2000): 217–234.

Gutmann, Amy. *Democratic Education.* Princeton: Princeton University Press, 1999.

Macedo, Stephen. *Diversity and Distrust: Civic Education in a Multicultural Democracy.* Cambridge, Mass.: Harvard University Press, 2000.

Civic Engagement

Civic engagement, as a concept, combines diverse forms of involvement, ranging from political to leisure activities, under one notion. The concept stresses activity oriented toward or originating from society. It emerged in the 1990s when it was used to refer to involvement in public affairs that creates network relations among citizens. Yet, despite its increased application, it lacks conceptual clarity. A narrow definition equates civic engagement with political participation. As a distinct concept, however, it is more useful when it more broadly refers to voluntary, public activities that are oriented toward society and carried out without the intention of profit.

In the Middle Ages, the notion of engagement referred to an oral commitment to a contract. Later, it was used when contracting artists, waging war, and purchasing stocks. In social sciences, it emerged in the context of the civil society discourse with the prefix "civic" indicating a commitment to public, nonviolent, self-organized, discursive, and pluralistic activities.

MODES AND FIELDS

Civic engagement is usually associated with citizen organizations active in the fields of politics, human services, culture, education, religion, sports, environment, development, or emergency aid. But it also occurs in informal groups, networks, and social movements that are more difficult to research and are often overlooked. In recent decades, a reflexive form of engagement has emerged that is characterized by choice, a biographical match in one's life, and the recognition of own aims, instead of tradition, life-long commitment, and determination by organizational needs. Further, semiprofessionalization substitutes lay experience, and the expectation of reciprocity includes the compensation of expenses.

RESEARCH AGENDA

Research typically focuses on the positive effects of civic engagement. Robert D. Putnam refers to networks of civic engagement as sources of social capital that promote good governance and economic development. Other possible outcomes are the production of social services and, as a by-product, the promotion of social integration. More sociologically oriented streams of research try to understand the occurrence of civic engagement and use surveys and register data to explain individual motives and societal structures. Policy research deals with infrastructures and policy measures that advance civic engagement.

PROBLEMS

The lack of conceptual clarity leads to problems with measurement and comparability. There is no conceptual study that links civic engagement to related concepts like volunteering, nonprofit associations, or civic activism. Second, reference to the common good accounts for much of the attraction the concept enjoys, but it also blurs its meaning because it combines commitment with moral standards. What constitutes the common good remains highly contested in plural societies. For example, nongovernmental organizations are sometimes seen as particularistic interest groups and other times as advancing the public interest. Third, whether civic engagement should be evaluated according to the deontological ethics of "well-meaning" or the consequential logics of "good results" remains unclear. Finally, the negative effects of civic engagement are often overlooked. Even well-meant engagement can increase the power difference between social groups, degrade the human object of engagement, or sacrifice the activist.

See also *Civic Education; Civic Humanism; Collective Action and Mobilization; Lesbian, Gay, Bisexual, and Transgender Political Participation; Political Participation; U.S. Politics and Society: African American Political Participation; U.S. Politics and Society: Latino Political Participation; U.S. Politics and Society: Women, Political Participation of; Voting Behavior.*

. . . . PETER HILGER

BIBLIOGRAPHY

Berger, Ben. "Political Theory, Political Science, and the End of Civic Engagement." *Perspectives on Politics* 7, no. 2 (2009): 335–350.

Hustinx, Leslie, and Frans Lammertyn. "Collective and Reflexive Styles of Volunteering: A Sociological Modernization Perspective." *Voluntas* 14, no. 2 (2003): 167–187.

Kendall, Jeremy. "The Mainstreaming of the Third Sector into Public Policy in England in the Late 1990s: Whys and Wherefores." *Policy and Politics* 28, no. 4 (2000): 541–562.

Pattie, Charles, Patrik Seyd, and Paul Whiteley. "Citizenship and Civic Engagement: Attitudes and Behaviour in Britain." *Political Studies* 51, no. 3 (2003): 443–468.

Putnam, Robert D. *Making Democracy Work: Civic Traditions in Modern Italy.* Princeton: Princeton University Press, 1993.

Skocpol, Theda, and Morris P. Fiorina. "Making Sense of the Civic Engagement Debate." In *Civic Engagement in American Democracy,* edited by Theda Skocpol and Morris P. Fiorina, 1–23. Washington, D.C.: Brookings Institution Press, 1999.

Uslaner, Eric M., and Mitchell Brown. "Inequality, Trust, and Civic Engagement." *American Politics Research* 33, no. 6 (2005): 868–894.

Verba, Sidney, Kay Lehman Schlozman, and Hery E. Brady. *Voice and Equality: Civic Voluntarism in American Politics.* Cambridge, Mass.: Harvard University Press, 1995.

Civic Humanism

Civic humanism is a political and philosophical orientation emphasizing the value and importance of the practical and moral virtues that may be inculcated in and passed along by citizens through their active participation in the political life of their polity. Its central aim is to defend and promote the qualities believed as necessary for communities to effectively, responsibly, and independently govern themselves; those qualities include the virtues of patience, tolerance, patriotism, self-sacrifice, duty, a commitment to the law, and forgiveness.

Civic humanism is closely entwined with ideals of education and moral formation that are most often associated with the humanist beliefs of Renaissance thinkers, as well as with the classical republican ideas of ancient Greece and Rome. In fact, *civic humanism* and *classical republicanism* are sometimes used interchangeably, as each are taken to refer to a view of public life that celebrates the role of, and places great seriousness upon, the duties and activities of citizenship. A variety of communitarian ideologies use civic humanist arguments extensively in advancing their beliefs.

DEBATE OVER ORIGINS

It is often claimed that civic humanism took shape as an intellectual orientation in Florence during the late fourteenth and early fifteenth centuries. It is certainly correct that, during these years, new translations of Greek and Roman philosophical and literary classics inspired many to reject the scholastic model of education that had become standard throughout much of Western Europe during the Middle Ages. As a result, a new model developed, the *studia humanitatis,* which connected the Christian improvement of oneself and one's community with the spread of knowledge of languages, grammar, rhetoric, philosophy, and history.

However, it is historically questionable as to what degree this movement involved a specific "civic humanist" orientation as a political and philosophical expression of its own. Both civic humanism and classical republicanism, as they are understood and used today, emerged through historiographic reconstruction: German and English scholars throughout the twentieth century (including Hans Baron, J. G. A. Pocock, Quentin Skinner, and Bernard Bailyn) looked to the traditions and behaviors of Renaissance Italy as a way to tie together a wide variety of political aspirations and philosophical convictions that, throughout the seventeenth and eighteenth centuries, periodically revived to inspire, guide, or frustrate different political actors. Civic humanism as an orientation, then, is a well-understood descriptive term uniting such figures across history as Francesco Petrarch, Thomas More, James Harrington, Giambattista Vico, and Baron de Montesquieu, not to mention many leaders of the American Revolution; yet, as a historical matter, the label itself probably owes more to the modern desire to assemble a genealogy of communitarian and republican thinkers. This modern assemblage aims more to support various attacks upon increasingly dominant liberal and individualist orientations than to align with anything that was actually expressed historically.

MODERN INTERPRETATIONS

Those who advocate civic humanism today most often to do so in conjunction with a push for educational as opposed to political reforms, thus grounding the orientation more firmly in its purported origin in the classic learning of the Renaissance. (Classical republicanism, by contrast, is usually, when the two terms are distinguished at least, more explicitly used as a tool of political critique.) The civic humanist argument generally asserts that human flourishing and happiness are most likely to be realized through autonomous (though not necessarily individualistic) moral action; yet, human beings are generally incapable of such responsible and independent moral choices without training in the language and worldview of classical authors. In addition, people need practical opportunities to see the value of those classical teachings in their own lives and the lives of others, and perhaps to put them into effect themselves. This would suggest the vital importance of an education in moral ideas, and similarly the importance of bringing those ideas to bear through direct service to and participation in political life. Both of these implications resonate with broadly communitarian perspectives: First, human beings are most likely to find fulfillment through participation in their respective groups, communities, or polities. Second, effective and responsible participation is most likely to occur when citizens are familiar with the history and traditions of their own communities.

Civic humanism may be linked to civic education of one sort or another, the reigning notion being that schools are, among other things, sites of character formation, and that if one assumes—as most advocates of civic humanism do—that responsible self-government depends upon, among other things, forming the necessary character attributes amongst the citizens, then clearly there must be a civic component to the education of the community members (and presumably future participating citizens). Interestingly, in the United States, the close identification of the civic humanism tradition with America's founding has made the label, in the minds of some, a more conservative project. This attaches to protecting the sort of traditional political and social arrangements, and divisions, that existed in eighteenth-century American life; as such, a traditional civic humanism may be hostile to more inclusive or progressive educational projects. As a result, civic education advocates who sympathize with liberal, democratic, or egalitarian goals rarely use the civic humanist label. On the other hand, those who often reject modern public schooling in favor of educating their children at home or through private religious schools, believing that the necessary character formation will be more likely to take place in those environments than others, closely embrace the label. Either way, however, both sides of the divide carry the essence of the civic humanist ideal forward: being a citizen in a free society requires a willingness to be involved in democratic discussion, to be tolerant of decisions one disagrees with, and to patriotically support one's country and its laws.

See also *Civic Education; Civic Engagement; Communitarianism; Republicanism, Classical.*

. . . . RUSSELL ARBEN FOX

BIBLIOGRAPHY

Appleby, Joyce. *Liberalism and the Republican Imagination:* Cambridge, Mass.: Harvard University Press, 1992.

Bailyn, Bernard Bailyn. *The Ideological Origins of the American Revolution.* Cambridge, Mass.: Harvard University Press, 1967.

Baron, Hans. *The Crisis of the Early Italian Renaissance: Civic Humanism and Republicanism in an Age of Classicism and Tyranny.* Princeton: Princeton University Press, 1966.

McDonough, Kevin, and Walter Feinberg, eds. *Citizenship and Education in Liberal-Democratic Societies*. New York: Oxford University Press, 2003.

Pocock, J. G. A. *The Machiavellian Moment: Florentine Political Thought and the Atlantic Republican Tradition*. Princeton: Princeton University Press, 1975.

Smith, Rogers. *Civic Ideals*. New Haven: Yale University Press, 1997.

Vetterli, Richard, and Gary Bryner. *In Search of the Republic: Public Virtue and the Roots of American Government*: Lanham, Md.: Rowman and Littlefield, 1987.

Civic Virtue

See *Virtue Theory*.

Civil and Political Rights

Modern societies and governments proclaim freedom as the foundation of their respective political and legal systems. However, some societies and governments are more free than others, and even the most free societies and governments have some laws that regulate the citizenry. The question centers upon what basis the citizenry can not only assert, but compel, the government to respect their theoretical freedoms. The answer is through civil and political rights.

A right, in its broadest sense, is a power, privilege, or protection granted or recognized by a legitimate authority, law, or usage. Power means the actual ability or authority to perform a certain act. An example of a power is the U.S. president's power to command the military forces. Privilege means a particular benefit or advantage that may be claimed or exercised. An example of a privilege is a permit for a handicapped person to park in a designated handicapped-parking place. Protection refers to an immunity or a shield from certain duties, responsibilities, or acts of others. An example of a protection is the right to receive a trial after being arrested for a crime.

A legitimate authority, law, or usage recognizes the source of rights. It is indisputable that the law can be a legitimate source of rights. *Usage* refers to the continued social recognition of a right. Once a particular right is commonly accepted and practiced in a society over a period of time, it is frequently considered binding. This is how the common law of ancient England developed over time. Common practices, frequently called *norms*, became accepted over time and eventually were considered to be law. The term *authority* refers to other sources of rights besides law or usage. The two most widely recognized sources in this sense are philosophy and religion. In philosophy, natural law is considered to be idealized expression of the morally correct way to act. It is a theoretical concept recognized by the mind as opposed to a written law created by a legislature. In religion, divine commands or laws, sometimes identified with natural law, are considered the source of rights.

What is fundamentally important about rights, as recognized by philosopher Ronald Dworkin, is that they are enforceable against the government or any other entity violating those rights. For example, many nations possess laws regulating voting, defining the requirements of who is eligible to vote. If a voter is mistreated in regard to these laws, the individual's rights have been violated and legal redress can be sought. Thinkers in the *human rights* or *natural rights* traditions may assert that individuals have certain inalienable rights by virtue of their humanity, but these rights are yet not civil or political rights and can be understood more as aspirations for those protections to become civil rights protected by law.

A civil right can be defined in many different ways. By the term *civil*, the right is usually meant to apply to all of the members of that society or political entity. However, some nations provide greater civil rights to their own citizens than they do to foreign nationals. The use of the term *civil* usually distinguishes civil law from criminal law. Although it can be argued that a civil right differs from a criminal right, in practice, in many countries, a right that protects a person from abuse in the criminal justice system is, nonetheless, referred to as a *civil right*. This is true in the criminal justice system of the United States. Although the Fourth, Fifth, and Sixth Amendments in the Bill of Rights of the U.S. Constitution address certain protections for persons charged with a crime, these rights are still called civil rights. Another aspect of civil rights is that such rights can usually be enforced in a nation's civil courts.

In contrast, political rights are usually considered a subcategory of civil rights. The term *political rights* generally refers to those activities related to the formation or creation of a political or legal system and the participation in the political process. The most frequently acknowledged political rights are the right to national self-determination, the right of citizenship, the right to free speech, the right to vote, the right to hold political office, and the right to petition.

Civil and political rights are also recognized internationally, as in the United Nations Charter, in Articles 1, 62, 68, and 76. Although many of the provisions of the UN Charter are considered merely aspirational and not binding, most of the world's nations have signed the International Covenant on Civil and Political Rights (a part of the International Bill of Rights), and this is considered binding under international law.

Civil and political rights are the mechanism by which people can attempt to ensure their basic freedoms and obtain fair treatment from their respective governments. However, if these civil and political rights lack any enforcement power, any civil or political rights usually become, as Chief Justice Earl Warren of the U.S. Supreme Court stated, a mere form of words and without meaning or substance. Some violations of internationally recognized civil and political rights, such as genocide, can be prosecuted in the International Criminal Court and limited international tribunals are sometimes established to enforce violations concerning specific situations.

See also *Asylum Rights; Bill of Rights; Children's Rights; Citizenship; Civil Rights Movement; Cultural Rights; Disability Rights; Human Rights; Intellectual Property Rights; International Bill of Rights; Natural Law; Natural Rights; Privacy Rights; Property Rights; Reproductive Rights; Right to Die; Right to Life; Universal Declaration of Human Rights; Voting Rights and Suffrage; Welfare Rights; Workers' Rights*.

. . . . WM. C. PLOUFFE JR.

BIBLIOGRAPHY
Dworkin, Ronald. *Taking Rights Seriously*. Cambridge, Mass.: Harvard University Press, 1977.
Epstein, Lee, and Thomas G. Walker. *Rights, Liberties, and Justice*, 5th ed. Washington, D.C.: Pearson, 2004.
Frohnen, Bruce, and Kenneth L. Grasso. *Rethinking Rights: Historical, Political, and Philosophical Perspectives*. Columbia: University of Missouri Press, 2009.
O'Brien, David M., ed. *The Lanahan Readings in Civil Rights and Civil Liberties*, 2nd ed. Baltimore: Lanahan, 2003.
Rotunda, Ronald, and John Nowak. *Treatise on Constitutional Law*, 3rd ed. St. Paul, Minn.: West Group, 1999.
Sullivan, Harold J. *Civil Rights and Liberties*, 2nd ed. Englewood Cliffs, N.J.: Pearson, 2005.

Civil Disobedience

Civil disobedience involves a conscientious, nonviolent, and public violation of law or government policy with the intent of affecting social change. Since acts of civil obedience involve nonviolence and publicness, they are distinguished from illegal acts, and therefore, easier to defend. The motivation for civil disobedience is conscientious, as opposed to considerations that are merely pragmatic or prudential. The decision to participate in such an act is typically for the benefit of society, such as causing attention or interest to be directed toward injustice, which thereby stimulates moral consciousness and initiates the vigorous activity of social change.

The concept of civil disobedience traces to antiquity. Socrates chose death rather than cease pursing truth and wisdom. Addressing his countrymen, he declared, "I shall obey God rather than you." Even the Bible provides lucid examples for civil disobedience. The Hebrew midwives refused the command of Pharaoh to violate the sanctity of life (Exod 1:15–22). Although the authority of a government may be vast, a Christian understanding of human authority is that none is absolute. Romans (13:1–12) teaches that the legal ordinances and statutes of the state must be obeyed because God ordains the powers. However, it would appear that Paul was referring to legitimate governments and just laws. There are illegitimate governments and unjust laws so that obedience to corrupt or immoral practices is not an option. Obedience to the law of God may require participation in civil disobedience, and those who engage in such acts must be willing to accept the consequences of disobedience from the authority of the state.

Although there are ancient and biblical examples of civil disobedience, the first modern exposition of such obligations is written by Henry David Thoreau in his famous essay of 1849, "Resistance to Civil Government." Thoreau refused to pay his poll tax as a protest against slavery and the United States–Mexico War (1848). He compared government to a machine and the problems of government to friction. When injustice is the major characteristic of government and people are forced to follow injustice, thereby becoming "the agent of injustice," then principled people must let their "life be a counter friction to stop the machine." Thoreau's act of civil disobedience was not the first in nineteenth-century America. During the years 1829 to 1839, missionaries to the Cherokee Indians were confronted with a Georgia state law that demanded an oath of allegiance to reside in the Cherokee territory of the state. The legislation against the missionaries required them to obtain a special permit from the governor, which would express their support of Indian territory forfeiture and removal of the Indians from their lands. The missionaries disobeyed the state law and were imprisoned. The concept of civil disobedience was later renewed in America as a result of groups that organized to nullify the Fugitive Slave Act of 1850. Also significant, the notion of a conscientious minority who could "clog the machine" of an unjust government was a tremendous influence upon Mahatma Gandhi and Martin Luther King Jr. in the twentieth century.

Civil disobedience contrasts with revolution. For instance, the colonial revolutionaries disobeyed English laws. As a development of the limited view of government advanced by the Protestant Reformers, John Locke's *Second Treatise of Government* (1690) provided intellectual justification for revolution. Revolution occurs suddenly and violently in sociopolitical processes, with the goal to defeat and seize control of government power. Revolution, then, is directed toward the complete overthrow of an existing government power. The first criterion for participation in revolution would be whether it is a just cause; revolution must not be engaged because of burden or inconvenience, or even for the benefit of a narrowly minded ideology. A just revolution should always consider the best interests of society as a whole (i.e., it should not serve the special interests of a private group). As such, it would be appropriate in defense of basic human rights, such as individual and religious liberties. However, a peaceful revolution must always be acted first, with violent means being only the final option. Another criterion rests on existence of evidence that the revolution will be successful. Considering the potential for loss of life and civil unrest, it would be foolish and irresponsible to engage in a revolution that has no hope for victory or that might make matters worse. Revolution must also be justly engaged through the use of just means. Though revolution may be justly engaged, there is never any rationale for unjust means, such as mutilation or torture. The essential requirements of justice must be a greater priority than the normal inclination for nonviolence and social constancy.

See also *Locke, John; Revolutions; Thoreau, Henry David.*

. . . . RON J. BIGALKE JR.

BIBLIOGRAPHY
Bay, Christian, and Charles C. Walker. *Civil Disobedience: Theory and Practice*. Montréal: Black Rose Books, 1975.
Billington, James H. *Fire in the Minds of Men: Origins of the Revolutionary Faith*. New York: Basic Books, 1975.
Childress, James F. *Civil Disobedience and Political Obligation*. New Haven: Yale University Press, 1971.
Davies, J. G. *Christians, Politics, and Violent Revolution*. London: S. C. M. Press, 1976.
Gandhi, Mahatma. *Non-violent Resistance*. New York: Schocken Books, 1961.
Griffiths, Brian, ed. *Is Revolution Change?* Downers Grove, Ill.: InterVarsity Press, 1971.
Grounds, Vernon C. *Revolution and the Christian Faith*. Philadelphia: J. B. Lippincott, 1971.

Gutierrez, Gustavo. *A Theology of Liberation*. Maryknoll, N.Y.: Orbis Books, 1971.

King, Martin Luther, Jr. *Letters from Birmingham City Jail*. Philadelphia: American Friends Service Committee, 1961.

Pennock, J. Roland, and John W. Chapman, eds. *Political and Legal Obligations*. New York: Atherton Press, 1970.

Scharlemann, Martin H. *The Ethics of Revolution*. St. Louis: Concordia, 1971.

Thoreau, Henry David. *Walden, or Life in the Woods, and On the Duty of Civil Disobedience*. New York: New American Library, 1980.

Zashin, Elliot M. *Civil Disobedience and Democracy*. New York: Free Press, 1972.

Civilizations, Clash of

See *Clash of Civilizations.*

Civil Law

There are two primary meanings for the term *civil law*. The first definition refers to that branch of law within the legal systems of common-law states such as the United States, Canada, Australia, and the United Kingdom, which centers on the noncriminal fields of law. Civil-law cases address disputes between individuals, rather than disputes involving the state. Examples of civil law in this context include torts, wills, property disputes, and contract disputes. The second meaning attributed to civil law, and the focus here, is as a legal tradition within the field of comparative law. Civil law in this instance describes the dominant legal family in the world—one historically tied to the Roman and Canon law, built on Enlightenment principles—that relies on written law and codification rather than judicial decision as its primary form of law.

There are more countries with civil-law systems around the world than any other system. France, Germany, Italy, Spain, and most of the countries of Western Europe maintain civil-law systems. Brazil, Mexico, Argentina, and most of the countries of South America also maintain civil-law systems. There are also many states that have adopted civil-law systems and mixed them with other legal traditions. These include Turkey, Egypt, Morocco, Tunisia, the states of French West Africa, Russia, Cambodia, and Vietnam. The widespread adoption of civil law as the legal tradition is largely the result of the civil law's unique characteristics, including its extensive, written form; minimal reliance on judge-made law; and ties to Roman and Canon law, which facilitated its early prevalence. Unlike the common law, which can be difficult to disseminate due to its reliance on judge-made law, empires and colonizers from Europe easily spread the civil-law tradition around the world. The written form of the civil-law tradition makes it much more portable and much more adaptable to different countries and different cultures. Today, it is estimated that approximately 154 states maintain, either in whole or in part, elements of the civil-law tradition (as opposed to 96 states with elements of the common-law tradition and 36 states with elements of the Islamic-law tradition).

HISTORICAL FOUNDATIONS

The civil-law tradition dates to the time of the Roman Empire and the *Corpus Juris Civilis,* and has three main periods of influence: Roman law, Canon law, and the *jus commune*. Compiled by the Emperor Justinian in the sixth century CE, the Corpus Juris Civilis was a comprehensive compilation of Roman law into a single, codified written form. This is the foundation from which the core of the civil-law tradition—written law and codification—originated. After the disintegration of the Roman Empire, much of Europe entered into the Dark Ages—a period in which legal systems were largely absent and law was predominantly customary. The rise to power of the Catholic Church, however, kept the Roman writings on law alive and scholars such as Augustine and Aquinas even added to these laws, updating and refining the legal rules, while at the same time incorporating elements of morality and a communal purpose into the largely secular Roman laws. Seeking to impose more significant order to facilitate the rise in commercial transactions as the Middle Ages ended, the University of Bologna, in the eleventh century, began to revive the study of law. A group of scholars, known as the glossators, began to lecture on Justinian's codes, and more significantly, they began to recodify the law in a manner which made it applicable to Renaissance Europe. The new law was called the *jus commune* because it was to be a law that was common to all of Europe. This was possible because scholars from all over Europe came to study law at Bologna, and when they left they took the jus commune with them, incorporating it into their own legal systems.

Modern civil-law systems maintain significant ties to this historical development, and many states' legal systems are even further linked as a result of one of Napoleon's primary accomplishments, which was to consolidate French laws into a number of comprehensive codes. Known as the Napoleonic codes, the foremost of these was the Napoleonic civil code, which addresses issues of personal status and property. Napoleon also directed the creation of a penal code, a code of civil procedure, a commercial code, and a code of criminal procedure. The goal of these codes, which codified all existing laws and legal customs, was to ensure the clarity of the law for all French citizens.

As the foundation of the civil-law tradition, codes are designed to be all-encompassing, providing not just a list of legal obligations, rights, punishments, and remedies, but also an overall guide for people on how to conduct their daily lives.

CIVIL LAW AND THE COURTROOM

This reliance on codes as the primary source of law precipitates what is perhaps the greatest difference between the states of the common law and the states of the civil law. Unlike common law, under the civil-law tradition, judges play a minimal role in the creation of law. Judicial review and judicial activism are generally minimized as the courts are not seen so much as an arena for creating new laws; they are instead simply a venue for resolving disputes based on preexisting code provisions. Judges within the civil-law tradition are often responsible for applying the law as written, and there is much less room for judicial creativity.

The judiciary role also influences the style of proceedings in the civil-law tradition. In the context of civil law, trials are conducted in an inquisitorial fashion, as opposed to the adversarial fashion of the common law. In an inquisitorial proceeding, the judge and two parties work more closely together to achieve a desirable outcome, with the judge often playing the role of lawyer, judge, and jury. These characteristics have led to the development of a legal tradition based on written law, in which the legislature is responsible for making legal rules, and the judiciary is responsible for enforcing them.

See also *Common Law; Roman Catholic Political Thought.*

. . . . DANA ZARTNER

BIBLIOGRAPHY

Berman, Harold J. *Law and Revolution: The Formation of the Western Legal Tradition.* Cambridge, Mass.: Harvard University Press, 1983.

David, René, and John C. Brierley. *Major Legal Systems in the World Today,* 3rd ed. London: Stevens and Sons, 1985.

Glendon, Mary Ann, Michael Wallace Gordon, and Christopher Osakwe. *Comparative Legal Traditions,* 2nd ed. St. Paul, Minn.: West Publishing, 1994.

Koch, Charles H., Jr. "The Advantages of the Civil Law Judicial Design as the Model for Emerging Legal Systems." *Indiana Journal of Global Legal Studies* 11 (Winter 2004): 139–160.

Merryman, John Henry. *The Civil Law Tradition: An Introduction to the Legal Systems of Western Europe and Latin America,* 2nd ed. Stanford: Stanford University Press, 1985.

University of Ottawa, Faculty of Law, Civil Law Section. "World Legal Systems." University of Ottawa. http://droitcivil.uottawa.ca/world-legal-systems/eng-monde.php.

Civil-military Relations

Civil-military relations concern the interaction of the military and the state or, more broadly, between armed forces and society. The relationship between civil authority and the military has evolved along with the nature of states, societies, war, and the military profession, but the basic dilemma remains the same: ensuring protection *by and from* the armed forces.

THE MILITARY AND THE STATE

Modern polities are governed by states, which possess a monopoly over the legitimate use of force within a defined territory to enforce its edicts on the population. The armed forces embody that monopoly and serve three primary purposes: external defense, internal security, and promotion of patriotism through indoctrination and provision of public goods.

Because states interact in a system in which one may use organized violence against another, external defense is the primary mission of the military. It is operated, trained, and equipped primarily for this purpose. In some states, the military also is used to maintain internal order, although this function tends to be assigned to other institutions as governments mature. Service of the population in the armed forces indirectly contributes to internal order as members are indoctrinated to serve the state. Goods provided to society by the military—including security, employment, and infrastructure—further promote the legitimacy of the state.

Yet, control over the means of coercion by a subset of the population poses a danger to the rest of the polity. The military may endanger the polity directly through predation upon society or indirectly by seizing control of civil authority, influencing civil authorities to provide more resources than required for external defense and internal security, or initiating conflict contrary to the interests of the state or polity as a whole. Imperial Japan saw the military directly control the government from 1926 to 1945, leading their state to conquest in Asia and ruin against the United States. Therefore, controlling the military is *the* central dilemma of civil-military relations, and most other issues, from institutional design to recruitment of personnel, derive from it.

CONTROLLING THE MILITARY

States have developed a number of solutions to address this dilemma of military control by reducing the ability or the desire of the military to threaten the polity. With regard to reducing its ability, states have established institutions that divide or dilute the military's powers, including multiple services, internal security forces, parallel chains of command, a cadre-reserve structure, and reliance on citizen soldiers. The United States has utilized all of these to ensure civil control over the military. States have also forgone training and educating their military personnel in ways that would increase the military's ability to threaten or influence the polity, such as training in urban warfare or education in matters of governance. Finally, some polities have emulated ancient Rome and physically separated military forces from political centers so as to limit opportunities to influence civil authority.

States also reduce the military's desire to endanger the polity. Many states have ensured that their militaries are well resourced and the leadership well paid and accorded status among the state's elites. Most states have also established procedures that encourage convergent preferences between civil authority and the military. Primary among these has been indoctrination to ensure loyalty to the political system or government. This task has been eased over time by the prevalence of nationalism and patriotism in modern societies, which inculcate general loyalty to the society and state respectively among the citizenry, including those who enter military service. States have also used selection criteria to guarantee a convergence of interests between the political leadership and military personnel, particularly the officer corps. Historically, accession has been based on class membership, religious beliefs, political views, and merit with criteria varying with the nature of the polity's elite. Throughout modern Europe, only nobles could serve as officers until Prussia eliminated this requirement in 1808, beginning the process of professionalization in Western militaries.

CIVIL CONTROL AND THE MILITARY PROFESSION

The professionalization of the military deserves special attention, as it has been a key determinant of the quality of civil-military relations. As states have matured, their constituent institutions have become more professional: merit-based entry and promotion, specialized work, bureaucratized organization, and the impersonal performance of duties. The military, the officer corps especially, has been at the forefront of this trend. Military members can make a career of their service, are given a degree of autonomy to perfect their expertise in the application and management of organized violence, share a corporate identity, and inculcate a self-image of apolitical service to the polity. These qualities have significantly shaped civil-military relations. At times, professional militaries have implemented ruinous civilian policies, as in Nazi Germany. In states such as Turkey and Pakistan, the military is professional but political and intervenes regularly in civil affairs, delimiting the policies that can be pursued, while in yet others, such as Honduras or Thailand, the military intervenes occasionally to remove civilian leaders it deems corrupt or inept.

The delegation of authority from the state's leadership to the military requires monitoring and enforcement mechanisms to guard against insubordinate behavior. The extent of oversight and enforcement should vary with the congruence of preferences between the civil authority and the military. It is generally argued that a professional military will inherently comply with the preferences of civil authorities and requires minimal oversight. Moreover, it is argued that civilian involvement in the military's sphere, in terms of monitoring or providing guidance below the level of policy, degrades military effectiveness and provides incentives for military involvement in politics.

Unfortunately, delineating the military's sphere is precisely the issue. Advances in the means of warfare that have increased the distance, speed, and lethality with which violence can be applied drove the development of the military profession and have expanded the areas in which military professionals must be proficient to include national security policy, diplomacy, state-building, and governance associated with military operations. But this expansion goes both ways. It has been argued that civilian involvement is required at all levels of activity to integrate military means with political purposes even with a professional military. Thus changes in warfare have resulted in friction between civil and military authorities on substantive and process issues, including who should make what decisions, and suggests that the parameters of the relationship will continue to evolve.

Finally, a recent challenge to the military's sphere has been the trend toward utilizing private armed forces in lieu of the military to perform tasks central to achieving state ends. It suggests that civil authorities are redefining the forms that its monopoly over the legitimate use of force may take—potentially to the detriment of the military.

Civil-military relations are central to the stability and quality of governance in polities, their propensity to utilize force internationally and domestically, the quality of the military strategies pursued to achieve diplomatic ends, and ultimately the nature and stability of international relations.

See also *Bureaucratic Authoritarianism; Class and Politics; Coup d'État; Military Rule; National Security Policy; Nationalism; Principal-agent Theory.*

. . . .   GARY SCHAUB JR.

BIBLIOGRAPHY

Avant, Deborah D. *The Market for Force: The Consequences of Privatizing Security.* New York: Cambridge University Press, 2005.

Caforio, Guisepe, ed. *The Sociology of the Military.* Cheltenham, UK: Edward Elgar, 1998.

Cohen, Eliot A. *Supreme Command: Soldiers, Statesmen, and Leadership in Wartime.* New York: Free Press, 2002.

Feaver, Peter D. *Armed Servants: Agency, Oversight, and Civil-military Relations.* Cambridge, Mass.: Harvard University Press, 2003.

Feaver, Peter D., and Richard Kohn, eds. *Soldiers and Civilians: The Civil-military Gap and American National Security.* Cambridge, Mass.: MIT Press, 2001.

Huntington, Samuel P. *The Soldier and the State: The Theory and Politics of Civil-military Relations.* Cambridge, Mass.: Belknap Press, 1957.

Janowitz, Morris. *The Professional Soldier: A Social and Political Portrait.* New York: Free Press, 1960.

Lasswell, Harold. *National Security and Individual Freedom.* New York: McGraw-Hill, 1950.

Civil Religion

Civil religion has been a political and theological problem of enduring concern across the centuries and has become a topic of renewed interest among social scientists in the last fifty years.

There is a rich heritage of philosophical, theological, and political reflection on the problem that extends at least as far back as Plato's *Laws*. There are at least two prominent views of civil religion that characterize this heritage. According to one view, civil religion is a civic ethos that recognizes and cultivates beliefs supporting a society's moral-political commitments. This version of civil religion employs the force of religious symbols, images, and language to garner political strength. This view of civil religion is manifested in some works of Plato, Baruch Spinoza, Francis Bacon, John Locke, and Jean-Jacques Rousseau.

Another view of civil religion presents it as a civic ethos that is driven by more explicitly theological beliefs, though it gains power by political means and maintains itself through political forms. This version of civil religion arises from an overlapping theological consensus within a society and promotes a wider recognition of its bond with God and his providence, typically appealing to the language of national destiny and sacred purpose. Some features of this view occur in certain ancient Roman and medieval thinkers, while its other features manifest variously in later figures such as Niccolò Machiavelli, Georg Wilhem Friedrich Hegel, and certain American Puritan writers.

The past fifty years have seen numerous scholarly studies on civil religion. Sociologists, historians, religious studies scholars, theologians, and political scientists have conducted most of this work. Scholars have sought to define and explain the phenomena of civil religion according to the contours of these respective disciplines. For example, Robert Bellah has been one of the most influential analysts and has invited a very welcome reconsideration of civil religion as a phenomenon, especially in its American historical and cultural context. One characteristic feature of his work as a sociologist has been his attention to the complexities and internal logic of religious and political associations across the political and religious spectrum. Bellah's supporters and critics alike recognize how well he classifies and interprets the attitudes and behavior of such groups without reducing their motivations to merely economic or class considerations nor inflating their religious and political dimensions to the exclusion of other factors. He also recognizes the limitations of secularization theory, prominent among sociologists, that predict religion to become increasingly private and individualistic as society becomes more secular.

Among religious studies scholars, Martin Marty offers perceptive analyses of civil religion that capture some important religious and political features of the phenomena. For example, he distinguishes priestly and prophetic strains of civil religion. His prophetic variety of civil religion appropriates the religious language of prophecy to highlight the progress of social and political change toward a future of greater peace and justice. He associates a priestly version of civil religion with a religious language that promotes and preserves "American values."

Political scientists have tended to focus on particular institutions of government, including the constitution and the presidency. Representative examples of this can be seen in Richard Pierard and Robert Linder's book, *Civil Religion and the Presidency*, and in Sanford Levinson's *Constitutional Faith*. These are detailed studies of particular institutions as they are altered by civil religious phenomena. There are a number of illuminating studies of civil religion through particular figures in the history of political philosophy. Some good examples of such work include Michael Zuckert's essay on "Locke and the Problem of Civil Religion," Sanford Kessler's book *Tocqueville's Civil Religion: American Christianity and the Prospects for Freedom*, and Ronald Beiner's essay "Machiavelli, Hobbes and Rousseau on Civil Religion."

While civil religion is often associated with premodern and presecular societies, it has been a recurring phenomenon in the modern period and occasioned considerable reflection in modern and contemporary thought.

See also *Hegel, Georg W. F.; Locke, John; Machiavelli, Niccolò; Plato; Religion and Politics; Rousseau, Jean-Jacques; Spinoza, Baruch.*

. . . . RONALD WEED

BIBLIOGRAPHY

Augustine. *City of God,* translated by Henry Bettenson. New York: Penguin, 1984.

Bellah, Robert. "Civil Religion in America." *Daedalus* 96, no. 1 (1997): 1–21.

Bacon, Francis. *New Atlantis.* Manchester: Manchester University Press, 2002.

Cicero. *The Republic,* translated by Neil Rudd. Oxford: Oxford University Press, 1998.

Levinson, Sanford V. *Constitutional Faith.* Princeton: Princeton University Press, 1989.

Linder, Robert D., and Richard V. Pierard. *Civil Religion and the Presidency.* Grand Rapids, Mich.: Zondervan, 1988.

McClay, Wilfred M. "Two Concepts of Secularism." In *Religion Returns to the Public Square: Faith and Policy in America,* edited by Hugh Heclo and Wilfred M. McClay. Baltimore: Johns Hopkins University Press, 2003.

Montesquieu. *The Spirit of the Laws,* translated and edited by Anne Cohler, Basia Miller, and Harold Stone. New York: Cambridge University Press, 1989.

Plato. *The Laws,* translated, with notes and an interpretive essay by Thomas L. Pangle. New York: Basic Books, 1980.

Rousseau, J. J. *Social Contract,* translated by Judith R. Bush, Roger D. Masters, and Christopher Kelly. Hanover, N.H.: University Press of New England, 1994.

Spinoza, Benedict. *A Theologico-Political Treatise,* translated with an introduction by R. H. M. Elwes. New York: Dover Publications, 1951.

Tocqueville, Alexis de. *Democracy in America,* translated and edited by Harvey C. Mansfield and Delba Winthorp. Chicago: University of Chicago Press, 2000.

Civil Rights Movement

Civil rights is a broad phrase that is used in several different contexts. Its most common usage refers to race discrimination, but in its broadest sense, a civil right is a power, privilege, or protection granted or recognized by a legitimate authority, law, or usage. Civil rights protect individual people and groups of people from discrimination or mistreatment. Civil rights, in modern times, also include, but are not limited to, protection against gender discrimination, disability discrimination, and religious discrimination. Civil rights can be contrasted with human rights, which are asserted to belong to individuals independent of legal recognition. Human rights imply that individuals *deserve* certain protections; civil rights are delineated in law so that individuals or groups actually *receive* these protections.

THE ADVENT OF THE CIVIL RIGHTS MOVEMENT

The *civil rights movement* is typically the term used in the United States to refer to the struggle of African Americans to obtain equal protection under the law. However, the term can also be used generally for any struggle for legal protection that has occurred since one group of people was first subjected to the rule of another.

Nevertheless, at the end of the eighteenth century, the American Revolution (1776–1783) and French Revolution (1789–1799)—influenced by Enlightenment thinkers like John Locke, Jean-Jacques Rousseau, and Montesquieu—essentially marked the beginning of the modern civil rights movement. The U.S. Constitution's Bill of Rights and the French National Assembly's Declaration of the Rights of Man and the Citizen, both issued in 1789, were watersheds in turning Enlightenment ideas of individual rights into law. (The French Declaration only came into force in a revised version in 1793, following the Revolution.) With these revolutions, the concept of civil rights was formally recognized and placed into practice, albeit incompletely, as illustrated by the struggles that followed in the United States.

EXTENDING CIVIL RIGHTS

Despite the high ideals of such documents as the Bill of Rights, civil rights were not available to many sectors of society, especially for African Americans and women. During the U.S. Civil War (1861–1865), in 1863, President Abraham Lincoln issued the Emancipation Proclamation, proclaiming the freedom of slaves, but only in rebellious territories. Despite the Emancipation Proclamation's limited scope, it tolled the death knell for slavery in the United States, but not for racial discrimination.

After the war, the Thirteenth, Fourteenth, and Fifteenth Amendments were enacted to the U.S. Constitution, prohibiting slavery, guaranteeing equal rights and due process under state laws, and guaranteeing the right to vote for African American males (women would not receive the vote until the Nineteenth Amendment in 1920). Regardless, through nonenforcement and selective interpretation of these rights, problems of racial discrimination persisted, as illustrated by the infamous case of *Plessey v. Ferguson* (1896), which approved a "separate but equal" doctrine despite the manifest inequality in society.

THE FLOWERING OF THE CIVIL RIGHTS MOVEMENT

The early 1900s saw the founding of African American rights organizations like the National Association for the Advancement of Colored People in 1909. Still, not until 1954, following *Brown v. Board of Education* (banning segregation in public schools) were significant inroads made against racial discrimination. In the late 1950s, resistance to racial discrimination increased, headlined by the 1955 Montgomery bus boycott, as the African American community showed that they had power and demanded change. Subsequently, the 1960s witnessed the flowering of the civil rights movement in America. In response to the movement, African Americans were granted significant civil rights with the 1964 Civil Rights Act (mandating desegregation), the 1965 Equal Voting Rights Act (eliminating hindrances to voting), and the 1968 Civil Rights Act (banning discrimination in housing).

After these public policy victories and Martin Luther King Jr.'s 1968 assassination, the African American civil rights movement splintered into a sometimes violent black power movement and more prosaic legal and individual struggles to consolidate the gains of the 1960s. Political scientists continue to analyze the factors which contributed to the success of the civil rights movement from a variety of perspectives (critical race theory, social movement theory, etc.), but one main factor is undeniable: the broader civil rights movement began with the U.S. Constitution, to which the African American civil rights movement was able to appeal to draw support from the country. If the American civil rights movement is considered by many a completed period in U.S. history, the broader civil rights movement is an ongoing struggle throughout the world, as other minorities vie for the powers, privileges, and protections they believe are due them.

See also *Bill of Rights; Civil and Political Rights; International Bill of Rights; Jim Crow; Race and Racism; Segregation and Desegregation; Slavery; U.S. Politics and Society: African American Political Participation; U.S. Politics and Society: African American Social Movements; U.S. Politics and Society: Minority Interest Groups; White Supremacy; Women's Rights.*

. . . . WM. C. PLOUFFE JR.

BIBLIOGRAPHY

McAdam, Doug. *Political Process and the Development of Black Insurgency, 1930–1970,* 2nd ed. Chicago: University of Chicago Press, 1999.

Morris, Aldon D. *The Origins of the Civil Rights Movement.* New York: Free Press, 1984.

Robnett, Belinda. *How Long, How Long: African American Women in the Struggle for Civil Rights.* Oxford: Oxford University Press, 1998.

Weisbrot, Robert. *Freedom Bound: A History of America's Civil Rights Movement.* New York: Norton, 1990.

Civil Service

Civil service systems are composed of individuals who attain their positions by virtue of their performance on competitive examinations or by holding of specific qualifications such as a bachelor's degree. In contrast to elected officials who are expected to be policy advocates, civil servants are expected to embody expertise and neutral competence. Typical citizens rarely come into direct contact with their elected officials—one reason for this is the often brief tenure of these officials. In contrast, typical citizens have a good chance of frequently personally encountering the multitudes of civil servants who carry out government policies. Civil servants are present at the national, state, and local levels and may hold their positions for long periods of time. While the size of the U.S. civil service has been stable for the past fifty years, and has declined as a percentage of the total U.S. workforce, the growth of state and local civil service workforces has been steady.

Government service was originally understood to be the domain of the educated gentry. Then in 1829, with the age of President Andrew Jackson, as the U.S. government vastly expanded and political parties took their largely present-day composition, the *spoils system* flourished. In such a system, the supporters of the winning political party receive government jobs or other material rewards such as government contracts. Anyone could do a government job, so the reasoning went, and the United States should have a representative bureaucracy that mirrors the people it serves. Many a U.S. president has lamented the performance of individuals whom he put in office. Harlan Hahn wrote, "Several years after he left the presidency, William Howard Taft endorsed the familiar political maxim that the distribution of patronage often breeds 'one ingrate and ten enemies'" (368).

The term civil service itself came into common usage in the United States following the assassination of President James Garfield by Charles Guiteau. Guiteau, a Stalwart Republican, was seeking a government post in Paris, and he believed that if he killed Garfield, a Mugwump Republican, Chester Arthur (Garfield's successor and a fellow Stalwart) would appoint Guiteau to his desired position. Instead, Guiteau was executed for his offense, and the spoils system was condemned with the cry, "Spoils equals murder." President Chester Arthur signed the Civil Service Reform Act of 1883, which was authored by U.S. senator George H. Pendleton (D-Ohio). Three months later, Democratic governor Grover Cleveland of New York signed into law a bill authored by Republican representative Theodore Roosevelt, which established the first state civil service system. Roosevelt would go on to serve as a U.S. civil service commissioner from 1889 to 1895, his tenure overlapping with the second administration of President Grover Cleveland.

The enactment of the Civil Service Reform Act of 1883, also known as the Pendleton Act, meant that loyalty to particular politicians or political parties would no longer be a prerequisite for government employment. The act prohibited mandatory campaign contributions and outlawed campaign and political party assessments of U.S. government employees. It established the bipartisan, three-member Civil

Service Commission vested with rule–making and investigatory authority. Members required nomination by the president and confirmation by the U.S. Senate in order to serve. The legislation institutionalized the competitive entrance examination as the standard requirement for individuals who aspired to become government bureaucrats.

Competitive examinations for civil service positions also have a long history in China and Korea. The National Museum of Korea exhibits detailed elaborations on the nature of examinations that were administered more than a millennia ago. Indeed, opponents of Pendleton's legislation denigrated its Chinese antecedents.

The civil service system has gradually expanded, in part because many presidents have converted political positions into civil service ones prior to leaving office. This ensures that officials whose policy views and implementation strategies reflect a president's own preferences can exercise power potentially for years after an administration has ended. President Jimmy Carter, who had campaigned vigorously for the presidency on his record of executive branch reorganization and innovation during his tenure as governor of Georgia, brought major changes to the civil service with his signing of the Civil Service Reform Act of 1978. This act abolished the Civil Service Commission and replaced it with the Office of Personnel Management and the Merit System Protection Board. It also established the Senior Executive Service in order to reward outstanding performance and facilitate appropriate lateral transfers between agencies. The Office of Personnel Management is tasked with recruiting the most capable person for each position, while the Merit System Protection Board protects the due process rights of government employees.

The Hatch Act, passed in 1939, placed limitations on the political activities of U.S. civil servants. The following year, further legislation extended these prohibitions to many state and local government employees whose agencies were recipients of federal grants-in-aid. Proponents of the Hatch Acts argue that these limitations promote the ideal of a neutral bureaucracy, whose employees are not subject to manipulation by public officeholders. Those opposed to the Hatch Acts counter that one should not have to surrender fundamental rights of citizenship in order to be a civil servant.

A major contemporary issue concerning the civil service is the extent to which it should be supplanted in favor of contracting out government services to private entities. Proponents of the increased contracting of government services typically tout its efficiency, while its opponents are skeptical about such purported savings and decry the reduced accountability that this practice fosters.

See also *Bureaucracy; Patronage; Spoils System.*

. . . .   HENRY SIRGO

BIBLIOGRAPHY

Alexander, Herbert E. *Financing Politics: Money, Elections, and Political Reform,* 3rd ed. Washington, D.C.: CQ Press, 1984.

Berman, Evan M., James S. Bowman, Jonathan P. West, and Montgomery Van Wart. *Human Resource Management in Public Service: Paradoxes, Processes, and Problems,* 3rd ed. Thousand Oaks, Calif.: Sage Publications, 2010.

Hahn, Harlan. 1966. "President Taft and the Discipline of Patronage." *Journal of Politics* 20, no. 2 (1966): 368–390.

Rosenbloom, David H., Robert S. Kravchuk, and Richard M. Clerkin. *Public Administration: Understanding Management, Politics, and Law in the Public Sector,* 7th ed. New York: McGraw-Hill Higher Education, 2009.

Taft, William Howard. *Our Chief Magistrate and His Powers.* New York: Columbia University Press, 1925.

Theriault, Sean M. "Patronage, the Pendleton Act, and the Power of the People." *Journal of Politics* 65, no. 1 (2003): 50–68.

U.S. Office of Personnel Management. *Biography of an Ideal: A History of the Federal Civil Service.* Washington, D.C.: Government Printing Office, 2003.

Civil Society

Having been dormant as a social science concept for most of the nineteenth and twentieth centuries, the term *civil society* emerged in the 1990s as almost as fashionable a buzzword as *globalization*. Yet there is nothing even resembling a commonly agreed definition of the concept. Scholars at the Centre for Civil Society, London School of Economics reflect some of these ambiguities in a cautiously worded "initial working definition." They define civil society as

> "the arena of uncoerced collective action around shared interests, purposes and values," but then go on to make a distinction between its theoretical separation from state, family and market and the blurred and negotiated boundaries between these spheres in practice. (Centre for Civil Society)

A nonexhaustive list of the sort of actors who populate this sphere may be a less contested way to describe the concept than a theoretical definition: Civil society is generally agreed to comprise nongovernmental organizations, community groups, faith-based institutions, professional associations, trade unions, self-help groups, social movements, academics, and activists. Following the genealogy of the concept of civil society and its recent resurgence, a problematic conceptualization of the "civility" of civil society emerged; civil society also relates to democracy and democratization and to capitalism, with modern the debates relating to the existence and nature of a global civil society.

HISTORY OF THE CIVIL SOCIETY CONCEPT

The term civil society has a direct equivalent in Latin (*societas civilis*), and a close equivalent in ancient Greek (*politike koinona*). These terms denoted the polity, with active citizens shaping its institutions and policies. The terms also represented unequivocally bounded concepts, implying exclusion of noncitizens. As such, translated as *société civil* or commonwealth, the terms were attractive to the contractarian thinkers who sought to explain and justify the emergence of modern nation-states in the seventeenth and eighteenth centuries. Preoccupations ranged from the bleak requirement of complete subjection of Thomas Hobbes, to the liberal individualism of John Locke, to the equivocation over the benefits of nature versus civilization in Jean-Jacques Rousseau, to the emphasis on civic virtue by Adam Ferguson. But for all of them, civil society denoted the social contract between citizens, providing for a nonviolent social space that facilitated the development of commercial, civic, and political activity by the (male, white, propertied) contracting citizens.

Ferguson was widely translated, and Immanuel Kant and Georg Hegel were among his readers. Kant holds a special place in the genealogy of civil society since he was the first to posit it as unbounded, and realizable only in a universal (or, today, global) form. Hegel's conception of civil society is not easily penetrable, and impossible to summarize, but one key aspect was that he saw civil society as something separate from, although symbiotic with, the state. Civil society, for Hegel, concerned men trading and interacting socially, but civil society was separate from government and purely public activity. For Karl Marx, civil society, in its German translation *Bürgerliche Gesellschaft*, is narrowed to only economic life, in which everyone pursues individual selfish interests and becomes alienated from one's own human potential and one's fellow people.

At the same time as Marx was developing this bleak interpretation of Hegel's concept, French aristocrat Alexis de Tocqueville became the first theoretical proponent of *associationalism*. During his extensive visit to the United States (1831–1833), Tocqueville was struck by the American habit of founding associations for all manner of political and public purposes, and came to the conclusion that this was the foundation stone for the successful functioning of democracy in America.

In the early twentieth century, Antonio Gramsci, general secretary of the Italian Communist Party, grappled with a theoretical question of vital practical concern: Why, under what Marx had identified as ideal conditions (advanced industrialization, frequent economic and political crises) was the revolution not occurring in Italy? Going back from Marx to Hegel, Gramsci then divorced the notion of civil society, as cultural superstructure, from economic interactions as material base, founding a long line of scholarship on the manufacture of consent for practices of domination. This consent is generated in the institutions of civil society, notably the church, but also in schools, associations, trade unions, media, and other cultural institutions. Gramsci primarily emphasized how it was through this cultural superstructure that the bourgeois class imposed its hegemony, weathering even economic and political crises. However, Gramsci has been widely read as implying that civil society is therefore also the site where a counterhegemony can be built, as a kind of wedge between the state and the class-structured economy, which has the revolutionary potential of dislodging the bourgeoisie.

After Gramsci, the term and indeed the concept of civil society very nearly died out in Western political thought. When the term resurfaced, it was with dissidents against the authoritarian state both in Latin America and Eastern Europe.

In Latin America, the situation of left-wing intellectuals of the 1970s and 1980s was very similar to Gramsci's, fighting fascist dictatorships, where capitalists were by and large colluding with the state, but where the state did not exercise complete control over everyday life. Latin American thinkers, first of all in Brazil, appear to have been attracted to the idea of civil society because it was a term that could unify entrepreneurs, church groups, and labor movements in their opposition to the regime. As a force in society, civil society also could be distinguished from political parties, which many felt had been discredited, as well as from the kind of populist mobilization that had been endemic in various Latin American countries. Most important, civil society appealed to these Latin American groups because it was associated with nonviolence.

With the self-styled central Europeans, the concept of civil society was somewhat different. While state terrorism was more spectacular in Latin America, with military regimes behind the "disappearing" of thousands of people in each country in a matter of months, civil society in the Gramscian sense may have been snuffed out more successfully by the longer rule and more totalitarian aspirations of communism in Eastern Europe and the Soviet Union. In a totalitarian state, where the distinction between the interests of the people and the interests of the state is categorically denied (hence people's republics), central European dissidents began to believe that conceiving a civil society, as an association between people away from the tentacles of the state, was the way to begin resisting the state. Intellectuals in Czechoslovakia, Hungary, and Poland during the mid-1980s, such as Adam Michnik, Gyorgi Konrad, and Vaclav Havel revived the term to mean autonomous spaces independent of the state; their understanding may owe as much to Tocqueville's as to Gramsci's, although they do not explicitly acknowledge either.

The central European and the Latin American thinkers had several things in common. They emphasized the values of solidarity, public truth telling, ideological plurality, and nonviolence as characteristics of civil society. The way in which they conceived of civil society, also, was not a means to achieve an overthrow of their regimes. They were more interested in reclaiming space that the authoritarian state had encroached upon than in taking over the reigns of power. This space had to be kept open and alive as a necessary complement to a healthy democracy—an antidote to narrow party politics and a bulwark against future threats to democracy. Based on the insight that modern authoritarianism requires ostensible adherence to legal norms, the central European and Latin American intellectuals made much use of appeals to the law, whether it be national law or international human rights standards, as a strategy of legitimate resistance. Finally, while demonstrating a vivid awareness of the world beyond their state, these groups firmly believed that democratization must come from within.

Also in the 1990s, Robert Putnam published his influential work on Italy, *Making Democracy Work: Civic Traditions in Modern Italy*, inspired by the more Tocquevillean tradition of civil society as associationalism, accumulating social capital in communities, and buttressing the functioning of democracy.

From then on, the civil society idea caught on like wildfire. It was apparently considered useful by prodemocracy activists in the Philippines, South Korea, and South Africa. But it also obtained a new lease of life, both in political theory and in policy practice, in entrenched democracies in Western Europe and North America as well as India. This related both to concern over the erosion of democracy through the apathy and disillusionment of the electorate, and to the end of the grand ideologies. The civil society idea was seen as a way of revitalizing democracy when both the socialist great hopes of the all-powerful, all-providing state, and the neoliberal belief that market logic delivers benefits to all, had lost appeal. For the developing world, there is also a rather more cynical explanation for the concept of civil society's sudden and ubiquitous popularity: Since donors adopted the dogma that strengthening civil society was good for democracy and development, using the language of civil society was good for funding applications.

With these usages, there was a tendency to conflation between Enlightenment, Gramscian, and Tocquevillean meanings of civil society as well conflation of an empirical category, which is often referred to as nongovernmental organizations (NGOs), or the nonprofit or voluntary sector, with various political projects of liberalization, democratization, or resistance.

THE CIVILITY OF CIVIL SOCIETY
As evidenced in the roots of the civil society idea, the Enlightenment concept of civil society is deeply imbued with a sense of the superior civility of European polities. While not very precisely defined, the term *civility* appears associated with nonviolence, good manners, and at a stretch, tolerance for others within one's own society. But this internal civilization process had a necessary corollary in war, or at least the threat of war, with others. Moreover, from Napoleonic times onwards, colonial projects were increasingly justified in terms of "civilizing" the natives, even as the methods of subjugation were allowed to be "uncivil" because the population in question was not yet within the "civil" realm of those who can be expected to understand and respect the modern rule of law. This historical baggage makes any reflection on the meaning of the "civil" in civil society, and what might constitute uncivility, politically loaded. Some authors, like John and Jean Comaroff, reject any substantive use of civil as having racist connotations.

Nonetheless, the disillusionment following earlier expectations of civil society's contribution to a liberal-democratic end of history has spawned recent debates about the term *uncivil society*. It has come to be used for manifestations of civil society that challenge liberal-democratic values. Violence is most often singled out as its characteristic, but exclusivist or dogmatic ideologies, predatory practices, and general rule breaking are also mentioned. The use of the term uncivil society is also not confined to any particular region. Scholarly articles apply the term to civil society manifestations in Africa, Eastern Europe, Western Europe, the Arab world, and Latin America, as well as globally. After 9/11, the term has been used increasingly to denote "illiberal" reactions to neoliberal globalization, such as the al-Qaida network.

The main academic argument in relation to uncivil society turns on whether uncivil society should be included in or excluded from a definition of civil society. Some political theorists exclude the uncivil: they insist on acting within the rules, respect for others, or willingness to compromise as elements of civil society. A majority of the literature takes the opposite view, however, insisting on an empirical definition of civil society that includes uncivil society as a tendency within it. Kopecky and Mudde, in their 2003 work, *Uncivil Society? Contentious Politics in Post-Communist Europe*, give the most extensive attention to this issue, adducing no less than five interrelated arguments for eschewing the exclusion of uncivil society from civil society. In summary,

1. To some extent, all civil society manifestations are exclusivist in that they claim the moral high ground for their own position in opposition to all others.
2. Civility towards the uncivil has historically been limited and hypocritical.
3. Adherence to liberal democratic goals does not necessarily equate with internal democracy, or vice versa. Uncivil movements may have civil outcomes and vice versa.
4. Adherence to legal or even societal norms is far from desirable in nondemocratic societies and proscribes challenges to the status quo even in democratic ones.
5. Finally, "narrow conceptions of civil society screen off potentially vital ingredients of associational life and democratic politics." Inclusion is therefore necessary to progress in empirical knowledge.

CIVIL SOCIETY AND DEMOCRACY
Much of the civil society literature of the last decade is devoted to critiques of the idea, so dominant in policy making in the 1990s, that strengthening civil society contributes to democratization. This idea, partly considered to have come out of the "1989 experience" in Eastern Europe, and partly attributed to Robert Putnam's influential work on Italy, requires civil society to be imbued with both democratic and liberal values, and for it to be easily distinguishable from "uncivil society" which lacks these values. The critiques of the *mutual strengthening theory*, based on numerous empirical studies from a variety of regions, make four counterpoints.

First, having a vibrant civil society is not to be conflated with having a "civil" civil society. This argument is most persuasively pursued in a historical article by Berman, which shows that Germans in the Weimar Republic, having lost confidence in the state, were "addicted to associating" in much the same way as Tocqueville observed of early Americans, but that these dense associational networks were rapidly and successfully infiltrated and captured by Nazi organizers, accelerating and buttressing the Nazi seizure of power "from below."

Second, religious or nationalist movements often have a democratic base, and sometimes seek the overthrow of a nondemocratic government, but their values are not necessarily democratic and certainly not liberal. Segments of civil society imbued with liberal, Western values on the other hand do not necessarily have democratic legitimacy in the form of a grassroots base.

Third, democracy in Western nations developed in the context of a global system that exploited and repressed other parts of the world. It is not surprising therefore that populations and civil society actors in these other parts sometimes have a more cynical, even hostile conception of the liberal democracy; they see the liberal democracy as being offered or even forced upon them by Western institutions in a continuing context of inequality.

Finally, the quality of civil society and the quality of the state and market are interdependent. Hence, civil society can only be as civil as the circumstances allow. Leonardo Avritzer (53–60), for instance, develops "uncivil society," as the prototype of civil society most likely to emerge when the state is too weak to guarantee either physical or material security: the market economy exists only in clientelist form, and political society is nonexistent or fragmented to the point of destruction. He cites Peru and Colombia as Latin American prototypes of this situation, whilst acknowledging that elements of it can be found in all Latin American countries. The challenge in these situations is "whether civil society can produce civility in spite of the state and the market."

CIVIL SOCIETY AND CAPITALISM

The classical theorists made no distinction between civil society and the market. For Locke, the civility of civil society consisted precisely in providing sufficient physical security for the individual so that one could, through one's industry and ingenuity, amass property. Hegel, on the other hand, has described particularly vividly the dynamic nature of what he called *Buergerliche Gesellschaft*—what we would nowadays call the *capitalist system*—but he did not at all believe it to be civil. Without checks and balances provided by the state, the system neglects or exploits the poor who cannot help themselves. Similarly, Marx thought of civil society as bourgeois society, a necessary stage in history, but inherently exploitative.

Since then, through the detour of Gramsci's insistence on dividing material base from cultural superstructure, civil society has come to mean the nonstate, nonmarket realm of society. However, capitalism is now generally accepted as the global background setting in which civil society operates. Recent work has begun to take into account the problematic relationship between civil society and capitalism both at the national level and globally, but this relation is as yet much less theorized than that between civil society and democracy.

TRANSNATIONAL OR GLOBAL CIVIL SOCIETY

While until recently, civil society was primarily thought of as a national concept, the reality of cross-border networking of nonprofit associations and social movements is much older, especially if we include forms of organization associated with the Catholic Church and organized Islam. The nineteenth century saw peace movements, antislavery campaigns, women's suffrage, and labor movements having continuous correspondence and international meetings, spawning intellectual and strategic cross-fertilization.

The last two decades, building on these earlier links, are qualitatively different, however. The intensity with which people network and link up across borders has exploded. But this is not just an empirical shift. In stark contrast to the Enlightenment concept, the discourses and identities of civil society actors have become more transnational and even global. Human rights defenders used a legal universalist frame to combat national injustices, peace groups challenged national security policies with concepts of solidarity across conflict divides, and environmentalists initiated talk of one world and global solutions. More recently, normative cosmopolitan concepts of global civil society have been opposed to ethnic nationalism and religious fundamentalism, as well as a counterforce against predatory globalization. At the same time, some of the most common forms of uncivil society in the twenty-first century may be based on what Manuel Castells has called a "resistance identity," based solely on being against various (perceived) aspects of globalization rather than on a positive project for society.

See also *Colonialism; Democracy and Democratization; Globalization; Gramsci, Antonio; Hegel, Georg W. F.; Kant, Immanuel; Latin American Politics and Society; Locke, John; Marx, Karl; Nongovernmental Organizations (NGOs); Rousseau, Jean-Jacques; Soviet Union, Former; Tocqueville, Alexis de.*

. . . . MARLIES GLASIUS

BIBLIOGRAPHY

Abdel Rahman, Maha. "The Politics of 'Uncivil' Society in Egypt." *Review of African Political Economy* 29 (June 2002): 21–36.

Avritzer, Leonardo. "Civil Society in Latin America: Uncivil, Liberal, and Participatory Models." In *Exploring Civil Society: Political and Cultural Contexts,* edited by Marlies Glasius, David Lewis, and Hakan Seckinelgin, 53–60. London: Routledge, 2004.

Baker, Gideon. *Civil Society and Democratic Theory: Alternative Voices.* London: Routledge, 2002.

Berman, Sheri. "Civil Society and the Collapse of the Weimar Republic." *World Politics* 49 (April 1997): 401–429.

Centre for Civil Society. "What is Civil Society?" The London School of Economics and Political Science. www.lse.ac.uk/collections/CCS/introduction/what_is_civil_society.htm.

Cohen, Jean L., and Andrew Arato. *Civil Society and Political Theory.* Cambridge, Mass: MIT Press, 1992.

Comaroff, John L., and Jean Comaroff. *Civil Society and the Political Imagination in Africa: Critical Perspectives.* Chicago: University of Chicago Press, 1999.

Fatton, Robert. "Africa in the Age of Democratization: The Civic Limitations of Civil Society." *African Studies Review* 38 (September 1995): 67–99.

Howell, Jude, and Jenny Pearce. *Civil Society and Development: A Critical Exploration.* Boulder: Lynne Rienner, 2002.

Kaldor, Mary. *Global Civil Society: An Answer to War.* Cambridge: Polity Press, 2003.

Kaldor, Mary, and Diego Muro. "Religious and Nationalist Militant Groups." In *Global Civil Society 2003,* edited by Mary Kaldor, Helmut Anheier, and Marlies Glasius, 151–184. Oxford: Oxford University Press, 2003.

Keck, Margaret E., and Sikkink, Kathryn. *Activists beyond Borders: Advocacy Networks in International Politics.* Ithaca: Cornell University Press, 1998.

Kopecky , Petr, and Cas Mudde, eds. *Uncivil Society? Contentious Politics in Post-Communist Europe.* London: Routledge, 2003.

Lipschutz, Ronnie. "Power, Politics and Global Civil Society." *Millennium* 33 (June 2005): 747–769.

Putnam, Robert. *Making Democracy Work: Civic Traditions in Modern Italy.* Princeton: Princeton University Press, 1993.

Seligman, Adam. *The Idea of Civil Society.* Princeton: Princeton University Press, 1995.

Civil Wars

In the debate over defining civil wars, factors taken into account include the territory where the conflict occurs, the parties involved, and the casualty rates. According to James D. Fearon, a *civil war* is a violent conflict within a country fought by organized groups aiming to take power at the center or in a region, or to change government policies. According to Fearon, if the threshold for a conflict to be labeled a civil war is at least one thousand killed during the fighting, approximately 125 civil wars had occurred by 2007 since the end of World War II (1939–1945). Scholars such as Nicolas Sambanis identify other criteria. This can make it difficult to examine why such conflicts occur, and to identify the best resolution methods and hopefully prevent them. It can also cause controversy over the legitimacy of international intervention.

OCCURRENCE OF CIVIL WARS

Civil wars have occurred around the world but have been more common in some regions. From 1950 to 2001, developing Asia (South and East Asia and Oceania) experienced a persistently high incidence of war. Latin America experienced much conflict in the 1980s, as did the former Soviet bloc in the 1990s, although most of these conflicts were short. The Middle East and North Africa have had a stable and high incidence of civil war since the late 1960s; moreover, the incidence of violent conflict in sub-Saharan Africa has increased. Until the 1980s, Africa had a below-average incidence, whereas now it is comparable to Asia and the Middle East and much higher than Latin America. According to the Stockholm International Peace Research Institute, sixteen major armed conflicts were active internationally in 2008. For the fifth consecutive year, all of the conflicts were intrastate, though troops from another state aided one of the parties in four conflicts.

Widespread casualties and violation of human rights are common features of civil wars. Casualties are particularly common among the civilian population and those most vulnerable, such as women, children (who are often recruited as fighters), and the elderly. Moreover, fleeing refugees are vulnerable to attack, disease, and malnourishment. Human rights are frequently violated as social mores against such crimes are weakened and law and order break down. This breakdown can provide the opportunity for violations to occur unhindered and without fear of punishment. Human rights may also be systematically violated, as terror and brutality are used as another means to win dominance and ensure the population's compliance. The violation of human rights is graphically shown by the war in the former Yugoslavia and conflict in Rwanda during the 1990s. The disastrous impact of civil war continues to be felt long after the fighting has subsided or ended. Higher rates of mortality often remain, for it takes time to rebuild the country's damaged infrastructure and the economy. War remnants such as mines also continue to cause casualties, as in Cambodia where conflict occurred from 1970 to the 1990s.

There is debate over whether the conflict in Iraq since the 2003 overthrow of President Saddam Hussein by U.S.-led coalition forces is a civil war, but there clearly have been widespread casualties and human rights violations. Fearon has defined the conflict as a civil war, and a January 2007 *U.S. National Intelligence Estimate* said that the term accurately described key elements of the conflict, including the hardening of ethno-sectarian identities, changes in the character of violence, ethno-sectarian mobilization, and population displacements. This debate continues, as does the violence; two bombs struck Baghdad in October 2009, killing at least 155 people, the deadliest attack in over two years. The Iraq Body Count, a nongovernmental organization with a public database including deaths caused by U.S.-led coalition forces and paramilitary or criminal attacks by others, estimated that as of February 4, 2010, there had been a minimum of 95,412 civilian deaths since U.S.-led coalition forces entered Iraq. As of February 16, 2010, there had been 4,697 coalition deaths. Overall though, violence had declined since peaking in early 2007.

Many groups have committed human rights abuses in Iraq. Basic rights to food and shelter have been threatened too, with many people forced to live in very poor conditions. Although there have been some positive developments, such as provincial elections in February 2009 followed by July 2009 parliamentary and presidential elections in the Kurdistan region, there is fear as to future stability and the protection of human rights after the United States withdraws.

EXPLAINING CIVIL WARS

Various factors can contribute to the outbreak of war. Scholars such as Barbara F. Walter have examined the recurrent nature of civil war. Once a country has experienced civil war, the threat of more conflict is elevated. One reason for this is that the same factors causing the initial war often remain. Indeed, these factors might have become stronger as a result of the war's destruction and casualties. The threat of ongoing conflict is illustrated in Angola where continuous conflict has occurred since independence in 1975. The presence of key political institutions that provide adequate and appropriate avenues to exercise rights, express opinions, and address grievances is vital in reducing the likelihood of war. Similarly, a central government that can adequately provide the basics of good governance is needed. However, this is not the case in many countries. The term *failed nation-state* indicates a dangerous post–cold war development—the breakdown of law, order, and basic services in a number of multiethnic states. This phenomenon is often accompanied by conflict, as in Somalia.

The issue of ownership of resources often arises when the resources are spread unevenly, and this can cause conflict. According to Paul Collier and Anke Hoeffler, the plundering of natural resources can finance opportunistic rebellions, and resources can motivate conflict. In particular, various scholars, including Paivi Lujala, have examined the link between diamonds and civil war. In addition, divisions such as those based on ethnicity, region, and religion can cause tension and, ultimately, conflict if the different groups clash and cannot resolve differences peacefully. The potentially destructive nature of ethnic divisions is illustrated by the conflict in Nigeria from 1967 to 1970. More recently, there has been fighting between the Shiites and Sunnis in post–Saddam Hussein Iraq. State and insurgency leaders alike can inflame and exacerbate tensions that lead to war. The key role of a leader in the outbreak and continuation of war is shown by the influential role taken by Serbian President Slobodan Milosevic in the conflict that engulfed the former Yugoslavia's during the 1990s. Finally, assistance to factions from external actors can exacerbate conflict. External involvement frequently occurred during the cold war when it was used as a tool by the superpowers and their allies to promote their rival strategic interests, as shown by Afghanistan's experiences in the late 1970s and 1980s.

See also *Ethnic Cleansing; Human Rights; War Crimes.*

. . . . PAUL BELLAMY

BIBLIOGRAPHY

Bellamy, Paul. "Cambodia: Remembering the Killing Fields," *New Zealand International Review* 30, no. 2 (March/April 2005): 17–20.

Britsih Broadcasting Corporation. "Timeline—Iraq." *BBC News,* October 28, 2009. www.news.bbc.co.uk/2/hi/middle_east/737483.stm.

Cable News Network. "U.S. and Coalition Casualties." *CNN World,* February 16, 2010. www.cnn.com/SPECIALS/2003/iraq/forces/casualties/.

DeRouen, Karl, Jr., and Paul Bellamy, eds. *International Security and the United States: An Encyclopedia.* Westport, Conn.: Praeger Security International, 2008.

DeRouen, Karl, Jr., and Uk Heo, eds. *Civil Wars of the World: Major Conflicts since World War II.* Santa Barbara, Calif.: ABC-CLIO, 2007.

Evans, Graham, and Jeffrey Newnham. *The Penguin Dictionary of International Relations.* London: Penguin Books, 1998.

Fearon, James D. "Iraq's Civil War," *Foreign Affairs* 86, no. 2 (March/April 2007): 2–15.

Iraq Body Count Database. February 4, 2010. www.iraqbodycount.org/.

International Institute for Strategic Studies. *Strategic Survey, 2009.* London: Routledge, 2009.

NGO Coordination Committee in Iraq and Oxfam. "Rising to the Humanitarian Challenge in Iraq." Briefing Paper. Oxfam International. http://oxfam.org/en/policy/briefingpapers/bp105_humanitarian_challenge_in_iraq_0707.

Office of the Director of National Intelligence and National Intelligence Council. *National Intelligence Estimate: Prospects for Iraq's Stability: A Challenging Road Ahead.* www.dni.gov/press_releases/20070202_release.pdf.

Stockholm International Peace Research Institute. *SIPRI Yearbook, 2009 Summary.* Stockholm, 2009. www.sipri.org/yearbook/2009/files/SIPRIYB09summary.pdf.

University of British Columbia. *Human Security Brief, 2007.* Human Security Report Project. www.humansecuritybrief.info/.

University of British Columbia. *Human Security Report, 2005.* Human Security Report Project. www.humansecurityreport.info/.

Clash of Civilizations

"The Clash of Civilizations" (1993) is the well-known work of Samuel P. Huntington, the late Harvard professor of political science, who argued that the primary cause of violent and nonviolent conflicts in the post–cold war period will be civilizational differences.

Huntington defined *civilization* as the "highest cultural grouping of people." While civilizations are dynamic entities and redefined with changes in the self-identification of people, they also involve objective attributes, such as language, history, customs, institutions, and especially religion, which make their differences "real." Based on this premise, Huntington identified eight civilizations: Western, Confucian, Japanese, Islamic, Hindu, Slavic-Orthodox, Latin American and "possibly" African. He predicted that the conflicts in the post–cold war era would erupt "along the cultural fault lines separating these civilizations from one another."

According to Huntington, the underlying reasons behind civilizational conflicts are manifold. First, cultural and religious differences are more fundamental than ideological or political ones. An individual can switch ideologies in a day, as happened after the collapse of the Soviet Union, but "Azeris cannot become Armenians." He also underlined that ethnic attachments lead to the kin-country syndrome, which is influential in determining states' sides especially in the post–cold war conflicts: Russia behind Serbia against Bosnia, Turkey behind Azerbaijan against Armenia, and the United States behind Israel against Syria and Iran. Furthermore, ethnic differences are likely to have implications on immigration and human rights policies.

Second, globalization brings nations closer, which does not necessarily lead to greater cooperation but potentially to a reaction against the Western economic and military dominance. Accordingly, Huntington has argued, religious fundamentalism is spreading especially among the young, educated, middle-class people beyond national boundaries but within civilizations. In this regard, the tension between the West and Islam is likely to be the most conflictive one due to the American influence in the Middle East.

Finally, Huntington envisaged the rise of regional, rather than global, economic cooperation, which would reinforce civilizational consciousness. Consequently, he predicted that the European Union (EU) would be consolidated not only around economic interests but also around the common culture, which will inevitably leave Turkey outside. Another implication of his thesis is a growing economic cooperation in East Asia that would center on China rather than on Japan.

Since its suggestion, the clash of civilizations has become a thesis that many academics and political figures have disagreed with but not ignored. Amartya Sen criticized it for disregarding diversity within civilizations. Bruce Russett and coauthors examined militarized interstate disputes in the period from 1952 to 1992 and found that relative power and regime type have greater explanatory power than civilizational differences on the incidence of interstate conflict. A more recent study by Andrej Tusicisny examined the same relationship in the period from 1946 to 2001 and found that civilizational fault lines are not more prone to conflict than any other place. The United Nations has put forward initiatives like the Year of Dialogue Among Civilizations (2001) and the Alliance of Civilizations (2005), which aim to investigate and address the causes of contemporary polarization between cultures.

Despite strong criticisms, theories embedded in the clash of civilizations are still alive today, and not for bad reasons. First, the empirical studies that have refuted the thesis suffer from multiple deficiencies. They either cover a short period of time in the post–cold war era; do not include post-9/11 conflicts, such as the U.S. military involvement in Iraq and Afghanistan and against al-Qaida; or disregard nonviolent cultural conflicts, such as the cartoon crisis in Denmark or the increasing resistance in Europe to Turkey's membership in the European Union. Second, recent studies by Alan Krueger and Marc Sageman have found that the popular explanations for international terrorism, such as poverty and lack of education, have no empirical basis as terrorists tend to come from well-educated, middle-class or high-income families; target people of a different religion in suicide attacks; and are motivated by the sufferings of Muslims in Bosnia, Chechnya, Iraq, and other places. Overall, the jihad of al-Qaida; discourses like President George W. Bush's "crusade"; and the rise of right-wing, anti-immigrant political parties in Western Europe, among other developments, seem to have kept Huntington's thesis at least partly valid in the post–cold war period.

See also *Al-Qaida; Conflict Resolution; Culture Wars; Huntington, Samuel.*

. . . . HOWARD J. WIARDA AND MURAT BAYAR

BIBLIOGRAPHY

Huntington, Samuel P. "The Clash of Civilizations?" *Foreign Affairs* 72, no. 3 (1993): 22–49.

Krueger, Alan B. *What Makes a Terrorist: Economics and the Roots of Terrorism.* Princeton: Princeton University Press, 2007.

Russett, Bruce M., John R. Oneal, and Michaelene Cox. "Clash of Civilizations, or Realism and Liberalism Déjà Vu?" *Journal of Peace Research* 37, no. 5 (2000): 583–608.

Sageman, Marc. *Leaderless Jihad: Terror Networks in the Twenty-First Century.* Philadelphia: University of Pennsylvania Press, 2008.

Sen, Amartya. "Civilizational Imprisonments: How to Misunderstand Everybody in the World." *The New Republic*, June 10, 2002, 28–33.

Tusicisny, Andrej. "Civilizational Conflicts: More Frequent, Longer, and Bloodier?" *Journal of Peace Research* 41, no. 4 (2004): 485–498.

Class and Politics

Class is one way individuals organize to effect political change. Political scientists also use class to explain political phenomena. The long history of examining the relationship between class and politics in political science dates back to the ancient Greeks. However, explaining what class as a concept means, and how it affects political phenomena, has changed over time. Debates over the meaning of class are torn between notions of the term sourced either in the work of German political philosopher Karl Marx and the Marxist tradition or that by German sociologist Max Weber.

CLASS IN ANCIENT GREEK, ROMAN, AND MEDIEVAL TIMES

The earliest uses of the concept of class date back to the ancient Greek political theorists. Plato's *Republic* uses the concept to explain the tripart division of labor that he constructs for his idealized polis. In this community, he distinguishes among classes of individuals—the philosopher kings, guardians, and the artisans—as the three groups that would inhabit the republic. For Plato, class refers to a type of intrinsic quality of individuals.

In Plato's *Republic*, the intrinsic distinctions among the three classes of individuals are revealed in an extensive educational process that breaks up families in order to determine who will be part of what class. The educational process, open to both men and women, determines which individuals have what aptitudes to do what in the republic. Thus, social class or roles are ultimately premised upon natural innate talents to reason and obtain true knowledge, and a just society is one where all individuals perform the functions for which they are best suited. In the *Republic* and his other writings, Plato also distinguishes among monarchy, aristocracy, and democracy, with each defined by which class rules. Overall, Plato's writings draw linkages among class, social roles, aptitudes, and political power, setting the stage for subsequent analysis of the concept.

Aristotle's *Politics* employs a class analysis when it comes to politics. Aristotle adopts Plato's conception of different types of governments, viewing monarchies, aristocracies, and democracies as types of polities governed by the one, the few, or the many. Aristotle's typology of governments rests upon a class analysis in terms of who rules. Yet unlike Plato, who clearly linked class to intrinsic talents, virtue, or knowledge, Aristotle connects the term to economics. In fact, his concept of a middle class appears modern, defining it as those who are economically well off and deeming its stability as critical to a well-run polity.

During the Roman Republic and Empire era (extending roughly from 264 BCE–476 CE), class continued to be an important concept. The division of Roman society into patricians and plebeians (rulers and subjects) was a common distinction made by Roman writers and seen in the practical politics of the day. In *On the Commonwealth* and *On Laws* Roman philosopher and statesman Cicero devises his ideal republic, which consists of classes of individuals. Drawing upon Plato, Cicero describes some individuals or magistrates as more fit to rule than others, with fitness resting in the natural aptitudes of individuals as revealed through education. In his writings, Cicero draws upon the tripart monarchy, aristocracy, and democracy distinction, describing them and their perversions (tyranny, oligarchy, and mob rule) in terms of which class rules. This sixfold distinction would remain tremendously influential throughout the Middle Ages as political thinkers employed it to explain political authority.

CLASS IN MODERN POLITICAL THOUGHT

The beginning of more modern conceptions of class begins with eighteenth-century French philosopher Jean-Jacques Rousseau. In his *Discourse on the Origins of Inequality*, he implicitly criticizes the social contract tradition of seventeenth-century English philosophers Thomas Hobbes and John Locke to explain the origins and legitimacy of political society.

Instead of seeing society resting upon the voluntary consent of individuals, either to protect themselves against the threat of anarchy (as with Hobbes), or to defend their natural rights against the inconveniences of the state of nature (Locke), Rousseau contends that political society finds its origins in private property and in the rich tricking the poor into believing that joining a political community would be to their advantage. Rousseau set the stage for describing political society as divided by class in economic terms, with the state serving the interests of the rich against the poor.

German philosopher Georg Friedrich Hegel's *Philosophy of Right* (1820) describes the state in class terms, seeing it as a mediator of class conflict. However, his *Phenomenology of Spirit* (1807) takes class analysis another step further, with self-consciousness becoming an important concept. Here, in his famous battle for supremacy between master and slave, each seeks to have the other recognize his superiority. It is not until the slave realizes that he is capable of seeing his own work as the source of his alienated existence that he becomes self-consciously aware of his role in society. This realization occurs as a result of his struggle with his master. Through struggle, in Hegel's view, one becomes aware of one's own existence, and with this self-consciousness, the slave can eventually subdue the master and reverse their roles.

Both Rousseau and Hegel argued that class underlines political divisions and that through struggle one group, the lower class, will acquire the knowledge or awareness of their servitude or subjection, paving the way for some liberation or revolution to free them. This is how Karl Marx came to understand the significance of the writings of Rousseau and Hegel.

MARX AND CLASS
Modern conceptions of class analysis really emerge with Marx. Near the beginning of his 1848 *Communist Manifesto,* Marx states that the "history of all hitherto existing society is the history of class struggles" (Tucker, 1978, 473). Here, as well as in the *German Ideology,* Marx develops a theory of history and politics rooted in class conflict, particularly analyzing such relations within an industrial capitalist society. In Marx's model of society, material economic forces of production are the driving force of history. Changing modes of production lead to new forms of class alignments, dominant ideologies, and political structures. Consistent with Hegel's master-slave struggle, Marx argues that class struggles produce dominant groups and ideologies. In capitalism, two classes have emerged—the bourgeoisie and the proletariat. Bourgeois society sprouted from feudal society and the bourgeoisie from its burghers. Capitalism had produced the proletariat.

In his *Grundrisse,* Marx argues that, in capitalism, class can be understood relationally. The bourgeoisie own the means of production whereas the proletariat, as Marx states in *Wage, Labor, and Capital,* sells its labor power for wages. Class thus is an objective term that can be defined via one's relationship to the ownership of the means of production. If, as Marx states in the *Manifesto,* the "history of all past society has consisted in the development of class antagonisms, antagonisms that

assumed different forms at different epochs," then class conflict in a capitalist society emerges in several ways. First, Marx asserts that the state serves class interests. The job of the state is to enforce bourgeois authority. Workers battle the bourgeoisie for state control. Second, the battle between workers and the owners of the means of production replicates Hegel's master-slave dialectic, with capitalism producing the seeds of its own destruction (i.e., proletarian class consciousness).

In Marx's view, the bourgeoisie seek profit maximization by purchasing the labor power of workers, extracting the surplus value from them for their profits. For Marx, surplus value is the difference between the value the bourgeoisie pay the workers for their labor power and what it is really worth. The competitive drive for profits forces owners constantly to revolutionize the modes of production. Capitalists replace workers with machines and other labor–saving devices. But as capitalism matures, the drive for profit accelerates, and there is a need to replace organic or human capital with machines. This process results in an increasing loss of jobs, producing increased misery and poverty among workers. The decline in the use of human labor power also leads to a falling rate of profit because surplus value cannot be extracted from machines in the same way it can be from workers. To offset declining profits, even more machines must be employed.

According to Marx, the displacement and resulting misery of workers encourages the demise of capitalism. It forces ownership into fewer and fewer hands, thereby negating the concept of private property. The development of monopolies undermines market competition. Finally, the struggle with the proletariat will cause the workers, who have developed consciousness of their class, to organize as a party. At some point, the proletariat, with the Communist Party to lead them, will develop the revolutionary self-awareness as a class and use their political power to take political power from the bourgeoisie. This final battle between the workers and owners results in a victory for the former, with socialism and eventually communism structuring the new, classless society.

Class struggle is the heart of a Marxist analysis of political society. In Marx's works, the economic struggle between workers and the owners of the means of production seems to produce the requisite class consciousness for revolution, but while Marx believed consciousness would emerge out of struggles and the changing modes of production, his use of the concept of class was more a tool of analysis than an iron law that history would follow. In the political views of Friedrich Engels, Marx's chief collaborator, there is more determinism as to how class antagonisms would lead to a revolution. Engels viewed Marx's claims about class struggles almost as if they were scientific laws that had to be followed. In his analysis, the class struggle of capitalism would necessarily produce a communist revolution.

CLASS AND THE MARXIST TRADITION AFTER MARX
After Marx, Marxists such as Karl Kautsky, Eduard Bernstein, and Rosa Luxembourg expressed differing views over

Workers in Tbilisi, Georgia, gather in 1986 before portraits of, from left, Karl Marx, Friedrich Engels, and Vladimir Lenin. Marx, Engels, and Lenin held class struggle at the heart of their political theories.

SOURCE: © John Van Hasselt/Sygma/Corbis

whether parliamentary politics or revolution was the direction of class conflict. Yet among Marxists, Russian Communist leader Vladimir Lenin is among the most important.

Lenin describes class struggle as a theoretical, political, and practical economic battle. In "What Is to Be Done? Burning Questions of Our Movement," Lenin contends that the development of class consciousness is not automatic as Marx, or at least Engels, suggest. Without outside intervention, class consciousness may never rise beyond a level of trade union consciousness, and it was the role of party to become the dialectic of change to bring class consciousness to workers. Class consciousness can be brought to workers only from outside the economic struggle (economism). In "Two Tactics of Social Democracy," Lenin proposes a role for the Communist Party: to transform the bourgeois revolution against the tzar into a proletarian revolution. This involved workers taking over the battle and changing it into one that first fells the tzar and then the bourgeoisie. Leon Trotsky, in his *Permanent Revolution,* makes similar arguments.

In "State and Revolution," Lenin contends that the state is the product and manifestation of the irreconcilability of class antagonisms. State power is used to oppress classes. The vote is not enough to destroy capitalism; violent revolution is needed. The Communist Party, upon seizing control, would need to institute a dictatorship of the proletariat to suppress bourgeois relations and power. Finally, Lenin's *Imperialism* depicts a new stage of international capitalism. The struggles for class control were not simply to be fought in one state at a time. If capitalism was to become international, so too would class battles.

Lenin's employment of Marxism was critical for class analysis. It justified the development of a vanguard to lead the workers to revolution, and beyond, after victory over the capitalists had succeeded. Second, it emphasized revolution over parliamentary tactics. Third, it saw class battles as international, even though the establishment of the Soviet Union demonstrated that socialism would or could be built one country at a time. While the First and Second Internationals demonstrated a class solidarity in terms of workers across national boundaries, such unity ended with the nationalism of World War I (1914–1918).

After Lenin, Marxists continued to use class as a basis of their analysis of politics and society, often disagreeing over how, exactly, class consciousness emerges. Italian political leader and political theorist Antonio Gramsci, between 1929 and 1935, wrote in his *Prison Notebooks* that the state is the entire ensemble of relations and activities by which the ruling class maintains power and control. The state itself cannot simply achieve consent with force, but must convince workers to obey its rules. The state represents an unstable equilibrium of power among classes, with the ruling class achieving a hegemony in civil society via its laws. Class battles are also over ideas in an effort to capture control of the state. Georgy Lukács, in his 1920 influential *History and Class Consciousness,* also sought to understand what it would take for workers to be moved to revolutionary activity. He asserts that once workers have developed consciousness for themselves, they will act.

Lukács states, "For a class to be ripe for hegemony means that its interests and consciousness enable it to organize the whole of society in accordance with those interests." Which class possesses consciousness at the decisive moment? This is the major question that determines who will secure political power. Theorist Nico Poulantzas asserts that social classes are not simply the product of the modes of production. They are part of superstructure along with the state. Only classes have power (ability to objectively realize self), and the state gets its power from classes. In the view of Poulantzas, the state is a power center, much like Gramsci asserts, and it represents the political interests of dominant class. The significance of these arguments by Gramsci, Lukács, and Poulantzas was not to deny class as a dominant force of conflict in politics, but instead to assert and analyze various ways this form of class conflict manifested and could be fought in capitalism. Specifically, class battles could be fought out ideologically, in the press and popular culture, and in other venues such as the arts or sporting events between the United States, the Soviet Union, and their allies.

MAX WEBER AND CLASS AS SOCIAL STATUS

While the concept of class in politics came to be dominated by a Marxist analysis from the middle of the nineteenth century, another conception of this term also emerged in writings of sociologists such as Émile Durkheim and Max Weber. Their use of class produced an analysis that conveyed more about life chances or social status than political action.

Max Weber's discussion in his 1924 work "Class, Status, and Party" offers the strongest and most powerful contrast to the Marxist conceptions of class. Weber defines *class* as a number of people who have in common a specific causal component of life chances, defined exclusively by economic interests under the conditions of the commodity or labor markets. Class is still defined in relation to the market, but class is about status. It is about the overall prospects one has for life success, regardless of whether one works or owns the means of production. Class is about one's social economic status (SES), which may include income, education, and other measures of status in a society.

Marx and Weber agreed that class was based in unequal distributions of economic power, but for Weber economics was not enough. Weber linked class to status and honor to produce a status group. Moreover, Weber rejected the concept of class interest and of Marxists who argued that individuals may be wrong about interests. Weber also was critical of the notion of a class struggle, particularly the idea that all in the same class will react the same way. A similar SES does not necessarily produce the same outlook in life. The implications of a Weberian in contrast to a Marxist class analysis are significant. For Marxists, class is a structural institution that divides and organizes political power and individuals. For Weberians, class is potentially one variable, along with gender, race, or religion, that describes society and provides insights into individual attitudes.

CLASS IN A POSTCOMMUNIST AND POSTMODERN ERA

In addition to facing competition from Weberians, Marxist notions of class were threatened by three events after World War II (1939–1945): the emergence of identity politics, the collapse of Soviet Marxism, and the rise of postmodernism.

The civil rights movements of the 1950s and 1960s in the United States and around the world brought new and renewed attention to racism and sexual domination. While Marxists depicted class as the primary form of conflict in society, others began to analyze ways to reconcile class with gender, race, and other forms of discrimination and exploitation. Iris Young and other feminists saw patriarchy as a problem in capitalism and did not find class analysis sufficient in discussions regarding sexual exploitation and the market. Feminist theorist Sandra Harding went further in claiming that perhaps Marxism was blind to sexism. Both asked if sexual exploitation was inherent to capitalism, not for reasons that class could explain, but for others. Efforts to merge Marxism with feminism thus produced new lines of inquiry that suggested possible inadequacies in traditional Marxist analysis. Scholars who analyzed race, and eventually those examining sexual orientation, made similar criticisms.

Political events in the 1980s and 1990s also damaged class analysis. First, British and American voting based on class declined in the era of British prime minister Margaret Thatcher and U.S. president Ronald Reagan. Second, the imposition of martial law in Poland to suppress the solidarity labor movement in the early 1980s demonstrated to many that class had not disappeared within socialist countries. Third, and conversely, the collapse of Soviet Marxism and the end of the cold war in the early 1990s dealt a serious blow to Marxist class analysis. The fall of the Berlin Wall and the demise of the Soviet Union suggested that Marx was wrong, and therefore his entire method of inquiry, including class analysis, was incorrect.

The rise of identity politics and the collapse of Soviet Marxism fed into supporting postmodern claims that grand narratives such as the analysis of class were dead. Postmodernism denied the objectivity of class interests and instead argued that the economy does not automatically produce this type of conflict. In *Hegemony and Socialist Strategy,* Ernesto Laclau and Chantal Mouffe argue that politics constitute and determine the type of conflicts and interests that will be given at any time. Thus, the antagonisms of capitalism do not necessarily give rise to class conflict. According to Laclau and Mouffe, Marxists were confused in that not all antagonisms are contradictions: Antagonisms are external to society, not internal as are contradictions. Social or political antagonisms, such as racism or sexism, are limits on society, dictating the types of struggles that will or can occur. Moreover, the political struggles in late capitalism differ from those of the nineteenth century. Past successes in addressing some of the worst economic problems of capitalism have made the struggle against capitalism less popular. There is no longer a center for political struggle but, instead, many points of conflict beyond class, including the new antagonisms of race and gender identity. Radical or progressive politics must reorient around numerous struggles and not simply class if they are to remain relevant to the lives of the oppressed at the end of the twentieth and beginning of the twenty-first centuries.

Contemporary conceptions of class are closer to Weberian than Marxist notions of the term. UK sociologist Gordon Marshall contends that class is no longer a political concept in the Marxist sense, but it is still used as an explanatory variable. In the use of class as a research program, there is no Marxist theory of history, class exploitation, class-based collective action, and no reductionist theory of political action based on a theory of class interests. Class is employed in a far more limited fashion that examines its connections to mobility, education, and political partisanship. In research by scholars such as J. H. Goldthorpe, one now finds differentiation of classes based on market positions similar to classifications of occupations. Class thus remains a useful concept in political analysis but it is used far more in terms of SES than as a structural force dividing society.

See also *Class Consciousness, Envy, and Conflict; Communism; Communism, Fall of, and End of History; Engels, Friedrich; Feminist Political Theory; Gramsci, Antonio; Hegel, Georg W. F.; Lenin,*

Vladimir Illich; Leninism; Lukács, Gyorgy; Marx, Karl; Marxism; Postmodernism; Poulantzas, Nicos; Proletariat; Socialism; Weber, Max.

. . . . DAVID SCHULTZ

BIBLIOGRAPHY

Abendroth, Wolfgang. *A Short History of the European Working Class.* New York: Monthly Review Press, 1973.

Bernstein, Eduard. *Evolutionary Socialism.* New York: Schocken Books, 1978.

Bloch, Ernst. "Nonsynchronism and the Obligation to Its Dialectics." *New German Critique* 11 (Spring 1977): 22–38.

Dahrendorf, Ralf. *Class and Class Conflict in Industrial Society.* Stanford: Stanford University Press, 1957.

Durkheim, Émile. *The Division of Labor in Society,* translated by George Simpson. New York: Free Press, 1964.

Erickson, R., and J. H. Goldthorpe. *The Constant Flux.* Oxford: Clarendon Press, 1992.

Gramsci, Antonio. *Selections From the Prison Notebooks of Antonio Gramsci,* Edited by Quintin Hoare and Geffrey Nowell Smith. New York: International Publishers, 1980.

Harding, Sandra. "What Is the Real Material Base of Patriarchy and Capital? In *Women and Revolution,* edited by Lydia Sargent, 135–163. London: Pluto Press, 1986.

Hegel, Georg W. F. *Hegel's Phenomenology of Spirit,* translated by A.V. Miller. New York: Oxford University Press, 1985.

———. *Hegel's Philosophy of Right,* translated by T. M. Knox. New York: Oxford University Press, 1967.

Kautsky, Karl. *The Class Struggle.* New York: W. W. Norton, 1971.

Laclau, Ernesto, and Chantal Mouffe. *Hegemony and Socialist Strategy: Toward a Radical Democratic Politics.* New York: Verso, 1985.

Lenin, Vladimir. "What Is to Be Done? Burning Questions of Our Movement." In *The Lenin Anthology,* edited by Robert C. Tucker, 12–114. New York: W. W. Norton, 1976.

Lukács, Georg. *History and Class Consciousness,* translated by Rodney Livingstone. Cambridge, Mass.: MIT Press, 1968.

Marshall, Gordon. *Repositioning Class: Social Inequality in Industrial Societies.* Thousand Oaks, Calif.: Sage Publications, 1997.

Marx, Karl. "Communist Manifesto." In *The Marx-Engles Reader,* edited by Robert C. Tucker, 473–500. New York: W. W. Norton, 1978.

Parsons, Talcott. *The Social System.* New York: Free Press, 1951.

Poulantzas, Nico. *Political Power and Social Classes.* New York: Verso, 1978.

Rousseau, Jean-Jacques. *The First and Second Discourses,* translated by Roger D. and Judith R. Masters. New York: St. Martin's Press, 1964.

Tucker, Robert C. *The Marx-Engels Reader.* New York: W. W. Norton, 1978.

Weber, Max. "Class, Status, Party." In *From Max Weber,* translated by H. H. Gerth and C. Wright Mills, 180–195. New York: Oxford University Press, 1979.

Wright, Eric Olin. *Class Counts: Comparative Studies in Class Analysis.* New York: Cambridge University Press, 1997.

Young, Iris. "Beyond the Unhappy Marriage: A Critique of the Dual Systems Theory. In *Women and Revolution,* edited by Lydia Sargent, 43–69. London: Pluto Press, 1986.

Class Consciousness, Envy, and Conflict

Throughout the twentieth century, class played a central role in the politics of the advanced capitalist democracies. The accommodation of an increasingly conscious working class was a major preoccupation of national politics, and the development of class compromises largely conditioned the development of the welfare state and industrial regulations. Industrial states sought to contain class conflict, which are ultimately distributive conflicts, in the political sphere to head off more revolutionary politics. Thus, the extent of working class mobilization and organization influences the development of welfare and regulative institutions.

MARX'S CLASS CONFLICT THEORY

Considerable debate exists over what constitutes a class, what class interests are, and what causes class conflicts to occur. The most well-known theory to advance a central role for class consciousness and conflict in politics is that of Karl Marx. Marx defines classes in terms of the nature of their relations to the means of production, leading to a two-part class structure. The bourgeoisie is the class that owns and controls the means of production, making it the class of capitalists. On the other hand, there is the proletariat, which consists of those who don't own capital and who are dependent on the sale of their labor for survival. The conflict between these two classes arises from the fact that the bourgeoisie depends on the exploitation of the proletariat for its income. Exploitation is understood here in the technical sense of extracting labor from the proletariat.

In the Marxist picture, class conflict will result from the proletariat's development of class consciousness. This occurs when the proletariat becomes aware of the objective interest rooted in its material position due to a worsening of its condition. The objective interest of the proletariat is to end its exploitation, which is due to their nonownership of the means of production, and to therefore abolish private property. For Marx, the development of class consciousness is a necessary aspect of capitalist logic and development that compels the increasing immiseration of the proletariat. Class conflict does not concern the distribution of wealth—which Marx considers false consciousness—but concerns the nature of the property regime itself. Thus, envy plays a small motivational role in Marxist class theory because the disadvantaged class does not crave what the advantaged class has, but wants to end its exploitation and create an *egalitarian* system of ownership. Marxist class conflict cannot be contained in the democratic politics of the liberal state. It is, rather, revolutionary in nature, compelling the overthrow of the capitalist state and property regime.

However, Marxist class theory failed to predict many of the dynamics of class consciousness and conflict working against class revolution. The working class did not mobilize on the basis of an interest regarding its relationship to the means of production but rather on the basis of its distributive share and treatment. As such, it did not lead to revolutionary politics but to a distributive conflict contained in democratic politics. Moreover, capitalist development in the twentieth century did not lead to the steady immiseration of the proletariat but instead to the uneven improvement of its material condition. The narrow definition of a class is at the heart of Marxism's problems in predicting and accounting for the nature of class consciousness or conflict. Its concept of class lacked a connection between class position and the actual life chances and experiences of its members. Defining class on the basis of relationships to the means of production cannot account for the interests of, for example, the salaried white-collar classes or for those of the industrial middle class.

WEBERIAN CLASS THEORY

The second major approach to class consciousness and conflict, that of Max Weber and neo-Weberians, attempts to make up for deficiencies in Marxist class theory. For Weber, ownership of capital—or lack of it—is one of a number of *market capacities* that determine individuals' class position, which also includes skills and education. The possession of market capacities constitutes one's market situation so that one's class position is "determined by the amount and kind of power, or lack of such, to dispose of goods or skills for the sake of income in a given economic order." For Weber, class positions are defined by an overlap of the objective features of individuals' class situations, life chances or "the typical chance for a supply of goods, external living conditions, and personal life experiences."

For Weber, class conflict arises on the basis of growing class consciousness. *Class structure* refers to objective positional categories based on the distribution of life chances—shared class situations. The class structure is the "raw material" of class interests rather than the conscious understanding of interests by a group of similarly situated people. *Class formation* refers to the processes in which subjective experience and awareness of the fatefulness of positions within the class structure come to be shared by its members. Class formation is, thus, the creation of a collective identity based on a mutually perceived interest in altering the class structure. *Class conflict* occurs through class formation and concerns the distribution of market capacities and life chances. Unlike Marx's theory of class conflict, Weberian class conflict can be contained in the liberal democratic state given because it does not concern relationships to the means of production and the distribution of life chances generated by the market and the capitalist state.

See also *Class and Politics; Marx, Karl; Marxism; Poverty; Weber, Max.*

. . . . NEIL HIBBERT

BIBLIOGRAPHY

Esping-Andersen, Gosta. *Politics Against Markets: The Social Democratic Road to Power.* Princeton: Princeton University Press, 1985.
Giddens, Anthony. *The Class Structure of the Advanced Societies.* London: Hutchinson, 1973.
Marx, Karl, and Frederick Engels. *The Communist Manifesto,* edited by E. Hobsbawm. New York: Verso, 1985.
Weber, Max. *From Max Weber.* New York: Oxford University Press, 1946.
Wright, Erik Olin. *Classes.* London: Verso, 1985.

Clericalism

Clericalism is generally used as a pejorative term to describe the position of church hierarchy in society and the attitude of clerics toward the laity. It often denotes undue influence in worldly affairs on the part of ordained religious functionaries, but most commonly—especially in contemporary usage—indicates an overemphasis on the status, privileges, and special role of religious officials, with an eye to the failings and abuses stemming therefrom. While this perception of church institutions and leadership has existed in various manifestations and with varying intensity across the centuries, the term itself did not arise until the second half of the nineteenth century, in juxtaposition to the similarly modern neologism *anticlericalism.* Its association with church critics is reflected in its most famous invocation, French politician Léon Gambetta's claim that "Le cléricalisme—voilà l'ennemi!" (Clericalism is the enemy!)

The concept of clericalism implies a distinction between ordained religious officials, or clergy, and nonordained members of the faith, or laity. Such a distinction is found to different degrees in many religions, though the Roman Catholic Church has been the principle target for the charge of clericalism. While some might identify the distinction between clergy and laity itself as the fundamental problem, the pejorative use of the term clericalism generally suggests that the clergy has overstepped or corrupted a theoretically legitimate role, usually at the expense of active lay participation in communal religious life.

Clericalism indicates excessive focus on ritual, hierarchy, and deference to clerical opinion, which is seen as fostering a conservative, self-seeking mentality on the part of clergy that distances them from the problems of everyday life, renders them hostile to human progress, and interferes with their responsibility to serve the religious community and ability to champion secular reform. Among those who are more sympathetic to the church, use of he term may imply a contrast between a somewhat idealized early church, closely attuned to the lifestyle and needs of the laity, and the subsequent abasement brought on by the accumulation of power and overly defensive reactions to the major secular and religious developments of the modern world. In recent times, clericalism has received renewed attention following the sex scandal within the Catholic Church and the evident lack of accountability facilitated by clerical status.

See also *Anticlericalism; Confessional Parties; Laicite; Secularism; Theocracy.*

. . . . BENJAMIN PAULI

BIBLIOGRAPHY

Flynn, Frederick E. "Clericalism, Anti-Clericalism." *Commonweal* 58 (April 1953): 43–47.
Sánchez, José. *Anticlericalism: A Brief History.* Notre Dame, Ind.: University of Notre Dame Press, 1972.
Taylor, Charles. "Clericalism." *Cross Currents* 10, no. 4 (1960): 327–336.

Clientelism

Clientelism is a form of political organization based on informal dyadic relationships between patrons and clients. The asymmetric relationship between patrons and clients has both instrumental and affective dimensions. In instrumental terms, patrons, typically powerful and wealthy, provide their relatively weaker and poorer clients with material benefits, protection, or both in exchange for political loyalty, personal services, or both. Political loyalty frequently means votes for the patron or the patron's chosen candidate; personal services can include labor. Besides security, patrons may offer clients access to public or party resources, ranging from jobs and scholarships to gifts of food.

Many scholars have argued that clientelism also rests on affective ties between patrons and clients, although American anthropologist and historian Eric Wolf has described clientelism as clearly a "lopsided friendship." Clientelist relations are highly personal; a critical norm in the relationship is loyalty. Clientelism can be contrasted to bureaucratic universalism and market rationality as forms of social organization, and hence is often found in areas of lesser socioeconomic development or in polities with weak states unable to provide protection and public service to ordinary people. In modern democracies and electoral authoritarian regimes, however, political machines practice clientelism in both urban and rural areas.

See also *Clientelistic Parties in Latin America; Latin American Politics and Society.*

. . . . JOSEPH L. KLESNER

Clientelistic Parties in Latin America

Clientelism is a pervasive feature of Latin American politics and is exhibited in varying degrees by most parties. Douglas Chalmers notes that clientelistic networks in Latin America are vertically organized from top to bottom and rely on the presence of *brokers*, political operatives who aggregate demands from their communities and distribute the benefits provided by the center. Although clientelism has been traditionally associated with face-to-face interactions, these brokers enable clientelistic parties to develop links with a broader segment of the population without establishing personal contact. After all, as Herbert Kitschelt argues, these face-to-face interactions are only one extreme of the patron-client relationship continuum; anonymous party machines provide the other extreme. In both cases, however, communities rich in votes but poor in resources receive selective material incentives in exchange for their votes. Clientelistic parties, Kitschelt contends, build multilevel political machines that go from the top of the political center down to remote municipalities. These parties do not purse specific political or ideological agendas (what Kitschelt calls "programmatic linkages") but instead rely on the provision of selective incentives to garner electoral support.

The best representative of clientelistic parties in Latin America is Mexico's Institutional Revolutionary Party, or PRI (its Spanish initials). Founded in 1928 under a different name, the PRI became the official party of the revolution and established a one-party rule regime that lasted until 2000. The PRI successfully combined clientelism with a corporatist mode of interest representation by incorporating many labor and civil society organizations into the party, thus turning them into de facto state organizations. The PRI used its governmental monopoly to dispense favors to key constituents groups including labor, peasant, and state employee unions. *Caciques*, local brokers with strong influence in their communities, became crucial to the longevity of PRI rule. But caciques were not total instruments of the party higher-ups as they retained significant sources of local power. Other examples of parties that built powerful clientelistic networks based on their access to state resources include Venezuela's *Acción Democrática,* Costa Rica's *Partido Liberación Nacional,* and the *Peronist* party in Argentina.

Many populist leaders created clientelistic parties as a result of their efforts to build durable electoral support. Some of these parties achieved a small degree of organizational consistency and managed to survive the death of their leaders. In other cases, the parties had no organizational structure and failed to outlast their founders. In Brazil, for instance, Getulio Vargas, a populist leader, created organizations that achieved some life of their own. In 1945, after leaving office, Vargas founded two parties (the *Partido Trabalhista Brasileiro* and the *Partido Social Democrático*) that relied largely on the clientelistic networks he developed during his *Estado Novo* (1937–1945) regime. In Ecuador, by contrast, José María Velasco Ibarra, populist leader *par excellence,* created vast clientelistic networks that supported his five successful bids for the presidency but failed to create a party of his own. His followers, known as *Velasquistas,* worked in alliance with different parties that offered electoral support to their leader at different points in time. Also in Ecuador, a more structured clientelistic party was founded in 1949 by a local caudillo in the city of Guayaquil under the name of *Concentración de Fuerzas Populares.*

The dramatic changes that the region has undergone in recent decades have weakened but not eliminated clientelism or clientelistic parties. In the 1990s, neopopulist leaders resorted to clientelistic practices in an effort to gain political support in a time of painful economic restructuring. In an ironic twist, radical market reforms implemented to reduce the role of the state in the economy then provided governments with the opportunity to establish state-funded food and job programs that turned into vast clientelistic operations. In Mexico and Peru, PRONASOL and FENDECODES, respectively, became the best-known examples of state clientelism in the neoliberal era, working in close association with the PRI in Mexico and Alberto Fujimori's electoral vehicles in Peru. The practices were not clientelistic in *all* communities, yet, especially when cash transfers were involved, clearly were clientelistic in some of them. They were clientelistic to the extent that they provided selective incentives (scholarships, credit, granaries, livestock, and minor consumption goods) to some rather than to all of the community members. In the Peruvian case, Norbert Schady shows that clientelistic practices became more prevalent as opposition to the Fujimori regime mounted. More recently, Hugo Chávez replicated this model in Venezuela. His social programs, known as the *Misiones,* resorted to clientelistic practices aiming to shore up his electoral support as he confronted a tough recall election in 2004.

The well-documented demise of political parties in the region has not eliminated clientelism; it has only decentralized the sources of patronage. Brokers now find it more convenient to establish their own political organizations, or strike alliances with other regional brokers, rather than to pledge allegiance to declining national parties. Even when they do link up with national parties, many of these brokers act as independent operators, sharing only a party label with other brokers. An extreme case of this frequent occurrence is found in Colombia with their Liberal Party.

See also *Latin American Political Thought; Latin American Politics and Society.*

. . . .   JULIO F. CARRIÓN

BIBLIOGRAPHY

Chalmers, Douglas. "Parties and Society in Latin America." In *Friends, Followers, and Factions: A Reader in Political Clientelism,* edited by Steffen W. Schmidt, James C. Scott, Carl Landé, and Laura Guasti, 401–421. Berkeley: University of California Press, 1977.

Cornelius, Wayne. *Politics and the Migrant Poor in Mexico City.* Stanford: Stanford University Press, 1975.

Kitschelt, Herbert. "Linkages between Citizens and Politicians in Democratic Politics." *Comparative Political Studies* 33, no. 6/7 (2000): 845–879.

Magaloni, Beatriz, Alberto Diaz-Cayeros, and Federico Estévez. "Clientelism and Portfolio Diversification: A Model of Electoral Investment with Application to Mexico." In *Patrons, Clients, and Policies,* edited by Herbert Kitschelt and Steven Wilkinson, 182–205. Cambridge: Cambridge University Press, 2007.

Penfold-Becerra, Michael. "Clientelism and Social Funds: Evidence from Chávez's Misiones." *Latin American Politics and Society* 49, no. 4 (2007): 63–85.

Pizarro, Eduardo. "La atomización partidaria en Colombia: el fenómeno de las microempresas electorales." In *Degradación o cambio. Evolución del sistema político colombiano,* edited by Francisco Gutierrez. Bogotá: Norma, 2002.

Roncagliolo, Rafael, and Carlos Meléndez. *La política por dentro: Cambios y continuidades en las organizaciones políticas de los países andinos.* Lima: IDEA Internacional, 2007.

Schady, Norbert. "The Political Economy of Expenditures by the Peruvian Social Fund, 1991–1995." *American Political Science Review* 94, no. 2 (2000): 289–304.

Climate Change Conferences, United Nations

The involvement of the United Nations in the issue of climate change began through its specialized agency, the World Meteorological Organization (WMO) that, in 1969, called for a global network for monitoring pollutants suspected of contributing to climate change. Increasing international scientific attention to climate change and severe, decadal drought in the Sahel region of Africa led the WMO to convene the First World Climate Conference in 1979. The conference statement called for international cooperation to advance understanding of climate and climate change and established the World Climate Program to collect data and coordinate climate change research at the domestic level. This served as an impetus for a number of countries to develop national climate research programs.

GROWING MOMENTUM IN 1980S

There were a number of smaller international meetings in the 1980s, the most important of which was held in Villach, Austria, in 1985. Sponsored by the WMO, United Nations Environment Program (UNEP), and the International Council of Scientific Unions, the conference is seen as a major turning point in climate change science and policy as it provided international scientific consensus as to the magnitude of the issue, potential social and economic consequences, and urged states to take action to develop policy recommendations to mitigate climate change.

A group of scientists emerging from the Villach conference became active in developing a science and policy network that was instrumental in organizing the 1988 World Conference on the Changing Atmosphere in Toronto, sponsored by the Government of Canada, WMO, and UNEP. The Toronto conference was the first with an explicit political dimension and a strong conference declaration; this included a proposal that governments cut the 1988 level of carbon dioxide emissions by 20 percent by 2005, and that eventually emissions would need to be stabilized at 50 percent of existing levels.

What is notable about these first climate conferences is that they were by invitation only and were predominantly attended by scientists. The attendees were not official delegates of their respective countries and the conference statements, while calls to action, were neither negotiated nor agreed to by the participants' home states, nor were they binding. Nevertheless, the Toronto recommendations are cited as the basis for Germany's 25 to 30 percent carbon dioxide reduction goal affirmed in 1990, a key factor in generating concern for climate change in Canada, and triggered congressional action in the Untied States.

INTERGOVERNMENTAL PANEL ON CLIMATE CHANGE

Recognizing the need for climate change policies and recommendations to go through diplomatic processes, the Intergovernmental Panel on Climate Change (IPCC) was formed through a United Nations General Assembly (UNGA) resolution after the Toronto Conference in 1988. Its goals were to organize scientific information, evaluate risk from climate change, and consider mitigation strategies to inform treaty negotiations in establishing a convention on climate change. Governments had much greater control over the IPCC, as they selected experts and placed high-ranking foreign ministry officials in key positions.

Subsequent to the release of the first IPCC report, the Second World Conference on Climate Change was held in 1990. This meeting had both scientific and diplomatic components, with declarations reflecting the two groups' positions. The scientific, or technical, declaration was a strong call for action. While the ministerial declaration advocated action, it did not set time frames as more formal treaty negotiating process had been scheduled by the time the conference was held. In December 1990, the UNGA established the Intergovernmental Negotiating Committee to negotiate the United Nations Framework Convention on Climate Change (UNFCCC). The convention was opened for signature at the Rio United Nations Conference on the Environment and Development Earth Summit in June 1992, where it received 155 signatures.

TABLE 1: MAJOR UNITED NATIONS CLIMATE CHANGE CONFERENCES, 1995 TO 2009

YEAR	COP	LOCATION	OUTCOME
1995	COP1	Berlin	Berlin Mandate established a two-year period to analyze and evaluate a suite of policy instruments from which member countries could choose initiatives to suit their needs and capabilities.
1996	COP2	Geneva	Parties endorsed the IPCC second assessment, agreed to flexible rather than harmonized solutions, and called for medium-term targets.
1997	COP3	Kyoto	Kyoto Protocol negotiated, and binding targets established through 2012.
1998	COP4	Buenos Aires	Talks fell short of addressing unresolved issues from Kyoto Protocol, yet established two-year Buenos Aires Plan of Action to develop implementation mechanisms.
1999	COP5	Bonn	Largely technical discussions surrounded implementation mechanisms.
2000	COP6	The Hague	Negotiations broke down over including areas as carbon sinks and appropriate sanctions. Meeting reconvened six months later in Bonn.
2001	COP6, resumed	Bonn	Agreement reached in significant areas: (1) carbon sinks including reforestation and cropland management; (2) sanctions for not attaining carbon reduction goals; (3) flexibility mechanisms, including emissions trading, joint implementation and clean development mechanisms.
2001	COP7	Marrakech	Marrakech Accords included operational rules for the Kyoto Protocol and set the stage for ratification.
2002	COP8	New Deli	Attempts by EU countries to increase obligations of parties to UNFCCC were unsuccessful.
2003	COP9	Milan	Primary focus was on technical details of the Kyoto Protocol.
2004	COP10	Buenos Aires	Technical details dominated, and discussions of post-Kyoto actions began.
2005	COP11/CMP1	Montreal	Kyoto Protocol came into force; first Meeting of the Parties (CMP) follows COP11. Parties to UNFCCC who had not ratified Kyoto Protocol were given observer status. Montreal Action Plan was developed, focusing on deeper cuts to emissions and what to do after Kyoto Protocol expires in 2012.
2006	COP12/CMP2	Nairobi	Final technical details of Kyoto Protocol were decided. Progress for post-Kyoto strategy continued.
2007	COP13/CMP3	Bali	Bali Action Plan was adopted, setting stage for negotiations for COP15 in Copenhagen where new agreement was to be negotiated.
2008	COP14/CMP4	Poznań	Agreements reached for work program and meeting plan for Copenhagen.
2009	COP15/CMP5	Copenhagen	Key elements of nonbinding Copenhagen Accord included: capping temperature rise to 2 degrees Celsius (3.6 F), verification procedures, US$10 billion/year transfer from richer countries to poorer countries for adaptation and mitigation strategies, rising to US$100 billion by 2020.

CONFERENCES OF THE PARTIES

Since coming into force, the parties to the UNFCCC have met annually at the Conference of the Parties (COP) to negotiate binding commitments, assess progress, and establish principles and mechanisms for addressing climate change (see Table 1). The relative success and impacts of these meetings have varied substantially over time. The outcome of third conference (COP3), the Kyoto Protocol, was perhaps the most significant as it established binding targets through 2012 to Annex 1 (industrialized) countries. However, the world's largest greenhouse gas emitter, the United States, failed to ratify the Kyoto Protocol, and it did not include commitments for major developing countries such as China and India.

With the Kyoto Protocol nearing expiration, the stage was set for a new round of negotiations at Copenhagen in 2009. The Copenhagen Accord fell short of expectations with a nonbinding agreement lacking firm targets for reductions in greenhouse gases. The accord was negotiated by the United States, Brazil, South Africa, India, and China on the final day of the conference and was "taken note of," not "adopted," by the parties to the UNFCCC. Blame for the failure of the negotiations has been attributed to the United States for continuing its stance of not agreeing to binding targets, to China and India for frustrating the process so as to not thwart economic growth, and to the nontransparent process that took place among a limited number of countries in drafting the accord.

See also *Environmental Policy; Environmental Political Theory; Kyoto Protocol; United Nations (UN).*

. . . . BETSI BEEM

BIBLIOGRAPHY

Aldy, J. E., and R. N. Stavins, eds. *Architectures for Agreement: Addressing Global Climate Change in the Post-Kyoto World.* Cambridge: Cambridge University Press, 2007.

Jäger, J. "From Conference to Conference." *Climatic Change* 20, no. 2 (1992): iii–vii.

Ministry of Climate and Energy of Denmark. "COP1–COP14." Ministry of Foreign Affairs of Denmark. www.en.cop15.dk/climate+facts/process/cop1+–+cop14.

Paterson, M. *Global Warming and Global Politics*. London: Routledge, 1996.

Social Learning Group. *Learning to Manage Global Environmental Risks. Vol. 1, A Comparative History of Social Responses to Climate Change, Ozone Depletion, and Acid Rain.* Cambridge, Mass: MIT Press, 2001.

United Nations Framework Convention on Climate Change (UNFCCC). "Decisions of the COP and the COP/CMP." UNFCCC Secretariat. www.unfccc.int/documentation/decisions/items/3597.php.

Cloture

Cloture is a legislative procedure used to stop debate on a motion or bill and force a vote. It was developed in France in order to counter the *filibuster*, a parliamentary tactic used to prevent passage of legislation through continued debate that precludes a final vote. Cloture was introduced into the British parliament in 1882 and requires a vote of at least one hundred members to invoke it. However, the speaker has the authority to disregard cloture. Within parliamentary systems, a restriction on the length of time, or number of sittings, in which a bill can be considered or debated is known as a *guillotine*. Program motions that establish legislative timetables for bills have increasingly replaced guillotines. In the United States, cloture was first used in 1919 and applied only to the Senate, since debate on a bill or motion can be limited in the House of Representatives by the Speaker of the House or the House Rules Committee. In the Senate, cloture initially required a two-thirds majority, or sixty-seven senators, but the rules were changed in 1975 to reduce the required majority to a three-fifths majority vote, or sixty senators. Once cloture is invoked in the Senate, a vote must be taken on the measure within thirty hours.

See also *Filibuster; Question Time; Rules of Order.*

. . . . TOM LANSFORD

Coalition Formation

Coalition formation occupies a central place in the study of party politics and behavior, as well as the formation of governments. Coalition formation in this context is understood as the result of the process of bargaining between political parties (and their leaders), either before or after elections, to form alliances in order to attain and preserve power.

Early scholarship adopted rational choice theory as its framework of reference to account for why and how coalitions form. A key concern appeared to be the importance of size in the formation of coalitions, with later studies shifting attention to the coalition's internal bargaining process. In this regard, *office-seeking* and *policy-seeking* theories have defined classical research on coalition formation from the postwar period to the early 1980s. In both approaches, the focus lies on who (or how many) will form the coalition and how long this will last.

The most influential office-seeking theories are the minimal-winning coalition theory, the minimum-winning coalition theory, and the bargaining proposition theory. According to John Von Neumann and Oskar Morgenstern's minimal-winning coalition theory, a coalition is expected to form at the minimal level below which the coalition government would fail if any of its members were to defect from the coalition itself. Building on the minimal-winning coalition theory, William Riker's minimum-winning coalition theory contends that parties would enter a coalition commanding just over 50 percent of legislative seats to secure office. In Michael Leiserson's bargain proposition theory, efficient coalitions would be those where only the smallest number of parties join the coalition.

Policy-seeking coalition theories have contributed a greater predictive and explanatory power to coalition formation scholarship. Robert Axelrod's minimal connected winning theory (MCW) showed how coalitions would be formed by those actors whose party of affiliation is minimally connected on a single ideological dimension; this kind of coalition would show greater durability, reducing the potential for conflict between the coalition members. Abram De Swaan's closed coalition theory builds on the MCW and highlights how coalitions would form between parties showing the smallest ideological distance.

Two main theoretical innovations have contributed to the growth of coalition formation scholarship in recent years. First, since the 1980s a neoinstitutionalist critique to the dominance of rational choice theory in the study of coalition formation has emphasised that coalition bargaining power is constrained by institutions, including cabinet formation and operation rules, legislative and party rules, and external veto players. Institutions influence the behavior of political actors in their bargaining or decision-making procedures when they form coalitions and allocate portfolios. According to Wolfgang Müller and Kaare Strøm, institutions such as investiture rules or other parliamentary rules have an effect on coalition formation and size.

In addition, multidimensional coalition formation models have moved beyond the traditional single dimension—left-to-right scale—and propose that coalitions would form among parties located within the smallest distance in multiple policies dimensions. According to the core theory, parties stay in the core area of two dimensional policy spaces, and policies can be predicted by observing the behavior of the core party. Ian Budge and Hans Keman contend that if the core party or parties are structurally stable, the coalition government would be able to remain longer in office; unstable core parties would otherwise generate short-lived coalitions and fluctuating policies. Seeking to identify the ideal points among parties' policy preferences in multidimensional policy spaces, Michael Laver and Kenneth Shepsle argue that the ideal point of the median voter is the only point where the majority of voters converge on a given policy issue.

Although the literature has traditionally paid attention to the formation of coalition governments in parliamentary systems, scholars have recently also begun to include the study of coalitions in presidential and semi-presidential systems. One of the central assumptions in coalition formation studies (that political parties be viewed as unitary actors) has also come under criticism due to its neglect of intraparty processes.

Empirically, attention is now being paid to systems outside the traditional geographic areas of interest (Western Europe and the United States). Since the advent of the third wave of democratization, coalition formation has become a tool for political parties to achieve electoral success in East Central Europe, East Asia, and Latin America, resulting in the creation of new empirical data and fresh theoretical insights into the study of why and how coalitions form.

See also *Cabinets and Cabinet Formation; Coalition Theory; Riker, William.*

. . . . YOUNGMI KIM

BIBLIOGRAPHY

Budge, Ian, and Hans Keman. *Parties and Democracy: Coalition Formation and Government Functioning in Twenty States.* Oxford: Oxford University Press, 1990.

Laver, Michael, and Norman Schofield. *Multi Government: The Politics of Coalition in Europe.* Oxford: Oxford University Press, 1990.

Laver, Michael, and Kenneth Shepsle. *Making and Breaking Governments: Cabinets and Legislature in Parliamentary Democracies.* Cambridge: Cambridge University Press, 1996.

Müller, Wolfgang, and Kaare Strøm. *Coalition Governments in Western Europe.* Oxford: Oxford University Press, 2000.

Coalition Theory

Coalitions are "governments in which different parties commit themselves to serving together in the same cabinet and sharing the portfolios that control of the chief executive affords them," according to Kaare Strøm, Wolfgang C. Müller, and Torbjörn Bergman, editors of the 2008 *Cabinets and Coalition Bargaining: The Democratic Life Cycle in Western Europe.* Between 1945 and 2003, nearly five-sixths of all cabinets in Europe's parliamentary and semi-presidential systems constituted such multiparty governments, usually formed in cases where elections did not result in an overall parliamentary majority for a single party.

Coalition theories are a body of propositions designed to explain the dynamics of interparty cooperation in making, running, and breaking multiparty governments. Most theoretical literature on coalitions focuses on their partisan composition; the distribution of executive offices between the participating parties, or *portfolio allocation*; and variations in their duration. Some of this scholarship has been inductive and empirical, often influenced by normative concerns, such as government stability and performance in representative democracies. The more influential tradition has been a deductive and formal one, usually based on game theory, a rationalist theory derived from mathematics focusing on interactive decision making involving at least two actors.

COALITION FORMATION

The key concerns of game-theoretic models of coalition formation have traditionally been (1) the partisan composition of the coalition formed after negotiations between the parties, and (2) the allocation of portfolios. Game theorists have usually modeled political parties in coalition bargaining as unitary actors, either seeking to maximize the number of

top executive offices they hold in government, or to get this government to adopt their preferred policies. Assuming politicians to be office seekers first and foremost, William I. Riker, in his 1962 work *The Theory of Political Coalitions*, predicted the number of parties likely to be included in the government: "In *n*-person, zero-sum games, where side payments are permitted, where players are rational, and they have perfect information, only minimal winning coalitions occur" (32). In other words, in any situation where three or more actors (n-persons) bargain over the formation over a coalition and where one actor's gains (e.g., seats in the cabinet) are exactly balanced by the losses of the other "players," only coalitions will form that control an overall majority of the parliamentary seats, but do not share the spoils of government office with more parties than necessary. The German coalition of Christian Democrats and Social Democrats formed in 2005 under Chancellor Angela Merkel is a minimum-winning coalition: Had only one coalition party withdrawn its support, the government would have lost its parliamentary majority. Although Riker acknowledges that "oversized" coalitions may be formed as an "insurance policy" where the parties operate in an uncertain environment, the "minimal-winning criterion" has remained an influential concept.

Empirical and theoretical critiques of Riker's perspective led to the addition of a policy dimension to many game-theoretic models. In his 1970 book *Conflict of Interest,* Robert Axelrod predicted the formation of *minimal-connected-winning coalitions,* that is, minimal-winning coalitions formed of ideologically adjacent parties. The Italian government formed in 2008 by Prime Minister Silvio Berlusconi, for example, was composed of ideologically "connected" parties of the political right and center right. Later work based on spatial notions of "median" or (ideologically) "central" parties as well as "strong" or "very strong" parties (e.g., Michael Laver and Kenneth Shepsle's 1996 *Making and Breaking Governments: Cabinets and Legislatures in Parliamentary Democracies*) demonstrated how sufficiently large parties could form and sustain even minority cabinets, if they occupied a pivotal position in the policy space. The social democratic Labor Parties of Denmark, Norway, and Sweden occupied such a pivotal position for most of the time since the 1930s. Such models reflected a shift of emphasis from office-seeking assumptions to models focusing on policy preferences as well as office motivations. While especially earlier models analyze patterns of interparty cooperation (e.g., coalitions) and competition in one ideological dimension—usually focusing on the ideological differences between the parties in economic policy—authors such as Norman Schofield made considerable progress in constructing models of coalition politics in two or more dimensions. Although the formation of stable coalitions becomes far more difficult if political competition includes more than one dimension, Schofield demonstrates in the 1995 article, "Coalition Politics," that such a situation does not necessarily lead to theoretical predictions of legislative chaos. Coalitions (and even minority governments) can be stable under such conditions, if there is a *core*—a point representing acceptable compromise policies for all winning coalitions—in the multidimensional ideological space, which the largest or dominant party prefers. Other models sought to add institutional and electoral variables to game-theoretic explanations without losing rigor and generality. Strøm, in *Minority Government and Majority Rule*, for example, demonstrated that the toleration of minority cabinets may be an alternative to direct government participation, if rational parties are modeled as policy-seeking actors, the institutional environment allows minorities to influence policy making, and government participation involves likely electoral costs.

PORTFOLIO ALLOCATION

Like the literature on cabinet composition, early work on portfolio allocation was based on the assumption that political parties can be modeled as motivated by the pursuit of government office, neglecting the possibility of differential values of different portfolios to different parties and possible trade-offs between policy and office benefits. Empirical studies generally confirmed William A. Gamson's 1961 law of proportionality: members of a coalition are predicted to receive cabinet portfolios in proportion to their contribution to the government's parliamentary majority. Models such as Laver and Shepsle's portfolio allocation model sought to overcome the limitations of purely quantitative, office-driven models. For them, parties are driven by policy as well as office motivations. Their model predicts that cabinets will form in equilibrium consisting of parties controlling the median legislator on the most important policy dimensions. These parties will be allocated the relevant portfolio(s), giving their ministers control of policy making in that particular area.

COALITION DURATION

Beyond questions of government membership and portfolio allocation, coalition theories have focused on the decisions of political leaders to continue coalitions to the end of their "natural" term (usually the next election) or, alternatively, to terminate them earlier by changing the coalition's partisan composition, or the person of the prime minister, or by bringing the election date forward, known as strategic parliamentary dissolutions. Early research largely followed the empirical tradition and attempted to identify the main sources of variations in coalition durability in the "structural attributes" of the coalitions themselves (e.g., number of parties or ideological disagreement between them), or in the coalitions' bargaining environment (e.g., the size and polarization of the party system). In the 1980s, influential work challenged this structural perspective, arguing that the duration of coalitions was largely a function of critical events such as crises or scandals. Since the 1990s, a number of game-theoretic models have sought to incorporate such "random shocks" to coalition government and explain variations in the duration of coalitions by modeling the party leaders' decisions to maintain or break coalitions as the result of strategic considerations, focusing on the utility of alternative opportunities of making or influencing policy, the opportunity cost of early terminations, the anticipated costs of early elections, and the anticipated transaction costs of alternative forms of government.

COALITION GOVERNANCE

Finally, there has been a growing body of scholarship in coalition governance since the 1990s, seeking rigorously to model the dynamics of coalition politics after cabinet formation. In such endeavors, ministers are not conceived of as "policy dictators" (as in Laver and Shepsle's model), nor do they have their hands entirely tied by coalition agreements between the parties in government. Their agenda powers may allow them some leeway to move the policy from the agreement initially reached in coalition bargaining towards their own preferred policy position. This potential for *agency loss* can be contained, depending on institutional constraints such as the prime minister's powers, the extent of ministerial autonomy enshrined in the constitution, and commitment and enforcement mechanisms agreed between the parties in coalition treaties (for a survey, see Strøm, Müller, and Bergman's *Cabinets and Coalition Bargaining: The Democratic Life Cycle in Western Europe*, chapters 5 and 8).

Despite its very considerable advances since the 1960s, coalition theory faces a number of challenges. Most importantly, there remains a significant gap between theoretical advances and empirical work, the latter often lagging behind the former in terms of measurement and appropriate statistical estimation techniques. Other challenges include a number of implausible and restrictive assumptions on which some models are still based, for example, the modeling of parties as unitary actors.

See also *Behavioral Game Theory; Cabinets and Cabinet Formation; Coalition Formation; Political Thought, Foundations of.*

. . . . THOMAS SAALFELD

BIBLIOGRAPHY

Axelrod, Robert. *Conflict of Interest.* Chicago: Markham, 1970.

Diermeier, Daniel. "Coalition Government." In *The Oxford Handbook of Political Economy,* edited by Barry R. Weingast and Donald A. Wittman, 162–179. Oxford: Oxford University Press, 2006.

Gamson, William A. "A Theory of Coalition Formation." *American Sociological Review* 26 (1961): 373–382.

Laver, Michael. "Government Termination." *Annual Review of Political Science* 6 (2003): 23–40.

Laver, Michael, and Norman Schofield. *Multiparty Government: The Politics of Coalition in Europe.* Cambridge: Cambridge University Press, 1990.

Laver, Michael, and Kenneth Shepsle. *Making and Breaking Governments: Cabinets and Legislatures in Parliamentary Democracies.* Cambridge: Cambridge University Press, 1996.

Riker, William I. *The Theory of Political Coalitions.* New Haven: Yale University Press, 1962.

Schofield, Norman. "Coalition Politics: A Formal Model and Empirical Analysis." *Journal of Theoretical Politics,* 7 (1995): 245–281.

Strøm, Kaare. *Minority Government and Majority Rule.* Cambridge: Cambridge University Press, 1990.

Strøm, Kaare, Wolfgang C. Müller, and Torbjörn Bergman, eds. *Cabinets and Coalition Bargaining: The Democratic Life Cycle in Western Europe.* Oxford: Oxford University Press, 2008.

Cognitive Theory and Politics

Many models of psychology have been applied to political attitudes and behavior. Psychodynamic models predominated in the early work of scholars such as Harold Lasswell, who sought to apply psychology to politics, and in psychobiographies such as the one conducted of Woodrow Wilson by Alexander and Juliette George. However, as such models were replaced in psychology by behaviorist and later humanist approaches, such analysis fell by the wayside. With the rise of cognitive psychology in the 1980s, new possibilities for application arose. The apex of cognitive theory reached its height in the early 1990s with the work of Amos Tversky and Daniel Kahneman on judgment and decision making. This work reflected a reaction against both behaviorist models that rejected a role for the cognitive processes of the mind, and humanist approaches that privileged affect over thought. The growth and development of such models was potentiated by rapid technological advances offering previously unprecedented ways of accessing mental processes through increasingly precise reaction time tests; electroencephalogram readings, which provided accurate temporal measurements of mental processes; and perhaps reaching their height with the widespread use of function magnetic resonance imaging, which afford tremendous spatial accuracy in brain topography. Ironically, the introduction of this technology served to begin a reintegration of affective models with previously more exclusively cognitive ones.

APPLICATIONS OF COGNITIVE THEORY

Cognitive theories have been employed to help analyze and explain a variety of political phenomena. The most prominent of these have included models used to generate insight into problems related to framing, decision making, identity, and ideology. Cognitive theory has incorporated many elements, including work on memory, attention, perception, and abstract problem solving.

The work on judgment and decision making has proved most relevant to the central questions and problems posed by political scientists. The work on judgmental heuristics includes work on three kinds of biases that affect individuals' assessments of probability, frequency, and likelihood. By and large, these cognitive shortcuts work efficiently and effectively to help organize the world, yet they can also lead to systematic and predictable biases in judgment. Representativeness encourages people to make evaluations based on similarity between a person or an event and the particular category to which it belongs. Robert Jervis has conducted work examining the effect of representativeness in decision making on foreign policy. Arguing against the experimental results based on real-world cases, Jervis argued that decision makers rely on base rate probabilities in rendering judgments about the future because such assessments allow them to make causal arguments to help direct their choices. Such inferences support and encourage theory driven interpretation of events. A second judgmental heuristic, called *availability,* demonstrates how estimates of likelihood become skewed by accessibility, including salience and recency effects. Anchoring constitutes the third heuristic, documenting how people fail to adequately adjust from often irrelevant anchors in evaluating probabilistic outcomes. Nancy Kanwisher provided clear illustration of how these heuristics, along with others, can help account for systematic and recurrent fallacies in U.S. national security policy, including providing an explanation for

the domino theory and why policy makers incorrectly assume that deterrence entails matching forces. Kurt Weyland, applying these models in a comparative arena, has explored how heuristics affect policy diffusion in such areas as health care reform in Latin American countries.

COGNITIVE THEORY AND PROSPECT THEORY

Applications of cognitive theory to politics also include work on prospect theory, a psychological theory of decision making under conditions of risk. This model incorporates two phases. The first phases encompasses framing effects, which describe the way individuals shift the substance of their choices based on the order, method, or form of the presented options. This work has proved quite influential in analyses of survey research and investigations of the instability of question answers. The second phase of prospect theory relates to the way that people choose among options once these prospects have been framed; this work suggests that individuals prove more prone take risks when confronting losses than when facing gains. Prospect theory has most commonly been used in political applications to examine decision making in the realm of international relations, including explorations of the Iranian hostage rescue mission and the Cuban missile crisis. Additional work has also applied prospect theory in the arena of comparative politics to look at public policy choices among Latin American leaders under conditions of crisis.

COGNITIVE THEORY AND IDENTITY

Other applications of cognitive theory to politics include work on identity. Cognitive models form one of the bases for defining the content of identity, by providing ideas around which to structure expectations of behavior and preferences. Such cognitive models can provide a consensus around which actor expectations can converge by providing representative stereotypes for exemplar members to embody and represent. Scholars Michael Stone and Roblyn Young have used the content of belief systems to measure the nature of collective identities among Iraqi leaders. In this way, cognitive models can help define and measure the way individual choices among competing identities can aggregate into a cohesive sense of collective identity.

COGNITIVE THEORY AND IDEOLOGY

Cognitive models have also been employed to inform our understanding of ideology by examining the way voter beliefs, attitudes, and opinions can influence choice. Sometimes this work invokes demographics such as party identification, which can also incorporate an affective dimension. Cognitive theory can inform the mechanisms people use to adopt particular ideologies by examining the consistency between their beliefs and actions, as cognitive dissonance theory does; this model too assimilates a motivated component. Theories concerning right-wing authoritarianism, or other belief structures that can inform political ideology, often similarly depend on either implicit or explicit models of cognition.

As psychology has moved into a more integrated understanding of the way the human brain processes political information and coalition politics, the bifurcation of cognitive and affective models in psychology will continue to diminish. As this occurs, the application of cognitive theory to politics should begin to reflect the intertwined nature of thought and feeling in driving political actions and decisions.

See also *George, Alexander L.; Heuristics; Judgment and Decision Making; Lasswell, Harold Dwight; Political Psychology; Prospect Theory; Social and Political Cognition.*

. . . . ROSE MCDERMOTT

BIBLIOGRAPHY
Jervis, Robert. 1986. "Representativeness in Foreign Policy Judgments." *Political Psychology* 7, no. 3 (1986): 483–505.
Kahneman, Daniel, Paul Slovic, and Amos Tversky. *Judgment Under Uncertainty: Heuristics and Biases.* Cambridge: Cambridge University Press, 1982.
Kanwisher, Nancy. "Cognitive Heuristics and American Security Policy." *Journal of Conflict Resolution* 33, no. 4 (1989): 652–675.
McDermott, Rose. "The Psychological Ideas of Amos Tversky and Their Relevance for Political Science." *Journal of Theoretical Politics* 13, no. 1 (2001): 5–33.
Weyland, Kurt. *Bounded Rationality and Policy Diffusion: Social Sector Reform in Latin America.* Princeton: Princeton University Press, 2007.

Cohabitation

Cohabitation is an arrangement of split-executive government in semi-presidential systems where the directly elected president is forced to nominate the prime minister from the opposition party that holds the majority in the national assembly. Cohabitation strongly impacts the power of the president, as the parliamentary component is reinforced and the prime minister takes on far-reaching decision powers. This arrangement contrasts markedly with that of *unified government,* in which a de facto presidential logic prevails: The president is the undisputed head of government and the prime minister is the president's chief of staff. Rather, in cohabitation, both officials—the president and the prime minister—hold a formal and informal veto power, which leads to coalition-like politics based on compromise. Consequently, the system oscillates between the two poles of presidential and parliamentary regime features.

French political scientist Maurice Duverger introduced the term cohabitation in 1980 by to explain divided government in the Fifth French Republic (1958–present). In its history, cohabitation has occurred three times: from 1986 to 1988 and from 1993 to 1995, when socialist president Francois Mitterand was confronted with a center-right majority and had to respectively nominate Jacques Chirac and Eduard Balladur, and from 1997 to 2002, when Gaullist president Chirac had to nominate Lionel Jospin, the leader of the victorious Socialist Party, as prime minister.

See also *Coalition Theory; Dual Executive.*

. . . . DANIEL STOCKEMER

BIBLIOGRAPHY
Duverger, Maurice. *La Cohabitation des Francais.* Paris: Press Universitaire de France, 1987.
Elgie, Robert. *Political Institutions in Contemporary France.* Oxford: Oxford University Press, 2003.

Cold War

The term *cold war* is often given to the period of rivalry and confrontation between the United States (and its allies) and the Soviet Union (and its allies) from the end of World War II (1939–1945) until relations thawed in the late 1980s, when Soviet leader Mikhail Gorbachev undertook reforms. Writer George Orwell used the term cold war, and Bernard M. Baruch, an adviser of U.S. president Harry S. Truman, in April 1947 said, "Let us not be deceived—we are today in the midst of a cold war. Our enemies are to be found abroad and at home." Baruch himself credited the phrase to Herbert B. Swope, the former editor of the *New York World,* and that same year the writer and journalist Walter Lippman also used the term.

ORIGINS

There is debate over the cold war's precise start: Some scholars identify its origins as predating 1945, but the period's initial years are often associated with the immediate post–World War II period. By 1945, the United States and Soviet Union had emerged as the two leading powers (they were frequently called the *superpowers*), and by 1947 a general East (Soviet)-West (American) division of states was developing. The West believed the Soviets sought to undermine democracy and establish "puppet" communist regimes in Eastern Europe, thus increasing influence in their zone of occupation in Germany. The Soviets defended their actions in terms of establishing broadly based antifascist governments friendly towards them. Other conflicts emerged elsewhere, and both states increasingly denounced each other. Events symbolic of the cold war's early years include the Berlin blockade (1948–1949), when the Soviets blocked access to West Berlin, and the 1949 Communist victory in China over the American-supported Nationalist government.

INTERNATIONAL TENSIONS

Tensions continued in the 1950s, and their impact was felt globally. This was particularly the case as both countries had nuclear weapons—the United States from 1945 and Soviet Union from 1949—and built alliances. These included the West's North Atlantic Treaty Organization, established in 1949, and the Soviet-Communist European Warsaw Pact (1955–1991). The Korean War (1950–1953) began in June 1950 when Soviet-aligned North Korea sent forces across the 38th parallel of latitude dividing the Korean peninsula and invaded South Korea. This led to U.S. and United Nations deployment of forces and China's involvement. Fighting ultimately ended along the original 38th parallel with an armistice agreement in July 1953. Soviet domination over Eastern Europe during this time was graphically illustrated by the crushing of the 1956 Hungarian Revolution.

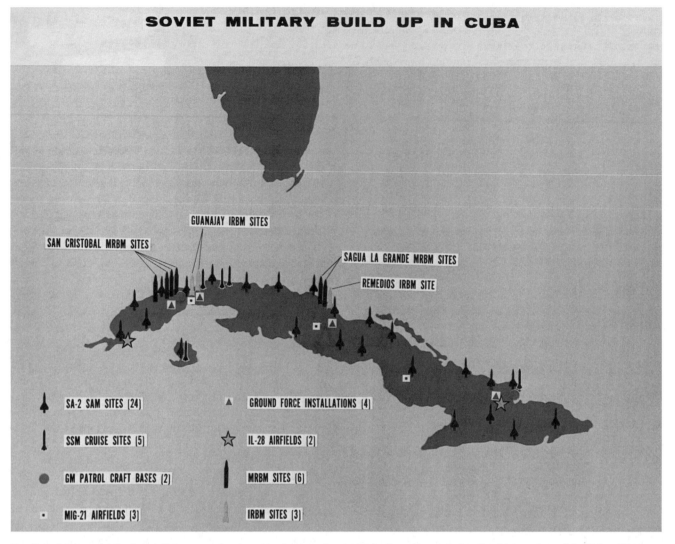

SOVIET MILITARY BUILD UP IN CUBA

GUANAJAY IRBM SITES

SAN CRISTOBAL MRBM SITES

SAGUA LA GRANDE MRBM SITES

REMEDIOS IRBM SITE

SA-2 SAM SITES [24]

SSM CRUISE SITES [5]

GM PATROL CRAFT BASES [2]

MIG-21 AIRFIELDS [3]

GROUND FORCE INSTALLATIONS [4]

IL-28 AIRFIELDS [2]

MRBM SITES [6]

IRBM SITES [3]

The United States and the Soviet Union came the closest to direct confrontation in the cold war during the thirteen days of the Cuban Missile Crisis. The Soviet Union had established missile sites in Cuba in response to a U.S. presence in Turkey.

SOURCE: © Corbis

Tensions increased in the early 1960s. In 1961, the Soviets constructed the Berlin wall separating East Germany from West Germany, and the following year the Cuban missile crisis occurred. This is generally regarded as the cold war's most dangerous event, with the superpowers coming close to a nuclear war. In October 1962, a U.S. spy plane photographed missile sites being built by the Soviets in Cuba. U.S. president John F. Kennedy established a naval blockade to prevent the arrival of additional Soviet military supplies, demanding the removal of the missiles and the destruction of the sites. For thirteen highly tense days, there was uncertainty over how the Soviet leader Nikita Khrushchev would respond to the naval blockade and U.S. demands. Khrushchev ultimately ordered Soviet ships to turn back and agreed to dismantle the weapon sites; in return, the United States agreed not to invade Cuba. In a separate, unpublicized deal, the United States agreed to remove its nuclear missiles from Turkey.

Cold war tensions decreased after the Cuban missile crisis, with a period of détente emerging. In 1963 the *hot line* was installed to provide direct communications between the superpowers, and the Partial Test Ban Treaty outlawing nuclear testing in the atmosphere was concluded. Preliminary discussions to limit long-range missiles and bombers began in 1967, but ended after the Soviets suppressed the 1968 Czechoslovakian Revolution. In 1969, the discussion resumed under the name of the Strategic Arms Limitation Talks (SALT) and concluded in 1972. The numbers of strategic launchers (missiles or bombers) were frozen for five years, although modernization and increases in the number of warheads carried by launchers were allowed. Relations between the United States and China improved, and in 1979, the SALT II Treaty, focusing on the total numbers and explosive power of warheads, was negotiated. Although it remained unratified after the 1979 Soviet invasion of Afghanistan, the superpowers largely continued to follow the treaty limits until the conclusion of the Strategic Arms Reduction Talks (START). Despite these events, conflict between the superpowers continued, especially in Africa and the Middle East. Moreover, the United States was involved in the Vietnam War, beginning in 1959 and lasting until the 1975 fall of South Vietnam to the Communist North.

FINAL DECADE

The early 1980s witnessed increased cold war rivalry until tensions declined during the decade's later years. The invasion of Afghanistan, Polish martial law from 1981 to 1983, the 1983 U.S. invasion of Grenada, and the Soviet destruction of a Korean airliner the same year set the context of a renewed arms race. U.S. president Ronald Reagan and British prime minister Margaret Thatcher strongly denounced the Soviet Union. Tensions began to ease after Gorbachev took power in 1985 and undertook reforms. The 1987 Intermediate-Range Nuclear Forces Treaty required the destruction of the parties' ground-launched ballistic and cruise missiles with ranges of between 500 and 5,500 kilometers (approximately 310–3,818 miles), their launchers, and associated support structures and support equipment. The Soviets withdrew from Afghanistan in 1989, and the first START talks concluded in 1991. These required reductions in each state's long-range launchers and warheads along with further limitations, especially on land-based missiles. During the late 1980s, Soviet domination over Eastern Europe fell, as symbolized by the 1989 fall of the Berlin wall. The Soviet Union itself collapsed in 1991.

There are various interpretations of the cold war, its origins, and why it ended. Factors often associated with the period include: the continuation of great power rivalry for domination and strategic advantage; the result of misperceptions of motives causing the alliance that defeated fascism to collapse and spur an arms race; events largely promoted by those standing to benefit from them, such as the military-industrial complex; and an ideologically driven conflict between capitalism and communism, or between democracy and totalitarianism.

See also *Communism; Russian Political Thought; Soviet Union, Former; U.S. Political Thought.*

. . . . PAUL BELLAMY

BIBLIOGRAPHY

British Broadcasting Corporation. "Word Wars: The Cold War." BBC News: World Wars in Depth. www.bbc.co.uk/history/worldwars/coldwar/.

Bealey, Frank. *The Blackwell Dictionary of Political Science.* Oxford: Blackwell, 1999.

Comfort, Nicolas. *Brewer's Politics: A Phrase and Fable Dictionary.* London: Cassell, 1995.

Gaddis, John. *The Cold War: A New History.* New York: Penguin Books, 2005.

Halliday, Fred. *The Making of the Second Cold War.* London: Verso, 1986.

Hanhimaki, Jussi, and Westad, Odd. *The Cold War: A History in Documents and Eyewitness Accounts.* Oxford: Oxford University Press, 2004.

John F. Kennedy Presidential Library and Museum. "The Cuban Missile Crisis." John F. Kennedy Presidential Library and Museum, Historical Resources. www.jfklibrary.org/Historical+Resources/JFK+in+History/Cuban+Missile+Crisis.htm.

McLean, Iain. *Oxford Concise Dictionary of Politics.* Oxford: Oxford University Press, 1996.

Robertson, David. *A Dictionary of Modern Politics,* 3rd ed. London: Europa Publications, 2002.

Walker, Martin. *The Cold War: A History.* New York: Holt, 1994.

Woodrow Wilson International Center for Scholars. "Cold War International History Project." The Wilson Center. www.wilsoncenter.org/index.cfm?fuseaction=topics.home&topic_id=1409.

Cole, George Douglas Howard

George Douglas Howard Cole (1889–1959) was an English political theorist. As a libertarian socialist, his career was dedicated to advancing the cause of labor. He was a founding member of Fabian Society and a strong defender of the cooperative movement.

Cole became a Fabian while studying at Oxford and joined its executive under Sidney Webb. He became a principal proponent of guild socialism, a libertarian alternative to orthodox Marxism. He expounded his ideas in *New Age* and the weekly founded by Beatrice and Sidney Webb and George Bernard Shaw, *New Statesman*. He wrote, "I became a Socialist because only a society of equals can set free from the twin evils of riches and poverty, mastership and subjection. That is the only kind of society that is consistent with human dignity and decency." Cole envisioned a socialism that is decentralized and participatory, with basic units in the workplace and the community. Both British Labour prime ministers Hugh Gaitskell and Harold Wilson were his students.

In his 1920 work, *Social Theory,* he advanced the theoretical basis of guild socialism, drawing on the ideas of J. N. Figgis and others. Earlier, in *The World of Labour* (1913), Cole argued for industrial democracy in which industry would be controlled by organized labor. On the principle that industrial power precedes political power, Cole said that direct action was more effective than winning elections and changing society through legislation. In his view, industry should be socialized, not nationalized, and production should be organized by national guilds and not by bureaucrats or technocrats. Each industry was to be a self-governing body, and interguild cooperation was to be channeled through coordinating agencies. Society was based on the principle of association and as a plurality of self-governing voluntary associations, and only through such associations could freedom be preserved. Any system in which a sovereign state regulated and administered every area of life was anathema to Cole.

By the mid-1920s, guild socialism fell out of favor. Cole spent the rest of his life rethinking his ideas. It was only at the end of the twentieth century that his ideas experienced a revival.

Cole was also a theorist of the cooperative movement and made a number of contributions to cooperative studies, cooperative economics, and cooperative history, including *Century of Co-operation* (1944) and *The British Co-operative Movement in a Socialist Society* (1951). His writings (over 130 books) may be divided into five broad and overlapping categories: guild socialism; history; biography; economic, political, and social analysis; and fiction. His strongest treatment of guild socialism was *Self-Government in Industry* (1917), a charter of the romantic socialism that inspired Cole all his life. He revised his ideas in *The Case for Industrial Partnership* (1957). His historical works include the five-volume *History of Socialist Thought* (1953–1960). His biographies include *The Life of William Cobbett* (1924) and *The Life of Robert Owen* (1925). Many of his seminal ideas were distilled in *Principles of Economic Planning and An Intelligent Man's Guide to the Post-War World* (1947).

See also *Fabianism; Guild Socialism; Socialism.*

. . . .   GEORGE THOMAS KURIAN

BIBLIOGRAPHY

Carpenter, Luther P. *G.D.H. Cole: An Intellectual Biography.* Cambridge: Cambridge University Press, 1973.

Cole, Margaret. *The Life of G.D.H. Cole.* London: MacMillan, 1971

Wright, Anthony W. *G.D.H. Cole and Socialist Democracy.* Oxford: Clarendon Press, 1979.

Collapsed and Failed States

State collapse and failure appeared as a common feature of the international system after the end of the cold war, though it is not a new phenomenon. *The State Failure Task Force: Phase III Findings* (Goldstone et al. 2000) identified 135 cases of state failure beginning between 1955 and 1998. The rate of state failures surged in the 1960s and again in the early 1990s, periods when new states were born following the withdrawal of imperial powers (e.g., from Africa in the 1960s) or collapse of a superpower (the Soviet Union in 1991).

Based on the state failure data set, several events are identified as state failure in the State Failure Task Force report: revolutionary wars, ethnic wars, adverse regime changes, genocides, and politicides. Since the 1980s, events such as the Islamic revolutions in Iran and Afghanistan; ethnic wars in Somalia and the former Yugoslavia; the collapse of the Soviet Union, the genocide in Rwanda; and the complex combination of ethnic and revolutionary conflicts in such places as Sierra Leone, Indonesia, and the Democratic Republic of Congo serve as examples of collapsed and failed states.

Today, many states are failing to provide security and public order, legitimate representation, and wealth or welfare services to their citizens. However, full-blown cases of state collapse, which involve the extreme disintegration of public authority and the metamorphosis of societies into a battlefield of all against all, remain relatively rare. The worst case of political disintegration is called a *collapsed state.* While a failed state can still have an official government, a fully collapsed state is characterized by a government's complete absence. Several features are central to a *failed state,* occurring when the state apparatus: is unable to uphold an effective monopoly of violence over its whole territory; lacks an effective judicial system and the rule of law; is unable or unwilling to fulfill international obligations, such as debt repayment; and cannot prevent various forms of transnational crime or the use of its territory for the perpetration of violence against other states in the international system. Generally, following the state failure, new local or regional governance structures are formed. The dynamics of governance structures emerge in the virtual or effective absence of a state.

WHY STATES FAIL OR COLLAPSE

There are several factors that cause states to fail and even collapse. *The Failed States Index 2007* applies twelve indicators of state vulnerability covering social, economic, and political factors that may trigger state failure: demographic pressures, massive movement of refugees and internally displaced peoples, a legacy of grievances among vengeance-seeking groups, chronic and sustained human flight, uneven economic development along group lines, sharp or severe economic decline, criminalization or delegitimization of the state, progressive deterioration of public services, widespread violation of human rights, the security apparatus functioning as a state within a state, the rise of factionalized elites, and the intervention of other states or external factors. The *Index* ranks states based on the total scores for these indicators on a scale of 0 to 10, with 0 being the lowest intensity (*most stable*) and 10 being the highest intensity (*least stable*). The objective of ranking the indicators is to measure a state's vulnerability to collapse or conflict, not to forecast when the state may experience violence or collapse.

Generally, states in early phases of state evolution come closest to the phenomenon of a failed state, since they are likely to face social and political problems that may trigger revolutionary wars, ethnic wars, regime changes, and even genocides. Rampant corruption, predatory elites who have long monopolized power, an absence of the rule of law, and severe ethnic or religious divisions can also cause state failure or collapse. For example, according to Transparency International, Burma (also known as Myanmar) and Haiti, which are on top of the most recent *Failed State Index,* are two of the most corrupt and repressive countries in the world. Burma's repressive junta persecutes ethnic minorities and subjects its population to forced resettlement, while Haiti experienced extreme poverty, lawlessness, and urban violence even before the 2010 earthquake destroyed the government's infrastructure and left over a million people homeless. On the other hand, Guinea, also one of the failed states according to the *Failed State Index,* has been experiencing some of the highest economic growth in sub-Saharan Africa, but the gap between the poor and rich is enormous. In the Democratic Republic of the Congo, the inability of the government to police its borders effectively or manage its vast mineral wealth has left the country dependent on foreign aid.

In *When States Fail: Causes and Consequences* (2004), Robert I. Rotberg and other contributors demonstrate that all failed states are by definition repressive, but not all repressive states have failed. The authors define several of the most repressive states as hollow states, failed but for the excessive security that prevents the state in question from being characterized as failed. No collapsed state can be repressive, because the apparatus of repression is by definition lacking.

State collapse does not occur spontaneously. It is likely that complex and conflict-ridden processes of deterioration, decline, and erosion of state functions precede state collapse. Actual collapse is likely to constitute the final phase of this process and it occurs when a point of no return is passed.

COLLAPSED AND FAILED STATES AND INTERNATIONAL SECURITY

In today's increasingly interconnected world, collapsed and failed states pose an acute risk to global security. Various types of state failure have posed major challenges to policy makers seeking to stabilize democratic regimes, prevent genocides, and provide humanitarian assistance during conditions of violence and political crisis. Terrorism, narcotics trade, weapons proliferation, and other forms of organized crime can flourish when chaos prevails. Internal conflict is more likely to arise in countries suffering from poverty, highly unequal income distribution, recent decolonization, weak institutions, ineffective police and counterinsurgency forces, and difficult terrain conditions that allow local armed groups to operate. Valuable raw materials, such as diamonds or oil, also tend to spark internal conflict among competitors who want to seize control of the wealth. Warring groups may even control territory, giving them a base for launching attacks on the state, its citizens, or its neighbors. Other nonstate actors, including transnational terrorist organizations, can also take root in failed states, posing a threat to global security.

See also *Arms Control; Caesarism; Corruption and Other Political Pathologies; Regional Security; State Failure.*

. . . . BEZEN BALAMIR COSKUN

BIBLIOGRAPHY

Bates, R. H. *When Things Fell Apart: State Failure in Late-Century Africa.* New York: Cambridge University Press, 2008.

The Fund for Peace. "The Failed States Index, 2007." *Foreign Policy,* July/August, 2007. www.foreignpolicy.com/story/cms.php?story_id=3865.

Global Policy Forum. *Failed and Collapsed States in the International System.* The African Studies Centre, the Transnational Institute, the Center of Social Studies, and the Peace Research Center. December, 2003. http://www.globalpolicy.org/images/pdfs/12failedcollapsedstates.pdf

Goldstone, J., et al. *State Failure Task Force Report: Phase III Findings.* McLean, Va.: Science Applications International Corporation, 2000.

Miliken, J., and K. Krause, K. "State Failure, State Collapse, and State Reconstruction: Concepts, Lessons, and Strategies." *Development and Change* 33, no. 5, (2002): 753–774.

Rotberg, R. I., ed. *When States Fail: Causes and Consequences.* Princeton: Princeton University Press, 2004.

Zartman, I. W., ed. *Collapsed States: The Disintegration and Restoration of Legitimate Authority.* Boulder: Lynne Rienner, 1995.

Collective Action

See *Collective Action and Mobilization.*

Collective Action, Theory of

Collective action theory attempts to address the problematic and uncertain character of individual participation in collective or collaborative efforts, especially those directed toward the provision of public goods such as social movements and political organizations. The foundational text of collective action theory is *The Logic of Collective Action: Public Goods and the Theory of Groups* (1965) by economist Mancur Olson. Collective action theory radically transformed studies of collective behavior by shifting the emphasis away from notions of irrational group instincts, mass agitation, or emotional spontaneity and toward the rational decision-making processes of participants.

The fundamentals of neoclassical economics inform Olson's work. In Olson's view, social undertakings arise from the choices of rational individuals. Individuals decide to partake in collective action primarily to maximize personal benefits while minimizing personal costs.

One primary problem facing theorists of collective activity is that collective action poses costs for the actor. Even more problematic, however, is the fact that collectively gained rewards are not divisible. Thus, no direct correspondence exists between the individual costs that one might incur by engaging in collective activity and the rewards that one might receive as a result of such action. A worker who refuses to join a union in the workplace will still be rewarded by a wage increase won by the union, if that worker's job falls within the bargaining unit in question. Because the individual collective member receives the collective rewards gained by group action, even if contributing nothing personally to the effort, rational choice theory would suggest that one would be likely to free ride on the efforts of others. Thus, for collective action theory, the issue of the free rider, who accepts the rewards of group membership without taking any of the risks involved in winning those rewards, becomes central.

For Olson, individuals are encouraged to act collectively where groups control and distribute selective incentives. Those who do not join the collective effort or contribute actively to achieve collective interests can be treated differently from those who do.

This raises some important considerations for political organizers. It is not enough to appeal to collective interests, values, or group goals to encourage people to engage in collective activity. Mobilizing people on collective actions, such as social movements, requires that the movement organizations be in a position to control rewards and distribute them selectively on the basis of participation. Mobilization is unlikely to occur in the absence of selective incentives, even where common interests are present. At the same time, the danger of undemocratic practices emerges where a minority that comes to control a preponderance of selective incentives comes to dominate the group's majority.

Olson's publication also provided the starting point for resource mobilization (RM) theories that have become the dominant perspective on social movements within American sociology. RM theorists have modified Olson's approach to lessen the individualist emphasis in favor of an analysis of organizational decision making and repertoires of action. Contemporary RM theorists have also looked more closely at emotional and cultural, rather than simply material, aspects of collective action.

See also *Group Theory; Rational Choice Theory.*

. . . . JEFFREY SHANTZ

BIBLIOGRAPHY

McCarthy, J. D., and M. N. Zald, eds. *The Dynamics of Social Movements.* Cambridge, Mass: Winthrop, 1977.

Oberschall, Anthony. *Social Conflict and Social Movements.* Englewood Cliffs, N.J.: Prentice-Hall, 1973.

Olson, Mancur. *The Logic of Collective Action: Public Goods and the Theory of Groups* Cambridge, Mass.: Harvard University Press, 1965.

Zald, M., and J. D. McCarthy, eds. . *Social Movements in an Organizational Society.* New Brunswick, N.J.: Transaction, 1987.

Collective Action and Mobilization

"You would not be reading this essay," writes Elinor Ostrom, "if it were not for some of our ancestors learning how to undertake collective action to solve social dilemmas." By *collective action,* scholars mean any situation that requires people to act jointly. "The theory of collective action," Ostrom continues, "is *the* central subject of political science." Solving collective action problems entails overcoming the potential costs and risks of acting collectively, and the possibility that potential cooperators will defect or decline to cooperate. Collective action problems pervade everything from international relations to budgeting in legislatures, decision making in bureaucracies, voting, interest group formation, and citizen control of government. "If political scientists do not have an empirically grounded theory of collective action," Ostrom concludes, "then we are hand-waving at our central questions." She goes on to list a bibliographic battery of the many fields to which collective action theory has made central contributions in the last fifty years: from economist and social scientist Mancur Olson's (1965) pathbreaking book to recent work ranging from epoch-making events (e.g., revolutions) to trivial issues (e.g., how cheerleaders solve their collective action problems). Social dilemmas, Ostrom concludes, "are found it all aspects of life."

In her recent work, Ostrom strives to specify a number of structural variables that affect cooperative behavior. However, she correctly observes that structure isn't everything and that "a theory of boundedly rational, norm-based human behavior is a better foundation for explaining collective action than a model of maximizing material payoffs to self." She makes clear that individuals *can* solve their collective action problems. Indeed, Ostrom cites abundant evidence from empirical work that individuals achieve better results—results beyond being rational—in confronting social dilemmas by building conditions in which reciprocity, reputation, and trust help to overcome the strong temptations of short-run self-interest.

Yet, while collective action problems are part of just about everything, this is not to say that they *are* everything. In literature surrounding the tragedy of the commons, the external "other" could be nature. The work of scholars Arun Agrawal, Robert Ellickson, Ronald Herring, Subir Sinha, and Robert Wade reveals that property systems; decisions of landlords, middlemen, and consumers; changes in climate and rainfall; and informal understandings all mediate commons' situations. But even more fundamentally, how close does the "solution" to the collective action problem come to the solution of the problem of mobilization? The problem of mobilization, subsequently, can be defined as the increase in a contender's available resources for collectively making claims in relation to some external actor or system of actors. Once mobilization occurs in relation to external actors, then the importance of the collective action problem becomes less than "everything" and may actually be affected by mobilization.

The efforts of states to cooperate against the prospective threat of a hostile state is one example of collective action and mobilization; their cooperation problem depends, among other things, on the other state's resource base, its strategic calculations, its own collective action problems, and the positioning of third parties. A high probability of aggressive intentions on the part of that state is likely to have more influence on the propensity of potential cooperators to cooperate than their inherent capacity to achieve cooperation. Uncertainties are equally critical in decisions to mobilize: the French revolutionaries who launched wars on their neighbors were driven more by fear of their intentions than by their own ability to solve their collective action problems; indeed, the fear of invasion increased their ability to overcome these problems.

In the social movement field, the solution to the problem of achieving internal cooperation is even more deeply imbricated with external factors. Unlike states facing external opponents, movements are never unitary actors. They depend on external support or opposition that cannot be predicted in advance, and movements must respond to shifts in the opportunities and threats that they face outside the group. These three issues come together in the problem of mobilization.

Mobilization is a process drawing on internal resources to connect actors with significant others outside the group and with the rules and repertoires of systemic politics. For connecting groups to effectively make claims on others who are significant to their external environments, more must be learned about mobilization as the link between internal group problems and that group's external environment. This means connecting what have been, until now, largely distinct traditions of research: research on collective action in the tradition from Olson to Ostrom and research on contentious politics from Charles Tilly to Doug McAdam.

COLLECTIVE ACTION THEORY

Olson made social movement scholars aware that there is such a thing as a collective action problem and that it could be used to explain the finding that actors who "should" act collectively often don't. Olson's work converges with the growing observation that grievances alone cannot explain mobilization because, if they did, social conflict and mobilization would be constant. Olson posits that, on average, no more than 5 percent of a given population could be expected to mobilize. Olson forced scholars of social movements to wrestle with the puzzle of the free rider. While Gerald Marwell and Pam Oliver focused on the critical mass that would enable collective action to mount, Norman Frohlich and Joe A. Oppenheimer extended the theory into hypotheses about the relations within groups; Samuel Popkin showed how revolutionary organization could combat the free-rider problem; Mark Lichbach shaped it into the "rebel's dilemma"; and Dennis Chong used it as the central puzzle in his work on the civil rights movement.

While influential, Olson's integration into the study of movements was slow and uneven because he wanted to explain why collective action was unlikely during a decade when contentious politics buzzed and bloomed. Empirically oriented economists, like Albert Hirschman, were quick to point to this paradox. Sociologists including William Gamson and his collaborators used quasi-experiments to examine the conditions in which the collective action problem is "solved"; they focused on the perception of the authorities' injustice. Others observed that the collective action problem is less intense for what they called "conscience constituents" than for self-oriented materialists. Finally, although he named his theory *collective action*, Olson had little to say beyond the aggregation of individual motivations. He gave little attention to the political and institutional contexts within which collective action episodes are launched, and the historical and cultural traditions that link actors to one another and guide their expectations. How could collective action theory be reconciled with the buzzing and blooming movement cycle of the 1960s?

Answers to this paradox were proposed, first, by Frohlich, Oppenheimer, and Oren Young and then by John McCarthy and Mayer Zald. The former argued that the collective action problem could be attacked successfully when someone (e.g., a political entrepreneur) finds it profitable to set up an organization (or make use of some existing organization), collect resources, and supply the goods in question. If the sum of resources collected is smaller than the value of the collective good to all recipients, yet larger than the entrepreneur's cost in supplying it, the collective action serves the interest of the entrepreneur as well as the collective interest. Similarly, while McCarthy and Zald agreed with Olson that the collective action problem was real, they argued that the expanded personal resources, professionalization, financial support, and organizations available to citizens in modern societies provide an answer to the dilemma—professional movement organizations.

This work led to three decades of productive theorizing and research on the organizational foundations of social movement organizations, but it also produced a cottage industry of criticism. First, like Frohlich and colleagues, McCarthy and Zald used the language of microeconomics (e.g., they wrote of movement entrepreneurs, movement industries, movement sectors), offending scholars who had come to social movement research from activist careers; second, they ignored the self-production of grassroots organizations in the process of mobilization. Soon, an alternative model, emphasizing informal participation and internal democracy, arose. The virtue of that approach was to show that mobilization can produce second-order organizations that continue after the initial impetus or threat has evaporated. This in turn led to the theory of cycles of contention that produce externalities that encourage collective action.

THREE FORMS OF MOBILIZATION

From both perspectives, attention centered on the process of mobilization, and this quickly bifurcated into three streams. They can be called *micromobilization, mesomobilization,* and *macromobilization.*

MICROMOBILIZATION

In their emphasis on organization as the solution to the collective action problem, McCarthy and Zald deflected attention from how individuals make the decision to adhere to a social movement. Dutch social psychologist Bert Klandermans tried to specify the process of adherence around both the propensity to participate and the probability of success. He eventually proposed a funnel of causation in which movement entrepreneurs look for support from within a broad but inert protest potential. This is through what Klandermans called "consensus mobilization," and it narrows by "action mobilization"; collective action then mounts with the support of a subset of the potential participants who were originally targeted.

MESOMOBILIZATION

But who is more likely to mobilize, and whose protest potential remains inert? This depends on more than individual propensities; it also depends on the individual's location in society. Social movement scholars soon observed that those who decide to engage in collective action do not do so as isolated individuals but from within networks of friends, family, roommates, and workmates. These scholars moved beyond the determined individualism of Olson and his followers to look at how groups themselves induce mobilization. Even in high-risk situations—like French insurrections, freedom summer during the civil rights movement, and the Tiananmen Square protests—participants embedding in social networks encouraged mobilization. For network scholars, the group, rather than being a source of collective action problems, actually helps to move individuals from inertia to mobilization.

MACROMOBILIZATION

Just as McCarthy and Zald, Klandermans, and the social network theorists were moving beyond Olson from the bottom, other theorists were building downward from a structuralist perspective. Social movement theory emerged in dialogue with Marxism, for which individuals mobilize as the outcome of impersonal macrostructural processes: exploitation, proletarianization, and concentration. States hovered on the margins of these processes, entering abstractly as the "executive committee of the capitalist class" or concretely as the agent of repression. From this mechanical Marxism, historians like E. P. Thompson and Eric Hobsbawm eventually departed, but it took a historically trained sociologist, Charles Tilly, to specify a number of mechanisms—organization, repression, facilitation, opportunity, threat, and mobilization—to connect the interests of a group with its collective action. A brief comment on each of Tilly's mechanisms is useful in placing work on the political process alongside the collective action tradition.

Tilly argued that any collective action begins with the interest of a group in acting collectively, which he defined as "the shared advantages or disadvantages likely to accrue to the population in question" as a result of "various possible interactions with other populations." But interest was just the beginning of Tilly's model. It continued with organization. More broadly than Olson, Tilly defined *organization* as "an increase in common identity and/or unifying structure." Unlike McCarthy and Zald, organization was not the single solution to the collective action problem—once participants left the precincts of the group, organizers encountered other actors, opponents, and the state. They encountered the environment through *repression,* defined as "any action by another group which raises the contender's cost of collective action." But other actors could also facilitate their actions via *facilitation,* which is "an action which lowers the contender's cost." Political repression and political facilitation relate to the relationship between contenders and governments. Repression and facilitation were specific forms of more general encounters, which Tilly summarized with the concepts of opportunity and threat: "the relationship between the population's interactions with other populations which favour/disfavour its interests in relation to those of others."

THE POLITICAL PROCESS TRADITION

Tilly's model launched an entire new stream of social movement research that focused more on the relations between a challenging group and its environment than on the group's particular grievances or its internal relations. Mobilization was at the center of this new paradigm. In contrast to collective action theorists who focused on the problem of internal cooperation, political process theorists emphasized a group's interaction with the constraints and resources it found in its external environment. If these constraints and resources could be successfully navigated, mobilization resulted, and in Tilly's terms, "an increase in the resources or in the degree of collective control."

The most fundamental difference between the political process approach and that of Olson and the post-Olsonians is that in this tradition, it is not the problem of cooperation within a group that is central to mobilization, but the relationship between members of that group and the outside environment. These relationships are channelled through a contender who, on the one hand, seeks to gain control of its internal resources, and, on the other, maneuvers in the external environment to effectively represent the interests of the group. To put this spatially: if the problem of mobilization for Olson and those who followed him was to overcome the obstacle to horizontal cooperation, for Tilly and the political process theorists it was the problem of achieving vertical control of the groups resources by a contender who uses these resources in facing external groups and institutions. In this way, the process of mobilization shifts from an internal process to one that connects the group to its environment as it makes claims on other actors, opponents, and the state.

The nub of the problem lies in how Tilly was interested in all kinds of contentious interactions, and the political process approach that grew out of his work came to focus almost exclusively on the mobilization of one kind of group—social movements—and has largely forsaken the problem of collective action within the group. Except for a few prominent outliers like Samuel Popkin and Dennis Chong, this has led to an increasing gap between the study of collective action internal to groups and the study of the encounter between groups and their external environments. The problem is to blend the insights of the relatively apolitical Olson approach with the more political approaches of political process or contentious politics. Only by doing so can the field interface with the core concerns of comparative politics.

A first step in bridging the two traditions would be for scholars of collective action to be reintroduced to one another. In Ostrom's otherwise wide-ranging review of collective action in the 1998 American Political Science Association presidential address, there was no recognition of the work on social movements that was simultaneously flowering in the political process tradition. Similarly, in the definitive *Blackwell Companion to Social Movements,* Olson is cited exactly twice in the index to this 754-page book, Ostrom is never cited, and the collective action problem is not even mentioned.

A second step would be to better specify the mechanisms in the mobilization process that are common to both traditions. Some of these, such as resource transfer from members of a group to the contender that seeks to represent it, are familiar from the collective action tradition but are also recognizable in the work of Klandermans, Tilly, and others. Other mechanisms—including the brokerage of a group's claims to represent its interests to third parties, allies, and opponents—developed in the contentious politics tradition, but are close to the concept of political entrepreneurship from the work of Frohlich, Oppenheimer, and Young. Still others, such as the way movement contenders frame the formation of claims, derive from the constructivist perspective on social movements, but are compatible with both perspectives.

A third step would be to try to build outward from the political process tradition's single-minded focus on social movements and inward from the collective action tradition's tendency to seek collective action solutions to everything, and thus form a bridge between the two traditions. The political process scholars have largely ignored other forms of collective action beyond social movements, like those we encounter in the collective action tradition. In contrast, collective action scholars seek general laws or necessary and sufficient conditions in which solutions to the collective action problems are sought, regardless of the site or the surrounding environment of the population being examined.

There are exceptions to the mutual indifference between collective action theorists and the political process tradition with respect to mobilization. The most prominent is found in the work of Mark Lichbach. In his monumental study *The Rebel's Dilemma,* Lichbach deduces four mechanisms of mobilization growing beyond the collective action tradition: market mechanisms, community mechanisms, contractual mechanisms, and hierarchical mechanisms. In a series of articles, he comes closer than any collective action theorist to building a bridge to what he calls "synthetic political opportunity theory." A second approach, starting from the political process side, is the contentious politics approach, which reaches beyond social movements to study the mechanisms of mobilization in revolutions, strike waves, nationalist episodes, and democratization. While this work does not seek to provide a theory of everything (indeed it deliberately excludes social movements that are not oriented toward public politics), like Lichbach, its proponents seek to identify mechanisms that are present across a range of forms of contention.

These are but the first steps in constructing a theory unifying mobilization and collective action.

See also *Mobilization, Political; Olson, Mancur; Social Movements.*

. . . . SIDNEY TARROW

BIBLIOGRAPHY

Agrawal, Arun. "Common resources and institutional sustainability." In *The Drama of the Commons,* edited by E. Ostrom et al., 41–85. Washington D.C.: National Academy Press, 2002.

Chong, Dennis. *Collective Action and the Civil Rights Movement.* Chicago: University of Chicago Press, 1991.

Davis, Gerald, Doug McAdam, W. Robert Scott, and Mayer N. Zald, eds. *Social Movements and Organization Theory.* Cambridge: Cambridge University Press, 2005.

Diani, Mario, and Doug McAdam, eds. *Social Movements and Networks: Relational Approaches to Collective Acton.* Oxford: Oxford University Press, 2003.

Ellickson, Robert. *Order Without Law: How Neighbors Settle Disputes.* Cambridge, Mass.: Harvard University Press, 1991.

Evans, Sara, and Harry C. Boyte. *Free Spaces: The Sources of Democratic Change in America.* Chicago: University of Chicago Press, 1992.

Fantasia, Rick. *Cultures of Solidarity: Consciousness, Action and Contemporary American Workers.* Berkeley: University of California Press, 1988.

Frohlich, Norman, and Joe A. Oppenheimer. "I Get By with a Little Help from My Friends." *World Politics* 23 (1970): 104–120.

Frohlich, Norman, Joe A. Oppenheimer, and Oren Young. *Political Leadership and Collective Goods.* Princeton: Princeton University Press, 1971.

Gamson, William, Bruce Fireman, and Stephen Rytina. *Encounters with Unjust Authority.* Homewood, Ill.: Dorsey Press, 1982.

Gould, Roger V. *Insurgent Identities: Class, Community, and Protest in Paris from the Commune.* Chicago: University of Chicago Press, 1995.

Hardy, Charles A., and Bibb Latané. "Social Loafing in Cheerleaders: Effects of Team Membership and Competition." *Journal of Sport and Excercise Psychology* 10 (1988): 109–114.

Herring, Ronald. "Resurrecting the Commons: Collective Action and Ecology. *Items* (Newsletter of the Social Science Research Council), December, 1989.

Herring, Ronald, and Subir Sinha. "Common Property, Collective Action, and Ecology. *The Economic and Political Weekly* 28 (1993): 1425–1433.

Hirschman, Albert O. *Shifting Involvements: Private Interest and Public Action.* Princeton: Princeton University Press, 1981.

Hobsbawm, Eric. *Primitive Rebels: Studies in Archaic Forms of Social Movement in the 19th and 20th Centuries.* Manchester: Manchester University Press, 1959.

Klandermans, Bert. "The Formation and Mobilization of Consensus." In *From Structure to Action,* edited by Bert Klandermans and Sidney Tarrow, 173–196. Greenwich, Conn.: JAI Press, 1988.

———. "Participation and Mobilization: Social Psychological Expansions of Resource Mobilization Theory." *American Sociological Review* 49 (1984): 583–600.

Lichbach, Mark I. "Contending Theories of Contentious Politics and the Structure-action Problem." *Annual Review of Political Science* 1 (1997): 401–424.

———. *The Cooperator's Dilemma.* Ann Arbor: University of Michigan Press, 1996.

———. "Internal Wars over the State: Rational Choice Institutionalism and Contentious Politics." In *Handbook of War Studies III,* edited by Manus Midlarsky. Ann Arbor: University of Michigan Press, 2009.

———. *The Rebel's Dilemma.* Ann Arbor: University of Michigan Press, 1995.

Marwell, Gerald, and Pam Oliver. *The Critical Mass in Collective Action: A Micro-social Theory.* New York: Cambridge University Press, 1993.

McAdam, Doug. "Conceptual Origins, Current Problems, Future Directions," In *Comparative Perspectives on Social Movements,* edited by Doug McAdam, John McCarthy, and Mayer N. Zald. Cambridge: Cambridge University Press, 1996.

———. *Freedom Summer.* Chicago: University of Chicago Press, 1998.

———. *Political Process and the Development of Black Insurgency,* 2nd ed. Chicago: University of Chicago Press, 1999.

McAdam, Doug, Sidney Tarrow, and Charles Tilly. *Dynamics of Contention.* Cambridge: Cambridge University Press, 2001.

McCarthy, John, and Mayer N. Zald. "Resource Mobilization and Social Movements: A Partial Theory." *American Journal of Sociology* 82 (1978): 1212–1241.

———. "The Trend of Social Movements in America: Professionalization and Resource Mobilization." In *Social Movements in an Organizational Society,* edited by Mayer N. Zald and John McCarthy. New Brunswick, N.J.: Transaction, 1987.

Olson, Mancur. *The Logic of Collective Action: Public Goods and the Theory of Groups.* Cambridge, Mass.: Harvard University Press, 1965.

Ostrom, Elinor. "A Behavioral Approach to the Rational Choice Theory of Collective Action." *American Political Science Review* 92 (1998): 1–22.

———. "Collective Action Theory." In *The Oxford Handbook of Comparative Politics,* edited by C. Boix and S. Stokes. Oxford: Oxford University Press, 2007.

Popkin, Samuel L. *The Rational Peasant: The Political Economy of Rural Society.* Berkeley: University of California Press, 1979.

Rosenthal, Naomi. B., and Michael Schwartz. "Spontaneity and Democracy in Social Movements." In *Organizing for Change: Social Movement Organizations in Europe and the United States,* edited by Bert Klandermans, 33–59. Greenwich, Conn.: JAI Press, 1988.

Snidal, Duncan. "Coordination vs. Prisoner's Dilemma: Implications for International Cooperation and Regimes." *American Political Science Review* 79 (1985): 923–947.

Snow, David A., Hanspeter Kriesi, and Sarah A. Soule, eds. *Blackwell Companion to Social Movements.* Oxford: Blackwell, 2004.

Snow, David, E., Burke Rochford Jr., Steven K. Worden, and Robert D. Benford. "Frame Alignment Processes: Micromobilization and Movement Participation. *American Sociological Review* 51 (1986): 464–481.

Tarrow, Sidney. *Power in Movement: Social Movements and Contentious Politics,* 2nd ed. Cambridge: Cambridge University Press, 1997.

Thompson, E. P. "The Moral Economy of the English Crowd in the Eighteenth Century." *Past and Present* 50 (1971): 76–136.

Tilly, Charles. *From Mobilization to Revolution.* Reading, Mass.: Addison-Wesley, 1978.

Tilly, Charles, and Sidney Tarrow. *Contentious Politics.* Boulder: Paradigm Press, 2007.

Wade, Robert. "The Management of Common Property Resources. Collective Action as an Alternative to Privatisation or State Regulation." *Cambridge Journal of Economics* 11 (1987): 95–106.

Walt, Stephen M. *Revolution and War.* Ithaca: Cornell University Press, 1996.

Zald, Mayer N., and John McCarthy, eds. *Social Movements in an Organizational Society: Collected Essays.* New Brunswick, N.J.: Transaction, 1985.

Zhao, Dinxao. "Ecologies of Social Movements: Student Mobilization During the 1989 Prodemocracy Movement in Beijing." *American Journal of Sociology* 103 (1995): 1493–1529.

Collectivization

Collectivization, a policy pursued in the Soviet Union and most other communist countries, refers to a process whereby private agricultural lands were seized by the state and transferred either to collective farms (*kolkhoz* in Russian) or state farms (*sovkhoz*). The policy was unpopular with farmers and was accompanied by violence. It also contributed to lower agricultural output. Nonetheless, politically it helped consolidate communist authority in the countryside.

RATIONALE

Collectivization had both an ideological and a practical purpose. Its ideological justification can be found in Karl Marx and Friedrich Engels's *Communist Manifesto* (1848), in which they argue that farmers, like factory workers, should be organized into large-scale collectives to eliminate private property and this, in their view, would lead to more efficient agricultural output. Collective farms would also foster the socialist ethos upon which communist society could be built. Privately owned farms and the emergence of a "richer peasant" class were seen as incompatible with communism.

The practical goals of collectivization were threefold. First, Soviet authorities wanted to ensure a steady supply of food to burgeoning cities. Experiments with partially market-based agriculture in the 1920s under the New Economic Policy had led to increases in agricultural output, but the supply of food depended on the willingness of Russian peasants to sell grain at prices set by the state. A serious crisis in 1928 in securing peasant cooperation compelled Soviet leaders to search for alternatives, including forced seizures of food supplies. Second, the Soviets wanted to launch a program of rapid industrialization but had little available resources to pay for such a program. Exporting food to pay for capital imports thus became a central plank in the Soviet industrialization program. Third, the Russian countryside traditionally had been the basis for revolts against central authority. Soviet authorities therefore wanted to ensure that they had political control over the rural population, which in the 1920s constituted the vast majority of the Soviet people.

COLLECTIVIZATION UNDER STALIN

In 1929, Soviet authorities embarked on a nationwide program of collectivization. Although collectivization had been encouraged, only 2 percent of peasants had voluntarily entered collective farms. Peasants did not like collectivization because it meant being forced to produce food at minimal prices set by the state and give up their land. Whereas production was organized around family households prior to collectivization, peasants in collective farms would have to join large production brigades working under the direction of farm managers. Collectivization therefore had to be pursued with rigorous force and violence. Those who refused to move into the collective farms were accused of sabotaging grain collection and labeled *kulaks.* Millions of kulaks were sent off to brutal labor camps, where many died. Frequently, peasants slaughtered their animals rather than transfer them to collective ownership, resulting in a massive drop in the supply of meat, milk, and eggs. The drastic impact of the program led Soviet leader Joseph Stalin to announce in 1930 that officials overseeing collectivization were "dizzy with success" and needed to rein in some of their efforts. Collectivization, however, was quickly pursued with renewed vigor. From 1932 to 1933, Soviet authorities forcibly seized grain from peasants in Ukraine, Russia, and Kazakhstan, resulting in the death by starvation of up to ten million people, an act labeled a genocide by many Ukrainians. At the same time its citizens were starving, the Soviet government was exporting grain to pay for industrialization. By 1936, 90 percent of Soviet agriculture was collectivized.

ECONOMIC IMPACT

Collective and state farms were far larger than small private holdings, and Soviet authorities brought in tractors and machinery to increase efficiency. Stalin predicted that the Soviet Union would become the world's leading producer of grain. However, because of poor infrastructure and distribution and lack of incentive for collective farm workers, grain production never met expectations. The numbers of livestock were still lower in 1950 than in 1928. Soviet authorities, in an ideological and practical concession, allowed collective farmers to cultivate small private plots of land, which produced a disproportionate amount of the Soviet total of fruits, vegetables, and milk. By the 1960s, the Soviets were compelled to import grain from the United States, and bread lines remained a constant in Soviet life. Although collectivization was a failure in economic terms, it was unquestioned on ideological grounds and did establish communist authority throughout the Soviet Union.

LEGACY

Collectivization became a key feature of the Soviet communist model and was pursued in many communist states, including most of Eastern Europe (except Yugoslavia and Poland), China, Vietnam, and Cambodia. As in the Soviet case, it was often resisted by farmers and was accompanied by violence.

China's economic reforms started in the 1970s by offering market-based incentives to collective farmers to increase food output. After the collapse of communism, land was eventually privatized in most postcommunist states, including Russia, although turning collective farm workers into successful independent farmers has proven difficult and most Russian farmers continue to work in large agricultural cooperatives.

See also *Communism; Communism, Fall of, and End of History; Marxism; Russian Political Thought; Stalinism.*

. . . . PAUL JAMES KUBICEK

BIBLIOGRAPHY

Conquest, Robert, ed. *Agricultural Workers in the USSR.* London: Bodley Head, 1968.

———. *Harvest of Sorrow: Soviet Collectivization and the Terror-Famine.* Oxford: Oxford University Press, 1986.

Davies, R. W. *The Socialist Offensive: The Collectivization of Soviet Agriculture 1929–1930.* Cambridge, Mass.: Harvard University Press, 1980.

Fitzpatrick, Sheila. *Stalin's Peasants: Resistance and Survival in the Russian Village after Collectivization.* Oxford: Oxford University Press, 1996.

Karcz, Jerzy. *The Economics of Communist Agriculture.* Bloomington: Indiana University Press, 1979.

Lewin, Moshe. *Russian Peasant and Soviet Power: A Study of Collectivization.* Evanston, Ill.: Northwestern University Press, 1968.

Colonialism

Colonialism is a particular relationship of domination between states, involving a wide range of interrelated strategies, including territorial occupation, population settlement, and extraction of economic resources by the colonizing state. Historically, colonialism also depended upon legal, cultural, and political justifications of the colonial project in the metropole and the colonized state. While colonialism and imperialism share many of these characteristics, colonialism involved significant amounts of settlement of citizens from the colonial center in the colonized territory, as well as formal relationships of law and governance between colonial states and their subjects. Variations in the colonizing power; the period and region of colonization; local conditions of polity, economy, society, religion, and culture; and global circumstances all contributed to enormous variations amongst and within colonies and colonial projects.

The term *colony* has a long history and has been applied to a wide range of state arrangements, beginning with the extension of the legal status of Roman citizens to the conquered territories they settled. It was later applied in the sixteenth century to refer to the conquest by competing European powers—initially Portugal and Spain, and in the seventeenth to nineteenth centuries the Dutch, French, English, and Germans—of territories in Africa, the Americas, India, and Asia. The era of formal colonialism is widely understood to have ended by the mid-twentieth century with waves of decolonization leading to independent nation states. However, the term has more recently been used to refer to informal relations of domination and economic exploitation by former colonial powers of previous colonies, and to the assertion of economic, military, and cultural dominance by ascendant global powers, the United States paramount among these.

While the practice of colonialism was undertaken by many powers at many times, including the Persians, Chinese, Mongols, Russians, Ottomans, and Japanese, scholarship and critique of colonialism has tended to focus on modern European

In this cartoon, English king Edward VII and French politician Theophile Delcasse negotiate their colonial holdings in Africa.

SOURCE: Getty Images

colonial powers and the settlement and exploitation of non-European territories and subjects. Scholars of world systems, colonialism, and state formation have sought in recent years to decenter Europe and formal state visions of colonization, by focusing on colonialism as a system whose local components, state and nonstate, were shaped by transnational processes and affected these processes in turn.

COMPONENTS AND GOALS

Early colonial settlement as practiced by the Greeks and Romans in the Mediterranean region involved the establishment of independent and self-governing city-states with close ties to the central colonial power. Their major functions included the facilitation of trade and economic growth and the securing of conquests. Beginning in the early modern period and reaching their apogee in the nineteenth century, changes in technological capacity allowed large-scale maritime trade and expansion, warfare, and migration. Later types of large-scale settler colonialism—as of the Spanish in South America; the British in North America and Australia; and other European powers in parts of South America, the Caribbean, Africa, and Asia—involved multiple modes of intervention, governance, and rule.

Another variant of colonialism, labeled *exploitation* colonialism because its major objectives were seen to be economic extraction rather than settlement, can further be divided into direct and indirect colonialism. The major distinguishing feature of direct colonialism was government and administration by colonial officials, such as the British in the American colonies. *Indirect* colonialism, by contrast, preserved (or constructed) some local governmental institutions and incorporated some local elites into colonial administrations, as in the princely states of British India, parts of Malaya, and Africa. For colonial administrations like the British in Africa, where a small amount of colonial manpower was extended over large territories and populations, indirect rule presented important advantages: Military, tax, and external relations were undertaken by British personnel, and all other areas of governance left, at least in name, to compliant local elites.

These categories of colonialism were never fully separate, and often overlapped across and within colonial territories, changed with time and with policy, and featured important exceptions. Even in indirectly ruled colonies, the areas left to the governance of local elites became part of the colonial project in critical ways, such as reorganizing regimes of land, labor and social life, religion and custom, as well as law and order. Some colonial powers, even though they exercised control over particular territories, worked in the shadow of more powerful imperial powers, such as Portugal's colonization of Brazil in the eighteenth century, dependent on British treaties for economic gain and British military protection in warfare.

The fundamental goal of modern European colonialism was economic gain—colonial possessions provided the raw materials (spices, cotton, silk, tea, opium) for trade and industry as well as markets into which goods produced from these materials would be sold. Competition and growth in the economies of empire fueled large flows of global exchange, precious metals for spices and textiles between Europe and Asia, but also interregional trade in Asia, and the development and extension of technologies of transport, manufacturing, and markets. Imperial economic organization included the ceding of territory and, in some cases, sovereignty, to merchant companies such as the British East India Company and the Dutch East India Company, who were granted particularly favorable rights and exemptions from their governments to conduct trade.

Companies were at times also given the right to exercise some of the functions of government such as war and treaty making, the establishment of colonies, the coining of currency and collection of taxes, as had the Dutch East India Company in Southeast Asia and South Africa in the seventeenth century—or the mandate to govern, as the British East India Company ruled in Bengal, Bihar, and Orissa from 1757 to 1858. When these companies faltered, due to economic and political problems at home and in the colonies, their territories became part of the colonial possessions of the home country (e.g., in the creation of the British raj in India, between 1858 and 1947).

LAW AND LEGAL INSTITUTIONS

Law played a critical role in the establishment, justification, and control of colonies, supplying the institutional and discursive mechanisms by which subject territories would be governed, their populations ordered, and their economic resources extracted. The reorganization of local land, labor, and production to achieve the economic aims of colonization took place through means of law, policing, and administrative ordering: Land title systems, inheritance and transfer of property, social and family organization, taxation, policing, criminality, order, and the differential rights and privileges of colonizer and colonized were constructed through law.

Law and legal institutions also provided one means by which the actions and aspirations of colonial settlers and agents could be limited, and provided one means, albeit limited, for colonized subjects to make claims against the colonial state. The provision of customary, personal status, and religious law based upon perceived or constructed traditional practices of native societies was a common feature of colonial governance, especially within British and French rule. These native legal forms were often placed within a hierarchical colonial legal system with laws, institutions, and legal personnel imported from the colonial metropole, interpreted within the overarching system of the colonial state, and transformed by both colonial actors and local elites for multiple ends.

IDEOLOGIES AND EFFECTS OF COLONIALISM

Ideologies of colonialism varied, depending on the specific colonial relationship; the interests and assumptions of multiple parties in the colonial project and outside it; and larger contemporary intellectual, philosophical, and political debates. One characteristic feature of the colony was the establishment of a distinct cultural group within the colonized territories, and the valorization of that group's difference from the "natives" along racial, moral, biological, and civilizational lines. A prominent justification of European colonization was that it represented the oversight by a stronger, advanced civilization over a weaker, backward people, for whom the introduction of stable institutions of government, rationalized economic relations, moral tutelage, and cultural example would result in increased civilizational maturity.

Other rationales included imperial competition amongst the great powers of Europe, social and cultural reformism, the spread of Christianity, and the achievement of more targeted objectives, such as the abolition of slavery, sexual purity, moral reform, education, health and hygiene, temperance, law, and order. This ideological orientation defined both the colonizing and the colonized society, established a moral justification for multiple interventions as well as rationalized their methods, and posited difference (racial and cultural) along developmental and historical lines.

The violence of colonialism was multiple, and an indispensable part of the colonial project. This included warfare conducted on behalf of the colonial state against its subjects, local opponents, and imperial competitors; the arming and support of some local elites against others; forced labor, collective punishment and later aerial bombardment; and the application of new techniques of biopower and knowledge. Brute force was both a component of state strength, controlling subjects and territories by superior force, and a symptom of its weakness, reflecting the failures of administrative and cultural discipline.

Colonial power was never total, and colonialism itself never a completed project; within the colonial center and in the colonies themselves, colonization had its opponents. Within European intellectual and moral debates, Christian theologians lent moral strength to imperialism by casting it as a conduit for Christianization, but also cast doubt upon the colonial impulse through theologies of natural law and universal humanity. Enlightenment figures such as Adam Smith, Denis Diderot, and Immanuel Kant opposed imperialism based upon ideas of justice, pluralism, and human nature. Local actors deployed varied strategies to resist, oppose, deflect, limit, and transform colonial efforts. Anticolonial struggles and nationalist movements advocated a range of approaches, including preemptive modernization and westernization; deeper religious, ethnic, and national commitments among colonized peoples; and appeals to ideals such as natural justice, democracy, and popular sovereignty. Anticolonial figures such as Frantz Fanon advocated uprising and violent resistance, arguing that the violence of colonialism was systemic, its effects both physical and psychological, and that its overthrow required anticolonial recruitment in the population least dependent on colonial resources.

The effects of colonialism extended to the colonial metropole and the global system as well as to colonized states and subjects. Efforts required to maintain empire, and attain the rewards—economic, political and moral—of colonial interventions were part of the domestic governing apparatus of European colonial states. The efforts allowed establishment of hierarchies of citizens and subjects, applying policies and experiences at home that were initially developed in the colony, and vice versa,

percolating into the self-perceptions, culture, and politics of the colonizing state as well as the colonized. The costs of maintaining colonial ambitions also had effects on the structure of the economies of colonial powers, investing heavily in some sectors and neglecting others, further increasing disparities between regions and sectors in the colonizing state itself.

In colonized states, these effects were even more pronounced, and reached into all areas of life—economy and administration, but also internal political dynamics, education, urban and rural divides, religious institutions and doctrines, language and culture, health and infrastructure, and education. Settler colonialism in the Americas, Australia, New Zealand, and South Africa had a particularly dire impact on the numbers of native peoples, and at times their continued existence, reducing populations through disease, warfare, resettlement, and forced integration. Indirect rule had particularly enduring effects on local power structures and institutions because colonial resources and policies were often passed down through certain local elites. These effects continued into postcolonial states in varied ways. They impacted governmental structures; long-term diplomatic, economic, and cultural relations; immigration; and national consciousness—and the effects have had enduring consequences.

THEORIES OF COLONIALISM

The study of colonialism has itself undergone multiple shifts over time, and also evolved as more scholarship has been produced by, or been based on, the former subjects of colonial rule. Political science, along with other social science and humanities disciplines, has studied, facilitated, and critiqued colonialism, while more recent scholarship like that by Edward Said has been acutely aware of the manner in which the production of knowledge is implicated in relationships of power. However, current theories of colonialism continue to occupy and draw from a wide range of philosophical, political, and empirical sources.

Developmental theories of colonialism have in common a sense that colonization was part of a historical progress from one form of statehood and subjectivity to another. Early studies of colonialism were produced as part of the European colonial project, and worked to justify, assess, compare, and improve colonial administration and policy, as well as communicate its experience to European readers. Many early scholars of colonialism, such as John Stuart Mill, were themselves employees of colonial companies (Mill of the British East India Company) or colonial officials. For thinkers like Mill—who combined a liberal view of individuals as capable and deserving of rational self-government with a belief in history as a progression along increasing levels of civilization—colonialism provided an essential bridge between the civilized and the savage subject, and the despotism of colonization the historical conduit from the uncivilized state to one capable of self-government.

Modernization theorists, including Marxist-Leninists, while they may reject the more paternalistic overtones of earlier developmentalists, have tended to see colonization as a part of the modernization process, through its integration of colonized states into the world economy; the extension of governmental administration, control, and bureaucracy over large areas of territory; and the regularization of systems and institutions. World-systems theorists see the extension of colonial divisions on a global scale, in which economic and political relations of dependency and coercion between core states and periphery states benefit the interests of core states, themselves colonial powers.

The progression from colonized states to independent nations, largely occurring after the end of World War II and into the 1950s and 1960s, has been seen as the end of the period of formal colonialism. However, scholars like Frederick Cooper question neat delineations between empire and nation, arguing instead for the overlap of political forms, institutional continuities, and discourses. France only became a nation-state after the end of rule in Algeria in 1962, for example, and many previously colonial states continue to have dependencies and territories; the Eurasian Habsburg, Ottoman, and Romanov empires persisted into the twentieth century, and panimperial identity became part of the repertoire of nationalist movements in these territories.

Postcolonial theory shifted the emphasis in the study of colonization and its effects from economy and diplomacy to the interrelationship between knowledge, culture, and power. Scholarship about, and knowledge of, the colonized subject and colonial societies, in which the cultural superiority of Europeans was assumed, and the casting of the "oriental" as radically different, as other, became part of the justification for colonial domination. Other postcolonial scholars like Gayatri Spivak and Homi Bhabha have emphasized language and discourses of identity, authenticity, and tradition as themselves implicated in colonial legacies.

The end of the cold war and further shifts in global power politics have given rise to academic reflections on the relationship between new forms of power, exercised primarily by the United States, and older patterns of colonialism. U.S. involvement in Hawaii and Puerto Rico, and more recent interventions in Iraq and Afghanistan, have been cited as examples of U.S. colonial projects, at different times, for different reasons, and different regions. Another widely discussed target of U.S. colonial power, albeit an informal and ambiguous form of colonial power, is the global system itself, control over which is exerted by allied nation states, international organizations and global capital. Scholarly treatments of U.S. colonialism occupy all the theoretical positions described here, with some distinct features including the following characteristics: informal rather than formal relations of economic, military, cultural, and diplomatic power; deeper ambiguities in jurisdiction, sovereignty, and control; and comparisons with Roman and other ancient imperial states.

See also Colonial Wars; Empire and Democracy; Globalization; Hegemony; Imperialism; Internal Colonialism; International System; Mill, John Stuart; Nation-building; Postcolonial Theory; South (Third World); Transnationalism.

·   IZA HUSSIN

BIBLIOGRAPHY

Abu-Lughod, Janet. *Before European Hegemony: The World System AD 1250–1350.* New York: Oxford University Press, 1991.

Adas, Michael. *Machines as the Measure of Men: Science, Technology, and Ideologies of Western Dominance.* Ithaca: Cornell University Press, 1989.

Benton, Lauren. "The Legal Regime of the South Atlantic World, 1400–1750: Jurisdictional Complexity as Institutional Order." *Journal of World History* 11, no. 1 (Spring 2000): 27–56.

Bhabha, Homi. *The Location of Culture.* New York: Routledge, 1993.

Calhoun, Craig, Frederick Cooper, and Kevin W. Moore, eds. *Lessons of Empire: Imperial Histories and American Power.* New York: New Press, 2006.

Cohn, Bernard. (1985) "The Command of Language and the Language of Command." In *Subaltern Studies: Writings on South Asian History and Society,* vol. 4, edited by R. Guha. Delhi: Oxford University Press.

Comaroff, John, and Jean Comaroff. *Of Revelation and Revolution. Vol. 1, Christianity, Colonialism, and Consciousness in South Africa.* Chicago: University of Chicago Press, 1991.

Cooper, Frederick. *Colonialism in Question: Theory, Knowledge, History.* Berkeley: University of California Press, 2005.

Fanon, Franz. *The Wretched of the Earth,* translated by Constance Farrington. New York: Grove Weidenfeld, 1963.

Mehta, Uday. *Liberalism and Empire: A Study in Nineteenth-Century British Liberal Thought.* Chicago: University of Chicago Press, 1999.

Merry, Sally. "Anthropology, Law, and Transnational Processes." *Annual Review of Anthropology* 21 (1992): 357–379.

Mill, John Stuart. *Principles of Political Economy,* Edited by J. Laurence Laughlin. New York: D. Appleton, 1891.

Mitchell, Timothy. *Colonising Egypt.* Cambridge: Cambridge University Press 1988.

Muthu, Sankar. *Enlightenment against Empire.* Princeton: Princeton University Press, 2003.

Said, Edward. *Orientalism.* New York: Vintage, 1979.

Spivak, Gayatri. "Can the Subaltern Speak?" In *Marxism and the Interpretation of Culture,* edited by Cary Nelson and Larry Grossberg, 271–313. Chicago: University of Illinois Press, 1988.

Colonialism, Internal

See *Internal Colonialism.*

Colonial Wars

The term *colonial war* is used to refer to conflicts fought to determine the future status of potential colonies, or currently held colonies, that generate at least one thousand battlefield casualties per year. This definition may be applied to two distinct categories of conflict: wars fought between great powers over a (potential) colony, and wars fought between a great power and a colony over its future status, otherwise referred to as asymmetric conflicts.

TRENDS IN THE LITERATURE

The political science literature on colonial wars concentrates on asymmetric conflicts. This literature focuses upon the causes of colonial wars and their outcome, with an emphasis upon great powers' losses to smaller powers, building upon Andrew Mack's balance-of-interests theory. Influenced by France's failed attempts to maintain its colonies in Indochina and Algeria, as well as the U.S. experience in Vietnam, Mack argues that the resolve of participants in asymmetric conflicts inversely relates to their relative capabilities. Weak powers have more to lose when fighting great powers and thus "fight harder," while great powers have fewer interests at stake in an asymmetric conflict, making domestic veto players more sensitive to losses.

Other authors have observed that explanations of asymmetric conflict such as Mack's cannot account for why and when great powers win small wars. Two theories based on strategic interaction have been put forward to account for why great powers win and lose asymmetric conflicts. One theory, advanced by Ivan Arreguín-Toft, argues that the outcome of asymmetric outcomes is contingent upon interaction between the strategies of great and lesser powers: "Every strategy has ideal counterstrategy" (104). Great powers lose when they choose the wrong counterstrategy. Patricia Sullivan argues that outcomes in asymmetric conflicts result from the war aims of great powers. Great powers are forced to terminate their participation in asymmetric conflicts when the "costs of victory exceed a state's prewar expectations" (Sullivan, 497). The costs of securing victory are determined by whether a great power's war aims require that its target comply with its demands; these costs are lower when the great power pursues conquest rather than compliance.

PROBLEMS WITH THE COLONIAL WAR CONCEPT

In response to the literature on colonial wars, there have been salient critiques of the very concept of a singular colonial war. First, this term conflates war with (one of) the issues or motivations responsible for its outbreak.

Second, in practice, it is difficult to distinguish between certain colonial wars and great power wars. The literature on colonial wars implicitly focuses on wars fought over territories located in the third world. However, there is little real distinction between wars fought by great powers to acquire or maintain colonial possessions in the third world and wars fought by great powers to either acquire or maintain territory within their locales. Wars fought by great powers to maintain or acquire additional territory only differ from colonial wars in that they are more likely to bring about war with other great powers. For example, efforts by great powers to attain regional dominance, such as Meiji Japan's pursuit of hegemony in Asia at the beginning of the twentieth century, may be indistinguishable from attempts to acquire colonies.

Third, war widening, along with the expansion of war aims, further blur the distinction between colonial and great power wars. Some conflicts that begin as disputes over extraregional territories may escalate and become hegemonic wars (i.e., a war that redistributes the overall international balance of power). One example is the transformation of the French and Indian War (1754–1763) into the Seven Years' War (1756–1763). Other conflicts may begin as wars between great powers, but the fighting may spread to great powers' extraregional territories. World War I (1914–1918) began in Europe, but the fighting spread to parts of the European powers' colonies in Africa.

A radical means to clarify the conceptual confusion now proposed is to abandon the term *colonial war*. Instead, the study of conflicts fought for control of territory would distinguish between the motivations that lead to the outbreak of war and the participants involved, allowing international relations theorists to focus upon the imperial motivation for war. This refers to states' utility for maintaining or acquiring additional territory. Rather than studying wars between great powers and wars between great and lesser powers under the same conceptual rubric, the strength of the imperial motivation for war could be studied across *symmetrical* (wars between great powers) and *asymmetrical* (war between a great and a lesser power) conflicts. It remains to be seen, however, whether this critique will become dominant in political science.

See also *Asymmetric Wars; Colonialism; Insurgency; Insurrection and Insurgency; Wars of Independence.*

. . . . ALBERT B. WOLF

BIBLIOGRAPHY

Arreguín-Toft, Ivan. "How the Weak Win Wars: A Theory of Asymmetric Conflict." *International Security* 26, no. 1 (2001): 93–128.

Mack, Andrew. "Why Big Nations Lose Small Wars." *World Politics* 27, no. 2 (January 1975): 175–200.

Sullivan, Patricia L. "War Aims and War Outcomes: Why Powerful States Lose Limited Wars." *Journal of Conflict Resolution* 51, no. 3 (2007): 496–524.

Commerce Clause

Article I, Section 8, of the U.S. Constitution lists the powers of the U.S. Congress. Under the original design of the Constitution, the Framers attempted to achieve the paradoxical objective of a *strong* government of *limited* powers by limiting the range of powers of the new legislative branch to those "enumerated powers" listed in Article I, Section 8, and then granting plenary power over that list by giving Congress the power "to make all laws which shall be necessary and proper for carrying into execution the foregoing powers."

From the beginning, one of the most important of the enumerated powers granted to Congress was the commerce clause, which grants Congress the power "To regulate commerce with foreign nations, and among the several states, and with the Indian tribes." Prior to the ratification of the Constitution, the national government did not have the legal authority under the Articles of Confederation to regulate commercial activity, thus causing state governments to engage in trade wars by placing tariffs and other taxes on out-of-state goods, and some states conducted their own trade policies with foreign nations. By granting the power to the federal government, the Framers apparently intended to facilitate a national economy and to minimize barriers to interstate commercial activity. Undoubtedly, the commerce power has turned out to be one the most important sources for the expansion of federal power over time.

Nonetheless, the exact scope of the commerce clause has long been a subject of debate and even controversy. In *Gibbons v. Ogden* (1824), Chief Justice John Marshall sided with the federal government over the issue of licensing navigation. Marshall found that Congress had the authority to regulate navigation between states pursuant to its commerce power, and the federal license trumped attempts by states to regulate in the same waters. By the time of the industrial revolution in the late nineteenth century and into the early twentieth century, the reach of the commerce power was again called into question. For example, the Supreme Court upheld the regulation of meat dealers and stockyards in *Swift & Co. v. Swift* (1905) and *Stafford v. Wallace* (1922), the shipment of lottery tickets in *Champion v. Ames* (1903), and the regulation of prostitution in *Hoke v. United States* (1913), as permissible legislation regulating items placed in the "current of commerce." However, the Supreme Court drew the line between purely local activities and those involving interstate commerce, and held that there exists an important distinction between "manufacturing" and commerce. For instance, the Court held that Congress could regulate neither the monopoly over the manufacturing of sugar in *United States. v. E.C. Knight & Co.* (1895) nor child labor in *Hammer v. Dagenhart* (1918) because manufacturing and labor are purely local activities outside the reach of the commerce clause. This period has been characterized as one of *judicial dualism* in which the Court allowed Congress to expand federal power over social or economic activity in some areas, but not others.

The debate over Congress's commerce power came to a head during the New Deal period in the 1930s. The Court initially struck down numerous statutes involving labor and other economic policies that it considered purely local activities outside the purview of the commerce clause. However, the Court eventually relented and upheld the regulation of manufacturing, labor, and similar activities that could be viewed has having a "substantial effect" on interstate commerce in *NLRB v. Jones & Laughlin Steel Corp.* (1937), *United States v. Darby* (1941), and *Wickard v. Filburn* (1942). While those decisions upheld and legitimized key New Deal legislation, the logic was used by Congress to support the passage of provisions in the Civil Rights Act of 1964, regarding discrimination in places of "public accommodation," which were upheld by the Court under the commerce clause in *Heart of Atlanta Motel v. United States* (1964), and *Katzenbach v. McClung* (1964). By the 1980s, Congress had built a large portion of the regulatory state—including forays into environmental policy and criminal law—on the back of its broad commerce power, and it was widely assumed that the Supreme Court would not attempt to draw lines around the commerce power.

But in the 1990s, the Supreme Court did find limits to Congress's commerce power. Applying the "substantial effects" test, the Court determined that Congress could not, pursuant to its commerce power, criminalize the possession of guns on school grounds in *United States v. Lopez* (1995) or provide a federal civil remedy for victims of gender-motivated violence in *United States v. Morrison* (2000). The Rehnquist Court's resurrection of judicially enforceable limits on Congress's commerce power has sparked a debate over the proper role of the Court in these and other federalism cases. Some have argued that the Court's recent decisions are proper and long overdue, and that only the Court can enforce

the constitutional federalism structures intended to place real limits on the scope of the national legislative powers. Others argue that Congress has the authority and means to engage in fact finding, policy evaluation, and constitutional deliberation; Congress also should not be subjected to judicial review over an area in which Congress has plenary powers.

See also *Checks and Balances; Constitutions and Constitutionalism; New Deal.*

. . . . J. MITCHELL PICKERILL

BIBLIOGRAPHY

Calabresi, Steven G. "A Government of Limited and Enumerated Powers: In Defense of *United States v. Lopez.*" *Michigan Law Review* 94 (1995): 752–831.

Colker, Ruth, and James J. Brudney. "Dissing Congress." *Michigan Law Review* 100, no. 1 (2001), 80–144.

McCloskey, Robert G. *The American Supreme Court.* Chicago: The University of Chicago Press, 1960.

NLRB v. Jones & Laughlin Steel Corp, 301 U.S. 1 (1937).

Pickerill, J. Mitchell. *Constitutional Deliberation in Congress: The Impact of Judicial Review in a Separated System.* Durham, N.C.: Duke University Press. 2004.

Common Goods

The term *common good,* or the term *commons,* both refer to resources as well as to property rights institutions that govern the appropriation, alienation, and management of the resource. Analytically, however, it is important to differentiate between the two concepts. A *common-pool resource* (natural or human constructed) is available for appropriation to multiple users. When one consumer uses a unit of these goods, this unit is no longer available to other users—a characteristic commonly referred to as *jointness* or *rivalry* in consumption. At the same time, it is difficult (or costly) to prevent other users from appropriating these goods—a characteristic commonly referred to as *nonexcludability.* Given its rivalry in use coupled with nonexcludability, these resources are often overused and degraded. In contrast, *common-property institutions* are rules regarding how members of a community may access a resource, how much they may appropriate or alienate the jointly owned resource, and how they can devise new rules regulating its use. Common-pool resources and their physical characteristics influence institutions devised to govern and manage them. Subsequently, common-property institutions have been devised to successfully protect many common-pool resources.

COMMON-POOL RESOURCES

While some may view common-pool resources as small scale, local resource systems and common-property institutions as archaic arrangements, the truth cannot be further from this notion. Though common-pool resources include prototypic local, natural resources such as village pastures and fish harvesting areas, large-scale resources such as the oceans, the gene pool, and the atmosphere all exhibit the characteristics of common-pool resources as well. Further, humans create new types of common-pool resources. Many urban families reside in condominiums—a combination of private and common property. Internet servers, with a finite storage capacity, exhibit the characteristics of common-pool resources because it is costly to prevent users from using a server, while, at the same time, an excessive number of users at a given time can result in the collapse of the server. Airport landing slots can be viewed as common-pool resources: The challenges faced by the U.S. Federal Aviation Administration in allocating these slots illustrate the complexities in managing common-pool resources, given that the demand for slots tends to exceed their availability.

Analytically, common-pool resources can be viewed as goods that exhibit rivalry in appropriation, akin to private goods, but low excludability in appropriation, akin to public goods. Several consumers can appropriate a given unit of a nonrival good (e.g., national defense), whereas only a single actor can appropriate a unit of a rival good. The loads of fish or mass of water withdrawn by one user are no longer available to others, hence rivalry in appropriation, or *consumption*. Similarly, the absorptive capacities of airsheds and watersheds decrease when one user emits pollutants into the air or water. Scholar Garrett Hardin suggested the race to appropriate first will lead to resource degradation, therefore the *tragedy of the commons*.

The second analytical characteristic of common-pool resources is their low levels of excludability. This implies that it is physically, institutionally, or economically difficult or costly to exclude users from appropriating the benefits of the good. The challenge is to devise and enforce institutions that assure resource users that others will not appropriate the resource first (i.e., they will not suffer the "sucker's payoff"). When institutions enforce excludability and limit access to the resource, the race to appropriate first can be thwarted. Consequently, the resource can be exploited in a sustainable manner. Indeed, overconsumption of a common-pool resource or the tragedy of the commons is not inevitable. In many ways, Hardin incorrectly equated open access resources, which do not have institutions to enforce excludability, with common-pool resources. Indeed, Hardin's famous pastures often have intricate institutions—often invisible to observers not familiar with the local culture—to govern resource appropriation.

While sharing the analytical attributes of rivalry and nonexcludability, common-pool resources differ on other attributes such as their size, boundary stability, negative externalities, complexity of the system in which the resource is located, uniformity in resource flows, and levels of resource use. Thus, any analysis of the governance of common-pool goods needs to take into account their analytical similarities and their differences. Some characteristics tend to be conducive to their successful governance. These characteristics are small-sized, stable, and well-delineated resource boundaries; small levels of negative externalities resulting from resource use; moderate levels of complexity so that the resource users can monitor resource stocks and flows at low cost; and resource users' solid understanding of the dynamics of the resource.

Common-pool resources of smaller size tend to support the establishment and maintenance of resource governance institutions. Researchers usually group common-pool resources into local, regional, and global resources. It is not clear, however, how the size alone affects institutional evolution and design. Rather, size may interact with other variables. Even though it is more difficult to design and enforce institutions to manage regional and global resources, several have been managed and protected. At this point, there are about two hundred international regimes addressing global common-pool resources. While some have been effective in curbing resource overuse—for example, the Montreal Protocol to protect the stratospheric ozone—the jury is out on others, such as the protection of biodiversity or the global atmosphere. The size of the resource tends to correlate with heterogeneity of resource users. Arguably, higher levels of heterogeneity impede the successful governance and management of common-pool resources as in the case of the global atmosphere, which is used as a sink for greenhouse gases.

Common-pool resources with well-delineated and stable boundaries are more conducive to the emergence and sustenance of institutions for managing these resources. If boundaries of the resource are understood and do not change over time, then it is easier to determine the users of the resource and the extent of their resource withdrawal. Inability to determine these characteristics is a fundamental problem that has led to overuse and degradation of many resources, including fisheries, watersheds, and airsheds. This problem is especially challenging when the common-pool resource is not extracted, but used as a sink for pollutants, leading to problems like acid rain, ozone hole, poor local air quality, low oxygen levels in watersheds, and others.

Externalities are the negative or positive effects of actions experienced by those not involved in the transaction. As a result, the social costs and benefits of a transaction differ from its private costs and benefits. For example, in fisheries, withdrawals by one user create negative externalities for other users. Withdrawing one unit of a resource reduces the number of resource units available to other resource users, thereby increasing the withdrawal costs. Resources with negative externalities tend to be overproduced or overappropriated, and those with positive externalities tend to be underproduced or underappropriated. Appropriation of common-pool resources associated with small levels of negative externalities is easier to manage.

The complexity of the system in which the resource is located creates challenges for devising institutions to manage the resource. Complexity may manifest in various ways such as levels of interconnectedness among various resources within a system, or the time lag after which the affects of resource appropriation can be observed, akin to information asymmetries in postexperience goods leading to market failures. For example, a harvest level of one fish species may affect levels of harvest of other species. Reducing the number of predator species may increase the stock of a given species; reducing the amount of species that constitute an important link in the food chain of the given species may reduce the stocks of this species. Further, the quality of the water may affect fish stock levels, and this is a function of the use of water as a pollution sink. In this case, multiple institutions must be devised, linked or nested, regulating multiple species or even ecosystems.

Resources that have nonuniform impacts of flows on the stocks are difficult to manage. For example, the impact of air pollutant emissions on pollution concentration is frequently nonuniform, dependent on airflows and topography. A unit of deposited air pollutant in one area may have more detrimental effects on the resource stocks than a unit deposited in other areas. Research on use of the atmosphere as a sink for air pollutants suggests this was a major problem in devising rules for maintaining air quality, especially for pollutants that remain in the close proximity of the emission point (e.g., nitrous oxides or lead).

Common-pool resources tend to be better managed when resource users can understand the dynamics of the resource flow and availability. Resources with time-dependent stocks are more difficult to manage than the resources that exhibit small levels of time dependence. Empirical research suggests that users of renewable resources pay close attention to the withdrawal rate and replacement rate. They are more likely to devise institutions to manage common-pool resources if they estimate that such institutions are necessary (i.e., replacement rate is not much higher than the resource withdrawal rate) and that they will be productive (i.e., the withdrawal rate is not much higher than the replacement rate). These relationships, however, are not stable. Replacement rates may change due to factors external to the institutional design. For example, replacement of a fish stock may drastically decline due to water pollution, or an introduction of a new predator or deposition of an air pollutant may skyrocket with a new technology (e.g., depletion of the ozone layer and global warming). If those changes are not monitored, the common-pool resource may be overconsumed. For resources that exhibit high uncertainty in these environmental factors, institutions have to be accordingly flexible.

INSTITUTIONS GOVERNING COMMON-POOL RESOURCES

Common-pool resources have the analytical attribute of nonexcludability. If users cannot be excluded, they have little incentives to defray the cost of maintaining and governing the resource. As economist and social scientist Mancur Olson pointed out, free riding impedes the supply of collective action. When nonexcludability couples with rivalry (e.g., "if I get the resource, you cannot"), it creates incentives to overharvest rapidly—a type of race to the overappropriation. For example, why would countries unilaterally incur costs to protect a global common-pool resource, the global atmosphere, from being overused as a sink for greenhouse gasses? Given its physical characteristics, users in other jurisdictions cannot be prevented from appropriating the benefits of this global pollution sink, a condition ripe for free riding. Thus, to manage common-pool resources, institutions (e.g., the Kyoto Protocol to mitigate global climate change) must be put in place to enforce exclusion. Indeed, as the rich literature on this subject attests, resource users at various scales, local to global, have sought to create institutions with varying levels of success to enforce excludability (i.e., regulate resource use), and thereby support resource governance.

As carefully documented by Nobel Prize-winning economist Elinor Ostrom in her book *Governing the Commons* as well as in several other volumes surveying common-pool resources, such as *The Questions of the Commons* edited by Bonnie McCay and James Acheson or in the *Drama of the Commons,* a volume edited by Elinor Ostrom and colleagues appropriate institutions can and have altered actors' incentives in the ways that they practice forbearance and appropriate resources sustainably. Communities across the world have devised rule systems to sustainably use communal pastures and forests for hundred of years; just because some these local institutions might have less visible, nontraditional features—such as a reliance on informal norms or cultural practices to encourage forbearance and regulate resource exploitation—external observers should not view them as open access resources.

Crafted institutions can increase the efficiency and sustainability of common-pool resource use over time. They can be thought of as the dos and don'ts that are commonly understood in regard to the entry, harvesting, and management of a resource, and how individuals acquire or transfer rights to use a resource. Three broad forms of ownership could be used to govern common-pool resources: government-, private-, or common-property ownership. There is no consistent evidence that any one of these ownership types is best suited for all types of common-pool resources, even though considerable debate about the relative advantages exists in the academic literature.

National governments have established a variety of institutions using government and private property ownership. Governments can decide to manage the resource on behalf of citizens in their jurisdictions. In the United States, federal, state, and city governments have established national parks, national forests, state forests, and city forests. Further, governments have regulated the use of common-pool resources by prescribing technologies users must employ either to withdraw the resource from the pool (e.g., fishing) or to deposit pollution in commons (e.g., emission filters and scrubbers to clean up exhausts). In addition, governments have adopted other instruments to influence responsible resource use. For example, governments have required for-profit organizations to provide information to consumers regarding the impact of their production processes and products on common-pool resources. Various labeling initiatives as well as pollution registries, such as the Toxics Release Inventory Program established by the U.S. Environmental Protection Agency, are examples of such initiatives. The idea behind such information-based regulation is that informed consumers will vote with their dollars and informed stakeholders will bestow goodwill benefits on firms that minimize use of environmental common-pool resources. Finally, governments have developed market incentives, such as taxes and fees to increase the cost of common-pool resource withdrawal. For some common-pool resources—such as fisheries, water bodies, and the air—governments have sought to partition the resource use and impose an upper limit to each user's overall appropriation by devising and allocating quantified rights to the use of this resource. The latter approach has drawn much attention, especially in the context of the ongoing global climate change debate.

One frequently recommended solution to the tragedy of the commons is to privatize the resource, as stated in John Dales's 1968 *Pollution, Property, and Prices:* "If it is feasible to establish a market to implement a policy, no policy maker can afford to do without one. Unless I am very much mistaken, markets *can* be used to implement any anti-pollution policy that you or I can dream up" (100). However, empirical analyses of individual common-pool resources suggest that this broad endorsement of privatization is somewhat optimistic. Tradable permit markets have been found to be thin and with high transaction costs. Data problems have impeded monitoring and enforcement of trading rules. Scholars question whether tradable permit systems stimulate innovation and have the ability to respond to sudden and substantial changes in the market. About thirty years after the implementation of the first tradable permit market in the United States, researchers are more careful in endorsing the tradable permit markets as a universal approach to solve the commons problem. As noted by A. Denny Ellerman and colleagues in *Markets for Clean Air,* "All of our analysis suggests one final observation: Experience with and lessons learned from the Acid Rain Program must be applied with care to other environmental objectives" (321). Instead of a one-size-fits-all approach across common-pool resources, the challenge is to devise institutional designs that ensure sustainability and efficiency in managing resources with specific characteristics located in given external legal and regulatory environments. The transfer of institutional designs across resources, regions, or scales must be undertaken with caution.

Globalization processes create additional challenges in devising institutions for common-pool resources. Globalization—the increased connectedness of markets and the increased levels of flows of goods, services, and factors of production across borders—can influence appropriation levels of common-pool resources. A local resource user might seek to appropriate a common-pool resource not only for individual use but to sell it to the world market. Farmers may shift from cultivation of traditional species, which are not, for instance, water intensive, to cash crops, which might be water intensive. This thereby potentially increases the pressure on the water table. The consequence of globalization is that the resource institutions that encouraged forbearance in resource use come under pressure. The opportunity and cost of complying with local norms seems to increase, sometimes dominate, in relation to the gains from violating the norms. Further, increased, low-cost access to world markets increases differentiation between those who have the resources (e.g., labor) to produce products and those who do not. This might put strain on traditional relationships, which were predicated on wealth and income equality and also sustained the resource use norms.

On the other hand, access to world markets can strengthen resource institutions by providing resource users the access to new technologies and providing them financial capital to regenerate common-pool resources. Also, globalization is not only about trade and investment; it is also associated with the global spread of common norms and ideas. With the diffusion of environmental and postmaterial values, globalization may provide users of common-pool resources in developing countries with a market for a sustainably harvested resource, if appropriately certified. For example, markets may develop for nuts from a tropical rainforest or for shade-grown coffee. Thus, globalization is both a blessing and a curse for the management of common-pool resources. Much depends on how actors can disrupt the traditional modes of social organization by making use of the opportunities and devising new ways to protect their institutions from the challenges of globalization.

With globalization, international donor agencies have become more involved in developing countries' resource use. Common-property institutions in developing countries can benefit from funds available from national and international donor agencies. In some cases, common-property institutions are even initiated by these donors. This brings a set of important new actors and dynamics that all pose challenges for the governance of common-pool resources. In particular, external funders might follow different time frames and operate on a much shorter cycle than required for the adaptive development of successful institutions. When common-property regimes are initiated with external donors' funding, a danger exists that the devised rules will not correspond to the social customs, norms, and value orientations. Further, the community may not be given authority to change the rules governing the resource; rather, this authority may be vested in the donor or national government of the country hosting the project. On the other hand, involvement of powerful international donors may bring legitimacy to communities that would otherwise, due to the local power structure, not be given the authority to govern the resource.

Finally, the subject of institutional change is particularly challenging for traditional common-pool resources. What if a particular institution is failing to stem resource overuse? How easily can a new one replace the former institution? One can seldom begin with an empty slate, since most traditional common-pool resources are likely to already have institutions in place. The challenge is to devise more effective institutions without becoming unduly distracted by path dependencies, while also responding to distributional consequences. Eventually, like any other governance systems, common-pool regimes need to have an economic and political logic to create incentive from their resource users.

See also *Environmental Policy; Environmental Political Theory; Globalization; Governability; International Cooperation; International Norms; Kyoto Protocol; New Institutionalism; Tragedy of the Commons.*

. . . . NIVES DOLŠAK

BIBLIOGRAPHY
Ascher, William. *Communities and Sustainable Forestry in Developing Countries.* San Francisco: ICS Press, 1995.
Axelrod, Regina S., David L. Downie, and Norman Vig, eds. *The Global Environment: Institutions, Law, and Policy,* 2nd ed. Washington, D.C.: Congressional Quarterly Press, 2005.
Bromley, Daniel W., David Feeny, Margaret McKean, Pauline Peters, Jere Gilles, Ronald Oakerson, C. Ford. Runge, and James Thomson, eds. *Making the Commons Work: Theory, Practice, and Policy.* San Francisco: ICS Press, 1992.

Coy, Carol, et al. (2001). *White Paper on Stabilization of NOx RTC Prices.* South Coast Air Quality Management District. www.aqmd.gov/hb/2001/010123a.html.

Dales, John. *Pollution, Property, and Prices: An Essay in Policy-Making and Economics.* Toronto: University of Toronto Press, 1968.

Dolšak, Nives. 2001. "Mitigating Global Climate Change: Why Some Countries are More Committed than Others?" *Policy Studies Journal* 29, no. 3 (2001): 414–436.

Dolšak, Nives and Elinor Ostrom. "The Challenges of the Commons." In *The Commons in the New Millennium: Challenges and Adaptations,* edited by N. Dolšak and E. Ostrom, 1–34. Cambridge, Mass.: MIT Press, 2003.

Driesen, David M. *The Economic Dynamics of Environmental Law.* Cambridge, Mass.: MIT Press, 2003.

Ellerman, Danny A., et al. *Markets for Clean Air: The U.S. Acid Rain Program.* Cambridge: Cambridge University Press, 2000.

Fung, Archon, Mary Graham, and David Weil. *Full Disclosure: The Perils and Promise of Transparency.* Cambridge, Mass.: Cambridge University Press, 2007.

Gangadharan, Lata. "Transaction Costs in Pollution Markets: An Empirical Study." *Land Economics* 76 (2000): 601–614.

Hahn, Robert W., and Gordon L. Hester. "Where Did All the Markets Go? An Analysis of EPA's Emissions Trading Program." *Yale Journal on Regulation* 6 (1989): 109–153.

Hardin, Garrett. "The Tragedy of the Commons." *Science* 162 (1968): 1243–1248.

Keohane, Robert, and Elinor Ostrom, eds. *Local Commons and Global Interdependence: Heterogeneity and Cooperation in Two Domains.* Thousand Oaks, Calif: Sage Publications, 1995.

Le Prestre, Philippe G., ed. *Governing Global Biodiversity: The Evolution and Implementation of the Convention on Biological Diversity.* Burlington, Vt.: Ashgate Publishing, 2002.

Long, Chun-Lin, Jefferson Fox, Lu Xing, Gao Lihong, Cai Kui, and Wang Jieru. "State Policies, Markets, Land-Use Practices, and Common Property: Fifty Years of Change in a Yunnan Village, China." *Mountain Research and Development* 19, no. 2 (1999): 133–139.

McCay, Bonnie J., and James M. Acheson, eds. *The Question of the Commons: The Culture and Ecology of Communal Resources.* Tucson: University of Arizona Press, 1987.

McCay, Bonnie J., and Svein Jentoft. "Market or Community Failure? Critical Perspectives on Common Property Research." *Human Organization* 57, no. 1 (1998): 21–29.

Montero, Juan-Pablo. "Pollution Markets with Imperfectly Observed Emissions." *RAND Journal of Economics* 36, no. 3 (2005): 645–660.

Morrow, Christopher E., and Rebecca W. Hull. "A Donor-Initiated Common Pool Resource Institution: The Case of Yanesha Forestry Cooperative." *World Development* 24, no. 10 (1996): 1641–1657.

Olsen, J. Rolf., and James S. Shortle. "The Optimal Control of Emission and Renewable Resource Harvesting under Uncertainty." *Environmental and Resource Economics* 7, no. 2 (1996): 97–115.

Olson, Mancur. *The Logic of Collection Action.* Cambridge, Mass.: Harvard University Press, 1965.

Ostrom, Elinor. *Governing the Commons: The Evolution of Institutions for Collective Action.* Cambridge, Mass.: Cambridge University Press, 1990.

Ostrom, Elinor, et al., eds. *The Drama of the Commons.* Washington, D.C.: National Academy Press, 2002.

Prakash, Aseem, and Matthew Potoski. *The Voluntary Environmentalists: Green Clubs, ISO 14001, and Voluntary Environmental Regulation.* Cambridge: Cambridge University Press, 2006.

Schlager, Edella, and Elinor Ostrom. 1992. "Property-Rights Regimes and Natural Resources: A Conceptual Analysis." *Land Economics* 68, no. 3 (August 1992): 249–262.

U.S. EPA. *Evaluation of the South Coast Air Quality Management District's Regional Clean Air Incentives Market: Lessons in Environmental Markets and Innovation,* 2002. www.epa.gov/region09/air/reclaim/report.pdf.

Young, Oran, ed. *The Effectiveness of International Environmental Regimes: Causal Connections and Behavioral Mechanisms.* Cambridge, Mass.: MIT Press, 1999.

Common Law

Common law developed not at a single moment by the proclamation of a single individual, but as a result of accumulated traditions and laws over many centuries. The first statement of common-law principles can be found in the Magna Carta. Embodied in these rules was protection of subjects from rulers by preserving the rule of law via a system of due process. It took nearly four centuries for Sir Edward Coke, who became lord chief justice of England, to create a theoretical understanding of the common law and place the courts at the center of the common-law system. Following Coke was Sir William Blackstone, author of *Commentaries on the Laws of England,* who made modifications in Coke's philosophy but stayed faithful nonetheless. American iterations of the common law were professed most famously by American jurist and Supreme Court justice Oliver Wendell Holmes Jr., who stated that the common law is judge-made law. However, this definition departs from the original conception of the common law. The role of judges within the original conception of the common law was to decide law in accordance with existing statements of the law. Common-law judges had to balance canon law, parliamentary law, and precedent. In the absence of a clear and authoritative statement of the law, judges would hand down decisions that filled in the gaps by interpreting the existing law. In addition to precedent, a number of institutional arrangements and legal principles characterize the common law, and these differentiate common-law legal systems from other legal systems.

COMMON FEATURES OF COMMON-LAW SYSTEMS

Common-law legal systems are generally found in those countries that were territories or colonies of the British Empire. They are adversarial systems in which an attorney represents the accused and another attorney represents the accuser. Each side presents their case to a judge and jury to determine fact, guilt, and sentence. The most identifiable feature of the common-law system is the use of jury trials. It is the presence of juries that creates a buffer between the state and the citizen as juries are made up of one's peers. In common-law systems, judges and attorneys are selected from the bar in order to provide a certain level of professionalization. The professionalization of the judiciary is necessary for the common-law court to function effectively since the judges must determine the relevancy of evidence in order to ensure that the evidence presented is relevant to the case at hand. Furthermore, in order to have a system in which judges are granted a great deal of latitude, the judges must be properly trained and have a firm grasp of the law as it has developed through precedent. In making their decisions, precedent guides judges in the common-law system. *Stare decisis* is another term for precedent that is used to reflect a judicial ruling that is binding in future cases.

CRITICISMS

The common-law system is often criticized for being wrought with procedural strictness that becomes burdensome to all involved. One of these features is the separation between courts of law and courts of equity. Charles Dickens's novel *Bleak House* criticized this cumbersome feature of the common-law system. Courts of law apply the law as established to a particular case. In some instances, the law may provide a remedy that is inadequate for a particular situation. When such an instance arises, then one of the party's may take the suit to be heard in an equity court, sometimes referred to as *courts of chancery.* Equity courts can exercise more latitude in granting rewards to the victim. Until 1873, England maintained separate courts of law and equity. The federal judiciary in the United States ended such a formal distinction with the ratification of the Constitution. Until 1937, with the passage of the Federal Rules of Civil Procedure in which law and equity were combined into one form of action, the courts of the U.S. federal judiciary maintained a distinction between law and equity in one court. This reform came one year before the landmark decision in *Erie Railroad Company v. Tompkins,* in which the Supreme Court stated there is no federal general common law.

CODIFICATION AND EVOLUTION OF COMMON LAW

In the United States, most of the common law has been codified. Codification is the process by which common-law principles are turned into statutes. Examples of federal codification include the Federal Rules of Civil Procedure, the Uniform Commercial Code, and the Federal Rules of Evidence. The change at the national level was the result of a similar change at the state level. The codification movement, inspired by English philosopher and legal theorist Jeremy Bentham, was put into action by nineteenth-century American lawyer David Dudley Field, whose field codes were implemented in New York. Nearly all states followed suit by codifying former common-law principles. Louisiana is the only state without a common-law background. Instead, its system of law is based on the Napoleonic Code, with France having first colonized the region.

The common law is a constantly evolving system of law. It is a body of general rules that prescribe social conduct. In the common law, the law is supreme and is placed above all institutions and actors. At its center is a judiciary who does not make law, but discovers law through a long and laborious study of the statutory law, tradition, and precedent. Judicial decisions, *stare decisis,* guide future decisions. Developing out of actual legal controversies, the common law is identified by its use of precedents, jury trials, adversarial proceedings, a professionalized bench and lawyers drawn from the bar, and the protection of individual rights. James Stoner, *Common-Law Liberty: Rethinking American Constitutionalism,* writes, "Common law emphasizes assent rather than domination, the community rather than the state, moral authority rather than physical power" (Stoner, 5).

See also *Civil Law; Due Process; Judicial Systems, Comparative; Precedent; Trial Courts.*

. . . . KYLE SCOTT

BIBLIOGRAPHY
Hogue, Arthur R. *Origins of the Common Law.* Reprint, Indianapolis, Ind: Liberty Fund, 1986.
Horwitz, Morton J. *The Transformation of American Law: 1780–1860.* Cambridge, Mass.: Harvard University Press, 1977.
Stoner, James R. *Common-Law Liberty: Rethinking American Constitutionalism.* Lawrence: University Press of Kansas, 2003.
Stoner, James R. *Common Law and Liberal Theory: Coke, Hobbes, and the Origins of American Constitutionalism.* Lawrence: University Press of Kansas, 1992.

Commonwealth

Dating from the fifteenth century, the phrase *common wealth* reflects the old meaning of well-being; hence commonwealth, as often used by seventeenth-century writers, meant an organized political community governed for the common good, on occasion implying an interest, or say, for all members. The term has evolved to denote a polity that is law-based, contractual, and consensually united with supreme authority vested in the populace; especially capitalized, it can also designate an association of sovereign states more or less loosely associated in a common *allegiance,* or an autonomous political unit voluntarily associated with another. Used most prominently at the international level today, a few cases of national and subnational commonwealths remain.

HISTORICAL COMMONWEALTHS

In various parts of the world, historical cases of commonwealths, to some extent, foreshadow their modern counterparts in displaying elements of contractual self-government. These cases include:

- The medieval Icelandic Commonwealth or Free State (930–1262), which ended with a pledge of fealty to the Norwegian king;
- The Polish-Lithuanian Commonwealth (1569–1791), one of the largest and most populous polities in seventeenth-century Europe, which, as a semifederal republic centered on a gentry-controlled parliament and an elected, contract-bound monarch, can be considered a precursor to modern concepts of constitutional monarchy and federation;
- The Commonwealth of England, which replaced the kingdoms of England and Scotland in the period of the English Interregnum (1649–1660) after the Civil War. Formally the first republic in the English-speaking world, under the rule of "Lord Protectors" Oliver and Richard Cromwell, the Commonwealth of England effectively amounted to military rule in the name of parliamentary supremacy;
- The Commonwealth of the Philippines (1935–1946), a transitional, self-governing political entity in free association with the United States, created in preparation for the Philippines's independence.

INTERNATIONAL LEVEL

The Commonwealth of Nations is the voluntary confederation of former parts of the British Empire (plus Mozambique), a group of fifty-three sovereign states and their dependencies linked by common objectives and interests. Members include both republics and monarchies, and in 2010 the (appointed, not hereditary) head of the Commonwealth of Nations is Queen Elizabeth II, who is also reigning monarch in the commonwealth realms, notably the United Kingdom, Australia, Canada, and New Zealand.

The roots of the modern commonwealth lie in the nineteenth and early twentieth centuries, when certain colonies—Canada (1867), followed by Australia (1900), New Zealand (1907), South Africa (1910), and the Irish Free State (1921)—became self-governing dominions, a newly constituted status implying equality with Britain. After World War I (1914–1918), the dominions' relationship with Britain was developed further, and in 1926 the Imperial Conference defined them as autonomous and equal communities within the British Empire, united by common allegiance to the Crown and freely associated as members of the British Commonwealth of Nations. After World War II (1939–1945), decolonization led to the London Declaration of 1949, which, in order to enable newly independent republics like India to join, dropped "allegiance to the Crown" as a requirement for membership as well as the designation "British." From the late 1950s, new members from the Mediterranean, Africa, the Caribbean, and the Pacific joined, extending the community's spectrum of activities, and in 1965 the establishment of the Commonwealth Secretariat in London furnished the organization with an independent civil service. The Commonwealth Foundation (1966), the Singapore Declaration of Commonwealth Principles (which, in 1971, introduced a formal code of ethics and a commitment to human rights, racial, and economic justice), and the Commonwealth Fund for Technical Cooperation completed the modern Commonwealth of Nations. Its biannual summits are the association's ultimate policy- and decision-making forum, at which it reviews international developments, issues positions, and decides on any action, particularly in terms of priorities and programs for development cooperation. These summits, held in a different member state each time, are also considered an opportunity to strengthen the idea of the Commonwealth of Nations as an association providing friendship, business partnership, and stabilization for its members.

The creation of the Commonwealth of Independent States (CIS) signaled the end of the Soviet Union in December 1991. A loose confederation of twelve of the fifteen former Soviet Republics on the basis of "sovereign equality," it has evolved from its initial purpose of facilitating their "civilized divorce" into a forum for economic, foreign policy, and defense cooperation, coordinated through an array of CIS institutions. Various institutional steps have been aimed at deepening integration among some of its members. In 1993, the CIS created an Economic Union modeled on the European Union's Common Market, notably also aiming for the coordination of tax and price policy. In 1995, Russia and Belarus agreed to form the Commonwealth of Sovereign Republics and to deepen integration in the humanitarian and economic fields with Kazakhstan and Kyrgyzstan with an interstate council, which later also included Tajikistan. In 2000, these five formed the Eurasian Economic Community, with which some other CIS members have associated themselves to various degrees.

In 2003, Russia, Belarus, Kazakhstan, and Ukraine created a common economic space. Unlike the Commonwealth of Nations, then, the CIS has been characterized by a certain incoherence due to members' strongly varying ambitions in terms of the desired levels of integration.

NATIONAL LEVEL

The Commonwealth of Australia was formed in 1901 with the federation of six states under a single constitution. After the first Europeans had begun exploration in the seventeenth century, Captain James Cook took possession for Great Britain in 1770, and subsequently, six colonies—New South Wales, Queensland, South Australia, Tasmania, Victoria, and Western Australia—were created. Early efforts at federation in the 1850s and 1860s, also involving Fiji and New Zealand who later decided to opt out, lacked popular support. The 1901 Commonwealth of Australia Constitution Act created a federal system dividing power between the national government and the six former colonies, designating Australia a constitutional monarchy where a governor-general represents the royal head of state at the federal level, and six governors represent at the state level.

Other national commonwealths include the Commonwealth of the Bahamas, which adopted the title upon independence from Britain in 1973 and also remains a commonwealth realm within the Commonwealth of Nations; and, since 1970, the Commonwealth of Dominica, after it obtained associated statehood (virtual independence from Britain) in 1968.

SUBNATIONAL LEVEL

The United States of America contains four commonwealths: Kentucky, Massachusetts, Pennsylvania, and Virginia. While not used in common parlance, the designation, which has no constitutional effect, emphasizes their government "based on the common consent of the people," as opposed to one legitimized through their earlier royal British colony status. In addition, commonwealth is also used to describe the political relationship between the United States and its unincorporated, self-governing overseas territories of Puerto Rico and the Northern Mariana Islands, indicating their consensual association as well as their status outside of the federal hierarchy.

In general, use of the term commonwealth has tended to underline the voluntary and consensual nature of a political community or an association among political entities; in some cases, it has additionally been used to indicate that such an association, while more than an alliance, constituted less than a confederation or federation.

See also *Allegiance; Federalism; Federation and Confederation.*

. . . . DOREEN K. ALLERKAMP

BIBLIOGRAPHY

Commonwealth Secretariat. *The Commonwealth Yearbook*. London: Nexus Strategic Partnerships, 2009.

Lloyd, Lorna. *Diplomacy with a Difference: The Commonwealth Office of High Commissioner, 1880–2006*. Leiden, the Netherlands: Martinus Nijhoff, 2007.

Lundan, Sarianna M., and Geoffrey Jones. "The 'Commonwealth Effect' and the Process of Internationalisation." *World Economy* 24, no. 1 (2001): 99–118.

MacCormick, Neil. *Questioning Sovereignty: Law, State, and Nation in the European Commonwealth.* Oxford: Oxford University Press, 1999.

Mayall, James. "Democratizing the Commonwealth." *International Affairs* 74, no. 2 (1998): 379–392.

Shaw, Timothy M. "The Commonwealth(s) and Global Governance." *Global Governance* 10, no. 4 (2004): 499–516.

Communalism

Communalism refers to a range of diverse perspectives, theories, and movements in which social change is founded in the redevelopment of community as a site of close, personal, face-to-face relationships as opposed to the anonymity and impersonal character of industrial capitalist society. One of the most influential early notions of communalism can be found in the works of German sociologist Ferdinand Tönnies, who presented the community as an alternative to the cold calculation of market-based society (*Gesellschaft*) that was replacing the close ties of rural life (*Gemeinschaft*).

The term communalism became increasingly popular in the late twentieth century, especially among progressive activists and leftists seeking an alternative discourse on communal societies beyond the discredited forms of authoritarian Communism, Marxism, Sovietism, and Leninism. It has become particularly popular among contemporary anarchists, notably those influenced by American anarchist philosopher Murray Bookchin's writings on social ecology and libertarian municipalism. Bookchin saw communalism not only as the development of a new public sphere that might oppose the state and capital, but also an alternative to the anticollectivist emphasis on individualism and personal autonomy in libertarianism and much of contemporary anarchism.

For communalism, social life is organized primarily in small communes where community decisions are based on consensus and participatory democracy in face-to-face meetings involving all members. In place of a national state—a central decision-making body consisting of professional governors who make decisions for communities they do not belong to—under communalism, local communes come together in a confederal association of recallable delegates to address issues of mutual interest and concern, such as trade.

Communalist movements have included communal living arrangements in urban centers, "back-to-the land" movements such as the hippie movement that began in the United States in the 1960s, utopian communities such as Scotland's New Lanark, and present-day land trusts, in which property is owned collectivity.

Anarchists view communalist arrangements as a precursor to a large-scale transformation of society, as the idea of a confederation of communes—the "commune of communes"—comes to pose an alternative to the state for a growing number of people. Eventually, having been rendered obsolete, the state will wither away.

Communalism has also gained popularity as a perspective within conservatism in North America. For conservatives, communalism offers an alternative to the cultural diversity, social fragmentation, and liberalization of contemporary society. Conservative communalists argue for what they view as a return to "traditional" community life, based on the neighborhood and often resting on a patriarchal view of the family, as an answer to broad social problems. Some conservative communalists point to the social movements of the 1960s and 1970s, especially those espousing feminism, black power, and gay and lesbian rights, as causes of a perceived breakdown of "traditional" community values. Among the most influential proponents of conservative communalism is German-Israeli-American sociologist Amitai Etzioni. In some areas of South Asia, including contemporary India, communalism refers to sectarian conflicts between religious communities and between people of the same religion but different regions.

See also *Anarchism; Bookchin, Murray; Communism; Community; Conservatism; Social Movements.*

. . . . JEFFREY SHANTZ

BIBLIOGRAPHY

Bookchin, Murray. *Free Cities: Communalism and the Left.* London: Pluto Press, 2009.

———. *The Politics of Social Ecology: Libertarian Municipalism.* Montreal: Black Rose, 1997.

———. *Social Ecology and Communalism.* San Francisco: AK Press, 2007.

Buber, Martin. *Paths in Utopia.* Syracuse, N.Y.: Syracuse University Press, 1996.

Etzioni, Amitai. *From Empire to Community: A New Approach to International Relations.* New York: Palgrave Macmillan, 2004.

———. *The Spirit of Community.* New York: Crown Books, 1993.

Commune

In its most technical sense, the term *commune* refers to a local level of social organization that became rooted in the administration of many European nations, especially France, where it represents the lowest level of government. When used in this sense, it is roughly equivalent to a township, civil parish, or municipality. In its more familiar usage, the term describes a voluntary association of people who seek to realize a common end through cooperative communal living.

Communes as vehicles of low-level social coordination flourished in medieval Europe, most notably in northern Italy. These communities initially banded together principally for the sake of common defense. Modern conceptions of commune reflect this notion of unity around a common end, though in more recent centuries this common end has tended to be spiritual or ideological rather than defensive. Consequently, modern communes are often referred to as *intentional communities* where "intent" implies not only the conscious design of living arrangements, but also a commitment to adopt a particular way of life; typically, this involves the pooling of property and consensus decision making. Usually communes are established and overseen by the grassroots initiative of a core group and supported by the like-minded consent of their membership, though occasionally the establishment has been imposed from above (like the Maoist "people's communes").

The vast majority of communes are short-lived, although in some instances, like the *kibbutzim* in Israel, they have proven extremely resilient.

The nineteenth century is often seen as the heyday of religious communes underpinned by shared faith, especially in the United States, where groups like the Shakers and the Hutterites established durable and influential settlements with thousands of members. The nineteenth century was also a time of secular social experimentation, however, spawning communal enterprises inspired by the works of Charles Fourier, Robert Owen, and Etienne Cabet, and informed by socialism and utopianism. In the twentieth century, the 1960s are particularly notable for the explosion of communal activity that took place in the context of the radical counterculture. The communes that were formed in this era often reflected, on one hand, the desire to "drop out" of mainstream society (like the hippie commune "Drop City") and, on the other hand, more self-conscious attempts to realize alternative lifestyles and provide models intended to influence future social arrangements.

When commune appears with a capital *C*, the intended reference is generally the Paris Commune of 1871, the most famous historical example of a commune, itself inspired by the commune that controlled Paris from 1792 until 1794 following the French Revolution. The Paris Commune was an administrative unit overseen by revolutionaries who sought autonomy from the national government of Adolphe Thiers, which ultimately suppressed the communards militarily.

See also *Communism; Social Movements; Utopias and Politics.*

. . . . BENJAMIN J. PAULI

BIBLIOGRAPHY

Jones, Philip. *The Italian City-State: From Commune to Signoria.* Oxford: Oxford University Press, 1997.

Kanter, Rosabeth Moss. *Commitment and Community: Communes and Utopias in Sociological Perspective.* Cambridge, Mass.: Harvard University Press, 1972.

Miller, Timothy. *The 60s Communes: Hippies and Beyond.* Syracuse, N.Y.: Syracuse University Press, 1999.

Pitzer, Donald E., ed. *America's Communal Utopias.* Chapel Hill: The University of North Carolina Press, 1997.

Shafer, David A. *The Paris Commune.* New York: Palgrave Macmillan, 2005.

Communication, Two-step Flow of

According to the two-step flow of communication theory, the mass media do not directly influence political behavior. Instead, opinion leaders—people in the community with more knowledge and expertise in politics and whom average citizens trust—take in information about politics in the media and share that information with others in the community. As such, mass-mediated information has little direct influence on most citizens, but interpretations of media messages provided by opinion leaders, who filter mass-mediated information along with other information available about politics, do influence the opinions of citizens. This theory is based on

Paul Lazarsfeld, Bernard Berelson, and Hazel Gaudet's 1948 Columbia University studies, *The People's Choice,* which found that the media have no real influence on vote choice. These findings were the beginning of the "era of minimal effects" in which political science researchers largely ignored the role of the mass media in political decision making. The Columbia findings have been criticized for exploring the effects of the media on a very narrow part of politics—vote choice in presidential elections—and for focusing on a homogeneous community. Subsequent research has demonstrated that the media do have direct, but subtle, effects on political behavior.

See also *Lazarsfeld, Paul F.; Media and Politics; Media Effect; Political Communication; Public Opinion.*

. . . . JANET L. DONAVAN

Communism

Communism (from the Latin *communis,* meaning "shared" or "common") advocates public ownership and communal control of the major means of production, distribution, transportation, and communication.

ORIGINS AND HISTORY

Although modern communism is associated with ideas advanced by German political philosophers Karl Marx and Friedrich Engels, and Russian Communist leader and theorist Vladimir I. Lenin, its intellectual roots are as old as Plato's *Republic* in the fourth century BCE. The vast disparities of wealth produced by the Industrial Revolution of the late eighteenth and early nineteenth centuries supplied the impetus and inspiration for modern communist theorizing, which consisted of (1) a critique of capitalism and (2) its replacement by an alternative social and economic system—communism.

THE CRITIQUE OF CAPITALISM

In *The Communist Manifesto* (1848) and other works, Marx (1818–1883) and Engels (1820–1895) criticized capitalism for alienating and exploiting workers (the proletariat), enriching capitalists (the bourgeoisie), and ensuring the rule of the latter over the former. All of human history, they wrote, is the history of struggles between classes—between slaves and masters; serfs and lords; and now, proletarians and capitalists. This epic struggle will be the final chapter in the story of class struggle. Out of it will emerge an egalitarian, just, and classless communist society.

Marx and Engels viewed capitalism as a historically necessary stage of development that had brought about remarkable scientific and technological changes—changes that greatly increased humankind's power over nature. Capitalism had also greatly increased aggregate wealth. In these respects, capitalism had been a positive and progressive force. The problem, in their view, was that wealth—and the political power and life chances that go with it—was unevenly and unfairly distributed. Workers are paid a pittance for long hours of hard labor. Moreover, it is they, not the capitalists, who are the creators of wealth. According to the labor theory of value, the worth of a commodity is determined by the amount of labor required to produce it. Under capitalism, workers are not paid fully or fairly for their labor. This enables capitalists to siphon off a portion that Marx calls "surplus value," the difference between what the workers are paid and the price paid by buyers of the product. This surplus is invested to yield even greater returns. This in turn enables the bourgeoisie to amass enormous wealth, while the proletariat falls further into poverty. The capitalist ruling class passes laws that benefit its members and disadvantage the proletariat. The state thus becomes an instrument for doing the bidding of the wealthy and powerful.

The exploitation of one class by another remains hidden, however, by a system or set of ideas that Marx and Engels call "ideology." "The ruling ideas of every epoch," they write in *The Communist Manifesto,* "are the ideas of the ruling class." That is, the conventional or mainstream ideas taught in classrooms, preached from pulpits, and communicated through the mass media are ideas that serve the interests of the dominant class and disserve those of the subordinate class.

THE COMING OF COMMUNIST SOCIETY

Marx predicted that a series of ever-worsening economic crises will produce ever-greater unemployment, lower wages, and increasing misery among the industrial proletariat. The proletariat will come to see that its interests are implacably opposed to the interests of the ruling bourgeoisie. Increasingly "immiserated" and motivated by "revolutionary class consciousness," the proletariat will seize state power and establish its own interim socialist state that Marx calls "the revolutionary dictatorship of the proletariat." That is, the proletariat will, as the bourgeoisie did before, rule in its own class interest in order to prevent a counter-revolution by the defeated bourgeoisie. Once this threat has passed there is no need for a state, and the state will "wither away" and make way for the emergence of a classless communist society.

Marx's vision of a communist society is remarkably (and perhaps intentionally) vague and sketchy. Unlike earlier "utopian socialists," whom he derided as unscientific and impractical, Marx did not produce detailed blueprints for a future society. Some features that he did describe, such as free public education for all and a graduated income tax (both considered radical in his day), are now commonplace. Other features—such as public ownership and control of the major means of production, and distribution of goods and services according to the principle in the 1875 "Critique of the Gotha Program," which states, "from each according to his ability, to each according to his need"—are anything but commonplace. Marx believed that the institutions of a future communist society should be designed and decided democratically by future people; it was not his task to "write recipes for the kitchens of the future" (preface to *Capital,* vol. 1). If Marx was reluctant to write such recipes, many of his followers were not. Among these was the Russian revolutionary Vladimir Ilyich Lenin.

COMMUNISM AFTER MARX

Lenin (1870–1924) made two important departures from the theory and practice of communism as Marx had envisioned it. The first is Lenin's view that communist revolution would not begin in advanced capitalist countries, as Marx had predicted, because workers there were imbued with reform-minded "trade union consciousness" instead of "revolutionary class consciousness." This led them to organize unions and workers' political parties to press for an ever-larger slice of the exploitative capitalist pie. Such workers had no interest in revolution. Communist revolution would begin instead in economically backward nations such as Russia and in the oppressed and exploited colonial countries of the capitalist periphery (now called the third world). This, Lenin argued, was because the scene of the most direct and brutal exploitation of workers had shifted from the first world to the third. Capitalists reaped "superprofits" from the cheap raw materials and labor available in the third world and were thus able to "bribe" workers at home with slightly higher wages, a shorter work week, and other reforms. Thus, contrary to Marx's expectation, it was not the industrial proletariat but the agricultural peasantry, directed by the Communist "vanguard," that was to make communist revolution.

A second major change is Lenin's view that revolution could not and should not be made "spontaneously" by the industrial proletariat—as Marx had held—but by the peasantry directed by an elite "vanguard party" composed of radicalized middle-class intellectuals like himself. Secretive, tightly organized, and highly disciplined, the Communist Party would educate, guide, and direct the masses. This was necessary, Lenin claimed, because the masses, suffering from "false consciousness" and unable to discern their true interests, could not yet be trusted to govern themselves.

In the bloody and violent revolution and its repressive aftermath there was, Lenin believed, no place for moral scruples. "You cannot make an omelette without breaking eggs," he was said to have remarked, meaning: you cannot make a revolution without breaking heads, or breaking promises: "Promises are like pie crusts—made to be broken." Immoral acts were justified in the name of a higher "socialist" morality, which held that the ultimate end—a classless communist society—justifies almost any means used to achieve it.

Marx's hopeful vision of a classless communist society in the nineteenth century turned toxic in the twentieth as a "new class" of party functionaries and bureaucrats rose to prominence. Regimes ruled by Josef Stalin (1879–1953) in the Soviet Union and Mao Zedong (1893–1976) in China, far from liberating workers, further exploited them.

See also *Capitalism and Democracy; Class and Politics; Communism, Fall of, and End of History; Engels, Friedrich; Ideologies, Political; Lenin, Vladimir Ilich; Leninism; Marx, Karl; Marxism; Proletariat.*

. . . .   TERENCE BALL

BIBLIOGRAPHY

Avineri, Shlomo. *The Social and Political Thought of Karl Marx.* Cambridge: Cambridge University Press, 1968.

Carver. Terrell. *Marx's Social Theory.* Oxford: Oxford University Press, 1982.

Cohen, G. A. *Karl Marx's Theory of History.* Princeton: Princeton University Press, 1978.

Djilas, Milovan. *The New Class.* New York: Praeger, 1957.

Harding, Neil. *Lenin's Political Thought,* 2 vols. London: Macmillan, 1981.

Kolakowski, Leszek. *Main Currents of Marxism.* 3 vols. Oxford: Oxford University Press, 1978.

Lenin, Vladimir Ilich. *Selected Works,* 4 vols. New York: International Publishers, 1968.

Mao, Zedong. *Selected Works,* 4 vols. Beijing: Foreign Languages Publishing House, 1965.

Marx, Karl, and Friedrich Engels. *Collected Works,* 50 vols. New York: International Publishers, 1975–2005. See esp. *The Communist Manifesto, The German Ideology,* "Preface to the Critique of Political Economy," *Capital,* and "Critique of the Gotha Programme."

McLellan, David. *Karl Marx: His Life and Thought.* London: Macmillan, 1973.

———, ed. *Karl Marx: Selected Writings.* Oxford: Oxford University Press, 2000.

Medvedev, Roy A. *Let History Judge: The Origins and Consequences of Stalinism.* New York: Knopf, 1971.

Stalin, Josef. *Selected Works.* Moscow: Progress Publishers, 1955.

Starr, John B. *Continuing the Revolution: The Political Thought of Mao.* Princeton: Princeton University Press, 1979.

Tucker, Robert C., ed. *Stalinism: Essays in Historical Interpretation.* New York: W. W. Norton, 1977.

Communism, Fall of, and End of History

During the summer of 1989, Francis Fukuyama published the now famous essay "The End of History?" in the conservative journal *The National Interest.* He argued that, with the end of the cold war, ideology had outlived its usefulness. Liberalism and capitalism had been victorious not only over the ideology of communism, but over ideology itself, and the phrase "the end of history" soon became part of the political lexicon. Fukuyama followed up with a book, The End of History and the Last Man, which contained a lengthy philosophical and historical expansion of his argument; as of the early twenty-first century, it had been translated into twenty languages.

THE SIGNIFICANCE OF IDEOLOGY

The term *ideology* arose during the French Revolution (1789–1799), and ideologies became central to European political life in the course of the nineteenth century. Ideologies incorporated the mobilized masses of urban industrial workers into the social fabric. They offered their adherents both a rational explanation of how the world works and an emotional-psychological sense of identity and meaning. The political and economic contradictions of liberalism gave birth to three rival ideologies—Soviet Communism on liberalism's left and Italian Fascism and German Nazism on its right. World War II (1939–1945) eliminated institutionalized Fascism, but Soviet Communism continued to battle liberalism for the next half-century in what came to be known as the cold war.

During the postwar decades, representative democracy and the market economy found a solution in the developed countries of the West (including Japan) to the problem of social cohesion that had dogged them over the previous century, in the form of the welfare state. In 1960, Daniel Bell published *The End of Ideology: On the Exhaustion of Political Ideas in the Fifties,* which made the case for the shift from ideology to pragmatism with regard to domestic politics in the United States. Political parties were no longer motivated by grand principles, and they had become shifting coalitions of interests. Shortly after the publication of Bell's book, there was the explosion of social mobilization and political idealism in the 1960s, including the civil rights movement, the antiwar movement, feminism, environmentalism, and gay rights. Bell's argument was discredited before the ink was dry.

At the same time Bell was declaring the death of ideology within the United States, the country was engaged in a struggle with Soviet communism. Even though democratic capitalism had sunk firm roots in the West, it was not clear that it would succeed in the newly independent former colonies of Africa and Asia. The Soviet model seemed to have worked in Russia, raising that country to the first rank of the world's industrial and military powers in less than a century. However, Soviet rule was deeply unpopular in the occupied countries of Eastern Europe. For example, as part of the Solidarity movement in Poland in 1980, industrial workers rose up against Communist rule. The invasion of Afghanistan in 1979 discredited the Soviet Union in the eyes of the third world. Within the Soviet Union itself, the appointment of Mikhail Gorbachev as general secretary in 1985 and his campaign of media openness, or *glasnost,* revealed that economic inefficiency, corruption, and ideological decay had undermined the foundations of Soviet power.

FUKUYAMA'S "END OF HISTORY"

Writing in the spring of 1989, Fukuyama read these events as showing that the end of communism was nigh. In his article he wrote about the "end of history," meaning the end of "History" in the Hegelian sense—as an integrated, rationally intelligible process with a beginning, a middle, and an end. In the United States, this translates into a familiar narrative of the founding of the Republic, the onward march of progress, and the American dream. For Marxists, it meant dialectical conflict and struggle, with the working classes ultimately persevering over the bourgeoisie, and culminating in the victory of communism—and the end of history.

In his conclusion, Fukuyama makes clear that the end of history "does not by any means imply the end of international conflict per se. . . . There would still be a high and perhaps rising level of ethnic and nationalist violence. . . ." While this implies that terrorism and wars of national liberation will continue to be an important item on the international agenda, Fukuyama also contended that "the end of history will be a very sad time." He wrote, "The struggle for recognition, the willingness to risk one's life for a purely abstract goal, will be replaced by economic calculation, the endless solving of technical problems, environmental concerns, and the satisfaction of sophisticated consumer demands" (18).

CRITICS OF FUKUYAMA'S THESIS

Fukuyama's work attracted worldwide attention at the time of publication but does have its detractors. In 1993 Fukuyama's former professor, Samuel Huntington, published "Clash of Civilizations?" in *Foreign Affairs,* in which he argued that far from disappearing, history seemed to be returning with a vengeance. Religious divides from the premodern era were fueling new violent social movements. Robert Kaplan, in the 2000 book *The Coming Anarchy: Shattering the Dreams of the Post–Cold War,* made similar arguments.

However, Fukuyama's analysis does seem to fit developments in Europe and most postsocialist societies, including China. In this context, ideology really does seem to have come to an end. In Eastern Europe, Communist parties have renamed themselves, shelved their millenarian rhetoric, and donned business suits. Nationalist parties have been established but rarely poll more than 10 percent of the vote—roughly what they get in Austria, France, or Italy. Elsewhere in the world, only a small number of rulers in the early twenty-first century directly challenged the idea that the market is the most efficient generator of wealth or that democracy is the best form of rule.

See also Clash of Civilizations; Communism; Huntington, Samuel; Leninism; Postcommunism.

. . . . PETER RUTLAND

BIBLIOGRAPHY
Bell, Daniel. *The End of Ideology: On the Exhaustion of Political Ideas in the Fifties.* Glencoe, Ill.: Free Press, 1960.
Fukuyama, Francis. "The End of History." *The National Interest,* no. 16 (Summer 1989).
———. *The End of History and the Last Man.* New York: Free Press, 1992.
———. "The 'End Of History' Twenty Years Later." *New Perspectives Quarterly* 27, no. 1 (2010): 7–10.
Huntington, Samuel. "Clash of Civilizations?" *Foreign Affairs* 72, no. 3 (Summer 1993): 22–49.
———. "The Clash of Civilizations Revisited." *New Perspectives Quarterly* 24, no. 1 (2007): 53–59.
Kaplan, Robert. *The Coming Anarchy: Shattering the Dreams of the Post–Cold War.* New York: Vintage, 2000.

Communitarianism

Communitarianism, like many political terms, has both a general and a specific meaning. In the general sense, a communitarian is anyone who believes that community is so vital to a worthwhile individual life that it must be protected against threatening trends and tendencies of the modern world. In the specific sense that emerged from the so-called liberal-communitarian debate of the 1980s and 1990s, a communitarian is someone who maintains that the excessively abstract and individualistic theories of liberal philosophers have been among the most threatening of these trends. This specific sense seems to be what most writers have in mind when they now refer to communitarianism.

A BRIEF HISTORY

The word *communitarian* first appeared in English in the early 1840s, when it was roughly synonymous with *socialism* and *communism.* These other words acquired more precise meanings in the ideological battles of the nineteenth and early twentieth centuries, but communitarianism remained a vague term, signifying little more than a desire to defend the traditional rural community or small town from the supposedly isolating and corrosive influences of capitalism, bureaucracy, and urban life. While socialists and communists came to be identified with the political left, communitarians were as likely to be to the right as the left of center.

According to one line of thought that developed in the late nineteenth century, the primary threat to community is the centrifugal force of modern life. Ferdinand Tönnies's distinction between two types of society, *gemeinschaft* (community) and *gesellschaft* (association or civil society), was especially influential in this regard, with gemeinschaft identified with the warmth of intimate, natural, and traditional life in contrast to the cold, calculating, and rational gesellschaft.

Concern for community took another direction in the twentieth century, as some saw the centripetal force of the modern state as the principal threat to community. In 1932, José Ortega y Gasset warned in *The Revolt of the Masses* against "the gravest danger that today threatens civilization: State intervention; the absorption of all spontaneous social effort by the State" (120). Less dramatically, Robert Nisbet argued in his 1953 book *The Quest for Community* that the free, spontaneous, and healthy life of community is increasingly difficult to sustain under the pressure of the modern state, with its impulses toward centralized power and bureaucratic regulation.

THE LIBERAL-COMMUNITARIAN DEBATE

These two themes persist in the writings of the communitarian political theorists of recent years, but they take the specific form of a series of objections to the community-dissolving tendencies of liberal individualism. Four books published in the early 1980s marked the emergence of this philosophical communitarianism: Alisdair MacIntyre's *After Virtue* (1981), Michael Sandel's *Liberalism and the Limits of Justice* (1982), Michael Walzer's *Spheres of Justice* (1983), and Charles Taylor's *Philosophical Papers* (1985). In general, the complaint was that liberal theories of justice and rights, such as those from John Rawls, have been too abstract and universalistic. Walzer thus called for a "radically particularist" approach that attends to "history, culture, and membership" by asking not what "rational individuals . . . under universalizing conditions of such-and-such a sort" (xiv) would choose, but what would "individuals like us choose . . . who share a culture and are determined to go on sharing it?" (5).

Communitarians have also complained that contemporary liberals rely on an atomistic conception of the self—an "unencumbered self," in Sandel's terms—that is supposedly prior to or independent of attachments to family, tradition, and community. This conception is both false and pernicious, communitarians claim, because individual selves are largely constituted by the communities that nurture them. Liberal theories of justice and rights thus contribute to the withdrawal into private life and the intransigent insistence on one's rights against others that threaten to undermine liberal democracies. There is little sense of a common good or even a common ground on which citizens can meet. As MacIntyre says, politics now "is civil war carried on by other means" (253).

The liberal-communitarian debate has not been clear-cut because some of those labeled communitarian have seen themselves as liberals trying to correct an atomistic tendency within liberalism (e.g., Taylor). Moreover, those who seemed the most severe critics of liberalism, MacIntyre and Sandel, have either forsaken communitarianism in favor of republicanism, like Sandel, or denied ever being a communitarian, like MacIntyre. Communitarianism in the specific sense survives, however, although it most often takes the form of a political communitarianism, less concerned with philosophical criticism of liberalism than with attempts to revive and defend community by calling attention to shared values, encouraging participation in civic life, and reinvigorating politics at the local level.

See also *Communism; Individualism; Socialism.*

. . . . RICHARD DAGGER

BIBLIOGRAPHY
Avineri, Shlomo, and Avner de-Shalit, eds. *Communitarianism and Individualism.* Oxford: Oxford University Press, 1992.
Bell, Daniel. *Communitarianism and Its Critics.* Oxford: Oxford University Press, 1993.
Etzioni, Amitai. *The New Golden Rule: Community and Morality in a Democratic Society.* New York: Basic Books, 1996.
Frazer, Elizabeth. *The Problems of Communitarian Politics: Unity and Conflict.* Oxford: Oxford University Press, 1999.
MacIntyre, Alisdair. *After Virtue: A Study in Moral Theory.* Notre Dame: University of Notre Dame Press, 1981.
Mulhall, Stephen, and Adam Swift. *Liberals and Communitarians.* Oxford: Blackwell, 1992.
Nisbet, Robert. *The Quest for Community.* Oxford: Oxford University Press, 1953.
Ortega y Gasset, José. *The Revolt of the Masses,* translated by T. Carey. New York: W. W. Norton, 1932.
Sandel, Michael. *Liberalism and the Limits of Justice.* Cambridge: Cambridge University Press, 1982.
Taylor, Charles. *Philosophical Papers,* 2 vols. Cambridge: Cambridge University Press, 1985.
Tönnies, Ferdinand. *Community and Civil Society,* translated by J. Harris and M. Hollis. Cambridge: Cambridge University Press, 2001.
Walzer, Michael. *Spheres of Justice: A Defense of Pluralism and Equality.* New York: Basic Books, 1983.

Community

Community usually refers to an integrated set of human relationships generally based on close ties, kinship, or ethical solidarities. These are often contrasted with the impersonal relations of modern society. *Political community* refers to ideas of political deliberation, solidarity, civic attachment, and common norms; political community also often rests upon ethical community.

HISTORICAL PERSPECTIVES

For Aristotle, political community was the highest goal of human activity. Community was rooted in human nature, and the ends of human nature were determined by the order of the cosmos. Political community rested on an ethos that guided practical activity, and aimed at more than mere protection or peaceful association. It required a deliberative community guided by reason. Political justice existed between these free and equal beings who sought self-sufficiency. For Plato, the citizen was not only a political animal by nature; the citizen was a member of an ongoing and historical community, not an independent individual.

Thomas Aquinas followed Aristotle in stressing the importance of community. Human's essentially social nature, however, included a variety of associations beyond the political, with *ordo* connecting both the order of the universe and the orders of social life. Relativizing and subordinating political community to religious community, Aquinas regarded the latter as the most perfect and saw its quest for perfect happiness as limited.

Early modern works like Thomas More's *Utopia* and Tommaso Campanella's *City of the Sun* formulated utopian communities based on communistic ideals like peace and happiness for all. These Renaissance theorists rejected the division of labor and the drudgery of work for socially purposeful activity. Utopias were the first instance of a modern discourse in which society or the social represented a sphere of self-organization, the willful creation of human activity and not of god or nature, and could be subject to human control and direction. In the nineteenth century, utopian socialists like Charles Fourier and Robert Owen founded experimental communities based on utopian ideals.

In industrial society, the idea of the social was more closely equated with the market over community. Ferdinand Tönnies formulated the standard distinction between two types of human association: community and society, or *Gemienschaft* and *Gesellschaft.* These, however, are not definitions of society but ideal types, which are found in combination in all societies. Gemeinschaft is a form of association based on strong ties such as family and kinship. The latter possess, according to Tönnies, a unity of will, a characteristic that might also be found in national identity or other group identities. Gesellschaft, in contrast, designates marketlike relations based on calculating self-interest.

Jean-Jacques Rousseau identified the alienation typical of modern commercial society. It created a pervasive inequality, bound humans to repressive institutions, and created artificial egoistic needs. Though Rousseau never advocated a return to a "state of nature," he did think that commercial society was egoistic and fragmented, lacking in community. It alienated humans from the sympathy for the suffering of others that such association required. Rousseau sought a solution in a more direct form of republican democracy, which could only be realized in smaller and integral communities.

NINETEENTH-CENTURY IDEAS OF COMMUNITY

Romantics mounted a critique of Enlightenment rationalism, its abstract universalism, and its mechanical and lifeless spirit that separated humans from nature and communal solidarities. While romanticism looked to the past, especially the medieval era, for models of integrated community, it was not uniformly conservative or backward looking. Early German romantics embraced republican political theories supportive of the French revolution, believing individual creativity and community could flourish through a renewed reason. Romantics also championed national identity. Johann Gottfried Herder, for example, saw national community as an integral unity based in a national language. Human nature, Herder argued, is historical, not an ideal of absolute, unchanging happiness. It is relative to linguistic, cultural, and social conditions. Early Marxist views can be seen as a variant of romanticism. Human alienation, which separated humans from their communal roots and the full development and expression of their creative powers, reached its greatest heights in industrial capitalism. The recovery of true community and creative human powers meant transcending the limits of nations for international communism.

Thinkers who rejected the achievements of French Revolution (1789–1799) looked to the failures of the terror as a caution against applying Enlightenment ideals to social life. Conservatives like Edmund Burke took a moderate path. Burke looked to the wisdom of tradition as source of gradual nonrevolutionary change. Tradition was the voice of history and community, which, while of human origin, was not a product of human will. Reactionary Joseph De Maistre saw the monarchy as the best form of association and rejected the Enlightenment idea of community as human artifice. God reveals constitutions, Maistre argued, according to god's plan. Others took the idea of national community in a less innocent direction believing that in the late nineteenth century, nationalism was linked to imperialism and power politics.

Developmental liberals such as John Stuart Mill, T. H. Green, and John Dewey recognized that the social conditions of modern freedom required not just civil rights but social rights. Rejecting the atomism of liberal theory, they argued that human life is essentially social and requires the guarantee of basic conditions such as education, social welfare, and protection from the fluctuations of the economy. While the latter aren't equivalent to the strong solidarities and moralities of the community, they are conditions that need to be in place for such communities to flourish.

Sociologist Émile Durkheim also sought to formulate a notion of community suitable for modern conditions. Mechanical solidarity was based on the similarity of tasks in older societies, while organic solidarity was the more complex integration of a modern division of labor and rested on pluralism. While not rejecting individualism, Durkheim held, like developmental liberals, that society needs to complete individualism. Political community, promoting a positive notion of liberty, differentiates from the state and community promotes a modernist sense of solidarity by integrating secondary groups (contra Rousseau) like the church, the family, labor, industry, and professions into the larger community. In contrast, anomie, in Durkheim's view, is a disconnection with community. Lacking in norms or attachments, Durkheim saw rootless, normless (largely urban) anomie as the main source of disorder and social disintegration.

CONTEMPORARY COMMUNITARIANS

The contemporary debate between communitarians and liberals has revived debate over the role community plays in political theory. Communitarians reject what they see as the atomism and abstract universalism of contemporary liberalism as exemplified by John Rawls. Communitarians, such as Michael Sandel, Alistair Macintyre, and Michael Walzer stress the idea that the good, rooted in specific political communities, takes priority over the right or claims of justice. Communitarians look to a prior community organized around the good life, with standards of morality and politics internal to community. Neither political order nor the identity of individuals, who are the bearers of rights, can be coherently conceived without reference to the constitutive conditions of community. American social theorists like Phillip Selznick and Amati Etzioni were also prominent in advocating a communitarian view of politics that balance individual rights and community responsibilities.

Multiculturalism has emerged as another element of the liberalism and communitarian debate. Charles Taylor, for example, has argued that cultural communities, such as those of the Quebecquois in Canada, are due cultural rights based on their character as linguistic communities. Reflecting the influence of Herder, Taylor holds that "the language I speak, the web which I can never fully dominate and oversee, can never be just my language, it is always our language." The integrity of language and culture precedes individual rights. This is not a matter of simply choosing a language but maintaining a community in which the language flourishes. Critics hold that Taylor views communities too holistically and his portrayal of liberalism is too narrow. Individuals are not simply members of unified language communities but of multiple and permeable social worlds. The "unified" self is constructed out of this plurality.

The central challenge for contemporary theories of political community remains to reconcile the forms of solidarity required by national and ethnic identities with the requirements of justice and universal human rights of cosmopolitan societies. This challenge examines how the local virtues of patriotism, civic virtue, and local theories of the good life are compatible with the plurality of value orientations—both within most cosmopolitan contemporary societies and as relations between nations and transnational associations.

See also *Communitarianism; Utopias and Politics.*

. . . . BRIAN CATERINO

BIBLIOGRAPHY

Aristotle. *The Politics.* New York: Oxford University Press, 1962.

Beiser, Frederick C., ed. *Early Political Writings of the German Romantics,* Cambridge: Cambridge University Press, 1996.

Etzioni, Amatai. *The Spirit of Community: Rights, Responsibilities and the Communitarian Agenda.* New York: Crown. 1993.

Giddens, Anthony. *Capitalism and Modern Social Theory: An Analysis of the Writings of Marx, Durkheim and Max Weber.* Cambridge: Cambridge University Press, 1973.

———, ed. *Durkheim on Politics and the State.* Stanford: Stanford University Press 1986.

Macintyre, Alastair. *After Virtue: A Study in Moral Theory,* 3rd ed. Notre Dame: University of Notre Dame Press, 2007.

More, Thomas. *Utopia.* New York: Penguin Books, 2003.

Rousseau, Jean-Jacques. *The Social Contract and the Discourses.* New York: BN Publishing, 2007.

Sandel, Michael. *Liberalism and the Limits of Justice.* Cambridge: Cambridge University Press, 1998.

Selznick, Phillip. *The Moral Commonwealth: Social Theory and the Promise of Community.* Berkeley: University of California Press, 1996.

Taylor, Charles. "Language and Human Nature." In *Philosophical Papers 1: Human Agency and Language.* Cambridge: Cambridge University Press, 1985.

———. *Multiculturalism.* Princeton: Princeton University Press, 1994.

Tönnies, Ferdinand. *Community and Society.* New York: Dover, 2002.

Yack, Bernard. *The Problems of a Political Animal: Community, Justice, and Conflict in Aristotelian Political Thought.* Berkeley: University of California Press, 1993.

Walzer, Michael. *Spheres of Justice: A Defense of Pluralism and Equality.* New York: Basic Books, 1984.

Community Power

Community power addresses the question of whether, and to what extent, power is distributed, and how power should be measured within local communities.

In the United States, the debate on community power coincided with the debate between elitists and pluralists. Elitist scholars took a stratification theory of power as a point of departure, viewing power as subsidiary to the social structure in a community. Thus, according to Floyd Hunter in 1953, a small financial and economical elite ruled the city of Atlanta, Georgia, at that time. Hunter arrived at this conclusion by first asking organizations representing four domains of Atlanta to provide him with a list of leaders in their domain. Subsequently, fourteen judges were asked who, from their individual perspectives, were "top leaders" on each of the lists of 175 persons. This resulted in a list of forty top leaders.

Similarly, in 1956, C. Wright Mills detected a "power elite" in the American society of his time. According to Mills, several developments taking place during and after World War II (1939–1945) resulted in increasingly enlarged, centralized, and interlocking hierarchies in the economic, political, and military realm of the United States. The power elite consisted of persons occupying the top positions in these three hierarchies and, as such, made or failed to make decisions with more consequences for more people than ever before. The methods Hunter and Mills applied to measure power are known as the reputation method and position method, respectively.

Pluralist scholars, however, criticized these studies for measuring actor properties and thus only potential power instead of actual, exerted power. The elitists' findings would follow from the methods they applied. Robert Alan Dahl and Nelson W. Polsby argued that studying the contribution actors make to specific decisions on key issues in a community could measure the actual, exerted power. In his study of New Haven, Connecticut, Dahl examined, for several decisions in three issue areas, which of the participating actors had most frequently initiated proposals that were later adopted (without or despite opposition of the other actors) or vetoed proposals of other participants. Only three of the fifty persons meeting the test of successfully initiating or vetoing proposals did so in more than one issue area. Among the actors who successfully initiated or vetoed proposals more than once, only a few were social or economic "notables." Thus, there appeared no one ruling elite in New Haven, drawn from a single homogeneous stratum that exerted power on all decisions in all three issue areas. Instead, power appeared to be distributed pluralistically: different actors exerted power concerning different decisions in different issue areas.

NONDECISION MAKING

Dahl's method became known as the *decision method,* and in 1970 Peter Bachrach and Morton Baratz upheld criticism for the method not providing an objective criterion to discriminate between important and unimportant issue areas. As the notables were not interested in two of the three issue areas Dahl had selected, it was not surprising that he ended up with pluralist rather than elitist conclusions. Bachrach and Baratz argued that power was exercised during the process of decision making, which they called the first face of power, and also during the process of nondecision making. This second face of power concerned setting the agenda of available options for decision making, where some issues become part of the agenda, whereas others—the nonissues—were kept from the agenda, resulting in nondecisions. Just as in case of the elitists, the pluralists' research method would thus predetermine their empirical findings.

In 1971, Matthew Crenson's comparative study of air pollution in American cities falsified the objection that nondecisions were nonevents and could thus not be empirically studied. His study examined two nearby urban areas with similar population characteristics and dirty air levels, and aimed at explaining why east Chicago's air pollution became an issue and resulted in local policy in 1949, whereas Gary, Indiana's, air pollution remained a nonissue, and no action was undertaken until 1962. Crenson argued that Gary was dominated by one steel company, U.S. Steel, and had a strong party organization, whereas east Chicago had several steel factories and no strong party organization. U.S. Steel managed to circumvent the dirty air issue, backed by its reputation for power, without having to do anything.

More recently, the debate on community power has been continued by regime theory scholars on the one hand, such as Davies and Imbroscio, and rational choice theory scholars on the other, such as Dowding and colleagues, from an increasingly integrative and comparative perspective.

See also *Elite Decision Making; Pluralism; Power; Power Indices; Rational Choice Theory; Regime; Regions and Regional Government; Relative Power.*

· · · · · · · · · · · · · · · · SANDER LUITWIELER

BIBLIOGRAPHY

Bachrach, Peter, and Morton S. Baratz. *Power and Poverty: Theory and Practice.* New York: Oxford University Press, 1970.

Clark, Terry N., ed. *Community Structure and Decision-Making: Comparative Analyses.* San Francisco: Chandler, 1968.

Crenson, Matthew A. *The Un-Politics of Air Pollution: A Study of Non-Decisionmaking in the Cities.* Baltimore: John Hopkins University Press, 1971.

Dahl, Robert A. *Who Governs? Democracy and Power in an American City*, 2nd ed. New Haven: Yale University Press, 2005.

Davies, Jonathan S., and David L. Imbroscio, eds. *Theories of Urban Politics*, 2nd ed. London: Sage, 2009.

Dowding, Keith, Patrick Dunleavy, Desmond King, and Helen Margetts. "Rational Choice and Community Power Structures." *Political Studies* 43, no. 2 (1995): 265–277.

Hunter, Floyd. *Community Power Structure. A Study of Decision Makers.* Chapel Hill: University of North Carolina Press, 1953.

Mills, C. Wright. *The Power Elite.* New York: Oxford University Press, 1956.

Polsby, Nelson W. *Community Power and Political Theory: A Further Look at Problems of Evidence and Inference*, 2nd ed. New Haven: Yale University Press, 1980.

Compacts, Interstate

See *Interstate Compacts.*

Compulsory Voting

Compulsory voting is the legal obligation for registered eligible voters to participate in elections. It is estimated that some thirty countries in the world have, or have had, such a legal obligation, including Australia, Belgium, Brazil, Greece, and Italy. Especially in Latin America, systems of compulsory voting are widespread, but usually only weakly enforced. Strictly speaking, compulsory voting only applies to the act of appearing in the polling station, since the vote itself is secret. In countries with this system, this can lead to a substantial percentage of spoiled or invalid votes.

Evidence suggests that a strictly enforced system of compulsory voting raises turnout, and in countries such as Australia or Belgium, turnout remains stable at well over 90 percent. When the Netherlands abolished compulsory voting in 1971, voter turnout decreased by almost 15 percent. Some nations, therefore, have considered adopting compulsory voting in order to stem the trend toward declining voter turnout. In recent history, however, not a single country has introduced compulsory voting. In some countries where the system exists, it is the topic of political controversy. Policy makers hesitate to implement sanctions against those who do not show up, while on a normative level, it is questioned whether states are entitled to impose this obligation on their citizens.

See also *Voter Registration Drive; Voting Behavior; Voting Procedures; Voting Rights and Suffrage.*

. . . . MARC HOOGHE

Computational Modeling

In political economy, computational models simulate the behavior of institutions or individuals, allowing researchers to explore emergent patterns in individual and institutional behavior over time. Computational models complement mathematical models, and also serve as a form of independent theory construction in their own right. This distinguishes computational models from statistical computation for data analysis, because although statistical models may involve simulation of mathematical functions, they use simulation to approximate known statistical models that are difficult or impossible to analyze analytically.

Although some scholars used computers to model political behavior in the early 1960s, many of the fundamental ideas now used in computational political economy appeared much later. In particular, Thomas Schelling's pioneering work in 1978, *Micromotives and Macrobehavior,* which created microsimulations of individuals without computers, showed dramatically how complex and unexpected patterns of behavior could emerge from individuals acting with simple motives and simple rules of individual behavior. This directly influenced the first major work of computational political economy in 1981, Robert Axelrod's "The Evolution of Cooperation," illustrating how cooperative behavior can emerge from self-interested agents operating with simple heuristics.

Modern computational models that describe the behavior of individual actors are sometimes known as *agent-based* simulations. In most modern agent-based simulations, local interactions are important: Individuals are modeled as acting on locally available information and as interacting with other local agents. Also, in typical agent-based simulations, individuals are modeled as being boundedly rational: Agents use heuristics to make decisions rather than acting optimally (in the game-theoretic sense). Moreover, the institutional environment in which individuals act is characterized as both stochastic and dynamic—evolving with, or coevolving in reaction to, the behavior of individual agents.

Computational models do not require individuals as the modeling unit. For example, models of international conflict, in which nations are the fundamental actors, date back to the early 1950s. Although used less frequently in political economy, institutional-level models are common in macroeconomics and finance.

Although initially opposed by formal theorists as too imprecise, and by qualitative theorists as too impoverished, computational models have gained a share of acceptance in the last decade. As a complement to mathematical theory, computational models are most often advocated as a way to generate both examples and counterexamples with which to probe the robustness of the mathematical model for changes in assumptions. Computational models may also be used as a constructive form of theory building, independent of a formal mathematical model, as the basis for making predictions and for generating qualitative insights. As such, they are often justified as a middle ground between purely mathematical formal models and purely textual qualitative models. Because computational models are far easier to construct than formal mathematical models, the researcher can use them to obtain, in the happiest of circumstances, the precision of a formal model with the realism of a qualitative model.

Proponents of computational models argue further that dynamic computational models are better-fitted models for studying dynamic patterns than standard mathematical equilibrium models. (Using equilibrium models to study dynamic behavior is sometimes likened to trying to understand Niagara Falls by staring into a collection bucket.) Still, even ardent proponents emphasize the need for caution in model building and interpretation. As in other forms of model building, seemingly innocuous assumptions may sometimes yield striking different patterns of outcomes. Thus, all models should be built with care, and researchers should actively seek cases in which competing models yield diverging predictions that may be directly compared.

See also *Simulation; Simultaneous Equation Modeling.*

. . . . MICAH ALTMAN

BIBLIOGRAPHY

Axelrod, Robert. "The Evolution of Cooperation." *Science* 211 (1981): 1390–1396.

Johnson, Paul E. "Simulation Modeling in Political Science." *American Behavioral Scientist* 42, no. 10 (1999): 1509–1530.

Page, Scott E. "Computational Models from A to Z." *Complexity* 5, no. 1 (1999): 35–41.

Schelling, Thomas C. *Micromotives and Macrobehavior.* New York: W. W. Norton, 1978.

Taber, Charles S., and Richard J. Timpone. *Computational Models.* Thousand Oaks, Calif: Sage, 1996.

Comte, Auguste

Isidore Auguste Marie Francois-Xavier Comte (1798–1857) was a French philosopher credited as the founder of positivism and, by many standards, considered the father of sociology. In Europe, and especially in France during his early years, there were no sociologists; rather, philosophers were beginning to venture into scientific and empirical terrain. It was Comte who laid the foundation for sociology to become a scientific discipline firmly embedded in empirical and theoretical grounds.

Though no monarchist himself, Comte was nonetheless critical of the French Revolution (1789–1799), its intellectual figures such as author Voltaire and philosopher Jean-Jacques Rousseau, and the chaos it unleashed. He was equally critical of the Catholic Church—which could not prevent the revolution—and what he termed the "metaphysical age (of uncertainty)." Yet Comte himself is an Enlightenment figure. His "positive philosophy" details a hierarchy of sciences in which, ultimately, sociology will become the scientific discipline through which all other sciences can be integrated into one systematic body of knowledge.

The idea of progress and development is also evident in his so-called law of three stages, which is perhaps Compte's most famous formulation of societal change. Accordingly, all societies develop along a path that includes three stages. Presumably, all societies depart from the same stage—the theological stage—and, given the "right" (scientific-sociological knowledge), arrive at the same end point of history: The positive society, once the intermediate metaphysical stage, is overcome. Despite its simplicity and its evidently Eurocentric view of societal change and development, Comte's law of three stages does invite serious questions from both political science and sociology: How do societies change, and what are the major forces of change? Are these forces primarily

Influential French philosopher Auguste Comte is known as the father of sociology.

SOURCE: The Granger Collection, New York

internal (domestic) or external (international)? To Comte, theological-spiritual, philosophical-metaphysical, and scientific-technological ideas are no doubt not only worldviews each in its own right; they also constitute major institutions and, as such, exert strong influence over the division of labor and the structural makeup of every society.

Due to Comte's efforts, science and especially scientific inquiry made a major step forward. His scientific method included observation, experimentation, and comparison, all of which are important elements in any introductory methods course and certainly part of political science and sociology. Of particular interest is his comparative method, itself composed of three different types: comparisons of human and nonhuman societies, comparisons of human societies at presumably the same development level, and comparisons of societies at different development levels.

Comte also wrote on the family, the individual, and society. Among those influenced by his ideas are English social philosopher Herbert Spencer and French sociologist Émile Durkheim. Scholars continue to debate the degree that Comte's particular understanding of positivism (especially his view of sociology and his faith in the scientific method) represents an extreme form of determinism.

See also *Durkheim, Émile; Empiricism; Positive Theory; Social Order.*

. . . . VOLKER K. FRANK

BIBLIOGRAPHY

Aron, Raymond. *Main Currents in Social Thought.* New York: Basic Books, 1965.

Comte, Auguste. *A General View of Positivism,* New York: R. Speller, 1957.

———. *The Positive Philosophy of Auguste Comte.* Kitchener, Ont.: Batoche, 2000.

Concept Analysis

Concept analysis, or formal concept analysis, allows researchers to identify and visualize specific structures in information. This data analysis method utilizes algebra and order theory and can enhance statistics and modeling analysis. When modeling through concept analysis, representations of concepts within a particular domain are derived from object-property matrices by using data-clustering algorithms. These algorithms use established and hierarchically ordered patterns to expose clusters within a larger data set, but the different algorithms delineate clusters in various ways. Concept analysis may be used to create concept lattices (known as Galois lattices) that allow identification and display of relationships. These lattices may further be developed into classification systems.

German scholar Rudolf Willie developed concept analysis in 1982, but its use initially remained limited because of its highly technical nature. In the 1990s, the popularity of concept analysis increased dramatically as new computer applications were integrated with the approach. By the twenty-first century, there were a variety of concept analysis software packages and open source software available for research. Fields ranging from medicine and psychology, to software engineering and library information science, use concept analysis, and it is also increasingly used in social sciences such as anthropology and sociology. Intelligence agencies in the United States and Western Europe have also used concept analysis as a means to possibly identify terrorist sleeper cells or other security threats, based on attributes and patterns.

See also *Qualitative Analysis; Qualitative Methodologies; Quantitative Analysis.*

. . . . TOM LANSFORD

Concordat

A *concordat* is an agreement between ecclesiastical and civil powers. The popes have widely used concordats to obtain recognition and privileges for the Roman Catholic Church and, in order to secure the state's promise to refrain from encroachment upon religious life, to terminate dissension with national civil powers by foregoing some of the church's traditional privileges and immunities. The concordats cover spiritual and temporal matters such as the nomination of bishops, the establishment of parishes, religious instruction, religious marriage, and church property.

The first concordat was *Pactum Callixtinum* of 1122, allowing the church to control the investiture of priests in exchange for important concessions permitting the emperor to assist at Episcopal elections and to exact an oath of vassalage from bishops that greatly restricted the rights and liberties of the church. In the nineteenth century, concordats became a preferred tool of the Roman Catholic Church to regulate ecclesiastical affairs in different lands. While concordats have provided the church with important benefits, the 1933 concordat with Germany granted international recognition to dictator Adolph Hitler's regime.

Since 1965, over 115 agreements have been concluded between the Vatican and various countries. This proliferation, and the implicit recognition concordats bestow on sometimes undemocratic political regimes, came under fire in the early twenty-first century.

See also *Religion and Politics; Roman Catholic Political Thought.*

. . . . LAVINIA STAN

Condorcet, Marquis de

Marie Jean Antoine Nicolas de Caritat, marquis de Condorcet (1743–1794), was an influential French philosopher, mathematician, political activist, and political scientist. Condorcet is a typical representative of the French Enlightenment tradition, bringing scientific and rational arguments into political and philosophical debates. Educated as a mathematician, he tried to promote moral and political progress by approaching political debates from a scientific point of view. Especially with regard to education and elections, his work has been hugely influential. Condorcet worked as a senior administrator before the French Revolution (1789–1799) and was elected a member of parliament in 1791. In the assembly, he championed moderate and liberal causes, argued in favor of equal rights for women, for the abolishment of slavery, and for the advancement of general education in France. In October 1793, he was prosecuted for his opposition to the death penalty for the former King Louis XVI. In March 1794 he died in prison, leaving the young philosopher Sophie de Grouchy (1764–1822) as his widow. In 1989, Condorcet was symbolically reburied in the Pantheon in Paris, the burial place for the most important figures in French history.

Condorcet is best known for his work on elections. In particular, his *Jury Theorem* states that large juries are an ideal mechanism to arrive at right answers to policy questions. The larger the number of votes being cast (in a jury or in a general election), the higher the probability the assembly will arrive at the right decision. The mathematical evidence for this claim basically rests in large numbers: If every single juror has slightly better than 50 percent chance of arriving at the right decision, a high number of jurors makes it all the more likely that there will be a majority for the right decision within the assembly. As such, the theorem has been used to legitimize the use of juries in courts, or to advance general suffrage (thus maximizing the number of voters). Condorcet himself indicated some limitations to the jury theorem, asserting that if the same jury has to reach a series of decisions, there is no guarantee that there will be logical order in these decisions. *Condorcet's paradox* claims that jury decisions are not necessarily transitive: If a jury prefers A over B, and B over C, it is still possible that in a third decision, C will be preferred over A. This caveat implies that in its pure form, the jury theorem only applies to single decisions, not to a series of decisions.

The same desire to use the cognitive possibilities of a large group led Condorcet to defend voting rights for women and general education for all children. His great hope was that if more people were introduced to logical reasoning, this would lead to a more humane society. In an ironic twist, Condorcet wrote his final work on the method to improve human moral progress while he was in hiding from his persecutors, just months before his death.

See also *French Political Thought; Voting Rights and Suffrage.*

. . . . MARC HOOGHE

BIBLIOGRAPHY
Badinter, Elisabeth, and Robert Badinter. *Condorcet, 1743–1794. Un intellectuel en politique.* Paris: Fayard, 1988.
Baker, Keith Michael. *Condorcet. From Natural Philosophy to Social Mathematics.* Chicago: University of Chicago Press, 1975.
Condorcet, Jean Antoine Nicolas de Caritat, marquis de. *Sketch for a Historical Picture of the Progress of the Human Mind,* translated by June Barraclough, with an introduction by Stuart Hampshire. London: Weidenfeld and Nicolson, 1955. Originally published as *Esquisse d'un tableau historique des progrès de l'esprit humain* (1795).
———. *Sur les élections et autres textes* [On Elections and Other Texts]. Fayard: Paris, 1986.
Goodell, Edward. *The Noble Philosopher: Condorcet and the Enlightenment.* Buffalo, N.Y.: Prometheus, 1994.

Confederation

See *Federation and Confederation.*

Confessional Parties

Confessional parties are parties organized around a shared religion. They can incorporate religious identity as an ethnic marker, socioeconomic agenda, or vehicle to advance an increased role for religion in the state. Although modernization theory predicted a decreasing relevance of religion, confessional parties continue to play an important role around the world. As a result, confessional parties are sometimes viewed as an anomaly and explained on an ad hoc basis, heavily emphasizing particular characteristics of faiths assumed to be resilient to reform (e.g., Catholicism and Islam). However, many recent scholars have instead treated confessional parties as explicable by a variety of social scientific theories—such as rational choice, social movement, and institutionalism—that apply to other aspects of sociopolitical life.

In Europe and Latin America, Christian Democratic parties are key actors; in South Asia, both Hindu and Islamic parties have eclipsed nationalist movements. In the Middle East, Islamic parties have participated extensively in the new electoral politics of the last two decades. Moreover, Lebanon and Iraq allocate political offices along sectarian lines, thus encouraging religious parties.

Since World War II (1939–1945), Christian Democratic parties have played a significant role in Europe, especially in Belgium, the Netherlands, Italy, Germany, Austria, and Switzerland. Historically holding a significant Catholic component, there are also now active Protestant elements in Christian Democratic parties. Generally speaking, the ideology of these parties is neither liberal nor socialist and instead focuses on solidarity based on a social reform agenda. Explanations of Christian Democracy range from primordialist accounts of a fixed Catholic identity to instrumentalist explanations that focus on the role of the Church or traditional elites, and to microeconomic rational choice explanations of party formation. In addition, Latin America (especially Chile, Venezuela, El Salvador, and Mexico) has Christian Democratic parties, although these are not as influential as in Europe.

Religious parties also play an important role in South Asia and the Middle East. In India's 1991 elections, the Hindu Nationalist Bharatiya Janata Party (BJP) emerged as the largest opposition party in India and continued on a trajectory of electoral growth until it became the ruling party in 1999; it's electoral fortunes were reversed slightly in 2004 and 2009 when the Indian congress made a comeback and the BJP returned to opposition. Islamic activism has also grown in the Middle East, and several Islamic parties have successfully contested elections throughout the region, including the 1991 interrupted ascension of the Islamic Salvation Front Algeria abrogated by a coup, the Hamas victory in the Palestinian national elections in 2006, and the main Islamist parties in Morocco and Jordan that operated as "loyal opposition" to the monarchies. This increased role in politics has led to the growth of literature on Islam and democracy, along with social movement literature explaining the moderating effect of political participation and accounts focusing more on institutions.

However, Lebanon is perhaps the best example of confessional parties due to the confessional underpinnings of the overall political system. The confessional allocation of parliamentary seats was institutionalized as a result of the 1943 National Pact at a six to five Christian-Muslim ratio and revised to one to one by the 1989 Taif Accord that ended the civil war. As a result, parties are organized along sectarian lines. Before the civil war, a few parties were nominally cross-confessional drawing on different religions, such as the Communist Party (with a largely Shia base) and the Constitutional Bloc Party. However, the development of militias from existing party apparatuses further entrenched the confessional nature of political parties. As a result, today there are few cross-confessional parties. For example, the Progressive Socialist Party is largely Druze, and the Future Movement Party is mostly Sunni. General Aoun's Free Patriotic Movement, which originally professed an anticonfessional agenda, has become a vehicle for advocating a Christian (largely Maronite) agenda. In addition, there are competing parties for some confessions. Among Maronites, the Lebanese Forces rival the Kataib (or Phlangist) from which it split. Similarly, Hezbollah is increasingly eclipsing the Amal Movement as the preeminent Shia party. Along a similar trajectory, political parties are organizing confessionally in postwar Iraq.

See also *Middle Eastern Politics and Society; Religion and Politics; Religious Parties.*

. . . .   MAREN MILLIGAN

BIBLIOGRAPHY

El-Khazen, Farid. "Political Parties in Post-War Lebanon: Parties in Search of Partisans." *Middle East Journal* 57, no. 4 (Autumn 2003): 605–624.

Kalyvas, Stathis. *The Rise of Christian Democracy in Europe.* Ithaca: Cornell University Press, 1996.

Lust-Okar, Ellen. *Structuring Conflict in the Arab World: Incumbents, Opponents, and Institutions.* Cambridge: Cambridge University Press, 2007.

Mainwaring, Scott, and Timothy Scully, eds. *Christian Democracy in Latin America: Electoral Competition and Regime Conflicts.* Stanford: Stanford University Press, 2003.

Schwedler, Jillian. *Faith in Moderation: Islamist Parties in Jordan and Yemen.* Cambridge: Cambridge University Press, 2006.

Conflict Resolution

Conflict resolution is the process of ending, changing, alleviating, or preventing conflict among different parties. In international politics, conflict is ever present in several forms, ranging from simple disagreement to outright genocide. Johan Galtung identified three components to conflict resolution: (1) peacemaking, (2) peacekeeping, and (3) peace building. According to William Zartman, conflict resolution depends upon "removing the causes as well as the manifestations of conflict between parties and eliminating the sources of incompatibility in their positions."

Because of the permanence of conflict in politics, conflict resolution specialists suggest that those engaged in a particular conflict must disconnect a given conflict from the concept of justice as well as accept that involved parties have legitimate concerns. Separating the legitimate concerns from the notion of justice is necessary because justice is subjective and sometimes clashes with the notion of peacemaking. Conflict resolution is a long-term prospect, and thus it can involve numerous methods such as mediation, negotiation, peacekeeping, and diplomacy. All of these methods have several prerequisites. First, the people engaged in conflict resolution need to recognize the legitimacy of claims of all parties involved in the conflict. Another prerequisite is for practitioners to recognize the impact of personalities, personal beliefs, and ideologies upon the conflict. Yet another prerequisite is to understand that conflicts can be transformed, albeit after the process of conflict resolution has started. Finally, people engaged in conflict resolution must recognize that third parties not directly involved in the conflict could be vital in the outcome of the resolution.

Various mediation strategies, according to Jacob Bergovich, can be grouped in the following categories. First, communication strategies include making contact with the parties, being neutral, gaining the trust and confidence of the parties, and clarifying the issues at stake. Second, formulation strategies include various protocol issues such as the time, place, and order of the meetings; controlling the physical environment; and establishing mutually accepted procedures. And third, manipulation strategies include altering the expectations held by the parties, manipulating the time, making the parties aware of the cost of nonagreement, promising resources for agreement, and threatening withdrawal.

Individuals comprise the first actor in conflict resolution by acting as mediators. For example, former president Jimmy Carter, on behalf of his Carter Center, has acted as a mediator in several conflicts, most recently in the Sudan. Groups such as the Quakers in the Cyprus dispute or organizations such as the International Negotiation Network (INN) can also provide assistance to the parties engaged in conflict resolution.

States are the most common actors in conflict resolution. States can be invited to become mediators in a given conflict such as former U.S. secretaries of state Warren Christopher and Cyrus Vance and former British foreign secretaries Peter Carrington and David Owen in Yugoslavia as well as several presidents of the United States in the Palestinian-Israeli conflict. Several world-renowned state mediated agreements have been reached, most famously the Camp David Accords, which led to the sharing of the Nobel Peace Prize by the leaders of Israel and Egypt.

Institutions and organizations can be engaged in conflict resolution, especially since some conflicts are complex and include several parties. International organizations have conducted conflict resolution negotiations, especially the United Nations (UN). Regional organizations have also played an active role in conflict resolution, such as the Organization for American States, which has been involved in conflict resolution between the United States and Venezuela, or the Arab League, which is involved in the Arab-Israeli conflict. Transnational organizations are also involved in conflict resolution; these include nongovernmental or quasi-governmental organizations such as Amnesty International, the International Committee of the Red Cross, or the INN. State sponsored organizations, such as regional or international courts, also conduct conflict resolution. For instance, the European Court of Human Rights and the International Court of Justice are entities that often help resolve conflicts after they have occurred by holding the perpetrators of human rights violations accountable.

Yet another group of theorists believe that war itself can be a tool of conflict resolution since the end of wars is ultimately peace. In his seminal work "Give War a Chance," Edward Luttwak argued that outside intervention to resolve conflicts usually tends to perpetuate war, not stop it. In Luttwak's opinion, most low intensity wars would run their normal course, ending in either capitulation on one side or the exhaustion of both and, thus, leading to a lasting peace. When the international community interrupts this, they basically allow the regrouping and rearming of warring factions and, thus, the war's continuation. Joseph Nye reached a similar conclusion, from a different perspective, in his call for the United States to scale down interventionism in small regional wars, which ultimately may not serve the U.S. "national interest." There is, however, serious disagreement on what constitutes a small war, and whether such wars pose a threat to the wider international community, as well as what constitutes national interest.

See also *Negotiations and Bargaining; United Nations (UN); War Termination.*

. . . . AKIS KALAITZIDIS

BIBLIOGRAPHY

Crocker, Chester. "A Poor Case for Quitting: Mistaking Incompetence for Interventionism." *Foreign Affairs* 79, no. 1 (2000): 183–186.

Galtung, Johan. "Three Approaches to Peace: Peacekeeping, Peacemaking, and Peacebuilding." In *Peace, War, and Defense: Essays in Peace Research,* edited by J. Galtung, vol. 2. Copenhagen: Christian Ejlers, 1976.

Kaufman, Stuart. "Escaping the Symbolic Politics Trap: Reconciliation Initiatives and Conflict Resolution in Ethnic Wars." *Journal of Peace Research* 43 (2001): 201–218.

Luttwak, Edward. "Give War a Chance." *Foreign Affairs* 78, no. 4 (1999): 36–44.

Nye, Joseph. "Redefining the National Interest." *Foreign Affairs* 78, no. 4 (1999): 22–35.

Zartman, William, and L. Rasmussen, eds. *Peacemaking in International Conflict: Methods and Techniques.* Washington, D.C.: United States Institute of Peace, 1997.

Confucian Political Thought

The tradition of Confucian political thought began over twenty-five hundred years ago and focused on the importance of ritual, roles, and virtue in creating a harmonious social order. With the unification of China by the Qin dynasty (221–206 BCE), Confucianism was initially persecuted, but with the collapse of the Qin and the rise of the Han dynasty (202 BCE–220 CE), Confucianism became the official ideology of the various dynasties occupying China through the collapse of the Qing dynasty in 1911. Confucianism as a ruling ideology also penetrated Korea, Japan, and Vietnam, and continues to exert social and political influence throughout East Asia.

THE FOUNDER AND HIS TEACHINGS

Confucian political thought began with the extraordinary personality Kongfuzi, latinized as Confucius (551–479 BCE). Though Confucius may have served briefly in minor or major governmental posts, his aspiration for governmental service went largely unfulfilled. His greatest success was as a teacher of scholars and those seeking positions in public service. Confucius did not believe his teaching was an innovation, but instead a transmission of the wisdom of the past with particular focus on the rituals of the Zhou dynasty (1022–256 BCE). The importance of ritual propriety (*li*) and its role in harmonizing human relationships is the central teaching of Confucianism.

Ritual propriety requires that individuals of different rank and status act appropriately according to their role in a given relationship. Confucius identified five relationships at the core of this harmonious community, including ruler-minister, father-son, husband-wife, elder-younger brother, and friend-friend. The senior partners of these relationships are obliged to show care and concern, whereas the junior partners of these relationships are obliged to be obedient and respectful. Filial piety (*xiao*), obedience, and concern toward parents and loyalty (*zhong*) to the ruler or state is the key to social order for Confucius. The balancing of these loyalties required the virtues of

humaneness or benevolence (*ren*) and personal responsibility toward social organizations and groups of people (*yi*).

The virtues necessary for realizing a harmonious community were to be cultivated within a cultural elite of exemplary persons (*junzi*), who through their example would guide the common people (*min*) to moral behavior. Such individuals needed to be deferential to persons in high position, perceptive of the will of heaven (*tian*), and attentive to the words of sages (*shengren*), the extraordinary founders of dynasties that exemplified harmonious human community.

The education of exemplary persons consisted of training in the six traditional arts of the aristocracy as well as rhetoric, public administration, and ethics. Confucius's willingness to teach all who were willing and able to learn, and his identification of some of his socially disadvantaged students as exemplary persons, led H. G. Creel, an American sinologist, to argue that Confucius carried out a major revolution against the existing aristocracy by opening the doors for high office to merit.

Another important legacy of Confucius revolves around his relationship to the supernatural. Though it would be inaccurate to argue that Confucius lived in a secular world, Confucius's relative silence on the spirits and his conception of a relatively rationalized heaven (*tian*) have focused the Confucian tradition on pragmatic social and ethical action as opposed to metaphysical speculation. This focus has led Herbert Fingarette to characterize Confucius as a figure who has treated human community as a holy rite and elevated it to become an arena of ultimate concern.

EVOLUTION OF THE CONFUCIAN TRADITION

The Warring States era (476–221 BCE), a period of disunity, produced two thinkers of great importance for the Confucian tradition, Mengzi (372–289 BCE) and Xunzi (312–230 BCE). These thinkers explored the problem of human nature and came to radically different conclusions. Mengzi believed human nature was good, whereas Xunzi concluded that human nature was evil. Both preserved the tradition's emphasis on the importance of learning and ritual practice to either realize human potential or curb human evil.

Other Warring States philosophers trained by Xunzi followed the implications of his characterization of human nature as evil and focused on a realist approach to governance emphasizing punishments and rewards known as *Legalism*. Legalism became the guiding ideology of the Qin dynasty that united China and later persecuted the Confucians and burnt their books. With the fall of the Qin and the rise of the Han dynasty, Confucianism combined with elements of Legalism to become the hegemonic doctrine of governance of China's succeeding dynasties.

Taoism and later Buddhism offered critical and complementary perspectives to the Confucian tradition. Taoist thinkers such as Zhuangzi (370–301 BCE) argued that the Confucian attention to benevolence and the artifice of ritual were acts against nature, deepening the troubles of the world.

Instead of seeking to serve in public office, Taoists preferred the free and easy living afforded by following the way (*Tao*) of nature. Buddhism, coming to China 67 CE, contradicted the Confucian values of loyalty to the emperor and family with its emphasis on monasticism and an otherworldly liberation. These traditions had moments of political influence, but practical orientation of Confucianism and the guidance of the two traditions away from worldly affairs minimized political conflicts among these traditions.

Neo-Confucians integrated Taoist and Buddhist metaphysical curiosity into the Confucian tradition. Zhu Xi (1100–1200), a scholar during the Song dynasty (960–1279), crafted a metaphysical system that focused Confucian self-cultivation on understanding the underlying principle (*li*) that ordered matter and energy (*qi*) through the investigation of things (*gewu*). Zhu's method of interpretation and the four books he selected as Confucian classics came to form the basis of the bureaucratic examination system, selecting scholar-officials to administer governmental affairs for the last three dynasties to govern China.

Wang Yangming (1472–1529) of the Ming dynasty (1368–1644) articulated a metaphysics that opposed Zhu's emphasis on the external world and focused the act of self-cultivation on internal experience and innate moral knowledge. He also argued that knowledge and action were unified, opposed to Zhu's conception that knowledge proceeded action. Thinkers who attacked existing social and gender hierarchies embraced Wang's metaphysics, leading to their own deaths and imprisonments, and his dangerous philosophical innovation to be declared unorthodox. The debate between followers of Zhu and Wang continues within Confucian circles even today.

THE CONFUCIAN TRADITION IN MODERN TIMES

The Qing dynasty (1644–1912), a dynasty founded by Manchu warriors from the north of China, like all other preceding dynasties, preserved the Confucian system. Yet, major disasters, internal rebellions of unprecedented scale, and invasion and impositions from colonial powers would break the ideology that had endured for over two thousand years. The resilience of the system may have been the factor that led the administrators of the empire to believe only minor adaptation of the contrivances (*yung*) of Western culture were necessary to respond to the crisis, while the essence (*ti*) of Chinese culture could still be preserved. The defeat by the Japanese, a culture previously looked down upon, in the Sino-Japanese War (1894–1895) convinced many that fundamental reform was necessary.

Reformers such as Kang Youwei (1858–1927) advocated the transformation to a constitutional monarchy. Practical reform was rejected, and entrenched conservative forces remained in place even as those forces lost control of the country. The Chinese Revolution of 1911, and numerous attempts to restore the Confucian ideal of the emperor of all under heaven, failed to establish a stable and lasting order. Kang later embraced the vision of a establishing a world government to realize the Confucian utopian ideal of the great harmony (*Datong*).

During the twenties and the thirties, a new culture movement evolved that challenged the legitimacy of the old ways in name of nationalism, democracy, and science. Lu Xun (1881–1936) argued that the tradition was eating its children, and Confucianism should not be saved because it was unable to save the Chinese people. Lu's criticisms occurred as warlords, Nationalists, and Communists battled to govern the land. The Nationalists, under Chiang Kai-shek (1887–1975), loosely embraced the Confucian tradition through the New Life Movement in 1934, whereas the Communists were more sympathetic to the radicalism of Lu.

The end of World War II in 1945 and the breakdown of the united front of Communists and Nationalists against Japanese aggression that started in 1937 unleashed a civil war in China that would send the followers of Confucius to Taiwan and leave his critics in control of mainland China. Confucianism was most aggressively attacked on the mainland during the Cultural Revolution (1966–1976). Mao Zedong (1893–1976), the chairman of the Communist Party and the founder and de facto political leader of the People's Republic of China, used Confucius as a symbolic stand-in for the forces that posed a political threat to him. Confucius was painted as desiring to return to the conditions of a feudal slave state, and his teachings and images were to be eradicated as emblems of counterrevolutionary forces.

RECENT DEVELOPMENTS

The rejection of Confucianism in the land of its origins raised questions about the tradition's viability into the future. On the surface, Confucianism appeared too complacent in dealing with authority in its search for social harmony, slow to reform and adapt to changing circumstances, antidemocratic, antifeminist, and anticapitalist. This pessimism about the potential of Confucianism to contribute to the modern world was rooted in a Western social science that identified Confucianism as being particularly antagonistic to capitalist development, and the experience of East Asians who viewed Confucianism as an impediment to modernization. The unexpected economic success of East Asian societies in the 1980s led Western scholars such as Ezra Vogel, a professor of East Asian studies at Harvard, to reappraise the economic and social potential of the Confucian tradition.

The movement to justify Confucianism on economic grounds was preceded by an attempt to redeem the humanistic value of the tradition. In 1958, Mou Zongsan, a major exponent of the neo-Confucian tradition, and several of his intellectual peers issued "A Declaration to the World for Chinese Culture," agreeing that Chinese culture needed to learn science and democracy from the West but also arguing the West needed to learn "a more all encompassing wisdom" from China. Tu Wei-ming, a Harvard professor of Chinese studies, is a prominent advocate of this holistic and humane vision of the Confucian tradition.

Academic commentators on Confucianism such as Roger Ames, William Theodore de Bary, Daniel Bell, Hahm Chaibong, Joseph Chan, Herbert Fingarette, David Hall, Philip

Ivanhoe, Henry Rosemont, and many more argue for a progressive and pragmatic understanding of the Confucian tradition. These thinkers not only challenge the sexism, elitism, and authoritarianism of the tradition, but they have pioneered Confucian ways of thinking about property rights, democracy, human rights, welfare policy, environmentalism, and more. The creative search for harmony and the cocreation of a meaningful aesthetic order from the perspective of all the participants within a community is the core of the Confucian tradition that they accentuate. Though this trend toward viewing Confucianism as a socially progressive and creative means of affirming human values is a very important trend in academic circles, not all professing Confucians embrace this vision.

The most visible controversy involving Confucianism in recent history challenging this progressive vision centers around the Asian values debate that emerged as many societies in Asia began to resent what they perceived to be the general permissiveness and decadence of Western liberal societies. The debate emerged in the 1990s, and it revolved around the question of whether universal human rights as they were conceived in the West should be applied to all societies.

Lee Kwan Yew, prime minister of Singapore during the time of the controversy, argued that individualistic Western values caused great harm to society and Eastern traditions such as Confucianism were correct to place society's interests above the rights of individuals. The economic success of many East Asian societies that had limited civil liberties gave this argument some strength, however Lee Teng-hui, former president of the Republic of China; Kim Dae Jung, former president of the Republic of Korea; and Amartya Sen, Nobel Prize-winning economist, among others, have been very critical of this authoritarian ideological framework that diminishes individual rights.

Some Western scholars, such as Samuel Huntington, a former Harvard political scientist, have perceived a fundamental incompatibility between Confucianism and liberal democracy because of the tradition's emphasis on the rights of groups over individuals. Other Western scholars such as Francis Fukuyama, a George Mason political scientist, argue that the tradition's commitment to education makes Confucianism quite compatible with liberal democracy. These debates are not only academic given the recent interest in Confucianism in the People's Republic of China.

Economic and political reforms initiated in 1978 within the People's Republic of China have led the Chinese Communist Party to reassess its relationship to the Chinese past and particularly the country's Confucian heritage. The decline in value of Marxist ideology in its international and national prestige following the collapse of communism in the Soviet Union and Eastern Europe have led China's top leaders to begin to rehabilitate Confucius as a source of the social values that will help them to manage a country experiencing rapid economic growth and development. Chinese president Hu Jintao quotes Confucius in his speeches emphasizing the value of harmonious relations, and the country's cultural outreach program to the rest of the world, the Confucius Institutes, bear the name

of the sage. Whether Confucianism will play an important role in the future governance of China and whether it will have an authoritarian or progressive form remain open questions.

See also *Chinese Political Thought; Communism.*

. . . . TODD MYERS

BIBLIOGRAPHY

Ames, Roger. *The Analects of Confucius: A Philosophical Translation,* translated by Henry Rosemont. New York: Ballantine, 1999.

Ames, Roger, and David Hall. *The Democracy of the Dead: Dewey, Confucius, and the Hope for Democracy in China.* Chicago: Open Court Publishing, 1999.

Angle, Stephen C. *Human Rights and Chinese Thought: A Cross-Cultural Inquiry.* Cambridge: Cambridge University Press, 2002.

———. *Thinking Through Confucius.* Albany: State University Press of New York, 1987.

Bell, Daniel A. *China's New Confucianism: Politics and Everyday Life in a Changing Society.* Princeton: Princeton University Press, 2008.

———, ed. *Confucian Political Ethics.* Princeton: Princeton University Press, 2008.

———. *Beyond Liberal Democracy: Political Thinking for an East Asian Context.* Princeton: Princeton University Press, 2006.

Bell, Daniel A., and Hahm Chaibong, eds. *Confucianism for the Modern World.* Cambridge: Cambridge University Press, 2003.

Berthrong, John. *Transformations of the Confucian Way.* Boulder: Westview Press, 1998.

Creel, Herlee G. *Confucius and the Chinese Way.* New York: Harper and Row, 1949.

de Bary, William Theodore, and Tu Wei-ming, eds. *Confucianism and Human Rights.* New York: Columbia University Press, 1999.

Fingarette, Herbert. *Confucius: Secular as Sacred.* New York: Torchbooks, 1972.

Holloway, Kenneth. *Guodian: The Newly Discovered Seeds of Chinese Religious and Political Philosophy.* New York: Oxford University Press, 2009.

Hua, Shipping. *Chinese Utopianism: A Comparative Study of Reformist Thought with Japan and Russia, 1898–1997.* Stanford: Stanford University Press, 2009.

Jensen, Lionel. *Manufacturing Confucianism: Chinese Traditions and Universal Civilization.* Durham, N.C.: Duke University Press, 1997.

Lau, D. C., trans. *Mencius.* New York: Penguin Classics, 1970.

Li, Chenyang. *The Sage and the Second Sex: The Sage and the Second Gender.* Chicago: Open Court Publishing, 2000.

Makeham, John. *New Confucianism: A Critical Appraisal.* New York: Palgrave-Macmillan, 2003.

Mitter, Rana. *A Bitter Revolution: China's Struggle with the Modern World.* New York: Oxford University Press, 2005.

Neville, Robert Cummings. *Boston Confucianism in a Late Modern World.* Albany: State University Press of New York, 2000.

Pines, Yuri. *Envisioning Eternal Empire: Chinese Political Thought of the Warring States Era.* Honolulu: University of Hawaii Press, 2009.

Tu, Wei-ming, ed. *Confucian Traditions in East Asian Modernity: Moral Education and Economic Culture in Japan and the Four Mini-Dragons.* Cambridge: Harvard University Press, 1996.

Watson, Burton, ed. *Xunzi.* New York: Columbia University Press, 2003.

———, ed. *Zhuangzi.* New York: Columbia University Press, 2003.

Congress, Contempt of

The two houses of the U.S. Congress, much like the courts, possess the power to protect their proceedings by deeming a person in contempt for obstructive or disorderly conduct. The power to hold nonmembers in contempt of Congress is not addressed in the U.S. Constitution but is an inherent congressional power, as recognized in 1821 by the U.S. Supreme Court in *Anderson v. Dunn.* (By contrast, each house's power to discipline its own members is expressly conferred by the Constitution.) A typical offense is the failure to provide testimony or documents requested by a congressional committee, but acts such as bribing or assaulting members have also been punished as contempts.

Although Congress has the power to impose contempt sanctions unilaterally—operating in effect as both prosecutor and judge—today Congress typically refers alleged contempts to federal prosecutors to pursue criminal proceedings in the courts under a federal contempt statute, which authorizes fines and imprisonment. Most persons charged with contempt of Congress are private citizens who refuse to cooperate with congressional investigations or hearings, but executive branch officials' reluctance to provide information to Congress sometimes results in threatened or actual contempt proceedings, especially in times of divided government.

See also *Parliamentary Privilege.*

. . . . AARON-ANDREW P. BRUHL

Conscience, Freedom of

See *Freedom of Conscience.*

Conscientious Objection

See *Pacifism and Conscientious Objection.*

Conseil d'État

Conseil d'État (Council of State) is the supreme judicial body in France for matters of government and public administration. The Conseil d'État decides cases on administrative or legislative issues and offers advice to the government and French National Assembly on constitutional affairs. It also serves as an appellate court for cases brought against the government by citizens or groups, including disputes arising from local or regional elections. Members of the Conseil d'État are senior or distinguished jurists, and the body is divided into six administrative sections. There are thirty-seven regional courts that serve as trial courts, and eight appellate courts under the Conseil d'Etat. The origins of the body date to the 1300s, but its modern functions and organization were established in 1799, with major reforms in 1872. The prime minister and the minister of justice formally preside over the Conseil d'État, but an appointed vice president oversees its day-to-day operations. As part of its advisory function, the Conseil d'État issues annual reports on legal and political matters and reviews draft legislation, decrees, and certain government projects or policies. A range of other countries have a Conseil d'État, or similar body, including Belgium, Spain, and Turkey.

See also *Judicial Review; Judicial Systems, Comparative.*

. . . . TOM LANSFORD

Consensus

Merriam-Webster's Collegiate Dictionary defines *consensus* as "general agreement: unanimity," or "the judgment arrived at by most of those concerned." Consensus may be used broadly to describe decisions reached in a spirit of compromise, regardless of what process is followed. More significant for political science, consensus denotes a specific *decision rule* whereby all participating agents possess veto rights over the collective outcome; the purpose is to ensure decisions that are genuinely supported by all members of a community. Consensus decision is designed as an alternative to majority rule, which permits the views or interests of the majority to override those of minorities. Whether consensus decision rules in practice produce more just outcomes than majority rule is debated.

Small groups often decide informally by consensus; consensus decision is formalized in some religious communities, including the Quakers; in Anglo-American law, jury verdicts must be unanimous. The practice in some ancient republics of voting by acclamation created the appearance of unanimity while veiling real divisions. Some contemporary anarchists insist that anything short of unanimous consent by all individuals to collective decisions violates personal autonomy.

None of these are adequate models for consensus decision making in large modern territorial states or federations. Most consensus theorists reject individual veto rights as impractical in large political communities and instead allocate veto powers to a relatively small number of corporate agents. The veto-bearing agents might be organized economic interests; religious, linguistic, or ethnic communities; or, in a federal system, states or provinces with their own peculiar history and traditions.

The most thorough advocate of the consensus model of government was John C. Calhoun of South Carolina (1782–1850). In *A Disquisition on Government* (1851), Calhoun argued that over time majority rule will inevitably produce entrenched, geographically concentrated majorities and minorities, and that the majority would systematically violate the rights and interests of the minority. Calhoun's proposed solution was to arm each significant interest with veto rights: to "give to each division or interest . . . either a concurrent voice in making and executing the laws, or a veto on their execution." He denied that this would produce deadlock or anarchy, claiming instead that it would force all interests to cooperate in the common good. Calhoun's principal successor among twentieth-century political scientists is Arend Lijphart, whose theory of *consociational democracy* bears a close though not exact resemblance to Calhoun's model.

Institutions practicing consensus decision have existed in the past and continue to exist today. The U.S. Articles of Confederation (1781–1788) enabled a single state to block decisions supported by all others. The United Nations Security Council allocates permanent veto rights to a handful of privileged powers. The 1998 Northern Ireland settlement grants the two largest parliamentary groups, the Nationalists and the

Unionists, veto rights over decisions. Consensus decision was seriously advocated, though not implemented, for postapartheid South Africa. The European Union operates according to a complicated and shifting blend of unanimity requirements and qualified majority rule.

Advocates of consensus decision claim that it prevents majority tyranny while encouraging minorities to wield veto rights with restraint and in a spirit of accommodation. Critics of consensus decision contend that it risks deadlock on urgent matters, entails arbitrary definitions of who or what is entitled to veto rights, and favors groups privileged by the status quo over those with a stake in change.

See also *Coalition Formation; Coalition Theory; Consociational Democracy; Decision Theory, Foundations of.*

. . . . JAMES H. READ

BIBLIOGRAPHY

Calhoun, John C. *A Disquisition on Government.* Columbia: General Assembly of the State of South Carolina, 1851.

Horowitz, Donald L. "The Northern Ireland Agreement: Clear, Consociational, and Risky." In *Northern Ireland and the Divided World,* edited by John McGarry. New York: Oxford University Press, 2001.

Lijphart, Arend. *Democracies: Patterns of Majoritarian and Consensus Government in Twenty-one Countries.* New Haven: Yale University Press, 1984.

McGarry, John, and Brendan O'Leary. *The Northern Ireland Conflict: Consociational Engagements.* New York: Oxford University Press, 2004.

Pinder, John, and Simon Usherwood. *The European Union: A Very Short Introduction,* 2nd ed. New York: Oxford University Press, 2008.

Rae, Douglas. "The Limits of Consensual Decision." *The American Political Science Review* 69, no. 4 (1975): 1270–1294.

Read, James H. *Majority Rule versus Consensus: The Political Thought of John C. Calhoun.* Lawrence: University Press of Kansas, 2009.

Schwartzberg, Melissa. "Shouts, Murmurs, and Votes: Acclamation and Aggregation in Ancient Greece." *Journal of Political Philosophy* (2010). Online publication date: 1-Apr-2010.

Wolff, Robert Paul. *In Defense of Anarchism.* New York: Harper and Row, 1970.

Consent of the Governed

The *consent of the governed* traditionally refers to acts of consent that people have performed in regard to their government. During the late Middle Ages, consent was viewed as central to political legitimacy, while since roughly the seventeenth century, individuals' own consent has been believed to be the main reason they are morally required to obey government. The main thrust of the doctrine is to limit the power of government and to make sure its actions are consistent with what people can accept.

The consent of the governed emerged as an important political idea in medieval Europe, as rulers of different territories began to consult with notable members of their polities. For example the English "model parliament" met for the first time in 1295 and the French Estates-Generals in 1302. Actions approved by such bodies literally had the consent of the governed—although only a small slice of the overall population. In subsequent centuries, amidst struggles to limit royal authority, arguments were developed according to which power originated in the people and was transferred to the

king (through the "social contract") conditionally. The people agreed to obey if the king ruled justly. Especially sophisticated statements were worked out in the church by "conciliar" theorists, attempting to limit the power of the pope, and during the religious and political turmoil of the Protestant Reformation. But in spite of the forcefulness of late medieval and sixteenth-century treatises, the theorists' views fell short of a modern conception. They conceive of the community as a whole consenting—through its representatives—opposed to the modern notion, which turns upon the consent of each individual.

The locus classicus for the modern view is John Locke's *Second Treatise of Government.* According to Locke, to avoid conflicts that arise in an otherwise relatively peaceful state of nature, people agree to common authority. Since individuals are naturally free, only their own consent can place them under political authority. They are not bound by agreements entered into by their forebears, such as an original contract at the founding of society. However, recognizing that most people have not "expressly" agreed to be governed, Locke turns to what he calls "tacit consent," which are other actions that constitute consent and thus capable of binding people. Most notable is simply remaining in a given territory. Although this would ground political obligations for virtually all inhabitants, in making consent accomplished so easily, Locke renders the need for actual acts of consent virtually insignificant. In spite of this and other problems, Locke's view was enormously influential, drawn upon, for example, in the preamble to the Declaration of Independence, which speaks of governments "deriving their just powers from the consent of the governed."

David Hume, in his essay "Of the Original Contract," classically—and fatally—criticized Locke's view of consent on historical grounds. Like Locke, Hume believes that most people have not consented expressly to government, since they have no recollection of doing so. Yet he rejects Locke's view of tacit consent. Since most people lack the resources and ability to leave their territories, their presence cannot be said to constitute consent.

Since the time of Hume, theorists have attempted to identify other actions performed by all or most citizens that constitute consent. Notable examples are voting or serving in the military. But none of these bears scrutiny. Immanuel Kant was responsible for an important theoretical advance in viewing consent as purely hypothetical, rather than an actual historical occurrence. According to this line of argument, a government is legitimate only if people *would* consent to it if given the opportunity. But in spite of difficulties in identifying acts of consent that have actually been performed, the idea continues to epitomize people's right to governments they accept, and to withdraw their consent, with possibly revolutionary implications, when they find government no longer acceptable.

See also *Hume, David; Kant, Immanuel; Locke, John.*

. . . . GEORGE KLOSKO

BIBLIOGRAPHY

Hume, David. "Of the Original Contract." In *Essays: Moral, Political, and Literary,* rev. ed., edited by E. Miller. Indianapolis, Ind.: Liberty Classics, 1985.

Kant, Immanuel. "On the Common Saying: 'This May Be True in Theory, But It Does Not Apply in Practice.'" In *Kant's Political Writings,* translated and edited by H. Reiss. Cambridge: Cambridge University Press, 1970.

Locke, John. *Two Treatises of Government,* edited by P. Laslett. Cambridge: Cambridge University Press, 1988.

Simmons, A. John. *Moral Principles and Political Obligations.* Princeton: Princeton University Press, 1979.

Consequentialism

Consequentialism is a philosophy that an act must be assessed as either good or bad depending upon its results. Hence, consequentialism holds that policies are good or just depending on their consequences. Undergirding consequentialism is the notion that values precede morality and even without a moral code, some things would still be good and others bad. Pleasure is judged to be the ultimate good result, and pain the ultimate bad. The main political strand of consequentialism was utilitarianism, as developed by the British philosopher Jeremy Bentham and later refined by British economist and philosopher John Stuart Mill. *Utilitarianism* posits that acts are morally correct only if they maximize the greatest good for the largest number of people. A variety of other forms of consequentialism have also emerged. Consequentialism as refined by the British philosopher G. E. Moore added intrinsic notions, such as beauty, to what could be considered good. Moore's ideas were dubbed ideal utilitarianism. In the preference utilitarianism of English philosopher R. M. Hare, acts are considered to be good if they meet or enhance the preferences of individuals or groups, whatever those preferences may be. Total consequentialism is predicated on the premise that goodness is dependent on the overall good of the action (even if it causes pain or displeasure to subsets of a group).

See also *Bentham, Jeremy; Mill, John Stuart; Utilitarianism.*

. . . . TOM LANSFORD

Conservatism

The disposition to preserve what one has attained, received, or inherited, and to defend against the losses that inevitably befall human beings in our time-bound existence, is undoubtedly observable universally in all times and places. This disposition to conserve, insofar as it is a natural response to contingent circumstances, is not conservatism. *Conservatism* is a self-conscious affirmation of this disposition with a self-conscious expression of resistance to the alternative, which welcomes change, by premeditated design, to the environment in which one finds oneself. Conservatism resists the readiness to explore, more or less adventurously, and the possibilities of an imagined, alternative future existence. Self-conscious conservatism theorizes the natural disposition to preserve, raising it to the level of a conscious affirmation that may lead to the formation of principles or rules that serve more or less as guides to one's conduct in personal life and political views and activities. A conservative disposition often manifests itself as considered points of view, even doctrines, engaging in

debate or argument with opposing alternative self-conscious doctrines. Today, common terms of political discourse such as conservatism, liberalism, and radicalism, and many other *-isms*, only reinforce the acutely self-conscious character of the modern age, which suggests that to be without such a doctrine is to be directionless and in need of guidance—a conclusion about which conservatives remain ambivalent.

ORIGINS OF CONSERVATISM

Traditionally, in histories of the concept, it is said that conservatism begins with Irish statesman and political theorist, Edmund Burke (1729–1797), especially in his critique of the French Revolution (1789–1799) in his celebrated *Reflections on the Revolution in France* (1790). There is no doubt Burke's critique was both powerful and prophetic about many of the consequences that would follow from the revolution's upheaval in Europe, and his work figures centrally in the study of the development of conservatism. Alongside Burke, we recognize Alexis de Tocqueville's analysis of *Democracy in America* (1835–1840), and his penetrating analysis of the French Revolution, as central to our understanding of these conditions.

However, prior to the French Revolution and Burke's theories, conservatism was conceptualized parallel to Europe's transformation from the Middle Ages in the fourteenth and fifteenth centuries to the religious Reformation in the sixteenth century, to the birth of the Age of Enlightenment and the Industrialism in the eighteenth and nineteenth centuries. These centuries saw the advent of a revolutionary era on every front, proceeding in varying forms in different regions and countries, but proceeding nonetheless to radically revise the reigning ideas of political order, symbolized profoundly in the emergence of the social contract theory with European philosophers, including Thomas Hobbes, John Locke, Jean-Jacques Rousseau, Immanuel Kant, and others.

Contractarian philosophy espoused a social order in which a community would be granted civil and social rights adhering to the rule of law of a political authority. The seventeenth- and eighteenth-century social contract theories complemented and influenced Europe's emerging modern commercial society and free market economy in what Scottish philosopher, Adam Smith, its greatest theorist, called, in *The Wealth of Nations* (1776), the "system of natural liberty." Smith proposed for the free, equal, and independent individual; the value of individual liberty as a common commitment; and the commitment to progress in terms of ever-expanding economic growth, all of which were increasingly accepted concepts in eighteenth-century Europe and the newly established America.

While conservatives were historically receptive with the evolving social contract theories and subsequent free market economics originating in the later seventeenth and eighteenth centuries, conservatives were—and remain—ambivalent on these economic concepts, given their historic affinity to the ancient and medieval ideas of virtue and noble character. Such modern propositions, stating wealth and virtue can be complementary, increasingly challenged the ancient prejudice that wealth and virtue conflict. Essentially, when an individual or society's wealth accumulates, the individual's moral virtue decays. According to conservatives, although economic growth is good and required, materialism and ostentation threaten society's moral virtue. Further, with the onset of advances in modern science and technology incited by Europe's modernization, it became plausible human beings could begin to take their destiny into their own hands, causing persons to either reject old theological doctrines of God's providence, or become self-determining agents who will fulfill that providence through creative renovation of human existence on earth. Conservatives have been historically reserved about such topics pertaining to science and religion.

The seventeenth and eighteenth centuries were also witness to increasingly centralized political authority as the modern state came to be seen as the primary political agent of world history. The division between Catholics and Protestants undermined the traditionally independent authority of the medieval church, rendering claims to independent ecclesiastical authority ambiguous or suspect. The creation of the modern state was as revolutionary a development as any of the other events of the aforementioned periods. This modern state was established by the aggregation, centralization, and deployment of power, together with increasingly sophisticated bureaucratic management, to an extent unimaginable in the medieval world.

Given these revolutionary changes in a relatively limited time span, it is not surprising that, as historical and philosophical assessments of what was happening evolved, extraordinary efforts to theorize the significance of these transformations appeared, either embracing or lamenting the events. Regardless of the responses, the changes between the seventeenth to nineteenth centuries were irreversible, as the democratic age supplanted the aristocratic age in Europe, America, and the European colonies worldwide. The American Revolution (1876–1883) and the French Revolution are revelatory of the implications of what had been developing over a long time. Notably, it can be understood conservatism was a response to this modern age—not merely as a rejection of the modern age, but as a response to certain terms and concepts of the modern age. Therefore, conservatism is a distinctly modern intellectual and political phenomenon.

CONSERVATISM IN POLITICS
SELF-CONSCIOUS CONSERVATISM

Burke did not use the term *conservatism*, as the word first came into use around 1819 by French writer François-René de Chateaubriand, following the rise and fall of French emperor Napoleon Bonaparte. Burke does offer, however, a deliberate or self-consciously chosen view—affirming the intention to conserve and, while allowing for necessary adjustments as circumstances alter, to respect traditional ways—more commonly referred to as *self-conscious conservatism*. A primary theme of self-conscious conservatism is requiring prudential judgment; it cannot be merely antiquarian or simply set in its way since with all modern conditions, conservative ideals must deal with the need of adjustment and alteration as one's environment and issues evolve. Conservatives must develop theoretical statements about what is to be preserved, or what it will mean to preserve something. Increasingly, it became difficult to be merely conservative in politics; one must be prepared to be "programmatically conservative." This indicates how the shape of modern life constrains what it can mean to be conservative, making it difficult to defend inherited practices without supplying arguments defending such inheritances, with the arguments themselves eliciting counterarguments.

CONSERVATISM AND GAUGING CENTRALIZED AUTHORITY

Conservatism as a political argument involves skepticism about the aggregation of power in governments, and a warning against diminishing the independence of traditional intermediate groups and influential organizations that soften or mitigate the power relation between the apparatus of the modern state and individuals and families who are subject to increasingly minute regulation from central governments. Further, conservatism involves respect, even veneration, for traditional manners and forms of living; an acceptance of the lives and the loyalties to groups and associations that were not created by, nor originally dependent on, the good will of the sovereign state; and to respect them simply because they are there and accepted by those who live in them. The enemy of this conserving attitude is the view that no practices or institutions should be accepted which are not thought through and given an independent rationale such that they could make sense even to those who have not lived within their terms. Such a rationale, of course, potentially undermines the independence of any entity in question because it is now eligible for assessment by those outside it as well as by those within. The age of acute self-consciousness demands to extend its self-consciousness to even more remote corners of human existence. A tradition's appeal cannot continue to rest solely on the fact that there are those who enjoy it. This stimulates what has been described as the "disenchantment" or "demythologization" of the modern world by such modern thinkers as Karl Marx, Fyodor Dostoevsky, Friedrich Nietzsche, Max Weber, T. S. Eliot, and Russell Kirk. Conservatives regret this obscuring of a sense of the transcendent or sacramental character of heritage, and so far as possible they wish to revivify that sense.

Politically speaking, a fundamental, recurrent conservative issue regarding modern political life has been, and continues to be, a debate over the scope of governmental power: What are governments supposed to do? Questioning the limits or scope of governmental power has become perennial and contentious. The social contract theory, in its numerous variations, has established itself as a primary device for testing the legitimacy of governments because it has taught us that political authority must rest on the consent of those over whom the authority will be exercised. No one, either by divine appointment or by natural authority, is entitled to rule. The revolutionary implication is that all governments not based on consent are inherently illegitimate and must be rectified by revolution or gradual reform. In this sense, the "democratic principle" seeks universality and remains unsatisfied to the extent that it has not yet achieved universality. However, even if conservatives express agreement on the democratic principle as the basis of political legitimacy, there is far less agreement on the scope of power to be exercised even by legitimate governments. While democracies can limit the exercise of political power, democracies can also serve as a plebiscite to empower governments to act virtually without limit.

Conservatism is skeptical about expanding the scope of governmental power beyond what is minimally required to maintain law and order. Since there is no fixed definition of the limits to governmental power, hence modern political life evidences incessant debates on what the limits are, and, since these debates are central to the way in which modern people understand political life, there can be no conceivable end to them. Conservatism is thus a manner of participating in these debates, and not simply a fixed and settled doctrine, as at times mistakenly characterized. The question for conservatives is not necessarily whether change is desirable, but a question about the means employed to affect change, coupled with skepticism about exaggerated claims as to how much good will result from change. It is precisely because conservatives understand that change is inevitable—there is no static world—which explains why conservatives tend to refrain from excessive enthusiasm about change. The conservative is sensitive to loss as well as gain, and believes that whatever the gains, there will be loss as well.

VARYING DEGREES OF CONSERVATISM
CASE STUDY: UNITED STATES OF AMERICA

To be conservative thus poses a choice either to opt out or to engage the modern game of politics with all of its uncertainties and open-endedness, and we see today that many conservatives are no less prone to reform and programmatic public policy than are their "liberal" and "radical" opponents. Today, in America the so-called *paleoconservatives* otherwise known as old-fashioned, antiquarian, and traditionalist tend to disdain the political scene; they criticize *movement conservatives*, or those who are oriented towards political success by gaining electoral office through compromises with their liberal opponents, and *neoconservatives*, proponents of an American welfare state, using U.S. resources to enforce improved social conditions globally. The latter term denotes, in America, reconstructed New Deal liberals, or former socialists, who take a more sober view of governmental power than they did in their earlier progressive days, who reject the left-wing of the Democratic Party especially on foreign policy issues, and who often have abandoned the Democratic Party for the Republican Party. How far conservatism can be identified with the Republican Party is itself a matter of debate among conservatives. There is in addition a divergence between those neoconservatives who focus on distrust of the growth of governmental power in domestic policy, and those who emphasize the projection of power in American foreign policy. To the degree that conservatism traditionally expressed skepticism about foreign involvement,

there is tension between traditional conservatives embracing isolationist policies and neoconservatives purporting foreign intervention.

Evolutionary conservatism is a profound feature of the American political tradition. It is also a source of intellectual controversy because there is a recurrent debate as to whether America even has a genuine conservative tradition at all. Such commentators as Louis Hartz, in *The Liberal Tradition in America* (1955), argued that there is in America no significant conservative tradition. However, Russell Kirk, in *The Conservative Mind* (1953), demonstrated such a tradition based on John Adams's American version of the Burkean idea and traced its path into the twentieth century. These are two classic expressions of the modern debate over the American political tradition. In addition, the word *tradition* can be, and is, appropriated by conservatives and liberals alike. Liberalism, too, has its traditions. One might conclude, then, with respect to America, there remains an amalgamation of traditional and enlightenment ideas such that America is both old and new, both conservative and liberal, at the same time.

EDMUND BURKE

Burke's conservatism, which was formed in the different conditions of the late eighteenth century in contrast to present times, was moderate in that he recognized the unavoidability of reform while seeking to keep it within limits. He was a reformer himself, not a "reactionary." For example, he acknowledged the legitimacy of the claims of the American revolutionaries as he rejected the aspirations of the French revolutionaries. While in Burke's view, the Americans appealed for their traditional rights as English citizens—and Burke respected this because he was devoted to defending liberty against the encroachments of governmental power—the French sought to remake the whole of society from the ground up, and this impelled their increasing use of greater force to overcome the natural resistance to wholesale change. Indeed, the American Revolution is often described as a "conservative" revolution precisely because it did not seek to reconstruct the whole of existing society, and in the framing of a new constitution in 1787, Americans preserved a certain skepticism about centralized government. This is most profoundly expressed in *The Federalist Papers* (1788–1789), especially those composed by James Madison, America's fourth President.

Burke's was not the only form of conservatism at his time. A variation on the theme is found in Joseph de Maistre (1753–1821), and in the romanticism of Chateaubriand (1768–1848). Here is conservatism as reaction against the transformation of modern Europe. Both embrace tradition in response to the upheavals of their time, but their emphasis differs from Burke's. Maistre and Chateaubriand regret the loss of the traditional forms of authority that accept a ruling elite and the authority of traditional, especially Catholic, religious figures.

Burke, in embracing traditional English liberties, for example, accepts the economic revolution that produced free markets and Adam Smith's system of natural liberty, rejecting government control of the economy as another perceived means in which governmental power will exceed its justifiable authority. In this respect, Burke maintains a strong defense of limited government, and is more compatible with what developed as *classical liberalism* in the nineteenth century, with its emphasis on free markets and international free trade. Today there is a strong affinity between classical liberals who defend free markets as the principal safeguard of liberty, and conservatives who, while prone to attack materialism, nevertheless acknowledge the importance of civil society and its foundation in the rights of private property and self-determination.

There is also a greater degree of individualism in Burke, and, ultimately, an acceptance of the need to come to terms with the new world post-1789; he is not a nostalgic, longing for a return to a vanished world; he deals with the new without glorifying it. In this sense, Burke's counterparts are John Adams in America, Alexis de Tocqueville in France, and Winston Churchill in England.

CONSERVATISM AS PRAGMATISM

Conservatism combines discernible characteristics in varying ways, with varying emphases, by different exponents. Conservatism, in its political skepticism, reflects the Augustinian Christian notion of original sin, sometimes expressed in theological terms, and sometimes transposed into more secular terms. Religious and secular conservatives can agree on human limitations, even though they may disagree on the importance of religious belief for a well-ordered society. Conservatism exhibits a moral imagination which, implicitly or explicitly, acknowledges a transcendent reality that is beyond human control; thus, scientific and technological innovation is to be treated with restraint because conservatives know that we can initiate many things but we cannot know in advance what all the consequences will turn out to be, nor how much we will like the results even of our successes. Untested innovation should be approached with caution. Conservatives typically stress to enjoy the opportunities of the present moment, to diminish the anxieties that follow from obsessive concern for, or guilt about, the past and, in addition, to restrain anxiety about what the future may bring.

This bespeaks a certain disposition of gratitude for what they have—defying resentment, envy, or alienation. This further suggests either a capacity for enjoyment of life, or Stoic patience with the human condition, or elements of both at once. It is these very characteristics that are criticized or commonly misinterpreted as complacency, as indifference to the plight of others, or as an unmerited sense of superiority or self-righteousness.

However, in the conservative's opinion, this is, rather, to acknowledge that human action is never complete by design. Conservatives deny political action can be made entirely rational to all of its public-serving interests. Therefore, the goal of the conservative is neither to be deceived nor to engage in self-deception and wishful thinking. If, as a result, conservatives are sometimes perceived as too reticent about change, conservatives will defend their stance citing it is because their opponents are too enthusiastic about claims, which allege to

know more than they actually know or can potentially achieve. Abstracting parts of the past from the whole—unavoidable, perhaps, as a condition of arguments for reform and perfection—carries always, as the conservative sees it, an unreliable optimism, which the record of human history teaches us to treat with considerable suspicion.

POPULAR CONSERVATIVE BELIEFS

RIGHT TO PROPERTY

Conservatism also defends the right of private property as fundamental. Conservatives take private property to be a bulwark against centralized power and an essential factor in the defense of the individual right to make something of one's self. Conservatives are not ashamed to possess property and, in principle, they do not resent that others have property, indeed even more property than they themselves have. Conservatives, while believing in the universal dignity of human beings, tend to value liberty more highly than equality. In their view, a society of free individuals will inevitably produce mixed results from the efforts of individuals to live for themselves. There will be successes and failures, and inequalities in outcomes, and the price of liberty is to accept responsibility for oneself, and to mind one's own business.

ORGANIC ARISTOCRACY

For those like John Adams, there is a *natural aristocracy*. The natural aristocrat demonstrates excellence not by holding high rank in a hierarchical social order based on inherited status. Indeed, except by convention, a member of an aristocratic class may not be excellent at all. A natural aristocrat is an individual of talent and energy who might spring from any social location, and a good society is one in which there is opportunity to show one's self, and to be acknowledged and rewarded for proven accomplishments. This distinction between two ideas of the aristocrat shows also the essential modernity of the idea of natural aristocracy. Conservatism does not necessarily defend classes or hierarchies, but it does defend the rewards that derive from accomplishment, protecting liberty from an excessive and destructive preoccupation with egalitarianism. Conservatives resist *social leveling* as a recipe for mediocrity. Thus, conservatives tend to emphasize the republican form of government, which incorporates the principle of equality in consent in a system of representative government wherein the natural aristocracy has the opportunity to achieve office and govern. In contemporary terms, they support *liberal democracy*, which symbolizes the primacy of liberty tempered by democratic consent.

Conservatives also argue that, while the promotion of equality is not in and of itself undesirable, efforts to equalize the conditions of individuals risk involving more and more government intervention (i.e., expanding government scope), taking away from some individuals for the sake of others, and that this will finally produce, in the name of liberal reform, a nonliberal society. In modern times, the compromise of the moderate welfare state is the practical approach to reconcile the claims of liberty and equality. This may not appeal to radical libertarians or to socialists, and it may irritate conservatives, but it is the meeting ground, wherein conservatives and modern liberals deal with each other—and it is the locus for the debate over the scope of governmental power, which is believed to be at the heart of modern politics.

ADVOCATING RULE OF LAW

Further, conservatives celebrate the rule of law and constitutional government. The rule of law is first and foremost a fundamental principle expressing a vision of how individuals should be formally organized in relation to each other. The principle suggests individuals should live in relation to each other as law-abiding citizens, free to enter into voluntary agreements with each other in pursuing their self-chosen lives. There need to be rules of this game. The rules are primarily procedural in character, as they do not tell individuals what to do; rather, they establish a set of limitations by informing individuals, whatever they are doing, to conduct themselves in a certain manner in the course of doing it. A classic and obvious example would be the rules of the road. The rules of the road do not tell one where to travel or, indeed, whether to travel at all. They do prescribe that, wherever one decides to go, one should observe basic procedures designed to facilitate getting there safely. All are equally subject to these rules; they do not favor one traveler over another, nor do they specify destinations.

As such, these rules are compatible and with a wide range of differing socioeconomic conditions among individuals, complementary to a modern world characterized by continuous diversity. These rules are practical implementations of the *idea* of the rule of law, meaning how individuals of widely differing backgrounds and interests may nevertheless interact with each other safely while pursuing what are often entirely different goals and aspirations. Adherence to the law is a fundamental idea in the conservative moral disposition.

For conservatives, the primary purpose of government will be to maintain the rule of law, to safeguard property rights, to provide a judicial structure for adjudicating disputes, and to provide a national defense. Of course, there must be an enforcement power to punish those who do not live up to the responsibility to be law-abiding. Law enforcement faculties are to focus on maintaining the rule of law, not to engage in imposing social changes deemed desirable by some, and not by all. As commonly associated with conservatism, the rule of law of the state should be strong but its scope limited and in contrast to the idea of the administrative state. An administrative state emphasizes the use of political power to renovate and perfect the social order, involving the supersession of rules by the exercise of discretionary judgment entrusted to bureaucratic agencies seeking to implement the goals of various policies in detail. For conservatives, this poses significant perils: first, forgetting or downplaying the limits to human wisdom and insight, and the danger of enabling specific persons to determine what is best for everyone else; and secondly, the aggregation of power to micromanage the manner in which individuals conduct their lives, compromising individual liberty for the potential but unlikely perfection of the social order.

See also *Burke, Edmund; Conservative Parties; Fiscal Conservatism; Neoconservatism; New Conservatism; Property Rights; Religious Right; Rule of Law; Social Conservatism; Social Order.*

. . . . TIMOTHY FULLER

BIBLIOGRAPHY

Allitt, Patrick. *The Conservatives, Ideas and Personalities Throughout American History.* New Haven: Yale University Press, 2009.

Burke, Edmund. *Freedom and Virtue: The Conservative/Libertarian Debate,* edited by George W. Carey. Wilmington, Del.: ISI Books, 1998.

———. *Reflections on the Revolution in France.* Oxford: Oxford World's Classics, 1790.

de Jouvenel, Bertrand. *The Ethics of Redistribution.* Indianapolis, Ind.: Liberty Fund, 1990.

Kirk, Russell. *The Conservative Mind: From Burke to Eliot.* New York: BN Publishing, 2008.

———. *Liberty for the 21st Century: Contemporary Libertarian Thought,* edited by Tibor Machan and Douglas B. Rasmussen. Lanham, Md.: Rowman and Littlefield, 1995.

Meyer, Frank S. *In Defence of Freedom and Related Essays.* Indianapolis, Ind.: Liberty Fund, 1996.

Muller, Jerry. *Conservatism: An Anthology of Social and Political Thought from David Hume to the Present.* Princeton: Princeton University Press, 1997.

Nashe, George. *The Conservative Intellectual Movement in America since 1945.* Wilmington, Del.: ISI Books, 1998.

Nisbet, Robert. *Conservatism: Dream and Reality.* Minneapolis: University of Minnesota Press, 1986.

Oakeshott, Michael. *The Politics of Faith and the Politics of Scepticism.* New Haven: Yale University Press, 1996.

———. *Rationalism in Politics.* Indianapolis, Ind.: Liberty Fund, 1991.

Pieper, Josef. *Tradition: Concept and Claim,* translated by E. Christian Kopf. Wilmington, Del.: ISI Books, 2008.

Schneider, Gregory, ed. *Conservatism in America Since 1930.* New York: New York University Press, 2003.

Stelzer, Irwin, ed. *The Neocon Reader.* New York: Grove Press, 2004.

Weaver, Richard. *Ideas Have Consequences.* Chicago: University of Chicago Press, 1984.

Conservative Parties

In the Western world, conservative parties are traditionally the parties of landed interest. They generally represent the preservation of traditional moral teaching and a belief in a transcendental order, a denial of uniformity and equalitarianism, an acceptance of the organic structure of society, and a subscription to evolutionary rather than revolutionary change in societies. In short, rather than being an ideology, conservatism represents a way of life or accumulation of values as opposed to those ideologies that emerged after the French Revolution (1989–1799) and Industrial Revolution in the late eighteenth and nineteenth centuries.

ORIGINS OF CONSERVATISM

The term *conservatism* is often used to describe tradition and traditional values, beliefs, and institutions. Although the origins of some conservative parties, such as the Conservative Party in the United Kingdom, can be traced back to the seventeenth century, the term conservative is exclusively modern, having developed after the Enlightenment and the French Revolution with its reactionary tone to occurrences in rapidly industrializing Western societies.

Anglo-Irish statesman and theorist Edmund Burke developed a conservative view against the Enlightenment and its reason-based progressive, utopian, and inorganic views, insisting on the importance of inherited values and customs in the survival and continuation of any given society. According to Burke, the proper formulation of government does not come from abstract views or individually developed ideologies, but from time-honored development of the state, piecemeal progress through experiences, and continuation of important societal institutions such as family and the church. Accordingly, tradition is experienced and deeply rooted in a society and has much more value and importance than abstract metaphysical assertions because it is tested by time and various people's experiences. Reason, on the other hand, may be a mask for the preferences of certain people or the untested and unreliable wisdom of only one generation. Therefore, change should come via organic methods rather than revolutionary movements because, in this conservative understanding of society, human society is not an aggregation of atomized individuals—it is an organic unity.

In Western political theory, there have not been systematic treaties about conservatism similar to Thomas Hobbes's *Leviathan* or John Locke's *Two Treaties of Government,* or even Karl Marx's *Communist Manifesto.* Therefore, conservatism is considered to be less a political doctrine than a habit of mind, a way of living or a mode of feeling. Traditionally, conservatives strongly support the right of property. For example, as Burke famously declared, nothing was more sacred to eighteenth century Whigs than property rights.

CONSERVATIVE VARIANTS: CULTURAL, RELIGIOUS, AND FISCAL

Many contemporary parties also represent conservative views that may very well be informally referred to as conservative parties, even if they are not explicitly named so. These parties have conservative agendas but represent a variety of conservative views in association with their country's historical development and cultural background. For example, conservative parties in the Western world have more or less adopted the Enlightenment ideas of the separation of church and state, while conservative parties in the Islamic world, such as the ruling Justice and Development Party in Turkey and Muslim Brotherhood in Egypt, proved to have problems with the Western notion of secularism. Conservative parties in the West also distinguish themselves from far-right ideologies and parties that often have a xenophobic and racist agenda. In Europe, conservative parties often ally with centrist and, in some cases, leftist parties rather than xenophobic far-right parties. However, some anti-immigration policies of the conservative parties in Europe often conflict with their free market economy views.

Among parties that do explicitly identify themselves as conservative, it is necessary to distinguish three different conservative approaches—cultural conservatives, religious conservatives, and fiscal conservatives—in order to understand the structures and contents of various conservative parties in the world. Instead of relying on universalistic moral codes, *cultural conservatives* rely on the moral values of their culture and argue that old institutions particular to place or culture should

persevere. However, *religious conservatives* may support or be supported by secular establishment, or they may find themselves at odds with the culture in which they live. In any case, their point of reference is mostly religious texts and people, and thus, unlike cultural conservatism, religious conservatism is not necessarily organic. Moreover, there is no clear-cut separation between these two conservative approaches, so they can intertwine, influencing conservative movements and parties accordingly. British prime minister John Major's back-to-the-basics campaign is an example of this. During the draft of the European Union's constitution, a conservative movement sought to imprint certain conservative values in the constitution.

Fiscal conservatism, on the other hand, reflects a prudent approach in government spending and debt. According to this approach, governments do not have the right to accumulate large debts and expect the public to pay them. Since this fiscal conservatism is an economic approach that has nothing to do with traditional values, beliefs, and institutions, a party can therefore be a fiscally conservative one that does not pursue a conservative agenda in its political action. However, from an economic perspective, many of today's conservative parties have adopted a neoliberal economic agenda. The term *liberal* often refers to free market policies outside the United States, and the term *liberal conservative* has become acceptable in the politics of many European countries. In fact, in today's era of globalization, conservative and neoliberal parties are allied against many common enemies, such as socialism.

THE ENLIGHTENMENT AND CONTEMPORARY CONSERVATISM

Many Enlightenment ideas and events, such as the French Revolution and Industrial Revolution, invariably affected many countries' traditional ways of living and thinking. Therefore, conservatism today cannot be considered an isolated approach immunized from the premises and approaches of other ideologies and modern movements. Accordingly, most conservative parties support the sovereign nation and patriotic values of duty and sacrifice, which are basically a result of the Enlightenment and subsequent events.

See also *Confessional Parties; Conservatism; Counter-Enlightenment Political Thought; Ethnic Parties; Family Values; Fascist Parties; Fiscal Conservatism; Liberal Parties; Nationalist Parties; Neoconservatism; New Conservatism; Political Parties; Religious Parties; Social Conservatism.*

. . . . SEZGIN S. CEBI

BIBLIOGRAPHY

Beyme, K. Von, and E. Martin. *Political Parties in Western Democracies.* Aldershot, UK: Gower Publishing, 1985.

Blake, R. *The Conservative Party from Peel to Thatcher.* London: Methuen, 1985.

MiddleBrook, Kevin J., *Conservative Parties, the Right and Democracy in Latin America.* Baltimore: John Hopkins University Press, 2000.

Muller, Jerry, Z. *Conservatism, an Anthology of Social and Political Thought from David Hume to the Present.* Princeton: Princeton University Press, 1997.

Seruton, Roger. *The Meaning of Conservatism.* London: St. Augustine Press, 2002.

Consociational Democracy

Consociational democracy is an electoral and civil arrangement that attempts to incorporate and share power throughout the various politically salient subgroups within a given society. Constitution writers and politicians in deeply divided countries such as Austria, Belgium, Canada, Colombia, Cyprus, India, Lebanon, Malaysia, the Netherlands, South Africa, and Switzerland used consociational arrangements to deal with the fragmentation within their societies many years before scholarly interest in power-sharing democracies developed. Consociational arrangements were implemented as a means of addressing internal, enduring conflicts that had frequently erupted into violence. These cleavages often form along class, linguistic, religious, or race lines. For the states mentioned above, and other countries throughout the world, consociationalism represented an alternative to majority-rule democracy and a belief that pursuing policies of accommodation could best reduce the potential for conflict within a given society.

Consociational democracy rests on four principles: (1) grand coalition as a means of achieving broad representation in political decision making, particularly at the executive level; (2) segmental autonomy in matters of self-interest for the subgroups (e.g., schools and culture); (3) proportional representation in the legislature; and (4) veto rights for all subgroups on matters of substantial importance to the subgroup. Although the first modern researcher to use the term as it is understood today was the economist Sir Arthur Lewis (1965), Arend Lijphart and Gerhard Lehmbruch introduced consociational democracy to political science in 1967. Emphasizing the importance of institutional configurations, they broke with the dominant belief within the discipline that ethnic homogeneity was the most important element in societal stability. The early work of these scholars focused on the consociational practices of several smaller countries in Europe. To date, political science research on consociational democracy is still most readily associated with Lijphart.

EMPIRICAL RESULTS

In Western Europe, the track record of consociational democracy has been largely successful (except perhaps in Belgium). Indeed, in several countries such as Austria, the Netherlands, and Luxembourg consociational arrangements proved so successful that the prominence of consociational democracy has receded as it has become less necessary to stem conflict. In other parts of the world, the record is mixed. While Colombian, Indian, Malaysian, and South African experiments with consociationalism can be seen as largely successful, Cyprus and Lebanon's consociational systems each ended in civil war. After shifting from consociational or semiconsociational systems to more majoritarian patterns of governance, Uruguay in 1973 and Suriname in 1980 each became subject to martial rule. In the case of Lebanon, outside factors brought extraordinary pressure to bear on the consociational system that had worked rather well up to that point. In Uruguay and Suriname, each country's movement toward majority rule complicates any attempt to point to consociationalism as having brought about failure.

A recent study concerning the ability of political institutions to promote state attachment in multiethnic societies has found that proportional electoral systems and federalism—each frequently a key component of consociational arrangements—have mixed effects, at best, as solutions to ethnic divisions. The mixed record of consociationalism outside of Europe raises the possibility that it works better in more developed countries than developing countries and that some combination of other factors such as literacy, strength of overall institutions, or level of development are a necessary precondition for deeply fissured societies to implement consociationalism properly.

Comparative research has uncovered several factors that facilitate the maintenance of consociational democracy. The two most important are the absence of a majority segment and the lack of large socioeconomic inequalities throughout the population. Other important factors include subgroups of roughly equal size, a small overall population size, foreign threats common to all subgroups, overarching loyalties to the state that counteract segmental loyalty, and preexisting traditions of consensus among elites.

CHANGING IDENTITIES OVER TIME

Critics fear that consociational arrangements carry a one-size-fits-all approach or that they risk segmenting identities to a dangerous extent. Lijphart, however, in his 2004 article "Constitutional Design for Divided Societies," points to substantial variation in the means employed by different countries in achieving the core principles of consociationalism, and the incorporation of recent constructivist scholarship focusing on questions of identity in comparative research has begun to address the concerns surrounding identity. The salient dimensions of identity are much more subject to change over time than previous generations of scholars had suspected, and this information is relevant to those who study consociational democracy as well. Lijphart, in a 2001 work "Constructivism and Consociational Theory," suggests that his own ideas about the nature of ethnicity have changed over the span of his career, from a more primordial view to one more consistent with constructivism. His beliefs, however, were not changed so much by constructivist scholarship as by events on the ground in Lebanon and South Africa.

In Lebanon, the implementation of a consociational system that allocated political power along predetermined lines of cleavage, further calcified by a fixing of that proportion despite demographic change, proved highly unstable as Lebanese politics changed over time eventually ending in civil war. In South Africa, the intense and negative social engineering during apartheid made it very difficult and politically sensitive to predetermine the subgroups of society. Consociationalism implemented in such a way as to let the relevant groups self-select, and form of their own accord does not predetermine identity in a way that can form overly constraining permanent political cleavages, nor leaves a potential subgroup outside of power.

The Netherlands represents an example of consociationalism of the self-selecting variety. There, all groups receive equal public funding to establish schools of their own, provided certain standards are met. Further, a very low threshold was established for representation in the legislature, which again allows for political parties to form of their own accord. Self-selecting consociationalism represents a potentially important innovation in the theory as it relates to the integration of newcomers, an issue of increasing importance in the industrialized democracies of the world, because it does not arbitrarily fix the predicted identities of subgroups. Groups are still most likely to form along the conventional lines of expected cleavages, but consociationalism has now opened itself up to accommodating the potentially changing nature of these identities within a given society over time. This is consistent with constructivist research on the nature of identity and an important institutional design in attempts to integrate newcomers.

See also *Coalition Formation; Federalism, Comparative; Identity, Politics of; Pillarization; Proportional Representation.*

. . . . . HOWARD J. WIARDA AND JONATHAN T. POLK

BIBLIOGRAPHY

Almond, Gabriel. "Comparative Political Systems." *Journal of Politics* 18, no. 3 (1956): 391–409.

Barry, Brian. "The Consociational Model and Its Dangers." *European Journal of Political Research* 3, no. 4 (1975): 393–412.

———. *Culture and Equality: An Egalitarian Critique of Multiculturalism.* Cambridge: Harvard University Press, 2001.

Bogaards, Matthijs. "The Favourable Factors for Consociational Democracy: A Review." *European Journal of Political Research* 33, no. 4 (1998): 475–496.

Chandra, Kanchan. "Cumulative Findings in the Study of Ethnic Politics." *APSA-CP* 12, no. 1 (2001): 7–11.

Crepaz, Markus M. L., and Jürg Steiner. *European Democracies.* New York: Longman, 2008.

Elkins, Zachary, and John Sides. "Can Institutions Build Unity in Multiethnic States?" *American Political Science Review* 101, no. 4 (2007): 693–708.

Horowitz, Donald L. "Constitutional Design: Proposals versus Processes." In *The Architecture of Democracy: Constitutional Design, Conflict Management, and Democracy,* edited by Andrew Reynolds. Oxford: Oxford University Press, 2002.

Kerr, Michael. *Imposing Power-Sharing: Conflict and Coexistence in Northern Ireland and Lebanon.* Dublin: Irish Academic Press, 2005.

Laitin, David D., and Daniel N. Posner. "The Implications of Constructivism for Constructing Ethnic Fractionalization Indices." *APSA-CP* 12, no. 1 (2001): 13–17.

Lehmbruch, Gerard. "A Noncompetitive Pattern of Conflict Management in Liberal Democracies: The Case of Switzerland, Austria, and Lebanon." In *Consociational Democracy: Political Accommodation in Segmented Societies,* Carleton Library 79, edited by Kenneth MacRae. Toronto: McClleland and Stewart. 1974.

Lewis, W. Arthur. *Politics in West Africa.* Oxford: Oxford University Press, 1965.

Lijphart, Arend. "Consociational Democracy." In *The Oxford Companion to Politics of the World,* edited by Joel Kreiger. New York: Oxford University Press, 2001.

———. "Consociational Democracy." *World Politics* 21, no. 2 (1969): 207–255.

———. "Constitutional Design for Divided Societies." *Journal of Democracy* 15, no. 2 (2004.): 96–109.

———. "Constructivism and Consociational Theory." *APSA-CP* 12, no. 1 (2001): 11–13.

———. *The Politics of Accommodation. Pluralism and Democracy in the Netherlands.* Berkeley: University of California Press, 1968.

Constant de Rebeque, Henri-Benjamin

French politician and writer Henri-Benjamin Constant de Rebeque (1767–1830), born in Switzerland and educated in Scotland and Germany, was an important advocate of liberal politics in postrevolutionary France.

Although Constant was not in France during the French Revolution (1789–1799), he returned soon after the Reign of Terror and dove into political life. He opposed Napoleon Bonaparte strongly enough that the dictator ousted him from the government and exiled him for more than ten years. During his exile, Constant wrote some of his most important political theory (including *Principles of Politics* in 1810), as well as an influential romantic novel (*Adolphe* in 1816) and much of his lifelong project on the history of ancient religion (*De la religion* from 1824–1831). He also wrote a powerful critique of Napoleon's rule in 1814 that would strike a chord with twentieth-century readers contemplating the totalitarianisms of their time (*The Spirit of Conquest and Usurpation*). Despite his long opposition to Napoleon, he agreed to write a constitution for the new imperial regime when Napoleon returned to power briefly in 1815. Although never implemented, his plan influenced later constitutional experiments in France and elsewhere. Following the Bourbon restoration in 1814, Constant returned to politics, occupying a seat in the Chamber of Deputies from 1819 to 1822 and 1824 to 1830, where his spirited rhetoric helped to create a strong opposition and foster a partisan style of politics on the British model.

Constant was one of the first writers to use the word *liberal* to describe his political stance. Strongly influenced by the example of Britain's constitutional monarchy, he spoke out forcefully on behalf of limited government, a free press, and religious toleration. In his more theoretical writings, he followed Scottish thinkers David Hume and Adam Smith in praising commercial society, but he was more interested in the political challenges of instituting and governing such societies than these thinkers had been, and he explored questions about institutional design in more detail. He defended a system of representative government that would be resistant to the consolidation of authority and the arbitrary use of power. His institutional scheme included checks and balances between parts of government, a gradual expansion of suffrage in conjunction with a property requirement, a "neutral power" in the monarch to help adjudicate among the various active powers, and a new style of federalism that would leave decisions in the hands of local institutions whenever practicable. The July Revolution of 1830, just months before his death, finally realized some of the measures that he had advocated.

Among political theorists, Constant is best known for his 1819 lecture "On the Liberty of the Ancients Compared with That of the Moderns," which argued that modern peoples should not pursue the form of liberty associated with ancient Sparta and Rome. Instead of requiring constant involvement in politics, sacrifice for the public good, and warlike virtues, modern nations should try to leave their citizens free to pursue private happiness and self-development. In other writings, he voiced anxiety about commercial society's tendency to foster utilitarianism and materialism, and he investigated the history of ancient religion, seeking insight into how religious feeling could escape the bonds of priestly and political authority and be made compatible with modern liberty.

See also *Liberalism, Classical; Liberal Theory.*

. . . . BRYAN GARSTEN

BIBLIOGRAPHY
Constant, Benjamin. *Political Writings,* edited by Biancamaria Fontana. Cambridge: Cambridge University Press, 1988.
———. *Principles of Politics Applicable to All Governments,* edited by Etienne Hofmann, translated by Dennis O'Keeffe. Indianapolis, Ind.: Liberty Fund, 2003.
Fontana, Biancamaria. *Benjamin Constant and the Post-revolutionary Mind.* New Haven: Yale University Press, 1991.
Holmes, Steven. *Benjamin Constant and the Making of Modern Liberalism.* New Haven: Yale University Press, 1984.
Rosenblatt, Helena. *Liberal Values: Benjamin Constant and the Politics of Religion.* Cambridge: Cambridge University Press, 2008.

Constituency

A *constituency* has two central meanings in the context of electoral systems. The first is also known as an electoral district, riding, or voting area. It refers to a geographical area of a country or region, or a local area, that is legislatively divided, usually for electoral purposes. Single-member districts elect one representative to a legislative body, while multimember districts elect more than one representative. The number of representatives elected per district is known as the *district magnitude.* The geographic size and number of representatives elected in each constituency are determined by the electoral system in place. Constituency boundaries, or electoral boundaries, are also often distributed and readjusted based on geographic and population considerations, including population parity or equality; regional population features; and in order to recognize community and diversity interests.

The second meaning of constituency refers to any particular group of electors, bound by a shared geography for the purposes of electoral districting, or bound by shared demographic characteristics, such as gender, age, ethnicity or nationality, culture, language, religion, or other attributes. Within this meaning, a *constituent* is a single individual who is part of the larger constituency, or group.

See also *District Magnitude; Districting; Electoral Geography; Gerrymandering.*

. . . . JENNIFER E. DALTON

Constituency Relations

When legislators are elected from specific geographic districts, significant resources are typically devoted to constituency relations—activity characterized by interaction between elected legislators and individual citizens or small groups of citizens. The nature of such interactions ranges from impersonal contact, mediated by legislative staff or conducted by correspondence, to direct encounters between representative and constituents.

REPRESENTATION
Constituency relations serve two distinct functions for a legislator. First, a legislator's interactions with constituents can facilitate representation by providing crucial information about the represented citizens. As political scientist Richard Fenno notes in his 1978 book *Home Style: House Members in Their Districts,* regarding constituents, it is critical for a member of Congress and, implicitly, a member of any representative body, to know "who they are, what they think, and what they want" (233). Constituency relations are an important way for legislators to gain such knowledge. Sometimes a legislator will gather information directly, meeting with constituents individually or in small groups.

When legislators are in their home districts, their schedules are filled with community events; for example, representatives often give speeches at graduation ceremonies, present awards for civic organizations, and hold town-hall-style meetings for the public. Such occasions give legislators ample opportunities to hear the views and concerns of the people they represent. They also offer opportunities to curry favor with the people they represent, thus serving a second purpose, helping legislators' reelection efforts.

CASEWORK AND REELECTION PROSPECTS
One significant form of constituency relations is known as *casework.* With casework, legislative aides receive and respond to particularized requests from individuals. Casework is thought to enhance legislators' reelection prospects in two ways: by creating satisfied customers who will support their representative out of a sense of gratitude and by giving the representative positive accomplishments to advertise. Notably, while studies of legislator attitudes provide ample evidence that representatives believe constituency service improves their reelection tallies, the actual effect of casework on reelection prospects has been quite difficult to pin down. Most recent studies, however, suggest that performing casework helps legislators win reelection.

The link between casework and representation is not quite as straightforward, as casework is generally divorced from ideological or policy content. The aggregation of citizens' requests, however, can provide representatives with important information about how the government is functioning (or malfunctioning) and thus facilitate the traditional legislative function of executive oversight. If a veterans' hospital is providing poor service, the representative from that district will hear about it from constituents seeking the representative's help. If the streets in a certain neighborhood are not regularly swept, residents will call their city counselor.

Members of the U.S. Congress consider service to be a core function of their congressional offices and make it very easy for constituents to request help. Every member of Congress features a link or button on the gateways to their Web sites labeled "How can I help you?" or "constituent services" or something similar; these links lead to pages that generally include detailed instructions on the range of services the member offers. A sample of such services includes arranging a tour of the Capitol or White House, nominating a constituent to one of the service academies, and providing a letter to support federal grant applications. But the meat-and-potatoes of constituency relations consists of intervening with a government agency on behalf of a specific individual. Typical requests seek help with an agency that provides benefits and services, such as the Social Security Administration or the Veterans Administration, but members of Congress are willing and eager to help in more unusual circumstances too. An example that received wide attention in early 2010 involved an eight-year-old boy from New Jersey who had the same name as an individual on the federal government's "selectee" list of persons who receive extra security screening at U.S. airports. Each time he traveled, the boy's family endured long delays, and he himself was aggressively frisked. The family asked their representative, Rep. Bill Pascrell (D-N.J.) to intervene on their behalf with the Transportation Security Administration (TSA). *The New York Times* reported Pascrell's response, arranging for a TSA agent to personally escort the family at Newark Airport. In this case, Pascrell's office earned the gratitude of an individual voter and attracted significant positive attention for Pascrell in a national news outlet.

While constituency relations are a key part of legislators' reelection efforts, two characteristics distinguish them from traditional campaign activity. First, constituency relations involve the conduct of official governmental business. Advertising one's positions on public issues or record of achievement, even when such achievement relates to helping individual constituents, is not an official act; intervening with a government agency on behalf of an individual, responding to constituents' inquiries about legislation, or appearing before a community group to discuss public issues are official acts. Second, constituency relations generally entail reciprocal communication, whereas campaign activity emphasizes the flow of information from legislator to constituency.

IMPORTANCE OF CONSTITUENCY RELATIONS

Emphasis on constituency relations varies across legislatures depending on the institutional context. The size of the constituency, in terms of both population and geography, the nature of the electoral system, and the availability of official resources are important factors determining a legislator's level of attention to constituency relations. For example, in the United States, members of the House emphasize constituency relations more than senators. Senators represent many more constituents than the House members (with a handful of exceptions). Their "districts" are geographically large and thus require more reliance on mass media. Furthermore, they are elected for longer terms and from two-member districts.

These factors all make constituency relations less important in the allocation of official resources. In electoral systems where parties play a stronger role, constituency relations are also less valuable to individual legislators, whose reelection prospects depend more on party label than on their individual appeal.

See also *Civic Engagement; Civil Service; Representation and Representative; Town Hall Meeting.*

. . . . JENNIFER A. STEEN

BIBLIOGRAPHY

Cain, Bruce E., John A. Ferejohn, and Morris P. Fiorina. *The Personal Vote: Constituency Service and Electoral Independence.* Cambridge, Mass.: Harvard University Press, 1987.

Fenno, Richard F., Jr. *Home Style: House Members in Their Districts.* Boston: Little, Brown, 1978.

Jewell, Malcolm E. "Legislator-Constituency Relations and the Representative Process." *Legislative Studies Quarterly* 8 (August 1983): 303–333.

King, Gary. "Constituency Service and Incumbency Advantage." *British Journal of Political Science* 21 (January 1991): 119–128.

McAdams, John C., and John R. Johannes. "Congressmen, Perquisites, and Elections." *Journal of Politics* 50 (May 1988): 412–439.

Norris, Pippa. "The Puzzle of Constituency Service." *Journal of Legislative Studies* 3 (Summer 1997): 29–49.

Serra, George, and David Moon. "Casework, Issue Positions, and Voting in Congressional Elections: A District Analysis." *Journal of Politics* 56 (February 1994): 200–213.

Constitutional Amendments

Article V of the U.S. Constitution provides two processes for proposing and two processes for ratifying amendments. Consistent with the role of the Constitution as a superior law designed to rein in legislative and other governmental powers, both processes are designed to be more difficult than the processes for ordinary legislation. Congress must either muster a two-thirds majority to propose amendments, or, in a still unused provision, two-thirds of the states can request Congress to call a convention to propose amendments. Three-fourths of the state legislatures, or special conventions within three-fourths of the states (a mechanism used only in the case of the amendment repealing national alcoholic prohibition), must subsequently approve them.

THE EARLY AMENDMENTS

During ratification debates over the Constitution, Federalist proponents of the document praised its amendment-making mechanisms as being superior to the process under the Articles of Confederation, which required congressional proposal and unanimous approval of the states. Federalist claims got an early test. Anti-Federalists had criticized the new Constitution for omitting a bill of rights to protect the people against the new national government. When James Madison, a prominent proponent of the new Constitution, agreed to work for a bill of rights, he hoped to protect individual rights, but he also wanted to ensure that amendments did not undo the work of the Constitutional Convention, which had provided for a more powerful national government. Madison fought a heroic and successful fight to get the first Congress to devote attention to introducing such rights to calm Anti-Federalist fears at a time when many of his colleagues thought that there were more pressing issues at state. Ultimately, Congress proposed twelve amendments, ten of which the states ratified in 1791. Although Madison had favored integrating these amendments into the constitutional text, Roger Sherman succeeded in convincing Congress to add them to the end of the document, which now provides a trail of constitutional alterations throughout American history.

The Bill of Rights continues to represent some of the nation's most important ideals. The First Amendment protects freedoms of religion, speech, press, peaceable assembly (linked to freedom of association), and petition. The Second Amendment provides for the right to bear arms, and the Third Amendment limits the quartering of troops in private homes. The Fourth Amendment prohibits unreasonable searches and seizures and requires probable cause for search warrants, and, in addition to providing for compensation for government takings, the Fifth and Sixth Amendments follow with a variety of rights for individuals accused of crimes or on trial for them. The Seventh Amendment provides for jury trials in civil cases, and the Eighth Amendment limits bail, fines, and prohibits cruel and usual punishments. The Ninth Amendment indicates that the list of rights is not exclusive, while the Tenth Amendment recognizes that states reserve some unspecified powers to themselves.

Congress proposed the Bill of Rights in 1789, which the states ratified in 1791. Similarly, states ratified the Eleventh Amendment in 1795, just two years after a Supreme Court decision in *Chisholm v. Georgia,* which had allowed out-of-state citizens to sue states without their consent and contrary to assurances that some Federalists had made during ratification debates.

Congress proposed the Twelfth Amendment in 1803, and the states ratified in 1804. Reacting both to presidential elections in which the president and vice president had been chosen from different parties and to the 1800 election in which Democratic and Republican presidential and vice presidential candidates tied, this amendment altered the electoral college mechanism so that electors began to cast separate votes for the top two offices.

POST–CIVIL WAR AMENDMENTS

The first twelve amendments suggested that the amending process was relatively easy, but subsequent experience proved otherwise. Despite rising tensions between the North and South, and numerous proposals for alterations that might head off conflict, Congress proposed only two amendments between 1803 and the Civil War (1861–1865), and both failed. The first would have disbarred individuals who accepted titles of nobility from citizenship, while the second would have exempted slavery from federal action.

The Civil War temporarily broke the amending logjam and resulted in the most consequential amendment in U.S. history. The Thirteenth Amendment (1865) prohibited involuntary servitude. The Fourteenth Amendment (1868) overturned the *Scott v. Sandford* (1857), by declaring that all persons, including blacks, who were born or naturalized in the United States were citizens. It also guaranteed all such citizens the privileges and immunities of U.S. citizens and protections of due process and equal protection. The Fifteenth Amendment (1868) further prohibited voting discrimination on the basis of race. Supreme Court decisions, culminating in the doctrine legitimizing "separate but equal" treatments in *Plessy v. Ferguson* (1896), however, narrowed interpretations of the Thirteenth and Fourteenth Amendments, while states embraced poll taxes, literacy tests, and other devices that limited African American voting rights.

PROGRESSIVE ERA AMENDMENTS

The years from 1868 to 1913 marked a period of amendment stalemate, followed by another period of reform associated with the Progressive Era. The Sixteenth Amendment overturned the Supreme Court decision in *Pollock v. Farmers' Loan & Trust Co.* (1895), and allowed for a national income tax, while the Seventeenth Amendment provided for direct election of U.S. senators (previously chosen by state legislatures). The Eighteenth Amendment (1919) inaugurated national alcoholic prohibition, while the Nineteenth (1920) prohibited discrimination on the basis of sex. Significantly, the Seneca Falls Convention had called for such a right, which both the Fourteenth and Fifteenth Amendments had ignored, in 1848.

MODERN AMENDMENTS

Subsequent amendments have been largely inconsequential by comparison. The Twentieth Amendment (1933) shortened the so-called lame-duck service of the president and members of Congress after new elections. The Twenty-first Amendment (1933) repealed the Eighteenth. The Twenty-second Amendment (1951), adopted in the wake of Franklin D. Roosevelt's unprecedented election to four terms, capped future presidential service at two full terms or no more than ten years. The Twenty-third Amendment (1961) provided for representation in the electoral college for the District of Columbia while the Twenty-fourth (1964) prohibited the poll tax in national elections. The Twenty-fifth Amendment (1967) made provision for presidential disability, the Twenty-sixth (1971) provided for national voting at age eighteen, thus effectively negating the Supreme Court decision in *Oregon v. Mitchell* (1970), which had ruled that Congress could only legislate on this matter relative to national elections. Finally, the Twenty-seventh amendment, originally proposed as part of the Bill of Rights and limiting the timing of congressional pay raises until after intervening elections, was putatively ratified in 1992.

MANY ARE CALLED, BUT FEW ARE CHOSEN

Members of Congress have introduced more than twelve thousand amending proposals, most of which have been redundant. Congress has only proposed thirty-three by the required majorities, and the states have ratified only twenty-seven. In addition to proposals discussed previously, states have failed to ratify an amendment relative to congressional representation proposed with the original bill of rights, a child labor amendment, an amendment that would have granted the District of Columbia voting representation in Congress, and a proposed equal rights amendment for women.

After comparing the U.S. amending process to those in eleven democratic nations that use a system of legislative supremacy to adopt constitutional changes—those in nine nations that have legislative supremacy with an intervening election; those in five nations that allow for an amendment referendum to bypass the legislature; and those in seven nations, including the United States, that *require* such a referendum or its equivalent in complexity—political scientist Donald Lutz found that the U.S. system was the second most difficult in the world behind Australia. Because the Constitution is interpreted capaciously, however, institutions of government, especially the courts, have been able to render many decisions that have adapted the constitution to changing times, short of formal amendments.

See also *Articles of Confederation; Bill of Rights; Constitution Amending Procedures; Constitutions and Constitutionalism.*

. . . . JOHN R. VILE

BIBLIOGRAPHY

Amar, Akhil Reed. *America's Constitution: A Biography.* New York: Random House, 2005.

Bernstein, Richard B., with Jerome Agel. *Amending America: If We Love the Constitution So Much, Why Do We Keep Trying to Change It?* New York: Times Books, 1993.

Grimes, Alan P. *Democracy and the Amendments to the Constitution.* Lexington, Mass.: Lexington Books, 1978.

Kyvig, David E. *Explicit and Authentic Acts: Amending the U.S. Constitution, 1776–1995.* Lawrence: University Press of Kansas, 1996.

Lutz, Donald S. "Toward a Theory of Constitutional Amendment." *American Political Science Review* 88 (June 1994): 355–370.

Palmer, Kris E. *Constitutional Amendments: 1789 to the Present.* Detroit, Mich.: Gale Group, 2000.

Pendergast, Tom, Sara Pendergast, and John Sousanis. *Constitutional Amendments: From Freedom of Speech to Flag Burning,* 3 vols. Detroit, Mich.: UXL, 2001.

Vile, John R. *Encyclopedia of Constitutional Amendments, Proposed Amendments, and Amending Issues, 1789–2002,* 2nd. ed. Santa Barbara, Calif.: ABC-CLIO, 2003.

———, ed. *Proposed Amendments to the U.S. Constitution, 1787–2001,* 3 vols. Clark, N.J.: Lawbook Exchange, 2003.

Constitutional Courts

Constitutional courts are judicial bodies that possess the authority to nullify or invalidate actions taken or laws enacted by governmental officials on the grounds that those actions or laws are violations of that country's constitution. This power of a court to authoritatively determine whether a legislative enactment or executive action is constitutional or unconstitutional is known as judicial review. The origin of judicial review is commonly considered to have come from the United States and the U.S. Supreme Court's landmark and politically critical decision in *Marbury v. Madison* (1803). It is in this case that Chief Justice John Marshall carved out this power of judicial review for the U.S. Supreme Court, even though the U.S. Constitution does not specifically enumerate this authority in the first place, nor does it attach such a power

as belonging to the federal courts or any other governmental actor. A variety of other nations have followed America's lead in placing this judicial check into their democratic governance structures, observed in the democratizing trends as manifested during the twentieth century—especially so after World War II (1939–1945) and in the post-1980s period.

CONSTITUTIONAL COURT STRUCTURES IN COMMON-LAW AND CIVIL-LAW COUNTRIES

The American orientation has been to give this function of constitutional adjudication to ordinary courts and to a supreme court—that is to say, they resolve disputes emanating from common law, statutory law, and the nation's constitution. However, the common practice seen in the contemporary era is for nations to construct special courts whose sole purpose and function is to engage in judicial review. These courts are called constitutional courts. Just under seventy nations now have such constitutional courts operating, and most of these nations make a point, unlike the United States, in directly establishing this authority of judicial review in their respective constitutions.

A clear pattern has emerged that shows that the U.S. form of judicial review—where ordinary courts possess judicial review authority; there are appellate courts in place to review lower court rulings; the supreme court serves as the court of last resort and final arbiter on these constitutional cases; and the dispute in question must be actual and concrete, not merely an hypothetical or abstract conflict—is often found in nations with common law backgrounds (e.g., Canada, Australia, Scandinavian countries, Pakistan, India, Burma, and a number of Latin American countries). Countries with a civil-law background are more likely to have a structure of constitutional courts separate from ordinary courts that decide constitutional cases and some of these countries allow these courts to produce advisory opinions on more abstract, less concrete disputes such as a proposed law in addition to resolving actual disputes arising from already enacted laws (e.g., Austria, France, Russia, Germany, Spain, and Italy).

DEBATE OVER THE PRIMARY PURPOSE AND FUNCTION OF CONSTITUTIONAL COURTS

In the European context of constitutional courts, the post–World War II constitutions of previously fascist states clearly stressed protections for fundamental human rights—constitutional courts would play a critical role in guaranteeing such rights and serving as a bulwark against the return of brutal autocrats. Thus, it has been argued that the overriding design of constitutional courts is to have them serve as inherently countermajoritarian institutions, working to ensure that the will of the majority would not and could not trample over basic liberties of the minority. In other words, the constitutional courts in their exercise of judicial review work to stabilize and temper forms of democratic governance. It is noteworthy that all of the postcommunist states in Eastern Europe after the fall of the Soviet Union in the early 1990s ended up opting for a structure of constitutional courts, directly modeled from the German system.

A counterargument to this human rights protection contention is that constitutional courts have become popular due to the motivations of political elites and the accompanying incentive structures in their respective countries. As political actors in newly developing democracies deal with elections and the high probability that at some point they will not win an election and thus be out of power for a period of time, they are duly motivated to designate institutions (such as constitutional courts) to legitimately test, challenge, and potentially hinder public policy of the advantaged political opposition. In other words, constitutional courts are established instrumentally by political elites as they recognize and respond to the intrinsic electoral uncertainty associated with democratic procedures.

JUDICIAL SELECTION FOR CONSTITUTIONAL COURTS

The mechanisms used in the recruitment and selection of judges to serve on these constitutional courts varies. A common practice in these methods of appointment is to place some degree of insulation between these judges and external political influence, but at the same time try to provide a modicum of judicial accountability and responsiveness to the public. This captures one of the leading criticisms of constitutional courts: The appointment processes in place do not provide adequate levels of accountability for these judges. A variety of countries use methods that necessitate a sharing of this judicial appointment power between the executive and legislative branches, with the executive nominating the appointee and the legislature consenting or rejecting (a prime example of a checks and balances effort in the structure). Other more complex systems involve even more actors in selection process, such as all three branches (legislative, executive, and judicial) responsible for nominating a proportion of constitutional court judges. Additional recruitment iterations, albeit less common, involve a single entity, such as the chief executive, making the appointment. The typical normal tenure for a constitutional court judge is one nonrenewable term, commonly between six to nine years of service.

CONTROVERSIES

There are several inherent controversies with constitutional courts (as well as supreme courts) as they engage in judicial review. The first revolves around unelected, relatively politically unaccountable judges striking down and invalidating actions or measures taken by the people's elected representatives. With its judicial second-guessing, this antimajoritarian posture strikes some as problematically antidemocratic. The second controversy engages the challenging conundrum of how exactly these judges are supposed to go about interpreting their nation's constitution to help them decide whether a statute or governmental activity is truly unconstitutional. The ongoing debate between judicial activism and judicial restraint manifests directly in these types of questions. How much deference these judges should show the elected

branches, and how close to the text of the constitution or to the specific intentions of the constitution's original writers these judges should cleave, remains uncertain.

See also *Constitutions and Constitutionalism.*

. . . . STEPHEN R. ROUTH

BIBLIOGRAPHY

Abraham, Henry J. *The Judicial Process: An Introductory Analysis of the Courts of the United States, England, and France,* 7th ed. New York: Oxford University Press, 1998.

Ginsburg, Tom. *Constitutional Interpretation,* 9th ed, edited by Craig R. Ducat. Boston: Wadsworth, 2009.

———. *Judicial Review in New Democracies: Constitutional Courts in Asian Cases.* New York: Cambridge University Press, 2003.

Hague, Rod, and Martin Harrop. *Political Science: A Comparative Introduction,* 5th ed. New York: Palgrave Macmillan, 2007.

Hirschl, Ran. *Towards Juristocracy: The Origins and Consequences of the New Constitutionalism.* Cambridge, Mass.: Harvard University Press, 2004.

Murphy, Walter F., C. Herman Pritchett, Lee Epstein, and Jack Night. *Courts, Judges, and Politics: An Introduction to the Judicial Process.* Boston: McGraw-Hill, 2006.

Tushnet, Mark. *Weak Courts, Strong Rights: Judicial Review and Social Welfare Rights in Comparative Constitutional Law.* Princeton: Princeton University Press, 2007.

Constitutional Democracy

A *constitutional democracy* is a form of representative, democratic governance, in which the constitution, or rule of law, is supreme. This type of democracy is premised on the doctrine of the separation of powers, resulting in a system of checks and balances. The separation of powers manifests through the constitutional authority that each branch of government exercises in checking and balancing the other branches of government. A constitutional democracy normally consists of three largely independent branches; the functions of each, however, do not operate in complete exclusivity. The executive branch is responsible for the administrative implementation of legislation; the legislature enacts and amends laws; and the judiciary interprets, and applies, the law based on precedence and legislative statutes. Each branch may be elected or appointed.

Constitutional democracies may be unitary, federal, or confederal, but most states are unitary. *Unitary states* are constitutionally governed as one single unit with authority stemming from a single legislature. In a unitary state, there may be subgovernmental units, but they are created and abolished by the central government. Any powers that subgovernmental units hold are granted and amended by the central government without the need for formal agreement from the subgovernmental units—a process known as *devolution*. A devolved state is unitary in nature, but the subgovernmental units have a great deal of autonomous decision-making authority, much like federal systems. Nevertheless, the subgovernmental units do not have any constitutional authority to override national legislation or to protect the powers they have been granted.

Federal governments consist of a central or national government alongside other autonomous legislatures, such as state or provincial governments. These different levels of government are constitutionally recognized, with constitutionally enshrined legislative distribution of sovereignty. Areas of jurisdiction can be exclusive or concurrent, depending on the requirements laid out in the constitution. Classical federalism mandates that the levels of government are equal; there is no imbalance between the jurisdictional authorities of each level. In this way, the central government normally retains exclusive jurisdiction over matters that are of relevance to the nation as a whole, while the provincial or state governments deal with issues that are localized or regional in nature. However, this rarely occurs because federal constitutions are usually biased in favor of one level of government. *Confederal states* are rare and mirror federal governments quite closely in structure, albeit with most authority vested in peripheral government bodies, while the central government holds little power.

Centralization occurs when the majority of authority lies with the national government, whereas *decentralization* describes a system where the subnational legislative bodies hold significant jurisdictional powers. *Asymmetrical federalism* occurs when the different levels of government have imbalanced degrees of jurisdictional authority. *Fiscal federalism* stems from the devolution of power over revenue sources divided among the different levels of government, including management of any fiscal imbalances among governments.

If a legislative body acts outside of its jurisdictional authority, it is beyond the legal scope of the constitution, while legislation or statutes that are within jurisdiction are within this power. However, there are residual powers to consider in a federal system. These residual powers are areas of authority not explicitly assigned in the constitution, which are comprehensively granted to one level of government.

In federal systems, there may be additional orders of government, such as local governments, but these are usually not given explicit constitutional jurisdiction. Instead, they are often creatures of the subnational governments, serving the needs and interests of specific cities, communities, or neighborhoods. Powers may include taxation and other limited autonomy granted by the constitutionally recognized levels of government.

Some federations are multinational in scope, including national minority populations within the federation. Canada is an especially useful example of a multinational state, most notably with regard to its francophone and indigenous peoples. Very basically, in the provincial context of Quebec, extensive autonomous governing authority, rooted in historical and cultural distinctiveness, has been recognized and ensured to protect Francophone culture. While the same progress is not evident for indigenous peoples in Canada, there has been implied judicial and explicit governmental acknowledgment of Aboriginal governance. While the Canadian constitution does not explicitly lay out a third order of Aboriginal governance, as would have been the case had the 1992 Charlottetown Accord been successfully ratified by the Canadian public, several governance agreements have been implemented, or are currently being negotiated, including some jurisdictional authority for indigenous communities.

See also *Centralization, Deconcentration, and Decentralization; Checks and Balances; Constitutions and Constitutionalism; Endangered Cultures; Federalism; Nationality; Rule of Law; Universal Jurisdiction.*

. . . . JENNIFER E. DALTON

BIBLIOGRAPHY

Bakvis, Herman, and Grace Skogstad, eds. *Canadian Federalism: Performance, Effectiveness, and Legitimacy.* New York: Oxford University Press, 2001.

Dalton, Jennifer E. "Aboriginal Self-Determination in Canada: Protections Afforded by the Judiciary and Government." *Canadian Journal of Law and Society* 21, no. 1 (2006): 11–38.

Murphy, Walter F. *Constitutional Democracy: Creating and Maintaining a Just Political Order.* Baltimore: Johns Hopkins University Press, 2006.

Rocher, François, and Miriam Smith, eds. *New Trends in Canadian Federalism,* 2nd ed. Peterborough, Ont.: Broadview Press, 2003.

Watts, Ronald L. *Comparing Federal Systems,* 2nd ed. Kingston, Ont.: Institute of Intergovernmental Relations, Queen's University, 1999.

Constitutional Law

From a formal point of view, constitutional law is a normative fountain from which all other secondary norms are derived. In a pure theory of law, a constitution is the fundamental norm of the state. It represents simply the basic authorizing norm of a legal system, being at the top of a coherent and hierarchical order, as described by legal philosopher and international jurist Hans Kelsen in his various works during the 1960s. Constitutional rules are often collected in a written chart, especially in countries with Roman legal tradition, characterized by a clear distinction between constitutional law and other branches of law. Yet, the presence of a code is not an essential element: As Italian political scientist Giovanni Sartori observed in 1962, although most countries have a constitutional text, only a few of them have a form of constitutionalism.

To understand such a key point—and paradox—the formal interpretation of constitutional law is not enough. Turning to a functional perspective, only the idea of restriction of powers connotes the specific function of constitutional law. First, modern constitutions interpret the liberal aspiration to protect citizens against the arbitrariness of political powers: They limit political power by defining rules of its exercise, and according to Samuel E. Finer in *Five Constitutions,* regulate "the allocation of functions, power, and duties among the various agencies and offices of government, and define the relationships between these and the public" (15). Starting from the eighteenth century, the presence of a *garantiste* component characterizes constitutional law on the basis of its *telos:* the constitution "guarantees" itself to the citizens by providing a frame of government and the institutional devices that would structure its observance. Modern constitutionalism is new in the sense that in any state in which the will of the government has no check upon it from the constitution, there is in reality no constitution, and that state is in fact a despotism, as explained by Charles H. McIlwain in his 1940 book *Constitutionalism: Ancient and Modern.*

Procedural conception of constitutional law has emphasized, especially in the new world, the definition of a system of separate institutions competing for powers. According to the U.S. Founders, any bill of rights represents a question to be inserted in a moral treatise more than a constitutional concern—the most important part of a constitution has to be found in its organization of powers. The Framers tried to contrast centrifugal tendencies in American political structure by embracing ideas of separation of powers, picked from Scottish philosopher David Hume and French Enlightenment thinker Montesquieu, and connected with a new conception of federalism adapted for a wide-ranging republic. In their view, a constitution had to pursue two objectives: the first one was to draw up a structure of government that could serve to protect people from government—from the danger of a tyranny of the majority in legislature; the second one was to protect people from themselves.

Only after the eruption of masses in politics, the twentieth-century constitutions acquired more focus on democratic rights. As charters superior in rank to ordinary law, they have come to represent a framework of citizen rights and duties, asking what democratic states ought to be doing and how they should design political institutions to make legitimate choices. Such second-generation democratic constitutions seem to move away from a solely pragmatic constitutional vision by including more ample declaratory preambles stating a true political manifesto for democratic states. However, the marriage between constitutionalism and democracy has been considered one of the most delicate arrangements in the modern world. As Walter F. Murphy noted in a 2001 article, a union between constitutionalism and democracy constantly endures tension because it brings together the notion that the people should rule through their freely chosen representatives, with the prescription that if the people govern, they should not govern too much. Even according to some scholars, such as Jürgen Habermas and William Rehg, constitutional democracy denotes a paradoxical union of contradictory principles, as in the idea that a "rule of law" comes on the scene alongside and together with popular sovereignty.

Constitutionalism, then, is always a difficult balance between allocation of sovereignty and limits in absolute discretion—a delicate equilibrium since constitutions are not fixed and immutable. As historical products, they adapt to their environment and reflect shifts in political forces of the states to which they refer. Any constitutional charter contains emendatory rules that permit modification of its contents. Furthermore, in addition to standard emendatory procedures, constitutional law is modified in another and probably more relevant way. Many scholars, such as Italian constitutional law scholar Costantino Mortati in 1940, have referred to the concept of *living constitution* or *material constitution* to describe how sociopolitical actors may partly drift away from static constitutional norms with no formal changes. If a constitution limits and regulates powers, political forces continuously redefine rules by interacting with each other and interpreting their own times. So, another paradox joins the concept of constitutional law: If it serves to provide regularized, and predictable, restraints upon those who exercise political power, it may also be shaped by concrete dynamics of power.

See also *Checks and Balances; Constitution Amending Procedures; Constitutional Democracy; Constitutions and Constitutionalism; Hume, David; Montesquieu, Charles-Louis.*

. . . . FORTUNATO MUSELLA

BIBLIOGRAPHY

Bogdanor, Vernon. *Constitutions in Democratic Politics.* Aldershot: Gower, 1988.

Elkin, Stephen L., and Karol E. Soltan. *New Constitutionalism: Designing Political Institutions for a Good Society.* Chicago: University of Chicago Press, 1993.

Finer, Samuel E. *Five Constitutions.* New York: Penguin Books, 1979.

Fredrich, Carl J. *Constitutional Government and Democracy: Theory and Practice in Europe and America,* 4th ed. Waltham, Mass.: Blaisdell, 1968.

Habermas, Jürgen, and William Rehg. "Constitutional Democracy: A Paradoxical Union of Contradictory Principles?" *Political Theory* 29, no. 6 (2001): 766–781.

Hamilton, Alexander, James Madison, and John Jay. *The Federalist Papers,* edited by Charles R. Kesler. New York: Signet, 1999.

Jennings, Ivor W. *The Law and the Constitution.* London: University of London Press, 1933.

Jones, Charles. "The Separated Presidency." *The New American Political System,* 2nd ed., edited by Anthony King. Washington, D.C.: American Enterprise Institute, 1990.

Kelsen, Hans. *General Theory of State and Law.* Cambridge, Mass.: Harvard University Press, 1945.

———. *Pure Theory of Law,* translated by Max Knight. Berkeley: University of California Press, 1967.

Marshall, Geoffrey. *Constitutional Theory.* Oxford: Oxford University Press, 1971.

McIlwain, Charles H. *Constitutionalism: Ancient and Modern.* Ithaca: Cornell University Press, 1940.

Mortati, Costantino. *La Costituzione in senso materiale.* Giuffré: Milano, 1940.

Murphy, Walter F. "Constitutionalism." In *International Encyclopedia of the Social and Behavioral Sciences,* edited by Neil J. Smelser and Paul B. Baltes, 2641–2643. Amsterdam: Elsevier Science, 2001.

Sartori, Giovanni. "Constitutionalism: A Preliminary Discussion." *American Political Science Review* 56, no. 4 (1962): 853–864.

Wills, Garry *Explaining America: The Federalist.* Garden City, N.Y.: Doubleday, 1981.

Constitutional Monarchy

Constitutional monarchy is a type of government in which a sovereign can rule under the limits of a constitution. The text of the constitution or its principles limit the sovereign power, and subsequently, government ministers formulate parliamentary acts and assume responsibility for the government. However, the sovereign has to sign these acts, and constitutionally, they are considered to be acts of the sovereign, which is politically neutral authority. Aligned with the idea that "the king can do no wrong," in a constitutional monarchy, the sovereign still keeps some ceremonial and formal powers (e.g., nomination of a prime minister or dissolution of parliament), as well as prerogative powers. The most important of the sovereign's rights are the following: the right to be consulted, the right to encourage, and the right to warn (from Walter Bagehot's "trinity of rights").

ORIGINS OF THE CONSTITUTIONAL MONARCHY

Constitutional monarchy developed from ancient and medieval types of monarchy; according to Aristotle's classification of states, the *monarchy* is "the good government by one." Generally, this type of governing is based on the premise of *paternalism,* the notion that a benevolent ruler is needed to care for the subjects of the kingdom. Monarchies have reflected the importance of conservatism and continuity in governance and in the institutions of a society and culture. In addition, monarchies have generally emphasized the importance of religion, with the monarch an agent of God, legitimized by the deity. Before the period of democratization, there were two types of European monarchies. The first was the *aristocratic monarchy* (e.g., feudal monarchy; it did not give the sovereign absolute power but only limited power regulated by the power of noblemen). The second was the *absolute monarchy,* which allowed kings to use nonregulated power. Absolute monarchy described, first, the European monarchies such as France and Spain from the sixteenth to the eighteenth centuries and later on included Prussia, Russia, and Austria. Nevertheless, none of these monarchies were really absolute; in all there were some limits to the king's power, mostly based on custom.

The division of powers characteristic of constitutional monarchy developed in connection with the emergence of the modern state in the seventeenth century in France (e.g., the centralized state with a well-defined territory and powerful governmental authority). In Britain, the absolute monarchy was introduced under the Tudor dynasty (Henry VIII and Elizabeth I); none of these monarchs were entirely absolute in authority, however, because they had "great regard for parliamentary conventions." During the English Civil War (1642–1651), the monarchy was abolished. Parliament technically ruled supreme, although, in reality, Oliver Cromwell ruled as the country's dictator. The monarchy was restored in 1660 after Cromwell's death, but the growing power of the king sparked the Glorious Revolution of 1688. From then on, under Britain's constitutional monarchy, the king was, and the sovereign still is, subordinated to the principles of a constitution (or constitutions, in other European monarchies). This means that Parliament, especially the House of Commons, shares the legislative power with the sovereign power and House of Lords.

With the development of the philosophy of rationalism, monarchy was justified by what was seen as its natural role as a governing institution, reflected in both history and tradition. This view was held until the period of democratization in the nineteenth century. According to Richard Rose and Dennis Kavanagh, there are two prerequisites that give monarchy a chance to function with democratic institutions: "the readiness" of the reigning family to withdraw from active politics (e.g., the willingness to self-impose these restraints) and, at the same time, "the repudiation" of its members from influence on politics without needing to reduce the symbolic role of the sovereign.

DEMOCRACY AND THE MONARCHY

In a democratic system with a hereditary monarch, the role of the king or queen is nonpolitical (e.g., it is symbolic and ceremonial; the sovereign is a head of the state, a symbol of national unity, continuity, and tradition). According to Vernon Bogdanor, during the twentieth century, the sovereign's constitutional power was reduced step by step in a number of areas critically important to the constitution, but the sovereign still kept a vast number of prerogative powers. The sovereign still holds a few formal executive powers that allow, for example, naming—but not choosing—the head of a cabinet who is not politically responsible to the sovereign but to the directly elected parliament. Nevertheless, decisions about government formation are left to politicians, so the sovereign plays no active role in them. The sovereign can use the granted power to appoint ministerial officeholders on the recommendation of the prime minister, too; the sovereign is politically nonresponsible but acts on the advice of the ministers, who are willing to assume responsibility for the sovereign's acts. The sovereign is inviolable, too, and can exercise influence by using, according to Bagehot, "the rights to be consulted"; for example, consultations were an important point of the political game in the United Kingdom during the second half of the twentieth century. The sovereign in all constitutional monarchies can dissolve the parliament (on request), and also has some power that can be used in a constitutional emergency. Other important powers of the sovereign include: nominating judges (in cooperation with the executive), directing the armed forces, declaring war, making treaties, and regulating the civil service.

Constitutional monarchy in democratic states can survive only when monarchs accept their limited powers based on the constitutional text. Currently, there are only a few democratic constitutional monarchies in Europe: the United Kingdom, Spain, Sweden, Denmark, Norway, the Netherlands, Belgium, Luxembourg, and Liechtenstein; there are also a few outside Europe, such as Japan. The influence of sovereigns in these countries differs according to historical circumstances. For example, in Scandinavia the sovereigns and their families are very popular because they stress egalitarianism over many of the ancient symbols of royalty and wealth; Richard Rose mentions that they are popularly called "bicycling monarchs." Spain, on the other hand, is unique among contemporary constitutional monarchies: after Francisco Franco's death, new political leaders accepted the politically well-balanced role of Juan Carlos in transition to democracy and gave a way to restoring monarchy instead of introducing a republic. Another, rather specific case in the contemporary world is the British Commonwealth, an association of free, independent states (mostly republics) like Canada, Australia, and India. The nominal head of this postcolonial international association is the English sovereign, whose symbolic role was accepted by a free decision of democratically elected leaders of these previous British dominions, contrary to the hereditary character of this post in the United Kingdom.

See also *British Political Thought; Monarchy; Constitutional Systems, Comparative.*

. . . .   BLANKA ŘÍCHOVÁ

BIBLIOGRAPHY

Blahož, Josef, Vladimír Balaš, and Karel Klíma. *Srovnávací ústavní právo* [Constitutional Law: Comparative Analysis], 2nd ed. Prague: ASPI Publishing, 2003.

Bogdanor, Vernon. *The Monarchy and the Constitution*. Oxford: Clarendon Press, 1995.

Brazier, Rodney. "The Monarchy." In *The British Constitution in the Twentieth Century*, edited by Vernon Bogdanor, 69–95. Oxford: Oxford University Press, 2005.

Klokočka, Vladimír. *Ústavní systémy evropských států* [Constitutional Governments in Europe], 2nd ed. Prague: Linde Praha , 2006.

Neubauer, Zdeněk. *Státověda a teorie politiky* [State, Law and Theory of Politics]. Prague: Slon, 2006.

Constitutional Systems, Comparative

COMPARATIVE CONSTITUTIONAL SYSTEMS

Most countries of the world have written constitutions establishing basic rights and regulating the relationships between public offices, and between these public offices and the public. During the late middle ages and early modern times, constitutions were mainly devices for establishing local, sectoral, or individual rights and limiting powers. But as those old powers to be limited were autocratic, constitutionalism almost naturally advanced with the expansion of suffrage rights and democratization. Nondemocratic constitutions are still relatively abundant in some parts of the world. As of 2005, of the 126 independent countries with information on their constitutional laws collected, only 62 percent were considered "electoral democracies"—and only 46 percent were called "free" countries, according to separate data lists provided by Axel Tschentscher and Freedom House. But the number of constitutional democracies rose enormously during the last quarter of the twentieth century, encompassing for first time a majority of total world population by 1996. (Major exceptions are China, the Arab region, and the Middle East.) Thus, constitutionalism has been increasingly linked to democratization.

MIXED CONSTITUTIONAL MONARCHY

A traditional constitutional model was a *mixed monarchy*, which united a one-person, nonelected monarch with executive powers and a multiple-person, elected assembly with legislative powers. This type of regime had already existed in certain medieval kingdoms in Europe in which an elected parliament limited the king's powers. It also existed in the German Empire, where the emperor was elected by the representative Diet, and in the Christian Church, where the pope shared powers with councils. The modern constitutional formulas of a mixed regime were formally shaped in England following the revolution of 1688 and in France by the constitution of 1791. They were replicated during the nineteenth century in monarchies such as those of Austria, Belgium, Brazil, Germany, Norway, Portugal, Spain, and Sweden. In more recent times, similar formulas have been adopted in some Arab monarchies, such as Jordan and Morocco.

With broadening suffrage and democratization, the nonelected monarch's powers were reduced, while those of the elected assembly expanded, especially regarding the control of executive ministers, thus moving towards a parliamentary regime. The powers of the one-person monarch were largely transferred to the prime minister elected by the parliament. In recent times, there are parliamentary regimes in about half of the democratic countries in the world. Some of these regimes are British-style monarchical variants, such as Australia, Belgium, Canada, Denmark, Japan, the Netherlands, New Zealand, Norway, Spain, and Sweden. Others are of the republican variant, such as Austria, Czech Republic, Estonia, Finland, Germany, Greece, Hungary, India, Ireland, Italy, Latvia, Slovakia, Slovenia, South Africa, and Switzerland.

CONSTITUTION WITH ELECTED CHIEF EXECUTIVE

In another democratic formula that originated with the 1787 constitution of the United States, it is not only the multiple-person legislative assembly that is popularly elected but also the one-person chief executive. In the United States, the nonelected English monarch ceased to be recognized and was replaced with an elected president with executive powers. (At the time, the monarch of England was actually already highly dependent on parliament's decisions.) This model of political regime implies separate elections for the chief executive and the legislative branch, divided powers, and checks and balances among the presidency, the House, the Senate, and the Supreme Court. The basic formulas of the U.S. Constitution have been replicated in a number of Asian countries under American influence, including Indonesia, South Korea, the Philippines, and Taiwan.

A variant usually called *presidentialism* emerged in almost all twenty republics in Latin American since the mid- or late nineteenth century. Some founding constitution makers in countries such as Argentina, Brazil, Chile, Colombia, Costa Rica, Mexico, Peru, Uruguay, and Venezuela claimed to be imitating the U.S. Constitution, but they were also influenced by the presidential Second Republic and the Second Empire in France. Some of them looked farther back to the absolutist monarchies that preceded mixed regimes and division of powers and aimed at having "elected kings with the name of presidents" (in Simón Bolívar's words). Instead of checks and balances, most Latin American constitutions promoted or favored high concentration of power in the presidency. Similar features can be observed in a number of postcolonial republics in East and Southern Africa.

DUAL-EXECUTIVE REGIMES

After World War I (1914–1918), Finland and Germany experimented with a different variant of political regime with separate elections and divided powers—usually called a *semipresidential* or *dual-executive regime*. This variant was more consistently shaped with the 1958 constitution of France. With this formula, the presidency and the assembly are elected separately, as in a checks-and-balances regime, but it is the assembly that appoints and can dismiss a prime minister, as in a parliamentary regime. The president and the prime minister share the executive powers in a *governmental diarchy*. Similar constitutional formulas have been more recently adopted in a few countries in Eastern Europe, including Lithuania, Poland, Romania, Russia, as well as in a few countries in Africa.

RECENT TRENDS

Recent trends favor democratic constitutional formulas permitting relatively high levels of social inclusiveness, political pluralism, policy stability, and democracy endurance. Actually, almost no new democracy established in the world during the broad "third wave" of democratization starting in 1974 has adopted the British-style constitutional model of parliamentary regime with majoritarian electoral rules and single-party cabinets. Of the democratic countries with more than one million inhabitants, fewer than one-sixth use parliamentary constitutional formulas with a majoritarian electoral formula, while more than one-third are parliamentary regimes with proportional representation electoral rules and multiparty coalition cabinets, and about one half are checks-and-balances regimes or its presidentialist and semi-presidential variants.

See also *Checks and Balances; Constitutional Democracy; Constitutional Monarchy; Constitutions and Constitutionalism; Dual Executive; Parliamentary Democracy; Presidencialismo; Prime Minister (Head of Government); Semi-presidential System.*

. . . . JOSEP M. COLOMER

BIBLIOGRAPHY

Bogdanor, Vernon, ed. *The British Constitution in the Twentieth Century.* Oxford: Oxford University Press, 2003.

Colomer, Josep M. *Political Institutions.* Oxford: Oxford University Press, 2001.

Dahl, Robert A. *How Democratic is the American Constitution?* New Haven: Yale University Press, 2002.

Duverger, Maurice, ed. *Les régimes semi-présidentiels.* Paris: Presses Universitaires de France, 1986.

Freedom House. *Freedom in the World 2005.* Washington: Freedom House, 2005.

Grofman, Bernard, ed. *The Federalist Papers and the New Institutionalism.* New York: Agathon, 1989.

Lijphart, Arend, ed. *Parliamentary versus Presidential Government.* Oxford: Oxford University Press, 1992.

Sartori, Giovanni. *Comparative Constitutional Engineering.* London: Macmillan, 1994.

Tschentscher, Axel. "International Constitutional Law." University of Bern, 2005. www.oefre.unibe.ch/law/icl.

Constitution Amending Procedures

From early Greek history, as scholar Melissa Schwartzberg has observed, democracies were associated with constant legal change. Like legislation, constitutions also require change as circumstances alter and as flaws reveal themselves.

TYPES OF AMENDING PROCESSES

Formal amending processes emerged in America with the birth of written constitutions. Although less than 4 percent of modern nations with written constitutions lack a constitutional amending process, the processes vary widely and require varying levels of difficulty. Donald Lutz divided such constitutions into four progressively more difficult categories. Parliamentary systems with written constitutions such as Austria, Botswana, Brazil, Germany, India, Kenya, Malaysia, New Zealand, Papua New Guinea, Portugal, and Samoa allow a single vote of the national legislature to enact such changes. Nations such as Argentina, Belgium, Columbia, Costa Rica, Finland, Greece, Iceland, Luxembourg, and Norway require at least two votes of the legislature with an intervening election. Chile, France, Italy, Spain, and Sweden permit bypassing the legislature through a referendum, whereas Australia, Denmark, Ireland, Japan, Switzerland, the United States, and Venezuela require a referendum or its equivalent. Lutz's research, on both national constitutions and on U.S. state constitutions, shows that longer documents are amended more frequently than shorter ones. Documents that are difficult to change also promote higher levels of judicial interpretation.

A convention of delegates from the states authored the U.S. Constitution. This distinguished the founding of United States from ancient states where laws had been created by a single lawgiver and were sometimes considered inviolate, and from those, like Great Britain, which traced its origins to a more continuous series of immemorial customs and usages that could be changed by new ones.

CONSTITUTIONAL MECHANISMS

Amending processes seek to promote deliberation and reflect consensus; federal systems also provide input for national and subnational actors. In the United States, for example, these goals are reflected in the mechanisms that Article V of the U.S. Constitution established for proposing and ratifying amendments. Two-thirds of the state legislatures under the Constitution have never yet requested that Congress call a convention to propose amendments. Instead, two-thirds majorities in both houses of Congress have proposed all twenty-seven U.S. amendments. They have all been ratified by three-fourths of the states, acting in all cases but one through their legislatures.

ENTRENCHMENT CLAUSES

Some constitutions attempt to entrench certain institutions or values against regular alteration. Article V of the U.S. Constitution, for example, prohibits any state from being deprived of its equal representation in the U.S. Senate without its consent. The U.S. Constitution does not mention any other substantive limits on the process, but courts in some countries—India and Germany, for example—have struck down some proposed constitutional changes as inconsistent with the document as a whole, and hence "unconstitutional."

JUDICIAL DECISIONS RELATIVE TO THE AMENDING PROCESS

Kemal Gozler has observed that the Turkish constitutions of 1961 and 1982, the Chilean Constitution of 1980, and the Romanian Constitution of 1991 specifically empowered constitutional courts to review the content of constitutional amendments, whereas others are silent on the subject. The

U.S. Supreme Court has never invalidated an amendment on the basis of its substance, and since *Coleman v. Miller* in 1939, the Court has generally deferred to Congress in ascertaining whether amendments have been legitimately ratified.

See also *Bills of Rights; Constitutional Amendments; Constitutional Courts; Parliamentary Government.*

. . . . JOHN R. VILE

BIBLIOGRAPHY

Dellinger, Walter. "The Legitimacy of Constitutional Change: Rethinking the Amending Process." *Harvard Law Review* 97 (December 1983): 280–432.

Gozler, Kemal. *Judicial Review of Constitutional Amendments.* Bursa, Turkey: Ekin Press, 2008.

Grimes, Alan P. *Democracy and the Amendments to the Constitution.* Lexington, Mass.: Lexington Books, 1978.

Kyvig, David E. *Explicit and Authentic Acts: Amending the U.S. Constitution, 1776–1995.* Lawrence: Kansas University Press, 1996.

Levinson, Sanford, ed. *Responding to Imperfection: The Theory and Practice of Constitutional Amendment.* Princeton: Princeton University Press, 1995.

Lutz, Donald S. "Toward a Theory of Constitutional Amendment." *American Political Science Review* 88 (June 1994): 355–370.

Schwartzberg, Melissa. *Democracy and Legal Change.* New York: Cambridge University Press, 2007.

Vile, John R. *Encyclopedia of Constitutional Amendments, Proposed Amendments, and Amending Issues, 1789–2002,* 2nd ed. Santa Barbara, Calif.: ABC-CLIO, 2003.

———. *The Constitutional Amending Process in American Political Thought.* Westport, Conn.: Praeger, 1992.

———. *Contemporary Questions Surrounding the Constitutional Amending Process.* Westport, Conn.: Praeger, 1993.

———. "Three Kinds of Constitutional Founding and Change: The Convention Model and Its Alternatives." *Political Research Quarterly* 46 (December 1993): 881–895.

Constitutions, Unwritten

An *unwritten constitution* is the body of legislation, rules, regulations, and common law recognized by legislators, executives, and courts as the binding laws that legitimize, guide, and limit a government's powers and authority as well as the public's rule of law. With an unwritten constitution, the body of laws are not enumerated within a single, formal document as witnessed in Israel, New Zealand, and the United Kingdom. Unlike a written constitution, an unwritten constitution is modified gradually, changing by accretion of new laws, often in response to the evolving needs and environment of its sovereign state. Of note, there are numerous statutes of an unwritten constitution that do exist in written form, causing some to prefer the term *uncodified constitution,* on the premise so much of these unwritten constitutions have been documented but not itemized. For example, the United Kingdom's Houses of Parliament have the ability to approve an act of Parliament, which is a specific primary written piece of legislature serving as an addendum to previous laws or establishment of an entirely new law.

A primary trait of the unwritten constitution is the flexibility by which these constitutions have to effectively adopt new statutes or modernize existing legislature addressing emerging political prerogatives. Governments ruled by unwritten constitutions do not typically have sovereign executives or legislators with constitutional supremacy; therefore, the political, legislative, and civic institutions grew up together as the result of continuous adaptation and accretion of customs rather than abiding to a deliberate, static set of limited powers. There is no singular institution designed specifically to control the principles and implementation of legislation as demonstrated by the U.S. Supreme Court, which not only is the highest appeals court but is responsible for upholding judicial review and the system of checks and balances on congressional and executive powers. Moreover, an evolutionary democratic system based on an unwritten constitution does not mean a flexible constitution equates to unstable governance as demonstrated by the United Kingdom. Stability prevails in this system by depending on the people's feeling about the fundamental political values the legal system ought to honor.

From a constitutional perspective, the U.K. unwritten constitution is a special case of combining legal and nonconventional rules that provide the framework of government and dictate the behavior of the main political institutions. Juridical supremacy is practiced among all the supreme powers of the state, to include the Crown, Parliament, and cabinet, which can modify or abrogate British constitutional institutions and rules. This parliamentary supremacy and sovereignty in lawmaking make it difficult to distinguish between laws considered to comprise the original unwritten constitution and those laws that have gradually become part of it. Many contemporary political scientists even question the possibility to enumerate the exact number of constitutional laws embodied in the British unwritten constitution.

CASE STUDY: UNITED KINGDOM AND THE EVOLUTION OF AN UNWRITTEN CONSTITUTION

The historical and political genesis of the United Kingdom's unwritten constitution is based on a gradual development of British parliament. This legislative institution grew out of the king's council (*curia regis*), in which the monarch originally consulted with the great magnates of the realm and later with commoners who represented the boroughs and shires. The locus of power in the constitution shifted gradually as a result of changes in the political and interest groups whose consent the government required in order to be effective. Parliament was, and is, a place in which to debate specific issues of disagreement between the Crown, on the one hand, and Parliament (the House of Commons and the House of Lords), on the other. The conflicts were settled in Parliament so that its original main function was that of a court (the High Court of Parliament during the sixteenth century). During the eighteenth century, the powers of the government passed more and more into the hands of he king's first minister and his cabinet, all of whom were also members of one the houses of Parliament. According to Marshall's *British Constitution,* an evolution of the constitution occurred when the transfer of prerogative powers from the Crown was given to the Crown's ministers in a way in which the Crown acted on advice about its executive functions. Today's parliamentary sovereignty originated from the powers of the king to make and approve law.

According to prevailing interpretations of the United Kingdom's unwritten constitution, the constitutional laws gradually incorporated significant and historical documents, including: Magna Carta Libertatum (1215), which is considered the founding step in evolution of parliamentary sovereignty; Petition of Right (1628); *Habeas Corpus* Act (1679); Bill of Rights (1689); electoral laws (1832, 1867, 1874, 1918, 1928, 1969); as well as laws transferring the power from the House of Lords to the House of Commons (1911 and 1949; the 1999 House of Lords Act eliminating Hereditary Peers for the House of Lords); and, recent devolution laws (considering Scotland, Wales, and Northern Ireland).

Moreover, this constitution embodies conventions that, according to Dicey's publication Introduction to the Study of *Law of the Constitution,* could be interpreted like "rules intended to regulate the exercise of the whole of the remaining discretionary powers of the Crown." However, the constitutional conventions do not have authoritative interpretations and the individual convention can be challenged by fresh arguments based on the interpretation of the precedence supporting them. Thus, the U.K. constitution includes the books of authority, for example Blackstone's *Commentaries on the Law of England*, which are commentaries and interpretation of the most prestigious jurists.

See also *British Political Thought; Common Law; Constitutional Monarchy; Constitutions and Constitutionalism; Parliamentary Government.*

. . . .   BLANKA ŘÍCHOVÁ

BIBLIOGRAPHY
Bogdanor, Vernon, ed. *The British Constitution in the Twentieth Century.* Oxford: Oxford University Press for the British Academy, 2003.
————. *Politics and the Constitution: Essays on the British Government.* Brookfield, Vt.: Dartmouth Publishing, 1996.
Dicey, A.V. *Introduction to the Study of the Law of the Constitution,* 10th ed. New York, Macmillan, 1987.
Marshall, G. *Constitutional Conventions: The Rules and Forms of Political Accountability.* Oxford, Clarendon Press, 1986.
Neubauer, Z. *Státověda a teorie politiky* [Theory of the State and Politics]. Prague: Slon, 2006.

Constitutions and Constitutionalism

A *constitution* is a set of basic rules for making collective decisions. Rules producing enforceable decisions can solve coordination and cooperation dilemmas, which may induce individuals to prefer constraining rules to settings in which every human interaction should be adjusted independently. However, different rules may favor different decisions with differently distributed benefits among individuals and groups.

TWO CATEGORIES OF CONSTITUTIONAL RULES

Two categories of constitutional rules can be distinguished: (1) those to regulate the division of powers among the various branches of government, and (2) those to define the relationships between these branches and the public, which in democracy are based on elections. Regarding the first category, virtually all the political regimes in world history have been based on a one-person office combined with multiple-person offices. The rationale for this is that, while a one-person institution may be highly effective at decision making, a few person council may be more capable of collecting information and deliberating, and a large assembly can be representative of different interests and values in the society and able to organize consent and facilitate the enforcement of decisions.

In classical political theory (as elaborated most prominently by Aristotle), the distinction between the rule of one, the few, or the many was sufficient to define basic types of political regime, such as monarchy, aristocracy, and democracy. In modern times, an analogous distinction can be made between dictatorship, semidemocratic regimes (typically holding multiple-candidate elections with restrictions on suffrage or on the offices submitted to electoral results), and democracy. Within democracy, the rules of one, the few, and the many—would correspond to the institutions of one-person prime minister or president, the few—member cabinet, and the many—member assembly. The relationships between these institutions define different types of democratic regime, as discussed in the following paragraphs.

The second category of constitutional rules mentioned above regulates the relationships between public officers and citizens by means of elections, which makes the classification of democratic regimes more complex. In particular, we can distinguish electoral systems based on simple plurality or absolute majority rule, which produce a single absolute winner and favor the concentration of power, and those using proportional representation rules, which are associated to multiparty systems and coalition governments.

TYPES OF CONSTITUTIONAL REGIME

PARLIAMENTARY CONSTITUTIONAL REGIMES

The parliamentary regime resulted historically from the process of enhancing the role of the elected assembly and limiting the monarch's powers. According to the English or *Westminster model,* parliament became the sovereign institution, also assuming the power of appointing and dismissing ministers, while the monarch remained a ceremonial although nonaccountable figure. The Third French Republic established in the late nineteenth century was the first democratic republic with a parliamentary regime. This type of regime produces political congruence between the legislative and the executive and some "fusion" of institutional powers.

Specifically, in parliamentary regimes with majoritarian electoral rules, a single party, even with a minority electoral support, usually can find sufficient institutional levers to win an assembly majority, appoint the prime minister, and form a government. In these situations, power tends to concentrate in the hands of the prime minister, which led to an interpretation of the development of political parties as a force eroding the central role of the parliament. In constitutional studies in the early twentieth century, the British model was provocatively labeled a "cabinet" of a "prime minister" regime, rather than "parliamentary." However, it has more recently been remarked that the growth of party was instrumental to reduce the influence of the monarch but not necessarily that of parliament. With the reduction of the monarch to a figurehead, the prime minister has indeed become the new one-person relevant figure, while the position of the cabinet has weakened. Still, the role of parliament has survived, and even, in a modest way, thrived.

The central role of parliament is more prominent in parliamentary regimes with proportional representation electoral rules, in which typically multiparty coalition governments are formed. The diffusion of power is wider in these than in regimes based on plurality or majority electoral rules. In contrast to electorally minority single-party governments, multiparty cabinets typically rely upon broad majority support both among parliamentarians and in the electorate. A multiparty coalition based on a majority of seats and popular votes is the typical government formula in most countries of continental Europe, including Belgium, the Czech Republic, Finland, Germany, Italy, Netherlands, Norway, Sweden, and Switzerland. Minority cabinets with additional parliamentary support are also formed in a few cases, as in Denmark and Spain.

PRESIDENTIAL CONSTITUTIONAL REGIMES

The second basic type of political regime resulted from the replacement of the executive monarch with an elected president, which should exert power in parallel to a representative congress. This model thus implies separate elections and divided powers between the chief executive and the legislative branch. It is usually called, in a rather confusing term, a *presidential regime*. In the original U.S. version, it implies a complex system of *checks and balances,* or mutual controls among separately elected or appointed institutions (presidency, the House, Senate, the Supreme Court). Interinstitutional relations are subjected to rules including term limits for the president, limited presidential veto of congressional legislation, Senate rules permitting a qualified minority to block decisions, senatorial ratification of presidential appointments, congressional appointment of officers and control of administrative agencies, congressional impeachment of the president, and judicial revision of legislation.

These counterweighting mechanisms play in favor of power sharing between institutions. As they induce negotiations and agreements between offices with different political orientation, they are equivalent devices to supermajority rules for decision making. The obstacles introduced by the numerous institutional checks to innovative decision making may stabilize socially inefficient status-quo policies, but they also guarantee that most important decisions are made by broad majorities able to prevent the imposition of a small or minority group's will. With similar analytical insight but a different evaluation, other analyses have remarked that separate elections and divided governments create a "dual legitimacy" prone to "deadlock," that is, legislative paralysis and interinstitutional conflict.

A *unified government* can exist when the president's party controls a majority of seats in the assembly. In the United States, there has been a situation of unified government with the president's party having a majority in both houses of Congress during less than 60 percent of time from 1832 to 2008, while *divided government* was more frequent during the second half of the twentieth century. However, U.S. congressional rules have traditionally included the ability of 40 percent of senators to block any decision by filibustering, which has almost always made the president's party unable to impose its decisions by its own. This could explain why no significant differences in legislative performances between periods of unified and divided governments have been observed.

Presidential dominance has been attempted in other countries, especially in several republics in Latin America and Africa, by supplementing the president's veto power over legislation and his control of the army, which do exist in the United States, with other constitutional mechanisms favoring the concentration of power. They include long presidential terms and reelections, the president's unconstrained powers to appoint and remove members of cabinet and other high officers, legislative initiative, capacity to dictate legislative decrees, fiscal and administrative authority, discretionary emergency powers, suspension of constitutional guarantees and, in formally federal countries, the right to intervene in state affairs. The other side of this same coin is weak congresses, which are not usually given control over the cabinet and are frequently constrained by short session periods and lack of resources. However, in democratic periods in the ten countries of South America since 1945, the president's party has not had a majority in congress 65 percent of the time; in about half of these cases, multiparty presidential cabinets have been formed by means of postelectoral, congressional negotiations (a formula which always applies, for instance, in the case of Brazil).

SEMI-PRESIDENTIAL CONSTITUTIONAL REGIMES

In another variant of regimes with division of powers, usually called *semi-presidentialism*, the presidency and the assembly are elected separately, like in a checks-and-balances regime, but it is the assembly that appoints and can dismiss a prime minister, like in a parliamentary regime. As a result, in parallel to the multiple-person assembly, two one-person offices, the president and the prime minister, share the executive powers in a *governmental dyarchy*, as in the current Fifth Republic of France.

At the beginning of the French experience, it was speculated that this constitutional model would produce an alternation between presidential and parliamentary phases, respectively favoring the president and the prime minister as a one-person dominant figure. The first phase of the alternation was indeed confirmed with presidents enjoying a compact party majority in the assembly. In these situations, the president becomes more powerful than in the classical presidential regimes, as well as more powerful than the British-style prime minister because the president accumulates the latter's powers plus those of the monarch. The second parliamentary phase was, in contrast, not confirmed, since, although in the so-called cohabitation experience the president faces a prime minister, a cabinet and an assembly majority with a different political orientation, the president usually retains significant powers, including the dissolution of the assembly, as well as partial vetoes over legislation and executive appointments, among others, depending on specific rules in each country. This makes the president certainly more powerful than any monarch or republican president in a parliamentary regime. There can, thus, be indeed two phases, depending on whether the president's party has a majority in the assembly and can appoint the primer minister or not; however, the two phases are not properly presidential and parliamentary, but they rather produce an even higher concentration of power than in a presidential regime and a dual executive, respectively.

CENTRALIZATION OR FEDERALISM

In addition to horizontal relationships between institutions above discussed, vertical relationships can be distinguished as corresponding either to unitary states or to decentralized, federal-type large states and empires. In the unitary model, a single, central government holds all relevant powers. In decentralized polities, the party in the central government may control different proportions of regional or local governments. Analogously to what has been discussed for vertical interinstitutional relationships, the degree of coincidence between the parties in central government and those in smaller territorial governments can produce different levels of unified or divided government. In contrast to unitary states, where only those citizens whose preferences coincide with the statewide majority obtain political satisfaction, in vertically divided governments global minorities can become local majorities. In multilevel political regimes, the number of total losers is likely to be smaller than in a unitary state and the aggregate amount of social utility should, thus, be higher, only depending on the intensity of preferences given by the citizens to different policy issues associated with each governmental level.

Horizontally unified governments, such as those that are typical of parliamentary regimes with majoritarian electoral rules, do not suit well with vertical division of powers. If a single party controls the central government, but does not control most noncentral governments, it may try to increase the concentration of power by replacing the constitutional scheme of vertical division of powers with a unitary formula (as happened in Britain throughout the nineteenth century). In contrast, an effective vertical division of powers of federal type is more likely to exist and survive in the framework of a divided central government, whether in the form of multiparty coalition cabinets (like in Germany and Switzerland) or with coexistence of different party majorities in the presidency and the congress (like in the United States).

CONSTITUTIONAL CONSEQUENCES

The more direct political consequences of different constitutional formulas regard the type, party composition, and degree of stability of governments. The rest of political, economic, and social consequences from constitutions should be considered relatively remote, indirect and identifiable in terms of constraints, limits, and opportunities, rather than determining specific decisions or outcomes. They may affect economic and other public policy making, as well as the corresponding performance. Also, different constitutional formulas may help democracy to endure or facilitate its shortening.

Single-party governments in parliamentary regimes and unified government in regimes with constitutional separation of powers can be compared for their high degree of concentration of powers around a one-person institution. Likewise, multiparty coalition cabinets in parliamentary regimes with proportional representation can be considered to be a variant of divided government. However, the two basic forms of constitutional regime differ because in a parliamentary regime, the prime minister can dissolve the parliament and call anticipated elections, while regimes with separation of powers typically have fixed terms and electoral calendars. Thus, in parliamentary regimes, while single-party governments tend to be relatively consistent and durable, multiparty coalition or minority governments are more vulnerable to coalition splits, censure or confidence-lost motions, and other events and strategies provoking anticipated elections. In contrast, in separation of powers regimes, situations of divided government—if they do not lead to the formation of multiparty coalitions between the president's and other parties with a sufficient congressional majority—may produce legislative paralysis and deadlock.

Relatively stable single-party parliamentary governments, as well as presidential governments with a president's party majority in the assembly and fixed terms, tend to produce more changing and unstable policies than those relying upon the support of multiple parties or interinstitutional agreements. A parliamentary regime with majoritarian electoral rules creating single-party governments on the basis of a minority of popular votes is the classical scene of *adversarial politics*. This implies two major consequences. First, electorally minority governments with a social bias are more prone to be captured by minority interest groups and to implement redistributive and protectionist policies hurting broad social interests. Second, frequent alternation of socially and electorally minority parties in government produces policy reversal and instability (including changes in regulations of prices, the labor market, or taxes), which may depress investment incentives.

In contrast, in multiparty elections producing coalition cabinets, as well as in interinstitutional relations involving different political majorities, each party can focus on a different set of issues, globally enlarging the electoral agenda and the corresponding debate. In the further institutional process, certain issues (typically including major domains such as macroeconomic policy, interior, and foreign affairs) can be the subject of a broad multiparty or interinstitutional agreement around a moderate position. This precludes drastic changes and induces mid- or long-term policy stability. Other issues can be negotiated in a way that the minority with more intense preferences on each issue may see its preferred policy approved, whether through the distribution of cabinet portfolios to parties focusing on different domains (such as finances for liberals, education for Christian Democrats, social policy or labor for Social Democrats, etc.) or through logrolling among different groups on different congressional issues. This second mechanism creates different but enduring political supports to decisions on each issue and also tends to produce relative policy stability.

A number of empirical studies show that parliamentary regimes with proportional representation perform better regarding electoral participation, low levels of politically motivated violence, women's representation, and social and environmental policies. They also appear to be associated to better growth-promoting policies, although they tend to imply relatively high taxes and public spending, which do not necessarily favor growth. Parliamentary regimes with proportional representation tend to develop broad programs benefiting a majority of the voters, including redistribution through social security and welfare policies, in contrast to narrower targets in both parliamentary regimes with majoritarian elections and presidential regimes. Other favorable conditions for economic growth include administrative effectiveness and an independent judiciary, which may be favored by a robust and pluralistic democratic regime. However, economic performance also depends on other factors, such as economic institutions (including those regulating property rights, contracts, and finances) and an educated population able to make technological innovation available and operational, which may not be directly associated with specific constitutional formulas.

Different constitutional alternatives have been linked to different rates of success in attempts of democratization and the duration of democratic regimes. Strategic choices of different constitutional formulas may be driven by actors' relative bargaining strength, electoral expectations, and attitudes to risk. Citizens and political leaders tend to support those formulas producing satisfactory results for themselves and reject those making them permanently excluded and defeated. As a consequence, those constitutional formulas producing widely distributed satisfactory outcomes can be more able to develop endogenous support and endure. Widely representative and effective political outcomes can feed social support for the corresponding institutions, while exclusionary, biased, arbitrary, or ineffective outcomes might foster citizens' and leaders' rejection of the institutions producing such results.

Generally, constitutional democracies favoring power sharing and inclusiveness should be able to obtain higher endogenous support and have greater longevity than those favoring the concentration of power. Empirical accounts show that democratic regimes are the most peaceful ones, while semi-democratic or transitional regimes are most prone to conflict, even more than exclusionary dictatorships (basically because the latter increase the costs of rebellion). Among democracies, parliamentary constitutional regimes are more resilient to crises and more able to endure than presidential ones. More specifically, parliamentary regimes with majoritarian electoral systems appear to be associated to higher frequency of ethnic and civil wars than presidential regimes, while parliamentary regimes with proportional representation are the most peaceful ones.

See also *Coalition Theory; Cohabitation; Constitutional Law; Constitutional Monarchy; Constitutional Systems, Comparative; Constitutions and Constitutionalism; Divided Government; Dual Executive; Parliamentary Democracy; Proportional Representation; Unitary Government; Westminster Model; Winner-Take-All.*

. . . . JOSEP M. COLOMER

BIBLIOGRAPHY

Brennan, Geoffrey, and James Buchanan. *The Reason of Rules. Constitutional Political Economy.* Cambridge: Cambridge University Press, 1985.

Buchanan, James, and Gordon Tullock. *The Calculus of Consent: Logical Foundations of Constitutional Democracy.* Ann Arbor: University of Michigan Press, 1962.

Cheibub, José A., and Fernando Limongi. "Modes of Government Formation and the Survival of Presidential Regimes." *Annual Review of Political Science* 5 (2002): 151–175.

Colomer, Josep M. *Political Institutions.* Oxford : Oxford University Press, 2001.

Colomer, Josep M., and Gabriel L. Negretto. "Can Presidentialism Work Like Parliamentarism?" *Government and Opposition* 40, no. 1 (2005): 60–89.

Cox, Gary W. *The Efficient Secret: The Cabinet and the Development of Political Parties in Victorian England.* Cambridge: Cambridge University Press, 1987.

Duverger, Maurice. *Les constitutions de la France,* 14th ed. Paris: Presses Universitaires de France, 1998.

Flinders, Matthew. "Shifting the Balance? Parliament, the Executive, and the British Constitution." *Political Studies* 50, no. 1: 23–42.

Hammond, Thomas H., and Gary J. Miller. "The Core of the Constitution." *American Political Science Review,* 81 (1987): 1155–1174.

Hardin, Russell. *Liberalism, Constitutionalism, and Democracy.* Oxford: Oxford University Press, 1999.

Krehbiel, Kenneth. *Pivotal Politics.* Chicago: University of Chicago Press, 1998.

Laver, Michael, and Norman Schofield. *Multiparty Government.* Oxford: Oxford University Press, 1990.

Laver, Michael, and Kenneth Shepsle. "Divided Government: America Is Not Exceptional." *Governance* 4, no. 3 (1991): 250–269.

Lijphart, Arend. *Patterns of Democracy.* New Haven: Yale University Press. 1999.

Linz, Juan J., and Arturo Valenzuela, eds. *The Failure of Presidential Democracy.* Baltimore: Johns Hopkins University Press, 1994.

Mueller, Dennis. *Constitutional Democracy.* Oxford: Oxford University Press, 1996.

Müller, Wolfgang, and Kaare Strom. *Coalition Governments in Western Europe.* Oxford: Oxford University Press, 2000.

Persson, Torsten, and Guido Tabellini. *The Economic Effects of Constitutions.* Cambridge, Mass.: MIT Press, 2003.

Powell, G. Bingham. *Elections as Instruments of Democracy.* New Haven: Yale University Press, 2000.

Reynal-Querol, Marta. "Ethnicity, Political Systems, and Civil Wars." *Journal of Conflict Resolution* 46, no. 1 (2002): 29–54.

Shugart, Matthew S., and John M. Carey. *Presidents and Assemblies.* Cambridge: Cambridge University Press, 1992.

Constructivism

The term constructivism encompasses several schools of thought that emphasize the role of social constructions in the study and practice of politics. Social constructions are defined as shared interpretations or ideas on how the material world is or should be ordered. Constructions are neither objective, since they exist only by virtue of being agreed on by more or less extended groups of individuals, nor subjective, given their collective nature. Rather, they are *intersubjective*.

Social constructions operate at the epistemological as well as the ontological level. On the one hand, they provide communities of scholars with common understandings of the reality they face; on the other hand, they are intersubjective structures influencing political life. While most, if not all, constructivists acknowledge the existence of both dimensions, they are divided as to which dimension should be assigned more weight in the analysis of political phenomena. This disagreement underlies the main cleavage in the constructivist camp—that between postmodern and modern constructivism.

POSTMODERN CONSTRUCTIVISM

The most radical of the two variants, postmodern constructivism, points to the role of constructions in the so-called scientific process to attack the positivist underpinnings of mainstream political science. Positivism asserts the existence of an objective political reality whose laws can be progressively discovered through the formulation and testing of theories. For postmodern constructivists, conversely, the presence of unobservable elements in any account of politics, and the need to replace these elements with assumptions and mental constructs, makes theory building necessarily a socially laden enterprise: one in which the formulation of hypotheses on the political world hinges to a large extent on the researcher's cultural, ideological, and political convictions. Empirical work, according to postmodern constructivists, can do very little to increase the objectivity of research. For one thing, the complexity of the sociopolitical reality, where perfect empirical tests are rare, and the ever-present possibility of formulating ad hoc explanations make it very hard, if not impossible, to disprove any theory. Second, and perhaps more important, most testing methods and procedures are themselves theory driven, and hence biased in favor of the hypotheses they are meant to evaluate.

The resulting view of science is very far from the positivist ideals of neutrality, universality, and progress. For postmodern constructivists, the subjects (i.e., researchers) and the objects of political research can never be fully separated. If there are dominant theories in certain historical periods, this is due less to their actual validity than to their consistency with prevailing cultures or professional orientations influencing scholars' interpretation of the political reality. To the extent that any meaningful political research can exist at all, the postmodern constructivists conclude that it can only be a theoretically and methodologically "anarchic" activity, in which no approach can be deemed more "scientific" than others and, ultimately, anything goes.

MODERN CONSTRUCTIVISM

Unlike their postmodern counterparts, modern constructivists do not take their concern with the intersubjectivity of the scientific process as far as rejecting positivism altogether. While partially constructed, they contend, competing accounts of the political world are not all the same, and careful empirical research, combined with theoretical debate, can help the scholarly community distinguish between plausible and untenable explanations. At least in the long run, in sum, positivist research methods can result in a faithful depiction of the sociopolitical reality.

Far more important than the constructions of the researcher are, for modern constructivists, those of the actors of domestic and international politics: voters, leaders, parties, bureaucracies, states, and so on. In contrast to rationalist approaches, which view political actors as constantly maximizing certain stable objectives (e.g., power, wealth, security, etc.), modern constructivism argues that the nature, identity, and preferences of individual and collective agents are not fixed and exogenously given, but formed through processes of socialization that shape their interpretation of the world, define appropriate behaviors and, ultimately, influence political action. The field of nuclear proliferation provides a good illustration of the differences between rationalists and constructivists: While rationalists focus on the material side of the issue and see weapons as, in principle, equally threatening regardless of who proliferates, for constructivists the consequences of nuclear armaments on international security cannot be assessed apart from the identity of the countries involved, the nature and history of their relations, and their perception of each other.

If social constructions influence the behavior of political actors, social interactions derive, by definition, from individual actions. So, while constructivism rejects individualism—the idea that the characteristics of society stem from those of the individual agents in it—it does not embrace its opposite, holism, entirely. Rather, constructivists posit the "mutual constitution" of intersubjective structures and sociopolitical agents, in which neither part logically precedes the other. As a result, the basic coordinates of politics are always subject to (more or less gradual) change.

So defined, constructivism is more of a "thin" theoretical framework than a substantive theory of politics: It draws attention to the role of social structures in the explanation of political behavior but is compatible with different specific sources of political agents' identities and preferences. Three such sources so far have received particular attention in the constructivist literature: culture, ideas, and institutions. Constructivists of the first branch emphasize the impact of consolidated cultural elements on the behavior of individuals, groups, and entire communities. Ideas, on the contrary, figure in many explanations of political change, which concentrate particularly on the ways in which cognitive and normative meanings are expressed and transmitted. Analyses focusing on institutions, finally, explain how certain social and political practices often acquire a self-reproductive character by shaping the worldviews and preferences of the actors involved.

Modern constructivism has acquired great popularity in Western academia in the past few decades, particularly in the subfields of comparative politics and international relations, where constructivists contribute to the main debates and have produced a substantial body of empirical work. Methodologically, constructivism is especially—though not exclusively—compatible with studies analyzing a few empirical observations (small-n studies) and inductive research strategies, which attempt to generalize from the examination of specific cases instead of using the latter to test previously formulated hypotheses. These methods allow constructivist researchers to better capture the qualitative variables they work with and to trace specific processes of agent constitution. In addition, constructivists make large use of several tools and techniques originally developed in other disciplines, such as fieldwork, participant observation, and discourse analysis. These methodological preferences have provoked the criticism of many rationalist scholars, who accuse constructivism of being unable to produce truly general and falsifiable explanations. To these allegations, constructivists respond mainly by pointing out their peculiar logic of inquiry, one that does not deny or underestimate the existence of universal social dynamics, but that is nonetheless more interested in the different and the unique in each political situation, process, or phenomenon.

See also *Cognitive Theory and Politics; Empiricism; Positive Theory; Small-n and Case Study.*

. . . .   PIER DOMENICO TORTOLA

BIBLIOGRAPHY

Adler, Emanuel. "Seizing the Middle Ground: Constructivism in World Politics." *European Journal of International Relations* 3, no. 3 (1997): 319–363.

Berger, Peter L., and Thomas Luckmann. *The Social Construction of Reality: A Treatise in the Sociology of Knowledge.* Garden City, N.Y.: Anchor Books, 1966.

Blyth, Mark. "Structures Do Not Come with an Instruction Sheet: Interests, Ideas, and Progress in Political Science." *Perspectives on Politics* 1, no. 4 (2003): 695–703.

Feyerabend, Paul K. *Against Method.* London: New Left Books, 1975.

Finnemore, Martha, and Kathryn Sikkink. "Taking Stock: The Constructivist Research Program in International Relations and Comparative Politics." *Annual Review of Political Science* 4 (2001): 391–416.

Giddens, Anthony. *The Constitution of Society: Outline of the Theory of Structuration.* Cambridge: Polity Press, 1984

Green, Daniel M. *Constructivism and Comparative Politics.* Armonk, N.Y.: M. E. Sharpe, 2002.

Kuhn, Thomas S. *The Structure of Scientific Revolutions.* Chicago: University of Chicago Press, 1962.

Price, Richard, and Christian Reus-Smit. "Dangerous Liaisons? Critical International Theory and Constructivism." *European Journal of International Relations* 4, no. 3 (1998): 259–294.

Ruggie, John G. "What Makes the World Hang Together? Neo-utilitarianism and the Social Constructivist Challenge." *International Organization* 52, no. 4 (1998): 855–885.

Sismondo, Sergio. *Science without Myth: On Constructions, Reality, and Social Knowledge.* Albany: SUNY Press, 1996.

Wendt, Alexander. *Social Theory of International Politics.* Cambridge: Cambridge University Press, 1999.

Consultants, Political

Political consultants are professionals who assist candidates running for office by providing one or more specialized services. They work on an ad hoc basis, taking a different set of clients each election cycle. The work is typically done on a fee-for-service basis and confined to the specific election cycle. Consultants may work individually, or more typically, as part of a political consulting firm comprised of many professionals who provide the variety of service(s) the firm offers.

Consultants are fixtures in campaigns at all levels in modern American electoral politics. Presidential candidates have stables of consultants working for their campaigns, sometimes with multiple firms providing the same service. In addition, most congressional candidates also hire consultants, though how many varies depending on whether the candidate is an incumbent, challenger, or open-seat candidate, as well as the estimated competitiveness of the campaign. While no serious candidate for office at the federal level would proceed with the assistance of one or more political consultants, the use of such consultants has even spread to state legislative campaigns, mayoral races, and school board contests.

ORIGINS OF POLITICAL CONSULTING

Political consultants are nothing new to political campaigns, although there is some disagreement as to how political consulting originated. Some scholars state that consultants were not strictly an American phenomenon and date as far back as 63 BCE, when ancient Roman Quintus Tullius Cicero advised his brother, orator and philosopher Marcus Tullius Cicero in an election for the consulship of Rome. In the American context, however, some scholars point to the founding of and debate over the ratification of the U.S. Constitution when the Federalists and Anti-Federalists engaged in political tactics that are reminiscent of those used today. In a more modern context, many observers consider Clem Whitaker and Leone Baxter as the founders of the political consulting industry, as they were the first individuals to try and make a living by providing campaign services to clients through their formation of their firm, Campaigns Inc., in 1933.

The consulting industry developed slowly after Campaigns Inc., but was helped along with technological advancements like scientific polling and electronic media, such as radio and television. These advancements meant that campaigning was no longer only a political endeavor: Candidates would need help with the sophisticated and technical tools now at their disposal. In fact, many of the first media consultants were advertisers from Madison Avenue in New York who found new clients in the form of candidates running for office.

Technical advancements also spurred another important development in the consulting industry in the form of specialization. Before this, a single person or a small group of individuals could run the entire campaign, but as the tactics of campaigning became more and more sophisticated, specialization of the industry and skills needed for campaigning developed. Today, political consulting is a highly specialized industry, with thousands of individuals working in many different fields.

SERVICES PROVIDED AND EFFECTS MEASURED

There is a core group of services that define the political consulting industry and others that support or supplement the work of these central elements. The heart of political consulting is the creation and delivery of a candidate's message, or the short statement that gives voters the reasons they should vote for this candidate rather than the opponent. The consultants typically responsible for developing and disseminating the candidate's message include a pollster, a media consultant, a direct mail specialist, and a campaign manager or general consultant. Additional consultants may include an opposition researcher, a fundraiser, and a field or get-out-the-vote specialist. Beyond this, other services that are not as central to the overall creation of the candidate's message, but are just as important to a modern political campaign, include Web site design, media buying, printing services, and culling data from voter files and other sources to help target voters. Individuals providing these services are sometimes called *vendors,* making the distinction between their role and true consultants. These specialists come together to provide candidates with all the information and assistance they need to run a sophisticated and modern campaign for office.

Political consultants produce tangible results for their candidates. Scholars have systematically examined consultants' presence in candidates' campaigns and found that candidates who hire consultants raise more money during their campaign and get more votes on election day than those candidates who do not hire professionals. In terms of fundraising, candidates who hire consultants raise more money from party committees, political action committees, and individual donors than do those candidates who run amateur campaigns. Scholars also believe that a candidate hiring one consultant or more signals to potential donors that their campaign is serious, viable, and worth the investment of a campaign contribution.

Consultants' impact on a candidate's vote share is slightly more complex. While Stephen Medvic, in his 2001 book *Political Consultants in U.S. Congressional Elections,* finds that both the presence of consultants as well as the actual number of consultants hired by a candidate impact the number of votes that challenger and open-seat candidates receive, the same relationship is not true for incumbents. Medvic also finds that the most valuable type of consultant challenger candidates can hire is the pollster, who provides the most bang for the campaign's buck. Again, however, the same is not true for incumbents. These results may seem to indicate that consultants are not as important for incumbent officeholders seeking reelection. While this may be true for safe incumbents, for embattled incumbents, there is another dynamic at work, as embattled incumbents worry only about winning and not about how many votes they get as long as they receive more than their opponent. For those incumbents who are in a difficult race, the impact of consultants may not be best measured in votes; it may be better measured in terms of simple victory.

See also *Campaign Advertising; Campaign Finance; Campaigns; Election Monitoring; Negative Campaigning.*

. . . .   DAVID A. DULIO

BIBLIOGRAPHY
Dulio, David A. *For Better or Worse? How Political Consultants Are Changing Elections in the United States.* Albany: SUNY Press, 2004.
Farrell, David M., Robin Kolodny, and Stephen Medvic. "Parties and Campaign Professionals in a Digital Age: Political Consultants in the United States and Their Counterparts Overseas." *Harvard Journal of Press/Politics* 6, no. 4 (2001): 11–30.
Grossmann, Matt. "Going Pro? Political Campaign Consultants and the Professional Model." *Journal of Political Marketing* 8, no. 2 (2009): 81–104.
Herrnson, Paul S. "Campaign Professionalism and Fundraising in Congressional Elections." *Journal of Politics* 53, no. 3 (1992): 859–870.
Johnson, Dennis W. *No Place for Amateurs: How Political Consultants Are Reshaping American Democracy.* New York: Routledge.
Medvic, Stephen K. *Political Consultants in U.S. Congressional Elections.* Columbus: Ohio State University Press, 2001.
———. "Professional Political Consultants: An Operational Definition." *Politics* 23, no. 2 (2006): 119–127.
Medvic, Stephen K, and Silvo Lenart. "The Influence of Political Consultants in the 1992 Congressional Elections." *Legislative Studies Quarterly* 22, no. 1 (1997): 61–77.
Nimmo, Dan. *The Political Persuaders: The Techniques of Modern Election Campaigns.* Englewood Cliffs, N.J.: Prentice Hall, 1970.
Petracca, Mark P. "Political Consultants and Democratic Governance." *PS: Political Science and Politics* 22, no. 1 (1989): 11–14.
Sabato, Larry J. *The Rise of Political Consultants: New Ways of Winning Elections.* New York: Basic Books, 1981.

Consumer Society

The term *consumer society* refers to modern capitalist societies that are organized around increasing levels of consumption. The key features generally include a culture dominated by fashion, advertising, and mass marketing; aspirations, lifestyles, and identities tied to conspicuous consumption; and a lack of traditional moral restraints on individual desires. While some scholars see the emergence of consumer societies as part of the natural trajectory of capitalist development, most who use the term critique what they see as the irrationality and wastefulness of consumer capitalism.

CRITICISMS OF THE CONSUMER SOCIETY

The *paradox of affluence*—the belief that accumulating more consumer goods does not make us better off—is one of the more prominent criticisms of a consumer society. Juliet Schor and Robert Frank depict a society caught in an endless cycle of emulation, in which attempts to raise our social status through increasing displays of wealth are constantly frustrated by our neighbors' efforts to match us. Consumption becomes a no-win situation, like trying to move forward by running on a treadmill. A study by Richard Easterlin, showing the residents of wealthy countries report being no happier than those from poorer countries, is frequently cited to provide empirical support for this position. More recently, some commentators have linked social pressures to increase consumption standards (even in the face of stagnant wages) to the explosion of personal debt that precipitated the global economic crisis of 2008.

The emulation perspective draws on Thorstein Veblen, an influential American social critic of the early twentieth century. Veblen dismissed the notion that optimizing individuals make consumer choices, and that these choices determine what capitalist firms produce, which economists call *consumer sovereignty.* He maintained that the bulk of what capitalist societies produced did not serve human needs but instead fueled "predatory" emulation. John Kenneth Galbraith adds to the critique by arguing that the advertising and marketing practices of large corporations largely determine consumer choices.

For environmentalists, ever-growing consumption creates ever-higher levels of pollution, waste, and resource depletion—to the point that continuing down this path becomes both unsustainable and immoral. Many religious traditions have long been critical of the morality of consumer societies in which secular, materialist values of pleasure seeking and profligacy crowd out traditional values of restraint, spirituality, and charity. The effects of advertising and consumer culture on the family, particularly children who are subjected to thousands of messages promoting consumption and instant gratification every day, have also traditionally been areas of concern. These criticisms have inspired a small but growing number of anticonsumerist rebels to reject the consumer society—to "get off the treadmill"—and embrace *voluntary simplicity*.

More radical critics paint a darker picture. German philosopher-sociologists Max Horkheimer and Theodor Adorno, seeking to understand why workers in capitalist nations were not revolutionary, found one answer in the ideological functions of consumer culture. In capitalist societies, the culture industry indoctrinates and manipulates consumers; creates false needs; and produces passive, alienated individuals who are incapable of critical thought or resistance. Taking the criticism to the next level, French sociologist Jean Baudrillard argues that consumer culture has imploded into every aspect of life to the extent that there are no longer true needs to be alienated from or manipulated.

REACTIONS

Theories of the consumer society have come under criticism from both the right and the left. For libertarians, these perspectives are elitist and paternalistic for asserting that consumers make choices that are not in their interest (i.e., if consumer goods do not make people happy, why do they buy them?), and moralistic for assuming that a simple life is superior to other freely chosen lifestyles. American sociologist Michael Schudson defends advertising from charges of manipulation by pointing out that many advertising campaigns are unsuccessful. These critics point to another paradox: If we are all manipulated by the forces of the consumer society, then how is it that an enlightened few have escaped its grasp, and can see how the rest of us are manipulated?

While the left largely accepts the critique of consumer capitalism, many are uncomfortable with what they see as the essentially conservative (or even puritanical) nature of perspectives that advocate simplicity and frugality. Others fear that the radical theories are fatalistic and disempowering, leaving little space for opposing the consumer society or constructing an alternative. Some feminists argue that the depiction of consumers is gendered—since women have historically been associated with consumption and have been stereotyped as irrational and easily manipulated.

See also *Critical Theory; Environmental Political Theory; Veblen, Thorstein.*

. . . . ALLAN MACNEILL

BIBLIOGRAPHY

Baudrillard, Jean. "Consumer Society." In *Jean Baudrillard: Selected Writings,* edited by Mark Poster. Stanford: Stanford University Press, 1988.
Durning, Alan. *How Much Is Enough? The Consumer Society and the Future of the Earth.* New York: W. W. Norton, 1992.
Easterlin, Richard. "Does Economic Growth Improve the Human Lot?" In *Nations and Household in Economic Growth,* edited by P. David and M. Reder. New York: Academic Press, 1974.
Frank, Robert. *Luxury Fever: Why Money Fails to Satisfy in an Era of Excess.* Princeton: Princeton University Press, 2000.
Galbraith, John Kenneth. *The Affluent Society.* New York: Mentor, 1958.
Horkheimer, Max and Theodor Adorno. "The Culture Industry: Enlightenment as Mass Deception." In *Dialectic of Enlightenment,* translated by John Cumming. New York: Continuum, 1987.
Schor, Juliet. *The Overspent American: Upscaling, Downshifting, and the New Consumer.* New York: Basic Books, 1998.
Schudson, Michael. *Advertising, The Uneasy Persuasion: Its Dubious Impact on American Life.* New York: Basic Books, 1984.
Veblen, Thorstein. *The Theory of the Leisure Class.* New York: Penguin Books, 1967.

Contagion of the Left

Political theorist Maurice Duverger argues that a right-wing party could change its organization and ideology to maintain its competitive position. Therefore, *contagion of the left* refers to those situations in which leftist oppositions force government to make policy decisions it otherwise would not make.

If all major political forces in a political system espouse identical policy alternatives, or all actors share political power through grand coalitions or consociational cases, then there is little or no room for policy contagion. If there is an ideologically polarized political conflict, there will be little chance for any policy influence or contagion of the left.

Considerable comprehensive and historical evidence exists to show that conditions of insecurity and socialist threat can lead political authorities to change their policies. In the late nineteenth century, Bismarck made comprehensive social reforms to undermine and ultimately destroy the popular appeal of the rising Social Democrats in imperial Germany. It was argued that fear of socialism was very real and profound for both the ruling classes and the bourgeoisie. Another example can be given from Britain. The reformist impulse labeled as "red toryism" within British conservatives materialized from the necessities of the emerging working class with their leftist political representatives.

. . . . SEZGIN S. CEBI

See also *Conservative Parties; Social Welfare; Welfare State.*

Containment

At the outset of the cold war, George F. Kennan developed the containment concept in a major formulation of how the United States should handle the threats posed by Joseph Stalin's Soviet Union. Kennan first discussed his ideas in "The Sources of Soviet Conduct," which he authored anonymously in 1947 under the name "X" in *Foreign Affairs.* In later years, there have been references to an American policy in the 1990s of a *dual containment* of both Iran and Iraq, as well as some debate about whether American policy toward China should amount to containment or to engagement.

Some interpreters of Kennan's formula vis-à-vis the Soviet Union might have seen this as nothing more than the traditional need to maintain a balance against the geopolitical power that Moscow could accumulate from its position at the center of Eurasia, that is, as nothing new. But, on a more positive note, Kennan was contrasting the Soviet dictatorship with that of Nazi Germany, arguing that the United States did not need to anticipate a preemptive or preventive war against the Soviets, who were more bound by ideology and not as adventurous or aggressive as Adolf Hitler had been. If Americans patiently held the line of containment, this would disprove the ideology by which the advance of communism was inevitable, and it would in the long run undermine the Soviet system.

See also *Cold War; Communism, Fall of, and End of History; Domino Theory.*

. . . . GEORGE H. QUESTER

Contempt of Congress

See *Congress, Contempt of.*

Content Analysis

Content analysis refers to a method for classifying textual material that involves reducing it to more manageable, categorical, or quantitative data for use in comparative analysis. The basic goal of content analysis is to apply a set of explicit procedures to the analysis of texts to make systematic inferences possible about the text, the authors, or the intended recipients of the text. Content analysis differs from discourse analysis in that the latter typically focuses more on the qualitative interpretation of the meaning of language in texts, paying special attention to how context and conventions are represented through language. While *text* typically refers to written documents, it applies quite generally to recorded verbal behavior of almost any kind. Commonly analyzed examples include political speeches, media broadcasts, newspaper editorials, court decisions, business reports, psychological diaries, draft legislation, correspondence with companies, and the transcripts of customer service phone calls.

Content analysis is commonly used in the study of politics, media, business, law, psychology, and public administration. For instance, a political scientist might be interested in analyzing the policy positions of political parties and would turn to content analysis of the official political programs, known as *manifestos*, published by the parties. In fact, the long-standing Comparative Manifesto Project does just this, unitizing party manifestos into discrete *quasi-sentence* units and then assigning each quasi sentence a policy category from a predefined, fifty-six-category coding scheme.

See also *Discourse Analysis; Qualitative Methodologies.*

. . . . KENNETH BENOIT

BIBLIOGRAPHY

Krippendorff, Klaus. *Content Analysis: An Introduction to Its Methodology,* 2nd ed. Thousand Oaks, Calif: Sage Publications, 2004.

Weber, Robert Philip. *Basic Content Analysis,* 2nd ed. Thousand Oaks, Calif: Sage Publications, 1990.

Contentious Politics

Contentious politics, in the context of political science, means episodic, public, collective interaction among makers of claims and their objects when: (1) at least one government is a claimant, an object of claims, or a party to the claims, and (2) the claims would, if realized, affect the interests of at least one of the claimants or objects of claims. Roughly translated, the definition refers to collective political struggle.

Of course, each term in the definition cries out for further stipulations. The term *episodic,* for example, excludes regularly scheduled events such as votes, parliamentary elections, and associational meetings. The term *public* excludes claim making that occurs entirely within well-bounded organizations, including churches and firms. Contention, of course, occurs both inside and outside of public politics, but political contention involves government, however peripherally, and thereby increases the likelihood of intervening coercive agents such as police and, on the average, increases the stakes of the outcome.

Not all forms of politics are necessarily contentious. Much of politics consists of ceremony, consultation, bureaucratic process, collection of information, registration of events, educational activities, and the like; these actions usually involve little if any collective contention. This does not imply that all forms of contention conform to a single general model. Drawing upon definitions from Charles Tilly and Sidney Tarrow's *Contentious Politics* (2006), Tilly's *European Revolutions, 1492–1992* (1993), and Nicholas Sambanis's "What Is a Civil War?" (2004) the differences among three major forms of contention clarify this lack of a general model:

- *Social movements:* sustained challenges to power holders in the name of a population living under the jurisdiction of those power holders by means of public displays of that population's worthiness, unity, numbers, and commitment;
- *Civil wars:* sustained large-scale reciprocal armed conflict between two or more social actors in a population—however defined—over control of a state or over the demand of one of the actors to establish its own state;
- *Revolutions:* attempted transfers of power over a state in the course of which at least two distinct blocs of contenders make incompatible claims to control the state, and some significant portion of the population mobilizes on behalf of the claims of each bloc.

These forms of contention have different dynamics, involve different combinations of performances, and produce different levels of violence. Although they can overlap empirically and easily shift from one to another, they are best understood by examining what they have in common; they share contentious interaction between makers of claims and others who recognize that these claims bear on their interests and bring in government as mediator, target, or claimant. Considering the forms of contention in the same framework helps to understand three important properties of contentious politics: (1) the rapid formation and transformation of different forms of contention; (2) the interactions between actors that form across institutional boundaries; and most important, (3) the common mechanisms and processes that underlie and drive contentious politics.

APPROACHES TO CONTENTIOUS POLITICS

Since the 1960s, the study of contentious politics has spawned a host of distinct topical literatures—on revolutions, social movements, industrial conflict, international war, civil war, interest group politics, nationalism, and democratization. Scholars in each group used different methodologies and mainly proceeded in cordial indifference to each other's findings. Yet different forms of contentious politics involve similar causal processes, such as mobilization, a central process in civil wars, revolutions, and social movements as well as in electoral campaigns, strikes, and warfare. As long as the same mechanisms and processes can be identified in different forms of contention, they should be studied together irrespective of the boundaries that scholars have established between these forms. Several general approaches to contentious politics have attempted to bring integration out of segmentation.

Until the late 1960s, the so-called *collective behavior approach* had dominated American studies of social movements. Best synthesized in the work of Neil Smelser in 1962, the approach emphasized the cognitive and emotional elements in collective action and focused heavily on grievances. In its extreme manifestations, it invited caricature by regarding collective action as the result of anomie, alienation, and even psychological disorder. But even more balanced proponents of the approach never solved the puzzle that there is no one-to-one relationship between the extent of people's grievances and their capacity and willingness to advance their claims. In the 1960s and after, the dominant approaches to contentious politics shifted from collective behavior to the structures that empower and constrain it.

STRUCTURAL APPROACHES

Structuralism took two forms: classical macrostructural models descended from Marx, in which major societal changes directly produce shifts in contention; and models of political structure focusing on the opportunities and threats, along with the facilitation and repression induced by political institutions and regimes. Macrostructural models were more popular in Europe, while political structural models developed in the United States, especially after the civil rights movement. But the *political process model* that resulted soon became the common property of Americans such as Doug McAdam and Europeans including Donatella della Porta, Dieter Rucht, and Hanspeter Kriesi.

Most scholars who focus on the political intermediation of contentious politics center on a cluster of variables called *political opportunity structure*. Opportunity structures are features of regimes that affect the likely outcomes of actors' possible claims. A reasonably consensual list of those features, noted by Charles Tilly and Sidney Tarrow, include:

1. Multiplicity of independent centers of power within the regime.
2. The regime's openness to new actors.
3. Instability of current political alignments.
4. Availability of influential allies or supporters for challengers.
5. Extent to which the regime represses or facilitates collective claim making.
6. Decisive changes in all of these features.

Threats are the converse of opportunities. But threats and opportunities occur simultaneously and most people engaging in contentious politics combine response to threat with seizing opportunities. Both threats and opportunities shift with fragmentation or concentration of power, changes in a regime's openness or closure, instability of alignments, and the availability of allies.

REPERTOIRES OF CONTENTION

The development of the political process approach was accompanied by systematic attention to the *repertoire* of contention—the sets of performances that people habitually use in mounting contention. Repertoires represent not only how people make claims, but also what they know about making claims and their reception by targets of their claims. Repertoires and performances evolved with the histories of industrialization and state-building. For example, the protest demonstration grew out of, and at first resembled, the religious procession to a place of worship. It turned contentious as demonstrators moved from a place of assembly to a site from which they could directly confront the targets of their claims. Later, the protest demonstration became the central form of action, mounted routinely to demonstrate a claim before the public. With the development of mass media, it could be staged to gain media attention. Change in social movement repertoires accelerated in the 1960s—as they do in any major wave of contention.

PROTEST EVENT ANALYSIS

After the 1960s, complementing the emphasis on repertoires, scholars developed a wide array of systematic methods and approaches to track the changes in the forms of contention in the public sphere. The systematic analysis of contentious events has become the closest thing to a core method for the study of contentious politics. Scholars enumerate and analyze the number of events, numbers and composition of participants, their targets and degree of violence, and the kinds of performances they involve. But in focusing on the *public politics* of contention, the new method ignored private forms of contention, such as the emotions in contentious politics, the construction of new collective actors (e.g., the new women's movement), and the study of motivations for collective action. These were the major starting points for new approaches in the 1980s and 1990s.

ALTERNATIVES TO STRUCTURALISM

In the 1980s, two alternative models began to challenge the hegemony of structuralism: a *culturalist model,* which focused on emotions, cognition, discourse, and the construction of collective action; and a *rationalist model* focusing on the dispositional microfoundations of collective action.

The culturalist model is part of the broader, cultural turn in the social sciences, but it also had social-psychological roots and led to a revived interest in Erving Goffman's important 1974 book, *Frame Analysis: An Essay on the Organization of Experience.* Cultural factors were also important to scholars of contention in the global South, where the cultural grounding of Western social movements could not be assumed. By the turn of the century, the culturalist approach had developed into a wholesale critique of structuralism.

The rationalist model has in common with culturalism a focus on individual motivations for collective action, but it had in common with structuralism a focus on external inducements to collective action. Building on the earlier insights of Mancur Olson in 1965, rationalists observed that rational people might very well avoid taking action when they see that others are willing to act on their behalf. To solve this *free-rider problem,* rationalist-oriented scholars focused on the microfoundations of collective action, on movement organizations, and on the social networks that underlie collective action. What remained obscure in both culturalism and rationalism were the specific links between individuals and their opposite numbers, significant third parties, and institutions. This led to an increased emphasis on relational models.

MECHANISM-AND-PROCESS APPROACHES

Mechanism-and-process-based accounts of contentious politics attempt to specify links among actors, their opponents, third parties, and institutions in studies of entire episodes of contention. Relevant mechanisms can be found in the general environment of the actors, in actors' dispositions toward significant others, or in their relations to significant others. Familiar environmental mechanisms include population shift or resource increase or depletion. Important dispositional mechanisms include the attribution of similarity (e.g., identification of another political actor as belonging to the same category as one's own, a key mechanism in coalition formation). Significant relational mechanisms include brokerage (e.g., the production of a new connection between previously unconnected or weakly connected sites). Processes can be either combinations of simultaneously developing mechanisms or regularly linked sequences of mechanisms.

Some combinations of mechanisms are fortuitous or idiosyncratic, but others combine regularly in robust processes that can be observed in a wide variety of contentious episodes. The most fundamental one is mobilization, or the shift of resources from individuals to collectivities through a combination of mechanisms.

MOVEMENTS AND INSTITUTIONS

In relating contentious politics to institutions, an earlier research tradition saw all political contention aimed against institutions. But properly seen, contention can occur outside of, within, and on the boundaries of institutions. Boundaries between institutionalized and noninstitutionalized politics are difficult to draw with precision. More important, the two sorts of politics involve similar causal processes. For example, the study of coalitions has almost always been operationalized

within legislative institutions, but coalitions occur widely in the disruptions of rebellions, strikes, and social movements. As long as the same mechanisms and processes can be identified in institutional and noninstitutional politics, they can be studied together irrespective of institutional boundaries.

Of course, institutions both constrain and enable contentious politics, and, subsequently, different kinds of regimes produce different configurations of contention. These connections among contention, political power, and institutions appear in both turbulent periods and in the more routine politics of both authoritarian regimes and settled democracies. However, the more violent forms of contention are most likely to develop in weak authoritarian regimes, or *anocracies,* as termed by James D. Fearon and David D. Laitin in 2003.

LETHAL CONFLICTS

Civil wars and most revolutions involve large-scale lethal conflicts with special features that set them off from other forms of contentious politics. Two features in particular make

The police detain a man who attempted to confront protestors during a 2007 rally in Chechnya marking the anniversary of the death of Chechen rebel leader Aslan Maskhadov. The Chechen conflict represents a large-scale lethal conflict with high stakes.

SOURCE: AP Images

a difference. First, killing, wounding, and damaging affect the survival of participants well after the immediate struggle has ended. Second, creating and maintaining armed force requires extensive resources. Large-scale lethal conflicts include inter-state wars, civil wars, revolutions, and genocides as well as a significant subset of struggles across religious, ethnic, linguistic, and regional boundaries. All of these involve high stakes and disciplined military organizations.

Yet there are significant commonalities between lethal conflicts and social movements. As in these more pacific conflicts, existing political opportunity structure interacts with established repertoires of contention to shape what sorts and degrees of large-scale violence occur within a given regime. When large-scale lethal contention is compared with social movements, similar mechanisms and processes emerge: environmental mechanisms, such as resource extraction or depletion; dispositional mechanisms, such as the hardening of boundaries between ethnic groups that formally lived together; and relational mechanisms, such as the brokerage of new connections between previously unconnected or weakly connected sites.

In contrast with social movements, which concentrate in high-capacity democratic or democratizing states, lethal conflicts concentrate in low-capacity authoritarian states. High-capacity states reduce the threat from challengers both by offering routine opportunities for making low-level claims and by making it difficult for anyone to create rival concentrations of coercive means within their territories. Low-capacity states fear that making concessions to low-level claims will trigger broader ones. They also more often face the threat that some rival actor will build up a major concentration of coercive means and use it to topple existing rulers.

OPEN QUESTIONS
As in any evolving field, a number of contested issues score the surface of the study of contentious politics. A brief sketch of the most important questions include:

• Do social movements that do not target the state fall outside the range of contentious politics?

• Are the major outcomes of contentious politics limited to the policy terrain, or do they also involve cultural change and biographical impacts?

• Do new forms of collective action—particularly Internet-based campaigns—challenge existing approaches to contentious politics, or will they eventually be absorbed into the repertoire of contention, much as the newspaper and television were?

• Does globalization shift the targets of contention from national states to something beyond the state, or does it simply add the possibility of "forum shopping" to claim-making strategies?

See also *Civil Wars; Collective Action, Theory of; Collective Action and Mobilization; Protests and Demonstrations; Olson, Mancur; Revolutions; Social Movements; Structuralism.*

. . . . SIDNEY TARROW

BIBLIOGRAPHY
Aminzade, Ron, and Doug McAdam. "Emotions in Contentious Politics." In *Silence and Voice in the Study of Contentious Politics,* edited by Ron Aminzade, Jack A. Goldstone, Doug McAdam, Elizabeth J. Perry, William H. Sewell Jr., Sidney Tarrow, Douglas McAdam, and Charles Tilly. New York: Cambridge University Press, 2001.

Bates, Robert H., Avner Greif, Margaret Levi, and Jean-Laurent Rosenthal. *Analytic Narratives.* Princeton: Princeton University Press, 1998.

Chong, Dennis. *Collective Action and the Civil Rights Movement.* Chicago: University of Chicago Press, 1991.

della Porta, Donatella. *Social Movements, Political Violence, and the State: A Comparative Analysis of Italy and Germany.* New York: Cambridge University Press, 1995.

Diani, Mario. *Green Networks: A Structural Analysis of the Italian Environmental Movement.* Edinburgh: Edinburgh University Press, 1995.

Fearon, James D., and David D. Laitin. "Ethnicity, Insurgency, and Civil War." *American Political Science Review* 97 (2003): 91–106.

Gamson, William. "Political Discourse and Collective Action." In *From Structure to Action: Comparing Social Movement Research Across Cultures,* edited by Bert Klandermans, Hanspeter Kriesi, and Sidney Tarrow, 219–244. Greenwich, Conn: JAI Press, 1988.

Goldstone, Jack, and Charles Tilly. "Threat and Opportunity." In *Silence and Voice in the Study of Contentious Politics,* edited by Ron Aminzade, Jack A. Goldstone, Doug McAdam, Elizabeth J. Perry, William H. Sewell Jr., Sidney Tarrow, Douglas McAdam, and Charles Tilly. New York: Cambridge University Press, 2001.

Goffmann, Erving. *Frame Analysis: An Essay on the Organization of Experience.* Cambridge, Mass.: Harvard University Press, 1974.

Goodwin, Jeff, and James Jasper, eds. *Rethinking Social Movements: Structure, Meaning, and Emotion.* Lanham, Md.: Rowman and Littlefield, 2004.

Klandermans, Bert. "Mobilization and Participation in a Social Movement: Social Psychological Expansions of Resource Mobilization Theory." *American Sociological Review* 49 (1984): 583–600.

Kriesi, Hanspeter, Ruud Koopmans, Jan Willem Duyvendak, and Marco G. Giugni. *New Social Movements in Western Europe: A Comparative Analysis.* Minneapolis: University of Minnesota Press, 1995.

McAdam, Doug. *Political Process and the Development of Black Insurgency, 1930–1970,* 2nd ed. Chicago: University of Chicago Press, 1999.

McAdam, Doug, Sidney Tarrow, and Charles Tilly. *Dynamics of Contention.* New York: Cambridge University Press, 2001.

McCarthy, John, and Mayer N. Zald. "Resource Mobilization and Social Movements: A Partial Theory." *American Journal of Sociology* 82 (1977): 1212–1241.

Melucci, Alberto. "Getting Involved." In *From Structure to Action: Comparing Social Movement Research Across Cultures,* edited by Bert Klandermans, Hanspeter Kriesi, and Sidney Tarrow. Greenwich, Conn.: JAI Press, 1988.

Olson, Mancur, Jr. *The Logic of Collective Action.* Cambridge, Mass.: Harvard University Press, 1965.

Piven, Frances Fox, and Richard Cloward. *Poor People's Movements: Why They Succeed; How They Fail.* New York: Vintage, 1977.

Rochon, Thomas R., and David S. Meyer, eds. *Coalitions and Political Movements: The Lessons of the Nuclear Freeze.* Boulder: Lynne Reinner, 1988.

Rucht, Dieter, ed. *Research on Social Movements: The State of the Art in Western Europe and the USA.* Frankfurt/Boulder: Campus Verlag/Westview Press, 1991.

Rucht, Dieter, Ruud Koopmans, and Friedhelm Neidhardt, eds. *Acts of Dissent: New Developments in the Study of Protest.* Lanham, Md.: Rowman and Littlefield, 1999.

Sambanis, Nicholas. "What is a Civil War? Conceptual and Empirical Complexities of an Operational Definition." *Journal of Conflict Resolution* 48 (2004): 814–858.

Scott, James. *Weapons of the Weak: Everyday Forms of Peasant Resistance.* New Haven: Yale University Press, 1985.

Smelser, Neil. *A Theory of Collective Behavior.* New York: Free Press, 1962.

Snow, David A., E. Burke Rochford Jr., Steven K. Worden, and Robert D. Benford. "Frame Alignment Processes, Micromobilization, and Movement Participation." *American Sociological Review* 51 (1986): 464–481.

Tilly, Charles. *European Revolutions, 1492–1992.* Oxford: Blackwell, 1993.
———. *From Mobilization to Revolution.* Reading, Mass.: Addison-Wesley, 1978.
———. *The Politics of Collective Violence.* New York: Cambridge University Press, 2003.
———. *Popular Contention in Great Britain, 1758–1834.* Cambridge, Mass.: Harvard University Press, 1995.
Tilly, Charles, and Sidney Tarrow. *Contentious Politics.* Boulder: Paradigm Press, 2006.

Contractarianism

Contractarianism is a theory of the development of social institutions and political morality based on the consent of free and equal people. It is primarily associated with both the descriptive and prescriptive elements of liberal political theory. Descriptively, it aims to explain the origins of political authority and why people form political communities. Prescriptively, contractarianism provides an account of the legitimate functions of the state and the conditions of political obligations. Its most well-known historical exponents are Thomas Hobbes, John Locke, and Jean-Jacques Rousseau. Its contemporary adherents include John Rawls and David Gauthier.

Contractarianism is an egalitarian approach to political morality because all individual interests are taken into account in the bargaining process. It provides a conventional view of politics and justice in which the state is created to advance individual interests, and it contrasts with naturalistic or organic accounts of politics. Despite these foundations, contractualists differ significantly as to the legitimate functions of the state and the extent of one's obligations in political society. Contractarianism is also the subject of significant critical treatment, including pluralist, associative, and feminist theories of political morality.

Contractualists theorize social cooperation and political institutions as systems of mutual advantage because rational people can be expected to consent only to arrangements from which they benefit. According to Hobbes, life without political institutions is insecure, violent, and underdeveloped. Sovereign individuals pursuing their own interests will inevitably come into conflict with one another, and without a coercive third party, find themselves in a ceaseless "war of all against all." In time, their interests and rationality will lead them to form a contract among each other to mutually transfer their natural rights to self-preservation, creating the sovereign state charged with maintaining the conditions of social peace. For Hobbes, the contract is constitutive of society, politics, property, and justice; it is also the precondition of people's capacities to pursue any human goods beyond survival. However, Hobbes's theory is not fully liberal because the social contract creates an absolute state as opposed to a constitutionally limited state.

Locke's state of nature, in contrast to Hobbes, is a much more developed situation and comes to include a fully functioning market economy. It is only after time, as inequality deepens and property becomes less secure, that individuals enter a social contract to create political authority to avoid the inconveniences of the state of nature. However, because individuals enter into the social contract in unequal circumstances, the contract solidifies differences in advantages by

protecting preexisting natural property rights. In this respect, contractarianism is widely criticized for unduly reflecting baseline inequalities in terms of social cooperation. It is seen as a mutually advantageous agreement between producers that leaves nonproducers and those lacking a threat capacity, such as the severely disabled, to the system of production outside the scope of political justice. However, not all contractualists understand the social contract in this way and seek to broaden its scope and transformative effects.

Rousseau's social contract criticizes the design of Locke's contract, which protects natural property rights and locks in initial advantage. Rousseau's contract is more deeply transformative. He argues that the social contract cannot attempt to preserve the freedom humans experienced in the state of nature as isolated and independent individuals, rather it must reconcile the "chains" of a coercive political society with a new sort of social freedom. To be free in society, people must subsume their individual wills to a common or general will, which is the outcome of a contract or an agreement among others. Sovereignty is created when people contract together to create a general will that concerns the common good. When a person disagrees with the general will, this individual is, in fact, mistaken and must be made to conform to its precepts. In reconciling social rules and coercion with individual liberty through the social contract, Rousseau famously suggests people can be "forced to be free."

John Rawls's version of the contract also seeks to eliminate initial bargaining advantages in shaping political agreement. Rawls's contract is explicitly hypothetical and imagines people seeking agreement on principles of justice in the "original position." In the original position, people deliberate behind a "veil of ignorance" such that they know nothing of their own personal traits, including their gender, ethnicity, capacities, or social class. This situation creates an equal baseline and compels impartial reasoning. From this contracting position, Rawls argues that people will agree on strong egalitarian and redistributive principles of justice.

See also *General Will; Hobbes, Thomas; Locke, John; Rawls, John; Rousseau, Jean-Jacques; Social Contract; State of Nature.*

. . . .   NEIL HIBBERT

BIBLIOGRAPHY
Gauthier, David. *Morals by Agreement.* Oxford: Oxford University Press, 1986.
Hobbes, Thomas. *Leviathan,* edited with an introduction by J. C. A. Gaskin. Oxford: Oxford University Press, 1996.
Locke, John. *Second Treatise of Government,* edited with an introduction by C. B. Macpherson. Indianapolis: Hackett Publishing, 1980.
Rawls, John. *A Theory of Justice.* Cambridge: Belknap Press, 1971.
Rousseau, Jean-Jacques. "On the Social Contract." In *The Basic Political Writings,* translated by Donald Cress. Indianapolis: Hackett Publishing, 1987.

Convenience Voting

Convenience voting is the term used to describe the broad array of methods used in contemporary democracies to make it easier for citizens to cast ballots. Types of convenience voting include absentee voting (and no-excuse absentee voting), early in-person voting, voting by mail, and various forms of electronic voting, such as voting by fax or Internet. An increasing number of countries also allow same-day voter registration. Convenience voting is perceived as a means to increase voter participation and reduce electoral costs. Opponents of convenience voting have raised concerns over the potential for voter fraud, and some studies have demonstrated no significant increase in turnout. Critics also contend that convenience voting disproportionately raises participation rates among the wealthier and better educated. Early voting also carries the risk that a major event or candidate problem could occur after citizens has cast their ballots but before the general election. Nonetheless, most developed democracies have adopted some form of convenience voting. For instance, Estonia utilized Internet voting in its 2007 parliamentary elections. Within the United States, most states utilize at least one form of convenience voting. For instance, following a 1998 referendum, Oregon initiated a system in which all elections are conducted by mail.

See also *Absentee Voting; E-governance, E-voting, E-Democracy, E-Politics; Electronic Voting; Voting Machines and Technology.*

. . . . TOM LANSFORD

Convergence Theory

The central questions for students of convergence begin with whether, after centuries of industrialization, currently rich countries become more alike in social structure, culture, and politics. If they converged, the specific ways that they became alike are then pondered, followed by explanations for deviations from the common patterns. In this theory, the driving force that moves modern societies toward common structures, values, and beliefs is continuing industrialization. *Industrialization* is defined as the increasing and widespread use of tools that multiply the effects of their initial applications of energy and inanimate sources of energy.

High-energy technology is similar to how a hoe increases the effects of human energy far more when digging a hole for planting than the stick that preceded it; how a horse-drawn plow continues to multiply the effects of the human hand; how the tractor continues the escalation of effects; and how an atomic bomb can move a mountain, or destroy a city, with a push of one finger. This idea also applies to recent information technology. The same fingers that operated the keyboard for a statistical report using the IBM mainframe of the 1950s can, with the same energy expenditure, now process gargantuan amounts of information—a continuous process of making smaller microprocessors do ever-increasing work. Before the early modern period, with inanimate sources of energy, perhaps 80 to 90 percent of the total energy consumed at any one time was derived from plants, animals, and humans—an intractable limit on their productivity.

The concept of industrialization is most attainable when confined to this technological idea. If all the correlates, along with organizational and demographic outcomes, of industrialization are encompassed in its definition, it cannot be invoked as a cause of the structures, cultures, and political patterns of interest; this is why so much of the early literature on industrialism, based on broader definitions, was tautological. For example, scholars have identified industrialism as including one or more of the following: high degrees of specialization, including the concomitant monetary system of exchange; complex organizations; mechanization; urbanization; extensive use of capital; frequent technological change; rational capital accounting; emergence of a working class; a reasonably predictable political order; demographic transition; and individual work ethics. There is no way to relate the underlying increases in high-energy technology and inanimate sources of power to these variable structures and values if they are all included in the concept. Most of the empirical studies of convergence therefore use the narrow definition, roughly measured by economic level, or gross national product or gross domestic product per capita.

The term *continuing industrialization* captures two essential facts about these technological-economic changes: They cover many centuries and, despite recurrent spurts of growth, they are continuous. A gong did not ring when the industrial revolution began; it was a long and gradual process, and as economic historians reiterate, it has continued since long before the nineteenth century. The High Middle Ages (ca. 1000–1350) saw substantial economic growth and much innovation (e.g., the inanimate power of windmills, invention in armaments, marine transportation and navigation, optics, the mechanical clock).

During the early modern period (ca. 1500–1800), imperial expansion and a global trade network, combined with the spread of literacy among craftsmen and the experimental method among the educated, increased standards of living in the West. Of course, the pace of technological change picked up in the eighteenth and nineteenth centuries, in the period we label the Industrial Revolution, and accelerated markedly after about 1850 wherever science was applied to agriculture and industry.

Finally, convergent tendencies have threshold effects. The process and effects of early industrialization are not the same as the process and effects of later continuing and accelerating industrialization. The threshold for fully modern is about the level of economic development where roughly three-quarters of the modern labor force no longer work in agriculture—due to the extraordinary increases in agricultural productivity—and 40 or 50 percent of adult women work in nondomestic settings. In 1910, the United States still had almost one-third of its labor force in farming. This is about the level where France was in 1946, Japan in the 1950s, and the Soviet Union in the mid-1960s.

CONVERGENT TENDENCIES OF INDUSTRIALIZATION

Nine major structural and demographic shifts, all rooted in industrialization, characterize what is truly modern about modern—*advanced industrial*—society. However, as the range of per capita income from developing to developed countries narrows, sheer levels of well-being fade as an explanation for national differences in structure, culture, politics, and policy. Types of political economy combining party ideology, power, and national bargaining arrangements among major economic interest groups and government explain persistent differences among equally modern nation-states that share these common trends. These convergent tendencies among the currently rich countries ignore differences in timing and concentrate on the amount, pace, and direction of change.

CHANGES IN FAMILY STRUCTURE

For over two centuries, there have been major changes in family size, composition, functions, and lifestyles; these have coincided with associated political demands and elite responses. By separating work from residence and changing the occupational and educational structure, industrialization increases mobility opportunity for both men and women, and inspires rising aspirations among parents for themselves and their children. Convergent tendencies also reduce the economic value of children and increase their cost, giving women both motive and opportunity to enter the nonagricultural labor force. This thereby increases their independence, reducing fertility rates, and increasing family breakup. Convergence also reduces the family's motivation and resources to care for aging parents and to meet the risks of invalidism, sickness, job injuries, and other shocks. The net effect is a dominant family type in industrial society—small and independent. The dramatic population response to rapid economic development, with birth rates and death rates both falling, has earned the label of *demographic transition*.

Declining birthrates and increased longevity are the product of public health measures—sanitation, control of epidemic diseases, better nutrition, and spacing of births—plus increasing access to medical care. The political responses to these structural changes include a mass demand for the welfare state, especially income and care for the aged; a family polity to help facilitate the balance between work and family; and finally, public policies that enhance gender equality. Rich democracies are moving toward the Swedish model, even Japan and Switzerland, the developed countries most resistant to gender equality.

MINORITIES' PUSH FOR EQUALITY ALONGSIDE GOVERNMENTS' INCREASING OPENNESS

Much change has occurred in equality for minorities over the last century, accelerating during and after World War II (1939–1945). Everywhere, discrimination on the basis of race, ethnicity, religion, language, gender, sexual preference, and physical disability has declined. Despite the occasional resurgence of minority-group militancy, structural and cultural integration of minority groups is increasing, even those based on race. Two sources of long-term integration are increased opportunities for education and the work, with the consequent increase in intermarriage. These trends foster some merger of values and tastes.

A recent convergence in social heterogeneity, rooted in a revival of massive migration of economic and political refugees, moves all rich democracies toward the American multicultural model. Yet, as governments respond to the demand for gender equality, the rich democracies move toward models in Scandinavia, however varied their specific policies and speed of response. The increase in equality of educational opportunity facilitates the considerable achievement of minority-group equality and the great changes in women's roles and family structure.

INCREASING EQUALITY IN HIGHER EDUCATION OPPORTUNITIES

For more than a century, education has been the main channel for upward mobility in occupation, income, and social status. The ambivalent mass demand for some combination of absolute equality and equality of opportunity—which often takes the form of demands for affirmative action or quotas for those groups presumed to be deprived—has had little effect on the essential character of higher education. Colleges and universities remain meritocratic, very much attuned to the demands of the economy, and quite vocational in emphasis. Education for alert citizenship and critical thought—for making moral judgments, for the pursuit of wisdom, for the enhancement of capacities of appreciation and performance in the arts, and for broader understanding of the individual in society—all tend to take second place. In recent decades, the laggards in mass higher education have moved toward the leader, the United States, and in a few cases have surpassed it in enrollment ratios. Finally, in response to the intensified demand for skilled or professional labor and the great variety of people to be processed, all rich countries now share the twin trends toward universality, along with specialization of institutions and curricula in higher education.

MASS MEDIA ASCENDANCE

Leaving aside nondemocracies, the convergence of rich democracies toward the American model is evident not only in mass higher education but also in the increased influence of mass communication and entertainment media in politics and culture. Industrialization links to the spread of expensive media technology and organizational forms, and also to the increase in income and leisure that it provides the audience. Despite national differences in the control, financing, and organization of the media, which persisted for decades, there is an unmistakable—recent and swift—convergence toward the commercialization and privatization of public broadcasting with a concomitant but somewhat slower shift toward American style and content. The media is now increasingly competitive, frantic, sensational, negative, aggressively interpretive, and anti-institutional. This talk-show style has itself become dominant in American print and broadcasting media only in roughly the last thirty-five years. In political campaigns, however, convergence toward the American model is quite slow—counterpressures in Europe and Asia that make the United States still exceptional among rich democracies include strong parties; government-assured access to television and radio for parties and candidates; restrictions on ads and the length of campaigns; and the well-financed, year-round public broadcasting news coverage.

INCREASED PREVALENCE AND INFLUENCE OF INTELLECTUALS

Scholars who emphasize changes in the mentality of masses or elites suggest that modernization produces a transformation toward a secular, rational, skeptical outlook. Max Weber, in 1918, spoke of "the disenchantment of the world." With a touch of irony, Joseph Schumpeter in 1942 observed that the abundance of critical, independent intellectuals might undermine the very affluent capitalist order that supports them. Plainly, scientists and intellectuals are a double-edged sword: Modern society evidences not only rational secular bureaucratic tendencies, but also periodic resurgence of backlash movements and parties among the losers and their ideological leaders (e.g., the creationist movement in the United States or the Christian right and Southern takeover of the Republican Party and its associated think tanks). In almost all of the most developed countries, populist-right protest movements and parties—sectarian religious, ethnic linguistic, or nativist—abound. The question for research is whether their incidence and influence increase or remain peripheral and cyclical.

SOCIAL STRATIFICATION AND MOBILITY

Continuing industrialization shapes social stratification—the class structure—and mobility in several ways. It blurs older class lines and creates increasing social, cultural, and political heterogeneity within each social class; the internal differences within classes then become greater than differences between them. Continuing industrialization also fosters the emergence of a politically restive *middle mass*—in the upper-working class or lower-middle class—whose behavior, values, beliefs, and tastes increasingly differ from those of the privileged college-educated, upper-middle class, the very rich above them, and the poor below. Increasing mobility adds to the heterogeneity of social classes. At every level, the mobile population and those with mobility aspirations contrast sharply with the nonmobile population at the same socioeconomic status. Finally, the persistence and even slight growth in the urban self-employed portion of the labor force—people who live in a separate world—adds another source of heterogeneity within each class.

In short, convergence theory exceeds explanations based on social class, however measured. Convergence in mass education and occupational structures; related increases in mobility among all rich countries; and multiple ladders for achieving income, status, or power all allow explanations for the behavior of modern populations of almost any major source of social differentiation. Although all affluent countries share these trends in class structure, they differ greatly in the cross-class solidarity fostered by labor-left parties and groups, and in the percentage of working and nonworking poor.

THE ORGANIZATION OF WORK

With all its variety within and across nations, the technical and social organization of work is still an area of convergence. Continuing industrialization brought a steady decline in annual average hours of work from the late nineteenth century up to about 1960, with a divergence since then as the long annual-hours countries like Japan and the United States reduced hours only slightly, while the short-hours countries like Germany, the Netherlands, and Norway continued their penchant for leisure. Within nations, the uneven distribution of work increased in recent decades; the most educated groups intensified their labor, while the rest of the population typically continued to reduce average annual hours, or suffered forced leisure. There has recently been a gradual spread of nonstandard work schedules, especially among women; and a sizable, rapid growth of contingent labor—part-time, temporary, or subcontracted work—equating to a source of widespread insecurity.

As for modern society becoming a *high-tech* or *postindustrial society*, evaluation of occupational and industrial trends shows that the vast majority of modern populations work in low-tech or no-tech jobs and that almost all of the large and fastest growing occupations are anything but high-tech positions.

GROWTH OF THE WELFARE STATE

For more than a century, since Bismarck in Germany, there has been gradual institutionalization of the social and labor market programs comprising the welfare state. The essence of the welfare state is government-protected minimum standards of income, nutrition, health and safety, education, and housing assured to every citizen as social right, not as charity. In the abstract, this is an ideal embraced by both political leaders and the mass of people in every affluent country, but in practice it becomes expensive enough and evokes enough ambivalence to become the center of political combat about taxes, spending, and the proper role of government in the economy. Because the welfare state is about shared risks that cross generations, localities, classes, ethnic and racial groups, and educational levels, it is a major source of social integration in modern society. Because it lends a measure of stability to household incomes, it has been an important stabilizer of the economy in the downswings of the business cycle, especially since World War II. Developing and developed countries, whatever the type of regime or elite motives, all move in this direction.

CHANGES IN THE POLITY

At first glance, change in the polity is an area of least convergence; a high level of economic development may not be a decisive determinant of political systems. But the first eight areas of most convergence may well foster some convergence in polities. Among the most solid findings in the literature of comparative politics are that affluence brings a decline in civil violence, a decline in coercion as a means of rule, an increase in persuasion and manipulation, an increase in pluralism, and less surely, an increase in democracy. All democracies focus on the market, though all market-oriented political economies are not democracies.

Economic development at the level of the rich democracies brings a sharp decline in internal collective political violence, and even a decline in the intensity of peaceful demonstrations. The most extensive analysis of this relationship, carried out by Ted Robert Gurr and published in his 1979 article "Political

Protest and Rebellion in the 1960s," covers the extent and intensity of civil conflict at three levels of economic development in eighty-seven countries. The first finding is that the higher the standard of living, the less deadly and extensive is civil conflict, but there may be a curvilinear relationship between economic level and collective political violence. The twenty-nine most violent countries are poor but not the poorest; they have begun a process of industrialization. Somewhat less violent are countries at very low and medium levels of development, and the twenty-nine richest countries are by far the least violent. The old idea that political violence and militant labor protest intensifies during the painful transformation of early industrialization from rural to urban, and from peasant to dependent industrial or service worker, is confirmed.

The second finding is that at low levels of development, personal dictatorships and modernizing oligarchies alike provoke the most civil violence. In contrast, the twenty-one pluralist regimes and the eight formerly communist regimes at relatively high levels of economic development yield the very least civil violence. Three forces are at work among the richer countries. Pluralist and democratic systems channel mass grievances and group protest into electoral politics while delivering abundant material benefits; communist or other centrist authoritarian regimes could keep the lid on for decades by comprehensive agencies of political and social control, including one-party domination of secret police, armed forces, mass media, schools, and workplaces.

Students of comparative politics have established that all democracies have market economies. Historically, liberal constitutional systems—the United States, Britain, and France—were established mainly to win and protect private property, free enterprise, free contract, and residential and occupational choice against government restrictions, not to achieve broad popular participation in governance. In the development of the older democracies, this emphasis on liberty to engage in trade was more prominent than the idea of equality of participation in selecting leaders. The expansion of civil liberties, the suffrage, and the rule of law in these countries was preceded or at least accompanied by the expansion of institutions supporting free markets. Yet, again, all market economies are not democracies. For instance, in periods following World War II, South Korea, Taiwan, Chile, Yugoslavia, Spain, Portugal, and Argentina were authoritarian and market oriented. To say that all the currently rich democracies have market economies does not say much about convergence, because democracies relying on the market vary greatly in the institutions in which markets are embedded—in the legal, political, economic, and social context in which finance, industry, labor, the professions, agencies of the executive, the judiciary, and the legislative interact and shape market transactions.

The interplay between modernization, markets, and democracy is complex and does not reflect any straight-line trend. Historically, as Samuel Huntington notes, democracy advanced in waves from early nineteenth century until now, and each wave was followed by reversals and new gains. Sometimes the reversals were drastic. Thus, several of the worst cases

of totalitarian or fascist rule emerged in relatively advanced industrializing societies—Hitler's Germany, Mussolini's Italy, Austria, Czechoslovakia, and Hirohito's Japan. Happily, both for democratic values and convergence theory, each reversal did not undo all previous gains: The net number of democracies by Huntington's reckoning went from zero before 1828 to fifty-nine in 1990. They are not, though, all rich or near rich, because the number includes poor Bangladesh, India, Costa Rica, Uruguay, and Botswana. It is clear, however, that the central tendency is for successfully industrializing countries to become more pluralistic and even more democratic as they become wealthier—for example, the cases of South Korea, Taiwan, Chile, Mexico, and South Africa. These countries may represent the threshold beyond which changing social structures rooted in industrialization strongly favor pluralism, and even some authoritarian regimes tolerate a few autonomous groups and limited cultural freedom. Among the relevant changes are the dominant convergent tendencies: growing middle- and upper-middle strata; accommodation of the minority-group thrust for equality; mobility out of the working class; rise of professionals and experts; growth of the welfare state; and the spread of commerce and industry, both of which require a rule of law.

Whatever the intermediate links between economic level and democracy, the two strongly correlate. Thus, the authoritarian countries that are mostly successful making the move to democracy were overwhelmingly middle income, moving toward upper-middle income. The strong causal relationship very likely runs from economic development to democracy, and not the other way round.

The level of economic development and its structural and demographic correlates help explain why democratic regimes in Greece, Portugal, and Spain by the 1980s, and the Czech Republic, the former East Germany, and Hungary by the late 1990s, successfully consolidated after their authoritarian regimes collapsed and why the transition to democracy has been so problematic in the less developed countries of Central and Latin America (except for Uruguay), and even worse in the poorer countries of Eastern Europe, including Romania, Bulgaria, Albania, and Serbia.

Ethnic warfare can further complicate the democratic transition, as it has in the former states of the Soviet Union and Yugoslavia, both of which also delivered drastic declines in standards of living. Consistent with convergence theory, however, it is the less developed countries in which ethnic conflict is most virulent and violent, especially where feeble authoritarian regimes face ethnonational rebellions, as in Bosnia, Georgia, Rwanda, and Haiti. In the early 1990s, there were about 120 shooting wars going on in the world, 90 of which involved states attempting to suppress ethnic minorities. None were among the rich democracies. In fact, economic development at above average levels and democratization together always channel such movements into nonviolent politics.

Rich democracies have both economic strength and a high degree of legitimacy—resources to use for any aspect of social peace. As Arend Lijphart suggests, dominant "majorities" do this by sharing power (coalitions), dispersing power (bicameralism and multiparty systems), distributing power more fairly (proportional representation in its various forms), delegating power (federalism), and limiting power formally (minority veto). The mix of these electoral and constitutional arrangements varies, but all modern democracies have found ways toward minority and majority accommodation. Some form of affirmative action in assignment of jobs, political positions, or college admissions is also common, although specific government policies vary. Finally, an obvious and well-traveled road to social peace is expansion of the franchise and a well-developed, universalistic welfare state.

DEMOCRATIC TRANSITION AND CONTEMPORARY RESEARCH

Research on the breakdown, emergence, or consolidation of democracy is a growth industry. Among scholars analyzing lengthy lists of conditions favorable to the democratic transition, such as Huntington, all note the importance of economic level or material conditions for the emergence and the consolidation of democracy. However, they all offer a list of noneconomic determinants of uncertain relative importance. Major contributors to knowledge in this area include S. M. Lipset, Robert Dahl, John Stephens, Larry Diamond, and Juan Linz and Alfred Stepan.

Among social scientists, convergence or modernization theory was most popular in the 1940s through the mid-1960s when it went out of fashion. But it has recently been revived. The scholars who early articulated these ideas include Wilbert Moore; Daniel Lerner; Neil Smelser; Clark Kerr and colleagues; Samuel Huntington; and, on the social psychological correlates of economic development, Alex Inkeles. A chorus of criticism emerged in response. Students of the organization of work, such as Ronald Dore and Reinhard Bendix, emphasized the national and sectoral variations in authority relationships in the workplace and society. Many political critics, including André Gunder Frank, emphasized what they saw as the Eurocentric or North America–centric, or the conservative bias, of convergence theory. Emmanuel Wallerstein, in 1974, counterposed the idea of a world system dominated by a core of imperial capitalist states including the United States; others, like Peter Evans in 1979, accented the related theme of dependent development. A few critics allege that convergence theorists ignore politics; they forget that theorists and critics are not contending camps at war—economic determinists versus political or social determinists. In fact, the most systematic and creative work in this area deals with the interplay of markets and politics (political economy) or the social bases of politics (political sociology) or both. The trick is to learn how much of the explanation of outcomes is attributable to industrialization and how much to alternative theories, including variation in political and social organization. Using both quantitative and comparative historical methods, much recent research does exactly that, for example the less polemical students of varieties of capitalism, including Peter Hall and David Soskice. Indeed, many contemporary scholars such as Ruth and David Collier, John Stephens,

and Harold Wilensky focus fruitfully on the interaction of economic and noneconomic forces shaping diverse paths of development among nations and regions of the world—a continuing challenge for researchers today.

See also *Democracies, Advanced Industrial; Democratic Transition; Equality and Inequality; Industrial Democracy; Postindustrial Society; Welfare State.*

. . . .   HAROLD L. WILENSKY

BIBLIOGRAPHY

Bendix, Reinhard. *Work and Authority in Industry: Ideologies of Management in the Course of Industrialization.* New York: John Riley, 1956.

Collier, Ruth Berins, and David Collier. *Shaping the Political Arena: Critical Junctures, the Labor Movement, and Regime Dynamics in Latin America.* Princeton: Princeton University Press, 1991.

Dahl, Robert A. *Democracy and Its Critics.* New Haven: Yale University Press, 1989.

———. "Some Explanations." In *Political Oppositions in Western Democracies,* edited by R. A. Dahl, 348–386. New Haven: Yale University Press, 1966.

Diamond, Larry. "Economic Development and Democracy Reconsidered." *American Behavioral Scientist* 35, 4–5 (1992): 450–499.

Dore, Ronald. *Flexible Rigidities: Industrial Policy and Structural Adjustment in the Japanese Economy, 1970–80.* London: Athlone, 1986.

Evans, Peter B. *Dependent Development: The Alliance of Multinational, State and Local Capital in Brazil.* Princeton: Princeton University Press, 1979.

Frank, Andre Gunder. *Capitalism Under Development in Latin America.* New York: Monthly Review Press, 1967.

Gurr, Ted Robert. "Political Protest and Rebellion in the 1960s: The U.S. in World Perspective." In *Violence in America,* edited by Hugh Davis Graham and Ted Robert Gurr, 49–76. London: Sage Publications, 1979.

Hall, Peter A., and David Soskice, eds. *Varieties of Capitalism: The Institutional Foundations of Comparative Advantage.* Oxford: Oxford University Press, 2001.

Huntington, Samuel P. *The Third Wave: Democratization in the Late Twentieth Century.* Norman: University of Oklahoma Press, 1991.

Inkeles, Alex, and David Smith. *Becoming Modern: Individual Change in Six Developing Countries.* Cambridge, Mass.: Harvard University Press, 1974.

Kerr, Clark, Frederick H. Harbison, John T. Dunlop, and Charles A. Myers. *Industrialism and Industrial Man: The Problem of Labor and Management in Economic Growth.* Cambridge, Mass.: Harvard University Press, 1960.

Lerner, Daniel. *The Passing of Traditional Society: Modernizing the Middle East.* Glencoe, Ill: Free Press, 1958.

Lijphart, Arend. *Democracies: Patterns of Majoritarian and Consensus Government in Twenty-One Countries.* New Haven: Yale University Press, 1984.

Lindblom, Charles E. *Politics and Markets: The World's Political Economic Systems.* New York: Basic Books, 1977.

Lipset, Seymour Martin. "The Social Requisites of Democracy Revisited." *American Sociological Review* 59 (1994): 1–22.

Moore, Barrington, Jr. *Social Origins of Dictatorship and Democracy.* Cambridge, Mass.: Harvard University Press, 1966.

Moore, Wilbert E. *Industrialization and Labor: Social Aspects of Economic Development.* Ithaca: Cornell University Press, 1951.

O'Donnell, Guillermo, and Philippe C. Schmitter. *Transitions from Authoritarian Rule: Tentative Conclusions about Uncertain Democracies.* Baltimore: John Hopkins University Press, 1986.

Przeworski, Adam. *Democracy and the Market: Political and Economic Reforms in Eastern Europe and Latin America.* Cambridge: Cambridge University Press, 1991.

Rueschemeyer, Dietrich, Evelyne Huber Stephens, and John D. Stephens. *Capitalist Development and Democracy.* Chicago: University of Chicago Press, 1992.

Schumpeter, Joseph A. *Capitalism, Socialism, and Democracy.* New York: Harper and Brothers, 1942.

Smelser, Neil. *Social Change in the Industrial Revolution.* Chicago: University of Chicago Press, 1959.

Stephens, John D. "Democratic Transition and Breakdown in Western Europe, 1870–1939: A Test of the Moore Thesis." *American Journal of Sociology* 94, no. 5 (1989): 1019–1077.

Wallerstein, Immanuel. *The Modern World System: Capitalist Agriculture and the Origins of the World Economy in Sixteenth Century.* New York: Academic Press, 1974.

Weber, Max. "Science as a Vocation." In *From Max Weber: Essays in Sociology,* translated by H. H. Gerth and C. Wright Mills, 129–158. Oxford University Press, 1946.

Wilensky, Harold L. *The "New Corporatism," Centralization, and the Welfare State.* London: Sage Publications, 1976.

———. *Rich Democracies: Political Economy, Public Policy, and Performance.* Berkeley: University of California Press, 2002.

Cooperation, International

See *International Cooperation.*

Cooperative Security

The concept of *cooperative security* arose in the United States during the later stages of the cold war period as it became apparent that the Soviet Union under Mikhail Gorbachev was not as inclined to imperial aggression as had been earlier assumed. Although Soviet forces in East Central Europe were evidently configured to attempt to occupy Western Europe in the event of war, it was conceded that such a posture could reflect an underlying intention not to initiate war, but simply to defend Soviet territory in a manner informed by the experience of World War II (1939–1945). If so, then it might be possible to stabilize the situation by negotiating measures designed to prevent surprise attack. These were officially termed *confidence-building measures,* but the phrase *cooperative security* was used as an expression of the underlying principle, namely, that each side would cede the legitimacy of territorial defense and would cooperate to impose restraint on offensive operations.

With the dissolution of the Soviet Union and its alliance system, the original focus of concern essentially disappeared. A combined arms assault was no longer possible on continental scale, and the engagement of nuclear weapons in such an event was no longer the potential trigger for global catastrophe it was once considered to be. Primary security concerns shifted to more localized forms of conflict and to the process of weapons proliferation. In particular, it was recognized that the Russian Federation as principal successor to the Soviet Union had inherited a nearly intractable set of security burdens—most notably, a contracting economy that could not support the remnants of Soviet conventional forces redeployed from East Central Europe, deterrent forces still actively engaged with the increasingly more capable American forces, and a fractured system for exercising managerial control over the massive arsenal of nuclear weapons the Soviet Union had assembled.

In this new context, the Carnegie Corporation of New York, a leading American foundation, initiated a special project to address the problems of nuclear weapons proliferation with the burdens of the Russian Federation specifically in mind. The initiative was inspired by the president of the foundation, David Hamburg, and by Sam Nunn, a U.S. senator from Georgia, with cooperative security explicitly advanced as the central concept of the project. The phrase connoted not merely a stabilization of residual confrontation but a fundamental transformation of security relationships whereby all governments, the Russian Federation and the United States in particular, would collaborate in assuring the legitimate defense of sovereign territory by measures designed to preclude attack, and in establishing higher standards of managerial control over the large arsenals of nuclear weapons and stockpiles of explosive isotopes that had accumulated during the cold war.

The practical effect of the Carnegie project was significant but more limited than the cooperative security concept envisaged. The project was directly instrumental in initiating and developing what came to be known as the Nunn-Lugar program through which the United States provided financial and technical assistance to the Russian Federation to secure some portion of the nuclear weapons, explosive materials, and delivery systems deactivated from the inherited Soviet arsenal. From 1991 to 2007 as the United States provided some $1.8 billion in financial assistance, approximately twenty-five hundred weapons delivery systems were jointly deactivated, and collaborative projects were undertaken at nearly all permanent installations involved in the operations of Russian nuclear forces. Originally administered by the U.S. Department of Defense, the scope of the effort grew to include programs managed by the Department of Energy, the Department of State, and other U.S. government agencies. The accomplishments of the program were nonetheless limited by the fact that fundamental security policy in both countries featured indefinite continuation of legacy deterrent practices, with decreasing emphasis in the United States on bilateral legal regulation and increasing emphasis on preemptive potential. Although the size of the U.S. deterrent force was reduced, it still preserved enough firepower on immediately available alert status to decimate the Russian Federation and to threaten the retaliatory capability of its deterrent forces. That operational fact preserved confrontation as the dominant security principle and limited the scope for direct cooperation.

In the academic literature, cooperative security was recognized as a departure from the self-styled realist perspective on security, which holds that national interests immutably conflict and can only be assured by superior military power—a perspective that appears to require the advantages that only the United States has recently enjoyed. With varying degrees of politeness, realist theorists rejected the cooperative security idea as indefinitely impractical in principle. In contrast, an emerging globalist perspective holds that the process of globalization has altered the scale and character of primary threat as well as fundamental interest. The contention is that the massive forms of aggression that have been the traditional concern are very unlikely to occur because no country has either the incentive or the capacity to undertake them. Instead, the primary source of threat is said to come from civil violence and associated terrorism, apparently arising from conditions of endemic economic austerity. Those forms of violence, the argument holds, undermine basic legal order necessary to support global economic performance and thereby threaten the dominant common interest all countries have in assuring their own economic performance. If so, then cooperation for mutual protection can be expected to emerge as the primary imperative of security policy, even for the United States.

It may take some time before the viability and endurance of the cooperative security idea can be reliably judged. Both its conceptual and its practical standing appear to depend on the eventual fate of the realist and the globalist perspectives—a contest that, at least in the United States, is yet to be decided.

See also *Cold War; Nuclear Proliferation and Nonproliferation; Soviet Union, Former.*

. . . . JOHN STEINBRUNER

BIBLIOGRAPHY
Carter, Ashton B., William J. Perry, and John D. Steinbruner. *A New Concept of Cooperative Security.* Washington, D.C.: Brookings Institution, 1992.
Goodby, James E. *The Stockholm Conference: Negotiating a Cooperative Security System for Europe.* Washington, D.C.: Center for the Study of Foreign Affairs, 1986.
Nolan, Janne E. *Global Engagement: Cooperation and Security in the 21st Century.* Washington, D.C.: Brookings Institution, 1994.
Posen, Barry R., and Andrew L. Ross. "Competing Visions for U.S. Grand Strategy." *International Security* 21, no. 3 (Winter 1996): 5–53.
Steinbruner, John "Consensual Security." *Bulletin of the Atomic Scientists* 64, no. 1 (2008): 23–27, 55.

Copyright

Copyright prohibits people from copying a wide range of works—music, books, movies photographs, computer code, and so on—without prior permission. By putting restrictions on use, copyright attempts to provide content creators with financial compensation in an effort to ensure they have an incentive and the means to continue creating work in the future. It also helps prompt investment in their works.

Copyright legislation creates intellectual property, which recognizes works as the expression of ideas; it is the physical manifestation that is protected through legislation—not the ideas themselves. The history of copyright is long and has been turbulent at times. The first copyright legislation was the United Kingdom's Statute of Anne passed in 1709, which gave authors control over the use of their work and took some power away from publishers.

INTERNATIONAL COPYRIGHT

Understanding copyright law is complicated as it varies from country to country. However, an international legal system exists to tackle disputes arising from differences in national legislation. International cooperation has been ongoing for more than two hundred years, starting, most notably, with the Berne Convention for the Protection of Literary and Artistic Works in 1886. Today, the World Intellectual Property Organization (WIPO) is tasked with administering international copyright agreements States belonging to the European Union are also subject to copyright regulations at the European level.

Two distinct attitudes toward copyright have emerged and are very much reflected in the evolution of legislation in different countries. On one hand, there is the view that once a work is made available for public consumption, people should have a certain freedom to use it as they please. According to this line of argument, copyright owners should receive only limited control over—and compensation for—use of their work. This view tends to underpin American and British attitudes and legislation toward copyright. On the other hand, there is the view that favors the natural, or moral, right of those who created a work to receive compensation for its every use, and such an attitude is often reflected in European legislation.

NEW CHALLENGES

While it was technological advancement that brought copyright into being, such advancements led to great challenges for owners of copyright. With technology like the printing press and the photocopier, exact copies of works could be reproduced relatively easily. Today, the Internet facilitates the ease of copying, lowering costs and making the process faster. As a result, the unauthorized copying of many works—or piracy—has been on the rise.

In spite of the challenges raised by technology and the concerns of copyright owners over piracy and loss of revenue, technological advancements have also contributed to ease when it comes to the management of copyright. Programs that allow for the legal downloading and purchasing of music not only make work easier to distribute, but also help to ensure that compensation is received when work is accessed. Growing attention has been paid to the development of digital rights management (DRM) strategies because many copyright owners look toward encryption as a means of protecting their work.

The protection of digital work has not been without controversy and complication. Critics claim that some DRM strategies undermine privacy and in some cases even compromise our personal property, as Sony BMG found out when its CDs were found to make computers vulnerable to viruses. DRM has also been frowned upon as it clashes with the fair use doctrine built into the copyright system that allows copyrighted material to be used for specific purposes such as teaching.

The challenges posed by new media prompted copyright owners to call for changes to copyright legislation, and WIPO responded with two Internet treaties in 1996: the WIPO Copyright Treaty and the WIPO Performances and Phonograms Treaty. Individual countries followed with legislative change to implement the measures outlined in the treaties. The United States, for example, passed the Digital Millennium Copyright Act in 1998. As technology continues to evolve, we can anticipate further changes to ensure a balance among the rights of copyright owners, creators, and consumers.

See also *Digital Democracy; Intellectual Property Rights.*

. . . . MARY FRANCOLI

BIBLIOGRAPHY

Gillespie, Tarleton. "Designed to 'Effectively Frustrate': Copyright, Technology and the Agency of Users." *New Media and Society*, 8, no. 4 (2006): 651–669.

Goldstein, Paul. *Copyright's Highway: From Gutenberg to the Celestial Jukebox.* Stanford: Stanford University Press, 2003.

Gurnsey, John. *Copyright Theft.* London: Aslib Gower, 1995.

Kretschmer, Martin. "Trends in Global Copyright." *Global Media and Communication* 1, no. 2 (2005): 231–237.

Litman, Jessica. *Digital Copyright.* New York: Prometheus Books, 2001.

Corporation

Large corporations affect the lives and livelihoods of hundreds of millions of people around the world. They employ a large portion of the world's population, own the rights to most global technology patents, and yield tremendous influence over governments. The history of the modern corporation reflects a continued path towards greater wealth, influence, and international power—a power that critics contend is wielded with little regard to the social, environmental, or public local costs. As such, a variety of advocacy groups, watchdog organizations, and nongovernmental organizations have mobilized against large corporations' intent to force corporate reforms toward more socially and environmentally conscious ends. While for some, social pressures may foreshadow a new age of tempered capitalism and diffuse power, for others, corporate changes are regarded as superficial and do not limit their power or influence nor alter their profit-seeking goals.

BRIEF HISTORY

In many ways, the nature of the corporation parallels the evolving political relationship between the state and the market. In the days of monarchic rule, as seen in sixteenth- and seventeenth-century Europe, the state's economy and resources were regarded as extensions of the state's authority. During this period, a corporation would have to obtain permission from the state to come into existence. In an attempt to curry favor with the monarch to ensure passage of its charter, corporate founders would frame their mission as being in the service of the state while highlighting explicit benefits to the monarch. Describing the role of the corporation during mercantilist time, Frederick Maitland in *Political Theories of the Middle Ages* (1900) noted, "The corporation is, and must be, the creature of the State. Into its nostrils the State must breathe the breath of a fictitious life."

This relationship evolved with philosophical developments in political and economic theory in subsequent centuries. In the eighteenth century, the Scottish Enlightenment philosopher, Adam Smith, extolled the virtues of a self-organizing marketplace unrestricted by the intrusive power of the monarch. Individual liberty within the marketplace was now cast as the necessary component for not only the individual's but the state's greater economic prosperity. While Smith's classical economics did not explicitly extend this concept to corporations, since Smith perceived corporations as a potential risk to market competition, free market advocates and neoclassical economists after him often refer to Smith's ideas to advocate limited government interference within a free marketplace and specifically on corporations. Toward the middle of the nineteenth century, obtaining a corporate charter became a matter of bureaucratic formality no longer contingent on the approval of rulers, and therefore corporations were no longer obligated on serving a goal or public interest for the state.

OPPOSING THEORIES OF THE CORPORATE FIRM

The now dominant neoclassic economic theory has firmly transformed the original role of the corporation and its relationship to the state. The purpose of the firm, as theorized by economist Ronald Coase, is to integrate various production operations into one organization in order to minimize external transaction costs. This pervasive and purely economic view of the corporation has overtaken the originating concept in which the firm should serve the greater goals of society. A purely economic view places little restraint on a corporation's dedication to minimize costs and increase shareholder wealth, encouraging the unbridled expansion of these integral organs of capitalism. The largest global corporations have influence spanning the globe, extending beyond economic powers, but exert influence well into international and political spheres. Of the largest one hundred economies in the world, fifty-three are corporations. The largest corporation in 2000 had revenue greater than the GDP of more than 180 countries, according to M. Gabel and H. Bruner in *Global Inc.: An Atlas of the Multinational Corporation*.

Today the relationship between the state and the firm has been described as a special relationship of mutual interdependence. This interdependent relationship between governments and powerful corporations was made evident during the worldwide economic crises during 2008 and 2009, following the housing market collapse. Criticisms were hurled at the U.S. government for bailing out major banks; however, counterarguments stated the large financial institutions were the pillars of the global economy and, if allowed to fail, the United States as well as global markets would suffer greater collective losses. Whereas once the corporation remained solidly under the authority of the state, today's corporations wield tremendous influence among government policy makers and politicians; this causes many to fear these singularly profit-seeking entities are overriding the publicly interested goals of the state.

The controversy surrounding the role of corporations in society can be summarized in two opposing theories of the firm. First, the classical economic or shareholder view of the firm insists on the absolute primacy of profit maximization as the goal of corporations. The well-known quote by economist Milton Friedman in "The Social Responsibility of Business Is to Increase Its Profits" (1970) states, "The social responsibility of business is to increase its profits"—a claim he made in response to the rising tide of another theory of the firm. The competing stakeholder theory does not deny the necessary goal of profit seeking, but insists that beyond the sole interests of shareholders, firms must also consider the interests of every stakeholder group impacted by its operations. The list of stakeholders includes employees, customers, the community within which it operates, and the environment within which it is located.

While these two theories have caused significant debate among scholars, policy makers, and corporate managers as to the actual objectives of a corporation, a simple deduction shows the two theories considerably overlap. When enough people, consumers, and corporate managers believe firms should be sensitive to interests of all stakeholders, it creates an incentive for firms to comply with this normative standard. In other words, adopting the stakeholder theory of corporate behavior may in fact be the best way to meet the goals of the shareholder theory.

NEW HORIZONS

Today we observe the proliferation of corporations engaged in voluntary self-regulation, self-auditing, and various other programs of corporate social responsibility (CSR). Even with little empirical evidence of a direct link between profits and CSR, corporations continue to adopt these practices, according to David Vogel in *The Market for Virtue: The Potential and Limits of Corporate Social Responsibility* (2005). Benjamin Cashore, in his 2002 article "Legitimacy and the Privatization of Environmental Governance," states the emergence of nongovernmental organizations, advocacy groups, corporate watchdog organizations, and nonstate market based governance systems create an institutional network of interests aiming to shift, yet again, the relationship between the corporation and the state. This shift, however, is not identical to the role corporations held centuries earlier, in which they were compelled to serve a role more aligned with larger public interests. While corporations may engage in more social and environmental responsibility, it is not necessarily born out of pressure or negotiations with states, but rather to appease the variety of actors and civil society groups, some of which are active stakeholders.

See also Business Pressure in Politics; Capitalism and Democracy; Economic Interdependence; Multinational Corporation (MNC).

. . . . RABIH HELOU

BIBLIOGRAPHY
Cashore, Benjamin. "Legitimacy and the Privatization of Environmental Governance: How Non-state Market-driven (NSMD) Governance Systems Gain Rule-making Authority." *Governance: An International Journal of Policy, Administration, and Institutions* 15, no. 4 (2002): 503–529.
Frederick W. Maitland. "Introduction." In *Political Theories of the Middle Ages,* edited by Otto von Gierke. Cambridge: Cambridge University Press, 1900.
Gabel, M., and H. Bruner. *Global Inc.: An Atlas of the Multinational Corporation.* New York: W.W. Norton, 2003.
Friedman, Milton. "The Social Responsibility of Business Is to Increase Its Profits," *New York Times Magazine,* September 13, 1970.
Vogel, David. *The Market for Virtue: The Potential and Limits of Corporate Social Responsibility.* Washington, D.C.: Brookings Institution Press, 2005.

Correlation

In political science, two variables are said to correlate when they tend to vary together. More precisely, correlation can be positive if the variables move in the same direction (they both increase or decrease at the same time), or negative if they move in opposite directions (when one variable increases, the other decreases).

In statistics, *correlation* is more specifically defined as a measure of the strength, or consistency, of the linear relationship between two variables in a population. Graphically, this statistic indicates how well the scatterplot obtained by representing the observations on a Cartesian plane with the two variables as dimensions fits along a straight line. Correlation is most commonly measured—or estimated, when only a sample is available—with the Pearson product-moment coefficient (ρ or r in statistical notation, respectively, for populations and samples), a standardized indicator whose value ranges between -1 (perfect negative correlation) and 1 (perfect positive correlation), and where 0 denotes the absence of correlation.

The correlation coefficient is an inadequate statistic when the relationship analyzed is believed to be nonlinear or when the variables of interest are nominal or ordinal. In these cases, alternative measures of association such as the chi-square, Spearman's ρ, or Kendall's τ might be more suitable.

See also Causation and Correlation; Partial Least Squares; Regression with Categorical Data; Statistical Analysis.

. . . . PIER DOMENICO TORTOLA

BIBLIOGRAPHY
Freedman, David, Robert Pisani, and Roger Purves. *Statistics,* 4th ed. New York: W.W. Norton, 2007.

Corruption

See *Democracy and Corruption.*

Corruption, Political

Most definitions of *corruption* emphasize the abuse of public power or resources for private benefit. Many basic terms of that definition, however, are themselves contested: Legal standards, public opinion or social values, or the public good may judge *abuse.* Terms such as *public, private, power,* and *benefit* may also be matters of dispute. Variations on the theme emphasize public office dimensions (duties, powers and their limits, process issues, accountability), market processes (using public power to extract rents, or allocating public goods on the basis of demand rather than need), and the public interest, among other factors, as defining characteristics. A continuing debate has to do with the role, if any, that cultural differences should play in defining corruption. Thus, there is no universally agreed upon definition of corruption.

As a concept, corruption has a long lineage. In classical times, it referred to a collective state of being. In this state, leaders forfeit, by their conduct, their claims to virtue and thus their right to lead; citizens or followers fail to play their roles in society; and the overall political order loses its moral structure and justifications. Modern conceptions of corruption originate not only in the works of thinkers like French philosopher Jean-Jacques Rousseau but also out of political contention over accountability and the limits of power. These conceptions tend to treat corruption as a property of a particular action or actor. An official might take bribes, for example, without corrupting the overall political order. While the modern conception dominates, classical ideas are still relevant. For example, citizens of many democracies perceive fundamental corruption in the process of financing campaigns, even where funds are raised and spent in legal, publicly disclosed ways. Corruption in that sense has less to do with rule breaking than with leaders and a political order made unresponsive and unaccountable—and citizen choices made meaningless—by factors such as money and favoritism. Whether or not analysts agree with such perceptions, they can pose a real problem for the vitality and credibility of democratic politics.

MODERN VIEWS OF CORRUPTION

Corruption was a significant issue among scholars and agencies concerned with development during the 1960s and 1970s, but received less attention between the mid-1970s and late 1980s. The reasons for that hiatus are unclear, but among them might be the reluctance of analysts to appear to blame developing countries for their own problems; resistance on the part of Western governments, international organizations, and businesses to the idea that their own activities might contain or encourage corruption; and the inability of analysts to devise effective reforms. Academic analysis during those early periods often *relativized* the issue—treating corruption and its consequences as matters of opinion, or as so diverse as to resist comparisons across societies—and focused on the *functionality* question—whether corruption might do more good than harm in developing societies despite its illegitimate status. Corrupt dealings occurring or originating within advanced societies often received insufficient attention. A related cultural critique held that corruption was a Western concept; and that some varieties, in developing societies, were extensions of longstanding acceptable social practices; and that corruption should not be viewed in negative terms.

The end of the cold war and economic globalization, however, brought corruption back to the fore. Governments and international lenders sought better results from aid and assistance, and corporations, faced with intensifying international competition, began to see corruption not as an overhead cost of doing business but as a deadweight loss. Research beginning during the 1990s led to new kinds of data, including a number of attempts to measure and compare levels of corruption internationally (usually based on perception surveys), and to much improved theory. As corruption is generally a clandestine phenomenon, however, any sort of measure will be imperfect. In his 2007 article, "What Have We Learned about the Causes of Corruption from Ten Years of Cross-National Empirical Research?" Daniel Treisman reviewed the literature regarding studies of corruption. He concluded that mature liberal democracies and market-oriented societies are regarded as less corrupt, while fuel-exporting countries and those with intrusive regulation and unpredictable inflation tend to be seen as more corrupt. While higher development does cause lower perceived corruption, when income is taken into account many predictors of perceptions are only weakly related to individuals' reported experiences with corruption. Strong evidence that corruption delays, diverts, and distorts economic and political development superseded functionality arguments—that corruption is not "grease for the wheels," but rather "sand in the gears." To a striking extent, this line of research places relatively little emphasis on definitions.

REFORM SOLUTIONS

The past generation's policy recommendations and reforms have often been broadly consistent with the Washington *consensus* view, and neoliberal outlooks that revived the debate. The worldview that emerged, first of all, sees corruption primarily as bribery, and thus as a transaction that is quid pro quo and amenable to economic modeling. It holds that smaller governments, by reducing interference in the marketplace, will produce less corruption as well as more growth; that democratic politics is another, parallel sort of market; and that the state's proper functions, often termed *good governance*, should be primarily technical and administrative—in effect, a referee role in liberalized societies. Much theory and data support such views, particularly to the extent that we conceptualize corruption in terms of rent-seeking, regard public institutions more as obstructions to market processes than as foundations for them, and idealize the ways markets and governments would work in the absence of corruption. Indeed, evidence does suggest that where corruption is apparently more common, inspections, delays, and red tape are more extensive, and economic processes less vibrant, than in societies where it is less extensive, and that corruption is a major factor keeping poor people poor.

More recent research, while accepting the basic view of corruption as broadly harmful, has reemphasized the value of politics and public institutions. It suggests that the consensus view—and international corruption indices—overlook variations among and within societies and in the kinds of corruption problems they experience. Cultural variables resurfaced too, less as definitions than as clues to the origins of certain forms, and clues to the social significance, of corruption. Mediating cultural institutions such as *guanxi* in Chinese societies and *middlemen* in India, have major implications at those levels. Such arguments remind us that active markets and democratic politics require social and institutional foundations, rather than just liberalized processes, and that we have no way of knowing how real economies and governments would function without corruption.

In the United States, reform has been a long-running research and policy concern shaped by both the abolitionist movement and the struggle against machine bosses like William M. Tweed of New York's Tammany Hall. Both that struggle, and the Progressive Era more generally, gave rise to administrative and civil service reforms that undercut many corrupt practices; New Deal social services likewise weakened the power of machine politicians' petty favors and gifts. Critics see these reforms, however, as introducing fragmentation, rigidity, and new costs into government.

Contemporary research issues associated with corruption include the further elaboration of Principal-Agent-Client (P-A-C) models, and other conceptions of incentives and constraints often drawing upon economics theories; improved measurement, including assessing corruption indirectly using indicators of government performance; and the analysis of reforms. Most democratic societies have instituted political finance rules and, less commonly, subsidies; many are also scrutinizing corporate governance, accounting standards, and the transparency of markets with renewed vigor. On the international front, organizations such as the Organization for Economic Cooperation and Development, Organization for American States, and the United Nations have ratified anticorruption treaties and conventions, usually backed up by ambitious intergovernmental scrutiny and assistance schemes. At all levels, major themes in reform include accountability, transparency, and the responsibilities and strength of civil society.

See also *Accountability; Corruption and Other Political Pathologies; Principal-agent Theory; Relativism; Rent-Seeking; Transparency.*

. . . . MICHAEL JOHNSTON

BIBLIOGRAPHY

Anechiarico, Frank, and James B. Jacobs. *The Pursuit of Absolute Integrity.* Chicago: University of Chicago Press, 1996.

Bardhan, Pranab. "Corruption and Development: A Review of Issues." *Journal of Economic Literature* 35 (1997): 1320–1346.

Bayley, David. "The Effects of Corruption in a Developing Nation." *Western Political Quarterly* 19 (1966): 719–732.

Heidenheimer, Arnold J., and Michael Johnston. *Political Corruption: Concepts and Contexts.* New Brunswick, N.J.: Transaction, 2002.

Johnston, Michael. *Syndromes of Corruption: Wealth, Power, and Democracy.* Cambridge: Cambridge University Press, 2005.

Klitgaard, Robert. *Controlling Corruption.* Berkeley: University of California Press, 1988.

Mbaku, John Mukum. *Corruption in Africa: Causes, Consequences, and Cleanups.* Lanham, Md.: Lexington Books, 2007.

Nye, Joseph. "Corruption and Political Development: A Cost-Benefit Analysis." *American Political Science Review* 61 (June 1967): 417–427.

Quah, Jon S. T. *Curbing Corruption in Asia: A Comparative Study of Six Countries.* Singapore: Eastern Universities Press, 2003.

Rose-Ackerman, Susan. *Corruption and Government: Causes, Consequences, and Reform.* Cambridge: Cambridge University Press, 1999.

Sampford, Charles, Arthur Shacklock, Carmel Connors, and Fredrik Galtung, eds. *Measuring Corruption.* Aldershot, UK: Ashgate, 2006.

Scott, James C. *Comparative Political Corruption.* Englewood Cliffs, N.J.: Prentice-Hall.

Treisman, Daniel. "What Have We Learned about the Causes of Corruption from Ten Years of Cross-National Empirical Research?" *Annual Review of Political Science* 10 (2007): 211–244.

Corruption and Other Political Pathologies

In an ideal democracy, the polity faithfully maps the preferences of citizens into public choices. Protections for individual rights constitutionally limit the range of democratic choice, but within those constraints, citizens' preferences rule. In practice, real governments fail to measure up. Some of this divergence is the result of disagreements among citizens over policy; other difficulties arise from the nature of representative government. If preferences diverge, the state must aggregate preferences to make choices using methods that are subject to strategic manipulation and that produce winners and losers. This will happen even in a direct democracy lacking any of the institutions of the modern state beyond elections. Furthermore, most democratic states require representative institutions in order to function, and under these structures some will have more power than others because of their geographical locations or their strategic positions. These are not pathologies but are, instead, inherent in the structure of representative government.

Such difficulties, which need to be acknowledged and managed, are distinguishable from others that represent direct challenges to the legitimacy of governments, however democratic their nominal structure. The tendency of political systems to provide narrowly focused goods and services, *pork barrel* projects, is a familiar complaint about democracy, but it is not pathological. It is the inevitable result of a political system that elects representatives from single-member districts. These representatives will try to satisfy the local demands of their constituents as well as work for broader public goals. Two types of political pathologies are, however, of concern: *corruption* and *clientalism*. The former involves the illicit personal enrichment of public officials, often combined with excess profits for those who pay bribes. The latter is a more subtle phenomenon occurring when public officials provide benefits to their supporters in a way that undermines general public values. As Jana Kunicová and Susan Rose-Ackerman argue in their 2005 article, past work has too often conflated pork barrel politics, clientalism, and corruption. It is important, however, to analyze them as separate, if overlapping, phenomena. For example, structural reforms designed to limit pork barrel politics may lead to higher levels of illegal corruption that diverts public money and power to the private benefit of politicians and their corrupt supporters.

The focus here is on states that have not descended into chaos and anarchy. States where corruption, clientalism, and other political pathologies are endemic may, of course, eventually collapse, but sometimes such states are quite stable and long lasting. As Robert Rotberg argues, the system may be pathological in the sense of not reflecting the interests of most citizens and of not providing security, but it does endure.

The line between pathology and normal democratic politics is not always easy to draw. Extreme cases are easy to identify—Zaire under the thirty-two year presidency of Mobutu Sese Seko, Cambodia under Khmer Rouge leader Pol Pot—but what should we make of democratic states where private wealth has a major impact on public choices? How much of this is the normal and predictable result of the fact that elections cost money, and when does the use of private funds to support political careers become corrupt or pathological? When is support for public works in one's home district an indication that a representative system is working well, and when does it tip over the line into dysfunctional clientalism?

In a political system that pays lip service to notions of public accountability and is, in fact, controlled by corrupt officials, the basic problem is the interaction between officials' venality and corrupt inducements offered by private groups and individuals. Alongside alternative models of corrupt public and private interactions, the more familiar case of a functioning democracy is, nevertheless, deeply influenced by clientelistic networks and concentrations of private wealth.

CORRUPTION

Corruption describes a relationship between the state and the private sector. Sometimes state officials are the dominant actors; in other cases, private actors are the most powerful forces. The relative bargaining power of these groups determines both the overall impact of corruption on society and the distribution of the gains between bribers and bribe payers. The nature of corruption depends not just on the organization of government but also on the organization and power of private actors. A critical issue is whether either the government or the private sector has monopoly power in dealing with the other.

In *Corruption and Government: Causes, Consequences and Reform* (1999), Susan Rose-Ackerman distinguishes between *kleptocracies,* where corruption is organized at the top of government, and other states, where bribery is the province of a large number of low-level officials. On the other side of the bribery "market," there is a difference between cases with a small number of major corrupt private actors and ones where the payment of bribes is decentralized across society. Table 1 from Rose-Ackerman's book illustrates four polar cases: kleptocracy, bilateral monopoly, mafia-dominated states, and competitive bribery.

KLEPTOCRACY

In the extreme case of a kleptocratic ruler who faces a large number of unorganized potential bribe payers, a powerful head of government can organize the political system to maximize its corrupt extraction possibilities. According to American economist and social scientist Mancur Olson in his 1993 article "Dictatorship, Democracy and Development," such a "stationary bandit" acts like a private monopolist, striving for productive efficiency, but restricting the output of the economy to maximize profits. The ruler sacrifices the benefits of patronage and petty favoritism to obtain the profits generated by a well run monopoly. Under this model, high-level corruption is not as serious a problem as low-level corruption under which officials "overfish" a "commons," according to Olson, in their search for private gain. However, this claim ignores the fact that kleptocratic rulers have more power than lower level officials and may use this power to expand the resources under state control. Furthermore, even if they expand the state, kleptocrats frequently have a weak and disloyal civil service, a poor resource base, and a vague and confusing legal framework. Such kleptocrats, described as "official moguls" by Michael Johnston in *Syndromes of Corruption: Wealth, Power, and Democracy* (2005), favor a bloated and inefficient state that maximizes corrupt possibilities.

Of course, some powerful rulers do manage to avoid inefficient policies. They enrich themselves and their families, but do not push rent-generating programs so far as to significantly undermine growth. Countries with a high degree of corruption that are politically secure and tightly controlled from the top may suffer from less inefficiency than those with an uncoordinated struggle for private gain. They have a long-run viewpoint and hence seek ways to constrain uncoordinated rent-seeking. This type of regime seems a rough approximation to some East Asian countries which have institutional mechanisms to cut back uncoordinated rent-seeking by both officials and private businesses. However, many corrupt rulers are not so secure. In fact, their very venality increases their insecurity. Furthermore, corruption at the top creates expectations among bureaucrats that they should share in the wealth and reduces the moral and psychological constraints on lower level officials.

BILATERAL MONOPOLIES AND MAFIA-DOMINATED STATES

The two cases where private interests exert power over the state differ depending upon whether or not the state is centrally organized to collect bribes. In the first, bilateral case, a corrupt ruler faces an organized oligarchy so that the rent extraction possibilities are shared between the oligarchs and the ruler. Their relative strength will determine the way gains are shared. Each side may seek to improve its own situation by making the other worse off through expropriating property, on the one hand, or engaging in violence, on the other.

In *The Sicilian Mafia* (1993), Diego Gambetta defines a *mafia* as an organized crime group that provides protective services that substitute for those provided by the state in ordinary societies. In some bilateral cases, the state and the mafia share the protection business and perhaps even have overlapping membership. Donatella della Porta and Alberto Vannucci, in *Corrupt Exchanges: Actors, Resources, and Mechanisms of Political Corruption* (1999), provide examples from Italy. Louise I. Shelley highlights this feature in a 2001 article, "Corruption and Organized Crime in Mexico in the Post-PRI Transition," and Shelly and Svante E. Cornell, in a 2006 article, document state and mafia interpenetration in "The Drug Trade in Russia."

A powerful corrupt ruler extorts a share of the mafias' gains and has little interest in controlling criminal influence. If the

TABLE 1: TYPES OF CORRUPT GOVERNMENTS

	MULTIPLE BRIBERS	FEW BRIBERS
BRIBE RECIPIENTS CONCENTRATED AT TOP OF GOVERNMENT	Kleptocracy	Bilateral monopoly
MULTIPLE BRIBE RECIPIENTS AT LOW LEVELS OF GOVERNMENT	Competitive bribery with a possibility of spirals	Mafia-dominated state

mafias get the upper hand, they will enlist the state in limiting entry through threats of violence and the elimination of rivals. Furthermore, organized crime bosses who dominate business sectors may be more interested in quick profits through the export of a country's assets and raw materials than in the difficult task of building up a modern industrial base. The end result is the delegitimation of government and the undermining of capitalist institutions.

Criminal mafias are only the most extreme form of private domination. Some states are economically dependent on the export of one or two primary products. These countries may establish long-term relationships with a few multinational firms. Both rulers and firms favor productive efficiency and the control of violent private groups, but the business and government alliance may permit firms and rulers to share the nation's wealth at the expense of ordinary people. The division of gains will depend upon their relative bargaining power. If investors have the upper hand, there may not be much overt corruption, but the harm to ordinary citizens may, nevertheless, be severe. The size of the bribes is not the key variable. Instead, the economic distortions and the high costs of public projects measure the harm to citizens.

In the case when officials of a weak and disorganized state engage in freelance bribery but face concentrations of power in the private sector, the monopolist could be a domestic mafia, a single large corporation, or a close-knit oligarchy. Yet in each case, private power dominates the state, buying the cooperation of officials. The private actors are not powerful enough to take over the state and reorganize it into a unitary body, and the very disorganization of the state reduces the ability of the private group to purchase the benefits it wants. Making an agreement with one official will not discourage another from coming forward. Such a state is very dysfunctional as officials compete for corrupt handouts.

COMPETITIVE BRIBERY

In cases of competitive bribery, many low-level officials deal with large numbers of citizens and businesses. This could occur in a weak autocracy or in a democratic state with weak legal controls on corruption and poor public accountability. The competitive corruption case is not analogous to an efficient competitive market. A fundamental problem is the possibility of an upward spiral of corruption. The corruption of some encourages additional officials to accept bribes until all but the unreconstructed moralists are corrupt. Two equilibria are possible—one with pervasive corruption and another with very little corruption.

Reform requires systemic changes in expectations and in government behavior to move from a high corruption to a low corruption equilibrium. Unfortunately, the states that fall into this fourth category, such as many states in sub-Saharan Africa and in South and Southeast Asia, are precisely those that lack the centralized authority needed to carry out such reforms. The decentralized, competitive corrupt system is frequently well-entrenched, and no one has the power to administer the policy shock needed for reform.

CLIENTALISM, CAMPAIGN FUNDS, AND PRIVATE WEALTH

More subtle and difficult pathologies arise in democracies with well-established competitive electoral systems. Democratic processes are expensive. Because the state can provide targeted benefits, award procurement contracts, and impose regulatory and tax costs, private interests seek political influence. Even if they only do this within the law, those with wealth are likely to do better than others. Of course, more diffuse interests have an impact both through the ballot box and through grassroots protests, but the well-off often can either co-opt mass opinion or counteract it through their own actions.

What can wealthy interests bring to the table beyond more pay for lobbyists and lawyers? In functioning democracies, a key resource is the provision of campaign funds and in-kind benefits, ranging from free media exposure to free travel and trips for volunteer campaign workers. Skirting close to the corrupt edge are the conflicts of interest that arise when government officials are given favorable access to investment opportunities, are promised private sector jobs, or are themselves associated with prominent business families. Even when there is no direct quid pro quo that runs afoul of anticorruption laws, ongoing connections and past patterns of favors can distort choices.

Clientalism operates in the other direction, as demonstrated in Junichi Kawata's edited volume, *Comparing Political Corruption and Clientalism* (2006). Powerful politicians, sometimes in alliance with wealthy private interests, develop vertical ties that make ordinary citizens dependent on them for jobs; they also help with regulatory hurdles and access to public services. The state does not provide benefits to citizens as a right. Rather, its benefits are dispensed as favors, and costs are imposed on those who do not show proper deference. The clients may then provide help during electoral campaigns. Masaya Kobayashi, in the article "A Typology of Corrupt Networks" (2006), makes the useful distinction between the long-term reciprocal relations typical of clientalism and the specific purchase of services that characterizes bribery. Clientalism may be more deeply entrenched and harder to counteract than individual instances of corruption.

Restrictions on campaign finance are one response to both clientalism and corruption in established democracies. Solutions approach the problem from four dimensions. First, reducing the length of time for campaigns and limiting the methods available can reduce the costs of political campaigns. Second, stronger disclosure rules can be established. Disclosure permits citizens to vote against candidates who receive too much special interest money. In *Voting with Dollars* (2000), Bruce Ackerman and Ian Ayres, however, suggest the opposite strategy; they recommend that all donations should be anonymous so that no quid pro quo is possible. This idea invites donors to find ways to cheat, but if successful, it would likely discourage contributions from all but the most ideological donors.

Third, laws can limit both individual donations and candidates' spending. In the United States, such limits are in tension with the constitutional protection of free speech. The basic issue, however, arises everywhere: To what extent can a democratic government interfere with citizens who wish to express their political interests through gifts to support political parties or individual candidates?

Fourth, alternative sources of funds can be found in the public sector. In the United States, the federal government provides funds for presidential candidates under certain conditions, and several American states provide public support for political campaigns. Also, a number of proposals have been made for more extensive public funding. One idea is to grant public funds to candidates who demonstrate substantial public support. Ackerman and Ayres, for example, argue that giving vouchers to voters to support the candidates of their choice could achieve this. This plan would combine public funding with an egalitarian system for allocating funds and, if combined with secrecy for private gifts, would reduce the influence of wealthy interests. If not well-monitored, however, it might increase illegal payments. Furthermore, their proposal does not respond to the pathologies of clientelistic systems where voters might still support entrenched incumbents who offer jobs and targeted services with little concern for broad public values.

CONCLUSIONS

All political systems fall short of the democratic ideal. Constitution writing and legislative drafting are pragmatic exercises requiring compromise and a realistic appreciation of the limits of institutions to control self-seeking behavior. Nevertheless, some political systems are worse than others. They have crossed the line into kleptocracy or into state capture—be it by mafias using intimidation and violence or by large business corporations leveraging their economic clout. Some states risk slipping into such pathologies and into outright failure, but one also needs to acknowledge the more subtle ways in which private wealth and public power can interact in more advanced systems. These interactions can undermine government legitimacy and divert the benefits of state action to narrow, unrepresentative groups. The policies required may not be as drastic and transformative as in kleptocratic or fully captured states, but they, nevertheless, require difficult confrontations with powerful vested interests both inside and outside of government.

See also *Accountability; Campaign Finance; Corruption, Political; Democracy and Corruption; Organized Crime and Mafia; Public Good; Public Interest Groups; Public-private Dichotomy.*

. . . . SUSAN ROSE-ACKERMAN

BIBLIOGRAPHY

Ackerman, Bruce, and Ian Ayres. *Voting with Dollars.* New Haven: Yale University Press, 2000.

della Porta, Donatella, and Alberto Vannucci. *Corrupt Exchanges: Actors, Resources, and Mechanisms of Political Corruption.* New York: Aldine de Gruyter, 1999.

Gambetta, Diego. *The Sicilian Mafia.* Cambridge, Mass.: Harvard University Press, 1993.

Jain, Arvind K., ed. *The Political Economy of Corruption,* London: Routledge, 2001.

Johnston, Michael. *Syndromes of Corruption: Wealth, Power, and Democracy,* Cambridge: Cambridge University Press, 2005.

Kawata, Junichi, ed. *Comparing Political Corruption and Clientalism.* Aldershot, UK: Ashgate, 2006.

Khan, Mushtaq H., and K. S. Jomo, eds. *Rents, Rent-Seeking, and Economic Development: Theory and Evidence in Asia.* Cambridge: Cambridge University Press, 2000.

Kobayashi, Masaya. "A Typology of Corrupt Networks." In *Comparing Political Corruption and Clientalism,* edited by Junichi Kawata, 1–23. Aldershot, UK: Ashgate, 2006.

Kunicová, Jana, and Susan Rose-Ackerman. "Electoral Rules and Constitutional Structures as Constraints on Corruption." *British Journal of Political Science* 35, no. 4 (2005): 573–606.

Olson, Mancur. "Dictatorship, Democracy, and Development." *American Political Science Review* 87, no. 3 (1993): 567–575.

Rose-Ackerman, Susan. *Corruption: A Study in Political Economy,* New York: Academic Press, 1978.

———. *Corruption and Government: Causes, Consequences, and Reform.* Cambridge: Cambridge University Press, 1999.

———. *International Handbook on the Economics of Corruption.* Cheltenham, UK: Edward Elgar, 2006.

Rotberg, Robert I., ed. *When States Fail: Causes and Consequences.* Princeton: Princeton University Press, 2004.

Shelley, Louise I. "Corruption and Organized Crime in Mexico in the Post-PRI Transition." *Journal of Contemporary Criminal Justice* 17, no. 3 (2001): 213–231.

Shelley, Louise I., and Svante E. Cornell. "The Drug Trade in Russia." In *Russian Business Power: The Role of Russian Business in Foreign and Security Relations,* edited by Andeas Wenger, Jeronim Perović, and Robert W. Orttung. London: Routledge, 2006.

Corwin, Edward Samuel

Edward S. Corwin (1878–1963) was a leading political scientist and constitutional law scholar during the first half of the twentieth century. He was widely recognized for his writings on a broad range of constitutional issues. Corwin also made significant contributions to the study of the U.S. Supreme Court and the presidency. Corwin's work has been referred to in U.S. Supreme Court opinions and continues to be cited in current academic scholarship.

Corwin completed his undergraduate studies at the University of Michigan in 1900, where he developed an interest in American constitutional thought. After spending two years teaching high school students, Corwin enrolled in the University of Pennsylvania and received his doctorate in early American history in 1905.

Corwin spent his entire academic career at Princeton. In 1911, at the age of thirty-three, he became a full professor. In 1918, he succeeded Woodrow Wilson as McCormick Professor of Jurisprudence. Corwin was also the first chair of Princeton's department of politics. He was active in the profession and became the president of the American Political Science Association (APSA) in 1931.

Corwin was a prolific writer and authored more than twenty books and over 150 scholarly articles. He is often noted for the advances he made by analyzing constitutional concepts in historical context. Many of his studies were considered landmark contributions when they were published and continue to be read today. For example, Corwin's book, *The*

Constitution and What It Means Today, was first published in 1920 and is now in its fourteenth edition.

One of Corwin's most famous essays is "The 'Higher Law' Background of American Constitutional Law," which was published in 1928. In this article, he examines the intellectual roots of American constitutional thought and explanations relating to the Constitution's dominance. The importance of this article is underscored by the fact that scholars continue to debate its merits many years after its publication.

Corwin was a frequent commentator on public issues of the day. He was not shy about writing for the popular press or granting newspaper interviews. He advocated U.S. entry into World War I (1914–1918) and was a vocal supporter of Franklin Roosevelt's New Deal.

Corwin provided guidance in different capacities to two presidents. The advice he gave to Woodrow Wilson was more informal and not always implemented. During Roosevelt's administration, Corwin served as an adviser to the Public Works Administration. Corwin then worked in a consulting capacity for the attorney general.

The most controversial aspect of Corwin's career was his defense of Roosevelt's court-packing plan, which included testifying before the Senate's Committee on Court Reorganization. He had difficulty defending his views before the committee because, earlier, he was quite critical of the plan. It has been suggested that Corwin's support of the court-packing plan and his lackluster Senate testimony ended any reasonable chance of him receiving an appointment to the Supreme Court. After these events, Corwin became more politically conservative and openly critical of Roosevelt.

Corwin retired from Princeton in 1946, but continued to pursue an active research agenda, publishing several books and a handful of articles. The APSA offers an annual award in his name for the best doctoral dissertation in public law.

See also *Constitutional Courts; Constitutional Law; New Deal; Supreme Court.*

. . . . ADAM W. NYE

BIBLIOGRAPHY

Clayton, Cornell W. "Edward S. Corwin as Public Scholar." In *The Pioneers of Judicial Behavior,* edited by Nancy Maveety. Ann Arbor: University of Michigan Press, 2003.

Corwin, Edward S. *Edward S. Corwin's the Constitution and What It Means Today,* 14th ed, edited by Harold W. Chase and Craig R. Ducat. Princeton: Princeton University Press, 1978.

———. *The President: Office and Powers.* New York: New York University Press, 1940.

Crews, Kenneth D., ed. *Corwin's Constitution: Essays and Insights of Edward S. Corwin.* Westport, Conn.: Greenwood Press, 1986.

———. *Edward S. Corwin and the American Constitution,* Westport, Conn.: Greenwood Press, 1985.

Loss, Richard, ed. *Corwin on the Constitution,* 3 vols. Ithaca: Cornell University Press, 1981–1998.

Mason, Alpheus T., and Gerald Garvey, eds. *American Constitutional History: Essays by Edward S. Corwin.* New York: Harper and Row, 1964.

McDowell, Gary L. "The Corrosive Constitutionalism of Edward S. Corwin." *Law and Social Inquiry* 14 (1989): 603–614.

Cosmopolitan Democracy

See *Cosmopolitanism.*

Cosmopolitanism

Cosmopolitanism, a term derived from the Greek word *kosmopolitês* meaning "citizen of the world," is used to refer to a variety of beliefs and attitudes about the relationship between the individual and humanity (or the world) as a whole.

From a Stoic point of view, the citizen of the world is indifferent to particular places and detached from particularistic commitments. In other words, the citizen of the world is at home nowhere, except perhaps in the realm of ideas, where goodness in its purist form is to be found and where justice reigns unchallenged by the ignorance and selfishness of humankind. In this light, cosmopolitanism has less to do with the transcendence of national boundaries than it does with an allegiance to the *kosmos*—meaning, the intelligible realm of forms—above and beyond the visible world of endless cruelty and conflict. This may be what Plutarch means when he attributes to Socrates the designation of citizen of the world in his essay "On Banishment."

From a cultural point of view, the world citizen is world traveler who appreciates variety in culture, art, literature, cuisine, and so on, and who is open to different ideas and ways of life. From this perspective, articulated by Jeremy Waldron, the citizen of the world is at home everywhere, including the realm of contested truths and hybridized identity. Like Stoic cosmopolitanism, cultural cosmopolitanism requires a level of detachment from one's own culture and context. But unlike Stoic cosmopolitanism, the wider world exists both to be appreciated and to be learned from by the world citizen, not to be renounced in its entirety in favor of a higher level of existence.

What is generally meant by political cosmopolitanism is the recognition that the activities of one's own state affect the lives of people living in another state and the belief that these people are worthy of consideration and respect. It does not mean that an individual is devoted to all states (or peoples) equally or to the idea of a world state. Immanuel Kant, in "Perpetual Peace," looked to humanity's unsociable sociability as the engine that would drive the emergence of political cosmopolitan and an international federation of free nations. But there is nothing inevitable about the historical development of political cosmopolitanism—or cosmopolitanism of any kind, although imagining rationally self-interested states as the drivers of cosmopolitan change, as Kant did, does go against a utopian basis for such speculation.

Some contemporary philosophers, including Martha Nussbaum, argue that people should owe their primary allegiance to the world, not to any association more limited or local, while others, such as Kwame Anthony Appiah, have argued more modestly for a rooted cosmopolitanism that allows individuals to preserve a special or prior obligation to a local or national community, rather than insisting on a potentially unlimited obligation to aid the worst off in the world. Another contemporary view of cosmopolitanism is offered by Seyla Benhabib, who recovers and expands upon the Kantian concept of hospitality, understood as a cosmopolitan right of individual members of a global civil society to be welcomed and protected by other nations. Since this right intersects with the sovereignty of states, Benhabib argues that citizens of democracies who are convinced of the validity of cosmopolitan norms must articulate it into positive law.

Critics of cosmopolitanism, including Richard Rorty, have argued that since the global moral community does not exist as an empirical reality, people cannot be morally attached to it or feel loyalty toward others as fellow members of it. Rorty goes further by arguing that cosmopolitan norms cannot emerge from anything like Kantian rationality, as Benhabib suggests, and that the only hope for the gradual emergence of a global moral community is for people to abandon the pretense of universality. Until that happens, citizens of more affluent, developed countries are unlikely to identify with or sacrifice their prosperity for the sake either of strangers living in a far corner of the world or strangers arriving on their shores.

See also *Greek Political Thought, Ancient; Kant, Immanuel.*

. . . . JASON SCORZA

BIBLIOGRAPHY

Appiah, Kwame Anthony. *Cosmopolitanism: Ethics in a World of Strangers.* New York: W. W. Norton, 2006.

Benhabib, Seyla. *Another Cosmopolitanism.* Oxford: Oxford University Press, 2006.

Nussbaum, Martha. *For Love of Country?* Boston: Beacon Press, 2002.

Rorty, Richard. "Justice as a Larger Loyalty." In *Philosophy as Cultural Politics: Philosophical Papers,* vol. 4. Cambridge: Cambridge University Press, 2007.

Waldron, Jeremy. "What Is Cosmopolitan?" *Journal of Political Philosophy* 8, no. 2 (2000): 227–243.

Cost-benefit Analysis

Cost-benefit analysis is a technique to determine the best alternative out of many available options by comparing the expected costs and benefits. It can be applied to the analysis of almost any course of action characterized in terms of its benefits and costs, including opportunity costs. The comparison of one alternative course of action to another is based on their net present values. The net present value of an alternative is the difference between the sum of all future benefits brought by the course of action and the sum of all future costs resulted from that course of action. A discount rate must be chosen in order to calculate future costs and benefits in present terms. For actions with long-term consequences, this choice is controversial because it requires predicting financial market performance, and often evaluating the value of the welfare of future generations.

The cost-benefit analysis is used in many areas. In finance applications, the cost-benefit technique helps to determine the most profitable projects. In government policy applications, the cost-benefit tool is often used to judge the effectiveness of government regulations for preventing market failures. The international relations between countries are also based on cost-benefit calculations. For example, the choice of a certain foreign policy action takes into account the expected subsequent positive and negative reactions of other countries, which generate the benefits and costs. However, where perfect markets for the inputs to the analysis do not exist, deriving the required costs and benefits is controversial.

. . . . TATIANA VASHCHILKO

Council, Constitutional

See *Constitutional Courts.*

Counter-Enlightenment Political Thought

Counter-Enlightenment political thought refers to a range of views that share the belief that the eighteenth century Age of Enlightenment in the West was fundamentally mistaken in ways that have seriously damaged religion, morals, and society. The Enlightenment was a period of reform when prominent and influential European and American philosophers, historians, economists, and politicians challenged many traditional beliefs and institutions in the name of reason, science, and progress. Critics of this movement's emphasis on the power and centrality of reason in human affairs have sought to depict it as both exaggerated and dangerous.

Over the past 250 years, the Enlightenment has attracted critics from across the ideological spectrum, ranging from devout conservative Catholics to radical feminists, from nineteenth-century romantic poets to twentieth-century neo-Marxists and even liberals. Most disagree on their interpretation of what the Enlightenment was; however, there is broad agreement among its adversaries that the period was socially and politically harmful, if not disastrous. There have been, and still are, many Counter-Enlightenments, from the eighteenth century to the present, covering not only a wide range of specific criticisms of the Enlightenment, but also many different, and sometimes incompatible, depictions of the Enlightenment by its critics, each of which suits their own beliefs, agendas, and interests.

EARLY CRITIQUES OF THE ENLIGHTENMENT

The first serious, systematic critique of the Enlightenment came from the eighteenth-century Swiss writer Jean-Jacques Rousseau, who had been a friend and ally of many of its leading proponents such as the writer Denis Diderot and the philosopher and mathematician Jean d'Alembert. Yet in his *Discourse on the Sciences and the Arts* (1750) Rousseau praises ignorance and associates the acquisition of knowledge of the arts and sciences with decadence and moral depravity. Many philosophers were shocked by this stance, which they saw as a betrayal of the ideals of the Enlightenment. D'Alembert sought to counter it in his *Preliminary Discourse to the Encyclopédie* (1751), which became the French Enlightenment's unofficial manifesto. This early skirmish over the effects of the arts and sciences on morals soon escalated into an epic clash between Rousseau and the philosophers of the Enlightenment, which has continued without interruption ever since.

In the decades preceding the French Revolution (1789–1799), Enlightenment philosophers sparred constantly with orthodox religious writers such as the conservative Jesuit Guillaume-François Berthier, who assaulted the *Encyclopédie* for attacking Christianity and for its alleged corrosion of traditional morals and beliefs. After 1789, many writers blamed the violent excesses of the French Revolution on the Enlightenment which, it was widely believed, had systematically destroyed the legitimacy of monarchy and aristocracy in Europe and plunged the continent into decades of political chaos and bloodshed. The most eloquent proponent of this view was the conservative Savoyard Catholic Joseph de Maistre, whose *Considerations on France* (*Considérations sur la France*, 1796) depicts the events of the 1790s as divine punishment for the sins of the Enlightenment. Its most popular advocates were the Anglo-Irish statesman and philosopher Edmund Burke, author of the influential *Reflections on the Revolution in France* (1790), and the Abbé Augustin Barruel. Barruel's bestselling *Memoirs Illustrating the History of Jacobinism* (*Mémoires pour servir à l'Histoire du Jacobinisme*, 1797) makes the case that a conspiracy of Enlightenment philosophers, Freemasons, and the secret Illuminati Order deliberately sought to overthrow established monarchs and governments in Europe in the name of reason and progress.

Many romantic writers at the end of the eigteenth century and early nineteenth century in France, Germany, and Britain condemned the Enlightenment as antireligious, although their own religious views were often far less orthodox than those of its earlier Enlightenment critics such as Berthier. The belief was widespread among these romantic poets and writers that the Enlightenment's allegedly narrow emphasis on reason at the expense of emotion and passion had led to a world devoid of beauty, imagination, and spirit. This is a central theme of François-René de Chateaubriand's enormously popular and influential book *The Genius of Christianity* (*Le Génie du Christianisme*, 1802), an aesthetic defense of Christianity that depicts the beauty and mystery of faith as a casualty of the Enlightenment's relentless assault on traditional religious beliefs in the name of reason. Many romantic writers shared the mistaken conviction of earlier religious opponents of the Enlightenment that the philosophers of the Enlightenment were mostly atheists; in fact, very few were.

TWENTIETH-CENTURY COUNTER-ENLIGHTENMENT THOUGHT

Attacks on the Enlightenment were common throughout the nineteenth century, most notably in the later works of the German philosopher Friedrich Nietzsche, who associated it with the French Revolution as its earlier critics

had done. But it was not until the end of World War II (1939–1945) that Counter-Enlightenment thought became as widespread as it had been during and after the French Revolution. According to a generation of intellectuals born at the turn of the century, the Enlightenment played a central role in the emergence of twentieth-century totalitarianism, epitomized by Adolf Hitler's Germany and Joseph Stalin's Soviet Union. After World War II, German critical theorists Max Horkheimer and Theodor Adorno associated the Western conception of Enlightenment with a narrowly instrumental form of reason that was repressive and totalitarian in their very influential book *Dialectic of Enlightenment* (1947). Cold–war liberals of the same generation, such as philosophers Jacob Talmon and Isaiah Berlin, saw the legacy of the Enlightenment as directly linked to twentieth-century communism. In addition, their conservative contemporaries Michael Oakeshott and Eric Voegelin restated earlier, orthodox attacks on Enlightenment rationalism for its disastrous political and spiritual effects.

Among later generations of thinkers, postmodernists have been the Enlightenment's most vociferous critics. Works such as *Madness and Civilization* (1961) and *Discipline and Punish* (1975), by French philosopher and historian Michel Foucault, chronicle the emergence in the late eighteenth and early nineteenth centuries of a new disciplinary society that was liberal and humane in name and rhetoric but sinister and highly controlling in practice. Postmodern feminists such as Sandra Harding have attacked the Enlightenment for its supposedly pure conception of reason in which important gender differences are suppressed in the interests of men.

New forms of Counter-Enlightenment thought continue to proliferate today, for example, among some environmentalists critical of the modern West's faith in science and technology. Given that so many of the values, practices, and beliefs of modern Western civilization are rooted in the eighteenth-century Enlightenment, it is certain that its assumptions and consequences will remain matters of deep and abiding contestation.

See also *Conservatism; Critical Theory; Enlightenment Political Thought; Foucault, Michel Paul; Rousseau, Jean-Jacques; Scottish Enlightenment.*

. . . . GRAEME GARRARD

BIBLIOGRAPHY

Berlin, Isaiah. "The Counter-Enlightenment." In *Against the Current: Essays in the History of Ideas.* Princeton: Princeton University Press, 2001.

Garrard, Graeme. *Counter-Enlightenments: From the Eighteenth Century to the Present.* London: Routledge, 2006.

Mali, Joseph, and Robeert Wokler, eds. *Isaiah Berlin's Counter-Enlightenment.* Philadelphia: American Philosophical Society, 2003.

Masseau, Didier. *Les ennemis des philosophes: L'antiphilosophie au temps des Lumières.* Paris: Albin Michel, 2000.

McMahon, Darrin. *Enemies of the Enlightenment: The French Counter-Enlightenment and the Making of Modernity.* Oxford: Oxford University Press, 2001.

Norton, Robert E. "The Myth of the Counter-Enlightenment." *Journal of the History of Ideas,* 68 (2007): 635–658.

Counterfactual

A *counterfactual,* also *contrafactual,* is a hypothetical situation usually created to examine what may have happened given a different course of events or set of conditions. Counterfactual experiments substitute variables of the historical context and analyze how these changes would have affected outcomes; for example, "If the United States had not gone to war against Iraq, it would have been able to fight terrorism worldwide more effectively." Counterfactual reasoning is used in any field in which researchers want to draw cause-effect conclusions but cannot perform controlled experiments in which they consider conditions that differ only in the presence or absence of the hypothesized cause. It is assumed that good counterfactuals should rest on multiple factuals, and, as sociologist Max Weber (1864–1920) claimed, they "should make as few historical changes as possible." Counterfactuals are often crucial for theory building and interpretations, may provide analytical insight, help to acknowledge the role of chance, and can facilitate, in Philip Tetlock's words, "learning from history." Limitations of this method are associated with the inherently subjective process and the certainty-of-hindsight effect.

See also *Critical Juncture; Forecasting, Political; Path Dependencies; Politics, Comparative; Qualitative Methodologies.*

. . . . JIRI S. MELICH

BIBLIOGRAPHY

Ferguson, Niall, ed. *Virtual History: Alternatives and Counterfactuals.* New York: Basic Books, 1999.

Tetlock, Philip, and Aaron Belkin. *Counterfactual Thought Experiments in World Politics.* Princeton: Princeton University Press, 1996.

Counterterrorism

See *Crime Policy.*

Coup d'État

A *coup d'état* involves the sudden, often violent, overthrow of an existing government by a small group. In contrast, revolutions are achieved by large numbers of people working for basic social economic and political change. In almost all cases, a coup d'état is essentially identical to military coup because it either replaces a civilian government with the military or one military group with another.

There are three kinds of coups. The first is a *breakthrough coup d'état* that occurs when a revolutionary group overthrows a civilian government and creates a new elite. Examples of this type of coup include China (1911), Egypt (1952), Greece (1967), and Liberia (1980). A *guardian coup d'état* takes place when a group comes to power to ostensibly improve public order, as occurred in Pakistan with Prime Minister Zulfikar Ali Bhutto's overthrow by Chief of Army Staff Muhammad Zia-ul-Haq in 1979. Finally, a *veto coup d'état* occurs when the army vetoes democracy. The most famous example took place in Chile in 1973 when the military overthrew the elected socialist President Salvador Allende Gossens.

There is a question whether attempted plots and failed coups should be included in a study of the causes and effects of coups. Failed coups may have as large an effect as a successful coup. For instance, if a group were to attempt a coup and fail, the response of the regime that survived the attempt would likely not be much different from the actions of a group that succeeded; political repression is the common outcome. This, in turn, ferments resentful out-groups prone to violence that often lead to countercoups or civil war.

By way of illustration, Patrick McGowan breaks down the analysis of coups in sub-Saharan Africa into two periods, from 1958 to 1979 and 1980 to 2001. The causes of these coups across both periods are clustered along four explanations: the characteristic of the military, the level of political development, social mobilization, and the national political economy. But, there is disagreement on how these various causes positively or negatively affect change. For instance, does pluralism abate or accelerate coup d'états?

The centrality of the military is almost always a key cause, and related to this is the characteristic of the military, such as its ethnic composition. Countries with large militaries, particularly where they have strong ethic affinities, are strong candidates for a coup d'état. There is also broad agreement that poor economic performance is a powerful catalyst. Coups, of course, in turn have a negative impact on gross domestic product, which creates a viscous circle. In both cases, the causes of coups can be associated with the hollowing out of the state that eventually cripples it—a process that always precedes state collapse.

There is more debate on the association between pluralism and coups, and there are two important points here. First, whatever impact the level of pluralism has on coups, once a coup occurs, the possibility of a subsequent coup is high, and therefore the lack of political development and coups will have a high correlation. The relationship between pluralism and coups may also depend on the time period. For example, in Africa, the coups that took place between 1958 and 1975 occurred mostly in civilian regimes and those between 1976 and 1984 occurred mostly in military regimes. The effect here is key. A coup d'état that overthrows a military regime is much more likely to lead to military factionalism, which not only predicts further coups, but also plants the seeds for competing militias that characterize state collapse. The possibility of further violence heightens if the military splits after a coup, with each side supporting a different faction of elites. One way back to power is a countercoup.

Finally, one of the most commonly accepted effects of coup d'états is the contagion effect—it spreads to contiguous states. However, there is no conclusive explanation for this. Nonetheless, in Africa—and elsewhere—there is a geographic pattern to coups. Of the five major regions, west and central Africa seem to have been most prone to coups, while southern Africa has been remarkably free of coups.

See also *Assassinations, Political; Authoritarianism, African; Autogolpe; Civil-military Relations; Civil Wars; Political Change; Regime Change; Revolutions; Revolutions, Comparative.*

. . . . JAMES J. HENTZ

BIBLIOGRAPHY

Decalo, Samuel. *Coups and Army Rule in Africa: Studies in Military Style.* New Haven: Yale University Press, 1976.

Gershoni, Yekutiel. "The Changing Pattern of Military Takeovers in Sub-Saharan Africa." *Armed Forces and Society* 23, no. 2 (1996): 234–248.

Kandeh, Jimmy. *Coups from Below Armed Subalterns and State Power in West Africa.* New York: Palgrave, 2004.

Mbaku, John. "Military Coups as Rent-Seeking Behavior." *Journal of Political and Military Sociology* 22 (1994): 241–284.

McGowan, Patrick. "African Military Coups d'État, 1965–2001: Frequency, Trends, and Distributions." *Journal of Modern African Studies* 41, no. 3 (2003): 339–370.

McGowan, Patrick, and Thomas Johnson. "Sixty Coups in Thirty Years—Further Evidence Regarding African Military Coups d'État." *Journal of Modern African Studies* 24, no. 3 (1986): 539–546.

Courts, Administrative

See *Administrative Courts.*

Courts, Constitutional

See *Constitutional Courts.*

Covenant

THE BIBLICAL COVENANT

The *biblical covenant* is a mutual and voluntary pledge between God and humankind for the attainment of the common good and justice. A congregation of equals (since people were created alike and in God's image) consents to a covenant; God does not force them to obey (Deuteronomy 4:1). A transcendent sovereign oversees the content of the covenant, and intervenes occasionally to ensure all act according to its terms. God submits to the same law he proposes for humans (Deuteronomy 7:12), limiting his omnipotence. Subsidiary covenants establish different sets of rights and obligations: between rulers and the ruled, under God's supervision (2 Samuel 5:3, Joshua 24), or international treaties (Genesis 21:27–32, Joshua 9).

Failure to comply with these stipulations leads to internal collapse, preceding the destruction of Israel by a foreign power. This causes the replacement of the original covenant (Jeremiah 31:31–32) and the introduction of a mediator between God and humankind, which warrants Christ, the new covenant in the New Testament (Hebrews 12:24). The new bond is anchored on grace and faith and sealed with baptism, which replaced circumcision.

COVENANT THEOLOGY IN THE REFORMED CHURCH

The Protestant theologians of the sixteenth century saw Reformed Christians as the new chosen people, a new Israel persecuted by a papal monarchy that identified them as "false teachers" (2 Peter 2:1). Reformation embodied the restoration of the covenant and the original purity of the religion of the patriarchs. The right to resistance to Catholic false idols and gods was therefore a religious obligation that extended to the civil domain through the duty to depose rulers who renounced true faith. The task was to govern according to God's will for the benefit of the population, which corresponded to a subsidiary double covenant between the people and the political leader and between the political leader and God. Violation of these conditions would lead to tyranny, which would contradict the biblical horizontal paradigm. This paradigm is based on a democratic republic moderated by the aristocracy of magistrates, such as Moses and pious kings. The Christian magistrate, a man of staunch faith answerable only before God, would adapt this model.

SECULAR VERSIONS

In the following two centuries, establishing a parallel between the biblical episodes prior to the covenant God made with Abraham and the condition without government, contractarians identified both with the state of nature. For Thomas Hobbes, this is a state of "war of one against the other" that can be overcome only by a covenant, through which people irreversibly deliver all rights to a sovereign whose powers are absolute. John Locke acknowledges the inconveniences of the state of nature, given the absence of a universally accepted law and coercive power. This creates a need to transfer certain rights to a sovereign with power that is conditional upon fulfillment of the compact with the people who can always depose the sovereign. For Jean-Jacques Rousseau, in the state of nature, humans were "noble savages" who were later corrupted by society. The social contract, signed by the people who collectively exercise sovereignty and obey no one but themselves, is the means to restore the freedom enjoyed in an idyllic state of nature.

AMERICAN SYNTHESIS

Religious and secular versions merged in the foundation of the early American Republic. The country was built by religious confessions—Puritans, Baptists, Presbyterians, Quakers, German Sectarians, Huguenots—in the name of liberty. The means to that end lay in the covenant paradigm; just as the Israelites had entered freely into a covenant with God, so did early Americans voluntarily agree to the creation of a church or a political society. That rationale was extended to all domains—labor unions, businesses, professional associations, towns, cities, states, the federal Union—through a network of secularized versions of the covenant. Saintly conduct—charity, interdependence, self-discipline, submission of the private interest to the community, obedience, virtue—ensured by influential churches, was translated in the political realm. This resulted in limited government, popular sovereignty, equity, and an equal share in the decision-making process.

See also *Contractarianism; Federalism; Protestant Political Thought; Reformation Political Thought; Social Contract; U.S. Political Thought.*

. . . . ISABEL DAVID

BIBLIOGRAPHY

Elazar, Daniel J., ed. *The Covenant Connection: From Federal Theology to Modern Federalism.* Lanham, Md.: Lexington Books, 2000.

Hobbes, Thomas. *Leviathan.* New York: Touchstone, 1997.

Holy Bible: Contemporary English Version. New York: American Bible Society, 2000.

Lindberg, Carter, ed. *The Reformation Theologians: An Introduction to Theology in the Early Modern Period (The Great Theologians).* Oxford: Blackwell, 2002.

Locke, John. *Two Treatises of Government.* Cambridge: Cambridge University Press, 1988.

Lutz, Donald. *Documents of Political Foundation Written by Colonial Americans.* Philadelphia: ISHI Press, 1986.

Rousseau, Jean-Jacques. *On The Social Contract.* Indianapolis, Ind.: Hackett Publishing, 1987.

Schmitt, Carl. *Théologie Politique.* Paris: Éditions Gallimard, 1988.

Spinoza, Baruch. *A Theologico-Political Treatise.* Indianapolis, Ind.: Hackett Publishing, 2001.

Credibility

See *Trust and Credibility.*

Crime against Humanity

See *Human Rights.*

Crime Policy

Government response to crime begins first with defining what constitutes criminal behavior. In totalitarian regimes, *crime* is often defined as any behavior that threatens the authority of the state. In liberal democracies, crime often mirrors the public's judgment of right and wrong behavior. Although these judgments may vary from state to state, most democratic nations condemn behavior that threatens the life, liberty, and property of others.

LIMITATIONS ON CRIME PREVENTION POLICIES

Social scientists and philosophers actively debate what causes people to commit crime. Some experts adhere to a medical model of crime, which posits that crime is a symptom of individual or societal dysfunction. Other experts assert that crime is a choice made by rational actors who act as free moral agents. Over time, lawmakers have incorporated both perspectives in their attempts to prevent crime: Officials will commit public funds to improve living conditions, educational opportunities, and vocational resources for their citizens while at the same time enacting tough sentencing laws that communicate the consequences of bad behavior.

Although public officials are concerned about the problem of crime, they are limited in their ability to stop it since many of the influences that impact criminal behavior are beyond government control. For example, research has shown that individuals with absent or dysfunctional families, negative peer relationships, and inadequate moral or religious training are more likely to commit crime; yet policy makers are often precluded from intervening in these private spheres. Similarly, studies have found that individuals with poor self-control are at higher risk for engaging in criminal behavior, but government policies can do little to change individual character traits. Nonetheless, when crime rates rise, increased public concern puts pressure on lawmakers to take immediate action to reduce crime. Accordingly, policy makers enact policies that alter the role of police, adjust the prosecutorial response, or amend the punishment scheme.

ALTERING THE ROLE OF POLICE

In most jurisdictions, local police agencies are charged with enforcing criminal statutes and maintaining social order. In the United States, police agencies have been transformed from loosely structured partisan organizations to professionalized bureaucratic agencies. Urban unrest in the 1960s and 1970s prompted a renewed interest in creating a community service role for police officers. Instead of patrolling neighborhoods in police cars—a practice that created distance between officers and citizens—offers were reassigned to foot patrol to encourage a stronger affinity between police and community residents. This also allowed officers to implement the zero tolerance theory of policing, which required officers to address minor disturbances in order to keep more serious crime at bay.

On occasion, lawmakers have enacted policies that change the way police officers do their jobs. When civil rights advocates complained that officers were indifferent to domestic violence and other crimes against women, policy makers curtailed traditional police discretion by enacting mandatory arrest policies and requiring certain procedural protections for victims of sexual violence. Similarly, police organizations with a history of racial prejudice have been the subject of targeted reforms, particularly with regard to the hiring, training, and evaluation of police officers. In some jurisdictions, civilian oversight of police agencies remains a source of contention as police officers view such policies as being unnecessarily restrictive or overly meddlesome.

Since the start of the modern war on terror, counterterrorism efforts have increasingly involved local police agencies. Many policy makers believe that police agencies are better suited than the military for counterterrorist operations because officers are regularly trained to detect, apprehend, and interrogate criminal suspects without compromising individual civil liberties or incurring civilian casualties. They are also in a better position to work with community leaders and other local agencies to prevent and respond to terrorist attacks. Other lawmakers, however, believe that counterterrorism efforts should be coordinated by national agencies because police agencies are ill-suited to handle the national security implications of terrorist related threats. They also lack the ability to direct personnel and resources outside of their local jurisdictions.

ADJUSTING THE PROSECUTORIAL RESPONSE

In liberal democracies, state attorneys are responsible for initiating judicial proceedings against criminal suspects. They weigh evidence collected from the police and file criminal charges with the court. In many instances, prosecutors have independent authority to decide whether to initiate proceedings against the suspect; in other jurisdictions, policy makers compel prosecutors to press charges in certain types of cases.

In recent years, governments have vacillated in their prosecutorial response to terrorism. Some governments have allowed terrorist suspects to have full due process rights, while others have treated terrorists as enemies of the state. Before the attacks against the United States on September 11, 2001, U.S. officials routinely prosecuted individual terrorists as criminal suspects in civilian courts; however, after the 2001 attacks, the George W. Bush administration began to treat some terrorist suspects as unlawful enemy combatants. Instead of facing criminal charges in regular court proceedings, these suspects were prosecuted and tried in military tribunals. Since the 2008 election of Barack Obama, however, federal Department of Justice officials have been authorized to selectively prosecute high-profile terrorism cases in civilian proceedings.

AMENDING THE PUNISHMENT SCHEME

In most liberal democracies today, convicted criminals are punished with loss of liberty or property, and occasionally, with loss of life. Although the death penalty remains a punishment option in some nations, its use has decreased dramatically in the last several decades. In most nations, government officials are more likely to punish criminals with alternative sanctions, such as monetary fines and restitution, compelled participation in rehabilitation programs and community service, and fixed terms of imprisonment. In some jurisdictions, judges have full discretion over criminal sentencing; elsewhere, lawmakers are responsible for determining the terms of punishment.

Since the early twentieth century, sentencing policies have reflected a variety of philosophical beliefs. Some lawmakers assert that offenders can be rehabilitated through compelled participation in educational and behavioral modification programs. Others contend that bad behavior can be deterred by more punitive sentences or prevented altogether by sentences that incapacitate incorrigible offenders. Still others insist that the government only impose sentences that are justly deserved. Since each position has its practical advantages and disadvantages, democratic lawmakers have struggled to find a policy mixture that can curb crime while minimizing costs and maximizing liberty. Accordingly, when crime rates fluctuate, officials will often try to amend the sentencing scheme first before examining other parts of the system.

See also *Capital Punishment; Civil Law; Due Process; Law and Society; Trial Courts; Universal Jurisdiction.*

. . . . JENNIFER E. WALSH

BIBLIOGRAPHY

Martin, Gus. *Understanding Terrorism: Challenges, Perspectives, and Issues.* Los Angeles: Sage Publications, 2010.

Scheingold, Stuart. *The Politics of Law and Order: Street Crime and Public Policy.* New York: Longman, 1984.

Tonry, Michael H. *Sentencing Matters.* New York: Oxford University Press, 1996.

Wilson, James Q. *Thinking about Crime,* rev. ed. New York: Basic Books, 1983.

Crisis Rhetoric

Rhetoric is the use of persuasive language or other symbols, while *crisis* is a type of rhetorical terminology that conveys a sense of urgency and suggests that a threatening event, different from routine events, has occurred.

GENERATIVE AND STRATEGIC CRISIS RHETORIC

Crises may be rhetorical in two senses: generative and strategic. First, the language that policy makers use to talk and write about issues, whether intentional or not, influences their perceptions of reality. They then convey these depictions of reality to journalists and citizens, often unconsciously, through their messages. When government officials choose to speak about armed conflict in another country as a "crisis," for instance, their language immediately heightens the importance of events there and generates perceptions of a particular political reality for themselves and others.

Crises also can be rhetorical in the strategic sense that Aristotle described in *The Rhetoric* as the ability to identify, in any situation, "the available means of persuasion." Leaders may intentionally adopt a crisis terminology and construct messages in order to win public opinion in line with their view that a crisis exists and that their policy choice is the best means to resolve the crisis. In 1947, most Americans did not view the Soviet Union as a threat, but U.S. president Harry S. Truman and his State Department embarked on a campaign to convince them otherwise and to gain support for the Truman Doctrine. Conversely, leaders may use language strategically to downplay perceptions of crisis, as when the Sudanese government in 2009 attempted to avoid Western intervention with claims, quoted by Reuters's news service, that the humanitarian crisis in Sudan was "absolutely under control."

U.S. PRESIDENTS AND CRISIS RHETORIC

In the United States, since the end of World War II (1939–1945), presidents have been particularly prone to employing rhetoric that encourages perceptions of foreign crisis, and their rhetoric tends to have a number of recurring characteristics. First, presidents depict dangerous scenes of crisis abroad that pose a threat to both American interests (e.g., American lives) and ideals (e.g., freedom). Presidents argue that these scenes, in turn, dictate particular actions and goals. The portrayal of crisis scenes serves to frighten listeners and usually represents the world in black-and-white terms that simplify complex issues. In so doing, presidents attempt to justify particular policies as the only options available by claiming that time is of the essence if devastating consequences are to be avoided.

A second aspect of presidential foreign crisis rhetoric is its depiction of the United States. In their messages, presidents usually portray a nation that is powerful and determined, yet also peaceful and patient. When presidents take military action, they describe the United States as reluctant to do so, but—in the face of grave threat—resolute. Presidents often draw upon the myths of mission (the idea that the United States should be a model for all the world) and manifest destiny (the idea that the United States is destined to spread American institutions and values) to depict the nation as a moral agent with sacred world responsibilities. Presidents also consistently depict crises as tests of character in which the United States must prove its credibility, often through acts of military intervention.

A third facet of presidential foreign crisis rhetoric is its treatment of the enemy. When presidents urge strong military action, they frequently depict an enemy that is too dangerous and too wicked to ignore. Conversely, presidents interested in diplomatic solutions choose to deemphasize enemy portrayals, for fear that such language will undermine public support for diplomacy or even lead to demands for a military response.

A fourth characteristic of presidential foreign crisis rhetoric is its reliance upon references to the president's office, title, and responsibilities as a way to legitimize policy decisions. Since the Korean War (1950–1953), U.S. presidents have regularly used crisis rhetoric to justify military actions that they already have taken, thereby deepening the need to appeal to presidential authority.

When presidents choose to convince citizens that foreign crises exist, they also can depend on a number of advantages to help them do so: Americans's limited knowledge of international relations, the institutional credibility of the presidency, and the rally around the president phenomenon in which citizens tend to support their presidents, at least in the short term, during crises.

In addition, presidents can rely upon a largely compliant mass media to convey their messages for two basic reasons. First, administrations have become adept at news management, an activity that began to accelerate during the latter half of the twentieth century and includes tactics to affect coverage positively, such as President John F. Kennedy's use of exclusive interviews and the Ronald Reagan administration's "line of the day." Second, as media companies have come to treat the purpose of news as profit, rather than public service, they have cut resources from news gathering and encouraged coverage that is entertaining in order to appeal to a wider audience. Such changes, along with a compressed news cycle, have encouraged journalists to rely on official sources, rather than investigating issues themselves, to fulfill the constant demand for stories easily and inexpensively.

From another vantage point, presidents may seem less able to influence public opinion today since the number of media outlets, and hence choices, has proliferated; electronic news coverage tends to summarize presidential messages rather than airing them as spoken; and media coverage, while not questioning facts, discusses politicians' motives cynically.

Nonetheless, when a foreign crisis appears to threaten the nation and citizens have rallied around the president as a representative of the nation, journalists still become especially deferential, thereby allowing presidents to convey their views readily, as President George W. Bush did after the September 11, 2001, attacks on the United States. Presidents find their persuasive task more difficult, however, when they cannot resolve a crisis or their personal credibility is badly damaged, as with Lyndon B. Johnson and Vietnam and Jimmy Carter and Iran.

Over time, the relationship between presidential power and foreign crisis rhetoric has tended to be symbiotic: presidents have used their power to support their rhetoric, and they have used their crisis rhetoric to expand their power. From 1990 to 1991, for example, George H. W. Bush sent 400,000 U.S. troops to Saudi Arabia without asking for congressional consent or invoking the War Powers Resolution of 1973. Presidents have regularly used crisis rhetoric to legitimize unilateral actions and, most often, Congress has assented, thereby ceding the executive branch greater control over foreign policy. If critics oppose military action, they may be attacked for not "supporting the troops."

Foreign crisis rhetoric also discourages careful deliberation by arguing that danger leaves no time for delay, as in George W. Bush's insistence that Congress complete any debate on Iraq prior to the November 2002 elections. Equally troubling, foreign crisis rhetoric may justify extreme measures that violate civil liberties to achieve security.

WORLD LEADERS AND CRISIS RHETORIC

While American presidents have been particularly prone to using crisis rhetoric, other world leaders have often been similarly inclined. Spanish prime minister José María Aznar, for example, engaged in crisis rhetoric before the Spanish parliament in 2003 to justify his support for an impending U.S.–led war against Iraq. According to Teun A. van Dijk in a 2005 article, Aznar depicted a crisis, created by Iraq, which threatened the entire international community, and portrayed his government's actions as peaceful and defensive in nature. In 2004, Russian president Vladimir Putin likewise used crisis rhetoric to represent Chechen hostage takers as part of an international terrorist threat and to bolster perceptions of his own leadership, thereby obscuring Chechen grievances. International leaders have also learned from the example of American presidents that news management techniques can be instrumental in attaining positive media coverage for their crisis interventions. When Israeli military forces invaded Gaza in January 2009, Israeli prime minister Ehud Olmert gave Western journalists easy access to Israeli locations where Hamas rockets had landed, but prevented them from covering the bloodshed in Gaza.

In an era when so many issues vie for public attention, the allure of crisis rhetoric remains strong. The government of North Korean leader Kim Jong-il demonstrated this point quite well with its March 2009 accusation, quoted in *The Boston Globe* and *The Wall Street Journal,* that U.S. president Barack Obama's administration "is now working hard to infringe upon the sovereignty" of North Korea "by force of arms in collusion with the South Korean puppet bellicose forces." According to analysts, this crisis rhetoric was both a response to the new, more conservative South Korean government and a bid to gain U.S. attention.

See also *Emergency Powers; Executive Privilege; Language and Politics; Media, Political Commentary in the; Media and Politics; Rhetoric.*

. . . .   DENISE M. BOSTDORFF

BIBLIOGRAPHY

Aristotle. *The Rhetoric,* translated by W. Rhys Roberts. New York: Modern Library, 1954.

Baum, Matthew A., and Samuel Kernell. "Has Cable Ended the Golden Age of Presidential Television?" *American Political Science Review* 93 (March 1999): 99–114.

Bagdikian, Ben H. *The New Media Monopoly.* Boston: Beacon Press, 2004.

Bostdorff, Denise M. "George W. Bush's Post-September 11 Rhetoric of Covenant Renewal: Upholding the Faith of the Greatest Generation." *Quarterly Journal of Speech* 89 (November 2003): 293–319.

———. *The Presidency and the Rhetoric of Foreign Crisis.* Columbia: University of South Carolina Press, 1994.

———. *Proclaiming the Truman Doctrine: The Cold War Call to Arms.* College Station: Texas A&M University Press, 2008.

Bostdorff, Denise M., Martin Carcasson, James M. Farrell, Robert L. Ivie, Amos Kiewe, and Kathleen B. Smith. "Report of the National Task Force on Presidential Rhetoric in Times of Crisis." In *The Prospect of Presidential Rhetoric,* edited by James Arnt Aune and Martin J. Medhurst, 355–378. College Station: Texas A&M University Press, 2008.

Cappella, Joseph N., and Kathleen Hall Jamieson. *Spiral of Cynicism: The Press and the Public Good.* New York: Oxford University Press, 1997.

Edelman, Murray. *Political Language: Words That Succeed and Policies That Fail.* New York: Academic Press, 1977.

Fallows, James. *Breaking the News: How the Media Undermine American Democracy.* New York: Pantheon, 1996.

Fisher, Louis. *Presidential War Power.* Lawrence: University Press of Kansas, 1995.

Glad, Betty, and Chris J. Dolan, eds. *Striking First: The Preventive War Doctrine and the Reshaping of U.S. Foreign Policy.* New York: Palgrave Macmillan, 2004.

Ivie, Robert L. *Democracy and America's War on Terror.* Tuscaloosa: University of Alabama Press, 2005.

Jamieson, Kathleen Hall, and Paul Waldman. *The Press Effect: Politicians, Journalists, and the Stories That Shape the Political World.* New York: Oxford University Press, 2003.

Kiewe, Amos. "The Crisis Tool in American Political Discourse." In *Politically Speaking: A Worldwide Examination of Language Used in the Public Sphere,* edited by Ofer Feldman and Christ'l De Landtsheer, 79–90. Westport, Conn.: Praeger, 1998.

———, ed. *The Modern Presidency and Crisis Rhetoric.* Westport, Conn.: Praeger, 1994.

Kim, Jack. "North Korea Accuses U.S. of Plotting Attack." *Boston Globe,* March 11, 2009. www.boston.com.

Hu, Fengyung. "Russian Crisis Communication: Interaction Between Federal Television and President Putin in the Beslan's Hostage Crisis." *China Media Research* 3 (2007): 43–52.

Medhurst, Martin J. "Introduction: The Rhetorical Construction of History." In *Critical Reflections on the Cold War: Linking Rhetoric and History,* edited by Martin J. Medhurst and H. W. Brands, 3–19. College Station: Texas A&M University Press, 2000.

Morus, Christina M. "Slobo the Redeemer: The Rhetoric of Slobodan Milosevic and the Construction of the Serbian 'People.'" *Southern Communication Journal* 72 (January–March 2007): 1–19.

Ramstad, Evan. "North Korea Scraps Seoul Accords." *Wall Street Journal,* January 31, 2009. www.online.wsj.com.

Sabato, Larry. *Feeding Frenzy: How Attack Journalism Has Transformed American Politics.* New York: Free Press, 1991.

van Dijk, Teun A. "War Rhetoric of a Little Ally: Political Implicatures and Aznar's Legitimatization of the War in Iraq." *Journal of Language and Politics* 4, no. 1 (2005): 65–91.

Windt, Theodore Otto, Jr. "The Presidency and Speeches on International Crises: Repeating the Rhetorical Past." *Speaker and Gavel* 11 (1973): 6–14.

Worsnip, Patrick. "Darfur Mediator Says Bashir Warrant Imperils Talks." Reuters, March 26, 2009. www.alertnet.org.

Critical Juncture

A *critical juncture* is an episode of pivotal transformation, during which an institution undergoes fundamental and revolutionary change. Critical junctures are unlike other changes because critical junctures are not incremental: They are one-time episodes with lasting consequences. The critical juncture secures a choice or a path through which the institution continues after the juncture has passed. The choice is secured, or "locked in," because other choices are either excluded from later analyses or because other options are eliminated through cost-benefit comparison. As part of the path-dependency analysis, a critical juncture helps establish the trajectory of a society.

Identifying a critical juncture is, strictly speaking, only possible after the fact. Analysts cannot know that a critical juncture is in fact critical until afterwards, because it requires that the institution(s) it fosters become self-reinforcing. Identifying an event as a critical juncture often involves creating counterfactual projections as to what might otherwise have occurred. In this way, an episode may be identified as critical to an institution's creation, it or contributes to how an institution has changed. Counterfactual arguments explain how a moment was critical by creating possible alternatives to history.

Of course, journalists and politicians often see particular movements as historic even as they happen, but a historic moment is not necessarily a critical juncture. At times, it seems that social forces move inexorably toward a certain outcome. For instance, given the preceding rise in women's status in the legal profession, the appointment of a woman to the U.S. Supreme Court in the twentieth century seemed inevitable at some point, if not exactly when it would occur.

By contrast, critical junctures are contingent on preceding events, but yield unexpected outcomes of these events. A crucial facet of critical junctures is that, though proceeded by enabling social conditions, they are context specific and differ from society to society. These episodes may last moments or linger on for years, depending on the circumstances. Critical junctures interrupt or profoundly influence existing institutions, but are unpredictable even by those familiar with a society's institutions.

Scholars who employ path dependency as an explanation of events therefore investigate antecedent conditions to a critical juncture, but rely more heavily on posterior events. Not only do different environments and actors within societies affect how critical junctures affect the development of an institution, but different institutions and processes are more susceptible to change than others. Antecedent conditions cannot reliably predict if there will be a critical juncture, what will change, or how the institution will change. Following a critical juncture is a period of *historical legacy* in which the effects of the juncture persist. This legacy may become evident directly after the juncture, or it may become evident only long after the event has transpired. For instance, the Magna Carta in 1215, which established certain rights of the nobility in England, is now recognized as a critical step toward universal human rights.

Critics of analyses that employ critical junctures argue that the concept is either too broad to be useful or too vague to explain anything. The idea of a critical juncture may be applied to different contexts, but it may also be so context specific that it cannot be generalized to other circumstances. The same scenarios, actors, and processes are unlikely to occur in and influence disparate processes. Likewise, the concept of a critical juncture leaves unanswered how long a juncture might last or specific attributes that a critical juncture must entrench before it becomes important.

Analyses that use the critical juncture framework are also criticized as being overly deterministic, and exclude the role of individual actors outside the critical juncture and may be unfalsifiable. Also, path dependent solutions work only in hindsight, and while most historical analysis allows analysts to develop predictions, a key component of a critical juncture is that the outcome is either random or unpredictable. In this way, critical junctures inhibit prediction. Lastly, deterministic arguments may create logical tautologies: Something is a critical juncture because it shaped an institution as such, and something was shaped as such because of the critical juncture.

Critical junctures are widely used within political science to explain important moments in the history of a society or institution. Scholars point to seemingly important events and attempt to show how an incident shaped an outcome that might not have been, no matter how entrenched it has become. While many argue that such analysis lacks scientific rigor, others argue that explaining these critical moments is important to understanding how institutions develop.

See also *Magna Carta; Path Dependencies.*

. . . . RYAN GIBB

BIBLIOGRAPHY
Collier, Ruth Berins, and David Collier. *Shaping the Political Arena: Critical Junctures, the Labor Movement and Regime Dynamics in Latin America.* Princeton: Princeton University Press.
Mahoney, James. "Path Dependence in Historical Sociology." *Theory and Society* 29, no. 4 (2000): 507–548.
Pierson, Paul. "Increasing Returns, Path Dependence, and the Study of Politics." *American Political Science Review* 94, 2 (2001): 251–267.
———. *Politics in Time: History, Institutions and Social Analysis.* Princeton: Princeton University Press, 2003.

Critical Legal Studies

See *Jurisprudence and Legal Theory.*

Critical Race Theory

ORIGINS AND DEVELOPMENT

Critical race theory (CRT) began in the early 1980s as an insurgent intellectual movement within the American legal academy. The movement's impetus was, according to Kimberlé Crenshaw, Neil Gotanda, Gary Peller, and Kendall Thomas, the editors of the 1995 book, *Critical Race Theory: The Key Writings That Formed the Movement,* "a deep dissatisfaction with traditional civil rights discourse" felt by students and younger professors, mostly of color, in top U.S. law schools. CRT students and scholars maintained that legal academic elites such as the Harvard Law faculty promulgated a naïve view of racial justice, which worked to preserve de facto white supremacy by underestimating the breadth and depth of racial injustice in the United States. CRT proponents held that an

implicit social compact existed between liberals and conservatives in the American intelligentsia about how racial justice would be debated and understood. As described by Kimberlé Crenshaw and her colleagues in *Critical Race Theory: The Key Writings that Formed the Movement,* liberals and conservatives together would exclude "radical or fundamental challenges to [the] status quo . . . by treating the exercise of racial power as rare and aberrational rather than as systemic and ingrained" (xiv). Racism would be conceived as the "intentional, albeit irrational, deviation by a conscious wrongdoer from otherwise neutral, rational, and just ways of distributing jobs, power, prestige, and wealth. The adoption of this perspective allowed a broad cultural mainstream both explicitly to acknowledge the fact of racism and, simultaneously, to insist on its irregular occurrence and limited significance" (xiv). The intended effect of this tacit agreement was to forestall radical challenges to de facto white supremacy and to confine racial reform to liberal incrementalism.

The radicalism of CRT's critique of American white supremacy elicited shock, outrage, and even ridicule from both the law school establishment and the American intelligentsia. But as CRT produced a steady stream of law review articles deconstructing the conventional wisdom of American legal liberalism—illustrating the gap between that conventional wisdom and real-life minority experience—the movement won adherents. Closely allied with critical legal studies (CLS), which sought to expose the ways American law systematically perpetuated and legitimated economic exploitation, CRT drew sustenance from the Marxist and poststructuralist insights of CLS while at the same time forcing it to move race closer to the center of its inquiry. CRT thus constituted of both "a left intervention into race discourse and a race intervention into left discourse" (Crenshaw et al., xix). Today CRT scholars hold tenured professorships in prestigious law schools and are making inroads in the disciplines of history, sociology, political science, and philosophy. While there is less resistance to CRT today than there was at its inception, many scholars and pundits still consider CRT to be conspiratorial and antiwhite.

PREMISES AND TENETS

CRT is a diverse intellectual movement without a rigid orthodoxy. Its adherents nevertheless share some premises and tenets. First, critical race theorists insist that though *race* is bankrupt as a biological concept, it is significant as a social concept. For five centuries, changing conceptions of race legitimized the enslavement, dispossession, colonization, and oppression of African, Native American, Latino and Latina, Asian, and Jewish peoples; though those conceptions of race have been discredited, they still organize inequality and infect modern thought. To diagnose the ways those conceptions of race continue to distort social perception and structure inequality, it is necessary to employ race as a social category. In addition, to avoid essentialism and overgeneralization, it is important to study the various ways different groups have been racially categorized and characterized at different points in time.

Second, critical race theorists consider white supremacy to be constitutive of, and not anomalous to, the American polity. This premise overturns the mainstream belief that civil rights advances of the 1950s and 1960s—*Brown v. Board of Education* (1954), the Civil Rights Act of 1964, and the Voting Rights Act of 1965—purged the laws of racial injustice, removed all obstacles to racial equality, and restored the legitimacy of an otherwise just system. Critical race theorists opt for their historical view not out of eagerness either to discount the triumphs of the civil rights movement or to be reflexively anti-American, but rather out of a carefully considered belief that (1) their view more accurately reflects American historical and sociological reality, and (2) any sugarcoating of that reality provides a false sense of comfort and forestalls the achievement of racial equality. Critical race theorists also wish to emphasize that America's achievement of racial justice is not destined and inevitable. History can and does move backward; realizing racial justice thus requires moral vigilance and political action.

Third, CRT is highly critical of the turn toward the ideal of *colorblindness,* both in the judiciary's interpretation of the Fourteenth Amendment and in American political culture generally. While many critical race theorists agree that a colorblind society is the ultimate goal, all are skeptical that social and economic white supremacy can be dismantled without color-conscious, results-oriented public policy. Maintaining that racial justice means substantive racial equality, they argue that those who opt for formalistic understandings of racial justice—intentionally or not—act to preserve the social and economic privileges white Americans accumulated over three centuries of de jure white supremacy. Against those who characterize prominority remediation as morally equivalent to antiminority discrimination, critical race theorists respond that the two are morally asymmetrical. They urge judges to consider social and historical context in adjudicating color-conscious public policies, and measure their constitutionality by whether they reinforce or undermine de facto white supremacy.

Fourth, CRT emphasizes the importance of attending to *intersectionality*—how individuals live within multiple identities. Because both antidiscrimination law and identity-based social movements typically are organized around single dimensions of identity—race *or* sex *or* sexual orientation, to name just three—our structures of law and protest are ill-equipped to address problems that arise from hybrid forms of oppression. If a black woman, for example, is denied a promotion because her boss feels special animus against black women, that boss can defuse her race-based or sex-based antidiscrimination claim by pointing to recent promotions of black men and white women. The law's insensitivity to the fact that people suffer hybridized forms of discrimination leaves these victims without legal recourse. Scholars of intersectionality analyze these dilemmas and develop conceptual frameworks capable of addressing them.

See also *Intersectionality; Race and Racism; Racial Discrimination; White Supremacy.*

. . . . JACK TURNER

BIBLIOGRAPHY
Bell, Derrick. *And We Are Not Saved: The Elusive Quest for Racial Justice.* New York: Basic Books, 1987.
———. *Faces at the Bottom of the Well: The Permanence of Racism.* New York: Basic Books, 1992.
Crenshaw, Kimberlé, Neil Gotanda, Gary Peller, and Kendall Thomas, eds. *Critical Race Theory: The Key Writings that Formed the Movement.* New York: New Press, 1995.
Delgado, Richard, and Jean Stefancic, eds. *Critical Race Theory: The Cutting Edge,* 2nd ed. Philadelphia: Temple University Press, 2000.
———. *Critical Race Theory: An Introduction.* New York: New York University Press, 2001.
Guinier, Lani. *Tyranny of the Majority: Fundamental Fairness in Representative Democracy.* New York: Free Press, 1994.
Guinier, Lani, and Gerald Torres. *The Miner's Canary: Enlisting Race, Resisting Power, Transforming Democracy.* Cambridge, Mass.: Harvard University Press, 2002.
Haney López, Ian F. *White by Law: The Legal Construction of Race,* rev. ed. New York: New York University Press, 2006.
Williams, Patricia J. *The Alchemy of Race and Rights: Diary of a Mad Law Professor.* Cambridge, Mass.: Harvard University Press, 1991.
———. *Seeing a Color-Blind Future: The Paradox of Race.* New York: Farrar, Straus, and Giroux, 1998.
Wing, Adrien Katherine. *Critical Race Feminism: A Reader,* 2nd ed. New York: New York University Press, 2003.

Critical Realignment Theory

Popularized in the 1960s and 1970s, critical realignment theory gained credibility through the efforts of such notable scholars as V. O. Key Jr., E. E. Schattschneider, James L. Sundquist, and Walter Dean Burnham. For years, critical realignment theory was considered conventional wisdom, and political scientists pondered over when the next critical realignment would occur. Not without its critics, critical realignment theory garners an important place in political science with its definition of eras and electoral politics.

Shortly before the end of World War II (1939–1945), the field of political science began toying with the idea of realigning elections. In *A Theory of Critical Elections,* Key provided the first conceptualization of a critical election. Having studied American presidential elections, Key suggested that two types of elections occur—a few defining *critical elections* and a larger number of quite ordinary and undistinguished elections. Key argued that the defining features of critical elections are (1) voters' involvement is more intense, (2) voters are concerned with the result of the election, (3) the results of the election produce a transformation in the electorate, and (4) the results of the transformation endure for several election cycles. These critical elections usher in a new era in which the electorate shifts as a whole and the dynamics of the electorate are redefined. Although Key identifies two elections that meet the criteria of critical elections, the U.S. presidential elections of 1896 and 1928, he fails to discuss periodicity or the affects these elections have on government processes or policies.

Sundquist builds on the work of Key and Schattschneider and illustrates the significance of the eras that mark the time in between critical elections. Sundquist finds that not all realignments occur in one election, but may be the result of several critical elections. Several features are characteristic of critical realignment theory. Again, in examining voter support of political parties over time, two types of elections are prevalent, realigning and nonrealigning. The existence of critical elections that foster a realignment in the electorate occur in regular intervals. The cycle between critical elections culminates with a transformation in the electorate approximately every thirty years. Many of the transformative effects are the result of oscillation between a weakening and strengthening party identification. As party identification strengthens so too does voters' concern with the election, and high turnout results. There is also evidence suggesting that third parties usually perform well right before a critical election and this may factor into the realignment. Furthermore, realigning elections or critical elections usually focus almost predominately on national issues. Those elections that are characterized as critical elections produce notable changes in the political order. Different interests are recognized as salient to the voters, new ideological issues act as cleavages between the parties, and a long span of unified government emerges. As a result, new government policies emerge that seek to address these new differences or salient issues.

Building on the work of Key and others, Burnham was the first to articulate a specific time period to identify the time span between elections that can best be categorized as a critical election. These critical elections serve to disrupt the current party system at the time and thereby usher in an era that identifies with different policies, ideologies, theories, and presuppositions. Burnham specifies that these critical elections occur every thirty to thirty-six years and, as a result, exhibit a cyclical quality.

Although critical realignment theory is customarily considered an influential theory of elections in political science, it does have its share of critics. Perhaps the greatest critique leveled at critical realignment theory is the failure of a critical election to occur in more than seventy years. The last election that scholars support and recognize as a critical election is the presidential election of 1932. A few scholars have posited the occurrence of a critical election in the 1970s, and perhaps the 1990s, but these elections fail to meet the criteria of a realigning election as established by the theory in the 1960s and 1970s. As David Mayhew states, " . . . the chief contemporary charge against the realignments genre is that it has ceased to be relevant: No certifiable electoral realignment has occurred since 1932." Several explanations exist. First, more than seventy years since a critical election results from the decay of the American parties in the 1960s and 1970s as a result of ticket splitting and increasing numbers of independents. Second, parties seek out the median voters in elections and actively attempt to be less polarizing in order to garner their support. Last, a critical election did not occur as per the schedule of every thirty years because there was not a strong enough event to cause realignment.

See also *Key, V. O., Jr.; Realignment, Partisan; Voting Behavior.*

. . . .   RICHARD M. YON

BIBLIOGRAPHY

Burnham, Walter Dean. *Critical Elections and the Mainsprings of American Politics.* New York: W. W. Norton.

Campbell, Bruce A., and Richard J. Trilling. *Realignment in American Politics: Toward a Theory.* Austin: University of Texas Press, 1980.

Key, V. O., Jr. *A Theory of Critical Elections.* New York: Irvington, 1993.

Mayhew, David. *Electoral Realignments.* New Haven: Yale University Press, 2002.

Schattschneider, E. E. *Party Government.* New York: Holt, Rinehart, and Winston, 1967.

Critical Theory

Critical theory as a philosophical tendency was formed within German culture, but the term was actually coined in the United States. The critical theory project took shape at the Institute for Social Research, founded in 1923 in Frankfurt. The first director of the institute, Carl Grunberg, and many of its early members like Henryk Grossman, Fritz Sternberg, and Felix Weill were primarily interested in the study of political economy, imperialism, and the history of the socialist labor movement.

MAX HORKHEIMER, WALTER BENJAMIN, AND THE FRANKFURT SCHOOL

Max Horkheimer, who took over as the new director of the Institute for Social Research in 1930, changed the orientation of critical theory. Seminars of an interdisciplinary sort were organized among the members of Horkheimer's inner circle and, ultimately, they would produce the major works of critical theory normally associated with the Frankfurt school. Participants included Leo Lowenthal, an expert in literary criticism who joined the institute in 1926, and Theodor W. Adorno, who was considered valuable for his knowledge of music, and who began his collaboration with the institute in 1928, yet only became an official member ten years later. There was also Erich Fromm, a gifted psychologist, who started his nine-year collaboration in 1930; Herbert Marcuse, a philosopher and former student of Martin Heidegger, who joined in 1933; and Walter Benjamin, the most unique of these thinkers, who never officially was a member at all.

Benjamin was completely unknown in the United States until the preeminent political theorist, Hannah Arendt, edited a collection of his essays, *Illuminations* (1969). Benjamin thereafter became celebrated as an iconoclastic thinker involved with investigating and meshing traditions as diverse as Jewish messianism, baroque, modernism, and Marxism. With the new popularity of the radically subjective postmodern movement during the 1980s, however, his fame reached extraordinary proportions: A library of secondary works has appeared and almost every volume of Benjamin's four-volume *Selected Writings* has become an academic bestseller. His critique of progress and optimistic illusions, his attempt to reconstruct theory through the assimilation of seemingly mutually exclusive traditions, his skepticism concerning traditional foundations and universal claims, and his preoccupation with subjectivity produced a transformation of the entire critical project. Benjamin's work spoke directly to many on the left who, following the collapse of the social and cultural movements associated with the 1960s, felt they were living in an age of ruins. Above all, however, his inability to decide whether to emigrate to Israel or the United States and his subsequent tragic death in 1940, while attempting to flee the Nazi invasion of France, put a particularly dramatic stamp on his life and the experience of exile.

Exile marked the work of the Institute for Social Research. Horkheimer, in fact, only coined the term *critical theory* in 1937, after having fled to the United States. His seminal essay on the subject, "Traditional and Critical Theory" (1937), treated it as an approach qualitatively different from "vulgar" materialism—that is to say positivism or behaviorism—and metaphysical idealism. Following the approach developed in the classic works of unorthodox Western Marxists like *Marxism and Philosophy* by Karl Korsch and *History and Class Consciousness* by Georg Lukács, Horkheimer insisted that critical theory should be understood neither as a philosophical system nor a fixed set of proscriptions. He instead viewed it as a method of liberation, a cluster of themes or concerns that would express an explicit interest in the abolition of social injustice and the psychological, cultural, and political reasons why the international proletarian revolution failed following the events of 1917 in Russia. With the publication of "Authority and the Family" (1934), for example, Horkheimer sought to analyze how a patriarchal familial structure inhibited the development of revolutionary consciousness among workers. "The Jews and Europe" (1938) insisted that confronting bigotry called for confronting economic exploitation: or, as Horkheimer put the matter in his essay, "he who wishes to speak of anti-Semitism must also speak of capitalism." Works like these set the stage for a new mode of *dialectical thinking*—a version of Marxism—that went beyond the economic interests of classes and elites as well as the institutional dynamics of the state.

THE CRITIQUE OF IDEOLOGY AND TOTALITARIANISM

Reactionary sexual mores, mass culture, the division of labor, and the need to grasp the universal through the particular would prove essential themes for the Institute for Social Research. Deeper issues mired in the anthropology of human existence also became matters of concern for critical theory. Indeed, the need for a response to these issues turned critical theory into an ongoing threat to the stultifying dogma and collectivism of "actually existing socialism." In the spirit of Marxism, critical theory leveled an attack on all ideological and institutional forms of oppression including those justified by Marxism itself. Critical theory was—from the first—intended to foster critical reflection, a capacity for fantasy, and new forms of political action in an increasingly bureaucratized world.

Most members of the institute remained suspicious of the different ways in which supposedly neutral formulations of science veiled repressive social interests. That is why they employed a methodological approach indebted to both the *critique of ideology* (*Ideologiekritik*) that derived from German idealism and Marx's sociology of knowledge. Ideals of freedom

and liberation thus provided the basis for the social critique of the existing order. In the United States, however, the character of this engagement changed dramatically from that of the early days. The most compelling reasons were connected with the failure of the proletarian revolution, the increasingly stark reality of totalitarianism, and the looming shadow of McCarthyism.

Major scholars associated with the Institute for Social Research—albeit often at the fringes—added much to an understanding of the ideological forces behind the new totalitarian phenomenon and its structure. Its emergence in Germany was analyzed in diverse works of an interdisciplinary character. *Escape from Freedom* (1941) by Erich Fromm, which proved enormously popular, analyzed the psychological appeal of Nazi totalitarianism. Siegfried Kracauer, who was close to Adorno and Benjamin, offered what would prove a classic examination of German film in the Weimar Republic in his work entitled *From Caligari to Hitler* (1947). In a more social scientific vein, Otto Kirchheimer contributed *Political Justice* (1961) and Franz Neumann, with *Behemoth* (1942), introduced the first significant work that analyzed the structure of the Nazi state. Horkheimer himself edited a five-volume work, *Studies in Prejudice* (1949), for the American Jewish Committee while Adorno led a team of researchers in producing the classic book *The Authoritarian Personality* (1950). In the context of the United States, both looking backward to the 1930s and forward to McCarthyism, *Prophets of Deceit: A Study of the Techniques of the American Agitator* (1948) by Leo Lowenthal and Norbert Guterman as well as Lowenthal's work on American anti-Semitism, *Images of Prejudice* (1945), are significant works.

Following the Hitler-Stalin Pact that unleashed World War II (1939–1945), the proletarian revolution ceased to serve as the ultimate aim of the critical enterprise. The working class lost its standing as the revolutionary subject of history and the Frankfurt school no longer saw its interests as sufficient for generating a critique of the status quo. A new phase in the development of critical theory began with the completion of *Dialectic of Enlightenment* (1944), including a sensational last chapter "Elements of Anti-Semitism," in 1947. Horkheimer and Adorno, its authors, called into question the old belief in progress, science, and the benefits of modernity. They insisted that by privileging mathematical reason, the Enlightenment not only assaulted reactionary forms of religious dogma, but also, whether intentionally or unintentionally, the more progressive normative ways of thinking. Scientific rationality divorced from ethical concerns was, indeed, seen as culminating in the number tattooed on the arm of the concentration camp inmate.

Dialectic of Enlightenment offers less the vision of a better world emerging from the Enlightenment than one increasingly defined by the commodity form and bureaucratic rationality, in which the individual is stripped of conscience and spontaneity. Stalinism on the left, Nazism on the right, and an increasingly bureaucratic and robotic mass society emerging in the United States inspired this book: mass society, the horror of war, and—perhaps above all—the concentration camp universe. The new reality demanded a significant revision in the more traditional understandings of critical and radical theory.

THEODOR ADORNO AND THE CRITIQUE OF THE BUREAUCRATIC ORDER

Communism had turned into a nightmare, Nazism was even worse, social democracy had been integrated into the status quo, and liberalism—with its emphasis upon the abstract individual of the social contract—had seemingly become anachronistic. For Horkheimer and Adorno, the possibility of revolutionary transformation faded in the face of an apparently seamless bureaucratic order buttressed by the culture industry intent on eliminating subjectivity and any genuinely critical opposition to the status quo. This development is what required rethinking of the usually positive view that progressives had traditionally accorded the Enlightenment. Not the *philosophe* or the political critic but the bohemian intellectual, who challenged society in its entirety, was seen as embodying whatever emancipatory hope existed for the future. Thus, for the proponents of critical theory, it had become necessary to supplement the dialectical framework of Hegel and Marx with the more modernist and subjectivist tenets of nineteenth-century German philosophers Arthur Schopenhauer and Friedrich Nietzsche in combating the collectivist strains within advanced industrial society.

It was now incumbent upon a genuinely critical theory to explore the ways in which civilization in general, and modernity in particular, were flawed from the beginning. The critical theory of society would thus require a more directly anthropological form of inquiry. According to Horkheimer and Adorno, indeed, it was now necessary to highlight not the needs of some class-bound and collectivist "revolutionary subject" like the proletariat, but the ways in which individual subjectivity might resist the conformity generated by an increasingly administered and culturally barbaric universe. Political resistance thus made way for a philosophico-aesthetic assertion of subjectivity in *Negative Dialectics* (1966) and *Aesthetic Theory* (1970), two monumental works by Adorno, while Horkheimer emphasized a philosophico-religious understanding of resistance in *The Longing for the Totally Other* (1970).

Adorno was probably the most talented proponent of this new turn in critical theory. His interests extended from musicology and literary analysis to sociology, metapsychology, and philosophy. Adorno's works evidence a rare standard of intellectual brilliance. They include extraordinary studies on modern music, in his masterful *Aesthetic Theory,* and *Minima Moralia: Reflections of a Damaged Life* (1947).

Adorno's work exemplifies the abstruse style that has become identified with the Frankfurt school. The heritage of dialectical philosophy surely had an impact on its formation and the complex use of complex concepts employed often demanded a complex articulation. Especially in the ideologically charged context of the war and its aftermath, however, members of the Institute for Social Research also self-consciously employed an *Aesopian* form of writing. As exiles living in the United States, they sought to hide their indebtedness to Marx by substituting the highly abstract language of Hegel. But also noteworthy about the style of Adorno and Horkheimer, their famous analysis of the culture industry developed in *Dialectic of Enlightenment,* written while they were living in Los Angeles, implied that popularity would necessarily "neutralize" whatever critical or emancipatory messages a work might retain. Nevertheless, there was nothing ambivalent about the willingness of Erich Fromm—or Herbert Marcuse—to engage the public in a radical fashion.

ERICH FROMM AND HERBERT MARCUSE

Erich Fromm was surely the most lucid stylist to emerge from the Institute for Social Research. He was also the most popular and, arguably, the most loyal to its original purpose insofar as he always sought to link theory with the practical demands of social change and individual transformation. Fromm grew up Orthodox and he studied with some of the leading rabbis in Europe. His dissertation dealt with the Jewish Diaspora and another of his early works with the Sabbath. The psychoanalytic institute he founded in Berlin with his first wife, Frieda Reichmann, soon became known as the Torah-peutikum. His interest in the psychological appeal and ethical impulse provided by religion, indeed, never fully disappeared.

Fromm was initially one of the most influential members of the institute and a close friend of Horkheimer. His concern was with how psychological attitudes mediated the relation between the individual and society. Even during the 1920s, he was intent upon linking Sigmund Freud's psychoanalytic theory with Marx's historical materialism. For this reason, when Adorno first insisted on developing an anthropological critique of civilization from the standpoint of Freud's instinct theory, he clashed with Fromm, who insisted upon the primacy of Freud's more practical clinical studies. The dazzling newcomer won the battle. Fromm divorced himself from the institute by 1940 and proceeded to write a number of bestsellers, including *Escape from Freedom.* Quickly enough, his former colleagues condemned him for the "superficial" quality of his writings even while his influence soared among left-wing intellectuals and a broader public from the 1950s to the 1970s.

As for Herbert Marcuse, while in the United States, he not only worked with the Office of Strategic Services as an expert on West European politics, but also wrote papers on totalitarianism and, in 1958, published a highly respected study entitled *Soviet Marxism.* In spite of his penchant for utopian thought, so prominent in *Eros and Civilization* (1955), Marcuse also remained faithful to the original practical impulse of critical theory. His most influential work, *One-Dimensional Man* (1964), actually anticipated the seminal role of the new social movements and a radical cultural politics in responding to the bureaucracy, commodification, and conformism of advanced industrial society. Pessimism concerning the future of a society in which all radical alternatives were being absorbed, and all ideological contradictions were being flattened out, combined with a utopian vision built upon the radical humanism of the young Marx, the *play principle* of Schiller with its utopian assault upon the repression demanded by reality, and the metapsychology of Freud. This tension, indeed, permeated all of Marcuse's writings.

THE LEGACY OF THE FRANKFURT SCHOOL AND FUTURE OF CRITICAL THEORY

In the United States, the popularity of Fromm and Marcuse contrasted strikingly with a virtually total ignorance of the work produced by the rest of the Frankfurt school. The legend that critical theory inspired the movement of the 1960s is, certainly in America, misleading; its major works were translated only in the 1970s. During that decade, journals like *Telos* and *New German Critique* helped publicize its ideas and the works of its most important representatives. In Europe, however, the influence of the Frankfurt school on the partisans of 1968 was strong. Its emphasis upon alienation, the domination of nature, the regressive components of progress, the mutability of human nature, and the stultifying effects of the culture industry and advanced industrial society made the enterprise relevant for young intellectuals who had come of age through the movement of the 1960s.

Horkheimer and Adorno, however, were appalled by what they had helped inspire. Following their return to Germany, the former became rector and the latter, somewhat later, a dean at the University of Frankfurt. It is somewhat ironic that these new stalwarts of the establishment should have anticipated the movement's concern with a cultural revolution and the transformation of everyday life demanded by so many of their students. These themes were as real for many activists of the 1960s, both in Europe and the United States, as the quest for racial justice and the anti-imperialist opposition to the Vietnam War (1959–1975). Nevertheless, these themes lost their salience in the general malaise that followed the collapse of the movement and the emergence of a neoconservative assault upon the so-called adversary culture.

A new set of academic radicals embraced instead the deconstructive and radically subjectivist elements in the thinking of the Frankfurt school in general, and in the work of Adorno and Benjamin in particular, with their emphasis upon the fragmentary character of reality, the illusion of progress, and the need to substitute experimental cultural for political resistance. All this fit the time in which radicalism retreated from the streets into the university. Critical theory of this new *deconstructive* or *poststructuralist* sort invaded the most prestigious journals and disciplines ranging from anthropology and film to religion, linguistics, and political science. Elements of it have, indeed, have become features of the very society that the Frankfurt school ostensibly wished to challenge.

But that time, too, is passing. If it is to remain relevant, especially in the United States, critical theory must begin taming its metaphysical excesses, mitigating its subjectivism, and affirming its repressed political character. These concerns inform much of the work undertaken by Jürgen Habermas, the brilliant student of Horkheimer and Adorno, who came to maturity in the aftermath of World War II. Of particular interest, in this vein, is his *Philosophical Discourse of Modernity: Twelve Lectures* (1985). Habermas was never in exile: He experienced the impact of totalitarianism directly in his youth, and it left him with a profound respect for the liberal political legacy, the *public sphere*, and the repressed possibilities of *communicative action*. Habermas has also gained a large academic following in the United States. Nevertheless, his work provides an important beginning for resurrecting the critical undertaking.

A *clash of civilizations*, globalization, new forms of imperialism, and a powerful tide of conservatism are creating new problems for a new generation of critical theorists. It is becoming increasingly necessary to begin reconstructing the practical impulse of the critical project, its repressed political purpose, and its speculative legacy for the present. Critical theory was originally intended to foster social justice, cultural experimentation, and human happiness. Its academic transformation into a form of metaphysics cannot remain immune from criticism. Remaining honest to the tradition of critical theory thus calls for confronting it from the critical standpoint. Whatever the other differences between them, all of its major representatives would assuredly—today—find themselves in agreement with that claim.

. . . .   STEPHEN ERIC BRONNER

BIBLIOGRAPHY

Adorno, Theodor W. *Minima Moralia: Reflections from Damaged Life*, translated by E. F. N. Jephcott. London: New Left Books, 1974.

Benjamin, Walter. *Illuminations*, edited by Hannah Arendt, translated by Harry Zohn. New York: Schocken Books, 1969.

Bronner, Stephen Eric. *Of Critical Theory and Its Theorists*, 2nd ed. New York: Routledge, 2002.

Bronner, Stephen Eric, and Douglas MacKay Kellner, eds. *Critical Theory and Society: A Reader*. New York: Routledge, 1989.

Habermas, Jürgen. *Knowledge and Human Interests*, translated by Jeremy J. Shapiro. Boston: Beacon Press, 1972.

Horkheimer, Max. *Critical Theory: Selected Essays*, translated by Matthew O'Connell. New York: Continuum, 1982.

Horkheimer, Max, and Theodor Adorno. *Dialectic of Enlightenment: Fragments*, translated by John Cumming. New York: Herder and Herder, 1972.

Jay, Martin. *The Dialectical Imagination: A History of the Frankfurt School and the Institute of Social Research, 1923–1950*. Berkeley: University of California Press, 1996.

Kellner, Douglas. *Critical Theory, Marxism and Modernity*. Oxford: Polity Press, 1989.

Marcuse, Herbert. *One-Dimensional Man*. Boston: Beacon Press, 1966.

Wiggershaus, Rolf. *The Frankfurt School: Its History, Theories, and Political Significance*, translated by Michael Robertson. Oxford: Polity Press, 1994.

Croce, Benedetto

Benedetto Croce (1866–1952) was an Italian philosopher of history and aesthetics who emphasized the importance of the human imagination, consciousness, and intuitive understanding in the concrete experiences of living. Born near Naples, Croce was raised in a wealthy family. In 1883, only Croce and his brother survived the earthquake of Casamicciola, which killed his parents and sister. At age sixteen, he went to Rome to live with his uncle, Silvio Spaventa, who introduced Croce to art and politics. He studied law at the University of Rome without taking a degree, returned to Naples, and enriched his intellectual life by traveling to Spain, Germany, France, and England.

In 1910, Croce was made a life member of the Italian Senate in honor of his work. When Mussolini rose to power, Croce left his one-year tenure as minister of education (1920–1921). Croce's 1925 *Manifesto of the Anti-Fascist Intellectuals* severed his relationship with philosopher Giovanni Gentile (1875–1944), who supported Mussolini's Fascism. Croce continued to be a critic of the Fascist regime, publishing his bimonthly review *La critica* from 1903 to 1944. Subsequently, the Fascists raided his personal library was raided, and his books were banned. Due to his international reputation, Croce avoided imprisonment. After the fall of Mussolini in 1943, Croce led the Liberal Party and remained its president until 1947, the same year he established the Italian Institute for Historical Studies.

Giambattista Vico, Giovanni Gentile, and G. W. F. Hegel were major influences. Croce applied Vico's cyclical theory of social progress to the relation between art, philosophy, and practice. Also, many scholars view Croce as neo-Hegelian because of his view of history as dialectical and progressive. Unlike Hegel, Croce opposed idealism as a systematic, utopian philosophy, because of human's lower nature. Croce also rejected materialism and positivism as morally bankrupt. Fighting against the ideological illusion of systematic certainty, he argued for moral ambiguity in knowing the ethical ideal. Since Croce believed logic rested on intuitive knowledge, the foundation of his philosophy as aesthetics was an ongoing process of moral experience and expression. Croce's core philosophical writings are *Aesthetic,* published in 1902, along with *Logic* and *The Philosophy of the Practical,* both published in 1908. Because of his stress on the arts and the power of symbols and language as the imaginative source for knowledge, Croce's liberalism was aristocratic.

In *History as the Story of Liberty,* published in 1938, Croce distinguishes four forms of history: politics or economy, ethics or religion, art, and thought or philosophy. The standard of judgment correlated to these forms are the useful, the true, the beautiful, and the good. Underlying these diverse forms is one individual human spirit of liberty activating its expression. The unity is organic as new realizations of particular premises revise earlier manifestations of the same type of knowledge. In Croce's view, political philosophy arises from the particular individual acts in society, which ideally express morality and truth. It is only in the concrete historical situation that one can realize one's higher nature in politics. Croce defined philosophy as historical, and hence aesthetic and practical, a view criticized as *historicism*—giving undue credence to immanence as if transcendence were not a separate metaphysical, spiritual reality.

See also *Hegel, Georg W. F.; Historicism.*

. . . . JOANNE TETLOW

BIBLIOGRAPHY

D'Amico, Jack, Dain A. Trafton, and Massimo Verdicchio, eds. *The Legacy of Benedetto Croce: Contemporary Critical Views.* Toronto: University of Toronto Press, 1999.

Orsini, Gian N. *Benedetto Croce: Philosopher of Art and Literary Critic.* Carbondale: Southern Illinois University Press, 1961.

Rizi, Fabio Fernando. *Benedetto Croce and Italian Fascism.* Toronto: University of Toronto Press, 2003.

Roberts, David D. *Benedetto Croce and the Uses of Historicism.* Berkeley: University of California Press, 1987.

Ryn, Claes. *Will, Imagination, and Reason: Babbitt, Croce, and the Problem of Reality.* New Brunswick, N.J.: Transaction, 1997.

Crosland, Charles Anthony Raven

Charles Anthony Raven Crosland (1918–1977) was a leading British socialist intellectual in the mid-twentieth century whose theories had a major influence on the evolution of the Labour Party. He also occupied key cabinet positions in several Labour governments.

Under Prime Minister Harold Wilson's first government in 1964, Crosland was deputy to George Brown, who had run against Wilson. In 1965, Crosland was appointed secretary of state for education and science and began a campaign for comprehensive education in England and Wales. In 1967, he moved to the Board of Trade as its president, remaining until 1969. He then became secretary of state for local government and regional planning until 1970.

In the 1970s, Crosland became the leader of the right wing of the Labour Party. After Roy Jenkins resigned, Crosland stood for the deputy leadership of the party but was eliminated in the first round. After Labour's return to power in 1974, he became secretary of state for the Department of the Environment. Following Wilson's retirement in 1976, Crosland contested the leadership but finished last in the poll. He then switched his support to the eventual winner, James Callaghan, who duly rewarded him by appointing him foreign secretary in 1976.

Crosland was an active member of the Fabian Society, an organization founded by Sidney and Beatrice Webb that sought the establishment of a democratic socialist state in the United Kingdom, and he contributed to their major publications.

Crosland expanded on his revisionism in *The Future of Socialism* (1956), in which he challenged the dominance of the Webbs in Fabian thinking and countered their ascetic top-down Fabianism with a more liberal version. Crosland was a revisionist in the manner of German political theorist Eduard Bernstein, who rejected the Marxist analysis of modern societies and defined socialism in terms of ethical goals rather than class and the common ownership of means of production. Crosland argued that classical capitalism was dead in the sense that robber barons no longer controlled the means of production as they did in the nineteenth century. State regulations had dispersed and curtailed ownership, and decision making now resided with managers and technocrats rather than capitalists. Power relations had irrevocably changed in society, and Marxism had to change as well. Socialism had to be redefined in terms of greater social equality and greater social justice, encompassing not merely economics but also other areas such as gender, race, and politics. Public ownership, until then one of the cardinal tenets of socialism, had to be jettisoned because it was no longer the essential component of a socialist society, but only one of a number of means to achieve economic equality. The desirability of public ownership depended on its effectiveness in advancing social justice.

In *Socialism Now* (1974), Crosland advocated for a "democratic equality," which he defined as a dynamic concept. He recognized that some inequality may be good for society or for an efficient economy because otherwise the have-nots might be worse off under equality of outcome. Incentives, Crosland asserted, are necessary to entice scarce talent and enlarge the common good. Equality is not a virtue in itself but only in relation to its efficacy as a means to social justice.

Crosland believed in leveling up rather than leveling down. Thus, without economic growth, everyone would be worse off than before and equally poor. Economic growth has fiscal dividends that enable governments to use public expenditure to redistribute or transfer wealth without impoverishing any sector of society. Growth in income ultimately equalized opportunity and access. It led to better lifestyles and improved efficiency. Crosland also placed emphasis on comprehensive education as a means to achieve greater social equality and reduce social disparities incrementally. He had little sympathy for the idealistic socialism that had dominated nineteenth-century thinking.

See also *British Political Thought; Socialism; Webb, Sidney and Beatrice Potter.*

. . . . GEORGE THOMAS KURIAN

BIBLIOGRAPHY
Crosland, Charles Anthony Raven. *The Conservative Enemy: A Programme of Radical Reform for the 1960's.* London: Jonathan Cape, 1962.
———. *The Future of Socialism.* London: Jonathan Cape, 1956.
———. *Socialism Now and Other Essays.* London: Jonathan Cape, 1974.
Jefferys, Kevin. *Anthony Crosland: A New Biography.* London: John Blake, 1999.
Lipsey, David, and Dick Leonard, eds. *The Socialist Agenda: Crosland's Legacy.* London: Jonathan Cape, 1981.

Crossman, Richard

Richard Howard Stafford ("Dick") Crossman (1907–1974) was a writer, diarist, and British Labour Party politician who served as member of British parliament for Coventry East from 1945 to 1974. He held high ministerial positions in Harold Wilson's Labour governments from 1964 to 1970, but his most lasting contribution to British political life was the publication of three volumes of his controversial ministerial diaries.

In his youth, Crossman won a scholarship to Winchester College and later a scholarship to Oxford University's New College to read classics. After taking first-class honors, in 1930 he became a don and tutor at New College, where he taught and published books on political philosophy. In the late 1930s, he left Oxford for Labour Party politics, working

as a writer and editor for the left-of-center *New Statesman.* During World War II (1939–1945), he served in the Ministry of Economic Warfare, coordinating political propaganda and psychological warfare. After the end of the war, he won the seat of Coventry East and began his career as a member of Parliament.

Despite his demonstrated abilities, Crossman remained on the Labour backbenches for nearly two decades, in part because of his contentious role in various Labour leadership challenges of the 1950s. His association with Aneurin Bevan and later with Harold Wilson marked him as a left-wing rebel, and it was not until the death of Hugh Gaitskell in 1963 that Crossman was able to use his close relationship with Wilson to help Wilson win his campaign for the party leadership. When the Labour Party won the general election of 1964, Crossman was named minister of Housing and Local Government.

Crossman served as housing minister until 1966, when a cabinet reshuffle gave him the position of lord president of the Privy Council and leader of the House of Commons, a position that he did not greatly enjoy. His diaries reveal that he missed the power and authority that the department had given him. In 1968 when Wilson combined the departments of health and social security to form the single Department of Health and Social Security, Crossman received the charge of the department. As its minister, he worked on a proposal to revise the existing flat-rate state pension program by adding a new earnings-related component.

When the Labour Party lost the 1970 election, Crossman resigned from his party's front bench to accept the editorship of the *New Statesman.* He also began to edit and format his political diaries for publication—a task that acquired a particular sense of urgency when he was diagnosed with cancer. Crossman's determination to give a full and complete account of his time within the Wilson cabinet ran into strong opposition from the cabinet office. Not only did his diaries flout the official secrets acts, which protected government documents from early release, but also his near-verbatim accounts of discussions in cabinet and between ministers and civil servants broke the long-standing tradition of confidentiality within the British political system. The ensuing legal battle to prevent publication was still unresolved when Crossman died in April 1974, but his ministerial diaries would eventually be published. To this day, the Crossman diaries remain a valuable resource for historians and politicians, and the precedent set by their publication opened the way for the printing of other political diaries, both by Crossman's contemporaries and by future politicians.

See also *British Political Thought; Political Philosophy.*

. . . . SHANNON GRANVILLE

BIBLIOGRAPHY
Crossman, R. H. S. *The Diaries of a Cabinet Minister,* 3 vols. London: Hamish Hamilton/Jonathan Cape, 1975–1977.
Dalyell, Tam. *Dick Crossman.* London: Weidenfeld and Nicolson, 1989.
Young, Hugo. *The Crossman Affair.* London: Hamish Hamilton/Jonathan Cape, 1976.

Cryptography

Cryptography, from the Greek *kruptō,* meaning "to conceal," and *graphō,* meaning "to write," is the science of concealed writing; it is a technical term referring to the translation of messages into ciphers or codes. *Cryptology* is the study of both cryptography and cryptanalysis. *Cryptanalysis* is the science of decrypting ciphers and codes without a key. Within modern cryptology, there are many theories and practices, particularly focusing on the basic infrastructure used in cryptographic systems.

The fundamental intention of cryptography is to enable two individuals, normally called "Alice" and "Bob," to communicate information securely. "Oscar" is the potential third-party adversary who wants to intercept the message.

A general model of a cryptosystem can be visualized as follows: Alice wants to communicate a plaintext message to Bob. She ciphers the plaintext message using a key according to the encryption rule of the system. Bob receives the ciphertext, which can also be received by Oscar, who can be either a passive observer intending to gain the key for reading all the communication messages or an adversary intending to impersonate the original messenger and to modify the message to the receiver. Cryptosystems are intended so only Bob is able to decode (decrypt) the ciphertext because he possesses the key that reconstructs the message into plaintext, thereby preventing Oscar from receiving any information from the message. The difference between enciphering and encoding is enciphering requires each letter (or numeral) of a message to be replaced by another letter (or numeral), whereas encoding replaces entire sentences, syllables, or words. The code is the predetermined rules for converting the messages from one representation to another. A cryptosystem using an encryption key for message communication is specified by a five-tuple representing P, C, K, E, and D. P is a finite set of every possible plaintext; C is a finite set of every possible ciphertext; K is a finite set of every possible key; E is the space of the encryption rule; D is the space of the decryption rule; therefore, $k \in K$, e_K: P $\rightarrow$ C. Conversely, each $k \in K$ and each $x \in P$ contain a d_K, such that $d_K(e_K(x)) = x$ for all plaintexts x.

The antiquity of cryptology is well attested in the history of civilization. The beautiful hieroglyphic script of ancient Egypt, for instance, would have been impossible to decipher without discovery of the Rosetta stone by French soldiers in 1799. The Spartans used a cryptographic device called a *scytale,* wherein a sheet of papyrus with a message relating to their military campaign was wound around a cylinder; to read the cipher, the recipient had to possess a staff of the same diameter on which the papyrus could be unwound. The Greek historian Polybius created a 5 × 5 grid using the twenty-four letters of the Greek alphabet, known as the Polybius square. During World War I (1914–1918), the Germans used the ADFGX cipher for communication. The German cipher used a 6 × 6 grid based on the Polybius square. The cipher of Julius Caesar encrypted messages in a rotated alphabet that used a shift of three letters to the immediate right. In the New Testament, the name *Babylon* was sometimes used as a designation for Rome. Jewish literature equated Edom, Egypt, Kittim, and Rome with Babylon as a type of cipher.

Ancient ciphers and codes, however, were much more simplistic than those of the computer age. Crypotological progress was essentially halted between the decline of the Roman Empire and the rise of Islam. Cryptanalysis among Arabs was pioneered in the eighth century and subsequently continued. The necessity of mathematical advances, which had not yet occurred, meant that cryptology would not be developed further until late in medieval history. In 1412, Arabic knowledge of cryptology was described in the *Subh al-Asha,* the classical fourteen-volume encyclopedia, with tremendous detail. Francis Bacon developed a biliteral alphabet, known as the biliteral cipher, in his *De Augmentis Scientiarum* (1624) using the two characters, *a* and *b,* in groups of five letters. Edgar Allan Poe, in his 1843 short story, "The Gold Bug," popularized cryptanalysis with a detailed description of methodology to decipher any monoalphabetic substitution cipher. Additional development in cryptology occurred in harmony with the emergence of modern armies and intelligence services throughout the nineteenth century. The end of the world wars and invention of the computer advanced cryptology even further. The ciphers and codes of the present age are so advanced that it is impossible to decode them without the combination of both human ingenuity and computer proficiency.

See also *Cybersecurity.*

. . . . RON J. BIGALKE JR.

BIBLIOGRAPHY

Beutelspacher, Albrecht. *Cryptology: An Introduction to the Art and Science of Enciphering, Encrypting, Concealing, Hiding, and Safeguarding Described without Any Arcane Skullduggery but Not Without Cunning Waggery for the Delectation and Instruction of the General Public.* Washington, D.C.: Mathematical Association of America, 1994.

Deavors, Cipher A., and Kruh, Louis. *Machine Cryptography and Modern Cryptanalysis.* Dedham, Mass.: Artech House, 1985.

Denning, Dorothy Elizabeth Robling. *Cryptography and Data Security.* Reading, Mass.: Addison-Wesley, 1982.

Gaines, Helen F. *Cryptanalysis: A Study of Ciphers and Their Solution.* New York: Dover, 1956.

Kahn, David. *The Codebreakers,* rev. ed. New York: Scribner, 1999.

Konheim, Alan G. *Cryptography: A Primer.* New York: Wiley, 1981.

Menezes, Alfred J., Paul C. van Oorschot, and Scott A. Vanstone. *Handbook of Applied Cryptography.* Boca Raton, Fla.: CRC Press, 1996.

Singh, Simon. *The Code Book: The Science of Secrecy from Ancient Egypt to Quantum Cryptography.* London: Fourth Estate, 1999.

Van der Lubbe, Jan C. A. *Basic Methods of Cryptography,* translated by Steve Gee. New York: Cambridge University Press, 1998.

Wolfe, James Raymond. *Secret Writing: The Craft of the Cryptographer.* New York: McGraw-Hill, 1970.

Cube Law

Cube law is a theory about democratic politics positing that in single-member electoral systems with two dominant parties, there is overrepresentation by the party or grouping that receives the most votes in elections. Concurrently, the party that secures the least number of votes is underrepresented.

Cube law is not applicable to systems with more than two parties or to electoral arrangements with proportional or cumulative voting. Articulated by J. P. Smith in the 1909 report of the British Royal Commission on electoral reform, cube law holds that if the ratio of votes gained by two parties is X/Y, then the proportion of seats gained by the respective groups should be X^3/Y^3. Hence, if party X secures 60 percent of the vote and party Y gains 40 percent, the ratio would be 60/40 or 1.5 votes for the majority party for every 1 for the minority. The seat ratio would be $60^3/40^3$ (3.375/1), which would give the majority party seventy-seven seats to the twenty-three for the losing party. Cube law has been fairly accurate in predicting elections in two-party systems, especially contests in the United States. Decomposed cube law was developed in the 1960s in an effort to apply the theory to multiparty systems.

See also *Minority Representation; Proportional Representation.*

. . . . TOM LANSFORD

Cue Taking

The cue taking model centers upon how a member of a legislative body makes thousands of decisions every term, including those on bills requiring a high level of technical expertise but falling outside particular areas of interest. There is an opportunity cost of time and resources if the representative tries to learn more about those issues. Hence, in order to cope with the volume of decisions, legislators need a technique to deal with the information overload.

There are two sets of actors in the system: *cue takers* and *cue givers.* When a members must cast a roll call vote on a complex issue outside their expertise, they behaves as cue takers. Cue takers look for cues provided by cue givers. Cue givers are trusted colleagues who—because of their formal position in the legislature or policy specialization—are more informed on the issue; in addition, cue givers are those individuals with whom the cue taker would probably agree if their own individual research was completed. In that sense, legislators efficiently allocate their resources since they do not need to know about every single bill being voted, and they can trust other legislators who know more about the issue. Many representatives act as cue givers on some issues and cue takers on others.

From this classical usage as proposed by Donald Matthews and James Stimson, political scientists have expanded the study of cue taking to include voters, who take cues from political elites, and *outer ring* media outlets, which take cues from "prestige" media outlets. These studies show that cue taking is a pervasive phenomenon, but the extent of its importance varies in different populations and must be verified empirically.

See also *Heuristics.*

. . . . MARCIO A. CARVALHO

BIBLIOGRAPHY
Bianco, William T. "Reliable Source or Usual Suspects? Cue-Taking, Information Transmission, and Legislative Committees." *Journal of Politics* 59, no. 3 (1997): 913.
Kuklinski, James H., and Norman L. Hurley. "On Hearing and Interpreting Political Messages: A Cautionary Tale of Citizen Cue-Taking." *Journal of Politics* 56, no. 3 (1994): 729–751.
Matthews, Donald R., and James A. Stimson. *Yeas and Nays: Normal Decision-Making in the U.S. House of Representatives.* New York: Wiley, 1975.
Shaw, Daron, and Bartholomew Sparrow. "From the Inner Ring Out: News Congruence, Cue-Taking, and Campaign Coverage." *Political Research Quarterly* 52, no. 2 (1999): 323–351.
Sullivan, John L., L. Earl Shaw, Gregory E. McAvoy, and David G. Barnum. "The Dimensions of Cue-Taking in the House of Representatives: Variation by Issue Area." *Journal of Politics* 55, no. 4 (1993): 975–997.

Cult of Personality

Cult of personality refers to the common practice among twentieth-century dictatorships of promoting religious types of devotion to their national leader. As described in George Orwell's novel *1984,* through skillful use of the mass media and pervasive secret police monitoring, a modern state can create fanatical mass adulation of its leader on a scale not possible in premodern dictatorships. In the absence of democratic elections, this provides a mechanism to secure the loyalty of a state's subjects.

The practice arguably began with Russian leader Joseph Stalin's decision to place the corpse of revolutionary Vladimir Lenin, the founder of the Russian Communist Party, on public display after Lenin's death in 1924. By 1930, the public veneration of Lenin had expanded to include Stalin. Similar cults developed in the fascist regimes of dictators Adolf Hitler in Germany and Benito Mussolini in Italy, and in the later communist regimes of China's Mao Tse-Tung, North Korea's Kim Il-Sung, Cuba's Fidel Castro, and others.

The term itself originated with the February 1956 speech by Soviet leader Nikita Khrushchev in which he denounced Joseph Stalin's "cult of personality." Although Leonid Brezhnev, the Soviet president from 1964 to 1982, did not wield Stalin's power, he did generate a so-called cult of personality, as did some post-Soviet leaders, notably Saparmurat Niyazov in Turkmenistan. One open question is to what extent *personality cults* are the result of pressure from below, from local officials and ordinary citizens, rather than being simply constructed from above by the national leadership.

See also *Caesarism; Charisma; Stalinism.*

. . . . PETER RUTLAND

Cultural Policy

Broadly defined, *cultural policy* deals with institutional support and guidance for ways of life or culture as understood in anthropology. Such support can include the diffusion of governance to make possible the cultivation of specific tastes and habits, through educational and other means. Examples of cultural policy include the support of particular languages and other symbols of nationhood to foster patriotism and nationalism. Cultural policy can be viewed in the narrow sense of institutional support for creative and aesthetic human expression, yet all cultural expressions, narrow or broad, are important for cultural identities and often emerge at the forefront of political debates.

Cultural policy studies in general are interdisciplinary and broad in focus, though public policy literatures in political science attending to cultural policy tend to confine their understanding to institutional support for creative and aesthetic human expression. These include fine and performing arts and creative or entertainment industry products such as films, music, and publishing. Beyond these core aesthetic expressions, cultural policy can often relate to cultural tourism exploring the tangible and intangible heritage of societies and design elements of industries, such as advertising, architecture, and textiles.

FROM PATRONAGE TO SUBSIDIES

Historically, support for cultural expressions depended on patronage from royalty, religious institutions, or the wealthy elite. In ancient India, the fine and performing arts flourished in and around temples; Indian classical dance and music, for example, had religious significance. The Florentine Renaissance, from the fourteenth to the seventeenth century, was spurred by the impetus given to the arts by the house of Medici. The modern era broadened the categories of the wealthy, in turn expanding patronage and thus encouraging new forms of art. The English bourgeoisie, which arose from the early Industrial Revolution in the late eighteenth century, gave a boost to English romantic painting through an emerging trend of private art collecting that spurred the romantic painters with a market for their works. Meanwhile, absolutist monarchies such as the Bourbons in France or the Hapsburgs in Austria preferred grand symbols of patronage, such as magnificent opera houses designed for imperial or national glorification.

After World War II (1939–1945), governments played an active role in cultural policy by giving various kinds of direct and indirect support to the arts and thus encouraging the growth of artists as a professional class. Historically, most artists had worked part-time, bringing about the popular image of the starving artist. Direct support for the arts came from government subsidies and grants and support for institutions such as museums, performing arts centers, and arts festivals and fairs. Indirect support for the arts came from tax, philanthropic incentives, and restrictions on creative industry products from other countries, ostensibly to encourage national ones.

CULTURAL POLICY IN THE UNITED STATES

The United States, in particular, has encouraged tax and philanthropy incentives to encourage arts financing. While the total budget of the National Endowment for the Arts (NEA) in the United States was only $132 million in 2006, charitable giving to the arts was $12.51 billion. The NEA budget was itself supplemented by other federal appropriations for arts institutions such as the Smithsonian ($517 million), Corporation for Public Broadcasting (CPB; $416 million), and the Kennedy Center ($18 million).

The United States does not have an official cultural policy because support for the arts comes from agencies such as the NEA, and the government keeps itself at arms length from issues of culture that are supposedly left for the citizens and private industry. In practice, the U.S. government does intervene in arts controversies, such as the reining in of the NEA or CPB when they were deemed too far to the left in the 1980s or, on the other hand, the quite visible impetus given to U.S. cultural products in public diplomacy initiatives. Despite these interventions, it is generally believed that independent arts agencies such as the NEA, or its role model, the UK's Arts Council, tend to keep direct political interference more to a minimum than when the support comes from ministries of culture. Nevertheless, public choice theorists often note that bureaucrats in arts agencies have an incentive to follow conservative policies in the arts so as to avoid highly charged controversies, especially around images of national heritage.

INTERNATIONAL MINISTRIES OF CULTURE

Most countries in the world boast of ministries of culture even though, as in the United Kingdom, they might have independent funding agencies for the arts. Thus, the ministry of culture in France has been historically important not only for inculcating a sense of French identity but also for supervising important funding organizations such as Centre National de la Cinématographie (CNC), a crucial pillar in the support of French cinema. Public support for the arts is difficult to calculate because of the myriad instruments and institutions involved, and thus comparative estimates are difficult. It is estimated that France and Austria have some of the highest yearly arts expenditure per capita at €180 and €179, respectively.

Ministries of culture are also gaining importance in the developing world after years of neglect in the postcolonial era, due to lack of resources or relegation of culture to recessive tradition, as opposed to the impetus given to modernization through industrialization. Countries like China and India have now prioritized creative industries in their economic development while cities that thrive on arts and creativity and derive their identity from it are coming up all over the world. Centers of music production are flourishing in places such as Bamako, Mali, and Bogotá, Colombia, while film production takes off in Mexico, South Africa, and India. The spectacular opening ceremonies at the XXIX Olympiad in Beijing directed by film director Zhang Yimou, choreographer Zhang Jigang, and composer Tan Dun presented a culturally confident China to an estimated global television audience of between two and four billion people.

At the international level, many countries feel threatened by foreign, especially U.S. or Hollywood, creative industry exports. The Uruguay Round of trade talks (1986–1994) at the General Agreement on Tariffs and Trade (GATT) galvanized the debates on cultural exports. The European Union (EU), especially with French backing, vigorously contested the market liberalization that would ensue from GATT's measures, fearing that Hollywood would further dominate their cultural markets and weaken the influence of domestic cultural products and policies. The EU, therefore, did not make any commitments in the audiovisual negotiations, the so-called cultural exception. The phrase was often used in European context to note that the importance of creative products to cultural identity was such that they needed a special exception to global norms governing international trade. The fear of future liberalization goaded Canada and Francophone countries led by France to assemble an international coalition of cultural ministries and civil society organizations to act concertedly to frame the United Nations Educational, Scientific and Cultural Organization (UNESCO) Convention on the Protection and Promotion on the Diversity of Cultural Expressions, which came in to force in March 2007. The purpose of this convention is to recognize the importance of cultural industries to national and societal cultural identities and diversity of cultural expressions. More importantly, the convention seeks to promote national autonomy in cultural policy and exempt it from global market norms. Nevertheless, UNESCO itself lacks effective enforcement powers and thus the future impact of the convention remains unclear.

CONCLUSION

Cultural policy is intricately tied with cultural identity and politicians, and cultural industry elite often exploit this link to their advantage in trying to restrict or ban particular cultural expressions or flows of cultural products. For example, the EU's Television Without Frontiers directive that went into effect in 1992 has tried to reserve a majority of the television broadcast content in its twenty-seven member states to national or EU programming for the explicit purpose of promoting European cultural identities. Nevertheless, cultural products and flows continue to grow globally. Cultural identities, as a result, continue to assimilate many influences—as they always have.

See also *Free Trade; Political Culture; Politics, Literature, and Film; Public Policy; Trade Diplomacy.*

. . . . J. P. SINGH

BIBLIOGRAPHY

Anheier, Helmut A., and Yudhishtir Raj Isar, eds. *Cultures and Globalization: The Cultural Economy.* London: Sage Publications, 2008.

Cherbo, Joni Maya, Ruth Ann Stewart, and Margaret Jane Wyzsomirski, eds. 2008. *Understanding the Arts and Creative Sector in the United States.* New Brunswick, N.J.: Rutgers University Press, 2008.

Cowen, Tyler. *Creative Destruction: How Globalization Is Changing the World's Culture.* Princeton: Princeton University Press, 2002.

Cummings, Milton C., Jr., and Richard S. Katz, eds. *The Patron State: Government and the Arts in Europe, North America, and Japan.* New York: Oxford University Press.

Florida, Richard. *The Rise of the Creative Class.* New York: Basic Books, 2002.

Miller, Toby, and George Yudice. *Cultural Policy.* London: Sage Publications, 2002.

Singh, J. P. *The Arts of Globalization.* New York: Columbia University Press, 2010.

Van Der Ploeg, Frederick. "The Making of Cultural Policy: A European Perspective." In *Handbook of the Economics of Art and Culture,* edited by Victor A Ginsburgh and David Throsby, 1183–1221. Amsterdam: North Holland, 2006.

Cultural Relations

In terms of foreign relations and policies, cultural relations exist at various levels. Cultural relations can be set between a given government and its artists, writers, and producers. Cultural relations can exist within the private sector; between countries; ministries between universities in different countries; or involve states, nongovernmental organizations and institutions like the United Nations Educational, Scientific and Cultural Organization (UNESCO) as a promoter and facilitator of cultural endeavors. Cultural relations may include the arts and artists, producers and distributors, but also museums and donors.

Over the past twenty years, the balance of cultural relations has been faced with the issue of diversity of cultural expressions, which seeks to promote—in a single place—a broader horizon of artists and works from various cultural backgrounds and countries. Since the 1990s, diversity of cultural expressions has become a significant issue for many states where the cultural landscape is heavily influenced by a significant proportion of products (movies, popular music, magazines, television programs) from the United States, in particular, through the phenomenon of cultural dumping. The commerce of culture is not like others because art and culture cannot be reduced only to mere merchandise. In 2005, UNESCO approved a Convention on the Protection and Promotion of the Diversity of Cultural Expressions in recognition of the importance of cultural diversity around the world.

The basic notion of cultural relations as a dialogue of cultures can take many forms of expression, sometimes unsuspected or unpredictable. The Olympic Games with official ceremonies and national anthems, an exhibition about a foreign country in a national museum, the world tour of the Red Army Choir, and the banning of Salman Rushdie's novel *The Satanic Verses* are all examples of cultural relations that simultaneously carry, at an international level, a strong political dimension within the expressions of art and culture. Here, culture is understood as the expression of a nation's specificity and uniqueness through its art, language, literature, history, symbols, and traditions.

Scholars in political science and international relations have mixed perspectives about cultural relations: Some academics in North America often neglect these aspects as being outside of their discipline, while others, especially in Europe, would likely consider cultural relations as a core, although overlooked, part of their field.

The relationship between power—that is, the governments—and artists, has sometimes been in conflict. In the former Soviet Union, Josef Stalin persecuted composer Dimitri Shostakovich (1906–1975), who had a love-hate relationship with the dictator. Incidentally, the genius composer once dedicated his Tenth Symphony as a musical tribute to the life of Stalin. Also in the former Soviet Union, abstract artists like Kazimir Malevich were rejected by the regime during the 1930s because their art was too far from the official social realist trend. During the same period, expressionist painters like

Max Beckmann also faced banning from the 1930s and were forced into exile from Nazi Germany.

THE HOLLYWOOD FILM INDUSTRY

The Hollywood film industry should is more than just a sector of the cultural industries; it ranks among the three most important exporters of the United States. Scholars like Thomas Guback, Manjunath Pendakur, Ian Jarvie, Toby Miller, John Trumpbour, and Janet Wasko have demonstrated that the Hollywood movie industry operates as an oligarchy, which explains why U.S. movies dominate the most lucrative markets (movie theatres, DVD rentals) in North America and in many countries, even though the United States is not the biggest film producer in terms of quantity (India produces a far greater number of feature films each year). The U.S. movie industry is political and linked with the highest power: Through the decades, the U.S. government has sometimes imposed boycotts of countries, such as England in 1949, which did not want to fully cooperate in terms of opening their markets to Hollywood movies.

Movies themselves can have a highly political content, especially documentaries. Some directors, like Leni Riefenstahl, used film to glorify Nazism and Hitler in her famous documentary *Triumph of the Will* (*Triumph des Willens,* 1935). But on the other hand, contemporary filmmakers like Australian Dennis O'Rourke (*Half Life,* 1985) and Peter Watkins (*The Journey,* 1987) masterfully demonstrated how politics, culture, and the media can hide the maneuvers of the most powerful leaders even when the media do provide news stories, which are often revealed to be uninformative. However, these important political documentaries about international issues are often available only through alternative networks and are hard to find in stores. For example, in the documentary *Half Life,* O'Rourke provides an impressive amount of archival footage about the side effects of the secret U.S. nuclear testing made in the Pacific Ocean during the 1950s, where hundreds of islanders were exposed to radioactivity without being protected or treated.

MUSEUMS AND MEMORIALS

Museums are not just houses for exhibitions about old objects and the past; in their narratives on history, these institutions acknowledge and interpret how past events, including conflicts and wars, should be understood now and tomorrow. Since any museum's mission is to educate citizens and visitors (in addition to preserving its collections), a country's history museum can be a challenging place to highlight and explain both sides of sensitive issues such as colonialism, slavery, ethnic tensions, and warfare. Hence, visitors can visit the Hiroshima Peace Memorial Museum, in Hiroshima; the Maison des esclaves (House of the Slaves) on the Gorée Island in Senegal; and the recent Museum of Genocide Victims in Vilnius, Lithuania. All of these sites serve as tangible proof of the human rights violations that occurred there. The transition from one political regime to another can be told by museums as well, as Steven Dubin explained in his analysis of the South African museums that dealt with colonialism and apartheid.

As French historian Pierre Nora has demonstrated, even places can have a history, even if a place's specific story is not always obvious; for instance, the location where President John F. Kennedy was shot in Dallas, or the site of a battle. The history of these places and events can be remembered and commemorated by memorials. Similar to a paraphrase, a memorial seems to say in symbolic terms: "something important happened here, even though you cannot tell or see any trace anymore." Sites of former concentration camps in Germany, Poland, and central Europe are notable examples; regardless of whether or not the original buildings remain intact, people ought to know that a significant part of world history has occurred there. For newcomers and younger observers, testimonies are just words; buildings and historical places are tangible. In his book *Memorial Museums: The Global Rush to Commemorate Atrocities,* Paul Williams analyzes the processes and uses of memorializing through the years. Today, a fundamental question remains for museums who own objects that are not tolerated anymore. How should the artifacts that were used to legitimate an oppressive system be displayed? Giant portraits of former dictators or symbols of a previous colonial presence can become disturbing exhibits for a new generation of visitors. Should these works be retired and hidden? Depending on their policies, institutions answer in various ways.

PEACE PARKS

Borders are sometimes seen as zones appropriate for cultural relations, as international frontiers can create special forums of exchange between countries. There are times, however, that frontiers are so imbued with conflict that the only possible use is a demilitarized zone, and sometimes a peace park. Such peace a park exists, for example, between the North and South Korea, which used to be considered a no-man's-land. Peace parks can exist either between "good neighbors" or between states in conflict; they are built by two countries (or sometimes more) that agree to dedicate a region to a common cause, in many cases in order to protect first the environment and wildlife, but sometimes to avoid unwanted uses.

CULTURES CONFIRM DIFFERENCES

In an era of new technologies, globalization, and the Internet, individuals can be in touch with others in just a few seconds, despite the distance between them. But as French sociologist Dominique Wolton demonstrated, this illusion of proximity should not hide the barriers created by the sometimes deep differences between people, that vary significantly from one culture to another, one country to another, or one continent to another. These sorts of differences can be seen, for example, when American businesspersons go abroad and experience different corporate cultures, rules of hospitality, and etiquette.

In the twenty-first century, cultural relations are not exclusively handled by political leaders and policy makers, as proven by the emergence of celebrity diplomacy, whenever rock stars and actors use their image to promote what they consider to be worthwhile causes, as did John Lennon (1940–1980) for peace during the late 1960s and 1970s. Some artists were even recognized as diplomats. In Europe, popular singers like Nana

Mouskouri and Salvatore Adamo were nominated as ambassadors of good will for the United Nation's Children's Fund. In 2009, Armenia named popular French singer Charles Aznavour as its ambassador to Switzerland.

Diplomacy schools are no longer the only road to becoming a world-class diplomat because some celebrities have gained levels of respect and credibility, not only in their country, but also from an international audience. Moreover, celebrities can sometimes attract awareness from the media for overlooked issues, thereby providing the issue with increased public exposure. This can often take the form of popular artists meeting with notable advocates or important political figures like Nelson Mandela, for example. For many observers unaware of current politics and international relations, these types of meetings are perhaps their only encounter with political and human rights issues.

See also *Cultural Policy; Politics, Literature, and Film; United Nations Educational, Scientific and Cultural Organization (UNESCO).*

. . . . YVES LABERGE

BIBLIOGRAPHY

Dubin, Steven C. *Transforming Museums: Mounting Queen Victoria in a Democratic South Africa.* New York: Palgrave Macmillan, 2006.

Kim, Ke Chung. "Preserving Korea's Demilitarized Corridor for Conservation: A Green Approach to Conflict Resolution." In *Peace Parks: Conservation and Conflict Resolution,* edited by Saleem H. Ali, 239–260. Cambridge, Mass.: MIT Press, 2007.

Marshall, P. David, ed. *The Celebrity Culture Reader.* London: Routledge, 2006.

Miller, Toby, Nitin Govil, John McMurria, Richard Maxwell, and Ting Wang. *Global Hollywood 2.* London: British Film Institute, 2005.

Nora, Pierre, ed. *Realms of Memory: The Construction of the French Past.* New York: Columbia University Press, 1998.

Trumpbour, John. *Selling Hollywood to the World: U.S. and European Struggles for Mastery of the Global Film Industry, 1920–1950.* Cambridge: Cambridge University Press, 2007.

Williams, Paul. *Memorial Museums: The Global Rush to Commemorate Atrocities.* Oxford: Berg, 2007.

Cultural Rights

DEFINING CULTURAL RIGHTS

Cultural rights as identified in the International Bill of Rights (Universal Declaration of Human Rights [UDHR 1948], the International Covenant on Civil and Political Rights [ICCPR 1966], and the International Covenant on Economic, Social and Cultural Rights [ICESC 1966]) appear as a discrete category of human rights, separate from political, civil, economic, and social rights. *Cultural rights* in international law include the right to education; the right to "take part in cultural life;" the right to "enjoy the benefits of scientific progress and its applications;" the right to "benefit from the protection of the moral and material interests resulting from any scientific, literary, or artistic production of which he [the person] is the author;" and the freedom to pursue "scientific research and creative activity" (UDHR, Articles 26 and 27; ICESC, Articles 13, 14 and 15).

Together these rights in effect point to an expansive notion of culture. Elsa Stamatopoulou, chief of the United Nation's Permanent Forum on Indigenous Issues and extensive advocate for cultural rights, identified three different meanings of the word *culture* as applied by international law in her 2004 article "Why Cultural Rights Now?" They are:

1. Culture in its *material sense,* as product, as the accumulated material heritage of mankind, either as a whole or part of particular human groups, including but not limited to monuments and artifacts;
2. Culture as *process* of artistic or scientific creation, that is, the emphasis being placed on the process and on the *creator(s) of culture;* and
3. Culture in its anthropological sense, that is, *culture as a way of life* or, in UNESCO's words, the "set of distinctive spiritual, material, intellectual and emotional features of society or a social group"; it encompasses "in addition to art and literature, lifestyles, ways of living together, value systems, traditions and beliefs."

GLOBAL PERSPECTIVES ON CULTURAL RIGHTS

In the arena of global human rights, political and civil rights are often referred to as the *first-generation rights* while economic, social, and cultural rights are referred to as the *second-generation rights.* This sequencing of rights has understandably led to endless debate over whether these rights can and should be ranked by way of priority. Yet regardless of where one stands on the issue, the reality is that cultural rights were a much neglected category of rights until the 1990s, especially as they pertain to culture in both the material and the anthropological senses of the word.

The change appeared to be closely associated with the dynamics of global politics since the collapse of communism in the early 1990s. The reign of free market economy has triggered an unprecedented scale of movement among people in search of economic opportunities and improved livelihood, while some are simply dislocated by development. In addition, with the end of the cold war, multifarious identity-based conflicts, often of ethnic origin, have emerged to replace the previous wars of polarized ideologies. Given the enormous changes that took place in the last two decades and the speed with which preindustrialized societies and nonmarket economies are being displaced, it is no wonder that cultural rights have quickly emerged as a category of human rights that need much rethinking.

POLITICS OF CULTURAL RIGHTS

Since the global debate over cultural rights evolved in the 1990s, one of the most contested issues is whether cultural rights are rights of groups or individuals. The issue is challenging for two reasons: (1) human rights are typically conceived of as individual rights, as they are first and foremost meant to affirm and protect the dignity of individuals qua individuals, especially against entities such as the state; and (2) in both its material and anthropological senses, culture is associated with a collectivity whose members appear to have something in common.

The tension thus generated is particularly challenging to liberalism, given its endorsement of the sanctity of the individual on the one hand, and the premium that it places on pluralism on the other. In the context of the contemporary Western world, this tension is articulated through the characterization of cultural rights as minority rights and they are typically associated with immigrants from the non-Western world. The political dynamics between the white majority and the nonwhite minorities is called the politics of multiculturalism, in which cultural differences are to be accommodated rather than obliterated.

Among the most influential theorists of multiculturalism is the Canadian philosopher Will Kymlicka. His distinctive contribution lies in reconciling the tension between cultural rights and individualism in liberalism by identifying cultural membership as a "primary good" in the Rawlsian sense, that is, a good that is essential to individuals in pursuit of a good life. At stake is Kymlicka's view that as individuals exercise their freedom to make choices that are deemed by them to be worthy of pursuit, they do not make their choices in a vacuum. Rather, in his 1989 book *Liberalism, Community, and Culture,* Kymlicka says they require "a context of choice," which he calls "culture". Thus considered, cultural membership plays a crucial role in the attainment of self-respect, which no good life can dispense with. Kymlicka's theory of minority rights maintains that if the preservation of group identity can foster the context within which individuals make choices, then in the end group rights are by no means antithetical to liberalism. Although these special rights are rights that individuals have qua members of a group, they are meant to enhance, rather than suppress, individual autonomy. Specifically, in the context of a multiethnic state, minority rights support the claim to self-government by national minorities while immigrants are entitled to what Kymlicka refers to as "polyethnic rights." In *Multicultural Citizenship: A Liberal Theory of Minority Rights,* Kymlicka states that the latter are "group-specific measures" that enable ethnic groups and religious minorities to "express their cultural particularity and pride" but with the intent "to promote integration into the larger society, not self-government."

Another controversial issue is whether the formulation of cultural rights as human rights is in effect an oxymoron. Human rights are by definition universalistic, whereas cultural rights are most often used to affirm differences. Culture understood as a way of life implies that there is more than one way to live a life. The right to participate in cultural life can therefore be interpreted to mean the right to be different to the point where differences can no longer be adjudicated by some common standard. In other words, cultural rights can lead to both cultural essentialism and cultural relativism, rendering human rights ineffective as global normative standards. This confrontation between universalistic human rights on the one hand, and particularistic cultures on the other, seems to be fuelling a new polarity that has emerged since the 1990s. Instead of the previous ideological divide between liberal democracy and communism, we now have a comparably uncompromising cultural divide between the West and the non-Western world.

See also *Civil and Political Rights; Economic, Social, and Cultural Rights; Human Rights; Individual and Society; International Bill of Rights; Multiculturalism; Relativism.*

. . . . THERESA M. LEE

BIBLIOGRAPHY
Appiah, K. Anthony. *The Ethics of Identity.* Princeton: Princeton University Press, 2004.
Bauer, Joanne R., and Daniel A. Bell, eds. *The East Asian Challenge for Human Rights.* New York: Cambridge University Press, 1999.
Benhabib, Seyla. *The Claims of Culture: Equality and Diversity in the Global Era.* Princeton: Princeton University Press, 2002.
Jones, Peter. "Human Rights, Group Rights, and Peoples' Rights." *Human Rights Quarterly* 21 (1999): 80–107.
Okin, Susan M. *Is Multiculturalism Bad For Women?* Princeton: Princeton University Press, 1999.
Taylor, Charles. *Multiculturalism and "The Politics of Recognition."* Princeton: Princeton University Press, 1992.
Tully, James. Strange *Multiplicity: Constitutionalism in an Age of Diversity.* Cambridge: Cambridge University Press, 1995.

Culture and Politics

See *Political Culture.*

Cultures, Endangered

See *Endangered Cultures.*

Culture Wars

Culture war refers to a situation of radical conflict between opposite values or worldviews. The term derives originally from the German *Kulturkampf*, which denotes the policies enacted between 1871 and 1878 by Otto von Bismarck, chancellor of the German Empire, to fight the influence of Catholicism. By extension, the term came to mean not just the opposition between secular and religious worldviews, but more generally all situations of confrontation of radically conflicting values. In the United States, the term has been used in this sense by sociologist James Davison Hunter, who argues that a culture war on divisive issues such as abortion, homosexuality, and guns is currently taking place in America.

METAPHOR OR REALITY

The objects of a culture war are potentially unlimited. All cultural values can become the object of a radical opposition among social actors, including both individuals and communities. A few possible objects of culture wars include diverging religious faiths; secularism as opposed to religious worldviews; contrasting political ideologies; arguments in favor of or against gender discrimination; same-sex marriages; and other controversial issues such as abortion, euthanasia, and stem-cell research.

Different forms of culture wars can be grouped according to the intensity of the conflict. The intensity of conflict ranges within a spectrum whose extremes are war as a metaphor for a cultural opposition between conflicting values, and war as a reality, that is, as an armed conflict. Discussion of either end of the spectrum relies on the concept of conflict.

In a broad sense, a conflict denotes a situation in which two or more social actors try to impose their will on objectives perceived as incompatible. The objectives of conflict can be material resources or ideals. The first case involves a conflict of interests, while the second entails a conflict of ideologies (or, more recently, of identities). These are ideal types that never appear in their pure form in social life. Most of the time, the different components of conflict are so intermingled with one another they can hardly be distinguished. All the same, it is helpful to distinguish them at the analytical level.

Conflicts differ, among other things, in the different means employed in them. In particular, nonviolent conflicts differ from conflicts based on violence, which can be understood as physical coercion. In nonviolent conflicts, the term *war* is a hyperbole—a rhetorical figure to denote the harshness of cultural conflict. Violent conflicts entail a real war, meaning an act of violence to compel the enemy to do act on the other's will. Examples of nonviolent conflicts abound in all multicultural societies characterized by a pluralism of values and where, therefore, a radical confrontation between conflicting values and worldviews is a common experience. The innumerable wars in history are all examples of violent conflict. Intermediate kinds of conflict are also possible, such as so-called "symbolic violence." The term refers to situations such as gender and racial discrimination, which do not necessarily imply the recourse to physical coercion, but nevertheless display high degrees of violence.

THE QUESTION OF A GLOBAL CULTURE WAR

Another possible criterion to characterize culture wars is their scale. Culture wars can take place within bigger or smaller political communities as well as among them. An example of culture war within community borders is the *Kulturkampf*, which took place within the German Empire at the end of the nineteenth century.

An example of culture wars on a larger scale is the alleged clash between civilizations—a confrontation between world civilizations that, according to some interpreters, now occurs. Since its publication in the early 1990s, Samuel P. Huntington's 1993 *Clash of Civilizations and the Remaking of the World Order* has ignited a lively debate. According to Huntington, in the post–cold war world, the critical distinctions between people are not primarily ideological or economic, but cultural. In particular, it would be the Islamic and Asian challenges to the supposedly universal Western ideals that would reconfigure the fault lines of world politics.

Although many saw in the September 11, 2001 attacks on the United States a confirmation of Huntington's concept, scholars continue to strongly criticize his thesis. Some question the scale of conflict Huntington described; others reject the thesis altogether. Among the former, some do not necessarily reject the idea of culture wars but view it on a different level than Huntington. According to Benjamin R. Barber, for instance, the struggle between the jihad and the "McWorld" is not a struggle between civilizations, but rather between two different worldviews. More radically, in *The Clash Within: Democracy, Religious Violence, and India's Future,* an analysis of contemporary India, Martha C. Nussbaum argues that the greatest threat does not come from the clash between civilizations, but from the clash "within" them and even within each of us as we oscillate between self-protective aggression and the ability to live in a world with others.

Among those who reject the thesis of a clash between civilizations, Charles A. Kupchan observes in *The End of the American Era* (2002) that Huntington tends to ignore politics while overemphasizing cultural factors. Kupchan contends that the ongoing struggle between the United States and Islamic radicals is not the result of a clash between civilizations, but rather of the behavior of extremist groups preying upon discontent within Muslim majority states. Others, such as Fawaz A. Gerges in *America and Political Islam: Clash of Cultures or Clash of Interests?,* criticize the very idea of a culture war by arguing that it is a clash of interests and not of cultures that is shaping contemporary world politics. In this view, the idea of a culture war is not only a mistaken metaphor, but an ideological cover for conflicts that find their true sources elsewhere.

See also *Clash of Civilizations; Conflict Resolution; Cultural Relations; Identity, Politics of; Ideologies, Political; Political Culture; Universalism.*

. . . . CHIARA BOTTICI

BIBLIOGRAPHY

Barber, Benjamin R. *Jihad Vs. McWorld.* New York: Ballantine Books, 1996.

Bottici, Chiara, and Benoit Challand. "Rethinking Political Myth: The Clash of Civilisations as a Self-Fulfilling Prophecy." *European Journal of Social Theory* 9, no. 4 (2006): 315–336.

Clark, Christopher, and Kaiser Wolfram. *Culture Wars: Secular-Catholic Conflict in Nineteenth-Century Europe.* Cambridge: Cambridge University Press, 2003.

Gerges, Fawaz A. *America and Political Islam: Clash of Cultures or Clash of Interests?* Cambridge: Cambridge University Press, 1999.

Hunter, James Davison. *Culture Wars: The Struggle to Define America.* New York: Basic Books, 1992.

Huntington, Samuel P. *The Clash of Civilizations and the Remaking of World Order.* New York: Simon and Schuster, 1996.

Kupchan, Charles A. *The End of the American Era.* New York: Knopf, 2002.

Nussbaum, Martha C. *The Clash Within: Democracy, Religious Violence, and India's Future.* Cambridge, Mass.: Belknap Press, 2007.

Ross, Ronald J. *The Failure of Bismarck's Kulturkampf: Catholicism and State Power in Imperial Germany, 1871–1887.* Washington, D.C.: Catholic University of America Press, 1998.

Taylor, Charles. *A Secular Age.* Cambridge, Mass.: Belknap Press, 2007.

Webb, Adam K. *Beyond the Global Culture War.* London: Routledge, 2006.

Cumulative Voting

Cumulative voting is an electoral procedure in which instead of being limited to casting a ballot for a single candidate, voters are given multiple votes and may divide those votes any way they chose. Voters may cast all of their votes for a single candidate or divide them among two or more office seekers. The number of votes given a citizen is dependent on the number of candidates. Hence, in an election with four candidates, a voter would receive four votes and could cast them in one of sixteen possible combinations.

By encouraging participation by small or minor parties, cumulative voting has been touted as a means to increase voter turnout and enhance the diversity of political systems. Voters do not face the dilemma of the wasted ballot in which they avoid voting for their preferred candidate because they don't believe that office seeker can win the election. In addition, the system lessens the negative impacts of the winner-take-all system. Proponents of cumulative voting argue that it can mitigate political gerrymandering. Some scholars have proposed using cumulative voting to increase the political representation or participation of disadvantaged groups by granting some voters additional points or votes during elections.

See also *Electoral Systems; Voting Behavior; Voting Procedures.*

. . . . TOM LANSFORD

Cybersecurity

Cybersecurity concerns keeping the space provided by the computer and the Internet safe for the various users of the technology. Section 2 of the Homeland Security Act of 2002 clearly outlines the concerns of the U.S. government when it comes to cybersecurity in the following words: "The term 'cybersecurity' means the prevention of damage to, the protection of, and the restoration of computers, electronic communications systems, electronic communication services, wire communication, and electronic communication, including information contained therein, to ensure its availability, integrity, authentication, confidentiality, and nonrepudiation." Such a concern operates on several different levels and indicates how various activities bordering on the illegal and the criminal are within the purview of what constitutes the concern of cybersecurity.

ISSUES

Protecting users from criminal and illegal activities in cyberspace necessitates determining what these activities are. Michael Margolis and David Resnick outline two types of cybercrimes: network crimes and computer crimes. *Network crimes* are activities that use the Internet but do not necessarily entail corrupting or breaking into computers. People are the victims of these crimes, such as gambling and pornography, in much the same way as those committed in the real world. Various crimes committed in cyberspace, such as consumer fraud, stock manipulation, and various types of sexual predation, resemble life offline with their share of scammers, crooks, and predators. Thus law enforcement officials and government agencies have had to develop expertise in fighting particular types of crimes that follow crooks into cyberspace, such as "hacker hunting."

In contrast, *computer crimes* may or may not employ the Internet in committing the crime; a computer is its target. People are victims only in the sense that the computer is the object of the activity, that is, hacking into computers to steal data, spread computer viruses or worms, and disable computer systems. As a result, policing the Internet has become a routine activity.

REMEDIES

Cybersecurity standards have also been created because sensitive information is now frequently stored on computers that are attached to the Internet. This affects the individual, businesses, and governments equally. Many tasks that were once done by hand are now carried out by computer, thus the need for security to guard against information theft, which leads to identity theft. Businesses need security to protect trade secrets, proprietary information, and customers' personal information. The government also needs to secure their information. This has been particularly critical after 9/11, since some terrorist acts are organized and facilitated by using the Internet.

Various protection programs address the protection of data against unauthorized access. Data can be secured by issuing passwords and digital certificates to authorized users. To go beyond authorization to authentication, the use of digital certificates and biometric techniques (fingerprints, eyes, voice, etc.) provide a more secure method. Beyond user authentication, sensitive data can be further protected through encryption, which prevents information from getting into the wrong hands.

Computer systems use various cybersecurity technologies to remedy threats; these include the use of routers, firewalls, antivirus protection software, intrusion detection systems, intrusion protection systems, and auditing and monitoring computer usage. Various risk management strategies and techniques, as well as training and education, are valued in protecting the network.

ORDER VERSUS FREEDOM

There are those, however, who view all of this protection as a threat to individual liberty, one's quality of life, and human dignity. There clearly is a struggle between the measures to protect privacy and safeguard intellectual property and the measures that are undertaken to ensure that law and order is enforced in cyberspace. It seems that self-regulation and voluntary enforcement procedures such as shunning, flaming, and blocking people from e-mail lists and forums can no longer be used as enforcement mechanisms. Closing down illegal operations and fining and imprisoning lawbreakers are now becoming necessary with the advent of laws governing relationships in cyberspace. However, state-sponsored surveillance and commercially motivated data collection done without the consent and knowledge of the entity under surveillance can lead to cries of lost freedom.

Thus the dilemma for those who are concerned with cybersecurity is whether the primary goal should be security and order first, and freedom and access second, or vice versa. For security advocates on the national defense level, where there is constant fear of giving away too much information about high-value targets, the goal is certainly law and order first. Freedom of access is secondary for security agencies but is not necessarily so for the ordinary user.

See also *Cyberterrorism; Intellectual Property Rights; National Security Policy; Privacy; Privacy Rights.*

. . . . CECILIA G. MANRIQUE

BIBLIOGRAPHY
Crumlish, Christian. *The Power of Many.* Alameda, Calif.: Sybex, 2004.
Klotz, Robert J. *The Politics of Internet Communication.* Lanham, Md.: Rowman and Littlefield, 2004.
Margolis, Michael, and David Resnick. *Politics as Usual.* Thousand Oaks, Calif.: Sage Publications, 2000.
Rheingold, Howard. *Smart Mobs.* Cambridge, Mass.: Perseus Group, 2002.
Speed, Tim, and Juanita Ellis. *Internet Security.* Amsterdam: Digital Press, 2003.
Thomas, Tom. *Network Security First-step.* Indianapolis, Ind.: Cisco Press, 2004.

Cyberterrorism

Cyberterrorism is the use of modern communication technology in the commission of terrorist activities. Although not strictly limited to the Internet, there is a strong bias toward using the Internet to exemplify the concept of cyberterrorism. Cyberterrorism does not have a single definition: In some instances, it refers to use of the Internet to disrupt information systems by formal, recognized terrorist organizations. In other instances, cyberterrorism refers to Internet use by recognized governments that may be seen as supporting or encouraging terrorist activities. When states launch attacks using the Internet, it is usually referred to as *cyberwarfare.* Sometimes cyberterrorism refers strictly to activities carried out by organizations, other times to activities carried out by individuals pursuing a common goal but without a formal organization. Cyberterrorism may refer to activities executed across international borders or within a single country.

Cyberterrorists go beyond the law and the general norms of the countries they attack to accomplish a political agenda agreed on by only a small minority within the country, and with which the majority of the country usually disagrees. Cyberterrorism is undertaken through such avenues as worms, viruses, and backdoors and has several important purposes for which it is undertaken, including extortion, the creation of economic disruption, and identity theft. The actual use of the Internet in cyberterrorism ranges from preparative acts to propaganda to carrying out an act of terrorism. Preparative acts of cyberterrorism include buying airline tickets, researching building plans, and acquiring weapons. Propaganda acts of cyberterrorism are generally limited to exhorting potential recruits into joining terrorist organizations and exhorting sympathizers to contribute money and resources. Carrying out acts of cyberterrorism on the Internet is generally limited to deluging opponents with threats or attacking computers and networks.

Much cyberterrorism is international in nature. Many groups recruit from and are active in a number of countries, and try to change the international activities of a specific country. Individuals within one country, or a small number of countries, use cyberterrorism to try to exact vengeance against another country for a perceived affront against either their homeland or their social group. Rebels fighting within one country who live and work outside of the country use the Internet to continue fighting against the government of the country through correspondence and recruitment and propaganda activities. This last situation usually occurs when a demographically identifiable group within a country fights for independence from that country or for equal or special rights. This does not negate the existence of cyberterrorist activities by groups within a single country. As a result of the frequently international nature of cyberterrorism, many countries have started working together to combat it.

Governments trying to stop cyberterrorism have used a combination of tools. Whenever possible, existing laws have been applied to stopping cyberterrorism. For example, purchasing illegal weapons on the Internet equates to purchasing illegal weapons in person or through other means. There are also specific treaties aimed at halting cyberterrorism internationally. The creator of *malware* (malignant software) is no longer punished solely according to the laws of the country of residence. Now, when malware goes international, the country that either suffered the most damage or has the harshest punishment, depending on the specifics of the treaty being applied, issues the punishment. Law enforcement agencies and sometimes militaries are now working much more closely when pursuing cyberterrorists.

Examples of cyberterrorism come from around the world. In the United States, abortion opponents use e-mail to harass doctors providing abortions. Al-Qaida operatives in Europe, the Middle East, and the United States have used the Internet to research bombing targets, purchase supplies, and recruit members. A female al-Qaida operative in Belgium used the Internet to exhort people to join and participate in bombings. Palestinians, Israelis, Chinese, Taiwanese, and Americans are known to have used the Internet to hack into and attack business and government Internet sites. Although the respective governments are sometimes blamed when this happens, complete evidence of this sort of cyberterrorism, often referred to as *hactivism,* or computer hacking as activism, is not available.

See also *Al-Qaida; Cybersecurity; Homeland Security; Internet and Politics; Terrorism, Political.*

. . . . DAVID B. CONKLIN

BIBLIOGRAPHY
Andrejevic, Mark. *iSpy: Surveillance and Power in the Interactive Era.* Lawrence: University Press of Kansas, 2007.
Brown, Lawrence V. *Cyberterrorism and Computer Attacks.* Hauppauge, N.Y.: Novinka Books, 2006.
Council of Europe. *Cyberterrorism: The Use of the Internet for Terrorist Purposes.* Brussels: Council of Europe, 2007.
Jordan, Tim, and Paul A. Taylor. *Hacktivism and Cyberwars: Rebels with a Cause.* New York: Routledge, 2004.
Verton, Dan. *Black Ice: The Invisible Threat of Cyberterrorism.* New York: McGraw-Hill, 2003.
Weimann, Gabriel. *Terror on the Internet.* Washington, D.C.: United States Institute of Peace Press, 2006.

INDEX
~

Illustrations are denoted by italic page numbers. Main entries are denoted by bold page numbers. Figures and tables are indicated by f and t following page numbers. Alphabetization is letter-by-letter (e.g., "Federalism" precedes "Federal mandates").

N

NAACP
in African American social movements, 1702–1703
civil rights movement and, 241
Garvey and, 649
as minority interest group, 1708
public interest groups and, 1384
NAACP Legal Defense and Education Fund, **1073–1074**
as minority interest group, 1708
Nader, Ralph, 410
NAFTA. *See* North American Free Trade Agreement
Nakumura, Robert, 1589
NAM (Non-Aligned Movement). *See* Nonalignment
Napoleon Bonaparte, 760, 904–905, 933
Napoleonic Codes
civil law and, 237
law, comparative, 925
Louisiana and, 281
NARA (U.S. National Archives and Records Administration), 1077
Narratives, political. *See* Politics, literature, and film
Nash, John, 646
Nash equilibrium, 646, 1012, 1095
Nasser, Gamal Abdel
Arab socialism and, 72
charisma, 211
military rule and, 1036
pan-Arabism and pan-Islamism and, 1031, 1171
Nast, Thomas, 197, 1510
Nation, **1074–1075**. *See also* Nationalism; Nationality; Nation-state
alternative conceptualizations, 1074–1075
primordialist perspectives, 1074
solutions to conceptualization conflicts, 1075
Nation, stateless, 1611–1612
The Nation (weekly magazine), 852
National American Woman Suffrage Association (NAWSA), 1786
National Annenberg Election Survey (NAES), 1385
National anthems, **1075–1076**
contents of, 1076
musical forms of, 1076
origins of, 1075–1076
unofficial and changing, 1076
National archives, **1076–1077**
National Assembly (France), 1479
National Association for the Advancement of Colored People. *See* NAACP
National Black Women's Health Project, 1779
National Convention of Newfoundland, 1769–1770
National critical discourse, 1564
National defense, 1380
National Election Studies (NES), 184, 1040

National Endowment for the Arts (NEA), 366
National identity, 765–766
Nationalism, **1077–1082**. *See also* Nation
African politics and society and, 26
Buddhism and, 155
chauvinism and, 212
competing theories of, 1079–1080
current debates on, 1080–1081
early modern African, 24
end of, 1078–1079
ethnic, 1579
immigration, 761
Kemalism and, 891
Marxism and, 1005
media bias and, 1018
modern African, 25
political anthropology and, 1228
quest for statehood and, 1079
the state, 1596
stateless, 1612
third world, 1579
Nationalism and Social Communication (Deutsch), 415
Nationalism Reframed (Brubaker), 1075
Nationalist music, 1070–1071
Nationalist parties, **1082–1083**
populist movement toward, 1082–1083
rise and decline of parties of class and religion, 1082
Nationality, **1083–1084**
citizenship vs., 1083
growing saliency of, 1083–1084
postmaterialism and politics of identity, 1084
Nationalization, **1084–1086**
Clegg's critique of socialist and communist approaches to, 1085
communist and socialist theories of, 1085
in practice, 1085
National Organization for Women (NOW), 1787
National Recovery Administration (NRA), 1106
National Research Council, 278
National Right to Life Committee
public interest groups and, 1384
right to life and, 1482
National Security Document 68, 1201–1202
National security policy, **1086–1087**. *See also* Homeland security; Occupation and annexation
foreign influences and assets under protection, 1086
means of protection, 1086
methods of deciding policy, 1086–1087
National socialism, **1087–1088**
appeal of, 1088
Hitler and rise of, 1087
National Socialist Workers Party (Nazi Party)
gleichshaltung, 674
national socialism, 1087–1088
political cartoons, 752
National Urban League (NUL), 1702, 1708

Nation-building, **1088–1089**. *See also* Nation; Nationalism; Nation-state
Nations as Zones of Conflict (Hutchinson), 1075
Nation-state, **1089–1090**
European politics and society, 533
formation of, 1089–1090
identity, politics of, 757–758
mercantilism and, 1023
modern, 1090
nationalism and, 1078, 1079
nation-building and, 1088–1089
nonstate actors and, 1118
sovereignty, 1582–1583
state formation, 1609
NATO. *See* North Atlantic Treaty Organization
Natural aristocracy, 304
Natural authority
foundations of political thought and, 1296–1297
patriarchy and, 1197
Naturalistic fallacy, 751
Naturalization, **1090–1092**. *See also* Citizenship
citizenship, 226
cross-national variation in, 1091
voluntary and involuntary, 1091
Naturalization Acts (1792 & 1795), 228
Naturalization of knowledge, 1251–1253
Natural law, **1092–1093**. *See also* Natural rights
Aquinas and, 1664
contemporary, 1092–1093
German political thought, 669
Greek and Medieval origins of, 1092
Greek political thought, 696
jurisprudence and, 880
Marisilius of Padua on, 1002
Maritain and, 999–1000
modern natural law and legal positivism, 1092
Pufendorf and, 1395
Roman Catholic social thought and, 1485
universalism and, 1720
Natural resources
civil wars and, 246
common-pool resources and, 277–279
Natural Resources Defense Council (NRDC)
nuclear club and, 1133
public interest groups and, 1384
Natural rights, **1093–1094**. *See also* Natural law
civil and political rights, 235
human rights, 745
public-private dichotomy, 1394
Nature, state of. *See* State of nature
Nazi Germany
anti-Semitism and, 63
appeasement and, 63–64
associationalism, 244
censorship, 204
civil-military relations, 239